MW00995373

# Substantive Criminal Law

*Carolina Academic Press*
*Law Advisory Board*

❦

Gary J. Simson, Chairman
*Dean, Mercer University School of Law*

Raj Bhala
*University of Kansas School of Law*

Davison M. Douglas
*Dean, William and Mary Law School*

Paul Finkelman
*Albany Law School*

Robert M. Jarvis
*Shepard Broad Law Center*
*Nova Southeastern University*

Vincent R. Johnson
*St. Mary's University School of Law*

Peter Nicolas
*University of Washington School of Law*

Michael A. Olivas
*University of Houston Law Center*

Kenneth L. Port
*William Mitchell College of Law*

H. Jefferson Powell
*Duke University School of Law*

Michael P. Scharf
*Case Western Reserve University School of Law*

Michael Hunter Schwartz
*Dean, William H. Bowen School of Law*
*University of Arkansas at Little Rock*

Peter M. Shane
*Michael E. Moritz College of Law*
*The Ohio State University*

# Substantive Criminal Law

## Cases, Comments and Comparative Materials

**Luis E. Chiesa**
Professor of Law, Vice Dean for Academic Affairs, and
Director of the Buffalo Criminal Law Center,
SUNY Buffalo Law School

Carolina Academic Press
Durham, North Carolina

Copyright © 2014
Luis E. Chiesa
All Rights Reserved

ISBN 978-1-61163-528-7
LCCN 2014937538

Carolina Academic Press
700 Kent Street
Durham, North Carolina 27701
Telephone (919) 489-7486
Fax (919) 493-5668
www.cap-press.com

Printed in the United States of America
2015 Printing

*To Karla, for selflessly allowing me to follow my passion for criminal law from the warm beaches of Puerto Rico to the cold and snowy shores of Lake Erie.*

# Contents

## Part Six · Specific Offenses

# Table of Cases

# Preface

This casebook differs from others in three obvious ways. First, given that the American Law Institute's Model Penal Code (MPC) has heavily influenced criminal law in the United States, each chapter contains one or more sections titled "Model Penal Code" that discuss the Code's approach to the chapter's topic. This sets the book apart, as many casebooks seldom highlight the MPC approach to a given criminal law doctrine in a separate section that clearly distinguishes it from the common law approach. As I have learned from teaching criminal law for many years, this sows a good deal of confusion amongst students, for professors—and bar examiners—expect them to neatly distinguish between MPC and common law doctrines, but the casebooks haphazardly combine discussion of both approaches in a rather unintuitive manner.

Another unique feature of this text is that—contrary to the prevailing trend in criminal law casebooks—the scholarly materials discussed in the text are not sprinkled throughout the different chapter sections. Instead, each chapter contains a section titled "Scholarly Debates" that discusses academic writings that illustrate the philosophical underpinnings of the doctrines discussed in the chapter. This is useful for both students and instructors.

Regarding students, it allows them to focus on learning the doctrines of criminal law before engaging with the scholarly writings on the subject. Understanding the basic doctrines of criminal law is a daunting task for even the most accomplished student. There is no need to make it more difficult by requiring them to engage with theoretical scholarly discussions while they are trying to master the basic rules. By making the "Scholarly Debates" section the last section of each chapter, this casebook introduces the student to the philosophical discussions after she has (hopefully!) learned the basic concepts. Although this makes much pedagogical sense, available criminal law casebooks do not follow this quite intuitive approach.

From the instructor's perspective, having a separate "Scholarly Debates" section allows for the flexibility of deciding not to assign this more philosophically laden section as required reading. Many professors approach criminal law from a theoretical perspective. For those who do, they will find discussion of rich philosophical materials in this section. Nevertheless, other professors downplay the philosophical underpinnings of criminal law. The way in which this casebook is structured allows such instructors to easily and painlessly skip the philosophical readings. In contrast, the vast majority of casebooks sprinkle philosophical discussions throughout all of the book's sections, making it very hard for instructors to eschew unwanted references to such debates.

The most distinctive aspect of this casebook is that each chapter includes a section titled "Comparative Perspectives" that discusses European and Latin American approaches to the doctrines discussed in the chapter. After years of teaching comparative criminal law both in the United States and Latin America, I have learned that comparative teaching materials can be profitably used in domestic criminal law courses. In my experience, use of such materials fosters both a better understanding of domestic criminal law and encourages students and professors to think about alternative ways of approaching basic concepts of criminal theory. I have translated the vast majority of the comparative materials included in these sections, as most have not been published in English. As a result, each "Comparative Perspective" section may include excerpts from foreign cases, statutes and scholarly writings, including materials from Germany, Spain, Argentina and Puerto Rico. Given that these materials are otherwise unavailable in English, the readings in this section should also prove useful as source material for scholarly research.

As with the "Scholarly Debates" section, the comparative materials are included in a separate section and only after the American approach to the black letter law has been discussed. Therefore, the student is ready to engage in comparative analysis once she reaches the "Comparative Perspectives" section. Furthermore, the instructor may omit the section if she is so inclined. This kind of flexibility is difficult to find, as the (infrequent) references to comparative criminal law in textbooks are usually sprinkled throughout the text as opposed to included in a separate section.

# Acknowledgments

This book would not have come to fruition without the able help of my research assistants Barbara Santisteban (Pace Law School), Anastasia Larios (Pace Law School), Trishe Ball (SUNY Buffalo Law School) and J.T. Hammons (SUNY Buffalo Law School). Professors Ernesto Chiesa and Oscar Miranda Miller's comments on various drafts of the casebook helped make the text considerably better than it was when they first laid hands on it. Finally, the text was dramatically improved by the feedback I received from my students when I assigned a draft version of the casebook in my Fall 2013 criminal law class at SUNY Buffalo Law School.

# Part One

# The Nature and Purposes of Criminal Law

# Chapter 1

# The Nature of Punishment

## § 1.01 Distinguishing Punishment from Civil Sanctions: In General

### Kennedy v. Mendoza-Martínez

Supreme Court of the United States, 1963
372 U.S. 144

Mr. Justice GOLDBERG delivered the opinion of the Court.

We are called upon in these two cases to decide the grave and fundamental problem, common to both, of the constitutionality of Acts of Congress which divest an American of his citizenship for '(d)eparting from or remaining outside of the jurisdiction of the United States in time of war or ... national emergency for the purpose of evading or avoiding training and service' in the Nation's armed forces.

I. The Facts.

A. Mendoza-Martinez-No. 2.

The facts of both cases are not in dispute. Mendoza-Martinez, the appellee in No. 2, was born in this country in 1922 and therefore acquired American citizenship by birth. By reason of his parentage, he also, under Mexican law, gained Mexican citizenship, thereby possessing dual nationality. In 1942 he departed from this country and went to Mexico solely, as he admits, for the purpose of evading military service in our armed forces. He concedes that he remained there for that sole purpose until November 1946, when he voluntarily returned to this country. In 1947, in the United States District Court for the Southern District of California, he pleaded guilty to and was convicted of evasion of his service obligations in violation of s 11 of the Selective Training and Service Act of 1940. He served the imposed sentence of a year and a day. For all that appears in the record, he was, upon his release, allowed to reside undisturbed in this country until 1953, when, after a lapse of five years, he was served with a warrant of arrest in deportation proceedings. This was premised on the assertion that, by remaining outside the United States to avoid military service after September 27, 1944 ... he had lost his American citizenship. Following hearing, the Attorney General's special inquiry officer sustained the warrant and ordered that Mendoza-Martinez be deported as an alien. He appealed to the Board of Immigration Appeals of the Department of Justice, which dismissed his appeal.

Thereafter, Mendoza-Martinez brought a declaratory judgment action in the Federal District Court for the Southern District of California, seeking a declaration of his status as a citizen, of the unconstitutionality of § 401(j), and of the voidness of all orders of deportation directed against him.

The District Court [ultimately held that] § 401(j) is unconstitutional [partially because] § 401(j) is 'essentially penal in character and deprives the plaintiff of procedural due process. '(T)he requirements of procedural due process are not satisfied by the administrative hearing of the Immigration Service nor in this present proceedings.' The Attorney General's current appeal is from this decision....

### IV. The Constitutional Issues.

### A. Basic Principles.

... We recognize at the outset that we are confronted here with an issue of the utmost import. Deprivation of citizenship—particularly American citizenship, which is 'one of the most valuable rights in the world today,' Report of the President's Commission on Immigration and Naturalization (1953), 235—has grave practical consequences....

### C. Sections 401(j) and 349(a)(10) as Punishment.

... We have come to the conclusion that there is a basic question in the present cases, the answer to which obviates a choice here between the powers of Congress and the constitutional guarantee of citizenship. That issue is whether the statutes here, which automatically—without prior court or administrative proceedings—impose forfeiture of citizenship, are essentially penal in character, and consequently have deprived the appellees of their citizenship without due process of law and without according them the rights guaranteed by the Fifth and Sixth Amendments, including notice, confrontation, compulsory process for obtaining witnesses, trial by jury, and assistance of counsel....

It is fundamental that the great powers of Congress to conduct war and to regulate the Nation's foreign relations are subject to the constitutional requirements of due process. The imperative necessity for safeguarding these rights to procedural due process under the gravest of emergencies has existed throughout our constitutional history, for it is then, under the pressing exigencies of crisis, that there is the greatest temptation to dispense with fundamental constitutional guarantees which, it is feared, will inhibit governmental action. 'The Constitution of the United States is a law for rulers and people, equally in war and in peace, and covers with the shield of ***566*** its protection all classes of men, at all times, and under all circumstances.' *Ex parte Milligan*, 4 Wall, 2, 120–121, 18 L.Ed. 281. The rights guaranteed by the Fifth and Sixth Amendments are 'preserved to every one accused of crime who is not attached to the army, or navy, or militia in actual service.' *Id.*, at 123. '(I)f society is disturbed by civil commotion—if the passions of men are aroused and the restraints of law weakened, if not disregarded—these safeguards need, and should receive, the watchful care of those entrusted with the guardianship of the Constitution and laws. In no other way can we transmit to posterity unimpaired the blessings of liberty, consecrated by the sacrifices of the Revolution.' *Id.*, at 124.

We hold § 401(j) invalid because in them Congress has plainly employed the sanction of deprivation of nationality as a punishment—for the offense of leaving or remaining outside the country to evade military service—without affording the procedural safeguards guaranteed by the Fifth and Sixth Amendments. Our forefathers 'intended to safeguard the people of this country from punishment without trial by duly constituted courts. And even the courts to which this important function was entrusted, were commanded to stay their hands until and unless certain tested safeguards were observed. An accused in court must be tried by an impartial jury, has a right to be represented by counsel, (and) must be clearly informed of the charge against him' *United States v. Lovett*, 328 U.S. 303,

317, 66 S.Ct. 1073, 1080, 90 L.Ed. 1252. As the Government concedes, § 401(j) automatically strips an American of his citizenship, with concomitant deprivation 'of all that makes life worth living,' *Ng Fung Ho v. White*, 259 U.S. 276, 284–285, 42 S.Ct. 492, 495, 66 L.Ed. 938, whenever a citizen departs from or remains outside the jurisdiction of this country for the purpose of evading his military obligations. Conviction for draft evasion is not prerequisite to the operation of this sanction. Independently of prosecution, forfeiture of citizenship attaches when the statutory set of facts develops. It is argued that the availability after the fact of administrative and judicial proceedings … to contest the validity of the sanction meets the measure of due process. But the legislative history and judicial expression with respect to every congressional enactment relating to the provisions in question dating back to 1865 establish that forfeiture of citizenship is a penalty for the act of leaving or staying outside the country to avoid the draft. This being so, the Fifth and Sixth Amendments mandate that this punishment cannot be imposed without a prior criminal trial and all its incidents, including indictment, notice, confrontation, jury trial, assistance of counsel, and compulsory process for obtaining witnesses. If the sanction these sections impose is punishment, and it plainly is, the procedural safeguards required as incidents of a criminal prosecution are lacking. We need go no further.

The punitive nature of the sanction here is evident under the tests traditionally applied to determine whether an Act of Congress is penal or regulatory in character, even though in other cases this problem has been extremely difficult and elusive of solution. Whether the sanction involves an affirmative disability or restraint, whether it has historically been regarded as a punishment, whether it comes into play only on a finding of scienter, whether its operation will promote the traditional aims of punishment-retribution and deterrence, whether the behavior to which it applies is already a crime, whether an alternative purpose to which it may rationally be connected is assignable for it, and whether it appears excessive in relation to the alternative purpose assigned are all relevant to the inquiry, and may often point in differing directions. Absent conclusive evidence of congressional intent as to the penal nature of a statute, these factors must be considered in relation to the statute on its face. Here, although we are convinced that application of these criteria to the face of the statutes supports the conclusion that they are punitive, a detailed examination along such lines is unnecessary, because the objective manifestations of congressional purpose indicate conclusively that the provisions in question can only be interpreted as punitive. A study of the history of the predecessor of § 401(j), which 'is worth a volume of logic,' coupled with a reading of Congress' reasons for enacting § 401(j), compels a conclusion that the statute's primary function is to serve as an additional penalty for a special category of draft evader.

### 1. The Predecessor Statute and Judicial Construction.

The subsections here in question have their origin in part of a Civil War 'Act to amend the several Acts heretofore passed to provide for the Enrolling and Calling out the National Forces, and for other Purposes.' Act of March 3, 1865, 13 Stat. 487. Section 21 of that Act, dealing with deserters and draft evaders, was in terms punitive, providing that 'in addition to the other lawful penalties of the crime of desertion,' persons guilty thereof 'shall be deemed and taken to have voluntarily relinquished and forfeited their rights of citizenship and their rights to become citizens and all persons who, being duly enrolled, shall depart the jurisdiction of the district in which he is enrolled, or go beyond the limits of the United States, with intent to avoid any draft into the military or naval service, duly ordered, shall be liable to the penalties of this section.'

The debates in Congress in 1865 confirm that the use of punitive language in § 21 was not accidental. The section as originally proposed inflicted loss of rights of citizenship only on deserters. Senator Morrill of Maine proposed amending the section to cover persons who leave the country to avoid the draft, stating, 'I do not see why the same principle should not extend to those who leave the country to avoid the draft.' Cong.Globe, 38th Cong., 2d Sess. 642 (1865). This 'same principle' was punitive, because Senator Morrill was also worried that insofar as the section as originally proposed 'provides for a penalty' to be imposed on persons who had theretofore deserted, there was question 'whether it is not an ex post facto law, whether it is not fixing a penalty for an act already done.' Ibid....

### 2. The Present Statutes.

The immediate legislative history of s 401(j) confirms the conclusion, based upon study of the earlier legislative and judicial history, that it is punitive in nature. The language of the section was, to begin with, quite obviously patterned on that of its predecessor, an understandable fact since the draft of the bill was submitted to the Congress by Attorney General Biddle along with a letter to Chairman Russell of the Senate Immigration Committee, in which the Attorney General referred for precedent to the 1912 reenactment of the 1865 statute. This letter, which was the impetus for the enactment of the bill, was quoted in full text in support of it in both the House and Senate Committee Reports.... The Senate Report stated that it 'fully explains the purpose of the bill.' The letter was couched entirely in terms of an argument that citizens who had left the country in order to escape military service should be dealt with, and that loss of citizenship was a proper way to deal with them. There was no reference to the societal good that would be wrought by the legislation, nor to any improvement in soldier morale or in the conduct of war generally that would be gained by the passage of the statute. The House Committee Report and the sponsors of the bill endorsed it on the same basis. The report referred for support to the fact that the FBI files showed 'over 800 draft delinquents' in the El Paso area alone who had crossed to Mexico to evade the draft. The obvious inference to be drawn from the report, the example it contained, and the lack of mention of any broader purpose is that Congress was concerned solely with inflicting effective retribution upon this class of draft evaders and, no doubt, on others similarly situated.

The Senate and House debates, together with Attorney General Biddle's letter, brought to light no alternative purpose to differentiate the new statute from its predecessor. Indeed, as indicated, the Attorney General's letter specifically relied on the predecessor statute as precedent for this enactment, and both the letter and the debates, consistent with the character of the predecessor statute, referred to reasons for the enactment of the bill which were fundamentally retributive in nature. When all of these considerations are weighed, as they must be, in the context of the incontestably punitive nature of the predecessor statute, the conclusion that § 401(j) was itself dominantly punitive becomes inescapable.... Our conclusion from the legislative and judicial history is, therefore, that Congress in these sections decreed an additional punishment for the crime of draft avoidance in the special category of cases wherein the evader leaves the country. It cannot do this without providing the safeguards which must attend a criminal prosecution.

### V. Conclusion.

We conclude, for the reasons stated, that § 401(j) is punitive and as such cannot constitutionally stand, lacking as they do the procedural safeguards which the Constitution commands. We recognize that draft evasion, particularly in time of war, is a heinous offense, and should and can be properly punished. Dating back to Magna Carta, however, it has been an abiding principle governing the lives of civilized men that 'no freeman shall be taken or imprisoned or disseised or outlawed or exiled ... without the judgment of his peers or by the law of the land....' What we hold is only that, in keeping with this cherished tradition, punishment cannot be imposed 'without due process of law.' Any lesser holding would ignore the constitutional mandate upon which our essential liberties depend. Therefore the judgments of the District Courts in these cases are affirmed.

Affirmed.

## *Notes and Questions*

1. The Sixth Amendment of the Constitution states that:

> In all criminal prosecutions, the accused shall enjoy the right to a speedy and public trial, by an impartial jury ... and to be informed of the nature and cause of the accusation; to be confronted with the witnesses against him; to have compulsory process for obtaining witnesses in his favor, and to have the Assistance of Counsel for his defence.

When does the Sixth Amendment apply? Does it apply in civil actions such as those that arise as a result of a tort? Does it apply in administrative proceedings? Does it apply in immigration proceedings? What difference does it make if it applies or not?

2. The Federal Government in *Mendoza-Martínez* obviously believed that § 401(j) did not impose punishment. The Supreme Court concluded, however, that it did. Who gets to define what counts as punishment? How much deference should be given to Congress and the Executive in determining whether a sanction ought to be treated as imposing punishment?

3. The Supreme Court in *Mendoza-Martínez* cited a number of factors that courts must take into account when determining whether a statute should be considered penal or regulatory (i.e., non-penal). Nevertheless, it also stated that "[a]bsent conclusive evidence of congressional intent as to the penal nature of a statute, these factors must be considered in relation to the statute on its face." What does this mean? Imagine that when Congress enacted § 401 they had expressly stated that "deportation pursuant to this statute is not considered punishment." Would that have changed the outcome in *Mendoza-Martínez*? Suppose that instead of deporting certain immigrants, Congress holds that "immigrants who violate the terms of their stay shall be deprived of their freedom of movement for a term that does not exceed ten years." Furthermore, Congress states in this imaginary statute that "the deprivation of freedom pursuant to this statute is not punitive in nature." In light of *Mendoza-Martínez,* does a person who is faced with sanctions pursuant to this imaginary statute have a right to the procedural protections safeguarded by the Sixth Amendment? Why or why not?

4. More recently, in *Padilla v. Kentucky,* 130 Sup. Ct. 1473 (2010), the Supreme Court held that counsel must advise non-citizen clients of the deportation risks of entering a guilty plea in a criminal proceeding. The Government of Kentucky argued in *Padilla* that the defendant had no Sixth Amendment right to counsel because this right extends only to assistance of counsel related to criminal matters and that the "collateral consequences" of criminal convictions (e.g., disenfranchisement, loss of professional licenses, eviction from public housing, etc.) are not criminal matters that counsel is required to convey to the defendant. The Government further argued that deportation is a "collateral consequence" that is not a criminal matter and that, as a result, counsel did not have a duty to inform the defendant about such consequences. The Supreme Court rejected this argument stating that:

> We have long recognized that deportation is a particularly severe "penalty," but it is not, in a strict sense, a criminal sanction. Although removal proceed-

> ings are civil in nature, deportation is nevertheless intimately related to the criminal process. Our law has enmeshed criminal convictions and the penalty of deportation for nearly a century. And, importantly, recent changes in our immigration law have made removal nearly an automatic result for a broad class of noncitizen offenders. Thus, we find it "most difficult" to divorce the penalty from the conviction in the deportation context. Moreover, we are quite confident that noncitizen defendants facing a risk of deportation for a particular offense find it even more difficult.
>
> Deportation as a consequence of a criminal conviction is, because of its close connection to the criminal process, uniquely difficult to classify as either a direct or a collateral consequence. The collateral versus direct distinction is thus ill-suited to evaluating a[n] [assistance of counsel] claim concerning the specific risk of deportation. We conclude that advice regarding deportation is not categorically removed from the ambit of the Sixth Amendment right to counsel. [The right] applies to Padilla's claim. *Id.*

Did the Supreme Court hold in *Padilla* that deportation that results as a consequence of engaging in a criminal offense amounts to "punishment"? If so, why did the Court state that deportation "is not, in a strict sense, a criminal sanction"? If the Court did not hold that deportation is a criminal sanction, then why is it that the Sixth Amendment right to counsel applies in *Padilla*? After all, the Sixth Amendment applies only "in all criminal prosecutions." Review once more the factors cited by the Supreme Court in *Mendoza-Martínez* as relevant to determining whether a sanction is "penal" or "regulatory." In light of these factors, is deportation that results as a consequence of a criminal conviction a "penal" or "regulatory" sanction? Why? Should it matter?

## § 1.02 Distinguishing Punishment from Civil Sanctions: Model Penal Code

### Model Penal Code
### Section 1.04. Classes of Crime. Violations.

(5) An offense defined by this Code or by any other statute of this State constitutes a violation if it is so designated in this Code or in the law defining the offense or if no other sentence than a fine, or fine and forfeiture or other civil penalty is authorized upon conviction or if it is defined by a statute other than this Code that now provides that the offense shall not constitute a crime. A violation does not constitute a crime and a violation shall not give rise to any disability or legal disadvantage based on conviction of a criminal offense.

### *Notes and Questions*

1. The Model Penal Code distinguishes between penal and non-penal penalties primarily on the basis of the type of sanction that is imposed. If the sanction imposed is imprisonment or probation, the Code automatically treats the penalty as punishment, with all of the procedural consequences that such a finding entails. The drafters of the Code considered and rejected an approach that would authorize imprisonment as a possible consequence of certain non-penal violations. According to the drafters, "this approach

was rejected … in the view that imprisonment ought not to be available as a punitive sanction, unless the conduct that gives rise to it warrants the type of social condemnation that is and ought to be implicit in the concept of 'crime.'" MPC and Commentaries, § 1.04, p. 72.

Thus, the Code treats the severity of the penalty as essential to determining whether it should be considered penal or non-penal. The more severe the penalty, the more powerful the argument in favor of considering the sanction to be "penal" becomes. In the case of imprisonment, the severity is so apparent, that the Code automatically treats it as a crime.

2. The Code states that violations are "noncriminal offenses." Furthermore, it states that an offense is a noncriminal violation if only a fine "or other civil penalty is authorized" for its commission. But how are courts supposed to determine whether a given penalty is civil or not? Is, for example, deportation a civil penalty? The Code is silent with regard to this issue. Does this open the door to arguing that penalties other than imprisonment or probation may be severe enough as to not qualify as civil penalties? Perhaps the Code drafters assumed that any penalty other than imprisonment or probation is civil. Would this make sense? Why or why not?

3. In the Commentaries to the Code, the drafters state that imprisonment should only be authorized as a penalty if "the conduct that gives rise to it warrants the type of social condemnation that is and ought to be implicit in the concept of 'crime.'" What do the drafters mean by this? And what exactly is implicit in the "concept of crime"? Is there a concept of crime? If so, what are the defining features of the "concept of crime" and how can we distinguish between conducts that fit within the "concept of crime" and conducts that fall outside the "concept of crime"? Does the Model Penal Code provide any guidance with regard to how to identify the concept of crime?

## § 1.03 Distinguishing Punishment from Civil Sanctions: Recent Developments

### Smith v. Doe

Supreme Court of the United States, 2003
583 U.S. 84

Justice KENNEDY delivered the opinion of the Court.

The Alaska Sex Offender Registration Act requires convicted sex offenders to register with law enforcement authorities, and much of the information is made public. We must decide whether the registration requirement is a retroactive punishment prohibited by the *Ex Post Facto* Clause.

I.

A.

The State of Alaska enacted the Alaska Sex Offender Registration Act (Act) on May 12, 1994. Like its counterparts in other States, the Act is termed a "Megan's Law." Megan Kanka was a 7-year-old New Jersey girl who was sexually assaulted and murdered in 1994 by a neighbor who, unknown to the victim's family, had prior convictions for sex offenses against children. The crime gave impetus to laws for mandatory registration of sex offenders and corresponding community notification.... By 1996, every State, the District of Columbia, and the Federal Government had enacted some variation of Megan's Law.

B.

Respondents John Doe I and John Doe II were convicted of sexual abuse of a minor, an aggravated sex offense. Although convicted before the passage of the [sex offender registration] Act, respondents are covered by it.... Both respondents, along with respondent Jane Doe, wife of John Doe I, brought an action seeking to declare the Act void as to them under the *Ex Post Facto* Clause of Article I, § 10, cl. 1, of the Constitution and the Due Process Clause of § 1 of the Fourteenth Amendment. The United States District Court for the District of Alaska granted summary judgment for petitioners. In agreement with the District Court, the Court of Appeals for the Ninth Circuit determined the state legislature had intended the Act to be a nonpunitive, civil regulatory scheme; but, in disagreement with the District Court, it held the effects of the Act were punitive despite the legislature's intent. In consequence, it held the Act violates the *Ex Post Facto* Clause. We granted certiorari.

II.

This is the first time we have considered a claim that a sex offender registration and notification law constitutes retroactive punishment forbidden by the *Ex Post Facto* Clause. The framework for our inquiry, however, is well established. We must "ascertain whether the legislature meant the statute to establish 'civil' proceedings." *Kansas v. Hendricks,* 521 U.S. 346, 361, 117 S.Ct. 2072, 138 L.Ed.2d 501 (1997). If the intention of the legislature was to impose punishment, that ends the inquiry. If, however, the intention was to enact a regulatory scheme that is civil and nonpunitive, we must further examine whether the statutory scheme is "'so punitive either in purpose or effect as to negate [the State's] intention' to deem it 'civil.'" *Ibid.* Because we "ordinarily defer to the legislature's stated intent," "'only the clearest proof' will suffice to override legislative intent and transform what has been denominated a civil remedy into a criminal penalty."

A.

Whether a statutory scheme is civil or criminal "is first of all a question of statutory construction." We consider the statute's text and its structure to determine the legislative objective. A conclusion that the legislature intended to punish would satisfy an *ex post facto* challenge without further inquiry into its effects, so considerable deference must be accorded to the intent as the legislature has stated it.

The courts "must first ask whether the legislature, in establishing the penalizing mechanism, indicated either expressly or impliedly a preference for one label or the other." Here, the Alaska Legislature expressed the objective of the law in the statutory text itself. The legislature found that "sex offenders pose a high risk of reoffending," and identified "protecting the public from sex offenders" as the "primary governmental interest" of the law. The legislature further determined that "release of certain information about sex offenders to public agencies and the general public will assist in protecting the public safety." As we observed in *Hendricks,* where we examined an *ex post facto* challenge to a postincarceration confinement of sex offenders, an imposition of restrictive measures on sex offenders adjudged to be dangerous is "a legitimate nonpunitive governmental objective and has been historically so regarded." In this case, as in *Hendricks,* "[n]othing on the face of the statute suggests that the legislature sought to create anything other than a civil ... scheme designed to protect the public from harm."

Respondents seek to cast doubt upon the nonpunitive nature of the law's declared objective by pointing out that the Alaska Constitution lists the need for protecting the public as one of the purposes of criminal administration. As the Court stated in *Flemming v. Nestor,* rejecting an *ex post facto* challenge to a law terminating benefits to deported aliens, where a legislative restriction "is an incident of the State's power to protect the health and safety of its citizens," it will be considered "as evidencing an intent to exercise that regulatory power, and not a purpose to add to the punishment." The Court repeated this principle in *89 Firearms,* upholding a statute requiring forfeiture of unlicensed firearms against a double jeopardy challenge. The Court observed that, in enacting the provision, Congress " 'was concerned with the widespread traffic in firearms and with their general availability to those whose possession thereof was contrary to the public interest.' " This goal was "plainly more remedial than punitive." These precedents instruct us that even if the objective of the Act is consistent with the purposes of the Alaska criminal justice system, the State's pursuit of it in a regulatory scheme does not make the objective punitive.

Other formal attributes of a legislative enactment, such as the manner of its codification or the enforcement procedures it establishes, are probative of the legislature's intent. In this case these factors are open to debate. The notification provisions of the Act are codified in the State's "Health, Safety, and Housing Code," § 18, confirming our conclusion that the statute was intended as a nonpunitive regulatory measure. The Act's registration provisions, however, are codified in the State's criminal procedure code, and so might seem to point in the opposite direction. These factors, though, are not dispositive. The location and labels of a statutory provision do not by themselves transform a civil remedy into a criminal one.

[Although the Act's registration provisions are codified in the code of criminal procedure], [t]he Act itself does not require the procedures adopted to contain any safeguards associated with the criminal process. That leads us to infer that the legislature envisioned the Act's implementation to be civil and administrative. By contemplating "distinctly civil procedures," the legislature "indicate[d] clearly that it intended a civil, not a criminal sanction."

We conclude, as did the District Court and the Court of Appeals, that the intent of the Alaska Legislature was to create a civil, nonpunitive regime.

B.

In analyzing the effects of the Act we refer to the seven factors noted in *Kennedy v. Mendoza-Martinez,* as a useful framework. These factors, which migrated into our *ex post facto* case law from double jeopardy jurisprudence, have their earlier origins in cases under the Sixth and Eighth Amendments, as well as the Bill of Attainder and the *Ex Post Facto* Clauses. Because the *Mendoza-Martinez* factors are designed to apply in various constitutional contexts, we have said they are "neither exhaustive nor dispositive," but are "useful guideposts." The factors most relevant to our analysis are whether, in its necessary operation, the regulatory scheme: has been regarded in our history and traditions as a punishment; imposes an affirmative disability or restraint; promotes the traditional aims of punishment; has a rational connection to a nonpunitive purpose; or is excessive with respect to this purpose.

A historical survey can be useful because a State that decides to punish an individual is likely to select a means deemed punitive in our tradition, so that the public will recognize it as such. The Court of Appeals observed that the sex offender registration and notification statutes "are of fairly recent origin," which suggests that the statute was not meant as a punitive measure, or, at least, that it did not involve a traditional means of punishing. Respondents argue, however, that the Act—and, in particular, its notification provisions—resemble shaming punishments of the colonial period.

Some colonial punishments indeed were meant to inflict public disgrace. Humiliated offenders were required "to stand in public with signs cataloguing their offenses." Hirsch, From Pillory to Penitentiary: The Rise of Criminal ***98** Incarceration in Early Massachusetts, 80 Mich. L.Rev. 1179, 1226 (1982). At times the labeling would be permanent: A murderer might be branded with an "M," and a thief with a "T." R. Semmes, Crime and Punishment in Early Maryland 35 (1938); see also Massaro, Shame, Culture, and American Criminal Law, 89 Mich. L.Rev. 1880, 1913 (1991). The aim was to make these offenders suffer "permanent stigmas, which in effect cast the person out of the community." ... Respondents contend that Alaska's compulsory registration and notification resemble these historical punishments, for they publicize the crime, associate it with his name, and, with the most serious offenders, do so for life.

Any initial resemblance to early punishments is, however, misleading. Punishments such as whipping, pillory, and branding inflicted physical pain and staged a direct confrontation between the offender and the public. Even punishments that lacked the corporal component, such as public shaming, humiliation, and banishment, involved more than the dissemination of information. They either held the person up before his fellow citizens for face-to-face shaming or expelled him from the community. By contrast, the stigma of Alaska's Megan's Law results not from public display for ridicule and shaming but from the dissemination of accurate information about a criminal record, most of which is already public. Our system does not treat dissemination of truthful information in furtherance of a legitimate governmental objective as punishment. On the contrary, our criminal law tradition insists on public indictment, public trial, and public imposition of sentence. Transparency is essential to maintaining public respect for the criminal justice system, ensuring its integrity, and protecting the rights of the accused. The publicity may cause adverse consequences for the convicted defendant, running from mild personal embarrassment to social ostracism. In contrast to the colonial shaming punishments, however, the State does not make the publicity and the resulting stigma an integral part of the objective of the regulatory scheme....

We next consider whether the Act subjects respondents to an "affirmative disability or restraint." *Mendoza-Martinez, supra.* Here, we inquire how the effects of the Act are felt by those subject to it. If the disability or restraint is minor and indirect, its effects are unlikely to be punitive.

The Act imposes no physical restraint, and so does not resemble the punishment of imprisonment, which is the paradigmatic affirmative disability or restraint. The Act's obligations are less harsh than the sanctions of occupational debarment, which we have held to be nonpunitive. *See ibid.* (forbidding further participation in the banking industry); *De Veau v. Braisted,* 363 U.S. 144, 80 S.Ct. 1146, 4 L.Ed.2d 1109 (1960) (forbidding work as a union official); *Hawker v. New York,* 170 U.S. 189, 18 S.Ct. 573, 42 L.Ed. 1002 (1898) (revocation of a medical license). The Act does not restrain activities sex offenders may pursue but leaves them free to change jobs or residences....

... [With regard to the purpose of the Act], The State concedes that the statute might deter future crimes. Respondents seize on this proposition to argue that the law is punitive, because deterrence is one purpose of punishment. This proves too much. Any number of governmental programs might deter crime without imposing punishment. "To hold that the mere presence of a deterrent purpose renders such sanctions 'criminal'... would severely undermine the Government's ability to engage in effective regulation."

The Court of Appeals was incorrect to conclude that the Act's registration obligations were retributive because "the length of the reporting requirement appears to be measured by the extent of the wrongdoing, not by the extent of the risk posed." The Act, it is true, differentiates between individuals convicted of aggravated or multiple offenses and those convicted of a single nonaggravated offense. The broad categories, however, and the corresponding length of the reporting requirement, are reasonably related to the danger of recidivism, and this is consistent with the regulatory objective.

The Act's rational connection to a nonpunitive purpose is a "[m]ost significant" factor in our determination that the statute's effects are not punitive. As the Court of Appeals acknowledged, the Act has a legitimate nonpunitive purpose of "public safety, which is advanced by alerting the public to the risk of sex offenders in their communit[y]." ...

Our examination of the Act's effects leads to the determination that respondents cannot show, much less by the clearest proof, that the effects of the law negate Alaska's intention to establish a civil regulatory scheme. The Act is nonpunitive, and its retroactive application does not violate the *Ex Post Facto* Clause. The judgment of the Court of Appeals for the Ninth Circuit is reversed, and the case is remanded for further proceedings consistent with this opinion.

*It is so ordered.*

## *Notes and Questions*

1. Many state courts have been asked to decide whether statutes requiring registration of released sex offenders may be applied retroactively to persons who committed sex offenses before the registration statutes were enacted. Like the Supreme Court in *Smith*, most state courts have decided that such statutes may be applied retroactively because they are not "penal" in nature. *See, e.g., People v. Picklesimer*, 48 Cal. 4th 330 (2010). Do you agree? Why or why not?

2. The *Smith* case demonstrates that the factors enumerated in *Mendoza-Martínez* for distinguishing between penal and regulatory laws are still relevant forty years after they were first put forth by the Supreme Court. Did you find the factors useful in determining whether sex registration laws are penal or civil? Which factors do you find more useful? Which do you find less useful? Why?

3. As the Court points out in *Smith*, determining whether a statute is penal or civil is relevant in many contexts. As *Mendoza-Martínez* illustrates, the civil or penal nature of the statute is important to Sixth Amendment right to counsel claims. It is also important—as in *Smith*—to *ex post facto* claims, given that the Constitution only bars the retroactive application of penal statutes. The penal-civil distinction is also important for double jeopardy purposes, for a person may not be criminally prosecuted twice for the same offense, but she may be tried both in civil court and in criminal court for the same offense. Think, for example, of the O.J. Simpson case, in which his acquittal in the criminal case did not bar him from being tried for the same conduct in a civil case.

4. The Court in *Smith* points out that the "act imposes no physical restraint, and so does not resemble the punishment of imprisonment, which is the paradigmatic affirmative disability or restraint." It would appear, then, that statutes that impose deprivation of freedom as a penalty are more likely to be considered penal than statutes that impose penalties that do not amount to physical restraints. What does this remind you of?

Nevertheless, in *Kansas v. Hendricks*, 521 U.S. 346 (1997), the Supreme Court decided that a Kansas statute that authorized the involuntary commitment of persons who due to a personality disorder or mental abnormality were "likely to engage in predatory acts of sexual violence" was not "penal" in nature and could thus be applied retroactively to involuntarily commit people who had engaged in sexual offenses before the passage of the act. Although commitment under the Kansas statute was potentially indefinite, the Supreme Court argued that such physical restraint did not amount to punishment because:

> [T]he mere fact that a person is detained does not inexorably lead to the conclusion that the government has imposed punishment. The State may take measures to restrict the freedom of the dangerously mentally ill. This is a legitimate non-punitive governmental objective and has been historically so regarded. The Court has, in fact, cited the confinement of "mentally unstable individuals who present a danger to the public" as one classic example of nonpunitive detention. If detention for the purpose of protecting the community from harm *necessarily* constituted punishment, then all involuntary civil commitments would have to be considered punishment. But we have never so held. *Id.*

Do you agree with the Supreme Court's analysis? Why or why not? Does the Kansas statute create a "crime" according to § 1.04(5) of the Model Penal Code?

5. Respondents in *Smith* argued that sex registration statutes are penal because they impose "shaming" sanctions and shaming sanctions have historically been considered punitive. While acknowledging that shaming sanctions are often considered punitive even if they do not involve the imposition of physical restraint, the Supreme Court rejected respondents' argument contending that the purpose of sex registration laws is not to shame or humiliate offenders, but rather to disseminate truthful information that the public can use to protect itself against potentially dangerous individuals. Do you agree with the Supreme Court that the primary purpose of sex registration laws is not to shame sex offenders? Why are shaming laws often considered punitive even when no physical restraint is imposed and no fine is levied against the offender?

## § 1.04. Distinguishing Punishment from Civil Sanctions: Comparative Perspectives

### Judgment of the Spanish Constitutional Court 32/1987

March, 1987

[Defendant was arrested in December, 1984 and was charged with several counts of falsifying documents. Defendant was subsequently committed awaiting trial. Six months after his commitment, defendant asked for his release citing a statute that authorized pretrial detention for a term not exceeding six months. The trial court denied his request, pointing out that subsequent to his arrest, the Spanish legislature enacted a law that authorized a two year term of pretrial detention for persons charged with felonies. The defendant appealed to the Spanish Constitutional Court alleging that retroactively applying the law that extends pretrial detention terms from 6 months to 2 years violates the *ex post facto* protections safeguarded by the Spanish Constitution. The state opposed defendant's motion stating, among other things, that laws governing the pretrial detention terms are not part of the "substantive criminal law", as they do not impact the defendant's punishment. Therefore, the state argued that they could be retroactively applied to the defendant. The Spanish Constitutional Court reasoned as follows:]....

In deciding the matter before us, it is necessary to reiterate ... that judicial decisions about pretrial detention are of great import, given that they have the potential of restraining defendant's freedom of movement. Therefore, such decisions have the potential of limiting defendant's constitutional right to liberty protected by virtue of Art. 17 of the Spanish Constitution.

As a result, this Court cannot agree with those who argue that decisions related to pretrial detention amount to a mere procedural step in the criminal trial without taking into account that such decisions may impact defendant's freedom of movement....

A non-formalist analysis of laws governing pretrial detention [reveals why such laws form part of the substantive criminal law]. The analysis draws upon the analogy between judicial decrees ordering the defendant to undergo pretrial detention and judicial decrees sentencing the defendant to serve time in prison as punishment. Both of these judicial determinations impact the defendant's freedom in the same way—negatively ... The law takes these similarities into account by establishing in Art. 33 of the Penal Code that "the term of pretrial detention served by the defendant must be subtracted from the term of imprisonment imposed by the sentencing judge."

In light of these arguments, we must decide the case in a way that is favorable to the accused. The judgment of the court of first instance is reversed.

## *Notes and Questions*

1. At first glance, pretrial detention is not punishment. However, the Spanish Constitutional Court argues that pretrial detention is similar enough to punishment to warrant treating it as if it were punishment for the purposes of the constitutional prohibition of *ex post facto* laws. After all, argues the Court, time served pursuant to pretrial detention is subtracted from the time that is to be served pursuant to a conviction. Do you agree with the Court's argument? Why or why not?

2. Do you think the Supreme Court of the United States would decide this case in the same way as the Spanish Constitutional Court? Why or why not?

3. In *Hendricks,* the Supreme Court of the United States concluded that involuntary confinement of those who suffer personality disorders and are likely to engage in predatory acts of sexual violence does not amount to punishment. It was essential to this holding that, according to the Court, the chief purpose of such statutes is not punitive. In other words, it is not to exact retribution or to deter individuals from engaging in similar conduct in the future. Rather, the main purpose of such statutes is to protect society from dangerous individuals. What is the main purpose of involuntarily confining someone pursuant to pretrial detention? If the purpose of doing so is not punitive, why do American and foreign jurisdictions invariably subtract time served during pretrial detention from the time that is to be served pursuant to a criminal conviction?

4. Suppose that a person is involuntarily confined pursuant to the Kansas statute discussed in *Hendricks.* Also assume that the person was judged to be likely to engage in predatory acts of sexual violence because she molested a seven-year-old child. Subsequently, the person is criminally charged and convicted of sexually assaulting the child. During the sentencing hearing, the defense argues that the court should subtract the thirty-six months that the defendant has been involuntarily committed pursuant to the Kansas statute from the term of imprisonment that she is now required to serve in light of her conviction. Do you agree with the defense? Why or why not?

## § 1.05 Distinguishing Punishment from Civil Sanctions: Scholarly Debates

### H.L.A. Hart, *Punishment and Responsibility*

pages 4–5 (Oxford, 1967, reprint 2008)
Reprinted by courtesy of the Editor of the Aristotelian Society:
© 1959

... I shall define the standard or central case of 'punishment' in terms of five elements:

(i) It must involve pain or other consequences normally considered unpleasant.

(ii) It must be for an offence against legal rules.

(iii) It must be for an actual or supposed offender for his offence.

(iv) It must be intentionally administered by human beings other than the offender.

(v) It must be imposed and administered by an authority constituted by a legal system against which the offense is committed....

### Joel Feinberg, *The Expressive Function of Punishment*

The Monist, *49: 397–423 (1965)*

... Recent influential articles have quite sensibly distinguished between questions of definition and justification [of punishment], between justifying general rules and particular decisions, between moral and legal guilt. So much is all to the good. When these articles go on to *define* "punishment," however, it seems to many that they leave out of their ken altogether the very element that makes punishment theoretically puzzling and morally disquieting. *Punishment is defined in effect as the infliction of hard treatment by an authority on a person for his prior failing in some respect (usually an infraction of a rule or command).* There may be a very general sense of the word "punishment" which is well expressed by this definition; but even if that is so, we can distinguish a narrower, more emphatic sense that slips through its meshes. Imprisonment at hard labor for committing a felony is a clear case of punishment in the emphatic sense. But I think we would be less willing to apply that term to parking tickets, offside penalties, sackings, flunkings and disqualifications. Examples of the latter sort *I propose to call penalties* (merely), so that I may inquire further what distinguishes punishment, in the strict and narrow sense that interests the moralist, from other kinds of penalties.

One method of answering this question is to focus one's attention on the class of non-punitive penalties in an effort to discover some clearly identifiable characteristic common to them all, and absent from all punishments, on which the distinction between the two might be grounded. The hypotheses yielded by this approach, however, are not likely to survive close scrutiny. One might conclude, for example, that mere penalties are less severe than punishment, but although this is generally true, it is not necessarily and universally so....

Rather than look for a characteristic common and peculiar to penalties on which to ground the distinction between penalties and punishments, we would be better advised, I think, to turn our attention to the examples of punishments. Both penalties and punishments are authoritative deprivations for failures; but, apart from these common features, penalties have a miscellaneous character, whereas punishments have an important additional characteristic in common. That characteristic, or specific difference, I shall argue, is a certain expressive function: *punishment is a conventional device for expression of attitudes of resentment and indignation,* and of judgments of approval and reprobation, on the part either of the punishment authority himself or of those "in whose name" the punishment is inflicted. Punishment, in short, has a *symbolic significance* largely missing from other types of penalties....

## Leo Zaibert, *Punishment and Retribution*

pages 112–114 (Ashgate, 2006)

... Feinberg's seminal "The Expressive Function of Punishment" contains elements which might indicate that the expressiveness of punishment is wholly a definitional affair.... Feinberg, for example, claims that:

> A philosophical theory of punishment that, through inadequate definition, leaves out the condemnatory function of punishment not only will disappoint the moralist and the traditional moral philosopher; it will seem offensively irrelevant as well to the constitutional lawyer, whose vital concern is both conceptual, and therefore genuinely philosophical, as well as practically urgent.

In other words, Feinberg is interested in the exact definition of (State) punishment because only if we are clear about this can we understand the safeguards of citizens' rights regarding potential punitive abuses by the State. Many things are painful to endure, and yet they are clearly not punishment. What renders some painful treatments punishment, in Feinberg's view, is that they express some sort of moral condemnation that the State, on behalf of the community at large, is interested in conveying to the criminal. Indeed, some praise these sorts of expressivist accounts insofar as they seek not only to "capture the meaning of punishment, but also, but itself, even to justify the practice." Yet, it is precisely this amalgam of definition and justification that is one of my main targets of criticism throughout this book.

I would like to contrast Feinberg's expressionist views with my own view regarding an irreducible emotional component in punishment. The basic difference between my account an Feinberg's is that I require that the punisher *feel* a certain indignation as a result of the instance of wrongdoing which she wishes to punish, but Feinberg requires that the punisher *communicate* this feeling.... [As a result] Feinberg claims that if the physical unpleasantness that the state inflicts upon a citizen is not meant to communicate moral condemnation then it simply is not punishment....

Feinberg ... explicitly denies [that some instances of harsh treatment are punishment], in the context of his discussion of the consequences of the Subversive Drivers Act of 1961, which, as Feinberg relates, prescribed the "suspension and revocation of the driver's license of anyone ... convicted ... of advocating the overthrow of the Federal government." And while Feinberg is aware of the potential abuse of this sort of practice, he nevertheless admits that, "strictly speaking, they [the victims of cruel laws] have not been *punished*; they have been treated much worse."

Pragmatically speaking, the most problematic aspect of Feinberg's view is that it opens up the possibility for the State to inflict painful treatment upon its citizens, a treatment which is usually "much worse than punishment", but for which the citizens have fewer defenses than they would if they had been "merely" punished....

... Contra Feinberg, and according to my definition of punishment, I am happy to admit that those convicted by the Subversive Drivers Act were *punished* by the State; and punished "strictly speaking", provided that either a government agent or a segment of the population feels some sort of indignation as a result of the actions exhibiting the punishee's desire to overthrow the government.

## *Notes and Questions*

1. According to H.L.A. Hart, a sanction counts as punishment only if it is imposed for "an offence against legal rules." While at first glance this feature of punishment might seem obvious, it amounts to a significant insight. It is important to distinguish between two interrelated but ultimately different questions. On the one hand, we may ask, "What is punishment imposed for?" A standard answer to this question—one inspired by Hart's musings on the subject—would be that an offense is imposed *for* the violation of a legal rule. This question asks about the conditions that *trigger* the imposition of punishment. And punishment is triggered by a violation of a rule, not by a desire to exact retribution or to deter or any other reason. On the other hand, one might ask "what is the purpose of punishment?" Unlike the former question, this query cannot be answered solely by pointing out that a legal rule has been violated. In addition to this, the answer to the question requires an explanation as to why the violation of the legal rule is relevant. The violation of the rule may signal, for example, the need to exact retribution. It may also signal a need to deter others from engaging in the same conduct or the offender from recidivating. Keep in mind the distinction between these two questions when you go over the materials in the next chapter. For more on this distinction, see George P. Fletcher, *What is Punishment Imposed For?*, 5 Journal of Contemporary Legal Issues 101 (1994) and Luis E. Chiesa, *Normative Gaps in the Criminal Law*, 10 New Crim. L. Rev. 102 (2007).

2. Review the different cases featured in this chapter. Was deportation in *Mendoza-Martínez* a sanction imposed for the violation of legal rules? Was the sex offender registration requirement in *Smith* imposed for the violation of a legal rule? What about the type of involuntary commitment at issue in *Hendricks*? Is pretrial detention imposed for the violation of a legal rule? Do you believe that focusing on whether the sanction is imposed for the violation of a legal rule as a way of distinguishing punishment from civil penalties is better than approaching the issue by applying the laundry list of factors cited by the Supreme Court in *Mendoza-Martínez* and *Smith*? Why or why not?

3. For Feinberg, the central feature of punishment is that it expresses or communicates moral condemnation. In contrast, nonpunitive penalties such as receiving a ticket for driving with a burned-out tail light or flunking a student on a test because she did not perform well do not express moral condemnation. While we might think that the driver should perhaps better maintain his vehicle or that the student should study more for her test, we do not think that the sanctions imposed communicate moral condemnation of the conduct or of the actors involved. At best, they might be bad drivers or car owners or bad students, but certainly not immoral people.

4. Does the deportation of a person express moral condemnation? Does requiring a sex offender to register certain information in a public document communicate moral condemnation? What about civil commitment? Pretrial detention? Do you believe that focusing on whether the sanction expresses moral condemnation as a way of distinguishing punishment from civil sanctions is better than approaching the issue by applying the laundry list of factors cited by the Supreme Court in *Mendoza-Martínez* and *Smith*? Why or why not?

5. Zaibert correctly points out that Feinberg's expressive dimension of punishment might be relevant to both defining punishment and to elucidating the purpose of pun-

ishment. On the one hand, Feinberg's theory might be construed to hold that in order for a sanction to count as punishment its imposition *must* express moral condemnation. If it does not, the sanction is simply not punishment. On the other hand, Feinberg's theory might be construed to hold that the proper purpose of punishment is to communicate that certain conduct and certain actors are worthy of moral condemnation.

6. Taken as a way of defining punishment, Zaibert takes issue with Feinberg's expressive theory of punishment. Why must a sanction express condemnation in order to count as punishment? Perhaps the imposition of certain types of sanctions should always count as punishment as long as they are imposed for a violation of legal rules (Hart). This might be the case with imprisonment. Regardless of whether the offender's imprisonment communicates moral condemnation, there might be good reasons to consider imprisonment that is imposed for the violation of a legal rule as an instance of punishment.

7. For Zaibert, a sanction that is imposed for the violation of a legal rule counts as punishment as long as the person who punishes or some segment of the population feels some sort of indignation as a result of the offender's conduct. Note that this is a subtly different view than Feinberg's. For Feinberg, the act of punishing must communicate or express condemnation to others. In contrast, for Zaibert the act of punishment need not express condemnation to others. It suffices that someone feels indignation as a result of the conduct that triggers punishment. In principle, such indignation may be felt even if it is not communicated to others. Think, for example, of a person who punishes her friend by refusing to talk to her again. Even if the friend (and others) do not understand why this silent treatment is meted out, it might still count as punishment as long as the punisher feels indignation at whatever conduct triggered the silent response. Similarly, a state might secretly punish someone without ever making such punishment public. Under Zaibert's account, these cases can count as punishment even if they are not designed to communicate anything, as long as the punisher feels indignation at the conduct that triggered the imposition of punishment. This might be the case, for example, with deportation. While deportation may not necessarily express moral condemnation of the conduct that gave rise to the sanction, it may very well be the case that the person who metes out the sanction or some segment of the population feels indignation toward the conduct that triggered the penalty. This might be enough to consider the sanction imposed to be punishment. See, for example, Leo Zaibert, *Uprootedness as (Cruel and Unusual) Punishment,* 11 New Crim. L. Rev. 384 (2008).

Still, is it possible to go beyond this? Can you imagine instances of punishment in which no indignation is aroused? Perhaps this is possible if you believe that the sole purpose of punishment is to deter future harmful conduct or to neutralize dangerous individuals. These and other purposes of punishment are discussed in the next chapter.

# Chapter 2

# Purposes of Punishment

## § 2.01 Purposes of Punishment: In General

### United States v. Irey

United States Court of Appeals, Eleventh Circuit, 2010
612 F.3d 1160

CARNES, Circuit Judge:

... The sentence that the district court imposed [in this case] is a clear error in judgment, a mistake, and it is our responsibility to "correct such mistakes when they occur." The sentence is substantively unreasonable primarily, but not solely, because of the nature and extent of William Irey's criminal conduct. The steady stream of criminal cases flowing through this Court brings us many examples of man's inhumanity to man, and we see a depressingly large number of crimes against children. But the sexual crimes that Irey committed against some of the most vulnerable children in the world set him apart. He raped, sodomized, and sexually tortured fifty or more little girls, some as young as four years of age, on many occasions over a four- or five-year period. He also scripted, cast, starred in, produced, and distributed worldwide some of the most graphic and disturbing child pornography that has ever turned up on the internet.

The horrific nature of Irey's crimes resulted in an adjusted offense level that would have led to an advisory [sentencing] guidelines range of life imprisonment. Because the government had charged all of Irey's crimes in just one count, the statutory maximum was 30 years and that had the effect of reducing the guidelines range to 30 years as well. The district court, however, did not impose that sentence. Instead, after deciding that pedophilia was an "illness" that had impaired Irey's volition, and pronouncing that Irey himself was a victim, like all of the little children he had sexually violated for so long, the district court deviated downward from the 30-year guidelines range and imposed a sentence of only 17½ years. Our duty to set aside unreasonable sentences requires that we set aside this one.

#### I. The Criminal Conduct

William Irey had a seemingly insatiable sexual appetite.... Starting in 2001 Irey began spending two weeks out of every month in China on business. On the weekends when he was there he would indulge himself in more "sexually disordered behavior" by traveling to brothels in different Asian countries. Early on he went to a brothel in Cambodia that featured underage girls and discovered that he enjoyed having sex with children. Over a period of four or five years, he "visited numerous brothels where they had underage children." Irey, who is 5'10" and weighs 200 pounds, was in his forties at the time. All of the children he sexually abused were underage girls; none of them was older than sixteen, and some of them were only four, five, or six years old.

Irey went to those brothels and had sex with the children "many many times," as he recounted it, during his numerous trips to that part of the world, and as time went on he became "more and more obsessed and was returning to Asia more and more often" to sexually abuse children. He paid the Cambodian brothels up to $1,500 for the use of each child, and he would typically buy two or three of the children at a time. When he was too busy in China on business to get away for weekend visits to Cambodia, Irey would sometimes pay to have some of the young girls flown to him so that he could sexually abuse them when he found the time. Irey's sexual violation of the children did not end until August of 2006 when law enforcement in this country finally caught up with him....

[Defendant was convicted and sentenced by the trial court to a 17½ year term of imprisonment.]....

### IV. Our Review of the Reasonableness of the Sentence

... The United States appealed [the 17½ year sentence], contending that in view of the facts and circumstances the sentence was unreasonably light, amounting to an abuse of discretion....

### C. Substantive Unreasonableness

... The statutory minimum sentence applicable to this case is 15 years and the maximum is 30 years. The advisory guidelines range is 30 years, top and bottom. The district court deviated downward 12½ years to a sentence of 17½ years, which is only 2½ years above the statutory minimum. The downward variance was 42 percent. Whether considered in absolute or percentage terms, it is a "major" variance in the legal parlance of sentencing law....

The district court's clear error in judgment becomes apparent when all of the facts and circumstances are considered in light of the § 3553(a) factors [that are supposed to guide the District Court's discretion in sentencing]. What § 3553(a) requires is "a sentence sufficient, but not greater than necessary, to comply with the purposes set forth in paragraph (2)" of that subsection....

We turn now to the sentencing factors set out in § 3553(a).24

#### 1. Section 3553(a)(1)

The first listed factor—it is actually two factors in one—that a district court must consider in sentencing, and that a court of appeals must consider in reviewing the sentence for substantive reasonableness, is "the nature and circumstances of the offense and the history and characteristics of the defendant." 18 U.S.C. § 3553(a)(1). To a large extent "the nature and circumstances of the offense" component of this factor overlaps with the next listed consideration, which is "the need for the sentence imposed—to reflect the seriousness of the offense, to promote respect for the law, and to provide just punishment for the offense," *id.* § 3553(a)(2)(A). For that reason, we will postpone some of our discussion of the nature and circumstances of the offense component of (a)(1) until we take up the (a)(2)(A) offense-related factor in the next section....

#### b. The "Illness" of Pedophilia

... [T]he district court insisted on describing Irey as suffering from the "illness" of pedophilia, while the two defense experts described it as a "treatable disorder." The district court found that because he suffered from pedophilia: "Mr. Irey's acts that bring him here today, I think it's safe to say, were not purely volitional. I think they were due in substantial part to a recognized illness. And while it does not excuse his conduct and he will be held accountable for it, I think it would be inappropriate to ignore that fact."

The record does not support the district court's finding that because he is a pedophile Irey could not much help raping, sodomizing, and sexually torturing little children, posing them as trophies, and smiling while he did it. The record actually contradicts that finding. Dr. Berlin reported: "Although it is not his fault that he has the disorder [of pedophilia], it is his responsibility to do something about it."...

The undisputed fact is that Irey was perfectly capable of not sexually abusing children where the risk of detection and punishment was high, which is why he consciously chose to commit his crimes against children halfway around the globe in a third world country where there was little or no risk from law enforcement. Irey's self-restraint when it was in his own best interest not to indulge his lust for children proves that his volition was not impaired to any extent worthy of weight in sentencing....

While in this country Irey refrained from committing any crimes against children, never once touching an American child in an inappropriate way, and instead consorted with adult prostitutes. It was while in Cambodia, where he could get away with sexually violating children, that he did it so "many many times." And he acted with cunning....

There is no sense in which reasonable people could view Garcia's pedophilia as morally mitigating of guilt, any more than reasonable people would find a defendant's uncontrollable compulsion to commit incest or eat human flesh "mitigating."...

### *2.* Section 3553(a)(2)(A)

... The second factor that a district court must consider in sentencing, and that a court of appeals must consider in reviewing the sentence for substantive reasonableness, is "the need for the sentence imposed ... to reflect the seriousness of the offense, to promote respect for the law, and to provide just punishment for the offense." 18 U.S.C. § 3553(a)(2)(A). This requirement extends beyond, but also overlaps to some extent with, the "nature and circumstances of the offense" component of § 3553(a)(1).

The § 3553(a)(2)(A) consideration is the "just deserts" concept, which carries the need for retribution, the need to make the punishment fit the crime, and the need not just to punish but to punish justly. In *Pugh* we quoted from the Senate Report regarding this provision:

> This purpose—essentially the "just deserts" concept—should be reflected clearly in all sentences; it is another way of saying that the sentence should reflect the gravity of the defendant's conduct. From the public's standpoint, the sentence should be of a type and length that will adequately reflect, among other things, the harm done or threatened by the offense, and the public interest in preventing a recurrence of the offense. From the defendant's standpoint the sentence should not be unreasonably harsh under all the circumstances of the case and should not differ substantially from the sentence given to another similarly situated defendant convicted of a similar offense under similar circumstances.

Because the punishment should fit the crime, the more serious the criminal conduct is the greater the need for retribution and the longer the sentence should be. The seriousness of a crime varies directly with the harm it causes or threatens. It follows that the greater the harm the more serious the crime, and the longer the sentence should be for the punishment to fit the crime. As we have stated before, "[c]hild sex crimes are among the most egregious and despicable of societal and criminal offenses." And Irey's criminal conduct, as we stated at the beginning, is virtually unparalleled in a "most egregious and despicable" field of crime. This circuit has seen few, if any, other criminals who have over such a long time span raped, sodomized, and tortured so many children, some of whom were very young, and all of whom were among the most helpless people in the world. Irey, a 200-pound man, subjected his helpless young victims not just to sexual intercourse but also to anal and oral sodomy and to sexual torture that went far beyond the heartland of depravity even for child molesters. Irey treated his child victims as objects, as his toys, which he bought and then did with as he pleased. He smiled as they cried out in pain. As if that were not enough, Irey also photographed and video recorded his debauchery and distributed it on the internet, thereby guaranteeing that the record of it would outlast him and all of us, inspiring other child molesters to commit crimes against children....

To be sure, the district court did describe the crime as "horrific," the victims as "numerous," and "perhaps the most vulnerable of the world's society," and it did state that it was "an offense that rises to the very top in terms of its seriousness and its effect on other human beings" who "may never, never overcome their abuse." The court also, in an incredible understatement, said that "the characteristics of the offense, the seriousness of it itself, the long-standing, long-term engagement in it certainly *does not mitigate in favor of any leniency*" (emphasis added). But the court then proceeded to show leniency anyway, in this worst of the worst crimes, by varying downward from the guidelines range by 12½ years to a sentence of 17½ years, which is only 2½ years above the statutory minimum. *See Irey*, 563 F.3d at 1227 (Hill, J., concurring) (noting how far the sentence was from the maximum and how close to the minimum).

The 17½-year sentence, if all of it were to be served, would amount to only 4 months and a week for each of the 50 distinguishable victims that Irey raped, sodomized, or sexually tortured. In light of 18 U.S.C. § 3624, Irey will likely serve only 15 years and 3 months of his sentence, which works out to less than four months for each of those 50 victims who can be distinguished from each other in the images that show some of Irey's crimes. And that calculation does not include any time for Irey's additional criminal behavior of producing and distributing the massive amount of extremely graphic child pornography. Four months per child raped, sodomized, or tortured is grossly unreasonable. In sentencing there should be no quantity discount for the sexual abuse of children.

### 3. Section 3553(a)(2)(B)

The third factor that a district court must consider in sentencing, and that a court of appeals must consider in reviewing the sentence for substantive reasonableness, is "the need for the sentence imposed ... to afford adequate deterrence to criminal conduct." *Id.* § 3553(a)(2)(B). The sentencing judge in this case referred to this important sentencing purpose as one ... that [is] "essentially are subjective in nature." He did say that "a serious sentence is hopefully going to deter others from conducting similar affairs," but then expressed his view that "when we're dealing with an illness like this, I'm not sure that that rationally follows." Even though the judge said that "nevertheless, deterrence is an appropriate consideration," it is apparent that his idiosyncratic doubts about whether pedophiles could be deterred from committing crimes involving the sexual abuse of children and child pornography affected the weight he gave to this important § 3553(a) factor.

The sentencing judge's skepticism about deterring these types of crimes is not shared by Congress, the Sentencing Commission, the Supreme Court, this Court, or other courts of appeals.

Far from questioning the value of deterrence, in *Pugh* we held that the deterrence objective of sentencing is "particularly compelling in the child pornography context." We explained that imposing a lighter sentence on one convicted of a child pornography offense "tends to undermine the purpose of general deterrence, and in turn, tends to increase (in some palpable if unmeasurable way) the child pornography market." The problem of a missed opportunity for deterrence, we observed, is compounded when the crime involves not just possession but also distribution of child pornography....

The defendant in *United States v. Goldberg* ... had been convicted of possessing child pornography and the guidelines range was 63 to 78 months. The district court varied downward to impose only a nominal prison sentence to be followed by a decade of supervised release. The Seventh Circuit reversed the sentence as substantively unreasonable ... The court explained why deterrence was so important in crimes involving the sexual abuse of children, including child pornography crimes:

> Young children were raped in order to enable the production of the pornography that the defendant both downloaded and uploaded—both consumed himself and disseminated to others. The greater the customer demand for child pornography, the more that will be produced. Sentences influence behavior, or so at least Congress thought when in18 U.S.C. § 3553(a) it made deterrence a statutory sentencing factor. The logic of deterrence suggests that the lighter the punishment for downloading and uploading child pornography, the greater the customer demand for it and so the more will be produced.

We would add that in this case not only were young children raped in the course of producing child pornography, but Irey is the one who actually did the raping.

The more serious the crime and the greater the defendant's role in it, the more important it is to send a strong and clear message that will deter others. In sentencing Irey the district court should not have under-weighed the § 3553(a)(2)(B) adequate deterrence factor based on a conclusory statement of its personal subjective views ... questioning the value of deterrence in crimes involving the sexual abuse of children....

### 4. Section 3553(a)(2)(C)

... The fourth factor that a district court must consider in sentencing, and that a court of appeals must consider in reviewing the sentence for substantive reasonableness, is "the need for the sentence imposed ... to protect the public from further crimes of the defendant." 18 U.S.C. § 3553(a)(2)(C). This is the specific deterrence or incapacitation factor.

Dr. Berlin, the defense psychiatrist, did not rate the risk of Irey committing more crimes against children as low or high, but instead gave his opinion that if Irey was "shown mercy and given the opportunity, he will be able to re-enter society as a safe and productive citizen." Dr. Shaw's report was more descriptive of the risk. It revealed that under one method of assessing risk, the Static-99 method, Irey's score placed him in "the Medium-Low risk category for sexually re-offending." ... Irey's score on another instrument used to assess the risk of recidivism, the Minnesota Sex Offender Screening Tool-Revised, placed him in "the Moderate Risk Range." The Shaw report concluded that all of the risk assessment factors "suggest a moderate to low moderate risk of a new charge," which could "be reduced through continued treatment and informed supervision upon his release." ...

The district court credited the opinions of the two experts, which it re-characterized as Irey having "a low risk of recidivism." But then the court added: "Of course, all of that is somewhat academic because by the time he gets out of prison, he'll be most likely at an age where recidivism would be unlikely, just from a physiological standpoint."

At the completion of the sentence that the district court imposed on him ... Irey would be 65 years old. There is no support in the record for a finding that a 65-year-old male with what Dr. Shaw called "deviant interests," who has a record of not just raping and abusing children but also of sexually torturing them, is too old to do it again, thereby rendering concern about recidivism "academic." That is not what Dr. Shaw said about the aging process. He said, when talking about whether he would advise drug therapy for Irey when he was released, that as they age men are "going to have experienced a reduction naturally in testosterone and a reduction in sex drive." That is different from saying that pedophiles in their sixties lose interest in sexually abusing children or are physically incapable of doing so. No one testified that the risk of recidivism is "academic" for a pedophile in his sixties or seventies, probably because that simply is not true....

[Furthermore,] supervised release is no guarantee that a criminal will not commit more crimes when he gets out of prison.

Part of the problem may be understaffing and the resulting high case loads of those who have the responsibility of doing the supervising ... The nationwide situation was summed up by Dr. Berlin (the same one who evaluated Irey for purposes of this case), when he testified before Congress that: "Many of these parole and probation people are stretched very thin. I think we want to be able to have them have smaller case loads." ...

Regardless of why so many convicted criminals on supervised release, including sex offenders, commit new crimes, the fact is that they do. Supervised release is better than unsupervised release, but it does not offer society the level of protection from a convicted criminal that incarceration does. Despite that undeniable fact, the district court found that Irey, one of the worst sex offenders ever prosecuted in this circuit, had a low risk of recidivism, or would pose a low risk when released at the end of the reduced sentence it imposed on him....

The district court imposed not one extra month over the statutory minimum for the purpose of protecting society and its children from further crimes by Irey, stating: "I don't think society needs further protection from him, at least beyond the statutory minimum sentence." Given the magnitude of the harm that will occur if Irey does commit more sexual crimes against children, that was a clear error in judgment....

### 7. What "It Comes Down To"

After discussing [the abovementioned] factors, the district court said [that the sentence imposed] "... comes down to my view of what promotes respect for the law and provides just punishment." The district court was right about the importance of the § 3553(a)(2)(A) factor, which requires consideration of the need for the sentence imposed "to reflect the seriousness of the offense, to promote respect for the law, and to provide just punishment for the offense." But the court was wrong, it committed a clear error in judgment, in deciding that those purposes could be served by a major downward variance to a point closer to the statutory minimum sentence than it is to the guidelines range. The district court's leap from the advisory guidelines sentence of 30 years down to a just-above-minimum sentence of 17½ years does not reflect the seriousness of and provide just punishment for Irey's rape, sodomy, and sexual torture of at least fifty children, acts that he committed "many many times" over a four- or five-year period, and his production and distribution of one of the worst series of child pornography on the internet. Nor does it promote respect for the law.

For all of the reasons we have explained, no downward variance from the guidelines range is reasonable in this case. Nothing less than the advisory guidelines sentence of 30 years, which is the maximum available, will serve the sentencing purposes set out in§ 3553(a)....

[W]e vacate the sentence the district court imposed and remand with instructions that the defendant is to be resentenced within the guidelines range.

## *Notes and Questions*

1. In an Opinion dissenting and concurring in part, Judge Tjoflat explained in *Irey* that the role of the courts of appeals in sentencing has varied widely throughout our history:

> Prior to the American Revolution, colonial courts fashioned sentences with three basic purposes in mind: to punish the offender for his crime, thereby satisfying society's desire for retribution; to deter others from committing the same crime by demonstrating its disadvantageous consequences ("general deterrence"); and to incapacitate the wrongdoer, so as to protect society from further criminal activity ("specific deterrence" or "incapacitation").
>
> In the 1800s, penological experts became "dissatisfied with the failure of prisons to rehabilitate inmates," and rehabilitation became a fourth basic purpose of sentencing. The American tradition thus embraced four purposes of sentencing—[retribution], general deterrence, specific deterrence, and rehabilitation; this tradition has continued to the present day.
>
> An early model of sentencing that combined these four purposes was the "medical model," so named because penological experts believed that proper measures taken during imprisonment could "cure" offenders, allowing them to reenter society as productive members. Accordingly, rehabilitation received more weight than the other three purposes of sentencing under the medical model. Under the medical model, sentencing responsibilities were divided between the district court and the Parole Board. District courts imposed indeterminate sentences that were monitored by a Parole Board, meaning that a judge would impose a sentence that had a minimum term of confinement and a maximum term of confinement, but "allow[ed for] the possibility of release sometime between the expiration of those terms[, with] the date and conditions of release before the maximum term" determined by the Parole Board.
>
> District courts fashioned the minimum and maximum bounds of the sentence in accordance with the four traditional purposes of sentencing.... Although the district court set the bounds of the sentence, the Parole Board was given discretion to determine when a prisoner ha[d] reached that point in his rehabilitation process at which he should be released under supervision to begin his readjustment to life in the community....
>
> The courts of appeals, on the other hand, had virtually no role under the medical model. So long as the sentence was within statutory limits, it "was, for all practical purposes, not reviewable on appeal." *Id.*

While rehabilitation was fashionable in the first half of the 20th century, it started coming under attack during the latter half of the century. This led to a rethinking of sentencing procedures and—ultimately—to a restructuring of the role of district courts and courts of appeals in sentencing. Judge Tjoflat's concurring and dissenting opinion summarizes this evolution:

By the 1970s, the medical model was falling out of favor. Congress had come to reject the medical model's core premise—that prison sentences could rehabilitate offenders—as well as its unfair results. Offenders who committed the same crime served wildly different sentences because of the district courts' unfettered discretion and because the Parole Board determined how much of a sentence would actually be served.

To address the vices of the medical model—mainly unwarranted sentencing disparity—Congress enacted the SRA [Sentencing Reform Act], which codified the traditional purposes of sentencing as the need for the sentence imposed—

(A) to reflect the seriousness of the offense, to promote respect for the law, and to provide just punishment for the offense;

(B) to afford adequate deterrence to criminal conduct;

(C) to protect the public from further crimes of the defendant; and

(D) to provide the defendant with needed educational or vocational training, medical care, or other correctional treatment in the most effective manner.

18 U.S.C. § 3553(a)(2).

These factors mapped onto [retribution], general deterrence, specific deterrence, and rehabilitation, respectively. Unlike under the medical model, however, rehabilitation was no longer the dominant concern; in fact, while rehabilitation could be a relevant factor in sentencing, it could not drive a prison sentence. 18 U.S.C. § 3582(a) (directing that the court, when considering a prison sentence, recognize that "imprisonment is not an appropriate means of promoting correction and rehabilitation"). Congress feared that allowing the district court to fashion a sentence based on these purposes in each individual case would perpetuate the unwarranted sentencing disparity that plagued the medical model. Congress therefore created the United States Sentencing Commission and tasked it with devising sentencing guidelines that would dictate offenders' sentences. *Irey*, 612 F.3d 1160.

2. The District Court sentenced the defendant in *Irey* to 17 ½ years of imprisonment followed by a period of supervised release under stringent conditions. The Court of Appeals overturned the lower court's decision arguing that a harsher sentence was warranted. As a result, the Court of Appeals resentenced the defendant, imposing a sentence of 30 years of imprisonment. What sentence do you believe is more appropriate? Why?

3. The District Court argued that pedophilia might sometimes serve as a mitigating factor. In contrast, the Court of Appeals suggested that pedophilia might sometimes serve as an aggravating factor. Explain both the District Court and Court of Appeals views regarding pedophilia as an aggravating or mitigating factor. Which view do you prefer?

4. The District Court argued that the sentence it imposed was adequate because the defendant would be 65 years old upon his release and at that age the risk of recidivism would be low, given that sexual urges diminish significantly with age. Do you agree? Why or why not?

5. A handful of states allow chemical castration as punishment for certain sexual offenders. In Florida, for example:

[T]he court:

(a) May sentence a defendant to be treated with medroxyprogesterone acetate (MPA) ... if the defendant is convicted of sexual battery ...

(b) Shall sentence a defendant to be treated with [chemical castration] ... if the defendant is convicted of sexual battery and the defendant has a prior conviction of sexual battery under.

If the court sentences a defendant to be treated with [chemical castration], the penalty may not be imposed in lieu of, or reduce, any other penalty ... However, in lieu of [chemical castration], the court may order the defendant to undergo physical castration upon written motion by the defendant providing the defendant's intelligent, knowing, and voluntary consent to physical castration as an alternative penalty. Florida Statutes Annotated § 794.0235

Assuming that castration suppresses or significantly reduces sexual urges, would the castration of defendants like *Irey* influence your intuitions regarding the appropriate punishment to be imposed? Should defendants who undergo castration be released earlier than those who do not? Why or why not?

6. After reading about the different theories of punishment, which theory do you believe better justifies punishment? Do you think that punishment should be imposed primarily for general or special deterrence (including rehabilitation or incapacitation)? Or do you think that punishment should be imposed primarily for desert-based retributive reasons, even when general or special deterrence reasons militate against punishment? Answer this question again when you finish reading the Chapter.

## § 2.02 Purposes of Punishment: Model Penal Code

### Model Penal Code (First Draft) Section 1.02(2). Purposes.

(2) The general purposes of the provisions governing the sentencing and treatment of offenders are:

(a) to prevent the commission of offenses;

(b) to promote the correction and rehabilitation of offenders;

(c) to safeguard offenders against excessive, disproportionate or arbitrary punishment;

(d) to give fair warning of the nature of the sentences that may be imposed on conviction of an offense;

(e) to differentiate among offenders with a view to a just individualization in their treatment;

### *Notes and Questions*

1. The Model Penal Code originally adopted a "mixed" or "hybrid" theory of punishment that combines elements of deterrence and retribution (just deserts). Never-

theless, Subsection (1) makes it clear that the chief purpose of punishment under the Code is to prevent the commission of future offenses. That is, the Code is primarily concerned with achieving general and specific deterrence. In contrast, Subsection (2) guards against "disproportionate" sentences. This suggests that the punishment that is deserved according to retributive theory may serve as the ceiling for the punishment to be imposed.

2. Although the Code adopted a mixed theory of punishment, it clearly established the prevention of offenses as the chief purpose of the Code. Therefore, it adopted a mostly forward-looking approach to punishment that justifies criminal liability on the basis of the good consequences that it produces (measured primarily in terms of the prevention of future offenses). It adopts, in sum, a primarily *consequentialist* approach to punishment. The American Law Institute is now working on a revised Model Penal Code approach to sentencing. According to the current version, the chief purpose of punishment is to give to the defender his just deserts (retribution). It remains to be seen what this change will mean in jurisdictions that follow the Model Penal Code.

3. Consequentialist theories of punishment (general and specific deterrence, incapacitation, rehabilitation) are often contrasted with non-consequentialist theories of punishment. Non-consequentialist theories of punishment are backward looking, for they justify the imposition of punishment on the basis of the offender's blameworthiness for having engaged in a wrongful act. The paradigmatic non-consequentialist theory of punishment is retribution. In a nutshell, retribution holds that punishing those who deserve to be punished is intrinsically good and may be justified regardless of whether good consequences flow from doing so.

## §2.03 Purposes of Punishment: Comparative Perspectives

### Günther Jakobs, *Derecho Penal: Parte General*

pages 18–19 (Marcial Pons, 1995)

The infraction of the norm does not give rise to a conflict that is relevant to the criminal law because of the harm that it inflicts, for the criminal law cannot undo the harm wreaked by the offender ... Nevertheless, human conduct is not only an event that impacts the natural world. To the extent that the actor is able to control her conduct, the actor's conduct has a certain meaning.... Thus, for example, the person who drives a car knowing that she is intoxicated and who culpably fails to take into account that her conduct may jeopardize the wellbeing of others communicates that she has more important things to worry about than caring about the wellbeing of those with whom she shares the road. The message that the driver communicates with his conduct is incompatible with the message represented by the legal norms that prohibit [driving recklessly or while intoxicated]. As a result, the infraction of the norm communicates a message that threatens to delegitimize the norm....

This gives rise to a social conflict that calls for a resolution, for the communicative meaning of the actor's conduct calls into question the norm's legitimacy as a source for shaping social interactions.... Punishment is the [state's] reaction to the conflict created by the infraction of the norm. [Given that norm infraction is relevant to the criminal law because of its communicative meaning rather than because of the evil that it inflicts], punishment ought to be conceived not as an event that changes the actor's situation by harming him, but rather as an act that communicates something. More specifically, punishment communicates that human interactions ought to be governed by the legal norm infringed rather than by whatever reasons or interests motivated the offender to infringe the norm. Punishment thus reveals that the perpetrator has not organized his affairs in a way that is consistent with the conventionally accepted rules of social interaction....

Given that the defining feature of punishment is the message that it communicates rather than the harm that it visits upon the offender, the purpose of punishment cannot be to prevent harm to legally protected interests. Its real purpose is to reaffirm the legitimacy of the norm that was infringed ... Punishment thus secures that the norm that was infringed is still looked at by the general citizenry as an adequate point of reference for organizing their conduct. In sum, the purpose of punishment is to react to the calling into question of the legitimacy of the norm that is represented by the perpetrator's conduct by reaffirming that the norm that was infringed is an appropriate vehicle for structuring social interactions.

### *Notes and Questions*

1. Jakobs—one of Germany's leading criminal theorists—espouses a theory of punishment that is known in Europe and Latin America as "positive general deterrence." This theory is defended by many civil law criminal theorists. According to the theory of "positive general deterrence," punishment protects society by reinforcing societal expectations that norms will be followed. It secures social interactions by reassuring law-abiding citizens that the trust that they place in legal norms is well founded and that calling the norm into question will not be tolerated. In Jakobs's words:

> Punishment must make itself felt at the level of social interaction ... It must protect the conditions that make such interactions possible. As a result, punishment has a preventive function. Punishment protects by reaffirming those who place their trust in legal norms that their trust [in the power of legal norms to shape social interactions] is well placed.

2. Positive general deterrence is contrasted with "negative general deterrence." According to the theory of "negative general deterrence," punishment protects society by coercing people into compliance with law by threatening them with the infliction of harm (punishment) if they fail to comply. The contrast between positive and negative general deterrence is explained by Jakobs in the following way:

> The power of [positive general deterrence] does not consist in that it prevents others from infringing legal norms or in that it will shape the perpetrator's future conduct, [as negative general deterrence would do]. The primary addressees of legal norms are not the pool of people who are potential future perpetrators, but rather all citizens, given that we all depend on the social interactions that punishment purports to protect. It is in this sense that punishment serves to reaffirm the trust that citizens place on legal norms as an essential vehicle for securing meaningful social interactions.

3. According to Jakobs (and other civil law criminal theorists), positive general deterrence is a consequentialist (forward looking) theory of punishment because it views punishment as a vehicle for protecting society by nurturing important social interactions.

4. In contrast, retributive (backward looking) theories of punishment posit that punishment ought to be imposed if the offender deserves it because doing so is good in itself. Since punishing those who deserve to suffer for what they have done has intrinsic value, society ought to punish wrongdoers regardless of whether doing so has instrumental value (e.g., protects society or promotes important interests or social interactions). The readings that follow explore the relative merits of different consequentialist and retributive theories of punishment.

## § 2.04 Purposes of Punishment: Scholarly Debates

### Dan Kahan, *What Do Alternative Sanctions Mean?*

63 U. Chi. L. Rev. 591, 598 (1996)

Under the expressive view, the signification of punishment is moral condemnation. By imposing the proper form and degree of affliction on the wrongdoer, society says, in effect, that the offender's assessment of whose interests count is wrong. It follows, moreover, that when society deliberately forgoes answering the wrongdoer through punishment, it risks being perceived as endorsing his valuations; hence the complaint that unduly lenient punishment reveals that the victim is worthless in the eyes of the law....

... [R]etributivism and deterrence theories can be analytically related to and distinguished from the expressive theory....

The core idea of retributivism—that an individual should be punished "because, and only because, (he) deserves it"—is vague. It is possible to give content to this notion without reference to expressive condemnation; one might say, for example, that an individual deserves punishment when "he renounces a burden which others have voluntarily assumed and thus gains an advantage which others ... do not possess," or when human beings naturally intuit that the individual has engaged in "a wrong action (that) ... calls for the infliction of suffering or de privation on the agent." But it is also possible to use the expressive view to inform desert. On this account, an individual deserves punishment when he engages in behavior that conveys disrespect for important values. The proper retributive punishment is the one that appropriately expresses condemnation and reaffirms the values that the wrongdoer denies.

The expressive theory can also be used to inform deterrence. One way in which it might do so is by supplying a consequentialist theory of value ... [For example], one might conclude that a white man who kills an African-American out of racial hatred should be punished more severely than a woman who kills the abuser of her child in anger, even if equal punishment would maximize social wealth; when expressive considerations are taken into account, racist killings are deemed to harm society more than are impassioned killings of child molesters.

Another way that the expressive theory might reinforce deterrence is through preference formation. The law can discourage criminality not just by "raising the cost" of such behavior through punishments, but also through instilling aversions to the kinds of behavior that the law prohibits. The latter is often referred to as the "moralizing" or "moral educative" effect of punishment.

The moralizing effect of criminal law depends on a variety of mechanisms, all of which are reinforced by the expressive character of the law. The first is preference adaptation. To avoid cognitive dissonance, citizens form aversions to the kinds of behavior—whether rape, theft, or insider trading—that the law tells them are unworthy of being valued. This sort of preference adaptation is most likely to take place when citizens perceive the law as expressing society's moral condemnation of such conduct.

The law also moralizes by shaping relevant "belief-dependent" preferences. Empirical studies show that the willingness of persons to obey various laws is endogenous to their beliefs about whether others view the law as worthy of obedience: if compliance is perceived to be widespread, persons generally desire to obey; but if they believe that disobedience is rampant, their commitment to following the law diminishes. Even a strong propensity to obey the law, in other words, can be under cut by a person's "desire not to be suckered." When the law effectively expresses condemnation of wrongdoers, however, it reassures citizens that society does indeed stand behind the values that the law embodies.

Finally, the law moralizes through goodwill. Individuals are more disposed to obey particular laws, whether or not those laws accord with their moral beliefs, when they perceive the criminal law as a whole to be basically just. They are more likely to have this perception when criminal punishment confirms, rather than disappoints, shared expectations about what behavior is worthy of moral condemnation....

## Michael Moore, *Closet Retributivism*

USC Cites, Spring–Summer 1982

[In order to determine whether we are retributivists or consequentialists], [c]onsider the case that Sanford Kadish and Stephen Schulhofer include in their leading criminal law casebook, *State v. Chaney,* a case that ... rouses our retributive juices. In *Chaney*, the defendant was tried and convicted of two counts of forcible rape, and one count of robbery. The defendant and a companion had picked up the prosecutrix at a downtown location in Anchorage. After driving the victim around in their car, the defendant and his companion beat her and forcibly raped her four times, also forcing her to perform an act of fellatio with the defendant's companion. During this same period of time, the victim's money was removed from her purse, and she only then was allowed to leave the vehicle after dire threats of reprisals if she attempted to report the incident to the police....

The thought experiment such a case begins to pose for us is as follows: Imagine in such a case that the defendant after the rape but before sentencing has got into an accident so his sexual and aggressive desires are dampened to such an extent that he presents no further danger of violence against women; if money was also one of his problems, suppose further that he has inherited a great deal of money, so that he no longer needs to rob. Suppose, because of both of these facts, we are reasonably certain that he does not present a danger of either forcible assault, rape, or robbery or related crimes in the future. Since Chaney is (by hypothesis) not dangerous, he does not need to be incapacitated, specially deterred, or reformed. Suppose further that we could successfully pretend to punish Chaney, instead of actually punishing him, and that no one is at all likely to find out. Our pretending to punish him will thus serve the needs of general deterrence and maintain social cohesion, and the cost to the state will be less than if it actually did punish him. Is there anything on [a consequentialist] theory of punishment which would urge that Chaney nonetheless should really be punished? I think not, so that if one's conclusion is that Chaney and people like him nonetheless should be punished, one will have to give up [consequentialist theories] of punishment.

## Victor Tadros, *The Ends of Harm: The Moral Foundations of Criminal Law*

pages 44–55 (Oxford, 2011)

In vindicating their view, retributivists often appeal to our emotional reactions about serious wrongdoers. Imagine a person who has committed a number of racially motivated murders. And suppose that once this has been discovered and he has been identified, punishing him would have no deterrent effects. Even though he has not been reformed, and continues to believe that he was right to commit his racist murders, we are now sure that he poses no further threat to us. Punishing him, in this case, would appear to lack instrumental benefits. And yet we would not wish him to go on living happily in society, going about his day-to-day business. We would want to see him suffer. But if his suffering has no good effects, we need another explanation for this intuition. We might wonder how powerful the intuition is that the wrongdoer should suffer in this case. Perhaps some people think: at least he's happy. If he enjoys happiness at no cost to anyone else, we should prefer him to be happy. This thought is, I think, too simple. I take it that many readers will share the judgment that when the racist murderer continues to live a happy life, something is out of joint....

Retributivists might reply ... that ... there [is] nevertheless something wrong in the person continuing to live in society without being deprived of any other goods of life.... I think that there is something behind this thought, but I don't think that we need to appeal to the idea that it is intrinsically good that wrongdoers suffer to explain it. We can distinguish between two explanations of why there is something amiss when wrongdoers do not suffer. One is the retributivist idea that we have failed to bring about something that is good in itself: the suffering of wrongdoers. The other is the idea that wrongdoers who do not suffer will have failed to fulfill a duty that they have incurred in virtue of their wrongdoing.

**i) A Duty to Bear a Cost**—In vindicating the idea that wrongdoers have a duty to bear a cost, we need not appeal to the intrinsic value of them bearing that cost. For in many other cases, we may think that a person has a duty to do something that is costly to them and nevertheless recognize that it is a bad thing that they must bear that cost. We might think about the racist murderer that we focused on in the previous section that he owes something to the victims and their families. Their lives have been shattered by his wrongdoing. If he is living a happy life we will suspect that he has not responded adequately to the harm that he has wrongfully caused. He bears a duty to the victims of his crime, a duty that it would take the rest of his life to fulfill. What is he doing living a happy life, we might wonder, when the effects of his wrongdoing continue and remain to be undone? The idea that wrongdoers owe a duty to their victims is quite distinct from the idea that their suffering is a good thing. It may be right that they bear a burden that causes them suffering without us valuing their suffering for its own sake. To see the distinction more clearly consider the following example. Suppose that I have culpably unleashed a threat on you, say by setting my dangerous dog on you. The only way to prevent the dog from harming you is to put myself in its way. But if I do that, the dog will harm me. I have a duty to protect you from the dog. Given that I have created the threat through my own wrongful action I must bear the burden of averting it. For if I were not to bear that burden the burden will fall on you. Hence, if you are harmed and I am not, we will think that something is amiss. I had a duty to bear a cost that I have not borne. If I fulfill my duty and put myself between you and the dog, we will not think that it is a good thing in itself that I am harmed, although it is of course good that I have done my duty.

The fact that it is my duty to accept being harmed will also have significance for the actions others. It will affect the way that the harm that I will suffer ought to figure in their decisions about what to do. For example, if I decide not to put myself between you and the dog, it may be permissible for others to force me in front of you to defend you against the threat. They can do that if there is no less costly way of averting the threat. Other people, including you, may not be required to bear a significant cost to avoid me being harmed. And even though I am harmed in order to prevent you from being harmed, you will not owe me compensation for the harm that I suffer. This does not, on its own, provide an alternative account of punishment of course. The example is intended to reveal two related things about our judgments concerning harm to others. The first is the distinction between the evaluation of the duties that people have and the way we should value the content of those duties. In this case, I have a duty to bear the cost if that is the only way of avoiding it falling on you. Obviously enough fulfilling one's duty is good. But that does not make the harm that I will suffer as a consequence of doing my duty itself a good. It is a bad thing that the dog bites me. It would have been better if I could have averted the threat in some less costly way, say by distracting the dog with a juicy steak. Had I been able to do that, I would not have needed to put myself between you and the dog. What is important is that I have averted the threat, not that I have suffered in the process. We might find that a similar idea lies behind the justification of punishment. It might be true that offenders have a duty to accept that they will be harmed. But in recognizing that they have such a duty we need not appeal to the idea that harming them will be in any way good, or even less bad, than the harm that would be inflicted on other people....

**ii) Choice and the Distribution of Harm**—Here is the obvious response that retributivists will make to this argument. In the earlier case involving the dog, I committed a wrong in setting the dog on you. And because I was wrong in doing so, it is I that deserve to suffer the harm rather than you. Desert surely has a role to play, then, in deciding whether it is either you or me who must bear the cost of my conduct. We might think that this provides us with a better account of desert. Desert does not make a difference to the quality of what is suffered. It makes a difference in determining how suffering ought to be distributed. If someone is going to be harmed, we might think, it is better that wrongdoers are harmed than innocent people....

The first thing to say is that even if this is true, it does nothing to vindicate the basic retributivist idea that the suffering of wrongdoers is good in itself. If we are to justify punishment in terms of the distribution of harms, it must be the case that there is someone whose harm is distributed away from. And that suggests that punishment must have an instrumental aim. We punish some people (those who deserve it) to ensure that others do not suffer. And we achieve that only if punishing those who deserve it will prevent suffering to those others. We can see that even more clearly from the dog case. I deserve to suffer more than you, the argument goes, so the harm must be distributed to me. The fact that harm is deserved would only be a selection criterion. It would do nothing to vindicate the view that the suffering of offenders is good in itself. Harm might simply be a bad thing that we must distribute either to offenders or to future victims. The idea that wrongdoers deserve to suffer would amount to the idea that we have good grounds to decide that suffering falls on wrongdoers, perhaps because it is less bad that they are harmed....

## Paul H. Robinson, *The Ongoing Revolution in Punishment Theory: Doing Justice as Controlling Crime*

42 Ariz. St. L. J. 1089 (2010–2011)

You probably remember from your first-year criminal law class the age-old tension between the retributivists who want to punish offenders because they deserve it, they see deserved punishment as a value in itself, and the utilitarians (or instrumentalists), who believe that punishment must have some more practical justification, such as avoiding future crime, perhaps through deterrence, incapacitation of the dangerous, or rehabilitation. The dispute between these two groups is classically thought to be irresolvable. The two are simply using different currencies and think different things to be important.

One of the most exciting developments in current punishment theory suggests that these two positions may not be entirely irresolvable, at least in a sense....

### IV. Empirical and Deontological Desert

... [D]esert as a distributive principle would give criminal liability and punishment according to an offender's blameworthiness, which would take account of the extent of the harm or evil of his conduct, his culpable state of mind at the time of the offense, an assessment of his personal capacities that might shape what we could reasonably have expected of him, and a variety of other factors.

I have distinguished ... the traditional deontological desert from what has been called "empirical desert." The former is an assessment of moral blameworthiness logically derived from principles of right and good, typically by moral philosophers. The latter is derived from social science studies of a community's shared intuitions of justice. Empirical desert is not "true justice" in a transcendent sense but only a representation of the principles by which the community actually makes judgments about justice.

It is obvious why one might care about doing justice in a deontological sense. Why might one care about empirical desert? Why might empirical desert be an attractive distributive principle for criminal liability and punishment? The short answer, we will say, is that it might make sense for instrumentalist crime control reasons. We will come back to that revolutionary idea—that doing justice, at least in an empirical desert sense, might be an effective crime control strategy—because it does put a new spin on the traditional view that the retributivist interest in doing justice and the instrumentalist interest in controlling crime are inevitably in conflict.

To work up to this conclusion, let me give some background from the social science studies of the past decade or more. Laypersons see punishment as something that is properly imposed according to desert, that is, blameworthiness. When they are asked to assign punishment, they don't look to the factors that determine dangerousness or deterrence, but rather to the offender's moral blameworthiness.

As discussed earlier, the traditional instrumentalist crime-control principles of deterrence, incapacitation, and rehabilitation each conflict with a desert distribution of punishment. If any of these principles were used for distributing criminal liability and punishment, the system would regularly do injustice and would often fail to do justice. Conversely, if the system adopted a desert distribution, it would not be optimizing deterrence, incapacitation of the dangerous, or rehabilitation.

However, a desert distribution of criminal liability and punishment would provide some significant opportunity for deterrence, incapacitation of the dangerous, and rehabilitation, albeit not the maximum that is possible. That is, deserved punishment can have a deterrent effect, can incapacitate, and can provide the opportunity for rehabilitation. The important point here is that to increase any of these instrumentalist effects, the distribution of criminal liability and punishment must deviate from desert, that is, it must do injustice or must fail to do justice.

Do crime-control instrumentalists have any reason to care about whether the criminal justice system regularly does injustice or fails to do justice? As instrumentalists, deviating from true justice (deontological desert) may be just an unfortunate necessity of fighting crime, one might argue. However, social science hints that there may be practical real-world crime-control complications that arise from regularly deviating from the community's perceptions of justice (that is, from empirical desert).

Here's how. We are becoming increasingly aware of the enormous power of social influence and internalized norms. The behavioral decisions that people are constantly making in their daily lives are driven primarily by a concern for what others, especially family and friends, will think of them and for what they think of themselves. The criminal law can harness these normative forces if it earns a reputation as a moral authority, that is, if people come to see it as a system that reliably punishes in ways consistent with people's intuitions of justice.

A criminal justice system that has earned moral credibility within the community is in a position to harness the power of stigmatization, for example, a highly efficient mechanism for influencing conduct. It lacks the high costs of imprisonment, yet can significantly influence people's conduct. In contrast, if the criminal law fritters away its moral authority by imposing criminal liability and punishment that deviates from empirical desert, it increasingly undermines its ability to stigmatize conduct through criminalization or punishment.

A criminal law that has earned a reputation as a moral authority also has a greater ability to avoid vigilantism, which is classically sparked when the community sees regular failures of justice that it finds intolerable. Similarly, a criminal justice system that regularly does injustice and/or fails to do justice is one that risks prompting resistance and subversion, and loses its ability to gain the acquiescence and cooperation that a criminal justice system relies upon, by witnesses, jurors, offenders, and most participants in the criminal justice and correctional process.

The criminal justice system that has earned moral authority also has a greater chance of gaining compliance in borderline cases where the actual condemnability of the conduct may be unclear. When insider trading first became a crime, for example, it may not have been immediately obvious to everyone that this conduct was qualitatively different from other forms of aggressive entrepreneurship that are tolerated and even encouraged. If the criminal justice system has earned a reputation as a reliable guide to what is and is not condemnable conduct, it is more likely to gain the deference of the community when it announces that insider trading has crossed a line and is indeed condemnable.

Perhaps the most powerful effect of gaining moral credibility is the influence that such credibility gives to the system in the larger public conversation by which societal norms are shaped. If we want to change people's thinking about the condemnability of domestic violence, or drunk driving, or downloading music from the Internet without a license, criminalization of that conduct or increasing the penalty to signal greater seriousness of the conduct can help reinforce the norm against it. In contrast, a criminal justice system that has squandered its moral authority by regularly deviating from desert is one that is more likely to be ignored during the public conversation because its view may be discounted as just one more example of how the system gets it wrong. (Understand that any criminal law, even one with moral credibility, may not be able to establish a strong societal norm by itself. That is the lesson of Prohibition. A strong, and eventually internalized, norm requires concurring views from a variety of sources of moral authority, including social institutions as well as circles of friends and acquaintances).

One may conclude, then, that the crime-control power of the criminal law depends in some significant part upon how well it tracks the community's shared intuitions of justice. Thus, let me say a few words of background about lay intuitions of justice. First, we have learned that people's intuitions of justice are quite nuanced and sophisticated. Small changes in facts can and do produce large and predictable changes in liability judgments. And sophistication does not depend upon people's education or intelligence; it seems to be the standard form.

Even more surprisingly, there appears to be an enormous amount of agreement about intuitions of justice across all demographics, at least with regard to the core of wrongdoing—physical aggression, taking property without consent, and deceit in exchanges. The agreement here is on the relative blameworthiness of different kinds of offenses and offenders, not on the absolute amount of punishment to be imposed. However, once a society commits itself to a punishment continuum endpoint, as every society must do (whether it is the death penalty, or life imprisonment, or twenty years), the large number of cases of distinguishable blameworthiness must be fit on this limited punishment continuum. Thus, each case will end up requiring a specific amount of punishment, not because of any magical connection between that amount of punishment and that offense but rather because that specific amount of punishment is required to put that case in its proper ordinal rank among all other cases. (If one changes the punishment continuum endpoint—different societies do have quite different endpoints—then the specific punishment required to put each case its proper ordinal rank would also change).

One may well ask how well current American criminal law matches the community's intuitions of justice. The short answer is: not well. Modern crime-control programs, such as three strikes, high drug-offense penalties, adult prosecution of juveniles, narrowing the insanity defense, strict liability offenses, and the felony-murder rule, all distribute criminal liability and punishment in ways that seriously conflict with lay persons' intuitions of justice.

To summarize, then, the strengths and weaknesses of the empirical and deontological desert might be presented this way:

| Distributive Principle | Strengths/Advantages | Weaknesses/Disadvantages |
|---|---|---|
| Empirical Desert | • most likely to be seen as just punishment, which can increase criminal law's moral credibility, thus crime control benefit | • may do injustice that is not apparent to the present community<br>• failure to deviate from empirical desert misses special crime control opportunities that can arise (e.g., deterrence prerequisites satisfied and high deterrent effect possible, reliable prediction of high probability of an offender's serious future offense) |
| Deontological Desert | • does justice | • fails to prevent avoidable crime<br>• difficulty in operationalizing because of common disagreement among moral philosophers |

## V. Selecting a Distributive Principle

What should be the principle by which we distribute criminal liability and punishment?

All of the alternative distributive principles are flawed in one way or another. Are we compelled to adopt the least flawed of the group? Or, could we combine two or more distributive principles in one way or another to create a hybrid? The following table summarizes the advantages and disadvantages of the different distributive principles of punishment:

| Distributive Principle | Strengths/Advantages | Weaknesses/Disadvantages |
|---|---|---|
| General Deterrence | • under right conditions can avoid crime<br>• can have effect beyond offender at hand | • works only when prerequisite conditions exist, which may not be common: knowledge of the deterrence-based rule, capacity and inclination to rationally calculate one's own best interest, perception that costs of crime (prob. x punishment) exceed benefits<br>• can give punishment other than what is deserved |
| Special Deterrence | • under right conditions can avoid crime by offender at hand | • works only on the offender at hand works only when prerequisite conditions exist<br>• can give punishment other than what is deserved |
| Rehabilitation | • if successful, can avoid crime by offender at hand<br>• may have value in itself, in making person's life better | • works only on the offender at hand<br>• only modest success in only limited cases<br>• can give punishment other than what is deserved<br>• problematic as sole distributive principle; must combine with another<br>• forcibly changing person's nature may raise ethical questions about intruding upon personal autonomy |
| Incapacitation | • no doubt that effective in reducing crime by offender at hand | • works only on the offender at hand<br>• commonly inaccurate in predictions, which causes wasted costs and unjustified detentions<br>• can give punishment other than what is deserved<br>• can better reduce prevention costs, reduce damage to system's moral credibility, and increase accuracy by operating as open civil preventive detention system apart from CJ system |
| Empirical Desert | • most likely to be seen as just punishment, which can increase criminal law's moral credibility, thus crime control benefit | • may do injustice that is not apparent to the present community<br>• failure to deviate from empirical desert misses special crime control opportunities that can arise (e.g., deterrence prerequisites satisfied and high deterrent effect possible, reliable prediction of high probability of an offender's serious future offense) |

A principled system must look to a distributive principle that defines the interrelation among alternatives.... [Choosing empirical desert as the dominant distributive principle] seems to resolve the traditional retributivist-instrumentalist "irresolvable tension"—but only in a sense. It suggests that there is good crime-control utility in doing justice, and in that sense rests upon an instrumentalist rather than a deontological perspective. However, given the practical realities of assessing desert principles, it may be that empirical desert offers the best practical approximation of deontological desert, and for that reason the position may be highly attractive to the retributivist perspective....

## Christopher Slobogin & Lauren Brinkley Rubinstein, *Putting Desert in Its Place*

65 Stan. L. Rev. 77 (2013)

The age-old debate among criminal law theoreticians over whether desert or prevention ought to drive criminal justice has taken on a new cast during the past few years. The old debate featured deontology against utilitarianism: put simply, should offenders be punished according to their moral blameworthiness or should concerns about protecting society be the focus of punishment? Numerous thinkers have staunchly staked out positions at opposite ends of the spectrum, while others have tried to reach some type of compromise between the two. But the consistent theme in the debate has been that a theory that bases punishment on the offender's degree of culpability is frequently in significant tension with the view that punishment should focus on how subsequent offending can be prevented.

In the new debate both sides are more optimistic about resolving this tension, perhaps because both sides are willing to abandon the deontological view of desert. In the new debate the value of a culpability-based punishment system is no longer assessed through the prism of moral philosophy but rather in terms of its utility at achieving the goals of the criminal justice system. Thus, where the two sides differ is not over methodology but over whether crime control and respect for the law is best achieved through a system focused on desert or through a prevention-based regime that is sensitive to desert only when ignoring it would have criminogenic impact.

Most of the literature in this new debate has favored the first stance. The principal proponent of that view has been Paul Robinson, who has coined the term "empirical desert" to capture the idea that a criminal justice system that tracks empirically derived societal views of desert may best facilitate the law's ability to assure compliance with legal prohibitions. Relying on a considerable amount of research, much of which he has helped conduct, Robinson contends that "a criminal justice system that distributes liability and punishment in concordance with the citizens' shared intuitions of justice ... may provide greater utility than a distribution following the more traditional instrumentalist approach of optimizing deterrence or incapacitation."

The competing view is not as well developed, and in fact has yet to be explicitly articulated. This Article aims to provide that articulation. The theory is that while liability rules should still depend primarily on desert, punishment rules that focus on the utilitarian goals of specific deterrence, rehabilitation, and incapacitation ("individual prevention" goals) are not only superior at accomplishing crime prevention but can also usually assuage society's urge for retribution well enough to avoid vigilantism, norm breakdown, and other negative effects. This Article presents original research that supports this approach to punishment, which could be called "preventive justice."

### III. Implications and Future Directions

The empirical desert project's effort to assess lay views about desert and the effect of the criminal law's divergence from those views is important for several reasons. First, it provides thought-provoking data for criminal law policymakers. Second, it calls into question the ability of lawmakers to represent the public's views. Third, and most importantly for our project, it begins to assess the instrumental value of adhering to desert. Deontological retributivists are presumably uninterested in this kind of data. But to utilitarians this assessment is crucial, because it helps determine the extent to which desert can be ignored or downplayed in arriving at dispositional decisions.

Empirical desert theory dictates that utilitarians not only try to measure the deterrent, incapacitative, and rehabilitative impact of punishment but also try to gauge the extent to which law's allegiance to societal views about desert affect "crime control," defined broadly in terms of preventing crime, assuring cooperation with the authorities, and reinforcing societal norms. The research Robinson has helped conduct suggests a relationship between these desiderata and a criminal justice system that is based on empirically derived desert. In contrast, the studies we have reported here tend to undermine all three hypotheses underlying empirical desert theory.

The consensus hypothesis is that consensus exists with respect to the relative ranking of a sizeable subset of crimes such as homicide, assault, and theft and that this consensus is based on desert considerations. Our research confirms that consensus about the ranking of core crimes exists, but it also shows that utilitarian concerns can change that ranking in ways inconsistent with desert. Moreover, lay views about specific punishments for crime—even for core crimes—can be multimodal rather than clustered around a mean, indicating significant disagreement about punishment preferences. This disagreement is most likely to occur in connection with serious crimes, ironically the only type of crime whose punishment is predominately driven by desert considerations. Thus, the consensus that is arguably most important to empirical desert theory does not exist.

The compliance hypothesis is that punishments that fail to adhere to desert can undermine the moral credibility of the law, and thus reduce compliance and cooperation with it. One of our studies suggests, to the contrary, that noncompliance effects are sometimes stronger the closer punishment conforms to desert-based results, perhaps because people are less worried that commission of trivial crimes will result in irrational sentences. Our other studies on this topic suggest that, to the extent that noncompliance effects result from criminal justice outcomes that diverge from societal views, they are as likely when the divergence is from utilitarian-oriented preferences as from desert-oriented preferences and, in any event, will dissipate quickly over time.

Finally, the crime control hypothesis is that the crime control benefits of a punishment system based on empirically derived desert are likely to be as great as or greater than the compliance generated by adhering to dispositions focused more directly on prevention. Our research does not directly test this hypothesis, which would be hard to do given the difficulty of measuring the extent of crime control and its causes. However, the studies testing the compliance hypothesis ... suggest that the crime control hypothesis is false to the extent that "crime control" is framed solely as the product of compliance that stems from following lay views about desert-based punishment. Furthermore, [other studies we conducted] suggest that, for all but the most serious crimes, most people are willing to change their assessments of punishment from what empirical desert would dictate if they think that preventive goals can be achieved through different means. Laypeople appear to believe that utilitarian considerations are at least as important as desert factors in fashioning sentences in the typical criminal case.

[In sum,] our research suggests that, if crime prevention is the objective, adherence to empirically derived desert is not likely to be the best way of achieving it. Even the less concrete goal of bolstering the moral credibility of the criminal justice system might be better pursued by following a mixture of desert and utilitarian goals. Of course, even if further research confirms that following empirically derived desert is not a superior crime prevention mechanism or the best way of shoring up the moral credibility of the criminal justice system, policymakers could still choose to make desert the lodestar of the criminal law on deontological grounds. The purpose of this Article is solely to evaluate the utility of desert, not its normative validity.

Furthermore, in assessing the relative merits of a desert- or prevention-based system, another type of utility, one that this Article has not evaluated, must also be considered. This second type of utility might be called the political economy of criminal justice. The choice between retributive and utilitarian goals in structuring the criminal justice system can not only have an impact on crime control and legitimization, but can also be driven by budgetary considerations, concerns about implementation, or the extent to which the choice can insulate the criminal justice system from the vagaries of the political process.

In The Disutility of Injustice, Robinson and his colleagues allude to this political economy concern. They describe a number of egregious "crime control" stories of the type alluded to earlier—life sentences for three minor offenses, extremely long sentences for possession of small amounts of drugs, tough sentences for strict liability crimes—and suggest that these punishments are not the product of reasoned judgments by the public and legislators, but rather the result of media and government distortions of the facts, unreasonable public fear of crime, and the incentives elections create for legislators to be "tough on crime." We tend to agree with this assessment. But by calling these "crime control" stories, Robinson et al. also imply that a preventive approach to criminal justice plays into the hands of irrational political forces and that a system based on empirical (or deontological) desert would avoid these travesties. In other words, the innuendo of The Disutility of Injustice is that, while politics may make any sensible system of criminal justice difficult to maintain, desert is more likely than other considerations to curb the worst impulses of the democratic process.

This is not the place to evaluate this controversy at length. But it should at least be pointed out that desert can also be misused and abused by a dysfunctional political system. Because desert is based on backward-looking assessments of the crime and the offender's mental state, it tends to be implemented by legislators and prosecutors. Because prevention—at least at the individual level—is based on forward-looking assessments of treatability and risk, it tends to be implemented by judges and parole authorities. The first set of decisionmakers is at least as susceptible as the second to the social and political pressures of the type described in The Disutility of Injustice.

In the end, the best way to reconcile retributive and preventive goals is probably through some sort of limiting retributivism, or what we are calling preventive justice, which allows utilitarian considerations to have significant impact within a range established by retributive principles. But much rides on the breadth of that range and the rationale for its endpoints. Desert theorists probably would not be happy with the broad ranges favored by many of our subjects in [one of our studies]. Yet not only are such ranges apparently popular, they probably offer the best method of preventing crime. In short, unless it represents a radical departure from desert, which is most likely to occur in cases involving serious crime, indeterminate punishment focused on prevention is neither likely to cause more noncompliance than it prevents (through the mechanisms of specific deterrence, incapacitation, and rehabilitation), nor likely to undermine the legitimacy of the system.

Furthermore, as one of us has argued at length, indeterminate sentencing within very broad ranges has many other advantages over determinate sentencing. Even in domains normally thought to be the province of desert-based systems—including accuracy, protection of offenders' liberty interests, respect for victims, and saving money—a prevention-oriented regime may well be superior to, or at least no worse than, a system that relies on narrower ranges. In other words, contrary to Robinson and Kurzban's claim, "justice" is not solely the province of desert.

## *Notes and Questions*

1. Note the striking resemblance between Jakobs's "positive general deterrence" theory of punishment (discussed in § 2.03) and Kahan's "expressive theory" of punishment (discussed at the beginning of the current section). It is remarkable that similar theories of punishment arose on both sides of the Atlantic in spite of the incredible lack of interaction between Anglo-American and European Continental scholars. It seems that great minds really do think alike! Imagine how much more progress scholars on either side of the Atlantic would have made had they only cared to figure out what their counterparts were doing.

2. Jakobs argues that his theory of "positive general deterrence" is consequentialist, for its ultimate aim is to achieve good consequences. More specifically, the goal of positive general deterrence is not to argue that punishment is intrinsically good, but rather to suggest that it is instrumentally good because it promotes certain interactions that are essential to organized society.

Kahan contends that his expressive theory of punishment may also promote consequentialist goals, given that it may be used to shape the beliefs and preferences of citizens in positive ways. Nevertheless, Kahan also notes that expressive theories may inform non-consequentialist retributive theories of punishment, as the theory may be invoked to identify the reasons why the offender deserves punishment. More specifically, expressive theories suggest that offenders deserve punishment because their conduct *expresses* disrespect for important values. Punishment, then, counteracts the offender's expression by reaffirming the primacy of the values disrespected by the offender.

Do you believe that the expressive theory is best conceived as a consequentialist or non-consequentialist (retributive) theory of punishment? Explain.

3. Read again Professor Michael Moore's thought experiment based on the *Chaney* case. Do you agree with Professor Moore that punishment ought to be imposed in that case even if there are no consequentialist reasons for doing so? Why or why not?

Go back to Note 6 in § 2.01 of this Chapter. It asked whether after reading about the different theories of punishment you considered yourself a consequentialist who cares primarily about deterrence and other methods of crime control or a retributivist who cares chiefly about punishing those who deserve it without consideration of the utility of doing so. If you considered yourself a consequentialist who cares mostly about deterrence, it would have been sensible for you to argue against punishing the defendant in Professor Moore's thought experiment. What if, however, you thought you were a consequentialist who cares primarily about deterrence but are in favor of punishing the defendant in Professor Moore's thought experiment? If you held those two views, perhaps you are a "closet retributivist"!

4. Retributivists—like Michael Moore—argue that punishing those who deserve it is intrinsically good. What this means is that the suffering that punishment inflicts on those who deserve it is good in itself, without regard to consequentialist considerations. Victor Tadros believes that this is incorrect. He argues that—in spite of the retributive intuitions stirred by thought experiments like the one devised by Michael Moore—visiting harm on wrongdoers is not instrinsically good. Upon close inspection, harm is generally visited on offenders for instrumental reasons. This is the case even in thought experiments like the one proposed my Moore. Can you explain Professor Tadros' position? Do you agree with his claim? Why or why not?

5. Professor Paul Robinson argues that there is a difference between so-called "deontological desert" and what he calls "empirical desert." What's the difference? What are the advantages and weaknesses of these two theories of desert?

6. Robinson argues that we should punish wrongdoers in accordance with their (empirical) desert not because doing so is intrinsically good (as retributivists like Michael Moore would argue), but rather because doing so produces good consequences. How is it that imposing desert-based retributive punishment may produce good consequences, such as controlling crime? Do you agree with Professor Robinson that "empirical desert" may dissolve the tension between retributive and consequentialist theories of punishment? Why or why not? What would a true retributivist who believes that punishing wrongdoers is intrinsically good (what Robinson calls a "deontological desert" theorist) have to say about empirical desert theory?

7. Professor Slobogin and Brinkley Rubinstein argue that empirical studies reveal that imposing punishment in accordance with "empirical desert" may not promote crime control as much as Robinson has argued. As a result, they suggest that if you believe that punishment's primary goal is to control crime, you are better off punishing people on the basis of consequentialist theories of punishment than you are punishing them on the basis of empirical desert. Do you find their arguments persuasive? What would a true retributivist who believes that punishing wrongdoers is intrinsically good (what Robinson calls a "deontological desert" theorist) have to say about Slobogin and Rubinstein's findings?

# Part Two

# Limits on the State's Power to Punish

# Chapter 3

# Principle of Legality

## § 3.01 Principle of Legality: In General

### John Calvin Jeffries, Jr., *Legality, Vagueness and the Construction of Criminal Statutes*

71 Va. L. Rev. 189, 190–201 (1985)

The principle of legality forbids the retroactive definition of criminal offenses. It is condemned because it is retroactive and also because it is judicial—that is, accomplished by an institution not recognized as politically competent to define crime. Thus, a fuller statement of the legality ideal would be that it stands for the desirability in principle of advance legislative specification of criminal misconduct.

Today, this understanding of the legality ideal is firmly established. It is, as Herbert Packer said, '*the* first principle' of the criminal law, of 'central importance' in academic discussions of the subject, and all-but-universally complied with in this country. Yet, for all its fundamentality, the principle of legality has a curiously obscure history. Although there may have been ancient antecedents, the categorical insistence on advance legislative crime definition is clearly a modern phenomenon. In fact, the legality ideal is an explicit and self-conscious rejection of the historic methodology of the common law. When a legal order rejects its past, one expects to find an obvious turning point, a crisis or revolution, some watershed event from which the currents begin to flow a different way. The triumph of legality, however, is not so clearly marked.

This much seems to be widely accepted: that the modern insistence on advance legislative crime definition sprang from the continental European intellectual movement known as the Enlightenment; that the legality ideal was exported to the emerging American nation along with other aspects of Enlightenment ideology; and that the idea was quickly taken up by American reformers who tried to replace the common law of crimes with systematic legislative codification. But these early codification efforts failed, and by the mid-nineteenth century the reform movement had spent its force in a largely futile attack on the American 'reception' of English common law. This reception seems to have embraced not only the roster of particular offenses defined by the English courts, but also the familiar and related assumption of residual judicial authority to create new crimes should the need arise. That such authority was widely recognized is suggested by some early cases and by the subsequent observations of leading commentators. Even as late as 1900, there seemed to be no shared and settled understanding of judicial incompetence to create new crimes.

The true explanation for the nineteenth-century decline of judicial crime creation may be not so much rejection as desuetude. Courts throughout the nineteenth century found frequent occasion to invoke previously defined non-statutory crimes, but a progressively infrequent need to define new ones. Both statute and precedent accumulated over time. Gaps in coverage were met by new legislation or filled in gradually by decisional accretion. In either event, the sources of law became more elaborate, detailed, and particularized, and the need to rely on very broad rubrics of common-law authority accordingly declined. By 1900 even those who asserted the continued vitality of judicial crime creation noted the paucity of recent example. A reasonably diligent search of the decisions of this century has not uncovered more than two clear-cut illustrations of acknowledged judicial creativity in the criminal law.

Thus, it is not surprising that Herbert Packer detected 'something of an academic ring' to discussions of legality, or that first-year law students often find the issue disturbingly remote. Judicial crime creation is a thing of the past. It is both unacceptable and unnecessary. That is not to say that the concerns of legality are never tested, but only that they arise under the subsidiary doctrines of vagueness and strict construction—doctrines that, although of very different origin, are used today to implement the legality ideal. In fact, it may be that the usual view of the vagueness doctrine as an offspring of the more general concept of legality turns history on its head. Academic celebration of the legality ideal seems to have flowered after, not before, judicial crafting of the modern vagueness doctrine. It seems likely, therefore, that the contemporary insistence on the principle of legality as the cornerstone of the criminal law may have sprung in part from the desire to establish a secure intellectual foundation for modern vagueness review.

In any event, the vagueness doctrine is the operational arm of legality. It requires that advance, ordinarily legislative crime definition be meaningfully precise—or at least that it not be meaninglessly indefinite. As the Supreme Court stated in an early and oft-quoted formulation, 'a statute which either forbids or requires the doing of an act in terms so vague that men of common intelligence must necessarily guess at its meaning and differ as to its application, violates the first essential of due process of law.' The connection to legality is obvious: a law whose meaning can only be guessed at remits the actual task of defining criminal misconduct to retroactive judicial decision making.

The difficulty is that there is no yardstick of impermissible indeterminacy. As Justice Frankfurter said, unconstitutional indefiniteness 'is itself an indefinite concept.' The inquiry is evaluative rather than mechanistic; it calls for a judgment concerning not merely the degree of indeterminacy, but also the acceptability of indeterminacy in particular contexts....

The second doctrine said to implement the ideal of legality is the rule that penal statutes must be strictly construed against the state. The origins of this policy lie in the legislative blood lust of eighteenth-century England. Faced with a vast and irrational proliferation of capital offenses, judges invented strict construction to stem the march to the gallows. Sometimes aptly called the rule of lenity, strict construction was literally 'in favorem vitae'—part of a 'veritable conspiracy for administrative nullification' of capital penalization.

By the mid-nineteenth century, death was no longer the usual sanction for lesser crimes, but the rule of strict construction lingered on despite the change in circumstance and, in many jurisdictions, despite explicit legislative rejection. Today, strict construction survives more as a makeweight for results that seem right on other grounds than as a consistent policy of statutory interpretation. Citation to the rule is usually pro forma.... [T]he construction of penal statutes no longer seems guided by any distinct policy of interpretation; it is essentially ad hoc....

## *Notes and Questions*

1. The requirements of the principle of legality are sometimes expressed by the Latin maxim *nulla poena sine lege* (no punishment without a previous law). As Professor Jeffries explains, the principle is associated with several doctrines, including the prohibition of retroactive definition of criminal offenses, the void for vagueness rule and the canon of strict construction of criminal statutes. One court explained the importance of the legality principle in the following manner:

> The principle that a person can be found guilty of a crime and punished for his acts only if the state beforehand has made the commission of those acts a crime and has authorized punishment to be imposed upon proof that a person has in fact committed those acts is at the heart of the "rule of law" characteristic of Anglo-American jurisprudence. Expressed in the maxim nulla poena sine lege: "[t]he essence of this principle of legality is limitation on penalization by the State's officials, effected by the prescription and application of specific rules." The principle of legality in this nations criminal law has historically found expression in the criminal law rule of strict construction of criminal statutes, and in the constitutional principles forbidding ex post facto operation of the criminal law, vague criminal statutes, [and] "courts from depriving persons of liberty or property as punishment for criminal conduct except to the extent authorized by state (or federal) law" ... In the absence of a rule of law making the conduct charged against a person a crime and authorizing the government to impose a punishment upon a person proven to have that conduct, a person cannot be criminally punished for having engaged in that conduct because he would not have violated any penal law. *United States v. Walker,* 514 F. Supp. 294, 317–319 (1981).

2. Both the void for vagueness doctrine and the prohibition of retroactively criminalizing conduct can be justified by appealing to the idea of "fair warning." Statutes that are too vague fail to provide "fair warning" to the citizenry about the elements of the prohibited conduct. Similarly, retroactive criminal statutes cannot provide fair warning, for the conduct retroactively criminalized was innocent at the time of the commission of the offense. As the materials that follow will show, the idea of "fair warning" is essential to the Supreme Court's approach to the legality principle. The prohibitions of retroactivity and vagueness are explored in § 3.03 and § 3.04 of this Chapter.

3. As Professor Jeffries notes, the legality principle is often associated with the so-called "rule of lenity," which requires that ambiguous criminal statutes be strictly construed in favor of the defendant. Can the rule of lenity be justified by appealing to the idea of "fair warning"? Why or why not?

4. In spite of the lip service that many courts pay to the rule of lenity and its connection to the principle of legality, many courts and scholars—including Professor Jeffries—consider that the rule of strict construction should be abandoned. This issue is explored in § 3.05 of this Chapter.

5. It is often said that the principle of legality also bars the judicial creation of criminal offenses. Judicially created offenses are known in Anglo-America as "common law crimes." Note that the prohibition of common law crimes cannot be justified by appealing to the idea of fair warning, for a judicially created crime that applies prospectively and that is defined with sufficient precision satisfies the fair warning requirement. What, then, explains the bar on the judicial creation of criminal offenses? It is to this issue that we now turn.

## § 3.02 Principle of Legality: Abolition of Common Law Crimes

### State v. Soto

Supreme Court of Minnesota, 1985
378 N.W.2d 625

KELLEY, Justice.

The Ramsey County Grand Jury indicted the respondent John Soto for the death of an 8½ month old fetus. [T]he indictment charged him with causing the death by negligent operation of a motor vehicle while under the influence of alcohol ... Holding that an 8½ month old viable fetus capable of sustained life outside the womb of the mother was not a "human being" within the meaning of the statute, the Ramsey County District Court dismissed the [charges]. We affirm.

On November 8, 1984, while operating a motor vehicle in the city of St. Paul, the respondent John Soto, when allegedly under the influence of intoxicating liquor, negligently drove into an intersection, violently striking a vehicle operated by Mrs. Jannet Anne Johnson who was at the time 8½ months pregnant.... [The fetus died as a result of the accident].

The Ramsey County Grand Jury returned a four count indictment ... Counts III and IV charged criminal vehicular operation resulting in death of the unborn child. In moving to dismiss Counts III and IV of the indictment, the defendant claimed that a motorist could not be convicted of criminal vehicular operation resulting in death unless the death was that of a "human being" and that the "human being" requirement could only be satisfied by proof the victim was "born alive and had an independent and separate existence from his mother." As indicated, the trial judge agreed with this contention, and thus the sole issue on appeal is whether a viable fetus capable of sustained life outside the womb is a "human being" within the meaning of [the offense charged]....

In the United States some jurisdictions recognize common law crimes as well as those crimes defined and proscribed by legislative enactment. Such states are known as "common law" states. Other states of the union have abolished common law crimes either by statute or constitution, and have provided that no act or omission constitutes a crime unless defined by statute. Such jurisdictions are known as "code states." Minnesota is a "code state." Thus, in Minnesota, the legislature has exclusive province to define by statute what acts shall constitute a crime and to establish sanctions for their commission. Notwithstanding abolishment of common law crimes, ... it is not impermissible to use common law rules of construction in the interpretation of penal statutes, but only in aid of statutory construction....

[We now] turn ... to an examination of our vehicular homicide statute. That statute uses the phrase "causes the death of a human being." Although it has never precisely been defined by statute, the term "human being" has been used in Minnesota homicide statutes since territorial days. The term "human being" was used in the state's first vehicular homicide statute [enacted in 1937] [and was] first codified in the highway code [in 1941]. The term "human being" has been used repeatedly in subsequent modifications of that statute.... Finally, the legislature amended the vehicular homicide provisions in 1983 and 1984 to make them read as they now exist.

Because none of the homicide statutes provide a statutory definition of the term "human being," this court may refer to common law rules as an aid to construction or interpretation of the phrase as it is used in the vehicular homicide statute.

At common law it is clear that only a living human being could be the victim of a homicide. To become a human being within the meaning of homicide statutes at common law, a child had to be born alive and have an existence independent of and separate from its mother ... The "born alive" rule dates back to at least the 17th century when the great common lawyer, Sir Edward Coke, wrote that the killing of an unborn quickened child "is a great misprision and no murder." The courts and commentators accepted Coke's views as authoritative on the common law. The "born alive" requirement was reiterated by Blackstone ... as has been elsewhere thoroughly documented, Blackstone had tremendous impact on the development of the common law in the original American colonies and in the early states of this new country. By 1850, the "born alive" rule had widespread general acceptance by all jurisdictions in the United States which had considered the issue.

We have been informed by brief and in oral argument, that of 25 jurisdictions in the United States which have considered the issue, both in so-called "common law" and in so-called "code" states, 23 have adopted the "born alive" rule. From the foregoing it is clear that the common law "born alive" rule is now well-established in the great majority of jurisdictions. In many jurisdictions the rule existed long before enactment of the vehicular homicide statutes by our own legislature.

While neither commentaries by renowned common law authorities nor precedents from foreign jurisdictions with respect to the interpretation of the words, "human being" are binding on us by principles of stare decisis, they are of considerable persuasion, particularly in view of their near unanimity....

The state, however, contends that instead of reliance on the common law of other jurisdictions, this court should confine itself to what the state considers to be the common law of Minnesota. The state argues that this court in *Verkennes v. Corniea* recognized that an unborn fetus could be a human being. The state then claims that *Verkennes* should provide the controlling authority for common law interpretation of "human being" in this case. In *Verkennes* we held the personal representative of an unborn but viable fetus, capable of a separate and independent existence, could maintain a civil action under the Minnesota Death by Wrongful Act Statute. The state ... asserts that by so ruling we implicitly rejected the "born alive" common law rule.... As support, the state cites Minn.Stat. § 645.17(4) which reads, "When a court of last resort has construed the language of a law, the legislature in subsequent laws on the same subject matter intends the same construction to be placed upon such language."

We decline to draw that inference ... It does not follow that because we held in *Verkennes* that next of kin might recover damages arising out of the destruction of a viable fetus in a civil action under Minn.Stat. § 573.02, that a viable fetus is a "human being" for purposes of the criminal law. This court may exercise its common law powers to fashion a remedy for a civil wrong, as it did in *Verkennes*.... However, this court is forbidden to use its common law power to fashion crimes for public wrongs by Minn.Stat. § 609.015 where the legislature has expressly stated "[c]ommon law crimes are abolished and no act or omission is a crime unless made so by this chapter or by other applicable statute." ... By asking us to infer that the legislature, in enacting Minn. Stat. § 609.21 in 1963, intended "human being" to include a viable fetus in the light of *Verkennes*, the state is, in reality, urging us to declare by judicial fiat that the time has now come to prosecute under homicide statutes one who kills an unborn but viable fetus. Were we to do so, we would be drastically rewriting the homicide statutes under the guise of "construing" them. The courts of our sister jurisdictions, when confronted with similar requests by prosecutors in vehicular homicide cases, have recognized, as we do, that a change of that magnitude would constitute substantive change in the criminal law within the province of the legislature....

The common law, case law from other jurisdictions, our rules on statutory interpretation of criminal statutes, and the statutory history have convinced us that it is not within our judicial province, under the guise of interpretation, to hold that the words "human being" as used in Minn.Stat. § 609.21 (1984) encompass a viable 8½ month old fetus. The enactment of criminal laws, the scope of those laws, and the sanctions for their violation, are solely within the legislative function and province.

Accordingly, we affirm.

## *Notes and Questions*

1. Common law crimes have by and large been abolished in America. In many jurisdictions this has been accomplished by statute. The New Jersey statute is representative:

> 2C:1-5. Abolition of common law crimes; all offenses defined by statute
>
> a. Common law crimes are abolished and no conduct constitutes an offense unless the offense is defined by this code or another statute of this State.

2. As the Court points out in *Soto,* the judiciary may legitimately "exercise its common law powers to fashion a remedy for a civil wrong." Courts may even go as far as creating new torts. This is, for example, what courts did with the tort of "intentional infliction of emotional distress" (IIED). The tort of IIED was created by courts to deal with what appeared to be a shortcoming in the tort of assault, which only allowed the plaintiff to recover damages for emotional harm caused as a result of an imminent threat of battery. The new tort of IIED increased the number of instances in which a plaintiff could recover damages for emotional harm. This was viewed as a salutary development. Nevertheless, as the *Soto* court also points out, judicial creation of criminal offenses is increasingly frowned upon. What difference, if any, is there between a judicially created tort and a judicially created crime? What is so problematic about judicially created crimes?

3. According to one federal court, the principle of legality is:

> ... a necessary feature of the separation of powers, and in this context, it reinforces the rule that there are no common-law crimes. "In our system, so far at least as concerns the federal powers, defining crimes and fixing penalties are legislative, not judicial, functions." *see Lanier,* 520 U.S. at 267 n. 6 ("Federal crimes are defined by Congress, not the courts...."). *United States v. Jones,* 689 F.3d 696 (2012).

Do you agree that there is a link between the principle of legality and the separation of powers doctrine? Why or why not? Does the judicial creation of torts infringe the separation of powers doctrine? If it doesn't, what is it about judicial creation of crimes that sparks separation of powers concerns?

4. The Court in *Soto* claims that it "may refer to common law rules as an aid to interpretation of the phrase 'human being' as it is used in the vehicular homicide statute." Why is a court barred from creating common law crimes while it is simultaneously allowed to refer to the common law when construing the terms of a statute? Is there tension between a rule that holds that common law crimes are abolished and a rule that allows a court to refer to the common law when interpreting statutes?

## § 3.03 Principle of Legality: Prohibition of Retroactive Punishment

### Stogner v. California

Supreme Court of the United States, 2003
539 U.S. 607

Justice BREYER delivered the opinion of the Court.

California has brought a criminal prosecution after expiration of the time periods set forth in previously applicable statutes of limitations. California has done so under the authority of a new law that (1) permits resurrection of otherwise time-barred criminal prosecutions, and (2) was itself enacted *after* pre-existing limitations periods had expired. We conclude that the Constitution's *Ex Post Facto* Clause, Art. I, § 10, cl. 1, bars application of this new law to the present case.

I.

In 1993, California enacted a new criminal statute of limitations governing sex-related child abuse crimes. The new statute permits prosecution for those crimes where "[t]he limitation period specified in [prior statutes of limitations] has expired".... The statute thus authorizes prosecution for criminal acts committed many years beforehand—and where the original limitations period has expired....

In 1998, a California grand jury indicted Marion Stogner, the petitioner, charging him with sex-related child abuse committed decades earlier—between 1955 and 1973. Without the new statute allowing revival of the State's cause of action, California could not have prosecuted Stogner. The statute of limitations governing prosecutions at the time the crimes were allegedly committed had set forth a 3-year limitations period. And that period had run 22 years or more before the present prosecution was brought.

Stogner moved for the complaint's dismissal. He argued that the Federal Constitution's *Ex Post Facto* Clause, Art. I, § 10, cl. 1, forbids revival of a previously time-barred prosecution. The trial court agreed that such a revival is unconstitutional. But the California Court of Appeal reversed.... We granted certiorari to consider Stogner's constitutional claims.

II.

The Constitution's two *Ex Post Facto* Clauses prohibit the Federal Government and the States from enacting laws with certain retroactive effects. The law at issue here created a new criminal limitations period that extends the time in which prosecution is allowed. It authorized criminal prosecutions that the passage of time had previously barred. Moreover, it was enacted after prior limitations periods for Stogner's alleged offenses had expired. Do these features of the law, taken together, produce the kind of retroactivity that the Constitution forbids? We conclude that they do.

First, the new statute threatens the kinds of harm that, in this Court's view, the *Ex Post Facto* Clause seeks to avoid. Long ago Justice Chase pointed out that the Clause protects liberty by preventing governments from enacting statutes with "manifestly *unjust and oppressive*" retroactive effects. *Calder v. Bull.* Judge Learned Hand later wrote that extending a limitations period after the State has assured "a man that he has become safe from its pursuit ... seems to most of us unfair and dishonest." In such a case, the government has refused "to play by its own rules," It has deprived the defendant of the "fair warning" that might have led him to preserve exculpatory evidence.

Second, the kind of statute at issue falls literally within the categorical descriptions of *ex post facto* laws set forth by Justice Chase more than 200 years ago in *Calder v. Bull*—a categorization that this Court has recognized as providing an authoritative account of the scope of the *Ex Post Facto* Clause ... Chase divided *ex post facto* laws into categories that he described in two alternative ways. He wrote:

> I will state what laws I consider *ex post facto* laws, within the words and the intent of the prohibition. 1st. Every law that makes an action done before the passing of the law, and which was innocent when done, criminal; and punishes such action. *2d. Every law that aggravates a crime, or makes it greater than it was, when committed.* 3d. Every law that changes the punishment, and inflicts a greater punishment, than the law annexed to the crime, when committed. *4th. Every law that alters the legal rules of evidence, and receives less, or different, testimony, than the law required at the time of the commission of the offence, in order to convict the offender.* All these, and similar laws, are manifestly unjust and oppressive.

In his alternative description, Chase traced these four categories back to Parliament's earlier abusive acts, as follows:

> Category 1: "Sometimes they respected the crime, by declaring acts to be treason, which were not treason, when committed."
>
> Category 2: "*[A]t other times they inflicted punishments, where the party was not, by law, liable to any punishment.*"
>
> Category 3: "[I]n other cases, they inflicted greater punishment, than the law annexed to the offence."
>
> Category 4: "*[A]t other times, they violated the rules of evidence (to supply a deficiency of legal proof) by admitting one witness, when the existing law required two; by receiving evidence without oath; or the oath of the wife against the husband; or other testimony, which the courts of justice would not admit.*"

The second category—including any "law that *aggravates a crime,* or makes it *greater* than it was, when committed,"—describes California's statute as long as those words are understood as Justice Chase understood them—*i.e.,* as referring to a statute that "inflict[s] *punishments,* where the party was not, by *law,* liable to *any punishment,*" ... After (but not before) the original statute of limitations had expired, a party such as Stogner was not "liable to any punishment." California's new statute therefore "aggravated" Stogner's alleged crime, or made it "greater than it was, when committed," in the sense that, and to the extent that, it "inflicted punishment" for past criminal conduct that (when the new law was enacted) did not trigger any such liability....

In finding that California's law falls within the literal terms of Justice Chase's second category, we do not deny that it may fall within another category as well. Justice Chase's fourth category, for example, includes any "law that alters the *legal* rules of *evidence,* and receives less, or different, testimony, than the law required at the time of the commission of the offence, *in order to convict the offender.*" This Court has described that category as including laws that diminish "the quantum of evidence required to convict."

Significantly, a statute of limitations reflects a legislative judgment that, after a certain time, no quantum of evidence is sufficient to convict. And that judgment typically rests, in large part, upon evidentiary concerns—for example, concern that the passage of time has eroded memories or made witnesses or other evidence unavailable. Indeed, this Court once described statutes of limitations as creating "a presumption which renders proof unnecessary."

Consequently, to resurrect a prosecution after the relevant statute of limitations has expired is to eliminate a currently existing conclusive presumption forbidding prosecution, and thereby to permit conviction on a quantum of evidence where that quantum, at the time the new law is enacted, would have been legally insufficient. And, in that sense, the new law would "violate" previous evidence-related legal rules by authorizing the courts to "receiv[e] evidence ... which the courts of justice would not [previously have] admit[ted]" as sufficient proof of a crime.

Third, likely for the reasons just stated, numerous legislators, courts, and commentators have long believed it well settled that the *Ex Post Facto* Clause forbids resurrection of a time-barred prosecution. [Editor's Note: The Court goes on to cite multiple sources in support of its contention.]...

[Furthermore, while some courts] have upheld extensions of *unexpired* statutes of limitations (extensions that our holding today does not affect), they have consistently distinguished situations where limitations periods have *expired*. Further, they have often done so by saying that extension of existing limitations periods is not *ex post facto* "provided," "so long as," "because," or "if" the prior limitations periods have not expired—a manner of speaking that suggests a presumption that revival of time-barred criminal cases is *not* allowed....

### IV.

The statute before us is unfairly retroactive as applied to Stogner. A long line of judicial authority supports characterization of this law as *ex post facto*. For the reasons stated, we believe the law falls within Justice Chase's second category of *ex post facto* laws. We conclude that a law enacted after expiration of a previously applicable limitations period violates the *Ex Post Facto* Clause when it is applied to revive a previously time-barred prosecution. The California court's judgment to the contrary is

Reversed.

**Justice KENNEDY, with whom THE CHIEF JUSTICE, Justice SCALIA, and Justice THOMAS join, dissenting.**

California has enacted a retroactive extension of statutes of limitations for serious sexual offenses committed against minors. The new period includes cases where the limitations period has expired before the effective date of the legislation. To invalidate the statute in the latter circumstance, the Court tries to force it into the second category of *Calder v. Bull*, which prohibits a retroactive law "that *aggravates a crime*, or makes it *greater* than it was, when committed." These words, in my view, do not permit the Court's holding, but indeed foreclose it. A law which does not alter the definition of the crime but only revives prosecution does not make the crime "greater than it was, when committed." Until today, a plea in bar has not been thought to form any part of the definition of the offense....

There are scholars who have considered with care the meaning of [the second] category; and they reached the conclusion stated in this dissent, not the conclusion embraced by the majority. In his treatise on retroactive legislation, William Wade defined the category as covering the law "which undertakes to aggravate a past offence, and make it greater than when committed, endeavors to bring it under some description of transgression against which heavier penalties or more severe punishments have been denounced: as, changing the character of an act which, when committed, was a misdemeanor, to a crime; or, declaring a previously committed offence, of one of the classes graduated, and designated by the number of its degree, to be of a higher degree than it was when committed." Joel Prentiss Bishop's work on statutory crimes concluded that a law reviving expired prosecution "is not within any of the recognized legal definitions of an *ex post facto* law." The author's explanation is an apt criticism of the Court's opinion: "The punishment which it renders possible, by forbidding the defense of lapse of time, is exactly what the law provided when "the fact" transpired. No bending of language, no supplying of implied meanings, can, in natural reason, work out the contrary conclusion.... The running of the old statute had taken from the courts the right to proceed against the offender, leaving the violated Law without its former remedy; but it had not obliterated the fact that the law forbade the act when it was done, or removed from the doer's mind his original consciousness of guilt."...

This definition of *Calder's* second category is necessary for consistency with our accepted understanding of categories one and three. The first concerns laws declaring innocent acts to be a crime; the third prohibits retroactive increases in punishment. The first three categories guard against the common problem of retroactive redefinition of conduct by criminalizing it (category one), enhancing its criminal character (category two), or increasing the applicable punishment (category three). The link between these categories was noted by Justice Paterson in *Calder* itself: "The enhancement of a crime, or penalty, seems to come within the same mischief as the creation of a crime or penalty; and therefore they may be classed together."...

The Court's opinion renders the second *Calder* category unlimited and the surrounding categories redundant. A law which violates the first *Calder* category would also violate the Court's conception of category two, because such a law would "inflic[t] punishments, where the party was not, by law, liable to any punishment."...

The majority seems to suggest that retroactive extension of expired limitations periods is "arbitrary and potentially vindictive legislation," but does not attempt to support this accusation. And it could not do so. The California statute can be explained as motivated by legitimate concerns about the continuing suffering endured by the victims of childhood abuse.

The California Legislature noted that "young victims often delay reporting sexual abuse because they are easily manipulated by offenders in positions of authority and trust, and because children have difficulty remembering the crime or facing the trauma it can cause."...

The Court tries to counter by saying the California statute is "unfair and dishonest" because it violated the State's initial assurance to the offender that "he has become safe from its pursuit" and deprived him of "the fair warning." The fallacy of this rationale is apparent when we recall that the Court is careful to leave in place the uniform decisions by state and federal courts to uphold retroactive extension of unexpired statutes of limitations against an *ex post facto* challenge.

There are two rationales to explain the proposed dichotomy between unexpired and expired statutes, and neither works. The first rationale must be the assumption that if an expired statute is extended, the crime becomes more serious, thereby violating category two; but if an unexpired statute is extended, the crime does not increase in seriousness. There is no basis in logic, in our cases, or in the legal literature to support this distinction. Both extensions signal, with equal force, the policy to prosecute offenders.

This leaves the second rationale, which must be that an extension of the expired statute destroys a reliance interest. We should consider whether it is warranted to presume that criminals keep calendars so they can mark the day to discard their records or to place a gloating phone call to the victim. The first expectation is minor and likely imaginary; the second is not, but there is no conceivable reason the law should honor it. And either expectation assumes, of course, the very result the Court reaches; for if the law were otherwise, there would be no legitimate expectation. The reliance exists, if at all, because of the circular reason that the Court today says so; it does not exist as part of our traditions or social understanding....

The California statute does not fit any of the remaining *Calder* categories: It does not criminalize conduct which was innocent when done; it allows the prosecutor to seek the same punishment as the law authorized at the time the offense was committed and no more; and it does not alter the government's burden to establish the elements of the crime. Any concern about stale evidence can be addressed by the judge and the jury, and by the requirement of proof beyond reasonable doubt. Section 803(g), moreover, contains an additional safeguard: It conditions prosecution on a presentation of independent evidence that corroborates the victim's allegations by clear and convincing evidence. These protections, as well as the general protection against oppressive prosecutions offered by the Due Process Clause, should assuage the majority's fear, that the statute will have California overrun by vindictive prosecutions resting on unreliable recovered memories....

The Court's stretching of *Calder's* second category contradicts the historical understanding of that category, departs from established precedent, and misapprehends the purposes of the *Ex Post Facto* Clause. The Court also disregards the interests of those victims of child abuse who have found the courage to face their abusers and bring them to justice. The Court's opinion harms not only our *ex post facto* jurisprudence but also these and future victims of child abuse, and so compels my respectful dissent.

## *Notes and Questions*

1. As both the Majority and Dissenting Opinions reveal, retroactive application of a criminal statute runs afoul of the Constitution if it falls within one of the four categories of *ex post facto* laws put forth over two hundred years ago in *Calder v. Bull.* In a nutshell, the first three categories of *ex post facto* laws consist of statutes that either criminalize conduct that was innocent when it was performed or retroactively increase the punishment that attaches for the commission of the offense. The fourth category includes laws that alter the rules of evidence in a way that waters down the sufficiency of the evidence needed to convict or lowers the quantum of evidence needed to secure a conviction.

2. The majority argues that laws that revive expired statutes of limitation are unconstitutional because they fall within the second category of *ex post facto* laws discussed in *Calder.* This category includes "[e]very law that aggravates a crime, or makes it greater than it was, when committed." The majority contended that these laws aggravate the crime retroactively because they "inflict punishment for past criminal conduct that (when the new law was enacted) did not trigger any such liability." The Dissent argues that laws that alter the statute of limitations do not fall within this category because they do not aggravate the crime or increase the punishment to be imposed. According to the Dissent, such laws merely regulate the amount of time that a suspect is subject to being prosecuted. Who has the better part of this argument? Why?

3. As is pointed out in *Stogner*, the enactment of *ex post facto* laws is objectionable—at least in part—because it deprives defendants of fair warning, given that citizens cannot reasonably know that conduct that is innocent when performed will later be retroac-

tively criminalized. The majority in *Stogner* suggests that retroactively reviving an expired statute of limitations may deprive citizens of a certain kind of fair warning. Do you agree? Did the defendant in *Stogner* lack fair warning that his conduct was prohibited at the time of the commission of the sexual acts?

4. Citizens obviously have a right to know in advance the conduct that the state deems unlawful. Should they also have a right to know in advance the rules governing statutes of limitation? Why or why not? If citizens have a right to know in advance what the statute of limitations is for a given offense, is this right more, less or equally important than the right that citizens have to know in advance the conduct that the criminal law prohibits? Why?

5. Regardless of the fair warning issue, do you think it's unfair to retroactively revive an expired statute of limitation? Explain. Assuming that it's unfair to do so, do you believe that the extent of the unfairness is such that the state should be categorically barred from reviving expired statutes of limitation? Or would you rather have courts decide on a case-by-case basis whether the unfairness caused by reviving an expired statute of limitation is of such a degree to justify barring prosecution of the defendant in that particular case?

6. The Supreme Court has held that the prohibition of *ex post facto* laws bars retroactive application of substantive criminal laws, but it does not prohibit the retroactive application of procedural and evidentiary criminal statutes. *Colling v. Youngblood,* 497 U.S. 37 (1990). Nevertheless, the Court subsequently clarified that laws that reduce the quantum of evidence required to convict an offender may not be given retroactive application. *Carmell v. Texas,* 529 U.S. 513 (2000). Such laws fall within the fourth category put forth by the Court in *Calder v. Bull.*

In *Carmell,* for example, the applicable rules of evidence when the crime was committed held that a defendant may not be convicted of the sexual offense charged solely on the basis of the victim's testimony. That is, the victim's testimony had to be corroborated by additional evidence in order for a conviction to stand. After the commission of the offense, a law was enacted that authorized a conviction for the offense with which defendant was charged solely on the basis of the victim's uncorroborated testimony. The new evidentiary law was applied retroactively to the defendant. The Supreme Court held the retroactive application of this new rule of evidence to be *ex post facto,* for it impermissibly altered the sufficiency of the evidence needed to convict in a way that was prejudicial to the defendant.

Why is it that retroactive application of procedural and evidentiary laws does not usually give rise to *ex post facto* concerns? Do citizens have a right to know in advance what the applicable rules of criminal procedure and evidence are? If they do, is this right more, less or equally important than the right that citizens have to know in advance the conduct that the criminal law prohibits? Explain.

Are laws governing statutes of limitation substantive or procedural? If they are substantive, then it would appear that their retroactive application runs afoul of the *ex post facto* clause. However, if they are procedural, then it would seem that applying them retroactively is lawful. The majority in *Stogner* suggests that laws that revive an expired statute of limitation may fall within the fourth category of *ex post facto* laws described in *Calder.* Why? Do you agree?

7. Most state jurisdictions and Federal Courts of Appeal have held that it is not *ex post facto* to retroactively change rules that govern the admissibility of evidence in a way will often or always be prejudicial to the defendant, for the only procedural and evidentiary rules that trigger the prohibition of *ex post facto* laws are those that affect the sufficiency

of the evidence or reduce the quantum of evidence needed for conviction. The California case of *People v. Flores*, 176 Cal. App. 4d 1171 (2009), illustrates this view. The defendant in *Flores* argued that a rule allowing evidence of his prior spousal battery convictions involving his former girlfriend could not be applied retroactively to his case because the admissibility of such evidence would always be prejudicial to defendants like him. The Court rejected his contention because:

> Appellant ... ignores that the fourth category [described in *Calder v. Bull*] bars the government from changing rules involving the *legal sufficiency* of the evidence, not the *admissibility* of a particular piece of evidence bearing upon a particular fact to be proved.... Admission of appellants history of domestic violence did not change the elements of the crime of murder or lower the prosecutions burden of proving those elements beyond a reasonable doubt in order to achieve a conviction.... Introduction of past domestic violence did nothing more than admit evidence upon an issue of fact which was not previously admissible. Appellant contends [that the new rule of evidence] always works in the prosecutions favor because the prosecutors ability to rely on propensity evidence strengthens the prosecutions hand.... As such, [the rule of evidence is], according to appellant, "unfair" and its unfairness violates the proscription against ex post facto application of laws, which has as its animating principle "fairness." [Appellant cites *Carmell* in support of his contention. Nevertheless, the following footnote from *Carmell* defeats appellant's argument]:
>
>> [Evidentiary] rules, by simply permitting evidence to be admitted at trial, do not at all subvert the presumption of innocence, because they do not concern whether the admissible evidence is sufficient to overcome the presumption. Therefore, to the extent one may consider changes to such laws as "unfair" or "unjust," they do not implicate the same *kind of unfairness implicated by* changes in rules setting forth a sufficiency of the evidence standard. Moreover, while the principle of unfairness helps explain and shape the Clause's scope, it is not a doctrine unto itself, invalidating laws under the *Ex Post Facto Clause by its own force. Carmell v. Texas,* footnote 23.
>
> Consequently, even if admission of evidence showing a history of domestic violence disadvantages appellant, it does not violate his constitutional right to be free of ex post facto application of the law. *Flores*, 176 Cal. App. 4d 1171.

Do you agree with the result in *Flores*? Why or why not?

## § 3.04 Principle of Legality: Prohibition of Vagueness

### Rose v. Locke

Supreme Court of the United States, 1975
423 U.S. 48

PER CURIAM.

Respondent was convicted in the Criminal Court for Knox County, Tenn., of having committed a "crime against nature" in violation of [Tennessee law]. The evidence showed that he had entered the apartment of a female neighbor late at night on the pretext of using the telephone. Once inside, he produced a butcher knife, forced his neighbor to partially disrobe, and compelled her to submit to his twice performing cunnilingus upon her. He was sentenced to five to seven years' imprisonment. The Tennessee Court of Criminal Appeals affirmed the conviction, rejecting respondent's claim that the Tennessee statute's proscription of "crimes against nature" did not encompass cunnilingus, as well as his contention that the statute was unconstitutionally vague. The Supreme Court of Tennessee denied review.

Respondent renewed his constitutional claim in a petition for a writ of habeas corpus filed in the District Court for the Eastern District of Tennessee. The District Court denied respondent's petition, holding that when considered in light of previous interpretations by the courts of Tennessee, the [offense charged] was "not unconstitutionally vague nor impermissibly overbroad."

Respondent appealed to the Court of Appeals for the Sixth Circuit, and that court sustained his constitutional challenge. Believing that the statutory term "crimes against nature" could not "in and of itself withstand a charge of unconstitutional vagueness" and being unable to find any Tennessee opinion previously applying the statute to the act of cunnilingus, the Court of Appeals held that the statute failed to give respondent "fair warning."

It is settled that the fair-warning requirement embodied in the Due Process Clause prohibits the States from holding an individual "criminally responsible for conduct which he could not reasonably understand to be proscribed." But this prohibition against excessive vagueness does not invalidate every statute which a reviewing court believes could have been drafted with greater precision. Many statutes will have some inherent vagueness, for "(i)n most English words and phrases there lurk uncertainties." Even trained lawyers may find it necessary to consult legal dictionaries, treatises, and judicial opinions before they may say with any certainty what some statutes may compel or forbid. All the Due Process Clause requires is that the law give sufficient warning that men may conduct themselves so as to avoid that which is forbidden.

Viewed against this standard, the phrase "crimes against nature" is no more vague than many other terms used to describe criminal offenses at common law and now codified in state and federal penal codes. The phrase has been in use among English-speaking people for many centuries and a substantial number of jurisdictions in this country continue to utilize it. Anyone who cared to do so could certainly determine what particular acts have been considered crimes against nature, and there can be no contention that the respondent's acts were ones never before considered as such. *See, e.g., Comer v. State*, 21 Ga.App. 306 (1917); *State v. Townsend*, 145 Me. 384 (1950).

Respondent argued that the vice in the Tennessee statute derives from the fact that jurisdictions differ as to whether "crime against nature" is to be narrowly applied to only those acts constituting the common-law offense of sodomy, or is to be broadly interpreted to encompass additional forms of sexual aberration. We do not understand him to contend that the broad interpretation is itself impermissibly vague; nor do we think he could successfully do so. We have twice before upheld statutes against similar challenges. In State v. Crawford, the Supreme Court of Missouri rejected a claim that its crime-against-nature statute was so devoid of definition as to be unconstitutional, pointing out that its provision was derived from early English law and broadly embraced sodomy, bestiality, buggery, fellatio, and cunnilingus within its terms. We dismissed the appeal from this judgment as failing to present a substantial federal question. And in Wainwright v. Stone, supra, we held that a Florida statute proscribing "the abominable and detestable crime against nature" was not unconstitutionally vague, despite the fact that the State Supreme Court had recently changed its mind about the statute's permissible scope.

The Court of Appeals, relying on language in Stone, apparently believed these cases turned upon the fact that the state courts had previously construed their statutes to cover the same acts with which the defendants therein were charged. But although Stone demonstrated that the existence of previous applications of a particular statute to one set of facts forecloses lack-of-fair-warning challenges to subsequent prosecutions of factually identical conduct, it did not hold that such applications were a prerequisite to a statute's withstanding constitutional attack. If that were the case it would be extremely difficult ever to mount an effective prosecution based upon the broader of two reasonable constructions of newly enacted or previously unapplied statutes, even though a neighboring jurisdiction had been applying the broader construction of its identically worded provision for years.

Respondent seems to argue instead that because some jurisdictions have taken a narrow view of "crime against nature" and some a broader interpretation, it could not be determined which approach Tennessee would take, making it therefore impossible for him to know if [the offense charged] covered forced cunnilingus. But even assuming the correctness of such an argument if there were no indication which interpretation Tennessee might adopt, it is not available here. Respondent is simply mistaken in his view of Tennessee law. As early as 1955 Tennessee had expressly rejected a claim that "crime against nature" did not cover fellatio, repudiating those jurisdictions which had taken a "narrow restrictive definition of the offense." And four years later the Tennessee Supreme Court reiterated its view of the coverage intended by [the offense at issue here]. Emphasizing that the Tennessee statute's proscription encompasses the broad meaning, the court quoted from a Maine decision it had earlier cited with approval to the effect that "the prohibition brings all unnatural copulation with mankind or a beast, including sodomy, within its scope." And the Maine statute, which the Tennessee court had at that point twice equated with its own, had been applied to cunnilingus before either Tennessee decision. Thus, we think the Tennessee Supreme Court had given sufficiently clear notice that [the offense charged] would receive the broader of two plausible interpretations, and would be applied to acts such as those committed here when such a case arose.

This also serves to distinguish this case from *Bouie v. City of Columbia*, a decision the Court of Appeals thought controlling. In Bouie, the Court held that an unforeseeable judicial enlargement of a criminal statute narrow and precise on its face violated the Due Process Clause. It pointed out that such a process may lull "the potential defendant into a false sense of security, giving him no reason even to suspect that conduct clearly outside the scope of the statute as written will be retroactively brought within it by an act of judicial construction." But as we have noted, respondent can make no claim that [the offense charged] afforded no notice that his conduct might be within its scope. Other jurisdictions had already reasonably construed identical statutory language to apply to such acts. And given the Tennessee court's clear pronouncements that its statute was intended to effect broad coverage, there was nothing to indicate, clearly or otherwise, that respondent's acts were outside the scope of [the offense]. There is no possibility of retroactive lawmaking here. Accordingly, the petition for certiorari and respondent's motion to proceed in forma pauperis are granted, and the judgment of the Court of Appeals is reversed.

**Mr. Justice BRENNAN, with whom Mr. Justice MARSHALL concurs, dissenting.**

I dissent from the Court's summary reversal. The offense of "crimes against nature" at common law was narrowly limited to copulation per anum. American jurisdictions, however, expanded the term some broadly and some narrowly to include other sexual "aberrations." Of particular significance for this case, as the Court of Appeals accurately stated, "courts have differed widely in construing the reach of 'crimes against nature' to cunnilingus."

The Court holds, however, that because "(o)ther jurisdictions had already reasonably construed identical statutory language to apply to (cunnilingus) ... given the Tennessee court's clear pronouncements that its statute was intended to effect broad coverage, there was nothing to indicate, clearly or otherwise, that respondent's acts were outside the scope of the [offense charged]." In other words the traditional test of vagueness whether the statute gives fair warning that one's conduct is criminal is supplanted by a test of whether there is anything in the statute "to indicate, clearly or otherwise, that respondent's acts were outside the scope of" the statute. This stands the test of unconstitutional vagueness on its head. And this startling change in vagueness law is accompanied by the equally startling holding that, although the Tennessee courts had not previously construed "crimes against nature" to include cunnilingus, respondent cannot be heard to claim that [the text of the offense charged], therefore afforded no notice that his conduct fell within its scope, because he was on notice that Tennessee courts favored a broad reach of "crimes against nature" and other state courts favoring a broad reach had construed their state statutes to include cunnilingus....

Nor will the Court's assertions that the Tennessee courts had in any event in effect construed the Tennessee statute to include cunnilingus withstand analysis. The Court relies on a 1955 Tennessee decision that had held that "crimes against nature" include fellatio, the Tennessee court rejecting the contention that the statute was limited to the common-law copulation-per-anum scope of the phrase. The Tennessee court in that opinion cited a Maine case, decided in 1938, where the Maine court had applied a "crimes against nature" statute to fellatio. But the Tennessee court did not also cite a 1950 Maine decision that applied Maine's "crimes against nature" statute to cunnilingus. Four years later, in 1959, in another fellatio case, the Tennessee court again made no mention of Townsend.... Despite this significant failure of the Tennessee court to cite Townsend, and solely on the strength of the Tennessee court's general "equating" of the Maine statute with the Tennessee statute, this Court holds today that respondent had sufficient notice that the Tennessee statute would receive a "broad" interpretation that would embrace cunnilingus.

This 1974 attempt to bootstrap 1950 Maine law for the first time into the Tennessee statute must obviously fail if the principle of fair warning is to have any meaning. When the Maine court in 1938 applied its statute broadly to all "unnatural copulation," nothing said by the Maine court suggested that that phrase reached cunnilingus. The common-law "crime against nature," limited to copulation per anum, required penetration as an essential element. In holding that a "broad" reading of that phrase should encompass all unnatural copulation including fellatio copulation per os Maine could not reasonably be understood as including cunnilingus in that category. Other jurisdictions, though on their State's particular statutory language, have drawn that distinction. Thus, when the Tennessee court in 1955 adopted the language of Maine's 1938 case, a Tennessee citizen had at most notice of developments in Maine law through 1938. That Maine subsequently in 1950 applied its statute to cunnilingus is irrelevant, for such subsequent developments were not "adopted" by the Tennessee court until the case before us. Indeed, the Tennessee court's failure in its 1955 Fisher opinion to cite Townsend, Maine's 1950 cunnilingus decision ... more arguably was notice that the Tennessee courts considered fellatio but not cunnilingus as within the nebulous reach of the Tennessee statute....

The principle that due process requires that criminal statutes give sufficient warning to enable men to conform their conduct to avoid that which is forbidden is one of the great bulwarks of our scheme of constitutional liberty. The Court's erosion today of that great principle ... reaches a dangerous level of judicial irresponsibility. I would have denied the petition for certiorari, but now that the writ has been granted would affirm the judgment of the Court of Appeals....

## *Notes and Questions*

1. As *Rose v. Locke* illustrates, excessively vague criminal laws run afoul of the *Due Process* clauses of the Fifth and Fourteenth Amendment. Such laws are unconstitutional because they fail to give the citizenry fair warning about the conduct proscribed by the statute. The offense charged in *Rose v. Locke* proscribed engaging in the "crime against nature." Do you believe that an average layperson would know what conduct is prohibited pursuant to this statute? The Court suggests that an average person may not know what the "crime against nature" proscribes. Nevertheless, it notes that citizens—and even trained lawyers—may need to "consult legal dictionaries, treatises, and judicial opinions before they may say with any certainty what some statutes may compel or forbid." Does a statute that requires an average person to consult case law, treatises and legal dictionaries in order to determine the scope of the prohibited conduct provide "fair warning"?

2. As both the majority and dissenting opinions note, at common law the "crime against nature" was limited to engaging in anal intercourse. Nevertheless, some jurisdictions later expanded the scope of the offense to encompass other kinds of intercourse, including oral sex. Others refused to expand the scope of the offense in this manner. At the time that the defendant engaged in the sexual act that gave rise to the charge in *Rose v. Locke*, the Supreme Court of Tennessee had not ruled that cunnilingus was an act that could give rise to prosecution for engaging in the "crime against nature," although it had decided that "fellatio" did trigger prosecution for the offense. The Supreme Court of the United States noted, however, that the Supreme Courts of Georgia and Maine had ruled that the "crime against nature" includes engaging in cunnilingus. Should the decisions of other jurisdictions be relevant to determining whether the statute with which the defendant is charged is excessively vague? Why or why not?

3. Which branch of government decided that performing oral sex satisfied the elements of the Tennessee offense that proscribed engaging in the "crime against nature"? It is difficult to argue that it was the legislature, for the common law definition of the crime against nature limited the offense to engaging in anal sexual intercourse. Ultimately, it was the Tennessee courts who decided that the crime against nature includes engaging in oral sex. Do you think that it is legitimate for courts to engage in this kind of expansion of criminal offenses? What is the difference between what the Tennessee courts did in *Rose v. Locke* and the judicial creation of common law crimes that was frowned upon by the Minnesota Supreme Court in *State v. Soto* (§ 3.02)? Do you believe that the kind of power that Tennessee courts wielded in *Rose v. Locke* raises separation of powers concerns? Why or why not? If you are troubled by courts exercising their power in this manner, can you articulate what exactly is it that is a cause for concern? Is it that this kind of judicial power raises fair warning issues? Something else? If so, what?

4. The Supreme Court has struck down as unconstitutionally vague statutes that afford unfettered and arbitrary discretion to police officers. In *Papchristou v. City of Jacksonville*, 405 U.S. 156 (1972), for example, the Court was asked to assess the constitutionality of the following vagrancy city ordinance:

> Rogues and vagabonds, or dissolute persons who go about begging; common gamblers, persons who use juggling or unlawful games or plays, common drunkards, common night walkers ... persons wandering or strolling around from place to place without any lawful purpose or object.... persons neglecting all lawful business and habitually spending their time by frequenting houses of ill fame, gaming houses, or places where alcoholic beverages are sold or served.... shall be deemed vagrants and, upon conviction in the Municipal Court shall be punished as provided for Class D offenses. *Id.*

The Supreme Court held the ordinance unconstitutional because it both "fail[ed] to give a person of ordinary intelligence fair notice that his contemplated conduct is forbidden by the statute," and because it "encourage[ed] arbitrary and erratic arrests and convictions." *Papchristou,* 405 U.S. 156. The Court was concerned that "the Jacksonville ordinance makes criminal activities which, by modern standards, are normally innocent," such as "nightwalking." The Court was also worried that the overly broad statute gave the police limitless discretion to decide whom to arrest without having to justify their decision. More specifically, the Supreme Court was troubled by the fact that "[a] vagrancy prosecution may be merely the cloak for a conviction which could not be obtained on the real but undisclosed grounds for the arrest." What are the "real but undisclosed grounds for arrest" that the court is worried that vagrancy prosecutions might legitimate?

5. For obvious reasons, vagrancy ordinances fell in disfavor after *Papachristou.* Nevertheless, states devised other mechanisms to grant broad discretion to police officers in deciding whom to arrest. During the 1990s, legislatures and city councils attempted to do this primarily by enacting Anti-Gang ordinances. In *City of Chicago v. Morales,* 527 U.S. 41 (1999), the Supreme Court was asked to pass upon the constitutionality of one such ordinance. The ordinance allowed a police officer to ask two or more persons to disperse and remove themselves from a public area if the officer "reasonably believed" that one or more of the persons present was a "gang member" and that they were "loitering." The ordinance defined "loitering" as "remaining in one place with no apparent purpose." Furthermore, it made it a crime to disobey the police officer's order to disperse.

The Supreme Court struck down the ordinance because—like the vagrancy ordinance in *Papachristou*—it criminalized "a substantial amount of innocent conduct" and it impermissibly provided the police with "absolute discretion" to determine what counts as "loitering." The Court also pointed out that:

> The broad sweep of the ordinance ... violates "the requirement that a legislature establish minimal guidelines to govern law enforcement." *Kolender* v. *Lawson,* 461 U.S., at 358. There are no such guidelines in the ordinance. In any public place in the city of Chicago, persons who stand or sit in the company of a gang member may be ordered to disperse unless their purpose is apparent. The mandatory language in the enactment directs the police to issue an order without first making any inquiry about their possible purposes. It matters not whether the reason that a gang member and his father, for example, might loiter near Wrigley Field is to rob an unsuspecting fan or just to get a glimpse of Sammy Sosa leaving the ballpark; in either event, if their purpose is not apparent to a nearby police officer, she may—indeed, she "shall"—order them to disperse. *Papchristou,* 405 U.S. 156.

What conduct did the Chicago ordinance prohibit? Was it "loitering" with a "gang member" or was it disobeying an officer's order to disperse? Did the ordinance in *Morales* fail to provide the citizenry with fair warning regarding prohibited conduct? Explain.

Assuming that the ordinance did provide fair warning, are there still cogent reasons for striking it down? Which branch of government ultimately decided what type of conduct would give rise to prosecution for violating the Chicago Anti-Gang ordinance? Does this kind of ordinance—or the one in *Papachristou*—raise separation of powers concerns?

## § 3.05 Principle of Legality: Prohibition of Retroactive Interpretation of Statutes and the Rule of Lenity

### McBoyle v. United States

Supreme Court of the United States, 1931
283 U.S. 25

Mr. Justice HOLMES delivered the opinion of the Court.

The petitioner was convicted of transporting from Illinois to Oklahoma, an airplane that he knew to have been stolen, and was sentenced to serve three years' imprisonment and to pay a fine of $2,000. The judgment was affirmed by the Circuit Court of Appeals for the Tenth Circuit. A writ of certiorari was granted by this Court on the question whether the National Motor Vehicle Theft Act applies to aircraft. That Act provides:

> Sec. 2. That when used in this Act: (a) The term 'motor vehicle' shall include an automobile, automobile truck, automobile wagon, motor cycle, or any other self-propelled vehicle not designed for running on rails.... Sec. 3. That whoever shall transport or cause to be transported in interstate or foreign commerce a motor vehicle, knowing the same to have been stolen, shall be punished by a fine of not more than $5,000, or by imprisonment of not more than five years, or both.

Section 2 defines the motor vehicles of which the transportation in interstate commerce is punished in Section 3. The question is the meaning of the word 'vehicle' in the phrase 'any other self-propelled vehicle not designed for running on rails.' No doubt etymologically it is possible to use the word to signify a conveyance working on land, water or air.... But in everyday speech 'vehicle' calls up the picture of a thing moving on land.... So here, the phrase under discussion calls up the popular picture. For after including automobile truck, automobile wagon and motor cycle, the words 'any other self-propelled vehicle not designed for running on rails' still indicate that a vehicle in the popular sense, that is a vehicle running on land is the theme. It is a vehicle that runs, not something, not commonly called a vehicle, that flies. Airplanes were well known in 1919 when this statute was passed, but it is admitted that they were not mentioned in the reports or in the debates in Congress. It is impossible to read words that so carefully enumerate the different forms of motor vehicles and have no reference of any kind to aircraft, as including airplanes under a term that usage more and more precisely confines to a different class....

Although it is not likely that a criminal will carefully consider the text of the law before he murders or steals, it is reasonable that a fair warning should be given to the world in language that the common world will understand, of what the law intends to do if a certain line is passed. To make the warning fair, so far as possible the line should be clear. When a rule of conduct is laid down in words that evoke in the common mind only the picture of vehicles moving on land, the statute should not be extended to aircraft simply because it may seem to us that a similar policy applies, or upon the speculation that if the legislature had thought of it, very likely the picture of vehicles moving on land.

Judgment reversed.

## Rogers v. Tennessee

Supreme Court of the United States, 2001
532 U.S. 451

Justice O'Connor delivered the opinion of the Court.

This case concerns the constitutionality of the retroactive application of a judicial decision abolishing the common law "year and a day rule." At common law, the year and a day rule provided that no defendant could be convicted of murder unless his victim had died by the defendant's act within a year and a day of the act. The Supreme Court of Tennessee abolished the rule as it had existed at common law in Tennessee and applied its decision to petitioner to uphold his conviction. The question before us is whether, in doing so, the court denied petitioner due process of law in violation of the Fourteenth Amendment.

### I.

Petitioner Wilbert K. Rogers was convicted in Tennessee state court of second degree murder. According to the undisputed facts, petitioner stabbed his victim, James Bowdery, with a butcher knife on May 6, 1994. One of the stab wounds penetrated Bowdery's heart. During surgery to repair the wound to his heart, Bowdery went into cardiac arrest, but was resuscitated and survived the procedure. As a result, however, he had developed a condition known as "cerebral hypoxia," which results from a loss of oxygen to the brain. Bowdery's higher brain functions had ceased, and he slipped into and remained in a coma until August 7, 1995, when he died from a kidney infection (a common complication experienced by comatose patients). Approximately 15 months had passed between the stabbing and Bowdery's death which, according to the undisputed testimony of the county medical examiner, was caused by cerebral hypoxia "secondary to a stab wound to the heart."

Based on this evidence, the jury found petitioner guilty under Tennessee's criminal homicide statute. The statute, which makes no mention of the year and a day rule, defines criminal homicide simply as "the unlawful killing of another person which may be first degree murder, second degree murder, voluntary manslaughter, criminally negligent homicide or vehicular homicide." Petitioner appealed his conviction to the Tennessee Court of Criminal Appeals, arguing that, despite its absence from the statute, the year and a day rule persisted as part of the common law of Tennessee and, as such, precluded his conviction. The Court of Criminal Appeals rejected that argument and affirmed the conviction....

The Supreme Court of Tennessee affirmed.... The court observed that it had recognized the viability of the year and a day rule in Tennessee in *Percer* v. *State*, 118 Tenn. 765, 103 S. W. 780 (1907), and that, "[d]espite the paucity of case law" on the rule in Tennessee, "both parties ... agree that the ... rule was a part of the common law of this State." Turning to the rule's present status, the court noted that the rule has been legislatively or judicially abolished by the "vast majority" of jurisdictions recently to have considered the issue.... After reviewing the justifications for the rule at common law, however, the court found that the original reasons for recognizing the rule no longer exist. Accordingly, the court abolished the rule as it had existed at common law in Tennessee. [Petitioner argued that the Supreme Court of Tennessee's decision to retroactively abolish the year and a day rule violates his rights under the *ex post facto* and *Due Process* clauses of the United States Constitution.]

We granted certiorari, and we now affirm.

## II.

Although petitioner's claim is one of due process, the Constitution's *Ex Post Facto* Clause figures prominently in his argument. The Clause provides simply that "[n]o State shall ... pass any ... ex post facto Law." ...

As the text of the Clause makes clear, it "is a limitation upon the powers of the Legislature, and does not of its own force apply to the Judicial Branch of government."

We have observed, however, that limitations on *ex post facto* judicial decisionmaking are inherent in the notion of due process. In *Bouie* v. *City of Columbia*, we considered the South Carolina Supreme Court's retroactive application of its construction of the State's criminal trespass statute to the petitioners in that case. The statute prohibited "entry upon the lands of another ... after notice from the owner or tenant prohibiting such entry." ... The South Carolina court construed the statute to extend to patrons of a drug store who had received no notice prohibiting their entry into the store, but had refused to leave the store when asked. Prior to the court's decision, South Carolina cases construing the statute had uniformly held that conviction under the statute required proof of notice before entry. None of those cases, moreover, had given the "slightest indication that that requirement could be satisfied by proof of the different act of remaining on the land after being told to leave."

We held that the South Carolina court's retroactive application of its construction to the store patrons violated due process. Reviewing decisions in which we had held criminal statutes "void for vagueness" under the Due Process Clause, we noted that this Court has often recognized the "basic principle that a criminal statute must give fair warning of the conduct that it makes a crime." Deprivation of the right to fair warning, we continued, can result both from vague statutory language and from an unforeseeable and retroactive judicial expansion of statutory language that appears narrow and precise on its face. For that reason, we concluded that "[i]f a judicial construction of a criminal statute is 'unexpected and indefensible by reference to the law which had been expressed prior to the conduct in issue,' [the construction] must not be given retroactive effect." We found that the South Carolina court's construction of the statute violated this principle because it was so clearly at odds with the statute's plain language and had no support in prior South Carolina decisions.

Relying largely upon *Bouie,* petitioner argues that the Tennessee court erred in rejecting his claim that the retroactive application of its decision to his case violates due process. Petitioner contends that the *Ex Post Facto* Clause would prohibit the retroactive application of a decision abolishing the year and a day rule if accomplished by the Tennessee Legislature. He claims that the purposes behind the Clause are so fundamental that due process should prevent the Supreme Court of Tennessee from accomplishing the same result by judicial decree. In support of this claim, petitioner takes *Bouie* to stand for the proposition that "[i]n evaluating whether the retroactive application of a judicial decree violates Due Process, a critical question is whether the Constitution would prohibit the same result attained by the exercise of the state's legislative power."

To the extent petitioner argues that the Due Process Clause incorporates the specific prohibitions of the *Ex Post Facto* Clause as identified in *Calder*, petitioner misreads *Bouie* ... Our decision in *Bouie* was rooted firmly in well established notions of *due process*. Its rationale rested on core due process concepts of notice, foreseeability, and, in particular, the right to fair warning as those concepts bear on the constitutionality of attaching criminal penalties to what previously had been innocent conduct. And we couched its holding squarely in terms of that established due process right, and not in terms of the *ex post facto* [clause]....

Petitioner observes that the Due Process and *Ex Post Facto* Clauses safeguard common interests—in particular, the interests in fundamental fairness (through notice and fair warning) and the prevention of the arbitrary and vindictive use of the laws. While this is undoubtedly correct, petitioner is mistaken to suggest that these considerations compel extending the strictures of the *Ex Post Facto* Clause to the context of common law judging. The *Ex Post Facto* Clause, by its own terms, does not apply to courts. Extending the Clause to courts through the rubric of due process thus would circumvent the clear constitutional text. It also would evince too little regard for the important institutional and contextual differences between legislating, on the one hand, and common law decision making, on the other.

Petitioner contends that state courts acting in their common law capacity act much like legislatures in the exercise of their lawmaking function, and indeed may in some cases even be subject to the same kinds of political influences and pressures that justify *ex post facto* limitations upon legislatures. A court's "opportunity for discrimination," however, "is more limited than [a] legislature's, in that [it] can only act in construing existing law in actual litigation." Moreover, "[g]iven the divergent pulls of flexibility and precedent in our case law system," incorporation of the *Calder v. Bull* categories into due process limitations on judicial decision making would place an unworkable and unacceptable restraint on normal judicial processes and would be incompatible with the resolution of uncertainty that marks any evolving legal system.

That is particularly so where, as here, the allegedly impermissible judicial application of a rule of law involves not the interpretation of a statute but an act of common law judging. In the context of common law doctrines (such as the year and a day rule), there often arises a need to clarify or even to reevaluate prior opinions as new circumstances and fact patterns present themselves. Such judicial acts, whether they be characterized as "making" or "finding" the law, are a necessary part of the judicial business in States in which the criminal law retains some of its common law elements. Strict application of *ex post facto* principles in that context would unduly impair the incremental and reasoned development of precedent that is the foundation of the common law system. The common law, in short, presupposes a measure of evolution that is incompatible with stringent application of *ex post facto* principles. It was on account of concerns such as these that *Bouie* restricted due process limitations on the retroactive application of judicial interpretations of criminal statutes to those that are "unexpected and indefensible by reference to the law which had been expressed prior to the conduct in issue."

We believe this limitation adequately serves the common law context as well ... Accordingly, we conclude that a judicial alteration of a common law doctrine of criminal law violates the principle of fair warning, and hence must not be given retroactive effect, only where it is "unexpected and indefensible by reference to the law which had been expressed prior to the conduct in issue."...

### III.

Turning to the particular facts of the instant case, the Tennessee court's abolition of the year and a day rule was not unexpected and indefensible. The year and a day rule is widely viewed as an outdated relic of the common law. Petitioner does not even so much as hint that good reasons exist for retaining the rule, and so we need not delve too deeply into the rule and its history here. Suffice it to say that the rule is generally believed to date back to the 13th century, when it served as a statute of limitations governing the time in which an individual might initiate a private action for murder known as an "appeal of death;" that by the 18th century the rule had been extended to the law governing public prosecutions for murder; that the primary and most frequently cited justification for the rule is that 13th century medical science was incapable of establishing causation beyond a reasonable doubt when a great deal of time had elapsed between the injury to the victim and his death; and that, as practically every court recently to have considered the rule has noted, advances in medical and related science have so undermined the usefulness of the rule as to render it without question obsolete.

For this reason, the year and a day rule has been legislatively or judicially abolished in the vast majority of jurisdictions recently to have addressed the issue. Citing *Bouie*, petitioner contends that the judicial abolition of the rule in other jurisdictions is irrelevant to whether he had fair warning that the rule in Tennessee might similarly be abolished and, hence, to whether the Tennessee court's decision was unexpected and indefensible as applied to him. In discussing the apparent meaning of the South Carolina statue in *Bouie*, we noted that "[i]t would be a rare situation in which the meaning of a statute of another State sufficed to afford a person 'fair warning' that his own State's statute meant something quite different from what its words said." This case, however, involves not the precise meaning of the words of a particular statute, but rather the continuing viability of a common law rule. Common law courts frequently look to the decisions of other jurisdictions in determining whether to alter or modify a common law rule in light of changed circumstances, increased knowledge, and general logic and experience. Due process, of course, does not require a person to apprise himself of the common law of all 50 States in order to guarantee that his actions will not subject him to punishment in light of a developing trend in the law that has not yet made its way to his State. At the same time, however, the fact that a vast number of jurisdictions have abolished a rule that has so clearly outlived its purpose is surely relevant to whether the abolition of the rule in a particular case can be said to be unexpected and indefensible by reference to the law as it then existed.

Finally, and perhaps most importantly, at the time of petitioner's crime the year and a day rule had only the most tenuous foothold as part of the criminal law of the State of Tennessee. The rule did not exist as part of Tennessee's statutory criminal code. And while the Supreme Court of Tennessee concluded that the rule persisted at common law, it also pointedly observed that the rule had never once served as a ground of decision in any prosecution for murder in the State. Indeed, in all the reported Tennessee cases, the rule has been mentioned only three times, and each time in dicta....

These [three] cases hardly suggest that the Tennessee court's decision was "unexpected and indefensible" such that it offended the due process principle of fair warning articulated in *Bouie* and its progeny. This is so despite the fact that, as Justice Scalia correctly points out, the court viewed the year and a day rule as a "substantive principle" of the common law of Tennessee. As such, however, it was a principle in name only, having never once been enforced in the State. The Supreme Court of Tennessee also emphasized this fact in its opinion, and rightly so, for it is surely relevant to whether the court's abolition of the rule in petitioner's case violated due process limitations on retroactive judicial decisionmaking. And while we readily agree with Justice Scalia that fundamental due process prohibits the punishment of conduct that cannot fairly be said to have been criminal at the time the conduct occurred, nothing suggests that is what took place here.

There is, in short, nothing to indicate that the Tennessee court's abolition of the rule in petitioner's case represented an exercise of the sort of unfair and arbitrary judicial action against which the Due Process Clause aims to protect. Far from a marked and unpredictable departure from prior precedent, the court's decision was a routine exercise of common law decisionmaking in which the court brought the law into conformity with reason and common sense. It did so by laying to rest an archaic and outdated rule that had never been relied upon as a ground of decision in any reported Tennessee case.

The judgment of the Supreme Court of Tennessee is accordingly affirmed.

**Justice Scalia, with whom Justice Stevens and Justice Thomas join, and with whom Justice Breyer joins as to Part II, dissenting.**

The Court today approves the conviction of a man for a murder that was not murder (but only manslaughter) when the offense was committed. It thus violates a principle—encapsulated in the maxim *nulla poena sine lege*—which "dates from the ancient Greeks" and has been described as one of the most "widely held value-judgment[s] in the entire history of human thought." Today's opinion produces, moreover, a curious constitution that only a judge could love. One in which (by virtue of the *Ex Post Facto* Clause) the elected representatives of all the people cannot retroactively make murder what was not murder when the act was committed; but in which unelected judges can do precisely that. One in which the predictability of parliamentary lawmaking cannot validate the retroactive creation of crimes, but the predictability of judicial lawmaking can do so. I do not believe this is the system that the Framers envisioned—or, for that matter, that any reasonable person would imagine.

I.

A.

To begin with, let us be clear that the law here was altered after the fact. Petitioner, whatever else he was guilty of, was innocent of murder under the law as it stood at the time of the stabbing, because the victim did not die until after a year and a day had passed. The requisite condition subsequent of the murder victim's death within a year and a day is no different from the requisite condition subsequent of the rape victim's raising a "hue and cry" which we held could not retroactively be eliminated in *Carmell* v. *Texas,* 529 U.S. 513 (2000). Here, as there, it operates to bar conviction. Indeed, if the present condition differs at all from the one involved in *Carmell* it is in the fact that it does not merely pertain to the "quantum of evidence" necessary to corroborate a charge, but is an actual *element* of the crime—a "substantive principle of law," the failure to establish which "entirely precludes a murder prosecution." Though the Court spends some time questioning whether the year-and-a-day rule was ever truly established in Tennessee, the Supreme Court of Tennessee said it was, and this reasonable reading of state law by the State's highest court is binding upon us....

B.

The Court's opinion considers the judgment at issue here "a routine exercise of common law decisionmaking," whereby the Tennessee court "brought the law into conformity with reason and common sense," by "laying to rest an archaic and outdated rule." This is an accurate enough description of what modern "common law decisionmaking" consists of—but it is not an accurate description of the theoretical model of common-law decisionmaking accepted by those who adopted the Due Process Clause....

It is not a matter, [as the majority argues], of "[e]xtending the *[Ex Post Facto]* Clause to courts through the rubric of due process," and thereby "circumvent[ing] the clear constitutional text." It is simply a matter of determining what due judicial process consists of—and it does not consist of retroactive creation of crimes. The *Ex Post Facto* Clause is relevant only because it demonstrates beyond doubt that, however much the acknowledged and accepted role of common-law courts could evolve (as it has) in other respects, retroactive revision of the criminal law was regarded as so fundamentally unfair that an alteration of the judicial role which permits *that* will be a denial of due process. Madison wrote that "*ex-post-facto* laws ... are contrary to the first principles of the social compact, and to every principle of social legislation." I find it impossible to believe, as the Court does, that this strong sentiment attached only to retroactive laws passed by the legislature, and would not apply equally (or indeed with even greater force) to a court's production of the same result through disregard of the traditional limits upon judicial power. Insofar as the "first principles of the social compact" are concerned, what possible difference does it make that "[a] court's opportunity for discrimination" by retroactively changing a law "is more limited than a legislature's, in that it can only act in construing existing law in actual litigation?" The injustice to the individuals affected is no less.

II.

Even if I agreed with the Court that the Due Process Clause is violated only when there is lack of "fair warning" of the impending retroactive change, I would not find such fair warning here. It is not clear to me, in fact, what the Court believes the fair warning consisted of. Was it the mere fact that "[t]he year and a day rule is widely viewed as an outdated relic of the common law?" So are many of the elements of common-law crimes, such as "breaking the close" as an element of burglary, or "asportation" as an element of larceny. Are all of these "outdated relics" subject to retroactive judicial rescission? Or perhaps the fair warning consisted of the fact that "the year and a day rule has been legislatively or judicially abolished in the vast majority of jurisdictions recently to have addressed the issue." But why not count in petitioner's favor (as giving him no reason to expect a change in law) those even more numerous jurisdictions that have chosen *not* "recently to have addressed the issue?" And why not also count in petitioner's favor (rather than *against* him) those jurisdictions that have abolished the rule *legislatively*, and those jurisdictions that have abolished it through *prospective* rather than *retroactive* judicial rulings (together, a large majority of the abolitions)? That is to say, even if it was predictable that the rule would be changed, it was *not* predictable that it would be changed *retroactively*, rather than in the *prospective* manner to which legislatures are restricted by the *Ex Post Facto* Clause, or in the *prospective* manner that most other courts have employed.

In any event, as the Court itself acknowledges, "[d]ue process ... does not require a person to apprise himself of the common law of all 50 States in order to guarantee that his actions will not subject him to punishment in light of a developing trend in the law that has not yet made its way to his State."...

Finally, the Court seeks to establish fair warning by discussing at great length, *ante*, at 12–15, how unclear it was that the year-and-a-day rule was ever the law in Tennessee. As I have already observed, the Supreme Court of Tennessee is the authoritative expositor of Tennessee law, and has said categorically that the year-and-a-day rule was the law. Does the Court mean to establish the principle that fair warning of impending change exists—or perhaps fair warning can be dispensed with—when the prior law is not crystal clear? Yet another boon for retroactively created crimes.

I reiterate that the only "fair warning" discussed in our precedents, and the only "fair warning" relevant to the issue before us here, is fair warning *of what the law is*. That warning, unlike the new one that today's opinion invents, goes well beyond merely "safeguarding defendants against *unjustified* and *unpredictable* breaks with prior law." It safeguards them against *changes in the law after the fact.* But even accepting the Court's novel substitute, the opinion's conclusion that this watered-down standard has been met seems to me to proceed on the principle that a large number of almost-valid arguments makes a solid case. As far as I can tell, petitioner had nothing that could fairly be called a "warning" that the Supreme Court of Tennessee would retroactively eliminate one of the elements of the crime of murder.

[In sum], [w]hat a court cannot do, consistent with due process, is what the Tennessee Supreme Court did here: avowedly *change* (to the defendant's disadvantage) the criminal law governing past acts.

For these reasons, I would reverse the judgment of the Supreme Court of Tennessee.

## People v. Cornett

Supreme Court of California, 2012
53 Cal.4th 1261

CANTIL-SAKAUYE, C.J.

Penal Code section 288.7 makes it a felony, punishable by an indeterminate life term, for any adult to engage in specified sexual conduct "with a child who is 10 years of age or younger." Does the phrase "10 years of age or younger" include within its protection a child victim who is 10 years of age but has not yet reached his or her 11th birthday? Or is the phrase limited, as the majority of the Court of Appeal held, to children molested prior to the day of or on the day of their 10th birthday? We conclude that the interpretation of the statutory phrase "10 years of age or younger" includes children younger than 10 years of age and children who have reached their 10th birthday but who have not yet reached their 11th birthday. That is, "10 years of age or younger" as expressed by the Legislature in Penal Code section 288.7 is another means of saying "under 11 years of age." We reverse the judgment of the Court of Appeal that concluded otherwise.

### I.

Defendant Michael David Cornett sexually molested his two stepdaughters. He was convicted of seven felony sex offenses, including one count of oral copulation of Jane Doe 1 in violation of Penal Code section 288.7. With respect to his conviction of violating section 288.7(b) as to Jane Doe 1, the trial court imposed, but stayed pursuant to section 654, a sentence of 50 years to life.

Defendant claimed on appeal, among other things, that his section 288.7(b) conviction must be reversed and the count dismissed because Jane Doe 1—who was 10 years and approximately 11 months old at the time of the molestation—was not "10 years of age or younger" within the meaning of section 288.7. The majority of the Court of Appeal panel agreed with defendant that victims who have passed their 10th birthday fall outside the scope of section 288.7. The Court of Appeal dissent reasoned that common parlance and common sense supported the interpretation of section 288.7 as covering children until they reached their 11th birthday. We granted the People's petition for review.

### II.

To determine whether defendant was properly convicted of violating section 288.7(b), we must determine the meaning of the phrase "10 years of age or younger" as stated in section 288.7. The basic rules for statutory construction are well settled.

"As in any case involving statutory interpretation, our fundamental task here is to determine the Legislature's intent so as to effectuate the law's purpose." "We begin with the plain language of the statute, affording the words of the provision their ordinary and usual meaning and viewing them in their statutory context, because the language employed in the Legislature's enactment generally is the most reliable indicator of legislative intent."...

### A. *The Ordinary Meaning of "10 Years of Age"*

In accordance with these principles, we begin our consideration of the language of section 288.7 by noting that, with the exception of infants, an individual ordinarily states his or her age as the year or number of years accumulated since the birth year. In common parlance, a person reaches a particular age on the anniversary of his or her birth and remains that age until reaching the next anniversary of his or her birth....

Defendant contends this ordinary understanding of age is not the only reasonable understanding of the phrase "10 years of age" used in section 288.7. In his view, individuals are "under" a specified age before their birthday and "over" the specified age starting on the day after their birthday. Technically, they are a specific age only on their actual birthday. He argues that because the Legislature used the phrase "10 years of age or younger" and not the phrase "under 11 years of age," a precise reading of the chosen language would at most cover children up to and including their 10th birthday.

Defendant's proposed technical reading of the phrase "10 years of age or younger" is sufficiently plausible to demonstrate a latent ambiguity in the statutory language....

### D. *The Rule of Lenity*

Defendant further insists that because there are two plausible interpretations of the statutory language "10 years of age or younger," we must apply the "rule of 'lenity," under which courts resolve doubts as to the meaning of a statute in a criminal defendant's favor. Defendant asserts that failure to apply the rule would constitute judicial "legislating" and would violate his right to fair notice of the scope of section 288.7.

"[W]e have frequently noted, '[the rule of lenity] applies 'only if two reasonable interpretations of the statute stand in relative equipoise.' '[A] rule of construction ... is not a straitjacket. Where the Legislature has not set forth in so many words what it intended, the rule of construction should not be followed blindly in complete disregard of factors ****845* that may give a clue to the legislative intent.' "

Here, defendant's proposed construction of the statutory language is improbable and would impede the protective function of the Act. It is, therefore, not in relative equipoise with the application of a commonsense understanding of the language, which understanding is consistent with and promotes the Legislature's protective purpose. "[I]f a statute is amenable to two alternative interpretations, the one that leads to the more reasonable result will be followed[.]"

We reject defendant's assertion that a failure to apply the rule of lenity here would amount to judicial "legislating." As we have explained before, courts have "the constitutional duty and function of ascertaining legislative intent and construing statutes in accordance therewith. By necessity, this function becomes significant only when a statute is unclear in some respect. It would be inappropriate to automatically conclude that, because a statute is ambiguous in some respect, we are not to attempt to construe its meaning and effect. Such overbroad reliance upon one principle of statutory construction would constitute an abdication of our responsibility as the final arbiter of the meaning of legislative enactments."

We likewise reject defendant's assertion that interpreting the phrase "10 years of age or younger" in section 288.7 to mean "under 11 years of age" would fail to give fair warning to defendants regarding the scope of the statute.... We cannot credit that anyone would reasonably believe sexual conduct with a 10-year-old victim would violate section 288.7 up to and only on the exact day of the victim's 10th birthday. Like the Court of Appeal's dissenting justice, "we have absolutely no doubt that when defendant committed the heinous crime on Jane Doe I, he knew that she was '10 years of age.' What else could he have thought? She had not reached her eleventh birthday."

*E. The Law of Other States*

We recognize that a split of authority has developed among courts of other states that have grappled with the statutory meaning of the phrase "X years of age or younger." A number of courts have construed such language or similar language in accordance with the common understanding we have adopted here—as including children who have reached the specified birthday but have not yet reached their next birthday....

Other courts have restricted the meaning of language similar to "X years of age or younger" to children who have not passed the specified birthday....

[E]ven to the extent there remains a split of authority, this does not require us to adopt defendant's proposed narrow construction of section 288.7. California's rule of lenity "does not automatically grant a defendant 'the benefit of the most restrictive interpretation given any statute by any court' when there is a split of authority." We are persuaded here that our Legislature intended "10 years of age or younger" as used in section 288.7 to be another means of saying "under 11 years of age" in accordance with the ordinary understanding of "age."

The judgment of the Court of Appeal is reversed to the extent it concluded defendant was improperly convicted of violating section 288.7, subdivision (b) with respect to Jane Doe 1.

## Notes and Questions

1. Do you agree with Justice Holmes' contention in *McBoyle* that an airplane should not have been considered a "vehicle" under the National Motor Vehicle Safety Act? Why or why not? Holmes suggests that ruling that an airplane is a vehicle under the Act could deprive defendants of fair warning. Do you agree?

2. Both the majority and dissenting opinions in *Rogers v. Tennessee* agree that the "year and a day rule" could not have been abolished retroactively had it been legislatively enacted. In dissent, Justice Scalia argues that there is little reason to allow the courts to retroactively abolish the rule in circumstances in which the legislature would not have been able to do so. Do you agree? Explain.

3. Justice Scalia claimed that the "year and a day rule" was part of the elements of the offense of homicide in Tennessee. He thus argued that retroactively eliminating the rule was tantamount to retroactively eliminating an element of the offense in prejudice of the defendant. Nevertheless, as the majority points out, the Tennessee statute makes no mention of the year and a day rule, for it defines criminal homicide simply as "the unlawful killing of another person." Given that the homicide statute makes no express reference to the year and a day rule, why does Justice Scalia argue that abolishing the rule

eliminates an element of the offense? Is the "year and a day rule" conceptually related to an element of the offense of homicide even if it is not expressly included in the statute? Should citizens who live in "year and a day" jurisdictions have a right to know in advance about the rule? If they do, is this right more, less or equally important than the right to know in advance the actual elements of the offense of homicide (i.e., unlawful killing of a human being)?

4. The majority in *Rogers* noted that the Supreme Court held in *Bouie v. City of Columbia* that the Due Process clause bars the retroactive application of unforeseeable and indefensible judicial expansions of criminal statutes. As a result, it appears that such interpretations of criminal statutes are constitutional as long as they are applied prospectively. Should courts be allowed to broaden the scope of criminal statutes unforeseeably as long as they do not do so retroactively? What reasons might militate against unforeseeably expanding the scope of statutes even when it is done prospectively?

5. In *People v. Cornett*, the Supreme Court of California refused to apply the rule of lenity to construe the sexual offense in the manner more favorable to the defendant in spite of the fact that the Court acknowledged that the statute was "ambiguous." Do you agree with the Court's refusal to apply the rule of lenity in this case? The Court further explained that applying the rule of lenity was not necessary to safeguard defendant's right to have fair warning of the prohibited conduct. Do you agree? Why or why not? If the rule of lenity is not necessary to safeguard the citizenry's right to have fair warning of the conduct prohibited by criminal statutes, should the rule be abandoned? This is the subject of the next section.

## § 3.06 Principle of Legality: Model Penal Code

### Model Penal Code
### Section 1.02. Purposes; Principles of Construction

(1) The general purposes of the provisions governing the definition of offenses are:

> … (d) to give fair warning of the nature of the conduct declared to constitute an offense;

(2) The general purposes of the provisions governing the sentencing and treatment of offenders are:

> … (d) to give fair warning of the nature of the sentences that may be imposed on conviction of an offense;

(3) The provisions of the Code shall be construed according to the fair import of their terms but when the language is susceptible of differing constructions it shall be interpreted to further the general purposes stated in this Section and the special purposes of the particular provision involved. The discretionary powers conferred by the Code shall be exercised in accordance with the criteria stated in the Code and, insofar as such criteria are not decisive, to further the general purposes stated in this Section.

## State v. Lukas

2012-240, __ N.H. __
N.H. Sup. Ct., March 13, 2013

HICKS, J.

The defendant, Robin Lukas, appeals a decision of the Superior Court denying her motion to dismiss the indictment against her for theft by unauthorized taking. We affirm.

The only issue on appeal is whether the defendant, having been twice previously convicted of a class A misdemeanor theft or felony theft in another state, may be charged with class B felony theft as a third offense under [New Hampshire law]. This question requires us to engage in statutory interpretation, a question of law that we decide *de novo*. In matters of statutory interpretation, we are the final arbiter of the intent of the legislature as expressed in the words of a statute considered as a whole. We do not follow the common law rule that criminal statutes are to be strictly construed; rather, we construe them according to the fair import of their terms and to promote justice.

Regardless of the value of the property stolen, [the New Hampshire larceny statute] makes a theft crime a class B felony if "[t]he actor has been twice before convicted of theft of property or services, as a felony or class A misdemeanor."

The defendant argues that her prior out-of-state convictions may not be considered for the purpose of the [statute] because the legislature's intent in enacting this provision was to "exclude out-of-state convictions." We disagree. The relevant definitions of a felony and a class A misdemeanor evince a clear legislative intent to include theft crimes committed outside of New Hampshire as predicate offenses triggering the sentence enhancement of [the statute]....

*Affirmed.*

### *Notes and Questions*

1. The Model Penal Code rejects the common law rule of strict construction. In its place, it adopts what it calls the "rule of fair import." The fair import rule mandates that ambiguities in statutes be resolved in a way that furthers the purposes of the code and the particular provision being construed. Many states have followed suit, including New Hampshire, as *State v. Lukas* demonstrates. This reveals that while the common law rule of lenity (rule of strict construction) is invoked by many courts, adherence to the rule is by no means unanimous and not constitutionally required. Is the Model Penal Code's "fair import rule" preferable to the common law's "rule of strict construction"? Why or why not?

2. The Model Penal Code lists "giving fair warning" of the criminal conduct as one of its chief purposes. Nevertheless, it declines to adopt the rule of lenity. Obviously, the Code drafters believed that giving fair warning does not require adoption of the rule of lenity. Do you agree? Why or why not?

3. The New Hampshire Supreme Court held in *State v. Lukas* that out of state convictions may be used to trigger the sentencing enhancement at issue in that case. In doing so, it refused to apply the rule of lenity to construe the statute in the way most favorable to the defendant. Would the result in *Lukas* have been different had the New Hampshire Supreme Court applied the rule of lenity as it was conceived by the California Supreme Court in *People v. Cornett* (§ 3.05)? Explain.

# § 3.07 Principle of Legality: Comparative Perspectives

## Judgment of the Spanish Constitutional Court 62/1982

October, 1982

... Defendant published a sex education book for young children titled "To See". The book was distributed to parents and teachers. Defendant was subsequently charged with public indecency [Editor's Note: literally translated, the offense would be called "public scandal"] ... He was eventually held liable and sentenced to a term of imprisonment of a month and a day. [On appeal to this Court], the defendant argues that he was convicted in violation of the rights secured by the principle of legality prescribed in Art. 25, num. 1 of the Spanish Constitution....

[Defendant argues that the principle of legality was infringed] because the offense charged requires proof that the defendant engage in conduct that is contrary to "morals, social mores and public decency" and that such elements are abstract, subjective and indeterminate. As a result, defendant contends that such elements fail to spell out the nature of the prohibited conduct with the specificity that is required by the principle of legality.

In addressing defendant's contention, we must recall that Art. 25.1 of the Spanish Constitution establishes that no one may be convicted of a crime for engaging in acts or omissions that did not amount to criminal offenses when the acts or omissions were performed. The right secured [by Art. 25.1] is essential to securing that the law provides those subject to it with the ability to regulate their conduct [and that people can organize their affairs without fear that the legal status of their conduct will be altered arbitrarily]. As a result, [the principle of legality] also requires that the legislature must make the utmost effort to ensure that criminal offenses are drafted in the most specific way possible. Nevertheless, this does not mean that the principle of legality is infringed if the criminal statute includes elements that leave some margin for judicial construction, especially when the elements are essential to safeguarding important legally protected interests. [This is precisely what happens in this case].

[Given that it is of great importance to protect minors from corrupting influences, the degree of vagueness of the criminal offense with which the defendant was charged ought to be tolerated. As a result, the judgment of the lower courts is affirmed].

### *Notes and Questions*

1. It is often said in European Continental jurisdictions that the principle of legality encompasses four interrelated doctrines. First, it requires that criminal laws be written down in a statute as opposed to being the product of judicial decisions or customary law. This is typically called the "written law principle." Second, it demands that the legislature draft criminal laws in the most specific way possible. This is frequently called the "principle of specificity." Third, the legality principle is thought to bar the retroactive application of criminal laws that are prejudicial to the defendant. Finally, the principle of legality requires that judges abstain from expanding the scope of a statute beyond the conventionally accepted meaning of its terms to encompass cases that can—by a process of analogical reasoning—be likened to the cases that actually fall within the clear scope of the rule. This is usually called the "prohibition of analogy." *See, generally,* Francisco Muñoz Conde & Mercedes García Arán, *Derecho Penal: Parte General* 102–108 (Valencia, 2010).

2. In the judgment excerpted in this section, the defendant challenged the constitutionality of the offense of "public indecency," arguing that the crime was drafted in an excessively indeterminate manner. As a result, he argued that the legislature drafted the offense in a way that ran afoul the specificity principle, which, in turn, is derived from the principle of legality. In assessing the defendant's claim, the Spanish Constitutional Court explained that the legality principle requires that legislatures write criminal statutes in the most specific way possible, so as to assure that citizens know what it is that the criminal law expects of them.

3. Compare and contrast the American approach to the void for vagueness doctrine as illustrated by the Supreme Court of the United States in *Rose v. Locke* ("crime against nature" case) with the specificity doctrine as espoused by the Spanish Constitutional Court in the judgment excerpted in the current section. Does the American void for vagueness doctrine require that the legislature draft the offense with as much specificity as possible? Does the Spanish specificity doctrine allow the judiciary to infuse a statute that was vaguely drafted by the legislature with the specificity that is needed for it to satisfy the principle of legality? Does the American void for vagueness doctrine allow the judiciary to specify the content of a statute that was originally drafted by the legislature in an unduly vague manner? Which approach do you prefer?

4. In European Continental jurisdictions, the principle of legality secures not only that citizens have fair warning regarding the prohibited conduct, but also that judges do not usurp the legislature's authority to enact laws. In such countries, it is believed that the legislature is the only branch of government that may legitimately criminalize conduct. As a result, the specificity principle is directed solely at the legislature, for it is the legislature's duty to enact criminal laws with sufficient specificity as to provide the citizenry with fair warning regarding the conduct prohibited by law. Furthermore, given that the specificity principle is directed at the legislature, the legislature's failure to draft criminal statutes with sufficient specificity cannot be remedied by judicial pronouncements that specify the nature of the prohibited conduct. As Diego Manuel Luzón Peña—one of Spain's leading criminal law scholars—explains:

> The principle of legality is infringed when the legislature drafts criminal offenses using vague, imprecise or indeterminate terms ... because doing so ends up leaving the task of determining the precise scope of the prohibited conduct to the judge. This is contrary to the principle that only the legislature may enact criminal statutes. Diego Manuel Luzón Peña, *Lecciones de Derecho Penal: Parte General* 59 (2nd ed., Valencia, 2012).

Is this view of the specificity principle compatible with the American approach to the void for vagueness doctrine? Explain.

5. In European Continental jurisdictions, the principle of legality also bars the legislature from enacting vague laws even when the legislature delegates to administrative agencies the power to specify the content of the prohibited conduct by promulgation of administrative regulations. Professors Muñoz Conde and García Arán explain:

> The power to enact criminal laws lies solely within the province of the legislature. Consequently, regardless of the exquisitely specific way in which an administrative regulation may define conducts that give rise to criminal liability, the principle of legality requires that such specificity in the definition of the criminal conduct stem from legislative action rather than from administrative regulation, for the legitimacy of criminal law flows from criminalization decisions that reflect the popular will of the people as expressed by their elected representatives. Muñoz Conde & García Arán, *supra*, at 105.

This approach stands in stark contrast with American law. The Supreme Court has held that the legislature may lawfully delegate to administrative agencies the power to define the prohibited conduct with specificity as long as the legislature establishes in the law an "intelligible principle" that channels the administrative agency's discretion. *See, e.g., United States v. Grimaud,* 220 U.S. 506 (1911). The "intelligible principle" standard is easily satisfied with vague legislative directives. Such vague "intelligible principles" would surely fail to satisfy the more stringent requirements of the specificity principle as it is conceived in European Continental jurisdictions. What interests are furthered by the more stringent European Continental approach to this issue? What interests are furthered by the more permissive American approach to this matter? Which approach do you prefer? Why?

6. Note that the Spanish Supreme Court upheld the constitutionality of the "public indecency" statute, contending that the vague drafting was necessary to accomplish the aim of protecting minors from corrupting influences. Do you agree that the statute complied with the specificity principle as explained by both the Court and the scholars cited in the previous notes? Explain. Would the public indecency statute be declared void for vagueness in America? Why or why not?

7. Many Spanish scholars have criticized the excerpted judgment, arguing that the "public indecency" statute should have been struck down because it infringed the legality principle. *See, e.g.,* Juan Cianciardo, *Los Límites de los Derechos Fundamentales,* in Reasonableness and Interpretation 209, fn. 33 (London, 2003). The "public indecency" offense was later eliminated in a reform of the Spanish Penal Code.

## § 3.08 Principle of Legality: Scholarly Debates

### Paul H. Robinson, *Fair Notice and Fair Adjudication: Two Kinds of Legality*

154 U. Pa. L. Rev. 335 (2005)

Our form of government and our legal system are distinguished from others by their commitment to the "rule of law." In the criminal law, in particular, this commitment is aggressively enforced through a series of doctrines that, taken together, demand a prior legislative enactment expressed with precision and clarity, traditionally bannered as the "legality principle." However, it is argued here that the traditional legality principle analysis actually conflates two distinct issues: one relating to the ex ante need for fair notice, the other to the ex post concern for fair adjudication. There are in fact two different kinds of legality—rules legality and adjudication legality—that suggest different, and sometimes conflicting, conclusions about the proper formulation and application of the legality doctrines. The criminal law would be better served, it is argued, by giving these two principles independent recognition and application.

The five rationales commonly offered in support of the legality principle do not apply evenly to the two functions of criminal law. Providing fair notice and gaining compliance, including providing effective deterrence and avoiding overdeterrence (the "chilling effect"), strictly address the ex ante rule articulation function. These rationales are designed to ensure that the rules of conduct can be known and understood and can guide individuals to remain law-abiding. In contrast, increasing uniformity in application and reducing the potential for abuse of discretion are rationales that apply directly to the adjudication function. They urge interpretations and applications of the principles of adjudication that avoid unnecessary discretion. The rationale of reserving the criminalization authority to the legislature applies to both functions....

Thus, both to best advance the legality rationales and to best perform the criminal law's functions, the legality doctrines ought to apply differently depending upon the function of the criminal law rule to which they are being applied. When applied to the conduct and circumstance elements of offense definitions and to the objective justification defenses, one set of rationales applies and urges one kind of application of the legality doctrines. When applied to the culpability element of offense definitions and excuse defenses, a different set of rationales applies and urges a different kind of application of the legality doctrines.

In truth, what traditionally has been thought of as a single legality principle is in proper practice two distinct principles. The first, the principle of "rules legality," (1) seeks primarily to advance the ex ante rules rationales of fair notice and gaining compliance, and (2) applies to those criminal law rules that serve to announce the rules of conduct. Therefore, these two rationales, together with that of reserving the criminalization authority to the legislature, should govern the application of legality doctrines to the conduct and circumstance elements of offense definitions—the definitions of prohibitions and duties—and to justification defenses.

In contrast, the second, the principle of "adjudication legality," (1) seeks primarily to advance the ex post adjudication rationales of increasing uniformity and reducing the potential for abuse by avoiding unnecessary discretion, and (2) applies to those criminal law rules that serve to adjudicate violations of the rules of conduct. Therefore, these two rationales, together with that of reserving the criminalization authority to the legislature, should govern the application of legality doctrines to the culpability requirements of offense definitions and to excuse defenses....

### IV. Applying Legality Doctrines to Serve Their Function: Rules Legality Versus Adjudication Legality

The effective operation of the rules of conduct calls for a somewhat different drafting form than one would use for the drafting of the principles of adjudication. The rules rationales of the legality principle would have the rules of conduct formulated to maximize fair notice and effective deterrence and to minimize overdeterrence of protected activities. For example, objective and simple criteria might be much preferred in the rules of conduct, for these rules generally are directed to the general public, who have no special training or background in the law and who must apply the rules in the course of their everyday lives. At the same time, there is realistically a limit to how much detail the average person can be expected to know and apply in guiding her daily conduct. Thus, one might tolerate simplified rules if necessary to make feasible a quick and untrained application.

In contrast, the adjudication rationales of the legality principle would formulate the doctrines of adjudication—those that assess the minimum conditions of liability and set the range of punishment—to maximize uniformity in application to similar cases and to minimize the potential for abuse of discretion. For example, a high degree of specificity might be desirable even if it created a degree of complexity that would be unreasonable to expect the public to master. The special training of decision makers and the more contemplative pace of the adjudication process means that greater complexity can be tolerated. At the same time, especially with the use of a jury system for adjudication, the rules may be formulated to call upon normative judgments about the principles of justice that are shared among the community.

Beyond such matters of general drafting form, consider precisely how the two forms of legality—rules legality and adjudication legality—translate into different applications of the ... legality doctrines to each of the four groups of criminal law rules that are relevant to function: the conduct rules of the definition of prohibitions and duties and of justification defenses, and the adjudication rules of culpability requirements and of excuse defenses....

### A. Rules Legality: Conduct and Circumstance Elements of Offense Definitions

It seems likely that it is this group of criminal law rules that scholars and courts had in mind when first formulating the legality doctrines.

Specifically, common law rules that define prohibited conduct or required duties should be invalidated, as should judicial decisions creating new prohibitions or new duties. Rules of construction should narrowly construe statutory definitions of prohibitions and duties. And if, for whatever reason, a judicial interpretation does broaden a prohibition or duty, the ruling should not be applied retroactively. Ex post facto application of statutory rules that create or broaden prohibitions or duties should be barred, and vague definitions of prohibitions or duties should be invalidated....

### B. Adjudication Legality: Culpability Requirements and Excuse Defenses

Quite a different picture arises in relation to the doctrines of adjudication: the offense culpability requirements and the general excuse defenses. The central rationales here—the adjudication ration ales—look to increasing uniformity in application and to limiting the potential for abuse of discretion, without undermining legislative decisions on the issues. These goals are not necessarily concerned with providing advance notice and guidance as much as assessing the complex issue of the offender's blameworthiness for a rule violation. This can require a good deal of subtlety and complexity. Luckily, because the adjudication doctrines are applied after the fact in settings that allow careful and thoughtful deliberation, the adjudication rules can tolerate greater subtlety and complexity. Because the goals of giving notice and gaining compliance have little application here, there is little need to insist on precise and objective formulations....

Because the adjudication rules do not trigger notice and compliance rationales, there is little reason to bar a legislature from creating and applying culpability and excuse defenses ex post. Finally, though the vagueness prohibition still has some value in advancing the adjudication rationales of increasing uniformity in application and decreasing abuse of discretion, the standard of vagueness must, as usual, be adjusted to take account of the extent to which precision is possible. Particularly in the context of excuse defenses, precision often is not possible if the excuses are to perform their function. Culpability defenses are subject to more precise definition, but there too some of the issues inevitably must defer to normative judgment....

### C. Rules Legality: Justification Defenses

It is worth reaffirming at the start that the criminal law rules at issue here are the objective requirements of the general justification defenses: rules that announce ex ante the special justifying circumstances under which a person may do what otherwise is prohibited....

The justification defenses present an interesting situation. On the one hand, as rules of conduct, they are similar in function to the objective conduct and circumstance elements of offense definitions, but on the other hand, as general exculpatory defenses, they are similar in form to excuse defenses. In this instance, function is more important than form.... [A]s a rule of conduct, the special function of the objective justification defenses is ... to announce ex ante the conduct rules that will govern when a person justifiably may do what otherwise is prohibited.

That function means that the legality doctrines ought to apply to justification defenses in much the same way as they apply to the definition of prohibitions and duties, the other half of the rules of conduct. Any other approach would fail to assure fair notice of what is criminal, would fail to accurately signal the criminal law's authorized response to future justifying circumstances, and would fail to ensure legislative control over defining the rules of conduct....

Because the goal of justification defenses as rules of conduct is to give future conduct guidance, not to adjudicate past violations, the primary goals of the legality doctrines when applied to justification defenses ought to be to assure fair notice of the conduct rules, to increase future compliance with them, and to ensure legislative control over them. Just as fair notice and legislative supremacy require fixed and clear statutory definitions of prohibitions and duties, so too do they require fixed and clear justification defenses....

## John Calvin Jeffries, Jr., *Legality, Vagueness and the Construction of Criminal Statutes*

71 Va. L. Rev. 189 (1985)

### III. Interpretation of Penal Statutes

... I have already said that strict construction no longer commands the allegiance of the courts. The rule is still invoked, but so variously and unpredictably, and it is so often conflated with inconsistencies, that it is hard to discern widespread adherence to any general policy of statutory construction. As should be clear by now, I find the rejection of strict construction in itself unobjectionable. The notion that every statutory ambiguity should be resolved against the government, no matter what the merits of the case, seems to me simplistic and wrong. Certainly, no such rule is required by a concern for political legitimacy. Separation of powers might be taken to mean that courts should make law only interstitially, but not that all change must move in one direction. Nor is strict construction required for fair warning. Of course, unfair surprise must be avoided, but that concern is rarely in issue. It does not apply to the generality of cases where there is no plausible suggestion that the actor either knew or cared what the law was. Finally, strict construction bears no necessary or dependable relation to the rule of law. In a great many cases the resolution of statutory ambiguity is very far removed from a concern for abusive enforcement.

Does this mean that the interpretation of penal statutes should be completely ad hoc, that a judge should do whatever looks right without regard to any general guidelines for decision? The answer is 'no.' In addition to considerations pertaining to the merits of the particular issue at hand, there are at least three generalized constraints that a judge might usefully keep in mind when confronting ambiguity in a penal statute. The first two are widely appreciated and understood, even if not often stated precisely. The third (and the principal topic of this discussion) is perhaps less obvious. In any event, it tends to get lost in the unconvincing explanations for traditional strict construction and, perhaps for that reason, is less dependably respected by the courts.

First, a court should avoid usurpation of legislative authority. As has been noted, separation of powers does not mean that judges lack the capacity to 'make law.' In many situations, interstitial judicial lawmaking is both politically legitimate and institutionally unavoidable. Considerations of political legitimacy do, however, require that (constitutional imperatives aside) judicial decisions be consistent with legislative choice, either express or implied. In some situations, this kind of concern will limit permissible responses to statutory ambiguity in the criminal law.

Second, a court should avoid interpretations that threaten unfair surprise. This concern should not be measured by the hypothetical construct of 'lawyer's notice,' which applies, albeit artificially, to a vast range of cases, but by the narrower and more focused inquiry identified by *Lambert*: Would an ordinarily law-abiding person in the actor's situation have had reason to behave differently? In the unusual case where that question would be answered 'no,' imposition of penal sanctions threatens genuine unfairness and must be avoided.

Last, ... a judge confronting ambiguity in a penal statute might usefully ask whether a proposed resolution makes the law more or less certain. Would this interpretation, taken as precedent, constrain future applications? Or would it merely multiply the possibilities? Would the decision resolve the ambiguity in the law, or merely exploit it? Of course, not every rule is a good rule, but the lack of any rule is usually a bad idea. To be avoided, therefore, is an interpretation that creates or perpetuates openendedness in the criminal law. Such an interpretation should be avoided not because it would be unfair or unwise in the instant case (that might or might not be true), but because it would invite abuse in the future....

Sometimes statutory ambiguity presents an essentially binary choice. The law is either A or B; whichever is chosen, future coverage is fairly clear. In such a case, strict construction would dictate exculpation, and this would be true even though the actor's conduct was both dangerous and reprehensible, even though there was no prospect of unfair surprise, and even though the result left an irrational gap in the law. In my view, this approach does not make sense. Faced with this kind of binary choice—where neither outcome is precluded by express or implied legislative decision, where there is no threat of *Lambert*-like surprise, and where neither construction embraces an open-ended commitment to ad hoc criminalization—a judge should do whatever seems right. That is, the judge should adopt whichever result more sensibly promotes the policies of the penal law. Deciding what is right may not be easy, but it should not be short-circuited by the strict-construction rule of thumb....

## *Notes and Questions*

1. Professor Robinson argues that the principle of legality applies differently to rules of conduct than it does to rules of adjudication. A conduct rule prescribes what the citizenry can or cannot do. The offense of homicide, for example, is a conduct rule. It prohibits the citizenry from killing human beings. Self-defense is also a conduct rule, for it conveys to the citizenry that they may kill a human being if doing so is necessary to protect themselves from imminent harm. Rules of conduct are thus directed to the general population. In contrast, rules of adjudication are directed to judges. They articulate the rules that judges will apply when deciding whether to hold someone criminally liable for violating a conduct rule. Thus, for example, the rules governing the insanity defense are adjudication rules. The insanity defense does not convey a message to the citizenry that they are allowed to kill people if they are insane. Rather, it directs judges to acquit those who violate the conduct rule that prohibits killing human beings (homicide) if the judge believes that the stringent standards of the insanity defense are satisfied. The distinction between conduct rules and rules of adjudication roughly maps unto the distinction be-

tween primary and secondary rules drawn by H.L.A. Hart in his famous *Concept of Law* (Oxford, 1961).

2. Robinson argues that legality requires that conduct rules provide fair warning. As a result, it demands that conduct rules be drafted in simple terms and with specificity. He also suggests that judicial expansions of conduct rules in ways that are prejudicial to the defendant should not be applied retroactively. Nevertheless, Robinson argues that legality does not require that adjudication rules provide the same kind of warning or that they be drafted in simple terms and with great specificity. Sometimes specificity in this context is demanded, but sometimes adjudication rules should be deliberately vague. Furthermore, judicial decisions significantly altering adjudication rules may sometimes be applied retroactively without implicating the same concerns that are raised by the retroactive application of expanded conduct rules. Do you agree? Explain.

3. Was the "year and a day" rule in *Rogers v. Tennessee* (§ 3.05) a conduct rule or an adjudication rule? Explain. In light of the nature of the "year and a day rule," does its retroactive abolishment raise the same issues that would be raised if the legislature retroactively abolished the defense of self-defense? Why or why not?

4. Professor Jeffries argues that the rule of strict construction is not essential to either securing the appropriate separation of powers or to providing the citizenry with fair warning. Do you agree? Explain.

5. Jeffries also argues that while courts should "avoid the usurpation of legislative authority," "interstitial judicial lawmaking is both politically legitimate and institutionally unavoidable." Can these two statements be reconciled? Why or why not?

# Chapter 4

# Proportionality

## § 4.01 Proportionality: Non-Capital Cases Involving Adult Defendants

### Harmelin v. Michigan

Supreme Court of the United States, 1991
501 U.S. 957

Justice SCALIA announced the judgment of the Court and delivered the opinion of the Court with respect to Part IV, and an opinion with respect to Parts I, II, and III, in which THE CHIEF JUSTICE joins.

Petitioner was convicted of possessing 672 grams of cocaine and sentenced to a mandatory term of life in prison without possibility of parole …

Petitioner claims that his sentence is unconstitutionally "cruel and unusual" for two reasons: first, because it is "significantly disproportionate" to the crime he committed; second, because the sentencing judge was statutorily required to impose it, without taking into account the particularized circumstances of the crime and of the criminal.

I

A

The Eighth Amendment, which applies against the States by virtue of the Fourteenth Amendment, provides: "Excessive bail shall not be required, nor excessive fines imposed, nor cruel and unusual punishments inflicted." In *Rummel v. Estelle*, we held that it did not constitute "cruel and unusual punishment" to impose a life sentence, under a recidivist statute, upon a defendant who had been convicted, successively, of fraudulent use of a credit card to obtain $80 worth of goods or services, passing a forged check in the amount of $28.36, and obtaining $120.75 by false pretenses. We said that "one could argue without fear of contradiction by any decision of this Court that for crimes concededly classified and classifiable as felonies, that is, as punishable by significant terms of imprisonment in a state penitentiary, the length of the sentence actually imposed is purely a matter of legislative prerogative." We specifically rejected the proposition asserted by the dissent … that unconstitutional disproportionality could be established by weighing three factors: (1) gravity of the offense compared to severity of the penalty, (2) penalties imposed within the same jurisdiction for similar crimes, and (3) penalties imposed in other jurisdictions for the same offense. A footnote in the opinion, however, said: "This is not to say that a proportionality principle would not come into play in the extreme example mentioned by the dissent, ... if a legislature made overtime parking a felony punishable by life imprisonment."

[Subsequently], we uttered what has been our last word on this subject to date. *Solem v. Helm*, set aside under the Eighth Amendment, because it was disproportionate, a sentence of life imprisonment without possibility of parole, imposed under a South Dakota recividist statute for successive offenses that included three convictions of third-degree burglary, one of obtaining money by false pretenses, one of grand larceny, one of third-offense driving while intoxicated, and one of writing a "no account" check with intent to defraud. In [*Solem,* this Court] decreed that a general principle of disproportionality exists, [and] the Court used as the criterion for its application the three-factor test that had been explicitly rejected in ... *Rummel* ...

It should be apparent from the above discussion that our 5-to-4 decision eight years ago in *Solem* was scarcely the expression of clear and well accepted constitutional law ... Accordingly, we have addressed anew, and in greater detail, the question whether the Eighth Amendment contains a proportionality guarantee—with particular attention to the background of the Eighth Amendment and to the understanding of the Eighth Amendment before the end of the 19th century. We conclude from this examination that *Solem* was simply wrong; the Eighth Amendment contains no proportionality guarantee....

C

... Wrenched out of its common-law context, and applied to the actions of a legislature, the word "unusual" could hardly mean "contrary to law." But it continued to mean (as it continues to mean today) "such as [does not] occu[r] in ordinary practice," Webster's American Dictionary (1828), "[s]uch as is [not] in common use," Webster's Second International Dictionary 2807 (1954). According to its terms, then, by forbidding "cruel *and unusual* punishments," the Clause disables the Legislature from authorizing particular forms or "modes" of punishment—specifically, cruel methods of punishment that are not regularly or customarily employed ...

The language bears the construction, however—and here we come to the point crucial to resolution of the present case—that "cruelty and unusualness" are to be determined not solely with reference to the punishment at issue ("Is life imprisonment a cruel and unusual punishment?") but with reference to the crime for which it is imposed as well ("Is life imprisonment cruel and unusual punishment for possession of unlawful drugs?"). The latter interpretation would make the provision a form of proportionality guarantee. The arguments against it, however, seem to us conclusive.

First of all, to use the phrase "cruel and unusual punishment" to describe a requirement of proportionality would have been an exceedingly vague and oblique way of saying what Americans were well accustomed to saying more directly. The notion of "proportionality" was not a novelty (though then as now there was little agreement over what it entailed). In 1778, for example, the Virginia Legislature narrowly rejected a comprehensive "Bill for Proportioning Punishments" introduced by Thomas Jefferson. Proportionality provisions had been included in several State Constitutions. See, *e.g.*, Pa.Const., § 38 (1776) (punishments should be "in general more proportionate to the crimes"); S.C.Const., Art. XL (1778) (same); N.H. Bill of Rights, Art. XVIII (1784) ("[A]ll penalties ought to be proportioned to the nature of the offence"). There is little doubt that those who framed, proposed, and ratified the Bill of Rights were aware of such provisions, yet chose not to replicate them ...

The Eighth Amendment received little attention during the proposal and adoption of the Federal Bill of Rights. However, what evidence exists from debates at the state ratifying conventions that prompted the Bill of Rights as well as the floor debates in the First Congress which proposed it "confirm[s] the view that the cruel and unusual punishments clause was directed at prohibiting certain *methods* of punishment." ...

II

We think it enough that those who framed and approved the Federal Constitution chose, for whatever reason, not to include within it the guarantee against disproportionate sentences that some State Constitutions contained. It is worth noting, however, that there was good reason for that choice—a reason that reinforces the necessity of overruling *Solem*. While there are relatively clear historical guidelines and accepted practices that enable judges to determine which *modes* of punishment are "cruel and unusual," *proportionality* does not lend itself to such analysis. Neither Congress nor any state legislature has ever set out with the objective of crafting a penalty that is "disproportionate"; yet as some of the examples mentioned above indicate, many enacted dispositions seem to be so—because they were made for other times or other places, with different social attitudes, different criminal epidemics, different public fears, and different prevailing theories of penology. This is not to say that there are no absolutes; one can imagine extreme examples that no rational person, in no time or place, could accept. But for the same reason these examples are easy to decide, they are certain never to occur. The real function of a constitutional proportionality principle, if it exists, is to enable judges to evaluate a penalty that *some* assemblage of men and women *has* considered proportionate—and to say that it is not. For that real-world enterprise, the standards seem so inadequate that the proportionality principle becomes an invitation to imposition of subjective values.

This becomes clear, we think, from a consideration of the three factors that *Solem* found relevant to the proportionality determination: (1) the inherent gravity of the offense, (2) the sentences imposed for similarly grave offenses in the same jurisdiction, and (3) sentences imposed for the same crime in other jurisdictions. As to the first factor: Of course some offenses, involving violent harm to human beings, will always and everywhere be regarded as serious, but that is only half the equation. The issue is *what else* should be regarded to be *as serious* as these offenses, or even to be *more serious* than some of them. On that point, judging by the statutes that Americans have enacted, there is enormous variation—even within a given age, not to mention across the many generations ruled by the Bill of Rights. The State of Massachusetts punishes sodomy more severely than assault and battery, compare Mass.Gen.Laws § 272:34 (1988) ("not more than twenty years" in prison for sodomy) with § 265:13A ("not more than two and one half years" in prison for assault and battery); whereas in several States, sodomy is not unlawful *at all*. In Louisiana, one who assaults another with a dangerous weapon faces the same maximum prison term as one who removes a shopping basket "from the parking area or grounds of any store ... without authorization." La.Rev.Stat.Ann. §§ 14:37, 14:68.1 (West 1986). A battery that results in "protracted and obvious disfigurement" merits imprisonment "for not more than five years," § 14:34.1, one half the maximum penalty for theft of livestock or an oilfield seismograph, §§ 14:67.1, 14:67.8. We may think that the First Congress punished with clear disproportionality when it provided up to seven years in prison and up to $1,000 in fine for "cut[ting] off the ear or ears, ... cut[ting] out or disabl[ing] the tongue, ... put[ting] out an eye, ... cut[ting] off ... any limb or member of any person with intention ... to maim or disfigure," but provided the death penalty for "run[ning] away with [a] ship or vessel, or any goods or merchandise to the value of fifty dollars." Act of Apr. 30, 1790, ch. 9, §§ 8, 13, 1 Stat. 113–115. But then perhaps the citizens of 1791 would think that today's Congress punishes with clear disproportionality when it sanctions "assault by ... wounding" with up to six months in prison, 18 U.S.C. § 113(d), unauthorized reproduction of the "Smokey Bear" character or name with the same penalty, 18 U.S.C. § 711, offering to barter a migratory bird with up to two years in prison, 16 U.S.C. § 707(b), and purloining a "key suited to any lock adopted by the Post Office Department" with a prison term of up to 10 years, 18 U.S.C. § 1704. Perhaps both we and they would be right, but the point is that there are no textual or historical standards for saying so.

The difficulty of assessing gravity is demonstrated in the very context of the present case: Petitioner acknowledges that a mandatory life sentence might not be "grossly excessive" for possession of cocaine with intent to distribute. But surely whether it is a "grave" offense merely to possess a significant quantity of drugs—thereby facilitating distribution, subjecting the holder to the temptation of distribution, and raising the possibility of theft by others who might distribute—depends entirely upon how odious and socially threatening one believes drug use to be. Would it be "grossly excessive" to provide life imprisonment for "mere possession" of a certain quantity of heavy weaponry? If not, then the only issue is whether the possible dissemination of drugs can be as "grave" as the possible dissemination of heavy weapons. Who are we to say no? The members of the Michigan Legislature, and not we, know the situation on the streets of Detroit.

The second factor suggested in *Solem* fails for the same reason. One cannot compare the sentences imposed by the jurisdiction for "similarly grave" offenses if there is no objective standard of gravity. Judges will be comparing what *they* consider comparable. Or, to put the same point differently: When it happens that two offenses judicially determined to be "similarly grave" receive significantly *dis* similar penalties, what follows is not that the harsher penalty is unconstitutional, but merely that the legislature does not share the judges' view that the offenses are similarly grave. Moreover, even if "similarly grave" crimes could be identified, the penalties for them would not necessarily be comparable, since there are many other justifications for a difference. For example, since deterrent effect depends not only upon the amount of the penalty but upon its certainty, crimes that are less grave but significantly more difficult to detect may warrant substantially higher penalties. Grave crimes of the sort that will not be deterred by penalty may warrant substantially lower penalties, as may grave crimes of the sort that are normally committed once in a lifetime by otherwise law-abiding citizens who will not profit from rehabilitation. Whether these differences will occur, and to what extent, depends, of course, upon the weight the society accords to deterrence and rehabilitation, rather than retribution, as the objective of criminal punishment (which is an eminently legislative judgment). In fact, it becomes difficult even to speak intelligently of "proportionality," once deterrence and rehabilitation are given significant weight. Proportionality is inherently a retributive concept, and perfect proportionality is the talionic law. Cf. Bill For Proportioning Punishments, 1 Writings of Thomas Jefferson, at 218, 228–229 ("[W]hoever ... shall maim another, or shall disfigure him ... shall be maimed or disfigured in like sort").

As for the third factor mentioned by *Solem*—the character of the sentences imposed by other States for the same crime—it must be acknowledged that that can be applied with clarity and ease. The only difficulty is that it has no conceivable relevance to the Eighth Amendment. That a State is entitled to treat with stern disapproval an act that other States punish with the mildest of sanctions follows *a fortiori* from the undoubted fact that a State may criminalize an act that other States do not criminalize *at all*. Indeed, a State may criminalize an act that other States choose to *reward*—punishing, for example, the killing of endangered wild animals for which other States are offering a bounty. What greater disproportion could there be than that? "Absent a constitutionally imposed uniformity inimical to traditional notions of federalism, some State will always bear the distinction of treating particular offenders more severely than any other State." Diversity not only in policy, but in the means of implementing policy, is the very *raison d'être* of our federal system. Though the different needs and concerns of other States may induce them to treat simple possession of 672 grams of cocaine as a relatively minor offense, see Wyo.Stat. §35-7-1031(c) (1988) (6 months); W.Va.Code §60A-4-401(c) (1989) (6 months), nothing in the Constitution requires Michigan to follow suit. The Eighth Amendment is not a ratchet, whereby a temporary consensus on leniency for a particular crime fixes a permanent constitutional maximum, disabling the States from giving effect to altered beliefs and responding to changed social conditions....

The judgment of the Michigan Court of Appeals is Affirmed.

**Justice KENNEDY, with whom Justice O'CONNOR and Justice SOUTER join, concurring in part and concurring in the judgment.**

... I write this separate opinion because my approach to the Eighth Amendment proportionality analysis differs from Justice SCALIA's ... *[S]tare decisis* counsels our adherence to the narrow proportionality principle that has existed in our Eighth Amendment jurisprudence for 80 years. Although our proportionality decisions have not been clear or consistent in all respects, they can be reconciled, and they require us to uphold petitioner's sentence.

I

A

Our decisions recognize that the Cruel and Unusual Punishments Clause encompasses a narrow proportionality principle. We first interpreted the Eighth Amendment to prohibit "'greatly disproportioned'" sentences in *Weems v. United States.* Since *Weems,* we have applied the principle in different Eighth Amendment contexts. Its most extensive application has been in death penalty cases. In *Coker v. Georgia,* we held that "a sentence of death is grossly disproportionate and excessive punishment for the crime of rape and is therefore forbidden by the Eighth Amendment as cruel and unusual punishment." We applied like reasoning in *Enmund v. Florida,* to strike down a capital sentence imposed for a felony-murder conviction in which the defendant had not committed the actual murder and lacked intent to kill.

The Eighth Amendment proportionality principle also applies to noncapital sentences. In *Rummel v. Estelle,* we acknowledged the existence of the proportionality rule for both capital and noncapital cases, but we refused to strike down a sentence of life imprisonment, with possibility of parole, for recidivism based on three underlying felonies. In *Hutto v. Davis,* we recognized the possibility of proportionality review but held it inapplicable to a 40-year prison sentence for possession with intent to distribute nine ounces of marijuana. Our most recent decision discussing the subject is *Solem v. Helm.* There we held that a sentence of life imprisonment without possibility of parole violated the Eighth Amendment because it was "grossly disproportionate" to the crime of recidivism based on seven underlying nonviolent felonies. The dissent in *Solem* disagreed with the Court's application of the proportionality principle but observed that in extreme cases it could apply to invalidate a punishment for a term of years.

B

Though our decisions recognize a proportionality principle, its precise contours are unclear. This is so in part because we have applied the rule in few cases and even then to sentences of different types. Our most recent pronouncement on the subject in *Solem,* furthermore, appeared to apply a different analysis than in *Rummel* and *Davis*. *Solem* twice stated, however, that its decision was consistent with *Rummel* and thus did not overrule it. Despite these tensions, close analysis of our decisions yields some common principles that give content to the uses and limits of proportionality review.

The first of these principles is that the fixing of prison terms for specific crimes involves a substantive penological judgment that, as a general matter, is "properly within the province of legislatures, not courts." Determinations about the nature and purposes of punishment for criminal acts implicate difficult and enduring questions respecting the sanctity of the individual, the nature of law, and the relation between law and the social order. "As a moral or political issue [the punishment of offenders] provokes intemperate emotions, deeply conflicting interests, and intractable disagreements." The efficacy of any sentencing system cannot be assessed absent agreement on the purposes and objectives of the penal system. And the responsibility for making these fundamental choices and implementing them lies with the legislature ... Thus, "[r]eviewing courts ... should grant substantial deference to the broad authority that legislatures necessarily possess in determining the types and limits of punishments for crimes." ...

The second principle is that the Eighth Amendment does not mandate adoption of any one penological theory. "The principles which have guided criminal sentencing ... have varied with the times." The federal and state criminal systems have accorded different weights at different times to the penological goals of retribution, deterrence, incapacitation, and rehabilitation. And competing theories of mandatory and discretionary sentencing have been in varying degrees of ascendancy or decline since the beginning of the Republic ...

Third, marked divergences both in underlying theories of sentencing and in the length of prescribed prison terms are the inevitable, often beneficial, result of the federal structure. ("The inherent nature of our federal system" may result in "a wide range of constitutional sentences"). "Our federal system recognizes the independent power of a State to articulate societal norms through criminal law." State sentencing schemes may embody different penological assumptions, making interstate comparison of sentences a difficult and imperfect enterprise. And even assuming identical philosophies, differing attitudes and perceptions of local conditions may yield different, yet rational, conclusions regarding the appropriate length of prison terms for particular crimes. Thus, the circumstance that a State has the most severe punishment for a particular crime does not by itself render the punishment grossly disproportionate. "[O]ur Constitution 'is made for people of fundamentally differing views.' ... Absent a constitutionally imposed uniformity inimical to traditional notions of federalism, some State will always bear the distinction of treating particular offenders more severely than any other State."

The fourth principle at work in our cases is that proportionality review by federal courts should be informed by "'objective factors to the maximum possible extent.'" The most prominent objective factor is the type of punishment imposed. In *Weems*, "the Court could differentiate in an objective fashion between the highly unusual *cadena temporal* and more traditional forms of imprisonment imposed under the Anglo-Saxon system." In a similar fashion, because "'[t]he penalty of death differs from all other forms of criminal punishment,'" the objective line between capital punishment and imprisonment for a term of years finds frequent mention in our Eighth Amendment jurisprudence. By contrast, our decisions recognize that we lack clear objective standards to distinguish between sentences for different terms of years.... Although "no penalty is *per se* constitutional," the relative lack of objective standards concerning terms of imprisonment has meant that "'[o]utside the context of capital punishment, *successful* challenges to the proportionality of particular sentences [are] exceedingly rare.'"

All of these principles—the primacy of the legislature, the variety of legitimate penological schemes, the nature of our federal system, and the requirement that proportionality review be guided by objective factors—inform the final one: The Eighth Amendment does not require strict proportionality between crime and sentence. Rather, it forbids only extreme sentences that are "grossly disproportionate" to the crime ...

II

With these considerations stated, it is necessary to examine the challenged aspects of petitioner's sentence: its severe length and its mandatory operation.

A

Petitioner's life sentence without parole is the second most severe penalty permitted by law. It is the same sentence received by the petitioner in *Solem.* Petitioner's crime, however, was far more grave than the crime at issue in *Solem.*

The crime of uttering a no account check at issue in *Solem* was "'one of the most passive felonies a person could commit.'" It "involved neither violence nor threat of violence to any person," and was "viewed by society as among the less serious offenses." The felonies underlying the defendant's recidivism conviction, moreover, were "all relatively minor." The *Solem* Court contrasted these "minor" offenses with "very serious offenses" such as "a third offense of heroin dealing," and stated that "[n]o one suggests that [a statute providing for life imprisonment without parole] may not be applied constitutionally to fourth-time heroin dealers or other violent criminals."

Petitioner was convicted of possession of more than 650 grams (over 1.5 pounds) of cocaine. This amount of pure cocaine has a potential yield of between 32,500 and 65,000 doses. From any standpoint, this crime falls in a different category from the relatively minor, nonviolent crime at issue in *Solem.* Possession, use, and distribution of illegal drugs represent "one of the greatest problems affecting the health and welfare of our population." Petitioner's suggestion that his crime was nonviolent and victimless, echoed by the dissent, is false to the point of absurdity. To the contrary, petitioner's crime threatened to cause grave harm to society.

Quite apart from the pernicious effects on the individual who consumes illegal drugs, such drugs relate to crime in at least three ways: (1) A drug user may commit crime because of drug-induced changes in physiological functions, cognitive ability, and mood; (2) A drug user may commit crime in order to obtain money to buy drugs; and (3) A violent crime may occur as part of the drug business or culture. Studies bear out these possibilities and demonstrate a direct nexus between illegal drugs and crimes of violence. To mention but a few examples, 57 percent of a national sample of males arrested in 1989 for homicide tested positive for illegal drugs. The comparable statistics for assault, robbery, and weapons arrests were 55, 73, and 63 percent, respectively. In Detroit, Michigan, in 1988, 68 percent of a sample of male arrestees and 81 percent of a sample of female arrestees tested positive for illegal drugs. Fifty-one percent of males and seventy-one percent of females tested positive for cocaine. And last year an estimated 60 percent of the homicides in Detroit were drug related, primarily cocaine related.

These and other facts and reports detailing the pernicious effects of the drug epidemic in this country do not establish that Michigan's penalty scheme is correct or the most just in any abstract sense. But they do demonstrate that the Michigan Legislature could with reason conclude that the threat posed to the individual and society by possession of this large an amount of cocaine—in terms of violence, crime, and social displacement—is momentous enough to warrant the deterrence and retribution of a life sentence without parole ...

The severity of petitioner's crime brings his sentence within the constitutional boundaries established by our prior decisions. In *Davis,* we upheld against proportionality attack a sentence of 40 years' imprisonment for possession with intent to distribute nine ounces of marijuana. Here, Michigan could with good reason conclude that petitioner's crime is more serious than the crime in *Davis.* Similarly, a rational basis exists for Michigan to conclude that petitioner's crime is as serious and violent as the crime of felony murder without specific intent to kill, a crime for which "no sentence of imprisonment would be disproportionate." ...

III

A penalty as severe and unforgiving as the one imposed here would make this a most difficult and troubling case for any judicial officer. Reasonable minds may differ about the efficacy of Michigan's sentencing scheme, and it is far from certain that Michigan's bold experiment will succeed. The accounts of pickpockets at Tyburn hangings are a reminder of the limits of the law's deterrent force, but we cannot say the law before us has no chance of success and is on that account so disproportionate as to be cruel and unusual punishment. The dangers flowing from drug offenses and the circumstances of the crime committed here demonstrate that the Michigan penalty scheme does not surpass constitutional bounds. Michigan may use its criminal law to address the issue of drug possession in wholesale amounts in the manner that it has in this sentencing scheme. For the foregoing reasons, I conclude that petitioner's sentence of life imprisonment without parole for his crime of possession of more than 650 grams of cocaine does not violate the Eighth Amendment.

## *Notes and Questions*

1. Justice Scalia argued that the constitutional prohibition of cruel and unusual punishments "contains no proportionality guarantee," at least in non-capital cases. Instead, Scalia argued that the Eighth Amendment "disables the Legislature from authorizing particular forms or 'modes' of punishment—specifically, cruel methods of punishment that are not regularly or customarily employed." According to this view, the Eighth Amendment may prohibit "torture" or "flogging" as forms of punishment (assuming they are cruel and unusual). Nevertheless, as long as a traditional and common method of punishment is used (e.g., imprisonment), the Constitution would not prohibit the imposition of such punishment regardless of how disproportional it may seem.

2. In contrast to Scalia, Justice Kennedy argued that the Eighth Amendment contains a "narrow proportionality" requirement. Under his view, the Constitution does not require that there be strict proportionality between the punishment imposed and the gravity of the offense. Nonetheless, the Eighth Amendment would bar the imposition of "extreme sentences" that are "grossly disproportional" to the crime. Although Kennedy argued that the Eighth Amendment prohibits grossly disproportional punishment, he concluded that imposing a life sentence without parole for the crime of possessing more than 650 grams of cocaine is not an extreme sentence that is constitutionally prohibited. Given that the crime charged in *Harmelin* was "serious and violent," Kennedy concluded that "no sentence of imprisonment would be disproportionate." Do you agree that the sentence imposed in *Harmelin* was not "extreme" and, therefore, not "grossly disproportional" to the crime? Explain.

3. As Justice Scalia pointed out, prior to *Harmelin* the Supreme Court applied a rather robust proportionality analysis in *Solem v. Helm.* According to *Helm,* in order to determine whether a sentence violates the Eighth Amendment, a court had to engage in three

inquiries. The first is an "inter-jurisdictional" inquiry in which the punishment imposed for the offense is compared with the punishment imposed for the same crime in other jurisdictions. If the punishment imposed for the offense was considerably harsher than the punishment imposed in other jurisdictions for the same crime, the argument in favor of finding a violation of the Eighth Amendment becomes more powerful. The second inquiry consisted in an "intra-jurisdictional" analysis in which the punishment imposed for the offense charged is compared with the punishment imposed in the same jurisdiction for more serious offenses. If the punishment imposed for the offense charged was harsher (or as harsh) as the punishment imposed for more serious offenses, the argument in favor of unconstitutionality becomes stronger (e.g., possession of cocaine is punished as severely as the more serious offense of murder). The final inquiry is required the court to independently assess whether the punishment imposed was excessive in light of the gravity of the offense. The more excessive that the punishment imposed appears to be when compared to the gravity of the offense, the stronger the argument in favor of finding the punishment to be cruel and unusual. The *Solem* approach garnered the support of four dissenting justices in *Harmelin*. How would *Harmelin* be decided if the Eighth Amendment analysis proceeded in the way suggested in *Solem v. Helm*? Why?

4. Since *Harmelin* was decided, the more robust proportionality analysis proposed in *Solem* has failed to garner majority support in the Supreme Court. Justice Scalia's approach simply rejects the three inquiries discussed in *Helm* as irrelevant to the Eighth Amendment. In contrast, Justice Kennedy argued that the factors discussed in *Solem may* be relevant to proportionality analysis, but should only come into play when the sentence is extreme and the underlying crime is neither serious nor violent. Given that the four dissenting justices in *Harmelin* would apply the more robust proportionality approach advocated for in *Solem*, it seems that they would side with Justice Kennedy's narrow proportionality standard if doing so is necessary to overturn a sentence as grossly disproportionate. Therefore, there is reason to conclude that a majority of the members of the Court agree that the Eighth Amendment bars the imposition of "grossly disproportionate" sentences, although there is no agreement as to the underlying rationale.

5. Note that neither Justice Scalia's opinion nor Justice Kennedy's concurrence garnered the support of a majority of the members of the Supreme Court in *Harmelin*. As a result, the Court has yet to articulate a majority position regarding proportionality analysis in non-capital cases involving adult defendants.

6. In *Ewing v. California*, 538 U.S. 11 (2003), the Supreme Court had to once again decide whether the punishment imposed on an adult defendant in a non-capital case was cruel and unusual. The defendant was charged with felony grand theft for stealing three golf clubs valued at $399 each. He was sentenced under California's "three strikes and you're out laws," which mandated the imposition of an indeterminate life sentence for anyone convicted of a felony that had previously been convicted of two or more serious or violent felonies. Given that the defendant had been previously convicted of four serious or violent crimes (three burglaries and a robbery), he was sentenced to twenty-five years to life imprisonment. The defendant appealed his sentence, contending that the punishment imposed was disproportional to the crime and, therefore, violated the constitutional prohibition against cruel and unusual punishment. A majority of the members of the Supreme Court agreed that the sentence imposed did not violate the Eighth Amendment, but they failed to agree on why this was the case.

7. Justice O'Connor, joined by then Chief Justice Rehnquist and Justice Kennedy, upheld the constitutionality of the punishment imposed in *Ewing*. In doing so, O'Connor first attempted to explain what the Court held in *Harmelin:*

> Eight years after *Solem*, we grappled with the proportionality issue again in *Harmelin*. *Harmelin* was not a recidivism case, but rather involved a first-time offender convicted of possessing 672 grams of cocaine. He was sentenced to life in prison without possibility of parole. A majority of the Court rejected Harmelin's claim that his sentence was so grossly disproportionate that it violated the Eighth Amendment. The Court, however, could not agree on why his proportionality argument failed. Justice SCALIA, joined by THE CHIEF JUSTICE, wrote that the proportionality principle was "an aspect of our death penalty jurisprudence, rather than a generalizable aspect of Eighth Amendment law." He would thus have declined to apply gross disproportionality principles except in reviewing capital sentences.
>
> Justice KENNEDY, joined by two other Members of the Court, concurred in part and concurred in the judgment. Justice KENNEDY specifically recognized that "[t]he Eighth Amendment proportionality principle also applies to noncapital sentences." He then identified four principles of proportionality review—"the primacy of the legislature, the variety of legitimate penological schemes, the nature of our federal system, and the requirement that proportionality review be guided by objective factors"—that "inform the final one: The Eighth Amendment does not require strict proportionality between crime and sentence. Rather, it forbids only extreme sentences that are 'grossly disproportionate' to the crime." Justice KENNEDY's concurrence also stated that *Solem* "did not mandate" comparative analysis "within and between jurisdictions."

Justice O'Connor then proceeded to apply the approach adopted by Justice Kennedy in his *Harmelin* concurrence:

> When the California Legislature enacted the three strikes law, it made a judgment that protecting the public safety requires incapacitating criminals who have already been convicted of at least one serious or violent crime. Nothing in the Eighth Amendment prohibits California from making that choice. To the contrary, our cases establish that "States have a valid interest in deterring and segregating habitual criminals." ...
>
> California's justification is no pretext. Recidivism is a serious public safety concern in California and throughout the Nation. According to a recent report, approximately 67 percent of former inmates released from state prisons were charged with at least one "serious" new crime within three years of their release. In particular, released property offenders like Ewing had higher recidivism rates than those released after committing violent, drug, or public-order offenses. Approximately 73 percent of the property offenders released in 1994 were arrested again within three years, compared to approximately 61 percent of the violent offenders, 62 percent of the public-order offenders, and 66 percent of the drug offenders....
>
> The State's interest in deterring crime also lends some support to the three strikes law. We have long viewed both incapacitation and deterrence as rationales for recidivism statutes: "[A] recidivist statute['s] ... primary goals are to deter repeat offenders and, at some point in the life of one who repeatedly commits criminal offenses serious enough to be punished as felonies, to segregate that person from the rest of society for an extended period of time." Four years after the passage of California's three strikes law, the recidivism rate of parolees returned to prison for the commission of a new crime dropped by nearly 25 percent....
>
> Against this backdrop, we consider Ewing's claim that his three strikes sentence of 25 years to life is unconstitutionally disproportionate to his offense of "shoplift-

> ing three golf clubs." We first address the gravity of the offense compared to the harshness of the penalty. At the threshold, we note that Ewing incorrectly frames the issue. The gravity of his offense was not merely "shoplifting three golf clubs." Rather, Ewing was convicted of felony grand theft for stealing nearly $1,200 worth of merchandise after previously having been convicted of at least two "violent" or "serious" felonies. Even standing alone, Ewing's theft should not be taken lightly. His crime was certainly not "one of the most passive felonies a person could commit." To the contrary, the Supreme Court of California has noted the "seriousness" of grand theft in the context of proportionality review. Theft of $1,200 in property is a felony under federal law, 18 U.S.C. § 641, and in the vast majority of States.
>
> In weighing the gravity of Ewing's offense, we must place on the scales not only his current felony, but also his long history of felony recidivism. Any other approach would fail to accord proper deference to the policy judgments that find expression in the legislature's choice of sanctions. In imposing a three strikes sentence, the State's interest is not merely punishing the offense of conviction, or the "triggering" offense: "[I]t is in addition the interest … in dealing in a harsher manner with those who by repeated criminal acts have shown that they are simply incapable of conforming to the norms of society as established by its criminal law." To give full effect to the State's choice of this legitimate penological goal, our proportionality review of Ewing's sentence must take that goal into account.
>
> Ewing's sentence is justified by the State's public-safety interest in incapacitating and deterring recidivist felons, and amply supported by his own long, serious criminal record. Ewing has been convicted of numerous misdemeanor and felony offenses, served nine separate terms of incarceration, and committed most of his crimes while on probation or parole. His prior "strikes" were serious felonies including robbery and three residential burglaries. To be sure, Ewing's sentence is a long one. But it reflects a rational legislative judgment, entitled to deference, that offenders who have committed serious or violent felonies and who continue to commit felonies must be incapacitated. The State of California "was entitled to place upon [Ewing] the onus of one who is simply unable to bring his conduct within the social norms prescribed by the criminal law of the State." Ewing's is not "the rare case in which a threshold comparison of the crime committed and the sentence imposed leads to an inference of gross disproportionality." *Harmelin*, (KENNEDY, J., concurring in part and concurring in judgment).
>
> We hold that Ewing's sentence of 25 years to life in prison, imposed for the offense of felony grand theft under the three strikes law, is not grossly disproportionate and therefore does not violate the Eighth Amendment's prohibition on cruel and unusual punishments …

Do you agree that imposing a sentence of twenty-five years to life imprisonment for stealing three golf clubs is not "grossly disproportional"? Why or why not? If the sentences imposed in *Harmelin* (life without parole for possession of over 650 grams of cocaine) and *Ewing* (twenty-five to life for stealing golf clubs aggravated by recidivism) are not "grossly disproportionate," are there any sentences currently imposed in the United States that would be unconstitutional under Kennedy's "narrow proportionality" approach?

8. Concurring in the judgment, Justice Scalia reiterated his *Harmelin* position that "the Eighth Amendment's prohibition of 'cruel and unusual punishments'" was aimed at

excluding only certain *modes* of punishment, and was not a "guarantee against disproportionate sentences." Furthermore, Scalia argued that the position espoused by Justices O'Connor and Kennedy in *Ewing* is incoherent because proportionality analysis is not consistent with assessing whether the sentence imposed is consistent with non-retributive justifications for punishment, such as deterrence and incapacitation. More specifically, Scalia contended that:

> Proportionality—the notion that the punishment should fit the crime—is inherently a concept tied to the penological goal of retribution. "[I]t becomes difficult even to speak intelligently of 'proportionality,' once deterrence and rehabilitation are given significant weight,"—not to mention giving weight to the purpose of California's three strikes law: incapacitation. In the present case, the game is up once the plurality has acknowledged that "the Constitution does not mandate adoption of any one penological theory," and that a "sentence can have a variety of justifications, such as incapacitation, deterrence, retribution, or rehabilitation." That acknowledgment having been made, it no longer suffices merely to assess "the gravity of the offense compared to the harshness of the penalty"; that classic description of the proportionality principle (alone and in itself quite resistant to policy-free, legal analysis) now becomes merely the "first" step of the inquiry. Having completed that step (by a discussion which, in all fairness, does not convincingly establish that 25-years-to-life is a "proportionate" punishment for stealing three golf clubs), the plurality must then *add* an analysis to show that "Ewing's sentence is justified by the State's public-safety interest in incapacitating and deterring recidivist felons."
>
> Which indeed it is—though why that has anything to do with the principle of proportionality is a mystery. Perhaps the plurality should revise its terminology, so that what it reads into the Eighth Amendment is not the unstated proposition that all punishment should be reasonably proportionate to the gravity of the offense, but rather the unstated proposition that all punishment should reasonably pursue the multiple purposes of the criminal law. That formulation would make it clearer than ever, of course, that the plurality is not applying law but evaluating policy.
>
> Because I agree that petitioner's sentence does not violate the Eighth Amendment's prohibition against cruel and unusual punishments, I concur in the judgment.

Do you agree with Justice Scalia that proportionality analysis is "inherently tied ... to the penological goal of retribution"? That is, does it make sense to argue that a sentence is "proportional" on the basis of something other than what the offender deserves, such as incapacitation or deterrence? Scalia believes that it does not, given that the concept of proportionality necessarily entails comparing the punishment imposed with the punishment that the defendant *deserves,* and such an analysis is inherently retributive. Consideration of deterrence or inapacitation as a reason for punishment may be relevant to determining whether punishment serves a useful purpose, but is—according to Scalia—irrelevant to assessing its proportionality. Do you agree? Why or why not? The coherence of taking into account non-retributive considerations when assessing proportionality is revisited in §4.07 of this Chapter.

9. In a dissenting opinion penned by Justice Breyer, four members of the Supreme Court compared the punishment that a *Ewing*-like defendant would receive in other jurisdictions and the sentences imposed in the same state for more serious crimes (i.e., the "intra" and "inter" jurisdictional factors proposed by the Supreme Court in *Solem*). After

engaging in this comparative analysis, Breyer concluded that "[o]utside the California three strikes context, Ewing's recidivist sentence is virtually unique in its harshness for his offense of conviction, and by a considerable degree." As a result, the dissenters argued that the sentence imposed in *Ewing* was grossly disproportionate and, therefore, violated the prohibition of cruel and unusual punishments.

10. Note that considerations of federalism play a significant role in shaping both Justice Scalia's and Justice Kennedy's approaches to Eighth Amendment proportionality analysis. As Justice Scalia pointed out in *Harmelin,* "[a]bsent a constitutionally imposed uniformity inimical to traditional notions of federalism, some State will always bear the distinction of treating particular offenders more severely than any other State." Given that "[d]iversity not only in policy, but in the means of implementing policy, is the very *raison d'être* of our federal system," Scalia noted that "[t]hough the different needs and concerns of other States may induce them to treat simple possession of 672 grams of cocaine as a relatively minor offense, nothing in the Constitution requires Michigan to follow suit." Similarly, as Justice Kennedy explained in his *Harmelin* concurrence, "the Eighth Amendment does not mandate adoption of any one penological theory." Therefore, "marked divergences both in underlying theories of sentencing and in the length of prescribed prison terms are the inevitable, often beneficial, result of the federal structure." As a result, Kennedy observed that "State sentencing schemes may embody different penological assumptions, making interstate comparison of sentences a difficult and imperfect enterprise."

11. If it is true—as virtually all members of the Supreme Court believe—that the Constitution "does not mandate adoption of any one penological theory," is it legitimate for the Supreme Court to strike down sentences based on proportionality grounds? The answer to this question depends on whether an assessment of proportionality necessarily entails adopting a retributive theory of punishment. If it is true—as Scalia argued in *Ewing*—that proportionality is a concept that is inherently tied to retributive theories of punishment, requiring proportionality between the punishment and the gravity of the offense may be tantamount to forcing states to punish in accordance to retributive justice as opposed to in furtherance of non-retributive goals such as deterrence and incapacitation. This would be incompatible with the flexibility in punishment theory that the American federal structure is designed to promote. Do you believe that proportionality is an inherently retributive concept? Explain. This issue is discussed in more detail in §4.07 of this chapter.

## §4.02 Proportionality: Death Penalty

### Kennedy v. Louisiana

Supreme Court of the United States, 2008
554 U.S. 407

Justice KENNEDY delivered the opinion of the Court.

The National Government and, beyond it, the separate States are bound by the proscriptive mandates of the Eighth Amendment to the Constitution of the United States, and all persons within those respective jurisdictions may invoke its protection. Patrick Kennedy, the petitioner here, seeks to set aside his death sentence under the Eighth Amendment. He was charged by the respondent, the State of Louisiana, with the aggravated rape of his then-8-year-old stepdaughter. After a jury trial petitioner was convicted and sentenced to death under a state statute authorizing capital punishment for the rape of a child under 12 years of age. This case presents the question whether the Constitution bars respondent from imposing the death penalty for the rape of a child where the crime did not result, and was not intended to result, in death of the victim. We hold the Eighth Amendment prohibits the death penalty for this offense. The Louisiana statute is unconstitutional.

I

Petitioner's crime was one that cannot be recounted in these pages in a way sufficient to capture in full the hurt and horror inflicted on his victim or to convey the revulsion society, and the jury that represents it, sought to express by sentencing petitioner to death. At 9:18 a.m. on March 2, 1998, petitioner called 911 to report that his stepdaughter, referred to here as L.H., had been raped. He told the 911 operator that L.H. had been in the garage while he readied his son for school. Upon hearing loud screaming, petitioner said, he ran outside and found L.H. in the side yard. Two neighborhood boys, petitioner told the operator, had dragged L.H. from the garage to the yard, pushed her down, and raped her. Petitioner claimed he saw one of the boys riding away on a blue 10-speed bicycle.

When police arrived at petitioner's home between 9:20 and 9:30 a.m., they found L.H. on her bed, wearing a T-shirt and wrapped in a bloody blanket. She was bleeding profusely from the vaginal area. Petitioner told police he had carried her from the yard to the bathtub and then to the bed. Consistent with this explanation, police found a thin line of blood drops in the garage on the way to the house and then up the stairs. Once in the bedroom, petitioner had used a basin of water and a cloth to wipe blood from the victim. This later prevented medical personnel from collecting a reliable DNA sample.

L.H. was transported to the Children's Hospital. An expert in pediatric forensic medicine testified that L.H.'s injuries were the most severe he had seen from a sexual assault in his four years of practice. A laceration to the left wall of the vagina had separated her cervix from the back of her vagina, causing her rectum to protrude into the vaginal structure. Her entire perineum was torn from the posterior fourchette to the anus. The injuries required emergency surgery.

At the scene of the crime, at the hospital, and in the first weeks that followed, both L.H. and petitioner maintained in their accounts to investigators that L.H. had been raped by two neighborhood boys ...

Eight days after the crime, and despite L.H.'s insistence that petitioner was not the offender, petitioner was arrested for the rape. The State's investigation had drawn the accuracy of petitioner and L.H.'s story into question. Though the defense at trial proffered alternative explanations, the case for the prosecution, credited by the jury, was based upon the following evidence: An inspection of the side yard immediately after the assault was inconsistent with a rape having occurred there, the grass having been found mostly undisturbed but for a small patch of coagulated blood. Petitioner said that one of the perpetrators fled the crime scene on a blue 10-speed bicycle but gave inconsistent descriptions of the bicycle's features, such as its handlebars. Investigators found a bicycle matching petitioner and L.H.'s description in tall grass behind a nearby apartment, and petitioner identified it as the bicycle one of the perpetrators was riding. Yet its tires were flat, it did not have gears, and it was covered in spider webs. In addition police found blood on the underside of L.H.'s mattress. This convinced them the rape took place in her bedroom, not outside the house.

Police also found that petitioner made four telephone calls on the morning of the rape. Sometime before 6:15 a.m., petitioner called his employer and left a message that he was unavailable to work that day. Petitioner called back between 6:30 and 7:30 a.m. to ask a colleague how to get blood out of a white carpet because his daughter had "'just become a young lady.'" At 7:37 a.m., petitioner called B & B Carpet Cleaning and requested urgent assistance in removing bloodstains from a carpet. Petitioner did not call 911 until about an hour and a half later.

About a month after petitioner's arrest L.H. was removed from the custody of her mother, who had maintained until that point that petitioner was not involved in the rape. On June 22, 1998, L.H. was returned home and told her mother for the first time that petitioner had raped her. And on December 16, 1999, about 21 months after the rape, L.H. recorded her accusation in a videotaped interview with the Child Advocacy Center.

The State charged petitioner with aggravated rape of a child under ... and sought the death penalty.

The trial began in August 2003. L.H. was then 13 years old. She testified that she "'woke up one morning and Patrick was on top of [her].'" She remembered petitioner bringing her "'[a] cup of orange juice and pills chopped up in it'" after the rape and overhearing him on the telephone saying she had become a "'young lady.'" L.H. acknowledged that she had accused two neighborhood boys but testified petitioner told her to say this and that it was untrue.

The jury having found petitioner guilty of aggravated rape, the penalty phase ensued. The State presented the testimony of S.L., who is the cousin and goddaughter of petitioner's ex-wife. S.L. testified that petitioner sexually abused her three times when she was eight years old and that the last time involved sexual intercourse. She did not tell anyone until two years later and did not pursue legal action.

The jury unanimously determined that petitioner should be sentenced to death. The Supreme Court of Louisiana affirmed ... The court rejected petitioner's reliance on *Coker v. Georgia*, noting that, while *Coker* bars the use of the death penalty as punishment for the rape of an adult woman, it left open the question which, if any, other nonhomicide crimes can be punished by death consistent with the Eighth Amendment. Because "'children are a class that need special protection,'" the state court reasoned, the rape of a child is unique in terms of the harm it inflicts upon the victim and our society....

On this reasoning the Supreme Court of Louisiana rejected petitioner's argument that the death penalty for the rape of a child under 12 years is disproportionate and upheld the constitutionality of the statute.

We granted certiorari. See 552 U.S. 1087, 128 S.Ct. 829, 169 L.Ed.2d 625 (2008).

II

The Eighth Amendment, applicable to the States through the Fourteenth Amendment, provides that "[e]xcessive bail shall not be required, nor excessive fines imposed, nor cruel and unusual punishments inflicted." The Amendment proscribes "all excessive punishments, as well as cruel and unusual punishments that may or may not be excessive." The Court explained in *Atkins* and *Roper*, that the Eighth Amendment's protection against excessive or cruel and unusual punishments flows from the basic "precept of justice that punishment for [a] crime should be graduated and proportioned to [the] offense." Whether this requirement has been fulfilled is determined not by the standards that prevailed when the Eighth Amendment was adopted in 1791 but by the norms that "currently prevail." The Amendment "draw[s] its meaning from the evolving standards of decency that mark the progress of a maturing society." This is because "[t]he standard of extreme cruelty is not merely descriptive, but necessarily embodies a moral judgment. The standard itself remains the same, but its applicability must change as the basic mores of society change."

Evolving standards of decency must embrace and express respect for the dignity of the person, and the punishment of criminals must conform to that rule. As we shall discuss, punishment is justified under one or more of three principal rationales: rehabilitation, deterrence, and retribution ... It is the last of these, retribution, that most often can contradict the law's own ends. This is of particular concern when the Court interprets the meaning of the Eighth Amendment in capital cases. When the law punishes by death, it risks its own sudden descent into brutality, transgressing the constitutional commitment to decency and restraint.

For these reasons we have explained that capital punishment must "be limited to those offenders who commit 'a narrow category of the most serious crimes' and whose extreme culpability makes them 'the most deserving of execution.'" Though the death penalty is not invariably unconstitutional, the Court insists upon confining the instances in which the punishment can be imposed.

Applying this principle, we held in *Roper* and *Atkins* that the execution of juveniles and mentally retarded persons are punishments violative of the Eighth Amendment because the offender had a diminished personal responsibility for the crime. The Court further has held that the death penalty can be disproportionate to the crime itself where the crime did not result, or was not intended to result, in death of the victim. In *Coker*, for instance, the Court held it would be unconstitutional to execute an offender who had raped an adult woman. And in *Enmund v. Florida,* the Court overturned the capital sentence of a defendant who aided and abetted a robbery during which a murder was committed but did not himself kill, attempt to kill, or intend that a killing would take place. On the other hand, in *Tison v. Arizona,* the Court allowed the defendants' death sentences to stand where they did not themselves kill the victims but their involvement in the events leading up to the murders was active, recklessly indifferent, and substantial.

In these cases the Court has been guided by "objective indicia of society's standards, as expressed in legislative enactments and state practice with respect to executions." The inquiry does not end there, however. Consensus is not dispositive. Whether the death penalty is disproportionate to the crime committed depends as well upon the standards elaborated by controlling precedents and by the Court's own understanding and interpretation of the Eighth Amendment's text, history, meaning, and purpose.

Based both on consensus and our own independent judgment, our holding is that a death sentence for one who raped but did not kill a child, and who did not intend to assist another in killing the child, is unconstitutional under the Eighth and Fourteenth Amendments.

### III

### A

The existence of objective indicia of consensus against making a crime punishable by death was a relevant concern in *Roper, Atkins, Coker,* and *Enmund,* and we follow the approach of those cases here. The history of the death penalty for the crime of rape is an instructive beginning point.

... 44 States have not made child rape a capital offense. As for federal law, Congress in the Federal Death Penalty Act of 1994 expanded the number of federal crimes for which the death penalty is a permissible sentence, including certain nonhomicide offenses; but it did not do the same for child rape or abuse ... Under 18 U.S.C. § 2245, an offender is death eligible only when the sexual abuse or exploitation results in the victim's death ...

Definitive resolution of state-law issues is for the States' own courts, and there may be disagreement over the statistics. It is further true that some States, including States that have addressed the issue in just the last few years, have made child rape a capital offense. The summary recited here, however, does allow us to make certain comparisons with the data cited in the *Atkins, Roper,* and *Enmund* cases.

When *Atkins* was decided in 2002, 30 States, including 12 noncapital jurisdictions, prohibited the death penalty for mentally retarded offenders; 20 permitted it. When *Roper* was decided in 2005, the numbers disclosed a similar division among the States: 30 States prohibited the death penalty for juveniles, 18 of which permitted the death penalty for other offenders; and 20 States authorized it. Both in *Atkins* and in *Roper,* we noted that the practice of executing mentally retarded and juvenile offenders was infrequent. Only five States had executed an offender known to have an IQ below 70 between 1989 and 2002, see *Atkins, supra,* at 316, 122 S.Ct. 2242; and only three States had executed a juvenile offender between 1995 and 2005.

The statistics in *Enmund* bear an even greater similarity to the instant case. There eight jurisdictions had authorized imposition of the death penalty solely for participation in a robbery during which an accomplice committed murder, and six defendants between 1954 and 1982 had been sentenced to death for felony murder where the defendant did not personally commit the homicidal assault. These facts, the Court concluded, "weigh[ed] on the side of rejecting capital punishment for the crime."

The evidence of a national consensus with respect to the death penalty for child rapists, as with respect to juveniles, mentally retarded offenders, and vicarious felony murderers, shows divided opinion but, on balance, an opinion against it. Thirty-seven jurisdictions—36 States plus the Federal Government—have the death penalty. As mentioned above, only six of those jurisdictions authorize the death penalty for rape of a child. Though our review of national consensus is not confined to tallying the number of States with applicable death penalty legislation, it is of significance that, in 45 jurisdictions, petitioner could not be executed for child rape of any kind. That number surpasses the 30 States in *Atkins* and *Roper* and the 42 States in *Enmund* that prohibited the death penalty under the circumstances those cases considered ...

## D

There are measures of consensus other than legislation. Statistics about the number of executions may inform the consideration whether capital punishment for the crime of child rape is regarded as unacceptable in our society. These statistics confirm our determination from our review of state statutes that there is a social consensus against the death penalty for the crime of child rape.

Nine States—Florida, Georgia, Louisiana, Mississippi, Montana, Oklahoma, South Carolina, Tennessee, and Texas—have permitted capital punishment for adult or child rape for some length of time between the Court's 1972 decision in *Furman* and today. Yet no individual has been executed for the rape of an adult or child since 1964, and no execution for any other nonhomicide offense has been conducted since 1963 ...

Louisiana is the only State since 1964 that has sentenced an individual to death for the crime of child rape; and petitioner and Richard Davis, who was convicted and sentenced to death for the aggravated rape of a 5-year-old child by a Louisiana jury in December 2007, are the only two individuals now on death row in the United States for a nonhomicide offense.

After reviewing the authorities informed by contemporary norms, including the history of the death penalty for this and other nonhomicide crimes, current state statutes and new enactments, and the number of executions since 1964, we conclude there is a national consensus against capital punishment for the crime of child rape ...

V

Our determination that there is a consensus against the death penalty for child rape raises the question whether the Court's own institutional position and its holding will have the effect of blocking further or later consensus in favor of the penalty from developing. The Court, it will be argued, by the act of addressing the constitutionality of the death penalty, intrudes upon the consensus-making process. By imposing a negative restraint, the argument runs, the Court makes it more difficult for consensus to change or emerge. The Court, according to the criticism, itself becomes enmeshed in the process, part judge and part the maker of that which it judges.

These concerns overlook the meaning and full substance of the established proposition that the Eighth Amendment is defined by "the evolving standards of decency that mark the progress of a maturing society." Confirmed by repeated, consistent rulings of this Court, this principle requires that use of the death penalty be restrained. The rule of evolving standards of decency with specific marks on the way to full progress and mature judgment means that resort to the penalty must be reserved for the worst of crimes and limited in its instances of application. In most cases justice is not better served by terminating the life of the perpetrator rather than confining him and preserving the possibility that he and the system will find ways to allow him to understand the enormity of his offense. Difficulties in administering the penalty to ensure against its arbitrary and capricious application require adherence to a rule reserving its use, at this stage of evolving standards and in cases of crimes against individuals, for crimes that take the life of the victim.

The judgment of the Supreme Court of Louisiana upholding the capital sentence is reversed. This case is remanded for further proceedings not inconsistent with this opinion.

*It is so ordered.*

## Notes and Questions

1. As *Kennedy v. Louisiana* illustrates, Eighth Amendment proportionality analysis is considerably more robust when the punishment imposed is the death penalty. According to Supreme Court precedent, the death penalty may not be imposed for a crime that does not involve the death of a person. It should be noted, however, that the conventional understanding of the Supreme Court's death penalty jurisprudence is that the death penalty may be imposed for certain crimes against the state, such as treason or espionage.

2. Justice Alito authored a dissenting opinion in *Kennedy* that was joined by Chief Justice Roberts and Justices Scalia and Thomas. In his dissent, Alito claimed that the majority's "principal ... justification" for holding that the death penalty may only be imposed for crimes involving the death of a human being is that homicides are "unique in its moral depravity and in the severity of the injury that it inflicts on the victim and the public" and—by implication—that child rape is not as morally depraved and, therefore, as worthy of condemnation as murder. Alito takes issue with this conclusion, arguing that:

> With respect to the question of moral depravity, is it really true that every person who is convicted of capital murder and sentenced to death is more morally

depraved than every child rapist? Consider the following two cases. In the first, a defendant robs a convenience store and watches as his accomplice shoots the store owner. The defendant acts recklessly, but was not the triggerman and did not intend the killing. In the second case, a previously convicted child rapist kidnaps, repeatedly rapes, and tortures multiple child victims. Is it clear that the first defendant is more morally depraved than the second?

... I have little doubt that, in the eyes of ordinary Americans, the very worst child rapists—predators who seek out and inflict serious physical and emotional injury on defenseless young children—are the epitome of moral depravity.

With respect to the question of the harm caused by the rape of a child in relation to the harm caused by murder, it is certainly true that the loss of human life represents a unique harm, but that does not explain why other grievous harms are insufficient to permit a death sentence. And the Court does not take the position that no harm other than the loss of life is sufficient. The Court takes pains to limit its holding to "crimes against individual persons" and to exclude "offenses against the State," a category that the Court stretches—without explanation—to include "drug kingpin activity." But the Court makes no effort to explain why the harm caused by such crimes is necessarily greater than the harm caused by the rape of young children. This is puzzling in light of the Court's acknowledgment that "[r]ape has a permanent psychological, emotional, and sometimes physical impact on the child." As the Court aptly recognizes, "[w]e cannot dismiss the years of long anguish that must be endured by the victim of child rape."

The rape of any victim inflicts great injury, and "[s]ome victims are so grievously injured physically or psychologically that life *is* beyond repair." "The immaturity and vulnerability of a child, both physically and psychologically, adds a devastating dimension to rape that is not present when an adult is raped." Long-term studies show that sexual abuse is "grossly intrusive in the lives of children and is harmful to their normal psychological, emotional, and sexual development in ways which no just or humane society can tolerate."

It has been estimated that as many as 40% of 7- to 13-year-old sexual assault victims are considered "seriously disturbed." Psychological problems include sudden school failure, unprovoked crying, dissociation, depression, insomnia, sleep disturbances, nightmares, feelings of guilt and inferiority, and self-destructive behavior, including an increased incidence of suicide.

The deep problems that afflict child-rape victims often become society's problems as well. Commentators have noted correlations between childhood sexual abuse and later problems such as substance abuse, dangerous sexual behaviors or dysfunction, inability to relate to others on an interpersonal level, and psychiatric illness. Victims of child rape are nearly 5 times more likely than nonvictims to be arrested for sex crimes and nearly 30 times more likely to be arrested for prostitution.

The harm that is caused to the victims and to society at large by the worst child rapists is grave. It is the judgment of the Louisiana lawmakers and those in an increasing number of other States that these harms justify the death penalty. The Court provides no cogent explanation why this legislative judgment should be overridden. Conclusory references to "decency," "moderation," "restraint," "full progress," and "moral judgment" are not enough.

Do you agree with the dissenters that some child rapes evince as much or more moral depravity than some murders? Assuming that some child rapes evince as much or more moral depravity than many murders, should punishing such rapes with the death penalty be upheld even if the historical practice has been not to impose capital punishment in these cases?

## § 4.03 Proportionality: Immature Defendants

### Miller v. Alabama

Supreme Court of the United States, 2012
132 S.Ct. 2455

Justice KAGAN delivered the opinion of the Court.

The two 14-year-old offenders in these cases were convicted of murder and sentenced to life imprisonment without the possibility of parole. In neither case did the sentencing authority have any discretion to impose a different punishment. State law mandated that each juvenile die in prison even if a judge or jury would have thought that his youth and its attendant characteristics, along with the nature of his crime, made a lesser sentence (for example, life *with* the possibility of parole) more appropriate. Such a scheme prevents those meting out punishment from considering a juvenile's "lessened culpability" and greater "capacity for change," and runs afoul of our cases' requirement of individualized sentencing for defendants facing the most serious penalties. We therefore hold that mandatory life without parole for those under the age of 18 at the time of their crimes violates the Eighth Amendment's prohibition on "cruel and unusual punishments."

I

A

In November 1999, petitioner Kuntrell Jackson, then 14 years old, and two other boys decided to rob a video store. En route to the store, Jackson learned that one of the boys, Derrick Shields, was carrying a sawed-off shotgun in his coat sleeve. Jackson decided to stay outside when the two other boys entered the store. Inside, Shields pointed the gun at the store clerk, Laurie Troup, and demanded that she "give up the money." Troup refused. A few moments later, Jackson went into the store to find Shields continuing to demand money. At trial, the parties disputed whether Jackson warned Troup that "[w]e ain't playin'," or instead told his friends, "I thought you all was playin'." When Troup threatened to call the police, Shields shot and killed her. The three boys fled empty-handed.

Arkansas law gives prosecutors discretion to charge 14-year-olds as adults when they are alleged to have committed certain serious offenses. The prosecutor here exercised that authority by charging Jackson with capital felony murder and aggravated robbery. Jackson moved to transfer the case to juvenile court, but after considering the alleged facts of the crime, a psychiatrist's examination, and Jackson's juvenile arrest history (shoplifting and several incidents of car theft), the trial court denied the motion, and an appellate court affirmed. A jury later convicted Jackson of both crimes. Noting that "in view of [the] verdict, there's only one possible punishment," the judge sentenced Jackson to life without parole. Jackson did not challenge the sentence on appeal, and the Arkansas Supreme Court affirmed the convictions.

Following *Roper v. Simmons,* in which this Court invalidated the death penalty for all juvenile offenders under the age of 18, Jackson filed a state petition for habeas corpus. He argued, based on *Roper*'s reasoning, that a mandatory sentence of life without parole for a 14-year-old also violates the Eighth Amendment. The circuit court rejected that argument and granted the State's motion to dismiss. While that ruling was on appeal, this Court held in *Graham v. Florida* that life without parole violates the Eighth Amendment when imposed on juvenile nonhomicide offenders. After the parties filed briefs addressing that decision, the Arkansas Supreme Court affirmed the dismissal of Jackson's petition. The majority found that *Roper* and *Graham* were "narrowly tailored" to their contexts: "death-penalty cases involving a juvenile and life-imprisonment-without-parole cases for nonhomicide offenses involving a juvenile." . . .

II

The Eighth Amendment's prohibition of cruel and unusual punishment "guarantees individuals the right not to be subjected to excessive sanctions." That right, we have explained, "flows from the basic 'precept of justice that punishment for crime should be graduated and proportioned'" to both the offender and the offense. As we noted the last time we considered life-without-parole sentences imposed on juveniles, "[t]he concept of proportionality is central to the Eighth Amendment." And we view that concept less through a historical prism than according to "'the evolving standards of decency that mark the progress of a maturing society.'"

The cases before us implicate two strands of precedent reflecting our concern with proportionate punishment. The first has adopted categorical bans on sentencing practices based on mismatches between the culpability of a class of offenders and the severity of a penalty. So, for example, we have held that imposing the death penalty for nonhomicide crimes against individuals, or imposing it on mentally retarded defendants, violates the Eighth Amendment. Several of the cases in this group have specially focused on juvenile offenders, because of their lesser culpability. Thus, *Roper* held that the Eighth Amendment bars capital punishment for children, and *Graham* concluded that the Amendment also prohibits a sentence of life without the possibility of parole for a child who committed a nonhomicide offense. *Graham* further likened life without parole for juveniles to the death penalty itself, thereby evoking a second line of our precedents. In those cases, we have prohibited mandatory imposition of capital punishment, requiring that sentencing authorities consider the characteristics of a defendant and the details of his offense before sentencing him to death. Here, the confluence of these two lines of precedent leads to the conclusion that mandatory life-without-parole sentences for juveniles violate the Eighth Amendment.

To start with the first set of cases: *Roper* and *Graham* establish that children are constitutionally different from adults for purposes of sentencing. Because juveniles have diminished culpability and greater prospects for reform, we explained, "they are less deserving of the most severe punishments." Those cases relied on three significant gaps between juveniles and adults. First, children have a "'lack of maturity and an underdeveloped sense of responsibility,'" leading to recklessness, impulsivity, and heedless risk-taking. Second, children "are more vulnerable . . . to negative influences and outside pressures," including from their family and peers; they have limited "contro[l] over their own environment" and lack the ability to extricate themselves from horrific, crime-producing settings. And third, a child's character is not as "well formed" as an adult's; his traits are "less fixed" and his actions less likely to be "evidence of irretrievabl[e] deprav[ity]." . . .

*Roper* and *Graham* emphasized that the distinctive attributes of youth diminish the penological justifications for imposing the harshest sentences on juvenile offenders, even when they commit terrible crimes. Because "'[t]he heart of the retribution rationale'" relates to an offender's blameworthiness, "'the case for retribution is not as strong with a minor as with an adult.'" Nor can deterrence do the work in this context, because "'the same characteristics that render juveniles less culpable than adults'"—their immaturity, recklessness, and impetuosity—make them less likely to consider potential punishment. Similarly, incapacitation could not support the life-without-parole sentence in *Graham* : Deciding that a "juvenile offender forever will be a danger to society" would require "mak[ing] a judgment that [he] is incorrigible"—but "'incorrigibility is inconsistent with youth.'" And for the same reason, rehabilitation could not justify that sentence. Life without parole "forswears altogether the rehabilitative ideal." It reflects "an irrevocable judgment about [an offender's] value and place in society," at odds with a child's capacity for change.

*Graham* concluded from this analysis that life-without-parole sentences, like capital punishment, may violate the Eighth Amendment when imposed on children. To be sure, *Graham*'s flat ban on life without parole applied only to nonhomicide crimes, and the Court took care to distinguish those offenses from murder, based on both moral culpability and consequential harm. But none of what it said about children—about their distinctive (and transitory) mental traits and environmental vulnerabilities—is crime-specific. Those features are evident in the same way, and to the same degree, when (as in both cases here) a botched robbery turns into a killing. So *Graham*'s reasoning implicates any life-without-parole sentence imposed on a juvenile, even as its categorical bar relates only to nonhomicide offenses.

Most fundamentally, *Graham* insists that youth matters in determining the appropriateness of a lifetime of incarceration without the possibility of parole. In the circumstances there, juvenile status precluded a life-without-parole sentence, even though an adult could receive it for a similar crime. And in other contexts as well, the characteristics of youth, and the way they weaken rationales for punishment, can render a life-without-parole sentence disproportionate ...

But the mandatory penalty schemes at issue here prevent the sentencer from taking account of these central considerations. By removing youth from the balance—by subjecting a juvenile to the same life-without-parole sentence applicable to an adult—these laws prohibit a sentencing authority from assessing whether the law's harshest term of imprisonment proportionately punishes a juvenile offender. That contravenes *Graham*'s (and also *Roper*'s) foundational principle: that imposition of a State's most severe penalties on juvenile offenders cannot proceed as though they were not children....

We therefore hold that the Eighth Amendment forbids a sentencing scheme that mandates life in prison without possibility of parole for juvenile offenders. By making youth (and all that accompanies it) irrelevant to imposition of that harshest prison sentence, such a scheme poses too great a risk of disproportionate punishment. Because that holding is sufficient to decide these cases, we do not consider [the] argument that the Eighth Amendment requires a categorical bar on life without parole for juveniles, or at least for those 14 and younger. But given all we have said in *Roper, Graham*, and this decision about children's diminished culpability and heightened capacity for change, we think appropriate occasions for sentencing juveniles to this harshest possible penalty will be uncommon. That is especially so because of the great difficulty we noted in *Roper* and *Graham* of distinguishing at this early age between "the juvenile offender whose crime reflects unfortunate yet transient immaturity, and the rare juvenile offender whose crime reflects irreparable corruption." Although we do not foreclose a sentencer's ability to make that judgment in homicide cases, we require it to take into account how children are different, and how those differences counsel against irrevocably sentencing them to a lifetime in prison ...

III

The States (along with Justice THOMAS) ... claim that *Harmelin v. Michigan* precludes our holding. The defendant in *Harmelin* was sentenced to a mandatory life-without-parole term for possessing more than 650 grams of cocaine. The Court upheld that penalty, reasoning that "a sentence which is not otherwise cruel and unusual" does not "becom[e] so simply because it is 'mandatory.'" We recognized that a different rule, requiring individualized sentencing, applied in the death penalty context. But we refused to extend that command to noncapital cases "because of the qualitative difference between death and all other penalties." According to Alabama, invalidating the mandatory imposition of life-without-parole terms on juveniles "would effectively overrule *Harmelin*."

We think that argument myopic. *Harmelin* had nothing to do with children and did not purport to apply its holding to the sentencing of juvenile offenders. We have by now held on multiple occasions that a sentencing rule permissible for adults may not be so for children. Capital punishment, our decisions hold, generally comports with the Eighth Amendment—except it cannot be imposed on children. So too, life without parole is permissible for nonhomicide offenses—except, once again, for children....

IV

*Graham*, *Roper*, and our individualized sentencing decisions make clear that a judge or jury must have the opportunity to consider mitigating circumstances before imposing the harshest possible penalty for juveniles. By requiring that all children convicted of homicide receive lifetime incarceration without possibility of parole, regardless of their age and age-related characteristics and the nature of their crimes, the mandatory sentencing schemes before us violate this principle of proportionality, and so the Eighth Amendment's ban on cruel and unusual punishment. We accordingly reverse the judgments of the Arkansas Supreme Court and Alabama Court of Criminal Appeals and remand the cases for further proceedings not inconsistent with this opinion.

*It is so ordered.*

## Notes and Questions

1. The Supreme Court adopts a relatively robust proportionality analysis when the defendant was immature at the time of the commission of the offense either because of her age or because of mental illness or defect. As *Miller* illustrates, the more meaningful proportionality analysis applied in these cases bars not only the imposition of the death penalty for offenses committed by juvenile or mentally ill defendants, but also prohibits imposing a sentence of life without parole for a crime committed by a juvenile defendant.

2. In *Atkins v. Virginia*, 536 U.S. 304 (2002), the Supreme Court concluded that executing a defendant with severe mental deficiencies amounts to cruel and unusual punishment. In doing so, the Court pointed out that "within the world community, the imposition of the death penalty for crimes committed by mentally retarded offenders is overwhelmingly disapproved." This—coupled with the fact that the vast majority of American jurisdictions prohibit the execution of mentally retarded offenders—helped support the Court's conclusion that the practice violated the Eighth Amendment. Subsequently, in

*Roper v. Simmons,* 543 U.S. 551 (2005), the high court was asked to assess the constitutionality of imposing the death penalty on a defendant who was a minor when he committed the offense. A majority of the members of the Supreme Court concluded that executing someone as punishment for a crime that was committed while under the age of 18 runs afoul the Eighth Amendment. In justifying its conclusion, the Court pointed out "that only seven countries other than the United States have executed juvenile offenders since 1990." While the Supreme Court conceded that the practices of other countries are not determinative of the meaning of the constitution of the United States, it also acknowledged that the Court frequently "refe[rs] to the laws of other countries and to international authorities as instructive for its interpretation of the Eighth Amendment's prohibition of 'cruel and unusual punishments.'"

3. In a strident dissent, Justice Scalia took issue with the majority's use of foreign materials in *Roper* to assess the constitutionality of executing a defendant who was a minor when he committed the offense. According to Scalia:

> [T]he basic premise of the Court's argument—that American law should conform to the laws of the rest of the world—ought to be rejected out of hand. In fact the Court itself does not believe it. In many significant respects the laws of most other countries differ from our law—including not only such explicit provisions of our Constitution as the right to jury trial and grand jury indictment, but even many interpretations of the Constitution prescribed by this Court itself. The Court-pronounced exclusionary rule, for example, is distinctively American ... Since then a categorical exclusionary rule has been "universally rejected" by other countries, including those with rules prohibiting illegal searches and police misconduct, despite the fact that none of these countries "appears to have any alternative form of discipline for police that is effective in preventing search violations." ...
>
> The Court has been oblivious to the views of other countries when deciding how to interpret our Constitution's requirement that "Congress shall make no law respecting an establishment of religion...." Most other countries—including those committed to religious neutrality—do not insist on the degree of separation between church and state that this Court requires ...
>
> And let us not forget the Court's abortion jurisprudence, which makes us one of only six countries that allow abortion on demand until the point of viability ...
>
> The Court should either profess its willingness to reconsider all these matters in light of the views of foreigners, or else it should cease putting forth foreigners' views as part of the *reasoned basis* of its decisions. To invoke alien law when it agrees with one's own thinking, and ignore it otherwise, is not reasoned decisionmaking, but sophistry.
>
> The Court responds that "[i]t does not lessen our fidelity to the Constitution or our pride in its origins to acknowledge that the express affirmation of certain fundamental rights by other nations and peoples simply underscores the centrality of those same rights within our own heritage of freedom." To begin with, I do not believe that approval by "other nations and peoples" should buttress our commitment to American principles any more than (what should logically follow) disapproval by "other nations and peoples" should weaken that commitment. More importantly, however, the Court's statement flatly misdescribes what is going on here. Foreign sources are cited today, *not* to underscore our "fidelity" to the Constitution, our "pride in its origins," and "our own [American]

> heritage." To the contrary, they are cited *to set aside* the centuries-old American practice—a practice still engaged in by a large majority of the relevant States—of letting a jury of 12 citizens decide whether, in the particular case, youth should be the basis for withholding the death penalty. What these foreign sources "affirm," rather than repudiate, is the Justices' own notion of how the world ought to be, and their diktat that it shall be so henceforth in America. The Court's parting attempt to downplay the significance of its extensive discussion of foreign law is unconvincing. "Acknowledgment" of foreign approval has no place in the legal opinion of this Court *unless it is part of the basis for the Court's judgment*—which is surely what it parades as today.

In her dissenting opinion, Justice O'Connor expressed disagreement with Justice Scalia's contention that foreign and international law are irrelevant to proportionality analysis under the Eighth Amendment. More specifically, she argued that:

> Over the course of nearly half a century, the Court has consistently referred to foreign and international law as relevant to its assessment of evolving standards of decency. This inquiry reflects the special character of the Eighth Amendment, which, as the Court has long held, draws its meaning directly from the maturing values of civilized society. Obviously, American law is distinctive in many respects, not least where the specific provisions of our Constitution and the history of its exposition so dictate. But this Nation's evolving understanding of human dignity certainly is neither wholly isolated from, nor inherently at odds with, the values prevailing in other countries. On the contrary, we should not be surprised to find congruence between domestic and international values, especially where the international community has reached clear agreement—expressed in international law or in the domestic laws of individual countries—that a particular form of punishment is inconsistent with fundamental human rights. At least, the existence of an international consensus of this nature can serve to confirm the reasonableness of a consonant and genuine American consensus. The instant case presents no such domestic consensus, however, and the recent emergence of an otherwise global consensus does not alter that basic fact.

Do you agree with Scalia's claim that foreign and international law have no place in the Supreme Court's cruel and unusual punishments jurisprudence or do you prefer O'Connor's view that such materials are relevant to assessing whether American punishment practices conform to "evolving standards of decency" as required by the Eighth Amendment? Explain.

## §4.04 Proportionality: Alternative Approaches under State Constitutions

### State v. Lewis

Supreme Court of Appeals of West Virginia, 1994
447 S.E.2d 570

WORKMAN, Justice:

Mabel Lewis appeals from a January 13, 1993, conviction for third offense shoplifting for which she was sentenced by the Circuit Court of Mercer County to an indeterminate term of not less than one nor more than ten years in the state penitentiary and fined $500 pursuant to mandatory sentencing laws. We reverse and remand this case for consideration by the circuit court of the alternative sentencing requested by Appellant.

On June 13, 1991, Appellant, a forty-five-year-old woman, entered the Princeton, West Virginia, Kroger store. The store's co-manager, Dan Watson, observed the Appellant placing boneless center loin chops and garlic powder into her purse while she was shopping throughout the store. While she paid for the items she placed in her cart at the checkout counter, she did not remove or pay for the pork chops and garlic powder, which were collectively valued at $ 8.83. After she proceeded past the checkout area, Mr. Watson stopped her to question her, whereupon the pork chops and garlic powder were discovered in her purse.

Appellant was indicted in October 1991 for the felony of third offense shoplifting. She had been on probation for second offense shoplifting at the time she committed the June 13, 1991, offense. Appellant was convicted for third offense shoplifting on January 13, 1993, and sentenced according to mandatory sentencing for such offense to one to ten years in the state penitentiary and fined $500.

As the basis for her appeal, Appellant assigns as error the trial court's failure to permit alternate sentencing in view of her health conditions and the nonviolent nature of the offense ...

Appellant's ... assignment of error arises from the trial court's failure to consider and utilize alternative sentencing. The State's position on this issue is that the statute, as written, does not permit the sentencing court any latitude in sentencing. West Virginia Code 61-3A-3(c) (1992) provides:

> Upon a third or subsequent shoplifting conviction, regardless of the value of the merchandise, the defendant shall be guilty of a felony and shall be fined not less than five hundred dollars nor more than five thousand dollars, and shall be imprisoned in the penitentiary for one to ten years. At least one year shall actually be spent in confinement and not subject to probation.

... In reviewing the criminal penalties imposed by other states for shoplifting, one glaring difference between our statute and those of other jurisdictions is readily apparent. Although several states impose similar mandatory periods of incarceration for subsequent shoplifting offenses, only one of the other statutes reviewed, contains a proscription against probation for a third or subsequent offense of shoplifting. Since West Virginia Code § 61-3A-3(c) expressly forbids the use of probation, it impliedly prohibits the use of an alternative sentence such as home confinement. The question that arises next is whether the purposeful effacement of alternative sentencing from the penalties imposed by West Virginia Code § 61-3A-3(c) is constitutional.

To resolve this issue, we review our holdings regarding the proportionality principle. In ... *State v. Vance,* we ruled that: "Article III, Section 5 of the West Virginia Constitution, which contains the cruel and unusual punishment counterpart to the Eighth Amendment of the United States Constitution, has an express statement of the proportionality principle: 'Penalties shall be proportioned to the character and degree of the offense.'" We also held ... that "our constitutional proportionality standards theoretically can apply to any criminal sentence...."

In *Bordenkircher,* we discussed at length the analysis for determining whether a statute survives constitutional muster on the grounds of proportionality. As we explained in *Bordenkircher,*

> [i]n determining whether a given sentence violates the proportionality principle found in Article III, Section 5 of the West Virginia Constitution, consideration is given to the nature of the offense, the legislative purpose behind the punishment, a comparison of the punishment with what would be inflicted in other jurisdictions, and a comparison with other offenses within the same jurisdiction.

Comporting with the analysis required by *Bordenkircher,* we first observe that the nature of the offense of shoplifting, as Appellant emphasizes, is nonviolent and necessarily limited in its ability to inflict harm on others. Given the absence of any legislative history regarding the intent underlying the imposition of mandatory incarceration for third offense shoplifting, we can only surmise that the statute's purpose was to create a strong deterrent against the commission of this particular crime. As discussed above, we have located only one other jurisdiction which carries the same express requirement that probation or other alternative sentencing cannot be utilized in sentencing for third or subsequent offense shoplifting. As contrasted to other offenses committed within this State, we note that probation and alternative sentencing are permitted for a variety of criminal offenses, many of which are viewed societally as warranting more severe penalties than shoplifting and certainly more in need of requiring incarceration as a penalty. *See e.g.,* W.Va.Code §§ 60A-4-401 (1992) (controlled substance manufacture, delivery, or possession); 61-2-2 (1992) (first degree murder); 61-2-12 (1992) (robbery); 61-3-1 (arson); 61-3-13 (Supp.1994) (grand larceny); 61-8B-3 (1992) (first degree sexual assault).

Even against this admittedly abbreviated *Bordenkircher* analysis, the penalty imposed by West Virginia Code § 61-3A-3(c) appears disproportionate in its removal of alternate sentencing from those penalties permitted for third offense shoplifting. The Legislature ultimately adopted this same view as the statute was amended in 1994 to insert the following new language to West Virginia Code § 61-3A-3(c): "Provided, That an order for home detention by the court pursuant to the provisions of article eleven-b [§ 62-11B-1 et seq.], chapter sixty-two of this code may be used as an alternative sentence to the incarceration required by this subsection." W.Va.Code § 61-3A-3(c) (1994). With the 1994 amendments to West Virginia Code § 61-3A-3(c), a court may now sentence a third offense shoplifter to home detention.

In *Bordenkircher,* when addressing whether the imposition of the life recidivist sentence, West Virginia Code § 61-11-18(Supp.1994), for a third felony of forging a $43 check violated the proportionality principle, this Court stated that:

> [w]e cannot conceive of any rational argument that would justify this sentence in light of the nonviolent nature of this crime and the similar nature of the two previous crimes, unless we are to turn our backs on the command of our proportionality clause and merely conclude that regardless of the gravity of the underlying offenses the maximum life sentence may be imposed. This would ignore the rationality of our criminal justice system where penalties are set according to the severity of the offense.

While this case does not involve a general recidivist statute such as West Virginia Code § 61-11-18, the rationale stated in *Bordenkircher* is equally applicable here in that statutes such as West Virginia Code § 61-3A-3(c) are specific recidivist statutes. Thus, notwithstanding the mandatory nature of the penalty enhancing language of West Virginia Code § 61-3A-3(c), this Court is still required to consider the gravity of the offense in determining whether the penalty imposed comports with the proportionality principle.

Without intending to minimize the criminal aspect of shoplifting and its attendant costs to society, we cannot, with a clear collective conscience, conclude that Appellant deserves to be imprisoned for a minimum of one year for failing to pay for $ 8.83 worth of groceries. Accordingly, we hold that prior to the 1994 amendments, West Virginia Code §61-3A-3(c) (1981) was unconstitutional in that it violated the cruel and unusual proscription of the Eighth Amendment to the United States Constitution and Article III, Section 5 of the West Virginia Constitution by imposing a disproportionate sentence to the crime committed by expressly prohibiting probation and implicitly prohibiting alternative sentencing.

Based on the foregoing, we reverse the decision of the Circuit Court of Mercer County and remand this case for consideration of the alternative sentencing requested by Appellant.

Reversed and remanded.

## Bult v. Leaply

Supreme Court of South Dakota, 1993
507 N.W.2d 325

MILLER, Chief Justice.

### ACTION

A jury convicted Justin Lloyd Bult (Bult) of kidnapping and sexual contact with a child under fifteen. He was sentenced to life imprisonment on the kidnapping conviction and to a concurrent ten year sentence on the sexual contact conviction by Circuit Court Judge Eugene L. Martin. This Court unanimously affirmed Bult's convictions; no issues regarding the sentence were raised on direct appeal. Bult filed an application for a writ of habeas corpus contending that his life sentence without the possibility of parole was constitutionally offensive under state and federal constitutional provisions prohibiting the imposition of cruel and unusual punishment. Circuit Court Judge Jon R. Erickson entered findings of fact, conclusions of law, and judgment denying the application for a writ of habeas corpus. Because we conclude that the sentence shocks the conscience, we reverse and remand for resentencing proceedings.

### FACTS OF THE OFFENSE

Bult does not dispute the factual allegations and evidence which supported them and led to his conviction. We summarize the facts of the offense from our statement of facts in *State v. Bult, supra.*

Over eleven years ago at 5:10 p.m. on September 15, 1982, Bult, an eighteen year old high school senior, forced a screaming and crying five-year-old girl off of her tricycle and into his automobile. He drove away at a high rate of speed. According to the victim, they drove to a corn field in the country where he held her down, removed her clothes, and "tried to put his wienie" in her while she was laying on the seat. At 5:35 p.m. that afternoon the victim's mother heard her daughter screaming in the yard and questioned her about what had happened.

Bult initially denied being implicated but later admitted to investigators that he abducted the victim and attempted to have sex with her. He refused to sign a written confession. At trial, Bult testified, denied all charges, and presented alibi witnesses. The jury reached guilty verdicts.

## SENTENCING

At sentencing the trial court had the benefit of a presentence report. According to the report, Bult was born on January 19, 1964. He was raised by his natural parents and felt that he had a good childhood except for the times that his parents were drunk.

Bult's criminal record involved an incident of alleged arson in 1975. He was adjudicated delinquent on October 16, 1975, and placed on indefinite probation which terminated on December 3, 1975. On September 14, 1981, Bult was placed on a ninety day diversion program because of a referral as a child in need of supervision alleging that he was a runaway and beyond parental control. This terminated on November 30, 1981.

Educationally, Bult was in the twelfth grade. Academically he was a poor student, a problem exacerbated by his short temper. Despite his low academic ability, he never missed a day and was never tardy for three years. With individualized educational instruction he showed considerable improvement in the area of self-concept although his social skills had not developed as dramatically.

[Bult was sentenced to life imprisonment without the possibility of parole]

## HABEAS CORPUS

In his application for a writ of habeas corpus Bult contended that the life sentence without the possibility of parole infringed upon his constitutional right to be free from cruel and unusual punishment. In addition, Bult presented the court with information regarding the sentences of inmates imprisoned in the South Dakota penitentiary for kidnapping.

## ISSUE

## WHETHER BULT'S SENTENCE OF LIFE WITHOUT THE POSSIBILITY OF PAROLE VIOLATES STATE AND FEDERAL PROHIBITIONS AGAINST CRUEL AND UNUSUAL PUNISHMENT?

"On appeal, we first determine whether the sentence 'shocks the conscience' or is so disproportionate to the crime that it activates the Eighth Amendment 'within and without jurisdiction' proportionality tests." "Absent a sentence which is so excessive in duration that it shocks the conscience of the court, it is well settled in South Dakota that a sentence within statutory limits is not reviewable on appeal." Stated alternatively, we will only engage in extensive review of a sentence where we have first determined the sentence was manifestly disproportionate to the crime. "If a sentence is manifestly disproportionate to the crime, [in light of the gravity of the offense and harshness of the penalty] ... then the other two factors listed in *Helm* [sentence imposed on others in the same jurisdiction and in other jurisdictions] become more focused and require extensive review."

The test to determine whether a sentence is so constitutionally offensive as to shock the conscience is two-fold.

First, is the punishment so excessive or so cruel "as to meet the disapproval and condemnation of the conscience and reason of men generally." And second, whether the punishment is so excessive or so cruel as to shock the collective conscience of this court.

The commonly accepted goals of punishment are 1) retribution, 2) deterrence, both individual and general, and 3) rehabilitation. We have recognized that while a life sentence without parole extracts retribution, deters the convict from committing crime, removes him from the street, and puts would-be felons on notice of the high penalty of recidivism, it completely eschews the goal of rehabilitation.

In *Weiker, supra,* we noted that a life sentence is exceeded in severity only by capital punishment. While we acknowledged that there are cases where the imposition of a life sentence without parole is meritorious, we cautioned:

> [T]hey are rare and should involve a history of much more serious offenses that by reason of their brutality or calculated destructiveness render irrelevant the goal of rehabilitation and require in vindication of public safety and the moral underpinnings of the criminal law that the offender forfeit his right to ever again be set free.
>
> * * * * * *
>
> But even more strongly, we recommend to the trial court that the maximum of life sentence be imposed only in such cases where it can determine from the facts of the principal offense and the previous convictions that rehabilitation is so unlikely as to be removed from consideration in sentencing; that the interests of society demand that the convict be kept off the streets for the rest of his life; and that society, speaking through the legislature, has clearly mandated that the offense or offenses involved are so malignant that a lifetime of incarceration is the only adequate retribution.

Bult was convicted of kidnapping, a Class 1 felony, and sexual contact with a child under fifteen, a Class 4 felony. The South Dakota Legislature gave trial courts broad discretion in determining the severity of the sentence that a defendant convicted of each crime receives. Neither crime carries a statutory minimum penitentiary sentence. The maximum penitentiary sentence for Class 1 kidnapping was life imprisonment without the possibility of parole while the maximum sentence for Class 4 sexual contact was ten years imprisonment. The trial court sentenced Bult to the maximum penitentiary sentence for each conviction. It is apparent from its remarks at Bult's sentencing that the trial court believed that any person committing the crimes Bult was convicted of was beyond rehabilitation.

We do not minimize or trivialize the seriousness of Bult's abduction and attempted rape of a five-year-old girl. However, this crime, although brutal and destructive, does not rise to a level rendering rehabilitation irrelevant. Bult did return the child to her home shortly after the abduction. Fortunately, the victim was not raped, nor did she sustain substantial physical injury.

In addition, the record reveals that at the time of the offense the eighteen year old Bult's criminal history consisted of two brushes with the law while he was a juvenile and resulted in a brief period of probation and a ninety day diversion program. While he had learning disabilities and self-image problems one-on-one counseling resulted in positive changes, a fact reflecting amenability to rehabilitation. In addition, there was no evidence of any prior sexual offenses or sexual disfunctionality which would lead to the conclusion that Bult was an incorrigible criminal incapable of rehabilitation.

In sentencing Bult to life imprisonment without the possibility of parole for kidnapping the trial court went beyond the facts of the case, the information contained in the presentence report, and the prosecutor's recommendation. Based upon this record, a life sentence without the possibility of parole for this eighteen year old defendant shocks the conscience of men generally and of this Court.

Finally Bult presented the habeas corpus court with all available information concerning individuals serving time in the penitentiary for a conviction of kidnapping. Because of our conclusion that Bult's sentence shocks the conscience, the need to determine whether the sentence is so disproportionate to the crime as to activate Eighth Amendment proportionality review is obviated. We only observe that this data validates our judgment that a life sentence in Bult's case shocks the conscience. Bult's case is distinguished from the cases presented where life terms for kidnapping were imposed by Bult's youth, his lack of significant prior convictions, and the fact that he did not inflict substantial bodily injury or use a deadly weapon.

Reversed and remanded for resentencing proceedings.

## *Notes and Questions*

1. The Supreme Court of Appeals of West Virginia held in *Lewis* that punishing third offense shoplifting with a mandatory one- to ten-year imprisonment term without the possibility of probation or alternatives to confinement ran afoul of the state's constitutional provision barring cruel and unusual punishments. Towards the end of its opinion, the Court also suggested that the punishment imposed would violate the Eighth Amendment of the United States. Do you agree? Would imposing such punishment violate the Eighth Amendment as construed by the Supreme Court in *Harmelin* and *Ewing*? Why or why not?

2. The Supreme Court of South Dakota held in *Bult* that imposing a sentence of life imprisonment without parole for a kidnapping committed by an eighteen-year-old offender violated the state's constitutional protection against cruel and unusual punishments. Would this sentence violate the **federal** constitutional provision barring cruel and unusual punishments? Explain.

3. Note that the Constitution of West Virginia contains a provision that expressly provides that "[p]enalties shall be proportioned to the character and degree of the offense." This gives the West Virginia courts a textual argument in favor of adopting a meaningful proportionality analysis. Several other state constitutions include provisions that expressly require proportionality between the punishment and the crime, including the constitutions of Illinois, Maine, Nebraska, Oregon and Vermont, among others. As Justice Scalia pointed out in *Harmelin*, the federal constitution lacks a similar provision. Do you believe that the lack of a provision in the federal constitution that expressly provides that punishments should be proportional to the crime reveals that the framers did not intend to prohibit disproportionate punishments? Why or why not?

4. The Supreme Court of Appeals of West Virginia engaged in an "intra" and "inter" jurisdictional comparison of punishments in order to assess whether the sentence imposed in the case was proportional to the crime. This analysis is similar to the one proposed by the United States Supreme Court in *Solem*. Do you find this approach to proportionality more or less appealing than the "gross proportionality" approach espoused by Justice Kennedy in his *Harmelin* concurrence and by Justice O'Connor in *Ewing*? Why?

5. According to the Supreme Court of South Dakota, punishment is cruel and unusual in violation of the state constitution if it meets "the disapproval and condemnation of the conscience and reason of men generally" and if it "is so excessive or so cruel as to shock the collective conscience of this court." The collective conscience of the North Dakota Supreme Court was apparently shocked by sentencing an eighteen-year-old guilty of kidnapping a child to life imprisonment without parole. Is your conscience shocked by this punishment? Is there a non-arbitrary way of determining whether a court's conscience is "shocked" or are such determinations irreducibly subjective? Are you comfortable with courts deciding cases on the basis of whether their "conscience is shocked"? Explain.

# § 4.05 Proportionality: Model Penal Code

## Model Penal Code: Sentencing

*Tentative Draft No. 1*
(April 9, 2007)

**§ 1.02(2). Purposes; Principles of Construction.**

(2) The general purposes of the provisions on sentencing, applicable to all official actors in the sentencing system, are:

(a) in decisions affecting the sentencing of individual offenders:

(i) to render sentences in all cases within a range of severity proportionate to the gravity of offenses, the harms done to crime victims, and the blameworthiness of offenders;

(ii) when reasonably feasible, to achieve offender rehabilitation, general deterrence, incapacitation of dangerous offenders, restoration of crime victims and communities, and reintegration of offenders into the law-abiding community, provided these goals are pursued within the boundaries of proportionality in subsection (a)(i); and

(iii) to render sentences no more severe than necessary to achieve the applicable purposes in subsections (a)(i) and (a)(ii); ...

### *Notes and Questions*

1. While the original draft of the Model Penal Code stated that the principal aim of punishment was to prevent and forbid harmful conduct, the revised tentative draft excerpted in this section points out that the chief purpose of punishment is to "render sentences in all cases within a range of severity proportionate to the gravity of offenses, the harms done to crime victims, and the blameworthiness of offenders." Proportionality is thus the central concern of the drafters of the most recent tentative draft of the Model Penal Code's sentencing provisions.

2. The comments to the tentative draft explain the scope and import of the Code's proportionality requirement in the following manner:

> The starting precept of subsections (2)(a)(i) and (2)(a)(ii) is that utilitarian goals such as rehabilitation, incapacitation, general deterrence, and victim and community restoration should not be allowed to produce sentences more or less severe than those deserved by offenders on moral grounds. Deontological concerns of justice or "desert" place a ceiling on government's legitimate power to attempt to change an offender or otherwise influence future events. So too, an appeal to utilitarian goals should not support a penalty that is too lenient as a matter of justice to reflect the gravity of an offense, the harm to a victim, and the blameworthiness of the offender ...
>
> Responsible decisionmakers in each sentencing system must strive toward informed moral judgments concerning those sentences that fall within, or outside, acceptable boundaries of proportionality. There are no tools in law or philosophy that can render this undertaking an exact science. Indeed, different communities, and different jurisdictions, may be expected to arrive at divergent

> judgments about the ranges of punitive severity that will be deemed proportionate in specific cases, or across classes of cases. Short of constitutional limitations on cruel or unusual sentences, which are generally quite distant, prudential—or subconstitutional—proportionality limitations in a democratic society are best derived through cooperative and collective assessments of community sentiment.

The drafters of the revised provisions were acutely aware of the particular challenge that the United States' commitment to federalism presents in the context of devising a meaningful and coherent proportionality doctrine. More specifically, the drafters pointed out that:

> Recognizing the inevitability—and desirability—of jurisdictional variations in a federalist system, the revised Penal Code does not recommend a single, lockstep approach to be followed in all states. Nor does the Code propound detailed benchmarks of what penalties may be considered proportionate for what crimes. Instead, the Code gives conceptual and institutional structure to the moral reasoning process for the derivation of proportionality limits. Subsection (2)(a)(i) instructs decisionmakers to give weight to familiar deontological indices: the gravity of offenses, the injuries done to crime victims, and the blame-worthiness of offenders. In speaking of "proportionality," the provision also directs attention to the comparative severity of punishments in other cases.

3. While the drafters do not provide much concrete guidance to decision makers in assessing proportionality, they do suggest that engaging in comparative analysis of punishments in other cases is relevant to proportionality. Although the Code drafters do not expressly approve of the proportionality analysis proposed in *Solem*, the comments excerpted in the previous note imply that "intra" and "inter" jurisdictional comparison of punishments is helpful in assessing the proportionality of punishment. This is compatible with the views espoused in many state jurisdictions, as the materials excerpted in the previous section highlight.

## § 4.06 Proportionality: Comparative Perspectives

### STS 68/1994

Supreme Court of Spain, 1994

The trial court convicted the defendant of committing a robbery during which physical injuries were caused. The court also found that the punishment should be aggravated because of the defendant's prior convictions. As a result, the court sentenced the defendant to a term of imprisonment of twelve years....

The defendant appeals his conviction alleging [that the punishment imposed was disproportionate to the gravity of the offense and, therefore, in violation of the principle of proportionality]. We hold that sentencing the defendant to twelve years of imprisonment is wholly disproportionate to the gravity of the offense, given that the defendant did not successfully dispossess the victim of his property and that the physical injuries caused by the defendant were minor.

[The disproportionate nature of the punishment imposed] is revealed by the fact that the defendant was sentenced to twelve years of imprisonment, which is the same punishment that would be imposed in this country on someone who is convicted of intentional homicide. Punishing these two offenses [robbery and intentional homicide] in the same way [is objectionable], for there is an important difference between the interests protected by these two crimes. Given that robbery protects property interests while the offense of homicide protects the more important interest of preserving human life, the former should be punished less than the latter. As a result, the sentenced imposed in this case is disproportional and the defendant's punishment should be mitigated so that the punishment imposed reflects the true gravity of the offense.

### *Notes and Questions*

1. The Supreme Court of Spain held that punishing a robbery with a term of imprisonment of ten years is grossly disproportionate. Would imposing such punishment violate the Eighth Amendment as construed by the Supreme Court in *Harmelin* and *Ewing*? Why or why not?

2. Note that the Spanish Supreme Court engaged in an "intra" jurisdictional comparison of punishments in order to hold that the sentence imposed in the case was disproportionate. The Court believed that imposing on the defendant a sentence for robbery that was as harsh as that which would be authorized for intentional homicide reveals the disproportionate nature of the punishment imposed. Do you agree with the Court's assessment? Why or why not?

3. This case helps illustrate how punitive American criminal law is when compared with the criminal laws of civil law jurisdictions. It is difficult, if not impossible, to imagine an American court striking down as grossly disproportional a sentence that punishes robbery with a twelve-year imprisonment term.

## § 4.07 Proportionality: Scholarly Debates

### John Stinneford, *Rethinking Proportionality under the Cruel and Unusual Punishments Clause*

97 Va. L. Rev. 899 (2011)

The evolving standards of decency test [adopted by the Supreme Court in its recent Eighth Amendment case law] has proven itself an unreliable and ineffective measure of cruelty. Sole reliance on the Court's "independent judgment," on the other hand, would be standardless and potentially antidemocratic. A new approach to the measurement of excessiveness is needed.

As will be discussed below, the text of the Cruel and Unusual Punishments Clause and the early case law suggest that excessiveness should be measured primarily against the boundaries established by prior practice. If a punishment is significantly harsher than prior practice would permit for a given crime, the punishment is unusual and therefore presumptively cruel. Such a punishment would only be upheld in the rare circumstance in which the increase could be justified as a matter of retribution.

1. Determining Whether the Punishment Is Unusual

The word "unusual" means "contrary to long usage," which is another way of saying "contrary to longstanding practice." This choice of wording reflects the common law ideology that predominated at the time the Eighth Amendment was adopted. The common law was predicated upon the idea that practices that enjoy long usage are presumptively reasonable and enjoy the consent of the people. Longstanding practices that were used throughout the jurisdiction attained the status of law, despite never being codified by a legislature. On the other hand, unusual practices—that is, new practices that ran contrary to long usage—were presumed to be unreasonable, particularly where they undermined traditional rights.

Under the Cruel and Unusual Punishments Clause, a punishment is unusual if it exceeds the bounds established by the punishment practices that preceded it. This may happen when the government employs a previously impermissible method of punishment (such as torture) or where it imposes a punishment that is excessive relative to the crime of conviction. Such punishments are presumptively cruel. Indeed, in this context, the word "unusual" is virtually a synonym for "cruel," for the fact that the punishment is significantly harsher than prior practice would permit is powerful evidence that the punishment is unjustly harsh (and thus cruel).

The Cruel and Unusual Punishments Clause focuses on "new" punishments because the core purpose of the Clause is to prevent government from acting on a temporarily enflamed desire to inflict pain on criminal offenders. The government has a pronounced tendency to react to perceived crises by ratcheting up the harshness of punishments. Such crises occur in a variety of circumstances. Sometimes a person commits a crime in an outrageous manner, provoking an outcry for extreme punishment. Sometimes the government "has it in for" a political enemy or a member of a disfavored group and inflicts cruel punishments out of animosity or prejudice. And sometimes there is a societal moral panic. A moral panic occurs when a given problem suddenly appears to be beyond the capacity of government to control via traditional means: the public is led to believe that crack cocaine is a powerful new drug that is instantly addicting and much more harmful than powder cocaine; or that a rising generation of superpredators will tear apart the fabric of society; or that all sex offenders are remorseless pedophiles who will never stop raping children until they are jailed, killed, or castrated. When such situations occur, enormous pressure is placed upon the legislature to do something to show that it is in control. The Cruel and Unusual Punishments Clause is meant to prevent the government from responding to such situations by drastically increasing punishments beyond their traditional bounds …

A focus on prior practice does not require courts to employ the standards of the eighteenth century in determining the constitutionality of a punishment. Under the common law, if a given practice fell out of usage, it was no longer a "usual" punishment and lost its presumption of validity. If the legislature later reintroduced such a punishment, it was regarded as a "new" or "unusual" punishment. Thus, in comparing a challenged punishment to prior practice, the Court should compare the practice to those that came immediately before it, not to those that fell out of usage in the eighteenth or nineteenth centuries.

Because the Eighth Amendment applies to both the federal government and the states, the Court should compare the challenged punishment to prior practice in all of these jurisdictions. This part of the inquiry is similar to the Court's current approach under the evolving standards of decency test, but its purpose is different. Under both approaches, the Court looks at sentencing statutes and jury verdicts in the fifty states and the federal system to serve as a point of comparison for the challenged punishment. The purpose of the evolving standards of decency test is to determine whether the punishment meets today's standards, but what the Court should really be asking is whether the punishment meets the standards that have prevailed up until today …

### 2. Determining Whether the Punishment Is Cruel

If a punishment is found to be unusual, the next question is whether it is cruel. To answer this question, a court should ask whether the departure from prior practice appears to be justified as retribution. If the punishment is unjustly harsh in light of the defendant's culpability, it is cruel.

This part of the inquiry involves an exercise of the Court's own judgment. Unlike the Court's current approach to exercising "independent judgment" under the Cruel and Unusual Punishments Clause, however, there are constitutional guideposts to assist the inquiry. The most important of these is the size of the gap between prior punishment practice and the new punishment being challenged. Because departures from prior practice are presumptively unjust, a large gap between the harshness of the new punishment and those that came before it would be strong evidence that the punishment is cruelly excessive.

The Court should also ask whether some change in circumstances relevant to the offender's culpability justifies an increase in the harshness of punishment beyond what prior practice permitted. For example, in an age of financial globalization, corporate executives bent on fraud can now create financial harm that is far greater than was possible in the past—a fact that might justify a significant increase in punishment. Given the presumption that punishments that exceed the bounds established by prior practice are unjust, however, a court should be reluctant to accept the argument that changed circumstances justify a drastic increase in the harshness of punishment.

### 3. Effect on the Court's Recent Proportionality Cases

... A focus on prior practice would provide the Court a sufficiently determinate standard to enable it to judge the proportionality of prison sentences. For example, in Ewing v. California, the Court upheld a mandatory sentence of twenty-five years to life in prison for a small-time recidivist convicted of shoplifting three golf clubs. Because the crime was a felony and because crimes by recidivists are more serious than those committed by first offenders, the Court upheld the sentence without making any effort to determine whether legislative enactments or jury verdicts showed it to be excessive in light of current standards of decency. Had the Court focused on prior practice, the result would likely have been different. The California three strikes law under which Ewing was convicted represented a drastic change from prior practice. As Justice Breyer noted in his dissent, prior to the enactment of this law "no one like Ewing could have served more than 10 years in prison." In other words, the minimum time Ewing would spend in prison under the three strikes law was 250% greater than the maximum sentence he could previously have received anywhere in the country. The statute authorizing this punishment was new, and the punishment was significantly harsher than prior practice had permitted. It was cruel and unusual.

Similarly, in Harmelin v. Michigan, the Supreme Court upheld a statute imposing a mandatory life sentence with no possibility of parole for a first-time offender convicted of possessing with intent to distribute 650 grams of cocaine. The punishment required by the statute was much harsher than had previously been required in Michigan or any other American jurisdiction. Prior to 1978, there was no mandatory minimum punishment for the crime in Michigan, and the maximum punishment available for the crime was twenty years. No other state's sentencing statute required a mandatory minimum sentence of more than fifteen years, and federal law required a mandatory minimum sentence of five years imprisonment. Although several state statutes theoretically permitted a maximum sentence of life in prison, they all permitted parole after a term of years.

There was no evidence that a life sentence without possibility of parole had ever been imposed on someone like Harmelin, a first-time offender with no aggravating factors. The statute requiring a minimum sentence of life imprisonment with no possibility of parole was new and was significantly harsher than prior practice would support. Nor was there any new evidence regarding the culpability of drug dealers. The Court should have found the punishment cruel and unusual.

A focus on prior practice would probably not support the Court's conclusion that several traditional applications of the death penalty were cruel and unusual. For example, in Coker v. Georgia, the Court struck down the death penalty for rape of an adult. The Court based its decision largely on the fact that Georgia was the only state that still imposed the death penalty for the crime of rape. This decision was almost certainly not correct in light of the original meaning of the Cruel and Unusual Punishments Clause. A punishment may be cruel and unusual only if it is significantly harsher than prior practice would permit, because only then is it both cruel and "contrary to long usage." It appears, however, that Georgia had a long and unbroken tradition of imposing the death penalty for this crime. There was no reasonable way to characterize the punishment as "unusual," at least when the case was decided in 1977. It could not be properly held to be unconstitutionally excessive.

In short, a focus on prior practice would significantly increase the scope of protection the Cruel and Unusual Punishments Clause provides to criminal offenders generally. It would provide a stronger foundation for several recent decisions striking down punishments that enjoyed strong popular support, but would not support the Court's decision to invalidate traditional applications of the death penalty that were still in use at the time of the Court's decision …

## William W. Berry III, *Separating Retribution from Proportionality: A Response to Stinneford*

97 Va. L. Rev. InBrief 61 (2011)

[Stinneford's] approach [to proportionality] first asks whether a particular punishment is "unusual," using the concept developed in his previous article that unusual punishments are ones that have not enjoyed "long usage." If a punishment is "unusual," Stinneford's model then requires a determination of whether the punishment is "cruel." The "cruel" inquiry encompasses the question of retributive proportionality, that is, whether for *just deserts* purposes, the punishment exceeds the culpability of the defendant....

Elsewhere, I have argued that the Supreme Court should apply a two-pronged Eighth Amendment analysis based on the two different types of proportionality identified here: relative ("unusual") and absolute ("cruel"). I think Stinneford is correct in recognizing that there needs to be consistency (that is, relative proportionality) in sentencing under the Eighth Amendment—this concern is at the heart of the Courts opinion in *Furman*—but it is equally clear that *relative* proportionality and *absolute* proportionality are unique, if not competing, concepts.

I depart from Stinneford in defining the concept of absolute proportionality. I believe that this concept is more robust than *just deserts* retributive proportionality. As the Courts evolving standards of decency jurisprudence emphasizes, utilitarian considerations such as deterrence, future dangerousness, and rehabilitation help define whether a punishment is excessive for Eighth Amendment purposes. In other words, a punishment violates the Eighth Amendment, in terms of absolute proportionality, where no penological justification can support the punishment given the circumstances. Finally, I suggest that the Court engage in the relative proportionality analysis, through robust state appellate court proportionality review, *subsequent to* the absolute proportionality analysis to further narrow the cases that satisfy the absolute proportionality requirement.

## *Notes and Questions*

1. Professor Stinneford proposes a more robust proportionality analysis than the one that a plurality of the members of the Supreme Court applied in *Harmelin* and *Ewing.* According to Stinneford, punishment violates the Eighth Amendment if it is significantly harsher than the punishment that has historically been imposed for the same conduct in the same and other jurisdictions. Departure from historical practice is what makes the punishment "unusual." Additionally, in order to violate the Eighth Amendment, the significantly harsher punishment must be retributively unjustified. The new punishment's deviation from deserved punishment under a retributive theory of punishment is what makes the punishment "cruel." Compare and contrast Professor Stinneford's approach to the Eighth Amendment with the approach currently favored by the Supreme Court. Compare and contrast Stinneford's approach with the approaches put forth by the high courts of West Virginia, South Dakota and Spain. Which of these approaches is preferable? Why?

2. The least objective feature of Professor Stinneford's proposal is the "cruelty" inquiry, which requires courts to assess whether the punishment imposed significantly deviates from the punishment that is retributively deserved. In order to make this inquiry more objective, Stinneford suggests that courts take into account "the size of the gap between prior punishment practice and the new punishment being challenged" in order to determine if the new punishment is incompatible with retributively deserved punishment. The greater the gap between prior punishment practice and the new punishment, the stronger the argument in favor of a finding of unconstitutionality. Do you find this argument persuasive? Why or why not?

3. In his reply to Stinneford, Professor Berry III suggests that courts should assess both the "relative" and "absolute" proportionality of punishments in order to determine whether they run afoul the Eighth Amendment's proscription of cruel and unusual punishments. An assessment of "relative" proportionality requires comparing the punishment imposed in the case with the sentence imposed for the same conduct in the same and different jurisdictions. This is equivalent to the "intra" and "inter" jurisdictional analysis proposed by the Supreme Court in *Solem* and to the analysis of the "unusual" nature of the punishment proposed by Professor Stinneford. In contrast, an analysis of the "absolute" proportionality of punishment requires asking whether the sentence imposed is unjustified pursuant to either retributive or non-retributive theories of punishment. The absolute proportionality analysis proposed by Professor Berry III differs from the assessment of "cruelty" defended by Professor Stinneford in that Berry III measures the excessiveness of punishment in light of both retributive and non-retributive considerations, whereas Stinneford measures the proportionality of punishment solely on the basis of retribution. Which of these approaches is preferable? Why?

4. Professor Berry III contends that "utilitarian considerations such as deterrence, future dangerousness, and rehabilitation help define whether a punishment is excessive for Eighth Amendment purposes." This, in turn, paves the way for distinguishing between "excessive" and "disproportionate" punishment. Even if—as Stinneford and Scalia (see § 6.01, Note 8) argue—"disproportionate" punishment ought to be measured in accordance with retributive desert, there is no reason why "excessive" punishment should also be

measured solely in accordance to deserved retributive punishment. It is perfectly coherent to state that punishing speeding with life imprisonment is "excessive" in light of non-retributive considerations, such as deterrence and incapacitation. In this context, "excessive punishment" simply means punishment that is unjustified from a consequentialist perspective. More specifically, excessive punishment is punishment that imposes more costs than the benefits that it generates. So conceived, punishing speeding with life imprisonment is "excessive" for non-retributive reasons because the costs of doing so (e.g., most people will simply stop driving) considerably exceed the benefits reaped by the practice. Is the difference between "excessive" and "disproportionate" punishments helpful in understanding the role of retributive and non-retributive considerations in Eighth Amendment analysis?

# Chapter 5

# Constitutional Limits on Criminalization Decisions

## § 5.01 Criminalization Decisions: Liberty Interests Protected by Substantive Due Process

### Lawrence v. Texas

Supreme Court of the United States, 2003
539 U.S. 558

Justice KENNEDY delivered the opinion of the Court.

Liberty protects the person from unwarranted government intrusions into a dwelling or other private places. In our tradition the State is not omnipresent in the home. And there are other spheres of our lives and existence, outside the home, where the State should not be a dominant presence. Freedom extends beyond spatial bounds. Liberty presumes an autonomy of self that includes freedom of thought, belief, expression, and certain intimate conduct. The instant case involves liberty of the person both in its spatial and in its more transcendent dimensions.

I.

The question before the Court is the validity of a Texas statute making it a crime for two persons of the same sex to engage in certain intimate sexual conduct.

In Houston, Texas, officers of the Harris County Police Department were dispatched to a private residence in response to a reported weapons disturbance. They entered an apartment where one of the petitioners, John Geddes Lawrence, *563 resided. The right of the police to enter does not seem to have been questioned. The officers observed Lawrence and another man, Tyron Garner, engaging in a sexual act. The two petitioners were arrested, held in custody overnight, and charged and convicted before a Justice of the Peace.

The complaints described their crime as "deviate sexual intercourse, namely anal sex, with a member of the same sex (man)." The applicable state law is Tex. Penal Code Ann. § 21.06(a) (2003). It provides: "A person commits an offense if he engages in deviate sexual intercourse with another individual of the same sex." The statute defines "[d]eviate sexual intercourse" as follows:

> (A) any contact between any part of the genitals of one person and the mouth or anus of another person; or

(B) the penetration of the genitals or the anus of another person with an object.

The petitioners exercised their right to a trial *de novo* in Harris County Criminal Court. They challenged the statute as a violation of the Equal Protection Clause of the Fourteenth Amendment and of a like provision of the Texas Constitution. Those contentions were rejected. The petitioners, having entered a plea of *nolo contendere,* were each fined $200 and assessed court costs of $141.25.

The Court of Appeals for the Texas Fourteenth District considered the petitioners' federal constitutional arguments under both the Equal Protection and Due Process Clauses of the Fourteenth Amendment. After hearing the case en banc the court, in a divided opinion, rejected the constitutional arguments and affirmed the convictions. The majority opinion indicates that the Court of Appeals considered our decision in *Bowers v. Hardwick* to be controlling on the federal due process aspect of the case. *Bowers* then being authoritative, this was proper.

We granted certiorari to consider three questions:

1. Whether petitioners' criminal convictions under the Texas 'Homosexual Conduct' law—which criminalizes sexual intimacy by same-sex couples, but not identical behavior by different-sex couples—violate the Fourteenth Amendment guarantee of equal protection of the laws.

2. Whether petitioners' criminal convictions for adult consensual sexual intimacy in the home violate their vital interests in liberty and privacy protected by the Due Process Clause of the Fourteenth Amendment.

3. Whether *Bowers v. Hardwick, supra,* should be overruled.

The petitioners were adults at the time of the alleged offense. Their conduct was in private and consensual.

## II.

We conclude the case should be resolved by determining whether the petitioners were free as adults to engage in the private conduct in the exercise of their liberty under the Due Process Clause of the Fourteenth Amendment to the Constitution. For this inquiry we deem it necessary to reconsider the Court's holding in *Bowers.*

There are broad statements of the substantive reach of liberty under the Due Process Clause in earlier cases ... but the most pertinent beginning point is our decision in *Griswold v. Connecticut.*

In *Griswold* the Court invalidated a state law prohibiting the use of drugs or devices of contraception and counseling or aiding and abetting the use of contraceptives. The Court described the protected interest as a right to privacy and placed emphasis on the marriage relation and the protected space of the marital bedroom.

After *Griswold* it was established that the right to make certain decisions regarding sexual conduct extends beyond the marital relationship. In *Eisenstadt v. Baird,* the Court invalidated a law prohibiting the distribution of contraceptives to unmarried persons. The case was decided under the Equal Protection Clause; but with respect to unmarried persons, the Court went on to state the fundamental proposition that the law impaired the exercise of their personal rights. It quoted from the statement of the Court of Appeals finding the law to be in conflict with fundamental human rights, and it followed with this statement of its own:

> It is true that in *Griswold* the right of privacy in question inhered in the marital relationship.... If the right of privacy means anything, it is the right of the

*individual,* married or single, to be free from unwarranted governmental intrusion into matters so fundamentally affecting a person as the decision whether to bear or beget a child.

The opinions in *Griswold* and *Eisenstadt* were part of the background for the decision in *Roe v. Wade.* As is well known, the case involved a challenge to the Texas law prohibiting abortions, but the laws of other States were affected as well. Although the Court held the woman's rights were not absolute, her right to elect an abortion did have real and substantial protection as an exercise of her liberty under the Due Process Clause. The Court cited cases that protect spatial freedom and cases that go well beyond it. *Roe* recognized the right of a woman to make certain fundamental decisions affecting her destiny and confirmed once more that the protection of liberty under the Due Process Clause has a substantive dimension of fundamental significance in defining the rights of the person.

In *Carey v. Population Services Int'l,* the Court confronted a New York law forbidding sale or distribution of contraceptive devices to persons under 16 years of age. Although there was no single opinion for the Court, the law was invalidated. Both *Eisenstadt* and *Carey,* as well as the holding and rationale in *Roe,* confirmed that the reasoning of *Griswold* could not be confined to the protection of rights of married adults. This was the state of the law with respect to some of the most relevant cases when the Court considered *Bowers v. Hardwick.*

The facts in *Bowers* had some similarities to the instant case. A police officer, whose right to enter seems not to have been in question, observed Hardwick, in his own bedroom, engaging in intimate sexual conduct with another adult male. The conduct was in violation of a Georgia statute making it a criminal offense to engage in sodomy. One difference between the two cases is that the Georgia statute prohibited the conduct whether or not the participants were of the same sex, while the Texas statute, as we have seen, applies only to participants of the same sex. Hardwick was not prosecuted, but he brought an action in federal court to declare the state statute invalid. He alleged he was a practicing homosexual and that the criminal prohibition violated rights guaranteed to him by the Constitution. The Court, in an opinion by Justice White, sustained the Georgia law. Chief Justice Burger and Justice Powell joined the opinion of the Court and filed separate, concurring opinions. Four Justices dissented.

The Court began its substantive discussion in *Bowers* as follows: "The issue presented is whether the Federal Constitution confers a fundamental right upon homosexuals to engage in sodomy and hence invalidates the laws of the many States that still make such conduct illegal and have done so for a very long time." That statement, we now conclude, discloses the Court's own failure to appreciate the extent of the liberty at stake. To say that the issue in *Bowers* was simply the right to engage in certain sexual conduct demeans the claim the individual put forward, just as it would demean a married couple were it to be said marriage is simply about the right to have sexual intercourse. The laws involved in *Bowers* and here are, to be sure, statutes that purport to do no more than prohibit a particular sexual act. Their penalties and purposes, though, have more far-reaching consequences, touching upon the most private human conduct, sexual behavior, and in the most private of places, the home. The statutes do seek to control a personal relationship that, whether or not entitled to formal recognition in the law, is within the liberty of persons to choose without being punished as criminals.

This, as a general rule, should counsel against attempts by the State, or a court, to define the meaning of the relationship or to set its boundaries absent injury to a person or abuse of an institution the law protects. It suffices for us to acknowledge that adults may

choose to enter upon this relationship in the confines of their homes and their own private lives and still retain their dignity as free persons. When sexuality finds overt expression in intimate conduct with another person, the conduct can be but one element in a personal bond that is more enduring. The liberty protected by the Constitution allows homosexual persons the right to make this choice.

[T]he Court in *Bowers* [also made] the broader point that for centuries there have been powerful voices to condemn homosexual conduct as immoral. The condemnation has been shaped by religious beliefs, conceptions of right and acceptable behavior, and respect for the traditional family. For many persons these are not trivial concerns but profound and deep convictions accepted as ethical and moral principles to which they aspire and which thus determine the course of their lives. These considerations do not answer the question before us, however. The issue is whether the majority may use the power of the State to enforce these views on the whole society through operation of the criminal law. "Our obligation is to define the liberty of all, not to mandate our own moral code."

Chief Justice Burger joined the opinion for the Court in *Bowers* and further explained his views as follows: "Decisions of individuals relating to homosexual conduct have been subject to state intervention throughout the history of Western civilization. Condemnation of those practices is firmly rooted in Judeao-Christian moral and ethical standards." ... [S]cholarship casts some doubt on the sweeping nature of the statement by Chief Justice Burger as it pertains to private homosexual conduct between consenting adults. In all events we think that our laws and traditions in the past half century are of most relevance here. These references show an emerging awareness that liberty gives substantial protection to adult persons in deciding how to conduct their private lives in matters pertaining to sex. "[H]istory and tradition are the starting point but not in all cases the ending point of the substantive due process inquiry."

This emerging recognition should have been apparent when *Bowers* was decided. In 1955 the American Law Institute promulgated the Model Penal Code and made clear that it did not recommend or provide for "criminal penalties for consensual sexual relations conducted in private." ALI, Model Penal Code §213.2, Comment 2, p. 372 (1980). It justified its decision on three grounds: (1) The prohibitions undermined respect for the law by penalizing conduct many people engaged in; (2) the statutes regulated private conduct not harmful to others; and (3) the laws were arbitrarily enforced and thus invited the danger of blackmail. ALI, Model Penal Code, Commentary 277–280 (Tent. Draft No. 4, 1955). In 1961 Illinois changed its laws to conform to the Model Penal Code. Other States soon followed....

Two principal cases decided after *Bowers* cast its holding into even more doubt. In *Planned Parenthood of Southeastern Pa. v. Casey*, the Court reaffirmed the substantive force of the liberty protected by the Due Process Clause. The *Casey* decision again confirmed that our laws and tradition afford constitutional protection to personal decisions relating to marriage, procreation, contraception, family relationships, child rearing, and education. In explaining the respect the Constitution demands for the autonomy of the person in making these choices, we stated as follows:

> These matters, involving the most intimate and personal choices a person may make in a lifetime, choices central to personal dignity and autonomy, are central to the liberty protected by the Fourteenth Amendment. At the heart of liberty is the right to define one's own concept of existence, of meaning, of the universe, and of the mystery of human life. Beliefs about these matters could not define the attributes of personhood were they formed under compulsion of the State.

Persons in a homosexual relationship may seek autonomy for these purposes, just as heterosexual persons do. The decision in *Bowers* would deny them this right.

The second post-*Bowers* case of principal relevance is *Romer v. Evans*. There the Court struck down class-based legislation directed at homosexuals as a violation of the Equal Protection Clause. *Romer* invalidated an amendment to Colorado's Constitution which named as a solitary class persons who were homosexuals, lesbians, or bisexual either by "orientation, conduct, practices or relationships," and deprived them of protection under state antidiscrimination laws. We concluded that the provision was "born of animosity toward the class of persons affected" and further that it had no rational relation to a legitimate governmental purpose.

As an alternative argument in this case, counsel for the petitioners and some *amici* contend that *Romer* provides the basis for declaring the Texas statute invalid under the Equal Protection Clause. That is a tenable argument, but we conclude the instant case requires us to address whether *Bowers* itself has continuing validity. Were we to hold the statute invalid under the Equal Protection Clause some might question whether a prohibition would be valid if drawn differently, say, to prohibit the conduct both between same-sex and different-sex participants.

Equality of treatment and the due process right to demand respect for conduct protected by the substantive guarantee of liberty are linked in important respects, and a decision on the latter point advances both interests. If protected conduct is made criminal and the law which does so remains unexamined for its substantive validity, its stigma might remain even if it were not enforceable as drawn for equal protection reasons. When homosexual conduct is made criminal by the law of the State, that declaration in and of itself is an invitation to subject homosexual persons to discrimination both in the public and in the private spheres. The central holding of *Bowers* has been brought in question by this case, and it should be addressed. Its continuance as precedent demeans the lives of homosexual persons.

The stigma this criminal statute imposes, moreover, is not trivial. The offense, to be sure, is but a class C misdemeanor, a minor offense in the Texas legal system. Still, it remains a criminal offense with all that imports for the dignity of the persons charged. The petitioners will bear on their record the history of their criminal convictions. Just this Term we rejected various challenges to state laws requiring the registration of sex offenders. We are advised that if Texas convicted an adult for private, consensual homosexual conduct under the statute here in question the convicted person would come within the registration laws of at least four States were he or she to be subject to their jurisdiction. This underscores the consequential nature of the punishment and the state-sponsored condemnation attendant to the criminal prohibition. Furthermore, the Texas criminal conviction carries with it the other collateral consequences always following a conviction, such as notations on job application forms, to mention but one example.

The foundations of *Bowers* have sustained serious erosion from our recent decisions in *Casey* and *Romer*....

The doctrine of *stare decisis* is essential to the respect accorded to the judgments of the Court and to the stability of the law. It is not, however, an inexorable command. In *Casey* we noted that when a court is asked to overrule a precedent recognizing a constitutional liberty interest, individual or societal reliance on the existence of that liberty cautions with particular strength against reversing course. The holding in *Bowers*, however, has not induced detrimental reliance comparable to some instances where recognized individual rights are involved. Indeed, there has been no individual or societal reliance on

*Bowers* of the sort that could counsel against overturning its holding once there are compelling reasons to do so. *Bowers* itself causes uncertainty, for the precedents before and after its issuance contradict its central holding.

The rationale of *Bowers* does not withstand careful analysis. In his dissenting opinion in Bowers Justice STEVENS came to these conclusions:

> Our prior cases make two propositions abundantly clear. First, the fact that the governing majority in a State has traditionally viewed a particular practice as immoral is not a sufficient reason for upholding a law prohibiting the practice; neither history nor tradition could save a law prohibiting miscegenation from constitutional attack. Second, individual decisions by married persons, concerning the intimacies of their physical relationship, even when not intended to produce offspring, are a form of 'liberty' protected by the Due Process Clause of the Fourteenth Amendment. Moreover, this protection extends to intimate choices by unmarried as well as married persons.

Justice Stevens' analysis, in our view, should have been controlling in *Bowers* and should control here.

*Bowers* was not correct when it was decided, and it is not correct today. It ought not to remain binding precedent. *Bowers v. Hardwick* should be and now is overruled.

The present case does not involve minors. It does not involve persons who might be injured or coerced or who are situated in relationships where consent might not easily be refused. It does not involve public conduct or prostitution. It does not involve whether the government must give formal recognition to any relationship that homosexual persons seek to enter. The case does involve two adults who, with full and mutual consent from each other, engaged in sexual practices common to a homosexual lifestyle. The petitioners are entitled to respect for their private lives. The State cannot demean their existence or control their destiny by making their private sexual conduct a crime. Their right to liberty under the Due Process Clause gives them the full right to engage in their conduct without intervention of the government. "It is a promise of the Constitution that there is a realm of personal liberty which the government may not enter." *Casey*. The Texas statute furthers no legitimate state interest which can justify its intrusion into the personal and private life of the individual.

Had those who drew and ratified the Due Process Clauses of the Fifth Amendment or the Fourteenth Amendment known the components of liberty in its manifold possibilities, they might have been more specific. They did not presume to have this insight. They knew times can blind us to certain truths and later generations can see that laws once thought necessary and proper in fact serve only to oppress. As the Constitution endures, persons in every generation can invoke its principles in their own search for greater freedom.

The judgment of the Court of Appeals for the Texas Fourteenth District is reversed, and the case is remanded for further proceedings not inconsistent with this opinion.

**Justice SCALIA, with whom THE CHIEF JUSTICE and Justice THOMAS join, dissenting.**

... I turn now to the ground on which the Court squarely rests its holding: the contention that there is no rational basis for the law here under attack. This proposition is so out of accord with our jurisprudence—indeed, with the jurisprudence of *any* society we know—that it requires little discussion.

The Texas statute undeniably seeks to further the belief of its citizens that certain forms of sexual behavior are "immoral and unacceptable,"—the same interest furthered by criminal laws against fornication, bigamy, adultery, adult incest, bestiality, and obscenity. *Bowers* held that this *was* a legitimate state interest. The Court today reaches the opposite conclusion. The Texas statute, it says, "furthers *no legitimate state interest* which can justify its intrusion into the personal and private life of the individual." The Court embraces instead Justice Stevens' declaration in his *Bowers* dissent, that "'the fact that the governing majority in a State has traditionally viewed a particular practice as immoral is not a sufficient reason for upholding a law prohibiting the practice.'" This effectively decrees the end of all morals legislation. If, as the Court asserts, the promotion of majoritarian sexual morality is not even a *legitimate* state interest, none of the above-mentioned laws can survive rational-basis review....

**Justice THOMAS, dissenting.**

I join Justice Scalia's dissenting opinion. I write separately to note that the law before the Court today "is ... uncommonly silly." If I were a member of the Texas Legislature, I would vote to repeal it. Punishing someone for expressing his sexual preference through noncommercial consensual conduct with another adult does not appear to be a worthy way to expend valuable law enforcement resources.

Notwithstanding this, I recognize that as a Member of this Court I am not empowered to help petitioners and others similarly situated. My duty, rather, is to "decide cases 'agreeably to the Constitution and laws of the United States.'" And, just like Justice Stewart, I "can find [neither in the Bill of Rights nor any other part of the Constitution a] general right of privacy," or as the Court terms it today, the "liberty of the person both in its spatial and more transcendent dimensions."

## *Notes and Questions*

1. The Supreme Court acknowledged in *Lawrence* that "for centuries there have been powerful voices to condemn homosexual conduct as immoral," that such "condemnation has been shaped by religious beliefs, conceptions of right and acceptable behavior, and respect for the traditional family" and that "these are not trivial concerns but profound and deep convictions accepted as ethical and moral principles to which they aspire and which thus determine the course of their lives." Nevertheless, the Court concluded that such beliefs do not provide the state with a constitutionally sufficient reason to criminalize the conduct. Citing from Justice Stevens' dissenting opinion in *Bowers,* the Supreme Court stated in *Lawrence* that "the fact that the governing majority in a State has traditionally viewed a particular practice as immoral is not a sufficient reason for upholding a law prohibiting the practice." Therefore, the Court reasoned that the interest in liberty protected by the Due Process Clause of the Fourteenth Amendment prohibits a governing majority from using the power of the State to enforce moral views on the whole society through operation of the criminal law. This is so because—as the Court stated in *Planned Parenthood v. Casey,* "[o]ur obligation is to define the liberty of all, not to mandate our own moral code." Do you agree that it is illegitimate to criminalize conduct solely because a majority of the population views the conduct as immoral? Why or why not?

2. If the fact that a governing majority views certain conduct as immoral is not a sufficient reason for upholding a law punishing such conduct, what reasons must a state adduce in order to justify criminalizing conduct? One possible answer is that a state may only criminalize conduct that causes "harm to others" and that harm to moral sensibilities does not count as "harm to others." Those who defend this proposition argue that the state should abide by the so-called "harm principle." According to philosopher H.L.A.

Hart's conception of the "harm principle," the distress caused to people when others behave in what they consider to be an immoral fashion cannot constitute a punishable harm since this would:

> [punish people] simply because others object to what they do; and the only liberty that could coexist with this extension of the [harm principle] is liberty to do those things to which no one seriously objects. Such liberty plainly is quite nugatory. H.L.A. Hart, Law, Liberty and Morality 47 (1963).

Do you believe that the Supreme Court intended to constitutionalize the "harm principle" in *Lawrence v. Texas*? Why or why not?

3. In his dissent, Justice Scalia suggests that *Lawrence* "effectively decrees the end of all morals legislation." As a result, he argued that the reasoning underlying the Court's holding in *Lawrence* calls into question laws "against fornication, bigamy, adultery, adult incest, bestiality, and obscenity." More specifically, Scalia argued that if the promotion of majoritarian sexual morality is not even a *legitimate* state interest, none of the above-mentioned laws can pass constitutional muster. Do you agree with Scalia that the constitutionality of laws prohibiting incest, bigamy, bestiality and obscenity is suspect in light of the holding of *Lawrence*? Explain.

4. While Justice Scalia argued that *Lawrence* would lead to the demise of so-called "morals legislation," both federal and state courts in the wake of *Lawrence* have adopted a much narrower reading of the case. In *Lowe v. Swanson,* 663 F.3d 258 (2011), for example, the United States Court of Appeals for the Sixth Circuit held that *Lawrence* does not require that the Ohio incest statute be struck down as a violation of Due Process. According to the Court:

> *Lawrence* did not address or clearly establish federal law regarding state incest statutes. Indeed, the *Lawrence* Court expressly distinguished statutes like [the Ohio incest statute] when it emphasized that "[t]he present case does not involve ... persons who might be injured or coerced or who are situated in relationships where consent might not easily be refused [.]" Unlike sexual relationships between unrelated same-sex adults, the stepparent-stepchild relationship is the kind of relationship in which a person might be injured or coerced or where consent might not easily be refused, regardless of age, because of the inherent influence of the stepparent over the stepchild.
>
> Moreover, the State of Ohio's interest in criminalizing incest is far greater and much different than the interest of the State of Texas in prosecuting homosexual sodomy. Ohio's paramount concern is protecting the family from the destructive influence of intra-family, extra-marital sexual contact. This is an important state interest that the *Lawrence* Court did not invalidate. For these reasons, we hold that the Ohio Supreme Court's decision was not contrary to and did not involve an unreasonable application of clearly established federal law.
>
> Lowe's remaining arguments are meritless. His claim that the Ohio law is contrary to *Lawrence* because it is morality-based fails for two reasons. First, the state has a legitimate and important interest in protecting families. *See, e.g., Camp v. State* ("[S]ociety is as concerned with the integrity of the family, including step and adoptive relationships as well as those of blood relationships, and sexual activity is equally disruptive, whatever the makeup of the family."). Second, the *Lawrence* Court did not categorically invalidate criminal laws that are based in part on morality. Finally, Lowe's assertion that Ohio's "generalized interest in protecting the family unit" cannot support the statute as applied in this

> case because "there is no evidence in the record that beyond [his] technical status as stepfather an actual family unit even existed" is also without merit. Ohio has an interest in protecting *all* families against destructive sexual contacts irrespective of the particular factual family dynamic. *Lowe,* 663 F.3d 258

Do you agree that *Lawrence* does not require striking down statutes that prohibit incest? Is engaging in incest criminalized because it causes "harm to others" or is the conduct solely criminalized because the governing majority views it as immoral? How does the Court of Appeals for the Sixth Circuit answer this question in *Lowe*? Do you think that it is legitimate to criminalize incest even in circumstances in which the conduct does not cause harm to others (e.g., adopted siblings have sexual intercourse with each other and all other family members have passed away at the time of the conduct)? Why or why not?

5. In *State v. Holm,* 137 P.3d 726 (2006) the Utah Supreme Court held that *Lawrence* did not call into question the constitutionality of the state statute prohibiting bigamy. More specifically, the Court held that:

> Despite its use of seemingly sweeping language, the holding in *Lawrence* is actually quite narrow. Specifically, the Court takes pains to limit the opinion's reach to decriminalizing private and intimate acts engaged in by consenting adult gays and lesbians. In fact, the Court went out of its way to exclude from protection conduct that causes "injury to a person or abuse of an institution the law protects." Further, after announcing its holding, the Court noted the following: "The present case does not involve minors. It does not involve persons who might be injured or coerced or who are situated in relationships where consent might not easily be refused. It does not involve public conduct...."
>
> In marked contrast to the situation presented to the Court in *Lawrence,* this case implicates the public institution of marriage, an institution the law protects ... In other words, this case presents the exact conduct identified by the Supreme Court in *Lawrence* as outside the scope of its holding.
>
> First, the behavior at issue in this case is not confined to personal decisions made about sexual activity, but rather raises important questions about the State's ability to regulate marital relationships and prevent the formation and propagation of marital forms that the citizens of the State deem harmful.
>
> Sexual intercourse ... is the most intimate behavior in which the citizenry engages. [*Lawrence*] spoke to this discreet, personal activity. Marriage, on the other hand, includes both public and private conduct. Within the privacy of the home, marriage means essentially whatever the married individuals wish it to mean. Nonetheless, marriage extends beyond the confines of the home to our society.
>
> The very "concept of marriage possesses 'undisputed social value.'" Utah's own constitution enshrines a commitment to prevent polygamous behavior. That commitment has undergirded this State's establishment of "a vast and convoluted network of ... laws ... based exclusively upon the practice of monogamy as opposed to plural marriage." Our State's commitment to monogamous unions is a recognition that decisions made by individuals as to how to structure even the most personal of relationships are capable of dramatically affecting public life.
>
> Moreover, marital relationships serve as the building blocks of our society. The State must be able to assert some level of control over those relationships to ensure the smooth operation of laws and further the proliferation of social unions our society deems beneficial while discouraging those deemed harmful. The peo-

> ple of this State have declared monogamy a beneficial marital form and have also declared polygamous relationships harmful. As the Tenth Circuit stated in *Potter,* Utah "is justified, by a compelling interest, in upholding and enforcing its ban on plural marriage to protect the monogamous marriage relationship."
>
> Given the above, we conclude that *Lawrence* does not prevent our Legislature from prohibiting polygamous behavior. The distinction between private, intimate sexual conduct between consenting adults and the public nature of polygamists' attempts to extralegally redefine the acceptable parameters of a fundamental social institution like marriage is plain.... Given the critical differences between the two cases, and the fact that the United States Supreme Court has not extended its jurisprudence to such a degree as to protect the formation of polygamous marital arrangements, we conclude that the criminalization of the behavior engaged in by Holm does not run afoul of the personal liberty interests protected by the Fourteenth Amendment. *Id.*

Do you agree that criminalizing bigamy does not run afoul the Due Process Clause as construed by the Supreme Court in *Lawrence*? Is bigamy criminalized because it causes "harm to others" or is it punished because it is considered immoral? How does the Supreme Court of Utah answer this question in *Holm*? Do you agree?

6. Does it violate the interest in liberty protected by the Due Process Clause to criminalize bestiality? A federal district court held that it does not in *Kulch v. Rapelje,* 2010 WL 3419823. According to the court:

> *Lawrence* does not prohibit all laws regulating sexual conduct in the absence of "injury to a person or abuse of an institution the law protects." Rather, it prohibits laws regulating sexual conduct to the extent that they impinge on the protected liberty interest in forming meaningful personal relationships. Nothing in *Lawrence* ... suggests that the application of bestiality laws ... under which petitioner was prosecuted, are ... unconstitutional. Such laws do not implicate a liberty interest possessed by consenting adults in forming meaningful, intimate relationships. *Id.*

The Court then addressed Scalia's claim that *Lawrence* casts doubt on the constitutionality of so-called "morals legislation," including statutes prohibiting bestiality:

> There is language in *Lawrence* which, when divorced from the context of that case, suggests as Justice Scalia feared that all morality based legislation is unconstitutional. Quoting from Justice Stevens's dissent in *Bowers,* the majority observed that "the fact that the governing majority in a State has traditionally viewed a particular practice as immoral is not a sufficient reason for upholding a law prohibiting the practice." As observed above, however, the context in which the Court decided *Lawrence* was one in which the law at issue was being used to target homosexuals specifically and denying them the right to enter into intimate personal relationships. Nowhere in *Lawrence* does the Court suggest that there is a fundamental constitutional right to engage in sodomy or any other particular sex act ...
>
> As observed by the Eleventh Circuit,
>
> > [T]he Supreme Court has noted on repeated occasions that laws can be based on moral judgments. *See Barnes v. Glen Theatre* (upholding a public indecency statute, stating, "This and other public indecency statutes were designed to protect morals and public order. The traditional police power of

the States is defined as the authority to provide for the public health, safety, and morals, and we have upheld such a basis for legislation"); *Paris Adult Theatre I v. Slaton* (holding that Georgia had a legitimate interest in regulating obscene material because the legislature "could legitimately act ... to protect 'the social interest in order and morality'"). One would expect the Supreme Court to be manifestly more specific and articulate than it was in *Lawrence* if now such a traditional and significant jurisprudential principal has been jettisoned wholesale (with all due respect to Justice Scalia's ominous dissent notwithstanding)

> Moreover, even accepting petitioner's reading of *Lawrence,* the Court's disapproval of morality-based legislation does not call into question the validity of a statute prohibiting bestiality. As noted above, at no point in *Lawrence* did the Court suggest that there is a fundamental constitutional right to engage in any particular sex acts, and the Court did not apply strict scrutiny to the Texas sodomy law at issue. By citing Justice Stevens's dissent in *Bowers,* the Court at most held that moral opprobrium alone does not provide a rational basis for legislation. Laws against bestiality, however, are supportable on rational bases apart from moral opprobrium. "There is a substantial public health concern that pervades the taboo against bestiality," and thus the commentators have uniformly concluded that *Lawrence,* even if read to prohibit all morals based legislation, does not call into question the validity of bestiality laws. *Kulch v. Rapelje,* 2010 WL 3419823.

Do you agree that criminalizing bestiality is compatible with the Supreme Court's holding in *Lawrence*? Is bestiality a crime because it causes "harm to others" or is it punished merely because it is considered immoral? Other than morality, what interest does the federal district court cite in *Kulch* as a possible justification for criminalizing bestiality? Assuming that at least some acts of bestiality cause harm to animals, would such harm qualify as "harm to others" for the purposes of the "harm principle"? Explain. Citing an Eleventh Circuit decision, the federal district court also suggests that statutes criminalizing public indecency and possession of obscene materials are not unconstitutional under *Lawrence* even if the purpose of such statues is to enforce morality. Do you agree? Why or why not?

7. In *United States v. Thompson,* 458 F.Supp.2d 730 (2006), the defendant argued that *Lawrence* "necessarily renders laws prohibiting prostitution ... unconstitutional." The court disagreed, contending that:

> Contrary to Defendant's belief, *Lawrence* held only that a state cannot enact laws that criminalize homosexual sodomy; it did not address the constitutionality of prostitution statutes. Notably, in striking down the Texas sodomy law, the Court was concerned about protecting personal relations in the home. The majority was not commenting on, or concerned with, governmental regulation of sexual acts in the commercial marketplace. Surely, laws prohibiting the commercial acts of prostitution do not have the same far-reaching consequences as laws that regulate private sex acts of consenting adults in the home. Moreover, *Lawrence* did not announce "a fundamental right protected by the constitution, for adults to engage in all manner of consensual sexual conduct." With this understanding in mind, it would be an untenable stretch to find that *Lawrence* necessarily renders (or even implies) laws prohibiting prostitution, including section 2422, unconstitutional. Tellingly, Defendant fails to cite to any instance where a court invalidated any law prohibiting prostitution by relying upon *Lawrence* or its progeny. *Thompson,* 458 F.Supp.2d 730.

Do you agree that statutes criminalizing prostitution are compatible with *Lawrence*? Why or why not? Is prostitution prohibited because it causes "harm to others" or because a majority of the population views it as immoral? Explain.

8. After reading the materials discussed in these notes, has Justice Scalia's prediction that *Lawrence* will lead to the "end of all morals legislation" come to fruition? Have state and federal courts construed *Lawrence* in a way that makes it coextensive with the "harm principle" as defined by H.L.A. Hart? In light of the way in which *Lawrence* has been applied by lower courts in recent years, how would you describe the limits that substantive due process imposes on the state's power to criminalize conduct?

## § 5.02 Criminalization Decisions: Freedom of Speech

### R.A.V. v. City of St. Paul

Supreme Court of the United States, 1992
505 U.S. 377

Justice Scalia delivered the opinion of the Court.

In the predawn hours of June 21, 1990, petitioner and several other teenagers allegedly assembled a crudely made cross by taping together broken chair legs. They then allegedly burned the cross inside the fenced yard of a black family that lived across the street from the house where petitioner was staying. Although this conduct could have been punished under any of a number of laws, one of the two provisions under which respondent city of St. Paul chose to charge petitioner (then a juvenile) was the St. Paul Bias-Motivated Crime Ordinance, which provides:

> Whoever places on public or private property a symbol, object, appellation, characterization or graffiti, including, but not limited to, a burning cross or Nazi swastika, which one knows or has reasonable grounds to know arouses anger, alarm or resentment in others on the basis of race, color, creed, religion or gender commits disorderly conduct and shall be guilty of a misdemeanor.

Petitioner moved to dismiss this count on the ground that the St. Paul ordinance was substantially overbroad and impermissibly content based and therefore facially invalid under the First Amendment. The trial court granted this motion, but the Minnesota Supreme Court reversed. That court rejected petitioner's overbreadth claim because, as construed in prior Minnesota cases, the modifying phrase "arouses anger, alarm or resentment in others" limited the reach of the ordinance to conduct that amounts to "fighting words," *i.e.*, "conduct that itself inflicts injury or tends to incite immediate violence...," and therefore the ordinance reached only expression "that the first amendment does not protect." The court also concluded that the ordinance was not impermissibly content based because, in its view, "the ordinance is a narrowly tailored means toward accomplishing the compelling governmental interest in protecting the community against bias-motivated threats to public safety and order." We granted certiorari.

I.

... The First Amendment generally prevents government from proscribing speech, or even expressive conduct, because of disapproval of the ideas expressed. Content-based regulations are presumptively invalid. From 1791 to the present, however, our society, like other free but civilized societies, has permitted restrictions upon the content of speech in a few limited areas, which are "of such slight social value as a step to truth that any benefit that may be derived from them is clearly outweighed by the social interest in order and morality." We have recognized that "the freedom of speech" referred to by the First Amendment does not include a freedom to disregard these traditional limitations. See, *e.g., Roth v. United States* (obscenity); *Beauharnais v. Illinois,* (defamation); *Chaplinsky v. New Hampshire,* ("'fighting' words")....

## II.

Applying these principles to the St. Paul ordinance, we conclude that, even as narrowly construed by the Minnesota Supreme Court, the ordinance is facially unconstitutional. Although the phrase in the ordinance, "arouses anger, alarm or resentment in others," has been limited by the Minnesota Supreme Court's construction to reach only those symbols or displays that amount to "fighting words," the remaining, unmodified terms make clear that the ordinance applies only to "fighting words" that insult, or provoke violence, "on the basis of race, color, creed, religion or gender." Displays containing abusive invective, no matter how vicious or severe, are permissible unless they are addressed to one of the specified disfavored topics. Those who wish to use "fighting words" in connection with other ideas—to express hostility, for example, on the basis of political affiliation, union membership, or homosexuality—are not covered. The First Amendment does not permit St. Paul to impose special prohibitions on those speakers who express views on disfavored subjects.

What we have here, it must be emphasized, is not a prohibition of fighting words that are directed at certain persons or groups (which would be *facially* valid if it met the requirements of the Equal Protection Clause); but rather, a prohibition of fighting words that contain (as the Minnesota Supreme Court repeatedly emphasized) messages of "bias-motivated" hatred and in particular, as applied to this case, messages "based on virulent notions of racial supremacy." One must wholeheartedly agree with the Minnesota Supreme Court that "[i]t is the responsibility, even the obligation, of diverse communities to confront such notions in whatever form they appear," but the manner of that confrontation cannot consist of selective limitations upon speech. St. Paul's brief asserts that a general "fighting words" law would not meet the city's needs because only a content-specific measure can communicate to minority groups that the "group hatred" aspect of such speech "is not condoned by the majority." The point of the First Amendment is that majority preferences must be expressed in some fashion other than silencing speech on the basis of its content....

The content-based discrimination reflected in the St. Paul ordinance comes within neither any of the specific exceptions to the First Amendment prohibition we discussed earlier nor a more general exception for content discrimination that does not threaten censorship of ideas. It assuredly does not fall within the exception for content discrimination based on the very reasons why the particular class of speech at issue (here, fighting words) is proscribable. As explained earlier, the reason why fighting words are categorically excluded from the protection of the First Amendment is not that their content communicates any particular idea, but that their content embodies a particularly intolerable (and socially unnecessary) *mode* of expressing *whatever* idea the speaker wishes to convey. St. Paul has not singled out an especially offensive mode of expression—it has not, for example, selected for prohibition only those fighting words that communicate ideas in a threatening (as opposed to a merely obnoxious) manner. Rather, it has proscribed fighting words of whatever manner that communicate messages of racial, gender, or religious intolerance. Selectivity of this sort creates the possibility that the city is seeking to handicap the expression of particular ideas. That possibility would alone be enough to render the ordinance presumptively invalid, but St. Paul's comments and concessions in this case elevate the possibility to a certainty....

Finally, St. Paul and its *amici* defend the conclusion of the Minnesota Supreme Court that, even if the ordinance regulates expression based on hostility towards its protected ideological content, this discrimination is nonetheless justified because it is narrowly tailored to serve compelling state interests. Specifically, they assert that the ordinance helps to ensure the basic human rights of members of groups that have historically been subjected to discrimination, including the right of such group members to live in peace where they wish. We do not doubt that these interests are compelling, and that the ordinance can be said to promote them. But the "danger of censorship" presented by a facially content-based statute requires that that weapon be employed only where it is "*necessary* to serve the asserted [compelling] interest".... The dispositive question in this case, therefore, is whether content discrimination is reasonably necessary to achieve St. Paul's compelling interests; it plainly is not. An ordinance not limited to the favored topics, for example, would have precisely the same beneficial effect. In fact the only interest distinctively served by the content limitation is that of displaying the city council's special hostility towards the particular biases thus singled out. That is precisely what the First Amendment forbids. The politicians of St. Paul are entitled to express that hostility—but not through the means of imposing unique limitations upon speakers who (however benightedly) disagree.

Let there be no mistake about our belief that burning a cross in someone's front yard is reprehensible. But St. Paul has sufficient means at its disposal to prevent such behavior without adding the First Amendment to the fire.

The judgment of the Minnesota Supreme Court is reversed, and the case is remanded for proceedings not inconsistent with this opinion.

### *Notes and Questions*

1. The First Amendment right to freedom of speech imposes considerable limitations on the government's power to criminalize conduct. Thus, for example, the right to free speech was invoked by the Supreme Court to strike down laws that criminalized "flag desecration." See *Texas v. Johnson,* 491 U.S. 397 (1989). Furthermore, in light of the First Amendment, the government is barred from criminalizing the possession of pornographic materials. It may, however, prohibit the possession of *obscene* pornographic materials. Pornography is obscene if it appeals to "a prurient interest," shows "patently offensive sexual conduct" and "lacks serious artistic, literary, political, or scientific value." *See, generally, Miller v. California,* 413 U.S. 15 (1973). An example of conduct that may be lawfully proscribed in light of the obscene nature of the material is possession of child pornography.

2. As *R.A.V. v. City of St. Paul* illustrates, the First Amendment also imposes considerable limitations on the criminalization of hate speech. Given that the ordinance challenged in the case only proscribed fighting words that contained messages of hatred "on the basis of race, color, creed, religion or gender," the Supreme Court concluded that the ordinance selectively prohibited conduct based on the content of the speech. Such content-based regulations of speech run afoul of the constitutional right to free speech.

3. The Supreme Court pointed out in *R.A.V. v. City of St. Paul* that advancing the state's interest in "ensur[ing] the basic human rights of members of groups that have his-

torically been subjected to discrimination" was not a sufficient reason for upholding the law challenged in the case. Do you agree? Why or why not?

4. In the more recent case of *Virginia v. Black,* 538 U.S. 343 (2003), the Supreme Court held that criminalizing the conduct of "cross burning with intent to intimidate" does not violate the First Amendment. The Court distinguished the case from *R.A.V. v. City of St. Paul* by pointing out that "[u]nlike the statute at issue in *R.A.V.*, the Virginia statute does not single out for opprobrium only that speech directed toward 'one of the specified disfavored topics.'"

5. Pursuant to the Supreme Court's decision in *Wisconsin v. Mitchell,* 508 U.S. 476 (1993), statutes that aggravate the punishment imposed for a crime whenever the perpetrator selects her victim on the basis of race (i.e., hate crimes) do not run afoul of the right to free speech protected under the First Amendment. The Supreme Court distinguished the case from *R.A.V. v. City of St. Paul,* by explaining that "whereas the ordinance struck down in *R.A.V.* was explicitly directed at expression (i.e., 'speech' or 'messages'), the statute in this case is aimed at conduct unprotected by the First Amendment."

## § 5.03 Criminalization Decisions: Model Penal Code

### Louis B. Schwartz, *Morals Offenses and the Model Penal Code*

63 Colum. L. Rev. 669 (1963)

... The Model Penal Code does not penalize the sexual sins, fornication, adultery, sodomy or other illicit sexual activity not involving violence or imposition upon children, mental incompetents, wards, or other dependents. This decision to keep penal law out of the area of private sexual relations approaches [the] suggestion that private morality be immune from secular regulation. The Comments in Tentative Draft No. 4 declared:

> The Code does not attempt to use the power of the state to enforce purely moral or religious standards. We deem it inappropriate for the government to attempt to control behavior that has no substantial significance except as to the morality of the actor. Such matters are best left to religious, educational and other social influences. Apart from the question of constitutionality which might be raised against legislation avowedly commanding adherence to a particular religious or moral tenet, it must be recognized, as a practical matter, that in a heterogeneous community such as ours, different individuals and groups have widely divergent views of the seriousness of various moral derelictions.

Although this passage expresses doubt as to the constitutionality of state regulation of morals, it does so in a context of "widely divergent views of the seriousness of various moral derelictions." Thus, it does not exclude the use of penal sanctions to protect a "moral consensus" against flagrant breach. The Kinsey studies and others are cited to show that sexual derelictions are widespread and that the incidence of sexual dereliction varies among social groups. The Comments proceed to discuss various secular goals that might be served by penalizing illicit sexual relations, such as promoting the stability of marriage, preventing illegitimacy and disease, or forestalling private violence against seducers. The judgment is made that there is no reliable basis for believing that penal laws substantially contribute to these goals. Punishment of private vice is rejected on this ground as well as on grounds of difficulty of enforcement and the potential for blackmail and other abuse of rarely enforced criminal statutes. The discussion with regard to homosexual offenses follows a similar course.

The Code does, however, penalize "Open Lewdness"—"any lewd act which [the actor] ... knows is likely to be observed by others who would be affronted or alarmed." The idea that "flagrant affront to commonly held notions of morality" might have to be differentiated from other sorts of immorality appeared in the first discussions of the Institute's policy on sexual offenses, in connection with a draft that would have penalized "open and notorious" illicit relations. Eventually, however, the decision was against establishing a penal offense in which guilt would depend on the level of gossip to which the moral transgression gave rise. Guilt under the open lewdness section turns on the likelihood that the lewd act itself will be observed by others who would be affronted.

Since the Code accepts the propriety of penalizing behavior that affects others only in flagrantly affronting commonly held notions of morality, the question arises whether such repression of offensive immorality need be confined to acts done in public where others may observe and be outraged. People may be deeply offended upon learning of private debauchery. The Code seems ready at times to protect against this type of "psychological assault," at other times not. Section 250.10 penalizes mistreatment of a corpse "in a way that [the actor] ... knows would outrage ordinary family sensibilities," although the actor may have taken every precaution for secrecy. Section 250.11 penalizes cruel treatment of an animal in private as well as in public. On the other hand, desecration of the national flag or other object of public veneration, an offense under section 250.9, is not committed unless others are likely to "observe or discover." And solicitation of deviate sexual relations is penalized only when the actor "loiters in or near any public place" for the purpose of such solicitation. The Comments make it clear that the target of this legislation is not private immorality but a kind of public "nuisance" caused by congregation of homosexuals offensively flaunting their deviance from general norms of behavior....

A penal code's treatment of private homosexual relations presents the crucial test of a legislator's views on whether a state may legitimately protect people from "psychological assault" by repressing not merely overt affront to consensus morals but also the most secret violation of that moral code. As is often wise in legislative affairs, the Model Penal Code avoids a clear issue of principle. The decision against penalizing deviate sexuality is rested not merely on the idea of immunity from regulation of private morality, but on a consideration of practical difficulties and evils in attempting to use the penal law in this way. The Comments note that existing laws dealing with homosexual relations are nullified in practice, except in cases of violence, corruption of children, or public solicitation. Capricious selection of a few cases for prosecution, among millions of infractions, is unfair and chiefly benefits extortioners and seekers of private vengeance. The existence of the criminal law prevents some deviates from seeking psychiatric aid. Furthermore, the pursuit of homosexuals involves policemen in degrading entrapment practices, and diverts attention and effort that could be employed more usefully against the crimes of violent aggression, fraud, and government corruption, which are the overriding concerns of our metropolitan civilization.

If state legislators are not persuaded by such arguments to repeal the laws against private deviate sexual relations among adults, the constitutional issue will ultimately have to be faced by the courts. When that time comes, one of the important questions will be whether homosexuality is in fact the subject of a "consensus." If not, that is, if a substantial body of public opinion regards homosexuals' private activity with indifference, or if homosexuals succeed in securing recognition as a considerable minority having otherwise "respectable" status, this issue of private morality may soon be held to be beyond resolution by vote of fifty-one per cent of the legislators. As to the status of homosexuality in this country, it is significant that the Supreme Court has reversed an obscenity conviction involving a magazine that was avowedly published by, for, and about homosexuals and that carried on a ceaseless campaign against the repressive laws. The much smaller group of American polygamists have yet to break out of the class of idiosyncratic heretic-martyrs by bidding for public approval in the same group-conscious way....

### *Notes and Questions*

1. As the excerpted article shows, the drafters of the Model Penal Code discouraged states from engaging in "morals legislation." The Code drafters thus had—in the words of Professor Schwartz—a preference for leaving "private morality ... immune from secular regulation." By stating that the government should "not attempt to use the power of the state to enforce purely moral or religious standards," the Code drafters decidedly pronounced themselves in favor of the "harm principle" as a postulate for guiding criminalization decisions. As a result of their commitment to leaving private morality immune from punishment, the Code does not punish fornication, adultery or sodomy.

2. The Code drafters distinguished between criminalizing private acts and punishing acts that amount to "flagrant affront[s] to commonly held notions of morality." They cite the crime of "open lewdness" as an example of the latter. Other examples are the crimes of "desecration of a corpse," "cruelty to animals" and "flag desecration." Is criminalization of these crimes compatible with the "harm principle"? Explain. Would punishment of these crimes violate the Due Process Clause as construed by the Supreme Court in *Lawrence*? Why or why not? Do you believe that it is legitimate to criminalize the "desecration of a corpse"? Explain. The Code drafters lump the crime of "cruelty to animals" with the offenses of "corpse desecration" and "flag desecration." Do you believe that these crimes are similar? Is cruelty to animals criminalized because it amounts to a "flagrant affront to commonly held notions of morality" or is it punished because it causes "harm to others"? Explain.

## § 5.04 Criminalization Decisions: Comparative Perspectives

### Argentine National Constitution, Article 19

Private actions that in no way offend order and public morals, or harm a third party, are exclusively reserved to God, and are exempt from the authority of judges. No inhabitant of the Nation will be obliged to do that which the law does not order, nor deprived of that which it does not prohibit.

### Arriola Case

Supreme Court of Argentina, 2009

[The five defendants were charged with possessing small quantities of marijuana (about three cigarettes per defendant). The defendants challenged their conviction for the charged offense contending that it was unconstitutional for the state to criminalize the possession of small quantities of marijuana for personal use. The case made all its way up to the Supreme Court of Argentina. Excerpted portions from the judgment follow:]

We hold that the state has the duty to treat all its inhabitants with equal concern and respect, and the majority's preference for a policy cannot trump an individual's personal preferences. This is the meaning that ought to be given to Article 19 of the Argentine Constitution, which was penned by men of liberal spirit who set out to create a catalogue of constitutionally protected fundamental liberties inspired by the principle that we are all free to choose how to live our lives....

We are aware that there is a presumption of constitutionality that applies to norms that are duly enacted by Congress. Nevertheless, judges should not approve of the decisions made by the governing majority simply because they command the support of a majority.

In light of these considerations, we declare that the [challenged law] is unconstitutional, for it violates Article 19 of the National Constitution insofar as it invades a sphere of personal liberty that may not be infringed by the government. In light of these considerations, we hold that it is contrary to the constitution to punish the possession of marijuana for personal use that does not cause or risk harm to third parties.

## German Penal Code § 130—Public Incitement

(1) Whoever, in a manner that is capable of disturbing the public peace:

1. incites hatred against segments of the population or calls for violent or arbitrary measures against them; or
2. assaults the human dignity of others by insulting, maliciously maligning, or defaming segments of the population, shall be punished to a term of imprisonment of imprisonment from three months to five years. ...

(3) Whoever publicly or in a meeting approves of, denies or belittles an act committed under the rule of National Socialism of the type indicated in Section 6 subsection (1) of the Code of Crimes against International Law, in a manner capable of disturbing the public peace shall be punished with imprisonment for not more than five years or a fine.

(4) Whoever publicly or in a meeting disturbs the public peace in a manner that assaults the human dignity of the victims by approving of, denying or rendering harmless the violent and arbitrary National Socialist rule shall be punished with imprisonment for not more than three years or a fine....

## *Notes and Questions*

1. The Argentine Supreme Court held in the *Arriola* case that it violated the national constitution to punish the possession of marijuana for personal use. In doing so, the Court argued that punishing such conduct would "invade a sphere of personal liberty" that the Constitution prohibits the government from interfering with. Do you agree that punishing the possession of small quantities of marijuana for personal consumption illegitimately interferes with the freedom of individuals? Would punishing such conduct violate the Due Process Clause of the Fourteenth Amendment as construed in *Lawrence*? Explain.

2. Is the possession of marijuana for personal use criminalized because the governing majority views it as immoral or because it causes "harm to others"? Explain. Does pun-

ishing such conduct run afoul of the "harm principle" as construed by H.LA. Hart? Why or why not?

3. Many continental criminal law theorists invoke the concept of "legal goods" (*bien jurídico* in Spanish and *rechtsgut* in German) in order to limit the state's power to criminalize conduct. A "legal good" is the interest that the law seeks to protect when it criminalizes conduct. If the state cannot show that the defendant's conduct harms the "legal good" sought to be protected by the offense charged, then no punishment can be imposed. The Spanish Supreme Court has invoked the concept of "legal goods" to hold that the possession of drugs for personal consumption may not be criminalized. In a 1993 case, for example, the Spanish high court concluded that the "legal good" protected by laws that prohibit the possession of drugs is the "public health." Given that the possession of drugs for personal consumption does not endanger the legal good that drug laws are designed to protect (i.e., "public health"), the Spanish Supreme Court held that the government could not punish such conduct. *See Judgment of the Spanish Supreme Court of 25-3-1993.* For a discussion of the meaning and scope of the concept "legal good" *see* Bernd Shunemann, *The System of Criminal Wrongs: The Concept of Legal Goods and Victim-based Jurisprudence As a Bridge between the General and Special Parts of the Criminal Code*, 7 Buff. Crim. L. Rev. 551 (2004).

4. The public incitement offense codified in § 130(3) of the German Penal Code has been invoked to punish defendants for denying the occurrence of the Holocaust. What is the harm sought to be prevented by the criminalization of this conduct? Explain. Could the conduct punished pursuant to § 130 of the German Penal Code be constitutionally criminalized in the United States? Why or why not?

## § 5.05 Criminalization Decisions: Scholarly Debates

### Bernard E. Harcourt, *The Collapse of the Harm Principle*

90 J. Crim. L. & Criminology 109 (1999)

... Pornography, prostitution, disorderly conduct, homosexuality, intoxication, drug use, and fornication: with regard to each of these, the proponents of legal enforcement are now deploying the harm argument in support of a conservative agenda. The arguments are powerful. It is hard to respond adequately to the harm to women caused by pornography and prostitution, to the threat of the spread of AIDS caused by high-risk activities like homosexual and heterosexual fornication, or to the neighborhood decline and loss of property value associated with prostitutes, smut shops, and liquor establishments. The harm arguments are particularly compelling when the conception of harm has been pared down to its bare bones and brackets out other normative values.

The proliferation of harm arguments in the debate over the legal enforcement of morality has effectively collapsed the harm principle. Harm to others is no longer today a limiting principle. It no longer excludes categories of moral offenses from the scope of the law. It is no longer a necessary (but not sufficient) condition, because there are so many non-trivial harm arguments. Instead of focusing on whether certain conduct causes harm, today the debates center on the types of harm, the amounts of harm, and our willingness, as a society, to bear the harms. And the harm principle is silent on those questions.

The harm principle is silent in the sense that it does not determine whether a non-trivial harm justifies restrictions on liberty, nor does it determine how to compare or weigh competing claims of harms. It was never intended to be a sufficient condition. It does not address the comparative importance of harms. Joel Feinberg's thorough discussion of the harm principle recognized this important fact. In discussing the relative importance of harms, Feinberg admitted that "[i]t is impossible to prepare a detailed manual with the exact 'weights' of all human interests, the degree to which they are advanced or thwarted by all possible actions and activities, duly discounted by objective improbabilities mathematically designated." Thus, Feinberg concluded, "in the end, it is the legislator himself, using his own fallible judgment rather than spurious formulas and 'measurements,' who must compare conflicting interests and judge which are the more important."

> Feinberg proposed a three-prong test to determine the relative importance of harms:
>
> Relative importance is a function of three different respects in which opposed interests can be compared:
>
> a. how 'vital' they are in the interest networks of their possessors;
>
> b. the degree to which they are reinforced by other interests, private and public;
>
> c. their inherent moral quality.

But what are the inherent moral qualities of interests affected by claims of harm? And how could the harm principle tell us what those inherent moral qualities are? In the end, it can not. The harm principle itself—the simple notion of harm—does not address the relative importance of harms. Once non-trivial harm arguments have been made, we inevitably must look beyond the harm principle. We must look beyond the traditional structure of the debate over the legal enforcement of morality. We must access larger debates in ethics, law and politics—debates about power, autonomy, identity, human flourishing, equality, freedom and other interests and values that give meaning to the claim that an identifiable harm matters. In this sense, the proliferation of conservative harm arguments and the collapse of the harm principle has fundamentally altered the structure of the future debate over the legal enforcement of morals.

## Eric Blumenson & Eva Nilsen, *Liberty Lost: The Moral Case for Marijuana Law Reform*

85 Ind. L. J. 279 (2010)

... [E]ven in the absence of criminal penalties, outlawing the use of marijuana raises separate liberty concerns. How that putative liberty should be described is a significant and consequential question; recall that the Supreme Court found no "right to engage in homosexual sodomy" in Bowers v. Hardwick but later overruled that case because the Constitution guarantees a "right to autonomy in intimate relations." Similarly, some people may dismiss the issue here as merely a question of whether there exists a fundamental "right to smoke marijuana," while others might describe the right at issue, with Justice Brandeis, as the right to be let alone absent good reason, or with Kant, as the right to self-rule. Other moral rights are arguably at stake, including the rights to control one's body, to freedom of thought, to privacy in one's home, and to the pursuit of happiness. If any such individual rights are involved, preventing marijuana use needs more justification than a collective cost-benefit analysis alone.

The idea common to all these descriptions is that each person has certain fundamental interests that must be under the individual's exclusive control and immune from state interference. The Supreme Court has expressed this idea using the rubric of a constitutional right to privacy (and the Alaska Supreme Court has found private marijuana use in one's home protected under its state version of the right). In Lawrence v. Texas, the case that overturned Bowers, the Court described that right in the following terms:

> Liberty protects the person from unwarranted government intrusions into a dwelling or other private places.... And there are other spheres of our lives and existence, outside the home, where the State should not be a dominant presence ...
>
> Liberty presumes an autonomy of self that includes freedom of thought, belief, expression, and certain intimate conduct ...
>
> At the heart of liberty is the right to define one's own concept of existence, of meaning, of the universe, and of the mystery of human life. Beliefs about these matters could not define the attributes of personhood were they formed under compulsion of the State.... The petitioners are entitled to respect for their private lives....

Obviously, one's right to privacy, or what we might more affirmatively describe as a right to self-ownership or self-rule, is limited. According to Mill, the right is limited only by the harm principle: we must be free to choose for ourselves up to the point we would harm or risk harm to others. Justice Kennedy's opinion in Lawrence can be read as adding a second limitation on the right of self-rule, one that would permit paternalism in some areas that are removed from the reasons for respecting individual autonomy. In Kennedy's opinion for the Court, the right to self-rule apparently protects only the realm most closely related to the essential attributes of personhood. Requiring drivers to use seatbelts may not interfere with these attributes, but denying individuals freedom of thought and expression, or the freedom to choose their intimate relations, clearly does.

In assessing where marijuana use falls on this spectrum, one must attend to the reasons individuals offer for using it. These reasons are almost completely absent from drug policy analyses. Here is naturalist Michael Pollan's description:

> All those who write about cannabis's effect on consciousness speak of the changes in perception they experience.... [T]hese people invariably report seeing, and hearing, and tasting things with a new keenness, as if with fresh eyes and ears and taste buds....
>
> It is by temporarily mislaying much of what we already know (or think we know) that cannabis restores a kind of innocence to our perceptions of the world....
>
> There is another word for this extremist noticing—this sense of first sight unencumbered by knowingness, by the already-been-theres and seen-thats of the adult mind—and that word, of course, is wonder.

Pollan finds using marijuana edifying because it opens the door to thoughts, insights, and experiences he finds valuable. Rick Steves, the Public Broadcasting Service travel guru, says that his outlook and writing have been sharpened by using marijuana. Some other users say that temporarily changing the way they perceive and experience the world increases their self-awareness, or frees up some creative potential within them, or opens them up to more spiritual feelings. In the past year, the Italian Court of Cassation reversed a marijuana conviction on such grounds, accepting the Rastafarian defendant's contention that marijuana helped him achieve a "psychophysical state connected to contemplative prayer." On the other hand, many former users and other critics would find these self-assessments to be delusional. Law professor Michael Moore considers most such claims to be "grandiose descriptions of what in fact is a pretty pathetic condition" and writes that "[o]ne has to be high on [drugs] already in order to be able to judge the states induced as any kind of path to profundity or 'authenticity.'"

One need not resolve this dispute concerning marijuana's value to recognize that at least for its users, banning marijuana does implicate their freedom of thought and sometimes even the "right to define one's own concept of existence, of meaning, of the universe, and of the mystery of human life." That is one reason why a ban on marijuana cuts so close to core aspects of personhood—to the freedom of thought and religion that are necessary to respect an autonomous being's ability to choose what to think and what kind of person to be. That such thoughts, and such an identity, are not esteemed by a majority of Americans and their government is really beside the point: the very idea of this liberty is to protect each individual's sovereignty in this realm (as the Supreme Court long ago recognized). Yet according to President Nixon's National Commission on Marijuana, the war against marijuana, then beginning in earnest, was fueled by fear that the drug caused users to reject the "established value system."

A more quotidian moral right, perhaps less exalted but no less important, is recognized in the Declaration of Independence as an inalienable right to the pursuit of happiness. This right should protect those who seek affective rather than cognitive benefits from marijuana-users for whom it serves as a relaxant, a social lubricant, an antidepressant, or a palliative. The right to pursue happiness in one's own way is worthy of respect, and many Americans disdain the Iranian government because it affords none. There, the government bans certain dress and music that it deems decadent. Here, the default position is that people should be free to pursue their individual and idiosyncratic tastes in recreation, including even such risky ones as boxing and mountain climbing. Only in a few cases does the majority presume to control the personal pleasures of a minority; marijuana use, even privately at home, is one of them.

This is not to say that the state should be unconcerned with marijuana use, because it does present risks to health and safety, and both state and federal governments have important roles to play in eliminating or reducing those risks. In liberal societies such as ours, where the presumption is that individuals have the right to decide how to live their lives for themselves, the government safeguards us not by making the decisions for us but by helping us to make wise decisions with full knowledge. Thus the government does not legislate your weight or dictate your diet, but it labels food and advises on its health effects. Political philosopher William Talbott argues that the fundamental idea underlying human rights is that people "should be guaranteed what is necessary to be able to make their own judgments about what is good for them [and] to be able to give effect to those judgments in living their lives."

Certainly, there are exceptions to this principle where the government properly places something beyond the reach of its citizens for good reason. Many would include among them instances where: (1) the dangers of a trivial activity are very great; (2) a safer alternative can equally satisfy the consumer; (3) the individual is a child or lacks rationality; (4) collective action is able to accomplish things impossible by individual choice; or (5) the activity would result in an addiction so powerfully destructive of autonomy as to amount to a form of slavery, which may be true of certain drugs. Liberty rights can be overcome by sufficiently compelling grounds. But marijuana does not present any such reason. As Pollan writes, "The war on drugs is in [reality] a war on some drugs, their enemy status the result of historical accident, cultural prejudice, and institutional imperative."

## *Notes and Questions*

1. Professor Harcourt argues that "[t]he proliferation of harm arguments in the debate over the legal enforcement of morality has effectively collapsed the harm principle." As Harcourt correctly points out, some scholars now argue that pornography ought to be criminalized because it causes non-trivial harm that goes beyond offending moral sensibilities. He explains:

> Professor Catharine MacKinnon, perhaps more than anyone else, has focused the debate on the harm to women caused by pornography. MacKinnon's work has emphasized at least three types of harm emanating from pornography. First, pornography inflicts harm on the women who are used to make the pornographic material. "It is for pornography," MacKinnon explains, "and not by the ideas in it that women are hurt and penetrated, tied and gagged, undressed and genitally spread and sprayed with lacquer and water so sex pictures can be made." Second, MacKinnon has argued, pornography harms the women who are assaulted by consumers of pornography. Men who consume pornography may be led—and in some cases are led—to commit crimes of sexual violence against women. "It is not the ideas in pornography that assault women," MacKinnon writes. "[M]en do, men who are made, changed, and impelled by it." Third, pornography supports and promotes a general climate of discrimination against women. It becomes a part of the identity of women and of women's sexuality. "As the industry expands," MacKinnon explains, "this becomes more and more the generic experience of sex, the woman in pornography becoming more and more the lived archetype for women's sexuality in men's, hence women's, experience." Pornography, in sum, causes multiple harms to women by shaping and distorting the modern subject.

Scholars also argue that prostitution causes non-trivial harm that warrants criminalization. Harcourt summarizes the argument as follows:

> The proponents of regulation or prohibition, instead of arguing about morality or offense, have turned to the harm argument, and thereby disarmed the traditional progressive position. This shift is the result again, at least in part, of Catharine MacKinnon's writings. MacKinnon has argued that prostitution is on par with rape, battery, sexual harassment, and pornography in its harm to women. The impact of MacKinnon's work has been to focus on the harm to the women who engage in commercial sex and to women's identity more generally. What also has transformed the debate over prostitution is the "broken windows" theory of crime prevention, first articulated in James Q. Wilson and George L. Kelling's article, Broken Windows, in the Atlantic Monthly in 1982.... [U]nder the broken windows argument, the potential harm to society in prostitution is not so much the harm to women, but rather the likelihood of increased serious criminal activity. The broken windows hypothesis provides that, if prostitution and other minor disorderly conduct in a neighborhood go unattended, serious crime will increase in that neighborhood. Disorder, such as prostitution, brings about increased criminal activity. According to the broken windows argument, prostitution causes harm to society by causing more violent crimes.

Do you agree with Professor Harcourt that many—if not most—of the classic examples of "morals legislation" can be justified on the basis of harm arguments? Revisit the post-*Lawrence* cases discussed in the Notes to § 5.01. Note that the courts in the cases discussed in those notes came up with harm arguments to justify the criminalization of crimes such incest, bigamy, bestiality and prostitution. In light of this, how successful is the harm principle in limiting the state's power to criminalize conduct?

2. In a recent article, John Darley and Avani Mehta Sood devised a series of experiments to test whether people will come up with harm arguments when they desire to criminalize certain conduct and are informed that it is legitimate to criminalize conduct only if it causes harm. The studies showed "that although the harm principle dominates people's intuitions about punishment, there are acts—like public nudity and flag defiling—that people want to criminalize even without finding harm." Furthermore—and more importantly—the experiments revealed "that when informed that the law requires a finding of harm in order to penalize such conduct, those who want to punish are significantly more likely to report the presence of harm, and report significantly greater levels of harm." John Darley and Avani Mehta Sood, *The Plasticity of Harm in the Service of Criminalization Goals,* 100 Cal. L. Rev. 1313 (2012). The authors explained the implications of their studies in the following way:

> Our results suggest that the concept of harm may not be as cognitively stable or reliable as the legal system assumes. This calls into question the laws and policies that are based on perceptions of harm, to the extent that those perceptions may be endogenous to the desired outcomes of legal decision makers. In the current U.S. justice system, "[t]he duty of lawmakers, judges, and citizens to justify their positions on grounds susceptible of affirmation by persons of diverse moral persuasions—paradigmatically, the prevention of harm—is deeply woven into prevailing norms of legal and political discourse." However, our studies demonstrate that while supposedly objective standards like the harm principle appear to provide a way to overcome sectarian biases in legal decision making, the rhetoric of harm can covertly become a conduit for morally or ideologically motivated agendas.
>
> In fact, rather than enforcing objectivity, seemingly neutral legal constraints like the harm principle could ironically just exacerbate people's illusions of objectivity about their own judgments. Telling decision makers that they are "satisfying the duty of impartiality when they sincerely articulate a secular ... justification can't make those persons genuinely impartial. It can only make them less aware of the influence that our cultural commitments exert ... a form of self-misunderstanding to which persons in general are already vulnerable."

In light of these findings, is the harm principle likely to curtail the state's power to criminalize conduct in a significant way? Explain.

3. In the second article excerpted in this section, Professors Blumenson and Nilsen mention a case in which the Supreme Court of Alaska held that punishing the possession of marijuana for personal purposes violated the state constitution. The case is *Ravin v. State,* 537 P.2d 494 (1975). The Alaskan high court explained its holding in the following way:

> Privacy in the home is a fundamental right, under both the federal and Alaska constitutions. We do not mean by this that a person may do anything at anytime as long as the activity takes place within a person's home.... [W]e think this right must yield when it interferes in a serious manner with the health, safety, rights and privileges of others or with the public welfare. No one has an absolute right to do things in the privacy of his own home which will affect himself or others adversely. Indeed, one aspect of a private matter is that it is private, that is, that it does not adversely affect persons beyond the actor, and hence is none of

their business. When a matter does affect the public, directly or indirectly, it loses its wholly private character, and can be made to yield when an appropriate public need is demonstrated.

Thus, we conclude that citizens of the State of Alaska have a basic right to privacy in their homes under Alaska's constitution. This right to privacy would encompass the possession and ingestion of substances such as marijuana in a purely personal, non-commercial context in the home unless the state can meet its substantial burden and show that proscription of possession of marijuana in the home is supportable by achievement of a legitimate state interest ...

[W]e conclude that no adequate justification for the state's intrusion into the citizen's right to privacy by its prohibition of possession of marijuana by an adult for personal consumption in the home has been shown. The privacy of the individual's home cannot be breached absent a persuasive showing of a close and substantial relationship of the intrusion to a legitimate governmental interest. Here, mere scientific doubts will not suffice. The state must demonstrate a need based on proof that the public health or welfare will in fact suffer if the controls are not applied.

The state has a legitimate concern with avoiding the spread of marijuana use to adolescents who may not be equipped with the maturity to handle the experience prudently, as well as a legitimate concern with the problem of driving under the influence of marijuana. Yet these interests are insufficient to justify intrusions into the rights of adults in the privacy of their own homes.

4. Blumenson and Nilsen identify the fundamental right conferred by the Supreme Court in *Lawrence* as a "right to self-rule" that "protects only the realm most closely related to the essential attributes of personhood." Given that engaging in consensual anal intercourse is an essential attribute of a homosexual lifestyle, criminalizing such conduct infringes on "essential attributes of personhood." In contrast, it is difficult to imagine that driving without a seatbelt or skiing without a helmet are activities that are essential to defining the personhood of individuals. Therefore, it may be argued that prohibiting driving without a seatbelt or skiing without a helmet does not infringe on the fundamental right to self rule that formed the basis of the Supreme Court's holding in *Lawrence.* Do you agree that there is a significant difference between laws that punish engaging in consensual sexual intercourse and laws that require people to wear helmets or seatbelts? Is the difference between these laws sufficiently significant to justify allowing the government to criminalize the latter (driving without a seatbelt or skiing without a helmet) but not the former (engaging in consensual sexual intercourse)? Explain. Do laws that prohibit smoking marijuana infringe on an "essential attribute of personhood"? Why or why not? Are laws that punish smoking marijuana more similar to laws that criminalize engaging in consensual sexual intercourse or to laws that punish driving without a seatbelt? Explain.

# Part Three

# The Elements of Punishable Crimes I—The Offense

# Chapter 6

# Conduct: Action, Omission & Possession

## §6.01 Conduct: The Voluntary Act Requirement

### State v. Newman

Supreme Court of Oregon, 2013
353 Or. 632

BALDWIN, J.

Defendant was convicted of felony driving under the influence of intoxicants (DUII). At trial, defendant sought to introduce evidence that he suffers from a sleepwalking disorder and was "sleep driving" at the time he was stopped in his vehicle. Defendant argued he did not voluntarily drive his vehicle, an element of proof necessary to establish criminal liability for DUII. The trial court excluded defendant's proffered evidence, concluding it was not relevant because DUII is a strict-liability offense. On appeal, the Court of Appeals agreed that DUII is a strict-liability offense and affirmed. We allowed defendant's petition for review. For the reasons that follow, we conclude defendant's proffered evidence was relevant to the driving element of the DUII charge. Accordingly, we reverse.

#### I. Background

We take the following facts from the Court of Appeals opinion.

"Defendant met his friends for dinner one evening and, anticipating that he would drink alcohol at dinner, left his car parked by his apartment and walked to the restaurant. Thereafter, defendant's friends drove him home, and he went to sleep. Later that evening, a police officer followed defendant's car and observed defendant make a left-hand turn without signaling or stopping, run a red light, and drive down the middle of a street, straddling the two traffic lanes. The officer then activated his overhead lights to initiate a traffic stop and, in response, defendant pulled into a parking lot. The officer approached defendant's car, smelled a strong odor of alcohol, and observed defendant's bloodshot, watery eyes and slow, slurred speech. Defendant agreed to perform field sobriety tests and, after failing them, was taken into custody. At the police station, defendant consented to a Breathalyzer test, which revealed that he had a blood alcohol level of 0.15 percent."

Defendant was charged with felony DUII, reckless driving, and recklessly endangering another person. Before trial, the state filed a motion seeking to exclude as irrelevant testimony regarding defendant's sleepwalking disorder and his "sleep driving on the night in question." Defendant argued that evidence of his sleepwalking was relevant to negate the requirements for criminal liability under [the Oregon Penal Law]—specifically, proof of a voluntary act with respect to the driving element of DUII. Defendant contended that he was not capable of performing the necessary volitional movements to consciously control his vehicle because he was asleep when the police stopped his vehicle.

As part of his offer of proof, defendant testified that he had sleepwalked within his apartment on a number of occasions in the past, but, to his knowledge, had not left his apartment while sleepwalking before this incident. A friend also provided testimony confirming defendant's sleepwalking behaviors. Defendant further testified that, after he went to sleep that evening, he had no recollection of leaving his apartment, getting behind the wheel of his car, or driving. Also, as part of defendant's offer of proof, Dr. Joshua Ramseyer, a physician certified in neurology and sleep medicine, provided expert testimony about the symptoms associated with parasomnia—a category of unwanted behavior that emerges during sleep. Within that category of sleep phenomenon, Dr. Ramseyer explained, exists somnambulism—which is also known as sleepwalking disorder. As Dr. Ramseyer explained:

> Sleep driving is thought of as being sort of a subtype of sleepwalking or an extension of sleepwalking. It's a motor behavior that occurs without consciousness ... that comes out during sleep....
>
> [J]ust as someone's capable of sort of walking around the house, doing goal-directed behavior, such as eating, people can get behind the wheel, start up the car, and drive.

Dr. Ramseyer emphasized that activities performed while sleepwalking, such as "sleep driving," are *unconscious* acts. He further noted that sleepwalking resulting in "sleep driving," while uncommon in the general population, is a well-established phenomenon. If permitted to testify, Dr. Ramseyer would have rendered an expert opinion that defendant was "sleep driving" when stopped by police.

In seeking to exclude defendant's proffered evidence, the state argued that the evidence was irrelevant because the state was required to prove only that defendant drove a vehicle with a blood alcohol content of .08 percent or greater or was otherwise under the influence of an intoxicant. The trial court agreed with the state. It concluded that DUII is a strict-liability offense under [state law], and excluded defendant's proffered "sleep driving" evidence as irrelevant. The state then dismissed the charges of reckless driving and reckless endangerment and proceeded solely on the charge of felony DUII. Defendant waived his right to a jury and was convicted of the charge.

On appeal, defendant and the state generally reprised the arguments made before the trial court. Defendant argued, in particular, that the only question decided in *Miller* was whether proof of a culpable mental state was required for the intoxication element of DUII. Defendant further asserted that proof of volition is required to find a person criminally liable for DUII.

The Court of Appeals affirmed the trial court's decision ... [and] concluded that DUII is a strict-liability offense.

In this court, defendant again asserts that, for the purposes of DUII prosecutions, [Oregon Law] requires proof that a person committed the voluntary act of driving for criminal liability to attach. In defendant's view, evidence of his sleepwalking disorder and his condition on the night in question is relevant to the issue of whether his driving was voluntary, and thus should have been admitted. We allowed review to examine whether the trial court committed legal error in excluding defendant's "sleep driving" evidence....

### II. Analysis

The relevant statutory provision defining felony DUII … provide[s], in pertinent part:

(1) A person commits the offense of driving while under the influence of intoxicants if the person drives a vehicle while the person:

a) Has 0.08 percent or more by weight of alcohol in the blood of the person….

b) Is under the influence of intoxicating liquor, a controlled substance or an inhalant; or

c) Is under the influence of any combination of intoxicating liquor, an inhalant and a controlled substance.

The [DUII statute] sets forth two essential elements. A person commits the crime of DUII when the person (1) "drives a vehicle" (2) while "under the influence" of an intoxicating substance….

As noted, when he was stopped, defendant admitted that he was intoxicated. He did not admit, however, that he had been consciously driving. He now contends, therefore, that he cannot be found criminally liable for *driving* his vehicle unless the voluntary act requirement [included in the Oregon Penal Law] is met in this case….

Defendant thus contends that he should have been allowed to show that he was not engaged in a volitional act when driving because he was unconscious….

#### B. Voluntary Act—ORS 161.095(1)

We now turn to the legislative determination that a person perform a voluntary act for imposition of criminal liability. ORS 161.095(1) provides that:

> The minimal requirement for criminal liability is the performance by a person of conduct which includes a voluntary act or the omission to perform an act which the person is capable of performing.

The legislature has defined a "voluntary act" as used in [this statute] to mean "a bodily movement performed consciously and includes the conscious possession or control of property." Applying that understanding to this case, defendant is not criminally liable under [Oregon law] if he did not perform a bodily movement consciously.

Although the legislature has defined "voluntary act," it has not further defined what constitutes a "conscious" bodily movement. We have recognized that "conscious" as used in [Oregon law] is a word of common usage. Accordingly, we turn to the dictionary for further guidance to determine whether defendant's movements, if done while sleepwalking or "sleep driving," would be consciously performed … The dictionary definition of "conscious" includes:

> 2: perceiving, apprehending, or noticing with a degree of controlled thought or observation: recognizing as existent, factual, or true: a: knowing or perceiving something within oneself or a fact about oneself … b: recognizing as factual or existent something external … 5 a: having rational power: capable of thought, will, design, or perception … 7: mentally active: fully possessed of one's mental faculties: having emerged from sleep, faint, or stupor: AWAKE: the patient becoming as the anesthesia wears off. *Webster's Third New Int'l Dictionary* 482 (unabridged ed. 2002) (boldface omitted).

That definition associates consciousness with a wakeful state and implies that a person in a state of sleep cannot execute a conscious action.

That understanding is consistent with the pertinent legislative history. The commentary accompanying the 1971 substantive criminal code revisions explains that ORS 161.095(1)

> ... enunciates the basic principle that, no matter how an offense is defined, the minimal requirement for criminal liability is conduct which includes a 'voluntary' act or omission. This excludes all 'involuntary' acts such as reflex actions, acts committed during hypnosis, epileptic fugue, etc. Criminal Law Revision Commission Proposed Oregon Criminal Code, Final Draft and Report § 11 Commentary (July 1970) (providing comments to §§ 7, 8).

That explanation discloses a legislative intent to exclude from the definition of voluntary acts any acts that are taken when a person is sleeping.

In drafting the criminal code's liability requirements, the legislature looked to analogous provisions of the Model Penal Code. Model Penal Code section 2.01 is the counterpart of ORS 161.095(1), and requires proof of volition to establish criminal liability. Section 2.01 provides examples of what is *not* a voluntary act. Those examples include a reflex or convulsion, a bodily movement during unconsciousness or sleep, conduct during or resulting from hypnosis, and movement that otherwise is not a product of the effort or determination of the actor. The commentary to section 2.01 clarifies that while "unconsciousness" may imply collapse or coma, there are "states of physical activity where self-awareness is grossly impaired or even absent,"—*i.e.*, what the commentary refers to as states of active automatism—that are subsumed within the meaning of the term. American Law Institute, Model Penal Code Comments ***643** § 2.01, 121 (Tentative Draft No. 4 1955). The commentary explains that sleepwalking activity "should receive the same treatment accorded other active states of true automatism." Thus, as the text and commentary suggest, the drafters of the Model Penal Code understood a person engaged in sleepwalking to lack the level of consciousness necessary for a volitional act.

Furthermore, the commentary to Model Penal Code section 2.01 states that criminal liability must be based on conduct that includes a voluntary act because

> [t]he law cannot hope to deter involuntary movement or to stimulate action that cannot physically be performed; the sense of personal security would be short-lived in a society where such movement or inactivity could lead to formal social condemnation of the sort that a conviction necessarily entails. People whose involuntary movements threaten harm to others may present a public health or safety problem, calling for therapy or even for custodial commitment; they do not present a problem of correction. American Law Institute, Model Penal Code Comments § 2.01, 119 (Tentative Draft No. 4 1955).

*See also* Wayne R. LaFave, 1*Substantive Criminal Law* § 6.1(c) ("The deterrent function of the criminal law would not be served by imposing sanctions for involuntary action, as such action cannot be deterred.") In sum, the deterrent function of criminal sanctions and basic fairness are not served by punishing a person whose acts are the result of unconscious movement because the person committed those acts while sleeping. Thus, in enacting ORS 161.095(1), the legislature requires proof of a voluntary act for criminal liability to attach.

### C. Operation of ORS 161.095(1) in DUII prosecutions

We next address the state's argument that ORS 161.095(1) requires that the prosecution only prove that defendant engaged in "a voluntary act," which, in the state's view, does not require that the voluntary act be limited to *driving* for purposes of a DUII prosecution.... The state points out that defendant voluntarily consumed alcohol resulting in his intoxication, and asserts that that conduct, which is linked to the intoxication element of DUII, satisfies the voluntary act requirement.

We disagree. Although intoxication is an element of the DUII offense, it is not the proscribed conduct; it is a condition necessary to establish the offense. The voluntary act that [the offense charged] requires must be linked not to a condition but to proscribed conduct. That does not mean, however, that the only relevant voluntary act is the act of driving. The commentary to the Model Penal Code indicates that the voluntary act may occur prior to the proscribed act as long as it is related to it. That is to say, although a prior voluntary act may suffice, not merely *any* act, however tenuously related, is sufficient. As the commentary to section 2.01 explains:

> It will be noted that the formulation does not state that liability must be based on the voluntary act or the omission *simpliciter*, but rather upon conduct which *includes* such action or omission. The distinction has some analytical importance. If the driver of an automobile loses consciousness with the result that he runs over a pedestrian, none of the movements or omissions that accompany or follow this loss of consciousness may in themselves give rise to liability. But a prior voluntary act, such as the act of driving, or a prior omission, such as failing to stop as he felt illness approaching, may, under given circumstances, be regarded as sufficiently negligent for liability to be imposed. In that event, however, liability is based on the entire course of conduct, including the specific conduct that results in the injury. American Law Institute, Model Penal Code Comments § 2.01, 120 (Tentative Draft No. 4 1955) (emphasis in original).

Professor LaFave similarly expresses that point:

> Although a voluntary act is an absolute requirement for criminal liability, it does not follow that every act up to the moment that the harm is caused must be voluntary. Thus, one may be guilty of criminal homicide (or battery) even though he is unconscious or asleep at the time of the fatal (or injurious) impact, as where *A*, being subject to frequent fainting spells, has such a spell while driving his car (or, after the becoming aware that he is sleepy, continues to drive and falls asleep at the wheel), with the result that the car, out of control, runs into and kills (or injures) *B* while *A* is unconscious or asleep. Here, *A's* voluntary act consists of driving the car. LaFave, 1 *Substantive Criminal Law* § 6.1(c) at 429.

Under that formulation, a defendant may be held criminally liable for a prior voluntary act if that act, through a course of related and foreseeable events, results in proscribed conduct.

In this case, the jury was required to find that defendant engaged in a volitional act that led to the proscribed act of driving, but was permitted to consider evidence that defendant engaged in volitional acts other than the act of driving. For instance, the jury could have considered evidence that defendant engaged in the volitional act of drinking, if there were evidence that drinking led to the driving. However, the jury also could have concluded that defendant's "sleep driving" would have occurred without regard to whether he consumed alcohol and, thus, that defendant did not engage in a voluntary act which led to the act of driving.

However, the sufficiency of the evidence of a volitional act is not the issue on appeal. The issue presented is whether defendant was entitled to adduce evidence that he did not commit a voluntary act by driving on the night in question. The evidence defendant proffered was relevant to that issue.

We conclude that the text, context, and legislative history of [the DUII statute] demonstrate a legislative intent to require that a defendant committed a voluntary act with respect to the driving element of DUII. This court's case law is not to the contrary. In *Miller,* the court examined how other statutes ... operate with respect to the offense of DUII in determining whether a defendant may be convicted of DUII without proof of a culpable mental state when under the influence of an intoxicant. The court concluded that the "being-under-the influence-of-an-intoxicant element of DUII, requires no proof of a culpable mental state." However, the court did not consider how the voluntary act requirement of ORS 161.095(1) applies to the driving element in a DUII prosecution. *Miller* simply did not address the issue of volitional driving presented in this case.

To summarize: We hold that the minimal voluntary act requirement of ORS 161.095(1) applies to the driving element of DUII in this case. Here, the trial court erred in not allowing defendant to adduce evidence that he was not conscious when he drove on the evening in question. The state was entitled to present evidence that defendant's drinking or other volitional act resulted in defendant driving his vehicle that evening. As noted, the state may also show a voluntary act with evidence that defendant had engaged in "sleep driving" prior to this incident and failed to take adequate precautions to remove access to his car keys.

The decision of the Court of Appeals is reversed. The judgment of the circuit court is reversed, and the case is remanded to the circuit court for further proceedings.

## *Notes and Questions*

1. Criminal liability is usually imposed for engaging in harmful actions. Nevertheless, as the next sections of this chapter illustrate, punishment may also be imposed for failing to act (omissions) and for being in possession of certain items. Although the "voluntary act" requirement is typically associated with actions, it also applies to omission and possession offenses. That is, a defendant will typically not be held liable for failing to act if he was not conscious of the facts that triggered liability for his omission. Similarly, a defendant will usually not be held liable for being in possession of a certain item if he did not voluntarily acquire the item or consciously refuse to get rid of it. Therefore, the "voluntary act" requirement cuts across all three forms of commission of criminal offenses.

2. It may be argued that if the defendant's involuntary conduct is the product of a mental disease or defect, it would be appropriate to excuse the conduct on the basis of the insanity defense rather than to acquit the defendant on the basis of the "voluntary act" doctrine. By grounding such convictions on the insanity defense, the defendant may be subjected to medical treatment and confinement after acquittal. English courts call this kind of involuntariness "insane automatism." *See, e.g., Regina v. Burgess,* 2 All E.R. 769, 774–75 (C.A. 1991). The distinction between sane and insane automatism has yet to be embraced by American courts.

3. Why did the defendant fail to act voluntarily in *Newman*? Note that the actions appeared voluntary to the police officer who stopped the defendant. After all, driving seems to be the kind of activity that is difficult to perform involuntarily.

4. Perhaps what makes the defendant's actions involuntary in this case is that they were performed while he was unconscious (in a sleep state). If that is the case, it raises many interesting questions. One has to do with the familiar phenomenon of driving in a semi-conscious or unconscious way. It happens quite often when experienced drivers take familiar routes while listening to music or otherwise engaging their conscious mind in an

activity other than driving (having a conversation, for example). In many such cases, drivers report arriving at their destination without having a clear recollection of how they got there. Scientists call this the "unconscious driving phenomenon." *See, generally,* Susan Blackmore, *Consciousness: A Very Short Introduction* (Oxford, 2005). Suppose that while a person is experiencing the "unconscious driving phenomenon" she has an accident and harms someone. May the person be held criminally liable for the harm that she caused? Did her conduct satisfy the criminal law's "voluntary act" requirement? Why or why not?

5. As the Supreme Court of Oregon points out in *Newman,* even if the defendant was unconscious while driving and did not therefore drive "voluntarily," he may be held criminally liable if the state proves that "the defendant's drinking or other volitional act resulted in defendant driving his vehicle that evening." The Court also points out that defendant may be held liable if the state shows "that defendant had engaged in 'sleep driving' prior to this incident and failed to take adequate precautions to remove access to his car keys." In both of these instances, defendant's possible liability would hinge not on the involuntary or unconscious act of driving, but rather on a previous voluntary act (drinking) or conscious omission (failing to take precautions to prevent sleep driving) that is sufficiently connected to the act of driving as to justify the imposition of criminal liability. As a general rule, defendant's prior voluntary act or omission will give rise to liability for a subsequent harm caused by an involuntary act if two conditions are satisfied. First, it must be reasonably foreseeable that defendant might engage in harmful or risky involuntary action in the future. Second, the defendant's prior voluntary act or omission must negligently create a risk that she might engage in such harmful or risky involuntary conduct in the future.

In *People v. Decina,* 157 N.Y.S.2d 558 (1956), for example, the court concluded that a defendant that causes harm as a result of involuntary conduct that is the product of a seizure may be held liable on the basis of prior voluntary conduct. According to the court:

> Assuming the truth of the indictment ... this defendant knew he was subject to epileptic attacks and seizures that might strike at any time. He also knew that a moving motor vehicle uncontrolled on a public highway is a highly dangerous instrumentality capable of unrestrained destruction. With this knowledge, and without anyone accompanying him, he deliberately took a chance by making a conscious choice of a course of action, in disregard of the consequences which he knew might follow from his conscious act, and which in this case did ensue. How can we say as a matter of law that this did not amount to culpable negligence within the meaning of section 1053-a?
>
> To hold otherwise would be to say that a man may freely indulge himself in liquor in the same hope that it will not affect his driving, and if it later develops that ensuing intoxication causes dangerous and reckless driving resulting in death, his unconsciousness or involuntariness at that time would relieve him from prosecution under the statute. His awareness of a condition which he knows may produce such consequences as here, and his disregard of the consequences, renders him liable for culpable negligence.... To have a sudden sleeping spell, an unexpected heart or other disabling attack, without any prior knowledge or warning thereof, is an altogether different situation ... and there is simply no basis for comparing such cases with the flagrant disregard manifested here. *Id.*

6. Sometimes conduct is involuntary because it is the product of overwhelming physical compulsion. This is what happened in the oft-cited case of *Martin v. State,* 17 So.2d 427 (1944). Police officers arrested the drunken defendant at his home and took him onto

the highway. The defendant was charged and convicted of being drunk on a public highway. The Court reversed the conviction stating that:

> Under the plain terms of this statute, a voluntary appearance is presupposed. The rule has been declared, and we think it sound, that an accusation of drunkenness in a designated public place cannot be established by proof that the accused, while in an intoxicated condition, was involuntarily and forcibly carried to that place by the arresting officer. Conviction of appellant was contrary to this announced principle and, in our view, erroneous. *Id.*

A similar principle was upheld more recently in *State v. Sowry,* 803 N.E.2d 867 (2004). The defendant was arrested and transported to the county jail by police officers, where a thorough search at the time of booking revealed a baggie of marijuana in his right front pants pocket. Defendant was charged with bringing drugs into a state jail. The conviction was reversed because:

> Exercising the power to control his person which their arrest of [the defendant] conferred on them, officers [transported the defendant] to and into the jail to facilitate his detention. That his "person" and the possessions on his person were in the jail was therefore not a product of a voluntary act on [the defendant's] part. Rather, those events were, as to him, wholly involuntary. *Id.*

7. It is often stated that the state should punish people for what they do rather than for who they are. That is, the state may legitimately punish people for acts, but not for character or status. Offenses that punish people for who they are instead of for what they do are typically referred to as "status crimes." In *Robinson v. California,* 370 U.S. 660 (1962), the United States Supreme Court struck down a California statute authorizing punishment for "being addicted to the use of narcotics." The Court held that the law impermissibly criminalized status and that doing so amounted to "cruel and unusual punishment" in violation of the Eighth Amendment.

8. In the wake of *Robinson,* state jurisdictions tried to circumvent the constitutional prohibition of creating status crimes by making it an offense to engage in conduct that is closely linked to a certain status. Thus, for example, states criminalized the act of "public intoxication" as opposed to the status of "being a chronic alcoholic." Defendants accused of such crimes argued that the prohibition amounted to punishing the status of being an alcoholic, for chronic alcoholics cannot control their conduct and will quite often end up intoxicated in a public place. In *Powell v. Texas,* 392 U.S. 514 (1968), the United States Supreme Court rejected the argument, concluding that such statutes do not criminalize the status of being a chronic alcoholic, but rather the discrete act of getting drunk in public. Alcoholics in such jurisdictions are free to intoxicate themselves in private. Consequently, what is criminalized—according to the Court—is public drunkenness rather than the condition of being an alcoholic.

9. It is often quite difficult to distinguish between offenses that punish status and crimes that punish conduct. The relatively recent case of *Jones v. City of Los Angeles,* 444 F.3d 1118 (2006), illustrates the issue. Six homeless persons were cited or arrested for violating an ordinance that criminalized "sit[ting], lying, or sleeping in or upon any street, sidewalk or other public way." They challenged the constitutionality of the ordinance arguing that it criminalized the status of being homeless, for—almost by definition—people without a home will end up sleeping or sitting on public thoroughfares. They further argued that the City of Los Angeles lacked enough shelters to accommodate all of the homeless people living within city limits. Do you believe that the Los Angeles Ordinance criminalizes status or conduct? Why?

The United States Court of Appeals for the Ninth Circuit struck down the ordinance as applied to the defendants, contending that it impermissibly criminalized status in violation of the Eighth Amendment's proscription of cruel and unusual punishment. In justifying its conclusion, the Court stated that:

> The Eighth Amendment prohibits the City from punishing involuntary sitting, lying or sleeping on public sidewalks that is an unavoidable consequence of being human and homeless without shelter in the City of Los Angeles. *Id.*

Do you agree with the Court of Appeals? Why or why not? Do you believe that the ordinance was enacted primarily to deal with the social ills that result as a consequence of homelessness or do you believe that it was primarily enacted to provide the police with a tool that could be used to harass a certain class of people? Or do you believe that it was enacted for some other reason? Explain.

## § 6.02 Conduct: Omissions

### West v. Commonwealth

Court of Appeals of Kentucky, 1996
935 S.W.2d 315

COMBS, Judge.

... Appellant Russell West [was found] guilty of reckless homicide and his co-defendant, Appellant Ann West, guilty of complicity to reckless homicide. Having considered the arguments of counsel, we affirm the convictions.

Prosecution of the Wests, husband and wife, was precipitated by the death of Lillian West, Russell's fifty-four-year-old disabled sister. The Wests were alleged to have caused Lillian's death by their failure to care adequately for her physical needs and to secure the medical assistance she required.

Lillian West was born with Down's Syndrome and a heart ailment. Throughout most of her life, she was cared for by her mother, Rebekah West.... In 1983, Rebekah passed away, and Russell and Ann accepted responsibility for Lillian's care....

Near Thanksgiving, 1992, according to Russell, Lillian became confined to her bed. He testified that it was at this time that her condition began to decline significantly and that she would not eat. On December 31, 1992, Russell delivered Lillian to the emergency room at Mary Chiles Hospital in Montgomery County....

On January 17, 1993, Lillian died at University of Kentucky Medical Center. On March 2, 1993, Russell was indicted for manslaughter in the second degree; Ann was indicted as a complicitor. The indictments were consolidated for trial. At trial, medical witnesses recounted Lillian's horrific physical condition, describing numerous decubitus ulcers (pressure or bedsores) in various stages of development (many severe enough to reveal muscle tissue and even bone), severe malnutrition, and the presence of dried tears and feces upon her body. Physicians attributed the cause of death to sepsis and confluent bronchial pneumonia precipitated by the decubitus ulcers. They testified that caretaker neglect led ultimately to Lillian's death.

[A relevant statute in this case] is KRS 501.030, which provides in part as follows:

> A person is not guilty of a criminal offense unless:

> 1) He has engaged in conduct which concludes a voluntary act or the omission to perform a duty which the law imposes upon him and which he is physically capable of performing....

The Wests present identical issues on appeal. First, they maintain that neither of them had a duty to care for Lillian or to provide her with medical assistance. Thus, they conclude, neither of them could be convicted of an offense based upon the failure to provide such care. In a related argument, they note that the reckless homicide statute underlying their convictions does not, by its terms, impose criminal liability based upon an omission or failure to act. Therefore, they assert, the legislature must have envisioned that an *act* would form the basis of a conviction under the reckless homicide statute rather than a mere omission.

*People v. Beardsley*, a commonly cited case, addresses the issue of criminal ramifications arising from the omission to act where one has a duty to take action to preserve the life of another and that omission results in the death of the person to whom the duty is owed. It provides as follows:

> The law recognizes that under some circumstances the omission of a duty owed by one individual to another, where such omission results in the death of the one to whom the duty is owing, will make the other chargeable with manslaughter. This rule of law is always based upon the proposition that the duty neglected must be a legal duty, and not a mere moral obligation. It must be a duty imposed by law or contract, and the omission to perform the duty must be the immediate and direct cause of death.... (citations omitted).

We agree that before defendants can be found guilty of either reckless homicide or manslaughter, there must exist a legal duty owed by the defendants to the victim. A finding of legal duty is a critical element of the crime charged. As stated in KRS 501.030 and demonstrated by case law, the failure to perform a duty imposed by law may create criminal liability. Clearly, in the case of reckless homicide or manslaughter, the duty must be found outside the definition of the crime itself. The duty of care imposed may be found in the common law or in another statute. In this case, that duty statutorily is defined at KRS 209.020(6) as follows:

> "Caretaker" means an individual or institution who has the responsibility for the care of the adult as a result of family relationship, or who has assumed the responsibility for the care of the adult person voluntarily, or by contract, or agreement....

The trial court's instructions required the jury to be convinced beyond a reasonable doubt that Russell West was under a duty to provide Lillian with appropriate care and that he had breached that duty of care before liability could be imposed. The Commonwealth presented substantial evidence from which the jury could have concluded that Russell had assumed the duty of care and that Russell was acting in the capacity of "caretaker" as that term is defined by [Kentucky law]. Accordingly, the trial court did not err by instructing the jury with respect to reckless homicide and complicity to reckless homicide.

In *Jones v. United States*, the court stated as follows:

> There are at least four situations in which the failure to act may constitute breach of a legal duty. One can be held criminally liable: first, where a statute imposes a duty to care for another; second, where one stands in a certain status relationship to another; third, where one has assumed a contractual duty to care for another; and fourth, where one has voluntarily assumed the care of another and so secluded the helpless person as to prevent others from rendering aid.

Russell met the last of the *Jones* tests particularly aptly in voluntarily accepting responsibility for Lillian's care *and thereafter isolating her* from contacts that might have resulted in her aid or assistance. Additionally, Kentucky's Protection of Adults statutes impose a duty on adult caretakers to avoid the abuse, neglect, and exploitation of their charges. Contrary to the appellants' suggestions, we find that Russell's duty of care is well-grounded in the law.

For the foregoing reasons, we affirm the judgments of the Montgomery Circuit Court.

## Notes and Questions

1. The Court pointed out in *West* that defendant Russell had a legal duty to act because he voluntarily assumed the care of his sister. Would the result have been different if Russell had not voluntarily assumed her care? Explain. Note that—citing from *Jones v. U.S.*—the Court asserts that legal duties may also arise "where one stands in a certain status relationship to another." Was defendant's family relationship with the victim sufficient in and of itself to create a legal duty to aid? Why or why not? What kinds of relationships should count as the sort of "status relationships" that give rise to legal duties to aid?

2. Courts agree that spouses owe a legal duty to aid each other. This includes the duty to summon medical aid when not doing so may cause harm to the spouse. *See, e.g., State v. Mally,* 366 P.2d 868 (1961). Should this duty also extend to unmarried couples who live together or spend considerable amounts of time together? In *People v. Beardsley,* 150 Mich. 206 (1907), the Michigan Supreme Court held that a man did not owe a legal duty to a woman with whom he spent two nights together. The precedential value of *Beardsley* with regard to this issue is questionable. More recently, in *State v. ex rel. Kuntz,* 298 Mont. 146 (2000), the Supreme Court of Montana held that a legal duty to act may also be imposed on unmarried couples that live together. In doing so, the Court stated that:

> [The defendant and the victim], having lived together for approximately six years, owed each other the same "personal relationship" duty as found between spouses under our holding in *Mally*. This duty, identified as one of "mutual reliance" by LaFave and Scott, would include circumstances involving "two people, though not closely related, [who] live together under one roof." LaFave & Scott, §3.3(a)(1), at 285–286. To hold otherwise would result in an untenable rule that would not, under the factual circumstances found in *Mally*, impose a legal duty to summon medial aid on persons in a relationship involving cohabitation. *State v. ex rel. Kuntz,* 298 Mont. 146.

3. There is no general legal duty to aid in the vast majority of American jurisdictions. The facts and holding of *Pope v. State,* 396 A.2d 1054 (1979), are illustrative. The defendant took into her house a mother and her three month old child for fear that they would spend the night "out on the street." Defendant subsequently witnessed the mother severely beating the child. The child died as a result of injuries sustained during the beating. Defendant was convicted of felony child abuse for failing to prevent the death of the child. The conviction was reversed on appeal. The Maryland Court of Appeals agreed that the conviction could not stand. It reasoned that the defendant did not have a special legal duty to aid the child and there is no general legal duty to help strangers. The Court explained:

> Under the present state of our law, a person has no legal obligation to care for or look after the welfare of a stranger, adult or child. "Generally one has no legal duty to aid another person in peril, even when that aid can be rendered without

> danger or inconvenience to himself.... A moral duty to take affirmative action is not enough to impose a legal duty to do so." W. LaFave & A. Scott, Criminal Law 183 (1972).
>
> The legal position is that "the need of one and the opportunity of another to be of assistance are not alone sufficient to give rise to a legal duty to take positive action." R. Perkins, Criminal Law. Ordinarily, a person may stand by with impunity and watch another being murdered, raped, robbed, assaulted or otherwise unlawfully harmed. "He need not shout a warning to a blind man headed for a precipice or to an absentminded one walking into a gunpowder room with a lighted candle in hand. He need not pull a neighbor's baby out of a pool of water or rescue an unconscious person stretched across the railroad tracks, though the baby is drowning, or the whistle of an approaching train is heard in the distance." LaFave & Scott at 183 ...
>
> In the face of this status of the law we cannot reasonably conclude that the Legislature, in bringing a person responsible for the supervision of a child within the ambit of the child abuse law, intended that such responsibility attach [in situations like this one]. Were it otherwise, the consequences would go far beyond the legislative intent. For example, a person taking a lost child into his home to attempt to find its parents could be said to be responsible for that child's supervision. Or a person who allows his neighbor's children to play in his yard, keeping a watchful eye on their activities to prevent them from falling into harm, could be held responsible for the children's supervision. Or a person performing functions of a maternal nature from concern for the welfare, comfort or health of a child, or protecting it from danger because of a sense or moral obligation, may come within the reach of the act. In none of these situations would there be an intent to grant or assume the responsibility contemplated by the child abuse statute, and it would be incongruous indeed to subject such persons to possible criminal prosecution. *Pope*, 396 A.2d 1054.

Do you agree with the Court's conclusion in this case? Why or why not? Why was there a legal duty to act in the leading case (*West v. Commonwealth*) but no legal duty to act in *State v. Pope*? What additional facts do you believe would be sufficient to create a legal duty to act *State v. Pope*?

4. Why do you think that in most American jurisdictions a person may "stand by with impunity and watch another being murdered, raped, robbed, assaulted or otherwise unlawfully harmed"? Do you think such omissions should be punished? Why or why not? Assuming that they should be punished, how much should they be punished? A handful of states impose liability for failures to rescue when the aid can be provided without unreasonably jeopardizing the actor's wellbeing. The punishment imposed in such statutes is, however, relatively mild. The Vermont law criminalizing failures to rescue as a misdemeanor is representative:

> A person who knows that another is exposed to grave physical harm shall, to the extent that the same can be rendered *without danger or peril to himself* or without interference with important duties owed to others, give reasonable assistance to the exposed person unless that assistance or care is being provided by others. 12 V.S.A. § 519(a)

5. A legal duty to act may also arise when the defendant engages in conduct that places the victim in danger and subsequently fails to do anything to prevent the harm from ma-

terializing. In *State v. ex rel. Kuntz, supra*, the principle was explained in the following manner:

> Undoubtedly, when a person places another in a position of danger, and then fails to safeguard or rescue that person, and the person subsequently dies as a result of this omission, such an omission may be sufficient to support criminal liability. *See* LaFave & Scott, § 3.3(a)(5), at 288; *State v. Morgan* (imposing criminal liability for supplying cocaine leading to victim's overdose); *United States v. Hatatley* (10th Cir.1997), 130 F.3d 1399,1406 (imposing criminal liability for leaving victim badly beaten and shirtless in a freezing, remote desert). This duty may include peril resulting from a defendant's criminal negligence, as alleged here. *State v. ex rel. Kuntz*, 298 Mont. 146.

Should this principle be applied when the act that creates the peril is not culpable (i.e., innocent)? Suppose, for example, that a driver accidentally (non-negligently) crashes into a cyclist. The driver refuses to stop and aid the cyclist even though the cyclist suffered serious injuries as a result of the accident. The cyclist died as a consequence of the driver's failure to summon help. Assuming that the cyclist would have survived had the driver summoned medical aid, should the driver be held liable for homicide? Why or why not? Assuming that the driver should be held liable for homicide, should he be held liable for negligent or intentional homicide? Explain.

6. Sometimes it is difficult to tell whether a given course of conduct is best described as an act or as an omission. This is especially the case in the medical context, where it is hotly debated whether discontinuing life support is active or omissive conduct. On the one hand, termination of life support is usually accomplished by engaging in a willed bodily movement (flipping a switch, for example). This sounds in the language of action. On the other hand, doctors who terminate life support treatment are failing to provide further treatment. This sounds in the language of an omission. The matter is of considerable practical import, given that in most states patients do not have a right to ask their doctors to actively kill them (active euthanasia), whereas they have a constitutional right to ask their doctors to abstain from providing them with further treatment (passive euthanasia). *See Cruzan v. Director*, 497 U.S. 261 (1990), *Washington v. Glucksberg*, 521 U.S. 702 (1997).

American courts describe discontinuing life support as an omission, probably because this allows them to conclude that a patient has a right to ask a doctor to terminate life-saving treatment. In other words, it gives patients a right to so-called "passive euthanasia." In *Barber v. Superior Court*, for example, the court held that:

> [T]he cessation of "heroic" life support measures is not an affirmative act but rather a withdrawal or omission of further treatment. Even though these life support devices are, to a degree, "self-propelled," each pulsation of the respirator or each drop of fluid introduced into the patient's body by intravenous feeding devices is comparable to a manually administered injection or item of medication. Hence "disconnecting" of the mechanical devices is comparable to withholding the manually administered injection or medication. Further, we view the use of an intravenous administration of nourishment and fluid, under the circumstances, as being the same as the use of the respirator or other form of life support equipment ...
>
> In the final analysis, since we view petitioners' conduct as that of omission rather than affirmative action, the resolution of this case turns on whether [the doctors] had a duty to continue to provide life sustaining treatment. *Id.*

The *Barber* court then concluded that doctors do not have a legal duty to continue life saving treatment either when doing so would be ineffective or when the patient or her legally appointed surrogate refuses continuation of such treatment. Do you agree that discontinuing life support is best described as an omission or as an action? Suppose that a stranger enters a patient's room and flips the switch that powers the ventilator. The patient dies. Did the stranger kill the patient or did he let him die? That is, did the stranger's flipping of the switch amount to an act or an omission? If the stranger's flipping of the switch in this case amounts to an act, why is it that when a doctor performs exactly the same conduct courts call it an omission? For a discussion of these issues *See* Luis E. Chiesa, *Actmissions,* 116 W. Va. L. Rev. 583.

7. Sometimes a special duty to protect a person entails doing what is reasonably possible to prevent that person from being harmed by third parties. Parents, for example, have a duty to protect their small children from the harmful acts of third parties. This principle has been invoked to impose responsibility on a parent who witnesses the physical or sexual abuse of their child and fails to do anything to prevent it. *See, e.g., State v. Williquette,* 385 N.W.2d 145 (1986).

8. Police officers clearly have a duty to prevent crime. A breach of this duty will often result in disciplinary measures being taken against the police officer. In extreme cases, the breach of the duty may also give rise to criminal liability for dereliction of duty. But may the police officer also be held liable as an accomplice to the consummated crime for a failure to prevent it? Suppose, for example, that a police officer witnesses a course of conduct that culminates with the murder of a person. Assuming that the police officer could have prevented the murder had she decided to do so, should the police officer be held liable not only for an offense of dereliction of duty, but also for complicity to the murder? This is an important but undertheorized question. In a recent case, the Puerto Rican Supreme Court held that a police officer may be held liable as an accomplice to murder if she fails to take steps to prevent the killing. *See Pueblo v. Sustache,* 2009 TSPR 119. While it is intuitively plausible to hold a police officer liable as an accomplice for failing to prevent a murder committed by another, matters get more complicated when police officers fail to prevent less serious offenses. Should a police officer's failure to prevent a beating generate liability as an accomplice to battery? What about a police officer who fails to prevent a drug sale? Does such an omission generate accomplice liability for the drug sale? Explain.

9. The examples discussed thus far present cases in which an actor's omission is the basis for holding the actor liable for a crime as if he had committed it by engaging in an affirmative act. In *West,* for example, the defendant's failure to take care of his sister gave rise to liability for homicide and was punished in the same way as a homicide accomplished by engaging in an action would have been punished. Similarly, the parent who contributes to the death of her child by letting the child drown will be punished for homicide in much the same manner as if she had actively drowned the child. What ultimately justifies punishment in these cases is thus not the omission (failure to take care of a sister or child) itself, but rather the harm that is brought about as a result of the omission (death of the sister or child). Scholars sometimes call such cases instances of "commission by omission," for they involve actors who "commit" a crime of harmful consequences by way of an "omission." Punishing cases of commission by omission is viewed as problematic for at least two reasons. First, in many cases it is unclear whether a special legal duty to act exists. Do grandparents have a special legal duty to rescue their grandchildren? Do aunts and uncles have a special duty to rescue their nieces and nephews? Reasonable minds will likely disagree regarding the answer to these questions, especially when finding that there

is a special duty may trigger omission liability for serious crimes such as homicide. Second, even when the existence of the special duty is not an issue, it is often unclear whether the actor's omission contributed to bringing about the proscribed harm in a way that justifies imposing liability as if the harm had been caused by way of an affirmative act. Does, for example, the police officer's failure to prevent a battery contribute to bringing about the victim's harm (physical injury) in a manner that justifies punishing the police officer as if he had physically assaulted the victim?

10. In some instances, the law punishes omissions regardless of whether they cause harm or not. The offense of failing to file a tax return is representative. This offense is consummated when the actor fails to perform the required act (filing the tax return) irrespective of whether harm ensues as a consequence of the omission. Punishing these kinds of omissions is not particularly problematic, for the legal duty that gives rise to liability is expressly prescribed in the law that punishes the failure to act. The law that requires drivers to stop at a traffic light, for example, expressly prescribes that a failure to stop amounts to an offense. Furthermore, these kinds of omissions do not generate causation problems, for they give rise to liability whether or not harm results as a consequence of the failure to act.

## § 6.03 Conduct: Possessions

### Florida v. Adkins

Supreme Court of Florida, 2012
96 So.3d 412

CANADY, J.

In this case we consider the constitutionality of the provisions of chapter 893, Florida Statutes (2011), the Florida Comprehensive Drug Abuse Prevention and Control Act, that provide that knowledge of the illicit nature of a controlled substance is not an element of any offenses under the chapter but that the lack of such knowledge is an affirmative defense ...

For the reasons explained below, we conclude that the circuit court erred in determining the statute to be unconstitutional. Accordingly, we reverse the circuit court's order granting the motions to dismiss.

#### I. Background

Section 893.13, part of the Florida Comprehensive Drug Abuse Prevention and Control Act, provides in part that except as otherwise authorized "it is unlawful for any person to sell, manufacture, or deliver, or possess with intent to sell, manufacture, or deliver, a controlled substance" or "to be in actual or constructive possession of a controlled substance." ...

Section 893.13 itself does not specify what mental state a defendant must possess in order to be convicted for selling, manufacturing, delivering, or possessing a controlled substance. In *Chicone v. State*, this Court ... determined that "guilty knowledge" was one of the elements of the crime of possession of a controlled substance and that the State was required to prove that Chicone knew he possessed the substance and knew of the illicit nature of the substance in his possession.

More recently, in *Scott v. State*, this Court clarified that the "guilty knowledge" element of the crime of possession of a controlled substance contains two aspects: knowledge of the presence of the substance and knowledge of the illicit nature of the substance.

In response to this Court's decisions, the Legislature enacted a statute now codified in section 893.101, Florida Statutes (2011).Section 893.101 provides in full:

1) The Legislature finds that the cases of *Scott v. State* and *Chicone v. State*, holding that the state must prove that the defendant knew of the illicit nature of a controlled substance found in his or her actual or constructive possession, were contrary to legislative intent.
2) The Legislature finds that *knowledge of the illicit nature of a controlled substance is not an element* of any offense under this chapter. *Lack of knowledge of the illicit nature of a controlled substance is an affirmative defense* to the offenses of this chapter.

The statute thus expressly eliminates knowledge of the illicit nature of the controlled substance as an element of controlled substance offenses and expressly creates an affirmative defense of lack of knowledge of the illicit nature of the substance. The statute does not eliminate the element of knowledge of the presence of the substance, which we acknowledged in *Chicone* and *Scott*.

Since the enactment of section 893.101, each of the district courts of appeal has ruled that the statute does not violate the requirements of due process.

The United States District Court for the Middle District of Florida recently concluded, however, that section 893.13 is unconstitutional because it does not require sufficient mens rea on the part of the defendant to sustain a conviction.

Citing *Shelton* as persuasive — not binding — authority, the circuit court in this case concluded that section 893.13 is facially unconstitutional because it violates the Due Process Clauses of article I, section 9 of the Florida Constitution and the Fourteenth Amendment to the United States Constitution. The circuit court reasoned that the Legislature did not have authority to dispense with a mens rea element for a serious felony crime.

The State now appeals the circuit court's decision in this Court. The State asserts that section 893.13, as modified by section 893.101, is facially constitutional and that the circuit court therefore erred in granting the motions to dismiss.

### II. Analysis

... Because there is no legally recognized use for controlled substances outside the circumstances identified by the statute, prohibiting the sale, manufacture, delivery, or possession of those substances without requiring proof of knowledge of the illicit nature of the substances does not criminalize innocuous conduct or "impinge[ ] on the exercise of some constitutionally protected freedom." Because the statutory provisions at issue here do not have the potential to curtail constitutionally protected speech, they are materially distinguishable from statutes that implicate the possession of materials protected by the First Amendment ... There is no constitutional right to possess contraband. "[A]ny interest in possessing contraband cannot be deemed 'legitimate.'"

Nor is there a protected right to be ignorant of the nature of the property in one's possession.... Just as "common sense and experience" dictate that a person in possession of Treasury checks addressed to another person should be "aware of the high probability that the checks were stolen," a person in possession of a controlled substance should be aware of the nature of the substance as an illegal drug. Because controlled substances are valuable, common sense indicates that they are generally handled with care. As a result, possession without awareness of the illicit nature of the substance is highly unusual.

Any concern that entirely innocent conduct will be punished with a criminal sanction under chapter 893 is obviated by the statutory provision that allows a defendant to raise the affirmative defense of an absence of knowledge of the illicit nature of the controlled substance. In the unusual circumstance where an individual has actual or constructive possession of a controlled substance but has no knowledge that the substance is illicit, the defendant may present such a defense to the jury.

Because we conclude that the Legislature did not exceed its constitutional authority in redefining section 893.13 to not require proof that the defendant knew of the illicit nature of the controlled substance, we likewise conclude that the Legislature did not violate due process by defining lack of such knowledge as an affirmative defense to the offenses set out in chapter 893....

Based on the foregoing, we conclude that the circuit court erred in granting the motions to dismiss and we reverse the circuit court's order.

**PERRY, J., dissenting.**

I respectfully dissent. I cannot overstate my opposition to the majority's opinion. In my view, it shatters bedrock constitutional principles and builds on a foundation of flawed "common sense."

### Innocent Possession

The majority pronounces that "common sense and experience" dictate that "a person in possession of a controlled substance should be aware of the nature of the substance as an illegal drug" and further that, "[b]ecause controlled substances are valuable, common sense indicates that they are generally handled with care. As a result, possession without awareness of the illicit nature of the substance is highly unusual."

But common sense to me dictates that the potential for innocent possession is not so "highly unusual" as the majority makes it out to be.

> [T]he simple acts of possession and delivery are part of daily life. Each of us engages in actual possession of all that we have on our person and in our hands, and in constructive possession of all that we own, wherever it may be located. Each of us engages in delivery when we hand a colleague a pen, a friend a cup of coffee, a stranger the parcel she just dropped. *State v. Washington.*

"[C]arrying luggage on and off of public transportation; carrying bags in and out of stores and buildings; carrying book bags and purses in schools and places of business and work; transporting boxes via commercial transportation—the list extends *ad infinitum.*" *Shelton v. Sec'y, Dep't of Corr.*, 802 F.Supp.2d 1289, 1305 (M.D.Fla.2011).

Given this reality, "[i]t requires little imagination to visualize a situation in which a third party hands [a] controlled substance to an unknowing individual who then can be charged with and subsequently convicted ... without ever being aware of the nature of the substance he was given."

For example, [c]onsider the student in whose book bag a classmate hastily stashes his drugs to avoid imminent detection. The bag is then given to another for safekeeping. Caught in the act, the hapless victim is guilty based upon the only two elements of the statute: delivery (actual, constructive, or attempted) and the illicit nature of the substance. The victim would be faced with the Hobson's choice of pleading guilty or going to trial where he is presumed guilty because he is in fact guilty of the two elements. He must then prove his innocence for lack of knowledge against the permissive presumption the statute imposes that he does in fact have guilty knowledge. Such an outcome is not countenanced under applicable constitutional proscriptions.

The trial court order presently under review provides even more examples of innocent possession: a letter carrier who delivers a package containing unprescribed Adderall; a roommate who is unaware that the person who shares his apartment has hidden illegal drugs in the common areas of the home; a mother who carries a prescription pill bottle in her purse, unaware that the pills have been substituted for illegally obtained drugs by her teenage daughter, who placed them in the bottle to avoid detection. *State v. Adkins.*

As the examples illustrate, even people who are normally diligent in inspecting and organizing their possessions may find themselves unexpectedly in violation of this law, and without the notice necessary to defend their rights. The illegal drugs subject to the statute include tablets which can also be and are commonly and legally prescribed. A medicine which is legally available, can be difficult for innocent parties to recognize as illegal, even if they think they know the contents. For example, the mother of the teenage daughter carries the pill bottle, taking it at face value as a bottle for the pills it ought to contain, even during the traffic stop at which she consents to [a] search of her belongings, confident in her own innocence. These examples represent incidents of innocence which should be protected by the requirement of [a] *mens rea* element, particularly given the serious penalties for the crime of drug possession required under Florida law.

Other examples of innocent possession spring easily and immediately to mind: a driver who rents a car in which a past passenger accidentally dropped a baggie of marijuana under the seat; a traveler who mistakenly retrieves from a luggage carousel a bag identical to her own containing Oxycodone; a helpful college student who drives a carload of a friend's possessions to the friend's new apartment, unaware that a stash of heroin is tucked within those possessions; an ex-wife who is framed by an ex-husband who planted cocaine in her home in an effort to get the upper hand in a bitter custody dispute. The list is endless.

The majority nevertheless states that there is not "a protected right to be ignorant of the nature of the property in one's possession," elaborating that "[c]ommon' sense tells us that those who traffic in heroin will inevitably become aware that the product they deal in is smuggled, *unless they practice a studied ignorance to which they are not entitled.*" Majority op. at 421 (quoting *Turner v. United States,* 396 U.S. 398, 417, 90 S.Ct. 642, 24 L.Ed.2d 610 (1970)). But the above examples, and surely countless others, do not involve such a "studied ignorance." Rather, they involve genuinely innocent citizens who will be snared in the overly broad net of section 893.13.

And therein lies the point:

Section 893.13 does not punish the drug dealer who possesses or delivers controlled substances. It punishes *anyone* who possesses or delivers controlled substances—however inadvertently, however accidentally, however unintentionally.... What distinguishes innocent possession and innocent delivery from guilty possession and guilty delivery is not merely what we possess, not merely what we deliver, *but what we intend.* As to that—as to the state of mind that distinguishes non-culpable from culpable possession or delivery—§ 893.13 refuses to make a distinction. The speckled flock and the clean are, for its purposes, all one.

... [I]f the Florida legislature can by edict and without constitutional restriction eliminate the element of *mens rea* from a drug statute with penalties of this magnitude, it is hard to imagine what other statutes it could not similarly affect....

The majority opinion sets alarming precedent, both in the context of section 893.13 and beyond. It makes neither legal nor common sense to me, offends all notions of due process, and threatens core principles of the presumption of innocence and burden of proof. I would find section 893.13 facially unconstitutional and affirm the trial court order under review.

## *Notes and Questions*

1. Many—if not most—prison inmates are serving time for possession offenses. Although states criminalize possession of all sorts of items, drug and weapon possession offenses are the most common possession crimes.

2. As the dissent in *Adkins* points out, a thorny problem raised by possession offenses is the possibility of so-called "innocent possession." The "innocent possession" problem arises when a person is in actual or constructive possession of a prohibited item but lacks awareness that she is in possession of the item. As the examples discussed in the dissent illustrate, innocent possession may happen quite often. A similar problem seldom arises in the context of actions, for people who perform proscribed acts are seldom "innocent" in the sense that they lack awareness of what they are doing. Barring an uncommon mental disease or defect, the person who stabs another has knowledge of what she is doing. This explains the need for ascertaining knowledge before punishing possession. Without a knowledge requirement, too many innocent possessions will be unjustly punished. Nevertheless, as *Adkins* demonstrates, there is a recent trend towards eliminating the knowledge requirement. While the Florida statute at issue in *Adkins* did not entirely eliminate the knowledge requirement, it shifted the burden of proving (absence of) knowledge to the defense. The consequence is that the prosecution may prove its case without having to demonstrate that the defendant was aware that she was in possession of the prohibited item. It is then up to the defendant to come forward with evidence of absence of knowledge and, ultimately, to demonstrate that she was not aware that she was in possession of the item. Other states have gone as far as eliminating the knowledge requirement altogether. Do you think that entirely doing away with the knowledge requirement in possession offenses is constitutional? Explain.

3. Is possession an act or an omission? On the one hand, a person may possess something because she acquired control over it. The conduct of "acquiring control over" an object sounds like an act. After all, typical ways of acquiring control over an item include "grabbing" or "taking" the object. However, a person may possess something if she fails to terminate control over an item. Assume, for example, that you give a ride to your best friend. The friend enters your vehicle carrying a gun. If you fail to remove the gun (or your friend) from your vehicle, you are now in possession of the gun. In this case, the possession of the item seems to be the product of an omission.

4. Perhaps possession is a state of affairs that is neither act nor omission. While you read this note you are surely in possession of many items (shoes, eyeglasses, socks, wallet, shirt, etc.). It would seem odd to conclude that the possession of these items amounts to an act. It would seem equally odd to conclude that the possession of the items is the product of your failure to terminate control over the objects by, for example, removing your shoes or your shirt. *See, generally*, Douglas Husak, *Rethinking the Act Requirement*, 28 Cardozo Law Review 2437 (2007).

5. While it makes sense to describe possessions as states of being that are neither acts nor omissions, doing so raises puzzling questions. Is it legitimate to punish states of affairs that do not amount to acts or omissions? If possession is not conduct, what is it about possession that warrants the imposition of criminal liability?

6. A way of explaining the criminalization of possession offenses is that the possession of the object gives rise to an inference that the item was either used in the past or will

be used in the future. Thus conceived, the offenses of unlawful possession of weapons or drugs are criminalized not because the possession of the objects is wrong in itself, but rather because possession of the items gives rise to an inference that either they were unlawfully used in the past or will be unlawfully used in the future.

## § 6.04 Conduct: Model Penal Code

### § 2.01. Requirement of Voluntary Act; Omission as Basis of Liability; Possession as an Act.

(1) A person is not guilty of an offense unless his liability is based on conduct that includes a voluntary act or the omission to perform an act of which he is physically capable.

(2) The following are not voluntary acts within the meaning of this Section:

(a) a reflex or convulsion;

(b) a bodily movement during unconsciousness or sleep;

(c) conduct during hypnosis or resulting from hypnotic suggestion;

(d) a bodily movement that otherwise is not a product of the effort or determination of the actor, either conscious or habitual.

(3) Liability for the commission of an offense may not be based on an omission unaccompanied by action unless:

(a) the omission is expressly made sufficient by the law defining the offense; or

(b) a duty to perform the omitted act is otherwise imposed by law.

(4) Possession is an act, within the meaning of this Section, if the possessor knowingly procured or received the thing possessed or was aware of his control thereof for a sufficient period to have been able to terminate his possession.

### *Notes and Questions*

1. The voluntary act requirement is codified in Subsection 1 of the excerpted Model Penal Code provision. For a discussion of the meaning and scope of this subsection, see *State v. Newman* (excerpted in § 6.01).

2. Note that Subsection 2(d) clarifies that any act that is not the product of the effort or determination of the actor is involuntary and, therefore, not punishable. Nevertheless, it also posits that habitual bodily movements are voluntary within the meaning of the Section. Does this provide a suitable answer to whether the conduct of drivers who experience the "unconscious driving phenomenon" satisfies the voluntary act requirement? Explain.

3. Subsection 3 distinguishes between the kinds of omissions that generate liability regardless of whether harm is caused as a result of the failure to act (e.g., failure to file a tax return) (Subsection 3[a]) and those that only generate "commission by omission" liability if harm results as a consequence of a breach of a legal duty to act (parent who fails to rescue child is liable for death of the child) (Subsection 3[b]). Note that the Code does not list the special duties to act that if breached will generate commission by omission li-

ability. The explanatory note merely lists parental duties as one such duty, but it remains silent with regard to other duties. Given that there is no enumeration of special legal duties that trigger omission liability for harmful results, who will decide which legal duties give rise to such liability? Does this raise principle of legality problems? Explain.

4. The Code drafters expressly state in Subsection 4 that possession is an act within the meaning of the Section. Conceptually speaking, this is problematic, for—as was discussed in the previous section (notes 3 & 4)—it is unclear whether possession is truly an act. Regardless, note that the Code treats possession as an act only when the possessor "knowingly procured or received the thing possessed" or "was aware of his control thereof for a sufficient period to have been able to terminate his possession." The Code's provision highlights the connection between knowledge and culpable possession and thus precludes punishment of most innocent possessions.

## § 6.05 Conduct: Comparative Perspectives

### Jesús María Silva Sánchez, *Criminal Omissions: Some Relevant Distinctions*

11 New Crim. L. Rev. 452 (2008)

... Courts and criminal theorists have always accepted that there are some cases of omission that should be punished as if the actor had caused the result by active commission (e.g., the classic case of a mother who allows her newborn baby to die by not breast-feeding the child). [European scholars call such cases instances of "commission by omission."] However, the prevailing view stems from the notion that there are omissions to avert harm that deserve the same punishment as instances of active causation of the result, even if the omissive conduct is not structurally identical to an instance of active conduct. Before reaching that conclusion, however, one should first ask whether all cases of omission that result in harm as a consequence of a breach of a special duty to act should be punished just as if the harm had been brought about by an act. It is also worth asking whether these breaches of special duties to act that result in harm should be punished more severely than cases of simple omission consisting of a breach of a general duty to act (e.g., the general omission of the duty to rescue punishable pursuant to Bad Samaritan legislation)....

The [conventional] approach to cases of commission by omission ... conceives of crimes of [commission by omission] as breaches of a [special] duty to act. The existence of a special ... duty to act distinguishes these types of omissions from the traditional crimes of omission whose essence lies in the breach of a *general* duty to act....

[This] bipartite system of punishable omissions that only distinguishes between cases of simple omissions [based on a breach of a general duty to act] and instances of commission by omission [grounded on a breach of a special duty to act] is not the most adequate. As a matter of fact, those that defend this approach do not deny that there are omissions that, although not [as blameworthy as cases of] active commission, are more serious than the typical omission involving the breach of a general duty to act (such as in the general duty to provide aid in an emergency). These types of omissions seem to be of intermediate gravity, for they are less serious than true cases of commission by omission and more serious than instances of simple omissions.

I believe that the best way to deal with the problem presented by these omissions of intermediate seriousness ... is by proposing the creation of an intermediate category of omissions that, being more serious than simple omissions, are not equivalent to cases of active commission. This intermediate category of omissions is not of sufficient seriousness to warrant charging the offender with the commission of a crime of harmful consequences as if he had caused the harm by way of affirmative conduct. In the past, I have called these types of omissions *qualified or aggravated omissions, omissions of intermediate seriousness*, or *crimes of omission of a [special] duty*. The need to identify this third category of omissions arises from a deeply felt, though undertheorized, intuition about the relative seriousness of different types of omissions. Specifically regulating this type of intermediate omission in criminal codes would halt any possible trend towards expanding liability in borderline cases of commission by omission. At the same time, it would lead to acknowledging the undeniable fact that there are omissions for which the punishment of crimes of omission of a general duty to rescue is insufficient, whereas punishing them as full-fledged instances of commission by omission is disproportionate and lacks theoretical basis. Criminalizing omissions of intermediate seriousness as a qualified type of simple omission would allow us to bridge the gap between instances of simple omissions and cases of commission by omission. In my opinion, this is an important and necessary step that must be taken if we are to approach the problem of criminal omissions in a coherent and fair manner.

Omissions of intermediate seriousness do not actively cause harm to a third party's autonomy, for the perpetrator does not have the same control over a potential source of danger as an actor in a case of active commission would have. Thus, these are ultimately cases that involve a breach of a [special] duty of solidarity by a person who is particularly obligated to act in light of this duty. This is the case, for example, of omissions to rescue a spouse who is in danger, of helping a family member who is in need of aid, or of a public officer's failure to help someone in need, *as long as these actors [have not created the risk that endangers the victim and that they do not have a duty to actively shield the person from sources of risk created by others]*. These situations are, on the one hand, different from those in which there is a real link between omission and active commission and, on the other, much more serious than those of a general omission of duty to rescue.

To summarize, I propose a tripartite classification of crimes of omission. On the one hand, there are crimes of omission that are identical to cases of active commission (for which we should reserve the term of commission by omission). These are based on the idea of ... responsibility for [the risks that we create]. On the other hand, there are instances of simple crimes of omission in which we punish a breach of a duty of minimum solidarity toward our fellow citizens. Somewhere between these two categories lies a third type of aggravated crimes of omission that are based on liability for a breach of a special duty (derived from specific ... relationships between people). However, it should be noted that this is not a rigid classificatory scheme in the mold of the classic bipartite approach to omissions. Rather, my threefold classification is based on the idea that differences between such omissions are a matter of degree. Thus, the difference between crimes of omission that imply a breach of a [general duty to act] (simple omissions) and those that imply a breach of duty of [special duty to act] (omissions of intermediate seriousness) lies in the intensity of the institutional tie that binds offender and victim. The difference between the class of omissions identical to cases of active commission and the class of omissions of intermediate seriousness is one of degree as well. In the latter cases the perpetrator does not have the same control over the source of danger as an actor in a case of active commission would have. However, he does stand in a certain special relationship to either the source of danger or the endangered person. This relationship is also a matter of degree, for the seriousness of the omission is dependent on whether the conduct is seen as more or less similar to cases in which the actor has control over the source of the danger.

### *Notes and Questions*

1. Professor Silva Sánchez argues that failures to rescue that amount to breaches of special duties to act should not necessarily be punished as severely as if the actor had caused the result by engaging in an affirmative act. The example he discusses is that of a person who fails to rescue her spouse. Assuming that the spouse dies, should the actor's failure to rescue her spouse generate liability for homicide in much the same way as if the actor had actively killed her spouse? Silva Sánchez argues that—in light of the close relationship between the actor and the victim—the actor deserves more punishment than someone who fails to rescue a stranger. Nevertheless, he suggests that the actor deserves less punishment than if he had actively killed her spouse. The omission to rescue the spouse would thus be of "intermediate gravity," for it is more blameworthy than the failure to help a stranger, but less worthy of condemnation than actively killing the spouse. Do you agree? Why or why not?

2. The solution suggested by Silva Sánchez is contrary to the standard American approach to such omissions. As the cases and materials discussed in § 6.02 and § 6.04 illustrate, breaches of special duties to rescue generate liability for the harm as if the actor had caused it by engaging in an affirmative act. Thus, in America, an actor's failure to rescue her spouse would generate liability for homicide if the spouse dies. Do you prefer the American approach to such omissions or the approach defended by Professor Silva Sánchez? Explain.

## § 6.06 Conduct: Scholarly Debates

### Joshua Dressler, *Some Thoughts (Mostly Negative) about Bad Samaritan Laws*

40 Santa Clara L. Rev. 971 (2000)

#### I. "Soulless Individuals" in Our Midst?

In 1997, seventeen-year-old Jeremy Strohmeyer entered a Las Vegas casino restroom holding the hand of seven-year-old Sherrice Iverson. He apparently raped and murdered the little girl in a restroom stall. While these horrendous crimes were being committed, Strohmeyer's high school buddy, David Cash, entered the restroom and discovered the crimes in progress. Cash reportedly entered the restroom a few minutes after Strohmeyer went in, peered over the wall of a bathroom stall, and observed his friend with his hand over Sherrice Iverson's mouth, muffling her cries for help. Cash left the restroom but failed to report the ongoing incident to a security guard or to the police. Cash's inaction was awful enough, but then he spoke to reporters and gave listeners a chance to look into his mind, heart, and soul:

> It's a very tragic event, okay? But the simple fact remains I do not know this little girl. I do not know starving children in Panama. I do not know people that

> die of disease in Egypt. The only person I knew in this event was Jeremy Strohmeyer, and I know as his best friend that he had potential.... I'm sad that I lost a best friend.... I'm not going to lose sleep over somebody else's problem.

Even read today, Cash's cold, remorseless words are shocking and infuriating. We are understandably affronted by his self-centeredness, and his narrow and skewed view of his moral duties to his "fellow man." Cash told a reporter that he did not report his friend's actions because, in a touching display of compassion, he "didn't want to be the person who takes away his [Strohmeyer's] last day, his last night of freedom." Cash, it seems, believes he does not owe anything to anybody except (perhaps) loyalty to his high school buddy who "only" committed crimes upon a young "stranger."...

What is to be done with persons like David Cash? He violated no Nevada criminal law when he purportedly left Sherrice Iverson in the clutches of Strohmeyer. But if some legislators get their way, future David Cashes will not get away so easily. Legislators of all political stripes may find it hard to resist the opportunity to enact Bad Samaritan ("BS") criminal laws. After all, who would possibly want to defend the "soulless" David Cashes... of this world?

I, too, have no intention of defending the indefensible. As a Jew, I have grown up in a culture that values community and believes that human relationships (and relationships with God) involve stringent obligations to others. It is a culture that does not glorify self-centered rights. But it is precisely because the case for punishing people like Cash seems so obvious and so comforting to our psyche—it allows us to express our moral revulsion and, perhaps less charitably, feel morally superior—that we should hesitate long and hard before enacting BS legislation. Although such laws are morally defensible, there are also powerful reasons for rejecting them....

### III. Why We Don't (Usually) Punish "Soulless Individuals"

#### B. Bad Samaritan Laws

##### 1. Justifying Bad Samaritan Laws

The best (and perhaps the only decent) argument for BS legislation is retributive in nature. There are two types of retributivists, both of whom could justify such laws. First, culpability-retributivists believe that punishment is deserved if a person behaves in a morally culpable manner. Imagine Blind Person ("BP") about to step off the curb and into the street just as a fast-moving truck with an unobservant driver approaches. Bystander, a foot away from BP, sees this occurring and can save BP from probable death or serious injury by the simple act of putting his arm out and pulling BP back from the precipice. Bystander does not help, however, because he hates disabled persons and wants BP to die.

In this situation, culpability-based retributivists can justify punishment. The decision by Bystander to let BP take what may be a fatal step into the road is a case of willed nonmotion. The decision not to act is as much a matter of free choice as would be a decision to shove BP into the road. Further, based on the facts stated, the reason for Bystander's decision is to see BP harmed. For culpability-retributivists, it does not matter whether actual harm befalls BP; it is enough that Bystander wants it to happen....

##### 2. Refuting the Justifications for Bad Samaritan Laws

Although these retributive arguments support punishment of a Bad Samaritan, there are significant reasons... that should give responsible lawmakers considerable pause before endorsing general duty-to-aid legislation.

Criticisms of BS laws begin with legalist concerns with retributive overtones. First, why is the offense called a "Bad Samaritan" law? The name suggests, I think, that we punish the bystander for being a bad person, i.e., for his "selfishness, callousness, or whatever it was" that caused him not to come to the aid of a person in need. However, the criminal law should not be (and, ordinarily, is not) used that way: criminal law punishes individuals for their culpable acts (or, perhaps here, culpable non-acts), but not generally for bad character. As mortals, we lack the capacity to evaluate another's soul. It is wrongful conduct, and not an individual's status as a bad person or even an individual's bad thoughts, that justify criminal intervention. BS laws may violate this principle. At a minimum, there is a serious risk that juries will inadvertently punish people for being (or seeming to be) evil or "soulless," rather than for what occurred on a specific occasion. One need only consider David Cash and the public's intense feelings of disgust and anger toward him to appreciate why jurors might convict Bad Samaritans less on the basis of the "technicalities" of a statute, and more on the basis of character evaluation....

There is one final reason to question the wisdom of BS statutes. Not only are positive duties [to act] morally less powerful than negative ones [to abstain from causing harm], but they also restrict human liberty to a greater degree. A penal law that prohibits a person from doing X (e.g., unjustifiably killing another person) permits that individual to do anything other than X (assuming no other negative duty). In contrast, a law that requires a person to do Y (e.g., help a bystander) bars that person from doing anything other than Y. The edict that "no student may laugh aloud at a fellow student's silly answers to a professor's questions" only marginally restricts a student's autonomy—she can silently laugh at her colleague, sleep through the answer, or walk out of the room to protest the student's stupidity, just to name a few examples. However, a rule requiring a student to "provide reasonable assistance to a fellow student in jeopardy of offering a silly answer to a professor's question," not only is less precise, but also prevents students from doing anything other than help.

What is the significance of this point? It is that the United States is a country that highly values individual liberty:

> Each person is regarded as an autonomous being, responsible for his or her own conduct. One aim of the law is to maximize individual liberty, so as to allow each individual to pursue a conception of the good life with as few constraints as possible. Constraints there must be, of course, in modern society: but freedom of action should be curtailed only so far as is necessary to restrain individuals from causing injury or loss to others.

Few people, except the most ardent libertarians, accept the latter statement in full. The point, however, is that in a society that generally values personal autonomy, we need to be exceptionally cautious about enacting laws that compel us to benefit others, rather than passing laws that simply require us not to harm others. The issue here, after all, is whether criminal law (as distinguished from tort law and religious, educational, and family institutions) should try to compel Good Samaritanism. Traditionally, Anglo-American criminal law sets only minimalist goals. The penal law does not seek to punish every morally bad act that we commit (aren't we glad of that?), and it leaves to other institutions the effort "to purify thoughts and perfect character."

### IV. Closing Reflections

It is difficult to believe that a person who talks like David Cash should be left untouched by the criminal law. However, the criminal law cannot make people virtuous, and it should not be used to punish everyone who acts—much less, not acts—immorally.

It certainly should not be used to punish people for being less than they should be. It is worth remembering that the criminal law is not a cure for all of our problems.

## David Hyman, *Rescue Without Law: An Empirical Perspective on the Duty to Rescue*

84 Tex. L. Rev. 653 (2006)

... During the past decade, there have been an average of 1.6 documented cases of non-rescue each year in the entire United States. Every year, Americans perform at least 946 non-risky rescues and 243 risky rescues. Every year, at least sixty-five times as many Americans die while attempting to rescue someone else as die from a documented case of non-risky non-rescue. If a few isolated (and largely unverified and undocumented) cases of non-rescues have been deemed sufficient to justify legislative reform, one would think a total of approximately 1,200 documented cases of rescue every year should point rather decisively in the opposite direction. When it comes to the duty to rescue, leaving well enough alone is likely to be sufficient unto the day.

What of the impact of statutes reversing the no-duty rule? Although three states have had generalized duties to rescue in effect for a combined total of almost 80 years, there is no evidence that these statutes have affected the number of rescues or non-rescues. At least in the United States, there is also no evidence that these statutes are being employed in the sweeping manner feared by critics. Further research will be required to determine whether the enactment of these statutes has led to the creation of broader affirmative duties within these states.

What do we know about rescue and rescuers? Controlled for population, the frequency of civilian rescue declined over the first 40 years of the twentieth century and stabilized or increased over the next 60 years. Rescuers tend to be young males, particularly when strangers are rescued. Rescue is frequently dangerous: a sizeable percentage of rescuers are killed or injured.

Non-rescues are tragic, but it is important to have a sense of proportion about the magnitude of the problem. In a nation of 291 million people, of whom approximately 200,000 die every year in accidents, it is inevitable that there will be occasional instances of non-rescue, just as there are occasional instances of people being decapitated by elevators, drowning in a flood of molasses, killed on amusement park rides, and otherwise dying under freakish and extraordinary circumstances. Given the rarity of non-rescue and the high frequency of rescue, creating a statutory duty to rescue seems unlikely to have any material impact on the number of rescues and non-rescues.

It is certainly possible that the measures employed are insufficiently sensitive to identify non-rescues and capture the effects of statutory reversal of the no-duty rule, and are overly sensitive to instances of rescue, but that seems unlikely given the number of distinct data sources employed, the differing measures employed, and the consistency of the results. This particular dog may not have barked in the night simply because there wasn't a dog to do any barking.

The argument that the absence of a statutory duty to rescue teaches bad morals by example also appears distinctly implausible. The data indicates that Americans have figured out that it is better to rescue someone in need than to stand by and watch him die. It is unlikely that additional moral instruction, in the form of a statutory duty to rescue, will do anything to reach those few individuals who do not understand this basic insight....

Of course, leaving rescue to the independent discretion of potential rescuers results in a world that is short of perfection, but the right question is whether imposing a duty to rescue will improve on the status quo. Despite the automatic "yes" offered by proponents of the duty to rescue, the evidence presented in this Article suggests that the answer to this question is almost certainly "no."

To be sure, there is room for improvement in the status quo. A substantial number of rescuers are injured or killed every year, and they, or their estates, must largely bear the consequences themselves. It is somewhat surprising that law professors, who have lavished such concern on the subject of what Americans owe one another, have completely ignored the plight of ordinary Americans who voluntarily choose to rescue and suffer injury or death as a result. Professor Norval Morris focused attention on this issue almost 40 years ago, but his insight has been widely ignored:

> It is so easy to talk about the failure of others; of how Good Samaritanship seems to be a dying art among others. There is another parable, something about a mote and an eye, which seems to me to have some relevance. Perhaps we should first talk about ourselves, and our failure to provide even minimum conditions financially to protect those amongst us who are willing to act the Good Samaritan.

The results presented in this Article suggest that this problem is a serious one, deserving of immediate attention. This issue may lack the glamour of taking yet another run at reversing the no-duty rule, but it is a much more serious problem than the one that has preoccupied scholars who have written on the subject of the duty to rescue for the past two centuries.

Another issue that requires attention is harm reduction. Danger does appear to "invite rescue," as Judge Cardozo noted in passing more than 80 years ago. Too many of those who accept the invitation to rescue are seriously injured or killed because the rescue is too dangerous or because they are inadequately trained. Rescuers are usually "self-assured people who are certain they will emerge victorious." Self assurance is one thing; overconfidence is another—and overconfidence increases the death toll. A superior strategy, from a harm-reduction perspective, would be to encourage rescuers to appreciate that they should "want to be involved, but [not] want to get hurt." At a minimum, potential rescuers should understand that multiple fatalities (the original victim, plus those who bravely but foolishly attempt to assist) are the likely result of an attempted rescue by someone without sufficient training. Such outcomes may be viewed as the price of success for those who believe non-rescue is a serious problem, but the results presented in this Article suggest that the real problem is excessive enthusiasm for rescue, and not non-rescue. As such, better education of rescuers (and of potential victims, to avoid getting into such situations) is likely to prove a more fruitful strategy than reversing the no-duty rule.

Finally, most scholars who have written on the no-duty rule in the past two centuries appear to have believed that non-risky non-rescue was a widespread problem—and that imposing a duty to rescue would result in significant changes in behavior and social norms. The results presented in this Article indicate that neither assumption was accurate and that injury and death among rescuers is a much more serious and frequent problem than non-risky non-rescue. Future discussions of the merits of the duty to rescue might more profitably begin with the "facts on the ground," instead of moving immediately to theories of justice and obligation.

Of course, debates over the duty to rescue implicitly involve these broader issues and theories, which is why cases of non-rescue are prominently featured in torts textbooks and why legal scholars have been arguing about such cases for more than two centuries. Yet, when neither the initial suppositions nor the expectations for change of proponents seem justified, it is fair to ask them what they believe is actually at stake when the issue of the duty to rescue is under discussion. More broadly, the results presented in this Article suggest that the standard "instrumentalist" conception of legal scholarship—in which a legal scholar identifies a significant social problem, analyzes it, and then offers a policy prescription to be implemented by government officials that promises to cure it—is poorly suited to the problem of non-rescue. Theorizing without data has obvious charms, but one of the risks—here fully realized—is that the data will embarrass both the theory and the theorizer.

Although the no-duty rule presents a vital intellectual puzzle for law professors, judges, and philosophers, the rule has no detectable influence on the behavior of ordinary people. Americans, motivated by the imperfect obligations of beneficence, have proven themselves more than up to the task of rescuing those in need, irrespective of whatever the law might happen to say on the subject. The evidence presented in this Article simply does not support the received wisdom that there "ought to be a law" imposing a duty to rescue.

## Ken Levy, *Killing, Letting Die, and the Case for (Mildly) Punishing Bad Samaritanism*

44 Ga. L. Rev. 607 (2010)

### XII. The Five Strongest Objections to Bad-Samaritan Laws

#### D. The Too-Rare Objection [To Bad Samaritan Laws]

... David Hyman argues on the basis of empirical data both that bad Samaritanism is extremely rare and prosecutions under bad-Samaritan laws in the few states that have them even rarer. Even without bad-Samaritan laws, most people probably do the right thing and respond to others' cries for help. This point alone militates against implementing bad-Samaritan laws ...

### XIII. Replies to the Five Strongest Objections

#### D. Replies to the Too-Rare Objection

... [E]ven if the incidence of ... lettings-die were extremely rare, bad-Samaritan laws would still be necessary. Given the concentration of most violent crimes in urban areas, it is likely that some, if not many, non-urban and suburban areas in the United States have not prosecuted a murder or rape in decades. Some more rural communities and small towns may have never seen one. Yet all criminal codes prohibit murder and rape. (And one can only imagine what message these communities would send by decriminalizing these acts simply because they are rarely performed.) So whether or not a particular criminal prohibition should be, or remain, "on the books" does not necessarily depend on the frequency of the corresponding criminal act or omission. Some acts and omissions are so heinous that they should be criminally prohibited no matter how infrequently people may perform them. Letting die is just one of those heinous omissions—again, assuming its incidence is rare. Indeed, children are twenty-six times more likely to die from automobile accidents than from kidnappings. Yet this fact hardly means that we should punish the latter much less severely. There simply is no correlation between the rarity of a crime on the one hand, and its moral severity or therefore the punishment that it deserves on the other.

[Furthermore], some acts should be criminally prohibited no matter how infrequently people perform them because bad-Samaritan laws serve symbolic purposes just as much as practical purposes. Not only are they designed to fulfill the practical purposes of motivating our more indifferent citizens to attempt easy rescues and to punish them if they still are not sufficiently motivated with such laws. They are also designed to make two statements. First, they make a (negative) statement that we find David-Cash-like inaction and indifference to a fellow human being to be morally despicable. Second, they make a (positive) statement that we all have a strong affirmative moral duty to attempt easy rescues rather than turning a blind eye to people we happen to find in grave danger.

## *Notes and Questions*

1. Do you believe that David Cash's failure to do something to prevent Sherrice Iverson's rape was morally blameworthy? Should such failures be criminalized? Assuming that they should be criminalized, how much should they be punished? The oft-cited Vermont statute that imposes a duty to rescue punishes failures to aid as a misdemeanor. Assuming that criminal liability is appropriate in a case like David Cash's, is a misdemeanor conviction appropriate or should such omissions be punished more severely? Explain.

2. Although the case in favor of punishing some failures to rescue is intuitively attractive, Professors Joshua Dressler and David Hyman put forth cogent retributive (Dressler) and consequentialist (Hyman) arguments against criminalizing omissions to aid. For Dressler, punishing failures to rescue when there is no special duty to act comes very close to punishing for bad character. He suggests that the reason why we want to punish someone like David Cash is not because his failure to aid Sherrice Iverson helped cause the rape (it clearly didn't), but rather because his omission reveals that he is a bad person. If so, this is problematic, for—as the materials surveyed in notes 7, 8 and 9 of § 6.01 illustrate—it is deeply ingrained in American criminal law that people should be punished for doing bad things rather than for being bad persons. Do you share Dressler's concerns? Why or why not?

3. Professor Hyman's empirical research demonstrates that Bad Samaritan laws have no discernible effect on how humans behave when they decide whether to effect rescue or not. In other words, enactment of Bad Samaritan laws does not increase the amount of attempted rescues when compared with jurisdictions that lack such laws. This provides a decisive consequentialist argument against criminalizing failures to rescue. For a consequentialist, punishment must pay its way by achieving some salutary consequence. If studies demonstrate that Bad Samaritan laws do not increase the number of rescues attempted, the consequentialist argument in favor of criminalizing such conduct weakens considerably. This is perhaps why Professor Dressler claims that "[t]he best (and perhaps the only decent) argument for [Bad Samaritan] legislation is retributive in nature." It is also why in his reply to Hyman, Professor Levy argues that Bad Samaritan laws should be enacted regardless of whether doing so produces good consequences. He suggests that such statutes are justified on non-consequentialist grounds because they make the important symbolic statement "that we find David-Cash-like inaction and indifference to a fellow human being to be morally despicable." Do you agree with Professor Levy? Why or why not?

# Chapter 7

# Causation

## § 7.01 Causation: Actual Causation

### State v. Muro

Supreme Court of Nebraska, 2005
269 Neb. 703

STEPHAN, J.

Susana Muro was convicted by the district court for Dawson County of child abuse resulting in the death of a child and sentenced to 20 years' imprisonment. The Nebraska Court of Appeals affirmed her conviction, finding there was sufficient evidence that she knowingly failed to secure necessary medical care for her daughter, Vivianna Muro, after becoming aware that the child had sustained a serious injury, and that such failure was a ... cause of the child's death. On further review, we conclude that while the evidence in the record is sufficient to support the finding that Muro knowingly and intentionally caused or permitted Vivianna to be deprived of medical care, it is insufficient as a matter of law to establish that such deprivation caused the child's death.

#### I. Background

... On October 27, 2002, Muro resided in Lexington, Nebraska, with her husband, Jose Muro (Jose), and their children, a 4-year-old son and 8-month-old Vivianna. At approximately 3:20 p.m. on that day, Muro left the children at home in the care of Jose while she ran errands. Vivianna appeared normal at that time. When Muro returned home sometime after 6 p.m., Jose was holding Vivianna but the child was not crying as she usually did when held by Jose. Muro inquired about Vivianna, and Jose replied that she was asleep. He placed her in her crib while Muro fed their son and performed various chores.

Between 7 and 7:30 p.m., Muro took Vivianna from her crib and noticed that something was wrong. Vivianna was unresponsive and appeared "dazed," and her eyes were "half open, half closed." Muro observed that Vivianna was "limp, kind of like a rag doll." Over the next several hours, both Muro and Jose called the Tri-County Hospital in Lexington for advice without identifying themselves or disclosing that Vivianna was limp and unresponsive. A nurse testified that she advised the unidentified callers to bring the baby to the emergency room if they had any concern or uncertainty regarding her condition. Muro then called her mother-in-law, who resided in another state, and asked for advice about a "friend's baby who appeared dazed and loose," specifically denying that she was referring to Vivianna. Muro's mother-in-law told her to tell her friend to take the baby to the hospital as soon as possible. Muro and Jose then took Vivianna to Tri-County Hospital.

When she arrived at the hospital at approximately 11 p.m., Vivianna was not breathing, her pupils were fixed and dilated, and she was limp and cold. Although medical personnel performing resuscitation were able to establish a heartbeat, they were never able to stabilize Vivianna or establish spontaneous respiration. [Vivianna was then transferred to Good Samaritan Hospital] Upon arrival at Good Samaritan Hospital at approximately 1:30 a.m., a CT scan was performed which revealed a slightly displaced skull fracture in the left parietal area with an overlying hematoma, as well as other signs of brain injury. After consulting a neurosurgeon who concluded that surgical intervention was not feasible, Parys and other physicians conducted tests from which they concluded that brain death had occurred. Parys explained Vivianna's condition to Muro and Jose, and they made the decision to discontinue life support. Death occurred at 6:28 a.m. on October 28, 2002.

An autopsy was performed by Dr. Blaine Roffman the next day. He made certain findings indicative of trauma, including torn skin over the right lateral thorax and the left anterior thorax, broken and hemorrhaged fingernails, recent bruising of the right side of the neck and the midline of the forehead, bruising to "the left of the oral cavity on the cheek," and a fracture of the left parietal skull. At trial, Roffman ultimately opined that the cause of death was "a fracture of the left parietal skull, which resulted in cerebral edema [swelling], which resulted in brain death."

There is no contention or evidence that Muro inflicted or witnessed the infliction of the fatal injuries. There is evidence that the injuries occurred during the period when Muro was away from the family home on October 27, 2002....

### IV. Analysis

Muro was charged with Class IB felony child abuse, which provides in relevant part:

1) A person commits child abuse if he or she knowingly, intentionally, or negligently causes or permits a minor child to be: ...

    c) Deprived of necessary food, clothing, shelter, or care;....

6) Child abuse is a Class IB felony if the offense is committed knowingly and intentionally and results in the death of such child.

... [T]he three gradations of felony child abuse set forth in [the statute] are all based upon the same proscribed conduct; the differentiating factor is the degree of harm caused by such conduct.

It is undisputed that Muro did not seek medical care for Vivianna for a period of approximately 4 hours after she first noticed the child's unresponsiveness and other abnormal symptoms. Muro argues in this appeal that the State failed to prove ... that the deprivation of care ... resulted in the death of Vivianna.

#### 2. Causation

It is clear from the record that Vivianna sustained a serious traumatic head injury inflicted by someone other than Muro. The issue, as accurately stated by the Court of Appeals, is whether, viewing the evidence in a light most favorable to the prosecution, the court was clearly erroneous in finding that Muro's failure to seek medical treatment for Vivianna was a ... cause of her death. In other words, does the evidence support a finding that Vivianna's death would not have occurred had Muro not failed to seek medical treatment for Vivianna?

### (a) Principles of Law

... "Conduct is a cause of an event if the event in question would not have occurred but for that conduct; conversely, conduct is not a cause of an event if that event would have occurred without such conduct."

... [I]n *State v. Doyle*, an appeal from a manslaughter conviction, we held that the evidence was insufficient to establish that the defendant's conduct was a ... cause of the death. A dead human infant was found on premises occupied by the defendant, but there was no evidence of internal or external trauma and a pathologist was unable to state the cause of death. Witnesses testified that the defendant appeared to be pregnant before the body was found and that she appeared not to be pregnant thereafter. In determining that this evidence was insufficient to support the manslaughter conviction, we reasoned that there was "no evidence offered by the State that had the defendant done something, which she did not do, the infant would have lived; nor that had she not done anything, which she did do, the infant would have lived."

### (b) Medical Testimony

In this case, the State attempted to prove through the testimony of two physicians that Muro's conduct was a ... cause of the death. Parys, the pediatrician who treated Vivianna during and after her transport to Good Samaritan Hospital, testified at trial that there was very little chance of saving her life while she was in his care. Parys did state, with reasonable medical certainty, that "[i]f treatment was sought earlier, then there would've been a chance of survival." On cross-examination, he testified that he could not give a percentage of what the chance for survival would have been. He stated that if treatment had been sought immediately, survival was possible, but he could not say it was probable. He opined that Vivianna "might have survived" if treatment was sought earlier. He further testified that a person's condition progressively worsens after the type of skull injury suffered by Vivianna.

Dr. Randell Alexander, a pediatrician and an expert on child abuse, testified that a brain could swell to the degree seen in Vivianna within an hour, or it could also take several hours. He testified that in most cases with this type of injury, a child will die within 1 to 2 hours even with medical care. He opined, based upon the fact that Vivianna was still alive 4 hours after the trauma was inflicted, that "this is an injury that might have been survivable." He further testified that because of the delay in seeking treatment, Vivianna's survival was hopeless, but that there may have been a small amount of hope if prompt treatment had been sought. He testified that there was an opportunity to save Vivianna if treatment had been sought earlier and that if 100 children survived this type of injury for 4 hours, "a substantial fraction" could be saved with early treatment.

On cross-examination, Alexander admitted the possibility that doctors may not have been able to save Vivianna even if Muro had sought immediate treatment. He could not say that she would have survived if treatment had been sought 3 hours earlier. Alexander testified there was a reasonable likelihood that Vivianna could have survived with early treatment, but declined to say whether survival was possible or probable. He testified that her chance of survival with early treatment was more than 5 percent but less than 95 percent. On redirect, he stated that the long delay in seeking treatment and the fact that most children would have died within 2 hours of the injury suggested that Vivianna's injury was not "invariably fatal." Thus, he opined that the delay in treatment "may have" contributed to her death.

### (c) Resolution by Court of Appeals

Based upon the foregoing evidence and legal principles, a majority of the Court of Appeals panel concluded that it was "sufficient that the evidence establish that the injury could have been survived but for a defendant's actions." The majority thus determined that evidence of an unquantified chance of survival with prompt treatment was sufficient to establish that Muro's conduct was a ... cause of Vivianna's death. The dissenting judge reasoned that because there was no evidence that survival would have been probable with prompt medical care, it cannot be said that Muro's failure to seek prompt care was a ... cause of Vivianna's death. The dissenting judge considered the "core question" to be "whether, with the requisite degree of probability, earlier treatment would have made a difference—meaning whether it was probable that Vivianna would have lived, because the proof must show that the delay caused her death." [T]he dissenting judge reasoned that in order to establish the element of ... cause, the State had the burden to prove that survival in the absence of the unlawful conduct would have been probable, i.e., more likely than not, noting that a criminal conviction which requires proof of guilt beyond a reasonable doubt should not be based upon medical evidence of ... cause which would, as a matter of law, clearly fall short of the proof needed to support a workers' compensation claim, a personal injury claim, or a medical malpractice claim.

#### (d) Disposition on Further Review

Our case law, as summarized above, establishes that criminal conduct is a ... cause of an event if the event in question would not have occurred but for that conduct; conversely, conduct is not a ... cause of an event if that event would have occurred without such conduct. The burden in a criminal proceeding is on the State to produce proof beyond a reasonable doubt of every element of a charged offense. Thus, to establish that Muro's unlawful conduct was a ... cause of Vivianna's death, the State was required to prove beyond a reasonable doubt that but for Muro's delay in seeking medical treatment, Vivianna would have survived her preexisting traumatic head injury. We agree with the dissenting judge that the State did not meet this burden. The State proved only the *possibility* of survival with earlier treatment. Such proof is insufficient to satisfy even the lesser civil burden of proof by a preponderance of the evidence.

Viewing the evidence in this case in the light most favorable to the prosecution, a finder of fact could not reasonably conclude beyond a reasonable doubt that but for Muro's unlawful conduct, Vivianna would have survived. Accordingly, the evidence is legally insufficient to establish that Vivianna's death resulted from the conduct in question.

The State's failure to prove that Muro's unlawful conduct caused the death, however, does not relieve her of criminal responsibility. As noted above, [the child abuse statute] includes multiple gradations of felony child abuse, depending upon the result of the abusive conduct. We agree with the trial court and the Court of Appeals that the State proved beyond a reasonable doubt that Muro knowingly and intentionally deprived Vivianna of necessary care. That finding is sufficient to sustain a conviction for Class IIIA felony child abuse under [the statute] without any proof of resulting harm to the child. Accordingly, Muro's sentence must be vacated and the cause remanded for imposition of an appropriate sentence for the Class IIIA felony.

## *Notes and Questions*

1. Criminal offenses typically include both subjective and objective elements. In Anglo American jurisdictions, the subjective element of the crime is usually called "*mens rea*" (Latin for "guilty mind"). In contrast, the objective elements of crimes are frequently referred to as the "*actus reus*" (Latin for "guilty act"). The felony child abuse offense charged in *State v. Muro*, for example, has both subjective (intentionally or knowingly) and ob-

jective elements (failing to provide food, clothing, shelter or care to a minor child and death resulting as a consequence of such failure).

2. The objective elements can be subdivided into conduct, circumstance and result elements. The conduct element of the child abuse offense in *Muro* is failing to provide food, clothing shelter or care to a child. The criminalized conduct is therefore an omission. Nevertheless, as Chapter 6 illustrates, the conduct element of an offense may also consist of an action. It may also be the possession of a certain item. On the other hand, circumstance elements describe things, beings or states of affairs that are neither acts nor results. In the case of the felony child abuse offense, the circumstance element is "minor child," for it describes a being that is neither an act nor a result. Finally, the result element of an offense describes a harmful consequence that the actor must bring about in order to be held liable. The result element of the felony child abuse statute is the death of the child. Not all offenses have result elements. Attempted crimes are the paradigmatic example. In the case of attempts, the offense—by definition—lacks a reference to a harmful result that must take place. The offense of rape also lacks a result element, for the consummation of the crime merely requires that certain conduct take place (sexual acts) under certain circumstances (without consent) regardless of whether a harmful result obtains.

3. The problem of causation in the law explores the link between the defendant's conduct and the resulting harm suffered by the victim. Expressed in more abstract terms, legal causation studies the connection between the conduct and result elements of the offense. In order for a defendant to be held liable for an offense that includes a result element, the state must demonstrate that his conduct is linked to the result in a special kind of way. Given that the causation problem focuses on examining the relationship between conduct and result elements, offenses that lack result elements do not raise causation issues. Once again, attempt offenses are illustrative. Since attempts do not require that a result take place, talk of causation in the context of these offenses is inapposite. The same can be said of the crime of rape. Because the offense of rape lacks a result element, no causation related issues arise during its prosecution.

4. In order to determine whether the defendant's conduct is linked to the resulting harm in the special kind of way that criminal liability demands, courts engage in a two step analysis. First, courts ask if the defendant's conduct was the "actual" or "but for" cause of the harm that resulted. Conduct is an "actual" or "but for" cause of a harm when the harm would not have taken place *but for* defendant's conduct. Expressed in negative terms, defendant's conduct is not an actual cause if the harm would have taken place even without the defendant's conduct. Suppose, for example, that Cain shoots Abel and Abel later dies from the gunshot injury. Cain's conduct is a "but for" cause of Abel's death, for Abel would not have died but for Cain's conduct. Note that Cain's mother is also a "but for" cause of Abel's death, given that had she not given birth to Cain, Abel would not have died from the gunshot injury. It is, of course, absurd to hold Cain's mother criminally liable for the offense committed by her son. As a way of avoiding such outcomes, the law requires that—in addition to being an actual cause—the defendant's conduct be a "legal" or "proximate" cause of the harm. Actual or but for causation is thus a *necessary, but not a sufficient* condition for criminal liability. Legal causation is discussed in §7.02 of this Chapter.

5. The defendant in *State v. Muro* argued that her conduct was not a "but for" cause of her child's death. The Supreme Court of Nebraska agreed, pointing out that medical experts were not sure whether the child would have survived had the defendant sought medical care earlier. Since actual causation is a necessary (but insufficient!) condition for

establishing the special causal relationship between conduct and result that the criminal law demands, the defendant could not be held liable for the offense charged. Nevertheless, the Court concluded that the defendant could be punished for the lesser offense of depriving a child of needed medical care. Note that this offense is comprised solely of conduct (omission consisting in failure to provide medical care) and circumstance elements (victim must be a minor child). Since a result element is lacking, the state did not need to prove causation in order to hold the defendant liable for the lesser offense.

6. As is well known, the prosecution has the burden of proving the elements of the offense beyond a reasonable doubt. The Court pointed out in *Muro* that this burden also applies to proof of but for causation. This makes conceptual sense, for causation is the element that links the defendant's conduct (failure to provide medical treatment) to the harm proscribed by the offense (death of child). Consequently, a failure to prove causation results in a failure to prove the harm that the offense prohibits. This proved determinative in *Muro,* for the state was unable to demonstrate *beyond a reasonable doubt* that the child would have survived had the defendant sought medical care earlier.

7. Sometimes multiple actors engage in conduct against the victim in circumstances in which the contributions of any of the actors would have been sufficient to cause the harm suffered by the victim. The paradigmatic example is that of a victim killed by a firing squad. The contributions of any individual member of the firing squad are not a "but for" cause of the victim's death because the victim would have died anyway from wounds suffered as a consequence of the shots fired by the other squad members. Considering "but for" causation a necessary condition for criminal liability in such cases would produce anomalous results, for it would lead to acquitting *all* of the members of the firing squad, given that no individual contribution was a but for cause of the victim's harm. Courts and scholars refer to this as the problem of "concurrent or alternative sufficient causes." In order to avoid incongruous results when there are concurrent sufficient causes, courts have developed special rules for these types of cases.

8. The approach adopted by the Arkansas Supreme Court in *Cox v. State,* 305 Ark. 244 (1991), is illustrative of the conventional way of dealing with these issues. One of the co-defendants in *Cox* fired three shots at the victim, hitting him in the chest and side. The co-defendant subsequently fired three shots at the victim's head. The victim died as a result of the gun shots. Both defendants argued that they could not be held liable for the death of the victim because the state could not demonstrate which one of them caused the death. The Court rejected the defendant's argument by pointing out that:

> Arkansas law defines causation for the purpose of determining criminal liability as follows:
>
> > Causation may be found where the result would not have occurred but for the conduct of the defendant operating either alone or concurrently with another cause unless the concurrent cause was clearly sufficient to produce the result and the conduct of the defendant clearly insufficient. Ark.Code Ann. § 5-2-205 (1987).
>
> Our law is well established that, where there are concurrent causes of death, conduct which hastens or contributes to a person's death is a cause of death. *See also,* W.R. LaFave & A.W. Scott, 1 *Substantive Criminal Law,* § 3.12 (1986); R.M. Perkins & R.N. Boyce,*Criminal Law,* 783–4 (3d Ed.1982).
>
> In the case at bar, the medical examiner who performed the autopsy on the victim testified, "Mr. Harrison was shot six times and he died as a result of these six wounds, which entered the brain, internal organs and caused

death of internal bleeding." The eyewitnesses to the murder described the manner in which the killing occurred. The medical examiner's testimony, coupled with that of the eyewitnesses, was sufficient to prove that the victim died as a result of internal bleeding from the shots fired by the appellants. Thus, there was substantial evidence they caused the death of their victim. *Cox*, 305 Ark 244.

9. According to the statute cited in *Cox*, the defendant's conduct will be considered a cause of the victim's harm in a case that presents the problem of multiple concurrent causes as long as it was *sufficient by itself* to cause the harm. The fact that other defendants engaged in conduct against the victim that were also sufficient to cause the harm is thus made legally irrelevant by the statute. Applied to the firing squad example, the conduct of each individual member would be considered a cause of the death because each individual shot fired was sufficient to cause the death of the victim. Consequently, all of the firing squad members could be held liable for the victim's death, although none of the individual members' acts are technically a but for cause of the victim's death. Do you agree with this solution? Explain.

## § 7.02 Causation: Legal (Proximate) Causation

### People v. Acosta

Court of Appeals of California, 1991
284 Cal.Rptr. 117

WALLIN, Associate Justice.

... At 10 p.m. on March 10, 1987, Officers Salceda and Francis of the Santa Ana Police Department's automobile theft detail saw Acosta in Elvira Salazar's stolen Nissan Pulsar parked on the street. The officers approached Acosta and identified themselves. Acosta inched the Pulsar forward, then accelerated rapidly. He lead Salceda, Francis and officers from other agencies on a 48-mile chase along numerous surface streets and freeways throughout Orange County. The chase ended near Acosta's residence in Anaheim.

During the chase, Acosta engaged in some of the most egregious driving tactics imaginable. He ran stop signs and red lights, and drove on the wrong side of streets, causing oncoming traffic to scatter or swerve to avoid colliding with him. Once, when all traffic lanes were blocked by vehicles stopped for a red light, he used a dirt shoulder to circumvent stationary vehicles and pass through the intersection. When leaving the freeway in Anaheim, he drove over a cement shoulder.

Throughout the pursuit, Acosta weaved in and out of traffic, cutting in front of other cars and causing them to brake suddenly. At one point on the freeway, he crossed three lanes of traffic, struck another car, jumped the divider between the freeway and a transition lane, and passed a tanker truck, forcing it to swerve suddenly to avoid a collision.

Acosta generally drove at speeds between 60 and 90 miles per hour, slowing only when necessary. During several turns, his wheels lost traction. When an officer was able to drive parallel to the Pulsar for a short distance, Acosta looked in his direction and smiled. Near the end of the chase, one of the Pulsar's front tires blew out, but Acosta continued to drive at 55 to 60 miles per hour, crossing freeway traffic lanes.

Police helicopters from Anaheim, Costa Mesa, Huntington Beach, and Newport Beach assisted in the chase by tracking Acosta. During the early part of the pursuit, the Costa Mesa and Newport Beach craft were used, pinpointing Acosta's location with their high beam spotlights. The Costa Mesa helicopter was leading the pursuit, in front of and below the Newport Beach helicopter. As they flew into Newport Beach, the pilots agreed the Newport Beach craft should take the lead. The normal procedure for such a maneuver is for the lead helicopter to move to the right and swing around clockwise behind the other craft while climbing to an altitude of 1,000 feet. At the same time, the trailing helicopter descends to 500 feet while maintaining a straight course.

At the direction of the Costa Mesa pilot, the Newport Beach helicopter moved forward and descended while the Costa Mesa helicopter banked to the right. Shortly after commencing this procedure, the Costa Mesa helicopter, having terminated radio communication, came up under the Newport Beach helicopter from the right rear and collided with it. Both helicopters fell to the ground. Three occupants in the Costa Mesa helicopter died as a result of the crash.

Menzies Turner, a retired Federal Aviation Administration (FAA) investigator, testified as an expert and concluded the accident occurred because the Costa Mesa helicopter, the faster of the two aircraft, made a 360-degree turn and closed too rapidly on the Newport Beach helicopter. He opined the Costa Mesa helicopter's pilot violated an FAA regulation prohibiting careless and reckless operation of an aircraft by failing to properly clear the area, not maintaining communication with the Newport Beach helicopter, failing to keep the other aircraft in view at all times, and not changing his altitude. He also testified the Costa Mesa pilot violated another FAA regulation prohibiting operation of one aircraft so close to another as to create a collision hazard.

Turner could not think of any reason for the Costa Mesa helicopter's erratic movement. The maneuver was not a difficult one, and was not affected by the ground activity at the time. He had never heard of a midair collision between two police helicopters involved in tracking a ground pursuit, and had never investigated a midair collision involving helicopters.

After his arrest Acosta told the police he knew the Pulsar was stolen and he fled the police to avoid arrest. He also saw two helicopters with spotlights, and turned off the Pulsar's lights to evade them. Acosta knew that his flight was dangerous "to the bone," but he tried to warn other cars by flashing the car lights and by otherwise being "as safe as possible."

## I.

Acosta claims there was insufficient evidence of two elements necessary to support the convictions for second degree murder: that he proximately caused the deaths of the victims, and that his state of mind constituted implied malice. He is correct on the latter claim.

As to the proximate cause issue, Acosta argues that although a collision between ground vehicles was a foreseeable result of his conduct, one between airborne helicopters was not, noting his expert had never heard of a similar incident. He also contends the Costa Mesa helicopter pilot's violation of FAA regulations was a superseding cause. Because the deaths here were unusual, to say the least, the issue deserves special scrutiny....

To determine whether Acosta's conduct was not, as a matter of law, a proximate cause of death of the Costa Mesa helicopter's occupants, I enter a legal realm not routinely considered in published California cases....

"Proximate cause" is the term historically used to separate those results for which an actor will be held responsible from those not carrying such responsibility. The term is, in a sense, artificial, serving matters of policy surrounding tort and criminal law and based partly on expediency and partly on concerns of fairness and justice. Because such concerns are sometimes more a matter of "common sense" than pure logic, the line of demarcation is flexible, and attempts to lay down uniform tests which apply evenly in all situations have failed. That does not mean general guidelines and approaches to analysis cannot be constructed.

The threshold question in examining causation is whether the defendant's act was an "actual cause" of the victim's injury. It is a sine qua non test: But for the defendant's act would the injury have occurred? Unless an act is an actual cause of the injury, it will not be considered a proximate cause.

The next inquiry is whether the defendant's act was a "substantial factor" in the injury. This test excludes those actual causes which, although direct, play only an insignificant role in the ultimate injury. Although there is no strict definition, the Restatement Second of Torts, *supra,* section 433, lists considerations in determining whether a factor is "substantial": (1) the number and extent of other factors contributing to the harm; (2) whether the forces created by the actor are continuous in producing the harm or merely create a condition upon which independent forces act; and (3) any lapse of time between the act and the harm....

To this point I have spoken only of *direct* causes, "[causes] which produce [ ] a result without the aid of any intervening cause."...

[Intervening causes can be dependent or independent.] An intervening cause is dependent if it is a normal or involuntary response to, or result of, the defendant's act. These include flight and other voluntary or involuntary responses of victims, as well as defense, rescue and medical treatment by third parties. Even where such responses constitute negligent conduct, they do not *supersede* the defendant's act; i.e., they are nevertheless considered proximate causes of the harm. *People v. Armitage, supra,* 194 Cal.App.3d at p. 420, 239 Cal.Rptr. 515 [victim foolishly chose to attempt to swim to shore after defendant capsized the boat].

Conversely, when the defendant's conduct merely places the eventual victim in a position which allows some other action to cause the harm, the other action is termed an *independent* intervening cause. It *usually* supersedes the defendant's act; i.e., precludes a finding of proximate cause. The issue usually arises when the victim has been subjected to the independent harm after being disabled by the defendant, or is somehow impacted by the defendant's flight. *People v. Harris, supra,* 52 Cal.App.3d at p. 426, 125 Cal.Rptr. 40 [pursuing officer kills third party while pursuing defendant]; Perkins & Boyce, *supra,* at pp. 809–811 [falling stone hits man disabled by defendant; girl recovering from gunshot wound contracts scarlet fever from treating physician; bystander kicks to death victim knocked down by defendant; decedent may have inexplicably run into fire caused by defendant].

An independent intervening variable will *not* be superseding in three instances: (1) where it is merely a contributing cause to the defendant's direct cause; (2) where the result was intended; or (3) where the resultant harm was reasonably foreseeable when the act was done. As to the third exception, "[t]he consequence need not have been a strong probability; a possible consequence which might reasonably have been contemplated is enough.... The precise consequence need not have been foreseen; it is enough that the defendant should have foreseen the possibility of some harm of the kind which might result from his act."

As Perkins and Boyce put it, "Foreseeability" is not a "test" which can be applied without the use of common sense; it presents one of those problems in which "we must rely on the common sense of the common man as to common things." It is employed in the sense of "appreciable probability." It does not require such a degree of probability that the intervention was more likely to occur than not; and on the other hand it implies more than that someone might have imagined it as a theoretical possibility. It does not require that the defendant himself actually thought of it. For the purposes of proximate cause "an appreciable probability is one which a reasonable man in ordering his conduct in view of his situation and his knowledge and means of knowledge, should, either consciously or unconsciously, take into account in connection with the other facts and probabilities then apparent." (Perkins & Boyce, *supra*).

Prosser and Keeton, in an in-depth discussion of the dynamics of foresight, conclude that although it is desirable to exclude extremely remarkable and unusual results from the purview of proximate cause, it is virtually impossible to express a logical verbal formula which will produce uniform results. I agree. The standard should be simply stated, exclude extraordinary results, and allow the trier of fact to determine the issue on the particular facts of the case using "the common sense of the common man as to common things."

The "highly extraordinary result" standard serves that purpose. It is consistent with the definition of foreseeability used in California. It does not involve the defendant's state of mind, but focuses upon the objective conditions present when he acts. Like numerous other legal definitions, what it means in practice will be determined as case law develops. Limitations arising from the mental state of the actor can be left to concepts like malice, recklessness and negligence.

Because the highly extraordinary result standard is consistent with the limitation on direct causes, it simplifies the proximate cause inquiry. The analysis is: (1) was the defendant's conduct the actual cause of the harm (but for his actions would it have occurred as it did)? (2) was the result an intended consequence of the act? (3) was the defendant's action a substantial factor in the harm? and (4) was the result highly extraordinary in light of the circumstances?

If the first question is answered no, proximate cause is lacking. If answered yes, the next question must be examined. If the second question is answered yes, proximate cause is established. If answered no, the next question must be examined. If the third question is answered no, proximate cause is lacking. If answered yes, proximate cause is established unless the fourth question is answered yes, in which case it is lacking. The analysis does away with the need to consider the distinction between direct, concurrent, contributory, and dependent and independent intervening causes. It focuses, as it should, upon the role the defendant's act played in the harm, limiting culpability only where the conduct was de minimis or the result highly extraordinary.

Here, but for Acosta's conduct of fleeing the police, the helicopters would never have been in position for the crash. However, there was no evidence he intended the harm, so I must examine questions three and four.

Although an extremely close question, Acosta's conduct was a substantial factor in causing the crash. He was fleeing when the accident occurred, and there was no lapse of time between his flight and the crash—his action had not "come to rest." The only other factor operating at the time was the improper flight pattern of the Costa Mesa pilot. Although Acosta's horrendous driving did not cause the helicopter's improper maneuver, his flight undoubtedly infused excitement and tension into the situation, which can be considered to be a substantial factor. No similar case has held otherwise, although the third party collisions all have involved accidents on the ground.

The result was not highly extraordinary. Although a two-helicopter collision was unknown to expert witness Turner and no reported cases describe one, it was "a possible consequence which reasonably might have been contemplated." Given the emotional dynamics of any police pursuit, there is an "appreciable probability" that one of the pursuers, in the heat of the chase, may act negligently or recklessly to catch the quarry. That no pursuits have ever before resulted in a helicopter crash or midair collision is more a comment on police flying skill and technology than upon the innate probabilities involved.

The undisputed facts of this case mandate the result. Contrary to Justice Moore's assertion [in his concurring opinion], I do not find the result extraordinary, but almost so. I presume he does not dispute that it was extremely unusual. In fact, he cites no similar instances of aircraft colliding during police pursuits. But neither does Justice Crosby cite any case to support his claim the result was highly extraordinary.

Neither concurring opinion offers case law "on all fours," suggesting this case is unique and presents a close question. Partly because this is so, it is appropriate to rely on two compelling factors: the jury found proximate cause based on proper instructions, and the dearth of case law to support a rejection of that finding. Given these circumstances, a finding of proximate cause is appropriate....

[Editor's Note: In part iii of the opinion, the court held that the defendant could not be punished for murder because he did not have the subjective element of "malice" that is necessary for a murder conviction.]

IV.

The judgment is reversed on the murder counts and is affirmed in all other respects.

**CROSBY, Associate Justice, concurring and dissenting.**

Whether the defendant may be held criminally culpable for the tragic deaths in this case is the key issue before us. Justice Wallin says yes, but not for murder. I disagree ... because the law does not assign blame to an otherwise blameworthy actor when neither the intervening negligent conduct nor the risk of harm was foreseeable.

Or, as Justice Cardozo put it, "We are told that one who drives at reckless speed through a crowded city street is guilty of a negligent act and, therefore, of a wrongful one irrespective of the consequences. Negligent the act is, and wrongful in the sense that it is unsocial, but wrongful and unsocial in relation to other travelers, only because the eye of vigilance perceives the risk of damage. If the same act were to be committed on a speedway or a race course, it would lose its wrongful quality. The risk reasonably to be perceived defines the duty to be obeyed, and risk imports relation; it is risk to another or to others within the range of apprehension." *Palsgraf v. Long Island R. Co.* The occupants of these helicopters were surely not "within the range of apprehension" of a fleeing criminal on the ground.

To be sure, defendant represented a threat to everyone traveling the same roads and would have been responsible for any injury directly or indirectly caused by his actions in those environs; but to extend that responsibility to persons in the air, whose role was merely to observe his movements, a simple enough task in far speedier helicopters, defies common sense. It was perfectly foreseeable that someone would be hurt on the ground via some sort of causal chain connecting to defendant's conduct; the opposite is true of the airborne observers. They were not in the zone of danger in this case by any stretch of the imagination, and the manner and circumstances of the collision could hardly have reasonably been foreseen. Indeed, the lead opinion admits no similar accident has ever occurred anywhere according to our own research, as well as the trial expert. Although less remote than a dispatcher suffering a coronary, perhaps, this was a "highly extraordinary result" by any measure and, properly viewed, beyond the long arm of the criminal law.

## *Notes and Questions*

1. As Justice Wallin's opinion explains, courts have come up with different ways of framing the "proximate cause" inquiry. Some talk about the need for the defendant's act to be a "sufficiently direct" cause of the resulting harm. *See, e.g., People v. Kibbe,* 35 N.Y.2d 407 (1974). Others prefer asking whether the actor's conduct was a "substantial factor" in bringing about the harm, although some courts refer to the "substantial factor" test as an alternative to "but for" causation in cases that involve concurrent sufficient causes. Compare, e.g., *State v. Spate,* 176 Conn. 227 (1978) (invoking the "substantial factor" test as a tool for assessing proximate or legal causation) with *State v. Christman,* 160 Wash.App. 741 (2011) (explaining that "the substantial factor test applies ... where multiple causes could have produced the identical harm, thus making it impossible to prove the 'but for' test").

2. Regardless of the name given to the test for determining legal (proximate) causation, courts usually approach the causation inquiry by asking whether the harm suffered by the victim was "reasonably foreseeable" in light of the defendant's conduct. More specifically, it is often stated that the defendant's conduct should not be considered the proximate cause of unforeseeable results. In his *Acosta* dissent, Justice Crosby argued that the defendant's conduct should not be considered a proximate cause of the death of the pilots because their death was not a reasonably foreseeable consequence of the defendant's acts. Do you agree? Why or why not?

3. Sometimes courts focus—as the California Court of Appeals did in *Acosta*—on whether the resulting harm was a "highly extraordinary" consequence of the defendant's act. According to this approach, defendant's conduct will not be considered a proximate cause if the harm that resulted is deemed a highly extraordinary consequence of the defendant's act. Do you believe that the death of the helicopter pilots in *Acosta* was a "highly extraordinary" consequence? Why or why not?

4. Justice Crosby's dissent discusses a risk-based or "zone of danger" focused analysis of proximate cause that he borrows from Justice Cardozo's famous *Palsgraf* opinion. According to this approach, a finding of legal causation requires a comparison of the danger that a reasonable person observing the course of conduct would believe that the defendant's act created with the danger that ended up bringing about the result. If the danger created by the defendant's conduct is the same danger that brought about the result, then a finding of proximate causation is appropriate. On the contrary, if the danger created by the defendant's act is different than the danger that produced the harm, then the court should hold that the defendant's conduct was not the proximate cause of the result. Justice Crosby described the danger created by the defendant in *Acosta* as "a threat to everyone traveling the same roads." Therefore, he asserted that the defendant "would have been responsible for any injury directly or indirectly caused by his actions" to those using the same roads. Nevertheless, Justice Crosby argued against a finding of proximate cause because the pilots "were not in the zone of danger in this case by any stretch of the imagination." That is, the defendant's conduct should not be considered a proximate cause

because the danger created by his conduct (threat to those using the road) was different from the danger that brought about the death of the pilots (threat to those travelling in the air). Do you agree with Justice Crosby's analysis? Why or why not?

5. Whether a given result is "reasonably foreseeable," "not highly extraordinary" or "within the zone of danger created by the defendant" (RF, NHE or within ZOD for short) may depend on how the question is framed. In *Acosta,* for example, the inquiry could be phrased in at least the following two ways:

> Description A—Is the death of a helicopter pilot as a consequence of an actor's reckless driving maneuvers RF, NHE or within ZOD?
>
> Description B—Is it RF, NHE or within ZOD that two helicopters within close proximity of each other that are giving chase to a recklessly operated vehicle will collide with each other?

The way in which the inquiry is formulated in "Description A" likely leads to the conclusion that the pilot's death is not RF, is highly extraordinary or within ZOD. However, the argument in favor of finding that the crash of the helicopters was RF, NHE or within ZOD is considerably stronger when the inquiry is phrased as it is in "Description B." What this reveals is that these kinds of inquiries may not be as objective as they appear at first glance, for the answer to the query is (at least partially) dependent on the degree of specificity with which the facts are described. The more specific the description of the facts is, the easier it is to find that the resulting harm was RF, NHE or within ZOD (in this case, Description B is more specific than Description A). In contrast, a more generic description of the facts makes it easier to conclude that the defendant's conduct should not be considered RF, within ZOD, or highly extraordinary.

6. In order to determine whether the defendant's conduct is a proximate cause, courts also frequently assess whether there are "intervening causes" of sufficient causal force to break the link between the defendant's conduct and the resulting harm. An intervening cause is a causal force that intervenes after the defendant's conduct but before the harm takes place. The intervening cause in *Acosta* was the pilot's careless operation of the helicopter, given that the pilot's reckless maneuver took place after the defendant's conduct (fleeing from the police) but before the resulting harm (death of both pilots).

7. Intervening causes that have enough causal force to break the link between the defendant's conduct and the harm that ensued are usually called "superseding causes." The existence of a superseding cause precludes a finding of proximate cause and, therefore, exonerates the defendant of liability for the resulting harm.

8. Although there is no fixed test for determining whether an intervening cause ought to be considered superseding, courts frequently assess whether the intervening cause was reasonably foreseeable in light of defendant's conduct. If the intervening cause is reasonably foreseeable, courts often conclude that it does not break the causal link between the defendant's conduct and the resulting harm. In contrast, unforeseeable intervening causes often preclude a finding of proximate cause. Do you believe that the pilot's careless operation of the helicopter was foreseeable? Explain.

9. It is often difficult to determine whether an intervening cause should exonerate the defendant of liability, especially when—as in *Acosta*—the intervening cause is a person's negligent act. It is also difficult to assess whether the victim's freely willed decision to risk harm should be considered an intervening cause that defeats a finding of proximate cause. The next two sections explore these issues in more detail.

# § 7.03 Causation: Third Party Conduct as an Intervening Cause

## State v. García

Supreme Court of Iowa, 2000
616 N.W.2d 594

LARSON, Justice.

Alejandro Garcia was convicted in a jury-waived trial of first-degree murder ... He appealed, and the court of appeals reversed. We granted the State's application for further review and now vacate the decision of the court of appeals and affirm the judgment of the district court.

### I. Facts and Prior Proceedings.

We recite the facts in the light most favorable to the verdict. Garcia and four others were hired for $100 each to beat up an individual named Daniel Hernandez Gonzales (Hernandez), who allegedly owed money for drugs. The four of them drove to the victim's home armed with a metal baseball bat, beer bottles, and a gun "just in case" Hernandez was armed. Garcia, with the gun and baseball bat, broke into the victim's trailer home and pushed him down on the couch. Three others followed, while another man remained in the vehicle. Garcia hit Hernandez with the baseball bat, and the others hit him with beer bottles. The victim was able to get loose and run outside. His attackers followed him and began kicking him. When the victim got up, Garcia shot him four times. Garcia and the others fled the scene but were soon apprehended.

The victim was immediately taken to a hospital. Two bullets had struck him in the leg and were not life threatening. The other two wounds would have been fatal without immediate medical attention. One bullet had entered his abdomen and pierced his stomach, liver, and left lung, coming to rest just outside his rib cage. Dr. Francis Garrity, the Polk County Medical Examiner, characterized this wound as "very serious" and would have resulted in the victim's death if not treated. The other wound was from a bullet that grazed the victim's aorta and perforated both lungs. This wound would also have resulted in death if not treated.

Doctors performed surgery on the victim's abdomen and chest. During surgery, there were problems in repairing the holes in the victim's stomach, and gastric contents spilled into the belly area. During surgery on his lower left lung, doctors were forced to remove a substantial portion of the lung.

As a result of the trauma to his lungs, the victim developed Adult Respiratory Disease Syndrome (ARDS), a serious condition that results in death in forty to eighty percent of adult cases. With this condition, the lung becomes so dysfunctional that oxygen is unable to properly move from the airways to the blood stream, requiring the use of mechanical devices such as ventilators. The victim was placed on a ventilator when he was no longer able to breathe on his own. As part of his treatment, he was also placed on a large quantity of fluids, causing him to develop severe swelling. Prior to his death, the victim's condition was steadily and rapidly deteriorating, with a number of organ systems failing.

While the victim was hospitalized and while he was being shaved by a hospital employee, a tracheotomy tube used to connect him to the ventilator was nicked, and the attending physician decided to change the tube to increase the efficiency of the oxygen getting into the lungs. Due to the victim's swollen neck, as the tube was being changed, his airway closed and the attending physician was unable to replace the tube. As a result, the victim asphyxiated. One doctor believed the victim would have died anyway, notwithstanding the tube change, within three or four days. It was this doctor's opinion that the gunshot wounds were the proximate cause of the victim's death and that the medical decisions relating to treatment were part of a chain of events set in motion by the wounds.

Garcia and the others were charged with first-degree murder....

As the trial date approached, the State filed a motion for adjudication of law points and a motion to exclude evidence that medical treatment, characterized by Garcia as grossly negligent, was an intervening and superseding cause of the victim's death. The court sustained the State's motion and found as a matter of law that the medical treatment was not a superseding cause of death.

Garcia was tried to the bench and convicted. He appealed, [objecting to] the district court's ruling that prevented him from introducing evidence of superseding cause.

**II. The Ruling Prohibiting Introduction of Evidence of Intervening Cause.**

Garcia argues the district court denied him due process of law by depriving him of a defense to which he was entitled. In an offer of proof his expert, Dr. Lawrence Repsher, testified that the doctors' actions in removing the tracheotomy tube from the victim was the cause of his death. Garcia argues this creates a jury question as to causation and that the district court erred in ruling prior to trial that he could not present this evidence. This is the basis on which the court of appeals reversed.

Pursuant to Iowa Rule of Evidence 104(a), the court held a hearing on the admissibility of evidence as to intervening and superseding causes of death. Although Dr. Repsher testified that the victim's death was caused by incompetent medical treatment, the district court held that, even if that were true, it would not "vitiate a causal nexus between the risk [of incompetent treatment] and the act which created it, the shooting." Citing Dr. Repsher's testimony, the court stated that "reasonable minds would not differ in concluding that both the medical decision and the shooting [were] contributing causes to the death of [the victim]." The court held because the removal of the tracheotomy tube was not the sole proximate cause of death, a defense of intervening and superseding cause was not relevant and Garcia could not call Dr. Repsher as an expert witness to establish that defense.

The principles of causation normally associated with civil tort litigation are pertinent in criminal cases. The rules restricting an actor's responsibility under theories of superseding cause are for the court to apply and not the jury. In determining the legal cause of death, we have endorsed the following principle:

> [A]n act is a cause of an event if two conditions are satisfied: the event would not have occurred without the act; [and] the act made the event more likely. The first condition is necessary to distinguish the attempted from the completed crime, the second to rule out cases in which, while the event in question would not have occurred but for the act, the act did not create the kind of dangerous condition that would make such events more likely to occur.

A defendant can be relieved of criminal responsibility if an intervening act breaks the chain of causal connection between the defendant's actions and the victim's death. However, for an intervening act to relieve a defendant of criminal responsibility for homicide, the intervening act must be the *sole* proximate cause of death. In deciding whether medical treatments are superseding causes, we have stated:

> The intervention of a force which is a *normal consequence* of a situation created by the actor's negligent conduct is not a superseding cause of harm which such conduct has been a substantial factor in bringing about. *Murray,* 512 N.W.2d at 551 (quoting Restatement (Second) of Torts §443 (1965)).

In the pretrial evidentiary hearing, Dr. Repsher's opinion as to the cause of death was that it was the result of medical negligence. In fact, he had harsh words for the treatment rendered the victim. Referring to the removal of the tracheotomy tube, he said "it was outrageous. I mean it was—there was just no—absolutely no reason to do it and all sorts of reasons not to do it. I mean it was just extraordinary."

At another point, the witness testified that removal of the tracheotomy tube (which apparently everyone agrees caused the victim to asphyxiate) was "completely irrational." On cross-examination, however, the doctor agreed the gunshot wounds were sufficient in themselves to cause death in the absence of medical intervention.

The defendant relies on Restatement (Second) of Torts section 443, quoted above, stating that an intervening force that is a "normal consequence" of a defendant's act cannot be a superseding cause of death. In this case, however, the intervening act was not normal according to the defendant; it was "outrageous," and due process demands he be allowed to present it as a defense....

The question is whether Garcia's superseding-cause defense is one recognized in our law under the facts of this case. He acknowledges several of our cases holding that medical care furnished a crime victim cannot be a superseding cause of death but distinguishes them on the basis they involved ordinary negligence, not gross negligence as he claims here. *See, e.g., Murray,*512 N.W.2d at 551 (death of comatose victim following withholding of nourishment and medication held as a matter of law to be normal consequence of criminal assault); *Davis v. State,* 520 N.W.2d 319, 320 (Iowa App.1994) (placement of feeding tube in victim resulting in bacterial peritonitis and death held to be normal consequence of stabbing).

The defendant cites no cases holding that gross negligence may constitute a superseding cause under the facts of this case. However, in a case not cited by the defendant, the New York Court of Appeals suggested such a rule in dictum. *See People v. Eulo,* 63 N.Y.2d 341, 482 N.Y.S.2d 436, 472 N.E.2d 286 (1984). The court said:

> If victims' deaths were prematurely pronounced due to a doctor's negligence, the subsequent procedures [removal of organs for transplant] may have been a cause of death, but that negligence would not constitute a superseding cause of death relieving defendants of liability. *If, however, the pronouncements of death were premature due to the gross negligence or the intentional wrongdoing of doctors, as determined by a grave deviation from accepted medical practices or disregard for legally cognizable criteria for determining death, the intervening medical procedure would interrupt the chain of causation and become the legal cause of death.* Thus, the propriety of the medical procedures is integral to the question of causation.

This dictum in *Eulo* was later discussed and impliedly rejected by the New York court, which held that even gross negligence is insufficient to relieve a defendant from criminal liability unless the treatment is the sole cause of death. *See People v. Griffin,* 80 N.Y.2d 723, 594 N.Y.S.2d 694, 610 N.E.2d 367 (1993). After discussing the dictum in *Eulo,*the court reaffirmed its traditional rule in such cases by saying:

> The test for relief from criminal responsibility for a death applicable to the facts of this case remains whether the death can be attributed solely to the negligent medical treatment.

The facts of *Griffin* are strikingly similar to the facts in the present case. In *Griffin*, as here, the issue was whether the trial court erred in excluding evidence of medical malpractice as a superseding cause of death. In *Griffin* the victim of the stabbing developed complications during treatment, including ARDS, as in this case. The defense attempted to introduce evidence that medical malpractice was a superseding cause of death. The court held that medical malpractice, even if gross, must be the sole cause of death to be a superseding cause. As a matter of law, the malpractice was held not to be the sole cause of death.

Other cases that have addressed the issue leave no doubt about the legal principle to be applied: even gross negligence will not relieve a criminal actor of liability unless it is the sole cause of death. A recent Connecticut case reaffirmed that principle. In *State v. Shabazz,* the defendant was charged with stabbing a victim to death. He relied on the defense of intervening medical malpractice and asserted that the medical treatment was grossly negligent. He attempted to use a physician who specialized in anatomic, clinical, and forensic pathology, who testified to that effect. The Connecticut court held that the trial court properly refused to allow that evidence because no rational fact finder could conclude the intervening medical treatment, even if grossly negligent, was the sole cause of death …

Negligent treatment or neglect of an injury will not excuse a wrongdoer unless the treatment or neglect was the sole cause of death; gross maltreatment by attending physicians or surgeons which was the sole cause of the alleged victim's death is a good defense to a charge of homicide. It has also been said that, in order to avoid liability, the defendant must show that erroneous or unskilled medical care became the efficient intervening cause of death and superseded the effect of the wounds inflicted by the defendant so as to become the proximate cause of death.

Obviously, under this restrictive rule of proximate cause, it will be a rare case in which a criminal defendant is relieved from responsibility for the death of the victim, based on intervening medical care. However, one case illustrates when intervening medical treatment *can* break the connection between the criminal act and the death. *See People v. Stewart.* In that case, during medical treatment for a knife wound, surgeons discovered the victim also had an incarcerated hernia. After they sutured the knife wound and completed surgery on the victim's stomach, they proceeded to correct the hernia. The patient died. The autopsy report stated death was caused by a stab wound of the abdomen, stomach, cardiac arrest during surgical correction of a stab wound *and another operation which was indicated during the surgical procedure* with sepsis, which means infection, and kidney shut down. Because treatment for the hernia was not necessitated by the criminal attack, the court held the prosecution had failed to show the cause of death was the knife wound, and it ordered the manslaughter conviction to be reduced to assault.

In the present case, the trial court properly ruled that evidence of malpractice, even if it was "outrageous" as the defendant's witness testified, was inadmissible. No reasonable fact finder could conclude the medical treatment was the sole proximate cause of death. In fact, the defendant's own witness testified it was not. We therefore affirm the district court on this issue.

We vacate the decision of the court of appeals and affirm the judgment of the district court.

## Commonwealth v. Moyer

Supreme Court of Pennsylvania, 1994
436 Pa.Super. 442

HESTER, Judge:

Peter David Moyer appeals from the Lehigh County Court of Common Pleas order which dismissed his petition for habeas corpus. The court determined that the Commonwealth had presented a prima facie case on the charges of involuntary manslaughter [and] operating a watercraft under the influence [among other charges]. Appellant argues that the Commonwealth failed to establish ... that he operated his motorcraft under the influence of alcohol, and maintains that there is insufficient evidence that his conduct caused the death of the victim. We are constrained to reverse in part and affirm in part.

The relevant facts and procedure follow. The Commonwealth's sole eyewitness, Robert Williams, established that on July 19, 1992, at about 6:30 p.m., appellant was operating a "runabout" on the Lehigh River in an area known as Kimmets Lock and was traveling at approximately twenty-five miles per hour. Mr. Williams, an acquaintance of both appellant and the victim, gauged the speed at which the victim, Eric Hennigh, drove his jet ski to be about the same as appellant's craft, and approximately forty feet to the right of appellant's path. The witness explained that both the victim and appellant were acquaintances and had gathered at the river with a group of friends for the day. Mr. Williams stated that while he had observed appellant drink one beer while cooking on the beach earlier in the day, he had observed nothing about appellant's behavior to indicate that he was intoxicated. On a trestle six to eight feet from the waterway, a group of swimmers had gathered, one of whom was Richard Moore. As the victim made what would be his last pass by the trestle, Moore, who was standing on exposed rocks near the trestle, swung a five to six foot stick at the victim as he drove past the trestle. Uncontradicted eyewitness testimony established that after Moore swung the stick at the victim, the victim turned sharply to the left, lost control of the jet ski, and veered directly into the path of appellant's craft. Appellant's boat collided with the jet ski. Mr. Williams admitted that he told appellant that appellant could not have avoided the accident, because it took only a "split second" for the jet ski to travel the forty feet into the path of appellant's boat. Moore fled the scene after the impact, but appellant, whose craft came to an abrupt halt following the collision, jumped into the river and swam over to aid the victim, who was floating face down.

The victim was pronounced dead three hours later at Lehigh Valley Hospital. The autopsy determined that the victim died as the result of multiple traumatic injuries....

[A]ppellant [was taken by police] to police headquarters and [was asked to] submit to a breathalyzer test. Appellant complied but was not told he could opt to decline and lose his operator's license. Appellant took the test at 9:05 p.m., two and one-half hours after the incident. The results were recorded at .18%. No blood test was requested. Appellant's boat and the victim's jet ski were seized and searched. Sixteen empty beer cans were found on appellant's boat, nine of which were appellant's brand of choice.

Based upon the above evidence, appellant was arrested and charged with one count each of involuntary manslaughter [and] operating a watercraft while under the influence [among other charges]. At appellant's preliminary hearing, Richard Williams, the Commonwealth's sole eyewitness and an acquaintance of both the victim and appellant ... testified that appellant drove the runabout in a straight line and could have done nothing to avoid hitting the victim since only a "split second" of time elapsed after Moore swung the stick and the jet ski traversed the forty feet between the two vehicles....

Based upon the information gathered and testimony offered, the magistrate found a prima facie case on all charges.... [Subsequently], appellant filed a petition for review to this court ... He now challenges the magistrate's finding based upon a lack of evidence concerning causation. He argues that he was operating his boat in a straight line at a safe speed and distance from the victim. Further, appellant maintains that he did nothing to cause the victim to swerve into his path, but it was the victim's evasive action with respect to Moore which caused the collision. He alleges that the Commonwealth's evidence wholly fails to establish that he could have avoided the collision. Therefore, appellant asserts that the Commonwealth failed to show that his conduct caused the victim's death. We agree....

Appellant first argues that the Commonwealth failed to sustain its burden of proof with regard to the element of causation on the involuntary manslaughter charge.... Our review of the record reveals that the Commonwealth has failed in this regard....

In order to sustain a charge of involuntary manslaughter, the Commonwealth must show that the appellant's conduct was directly and substantially linked to the victim's death. We have determined that in order to sustain a conviction for involuntary manslaughter, a defendant's conduct must be the antecedent but-for which the result in question would not have occurred. Specifically, it would be unfair to hold an individual responsible for the death of another if his actions are remote or attenuated and the victim's death was attributable to other factors....

A review of the record reveals that there was *no* evidence that appellant could have avoided this tragic accident. The Commonwealth presents *no* support for its conclusion that appellant could have swerved to avoid striking the victim. Specifically, the Commonwealth eyewitness testimony established that appellant and the victim were traveling between twenty-five and thirty miles per hour. Simple calculations indicate that at 30 miles per hour, a vehicle travels at the rate of forty-four feet-per-second, while traveling at 25 miles per hour, a vehicle travels at thirty-six feet-per-second. Eyewitness testimony also established that the victim was located ten to forty feet to the right of appellant's motorboat when Moore struck him with the stick. In other words, in less than a second, two objects traveling about forty feet-per-second crossed paths. The Commonwealth presented no testimony on reaction time, either eyewitness or expert, to support its claim that any person *could* have swerved their boat, given the time frame that it established. Yet, the Commonwealth's case on causation consists solely of its position that defendant caused the death by failing to swerve his boat. The evidence it presented, however, is inadequate to demonstrate that this inaction caused the victim's death due to the fact that there is serious doubt as to whether any reasonable person could have avoided the unfortunate collision....

In conclusion, we are constrained to conclude that the Commonwealth failed to establish a prime facie case to sustain the charges of involuntary manslaughter, reckless operation of a watercraft, and homicide by watercraft under the influence. Consistent with this memorandum, however, the Commonwealth has presented a prima facie case of boating while under the influence of alcohol, and appellant must face proceedings on this charge.

## *Notes and Questions*

1. In *García,* the Supreme Court of Iowa concluded that a physician's medical treatment should not be deemed a superseding cause even if it is considered grossly negligent or outrageous. It argued, however, that negligent medical treatment amounts to a super-

seding cause when it is the *sole* cause of death. The Court cites the *Stewart* case as an example of the latter. The defendant in *Stewart* stabbed the victim, causing her life threatening injuries that required surgery. After successfully completing the surgery to treat the injuries caused by the stabbing, the attending physicians decided to operate on a hernia that was unrelated to the stabbing injuries. The autopsy report "stated death was caused by a stab wound of the abdomen, stomach, cardiac arrest during surgical correction of a stab wound *and another operation which was indicated during the surgical procedure* with sepsis, which means infection, and kidney shut down."

It was held that the physician's decision in *Stewart* to operate on the hernia amounted to a superseding cause because it was the sole cause of death rather than because it was grossly negligent. As a result, the defendant could not be held criminally liable for the victim's death. Do you agree that the physician's medical treatment was the sole cause of death? Does the autopsy report suggest that the surgery of the hernia was the only cause of death? Regardless of your answer to these questions, do you believe that the defendant who stabbed the victim in *Stewart* should have been held liable for the victim's death? Or do you believe that the doctor's conduct amounted to a superseding cause that should exonerate the defendant? Explain.

2. While the vast majority of courts agree that negligent medical treatment should not be considered a superseding cause, not all courts agree that grossly negligent malpractice should not be considered a superseding cause unless it is the sole cause of death. Instead of focusing on whether the treatment is the sole cause of death, some jurisdictions focus on whether the medical treatment was reasonably foreseeable. The Supreme Court of Michigan's approach to the issue in *People v. Shaefer,* 473 Mich. 418 (2005) is representative:

> For a defendant's conduct to be regarded as a proximate cause, the victim's injury must be a "direct and natural result" of the defendant's actions. In making this determination, it is necessary to examine whether there was an intervening cause that superseded the defendant's conduct such that the causal link between the defendant's conduct and the victim's injury was broken. If an intervening cause did indeed *supersede* the defendant's act as a legally significant causal factor, then the defendant's conduct will not be deemed a proximate cause of the victim's injury.
>
> The standard by which to gauge whether an intervening cause supersedes, and thus severs the causal link, is generally one of reasonable foreseeability. For example, suppose that a defendant stabs a victim and the victim is then taken to a nearby hospital for treatment. If the physician is negligent in providing medical care to the victim and the victim later dies, the defendant is still considered to have proximately caused the victim's death because it is reasonably foreseeable that negligent medical care might be provided. At the same time, *gross* negligence or intentional misconduct by a treating physician is not reasonably foreseeable, and would thus break the causal chain between the defendant and the victim.
>
> The linchpin in the superseding cause analysis, therefore, is whether the intervening cause was foreseeable based on an objective standard of reasonableness. If it was reasonably foreseeable, then the defendant's conduct will be considered a proximate cause. If, however, the intervening act by the victim or a third party was not reasonably foreseeable—e.g., *gross* negligence or intentional misconduct—then generally the causal link is severed and the defendant's conduct is not regarded as a proximate cause of the victim's injury or death. *Id.*

What result if the approach to superseding causes espoused by the Supreme Court of Michigan in *Shaefer* is applied to the facts of the *García* case? Explain. Do you prefer the

*Shaefer* approach to whether grossly negligent malpractice amounts to a superseding cause or do you prefer the *García* approach? Explain.

3. The defendant's conduct in *Commonwealth v. Moyer* was an actual cause of the resulting harm, for the victim would not have died but for the defendant's acts. In other words, had the defendant not been operating his boat there and then, the victim would still be alive. Why, then, did the Court hold that the prosecution failed to prove that the defendant's operation of the boat caused the victim's death? Do you agree with the result in *Moyer*? Explain.

4. What was the intervening cause in *Moyer*? Was it the victim's decision to suddenly swerve his jet ski in the direction of the defendant's boat? Was it Moore's swinging of the 5 or 6 foot stick at the victim as he drove past the trestle? Both? Was it reasonably foreseeable for the defendant that a motorist driving past the trestle would swing a stick at a person operating a jet ski in the vicinity? Was it highly extraordinary? Should Moore's swinging of the stick be considered a superseding cause that severs the link between defendant's conduct and the death of the victim? Who do you think was primarily responsible for the victim's death in *Moyer*? The defendant, the victim or Moore? Explain.

## § 7.04 Causation: Victim Conduct as an Intervening Cause

### State v. Murray

Supreme Court of Oregon, 2007
343 Or. 48

GILLETTE, J.

This criminal case requires this court to visit once again an old conundrum respecting the permissibility of punishing an individual criminally for reckless activity when the "victim" of that activity to some degree participated in the reckless conduct. Defendant argues that, under such circumstances, no criminal liability can be assigned to either participant. The trial court disagreed, convicting defendant of assault in the third degree, together with two counts of criminal mischief. On defendant's appeal, the Court of Appeals affirmed the decision of the trial court without opinion. We allowed defendant's petition for review and now affirm the decision of the Court of Appeals.

Although the parties state the essential facts somewhat differently, they do not appear to dispute them. Defendant owns an automobile shop where he converts conventional cars into racing machines by modifying a car's body, suspension, brakes, and engine. The victim, Harris, was defendant's employee at the shop. On the night of February 24, 2001, defendant was "test-driving" a Volkswagen GTI that defendant and Harris had modified for racing. Defendant was driving; Harris was in the front passenger's seat, monitoring the car's performance in various respects both by using his own senses and by using a laptop computer. Defendant drove the car into a residential neighborhood where the speed limit was 35 miles per hour and accelerated the car to a speed in excess of 90 miles per hour. At that point, defendant lost control of the vehicle, which skidded into a power pole, sheared off the pole, and burst into flames. Defendant, who suffered a concussion, was able to get out on his own. Harris was severely injured; passersby pulled him out of the burning car.

Although Harris was defendant's employee, he did not feel coerced to participate in the test drives that defendant would make with cars on which the pair worked. Indeed, there were times when Harris drove and defendant observed. Thus, there is no question in this case that Harris's participation in the test drive of the Volkswagen on the night in question was voluntary.

As noted, defendant was charged, *inter alia,* with assault in the third degree in connection with the crash of the Volkswagen. Assault in the third degree is defined in [Oregon Penal Law as follows]:

1) A person commits the crime of assault in the third degree if the person:

    a) Recklessly causes serious physical injury to another by means of a deadly or dangerous weapon.

At trial, defendant stipulated that Harris, the victim, was seriously physically injured in the crash, that defendant's own conduct in driving the car at the time was reckless, and that his recklessness led to Harris's injuries. Nonetheless, at the close of the state's case, defendant moved for a judgment of acquittal on the assault charge on the ground that, viewing the facts in the light most favorable to the state, the evidence established that the victim had been a knowing participant in the recklessness and, as a consequence, there was no "legal causation" on which to base a conviction ... As noted, the trial court disagreed with defendant and found him guilty, and the Court of Appeals affirmed the conviction without opinion.

We begin by examining the statute that defendant was convicted of violating. Under that statute, a person is guilty of third-degree assault if he recklessly "causes" injury to "another" using a dangerous weapon. To discern the meaning of [the statute], we ... first examine the words of the statute in context. If the meaning of the statute is clear at that first level of analysis, then we proceed no further.

The word "cause" is not defined in the criminal statutes. It is, however, a word of common usage, which we presume the legislature intended to be given its plain, natural, and ordinary meaning. The dictionary defines the verb "cause" as follows: "1: to serve as a cause or occasion of: bring into existence: MAKE (careless driving accidents) 2: to effect by command, authority or force." *Webster's Third New Int'l Dictionary* 356 (unabridged ed. 2002).

In addition, what a person must cause under [the statute defining the offense charged], in order to be guilty of third-degree assault, is a serious physical injury to "another." The statute contains no express limitation on who the victim might be and contains no provision respecting the victim's mental state. Nothing in the foregoing text (or the context) of [the statute] suggests that the legislature intended to carve out an exception for harm done to willing participants in the conduct. Based on our review of the text and context to this point, therefore, a person commits third-degree assault ... if he or she recklessly brings about, makes, or effects by force the serious injury of another person with a dangerous weapon, no matter the role of the other person in the reckless conduct.

At the first level of analysis of a statute, this court also considers case law interpreting that statute. In that regard, defendant suggests that this court in *Petersen* effectively redefined the concept of legal responsibility in cases of this kind. After that case, according to defendant, a person cannot be said to have legally caused a result to a victim if the victim was a willing participant in the conduct that led to the harm to the victim. As we shall show, however, defendant reads too much into this court's decision in *Petersen.*

In *Petersen,* two cars were involved in a speed contest. The defendant was the driver of one of the vehicles; the victim was a passenger in the other and a willing participant in the race. The two vehicles raced through city streets in Portland, reaching speeds of 60 to 80 miles per hour. After about a half-mile, the two vehicles approached an intersection with Powell Boulevard. The defendant, whose pickup truck had been in the lead for most of the race, decelerated as he approached Powell, coming to a complete stop at the intersection. The driver of the car in which the victim was riding passed defendant and proceeded, without slowing down, into the intersection, where his car was struck by a truck traveling west on Powell. Both the driver of that car and the victim were killed in the collision.

The defendant was charged with, among other offenses, second-degree manslaughter, for recklessly causing the death of the passenger in the other racing car. Under [Oregon Penal Law], a person commits the crime of second-degree manslaughter if he or she recklessly "causes the death of another human being." The defendant was convicted of that crime in the trial court. He appealed his conviction to the Court of Appeals, which affirmed in a divided decision. The Court of Appeals majority held that the defendant's conduct was the "cause in fact" of the victim's death, insofar as it was a substantial factor in bringing it about. In addition, the court held that the defendant's conduct was the legal cause of the accident, because the victim's death had been within the area of risk that the rules of caution that the defendant had violated were intended to minimize.

Chief Judge Schwab dissented. Judge Schwab began by defining the pertinent inquiry as whether the defendant's conduct was the legal cause of the victim's death, which, he opined, is "ultimately a policy question." He then went on to state that, in his view, "policy considerations are against imposing responsibility for the death of a *participant* in a race on the surviving racer when his sole contribution to the death is the participation in the activity mutually agreed upon."

In support of his basic proposition, Chief Judge Schwab described several other scenarios that could lead to the death of one of the participants, but in which he would not find a survivor legally responsible: a game of Russian roulette where one of the participants shoots and kills himself; an automobile race at a race track where one of the racers is involved in a fatal crash; and risky recreational activities such as skydiving, deep sea diving, or even ocean fishing in inclement weather, where all involved know that there is a risk of death and one of the participants in fact dies. Chief Judge Schwab concluded,

> My point is that people frequently join together in reckless conduct. As long as all participants do so knowingly and voluntarily, I see no point in holding the survivor(s) guilty of manslaughter if the reckless conduct results in death. Contrary to the majority, I find no expression of legislative policy on this issue in the manslaughter statute, or in any other statute. The issue here is 'legal causation,' an issue which has been traditionally left to the courts.

After the Court of Appeals affirmed the defendant's manslaughter conviction in *Petersen*, the defendant sought review in this court. In a very short opinion, this court reversed. As pertinent here, this court, after briefly reviewing the majority holding below, stated,

> Chief Judge Schwab dissented, expressing the opinion that [Oregon Penal Law] should not be interpreted to extend to those cases in which the victim is a knowing and voluntary participant in the course of reckless conduct. We agree with the reasoning in the dissenting opinion and adopt it as the opinion of this court.

[A]s this court has had occasion to state, in one form or another, on many occasions, considerations of *stare decisis* weigh particularly heavily when this court has purported to interpret a statute. Accordingly, to the extent that this court, in *Petersen*, truly and authoritatively interpreted the scope of the word "cause" in the manslaughter statute (and to the extent that that interpretation is equally applicable in other criminal statutes, including, as pertinent here, [the Oregon assault statute]), then this court considers itself bound by that interpretation, because the legislature has not changed that statute in any material respect since the court announced its opinion in *Petersen* in 1974.

That said, we turn to examine what was actually before the court in *Petersen* and what the court actually held there. In *Petersen*, the defendant's conduct—even if it was reckless—did not cause the victim's death; the defendant's contribution was limited to participation in the speed contest. The victim was killed when a different person—the driver of the car in which the victim was riding—recklessly chose to speed into a busy intersection. Similarly, none of the examples that Chief Judge Schwab gave to illustrate his view of legal causation in the manslaughter statute are ones in which a potential defendant, by his or her own conduct other than mere participation in the risky activity, caused a victim's death. Thus, as we read Chief Judge Schwab's dissent in *Petersen*—and this court's adoption of it—that case stands for the proposition that the mere fact that two people both participate in reckless conduct at the same time and place does not mean that one of the participants necessarily brings about, makes, or effects by force a harm to the other participant; that result requires something more. Chief Judge Schwab succinctly articulated that precise point when he stated that, in his view, the court should not impose legal responsibility "for the death of a *participant* [ ] in a race on a surviving racer *when his sole contribution to the death* is the participation in the activity mutually agreed upon."

The foregoing discussion shows that nothing in *Petersen* holds that a participant in a reckless activity whose recklessness *does* bring about, make, or effect by force an injury to or the death of another person would not be criminally liable for the consequences of his or her conduct, even if the victim voluntarily placed himself or herself in a position to be so injured or killed. It follows that the court's holding in *Petersen* does not absolve defendant of criminal liability for his conduct in this case. Rather, after examining the text of [the assault statute], in context, including this court's decision in *Petersen*, it is clear at the first level of our analysis of [the law] that a person commits third-degree assault if, in addition to participation in the reckless activity, that person's own recklessness causes—*i.e.*, brings about, makes, or effects by force—serious physical injury to another by means of a deadly or dangerous weapon, regardless of the other person's willing participation in the reckless activity. Here, it is undisputed that, in that sense, defendant caused Harris's serious physical injuries; he stipulated that he was driving recklessly and that his reckless driving led directly to the crash that injured Harris. Under [Oregon law], defendant is guilty of third-degree assault.

The decision of the Court of Appeals and the judgment of the circuit court are affirmed.

## *Notes and Questions*

1. The standard superseding cause analysis fails to fully capture the complexity of cases in which the intervening cause is the victim's voluntary decision to suffer harm or risk suffering harm. Take, for example, the case of an actor who successfully encourages another to commit suicide. Should the actor be liable for the death of the person who committed suicide? That is, should the actor be held liable for homicide? If the question is answered by applying the conventional superseding cause principles discussed in the previous section, the answer is likely to be that such actors ought to be held liable for homicide. After all, that a person will commit suicide is a reasonably foreseeable consequence of the act of encouraging someone else to commit suicide. Not only is such a result reasonably foreseeable, but it is also precisely the result that the defendant intended. According to the

conventional foreseeability-based analysis of proximate cause, this militates in favor of finding that the victim's decision to commit suicide is not a superseding cause that severs the nexus between the defendant's conduct and the resulting harm.

Nevertheless, courts almost unanimously resist imposing liability on defendants for harm that results as a consequence of the victim's voluntary decision to suffer self-inflicted harm. The standard approach to these cases is illustrated by *People v. Kevorkian*, 527 N.W.2d 714 (Mich. 1994). Doctor Kevorkian provided patients who were terminally ill or in extreme pain with the means to commit suicide. He was charged with murdering a victim that committed suicide using the means that he provided. The Michigan Supreme Court held that the defendant could not be held liable for murder because the victim's decision to commit suicide was the true cause of the death and therefore severed the link between the defendant's conduct and the death of the victim. The Court further explained that:

> In the context of participation in a suicide ... a conviction of murder is proper if a defendant participates in the final overt act that causes death, such as firing a gun or pushing the plunger on a hypodermic needle. However, where a defendant is involved merely "in the events leading up to the commission of the final overt act, such as furnishing the means" ... a conviction of assisted suicide is proper....
>
> Only where there is probable cause to believe that death was the direct and natural result of a defendant's act can the defendant be properly bound over on a charge of murder. Where a defendant merely is involved in the events leading up to the death, such as providing the means, the proper charge is assisting in a suicide. *Id.*

Do you agree with the outcome in *Kevorkian*? Explain. Why does the victim's decision to commit suicide exonerate the defendant of liability for the resulting harm when the decision to commit suicide is both reasonably foreseeable and subjectively foreseen (and encouraged) by the defendant?

2. The preceding analysis does not apply when the victim's decision to suffer harm is not voluntary. In *Stephenson v. State,* 205 Ind. 141 (1932), for example, the defendant kidnapped the victim and subjected her to physical and emotional abuse. Desperate to escape the abuse, the victim committed suicide by ingesting poison. Defendant was charged and convicted of murdering the victim. The Supreme Court of Indiana upheld the conviction. Addressing whether the victim's decision to commit suicide severed the causal link between the defendant's conduct and the resulting harm, the Court stated that:

> So if it be true, as appellant contends, that the indictment alleges that [the victim] voluntarily committed suicide, that is, that she took her own life while in sound mind, such an act on her part would constitute an intervening responsible agent such as would break the causal connection between the acts of appellant and the death of [the victim]. But we cannot agree with appellant in this construction of the first count of the indictment, for it is alleged in said count, in effect, that [the victim] was, at the time she swallowed the poison, distracted with the pain and shame inflicted upon her by appellant. If the allegations be true, and we must so consider them on a motion to quash, then the act of [the victim] in taking the poison was not the act of a responsible agent, and the chain of cause and effect between the acts of appellant and the death would not be broken, and appellant would be guilty of murder. *Id.*

When is the victim's decision to harm herself not sufficiently voluntary to be considered a superseding cause? Is an actor who successfully encourages a five year old to commit suicide guilty of homicide or merely of assisting in suicide? What about someone who successfully encourages a sixteen year old to kill herself? Is a person who successfully convinces a depressed person to commit suicide guilty of murder or assisting in suicide? What about an actor who convinces a drunk person to commit suicide? In *People v. Campbell,* 124 Mich.App. 333 (1982), defendant and victim were drinking heavily at a bar. Defendant then suggested that the victim kill himself and provided him with the gun to do so. After defendant left the bar, the victim committed suicide. The Court ruled that defendant could not be held liable for homicide. Do you agree with the outcome? Why or why not?

3. Although there is general agreement that the victim's voluntary decision to suffer harm severs the link between the defendant's conduct and the resulting harm, there is much debate regarding whether the victim's decision to *risk* suffering harm should be treated the same way. This is the issue addressed in *State v. Murray,* the leading case included in this section. The defendant in *Murray* was held liable for the physical injuries suffered by the victim even though the victim voluntarily decided to participate in the test drive of the vehicle with full knowledge that defendant would be driving recklessly and at excessive speeds. Why did the victim's decision to voluntarily risk suffering harm not amount to a superseding cause in this case? Why is the victim's decision to suffer harm treated differently than the victim's decision to risk suffering harm? Do you agree with the outcome in *Murray*? Explain.

4. According to the dissenting opinion that the Supreme Court of Michigan adopted in full in *Petersen* and which later served as the basis for its decision in *Murray,* when "participants knowingly and voluntarily [engage in reckless conduct], [there is] no point in holding the survivor(s) guilty of manslaughter if the reckless conduct results in death." This would lead to exonerating those who engage in "a game of Russian roulette where one of the participants shoots and kills himself; an automobile race at a race track where one of the racers is involved in a fatal crash; and risky recreational activities such as sky-diving, deep sea diving, or even ocean fishing in inclement weather, where all involved know that there is a risk of death and one of the participants in fact dies." Do you agree that it is pointless to hold the survivors of these reckless endeavors liable for the resulting harms? Do those that emerge unscathed deserve to be punished for the harm suffered by the participants who were not so lucky? Are there good consequentialist reasons for holding such actors liable regardless of whether the victim consented to the reckless conduct? Explain.

5. In the oft-cited case of *Commonwealth v. Atencio,* 189 N.E.2d 323 (1963), the defendants were convicted of manslaughter for the death of the victim who shot himself while playing Russian roulette with the defendants. The Supreme Court of Massachusetts rejected the defendants' argument that they should not be held liable because the victim voluntarily decided to play the game. According to the Court:

> [T]he defendants could properly have been found guilty of manslaughter.... Here the Commonwealth had an interest that the deceased should not be killed by the wanton or reckless conduct of himself and others. Such conduct could be found in the concerted action and cooperation of the defendants in helping to bring about the deceased's foolish act.
>
> The testimony does not require a ruling that when the deceased took the gun from Atencio it was an independent or intervening act not standing in any rela-

tion to the defendants' acts which would render what he did imputable to them.... In the abstract, there may have been no duty on the defendants to prevent the deceased from playing. But there was a duty on their part not to cooperate or join with him in the "game." *Id.*

Do you agree with the result in *Atencio*? Why or why not? What is achieved by holding defendants like those in *Atencio* liable for the harms that result as a consequence of engaging in reckless endeavors like Russian roulette? What is the most persuasive argument against liability in cases like these?

6. Another much debated question is whether participants in drag races should be held liable for the harms suffered by other participants. The question was answered affirmatively in *State v. Mcfadden,* 320 N.W.2d 608 (1982), where the Supreme Court of Iowa rejected defendant's argument that he should not be held liable because "competitor[s] in [a] drag race ... assume the risk of [their] own death." Citing another case, the Court stated that:

> Defendants by participating in the unlawful racing initiated a series of events resulting in the death of [the victim]. Under these circumstances, decedent's own unlawful conduct does not absolve defendants from their guilt. The acts of defendants were contributing and substantial factors in bringing about the death of [the victim]. The acts and omissions of two or more persons may work concurrently as the efficient cause of an injury and in such case each of the participating acts or omissions is regarded in law as a proximate cause. *Id.*

In contrast, in *Commonwealth v. Root,* 430 Pa. 571 (1961)—another drag racing case—the Supreme Court of Pennsylvania absolved the defendant of liability because:

> [T]he deceased was aware of the dangerous condition created by the defendant's reckless conduct in driving his automobile at an excessive rate of speed along the highway but, despite such knowledge, he recklessly chose to swerve his car to the left and into the path of an oncoming truck, thereby bringing about the head-on collision which caused his own death. *Id.*

A dissenting opinion in *Root* challenged the majority's conclusion by pointing out that:

> If the defendant did not engage in the unlawful race and so operate his automobile in such a reckless manner, this accident would never have occurred. He helped create the dangerous event. He was a vital part of it. The victim's acts were a natural reaction to the stimulus of the situation. The race, the attempt to pass the other car and forge ahead, the reckless speed, all of these factors the defendant himself helped create. He was part and parcel of them. That the victim's response was normal under the circumstances, that his reaction should have been expected and was clearly foreseeable, is to me beyond argument. That the defendant's recklessness was a substantial factor is obvious. All of this, in my opinion, makes his unlawful conduct a direct cause of the resulting collision. *Id.*

Do you agree with the majority or the dissent? Explain. Note that the harm of a participant in a drag race is clearly a reasonably foreseeable consequence of engaging in the drag race. Therefore, if the drag racing cases (and the Russian roulette cases) are approached from the perspective of foreseeability, the arguments in favor of holding defendants liable is powerful. Nevertheless, those who argue in favor of exonerating defendants in these types of cases do so in spite of the reasonable foreseeability of the harms that ensue. Rather than foreseeability, what explains this position is respect for the victim's autonomy. Part of being a morally accountable agent is accepting responsibility for the consequences of our voluntary acts. Respecting this principle entails recognizing that the responsibility for the harm suffered by the victim in the cases discussed in these Notes lies with the victim rather than with the defendants. This argument points in the direction of absolving the defendants of liability. On the other hand, punishing defendants in cases such as these may deter others from engaging in similarly foolish activities. This suggests that liability should be imposed in these cases. Which of these arguments do you find more convincing? Why?

## § 7.05 Causation: Model Penal Code

### § 2.03. Causal Relationship Between Conduct and Result; Divergence Between Result Designed or Contemplated and Actual Result or Between Probable and Actual Result.

(1) Conduct is the cause of a result when:

(a) It is an antecedent but for which the result in question would not have occurred; and

(b) The relationship between the conduct and result satisfies any additional causal requirements imposed by the Code or by the law defining the offense.

(2) When purposely or knowingly causing a particular result is an element of an offense, the element is not established if the actual result is not within the purpose or the contemplation of the actor unless:

(a) The actual result differs from that designed or contemplated, as the case may be, only in the respect that a different person or different property is injured or affected or that the injury or harm designed or contemplated would have been more serious or more extensive than that caused; or

(b) The actual result involves the same kind of injury or harm as that designed or contemplated and is not too remote or accidental in its occurrence to have a [just] bearing on the actor's liability or on the gravity of his offense.

(3) When recklessly or negligently causing a particular result is an element of an offense, the element is not established if the actual result is not within the risk of which the actor is aware or, in the case of negligence, of which he should be aware unless:

(a) The actual result differs from the probable result only in the respect that a different person or different property is injured or affected or that the probable injury or harm would have been more serious or more extensive than that caused; or

(b) The actual result involves the same kind of injury or harm as the probable result and is not too remote or accidental in its occurrence to have a [just] bearing on the actor's liability or on the gravity of his offense.

(4) When causing a particular result is a material element of an offense for which absolute liability is imposed by law, the element is not established unless the actual result is a probable consequence of the actor's conduct.

## *Notes and Questions*

1. Subsection (1) of the excerpted Model Penal Code provision requires that the defendant's conduct be a "but for" cause of the victim's harm. In addition to this, the remaining subsections state that it is no defense to criminal liability that the result differs from what the actor subjectively foresaw only in that a different person or property interest was affected. Strictly speaking, this is a problem of "transferred intent" that is more appropriately discussed in the context of subjective offense elements (*mens rea*). Transferred intent is discussed in the chapter devoted to subjective elements of the offense (Chapter 8).

2. Perhaps more importantly, the Code precludes liability when the actor's conduct is "too remote or accidental in its occurrence to have a just bearing on the actor's liability." Note that the Code drafters refused to make direct reference to the tests traditionally invoked by courts when assessing legal or proximate causation. The Code's causation provision does not mention foreseeability, whether the result is highly extraordinary or the concepts of intervening and superseding causes. Instead, it merely requires that the result not be too remote or accidental to have a just bearing on the liability of the defendant. The decision to address the causation inquiry in such broad terms was explained in the following manner in *State v. Martin*, 573 A.2d 1359 (1990):

> Neither the Model Penal Code nor the New Jersey Code attempts to deal with every possible problem of causation. The New Jersey Criminal Law Revision Commission (the New Jersey Commission or the Commission) explained:
>
> ... [The] Code makes no attempt to catalogue the possibilities, *e.g.*, to deal with the intervening or concurrent causes, natural or human; unexpected physical conditions; distinctions between the infliction of mortal or non-mortal wounds. It deals only with the ultimate criterion by which the significance of such possibilities ought to be judged, *i.e.*, that the question to be faced is whether the actual result is too accidental in its occurrence or too dependent on another's volitional act to have a just bearing on the actor's liability or on the gravity of his offense. *Id.*

Ultimately, then, as the Supreme Court of Kentucky observed in *Robertson v. Commonwealth*, 82 S.W.3d 832 (2002), the Code's causation provision "operates to exclude criminal liability in cases where the defendant would otherwise have committed an offense, but common sense notions of responsibility for the occurrence of results dictate that the imposition of criminal liability is inappropriate." Consequently, the approach to legal causation adopted in the Code is eminently normative in nature, focusing on whether it is fair or just to hold the defendant liable for the resulting harm rather than on factual questions regarding scientific causation or doctrinal inquiries regarding foreseeability or superseding causes.

3. According to the Code's approach, the relevant question in cases like the ones discussed in the previous sections is not whether the "medical malpractice was grossly negligent" or the "sole cause of the harm" or if the victim voluntarily consented to engaging in a reckless endeavor. Instead, the determinative question is whether it is *fair* or *just* to hold the defendant liable for the victim's harm in spite of the "outrageous" medical treatment or despite the victim's decision to risk suffering harm. This is not to say that foreseeability, the victim's autonomy or any of the other factors typically considered by courts when assessing legal causation are irrelevant under the Model Penal Code. What it means, however, is that none of these factors is determinative and that the judge or jury must make peace with the fact that the legal causation inquiry is ultimately dependent on intuitions of justice and fairness that cannot be reduced to neat formulas or rigid doctrinal prescriptions.

4. Reconsider the cases discussed in the previous sections. Was the death of the helicopter pilots "too remote or accidental to have a just bearing on the defendant's liability" in *Acosta*? Is it fair or just to hold defendants liable for harm that results as a consequence of the victim's decision to risk suffering harm? Why or why not? Would you rather look at these cases through the prism of foreseeability or superseding causes or do you prefer the purely normative inquiry that the Model Penal Code prescribes? Explain.

## § 7.06 Causation: Comparative Perspectives

### Claus Roxin, *The Controversy over Cases in Which an Actor Consents to Being Endangered by Someone Else's Conduct*

(originally published in Spanish in InDret 1/2013)

The starting point for my argument is the distinction between helping someone else engage in conduct that risks causing him harm and endangering someone else by engaging in reckless conduct with that person's consent. The former scenario takes place when an actor suffers harm as a result of his own risky conduct in circumstances in which someone else has helped him engage in the risky undertaking. For example, A and B engage in a dangerous motorcycle race in which A dies as a result of an accident. Although in this case B has cooperated to causing A's death, he cannot be held liable for negligent homicide. Since A's decision to endanger his own life is not punishable, it cannot be criminal for B to help A engage in conduct that does not give rise to criminal liability....

We have a different case when an actor consents to being endangered by someone else's conduct. The type of case that I have in mind is that in which an actor endangers someone else in circumstances when the person that is endangered by the actor's conduct assumes the risk with full knowledge of the dangerous nature of the conduct. Perhaps the most frequent real life case of this type is that of someone who—after a night of partying—agrees to take a ride with someone who is intoxicated, knowing full well that the driver is not capable of driving properly. Is the driver liable of negligent homicide if, because of his state of intoxication, he gets in an accident and the passenger riding with him dies? In what follows, I will present the reader with five additional cases taken out of German case law that illustrate the many real life situations in which this type of case may arise.

**(1) The Memel River case**

This case is still famous today, even though it was decided by the Imperial Supreme Court before World War II. A boat captain warned two travelers about the dangers of crossing the Memel River in inclement weather. The travelers insisted in crossing the river. The boat captain acquiesced. The boat capsized and the travelers drowned. Is the boat captain liable for negligent homicide?

**(2) The AIDS case**

... A woman voluntarily decides to have unprotected sexual intercourse with a male, knowing that the male has AIDS. The women is infected with AIDS as a result of the conduct. Is the male liable for negligent battery?

(3) **The pick-up truck case**

Against the advice of the driver, a construction worker hopped on the bed of the driver's pick-up truck. The construction worker was killed when the pick-up truck got in an accident. He died because he was traveling unrestrained in the back of the truck. The accident was not the driver's fault. Is the driver liable for negligent homicide?

(4) **The "car surfer" case**

According to the driver of the car, several young adults were engaging in the "sport" of standing on top of the roof of his car while it was traveling at 45 to 50 miles per hour. One of the young adults suffered serious bodily injury when he fell from the roof of the car. Is the driver criminally liable for the injuries?

(5) **The drag race case**

This case, which was decided by the Federal Supreme Court in 2008, has generated ample and intense debate in Germany. Several young adults planned a car race in which two cars would race each other at speeds nearing 150 miles per hour. The cars would then try to overtake a third vehicle that was not involved in the race. While dangerously trying to overtake the vehicle in a very narrow strip of road, one of the cars competing in the race crashed and one of the car's passengers died. The issue was whether the drivers of both cars involved in the competition were liable of negligent homicide in spite of the fact that the passengers agreed to riding in the cars, were filming the race and the passenger who actually died had even given the signal to start the race....

### 5. The Solution to the Cases

[Several decades ago], I proposed treating cases in which someone endangers another by engaging in reckless conduct with that person's consent as instances that preclude a finding of legal causation when ... "the actor who consents to being endangered by someone else's reckless conduct is as responsible [or more responsible] for the reckless conduct than the person who actually engaged in the reckless conduct." ...

According to this approach, the case of someone who encourages an intoxicated driver to give him a ride should be treated differently than the case of someone who is reluctant to ride with the intoxicated driver but eventually yields to the driver's insistent pleas that he ride along with him. If the passenger suffers an accident in the first case, the passenger is as responsible for his own injuries as the driver is. Consequently, the driver should not be held liable for the passenger's injuries. In the second case, however, the driver should be held liable, for he is more responsible for the passenger's injuries than the passenger.

This approach is similar to the one taken by the Imperial Supreme Court in the Memel River case, for the Court considered it determinative to the outcome of the case (exonerating the boat captain of liability) that the boat captain had "repeatedly cautioned the two travelers about the dangers of the voyage and tried to dissuade them from crossing the river". The Court further emphasized that "it was only because the travelers insisted in crossing the river that the boat captain decided to do so, knowing that he would be risking his own life in order to please the travelers". A case like this should be equated to a case in which the victims themselves engage in the reckless conduct that caused them harm. In contrast, had the boat captain been the one who convinced the travelers to cross the river in spite of their reservations about doing so, he should have been convicted of negligent homicide.

In the AIDS case, the Superior Court emphasized that the woman that engaged in unprotected sexual intercourse "had been warned several times by the defendant about his condition and about the dangers of engaging in unprotected sexual intercourse". Eventually, the woman's insistence to carry on in spite of such warnings "overcame the defendant's initial reluctance". The Court thus concluded that the woman's injuries were self-inflicted and, as a result, the defendant should not be held liable. The outcome of the case strikes me as the correct one....

The case would be different if the defendant had been the one that proposed engaging in unprotected sexual intercourse. It would have been even more different had the defendant ... asked the woman to engage in unprotected sexual intercourse as proof of her unconditional love for him. In such cases, the male should be held liable because he is more responsible for the injuries than she is....

The pick-up truck case should be decided in the same manner. Given that the injured construction worker insisted to ride in the bed of the truck over the driver's objections, he assumed the risk and the driver should be acquitted. Similarly, in the case of the "car-surfers", the injured parties desired to engage in the dangerous game, and were thus at least as responsible for their injuries as the driver was. As a result,—contrary to what the Superior Court held in the case—the driver should have been acquitted....

The car race case presents a different situation. Although both passengers and drivers agreed to the race and were thus equally responsible for it, the agreement did not encompass the driver's dangerous maneuver to overtake the third vehicle. But even if the agreement is construed to include acquiescence to the driver's dangerous overtaking maneuver, the driver had much more responsibility than the passenger for engaging in such conduct. As the Federal Supreme Court pointed out, the passengers were "exposed to the consequences of the actions taken by the drivers" and they "lacked the capacity to prevent the drivers from engaging in risky maneuvers." For these reasons, the drivers should be held liable for the death of the passenger. The case would have been different had the deceased passenger been as responsible of the dangerous maneuver as the driver, by, for example, encouraging the driver to engage in such risky conduct. In such a case, the injuries can be fairly attributed to the passenger's conduct and, as a result, the driver ought to be exonerated of liability.

## *Notes and Questions*

1. The German professor Claus Roxin is the most influential European criminal law scholar of the last several decades. In the excerpted article, he argues that cases in which an actor helps another to engage in risky conduct should be distinguished from cases in which an actor endangers another by engaging in reckless conduct with that person's consent. The *Atencio* case (§ 7.04, Note 5) is an example of the former, for the defendant encouraged the victim to engage in risky conduct (playing Russian roulette). In contrast, the *Murray* case (§ 7.04, leading case) is an example of the latter, for the defendant driver endangered the life of the passenger by engaging in risky conduct (driving car at 90 miles per hour) with the passenger's consent. The difference between these cases is that in the former the victim actually engages in the risky conduct (victim pulled the trigger in *Atencio*), whereas in the latter the victim consents to being endangered by someone else's risky conduct (victim agreed to ride as passenger while defendant drove recklessly).

2. Roxin argues that defendants in the first type of cases should be exonerated, given that the harm suffered by the victim in these instances should be entirely attributed to the

victim's freely willed decision to engage in the risky conduct. This would lead to acquitting the defendant in *Atencio*. This is the position defended by most European and Latin American courts and scholars. On the contrary, Roxin argues that defendants in the second group of cases should be convicted, but only if they heavily influenced the victim's decision to acquiesce to being endangered by the actor's risky conduct. Thus, he would convict the defendant in *Murray* only if the passenger's decision to ride in the car was prompted by the defendant's insistent pleas that he do so. More specifically, Roxin is inclined to hold defendants liable in these cases when the victim is initially skeptical about agreeing to the defendant's conduct, but is eventually convinced by the defendant to acquiesce. In contrast, Roxin would acquit the defendant if the victim convinced the defendant to engage in the dangerous conduct. He would also oppose liability when the defendant did not encourage the victim to consent and the victim nevertheless freely acquiesced to being endangered by the defendant's conduct. Given that the victim in *Murray* did not initially object to riding as a passenger and that there was no evidence that defendant went out of his way to convince the victim to ride with him, the defendant would likely by acquitted according to Roxin's theory.

3. Do you agree that there are important differences between cases in which the victim actually engages in the risky conduct and those in which the victim consents to being endangered by someone else's conduct? Explain. Do you agree with the outcomes that Roxin's theory would likely dictate in *Atencio* and *Murray*? Why?

4. Was the death of the passengers in the Memel River case foreseeable? Was it highly extraordinary? Roxin argues that it was appropriate to acquit the boat captain. Do you agree? Explain. Do you agree with the solutions that Roxin proposes for the AIDS, pick-up truck, car-surfer and car race cases? Why? How do you think American courts would decide these cases? Explain.

5. Roxin argues that an intoxicated driver who insists on giving a ride to a friend who is initially skeptical about accepting the ride should be held liable for the harms that the passenger may suffer as a result of his reckless driving. Nevertheless, he suggests a different outcome if the friend convinces the intoxicated driver to give him a ride. In this case, Roxin would not hold the intoxicated driver liable for the harms that the friend may suffer as a consequence of his careless driving. Do you agree that these two cases should be treated differently? Why or why not?

# § 7.07 Causation: Scholarly Debates

## Vera Bergelson, *Victims and Perpetrators: An Argument for Comparative Liability in the Criminal Law*

8 Buff. Crim. L. Rev. 385 (2005)

### C. How Can Victims' Conduct Mitigate Perpetrators' Liability?

#### 1. Principle of Conditionality of Rights

... The right not to be harmed is a fundamental human right and, as such, may very rarely, if ever, be lost completely; it, however, may be reduced. By that, I do not mean that the right not to be harmed may suddenly drop from 100% to 70%. Instead, I view the right not to be harmed as bunch of stick-like rights—not to be killed, not to be injured, not to be deprived of liberty, property etc. A person's actions may trigger the loss of some of those specific rights and, in this sense, reduce the overall right not to be harmed.

Accordingly, a person who, with the owner's consent, destroyed a valuable piece of property, has violated no rights of the owner and is usually guilty of no offense. And a person who, while acting in self-defense, applied more force than reasonably necessary, is responsible only for that "extra" force because the attacker has lost his right not to be attacked at all, but retained a right not to be attacked with a disproportionate amount of force.

This conclusion, naturally, leads to an important question: how can victims lose their rights to life, liberty, or property? Do car owners lose their right not to have their cars stolen by leaving keys in the ignition? Do women lose their right not to be raped by wearing mini-skirts?...

[What I call in this article] the conditionality of rights principle provides both the methodology and specific answers to the question of how the victim's conduct may reduce the perpetrator's criminal liability. Pursuant to that principle, there are two relevant inquiries: (i) what rights did the parties possess prior to the criminal encounter? and (ii) has the victim reduced his rights, voluntarily or involuntarily?

The first question includes legal as well as factual considerations. The answer to it depends on whether the law recognizes that a particular individual is entitled to a particular right under particular circumstances.... Among other things, it has been noted that the law may deny certain rights either completely (e.g., the right to enter into incestuous relations) or to some groups of citizens (e.g., the right of minors to sexual intercourse). Naturally, if the victim does not possess the relevant right (or the right is deemed inalienable), he may not reduce it either. In that case, the victim's conduct should not affect the perpetrator's liability. However, laws that deny people liberty or property rights are rather rare. The following discussion relates to the second inquiry, namely, to the victim's reduction of legally recognized rights.

### 2. Voluntary Reduction of Rights

Provided the victim had relevant alienable rights, he may reduce or waive them by consent. To be valid, consent has to be freely given and rational. To the extent the voluntary and rational nature of consent can be ensured, there is a strong argument for not punishing a person who caused harm pursuant to the valid consent of the victim. Such arguments have often been made in connection with assisted suicide.

Assumption of risk is a form of consent. Specifically, it constitutes express or implied consent to undertake a certain risk of harm. Implied consent is given by, or may be imputed to, the victim when he undertakes a substantial risk of harm—whether recklessly, negligently, or even non-culpably (e.g., in a situation when the dangerous conduct may be justified or excused by the circumstances). The less conscious the victim's decision to engage in a dangerous activity is, the more appropriate it may be to treat his behavior as an involuntary, rather than a voluntary, reduction of rights.

The requirements for the valid assumption of risk are essentially the same as for consent in general. Under the tort law, in order to be effective, consent must be given for the particular, or substantially the same, conduct of the actor. "Thus consent to a fight with fists is not consent to an act of a very different character, such as biting off a finger, stabbing with a knife, or using brass knuckles." Similar criteria applied to a criminal case would explain why consent to date Mike Tyson may not be viewed as consent to rape, just as consent to fighting may not be viewed as consent to being stabbed with a knife.

Conversely, if the scope of otherwise valid consent matches the scope of the parties' actions, the consent of the victim should be regarded as a liability mitigator. Examples of situations in which this principle should be applied include those where defendants are held liable for a death resulting from a duel, a fatal round of Russian roulette, or a drag race, i.e., cases in which we can speak about the victim's explicit consent to or disregard of substantial risk. The mitigating argument would be particularly strong in a situation in which the defendant was not a direct cause of the deadly accident. Consider Commonwealth v. Peak. In that case, three buddies, John Young, George Ramsey, and Charles Peak, "after discussions in two barrooms, agreed to race their cars." Young lost control of his car and was killed in an accident. There were no other casualties. Ramsey and Peak were found guilty of involuntary manslaughter of Young. The court opined:

> Defendants by participating in the unlawful racing initiated a series of events resulting in the death of Young. Under these circumstances, decedent's own unlawful conduct does not absolve defendants from their guilt. The acts of defendants were contributing and substantial factors in bringing about the death of Young.

It seems fair that the victim's own unlawful conduct should not completely absolve defendants from their guilt. The question is: their guilt for what? Ramsey and Peak are certainly guilty of violating the law prohibiting speeding contests but are they guilty of killing Young? Wasn't it Young himself who agreed to participate in the race? Wasn't it his own lack of judgment or poor driving skills that cost him his life? Some courts, after struggling with similar questions, have found no liability because the defendants' conduct was not the direct cause of the victim's death. But is it fair to say that the defendants bear no responsibility for what happened?

A more realistic and fair approach would be to apportion responsibility among all parties who have contributed to the criminal outcome, i.e., to hold Ramsey and Peak liable for the death of Young but reduce their level of liability. For instance, if negligent homicide is a felony of the third degree, Ramsey's and Peak's participation in a dangerous activity that resulted in negligent homicide could bring them the conviction of a misdemeanor. In fact, the MPC already has a provision that may be used for that purpose. Section 211.2 prohibits reckless conduct that "places or may place another person in danger of death or serious bodily injury." Convicting Ramsey and Peak under that section would reflect the level of their fault better than either finding them guilty of homicide by twisting the concept of proximate causation or relieving them of any responsibility....

#### 4. Factors Important to Mitigation

##### b. Comparative Causation

The question of responsibility is closely tied to the problem of causation....

All our experience tells us that causation is almost never an all-or-nothing issue. Many factors work together to bring about a result. Thus, in the words of Judith Jarvis Thomson, it is "[n]o wonder it has seemed such a hard problem to work out the truth-conditions for 'X is the cause of Y'—for it is doubtful that 'X is the sole cause of Y' can ever be true." Yet criminal law has chosen to ignore the causative role of the victim and instead has attributed the entire responsibility for harm to the defendant who was just a "but for" cause and a proximate cause of the victim's injury or loss. To overcome this simplistic model, the law needs to adopt a comparative approach to causation, not stay with a black-and-white dichotomy....

Can the causative importance of various events ever be compared? There is a view that denies that possibility. Under that view, causation is not a relative concept; it either exists or it does not, and if it does exist, one may not speak of degrees of causation. If certain events were necessary to produce a result, it is impossible to tell which event was more necessary. Thus, if "it took malaria-bearing mosquitoes and the spread of Christianity to undo the Roman Empire, the mosquitoes were as necessary as the Christians and neither is paramount to the other."

Although it is sometimes difficult to distinguish the determinative cause among other causes, nevertheless, in many contexts, we compare events as being more or less important for certain consequences. The following examples demonstrate our everyday experience in comparing the significance of various events:

> We might wish to say, for instance, that Lenin's participation in the Bolshevik Revolution was a more important cause of its success than was Stalin's, or that the absence of a skilled labor force is a more important cause of economic backwardness than is limited natural resources. Or, we might have reason to say that James is happier today than he was last week partly because he earned an A on his torts exam, but more because his love life has improved.

... We measure the importance of a cause by (i) the difference it makes ... and (ii) the legal and moral weight we assign to different types of behavior. The famous case of Stephenson v. State provides good material for showing how these considerations may work.

In that case, the victim, Madge Oberholtzer, took poison after being kidnapped, beaten, humiliated, and nearly raped. She was denied medical help by her kidnapper and eventually died. In summary, factors that contributed to Madge Oberholtzer's death apparently were: "shock, loss of food, loss of rest, action of the poison on her system and her lack of early treatment." According to medical testimony, it was unlikely that any one factor would have resulted in death on its own.

The jury found the defendant guilty of second-degree murder, and the Supreme Court of Indiana affirmed the verdict. Some commentators have harshly criticized that decision, which, in their view, undermined the requirement of proximate causation by holding Stephenson responsible for an intervening act of the victim. However, if we recognize the principle of comparative causation, that decision would be much more convincing. The question of liability would not be reduced to physical acts of the victim and the perpetrator. Instead, the jurors would be instructed to evaluate all evidence in order to determine (a) whether Madge Oberholtzer's death would have occurred in the absence of (i) her actions and (ii) the defendant's actions, and (b) who is more accountable for her death.

As for the first question, the jurors would be likely to conclude that Stephenson's actions were at least as important a cause of Madge Oberholtzer's death as her own—but for him, she would not have taken the poison. More importantly, even after she took the poison, she still could be saved had he not denied her medical treatment.

As for the second question, the jurors would have to compare the legal and moral significance of cold-blooded, premeditated criminal acts committed by Stephenson and hysterical, semi-rational acts of Madge Oberholtzer committed in response to the attack she had suffered. They would also have to include into the calculation the fact that Stephenson had not just the moral, but also the legal duty to rescue his victim—he was the one who created peril and who took her to a place of isolation where other people could not help her. If the question of causation were regarded this way, the Supreme Court of Indiana would have a much stronger legal basis to affirm the conviction and conclude that "[t]o say that there is no causal connection between the acts of appellant and the death of Madge Oberholtzer, and that the treatment accorded her by appellant had no causal connection with the death of Madge Oberholtzer would be a travesty on justice."

## Kenneth Simons, *The Relevance of Victim Conduct in Tort and Criminal Law*

8 Buff. Crim. L. Rev. 541 (2005)

... [S]hould consent have mitigating significance in the criminal law? One reason for doubt is that consent is not ordinarily understood to vary by degrees. Unlike victim fault, which can readily be characterized as varying from slight to extreme, consent appears to be an all-or-nothing concept. If all of its prerequisites are satisfied (sufficient awareness of the risks, lack of duress, and so forth), then it is often a complete defense; but if they are not quite satisfied, we do not ordinarily say that the victim partially or almost consented. Rather, consent simply drops out of the picture. Note, too, that consent is not considered a matter of degree in tort law. For example, although the range of factors considered in the Restatement Third of Apportionment's comparative fault formula is quite broad, the factors do not include consent.

On the other hand, perhaps criminal law (unlike tort law) has reason to give consent mitigating significance. Bergelson points out that many states have explicitly graded assisted suicide as manslaughter, rather than murder. She also notes that consent often has mitigating significance in determining a murderer's eligibility for the death penalty. And it might be appropriate to give consent mitigating weight in some other circumstances, too—for example, in sadomasochistic assaults, or in duels, Russian roulette, or drag races (the three examples that Bergelson cites).

Still, when and whether this is appropriate does not, I believe, depend on applying Bergelson's proposed ... framework. Indeed, Bergelson herself does not include "degree of consent" as one of the elements in her multifactor analysis. Rather, the advisability of mitigating punishment because of consent should consider at least the following four factors.

First, how strong is the state's paternalistic interest in protecting the victim? If a victim foolishly risks his own death simply to obtain a thrill, as in a game of Russian roulette, the state might justifiably ignore his consent. Moreover, if statutory rape is a defensible crime, obviously it would make little sense to permit a consent mitigation (except, perhaps, when consent has been obtained from the most mature victims who are less in need of state protection).

A second point is related: to a limited extent, consent can be a question of degree. Even when criminal liability is imposed despite the victim's consent, the proper punishment could depend on whether the victim is especially immature or especially mature. And when criminal liability is imposed because of the victim's lack of legally valid consent, perhaps the punishment should reflect whether the victim has to some extent consented—for example, whether the victim agreed to some degree of interaction with the perpetrator. On this approach, if a victim agrees to very intimate sexual contact short of intercourse, arguably the defendant who engages in nonconsensual intercourse should be considered partly justified in his conduct and should receive a lesser punishment.

But this last example suggests a third and important point. We should not assume that consent is relevant to mitigation only insofar as it demonstrates that the actor was at least partly justified. For consent is often relevant instead in demonstrating that the actor possessed a less culpable state of mind or was at least partially excused. A clear example is the death penalty mitigation provided to a killer who acted at a victim's request in order to relieve the victim's suffering. Such a motive is obviously far less culpable than the pecuniary or cruel motives that serve as aggravating death penalty factors. Similarly, if a rape victim's consent to sexual intimacies has any mitigating significance (and one might well argue that it should not, insofar as proceeding with intercourse in these circumstances is an especially wrongful breach of trust), the significance might lie more in the lesser culpability of the defendant than in the lesser harm or wrong to the victim.

A fourth and final point is this: we should have a special concern about using consent or assumption of risk as a complete defense in criminal law, because criminal behavior to which the victim has consented very often poses risks to third parties who did not consent. So even if a voluntary participant is injured by that behavior, and even if tort law would not permit the participant to recover, there are good reasons (both retributive and consequentialist) for still severely punishing the other participants. Indeed, there are cases in which both victims and injurers pose risks to third parties (such as a drag-race in which a participant suffers harm). In such cases, the zero-sum nature of tort liability requires an award ranging from no to full damages, but criminal law can and often should impose punishment on both the victim and the injurer.

Of course, in some cases, such as suicide pacts and consensual sadomasochism, there are no effects on third parties (at least, no physical or other direct tangible effects). Accordingly, there is much more reason to treat consent as a significant or complete mitigation here than in the case of a speeding driver who happens to run over a pedestrian who used the occasion to commit suicide. In the latter case, others are or easily could be endangered.

### IV. Genuine Victim Fault: The Tort (Dis)analogy

Much of Bergelson's analysis, including the multifactor test that she ultimately proposes, relies on the analogy to comparative fault in tort law. The predominant approach to victim fault in modern tort law is a rejection of traditional all-or-nothing rules (under which victim fault was either ignored or was a complete bar to recovery) and an endorsement of comparative responsibility (under which the victim recovers a portion of her recovery, depending on her share of total fault or responsibility).

The tort analogy is much less helpful than Bergelson believes it to be. First, insofar as Bergelson treats the analogy as a matter of comparative causal contribution, this reflects a misunderstanding. Second, insofar as she focuses on comparative fault or responsibility, there are powerful reasons for resisting that approach in the criminal law, except under very narrow circumstances.

#### A. Comparative Causation

On several occasions, Bergelson says or implies that the real foundation of a comparative responsibility assessment is causal: if a victim is more at fault, he is somehow more of a cause of the ultimate harm. For example, she relies in part on what she (misleadingly) calls the "just desert" principle, the view that "individuals should be responsible only for the amount of harm caused by them and not by the victim." Unfortunately, her discussion is marred by a failure to differentiate and carefully apply the criteria of factual and proximate cause. And on closer inspection, it becomes clear that causal criteria alone almost never justify a victim conduct mitigation.

In virtually all of the examples that she discusses, both the perpetrator and the victim are factual or "but for" causes of the harm: the ultimate harm (typically, an indivisible injury such as death or serious injury) would not have occurred if not for the causal contribution of each actor. And in most of the examples, both the perpetrator and the victim are proximate causes, as well, i.e., the resulting harm is a foreseeable and relatively direct consequence of their acts.

Consider her analysis of one example:

> If the victim is completely innocent and there is no other independent intervening cause, it is clear that the perpetrator is responsible for all the harm. But what about a victim who was at least as instrumental as the offender in causing the resulting injury or loss? Consider, for example, the victim who was a willing participant in a fatal drag race, or the victim who killed herself while playing a game of Russian roulette. Is it fair to say that, although there were two equally reckless participants, the defendant caused all the harm?

This passage contains a number of confusions. In both scenarios, most likely the defendant was a but for cause of the entire harm; but so was the victim. And both might well be considered proximate causes of the harm. Even if we conclude, under a restrictive version of proximate cause, that the voluntary act of the victim usually or always renders the defendant no longer a proximate cause, that judgment is typically a categorical one: the defendant is not a proximate cause of any of the harm. And in that case, causation cannot be employed as Bergelson wishes—to mitigate but not eliminate liability. (Although one can imagine cases in which a defendant is a proximate cause of some but not all of the victim's harm—suppose he runs over the victim, and the victim, in distress, commits suicide many years later—Bergelson's examples do not fit this category).

To be sure, in some cases (such as a drag race or Russian roulette), the victim's participation in and instigation of a crime are so pronounced that arguably the defendant's own responsibility should be less. But these are special cases. And even here, I do not believe that the sole or dominant reason for considering the victim's conduct is that the victim is a more significant "cause" than in other cases....

On the other hand, it is indeed possible to compare the causal contributions of different parties to an indivisible result (such as death) by comparing how "proximate" the causal contributions were (in terms of comparative foreseeability, or comparative directness). In tort law, comparative fault principles often consider both the extent of the causal relation and the extent of fault; however, when they do consider cause, it is presupposed that both parties are factual causes, an issue that is not one of degree and not subject to comparison. Bergelson's final formulation includes relative causal contribution, and this is indeed a coherent and plausible approach, if limited to proximate rather than factual cause. Criminal law doctrine currently employs proximate cause criteria in an all-or-nothing manner, but it would indeed be possible to employ such criteria flexibly, not dichotomously....

## *Notes and Questions*

1. Professor Bergelson asks whether car owners lose their right not to have their cars stolen by leaving keys in the ignition. Do they? Why? How would the question be answered according to Bergelson's theory?

2. Bergelson argues that the victim's assumption of risk in drag racing and Russian roulette cases should mitigate the defendant's liability without generating a full-blown acquittal. She thus argues for comparative liability in the criminal law. Do you find the idea of comparative liability in the criminal law appealing? Explain. Do you find her solution to the drag racing and Russian roulette cases appropriate? Why or why not?

3. Professor Simons argues that it is odd to think of the victim's consent to risk or harm as a mitigating factor rather than as something that completely precludes imposing liability on the defendant. He explains that, as a general rule, consent is either legally

relevant and thus generates an acquittal, or it is legally irrelevant and allows for no mitigation. Think of the offense of rape. Either there was legally valid consent, in which case no liability is imposed, or there was no consent, in which case full liability is appropriate. The same thing happens with the offense of theft. If the property owner consented to the taking, there is no liability. If the owner did not consent, then unmitigated liability for theft is warranted. Similarly, the victim's consent to discontinuing life support exonerates the doctor of liability for homicide. If, however, the victim does not consent, the doctor is fully liable for the patient's death. According to Professor Simons, this reveals that consent is not a matter of degree. And since it is not a matter of degree, it is difficult to argue that consent should mitigate without fully exonerating. Do you agree? Why or why not?

4. Professor Simons suggests that "[i]f a victim foolishly risks his own death simply to obtain a thrill, as in a game of Russian roulette, the state might justifiably ignore his consent." Do you agree? What reasons might the state have for justifiably ignoring the consent of the victim in such cases?

5. Another problem raised by comparative liability in the criminal law is determining how to distribute fault between the defendant and the victim. Bergelson suggests that fault may be apportioned on the basis of "comparative causation." More specifically, she argues that "causation is almost never an all-or-nothing issue" and that some causes may be more important than others. But—as Simons points out—there is a sense in which causes are both all-or-nothing and of equal importance. This is how "but for" causation is conceived. All "but for" causes are equally important because the resulting harm would not take place if any of the other "but for" causes is eliminated. Furthermore, all "but for" causes work in all-or-nothing fashion, for you need them all to produce the result, and if you eliminate one the resulting harm would fail to take place. As a result, Bergelson's "comparative causation" must be refined. As far as "but for" causation is concerned, causation must be all or nothing and all causes must be of equal importance. That is, there can be no "comparative causes" in this context.

6. Nonetheless—as Simons also points out—the notion of comparative causation is "a coherent and plausible approach, if limited to proximate rather than factual cause." Given that the proximate causation inquiry is designed to select which of the many "but for" causes are morally significant, there is room in this context for considering some "but for" causes to be more important than others. The problem, as the materials in this chapter illustrate, is how to non-arbitrarily discriminate between different causal contributions. Simons suggests that one possible approach is to give more weight to causes that are more "proximate" to the harm. Proximity would be judged "in terms of comparative foreseeability, or comparative directness." Comparative liability would then be distributed on the basis of how proximate the causal contributions of the defendant and the victim were. But how workable is this approach? Was the defendant's causal contribution in *Atencio* more proximate than the victim's? Were the causal contributions of the two travelers in the Memel River case more proximate than the boat captain's? Does engaging in an analysis of "comparative foreseeability" and "comparative directness" help figure out whether the defendant or the victim contributed more to the resulting harm in these cases? Explain.

# Chapter 8

# Subjective Offense Elements

## § 8.01 Subjective Offense Elements (*Mens Rea*): Common Law

### Morissette v. United States

Supreme Court of the United States, 1952
342 U.S. 246

Mr. Justice JACKSON delivered the opinion of the Court.

This would have remained a profoundly insignificant case to all except its immediate parties had it not been so tried and submitted to the jury as to raise questions both fundamental and far-reaching in federal criminal law, for which reason we granted certiorari.

On a large tract of uninhabited and untilled land in a wooded and sparsely populated area of Michigan, the Government established a practice bombing range over which the Air Force dropped simulated bombs at ground targets. These bombs consisted of a metal cylinder about forty inches long and eight inches across, filled with sand and enough black powder to cause a smoke puff by which the strike could be located. At various places about the range signs read "Danger—Keep Out—Bombing Range." Nevertheless, the range was known as good deer country and was extensively hunted.

Spent bomb casings were cleared from the targets and thrown into piles 'so that they will be out of the way.' They were not sacked or piled in any order but were dumped in heaps, some of which had been accumulating for four years or upwards, were exposed to the weather and rusting away.

Morissette, in December of 1948, went hunting in this area but did not get a deer. He thought to meet expenses of the trip by salvaging some of these casings. He loaded three tons of them on his truck and took them to a nearby farm, where they were flattened by driving a tractor over them. After expending this labor and trucking them to market in Flint, he realized $84.

Morissette, by occupation, is a fruit stand operator in summer and a trucker and scrap iron collector in winter. An honorably discharged veteran of World War II, he enjoys a good name among his neighbors and has had no blemish on his record more disreputable than a conviction for reckless driving.

The loading, crushing and transporting of these casings were all in broad daylight, in full view of passers-by, without the slightest effort at concealment. When an investigation was started, Morissette voluntarily, promptly and candidly told the whole story to the authorities, saying that he had no intention of stealing but thought the property was abandoned, unwanted and considered of no value to the Government. He was indicted, however, on the charge that he 'did unlawfully, wilfully and knowingly steal and convert' property of the United States of the value of $84, in violation of 18 U.S.C.A. s 641, which provides that 'whoever embezzles, steals, purloins, or knowingly converts' government property is punishable by fine and imprisonment. Morissette was convicted and sentenced to imprisonment for two months or to pay a fine of $200. The Court of Appeals affirmed, one judge dissenting.

On his trial, Morissette, as he had at all times told investigating officers, testified that from appearances he believed the casings were cast-off and abandoned, that he did not intend to steal the property, and took it with no wrongful or criminal intent. [Defendant was convicted. He appealed his conviction, which was then affirmed by the Court of Appeals.] The court [of appeals] ruled that this particular offense requires no element of criminal intent. This conclusion was thought to be required by the failure of Congress to express such a requisite.

I.

... The contention that an injury can amount toa crime only when inflicted by intention is no provincial or transient notion. It is as universal and persistent in mature systems of law as belief in freedom of the human will and a consequent ability and duty of the normal individual to choose between good and evil. A relation between some mental element and punishment for a harmful act is almost as instinctive as the child's familiar exculpatory 'But I didn't mean to,' and has afforded the rational basis for a tardy and unfinished substitution of deterrence and reformation in place of retaliation and vengeance as the motivation for public prosecution. Unqualified acceptance of this doctrine by English common law in the Eighteenth Century was indicated by Blackstone's sweeping statement that to constitute any crime there must first be a 'vicious will.' Common-law commentators of the Nineteenth Century early pronounced the same principle, although a few exceptions not relevant to our present problem came to be recognized.

Crime, as a compound concept, generally constituted only from concurrence of an evil-meaning mind with an evil-doing hand, was congenial to an intense individualism and took deep and early root in American soil. As the state codified the common law of crimes, even if their enactments were silent on the subject, their courts assumed that the omission did not signify disapproval of the principle but merely recognized that intent was so inherent in the idea of the offense that it required no statutory affirmation. Courts, with little hesitation or division, found an implication of the requirement as to offenses that were taken over from the common law. The unanimity with which they have adhered to the central thought that wrongdoing must be conscious to be criminal is emphasized by the variety, disparity and confusion of their definitions of the requisite but elusive mental element. However, courts of various jurisdictions, and for the purposes of different offenses, have devised working formulae, if not scientific ones, for the instruction of juries around such terms as "felonious intent," "criminal intent," "malice aforethought," "guilty knowledge," "fraudulent intent," "willfulness," "scienter," to denote guilty knowledge, or "mens rea," to signify an evil purpose or mental culpability. By use or combination of these various tokens, they have sought to protect those who were not blameworthy in mind from conviction of infamous common-law crimes.

However, the [there are certain] offenses [that] belong to a category of another character, with very different antecedents and origins. The crimes there involved depend on no mental element but consist only of forbidden acts or omissions. This ... is made clear from examination of a century-old but accelerating tendency, discernible both here and in England, to call into existence new duties and crimes which disregard any ingredient of intent. The industrial revolution multiplied the number of workmen exposed to injury from increasingly powerful and complex mechanisms, driven by freshly discovered sources of energy, requiring higher precautions by employers. Traffic of velocities, volumes and varieties unheard of came to subject the wayfarer to intolerable casualty risks if owners and drivers were not to observe new cares and uniformities of conduct. Congestion of cities and crowding of quarters called for health and welfare regulations undreamed of in simpler times. Wide distribution of goods became an instrument of wide distribution of harm when those who dispersed food, drink, drugs, and even securities, did not comply with reasonable standards of quality, integrity, disclosure and care. Such dangers have engendered increasingly numerous and detailed regulations which heighten the duties of those in control of particular industries, trades, properties or activities that affect public health, safety or welfare.

While many of these duties are sanctioned by a more strict civil liability, lawmakers, whether wisely or not, have sought to make such regulations more effective by invoking criminal sanctions to be applied by the familiar technique of criminal prosecutions and convictions. This has confronted the courts with a multitude of prosecutions, based on statutes or administrative regulations, for what have been aptly called 'public welfare offenses.' These cases do not fit neatly into any of such accepted classifications of common-law offenses, such as those against the state, the person, property, or public morals. Many of these offenses are not in the nature of positive aggressions or invasions, with which the common law so often dealt, but are in the nature of neglect where the law requires care, or inaction where it imposes a duty. Many violations of such regulations result in no direct or immediate injury to person or property but merely create the danger or probability of it which the law seeks to minimize. While such offenses do not threaten the security of the state in the manner of treason, they may be regarded as offenses against its authority, for their occurrence impairs the efficiency of controls deemed essential to the social order as presently constituted. In this respect, whatever the intent of the violator, the injury is the same, and the consequences are injurious or not according to fortuity. Hence, legislation applicable to such offenses, as a matter of policy, does not specify intent as a necessary element. The accused, if he does not will the violation, usually is in a position to prevent it with no more care than society might reasonably expect and no more exertion than it might reasonably exact from one who assumed his responsibilities. Also, penalties commonly are relatively small, and conviction does not grave damage to an offender's reputation. Under such considerations, courts have turned to construing statutes and regulations which make no mention of intent as dispensing with it and holding that the guilty act alone makes out the crime. This has not, however, been without expressions of misgiving....

[F]or diverse but reconcilable reasons, state courts converged on the same result, discontinuing inquiry into intent in a limited class of offenses against such statutory regulations.

It was not until recently that the Court took occasion more explicitly to relate abandonment of the ingredient of intent, not merely with considerations of expediency in obtaining convictions, nor with the malum prohibitum classification of the crime, but with the peculiar nature and quality of the offense. We referred to "... a now familiar type of legislation whereby penalties serve as effective means of regulation," and continued, "such legislation dispenses with the conventional requirement for criminal conduct—awareness of some wrongdoing. In the interest of the larger good it puts the burden of acting at hazard upon a person otherwise innocent but standing in responsible relation to a public danger." But we warned: "Hardship there doubtless may be under a statute which thus penalizes the transaction though consciousness of wrongdoing be totally wanting."

Neither this Court nor, so far as we are aware, any other has undertaken to delineate a precise line or set forth comprehensive criteria for distinguishing between crimes that require a mental element and crimes that do not. We attempt no closed definition, for the law on the subject is neither settled nor static....

Stealing, larceny, and its variants and equivalents, were among the earliest offenses known to the law that existed before legislation; they are invasions of rights of property which stir a sense of insecurity in the whole community and arouse public demand for retribution, the penalty is high and, when a sufficient amount is involved, the infamy is that of a felony, which, says Maitland, is "... as bad a word as you can give to man or thing." State courts of last resort, on whom fall the heaviest burden of interpreting criminal law in this country, have consistently retained the requirement of intent in larceny-type offenses. If any state has deviated, the exception has neither been called to our attention nor disclosed by our research.

Congress, therefore, omitted any express prescription of criminal intent from the enactment before us in the light of an unbroken course of judicial decision in all constituent states of the Union holding intent inherent in this class of offense, even when not expressed in a statute. Congressional silence as to mental elements in an Act merely adopting into federal statutory law a concept of crime already so well defined in common law and statutory interpretation by the states may warrant quite contrary inferences than the same silence in creating an offense new to general law, for whose definition the courts have no guidance except the Act.... Nor do exhaustive studies of state court cases disclose any well-considered decisions applying the doctrine of crime without intent to such enacted common-law offenses, although a few deviations are notable as illustrative of the danger inherent in the Government's contentions here.

The Government asks us by a feat of construction radically to change the weights and balances in the scales of justice. The purpose and obvious effect of doing away with the requirement of a guilty intent is to ease the prosecution's path to conviction, to strip the defendant of such benefit as he derived at common law from innocence of evil purpose, and to circumscribe the freedom heretofore allowed juries. Such a manifest impairment of the immunities of the individual should not be extended to common-law crimes on judicial initiative.

The spirit of the doctrine which denies to the federal judiciary power to create crimes forthrightly admonishes that we should not enlarge the reach of enacted crimes by constituting them from anything less than the incriminating components contemplated by the words used in the statute. And where Congress borrows terms of art in which are accumulated the legal tradition and meaning of centuries of practice, it presumably knows and adopts the cluster of ideas that were attached to each borrowed word in the body of learning from which it was taken and the meaning its use will convey to the judicial mind unless otherwise instructed. In such case, absence of contrary direction may be taken as satisfaction with widely accepted definitions, not as a departure from them.

We hold that mere omission from [the text of the offense charged] of any mention of intent will not be construed as eliminating that element from the crimes denounced.

## II.

... In the case before us, whether the mental element that Congress required be spoken of as knowledge or as intent, would not seem to alter its bearing on guilt, for it is not apparent how Morissette could have knowingly or intentionally converted property that he did not know could be converted, as would be the case if it was in fact abandoned or if he truly believed it to be abandoned and unwanted property.

III.

> ... However clear the proof may be, or however incontrovertible may seem to the judge to be the inference of a criminal intention, the question of intent can never be ruled as a question of law, but must always be submitted to the jury. Jurors may be perverse; the ends of justice may be defeated by unrighteous verdicts, but so long as the functions of the judge and jury are distinct, the one responding to the law, the other to the facts, neither can invade the province of the other without destroying the significance of trial by court and jury....

Of course, the jury, considering Morissette's awareness that these casings were on government property, his failure to seek any permission for their removal and his self-interest as a witness, might have disbelieved his profession of innocent intent and concluded that his assertion of a belief that the casings were abandoned was an afterthought. Had the jury convicted on proper instructions it would be the end of the matter. But juries are not bound by what seems inescapable logic to judges. They might have concluded that the heaps of spent casings left in the hinterland to rust away presented an appearance of unwanted and abandoned junk, and that lack of any conscious deprivation of property or intentional injury was indicated by Morissette's good character, the openness of the taking, crushing and transporting of the casings, and the candor with which it was all admitted. They might have refused to brand Morissette as a thief. Had they done so, that too would have been the end of the matter.

Reversed.

## *Notes and Questions*

1. As Justice Jackson famously asserted in *Morissette,* "[t]he contention that an injury can amount to a crime only when inflicted by intention is no provincial or transient notion." The requirement that there can be no punishment without proof of a subjective element or *mens rea* (guilty mind) is thus deeply ingrained in American criminal law. Note, however, that the Court did not hold that it is unconstitutional for Congress to criminalize conduct without making reference to subjective elements. Instead, it was held that—as a matter of statutory construction—federal courts ought to assume that the imposition of punishment requires proof of *mens rea,* unless Congress makes it very clear that it desires to impose liability without such proof (i.e., *strict liability*).

2. The Court distinguishes between traditional common law crimes, such as murder, rape and theft and more modern "public welfare" offenses. Public welfare offenses are mostly crimes that are enacted to regulate certain industries or to promote public safety or order. An example of a public welfare offense is the much derided crime of "tearing a tag off a mattress." Although nominally criminal in nature, these regulations resemble administrative violations, for—as the Supreme Court points out—"penalties [for such crimes] commonly are relatively small, and conviction does not [do] grave damage to an offender's reputation." Given the relatively benign nature of these criminal offenses, state legislatures frequently draft the crimes without reference to *mens rea* and courts uphold the legislature's power to do so. In contrast, as *Morissette* demonstrates, courts are generally reluctant to allow convictions for more serious common law crimes without proof of a guilty mind.

3. The Supreme Court also draws a distinction between *malum prohibita* offenses and crimes that are *malum in se*. A crime is *malum prohibitum* if the act it proscribes is not immoral or evil in itself. Public welfare offenses typically fall in this category. In contrast, an offense is *malum in se* when the act that it prohibits is immoral or evil in itself. The crimes of murder, rape, assault and kidnapping are obvious examples. As a general rule, courts frown upon punishing defendants for *malum in se* crimes without proof of *mens rea*. On the contrary, imposing strict liability (i.e., liability without proof of *mens rea*) is generally acceptable when the crime charged is *malum prohibitum* and the legislature omitted reference to a mental state that must be proved in order to hold defendant liable.

4. The common law approach to *mens rea* is not a model of clarity. As the Supreme Court pointed out in *Morissette,* the common law reveals "variety, disparity and confusion" in the "definitions of the requisite but elusive mental element" of the crime. This haphazard approach led "courts of various jurisdictions [to invoke] terms [such] as 'felonious intent,' 'criminal intent,' 'malice aforethought,' 'guilty knowledge,' 'fraudulent intent,' 'wilfulness,' [and] 'scienter,' to denote [the] guilty knowledge, or 'mens rea,'" of criminal offenses. It is unclear what each of these terms mean and how they differ from each other, if they differ at all. At a minimum, these terms denote conscious as opposed to inadvertent wrongdoing.

5. One of the most frequently used common law *mens rea* terms is "malice." Contrary to what might appear at first glance, a defendant may act with "malice" even if he does not have the purpose of causing harm and regardless of whether he has evil motives or a wicked intent. The word "malice" is thus a legal term of act that is currently defined by courts in a way that differs significantly from its conventionally accepted meaning. The legal definition of malice was fleshed out by the Queen's Bench in *Regina v. Cunningham,* 2 QB 396, [1957]. Defendant was convicted of "maliciously" endangering the victim's life when he stole a gas meter from a house, thereby releasing noxious coal gas into the victim's residence. He argued that he did not act maliciously because he was not aware that stealing the meter could endanger the life of the victim. The trial court instructed the jury the that the defendant could be deemed to have acted maliciously if his intent to steal the gas meter was "wicked" and even if he was not aware that stealing the meter could endanger the life of the victim. The Queen's Bench reversed. Citing from various criminal law treatises, the court held that:

> ... in any statutory definition of a crime "malice" must be taken not in the old vague sense of "wickedness" in general, but as requiring either (i) an actual intention to do the particular kind of harm that in fact was done, or (ii) recklessness as to whether such harm should occur or not (i.e., the accused has foreseen that the particular kind of harm might be done, and yet has gone on to take the risk of it). It is neither limited to, nor does it indeed require, any ill-will towards the person injured.... In our opinion, the word "maliciously" in a statutory crime postulates foresight of consequence. *Id.*

Malice thus requires conscious awareness that the act creates a risk of harm. It does not require, however, that the defendant act with purpose to cause the harm or that he know that the harm is practically certain to take place.

6. The common law also distinguished between general intent and specific intent crimes. The distinction is often relevant to determine whether the defendant may present evidence of voluntary intoxication in order to negate a subjective element of the offense charged. The traditional common law rule was that evidence of voluntary intoxication is admissible to negate specific intent but inadmissible to negative general intent. In *Frey*

*v. State,* 708 So.2d 918 (1998), the Supreme Court of Florida explained the traditional approach to this issue:

> Voluntary intoxication has long been recognized in Florida as a defense to specific intent crimes.... The defense, however, is unavailable for general intent crimes.
>
> Professor LaFave describes the general contours of specific intent, as opposed to general intent, crimes:
>
>> [T]he most common usage of "specific intent" is to designate a special mental element which is required above and beyond any mental state required with respect to the *actus reus* of the crime. Common law larceny, for example, requires the taking and carrying away of the property of another, and the defendant's mental state as to this act must be established, but in addition it must be shown that there was an "intent to steal" the property. Similarly, common law burglary requires a breaking and entry into the dwelling of another, but in addition to the mental state connected with these acts it must also be established that the defendant acted "with intent to commit a felony therein." The same situation prevails with many statutory crimes: assault "with intent to kill" as to certain aggravated assaults; confining another "for the purpose of ransom or reward" in kidnapping; making an untrue statement "designedly, with intent to defraud" in the crime of false pretenses; etc. Wayne R. LaFave & Austin W. Scott, Jr., *Substantive Criminal Law* § 3.5(e) (1986), *Frey,* 708 So.2d 918.

The Court then applied this definition of specific intent to determine whether the offense of "resisting arrest with violence" was a specific or general intent crime. According to the Court:

> To determine whether resisting arrest with violence is a general intent or specific intent crime, we look to the plain language of the statute:
>
>> Resisting officer with violence to his person.—Whoever knowingly and willfully resists, obstructs, or opposes any officer ... in the lawful execution of any legal duty, by offering or doing violence to the person of such officer ... is guilty of a felony of the third degree.... *Frey,* 708 So.2d 918.
>
> The statute's plain language reveals that no heightened or particularized, i.e., no specific, intent is required for the commission of this crime, only a general intent to "knowingly and willfully" impede an officer in the performance of his or her duties.... Only if the present statute were to be recast to require a heightened or particularized intent would the crime of resisting arrest with violence be a specific intent crime.

Do you agree with the Court's conclusion that "resisting arrest with violence" is not a specific intent crime? Explain.

7. If you are confused about the general intent/specific intent distinction, you are not alone. Justice Anstead wrote an opinion concurring in part and dissenting in part in the *Frey* case cited above arguing that the Court should abolish the general/specific intent distinction. More specifically, Justice Anstead opined that:

> This case presents an ideal opportunity for this Court to act on Justice Shaw's cogent observation that "the nebulous distinction between general and specific intent crimes and the defense of voluntary intoxication bear reexamination in a suitable case." In my view, this is that "suitable case."

I believe that the artificial distinction we have established between general and specific intent, with only specific intent crimes warranting additional defenses such as voluntary intoxication, often leads to incongruous and harsh results. Countless commentators and courts have criticized the lack of a principled and useful basis for maintaining this distinction....

Since this perplexing division between "general" and "specific" is judicially created, we should seriously consider whether now is the time to revise this ill-conceived framework. Rather than splitting hairs and attempting to draw a bright line through the murky and ill-defined netherworld that separates general from specific intent, our time would be better spent giving effect to the legislative intent behind a particular statute and focusing on the degree of culpability along the lines clearly delineated in the Model Penal Code. Other than the "nebulous distinction" separating general from specific intent crimes, no compelling policy reasons exist which support the availability of additional defenses in Florida to "specific" intent crimes such as first-degree murder, robbery, kidnapping, aggravated assault, battery, aggravated battery, burglary, escape, and theft, while denying the application of such defenses to "general" intent crimes such as resisting a police officer with violence or arson. The only difference I can see is that, for the most part, the statutes defining the former category have the magic words "with intent to," while the latter crimes do not....

In *State v. Stasio,* 78 N.J. 467, 396 A.2d 1129 (1979), the New Jersey Supreme Court ... explained that:

> [D]istinguishing between specific and general intent gives rise to incongruous results by irrationally allowing intoxication to excuse some crimes but not others. In some instances if the defendant is found incapable of formulating the specific intent necessary for the crime charged, such as assault with intent to rob, he may be convicted of a lesser included general intent crime, such as assault with a deadly weapon. In other cases there may be no related general intent offense so that intoxication would lead to acquittal....
>
> [W]here the more serious offense requires only a general intent, such as rape, intoxication provides no defense, whereas it would be a defense to an attempt to rape, specific intent being an element of that offense. Yet the same logic and reasoning which impels exculpation due to the failure of specific intent to commit an offense would equally compel the same result when a general intent is an element of the offense.

... Even the United States Supreme Court has recognized that "the mental element in criminal law encompasses more than the two possibilities of 'specific' and 'general' intent." *See Liparota v. United States,* 471 U.S. 419, 423 n. 5, 105 S.Ct. 2084, 2087 n. 5, 85 L.Ed.2d 434 (1985). Indeed, the Court has explained that:

> This ambiguity [in the terms specific intent and general intent] has led to a movement away from the traditional dichotomy of intent and toward an alternative analysis of *mens rea.* This new approach [is] exemplified by the American Law Institute's Model Penal Code.... *Frey,* 708 So.2d 918.

The issue of voluntary intoxication is discussed in more detail in Chapter 9.

8. As Justice Anstead pointed out in *Frey,* many courts and commentators expressed deep reservations about the coherence of the common law distinction between general and specific intent crimes. This dissatisfaction eventually blossomed into a desire to not only

abandon the general/specific intent dichotomy, but also to overhaul the common law's haphazard approach to *mens rea* in its entirety. A fresh start was clearly needed. And that is exactly what § 2.02 of the Model Penal Code delivered. The remaining sections of this Chapter focus on the Code's influential approach to subjective offense elements.

## § 8.02 Subjective Offense Elements (*Mens Rea*): Purpose and Knowledge under the Model Penal Code

### Model Penal Code § 2.02. General Requirements of Culpability.

(1) **Minimum Requirements of Culpability.** Except as provided in Section 2.05, a person is not guilty of an offense unless he acted purposely, knowingly, recklessly or negligently, as the law may require, with respect to each material element of the offense.

(2) **Kinds of Culpability Defined.**

(a) **Purposely:**

A person acts purposely with respect to a material element of an offense when:

(i) if the element involves the nature of his conduct or a result thereof, it is his conscious object to engage in conduct of that nature or to cause such a result; and

(ii) if the element involves the attendant circumstances, he is aware of the existence of such circumstances or he believes or hopes that they exist.

(b) **Knowingly:**

A person acts knowingly with respect to a material element of an offense when:

(i) if the element involves the nature of his conduct or the attendant circumstances, he is aware that his conduct is of that nature or that such circumstances exist; and

(ii) if the element involves a result of his conduct, he is aware that it is practically certain that his conduct will cause such a result.

### Vermont v. Jackowski

Supreme Court of Vermont, 2006
181 Vt. 73

JOHNSON, J.

Defendant Rosemarie Jackowski appeals her conviction for disorderly conduct. Defendant argues that the trial court improperly instructed the jury to consider whether defendant was "practically certain" that her conduct would cause public inconvenience or annoyance, when she was charged with intentionally causing public inconvenience or annoyance....

Defendant was arrested on March 20, 2003, during an anti-war demonstration at the intersection of Routes 7 and 9 in Bennington. During the demonstration, protesters blocked traffic at the intersection for approximately fifteen minutes. Defendant stood in the intersection, praying and holding a sign bearing anti-war slogans and newspaper clippings, including an article accompanied by a photograph of a wounded Iraqi child. Police officers repeatedly asked defendant to leave the intersection, and when she refused, she was arrested, along with eleven other protesters. The State charged them with disorderly conduct, alleging that defendant and the other protesters, "with intent to cause public inconvenience and annoyance, obstructed vehicular traffic, in violation of 13 V.S.A. § 1026(5)."

Defendant's intent was the only issue contested during her one-day jury trial. After several police officers testified for the State, defendant took the stand, admitting to blocking traffic, but stating that her only intention in doing so was to protest the war in Iraq, not to cause public inconvenience or annoyance.... At the conclusion of the trial, the court instructed the jury on the issue of intent. The court first instructed the jury that the State could establish defendant's intent to cause public inconvenience or annoyance by proving beyond a reasonable doubt that she acted "with the conscious object of bothering, disturbing, irritating, or harassing some other person or persons." The court then added, "This intent may also be shown if the State proves beyond a reasonable doubt that the defendant was practically certain that another person or persons ... would be bothered, disturbed, irritated, or harassed." The jury convicted defendant of disorderly conduct. Defendant appeals.

Defendant first argues that the jury charge was improper because the trial court failed to instruct the jury to consider whether defendant acted with the requisite criminal intent.... Defendant relies on *State v. Trombley* to draw a distinction between offenses that require purposeful or intentional misconduct and those that require only knowing misconduct.

In *Trombley,* we held that it was error for the trial court to instruct the jury to consider whether the defendant in an aggravated assault case acted "knowingly" or "purposely," when he was charged with "purposely" causing serious bodily injury. The aggravated assault statute in *Trombley* had been amended in 1972 to adopt the Model Penal Code's approach to mens rea, which distinguishes among crimes that are committed "purposely," "knowingly," and "recklessly." Under this approach, a person acts "purposely" when "it is his conscious object to engage in conduct of that nature or to cause such a result." MPC § 2.02(2)(a)(i). A person acts "knowingly" when "he is aware that it is practically certain that his conduct will cause such a result." MPC § 2.02(2)(b)(ii). While the Code's provisions are not binding on this Court, they are "indicative of what the General Assembly intended in adopting the legislation modeled on the Code." Thus, the trial court in *Trombley* erred in instructing the jury that it could find that the defendant acted "purposely" if "he was practically certain that his conduct would cause serious bodily injury."

Defendant argues that *Trombley* controls here, as the trial court used a similarly worded jury charge, and the disorderly conduct statute was amended at the same time, and for the same reasons, as the aggravated assault statute in *Trombley.* The State attempts to distinguish *Trombley* based on differences in the language of the aggravated assault and disorderly conduct statutes. Unlike the aggravated assault statute, the disorderly conduct statute contains the words "with intent" and not "purposely." Compare13 V.S.A. § 1026 (establishing mens rea for disorderly conduct as "with intent to cause public inconvenience, or annoyance or recklessly creating a risk thereof") with 13 V.S.A. § 1024(a)(1) (listing "purposely," "knowingly," and "recklessly" as culpable states of mind for aggravated assault). This is a purely semantic distinction, and it does not indicate a departure from the Code's approach to mens rea, the adoption of which was "the major statutory change" accomplished by the Legislature's 1972 amendments. The Code does not differentiate between "with intent" and "purposely"; instead, it uses the two terms interchangeably, explaining in its definitions that "'intentionally' or 'with intent' means purposely." MPC § 1.13(12). There is no indication that the Legislature used the phrase "with intent" to register disagreement with the Code's approach to disorderly conduct, and such disagreement seems unlikely in the context of an otherwise unqualified adoption of the Code's approach.

The State cites several cases supporting the proposition that both "purposely" and "knowingly" causing harm involve some element of "intent," and thus, that *Trombley*'s distinction between "purposely" and "knowingly" is illusory. Each of [the cases cited by the state] predates our decision in *Trombley,* however, and each adheres to an outmoded distinction between "specific intent" and "general intent" crimes—the distinction that the Legislature rejected in adopting the Code's approach to mens rea. See *Trombley,* 174 Vt. at 460–61 (linking the Legislature's adoption of the Code's approach to mens rea to the demise of the common-law distinction between general and specific intent offenses). At common law, crimes committed "purposely" and those committed "knowingly" would both have been specific intent offenses. In the cases the State cites, the defendants did not raise the question of statutory construction at issue in *Trombley,* so this Court had no opportunity to effectuate the Legislature's adoption of a more modern approach to mens rea. These cases provide no basis for distinguishing or limiting *Trombley* here. It was therefore error for the trial court to charge the jury to consider whether defendant was "practically certain" that her actions would cause public annoyance or inconvenience....

The error [in the present case was prejudicial]. The trial judge essentially instructed the jury that it could presume defendant intended to cause public annoyance or inconvenience if it found that defendant knew that such annoyance or inconvenience would occur. The instruction may have led the jury to ignore any evidence of defendant's intent and to convict solely based on her knowledge. Particularly in a case such as this, where intent was the only contested issue at trial, we are persuaded that the effect of the erroneous instruction was analogous to a directed verdict for the State. In light of defendant's right to a jury trial, we find that such an error cannot be harmless....

*Reversed and remanded for further proceedings consistent with the views expressed herein.*

## Notes and Questions

1. The most influential provision of the Model Penal Code is § 2.02, which defines subjective offense elements. The Code does away with the myriad common law *mens rea* terms, including notoriously difficult to define mental states like malice and general and specific intent. The Code reduces subjective elements to four kinds of culpability, namely: purpose, knowledge, recklessness and negligence.

2. The defendant in *Jackowski* argued that in order to convict her of disorderly conduct as defined in the Vermont Penal Law, the prosecution needed to prove that she *purposely* caused public inconvenience rather than merely demonstrating that she *knowingly* caused such annoyance. As the court pointed out in *Jackowski,* Vermont adopted the Model Penal Code's approach to subjective offense elements (*mens rea*). According to the Code, a person acts purposely with regard to a result if it is her conscious desire to bring about the result. In contrast, a person acts knowingly if she is aware that the result is practically certain to occur as a consequence of her conduct. What did the defendant in *Jackowski* desire to achieve by participating in the anti-war demonstration that gave rise to her arrest? Do you think that her desire was to cause public inconvenience or to raise awareness about what she perceived to be abuses committed during the Iraq War? Do you think the defendant was aware that her conduct would cause public inconvenience? Do you believe that she caused public inconvenience purposely or knowingly?

3. As the Supreme Court of Vermont explains in *Jackowski,* the term "intent" is frequently used as synonymous with "purpose." This is the case in many states, including New York, which follows the Model Penal Code definitions of subjective offense elements, but uses the term "intentionally" instead of "purposely." The relevant New York Penal Law provision states:

> *Section 15.05 Culpability; definitions of culpable mental states*
>
> The following definitions are applicable to this chapter:
>
> 1. "Intentionally." A person acts intentionally with respect to a result or to conduct described by a statute defining an offense when his conscious objective is to cause such result or to engage in such conduct.
> 2. "Knowingly." A person acts knowingly with respect to conduct or to a circumstance described by a statute defining an offense when he is aware that his conduct is of such nature or that such circumstance exists....

4. Suppose that X plants a bomb inside a plane with the desire to kill passenger Y. Although X does not desire anyone other than Y to die, he is aware that all other airplane passengers will die when the bomb explodes. The bomb explodes, killing all passengers instantly. Assuming the Model Penal Code applies, what culpability does X have with regard to the death of passenger Y? What culpability does X have with regard to the death of the rest of the passengers?

5. Suppose that X shoots at Y from a distance of 300 yards with the desire to kill Y, but knowing that it is highly unlikely that he will succeed in doing so. The shot reaches Y and kills her. What culpability does X have with regard to Y's death?

6. What happens when the defendant purposely tries to harm Juan but his conduct ends up harming Mary instead? This raises the problem of "transferred intent." The issue is addressed in §2.03 of the Model Penal Code, which prescribes that:

> When purposely or knowingly causing a particular result is an element of an offense, the element is not established if the actual result is not within the purpose or the contemplation of the actor unless:
>
> a) the actual result differs from that designed or contemplated, as the case may be, only in the respect that a different person or different property is injured or affected or that the injury or harm designed or contemplated would have been more serious or more extensive than that caused, or
>
> b) the actual result involves the same kind of injury or harm as that designed or contemplated....

Application of this provision will usually lead to holding the defendant liable for the harms suffered by Mary even if his purpose was to harm Juan, for the actual result (harm to Mary) differs from the harm intended by the defendant (harm to Juan) "only in the respect that a different person ... is injured" by the conduct. The intent or purpose to harm Juan "transfers" so that defendant may be held liable for the harm suffered by Mary as if he had intended to harm her. The common law solution to the problem is essentially the same.

7. A particularly thorny problem arises when the defendant causes a more serious injury than the one he intended. In *State v. Higgins,* 265 Conn. 35 (2003), the defendant fired his gun at an adult with the purpose of killing him, but the shot reached and killed a minor child instead. Defendant was convicted of the capital felony of murdering a person under sixteen years of age. He appealed his conviction, arguing that he could not be

convicted of murdering a minor because he intended to kill an adult. Furthermore, the defendant argued that the doctrine of transferred intent "may not be applied to impose a greater degree of liability than that which would have been imposed had the defendant committed the intended crime." The Supreme Court of Connecticut rejected the defendant's argument:

> [S]cholarly opinion is unsettled on whether "the transferred-intent theory will be applied even when the result is a greater degree of criminal liability than if the intended victim had been hit, as where ... the law makes harm to [an unintended victim] a more serious offense than harm to [the intended victim]." 1 W. LaFave & A. Scott, Substantive Criminal Law (Sup.2003) § 3.12, p. 76....
>
> Several courts ... have concluded that a defendant may be convicted under the doctrine of transferred intent of a more serious offense than that of which he would have been convicted had he committed the intended harm. *See* ... *State v. Cantua-Ramirez,* 149 Ariz. 377, 380, 718 P.2d 1030 (1986) (construing Arizona transferred intent statute that is similar to Model Penal Code and concluding that, because liability may be imposed when "the harm which occurred was not more extensive than the harm intended, it merely imposed a greater penalty," defendant who intended to strike adult but struck baby may be convicted of more serious offense of striking child). At least one court, however, has concluded that, for the doctrine to apply, the offense charged and the offense contemplated must be the same. See *United States v. Montoya,* 739 F.2d 1437 (9th Cir.1984) (defendant who intended to strike civilian but struck federal officer could not be convicted under common-law doctrine of transferred intent of more serious offense of assault on federal officer).
>
> We are persuaded that, contrary to the defendant's argument, the weight of authority supports the proposition that the common-law doctrine of transferred intent may be applied when the defendant's actual mental state and wrongful conduct are equivalent to the mental state and wrongful conduct that must be proved under the offense with which he is charged, even if that offense is more serious than the contemplated offense.
>
> We conclude that the trial court properly instructed the jury that it could apply the doctrine of transferred intent to convict the defendant of capital felony under [Connecticut law]. *Higgins,* 265 Conn. 35.

Is it fair to convict the defendant of the more serious crime of purposely killing a child when the harm that he intended to inflict was the killing of an adult? Do you agree with the outcome in *Higgins*? Explain.

8. The defendant in *Higgins* attempted but failed to kill an adult. Furthermore, while he did not intend to cause the child's death, he may very well have negligently created a risk that the child may die. If so, why not convict the defendant of attempted murder for unsuccessfully trying to kill an adult and of negligent homicide for the death of the child? While this solution is widely defended in Europe and Latin America, it has not been embraced (or seriously discussed) by American courts. The European and Latin American position is summarized in Hans Heinrich Jescheck & Thomas Weigend, Tratado de Derecho Penal parte general 335–336 (Miguel Olmedo Cardenete trad., 5th ed. 2002). For a defense of this approach in Anglo-America, *see* Anthony Dillof, *Transferred Intent: An Inquiry into the Nature of Criminal Culpability,* 1 Buff. Crim. L. Rev. 501 (1998).

9. Sometimes a defendant is charged with an offense that requires that the defendant have knowledge of a particular circumstance. May a defendant who lacks such knowledge but is aware that it is likely that the circumstance exists be convicted of this kind of offense? As a general rule, defendant may not be convicted because the subjective offense element of knowledge is missing. But what if the defendant took affirmative steps to avoid acquiring knowledge of the circumstance? May such an attitude be equated with knowledge even though, strictly speaking, the defendant lacks awareness of the circumstance? This type of case raises the problem of so-called "willful blindness." The facts of *State v. Nations,* 676 S.W.2d 282 (1984), are illustrative. Defendant was charged and convicted of "knowingly endangering the welfare of a child less than seventeen years old" for owning and operating a bar in which police officers found a scantily clad sixteen-year-old girl "dancing" for "tips." The defendant appealed her conviction, contending that the prosecution failed to prove that she knew that the child was under seventeen years old. The appellate court concluded that, "[a]t best, [the prosecution] prove[d] [that] defendant did not know or refused to learn the child's age." The court concluded that ignorance of the child's age—even if coupled with a refusal to learn the child's age—was not sufficient to establish that defendant had knowledge of the child's age. Consequently, defendant's conviction was reversed. According to the court:

> [The offense charged] requires the state to prove the defendant "knowingly" encouraged a child "less than seventeen years old" to engage in conduct tending to injure the child's welfare, and "knowing" the child to be less than seventeen is a material element of the crime.
>
> "Knowingly" is a term of art, whose meaning is limited to the definition given to it by our present Criminal Code. Literally read, the Code defines "knowingly" as actual knowledge—"A person '*acts knowingly,*' or with knowledge, (1) with respect ... to attendant circumstances when he is aware ... that those circumstances exist."... So read, this definition of "knowingly" or "knowledge" excludes those cases in which "the fact [in issue] would have been known had not the person wilfully 'shut his eyes' in order to avoid knowing." Perkins, *Criminal Law* 942 (2d ed. 1969).
>
> The Model Penal Code, the source of our Criminal Code, does not exclude these cases from its definition of "knowingly." Instead, the Model Penal Code proposes that "[w]hen knowledge of the *existence of a particular fact* is an element of an offense, such knowledge is established if a person is aware of a high probability of its existence."... Model Penal Code § 2.02(7) (Proposed Official Draft 1962). This definition sounds more like a restatement of the definition of "recklessly" than "knowingly." The similarity is intentional. The Model Penal Code simply proposes that willful blindness to a fact "be viewed as one of acting knowingly when what is involved is a matter of existing fact."...
>
> Our legislature, however, did not enact this proposed definition of "knowingly." Although the definitions of "knowingly" and "recklessly" in our Criminal Code are almost identical to the primary definitions of these terms as proposed in the Model Penal Code, the Model Penal Code's proposed expanded definition of "knowingly," encompassing willful blindness of a fact, is absent from our Criminal Code. The sensible, if not compelling, inference is that our legislature rejected the expansion of the definition of "knowingly" to include willful blindness of a fact and chose to limit the definition of "knowingly" to actual knowledge of the fact. Thus, in the instant case, the state's burden was to show defendant

> actually was aware the child was under seventeen, a heavier burden than showing there was a "high probability" that defendant was aware the child was under seventeen. In short, the state's burden was to prove defendant acted "knowingly," not just "recklessly." The state proved, however, that defendant acted "recklessly," not "knowingly." *Nations,* 676 S.W.2d 282.

Do you agree with the outcome in this case? Why or why not? Note that—as the court pointed out in *Nations*—Model Penal Code § 2.02(7) allows for a finding that defendant acted "knowingly" with regard to a circumstance as long as he was aware that there was a high probability of its existence. Do you agree with the Code's equation of "knowledge of a circumstance" and "awareness of a high probability of its existence"? Explain. What result in *Nations* if § 2.02(7) of the Model Penal Code is applied?

10. In *United States v. Heredia,* 483 F.3d 913 (2007), the defendant was driving her aunt's car when she was stopped at an inland Border Patrol checkpoint. A search of the car revealed 349 pounds of drugs inside the trunk of the vehicle. Defendant was charged with knowingly possessing a controlled substance with intent to distribute in violation of federal law. Defendant admitted "that she suspected there might be drugs in the car." Nonetheless, she maintained that "her suspicions were not aroused until she had passed the last freeway exit before the checkpoint, by which time it was too dangerous to pull over and investigate." As a result, defendant argued that she lacked knowledge that she was in possession of drugs. Defendant was convicted. On appeal, defendant contended that it was reversible error for the jury to have been instructed that they "may find that the defendant acted knowingly if [they] find ... that the defendant was aware of a high probability that drugs were in the vehicle driven by the defendant and deliberately avoided learning the truth." The Federal Court of Appeals for the Ninth Circuit rejected the defendant's argument and affirmed the conviction. Judge Kozinsky explained the Court's decision:

> While [our decision in *United States v. Jewell,* 532 F.2d 397 (1976)] has spawned a great deal of commentary and a somewhat perplexing body of case law, its core holding was a rather straightforward matter of statutory interpretation: "'[K]nowingly' in criminal statutes is not limited to positive knowledge, but includes the state of mind of one who does not possess positive knowledge only because he consciously avoided it." In other words, when Congress made it a crime to "knowingly ... possess with intent to manufacture, distribute, or dispense, a controlled substance," it meant to punish not only those who know they possess a controlled substance, but also those who don't know because they don't want to know....
>
> Since *Jewell* was decided in 1976, every regional circuit—with the exception of the D.C. Circuit—has adopted its central holding. Indeed, many colloquially refer to the deliberate ignorance instruction as the "*Jewell* instruction." ...
>
> The parties have pointed out one area where our cases have not been consistent: Whether the jury must be instructed that defendant's motive in deliberately failing to learn the truth was to give himself a defense in case he should be charged with the crime. *Jewell* itself speculated that defendant's motive for failing to learn the truth in that case was to "avoid responsibility in the event of discovery." Yet the opinion did not define motive as a separate prong of the deliberate ignorance instruction. And we affirmed, even though the instruction given at Jewell's trial made no mention of motive....

> Heredia argues that the motive prong is necessary to avoid punishing individuals who fail to investigate because circumstances render it unsafe or impractical to do so. She claims that she is within this group, because her suspicions did not arise until she was driving on an open highway where it would have been too dangerous to pull over. She thus claims that she had a motive *other* than avoiding criminal culpability for failing to discover the contraband concealed in the trunk.
>
> We believe, however, that the second prong of the instruction, the requirement that defendant have *deliberately* avoided learning the truth, provides sufficient protections for defendants in these situations. A deliberate action is one that is "[i]ntentional; premeditated; fully considered." *Black's Law Dictionary* 459 (8th ed. 2004). A decision influenced by coercion, exigent circumstances or lack of meaningful choice is, perforce, not deliberate. A defendant who fails to investigate for these reasons has not deliberately chosen to avoid learning the truth.
>
> We conclude, therefore, that the two-pronged instruction given at defendant's trial met the requirements of *Jewell* and, to the extent some of our cases have suggested more is required, they are overruled. A district judge, in the exercise of his discretion, may say more to tailor the instruction to the particular facts of the case. Here, for example, the judge might have instructed the jury that it could find Heredia did not act deliberately if it believed that her failure to investigate was motivated by safety concerns. Heredia did not ask for such an instruction and the district judge had no obligation to give it sua sponte. Even when defendant asks for such a supplemental instruction, it is within the district court's broad discretion whether to comply. *Heredia,* 483 F.3d 913.

The Court also explained that their deliberate ignorance rule does not equate knowledge of a fact with recklessness with regard to the existence of the fact:

> [D]eliberate ignorance, otherwise known as willful blindness, is categorically different from ... recklessness. A willfully blind defendant is one who took *deliberate* actions to avoid confirming suspicions of criminality. A reckless defendant is one who merely knew of a substantial and unjustifiable risk that his conduct was criminal. *Id.*

Do you agree with the outcome in *Heredia*? Explain.

11. What result if the "deliberate ignorance" rule had been applied in *State v. Nations* (Note 9)? Compare and contrast the "deliberate ignorance" approach to willful blindness with the "high probability" approach adopted in § 2.02(7) of the Model Penal Code. Are they essentially the same? If you believe they are different, which approach is preferable? Would the defendant's conviction in *Heredia* stand had Model Penal Code § 2.02(7) been applied to her case?

12. The court in *Nations* (Note 9) argued that the Model Penal Code's definition of "knowingly" in § 2.02(7) "sounds more like a restatement of the definition of 'recklessly' than 'knowingly.'" Do you agree? In contrast, the court in *Heredia* emphatically stated that the deliberate ignorance approach to acting "knowingly" does not redefine the concept in a way that makes it indistinguishable to acting "recklessly." Do you agree? Why or why not? Perhaps knowing more about what it means to act recklessly will help inform your answer to this question. Fortunately, recklessness is the subject of the next section.

# § 8.03 Subjective Offense Elements (*Mens Rea*): Recklessness under the Model Penal Code

## Model Penal Code § 2.02. General Requirements of Culpability.

(2) **Kinds of Culpability Defined.**

. . .

(c) **Recklessly:**

A person acts recklessly with respect to a material element of an offense when he consciously disregards a substantial and unjustifiable risk that the material element exists or will result from his conduct. The risk must be of such a nature and degree that, considering the nature and purpose of the actor's conduct and the circumstances known to him, its disregard involves a gross deviation from the standard of conduct that a law-abiding person would observe in the actor's situation....

(3) **Culpability Required Unless Otherwise Provided:** When the culpability sufficient to establish a material element of an offense is not prescribed by law, such element is established if a person acts purposely, knowingly or recklessly with respect thereto.

## In re D.G., Juvenile

Supreme Court of Vermont, 2003
2003 WL 25746107

D.G. appeals from an adjudication of delinquency based on a finding that he recklessly placed another person in danger of death or serious bodily injury. D.G. contends: (1) the evidence failed to demonstrate that he consciously disregarded a substantial and unjustifiable risk of injury.... We agree ... and therefore reverse.

Viewed in a light most favorable to the judgment, the record evidence may be summarized as follows. D.G., who was fourteen years old at the time of the events in question, lived in a foster home with three other boys. On the date in question, he entered the bedrooms of two of the other boys and used a lighter to ignite the spray from an aerosol can of deodorant. Both of the boys were playing on their Playstations at the time. One of the boys, C.C., testified that he felt the heat from the flame, but otherwise ignored D.G. until he left. The other boy also stated that he felt some heat and told D.G. to stop, but also continued to play uninterrupted. Both testified that D.G. was fooling around. D.G. testified in his own behalf, asserting that he was "just fooling around [and] didn't think I'd actually hurt anybody." He explained that he had sprayed his own hands and pants with the lit flame, without experiencing any pain. He testified further that he was not aware the can could explode, and had no intention to hurt anyone. A fourth boy, M.S., also apparently ignited the aerosol spray, but was not charged.

The boys' foster mother later learned of the incident and called the Department of Social and Rehabilitation Services. The State subsequently filed a delinquency petition, alleging that D.G. had engaged in reckless endangerment, under [Vermont law]. At the conclusion of the evidentiary hearing, the court entered oral findings as follows: "[Y]ou consciously disregarded the dangers. You knew it was a dangerous thing to do, you knew that the can could blow up. You knew that you were quote playing with fire. Close enough to other people, so that they felt the heat. And you knew that you were putting them in danger, and you did it anyway." Based on these findings, the court concluded that D.G.

had recklessly placed others in danger of serious bodily injury or death, and entered a finding of delinquency. This appeal followed.

The reckless endangerment statute applies to any "person who recklessly engages in conduct which places or may place another person in danger of death or serious bodily." We have endorsed the Model Penal Code definition of recklessness, which provides, in part, as follows: "A person acts recklessly with respect to a material element of an offense when he *consciously* disregards a substantial and unjustifiable risk that the material element exists or will result from his conduct." Thus, as we explained in [our cases], "recklessness requires a *conscious disregard* of the risk," while criminal negligence "results when an actor is unaware of the risk which the actor *should have perceived.*" Thus, to establish recklessness the State must prove the defendant knew of the risk of death or serious bodily injury, although courts have held that such knowledge "may be inferred from circumstances such as the actor' s knowledge and experience, or from what a similarly situated reasonable person would have understood about the risk under the particular circumstances."

All of the record evidence in this case tended to show that D.G. was unaware of any risk "much less a risk of serious bodily injury or death—from igniting the aerosol spray." He testified that he did not think he was putting anyone at risk, and claimed that he did not experience any pain when he sprayed himself with the flame. His playful demeanor as described by the other boys plainly supported his assertion that he did not believe there was any serious risk, and the boys' response to D.G.'s behavior "they simply ignored him or told him to go away" would not have alerted him to any more serious danger. Nor was there any evidence suggesting that any reasonable person in D.G.'s circumstances would have known that his behavior created a substantial and unjustifiable risk of death or serious bodily injury ... [T]he record contains no evidence to support the court's findings that D.G. knew of, and consciously disregarded, the risks that the can could blow up or otherwise cause death or serious bodily injury. Accordingly, we conclude that the judgment must be reversed.

## State v. Loeffel

Court of Appeals of Utah, 2013
300 P.3d 336

ORME, Judge:

Defendant Michael Dennis Loeffel appeals his conviction for three counts of aggravated assault, a third degree felony. We affirm.

On April 24, 2008, the police were notified of a public disturbance and possible domestic dispute between Defendant and his girlfriend....

[Several] officers arrived at the [defendant and girlfriend's] home soon after, and they began calling out to Defendant and his girlfriend with a loudspeaker. This prompted Defendant to come back out of his house and begin swearing and yelling very loudly at the officers from the enclosed porch. The officers repeatedly asked Defendant to come out of the porch area to speak with them, but Defendant refused each time. While he was screaming at the officers, Defendant referred to a gun and said that the officers were "fair game" if they tried to enter his house. Defendant also told the officers that if they approached, "it's on." During the commotion, Defendant's girlfriend came out onto the porch. The officers started encouraging her to come out of the porch area to talk and informed Defendant that if he prevented her from coming out to speak to them, he could be charged with kidnapping. Defendant's girlfriend eventually agreed to speak with the officers outside, and as she moved to unlock the screen door, Defendant went back inside his house and slammed the door.

Concerned that Defendant had gone in to retrieve the gun he had referred to, the officers drew their weapons and proceeded through the screen door that Defendant's girlfriend had unlocked and through which she had just exited. The officers kicked the front door of the house open and found Defendant in the entryway holding what turned out to be a loaded rifle with the safety off. One officer testified that Defendant was holding the rifle at the "low ready" position, and two of the officers testified that he started to raise the rifle toward them when they entered the house. As soon as he began to raise the rifle, the officers opened fire on Defendant, hitting him twice.

Because Defendant stated that he would shoot the officers if they entered his home and then pointed a rifle at them when they actually entered, Defendant was arrested and charged with, inter alia, three counts of aggravated assault. At the close of evidence at trial, the court instructed the jury on the elements of aggravated assault and included an instruction on a reckless mental state. Defendant objected to the instruction, arguing that recklessness was insufficient to satisfy the offense's mens rea requirement. The court overruled the objection and allowed the instruction. Defendant was ultimately convicted. He now appeals.

Defendant argues that the trial court erred by instructing the jury that aggravated assault can be committed by recklessly threatening to do bodily injury to another....

A person is guilty of aggravated assault if [he makes] "(a) an attempt, with unlawful force or violence, to do bodily injury to another"; or (b) a threat, accompanied by a show of immediate force or violence, to do bodily injury to another." *Id.* § 76-5-102(1)(a), (b). Under our criminal code, every offense not involving strict liability requires a prescribed culpable mental state. *See id.* § 76-2-102. However, if the definition of an offense "does not specify a culpable mental state and the offense does not involve strict liability, [then] intent, knowledge, or recklessness shall suffice to establish criminal responsibility." *Id.*

Nothing in the text of either assault provision explicitly prescribes a culpable mental state. Therefore, our statutory framework prescribes that section 76-2-102 controls and that the mens rea requirement defaults to "intent, knowledge, or recklessness." *See id.* § 76-2-102. Contrary to Defendant's assertion, section 76-2-102 is not merely a canon of interpretation or a non-binding suggestion that gives way to educated guesswork based upon inferences drawn from the language of a criminal offense. Rather, our cases confirm that section 76-2-102 controls when criminal offenses do not explicitly identify the applicable mens rea requirement ... Because neither the aggravated assault statute nor the underlying simple assault statute specified a more culpable mental state, section 76-2-102 controls. Accordingly, the trial court did not err in giving the jury a recklessness instruction.

## People v. Hall

Supreme Court of Colorado, 2000
999 P.2d 207

Justice BENDER delivered the Opinion of the Court.

### I. Introduction

We hold that Nathan Hall must stand trial for the crime of reckless manslaughter. While skiing on Vail mountain, Hall flew off of a knoll and collided with Allen Cobb, who was traversing the slope below Hall. Cobb sustained traumatic brain injuries and died as a result of the collision. The People charged Hall with felony reckless manslaughter.

At a preliminary hearing to determine whether there was probable cause for the felony count, the county court found that Hall's conduct "did not rise to the level of dangerousness" required under Colorado law to uphold a conviction for manslaughter, and the court dismissed the charges. On appeal, the district court affirmed the county court's decision. The district court determined that in order for Hall's conduct to have been reckless, it must have been "at least more likely than not" that death would result. Because the court found that "skiing too fast for the conditions" is not "likely" to cause another person's death, the court concluded that Hall's conduct did not constitute a "substantial and unjustifiable" risk of death. Thus, the district court affirmed the finding of no probable cause.

The charge of reckless manslaughter requires that a person "recklessly cause [ ] the death of another person." For his conduct to be reckless, the actor must have consciously disregarded a substantial and unjustifiable risk that death could result from his actions. We hold that, for the purpose of determining whether a person acted recklessly, a particular result does not have to be more likely than not to occur for the risk to be substantial and unjustifiable. A risk must be assessed by reviewing the particular facts of the individual case and weighing the likelihood of harm and the degree of harm that would result if it occurs. Whether an actor consciously disregarded such a risk may be inferred from circumstances such as the actor's knowledge and experience, or from what a similarly situated reasonable person would have understood about the risk under the particular circumstances.

We hold that under the particular circumstances of this case, whether Hall committed the crime of reckless manslaughter must be determined by the trier of fact. Viewed in the light most favorable to the prosecution, Hall's conduct-skiing straight down a steep and bumpy slope, back on his skis, arms out to his sides, off-balance, being thrown from mogul to mogul, out of control for a considerable distance and period of time, and at such a high speed that the force of the impact between his ski and the victim's head fractured the thickest part of the victim's skull-created a substantial and unjustifiable risk of death to another person. A reasonable person could infer that the defendant, a former ski racer trained in skier safety, consciously disregarded that risk. For the limited purposes of a preliminary hearing, the prosecution provided sufficient evidence to show probable cause that the defendant recklessly caused the victim's death. Thus, we reverse the district court's finding of no probable cause and we remand the case to that court for trial....

### III. Discussion

#### ... B. Manslaughter and Recklessness....

To provide background for our explanation of recklessness, we review the history of culpable mental states under our criminal code. We then examine the separate elements of recklessness, which require that an actor consciously disregard a substantial and unjustifiable risk that a result will occur or that a circumstance exists. Based on this review, we hold that to determine whether a risk is substantial and unjustified, a trier of fact must weigh the likelihood and potential magnitude of harm presented by the conduct and consider whether the conduct constitutes a gross deviation from the reasonable standard of care. Whether a person consciously disregards such a risk may be inferred from either the actor's subjective knowledge of the risk or from what a reasonable person with the actor's knowledge and experience would have been aware of in the particular situation.

With the exception of strict liability crimes, a person is not subject to criminal sanctions unless the prosecution establishes that, in addition to committing a proscribed act, the person acted with the culpable mental state required for the particular crime. In other words, except for strict liability crimes, our criminal justice system will not punish a defendant for her actions unless she acted with a state of mind that warrants punishment.

In the past, courts and legislatures developed a variety of definitions for different mental states, creating confusion about what the prosecution had to prove in a criminal case. Depending on the specific crime charged and the jurisdiction, juries might be instructed to determine whether the defendant acted with "'felonious intent,' 'criminal intent,' 'malice aforethought,' 'guilty knowledge,' 'fraudulent intent,' 'willfulness,' 'scienter,' ... or 'mens rea,' to signify an evil purpose or mental culpability." ...

In order to eliminate the confusion created by this variety of ill-defined mental states, the Model Penal Code suggested that criminal codes articulate and define the specific culpable mental states that will suffice for criminal liability. As part of a complete revision of Colorado's criminal code in 1971, the General Assembly followed the Model Penal Code's suggestion and adopted a provision specifically defining four culpable mental states: "intentionally," "knowingly," "recklessly," and "criminal negligence." ...

To demonstrate that Hall committed the crime of manslaughter, the prosecution must provide sufficient evidence to show that the defendant's conduct was reckless. Thus, we focus on describing the mental state of recklessness and determining whether Hall's conduct meets that definition.

As Colorado's criminal code defines recklessness, "A person acts recklessly when he consciously disregards a substantial and unjustifiable risk that a result will occur or a that circumstance exists." § 18-1-501(8). Thus, in the case of manslaughter, the prosecution must show that the defendant's conduct caused the death of another and that the defendant:

1) *consciously disregarded*
2) a *substantial* and
3) *unjustifiable risk* that he would
4) *cause the death of another.*

We examine these elements in detail.

**Substantial and Unjustifiable Risk**

To show that a person acted recklessly, the prosecution must establish that the person's conduct created a "substantial and unjustifiable" risk. The district court construed some of our earlier cases as requiring that the risk of death be "at least more likely than not" to constitute a substantial and unjustifiable risk of death. In interpreting our cases, the court relied on an erroneous definition of a "substantial and unjustifiable" risk. Whether a risk is substantial must be determined by assessing both the likelihood that harm will occur and the magnitude of the harm should it occur. We hold that whether a risk is unjustifiable must be determined by assessing the nature and purpose of the actor's conduct relative to how substantial the risk is. Finally, in order for conduct to be reckless, the risk must be of such a nature that its disregard constitutes a gross deviation from the standard of care that a reasonable person would exercise.

A risk does not have to be "more likely than not to occur" or "probable" in order to be substantial. A risk may be substantial even if the chance that the harm will occur is well below fifty percent. Some risks may be substantial even if they carry a low degree of probability because the magnitude of the harm is potentially great. For example, if a person holds a revolver with a single bullet in one of the chambers, points the gun at another's head and pulls the trigger, then the risk of death is substantial even though the odds that death will result are no better than one in six.

Conversely, a relatively high probability that a very minor harm will occur probably does not involve a "substantial" risk. Thus, in order to determine whether a risk is substantial, the court must consider both the likelihood that harm will occur and the magnitude of potential harm, mindful that a risk may be "substantial" even if the odds of the harm occurring are lower than fifty percent....

As well as being substantial, a risk must be unjustifiable in order for a person's conduct to be reckless. Whether a risk is justifiable is determined by weighing the nature and purpose of the actor's conduct against the risk created by that conduct. If a person consciously disregards a substantial risk of death but does so in order to advance an interest that justifies such a risk, the conduct is not reckless. For example, if a surgeon performs an operation on a patient that has a seventy-five percent chance of killing the patient, but the patient will certainly die without the operation, then the conduct is justified and thus not reckless even though the risk is substantial.

In addition to the separate analyses that are applied to determine whether a risk is both "substantial" and "unjustified," the concept of a "substantial and unjustifiable risk" implies a risk that constitutes a gross deviation from the standard of care that a reasonable law-abiding person would exercise under the circumstances. Both the Model Penal Code and the New York Code, which the General Assembly followed in drafting the Colorado criminal code, expressly define a "substantial and unjustifiable risk" as one that is a gross deviation from the reasonable standard of care. *See* MPC, § 2.02 at 226; N.Y. Penal Law, § 15.05. A substantial and unjustifiable risk must constitute a "gross deviation" from the reasonable standard of care in order to justify the criminal sanctions imposed for criminal negligence or reckless conduct, as opposed to the kind of deviation from the reasonable standard of care that results in civil liability for ordinary negligence....

### Conscious Disregard

In addition to showing that a person created a substantial and unjustifiable risk, the prosecution must demonstrate that the actor "consciously disregarded" the risk in order to prove that she acted recklessly. A person acts with a conscious disregard of the risk created by her conduct when she is aware of the risk and chooses to act despite that risk. In contrast to acting "intentionally" or "knowingly," the actor does not have to intend the result or be "practically certain" that the result will occur, he only needs to be "aware" that the risk exists.

Although recklessness is a less culpable mental state than intentionally or knowingly, it involves a higher level of culpability than criminal negligence. Criminal negligence requires that, "through a gross deviation from the standard of care that a reasonable person would exercise," the actor fails to perceive a substantial and unjustifiable risk that a result will occur or a circumstance exists. An actor is criminally negligent when he should have been aware of the risk but was not, while recklessness requires that the defendant actually be aware of the risk but disregard it. *See Shaw,* 646 P.2d at 380. Thus, even if she should be, a person who is not actually aware that her conduct creates a substantial and unjustifiable risk is not acting recklessly....

## IV. Application of Legal Principles to Hall's Conduct

### ... B. Review of Hall's Conduct

The district court's conclusion that Hall's conduct did not represent a substantial and unjustifiable risk of death rested on an erroneous construction of recklessness. Relying on two of our earlier cases, the court found that for a risk to be "substantial" it must "be *at least more likely than not* that death would result." As discussed, a risk of death that has less than a fifty percent chance of occurring may nonetheless be a substantial risk depending on the circumstances of the particular case. Because the district court applied a flawed interpretation of the law, we hold that the district court's assessment of probable cause was in error....

We first ask whether the prosecution presented sufficient evidence to show that Hall's conduct created a substantial and unjustifiable risk of death. Like other activities that generally do not involve a substantial risk of death, such as driving a car or installing a heater, "skiing too fast for the conditions" is not widely considered behavior that constitutes a high degree of risk. However, we hold that the specific facts in this case support a reasonable inference that Hall created a substantial and unjustifiable risk that he would cause another's death.

Several witnesses stated that Hall was skiing very fast. Allen and the other eyewitnesses all said that Hall was travelling too fast for the conditions, at an excessive rate of speed, and that he was out of control. Allen said that Hall passed him on the slope travelling three times faster than Allen, himself an expert skier. Sandberg presented testimony that Hall was a ski racer, indicating that Hall was trained to attain and ski at much faster speeds than even skilled and experienced recreational skiers. The witnesses said that Hall was travelling straight down the slope at such high speeds that, because of his lack of control, he would not have been able to stop or avoid another person.

In addition to statements of witnesses, the nature of Cobb's injuries and other facts of the collision support the inference that Hall was skiing at an inordinately high speed when he struck Cobb. As Dr. Galloway testified, the severe injuries Cobb sustained were consistent with a person being thrown from a moving automobile during a crash. The coroner said that although he could not estimate Hall's speed from Cobb's injuries, Hall must have been travelling with "a significant amount of speed" to generate sufficient force to cause a basal skull fracture and brain injuries like Cobb's. Additionally, Hall crashed through Lemaner's skis and poles after he struck Cobb-breaking one of the poles in half-indicating a very high speed and great deal of force. Hall came to rest over eighty feet past Cobb's body, further suggesting that Hall was skiing at exceptionally high speeds. Thus, based on the testimony of the witnesses and the coroner's examination of Cobb's body, a reasonable person could conclude that Hall was skiing at very high speeds, thereby creating a risk of serious injury or death in the event of a skier-to-skier collision.

In addition to Hall's excessive speed, Hall was out of control and unable to avoid a collision with another person. All the witnesses said Hall was not traversing the slope and that he was skiing straight down the fall line. Hall was back on his skis, with his ski tips in the air and his arms out to his sides to maintain balance. Allen said that Hall was bounced around by the moguls on the slope rather than skiing in control and managing the bumps. Hall admitted to Deputy Mossness that he first saw Cobb when he was airborne and that he was unable to stop when he saw people below him just before the collision. Hence, in addition to finding that Hall was skiing at a very high rate of speed, a reasonably prudent person could have concluded that Hall was unable to anticipate or avoid a potential collision with a skier on the trail below him.

While skiing ordinarily carries a very low risk of death to other skiers, a reasonable person could have concluded that Hall's excessive speed, lack of control, and improper technique for skiing bumps significantly increased both the likelihood that a collision would occur and the extent of the injuries that might result from such a collision, including the possibility of death, in the event that a person like Cobb unwittingly crossed Hall's downhill path. McWilliam testified that he was aware of only two other deaths from skier collisions on Vail mountain in the past eleven years, but a reasonable person could have determined that Hall's conduct was precisely the type of skiing that risked this rare result.

We next ask whether a reasonable person could have concluded that Hall's creation of a substantial risk of death was unjustified. To the extent that Hall's extremely fast and unsafe skiing created a risk of death, Hall was serving no direct interest other than his own enjoyment. Although the sport often involves high speeds and even moments where a skier is temporarily out of control, a reasonable person could determine that the enjoyment of skiing does not justify skiing at the speeds and with the lack of control Hall exhibited. Thus, a reasonable person could have found that Hall's creation of a substantial risk was unjustifiable.

In addition to our conclusion that a reasonable person could have entertained the belief that Hall's conduct created a substantial and unjustifiable risk, we must ask whether Hall's conduct constituted a "gross deviation" from the standard of care that a reasonable law-abiding person (in this case, a reasonable, law-abiding, trained ski racer and resort employee) would have observed in the circumstances.

As we noted, the nature of the sport involves moments of high speeds and temporary losses of control. However, the General Assembly imposed upon a skier the duty to avoid collisions with any person or object below him. *See* § 33-44-109(2). Although this statute may not form the basis of criminal liability, it establishes the minimum standard of care for uphill skiers and, for the purposes of civil negligence suits, creates a rebuttable presumption that the skier is at fault whenever he collides with skiers on the slope below him. A violation of a skier's duty in an extreme fashion, such as here, may be evidence of conduct that constitutes a "gross deviation" from the standard of care imposed by statute for civil negligence. Hall admitted to Deputy Mossness that as he flew off a knoll, he saw people below him but was unable to stop; Hall was travelling so fast and with so little control that he could not possibly have respected his obligation to avoid skiers below him on the slope. Additionally, Hall skied in this manner for some time over a considerable distance, demonstrating that his high speeds and lack of control were not the type of momentary lapse of control or inherent danger associated with skiing. Based on the evidence, a reasonable person could conclude that Hall's conduct was a gross deviation from the standard of care that a reasonable, experienced ski racer would have exercised knowing that other people were on the slope in front of him and that he could not see the area below the knolls and bumps over which he was jumping.

Having determined that Hall's conduct created a substantial and unjustified risk of death that is a gross deviation from the reasonable standard of care under the circumstances, we next ask whether a reasonably prudent person could have entertained the belief that Hall consciously disregarded that risk. Hall is a trained ski racer who had been coached about skiing in control and skiing safely. Further, he was an employee of a ski area and had a great deal of skiing experience. Hall's knowledge and training could give rise to the reasonable inference that he was aware of the possibility that by skiing so fast and out of control he might collide with and kill another skier unless he regained control and slowed down.

In addition to inferring Hall's awareness of the risk from Hall's training and experience, a reasonable person with expert training and knowledge of skiing may have realized that skiing at very high speeds without enough control to stop or avoid a collision could seriously injure or kill another skier. A reasonable expert and experienced skier also might understand that in view of his duties under section 33-44-109, he must maintain enough control to avoid collisions with skiers below him on the slope. Thus, both Hall's subjective knowledge and the awareness that a reasonable person with Hall's background would have had support the inference that Hall consciously disregarded the risk he created by acting despite his awareness of the risk.

Although the risk that he would cause the death of another was probably slight, Hall's conduct created a risk of death. Hall's collision with Cobb involved enough force to kill Cobb and to simulate the type of head injury associated with victims in car accidents. Even though it is a rare occurrence, the court heard testimony that two skiers in the past eleven years died on Vail mountain alone from skier-to-skier collisions. Based on the evidence presented at the preliminary hearing, a reasonable person could conclude that Hall's conduct involved a risk of death.

Thus, interpreting the facts presented in the light most favorable to the prosecution, we hold that a reasonably prudent and cautious person could have entertained the belief that Hall consciously disregarded a substantial and unjustifiable risk that by skiing exceptionally fast and out of control he might collide with and kill another person on the slope.

Obviously, this opinion does not address whether Hall is ultimately guilty of any crime. Rather, we hold only that the People presented sufficient evidence to establish probable cause that Hall committed reckless manslaughter, and the court should have bound Hall's case over for trial.... Thus, we remand this case to the district court for trial.

## *Notes and Questions*

1. As was explained in both *In re D.G.* and *People v. Hall,* a person acts recklessly only if he is aware that his conduct creates a substantial and unjustifiable risk of harm. A person who lacks such awareness does not act recklessly, although he acts negligently if his conduct creates a significant risk of harm.

2. Recklessness is a central concept in American criminal law, for it defines the limits between advertent and inadvertent wrongdoing. The distinction is important, given that inadvertent (negligent) wrongdoing is seldom criminalized. Moreover, in the few instances in which inadvertent wrongdoing is punished it is usually punished much less severely than advertent wrongdoing. Most state jurisdictions exclude negligent wrongdoing from punishment by prescribing a default culpability level that applies when no mental state is referenced in the definition of the offense. As § 2.02(3) of the Model Penal Code and *State v. Loeffel* illustrate, that default mental state is typically recklessness. The practical import of this default rule is that offenses may not be committed negligently, unless the definition of the offense expressly states that negligence suffices for the imposition of criminal liability.

3. The Supreme Court of Colorado held in *People v. Hall* that a defendant may act recklessly even if his conduct is not more likely than not to result in harm. More specifically, the Court held that the defendant may be held liable for reckless manslaughter even if the risk of death created by his careless skiing was "slight" and in spite of the fact that recklessness is defined by law as conduct that creates a "substantial" risk of harm. Do you think that the risk of death created by the defendant in *Hall* was substantial? Why or why not? The Court also suggested that a slight risk of great harm may be substantial, whereas a significant risk of trivial harm may not be substantial. Do you agree?

4. Is there a connection between the substantiality of the risk and its unjustifiable nature? That is, is it plausible to suggest that a slight but extremely unjustified risk of harm may be substantial, while a significant but extremely justified risk of harm may not be substantial? Explain.

# § 8.04 Subjective Offense Elements (*Mens Rea*): Negligence under the Model Penal Code

## Model Penal Code § 2.02. General Requirements of Culpability.

(2) Kinds of Culpability Defined.

...

(d) Negligently:

A person acts negligently with respect to a material element of an offense when he should be aware of a substantial and unjustifiable risk that the material element exists or will result from his conduct. The risk must be of such a nature and degree that the actor's failure to perceive it, considering the nature and purpose of his conduct and the circumstances known to him, involves a gross deviation from the standard of care that a reasonable person would observe in the actor's situation.

## State v. Strescino

Supreme Court of New Hampshire, 1965
106 N.H. 554

KENISON, Chief Justice.

As stated by the defendant the "issue in this case is whether or not the two indictments against the defendant ... charging him with second degree manslaughter are sufficient as a matter of law." The second-degree manslaughter statute reads as follows: "Every killing of one human being by the act, procurement, or culpable negligence of another, which is not murder, nor excusable nor justifiable homicide, nor manslaughter of the first degree, is manslaughter of the second degree."

"Culpable negligence" as used in the manslaughter law is not defined therein or by any other statute. The definitions of 'culpable negligence' have been many and varied in other jurisdictions. This phrase in its criminal context has escaped definition in our cases and was expressly left undecided in *State v. Karvelos.* Although there are some cases to the contrary, it is the general rule that culpable negligence as used in manslaughter statutes means something more than negligence sufficient as a basis for the recovery of damages in a civil action. In the manslaughter statute, as in the statute prohibiting reckless driving "Something more than mere negligence is required however."

The time has come to give the phrase 'culpable negligence' some concrete meaning in our statute even though any definition is difficult and runs the risk of defining culpability in terms of culpability. The definition of "negligently" in the Model Penal Code, s. 2.02(2)(d) (Proposed Official Draft, p. 26 (1962) provides a standard. "Negligently" is defined therein as follows: "A person acts negligently with respect to a material element of an offense when he should be aware of a substantial and unjustifiable risk that the material element exists or will result from his conduct. The risk must be of such a nature and degree that the actor's failure to perceive it, considering the nature and purpose of his conduct and the circumstances known to him, involves a *gross deviation* from the standard of care that a reasonable person would observe in the actor's situation" (emphasis supplied). A person charged with culpable negligence may not be convicted on evidence which establishes only ordinary negligence but may be convicted on evidence of acts which are done negligently as defined above.

The test to determine the sufficiency of an indictment which will satisfy constitutional and statutory requirements was succinctly stated in *State v. Rousten*. "In the light of modern conditions, any complaint or indictment should be considered adequate, if it informs the defendant 'of the nature and cause of the accusation with sufficient definiteness' so that he can prepare for trial." In the present case the defendant is not in doubt as to the offense with which he is charged. However, he claims that the allegations in the indictment constitute "mere simple negligence" and are therefore insufficient as a matter of law. This overlooks the fact that the indictment charges the defendant with conduct that is "culpably negligent" and then describes the acts which are alleged to constitute the culpable negligence. This is sufficient....

Whether the defendant created a "dangerous obstruction" to motor traffic, why he left his motor vehicle in the highway "dark and unlighted" and for how long a period are matters to be proved at the trial. As far as the indictment is concerned it alleges conduct which could be found to constitute culpable negligence by a court or a jury within the meaning of [the manslaughter statute].

### *Notes and Questions*

1. As the Supreme Court of New Hampshire notes in *Strescino*, there is some debate as to whether the negligence that suffices for imposition of tort liability also suffices for the imposition of criminal liability. A considerable number of courts—including the Court in *Strescino*—hold that criminal negligence "means something more than negligence sufficient as a basis for the recovery of damages in a civil action." What explains the reluctance to construe criminal negligence in accordance with how it has traditionally been conceived in the tort law context?

2. While courts will often state that criminal negligence requires something more than civil law negligence, it is not clear what exactly that "something more" is. It is also unclear whether courts and juries are capable of non-arbitrarily distinguishing between traditional negligence and criminal negligence. The Model Penal Code qualifies its conception of negligence in two ways. First, it does not criminalize all unreasonable risk creation. Rather, it prohibits only the creation of a *substantial* risk of harm. Second, it does not punish any deviation the reasonable person standard. Instead, it criminalizes acts only when they involve a *gross* deviation from the standard of conduct that a reasonable person would observe under the circumstances. Does the Code's way of defining negligence clarify the difference between civil law negligence and criminal negligence? Explain.

## § 8.05 Subjective Offense Elements (*Mens Rea*): Comparative Perspectives

### Eugenio Raúl Zaffaroni, Alejandro Alagia & Alejandro Slokar, *Derecho Penal: Parte General*

(Ediar, 2002)

[A person acts with] *dolus eventualis* when he accepts the causation of harm as a possible outcome of his conduct and acts in spite of such awareness.... Nonetheless, an actor who is aware that his conduct may bring about a legally proscribed harm but trusts that he will be able to prevent the harm acts with conscious negligence rather than with *dolus eventualis.* It should be noted, however, that merely leaving the outcome to chance in the unfounded hope that the harm will not ensue is not enough to preclude a finding of *dolus eventualis.* The actor's trust or confidence in his ability to prevent the harm from taking place must be confirmed in some way by objective facts [even if his confidence is mistakenly placed].

The famous case of the Russian beggars [illustrates the differences between *dolus eventualis* and conscious negligence]. The Russian beggars maimed small children so that they could then use the disfigured children to incite compassion and, hopefully, get people to give them money. Some of the children died as a result of the maiming. Obviously, had the beggars known that the children were going to die, they would not have maimed them, for the children are more valuable to them alive. Therefore, the beggars *did not accept or acquiesce to the death of the children.* However, by continuing to maim the children in spite of being aware that some might die as a result of doing so, the beggars did accept the possibility of the children dying, which is enough to hold them liable for a homicide produced with *dolus eventualis.* On the other hand, if the beggars trusted that they would be able to prevent their death, they act with conscious negligence and should be convicted of negligent homicide even if they were aware that the children may die as a result of their conduct.

## *Notes and Questions*

1. Differentiating *dolus eventualis* from conscious negligence is essential to discriminating between intentional and negligent conduct in civil law countries, for *dolus eventualis* is considered the most watered down form of intent, whereas conscious negligence is considered a type of negligence. Consequently, the difference between acting with *dolus eventualis* or conscious negligence is of significant practical import. This is because in continental jurisdictions negligent conduct usually remains unpunished. Furthermore, when negligent wrongdoing is criminalized, it is typically punished significantly less than intentional wrongdoing.

2. In order for a defendant to act with *dolus eventualis* he must be aware that his conduct creates a risk of harm. In addition to awareness, however, acting with *dolus eventualis* has traditionally required a certain kind of attitude with regard to the risk created. There is no consensus regarding the kind of attitude that is relevant. For some, the actor must convince himself that he would act even if the consequence of the act is producing the proscribed harm. Others—like the authors of the excerpted material—suggest that the actor must "accept" the causation of harm as a possible outcome and act in spite of such awareness. For others, what matters is indifference rather than acceptance. According to this view, a defendant acts with *dolus eventualis* if he is aware that his conduct creates an unjustifiable risk of harm *and* he is indifferent as to whether the harm takes place. If the defendant does not act with the special kind of attitude that *dolus eventualis* demands, he acts with conscious negligence even if he is aware that his conduct risks harm. On the other hand, an actor who is unaware that his conduct creates a risk of harm acts with what European Continental scholars call "unconscious negligence."

3. Compare and contrast *dolus eventualis* and conscious negligence with "recklessness" and "negligence" as defined in the Model Penal Code. What are the similarities and differences between these mental states?

4. With what form of culpability as defined in § 2.02 of the Model Penal Code do you believe that the Russian beggars acted with regard to the death of the children? The au-

thors of the excerpted material argue that "if the beggars trusted that they would be able to prevent [the children's death], they act with conscious negligence and should be convicted of negligent homicide even if they were aware that the children may die as a result of their conduct." Would the beggars be convicted of negligent homicide under the Model Penal Code if they were aware that their conduct created a risk of death but they trusted that they could prevent the death of the children?

5. In light of the differences between *dolus eventualis/conscious negligence* and recklessness/negligence as defined in the Model Penal Code, do you believe that certain cases may generate significantly different criminal liability depending on whether they are approached from the European Continental or the Anglo-American perspective? Take, for example, the facts that gave rise to the Puerto Rican case of *Pueblo v. Colón Soto,* 109 D.P.R. 545 (1980). Two friends were having drinks at a local bar. After a couple of cocktails, the defendant suggested that he could shoot his friend's hat off with a single gunshot. The friend agreed to stand motionless and allow the defendant to shoot. The defendant's shot missed the hat, but reached the friend's head, killing him. Defendant was charged with intentional homicide. Defense counsel argued, however, that he should be convicted of negligent homicide. Did the defendant act with *dolus eventualis* or conscious negligence? Was defendant's act reckless or negligent under the Model Penal Code?

# § 8.06 Subjective Offense Elements (*Mens Rea*): Scholarly Debates

## Larry Alexander, *Insufficient Concern: A Unified Conception of Criminal Liability*

88 Cal. L. Rev. 931 (2000)

### C. Negligence

Negligence involves inadvertence to a risk that, if adverted to, would render the actor reckless. I have argued elsewhere that negligence as inadvertent risk-taking is not culpable conduct. I have further argued that because such negligence is nonculpable, it cannot be defined nonarbitrarily, nor can it be distinguished from cases of strict liability or involuntariness. For these reasons, [which I will briefly sketch in the following subsections], I have urged that negligence be dropped from criminal codes as a form of criminal culpability.

#### 1. The Moral Immateriality of Failure to Advert to Risk

The world is full of risks to which we are oblivious. Or more accurately, because risk is an epistemic, not ontic, notion, we frequently believe we are creating a certain level of risk when someone in an epistemically superior position to ours would assess the risk to be higher or lower than we have estimated. Sometimes the epistemically superior position is the product of better information: For example, the doctor knows that what we believe is just a mole is in fact a life-threatening melanoma. At other times we have failed to notice something that another might have noticed, or we have forgotten something that another might have remembered. And once in a while, our lack of information, failure to notice, or forgetfulness results in our underestimating the riskiness of our conduct and causing harm.

We are not morally culpable for taking risks of which we are unaware, or so I contend. At any point in time we are failing to notice a great many things, we have forgotten a great many things, and we are misinformed or uninformed about many things. An injunction to notice, remember, and be fully informed about anything that bears on risks to others is an injunction no human being can comply with, so violating this injunction reflects no moral defect. Even those most concerned with the well-being of others will violate this injunction constantly.

Of course, inadvertence to risk may reflect moral culpability in the sense that it is the product of a prior reckless act. I may have failed to take the free course on medical problems of children, realizing at the time that I was taking a substantial risk that I might someday fail to recognize a child's serious medical problem. I may have failed to take the course on Japanese for sailors, realizing at the time that I was taking a substantial risk that I might someday cause harm because of a misunderstanding. I may have failed to write a note to myself to get the brakes fixed, realizing at the time that I was taking a substantial risk of forgetting. Or I may have engaged in a heated discussion with the passenger in my car, realizing at the time the discussion began that I was taking a substantial risk of having my attention diverted from my driving. In all of these examples I might be acting recklessly toward others, and hence culpably, by taking a risk that I would later fail to advert to a risk to others.

Even if inadvertence to risk is sometimes the product of a culpable act, it is still not culpable. It is merely the nonculpable product of some prior culpable act. And most often, inadvertent risk imposition cannot be traced to any prior act that we would deem morally culpable.

I realize that both the criminal law and most people's intuitions run against me on the issue of whether inadvertent negligence is culpable, so I would like to construct what I believe is the strongest example on the side of majority opinion. Sam and Ruth are a self-absorbed yuppie couple with a small child. They are throwing a dinner party for some socially prominent people who can help both Sam's and Ruth's careers and their social standing, and they are quite obsessed with making sure the party is a success. They put their child in the bathtub and begin drawing bathwater, but just then the first guests begin to arrive. Sam and Ruth both go downstairs to greet the guests, both realizing that the child would be in grave danger if they failed to return and turn off the water, but both believing correctly that at the rate the tub is filling, they will have plenty of time to return to the child after they have welcomed the guests. Of course, when they greet their guests they become so absorbed with making the right impression that both forget about the child, with tragic consequences.

If there is ever a case of culpable negligence, this is it. Sam and Ruth are not morally attractive people. And their moral shortcomings have played a role in their child's death. Still, I would argue, they did not act culpably. When they went downstairs they did not believe they were taking any substantial risk with their child, perhaps no more substantial a risk than we believe we are taking (for the sake of our careers) when we attend a workshop and leave our children with a sitter. Of course, once Sam and Ruth became engaged with their guests, the child's situation slipped out of their minds. And once the thought was out of their minds, they had no power to retrieve it. They were at the mercy of its popping back into mind, which it did not.

As Michael Zimmerman and Ishtijaque Haji have recently written, one is culpable only for acts over which one has control. If one is unaware that, say, someone has replaced the sugar on the table with poison, then one is not culpable for placing that poison in another's coffee and thereby killing her. For although one is in control of the conduct of placing the white substance in the coffee, the mistaken belief that it is sugar deprives one of the kind of control necessary for culpability. And what holds true for conduct taken in ignorance of its nature or likely consequences also holds true for the ignorance itself. One is not culpable for one's ignorance unless one is in control of it. And one can be in control of one's ignorance only indirectly, say, by deliberately refraining from learning something while being aware that one is running an unjustifiable risk of dangerous ignorance.

Because the actor who fails to advert to a risk acts in ignorance of that risk, he is not culpable for taking it. He may or may not be culpable for some earlier act that he realized at the time could result in further ignorance of the kind that did result. But even if he were culpable, he would be culpable only for the earlier recklessness, not the consequential negligence.

### 2. The Arbitrariness of the Definition of Negligence and the Lines Between Negligence, Strict Liability, and Involuntariness

If one accepts my argument in the previous subsection that negligence is nonculpable, then the very concept of negligence, in contradistinction to strict liability and involuntariness, collapses. The "reasonable actor," the construct by which negligence is gauged, is supposed to be somewhere between God, who knows with certainty whether conduct will cause harm, and the negligent defendant, who underestimated a particular risk. That is, the reasonable actor is supposed to be aware of more than the negligent actor but less than God.

There is, however, no way to construct the reasonable person nonarbitrarily. All of us are ignorant of many risks. When is that ignorance the kind that the reasonable person would possess, when is it not, and why? If negligence were culpable, then we could give an answer: The reasonable person would not be ignorant of those risks the ignorance of which would render him culpable. But if ignorance is never culpable because we lack direct control over it, then we have no materials from which to construct a nonarbitrary "reasonable person."

For the very same reason, negligence must collapse into strict liability and involuntariness. Take the person who drives a new car off the lot, sets the cruise control at the speed limit, and then, when the speed limit changes, cannot disengage the cruise control in time to avoid speeding. If he were deemed guilty of a traffic offense and punished, would this represent punishment for involuntary conduct, strict liability punishment, or punishment for negligence? The case for involuntariness is that for the period the cruise control was stuck, the defendant was a passenger in a runaway vehicle and had no control over its movement. On the other hand, he did voluntarily bring the car to its original speed and engage the cruise control, which from that standpoint makes his case seem like one of strict liability. In other words, depending on the point in time from which we begin to tell the story of the crime—the time at which the driver engages the cruise control versus the time at which he tries to slow down—his conduct can appear to be either one thing or the other. Without a culpable act to mark the beginning of the story of the crime, the choice of when to begin it, and thus whether it is a case of strict liability or a case of involuntariness, is purely arbitrary.

For the very same reason, given that negligence is nonculpable, the case could also be characterized as one of negligence. The defendant failed to advert to the condition of his cruise control that would cause it to malfunction. The risk of malfunction was high—in fact, one. His failure so to advert—his ignorance—was nonculpable; but so is all ignorance.

## George Fletcher, *The Fault of Not Knowing*

3 Theoretical Inq. L. 265 (2002)

A good transitional case for illustrating the general problem [of why we punish negligence] came before [Justice] Holmes when he was a Massachusetts Supreme Court judge. A doctor named Pierce treated a patient by applying kerosene-soaked rags to her skin. The patient died from the treatment, and though there was no suggestion of ill will on the doctor's part, the state prosecuted him for murder. Holmes wrote the opinion confirming the conviction on the ground that as judged against an "external" standard, the doctor had been reckless (meaning: grossly negligent) in providing this treatment. [T]he culpability of [the doctor] lies in not understanding the dangers latent in [his] conduct. Arguably, the doctor was more culpable because he presumably received stronger signals that there might be something harmful in using kerosene-soaked rags as a method of medical treatment. Yet the brunt of Holmes' opinion for conviction was that the doctor's good faith could not be a justification for his conduct. This was the relevance of an external standard in judging Pierce's conduct against an external standard.

It is not clear from the facts in *Pierce* whether the defendant had simply been oblivious to the danger of using kerosene-soaked rags or whether he had made the wrong cost/benefit judgment about whether the danger outweighed the potential benefit. In the pure case of not knowing of the danger, the fault lies in having failed to investigate the risks attendant upon his affirmative conduct of treating the patient.

Looking at the doctor's fault as an aspect of a larger activity says something important about how we have to think about negligence in torts and criminal law. If we look just at the doctrines of negligence, the structuring of issues very much resembles liability for omissions. That is, as every first-year law student knows, a finding of negligence requires a finding of duty and breach of duty. The analysis of intentional torts and of intentional (affirmative) crimes does not require a finding of duty. The only field of law that is structured in the same way as the standard analysis of negligence in torts is liability for omissions—both in torts and criminal law. No one is liable for an omission unless there is a duty to intervene and prevent the harm from occurring....

As the law of negligence evolved, however, the failure to exercise due care—an omission—came to be seen as part of affirmative risks to others—the risks of driving, of medical care, of handling weapons, of manufacturing goods. In the context of these larger activities, the omission is but an epicycle on the arc of risk generated by the affirmative conduct. The omission becomes a minor part of the actor's assertive conduct. This is the way criminal lawyers think of negligence—as a way of killing or committing assault or destroying property. Thus, Dr. Pierce created a risk of death by the way he administered medical treatment. His gross negligence appeared to be less of a failure to realize a certain risk and more, as the MPC would describe it, of introducing in the world a "substantial and unjustified risk" for which there was no excuse. The fault was not the passivity of an omission, but the affirmative wrong of creating an unreasonable risk.

It is not surprising, then, that criminal lawyers rarely speak of duty and breach when they discuss negligence. The survival of this terminology in torts reflects a throwback to a previous way of looking at risk-creation as a wrong that inheres in the fault of not knowing of a danger lurking in one's conduct.

The doctrine of unforeseeability reflects, I believe, the former way of looking at negligence as a fault of not knowing. Thus when the risk is too bizarre and the outcome so unexpected that no one can be faulted for running it, the appropriate way of talking about fault is to focus on the difficulty of knowing the unforeseeable. A good example is the nitroglycerine case decided by the Supreme Court. At about the time TNT was invented, agents for the Wells-Fargo Company received a mysterious crate that was leaking a liquid that they could not identify. They tried to open the case with a hammer and chisel. After the crate exploded and caused injury to bystanders, the company found itself being sued. The Court affirmed a finding of non-liability on the ground that the explosion was unforeseeable.

In these [two] cases—*Pierce* and *Wells-Fargo*—the defendants acted on a good-faith belief that there was nothing wrong, nothing risky, with their conduct ... [One way] to account for the attribution of wrongdoing and guilt [in *Pierce*] ... is based on the observation that a little effort in consulting people in the neighborhood can avert the risks that led to the ... use of kerosene-soaked rags in medical treatment ... The idea that the harm was "foreseeable" means that the actor was put on notice that there might be something risky in his conduct or in the state of the things in his charge. There is warrant for talking to others, for being open to advice about the correct path of conduct. When, as in the nitroglycerine case, it is extremely unlikely that anyone would know of the danger, the case falls under the excuse of "unforeseeability." ...

Our moral lives are not so different from our learning about the risks latent in our conduct. If we are open to the opinions of others, we increase our capacity for self-correction. And having the opportunity to correct one's belief and failing to exercise that capacity lie at the foundation of the fault of not knowing.

## *Notes and Questions*

1. Larry Alexander makes a philosophically sophisticated argument against punishing negligence. Ultimately, the argument hinges on a very simple proposition. Actors can only be blamed for what they freely choose to do. But actors do not freely choose to act negligently, given that the negligent actor is—by definition—not conscious or aware that he is acting negligently. Therefore, criminalizing negligence is unfair, for doing so punishes actors for generating risks that they did not freely choose to create. Are you persuaded by this argument? Explain.

2. Reconsider the hypothetical case of the self-absorbed yuppie couple that forgets that their child is alone in the bathtub. Professor Alexander argues that they should not be punished for contributing to their child's death. The parents cannot be faulted for forgetting about the child, given that they did not freely choose to forget about him. Furthermore, they cannot be faulted for not remembering, for they did not freely choose to not remember either. Since they did not freely choose to forget (or not think) about the child, it would be unfair to punish them for forgetting. Do you agree with this argument? If you do not, what is wrong with it?

3. Professor George Fletcher suggests that in order to understand why negligence should be punished it is necessary to focus on what the actor did as opposed to focusing on what the actor failed to do. And what the actor does in cases of negligence is create a risk of harm. The wrongfulness of negligent conduct is thus not the failure to do something, but rather actively putting in motion a course of conduct that risks causing harm. So conceived, the self-absorbed parents should not be faulted for forgetting about their child. Rather, they should be faulted for drawing bathwater with their child in the bathtub and leaving the child alone in order to greet their guests. Once the focus is on the creation of the risk instead of on failing to remember about their child, the relevant question becomes whether they had good reasons to create the risk (i.e., whether they

had good reasons for drawing the bathwater and leaving the child in the bathtub). Given that they did not have good reasons for creating the risk (greeting guests is not a good reason for leaving the baby alone in the bathtub), their negligent risk creation is culpable. What is blameworthy is the inexcusable (i.e., culpable) creation of the risk, not the failure to remember that the child was left in the bathtub. Does this account adequately explain why the parents should be punished for their negligence? How do you think Alexander would reply to this argument?

4. Does punishing negligence deter persons from acting negligently in the future? Does punishing negligence encourage actors to inform themselves more about the risks inherent in their conduct? Does criminalizing negligence encourage actors to take more precautions than they would otherwise take if negligence were not criminalized? If you answered some or all of these questions affirmatively, do you think that the consequentialist benefits that are reaped by criminalizing negligence justify punishing negligence even if Professor Alexander is right that negligent actors do not deserve retributive punishment? Explain.

# Chapter 9

# Negating Subjective Offense Elements

## § 9.01 Negating Subjective Offense Elements (*Mens Rea*): Common Law Approach to Mistake of Fact

### Louisiana Revised Statutes 14–16

*§ 16. Mistake of fact*

Unless there is a provision to the contrary in the definition of a crime, reasonable ignorance of fact or mistake of fact which precludes the presence of any mental element required in that crime is a defense to any prosecution for that crime.

### Busby v. State

Court of Criminal Appeals of Texas, 1921
89 Tex.Crim. 213

MORROW, P. J.

The appellant was convicted of bigamy. He first married Gracie Leona Rogers, and later married Ollie Gibson. The defense relied upon and submitted to the jury was a mistake of fact.

Appellant claimed and testified that at the time of the second marriage he believed that a decree of divorce had been entered dissolving the former marriage. He sought, by certain proof made and by certain evidence offered and excluded, to show the ground for this belief; that his mistake of fact did not arise from a want of proper care. He had brought suit against his wife for a divorce, and there was evidence that his sister had received a letter from his first wife, the contents of which letter were made known to him and in which the statement was made that she was divorced, that she was glad to be free, and that she did not want any longer to be called by the name of Grace Busby.

Appellant offered to prove by the bigamous wife that prior to the marriage, she had related to the appellant that she had had a conversation with one Hooker, a lawyer, whom appellant had employed to bring suit for divorce, and that Hooker had told her that the divorce had been granted. This appears to have been rejected as hearsay. As to establishing what the witness related to the appellant, it was improperly excluded under the hearsay rule. It was original testimony going to show the information upon which the appellant acted in entering into the second marriage.

Our statute, articles 46 and 47 of the Penal Code, makes a mistake of fact a defense when the mistake does not arise from the want of proper care.

"Whenever it is material to ascertain the condition of a party's mind at a particular time, statements made to him which account for his attitude are not excluded because they are hearsay." Wharton's Crim. Evidence, vol. 1, § 257.

It was material in the instant case to determine the state of the appellant's mind; that is, whether at the time he entered into the bigamous marriage he was under the mistaken belief that his first wife had been divorced from him, and whether in acting upon the mistake of fact he used proper care was a matter which the jury was called upon to determine from the evidence before them. As said by Judge Willson, in Watson v. State, 13 Tex. App. 82:

> The question as to proper care, we think, depends upon the facts in each particular case. No general rule can be prescribed in relation to it. What would be proper care in one case might be gross negligence in another. What would be proper care when considered with reference to one individual might not be when applied to another.

The statute declares that the mistake must not arise from a want of proper care on the part of the person committing the offense. Article 47, Penal Code. In the instant case the person committing the offense was a negro about 22 years of age. He appeared and testified before the jury. It was within their province to weigh the evidence in connection with their knowledge of the appellant, gathered from his appearance and demeanor in giving his testimony; and it was clearly his right to have before them the testimony of the bigamous wife that she had reported to him that his lawyer had told her that a divorce had been granted. The weight that the jury would have given to this testimony or the credit they would accord the witness are not for this court or the trial court to determine. In view of the other facts in the case, they might have determined the issue of mistake against him; but this evidence was clearly admissible and material upon a vital issue in the case, and its exclusion was, in our judgment, error which must result in a reversal of the judgment.

## Granger v. State

Court of Criminal Appeals of Texas, 1999
3 S.W.3d 36

MEYERS, J.,

Appellant was convicted of murder and sentenced by a jury to a term of fifty-five years confinement. The Court of Appeals affirmed appellant's conviction.... We granted review to determine whether the Court of Appeals erred in holding that appellant was not entitled to an affirmative "mistake of fact" instruction pursuant to § 8.02 of the Texas Penal Code.

In the early hours of February 4, 1995, appellant and three companions were ejected from a Dallas nightclub for "dancing dirty." The club's security guard testified that a young man who was with appellant became angry at the prospect of being thrown out of the club and argued with the security guard. The guard escorted the four young people out and then went back inside the club.

A few minutes later, the security guard went back outside to see if the group had left the area. In a parking lot across the street, the guard saw appellant and the other young man walking back toward the club. The security guard stepped back inside. The guard told the doorman that the two men were still out there and that he suspected that "they might be up to something." After about five minutes, the security guard again went outside and immediately heard two or three gunshots. He looked up to see where the shots were coming from and saw appellant and his companion standing on the passenger side of a car parked across the street from the club. The two men were standing on the curb looking down into the car with their arms extended toward the car. The security guard then saw two or three "flashes" accompanied by the sound of additional gunshots. The guard testified that at first he thought they were shooting into an empty car and started to walk toward the men. But when he got about half way across the street, he noticed the victim sitting in the driver's seat of the car. The guard yelled at the men. The two men then looked up and ran down a nearby alley. The victim later died of multiple gunshot wounds....

[Several] months later, the police arrested appellant, at which time he gave a second written statement. That statement provided:

> That night in February when me and Pam, Debbie, and Jerome went to the R.L. Blues Palace, we all got kicked out and walked over to Pam's car. Jerome was mad at the security guard for kicking us out, and he kept arguing with him. I tried to tell him to come on, and let's go but he grabbed a gun from inside Pam's car. I seen him grab his gun so I grabbed mine. It was a .32 or .380 automatic. We walked over across the street towards the security guard but he was already back inside the club. We turned and started walking back to Pam's car. Jerome then saw this car parked on the side of the street and that's when he started saying, "I know that car." We walked right past the car and Jerome started shooting at the car. When he started shooting *I didn't think that anybody was in side the car* so I started shooting at the car also. I fired about four shots. We then ran off and flagged down Pam's car over on the next street.

The State offered ... appellant's written [statement] into evidence at trial.

The court's proposed jury charge included an instruction on murder and the lesser included offenses of manslaughter and criminally negligent homicide. Defense counsel objected to the proposed charge inasmuch as it did not contain an instruction on mistake of fact. The trial court overruled the objection. Appellant was convicted of murder.

In the Court of Appeals, appellant claimed the trial court erred in denying his request for an affirmative instruction on mistake of fact. Specifically, appellant argued that the portion of his statement in which he claimed that he thought he was firing into an empty car was sufficient to raise the statutory defense under § 8.02.... [T]he Court of Appeals affirmed appellant's conviction. While the Court of Appeals acknowledged the general rule that an accused has the right to an instruction on any defensive issue raised by the evidence, the court nevertheless concluded that the defense of mistake of fact was not "raised" by the record because appellant had failed to present any evidence that his mistaken belief was "reasonable." The lower court stated, "appellant's purported mistaken belief that the car was empty was formed not through mistake, but by indifference. Given this, there is also no evidence that appellant's purported mistaken belief that the car was unoccupied was one that a reasonable and prudent person would have had under the same circumstances." Because appellant's mistake was "unreasonable," reasoned the lower court, he was not entitled to an affirmative instruction under § 8.02 of the Penal Code....

The general defense of mistake of fact, as codified in § 8.02(a) [of the Texas Penal Code], provides: "It is a defense to prosecution that the actor through mistake formed a reasonable belief about a matter of fact if his mistaken belief negated the kind of culpability required for the commission of the offense." This case pivots on the phrase "reasonable belief." The question we are faced with is whether the reasonableness requirement is a preliminary issue for the judge to decide in determining whether each element of the defense was "raised" by the evidence, or whether it is a fact issue that should be left to the jury.

The State argues, and the Court of Appeals held, that the reasonableness of an accused's mistaken belief may be evaluated by the trial judge in determining whether the statutory defense is raised. But the appellate court's holding is contrary to this Court's previous decision in *Hayes. Hayes* dealt with a defendant's "reasonable belief" in the related context of a jury instruction involving "Deadly Force in Defense of Person" under § 9.32 of the Penal Code. There, we held that whether the defendant's belief was "reasonable" was a fact issue for the jury to decide.

We see no reason to depart from the *Hayes* holding here. Whether appellant's mistaken belief was "reasonable," so as to comport with the requirements of § 8.02, should have been left for the jury to decide as trier of fact. By failing to give the appropriate instruction, the trial court denied the jury the opportunity to decide this issue....

Moreover, a holding in accordance with the State's position would tend to undermine the general rule that the jury should be responsible for gauging the credibility and veracity of the defensive evidence.... Trial court judges charged with evaluating the "reasonableness" of an accused's beliefs, no matter how well intentioned, would inevitably be placed in a position in which they were required to make their own decisions about the weight and believability of the defensive evidence. The Court of Appeals' opinion illustrates this dilemma. In reaching its conclusion that there was no evidence to support a "reasonable belief" that the car was empty, the court was forced to engage in its own subjective evaluation of the evidence:

> The victim's car was parked on the street in a line of cars directly opposite the front door of a nightclub that was open for business. Photographs admitted into evidence indicate the car's windows were clear and transparent. Photographs and testimony of the security guard indicate the area was well lit with street lights and lights from the club. There is no evidence in the record that appellant looked into the car—or did anything else—to determine whether the car was occupied before shooting into it. Given the fact that appellant had walked "right past" the car before he started shooting, he could easily have discovered the victim's presence. Thus, appellant's purported mistaken belief that the car was empty was formed not through mistake, but by indifference.

But whether appellant had the *opportunity* to correct his mistake is precisely the sort of fact issue properly left to the jury. The condition of the car's windows, the lighting on the street at the time of the shooting and appellant's failure to take advantage of a chance to look inside the car are all details that the State may argue in its closing statement. But the use of those factual details to bolster a court's conclusion that an accused's belief is unreasonable as a matter of law does exactly what the law forbids—it effectively substitutes the court's judgment on the weight of the evidence for that of the jury.

"When an accused creates an issue of mistaken belief as to the culpable mental element of the offense, he is entitled to a defensive instruction of 'mistake of fact.'" Therefore, in the instant case, the issue before the trial court was whether appellant's purported belief, if accepted as true, negated the culpability required for murder. Clearly, it does. Section 19.02(b) of the Texas Penal Code provides, in relevant part:

b) A person commits an offense if he:

1) intentionally or knowingly causes the death of an individual;

2) intends to cause serious bodily injury and commits an act clearly dangerous to human life that causes the death of an individual....

Accepting appellant's statement to the police as true, he could not have "intentionally or knowingly" caused the death of the victim, or "intend[ed] to cause serious bodily injury" to the victim if appellant did not know that the victim was in the car. Appellant was therefore entitled to a jury instruction on mistake of fact pursuant to § 8.02 of the Penal Code.

The Court of Appeals erred in denying appellant's request for a mistake of fact instruction. Whether appellant's purported belief that the car was unoccupied was reasonable and credible was a question for the jury in considering the affirmative mistake of fact instruction. Reversal is required if appellant suffered harm as a result of the error. *Almanza v. State.* We therefore remand the case to the Court of Appeals for further proceedings consistent with *Almanza.*

## People v. Russell

Court of Appeal, Sixth District, California, 2006
51 Cal.Rptr.3d 263

McADAMS, J.

Defendant Philip Russell was convicted by jury of one count of receiving a stolen motor vehicle, a felony.... The court denied defendant's motion for new trial and his request to reduce the receiving stolen property count to a misdemeanor.

On appeal, defendant contends there was insufficient evidence to support his conviction for receiving a stolen vehicle because his honest, even if mistaken, belief that the motorcycle was abandoned negated the felonious intent element of the offense. Defendant also contends the court prejudicially erred when it failed to instruct the jury on the mistake-of-fact ... [defense], which would have negated the intent element of the offense ... We conclude there was prejudicial instructional error and reverse the judgment....

### Mistake-of-Fact Defense

To sustain a conviction for receiving stolen property, the prosecution must prove: (1) the property was stolen; (2) the defendant knew the property was stolen (hereafter the knowledge element); and, (3) the defendant had possession of the stolen property.

Although receiving stolen property has been characterized as a general intent crime, the second element of the offense is knowledge that the property was stolen, which is a specific mental state. With regard to the knowledge element, receiving stolen property is a "specific intent crime".... The defendant therefore should have an opportunity to request instructions regarding the lack of requisite knowledge.

At common law, an honest and reasonable belief in the existence of circumstances, which, if true, would make the act with which the person is charged an innocent act, was a good defense.... A person who commits an act or makes an omission under a mistake of fact which disproves his or her criminal intent, is excluded from the class of persons who are capable of committing crimes.

The standard jury instruction on the mistake-of-fact defense, Judicial Council of California Criminal Jury Instructions provides:

> The defendant is not guilty of _____ *<insert crime[s]>* if (he/she) did not have the intent or mental state required to commit the crime because (he/she) [reasonably] did not know a fact or [reasonably and] mistakenly believed a fact.
>
> If the defendant's conduct would have been lawful under the facts as (he/she) [reasonably] believed them to be, (he/she) did not commit _____ *<insert crime[s]>*.
>
> If you find that the defendant believed that _____ *<insert alleged mistaken fact[s]>* [and if you find that belief was reasonable], (he/she) did not have the specific intent or mental state required for _____ *<insert crime[s]>*.
>
> If you have a reasonable doubt about whether the defendant had the specific intent or mental state required for _____ *<insert crime[s]>*, you must find (him/her) not guilty of (that crime/those crimes).

The bench notes instruct:

> If the defendant is charged with a general intent crime, the trial court must instruct with the bracketed language requiring that defendant's belief be both actual and reasonable.
>
> If the intent at issue is specific criminal intent, do not use the bracketed language requiring the belief to be reasonable.

Since receiving stolen property is a specific intent crime with regard to the knowledge element, the jury need not be instructed that the mistake of fact had to be objectively reasonable for the defense to apply.

The mistake-of-fact defense has been applied in a case involving the belief that property has been abandoned. In *People v. Navarro*, an oft-cited appellate department case, the defendant was charged with grand theft for taking four wooden beams from a construction site. There was evidence "from which the jury could have concluded that [the] defendant believed the wooden beams had been abandoned and that the owner had no objection to his taking them...." In light of the evidence, the defendant requested special mistake-of-fact instructions. The proposed instructions informed the jury that someone who takes personal property with the good faith belief that the property has been abandoned or that he has permission to take the property is not guilty of theft even if that good faith belief is unreasonable. Although the trial court instructed on the mistake-of-fact defense, it modified the defendant's proposed instructions by instructing that the good faith belief, either that the property was abandoned or that the person had permission to take the property, had to be reasonable.

The jury convicted the defendant of theft, but the appellate department of the superior court reversed. The court explained that "an honest mistake of fact ... is a defense when it negates a required mental element of the crime."... Quoting from LaFave and Scott, which used the crime of receiving stolen property as an example, the opinion reasoned "if the defendant by a mistake of either fact or law did not know the goods were stolen, even though the circumstances would have led a prudent man to believe they were stolen, he does not have the required mental state and thus may not be convicted of the crime." Applying these rules to the facts before it, the *Navarro* court concluded that "the trial court in effect instructed the jury that even though defendant in good faith believed he had the right to take the beams, and thus lacked the specific intent required for the crime of theft, he should be convicted unless such belief was reasonable. In doing so it erred. It is true that if the jury thought the defendant's belief to be unreasonable, it might infer that he did not in good faith hold such belief. If, however, it concluded that defendant in good faith believed he had the right to take the beams, even though such belief was unreasonable as measured by the objective standard of a hypothetical reasonable man, defendant was entitled to an acquittal since the specific intent required to be proved as an element of the offense had not been established."

The court has a sua sponte duty to instruct on mistake of fact if the defendant relies on the defense or if there is substantial evidence that supports the defense and the defense is not inconsistent with the defendant's theory of the case....

### E. Sufficiency of Evidence to Support Mistake-of-Fact [Defense]

We next consider whether there was evidence that supported giving the mistake-of-fact instructions in this case....

Although the jury was not required to believe it, defendant presented substantial evidence from which the jury could have inferred that he had a good faith belief that the motorcycle was abandoned. First, defendant testified repeatedly that he thought the motorcycle was abandoned.

Second, the condition and location of the motorcycle supported an inference that it had been abandoned. According to defendant, the 23-year-old motorcycle was rusty, the turn signal was covered with packing tape, there were cobwebs and leaves in the front wheel, the motor blocks were tarnished, and the registration had expired 22 months before. The apartment manager described it as "beat up" and said the starter was about to go. When defendant found it, the motorcycle was located near the trash area and was not inside the repair shop. It was not locked. In addition, defendant knew the repair shop's practice was to bring the motorcycles in at night.

Third, defendant's conduct could lead the jury to conclude that he had a good faith belief the motorcycle had been abandoned. Defendant went to Cycle Gear to inquire about the motorcycle after he took it to his camp. He assumed the repair shop and Cycle Gear were related businesses and a Cycle Gear employee told him the motorcycle did not belong to Cycle Gear. When he was [issued a traffic violation] by Officer Reyes, he told her he had found the motorcycle "abandoned," he had punched the ignition to get it running, and intended to register it in his own name. Officer Reyes told him the motorcycle had *not* been reported stolen. After he learned the identity of the registered owner, he went to [the owner's] apartment, hoping to persuade Foster to sign the motorcycle over to him. He told the apartment manager he had found the motorcycle "abandoned." He did not sell the motorcycle, remove its license plate, or try to disguise it. Instead, he invested time and money to fix it up. He left the motorcycle parked in an open lot near his tent in broad daylight and told the police officer it belonged to him. He told Officer Ciaburro he thought the motorcycle was "abandoned" and that he had "punched the ignition." After Officer Ciaburro told him the motorcycle had been reported stolen, he did not attempt to flee. He was friendly, cooperative, and eager to talk to the officer about the motorcycle....

In summary, defendant acted as if he believed he was entitled to possess the motorcycle. He did not behave in a furtive manner or attempt to conceal the fact that he had taken the motorcycle or punched its ignition. Moreover, this evidence was not minimal or insubstantial.

At trial, defendant's primary defense was that he did not know the motorcycle was a stolen vehicle because he believed the motorcycle had been abandoned. Defense counsel did not request mistake-of-fact ... instructions. However, the trial court had a sua sponte duty to instruct on [the defense] if it appeared defendant was relying on the [defense], or if there was substantial evidence supportive of the [defense] and [it] [was] not inconsistent with defendant's theory of the case. [T]he mistake-of-fact [defense] [was] implicated by defendant's claim that he did not have the requisite knowledge that the motorcycle was stolen because at all times he held a good faith belief that it had been abandoned.

For these reasons, we conclude there was substantial evidence that supported instructing the jury on the ... mistake-of-fact [defense] and that the trial court erred when it failed to instruct the jury on [the defense]....

[W]e [further] conclude it is reasonably probable defendant would have obtained a more favorable result if the jury had been instructed [about mistake of fact].

The judgment is reversed.

## *Notes and Questions*

1. As the three leading cases reveal, the common law approach is that a reasonable mistake of fact is usually a defense to criminal liability. Furthermore, as the excerpted Louisiana statute illustrates, a mistake of fact defeats liability when it "precludes the presence of any mental element required in that crime." In contrast, "[n]o mistake of law excuses one committing an offense." *Hailes v. State,* 15 Tex.App. 93 (1883). It is thus important to distinguish between mistakes of *fact* that are usually relevant to assessing defendant's liability and mistakes of *law,* which are generally irrelevant for the criminal law. This chapter focuses on mistakes of fact. Mistakes of law are discussed in Chapter 20.

2. It is sometimes difficult to determine whether an incorrect belief is a mistake of fact or law. The facts of *Busby v. State* are illustrative. Defendant argued that he should not be held liable of bigamy because "at the time of the second marriage he [mistakenly] believed that a decree of divorce had been entered dissolving the former marriage." The Court found that defendant's incorrect belief that his former marriage was dissolved was a mistake of fact. As such, the Court concluded that the mistake would preclude liability if reasonable. Nevertheless, as another court observed, "in prosecutions for bigamy it has been held that the alleged bigamist's mistake *in* law as to the former marriage having been legally dissolved is no defense." *Commonwealth ex rel Thompson v. Yarnell,* 313 Pa. 244 (1933). Consequently, many courts hold that such mistakes do not preclude liability for bigamy even if reasonable. See, e.g., *Burnley v. State,* 201 Miss. 234 (1947). Do you believe that a mistake regarding the validity of a marriage is a mistake of fact or law? Explain.

3. In order to sort out the mistake of fact/mistake of law distinction in cases like the ones highlighted in the prior note, it may be helpful to distinguish between mistakes of criminal law and mistakes of non-criminal law. A mistake of criminal law is a mistake about whether certain conduct is prohibited by the criminal law. A person who receives stolen goods incorrectly believing that receipt of such property is not prohibited makes a mistake about the criminal law because she ignores what the penal law criminalizes. In contrast, a person makes a mistake of non-criminal law when she receives abandoned goods incorrectly believing that she is not receiving stolen property because abandoned goods belong to the person who found them. In fact, abandoned goods in that jurisdiction belong to the state. In this case, the actor is not mistaken about what the criminal law prohibits, for she knows that receiving stolen goods is against the penal law. Nevertheless, she incorrectly believes that the goods are not stolen because she makes a mistake about the rules governing property law (i.e., she makes a mistake about non-criminal law).

Should either of these mistakes exculpate? As a general rule, it can be said that mistakes of criminal law will not exculpate even if reasonable. On the contrary, many courts will find that mistakes of non-criminal law will exculpate, given that they are conceptually analogous to mistakes of fact. As one court noted:

> The concepts of "mistake of fact" and "mistake of non-penal law" are often very close to one another. For example, trespassers may be excused for lack of criminal intent because they mistakenly but reasonably believed they had entered on to someone else's property under a prescriptive easement. The mistake may be as to the actual length of time that adverse use has continued (mistake of fact) or as to the time required to establish a prescriptive easement (mistake of law). *See* R. Perkins & R. Boyce, SUPRA, at 1031, 1044–45. *Morgan v. District of Columbia,* 476 A.2d 1128 (1984).

Is a defendant's claim that she should not be found guilty of bigamy because she incorrectly believed that it was lawful to marry more than one person at a time a mistake of criminal law or a mistake of non-criminal law? Is a defendant's claim that she should not be held liable for bigamy because she incorrectly believed that her first marriage had been legally dissolved a mistake of criminal law or a mistake of non-criminal law? Which of these two claims was the defendant making in *Busby v. State*? Should these two types of mistakes be treated equally or differently? For a sophisticated analysis of mistakes of criminal law and non-criminal law, see Kenneth W. Simons, *Ignorance and Mistake of Criminal Law, Noncriminal law and Fact*, 9 Ohio St. J. Crim. L. 487 (2012).

4. The link between mistakes of fact and subjective offense elements (*mens rea*) is illustrated quite well by *Granger v. State*. Defendant claimed that at the time he shot at the car he was unaware that there was a person inside the car. Given that the shots he fired killed a person who was inside the car, defendant was charged with murder, which was defined by the Texas Penal Code as "intentionally or knowingly caus[ing] the death of an individual" or as "intending to cause serious bodily injury [while] committ[ing] an act clearly dangerous to human life that causes the death of an individual." The Court concluded that if defendant mistakenly believed that the car he was shooting was unoccupied, then he could not have "intentionally or knowingly caused the death of the victim, or intend[ed] to cause serious bodily injury." Defendant's mistake would thus negate the mental element required by the offense charged.

5. Since mistake of fact negates *mens rea*, courts unanimously hold that defendant's mistake regarding a fact that is constitutive of the offense is legally irrelevant if she is charged with a strict liability crime. Given that strict liability crimes do not include a *mens rea* requirement, proof that the defendant incorrectly believed that her conduct did not satisfy the elements of the offense is not material to criminal liability. In *Garnett v. State,* 332 Md. 571 (1993), for example, defendant argued that he should not be convicted of the crime of "engaging in sexual intercourse with a person under 14 years of old (statutory rape)" because he mistakenly believed that the victim was 16 years old. The court rejected defendant's argument, explaining that "Maryland's [statutory] rape statute defines a strict liability offense that does not require the State to prove *mens rea;* it makes no allowance for a mistake-of-age defense." A considerable number of states have similarly held that statutory rape is a strict liability offense and mistake of fact is thus no defense to liability. *See, e.g., Jenkins v. State,* 110 Nev. 865 (1994). Other courts, however, have held that statutory rape is not a strict liability crime and thus defendant must be allowed to raise mistake of fact regarding the victim's age as a defense. See, e.g., *State v. Guest,* 583 P.2d 836 (1978). The issue of mistake of fact in rape prosecutions is revisited in §9.05 & 9.06.

6. A handful of courts follow the old common law "moral wrong" doctrine, which originated well over a hundred years ago in the English case of *R v. Prince,* 2 L.R.C.C.R. 154 (1875). The doctrine disallows a mistake of fact defense even if the mistake is reasonable when the defendant's act would still be considered morally wrong even had the circumstances been as the defendant (mistakenly) believed them to be. The doctrine was explained by a court in the following manner:

> [W]e take the view that a husband abandoning his wife is guilty of wrongdoing. It is a violation of his civil duty. He is charged with her support and protection. If he abandons her, he does so at his peril, and, if she be in fact at the time pregnant, though he may not have known it, he cannot plead that ignorance as a defense [to the crime of leaving a pregnant woman with the intent of abandoning her]. He must make sure of his ground when he commits the simple wrong of leaving her at all.
>
> We conclude, therefore, that ... when the accused is brought within the letter of the law [prescribing the offense charged], he cannot exculpate himself by showing his ignorance of the character of his act. *White v. State,* 185 N.E. 64 (1933).

Even in the few states that once followed the moral wrong doctrine, it is unclear how much of the doctrine is still followed today. The doctrine only seems to apply when the offense does not make reference to a mental state. If the offense prescribes a mental state, courts that apply the doctrine would likely allow a mistake of fact defense if the mistake negates the prescribed mental state. Furthermore, English courts abandoned the doctrine in its entirety in *B. (A Minor) v. Director of Public Prosecutions,* 1 All E.R. 833 (2000).

7. Note that the mistake of fact statute discussed in *Granger* exempts a defendant of liability only if "the actor through mistake formed a *reasonable belief* about a matter of fact if his mistaken belief negated the kind of culpability required for the commission of the offense." Similarly, in *People v. Russell* the court observed that "[a]t common law, an honest and *reasonable belief* in the existence of circumstances, which, if true, would make the act with which the person is charged an innocent act, was a good defense." The Louisiana statute excerpted at the beginning of this section also prescribes that only "*reasonable ignorance of fact* or mistake of fact" is a defense to criminal liability. Why is it that only reasonable mistakes of fact exculpate at common law? Don't some unreasonable mistakes of fact "negate the kind of culpability required for the commission of the offense"? Assuming that the defendant in *Granger* mistakenly but unreasonably believed that the car he was shooting at was unoccupied, did he "intentionally or knowingly cause the death" of the car's occupant or did he "intend to cause him serious bodily injury"?

8. In *People v. Russell,* the court stated that only reasonable mistakes of fact preclude liability for a general intent crime. It held, however, that reasonable and unreasonable mistakes of fact bar the imposition of liability for a specific intent crime if the mistake negates the specific intent required by the offense. This was the approach generally followed at common law. Thus, it is a defense to the crime of "intentionally taking property with intent to permanently deprive the owner of his property" (i.e., theft), that the defendant mistakenly believed that he was the lawful owner of the property. Such a mistake precludes liability even if unreasonable, given that the defendant's good faith belief that he owns the property negates that he had the specific intent of "permanently depriving the owner of the property."

9. The *Russell* court concluded that the defendant's mistaken belief that the motorcycle was abandoned would preclude liability even if unreasonable, for the offense of know-

ingly receiving stolen property is a specific intent crime. Do you agree that this is a specific intent offense? Was the offense charged in *Granger* (intentionally or knowingly causing death or causing the death of the victim by an act intended to cause serious bodily harm) a specific or a general intent crime? Explain. What if the defendant in *Granger* had been charged with "intentionally or knowingly causing death," would such an offense be a general or specific intent crime? Note that the answer to these questions is essential to sorting out the kinds of mistakes of fact that are relevant to criminal liability at common law. If the offense charged in *Granger* is considered a specific intent crime, then the defendant's mistaken belief that he was shooting at an unoccupied vehicle would preclude liability even if unreasonable. In contrast, if the offense charged is considered a general intent crime, then only a reasonable mistake would defeat liability. Is this approach defensible? Why or why not? As the next section illustrates, the Model Penal Code rejects both classifying mistakes as either reasonable or unreasonable and the relevance of the general/specific intent distinction to assessing whether mistakes of fact should exculpate.

## § 9.02 Negating Subjective Offense Elements (*Mens Rea*): Model Penal Code Approach to Mistake of Fact

### *Model Penal Code § 2.04. Ignorance or Mistake.*

1) Ignorance or mistake as to a matter of fact or law is a defense if:
   a) the ignorance or mistake negatives the purpose, knowledge, belief, recklessness or negligence required to establish a material element of the offense; or
   b) the law provides that the state of mind established by such ignorance or mistake constitutes a defense.
2) Although ignorance or mistake would otherwise afford a defense to the offense charged, the defense is not available if the defendant would be guilty of another offense had the situation been as he supposed. In such case, however, the ignorance or mistake of the defendant shall reduce the grade and degree of the offense of which he may be convicted to those of the offense of which he would be guilty had the situation been as he supposed.

### State v. Sexton

Supreme Court of New Jersey, 1999
160 N.J. 93

O'HERN, J.

"Once again, we must reconcile anomalies and ambiguities that inhere in the Code of Criminal Justice ... occasioned by the Legislature's selective inclusion and omission of provisions of its conceptual source, the Model Penal Code (MPC)." *Richardson v. Nickolopoulos,* 110 *N.J.* 241, 242, 540 *A.*2d 1246 (1988).

The "anomalies and ambiguities" presented in this appeal concern the meaning of *N.J.S.A.* 2C:2-4, governing the so-called mistake-of-fact defense to a criminal charge. Specifically, the question is how to explain to the jury the effect of a mistake of fact on a

charge of reckless conduct. The context is that of an accusation of aggravated or reckless manslaughter, after a gun went off, killing the seventeen-year-old victim, Alquadir Matthews. From the evidence, a jury could have found that the then fifteen-year-old defendant had pointed a gun at another and pulled the trigger. Defendant claims that he mistakenly believed the gun was not loaded.

I.

The facts of the case are more fully set forth in the opinion below. We repeat those facts essential to our ruling.

On May 10, 1993, Shakirah Jones, a seventeen-year-old friend of defendant and decedent, overheard the two young men having what she described as a "typical argument." The two young men walked from a sidewalk into a vacant lot. Jones saw defendant with a gun in his hand, but she did not see defendant shoot Matthews.

Jones heard Matthews tell defendant, "there are no bullets in that gun," and then walk away. Defendant called Matthews back and said, "you think there are no bullets in this gun?" Matthews replied, "yeah." Jones heard the gun go off. A single bullet killed Matthews....

Defendant's version was that when the two young men were in the lot, Matthews showed defendant a gun and "told me the gun was empty." Defendant "asked him was he sure," and "he said yes." When Matthews asked if defendant would like to see the gun, defendant said "yes." Defendant "took the gun and was looking at it, and "it just went off." He never unloaded the gun or checked to see if there were any bullets in the gun. He had never before owned or shot a gun.

A grand jury indicted defendant for purposeful or knowing murder, possession of a handgun without a permit, and possession of a handgun for an unlawful purpose. At the close of the State's case, defendant moved to dismiss the murder charge because the victim had told him that the gun was not loaded. The court denied the motion.

The court charged murder and the lesser-included offenses of aggravated manslaughter and reckless manslaughter.... The jury found defendant not guilty of murder, aggravated manslaughter, or possession of a handgun for an unlawful purpose, but guilty of reckless manslaughter and unlawful possession of a handgun without a permit.

On the charge of reckless manslaughter, the court sentenced defendant to the presumptive term of seven years, three of which were parole ineligible....

On appeal, the Appellate Division reversed defendant's conviction ... [because] the trial court should have charged the jury that the State bore the burden of disproving beyond a reasonable doubt defendant's mistake-of-fact defense, and that the failure to do so was plain error....

We granted the State's petition for certification, limited to the issue of whether "mistake of fact was a defense to the charge of reckless manslaughter."

II.

A.

On an earlier occasion, the Court wrote: "Twelve centuries of debate have yet to resolve the law's attitude about the criminal mind." *State v. Breakiron*, 108 *N.J.* 591, 595, 532 *A.*2d 199 (1987). At common law, proof of an *actus reus* and *mens rea* sufficed to establish criminal liability. Today's statutes require a voluntary act and a culpable state of mind as the minimum conditions for liability. At its earliest stages, the common law imposed liability without regard to a *mens rea* or culpable state of mind. "If someone caused harm, the person was accountable for it without any consideration of intent." At early common law, all homicides were capital. By examining the mental states involved, such as deliberation, premeditation, or malice, English common law gradually sought to distinguish homicides that were murder from those that were manslaughter, differentiating "criminal from non-criminal homicides, and [capital] homicides from those that were not." The common law had frequently focused on the conduct of the reasonable person as the measure of responsibility. To resolve the variety, disparity, and confusion concerning the mental elements of crime, the drafters of the MPC attempted to establish distinct levels of culpability applicable to all criminal offenses. The MPC "obliterated ill-defined, confusing common law language and concepts and replaced them with four specifically defined hierarchical levels of culpability in relation to the three objective element types used to define crimes."

The 1979 New Jersey Code of Criminal Justice (the Code) followed the mental-state formulation of the MPC. The Code provides generally that no person should be guilty of an offense unless the person "acted purposely, knowingly, recklessly or negligently, as the law may require, with respect to each material element of the offense." The precise delineation of these four states of criminal culpability, each drawn from the MPC..., represented an effort, as a framer of the Code described it, "to achieve greater individual justice through a closer relation between guilt and culpability, requiring workable definitions of the various culpability factors. These factors must be related precisely to each element of an offense, defense, or mitigation, and all unnecessary limitations upon individual culpability should be eliminated." "[T]he material elements of an offense vary in that they may involve (1) conduct per se, (2) the attendant circumstances of conduct, or (3) the result of conduct. The MPC attempts to define culpability status for each."

The MPC also contains an express provision for mistake-of-fact defenses. "Its mistake of fact provision, while creating potential for conceptual confusion by continuing the common law characterization of the doctrine as a 'defense,' in fact sought to clarify the common law." The MPC expressly recognized that the doctrine did not sanction a true defense, but rather was an attack on the prosecution's ability to prove the requisite culpable mental state for at least one objective element of the crime. Hence, unlike enactments in many pre-MPC states, "the MPC expressly recognizes that the mistake of an accused need not be a reasonable mistake unless the Legislature has expressly decided that the requisite culpable mental state was minimal-'negligence' or perhaps, 'recklessness.'"

The MPC provides that, "Ignorance or mistake as to a matter of fact or law is a defense if: (a) the ignorance or mistake negatives the purpose, knowledge, belief, recklessness or negligence required to establish a material element of the offense; or (b) the law provides that the state of mind established by such ignorance or mistake constitutes a defense." Model Penal Code § 2.04 (1962).

Whether a mistake would negate a required element of the offense, depended, of course, on the nature of the mistake and the state of mind that the offense required. This led commentators to observe:

> Technically, such provisions [for a mistake of fact defense] are unnecessary. They simply confirm what is stated elsewhere: 'No person may be convicted of an offense unless each element of such offense is proven beyond a reasonable doubt.' If the defendant's ignorance or mistake makes proof of a required culpability element impossible, the prosecution will necessarily fail in its proof of the offense. Paul H. Robinson & Jane A. Grall, *Element Analysis in Defining*

*Criminal Liability: The Model Penal Code and Beyond,* 35 *Stan. L.Rev.* 681, 726–27 (1983) (quoting Model Penal Code § 1.12(1) (Proposed Official Draft 1962)).

*See also* Wayne R. LaFave & Austin W. Scott, Jr., *Substantive Criminal Law,* § 5.1a (2d ed. 1986) ("Instead of speaking of ignorance or mistake of fact ... as a defense, it would be just as easy to note simply that the defendant cannot be convicted when it is shown that he does not have the mental state required by law for commission of that particular offense.")

The Commentary to the Hawaii Criminal Code gives an easy example of how, under the MPC, a mistake of fact may negate culpability.

> [I]f a person is ignorant or mistaken as to a matter of fact ... the person's ignorance or mistake will, in appropriate circumstances, prevent the person from having the requisite culpability with respect to the fact ... as it actually exists. For example, a person who is mistaken (either reasonably, negligently, or recklessly) as to which one of a number of similar umbrellas on a rack is the person's and who takes another's umbrella should be afforded a defense to a charge of theft predicated on either intentionally or knowingly taking the property of another.... A reckless mistake would afford a defense to a charge requiring intent or knowledge—but not to an offense which required only recklessness or negligence. Similarly, a negligent mistake would afford a defense to a charge predicated on intent, knowledge, or recklessness—but not to an offense based on negligence. *State v. Cavness,* 80 *Hawai'i* 460, 911 *P.*2d 95, 99--100 (Ct.App.1996).

B.

State legislatures, however, "in emulating the Model Penal Code's three culpability provisions (its culpability definitions, its guidelines for resolving the requisite culpable mental state, and its mistake of fact doctrine), have not always understood their interrelationship. Hence, these states have failed to coordinate the enactment of these three types of culpability provisions." States have restricted the mistake-of-fact doctrine by imposing a reasonableness requirement. By thinking in terms of the reasonable person while failing to appreciate that the MPC's mistake-of-fact and culpability provisions are interrelated, these states have undermined the structure of the MPC.

To explain, we may consider again the case of the absent-minded umbrella thief. If only a reasonable mistake will provide a defense to the charge of theft, the absent-minded but careless restaurant patron will have no defense to a charge of theft. *People v. Navarro* explains how a mistake of fact, even though it is unreasonable, may constitute a defense to a crime requiring a culpable mental state higher than recklessness or negligence. In *Navarro,* defendant took some wooden beams from a construction site. He was charged with theft. He claimed that he thought the owner had abandoned the beams. The trial court instructed the jury that this would be a valid defense only if the scavenger's belief was reasonable. The reviewing court held that such an instruction was erroneous because if the jury "concluded that defendant in good faith believed that he had the right to take the beams, even though such belief was unreasonable..., defendant was entitled to an acquittal since the specific intent required to be proved as an element of the offense had not been established." Otherwise, one would end up imposing liability for theft on a lesser basis than knowledge or purpose to steal the property of another.

How then shall we resolve the problem created by the selective inclusion and exclusion of the culpability provisions of the MPC?

### III.

The issue posed by our grant of certification was whether a mistake of fact was a defense to the charge of reckless manslaughter. The short answer to that question is: "It depends." The longer answer requires that we relate the type of mistake involved to the essential elements of the offense, the conduct proscribed, and the state of mind required to establish liability for the offense. Defendant insists that the State is required to disprove, beyond a reasonable doubt, his mistake-of-fact defense. Most states would agree with that statement.... In *State v. Savoie,* the Court ... said that once the defense of mistake of fact is raised, the burden of persuasion is on the State. Just what does that mean? Does it mean that the State must prove that the mistake was unreasonable? We must begin by examining the language of the statute.

*N.J.S.A.* 2C:2-4a allows a defense of ignorance or mistake "if the defendant reasonably arrived at the conclusion underlying the mistake and" the mistake either "negatives the culpable mental state required to establish the offense" or "[t]he law provides that the state of mind established by such ignorance or mistake constitutes a defense." The crime of manslaughter is a form of criminal homicide. "A person is guilty of criminal homicide if [the actor] purposely, knowingly [or] recklessly ... causes the death of another human being." Criminal homicide constitutes aggravated manslaughter, a first-degree offense with special sentencing provisions, when the actor "recklessly causes death under circumstances manifesting extreme indifference to human life." Criminal homicide constitutes manslaughter, a second-degree crime, "when ... [i]t is committed recklessly," that is, when the actor has recklessly caused death.

In this case, the jury has acquitted defendant of aggravated manslaughter. He can be retried only for reckless manslaughter. The culpable mental state of the offense is recklessness. *N.J.S.A.* 2C:2-2b(3) states:

> A person acts recklessly with respect to a material element of an offense when [the actor] consciously disregards a substantial and unjustifiable risk that the material element exists or will result from [the actor's] conduct. The risk must be of such a nature and degree that, considering the nature and purpose of the actor's conduct and the circumstances known to [the actor], its disregard involves a gross deviation from the standard of conduct that a reasonable person would observe in the actor's situation....

The State argues that "[i]t is obvious that the firing of a gun at another human being without checking to see if it is loaded disregards a substantial risk." The State argues that at a minimum there must be some proof establishing that defendant "reasonably arrived at the conclusion underlying the mistake." *N.J.S.A.* 2C:2-4a. To return to the language of *N.J.S.A.* 2C:2-4a, does the mistake about whether the gun was loaded "negative the culpable mental state required to establish the offense," or does "the law provide that the state of mind established by such ignorance or mistake constitutes a defense?" Of itself, a belief that the gun is loaded or unloaded does not negate the culpable mental state for the crime of manslaughter. Thus, one who discharges a gun, believing it to be unloaded, is not necessarily innocent of manslaughter.

The State notes that under *N.J.S.A.* 2C:12-1b(4), a defendant is criminally liable for fourth-degree aggravated assault when the actor, "[k]nowingly under circumstances manifesting extreme indifference to the value of human life points a firearm ... at or in the direction of another, whether or not the actor believes it to be loaded." The State contends that a defendant should not be able to assert a mistake-of-fact defense when charged with manslaughter, if such a defense would not be available against a charge of aggravated assault. In the case of certain offenses, state of mind is simply not an essential or material element.

On the other hand, the Sixth Amendment allows a defendant to assert any fact that will negate a material element of a crime. The material elements of manslaughter are the killing of another human being with a reckless state of mind. The culpable mental state is recklessness—the conscious disregard of a substantial and unjustified risk that death will result from the conduct. What mistaken belief will negate this state of mind?

> [T]he translation is uncertain at its most critical point: in determining the kind of mistake that provides a defense when recklessness, the most common culpability level, as to a circumstance is required. Recall that a negligent or faultless mistake negates ... recklessness. While a "negligent mistake" may be said to be an "unreasonable mistake," all "unreasonable mistakes" are not "negligent mistakes." A mistake may also be unreasonable because it is reckless. Reckless mistakes, although unreasonable, will not negate recklessness. Thus, when offense definitions require recklessness as to circumstance elements, as they commonly do, the reasonable—unreasonable mistake language inadequately describes the mistakes that will provide a defense because of the imprecision of the term "unreasonable mistake." Reckless-negligent-faultless mistake language is necessary for a full and accurate description. Robinson & Grall, *supra,* 35 *Stan. L.Rev.* at 729.

Thus, to disprove a reasonable mistake by proving that it is unreasonable, will turn out to be a mixed blessing for defendant. If the State may disprove a reasonable mistake by proving that the mistake was unreasonable, defendant may be convicted because he was negligent, as opposed to reckless, in forming the belief that the gun was unloaded. If recklessness is required as an element of the offense, "a merely negligent or faultless mistake as to that circumstance provides a defense." *Id.* at 728.

Correctly understood, there is no difference between a positive and negative statement on the issue—what is required for liability versus what will provide a defense to liability. What is required in order to establish liability for manslaughter is recklessness (as defined by the Code) about whether death will result from the conduct. A faultless or merely careless mistake may negate that reckless state of mind and provide a defense.

How can we explain these concepts to a jury? We believe that the better way to explain the concepts is to explain what is required for liability to be established. The charge should be tailored to the factual circumstances of the case. The court should explain precisely how the offered defense plays into the element of recklessness. Something along the following lines will help to convey to the jury the concepts relevant to a reckless manslaughter charge:

> In this case, ladies and gentlemen of the jury, the defendant contends that he mistakenly believed that the gun was not loaded. If you find that the State has not proven beyond a reasonable doubt that the defendant was reckless in forming his belief that the gun was not loaded, defendant should be acquitted of the offense of manslaughter. On the other hand, if you find that the State has proven beyond a reasonable doubt that the defendant was reckless in forming the belief that the gun was not loaded, and consciously disregarded a substantial and unjustifiable risk that a killing would result from his conduct, then you should convict him of manslaughter.

Undoubtedly, our Committee on Model Criminal Charges can improve the formulation.

To sum up, evidence of an actor's mistaken belief relates to whether the State has failed to prove an essential element of the charged offense beyond a reasonable doubt. As a practical matter, lawyers and judges will undoubtedly continue to consider a mistake of fact as a defense. When we do so, we must carefully analyze the nature of the mistake in relationship to the culpable mental state required to establish liability for the offense charged. Despite the complexities perceived by scholars, the limited number of appeals on this subject suggests to us that juries have very little difficulty in applying the concepts involved. We may assume that juries relate the instructions to the context of the charge. For example, in the case of the carelessly purloined umbrella, we are certain that juries would have no difficulty in understanding that it would have been a reasonable mistake (although perhaps a negligent mistake) for the customer to believe that he or she was picking up the right umbrella.

To require the State to disprove beyond a reasonable doubt defendant's reasonable mistake of fact introduces an unnecessary and perhaps unhelpful degree of complexity into the fairly straightforward inquiry of whether defendant "consciously disregard[ed] a substantial and unjustifiable risk" that death would result from his conduct and that the risk was "of such a nature and degree that, considering the nature and purpose of the actor's conduct and the circumstances known to him, its disregard involve[d] a gross deviation from the standard of conduct that a reasonable person would observe in the actor's situation." *N.J.S.A.* 2C:2-2b(3);*N.J.S.A.* 2C:11-4b.

The judgment of the Appellate Division is affirmed. The matter is remanded to the Law Division for further proceedings in accordance with this opinion.

## *Notes and Questions*

1. As the Supreme Court of New Jersey points out in *Sexton,* mistake of fact defeats liability under the Model Penal Code as long as the mistake negates the "purpose, knowledge, belief, recklessness or negligence required to establish a material element of the offense." As a result, the determinative question under to Code is not whether the defendant's mistake is reasonable or unreasonable, but instead whether the mistake negates a subjective element of the offense charged. Furthermore, as the Court also points out in *Sexton,* the Code treats mistake of fact as a way of negating an element of the offense rather than as a freestanding defense to criminal liability. That is, a defendant who successfully pleads mistake of fact does not demonstrate that he committed the offense but has a valid defense of justification or excuse. Properly understood, a valid mistake of fact claim reveals that the defendant simply did not engage in conduct that is constitutive of the (subjective) elements of the offense. As a result, the trier of fact must acquit if she has reasonable doubts about whether the defendant has a valid mistake of fact claim, for this translates into having reasonable doubt about whether the prosecution proved the *mens rea* required by the offense.

2. The issue in *Sexton* was whether an unreasonable mistake of fact defeats liability for a crime that prescribes recklessness as the required form of culpability. More specifically, the issue was whether defendant's belief that the gun was unloaded and therefore not capable of killing the victim would defeat liability for reckless manslaughter even if the belief is deemed unreasonable. As the Court points out, asking whether the defendant's belief was reasonable or unreasonable is unhelpful to determining if the mistake negates recklessness, as both the New Jersey Penal Code and Model Penal Code require. The reason for this difficulty is that both negligent and reckless mistakes are "unreasonable," for they both entail "creating a substantial and unjustifiable risk" in situations in which the

conduct involves a "gross deviation from the standard of conduct" that a reasonable person would observe under the circumstances. Nevertheless, in a prosecution for a reckless offense, only mistakes that are unreasonable because they are negligent will defeat liability because they preclude a finding of recklessness. In contrast, mistakes that are unreasonable because they are reckless will not defeat liability in a prosecution for a reckless offense, since the recklessness of the mistake reveals that the defendant's conduct satisfies the culpability prescribed by the offense. This explains why the court concluded in *Sexton* that the defendant should be acquitted of reckless manslaughter if the "State [does not prove] beyond a reasonable doubt that the defendant was reckless in forming his belief that the gun was not loaded." Given that the kind of culpability required by the offense charged was recklessness, what is ultimately determinative of defendant's liability is whether his belief was reckless rather than whether it was reasonable or unreasonable. If his belief was negligent but not reckless, he must be acquitted. On the other hand, if his belief was reckless, he should be convicted.

3. The following chart attempts to translate the common law mistake terminology into Model Penal Code terms:

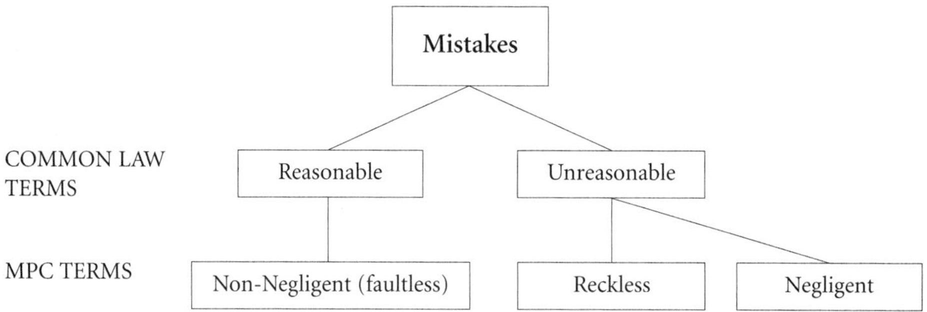


# §9.03 Negating Subjective Offense Elements (*Mens Rea*): Common Law Approach to Voluntary Intoxication

## People v. Hood

Supreme Court of California, 1969
1 Cal.3d 444

TRAYNOR, Chief Justice.

An indictment charged defendant in Count I with assault with a deadly weapon upon a peace officer, in Count II with battery upon a peace officer, and in Count III with assault with intent to murder [an officer]. A jury found him guilty on Counts I and III and not guilty on Count II, and the trial court entered judgment on the verdicts.... Defendant appeals.

On September 11, 1967, at about 2:00 a.m., defendant, his brother Donald, and a friend, Leo Chilton, all of whom had been drinking for several hours, knocked on the door of the house of Susan Bueno, defendant's former girlfriend, and asked if they could use the bathroom. Susan said no, but defendant forced his way in and started to hit her. He knocked her to the floor and kicked her. Donald Hood then took Susan aside, and defendant, Chilton, and Gene Saunders, a friend of Susan's who was staying at the house, went to the kitchen and sat down.

Gilbert A. Nielsen, Susan's next-door neighbor, was awakened by the sound of Susan's screams and called the police.

[Editor's Note: Three officers responded to the call. Upon arriving, they were invited inside the house by Susan Bueno. Once inside, the following scuffle ensued between the defendant and the police officers:]

... Defendant swung at [Officer Elia] with his fist. When Officer Kemper attempted to go to Officer Elia's assistance, [defendant] jumped on him from behind. During the ensuing struggle, Officer Elia fell with defendant on top of him in a corner of a pantry adjoining the kitchen at the rear. While struggling on the floor, Officer Elia felt a tug at his gun belt and then heard two shots fired....

[The officers] testified that after the shots, defendant's arm came up over his head with the revolver in his hand. The struggle continued into the bathroom. Defendant was finally subdued when Officer Elia regained possession of the gun and held it against the side of defendant's neck. Officer Elia then noticed that defendant had shot him once in each leg.

The foregoing evidence is clearly sufficient to support the verdicts.

Defendant contends that the court failed properly to instruct the jury ... on the effect of intoxication with respect to the offenses charged in both Counts I and III....

The judgment must [be] reversed as to Count III, for the court gave hopelessly conflicting instructions on the effect of intoxication. Although the court correctly instructed the jury to consider the evidence that defendant was intoxicated in determining whether he had the specific intent to commit murder, it followed that instruction with the complete text of CALJIC No. 78(revised), which applies to crimes that require proof only of a general criminal intent. The court in no way made clear to the jury that the latter instruction did not apply to the charge of assault with intent to commit murder. The giving of such conflicting instructions with respect to a crime requiring proof of a specific intent is error. That error was clearly prejudicial in this case. There was substantial evidence that defendant was drunk. He testified that he was not aware that he ever had the gun in his possession or fired it. Its discharge during the scuffle could be reconciled with an intent to kill, an intent to inflict only bodily injury, or with no intent to fire it at all. Had the jury not been given conflicting instructions on the significance of defendant's intoxication, it is reasonably probable that it would have reached a result more favorable to defendant on Count III.

To guide the trial court on retrial, we consider the question of the effect of intoxication on the crime of assault with a deadly weapon....

[Editor's Note: The Court goes on to explain that some California cases suggest that assault is a specific intent crime, whereas other cases suggest that it is a general intent crime. after surveying these cases and pointing out the tension between them, the Court stated:]

The distinction between specific and general intent crimes evolved as a judicial response to the problem of the intoxicated offender. That problem is to reconcile two competing theories of what is just in the treatment of those who commit crimes while intoxicated. On the one hand, the moral culpability of a drunken criminal is frequently less than that of a sober person effecting a like injury. On the other hand, it is commonly felt that a person who voluntarily gets drunk and while in that state commits a crime should not escape the consequences. (See Hall, General Principles of Criminal Law (2d ed. 1960), p. 537).

Before the nineteenth century, the common law refused to give any effect to the fact that an accused committed a crime while intoxicated. The judges were apparently troubled by this rigid traditional rule, however, for there were a number of attempts during the early part of the nineteenth century to arrive at a more humane, yet workable, doctrine. The theory that these judges explored was that evidence of intoxication could be considered to negate intent, whenever intent was an element of the crime charged. As Professor Hall notes, however, such an exculpatory doctrine could eventually have undermined the traditional rule entirely, since some form of mens rea is a requisite of all but strict liability offenses. (Hall, Intoxication and Criminal Responsibility, 57 Harv.L.Rev. 1045, 1049). To limit the operation of the doctrine and achieve a compromise between the conflicting feelings of sympathy and reprobation for the intoxicated offender, later courts both in England and this country drew a distinction between so-called specific intent and general intent crimes.

Specific and general intent have been notoriously difficult terms to define and apply, and a number of textwriters recommend that they be abandoned altogether. (Hall, General Principles of Criminal Law, supra, p. 142; Williams, Criminal Law—The General Part (2d ed.1961) s 21, p. 49). Too often the characterization of a particular crime as one of specific or general intent is determined solely by the presence or absence of words describing psychological phenomena—"intent" or "malice," for example—in the statutory language of defining the crime. When the definition of a crime consists of only the description of a particular act, without reference to intent to do a further act or achieve a future consequence, we ask whether the defendant intended to do the proscribed act. This intention is deemed to be a general criminal intent. When the definition refers to defendant's intent to do some further act or achieve some additional consequence, the crime is deemed to be one of specific intent. There is no real difference, however, only a linguistic one, between an intent to do an act already performed and an intent to do that same act in the future.

The language of Penal Code section 22, drafted in 1872 when "specific" and "general" intent were not yet terms of art, is somewhat broader than those terms:

> No act committed by a person while in a state of voluntary intoxication is less criminal by reason of his having been in such condition. But whenever the actual existence of any particular purpose, motive, or intent is a necessary element to constitute any particular species or degree of crime, the jury may take into consideration the fact that the accused was intoxicated at the time, in determining the purpose, motive, or intent with which he committed the act.

Even this statement of the relevant policy is no easier to apply to particular crimes. We are still confronted with the difficulty of characterizing the mental element of a given crime as a particular purpose, motive, or intent necessary to constitute the offense, or as something less than that to which evidence of intoxication is not pertinent.

Even if we assume that the presence or absence of words clearly denoting mental activity is a valid criterion for determining the significance of intoxication, our present problem is not resolved. The difficulty with applying such a test to the crime of assault or assault with a deadly weapon is that no word in the relevant code provisions unambiguously denotes a particular mental element, yet the word "attempt" in Penal Code section 240 strongly suggests goal-directed, intentional behavior. This uncertainty accounts for the conflict over whether assault is a crime only of intention or also of recklessness.

We need not reconsider our position in [a prior case] that an assault cannot be predicated merely on reckless conduct. Even if assault requires an intent to commit a battery on the victim, it does not follow that the crime is one in which evidence of intoxication ought to be considered in determining whether the defendant had that intent. It is true that in most cases specific intent has come to mean an intention to do a future act or achieve a particular result, and that assault is appropriately characterized as a specific intent crime under this definition. An assault, however, is equally well characterized as a general intent crime under the definition of general intent as an intent merely to do a violent act. Therefore, whatever reality the distinction between specific and general intent may have in other contexts, the difference is chimerical in the case of assault with a deadly weapon or simple assault. Since the definitions of both specific intent and general intent cover the requisite intent to commit a battery, the decision whether or not to give effect to evidence of intoxication must rest on other considerations.

A compelling consideration is the effect of alcohol on human behavior. A significant effect of alcohol is to distort judgment and relax the controls on aggressive and anti-social impulses. Alcohol apparently has less effect on the ability to engage in simple goal-directed behavior, although it may impair the efficiency of that behavior. In other words, a drunk man is capable of forming an intent to do something simple, such as strike another, unless he is so drunk that he was reached the stage of unconsciousness. What he is not as capable as a sober man of doing is exercising judgment about the social consequences of his acts or controlling his impulses toward antisocial acts. He is more likely to act rashly and impulsively and to be susceptible to passion and anger. It would therefore be anomalous to allow evidence of intoxication to relieve a man of responsibility for the crimes of assault with a deadly weapon or simple assault, which are so frequently committed in just such a manner. As the court said in *Parker v. United States*:

> Whatever ambiguities there may be in distinguishing between specific and general intent to determine whether drunkenness constitutes a defense, an offense of this nature is not one which requires an intent that is susceptible to negation through a showing of voluntary intoxication.

Those crimes that have traditionally been characterized as crimes of specific intent are not affected by our holding here. The difference in mental activity between formulating an intent to commit a battery and formulating an intent to commit a battery for the purpose of raping or killing may be slight, but it is sufficient to justify drawing a line between them and considering evidence of intoxication in the one case and disregarding it in the other. Accordingly, on retrial the court should not instruct the jury to consider evidence of defendant's intoxication in determining whether he committed assault with a deadly weapon on a peace officer or any of the lesser assaults included therein....

## *Notes and Questions*

1. As Chief Justice Traynor explained in *Hood,* evidence of voluntary intoxication was admissible at common law only to negate a specific intent. Therefore, evidence of voluntary intoxication is not admissible at common law if defendant was charged with a general intent crime. The distinction between specific and general intent crimes was discussed in Notes 6, 7 and 9 of § 8.01.

2. The discussion in *Hood* regarding whether assault is a specific or general intent crime illustrates how difficult and confusing making this determination can be. The best way of approaching the distinction is by discriminating between crimes that merely require that the defendant intend to do the prohibited act from offenses that—in addition to the intent to do the prohibited act—require proof of an additional mental state that

does not directly refer to the act proscribed by the statute. The former kinds of crime merely require a general intent, whereas the latter types of offenses demand proof of a specific intent. As the Court observed in *Hood:*

> When the definition of a crime consists of only the description of a particular act, without reference to intent to do a further act or achieve a future consequence, we ask whether the defendant intended to do the proscribed act. This intention is deemed to be a general criminal intent. When the definition refers to defendant's intent to do some further act or achieve some additional consequence, the crime is deemed to be one of specific intent. *Hood*, 1 Cal.3d 444.

According to this definition, the crime of robbery would be a general intent offense, for it only demands proof of intent to engage in the proscribed act of taking the property of another by force or violence. In contrast, the crime of "robbery with intent to kill" is a specific intent crime, given that it requires proof of two different mental states. First, it demands proof that the defendant intended to take the property of another by way of force. Second, it requires evidence that the defendant also intended to kill the victim. The first mental state required by the offense of "robbery with intent to kill" is the general intent to rob the victim. On the other hand, the additional mental state required by the crime of "robbery with intent to kill" is the specific intent of intending to kill the victim. As a result, in a prosecution for robbery with intent to kill, evidence of voluntary intoxication would be admissible at common law to negate the intent to kill but not to negate the general intent to rob. Reconsider whether the offenses with which the defendant was charged in *Hood* were general or specific intent crimes. The Court concluded in *Hood* that evidence of voluntary intoxication was admissible with regard to the charge of "assault with intent to kill" but not admissible regarding the charge of "assault with a deadly weapon." Do you agree? Explain.

3. As the Court pointed out in *Hood,* a specific intent is often the "intent to do some further act or achieve some additional consequence" other than the specific act or consequence prohibited by the offense. It is precisely this "intent to do some further act" that makes the offense of "robbery with intent to kill" a specific intent offense. However, a specific intent may also be a mental state in addition to the intent to engage in the proscribed act that describes the defendant's state of mind at the time of the commission of the offense. Thus, the element of "premeditation" is often considered a "specific intent" in a prosecution for murder in spite of the fact that "premeditation" is not an "intent to do a further act or achieve some additional consequence." *See, e.g., State v. Skidmore,* 228 W.Va. 166 (2011). What makes premeditation a specific intent is that it is a mental state in addition to the intent to engage in the proscribed act (i.e., intent to kill).

4. Chief Justice Traynor observed in *Hood* that "[s]pecific and general intent have been notoriously difficult terms to define and apply, and a number of textwriters recommend that they be abandoned altogether." The confusion generated by these terms is at least partially due to the fact that some courts and commentators sometimes state that crimes requiring that the defendant act "purposely" or "knowingly" are specific intent crimes, whereas offenses demanding that the defendant act "recklessly" or "negligently" are not. Under this definition, the offense of robbery may be considered a specific intent crime, for a victim may only be robbed "purposely." Nevertheless, as explained in the previous Note, robbery is not a specific intent crime in the sense that it does not require proof of a mental state in addition to the purpose (intent) to rob the victim. Much of the confusion in this context is due to courts and lawyers mixing up these two different ways of defining specific and general intent crimes. As the next section illustrates, the drafters of the Model Penal Code

attempted to avoid this confusion by dealing with the problem of voluntary intoxication without making reference to the general/specific intent distinction.

## § 9.04 Negating Subjective Offense Elements (*Mens Rea*): Model Penal Code Approach to Voluntary Intoxication

### State v. Cameron

Supreme Court of New Jersey, 1986
104 N.J. 42

CLIFFORD, J.

This appeal presents a narrow, but important, issue concerning the role that a defendant's voluntary intoxication plays in a criminal prosecution. The specific question is whether the evidence was sufficient to require the trial court to charge the jury on defendant's intoxication, as defendant requested. The Appellate Division reversed defendant's convictions, holding that it was error not to have given an intoxication charge. We granted the State's petition for certification and defendant's cross-petition and now reverse.

I.

Defendant, Michele Cameron, age 22 at the time of trial, was indicted for second degree aggravated assault; possession of a weapon, a broken bottle, with a purpose to use it unlawfully; and fourth degree resisting arrest. A jury convicted defendant of all charges. After merging the possession count into the assault charge, the trial court imposed sentences aggregating seven years in the custody of the Commissioner of the Department of Corrections, with a three year period of parole ineligibility and certain monetary penalties.

The charges arose out of an incident of June 6, 1981, on a vacant lot in Trenton. The unreported opinion of the Appellate Division depicts the following tableau of significant events:

> The victim, Joseph McKinney, was playing cards with four other men. Defendant approached and disrupted the game with her conduct. The participants moved their card table to a new location within the lot. Defendant followed them, however, and overturned the table. The table was righted and the game resumed. Shortly thereafter, defendant attacked McKinney with a broken bottle. As a result of that attack he sustained an injury to his hand, which necessitated 36 stitches and caused permanent injury.
>
> Defendant reacted with violence to the arrival of the police. She threw a bottle at their vehicle, shouted obscenities, and tried to fight them off. She had to be restrained and handcuffed in the police wagon.

The heart of the Appellate Division's reversal of defendant's conviction is found in its determination that voluntary intoxication is a defense when it negates an essential element of the offense—here, purposeful conduct. We agree with that proposition. Likewise are we in accord with the determinations of the court below that all three of the charges of which this defendant was convicted—aggravated assault, the possession offense, and resisting arrest—have purposeful conduct as an element of the offense; and that a person acts purposely "with respect to the nature of his conduct or a result thereof if it is his conscious object to engage in conduct of that nature or to cause such a result" (quoting *N.J.S.A.* 2C:2-2(b)(1)). We part company with the Appellate Division, however, in its conclusion that the circumstances disclosed by the evidence in this case required that the issue of defendant's intoxication be submitted to the jury.

The court below noted that every witness who testified gave some appraisal of defendant's condition. On the basis of that evidence the Appellate Division concluded that:

> Defendant's conduct was both bizarre and violent. She had been drinking and could not be reasoned with. The victim thought she was intoxicated and two police officers thought she was under the influence of something. Not one witness who testified thought that her conduct was normal. Therefore, it was for the jury to determine if she was intoxicated, and if so, whether the element of purposefulness was negated thereby.

The quoted passage reflects a misapprehension of the level of proof required to demonstrate intoxication for purposes of demonstrating an inability to engage in purposeful conduct.

### II.

Under the common law intoxication was not a defense to a criminal charge ... Notwithstanding the general proposition that voluntary intoxication is no defense, the early cases nevertheless held that in some circumstances intoxication could be resorted to for defensive purposes—specifically, to show the absence of a specific intent.

> The exceptional immunity extended to the drunkard is limited to those instances where the crime involves a specific, actual intent. When the degree of intoxication is such as to render the person incapable of entertaining such intent, it is an effective defence. If it falls short of this it is worthless. *Warner v. State, supra,* 56 *N.J.L.* at 690, 29 *A.* 505.

The principle that developed from the foregoing approach—that intoxication formed the basis for a defense to a "specific intent" crime but not to one involving only "general" intent—persisted for about three-quarters of a century [until the most recent version of the New Jersey Penal Code was adopted ...]

### III.

[According to the New Jersey Penal Code]:

> a) Except as provided in subsection d. of this section, intoxication of the actor is not a defense unless it negatives an element of the offense.
>
> b) When recklessness establishes an element of the offense, if the actor, due to self-induced intoxication, is unaware of a risk of which he would have been aware had he been sober, such unawareness is immaterial....

As is readily apparent, self-induced intoxication is not a defense unless it negatives an element of the offense. *Code Commentary* at 67–68. Under the common-law intoxication defense, as construed by the Commission, intoxication could either exculpate or mitigate guilt "if the defendant's intoxication, in fact, prevents his having formed a mental state which is an element of the offense and if the law will recognize the proof of the lack of that mental state." Thus, the Commission recognized that under pre-Code law, intoxication was admissible as a defense to a "specific" intent, but not a "general" intent, crime.

The original proposed Code rejected the specific/general intent distinction, choosing to rely instead on the reference to the four states of culpability for offenses under the

Code: negligent, reckless, knowing, and purposeful conduct, *N.J.S.A.* 2C:2-2(b). Although the Code employs terminology that differs from that used to articulate the common-law principles referable to intoxication, the Commission concluded that the ultimately-enacted statutory intoxication defense would achieve the same result as that reached under the common law. In essence, "[t]hat which the cases now describe as a 'specific intent' can be equated, for this purpose, with that which the Code defines as 'purpose' and 'knowledge.' *See* § 2C:2-2b. A 'general intent' can be equated with that which the Code defines as 'recklessness,' or criminal 'negligence.'" *Code Commentary* at 68. Therefore, according to the Commissioners, *N.J.S.A.*2C:2-8(a) and (b) would serve much the same end as was achieved by the common-law approach. Specifically, *N.J.S.A.* 2C:2-8(a) permits evidence of intoxication as a defense to crimes requiring either "purposeful" or "knowing" mental states but it excludes evidence of intoxication as a defense to crimes requiring mental states of only recklessness or negligence.

*N.J.S.A.* 2C:2-8 was modeled after the Model Penal Code (MPC) § 2.08. See *N.J.S.A.* 2C:2-8 (Historical Note). The drafters of the MPC, as did the New Jersey Commission, criticized the specific-general intent distinction, *MPC Commentaries* § 2.08 comment at 353–54 and 357–58, and adopted instead the same four states of culpability eventually enacted in the Code. *MPC Commentaries* § 2.02 comment at 230. In the commentary, the drafters of the MPC expressly stated their intention that intoxication be admissible to disprove the culpability factors of purpose or knowledge, but that for crimes requiring only recklessness or negligence, exculpation based on intoxication should be excluded as a matter of law. *MPC Commentaries* § 2.08 comment at 354.

The drafters explicitly determined that

> Intoxication ought to be accorded a significance that is entirely co-extensive with its relevance to disprove purpose or knowledge, when they are the requisite mental elements of a specific crime.... [W]hen the definition of a crime or a degree thereof requires proof of such a state of mind, the legal policy involved will almost certainly obtain whether or not the absence of purpose or knowledge is due to the actor's self-induced intoxication or to some other cause. *Id.* at 357.

The policy reasons for requiring purpose or knowledge as a requisite element of some crimes are that in the absence of those states of mind, the criminal conduct would not present a comparable danger, or the actor would not pose as significant a threat. Moreover, the ends of legal policy are better served by subjecting to graver sanctions those who consciously defy legal norms. It was those policy reasons that dictated the result that the intoxication defense should be available when it negatives purpose or knowledge. The drafters concluded: "If the mental state which is the basis of the law's concern does not exist, the reason for its non-existence is quite plainly immaterial."

Thus, when the requisite culpability for a crime is that the person act "purposely" or "knowingly," evidence of voluntary intoxication is admissible to disprove that requisite mental state. The language of *N.J.S.A.* 2C:2-8 and its legislative history make this unmistakably clear....

## IV.

The foregoing discussion establishes that proof of voluntary intoxication would negate the culpability elements in the offenses of which this defendant was convicted. The charges—aggravated assault, possession of a weapon with a purpose to use it unlawfully, and resisting arrest—all require purposeful conduct (aggravated assault uses "purposely" or "knowingly" in the alternative). The question is what level of intoxication must be demonstrated before a trial court is required to submit the issue to a jury. What quantum of proof is required?

The guiding principle is simple enough of articulation. We need not here repeat the citations to authorities already referred to in this opinion that use the language of "prostration of faculties such that defendant was rendered incapable of forming an intent." Justice Depue's instruction to a jury over a century ago, quoted with approval in *State v. Treficanto* remains good law:

> You should carefully discriminate between that excitable condition of the mind produced by drink, which is not incapable of forming an intent, but determines to act on a slight provocation, and such prostration of the faculties by intoxication as puts the accused in such a state that he is incapable of forming an intention from which he shall act.

*See also State v. Stasio, supra:*

> [I]t is not the case that every defendant who has had a few drinks may successfully urge the defense. The mere intake of even large quantities of alcohol will not suffice. Moreover, the defense cannot be established solely by showing that the defendant might not have committed the offense had he been sober. What is required is a showing of such a great prostration of the faculties that the requisite mental state was totally lacking. That is, to successfully invoke the defense, an accused must show that he was so intoxicated that he did not have the intent to commit an offense. Such a state of affairs will likely exist in very few cases. 78 *N.J.* at 495, 396 *A.*2d 1129 (Pashman, J., concurring and dissenting)....

## V.

Measured by the foregoing standard and evidence relevant thereto, it is apparent that the record in this case is insufficient to have required the trial court to grant defendant's request to charge intoxication....

True, the victim testified that defendant was drunk, and defendant herself said she felt "pretty intoxicated," "pretty bad," and "very intoxicated." But these are no more than conclusory labels, of little assistance in determining whether any drinking produced a prostration of faculties.

More to the point is the fact that defendant carried a quart of wine, that she was drinking (we are not told over what period of time) with other people on the vacant lot, that about a pint of the wine was consumed, and that defendant did not drink this alone but rather "gave most of it out, gave some of it out." Defendant's conduct was violent, abusive, and threatening. But with it all there is not the slightest suggestion that she did not know what she was doing or that her faculties were so beclouded by the wine that she was incapable of engaging in purposeful conduct. That the purpose of the conduct may have been bizarre, even violent, is not the test. The critical question is whether defendant was capable of forming that bizarre or violent purpose, and we do not find sufficient evidence to permit a jury to say she was not....

Because the evidence was insufficient to justify submission of he intoxication issue to the jury, the trial court's refusal to charge intoxication was correct ...

The judgment below is reversed and the cause is remanded to the Appellate Division for further proceedings consistent with this opinion.

### *Notes and Questions*

1. As the court points out in *Sexton,* the Model Penal Code rejects the general/specific intent distinction. As we saw in Chapter 8, the Code rejects specific and general intent not only for the purposes of intoxication, but also for defining the subjective offense elements. Instead of focusing on the elusive (and confusing) distinction between general and specific intent, the Code prescribes four well defined forms of culpability (purpose, knowledge, recklessness and negligence) and holds that evidence of voluntary intoxication is relevant only if it negates purpose or knowledge. In contrast, evidence of voluntary intoxication is not admissible to negate recklessness or negligence under the Model Penal Code.

2. The underlying justification for the Code's rules regarding voluntary intoxication is the assumption that getting drunk is sufficiently culpable to justify holding intoxicated offenders liable for recklessness or negligence but not sufficiently culpable to hold them liable for purpose or knowledge. In other words, proof of voluntary intoxication may not be used to disprove recklessness, given that the decision to get drunk is reckless in itself. Do you agree with this analysis? Why or why not?

3. The court in *Sexton* observed that although both the New Jersey Penal Code and the Model Penal Code reject the common law distinction between general and specific intent, the approach to voluntary intoxication adopted in both codes would "achieve the same result as that reached under the common law." Do you agree? Why or why not? Even if both approaches would achieve the same results, are there still good reasons to prefer the Model Penal Code's framework over the common law's approach to the intoxicated offender? Explain.

4. Some states have prescribed by statute that voluntary intoxication may not be taken into account to determine whether the defendant acted with the mental state required by the offense. Evidence of voluntary intoxication is always inadmissible in these states, even when the offense charged is a "specific intent" crime or when the prescribed mental state is "purpose" or "knowledge." In *Montana v. Egelhoff,* the Supreme Court of the United States upheld the constitutionality of such statutes. 518 U.S. 37 (1996).

## § 9.05 Negating Subjective Offense Elements (*Mens Rea*): Comparative Perspectives

### Judgment of the Sixth Criminal Tribunal of Santiago, Chile (2007)

There can be no liability for engaging in a harmful act if the conduct is not performed in a subjectively culpable manner. There are two general kinds of culpability, namely: intent and negligence.... In order for a defendant to act intentionally, he must know that he is engaging in an act that is proscribed by law. That is, he must know that his conduct satisfies the elements of the offense. Therefore, a person who is unaware of the circumstances that make his conduct fall within the scope of the offense acts without intent. The ignorance of the existence of an offense element or the incorrect belief that the offense element doesn't exist is called a "mistake regarding offense elements." When the defendant is mistaken about the offense elements he cannot be said to have intentionally engaged in conduct constitutive of the offense. Therefore, such mistakes preclude a finding of intentional conduct. The defendant should be acquitted if his mistake is unavoidable. If his mistake is avoidable, the defendant cannot be held liable for an intentional offense, but he may be liable for negligence, albeit only if there is a negligent version of the offense charged. Chilean commentators discuss the following case as an example of a mistake regarding the offense definition:

> If A has sexual intercourse with B, believing that B is 16 years old when she is actually 13, the intent with which the offense of rape must be committed does not exist. It does not matter whether A should have known that the victim was underage, for the law does not contemplate an offense of negligent rape.

In the case that gave rise to the present judgment, the defendant incurred in a mistake regarding the offense definition (the same kind of mistake made in the abovementioned example), for he believed that he was having intercourse with a person over the age of 14. The age of the victim is an element of the offense charged. Given that the defendant mistakenly believed that this essential element did not exist, he cannot be said to have acted intentionally. We consider that the defendant's mistake in this case was avoidable, for had he been more diligent he would have realized that the victim was not over 14 years old. As a result, defendant's mistake precludes holding him liable for an intentional offense, but allows—in principle—for the imposition of liability for a negligent version of the offense charged. Nevertheless, given that negligent rape is not criminalized under Chilean law, the conduct of the defendant is not punishable.

## *Notes and Questions*

1. As was pointed out in Note 5 of § 9.01, statutory rape is considered a strict liability offense in many American jurisdictions. Mistake as to the victim's age is thus not a defense to liability in these states even if it is reasonable. In contrast, mistake as to the victim's age is a defense in a handful of states, but only if reasonable. *See, e.g., Pérez v. State,* 111 N.M. 160 (1990). Similarly, the Model Penal Code allows for a mistake as to age defense only if "the actor ... prove[s] by a preponderance of the evidence that he reasonably believed the child to be above the critical age." *See* MPC § 213.6(1). Interestingly, the Model Penal Code disallows the mistake of fact defense altogether if the child is less than 10 years old. *Id.*

2. On the other hand, courts in Great Britain currently hold that an honest mistake of fact regarding age defeats liability for rape even if it is unreasonable. The current English approach is summarized in Lord Nicholls of Birkenhead's opinion in *B. (A Minor) v. Director of Public Prosecutions*:

> The "reasonable belief" school of thought held unchallenged sway for many years. But over the last quarter of a century there have been several important cases where a defence of honest but mistaken belief was raised. In deciding these cases the courts have placed new, or renewed, emphasis on the subjective nature of the mental element in criminal offences. The courts have rejected the reasonable belief approach and preferred the honest belief approach. When mens rea is ousted by a mistaken belief, it is as well ousted by an unreasonable belief as by a reasonable belief. In the pithy phrase of Lawton L.J. in *Regina v. Kimber*: it is the defendant's belief, not the grounds on which it is based, which goes to negative the intent. This approach is well encapsulated in a passage in the judgment of Lord Lane C.J. in Regina v. Williams (Gladstone):
>
> > The reasonableness or unreasonableness of the defendant's belief is material to question of whether the belief was held by the defendant at all. If the

> belief was in fact held, its unreasonableness, so far as guilt or innocence is concerned, is neither here nor there. It is irrelevant. Were it otherwise, the defendant would be convicted because he was negligent in failing to recognize that the victim was not consenting ... and so on.
>
> Considered as a matter of principle, the honest belief approach must be preferable. By definition the mental element in a crime is concerned with a subjective state of mind, such as intent or belief. To the extent that an overriding objective limit ('on reasonable grounds') is introduced, the subjective element is displaced. To that extent a person who lacks the necessary intent or belief may nevertheless commit the offence. When that occurs the defendant's 'fault' lies exclusively in falling short of an objective standard. A statute may so provide expressly or by necessary implication. But this can have no place in a common law principle, of general application, which is concerned with the need for a mental element as an essential ingredient of a criminal offence. 1 All E.R. 833 (2000).

The approach adopted in the House of Lords in *B. (A Minor) v. Director* is essentially the same that is followed both by the Chilean court in the judgment excerpted at the beginning of this section and by the overwhelming majority of courts and commentators in Latin American and European jurisdictions. Which of the three approaches (mistake as to age is no defense, it is a defense only if reasonable, or it's a defense even if unreasonable) do you prefer? Why?

3. Note that the Chilean court concluded that the defendant's mistake regarding the victim's age was "avoidable," which in common law terms is equivalent to holding that the mistake was unreasonable. Given that the defendant's mistake was unreasonable, the court suggests that it would be appropriate to hold him liable for a crime of negligence. The position is tenable, for the essence of negligence is engaging in "objectively unreasonable" behavior, which is precisely the type of conduct that an unreasonably mistaken actor performs. Alas, the Chilean court acquitted the defendant because Chilean law—like American law—does not criminalize "negligent" rape. Should unreasonable mistakes regarding the victim's age (or consent in the case of an adult victim) defeat liability for rape? Should a negligent offense of rape be created to deal with the problem of unreasonable mistakes in this context? Why or why not? If so, should "negligent" rape be punished the same or less than traditional "intentional" rape? The materials that follow examine these issues.

## § 9.06 Negating Subjective Offense Elements (*Mens Rea*): Scholarly Debates

### Kyron Huigens, *Fletcher's Rethinking: A Memoir*

39 Tulsa L. Rev. 803 (2004)

... III.

... Morgan, an officer in the British Army, invited a group of his junior officers to have sex with his wife. He told them to ignore any objections from her, because his wife enjoyed rape fantasies and wanted to have sex with a number of men at one time. Mrs. Morgan did object when the officers raped her, and the officers duly ignored her. On trial for rape, they requested an instruction to the effect that their good faith belief in Mrs. Morgan's consent was a ground for acquittal. If the offense of rape requires an intentional state of mind regarding non-consent, then their genuine good faith belief in her consent precluded their having any such state of mind. The trial court refused to give this instruction, the Morgan defendants were convicted, and the Law Lords affirmed the conviction. But the appellate court affirmed the conviction only under a harmless error rule. The trial court did err in refusing to give the instruction, the Lords said, because rape requires an awareness of at least the risk of non-consent. In American terms, the Morgan defendants were entitled to their instruction because the law requires at least recklessness regarding non-consent to sexual intercourse, in accordance with the principle of Model Penal Code section 2.02(3).

Clearly, something has gone wrong here. If the Morgan defendants raped Mrs. Morgan out of callousness, immaturity, self-absorption, and stupidity, then the law grants them an acquittal because they were callous, immature, self-absorbed, and stupid. The Law Lords in Morgan confronted an apparently insoluble dilemma. They were simultaneously committed to the principle of intentional states (or "descriptive") fault and to the notion that such morally bad men should not escape criminal liability. However, the former commitment made it impossible to keep the latter. The Law Lords jumped between the horns of the dilemma by disposing of the case under a harmless error rule. As I will explain below, I think the dilemma should have been resolved by grabbing one of the horns—by rejecting the intentional states conception of criminal fault....

My solution to the problem of the Morgan case takes it to reflect the choices we make between intentional and non-intentional fault criteria in the definition of offenses. The paradox of Morgan arises only because the Law Lords (and the Model Penal Code) insisted on proof of an intentional state of mind—consciousness of a risk—with regard to the element of non-consent. There are at least three alternatives to this intentional states approach to proof of fault regarding non-consent in rape. One is not to require any formal proof of fault at all: to make rape a crime of strict liability where non-consent is concerned. We can achieve this rule if we refuse to accept even a reasonable mistake about non-consent as a defense, as some courts have done. The second possibility is to require proof only of negligence, a non-intentional kind of fault, regarding non-consent. Most jurisdictions have adopted this approach under the guise of requiring a mistake about non-consent to be reasonable. The third possibility is to use a different kind of non-intentional fault criterion, such as extreme indifference, that turns not on the reasonableness of the mistake, but instead on the defendant's attitude toward non-consent. This set of alternatives can be seen as stretching along a continuum of fault conceptions: from no formal proof of fault; to proof of an attitude indicative of fault; to a flawed course of practical reasoning indicative of fault; to proof of an intentional state of mind that is indicative of fault. Only the last option is an intentional state of mind fault criterion; the others are different versions of non-intentional fault.

What point along this continuum is the "right" point? As always, the question is more interesting than the answer.

... Where the stakes for both the victim and the defendant are so high, the legal system needs to produce morally palatable outcomes and to avoid over- and under-inclusion relative to our background moral judgments about autonomy, sex, and punishment. Mrs. Morgan was raped, because the defendants were at fault regarding her non-consent, and they were at fault for rape because they were callous, immature, self-absorbed, and stupid. We resort to non-intentional fault criteria in rape because unless the law captures compelling moral judgments, such as the one we make in cases such as Morgan, the law would lose essential credibility and public support.

## Susan Estrich, *Rape*

95 Yale L. J. 1087 (1986)

... While American courts have unwisely ignored the entire issue of *mens rea* or mistake of fact, the British courts may have gone too far in the other direction. To their credit, they have squarely confronted the issue, but their resolution suggests a highly restrictive understanding of criminal intent in cases of sexual assault. The focal point of the debate in Great Britain and the Commonwealth countries was the House of Lord's decision in *Director of Public Prosecutions v. Morgan,* in which the certified question was: "Whether in rape the defendant can properly be convicted, notwithstanding that he in fact believed that the woman consented, if such belief was not based on reasonable grounds." The majority of the House of Lords answered the question in the negative.

The Heilbron Committee was created to review the controversial *Morgan* decision. The Committee's recommendation, ultimately enacted in 1976, retained the *Morgan* approach in requiring that at the time of intercourse the man knew or at least was aware of the risk of nonconsent, but provided that the reasonableness of the man's belief could be considered by the jury in determining what he in fact knew. In situations where a "reasonable man" would have known that the woman was not consenting, most defendants will face great difficulty in arguing that they were honestly mistaken or inadvertent as to consent. Thus, in *Morgan* itself, the House of Lords, although holding that negligence was not sufficient to establish liability for rape, upheld the convictions on the ground that no properly instructed jury, in the circumstances of that case, could have concluded that the defendants honestly believed that their victim was consenting. Still, in an English case decided shortly after *Morgan,* on facts substantially similar (a husband procuring a buddy to engage in sex with his crying wife), an English jury concluded that the defendant had been negligent in believing, honestly but unreasonably, in the wife's consent. On the authority of *Morgan,* the court held that the defendant therefore deserved acquittal.

My view is that such a "negligent rapist" should be punished, albeit—as in murder—less severely than the man who acts with purpose or knowledge, or even knowledge of the risk. First, he is sufficiently blameworthy for it to be just to punish him. Second, the injury he inflicts is sufficiently grave to deserve the law's prohibition.

The traditional argument against negligence liability is that punishment should be limited to cases of choice, because to punish a man for his stupidity is unjust and, in deterrence terms, ineffective. Under this view, a man should only be held responsible for what he does knowingly or purposely, or at least while aware of the risks involved. As one of *Morgan*'s most respected defenders put it:

> To convict the stupid man would be to convict him for what lawyers call inadvertent negligence—honest conduct which may be the best that this man can do but that does not come up to the standard of the so-called reasonable man. People ought not to be punished for negligence except in some minor offences established by statute. Rape carries a possible sentence of imprisonment for life, and it would be wrong to have a law of negligent rape. Professor Glanville Williams in a letter to THE TIMES (London), May 8, 1975, at 15, col. 6.

If inaccuracy or indifference to consent is "the best that this man can do" because he lacks the capacity to act reasonably, then it might well be unjust and ineffective to punish him for it. But such men will be rare, and there was no evidence that the men in *Morgan* were among them, at least as long as voluntary drunkenness is not equated with inherent lack of capacity. More common is the case of the man who could have done better but didn't could have paid attention, but didn't; heard her say no, or saw her tears, but decided to ignore them. Neither justice nor deterrence argues against punishing this man.

Certainly, if the "reasonable" attitude to which a male defendant is held is defined according to a "no means yes" philosophy that celebrates male aggressiveness and female passivity, there is little potential for unfairness in holding men who fall below *that* standard criminally liable. Under such a low standard of reasonableness, only a very drunk man could honestly be mistaken as to a woman's consent, and a man who voluntarily sheds his capacity to act and perceive reasonably should not be heard to complain here—any more than with respect to other crimes—that he is being punished in the absence of choice.

But even if reasonableness is defined—as I argue it should be—according to a rule that "no means no," it is not unfair to hold those men who violate the rule criminally responsible, provided that there is fair warning of the rule. I understand that some men in our society have honestly believed in a different reality of sexual relations, and that many may honestly view such situations differently than women. But, it is precisely because men and women may perceive these situations differently, and because the injury to women stemming from the different male perception may be grave, that it is necessary and appropriate for the law to impose a duty upon men to act with reason, and to punish them when they violate that duty.

In holding a man to such a standard of reasonableness, the law signifies that it considers a woman's consent to sex to be significant enough to merit a man's reasoned attention. In effect, the law imposes a duty on men to open their eyes and use their heads before engaging in sex—not to read a woman's mind, but to give her credit for knowing her own mind when she speaks it. The man who has the inherent capacity to act reasonably, but fails to do so, has made the blameworthy choice to violate this duty. While the injury caused by purposeful conduct may be greater than that caused by negligent acts, being negligently sexually penetrated without one's consent remains a grave harm, and being treated like an object whose words or actions are not even worthy of consideration adds insult to injury. This dehumanization exacerbates the denial of dignity and autonomy which is so much a part of the injury of rape, and it is equally present in both the purposeful and negligent rape.

By holding out the prospect of punishment for negligence, the law provides an additional motive for men to "take care before acting, to use their faculties and draw on their experience in gauging the potentialities of contemplated conduct." We may not yet have reached the point where men are required to ask verbally. But if silence does not negate consent, at least the word "no" should, and those who ignore such an explicit sign of non-consent should be subject to criminal liability.

## *Notes and Questions*

1. Reconsider the question posed in the previous section regarding whether negligent rape should be punished. Note that a defendant who mistakenly but unreasonably believes that the victim consented behaves negligently. As a result, punishing such a defendant—as many American jurisdictions do —imposes liability for negligence. This point is succinctly made by Professor Huigens in the article excerpted above:

> The second [way of punishing rape] is to require proof only of negligence ... regarding non-consent. Most jurisdictions have adopted this approach under the guise of requiring a mistake about non-consent to be reasonable.

Given that there is no freestanding offense of negligent rape, such negligently mistaken defendants could be punished as severely as defendants who engage in "intentional" rape. Is this appropriate? Why or why not?

2. Professor Estrich suggests that defendants who negligently (unreasonably) believe that the victim consented "should be punished, albeit—as in murder—less severely than the man who acts with purpose or knowledge, or even knowledge of the risk" of non-consent. Do you agree with Estrich's proposal? Assuming that the defendants in *Morgan* believed in good faith that the victim consented to sexual intercourse, would Professor Estrich's proposal lead to punishing them less severely than a defendant who has sexual intercourse knowing that the victim does not consent? If so, do you find this solution acceptable? Why or why not?

3. Huigens argues that it is misguided to discriminate between more and less blameworthy conduct solely on the basis of whether the defendant was aware of a circumstance or not. Sometimes inadvertent wrongdoing is more (or equally) blameworthy than advertent wrongdoing. In the context of *Morgan,* Huigens argues that the defendants ought to be held liable for rape in spite of their mistake because their conduct revealed that they "were callous, immature, self-absorbed, and stupid." Whether the defendants were aware that there was a risk of non-consent should not be determinative, for conduct that reveals the aforementioned traits is as deserving of punishment as "advertent" (reckless) wrongdoing. Do you agree? Why or why not?

4. How would the *Morgan* case be decided in most American jurisdictions? Assuming that rape is defined as "engaging in non-consensual sexual intercourse," how would the case be decided under the Model Penal Code? What result if the case were tried in a European Continental or Latin American country? Do you find any of these solutions acceptable?

# Chapter 10

# Complicity

## § 10.01 Complicity: Common Law Distinction between Principals and Accessories and Its Abrogation

### Potts v. Florida

Supreme Court of Florida, 1982
430 So.2d 900

EHRLICH, Justice.

This cause is before the Court on petition for review of a district court of appeal decision on the ground of express and direct conflict. We have jurisdiction. At issue is whether or not an aider or abettor to the substantive crime may be convicted of a greater crime than his confederate/principal. The decision under review, *Potts v. State*, conflicts with *Turner v. State*. We affirm *Potts* and disapprove *Turner*.

Petitioner and one Lawrence Scott Ramirez participated in the burglary of a Clearwater car dealer. Ramirez actually conducted the burglary during which he placed his hand on an employee, guided him to a restroom, and instructed him to remain there. Petitioner's participation in the crime consisted of driving Ramirez to the scene, waiting nearby until summoned by Ramirez, then driving the get-away vehicle.

Both were charged with burglary ... Ramirez was tried separately, found guilty of simple burglary, and received a maximum sentence of five years. Petitioner was tried and found guilty of burglary of a structure wherein an assault was committed and received a sentence of thirty years.

The Second District Court of Appeal rejected petitioner's contention that he could not be convicted of being a principal in the first degree to the crime of aiding and abetting a burglary with assault when the principal perpetrator was only convicted of simple burglary. The judgment and sentence were set aside and remanded for a new trial on other grounds, but Potts nevertheless sought review in this Court on that issue only. Petitioner makes two arguments to which we will respond.

Potts was charged under the aider-abettor statute which makes all participants in a crime principals in the first degree. The correct interpretation of that statute, he argues, is the one given by the first district in its opinion in *Turner*.

The history of the culpability of the aider-abettor is an intricate and involved one. The courts have waivered on the issue. At common law jurists went to great lengths to classify and define the degree of culpability of each of the actors in the crime and four categories arose. These were: a) principals in the first degree, who actually committed the offense; b) principals in the second degree, who were actually or constructively at the scene of the crime and aided or abetted in its commission; c) accessories before the fact, who aided or abetted the crime but were not present at its commission; and d) accessories after the fact, who rendered assistance after the crime was committed.

Because at early common law all felonies were punishable by death, judges found it particularly hard to apply this harsh penalty to the aider or abettor who was an accessory before the fact. Consequently, procedural rules developed that tended to shield the accessories from prosecution in certain instances. Among these rules was the one that an accessory could not be convicted without the prior conviction of the principal offender. Therefore, the principal's disappearance, death or acquittal automatically served to release the accessory, and the pardon or reversal of a conviction of the principal operated in the same fashion. Indeed, "[a]n accessory follows, like a shadow, his principal." 1 J. Bishop, Criminal Law §666 (8th ed. 1892).

As the law developed and punishment for felony convictions became less harsh the necessity for this equitable procedural bar became a nullity. Statutes in England and the United States were enacted to overcome these judge-made rules and permit the trial and conviction of accessories before the fact independent of their principals. Florida ventured into the legislative arena as early as 1868 to pass legislation defining the accessory before the fact and the aider-abettor, and providing for punishment independent of the conviction of the principal.

Despite the legislature's efforts the courts continued to draw the line between the principal in the second degree and the accessory before the fact. *Montague v. State.* Another distinction began to develop as to whether or not the accessory was charged under the statute or at common law. *Flynn v. State.* And though the courts were willing to place the principal in the first degree and the principal in the second degree in the same shoes, the accessory before the fact was treated quite differently. *Neumann v. State.*

In an apparent effort to clear up this growing problem of distinguishing between the accessories and principals, the legislature passed Ch. 57-310, Laws of Florida, in 1957. This declared that principals in the first and second degree and accessories before the fact were treated equally and all were made principals in the first degree.

This statute was interpreted by *Blackburn v. State.* The age-old argument about whether or not the aider or abettor could be convicted while the principal was acquitted was dealt with by the *Blackburn* court as follows:

> Some of the cases cited by appellant appear to require a conviction of the original offender as a predicate to conviction of an aider and abettor. However, this is no longer the law. Those cases were limited to prosecution of accessories before the fact. The enactment of §776.011 of the Florida Statutes eliminated this requirement, under the peculiar circumstances where it existed.

That statute remained intact until 1974 when as part of a major revision of the criminal code the language was changed. The following underscored language was added:

> Principal in first degree.—Whoever commits any criminal offense against the state, whether felony or misdemeanor, or aids, abets, counsels, hires, or otherwise procures such offense to be committed, *and such offense is committed or is attempted to be committed,* is a principal in the first degree and may be charged, convicted, and punished as such, whether he is or is not actually or constructively present at the commission of such offense.

It is this amending language that is the crux of the holding in *Turner*, and the cornerstone of petitioner's argument. Petitioner asserts that by adding this language the legislature intended to change the statute and add a new element to the crime. He further argues that in order for the aider-abettor to be convicted of a particular crime, the primary perpetrator also has to be convicted of the same crime. In this case, the argument continues, since the primary perpetrator, Ramirez, was acquitted of burglary with assault and only convicted of simple burglary, the crime of burglary with an assault was not in fact committed and therefore, under the statute as amended, the petitioner himself cannot be convicted of any crime greater than simple burglary. In conclusion, petitioner's argument is that we should once again adopt the common law rule.

We disagree. First, after a due and diligent search we are unable to track down the illusory legislative intent relied upon by the petitioner. We are thus compelled to conclude that the reasons for the change were simply technical and designed to make the statute compatible with other sections of that chapter. Therefore, we interpret that statute to mean that it is sufficient at the trial of the aider-abettor only to show that a crime was committed. In order to convict the aider-abettor it is not necessary to show that the principal perpetrator was convicted of the same crime, nor is it even necessary to show that he was convicted at all.

We now address petitioner's second argument which is harder to reject because it is based on policy. He asks that we adopt either a collateral estoppel rationale or "consistency of judgments approach." We realize that both are doctrines logically developed and based on the appearance of equity and justice. We reject them, however, for several reasons.

We find illuminating the U.S. Supreme Court's opinion in *Standefer v. United States*. We are aware that that decision does not prevent a state from adopting a contrary position, but we feel that the reasoning is sound and compelling. That court refused to adopt the doctrine of non-mutual collateral estoppel in criminal cases because acquittals can result from many factors other than guilt or innocence, the procedural elements pertaining to one defendant can be totally different than those applying to another, and there is no procedure for retrying a defendant once acquitted even though the verdict might be clearly erroneous....

We therefore hold that 1) this statute makes an aider or abettor, principals of the first or second degree, and accessories before the fact equally responsible for the entire transaction, and all are principals in the first degree; 2) the language added to the statute means that at the trial of the aider or abettor, accessory or principal, it is only necessary to show that there was an attempt to commit a crime or that a crime was committed during the transaction; and 3) if any of the perpetrators are tried in separate trials the judgments and sentences, even though inconsistent, are independent of one another and stand or fall on their own merits.

The decision of the district court is affirmed.

## Notes and Questions

1. As *Potts v. Florida* illustrates, both principals in the second degree and accessories before the fact are now treated in the same way than principals in the first degree. Furthermore, the procedural hurdles that existed at common law for prosecuting and convicting accessories no longer exist. As a result, an accessory may be convicted even if the principal was never tried or was tried and acquitted. Accessories may also be convicted of a more serious offense than the principal, as illustrated by *Potts*. Nevertheless, acces-

sories *after* the fact continue to be treated differently than accessories before the fact and principals in the first and second degree.

2. An actor is an accomplice (i.e., accessory) if she contributes in any way to the commission of the offense. While the accomplice's contribution will often consist of physically assisting the perpetrator, moral support and encouragement are also considered forms of complicity. As the materials in the next section show, it is also possible become an accomplice by omission. Most American jurisdictions define complicity in very broad and general terms. The federal complicity statute is representative:

> Whoever commits an offense against the United States or aids, abets, counsels, commands, induces or procures its commission, is punishable as a principal. 18 USCS § 2 (2008).

According to the Supreme Court of the United States, this statute:

> "[A]bolishe[d] the distinction between principals and accessories and [made] them all principals." Read against its common law background, the provision evinces a clear intent to permit the conviction of accessories to federal criminal offenses despite the prior acquittal of the actual perpetrator of the offense. It gives general effect to what had always been the rule for second-degree principals and for all misdemeanants.
>
> The legislative history of [the statute] confirms this understanding. The provision was recommended by the Commission to Revise and Codify the Criminal and Penal Laws of the United States as "[i]n accordance with the policy of recent legislation" by which "those whose relations to a crime would be that of accessories before the fact according to the common law are made principals." 1 Final Report of the Commission to Revise and Codify the Laws of the United States 118–119 (1906). The Commission's recommendation was adopted without change. The House and Senate Committee Reports, in identical language, stated its intended effect:
>
> > The committee has deemed it wise to make those who are accessories before the fact at common law principal offenders, thereby permitting their indictment and conviction for a substantive offense.
> >
> > At common law, an accessory cannot be tried without his consent before the conviction or outlawry of the principal except where the principal and accessory are tried together; if the principal could not be found or if he had been indicted and refused to plead, had been pardoned or died before conviction, the accessory could not be tried at all. This change of the existing law renders these obstacles to justice impossible.
>
> This history plainly rebuts petitioner's contention that § 2 was not intended to authorize conviction of an aider and abettor after the principal had been acquitted of the offense charged. With the enactment of that section, all participants in conduct violating a federal criminal statute are "principals." As such, they are punishable for their criminal conduct; the fate of other participants is irrelevant.

3. Is it fair to punish an accomplice when the principal was tried and acquitted? Suppose that a mentally disturbed principal is acquitted of homicide because she was insane when she killed the victim. Should a mentally sane accessory that helped the principal kill the victim be convicted as an accomplice to homicide even if the principal is acquitted by reason of insanity? Explain. Although the perpetrator's acquittal or non-prosecution

is no longer a bar to trying and convicting accessories, note that—as the court pointed out in *Potts*—the state must show "at the trial of the aider-abettor ... that a crime was committed." That is, an actor may only be held liable as an accomplice if the prosecution demonstrates that she aided or abetted a crime committed by another. The reason for this is that accomplice liability is conventionally viewed as parasitic of the perpetrator's liability and, as such, requires proof that the actor helped someone else engage in criminal conduct, even if it does not require evidence that the perpetrator was convicted of the offense.

## § 10.02 Complicity: Objective Elements (*Actus Reus*)

### State v. Vaillancourt

Supreme Court of New Hampshire, 1982
122 N.H. 1153

PER CURIAM.

The only issue presented in this case is whether the Trial Court erred in ruling that the indictment against the defendant was sufficient on its face. We hold that the court's ruling was erroneous, and we reverse.

The factual backdrop of the case involves an attempted burglary on the morning of December 8, 1980, at the O'Connor residence in Manchester. On that day, a neighbor observed two young men, allegedly the defendant, David W. Vaillancourt, and one Richard Burhoe, standing together on the O'Connors' front porch. The men were ringing the doorbell and conversing with one another. Because they remained on the porch for approximately ten minutes, the neighbor became suspicious and began to watch them more closely. She saw them walk around to the side of the house where Burhoe allegedly attempted to break into a basement window. The defendant allegedly stood by and watched his companion, talking to him intermittently while the companion tried to pry open the window. The neighbor notified the police, who apprehended the defendant and Burhoe as they were fleeing the scene.

Shortly thereafter, a grand jury indicted the defendant for accomplice liability under [state law]. The indictment alleged, in pertinent part, as follows:

> "[T]hat David W. Vaillancourt ... with the purpose of promoting and facilitating the commission of the offense of attempted burglary, did purposely aid Richard Burhoe ... *by accompanying him to the location of said crime and watching* as the said Richard Burhoe [attempted to commit the crime of burglary]....

Prior to trial, the defendant filed a motion to dismiss, claiming that the indictment failed to allege criminal conduct on his part. The trial court denied the motion, and a jury subsequently found the defendant guilty as charged. The defendant now contests the sufficiency of his indictment.

The defendant bases his argument on the axiomatic principle that an indictment must allege some criminal activity. He specifically contends that his indictment was insufficient because, even if the facts alleged in it were true, they would not have satisfied the elements necessary for accomplice liability or for any other crime. We agree.

The crime of accomplice liability ... requires the actor to have solicited, aided, agreed to aid, or attempted to aid the principal in planning or committing the offense. The crime thus necessitates some active participation by the accomplice. We have held that knowledge and mere presence at the scene of a crime could not support a conviction for accomplice liability because they did not constitute sufficient affirmative acts to satisfy the *actus reus* requirement of the accomplice liability statute.

In the instant case, other than the requisite *mens rea*, the State alleged only that the defendant aided Burhoe "by accompanying him to the location of the crime and watching ...". Consistent with our rulings with respect to "mere presence," we hold that accompaniment and observation are not sufficient acts to constitute "aid" under [state law]. We conclude that the trial court erred in upholding the defendant's indictment.

**BOIS, Justice, with whom BROCK, Justice, joins, dissenting:**

I cannot accept the majority's conclusion that accompaniment and observation are insufficient acts to constitute "aid" under the accomplice liability statute. Although I agree that "mere presence" would be an insufficient factual allegation, *see State v. Goodwin,* the indictment in this case alleged more than "mere presence." As the majority concedes, the indictment alleged the requisite *mens rea.* It also alleged accompaniment, which connotes presence *and* some *further connection* between the accomplice and the principal. While not a customary form of assistance, "accompaniment with the purpose of aiding" implies the furnishing of moral support and encouragement in the performance of a crime, thereby "aiding" a principal in the commission of an offense. *Cf. id.* (jury could reasonably have concluded that defendant's presence facilitated and encouraged principal to commit rape). I would therefore hold that the indictment in this case sufficiently alleged criminal conduct on the part of the defendant.

## Porter v. State

Court of Criminal Appeals of Alabama, 1990
580 So.2d 823

PATTERSON, Judge.

Appellant, Charlotte K. Porter, and her husband, Darrell Porter, were jointly indicted in a two-count indictment for possession of cocaine and possession of marijuana for other than personal use. The cases were severed, and the state proceeded to trial against appellant. A jury found her guilty of possession of cocaine and guilty of the lesser—included offense of possession of marijuana for personal use. The trial court sentenced her to eight years' imprisonment for the possession of cocaine conviction and twelve months' confinement in the county jail for the possession of marijuana for personal use conviction. The sentences were ordered to run concurrently. Darrell Porter was never tried; the state entered a nolle prosequi as to the charges against him. Appellant appeals, raising two issues.

The state's evidence disclosed that appellant's residence was searched by officers of the Chambers County sheriff's department pursuant to a search warrant. The officers discovered five marijuana plants in the back yard, one marijuana plant in the kitchen, equipment in the barn for growing marijuana, and marijuana in small amounts in various other places in the residence. Also, they found a plastic bag containing cocaine on a shelf in the bedroom closet; various items of drug paraphernalia with cocaine residue in a box in the bedroom; two bottles of inositol in plain view on the bedside table; a set of electronic scales on the floor beside the bed; and packaging equipment, including plastic sandwich bags and "twist" ties, in a box on the floor in the bedroom. A small notepad with "dates, names, ... amounts in weights and also dollar amounts out to the side with markings of 'paid'" along with four one-hundred dollar bills, was found under the mattress. Appellant and her husband were separated at the time, and he did not live at the residence, even though he paid the utility bills and the rent. Appellant apparently had exclusive possession of the residence at the time; however, Mr. Porter was a frequent visitor. The bedroom in which the cocaine was seized was occupied by appellant, and her clothing was in the closet. She told the officers at the time of the search that the marijuana belonged to her and that she grew it for her personal use. She made no statement in reference to the cocaine and did not testify at her trial. In defense she called her husband as a witness and asked him if the cocaine was his. He refused to answer the question, invoking his rights under the Fifth Amendment. She also presented witnesses to show that her husband paid the rent and utility bills for the residence.

## I.

Appellant's first contention arises out of the following instructions given the jury by the trial court pursuant to a written request by the prosecution:

> I charge you, also, ladies and gentlemen of the jury, that under the law of the State of Alabama a person is legally accountable for the behavior of another person constituting a criminal offense if with intent to promote or assist in the commission of an offense, one, he or she procures or induces or causes such other person to commit the offense. Or, two, he or she aids or abets such other person in committing the offense. Or, three, he or she has a legal duty to prevent the commission of the offense and fails to make such effort as he or she is legally required to make to prevent it.

The instruction is in the language of the statute defining complicity. Ala.Code § 13A-2-23 (1975).

Appellant objects to the portion of the court's instruction [that imposes accomplice liability for failing to prevent the commission of the offense when she had a legal duty to prevent it.]....

Appellant argues that her mere presence at the time and place of the charged crime of possession of cocaine is not sufficient to make her guilty of the crime. She argues that the instruction gave the jury the false impression that she could be found guilty simply because she did not prevent her husband from committing the crime. She contends that there is no provision in our criminal code that provides that a person can be convicted of possession of a controlled substance by failing to prevent possession by another.

The commentary to § 13A-2-23 states, in pertinent part, as follows:

> This section formalizes in simple terms the basic principles for determining criminal liability where based upon the behavior of another person or persons. It delineates both the type of action or omission required and the necessary mental state....
>
> ... What this section does is define complicity in clear, direct and explicit terms, rather than attempt to accommodate the common-law concepts in defining accessorial liability. The test will be whether the accused with the intent to promote or assist the perpetration of an offense did any of certain enumerated acts in subdivisions (1) or (2) or failed to act (3)....
>
> The three subparagraphs delineate various types of action or omission which might hold one to accountability. Subdivision (1) imposes liability in the situa-

tion where the defendant is the party who instigates or starts the complicitous conduct....

Subdivision (2) imposes liability in the situation where one joins in the complicitous action. The classic words "aid and abet" are used. Aiding and abetting comprehends all assistance rendered by acts, or words of encouragement, or support or presence actual or constructive to render assistance should it become necessary, and no particular acts are necessary....

Subdivision (3) places liability in the situation where the defendant who has a legal duty to prevent the crime fails to do so with the intent to further the crime. Although apparently there is no recent Alabama case law on this point, it has been established in other common law jurisdictions. *See, e.g., People v. Chapman,* 62 Mich. 280, (1886) (husband who had induced another to seduce his wife stood by and did not interfere with subsequent rape). This would also comprehend the situation where a nightwatchman or policeman, if with an intent to aid the perpetrating party, stands by and neglects his duty to intervene. It should be noted that mere negligence in the night watchman situation would be insufficient for liability; one must also have the "intent to promote or assist the commission of the offense."

... Under subsections (1) and (2) of § 13A-2-23, an affirmative act on the part of the accused is required, while subsection (3) is concerned with the situations in which a person may be criminally responsible for the conduct of another by failing to act. Subsection (3) makes one a party who aids the commission of the offense by inaction. In other words, having a legal duty to prevent commission of the offense, and acting with intent to promote or assist its commission, he or she fails to make a reasonable effort to prevent commission of the offense....

There was overwhelming evidence presented by the state from which the jury could have found beyond a reasonable doubt that appellant was in knowing possession of the cocaine. The cocaine, drug paraphernalia, and related items were in her residence, indeed, in her bedroom, and since she was separated from her husband at the time, it was reasonable to infer that she had exclusive possession of the premises, even though her husband was still paying the rent and utility bills. The cocaine and related items were so situated in her bedroom and closet that it would have been almost impossible for her not to have known about them.

The question to be answered here, however, is whether the portion of the instructions objected to was a proper instruction under the facts and law of the case. We think that it was. Appellant's defense to the cocaine charge was to infer that the cocaine belonged to her husband, and this inference was based solely on her husband's refusal to answer a question, when called as a defense witness, as to whether the cocaine belonged to him, by invoking his rights against self-incrimination under the Fifth Amendment, and on his paying the rent and utilities on the residence. Assuming that the cocaine and related items belonged to Mr. Porter, did appellant have a legal duty under the circumstances of this case to prevent the commission of the offense? We say, yes. It was obvious that an illegal drug operation was being conducted on the premises. Cocaine, cutting agents, scales, packaging equipment, lists of names, and money were present. "At common law the owner of premises was under the duty, and upon him rested a primary obligation, to keep his premises from becoming a public nuisance." *State ex rel. Bailes v. Guardian Realty Co.*

What then is the relation and significance of nuisance to the general discussion of omission crimes? First, we may note that, although in discussing the law

> of nuisance courts talk in terms of a general duty on every member of society to so conduct his activities and so use his property as not to unreasonably annoy other persons, the law of nuisance is by and large limited to situations where the actor or omitter can be expected to realize the effects of his conduct on others. That is, it focuses on affirmative activities and deals with omissions only with regard to the individual's actions, property and things. In this sense the duty to avoid annoyance or injury to others is not fortuitous, but one which is closely assimilable to exercising care in affirmative conduct. Frankel, supra, at 412–413 (footnotes omitted).

A residence maintained as a place of business for selling and storing cocaine on a continuing and recurring basis constitutes a public nuisance. Clearly the operation here constituted a public nuisance, and appellant, with knowledge of the illegal activities, had a legal duty to prevent her property from being used in such a manner.

Thus, the evidence supported a factual basis on which to present to the jury the legal theory that appellant had a legal duty to prevent the commission of the offense, and with intent to promote or assist in the commission, failed to make an effort she was legally required to make to prevent the offense.

While it would probably be better practice for the trial judge to give more detailed and clarifying instructions when giving a charge concerning crimes of omission, we do not believe that the charge as given in the instant case was improper. However, trial courts should be cautious in giving this charge and should not give it when defining complicity except where there is a factual and legal basis to support it....

For the above reasons, this case is due to be, and it is hereby, affirmed.

## *Notes and Questions*

1. The defendants in both *Vaillancourt* and *Porter* argued that they should not be held liable as accomplices because "mere presence" at the scene of the crime is not enough to establish criminal complicity. Nevertheless, as the discussion in both cases illustrates, presence at the scene of the offense coupled with some act or omission intended to facilitate the consummation of the crime is enough to establish accomplice liability.

2. The court held in *Vaillancourt* that the conduct charged in the indictment was not sufficient to establish that the defendant was an accomplice to attempted burglary. The indictment charged defendant with accompanying the perpetrator to the location of the crime and watching as the perpetrator attempted to commit burglary. The dissent took issue with the majority's conclusion, arguing that "[w]hile not a customary form of assistance, 'accompaniment with the purpose of aiding' implies the furnishing of moral support and encouragement in the performance of a crime, thereby 'aiding' a principal in the commission of an offense." Who has the better part of this argument?

3. The oft-cited British case of *Wilcox v. Jeffery,* [1951] 1 All E.R. 464, illustrates the difficulties inherent in drawing the line between mere presence that is not punishable as complicity and presence that gives rise to accessorial liability because it amounts to moral support and encouragement of the offense. The defendant was charged with being an accomplice to the perpetrator's crime of staging an illegal concert. The perpetrator was a famous musician who held a concert although he knew that he had been denied the visa that was necessary for him to lawfully enter the country and perform. The defendant was aware of this fact, but nevertheless bought a ticket to assist the concert. He also seemed to enjoy the performance. The court held that defendant was liable as an accomplice. Li-

ability followed from his presence at the concert hall *plus* his various acts of encouragement such as buying the ticket and seemingly enjoying the performance as opposed to objecting or protesting to it. Do you agree with the outcome in *Wilcox*? Why or why not? If the defendant's conduct in *Wilcox* amounted to enough "moral support" to generate accomplice liability, why didn't the defendant's presence at the scene in *Vaillancourt* satisfy the *actus reus* of complicity?

4. Given that mere presence alone is typically not enough to establish accessorial liability, an actor's failure to prevent the commission of a crime by another is generally not punishable as complicity. Nevertheless, liability may be imposed if the person who fails to prevent the offense had a legal duty to make a proper effort to do so. A typical case is that of the parent who witnesses someone else assault the parent's child and does nothing to prevent the abuse. In the excerpted case of *Porter v. State,* the court held that the perpetrator's wife had a duty to prevent her husband from using her residence as a place for conducting drug operations. Do you agree with the court's conclusion? Note that at the time of the commission of the offense the defendant was separated from her husband and she had exclusive possession over the residence where the offense took place. Do you believe that the outcome would be different if both spouses shared possession over the premises? What result if the perpetrator was merely a friend of the person with exclusive possession over the premises? Would the exclusive possessor of the property have a special duty to prevent the offense even if he is not related to the perpetrator?

5. A more complicated case of complicity by omission arises when a police officer witnesses and fails to prevent the commission of a serious crime such as robbery, burglary or homicide. The court in *Porter* pointed out that the drafters of the Model Penal Code suggested that a "police officer or watchman who closes his eyes to a robbery or burglary [and] fails to present an obstacle to its commission" should be held liable as an accomplice as long as they act with the purpose of promoting or facilitating the perpetration of the crime. While there is scant case law on this issue, the high court of Puerto Rico held in *Pueblo v. Sustache,* 176 D.P.R. 250 (2009), that a police officer may be held liable as an accomplice to homicide if he failed to prevent the killing of an innocent human being and he had enough time to do so. Note that the examples mentioned in *Porter* involve police officers who fail to prevent serious crimes, such as robbery and burglary. Similarly, the aforementioned Puerto Rican case dealt with a police officer who failed to prevent a murder. In light of the gravity of such offenses, it is fairly easy to impose accessorial liability in these cases. Nevertheless, should an officer be held liable as an accomplice for failing to prevent less serious offenses, such as simple assaults or petty thefts? Explain.

6. The accomplice's conduct does not have to be a "but for" cause of the resulting harm in order for accessorial liability to attach. An actor is thus liable as an accomplice even if the perpetrator would have committed the offense without his help. The leading case in this regard is *State ex rel. Attorney General v. Tally, Judge,* 102 Ala. 25, 15, So. 722 (1894). Two brothers set out to kill the victim. A relative of the victim sent him a telegram warning him that the two brothers were looking for him. Judge Tally intercepted the telegram and prevented it from reaching the victim. The two brothers caught up with the victim and killed him. Judge Tally was charged with aiding and abetting the killing. Judge Tally argued that he should not be convicted as an accomplice because the victim would have likely been killed regardless of whether he intercepted the telegram. The court rejected the argument because:

> The assistance given ... need not contribute to the criminal result in the sense that but for it the result would not have ensued. It is quite sufficient if it facilitated a result that would have transpired without it. It is quite enough if the aid

> merely rendered it easier for the principal actor to accomplish the end intended by him and the aider and abettor, though in all human probability the end would have been attained without it. If the aid in homicide can be shown to have put the deceased at a disadvantage, to have deprived him of a single chance of life which but for it he would have had, he who furnishes such aid is guilty, though it cannot be known or shown that the dead man, in the absence thereof, would have availed himself of that chance; as, where one counsels murder, he is guilty as an accessory before the fact, though it appears to be probable that murder would have been done without his counsel; and as, where one being present by concert to aid if necessary is guilty as a principal in the second degree, though, had he been absent murder would have been committed, so, where he who facilitates murder even by so much as destroying a single chance of life the assailed might otherwise have had, he thereby supplements the efforts of the perpetrator, and he is guilty as principal in the second degree at common law, and is principal in the first degree under our statute, notwithstanding it may be found that in all human probability the chance would not have been availed of, and death would have resulted anyway. *Tally, Judge,* 102 Ala. 25, 15, So. 722.

Do you agree that accomplice liability is appropriate even when the resulting harm would have taken place without the accomplice's conduct?

7. Not only is it not necessary that the accomplice's conduct be a "but for" cause of the resulting harm, but the modern trend is to impose accomplice liability on actors who try to render assistance to the perpetrator even if they did not actually facilitate the commission of the offense. In *State v. Doody,* for example, the defendant argued that she could not be held liable as an accomplice to murder because the principal did not use the car that she made available to him for the execution of his plans. The court rejected the argument, holding that "it is immaterial that, in the course of actually committing the crime, [the defendant] did not have occasion to avail himself of appellant's proffered aid." 434 A.2d 253 (1981). The same result is accomplished in many state jurisdictions by statutes that expressly punish "attempts to aid" as complicity. The Hawaii complicity statute, for example, prescribes that:

> HRS § 702-222—A person is an accomplice of another person in the commission of an offense if:
>
> 1) With the intention of promoting or facilitating the commission of the offense, the person:
>
>     b) ... Aids or agrees or *attempts to aid* the other person in planning or committing it....
>
> According to the comments to the statute,
>
> "[T]he [criminalization] of attempts to aid seems entirely proper." Acquittal should not be had upon a showing of ineffective aid. "Where complicity is based upon agreement or encouragement, one does not ask for evidence that they were actually operative psychologically on the person who committed the offense; there ought to be no difference in the case of aid." HRS § 702-222.

Do you agree that attempts to aid should be criminalized? Assuming that they should, do you believe that attempts to aid ought to be punished as severely as providing actual assistance? Explain.

8. Accessorial liability is also imposed when an actor incites, counsels, commands, procures or solicits another to commit an offense. Furthermore, those who request an-

other to commit a crime may be held liable for the freestanding inchoate offense of "solicitation" if the offense is not actually carried out by the solicited person.

9. A person who incites or causes an innocent or irresponsible agent to commit a crime is typically held liable for the offense as a perpetrator rather than as an accomplice. This is often referred to as the "innocent agent doctrine." *See, e.g., McAlevy v. Commonwealth,* 44 Va.App. 318 (2004). The irresponsible agent may be innocent for various reasons. The most common are either because his conduct is excused as a result of a defense of insanity or infancy, or because he fails to act with the degree of culpability that is necessary to satisfy the elements of the offense charged. An example of the former is the case of *Johnson v. State,* 38 So. 182 (1904), in which an Alabama court held that the person who incited an insane person to kill is guilty as a perpetrator in much the same way as if he had committed the crime himself. Another example is *Rouse v. Commonwealth,* 303 S.W.2d 265 (Ky. 1957), which involved a child who was forced to operate a vehicle recklessly. An example of the latter is *United States v. Kenofskey,* 243 U.S. 440 (1917), in which a person was held to commit mail fraud by causing a person to mail a letter that unbeknownst to him contained a fraudulent life insurance death claim.

10. The actor who causes an innocent person to commit the crime is liable on the basis of his own culpability rather than on the basis of the culpability of the person that he used to commit the offense. Thus, for example, a person who recklessly causes a child to kill purposely (by giving the child a gun, for example) is liable for reckless homicide rather than for a purposeful homicide. Similarly, a person who negligently causes an innocent person to make false statements in exchange for property is not liable for theft by false pretenses because he does not act with the purpose to make false statements (or cause someone else to make false statements).

## § 10.03 Complicity: Subjective Elements (*Mens Rea*) with Regard to the Conduct Element of the Offense

### People v. Beeman

Supreme Court of California, 1984
35 Cal.3d 547

REYNOSO, Justice.

Timothy Mark Beeman appeals from a judgment of conviction of robbery, burglary, false imprisonment, destruction of telephone equipment and assault with intent to commit a felony. Appellant was not present during commission of the offenses. His conviction rested on the theory that he aided and abetted his acquaintances James Gray and Michael Burk.

The primary issue before us is whether the standard California Jury Instructions (CALJIC Nos. 3.00 and 3.01) adequately inform the jury of the criminal intent required to convict a defendant as an aider and abettor of the crime.

We hold that instruction No. 3.01 is erroneous. Sound law, embodied in a long line of California decisions, requires proof that an aider and abettor rendered aid with an intent or purpose of either committing, or of encouraging or facilitating commission of, the target offense. It was, therefore, error for the trial court to refuse the modified instruction requested by appellant. Our examination of the record convinces us that the error in this case was prejudicial and we therefore reverse appellant's convictions.

James Gray and Michael Burk drove from Oakland to Redding for the purpose of robbing appellant's sister-in-law, Mrs. Marjorie Beeman, of valuable jewelry, including a 3.5 carat diamond ring. They telephoned the residence to determine that she was home. Soon thereafter Burk knocked at the door of the victim's house, presented himself as a poll taker, and asked to be let in. When Mrs. Beeman asked for identification, he forced her into the hallway and entered. Gray, disguised in a ski mask, followed. The two subdued the victim, placed tape over her mouth and eyes and tied her to a bathroom fixture. Then they ransacked the house, taking numerous pieces of jewelry and a set of silverware. The jewelry included a 3.5 carat, heart-shaped diamond ring and a blue sapphire ring. The total value of these two rings was over $100,000. In the course of the robbery, telephone wires inside the house were cut.

Appellant was arrested six days later in Emeryville. He had in his possession several of the less valuable of the stolen rings. He supplied the police with information that led to the arrests of Burk and Gray. With Gray's cooperation appellant assisted police in recovering most of the stolen property.

Burk, Gray and appellant were jointly charged. After the trial court severed the trials, Burk and Gray pled guilty to robbery. At appellant's trial they testified that he had been extensively involved in planning the crime.

Burk testified that he had known appellant for two and one-half years. He had lived in appellant's apartment several times. Appellant had talked to him about rich relatives in Redding and had described a diamond ring worth $50,000. According to Burk the feasibility of robbing appellant's relatives was first mentioned two and one-half months before the incident occurred. About one week before the robbery, the discussions became more specific. Appellant gave Burk the address and discussed the ruse of posing as a poll taker. It was decided that Gray and Burk would go to Redding because appellant wanted nothing to do with the actual robbery and because he feared being recognized. On the night before the offense appellant drew a floor plan of the victim's house and told Burk where the diamond ring was likely to be found. Appellant agreed to sell the jewelry for 20 percent of the proceeds.

After the robbery was completed, Burk telephoned appellant to report success. Appellant said that he would call the friend who might buy the jewelry. Burk and Gray drove to appellant's house and showed him the "loot." Appellant was angry that the others had taken so much jewelry, and demanded that his cut be increased from 20 percent to one-third....

Appellant Beeman's testimony contradicted that of Burk ... as to nearly every material element of his own involvement. Appellant testified that he did not participate in the robbery or its planning. He confirmed that Burk had lived with him on several occasions, and that he had told Burk about Mrs. Beeman's jewelry, the valuable diamond ring, and the Beeman ranch, in the course of day-to-day conversations. He claimed that he had sketched a floor plan of the house some nine months prior to the robbery, only for the purpose of comparing it with the layout of a house belonging to another brother. He at first denied and then admitted describing the Beeman family cars, but insisted this never occurred in the context of planning a robbery.

Appellant stated that Burk first suggested that robbing Mrs. Beeman would be easy some five months before the incident. At that time, and on the five or six subsequent occasions when Burk raised the subject, appellant told Burk that his friends could do what they wanted but that he wanted no part of such a scheme.

Beeman admitted Burk had told him of the poll taker ruse within a week before the robbery, and that Burk told him they had bought a cap gun and handcuffs. He further admitted that he had allowed Burk to take some old clothes left at the apartment by a former roommate. At that time Beeman told Burk: "If you're going to do a robbery, you can't look like a bum." Nevertheless, appellant explained that he did not know Burk was then planning to commit this robbery. Further, although he knew there was a possibility Burk and Gray would try to rob Mrs. Beeman, appellant thought it very unlikely they would go through with it. He judged Burk capable of committing the crime but knew he had no car and no money to get to Redding. Appellant did not think Gray would cooperate.

Appellant agreed that he had talked with Gray on the phone two days before the robbery, and said he had then repeated he did not want to be involved. He claimed that Burk called him on the way back from Redding because he feared appellant would report him to the police, but knew appellant would want to protect Gray, who was his closer friend.

Appellant claimed he told the others to come to his house after the robbery and offered to sell the jewelry in order to buy time in which to figure out a way to collect and return the property. He took the most valuable piece to make sure it was not sold. Since Burk had a key to his apartment, appellant gave the diamond ring and a bracelet to a friend, Martinez, for safekeeping. After Burk fled to Los Angeles, appellant showed some of the jewelry to mutual acquaintances in order to lull Burk into believing he was attempting to sell it. During this time Burk called him on the phone several times asking for money and, when appellant told him of plans to return the property, threatened to have him killed.

When confronted with his prior statement to the police that he had given one of the rings to someone in exchange for a $50 loan, appellant admitted making the statement but denied that it was true....

Appellant requested that the jury be instructed in accord with *People v. Yarber* that aiding and abetting liability requires proof of intent to aid. The request was denied.

After three hours of deliberation, the jury submitted two written questions to the court: "We would like to hear again how one is determined to be an accessory and by what actions can he absolve himself;" and "Does inaction mean the party is guilty?" The jury was reinstructed in accord with the standard instructions, CALJIC Nos. 3.00 and 3.01. The court denied appellant's renewed request that the instructions be modified as suggested in *Yarber,* explaining that giving another, slightly different instruction at this point would further complicate matters. The jury returned its verdicts of guilty on all counts two hours later.

Penal Code section 31 provides in pertinent part: "All persons concerned in the commission of a crime, ... whether they directly commit the act constituting the offense, or aid and abet in its commission, or, not being present, have advised and encouraged its commission, ... are principals in any crime so committed." Thus, those persons who at common law would have been termed accessories before the fact and principals in the second degree as well as those who actually perpetrate the offense, are to be prosecuted, tried and punished as principals in California. The term "aider and abettor" is now often used to refer to principals other than the perpetrator, whether or not they are present at the commission of the offense.

CALJIC No. 3.00 defines principals to a crime to include "Those who, with knowledge of the unlawful purpose of the one who does directly and actively commit or attempt to commit the crime, aid and abet in its commission..., or ... Those who, whether present or not at the commission or attempted commission of the crime, advise and encourage its commission...." CALJIC No. 3.01 defines aiding and abetting as follows: "A person aids and abets the commission of a crime if, with knowledge of the unlawful purpose of the perpetrator of the crime, he aids, promotes, encourages or instigates by act or advice the commission of such crime."

Prior to 1974 CALJIC No. 3.01 read: "A person aids and abets the commission of a crime if he knowingly and with criminal intent aids, promotes, encourages or instigates by act or advice, or by act and advice, the commission of such crime."

Appellant asserts that the current instructions, in particular CALJIC No. 3.01, substitute an element of knowledge of the perpetrator's intent for the element of criminal intent of the accomplice, in contravention of common law principles and California case law. He argues that the instruction given permitted the jury to convict him of the same offenses as the perpetrators without finding that he harbored either the same criminal intent as they, or the specific intent to assist them, thus depriving him of his constitutional rights to due process and equal protection of the law. Appellant further urges that the error requires reversal because it removed a material issue from the jury and on this record it is impossible to conclude that the jury necessarily resolved the same factual question that would have been presented by the missing instruction.

The People argue that the standard instruction properly reflects California law, which requires no more than that the aider and abettor have knowledge of the perpetrator's criminal purpose and do a voluntary act which in fact aids the perpetrator. The People further contend that defendants are adequately protected from conviction for acts committed under duress or which inadvertently aid a perpetrator by the limitation of the liability of an aider and abettor to those acts knowingly aided and their natural and reasonable consequences. Finally, the People argue that the modification proposed by *Yarber, supra,* is unnecessary because proof of intentional aiding in most cases can be inferred from aid with knowledge of the perpetrator's purpose. Thus, respondent argues, it is doubtful that the requested modification would bring about different results in the vast majority of cases.

## II.

There is no question that an aider and abettor must have criminal intent in order to be convicted of a criminal offense. Decisions of this court dating back to 1898 hold that "the word 'abet' includes knowledge of the wrongful purpose of the perpetrator *and* counsel and encouragement in the crime" and that it is therefore error to instruct a jury that one may be found guilty as a principal if one aided *or* abetted. The act of encouraging or counseling itself implies a purpose or goal of furthering the encouraged result. "An aider and abettor's fundamental purpose, motive and intent is to aid and assist the perpetrator in the latter's commission of the crime."

The essential conflict in current appellate opinions is between those cases which state that an aider and abettor must have an intent or purpose to commit or assist in the commission of the criminal offenses and those finding it sufficient that the aider and abettor engage in the required acts with knowledge of the perpetrator's criminal purpose....

[Editor's Note: After surveying the conflicting California case law regarding whether accomplice's need to act with knowledge or purpose to assist the perpetrator, the Court held that:]

[Liability for complicity] requires that in addition to knowing of the perpetrator's criminal purpose the aider and abettor *at least realize* he or she is aiding commission of the crime. Moreover, the opinion states the general legal principles governing accomplice liability in the language of the older pre-1974 cases:

> Criminal liability as a principal attaches to those who aid in the commission of a crime only if they also share in the criminal intent, or, in the language of section 31, abet the crime. [Defendant] was thus an accomplice only if at the time she acted she had "guilty knowledge and intent with regard to the commission of the crime."

We agree with [what was held by the court in the *Yarber* case] that the facts from which a mental state may be inferred must not be confused with the mental state that the prosecution is required to prove. Direct evidence of the mental state of the accused is rarely available except through his or her testimony. The trier of fact is and must be free to disbelieve the testimony and to infer that the truth is otherwise when such an inference is supported by circumstantial evidence regarding the actions of the accused. Thus, an act which has the effect of giving aid and encouragement, and which is done with knowledge of the criminal purpose of the person aided, may indicate that the actor intended to assist in fulfillment of the known criminal purpose. However, as illustrated by *Hicks v. U.S.* (1893) (conviction reversed because jury not instructed that words of encouragement must have been used with the intention of encouraging and abetting crime in a case where ambiguous gesture and remark may have been acts of desperation) and *People v. Bolanger* (1886) (feigned accomplice not guilty because lacks common intent with the perpetrator to unite in the commission of the crime), the act may be done with some other purpose which precludes criminal liability....

Thus, we conclude that the weight of authority and sound law require proof that an aider and abettor act with knowledge of the criminal purpose of the perpetrator *and* with an intent or purpose either of committing, or of encouraging or facilitating commission of, the offense.

When the definition of the offense includes the intent to do some act or achieve some consequence beyond the *actus reus* of the crime (*See, People v. Hood* (1969)), the aider and abettor must share the specific intent of the perpetrator. By "share" we mean neither that the aider and abettor must be prepared to commit the offense by his or her own act should the perpetrator fail to do so, nor that the aider and abettor must seek to share the fruits of the crime. Rather, an aider and abettor will "share" the perpetrator's specific intent when he or she knows the full extent of the perpetrator's criminal purpose and gives aid or encouragement with the intent or purpose of facilitating the perpetrator's commission of the crime. The liability of an aider and abettor extends also to the natural and reasonable consequences of the acts he knowingly and intentionally aids and encourages.

CALJIC No. 3.01 inadequately defines aiding and abetting because it fails to insure that an aider and abettor will be found to have the required mental state with regard to his or her own act. While the instruction does include the word "abet," which encompasses the intent required by law, the word is arcane and its full import unlikely to be recognized by modern jurors. Moreover, even if jurors were made aware that "abet" means to encourage or facilitate, and implicitly to harbor an intent to further the crime encouraged, the instruction does not *require* them to find that intent because it defines an aider and abettor as one who "aids, promotes, encourages *or* instigates" (emphasis added). Thus, as one appellate court recently recognized, the instruction would "technically allow a conviction if the defendant knowing of the perpetrator's unlawful purpose, negligently or accidentally aided the commission of the crime." ...

We suggest that an appropriate instruction should inform the jury that a person aids and abets the commission of a crime when he or she, acting with (1) knowledge of the unlawful purpose of the perpetrator, and (2) the intent or purpose of committing, encouraging, or facilitating the commission of the offense, (3) by act or advice aids, promotes, encourages or instigates, the commission of the crime.

III.

... The jury certainly could have believed Burk and Gray while disbelieving appellant, and thus found that appellant intentionally aided and encouraged his friends in their crimes. However, the fact that the jury interrupted its deliberations to seek further instruction regarding accomplice liability indicates that the jurors did not dismiss appellant's testimony out of hand. Rather, the questions asked indicate the jury's deliberations were focused on the very issue upon which the defense rested and upon which the court's instructions were inadequate: the elements—including the mental element—of aiding and abetting. When it reinstructed the jury according to the standard instructions and again refused the *Yarber* modification requested by appellant, the court repeated its original mistake.

Under these circumstances, where the defense centered on the very element as to which the jury was inadequately instructed and the jurors' communication to the court indicated confusion on the same point, we cannot find the error harmless.... [W]e find that in this case it is reasonably probable that the jury would have reached a result more favorable to appellant had it been correctly instructed upon the mental element of aiding and abetting....

The convictions are reversed.

## Backun v. United States

United States Court of Appeals, Fourth Circuit, 1940
112 F.2d 635

PARKER, Circuit Judge.

This is an appeal from a conviction and sentence under an indictment charging the appellant Backun and one Zucker with the crime of transporting stolen merchandise of a value in excess of $5,000 in interstate commerce, knowing it to have been stolen, in violation of the National Stolen Property Act, 18 U.S.C.A. 415. Zucker pleaded guilty and testified for the prosecution. There was evidence to the effect that he was apprehended at a pawnshop in Charlotte, N.C., in possession of a large quantity of silverware, a portion of which was shown to have been stolen a short while before. He testified that he purchased all of the silverware from Backun in New York; that the purchase was partly on credit; that Backun had the silverware concealed in a closet and in the cellar of his residence; that there was no sale for second hand silverware in New York but a good market for it in the South; that Backun knew of Zucker's custom to travel in the South and was told by Zucker that he wished to take the silverware on the road with him; and that Backun sold to him for $1,400 silverware which was shown by other witnesses to be of a much greater value. A part of the silverware was wrapped in a laundry bag which was identified by means of a laundry ticket as having been in the possession of Backun....

There is no serious controversy as to the evidence being sufficient to show that Backun sold the property to Zucker knowing it to have been stolen. It is contended, however ... that there is no evidence that Backun had anything to do with the transportation in interstate commerce....

Whether one who sells property to another knowing that the buyer intends to use it for the commission of a felony renders himself criminally liable as aiding and abetting in its commission, is a question as to which there is some conflict of authority. *See United States v. Falcone.* It must be remembered, however, that guilt as accessory before the fact has application only in cases of felony; and since it is elementary that every citizen is under moral obligation to prevent the commission of felony, if possible, and has the legal right to use force to prevent its commission and to arrest the perpetrator without warrant, it is difficult to see why, in selling goods which he knows will make its perpetration possible with knowledge that they are to be used for that purpose, he is not aiding and abetting in its commission within any fair meaning of those terms. Undoubtedly he would be guilty, were he to give to the felon the goods which make the perpetration of the felony possible with knowledge that they would be used for that purpose; and we cannot see that his guilt is purged or his breach of social duty excused because he receives a price for them. In either case, he knowingly aids and assists in the perpetration of the felony.

Guilt as an accessory depends, not on "having a stake" in the outcome of crime, as suggested in the Falcone case, supra, but on aiding and assisting the perpetrators; and those who make a profit by furnishing to criminals, whether by sale or otherwise, the means to carry on their nefarious undertakings aid them just as truly as if they were actual partners with them, having a stake in the fruits of their enterprise. To say that the sale of goods is a normally lawful transaction is beside the point. The seller may not ignore the purpose for which the purchase is made if he is advised of that purpose, or wash his hands of the aid that he has given the perpetrator of a felony by the plea that he has merely made a sale of merchandise. One who sells a gun to another knowing that he is buying it to commit a murder, would hardly escape conviction as an accessory to the murder by showing that he received full price for the gun; and no difference in principle can be drawn between such a case and any other case of a seller who knows that the purchaser intends to use the goods which he is purchasing in the commission of felony. In any such case, not only does the act of the seller assist in the commission of the felony, but his will assents to its commission, since he could refuse to give the assistance by refusing to make the sale. This is the view taken of the matter in a number of well considered cases in the federal courts. It is in harmony with the well settled rule that one who, with knowledge of the existence of a conspiracy, aids in carrying out its unlawful design makes himself a party thereto.

A case very much in point is *Anstess v. United States*, 7 Cir., 22 F.2d 594, 595. In that case it was held that one who sells contraband whiskey to another with knowledge that the purchaser intends to transport it unlawfully participates in the purchaser's plan to transport. The court said: "If one, having possession of contraband goods, knowing that another desires to purchase those goods for the purpose of unlawfully transporting them, sells them to that person, he furnishes him the means for committing the crime. One who, with full knowledge of the purpose with which contraband goods are to be used, furnishes those goods to another to so use them, actively participates in the scheme or plan to so use them."...

[Editor's Note: In an omitted portion of the opinion, the court reversed defendant's conviction and remanded case for a new trial because the State failed to prove that defendant knew stolen goods were worth more than $5,000.]

## United States v. Peoni

United States Court of Appeals, Second Circuit, 1938
100 F.2d 401

L. HAND, Circuit Judge.

Peoni was indicted in the Eastern District of New York upon three counts for possessing counterfeit money, and upon one for conspiracy to possess it. The jury convicted him on all counts, and the only question we need consider is whether the evidence was enough to sustain the verdict. It was this. In the Borough of the Bronx Peoni sold counterfeit bills to one, Regno; and Regno sold the same bills to one, Dorsey, also in the Bronx. All three knew that the bills were counterfeit, and Dorsey was arrested while trying to pass them in the Borough of Brooklyn. The question is whether Peoni was guilty as an accessory to Dorsey's possession, and whether he was party to a conspiracy by which Dorsey should possess the bills.

The prosecution's argument is that, as Peoni put the bills in circulation and knew that Regno would be likely, not to pass them himself, but to sell them to another guilty possessor, the possession of the second buyer was a natural consequence of Peoni's original act, with which he might be charged. If this were a civil case, that would be true; an innocent buyer from Dorsey could sue Peoni and get judgment against him for his loss. But the rule of criminal liability is not the same; since Dorsey's possession was not de facto Peoni's, and since Dorsey was not Peoni's agent, Peoni can be liable only as an accessory to Dorsey's act of possession....

It will be observed that [liability as an accessory has] nothing whatever to do with the probability that the forbidden result would follow upon the accessory's conduct; and that [it] demand[s] that [the actor] in some sort associate himself with the venture, that he participate in it as in something that he wishes to bring about, that he seek by his action to make it succeed. [T]he words used [to describe accessorial liability]—even the most colorless, "abet"—carry an implication of purposive attitude towards it. So understood, Peoni was not an accessory to Dorsey's possession; his connection with the business ended when he got his money from Regno, who might dispose of the bills as he chose; it was of no moment to him whether Regno passed them himself, and so ended the possibility of further guilty possession, or whether he sold them to a second possible passer. His utterance of the bills was indeed a step in the causal chain which ended in Dorsey's possession, but that was all....

Conviction reversed; accused discharged.

### *Notes and Questions*

1. The conflicting jury instructions that the Supreme Court of California court had to reconcile in *People v. Beeman* highlight an issue that has generated considerable debate amongst American courts and commentators. According to California Jury Instruction (CALJIC) 3.00, a person is guilty of complicity if he aids or abets in the commission of an offense "*with knowledge* of the unlawful purpose of the one who does directly and actively commit or attempt to commit the crime." In contrast, CALJIC 3.01 defined an accomplice as a person who "knowingly and *with criminal intent* aids, promotes, encourages or instigates ... the commission of [a] crime." Is it enough for accomplice liability that—as CALJIC 3.00 holds—the actor render aid *with knowledge* that he is helping the perpetrator consummate the offense? Or must he have—as CALJIC 3.01 requires—the *purpose or intent* of assisting the commission of the crime? In *Beeman* the court opted for

the latter view of accomplice liability. That is, the court concluded that an actor may be held liable as an accessory only if has "the intent or purpose of committing, encouraging, or facilitating the commission of the offense." Mere knowledge that the conduct facilitates the commission of the offense is thus not sufficient to generate accessorial liability.

2. The view espoused by the court in *Beeman* is followed in the vast majority of American jurisdictions. Nevertheless, there is authority in a handful of states in favor of the proposition that an actor may be held liable as an accomplice if she has knowledge that her conduct aids the principal in the commission of the offense. The Indiana complicity statute, for example, defines an accessory as "[a] person who *knowingly* or intentionally aids, induces, or causes another person to commit an offense" (emphasis added). IC 35-41-2-4. The statute imposes accomplice liability for "(1) doing some act, (2) knowing that the act will aid the perpetrator." *Tippit v. State,* 266 Ind. 517 (1977). The position was forcefully defended in the excerpted case of *Backun v. United States,* where it was stated that:

> One who sells a gun to another knowing that he is buying it to commit a murder, would hardly escape conviction as an accessory to the murder by showing that he received full price for the gun; and no difference in principle can be drawn between such a case and any other case of a seller who knows that the purchaser intends to use the goods which he is purchasing in the commission of felony. *Id.*

Note that selling a handgun knowing that it will be used to commit a murder would not give rise to accessorial liability under the view put forth in *Beeman,* which is followed in most states. Should such knowing assistance be punishable even if not done with the purpose to assist the commission of an offense? Explain. According to Judge Learned Hand's opinion in *Peoni*, knowledge is not sufficient to establish accessorial liability because the terms "aiding" and "abetting" the crime "carry an implication of purposive attitude towards" the commission of the offense. As a result, Judge Hand argues that complicity "demand[s] that [the actor] in some sort associate himself with the venture, that he participate in it as in something that he wishes to bring about, that he seek by his action to make it succeed." Do you find this argument convincing? Why or why not?

3. Whether knowing assistance should give rise to criminal liability is a pressing issue in international criminal law. Suppose that someone sells weapons to a military leader knowing that they will be used to commit genocide or a crime against humanity. Assuming that the weapons are in fact used to commit such crimes, may the supplier of weapons be held liable as an accomplice even if he did not have the desire or purpose to aid in the commission of the atrocities? There is authority in support of punishing knowing assistance in circumstances such as these. In *Prosecutor v. Akayesu,* for example, the Trial Chamber of the International Criminal Tribunal for Rwanda held that "anyone who knowing of another's criminal purpose, voluntarily aids him or her in it, can be convicted of complicity even though he regretted the outcome of the offence." *Prosecutor v. Akayesu*, Judgment, No. ICTR-96-4-T (ICTR Trial Chamber Sept. 2, 1998) (P. 539). Do you agree that knowing assistance should be punished under international criminal law? For a discussion of the *mens rea* of accomplice liability for international crimes, *see generally*, Jens David Ohlin, *The Torture Lawyers,* 51 Harv. Int'l. L. J. 193, 196–197 (2010).

4. A few states have adopted the compromise position of creating separate offenses that punish knowing assistance less severely than purposeful complicity. The Kentucky "criminal facilitation" statute is representative:

> A person is guilty of criminal facilitation when, acting with knowledge that another person is committing or intends to commit a crime, he engages in con-

> duct which knowingly provides such person with means or opportunity for the commission of the crime and which in fact aids such person to commit the crime. KRS § 506.080

The origins and scope of the criminal facilitation provision are explained by the Kentucky Crime Commission as follows:

> This provision, borrowed from the New York Penal Law, provides sanctions for conduct such as that reflected in the following two hypothetical cases. In the first, the "offender" sells large quantities of sugar and malt to illegal distillers with knowledge of their illegal intentions. He knows that his conduct makes it possible for the offense to be committed, but, at the same time, he has no intention to further the criminal objective. In the second, the "offender," a druggist, sells poisonous substances to a woman with knowledge that she intends to poison her husband. As in the first case, the actor knows that his conduct facilitates commission of the offense but he has no intention to promote or contribute to its fruition.
>
> To be guilty of the offense of facilitation, an individual must facilitate the commission of a crime that is actually committed. If that crime is one defined in this Code as a Class A or B felony, the facilitation offense is classified as a Class D felony; if the crime is one defined as a Class C or D felony, the facilitation offense is a Class A misdemeanor; and if the crime is one defined as a misdemeanor, the facilitation offense is a Class B misdemeanor. The culpable mental state for the offense of facilitation is twofold: knowledge of the criminal purpose of the person facilitated and knowledge that the conduct in question is providing the means or opportunity for commission of the underlying offense.

Which of the following approaches is the best way of dealing with knowing facilitation: (1) not punishing it (*Beeman* and *Peoni* approach), (2) punishing it as severely as purposeful assistance (*Backun* approach), or (3) criminalizing it but punishing it less than purposeful complicity (separate criminal facilitation offense approach)? Explain.

5. Note that the conduct element of criminal facilitation is heightened in comparison to the conduct element of standard accomplice liability. While any assistance, however trivial, suffices to satisfy the conduct element of standard accomplice liability, criminal facilitation statutes require that the aid rendered consist in either providing the means to commit the offense or the opportunity to do so. This reflects the anxiety that watering down the *mens rea* for punishing someone for assisting another's crime may cast the net of criminal liability too wide. In response, the lowered *mens rea* is met with a corresponding increase in the stringency of the *actus reus* requirement.

6. The Supreme Court of California asserted in *Beeman* that "[t]he liability of an aider and abettor extends also to the natural and reasonable consequences of the acts he ... intentionally aids and encourages." Pursuant to this doctrine, an actor who purposely aids a robbery may be held liable not only for the robbery, but also for the death of the victim of the crime, given that it is reasonably foreseeable that the victim of the robbery may be harmed or killed if he resists. The holding in *People v. Luparello*, 231 Cal.Rptr. 832 (1986), is illustrative of the scope of this doctrine. The defendant asked several acquaintances to extract information from the victim "at any cost." After unsuccessfully trying to get the information, the defendant's acquaintances killed the victim. Defendant was charged with being an accomplice to murder. The defendant claimed that his plan was merely to scare the victim. He further argued that he should not be held liable as an accomplice to murder because he did not have the purpose of killing the victim. The California Court of Appeals affirmed his conviction as an accomplice to murder, arguing that:

> [T]he aider and abettor in a proper case is not only guilty of the particular crime that to his knowledge his confederates are contemplating committing, but he is also liable for the natural and reasonable or probable consequences of any act that he knowingly aided or encouraged.... Applying this theory [to the facts of the present case], we again find factual support for [defendant's] criminal liability: he aided and abetted [his acquaintances] in the planned confrontation of [the victim] and the consequential assault naturally and reasonably resulted in [the victim's] death....
>
> Here, the evidence shows [defendant] had knowledge of [his acquaintance's] planned assault of [the victim], but does not clearly reveal his knowledge of the eventual murder. However, this knowledge, in contrast to [defendant's] contention, is not necessary. As an aider and abettor, [he] is responsible for the natural and probable consequences of the acts which he intentionally encourages. *Id.*

This approach has come to be known as the "natural and probable consequences doctrine." The doctrine is followed in several American jurisdictions. Thus, for example, the complicity statute in Maine prescribes that "[a] person is an accomplice ... to any crime the commission of which was a reasonably foreseeable consequence of the person's conduct." 17-A M.R.S.A. § 57(3)(a). Nevertheless, several courts reject the natural and probable consequences doctrine. According to one such court:

> Although, as we have noted, the courts in a minority of jurisdictions have applied a "natural and probable consequences" approach to accomplice liability, it is significant that some of these courts have recently shifted to a standard consistent with *Peoni.* In *Sharma,* for example, the Supreme Court of Nevada reversed the conviction of an alleged aider and abettor for attempted murder (which required a showing of specific intent to kill) because the jury received a "natural and probable consequences" instruction but was not told that the accomplice "must have aided and abetted the attempt *with the specific intent to kill*" (emphasis added). The court noted that the natural and probable consequences doctrine:
>
>> Has been harshly criticized by most commentators as both incongruous and unjust because it imposes accomplice liability solely upon proof of foreseeability or negligence when typically a higher degree of *mens rea* is required of the principal. It permits criminal liability to be predicated upon negligence even when the crime involved requires a different state of mind. Having reevaluated the wisdom of this doctrine, we have concluded that its general application in Nevada to specific intent crimes is unsound precisely for that reason: it permits conviction without proof that the accused possessed the state of mind required by the statutory definition of the crime.
>
> Thus, "in order for a person to be held accountable for the specific intent of another under an aiding and abetting theory of principal liability, the aider or abettor must have knowingly aided the other person with the intent that the other person commit the charged crime." *Id.* at 872. The court relied on the decision of the Supreme Court of New Mexico in *State v. Carrasco,* 124 N.M. 64, 946 P.2d 1075 (1997), in which the court likewise disavowed the "natural and probable consequences" doctrine and held that "an accessory must share the criminal intent of the principal." *Wilson Bey v. U.S.,* 903 A.2d 818 (2006).

Jurisdictions that reject the natural and probable consequences doctrine hold that "guilt or the degree of guilt should turn on the mental state of each participant in the crime" rather than on whether the crimes were reasonably foreseeable. *Id,* at 838. In other words, an accomplice is liable under this approach only for the crimes committed by the perpetrator that he intended to aid. If, on the other hand, the accomplice did not intend to aid the additional crimes, he can only be held liable for a less culpable version of the additional crimes committed by the perpetrator. If the accomplice was aware that the perpetrator might commit the additional crime, he could be held liable for a reckless version of the offense (if it exists). In contrast, if the accomplice should have been aware that the perpetrator might engage in the additional offense, he can be held liable for a negligent version of the offense (once again, if such an offense exists). Is this preferable than holding the accomplice liable for reasonably foreseeable crimes regardless of whether he intended them? Explain.

## § 10.04 Complicity: Subjective Elements (*Mens Rea*) with Regard to the Result and Circumstance Elements of the Offense

### Méndez v. State

Court of Criminal Appeals of Texas, 1979
575 S.W.2d 36

DOUGLAS, Judge.

Guadalupe Mendez was indicted for murder. The court directed a verdict of acquittal on the murder charge and the jury found him guilty of the lesser included offense of involuntary manslaughter. Punishment was assessed by the court at five years.

Mendez appeals contending essentially that the law of parties does not apply to the offense of involuntary manslaughter. In this respect he challenges both the charge and the sufficiency of the evidence.

The conviction arises out of a senseless and tragic series of events which occurred in suburban Houston on July 30, 1974. Mendez, William Robinson and Alfred Fuschak were drinking beer when Robinson suggested they shoot Ray Richmond because he had dated Robinson's girl friend. Appellant got a shotgun, the other two got rifles. They drove to Richmond's parents' house where Richmond lived. Richmond was not home at the time. They shot up a car outside the Richmond house and fired at least eight shots at the house. The trio then drove to the house of Tommy DeArman, an acquaintance who was "tight" about lending his car, and shot up his car. As they left DeArman's house, Robinson shot his rifle randomly at several houses. One of these shots hit Rafael Martinez as he slept in bed next to his wife. Martinez was able to ask his wife to call an ambulance and managed to get to the dining room before he slumped against the wall and died. When the police arrived, they found Martinez and observed a trail of blood from his bed to the dining room.

Appellant's confession was introduced. He and Fuschak testified that they tried to talk Robinson out of the shooting spree and that appellant did not shoot at the houses. According to their testimony, they continued in the shooting spree after trying to get Robinson to stop....

Appellant argues ... that there can be no accomplice to an involuntary manslaughter. He contends that since the principal who commits an involuntary manslaughter does not act with a specific intent he cannot be assisted by another.

In other jurisdictions which have considered this precise question, there is a clear trend to hold the law of parties applicable to involuntary manslaughter. In Wade v. State (Tennessee), the court had to decide if an individual could aid and abet in an involuntary manslaughter case. The court concluded:

> Involuntary manslaughter necessarily negatives, of course, any intent on the part of the accused to kill another, but does not negative an intent to do the unlawful act, or the act not strictly unlawful in itself, but done in an unlawful manner and without due caution. Hence, one may be an aider and abettor in involuntary manslaughter because of a common purpose to participate in the unlawful act the natural and probable result of which was to kill another.

Similarly, in *Black v. State* (Ohio), the court dealt with a situation where several police officers were engaged in target practice in a saloon, an act which was prohibited by statute. An innocent passerby was killed by one of the shots. The Black court sustained an involuntary manslaughter conviction and concluded:

> [I]n such a case the act of each while engaged in the unlawful act becomes the act of all, not merely as to the unlawful act, but as to all the proximate results that naturally and logically follow there from....

While other jurisdictions have dealt with this question, it is one of first impression before this Court. We must first look to our statutes. The gist of our involuntary manslaughter offense is reckless conduct. An individual is criminally responsible for the acts of another if he acts "with intent to promote or assist the commission of the offense" and in so doing "solicits, encourages, directs, aids, or attempts to aid the other person to commit the offense."...

In the instant case we are dealing with three individuals. It is entirely possible to intentionally solicit or assist an individual in committing a reckless act. We hold that the law of parties does apply to the substantive offense of involuntary manslaughter.

In the case at bar the evidence reflects that all three individuals were drinking, armed themselves, shot up two cars and then Robinson shot randomly at houses killing the deceased. Considering this evidence in the light most favorable to the prosecution, we conclude the jury was free to believe that appellant's actions involved him as a party to the offense.

There is no reversible error. The judgment is affirmed.

## *Notes and Questions*

1. Many—if not most—American jurisdictions hold that an actor may be held liable as an accomplice to the commission of an unintentional offense such as involuntary manslaughter. Properly understood, this does not dispense with the traditional requirement that the accomplice purposely encourage the commission of the crime. Rather, it clarifies that the accomplice need only purposely assist, facilitate or encourage the *conduct* that gives rise to the offense. In *Méndez,* for example, the defendant was held to have purposely encouraged the perpetrator's *shooting spree,* although he clearly did not have the purpose of killing the victim. Courts quite often rule that an actor can also be held liable as an accomplice to the commission of a negligent offense, as long as he purposely encouraged the conduct that gave rise to the harm and was negligent with regarding to the possibility of harm taking place. According to one court, complicity for a crime of negligence is appropriate when:

> [T]he complicitor [is] aware that the principal is engaging in conduct that grossly deviates from the standard of reasonable care and poses a substantial and

> unjustifiable risk of [harm] to another. In addition, he must aid or abet the principal in that conduct and, finally, [harm] must result from that conduct. A verdict of guilty of [a] criminally negligent [offense] on a theory of complicity, therefore, does not involve an intent to promote or facilitate an unintentional act. *People v. Wheeler,* 772 P.2d 101, 105 (Colo., 1989).

In contrast, some courts argue that it is logically inconsistent to hold that an actor can be held liable as an accomplice to a negligent crime. The view was expressed by the Supreme Court of Alabama in the following manner:

> The legislature has written that criminal negligence involves a failure to "perceive a substantial and unjustifiable risk." In contrast, an offense committed by way of complicity requires the specific "intent to promote or assist" in the commission of an offense. On the facts before us, it is clear to the Court that criminal liability based upon complicity and criminally negligent homicide are inconsistent. That is, specific intent to commit an offense is required to show complicity but is rejected by the statute on criminal negligence. Since, in this case, we find these two sections to be in conflict we hold that the conviction based on this theory is improper. *Ex Parte Howell,* 431 So.2d 1328 (1983).

Do you agree that it is logically problematic to punish an actor for purposely aiding a negligent crime? Explain.

2. What mental state must an accomplice have with regard to attendant circumstances? Suppose that a priest marries A and B without knowing that at the time of the ceremony B was still legally married to another person. While B is clearly guilty of bigamy, may the priest be held liable as an accomplice to bigamy if he was unaware that B was already married? Surprisingly, there is limited case law on the subject. In *Bowell v. State,* 728 P.2d 1220 (1986), the Court of Appeals of Alaska asserted that:

> In *Reynolds v. State,* we held that the state must prove a culpable mental state regarding the "circumstance"—lack of consent—in order to convict a principal of the offense of first-degree sexual assault. "In order to prove [sexual assault], the state must prove that the defendant knowingly engaged in sexual intercourse and recklessly disregarded his victim's lack of consent." Similar reasoning leads us to conclude that the state must prove the same element in order to convict a person of first-degree sexual assault as an accomplice. In other words, in order to convict Bowell as an accomplice of Thomas' first-degree sexual assault of B.S., the state was required to prove that Bowell knew that Thomas intended to engage in sexual intercourse with B.S., that he intentionally engaged in conduct facilitating Thomas' efforts, and that at the time he aided Thomas, he recklessly disregarded B.S.'s lack of consent to Thomas' overtures. *Bowell,* 728 P.2d 1220.

Returning to the bigamy example, if the prosecution must prove that the principal was aware that he was previously married in order to convict him of bigamy, the state must also prove that the accomplice had such awareness in order to convict him of complicity to bigamy. This assumes, of course, that the rule put forth in *Bowell* is applied to the bigamy case. By the same token, an accomplice must be allowed to raise any defense that the principal would be allowed to raise in order to negate the *mens rea* of the crime charged. Therefore, if someone tried for bigamy is allowed to raise a mistake defense based on the fact he was unaware that his previous marriage was still legally valid, an accomplice to bigamy must also be allowed to raise the same type of mistake defense. Thus, a California Court of Appeals stated in *People v. Yarber,* 153 Cal.Rptr. 975 (1979), that:

> The alleged aider and abettor may know the purpose of the perpetrator and take an action which aids him, and yet not be guilty of aiding and abetting because of the existence of a state of mind which negates intent, such as mistake of fact or mistake of law.... Thus, in a robbery case ... if A intends to rob a store of property which B (but not A) believes (honestly but mistakenly) is rightfully B's, and B knows A's purpose and aids him to rob the store, A would be guilty of robbery but B would not because B's mistake of law would negate an intent on his part to steal. Similarly, in a rape case, if A had sexual relations with C, a female, and B aided A with knowledge of his purpose but with the good faith belief, not shared by A, that C had consented to have sexual relations with A, A would be guilty but B would not because B's mistake of fact would negate his intent. *Id.*

## § 10.05 Complicity: Model Penal Code

### Model Penal Code § 2.06. Liability for Conduct of Another; Complicity

(1) A person is guilty of an offense if it is committed by his own conduct or by the conduct of another person for which he is legally accountable, or both.

(2) A person is legally accountable for the conduct of another person when:

(a) acting with the kind of culpability that is sufficient for the commission of the offense, he causes an innocent or irresponsible person to engage in such conduct; or

(b) he is made accountable for the conduct of such other person by the Code or by the law defining the offense; or

(c) he is an accomplice of such other person in the commission of the offense.

(3) A person is an accomplice of another person in the commission of an offense if:

(a) with the purpose of promoting or facilitating the commission of the offense, he

(i) solicits such other person to commit it, or

(ii) aids or agrees or attempts to aid such other person in planning or committing it, or

(iii) having a legal duty to prevent the commission of the offense, fails to make proper effort so to do; or

(b) his conduct is expressly declared by law to establish his complicity.

(4) When causing a particular result is an element of an offense, an accomplice in the conduct causing such result is an accomplice in the commission of that offense if he acts with the kind of culpability, if any, with respect to that result that is sufficient for the commission of the offense.

(5) A person who is legally incapable of committing a particular offense himself may be guilty thereof if it is committed by the conduct of another person for which he is legally accountable, unless such liability is inconsistent with the purpose of the provision establishing his incapacity.

(6) Unless otherwise provided by the Code or by the law defining the offense, a person is not an accomplice in an offense committed by another person if:

(a) he is a victim of that offense; or

(b) the offense is so defined that his conduct is inevitably incident to its commission; or

(c) he terminates his complicity prior to the commission of the offense and

(i) wholly deprives it of effectiveness in the commission of the offense; or

(ii) gives timely warning to the law enforcement authorities or otherwise makes proper effort to prevent the commission of the offense.

(7) An accomplice may be convicted on proof of the commission of the offense and of his complicity therein, though the person claimed to have committed the offense has not been prosecuted or convicted or has been convicted of a different offense or degree of offense or has an immunity to prosecution or conviction or has been acquitted.

## Commonwealth v. Roebuck

Supreme Court of Pennsylvania, 2011
612 Pa. 642

Justice SAYLOR.

In this appeal, we consider whether it is possible, as a matter of law, to be convicted as an accomplice to third-degree murder.

The complete factual background is somewhat cumbersome. For present purposes, it is enough to say the Commonwealth presented evidence that the victim was lured to an apartment complex, where he was ambushed, shot, and mortally wounded. Appellant participated, with others, in orchestrating the events, but he did not shoot the victim.

For his role, Appellant was charged with, among other offenses, murder of the third degree. As he did not physically perpetrate the homicide, the Commonwealth relied upon accomplice theory, which is codified in Section 306 of the Crimes Code along with other complicity-based accountability principles. The matter proceeded to a bench trial, and a verdict of guilt ensued.

On appeal, Appellant argued that there is no rational legal theory to support accomplice liability for third-degree murder. He rested his position on the following syllogism: accomplice liability attaches only where the defendant *intends* to facilitate or promote an underlying offense; third-degree murder is an *unintentional* killing committed with malice; therefore, to adjudge a criminal defendant guilty of third-degree murder as an accomplice would be to accept that the accused *intended* to aid an *unintentional* act, which is a logical impossibility.

The Superior Court did not directly refute either of the two premises underlying Appellant's argument, but it differed with the conclusion. Initially, the court recognized that the complicity statute defines "accomplice" in terms of intentional promotion or facilitation of "the commission of the offense." Nevertheless, the court highlighted the following statutory prescription pertaining to the requisite *mens rea* (or mental state):

> When causing a particular result is an element of an offense, an accomplice in the conduct causing such result is an accomplice in the commission of that offense, if he acts with the kind of culpability, if any, with respect to that result that is sufficient for the commission of the offense.

... In effect, the intermediate court held that complicity theory applies in third-degree murder scenarios—even if homicide was not the intended underlying crime—

where the intentional acts demonstrate a disregard for human life amounting to malice. Upon the appellate review of this and other claims, the judgment of sentence was affirmed.

This discretionary appeal was allowed to resolve Appellant's legal challenge to the application of complicity theory to murder of the third degree.

Presently, Appellant maintains that accomplice liability for third-degree murder is a legal anomaly in view of his impossibility syllogism. In passing, Appellant observes that Section 306 of the Pennsylvania Crimes Code was derived from the Model Penal Code (the "MPC" or the "Code")....

To provide appropriate context in considering the MPC's treatment of complicity theory, it is helpful to review some of the Code's core theoretical underpinnings. Also impacting on this discussion, the MPC does not employ the term "malice" in its treatment of the crime of murder, but rather, expresses the concept as "reckless[ness] under circumstances manifesting extreme indifference to the value of human life." Model Penal Code § 210.2(1)(b). To streamline the discourse, and particularly since Appellant's impossibility logic is grounded on the presence of unintended consequences flowing from an intentional act—and thus extends to any crime in which the *mens rea* pertaining to a necessary result is recklessness—much of the discussion below is framed in terms of recklessness.

## I. The Model Penal Code

### A. The Code Generally

In addressing the terms of the Model Penal Code, it is important to bear in mind that the Code employs an elements approach to substantive criminal law, which recognizes that a single offense definition may require different culpable mental states for each objective offense element. § 2.02, Explanatory Note ("The requirement of culpability applies to ***618* each 'material element' of the crime."). The MPC further narrows *mens rea* analysis by pruning from the lexicon a plethora of common-law culpability terms, leaving four core terms. *See id.* § 2.02(1) (indicating, subject to one express exception, that "a person is not guilty of an offense unless he acted purposely, knowingly, recklessly or negligently, as the law may require").

Conceptually, the MPC also recognizes three objective categories of offense elements—conduct, attendant circumstances, and result. The Code frequently distinguishes among these offense-element categories in its various prescriptions regarding which of the four levels of culpability must be established for any given offense element. *See generally id.* at 229–30 ("The question of which level of culpability suffices to establish liability must be addressed separately with respect to each material element, and will be resolved either by the particular definition of the offense or the general provisions of [Section 2.02].").

The Model Penal Code has had its share of detractors, and, certainly, it does not provide perfect formulations. For example, as relevant to Appellant's arguments, the Code has been criticized for failing to provide an adequate description and overlay relating the four levels of culpability (purposeful, knowing, reckless, negligent) to the objective element categories (conduct, attendant circumstances, result) in the context of particular offense elements. Such criticism has been leveled in the accomplice-liability setting. ("The greatest flaw in the Model Penal Code provision [directed to accomplice liability], and those provisions modeled after it, is their failure to specify all of the culpability requirements of the substantive offense that the accomplice must satisfy."). We bear these observations in mind in proceeding to address the Code's treatment of complicity theory.

### B. MPC Treatment of Accomplice Liability

The legal accountability of accomplices for the conduct of others is treated in 2.06 of the Code. *See* MODEL PENAL CODE § 2.06(2)(c) ("A person is legally accountable for the conduct of another person when ... he is an accomplice of such other person in the commission of the offense."). Two material passages follow, developing the meaning of the term "accomplice" and the requisite *mens rea,* as relevant to the present case:

3) A person is an accomplice of another person in the commission of an offense if ... with the purpose of promoting or facilitating the commission of the offense, he ... aids or agrees or attempts to aid such other person in planning or committing it.

4) When causing a particular result is an element of an offense, an accomplice in the conduct causing such result is an accomplice in the commission of that offense if he acts with the kind of culpability, if any, with respect to that result that is sufficient for the commission of the offense. *Id.* § 2.06 3, 4.

Section 206(4) thus prescribes that an accomplice may be held legally accountable where he is an "accomplice in the conduct"—or, in other words, aids another in planning or committing the conduct with the purpose of promoting or facilitating it—and acts with recklessness (*i.e.,* the "kind of culpability ... sufficient for the commission of" a reckless-result offense).

To the extent any aspect of this accountability scheme is unclear, ample clarification is provided in the explanatory note and commentary. As a threshold matter, the commentary explains that the term "commission of the offense," as used in Section 2.06(3), focuses on the *conduct,* not the result. *See id.* § 2.06, cmt. 6(b), at 310 ("Subsection 3(a) requires that the actor have the purpose of promoting or facilitating the commission of the offense, i.e., that *he have as his conscious objective the bringing about of conduct* that that the Code has declared to be criminal[.]" (emphasis added)). This diffuses any impression that an accomplice must always intend results essential to the completed crime. *See Wheeler,* 772 P.2d at 103 (explaining that the "'intent to promote or facilitate the commission of the offense'... does not include an intent that death occur even though the underlying crime ... has death as an essential element." The commentary then points to the fourth subsection as supplying the essential culpability requirement, as follows:

> One who solicits an end, or aids or agrees to aid in its achievement, is an accomplice in whatever means may be employed, insofar as they constitute or commit an offense fairly envisaged in the purposes of the association. But *when a wholly different crime has been committed, thus involving conduct not within the conscious objectives of the accomplice, he is not liable for it unless the case falls within the specific terms of Subsection (4).* MODEL PENAL CODE § 2.06, cmt. 6(b), at 311 (emphasis added).

According to the commentary, the purport of the fourth subsection is to hold the accomplice accountable for contributing to the conduct to the degree his culpability equals what is required to support liability of a principal actor....

For the above reasons, at least under the regime of the Model Penal Code, holding an accomplice criminally liable for a result requiring a mental state of recklessness is not theoretically impossible, as Appellant asserts. To the contrary, it is precisely the norm. *Accord Riley,* 60 P.3d at 221 ("With respect to offenses that require proof of a particular result, the government must prove that the accomplice acted with the culpable mental state that applies to that result, as specified in the underlying statute.").

**II. The Pennsylvania Crimes Code**

As Appellant indicates (albeit lacking the above elaboration), Section 306 of the Pennsylvania Crimes Code derives from the Model Penal Code. Furthermore, the provisions of the Crimes Code establishing legal accountability for accomplice conduct are materially identical to the corresponding terms of Section 206 of the MPC in all relevant respects.

We recognize that the Crimes Code does not contain the wealth of collateral explanatory material which accompanies the Model Penal Code, including the latter's extensive notes and commentaries. Nevertheless, we believe the text of the Pennsylvania statute is clear enough. In terms identical to those of Section 206 of the MPC, Section 306(d) of the Crimes Code directs the focus, for result-based elements, to the level of culpability required of a principal. *See* 18 Pa.C.S. § 306(d). *See generally Riley,* 60 P.3d at 214(explaining that a "great majority" of judicial decisions have followed the MPC in holding that an accomplice must not necessarily intend to cause the prohibited result (citations omitted)). In the present factual scenario, the purport is to avoid elevating a recklessness-oriented culpability requirement to a purposeful one relative to an accomplice. *Accord Anthony,* 861 A.2d at 775 ("[I]f the offense's mental state with respect to the result is something less than purposeful, the State need only establish the lesser *mens rea* on the part of the accomplice to prove him or her guilty of the offense."). The policy basis for such treatment is readily discernable, and a homicide committed with the degree of recklessness predicate to murder provides a paradigmatic example....

**V. Summary and Holding**

In summary, a conviction for murder of the third degree is supportable under complicity theory where the Commonwealth proves the accomplice acted with the culpable mental state required of a principal actor, namely, malice. In other words, the Pennsylvania Crimes Code legally, logically, and rationally imposes accomplice liability for depraved heart murder.

The judgment of the Superior Court is affirmed and jurisdiction is relinquished.

## *Notes and Questions*

1. As *Commonwealth v. Roebuck* illustrates, pursuant to Model Penal Code § 2.06(4) an actor may be held liable as an accomplice as long as he purposely encourages or assists the perpetrator's *conduct* and acts with whatever culpability regarding the result suffices for holding the principal liable for the offense. Consequently, the Code allows holding an accomplice liable for the commission of a negligent offense. This is compatible with the approach exemplified by the *Méndez v. State* decision, which was excerpted in the previous section.

2. The Code drafters deliberately decided to not express an opinion regarding what kind of culpability should be required of an accomplice with regard to offense elements that consist of attendant circumstances. The issue was discussed in Note 2 of § 10.04.

3. In accordance with § 2.06(7) of the Code, "[a]n accomplice may be convicted ... though the person claimed to have committed the offense has ... been convicted of a dif-

ferent offense or degree of offense." As a result, the accomplice can be convicted of a more serious offense than the perpetrator depending on whether he acted with a more culpable mental state than the perpetrator. This approach is best illustrated by the California case of *People v. McCoy*, 24 P.3d 1210, at 1216 (2001). The perpetrator in *McCoy* shot and killed the victim in the good faith but unreasonable belief that he was doing so in self-defense. Consequently, the perpetrator could at most be held liable for manslaughter because in California an unreasonable but good faith belief that force is necessary pursuant to self-defense reduces what would otherwise be murder to manslaughter. Does this mean that the defendant charged as an accomplice to the perpetrator's killing in *McCoy* may not be convicted of a more serious offense than manslaughter? The *McCoy* court ruled that there was no such bar and that the accomplice could be convicted of a more serious offense than the perpetrator because "when a person, with the mental state necessary for an aider and abettor, helps or induces another to kill, that person's guilt is determined by the combined acts of all the participants as well as that person's own *mens rea*." *Id.* Consequently, the Court held that "if that person's mens rea is more culpable than another's, that person's guilt may be greater even if the other might be deemed the actual perpetrator." *Id.* Do you find it appropriate to sometimes hold an accomplice liable for a more serious offense than the perpetrator? Explain.

4. An accomplice may also be liable for a less serious crime than the perpetrator. In *Moore v. Lowe,* for example, defendant hired an assassin to kill her husband. The court held that even if the perpetrator (the hired assassin) is guilty of murder because he acted with malice, the accomplice (the spouse who hired the killer) may be liable for the lesser offense of manslaughter if she hired the killer while under the heat of passion. 180 S.E. 1 (W. Va. 1935).

5. Subsection 6 of the Code's complicity provision provides a defense to an accomplice who terminates his participation in the crime in a timely fashion. In order for the accomplice's termination to defeat liability it must take place before the perpetrator consummates the crime. Furthermore, it must either "wholly deprive [his complicity] of effectiveness in the commission of the offense or give timely warning to law enforcement authorities or otherwise make proper efforts to prevent the commission of the offense." What amounts to sufficient termination depends on the type of assistance given by the perpetrator. If the aid given by the perpetrator consists in providing goods or services, a statement of withdrawal from the criminal enterprise is not generally sufficient to constitute termination. *See,* Comments to Model Penal Code § 2.06(6)(c), at 326. In such cases the accomplice must do what is necessary to get back the goods that he supplied or to deprive the services that he provided of effectiveness. In contrast, when the assistance provided by the accomplice was requesting that a crime be committed or encouraging the commission of an offense, "countermanding disapproval may suffice to nullify its influence, provided it is heard in time to allow reconsideration by those planning to commit the crime." *Id.* Sometimes the only thing that an accomplice can do to prevent the crime is to make independent efforts to stop the commission of the offense. In such cases, the accomplice may establish termination by alerting the police in a timely manner or by making other proper efforts to prevent the crime. *Id.*

6. Note that according to § 2.06(a)(3)(ii) of the Code, attempts to aid are punished as complicity regardless of whether they are successful. It is thus no defense that the perpetrator did not take advantage of the assistance provided by the accomplice or that the offense would have taken place regardless of the accomplice's help. Attempts to aid were discussed in § 10.02, Note 7.

## § 10.06 Complicity: Comparative Perspectives

### Spanish Penal Code
### On persons criminally responsible for felonies and misdemeanors

**Article 27**

Those criminally responsible for felonies and misdemeanors are ... principals and their accessories.

**Article 28**

Principals are those who perpetrate the [offense] themselves, [either on their own], jointly, or by [using another as an instrument for the commission of the offense].

The following shall also be deemed principals:

a) Whoever directly induces another or others to commit a crime;

b) Whoever cooperates in the commission [of a crime] by an act without which [the offense] crime could not have been committed.

**Article 29**

Accessories are those who, not being included in the preceding Article, cooperate in carrying out the offence....

**Article 63**

Accessories of a consummated or attempted crime shall be sentenced to a lower degree of crime than the principals of the same offence.

### *Notes and Questions*

1. Spanish criminal law punishes those who assist with "acts without which the offense would not have been committed" (Art. 28[b]) more than those who aid with conduct without which the offense would still have been consummated (Art. 29). Spanish courts and scholars thus distinguish between what they call "essential" or "necessary" accomplices and "non-essential" accomplices. Essential accomplices are punished as severely as the perpetrators of the offense. In contrast, non-essential accomplices are punished less than the perpetrators. *See, generally*, Santiago Mir Puig, *Derecho Penal: Parte General* 408–410 (B de F, 2004).

2. Many—if not most—civil law jurisdictions punish some types of complicity more severely than others. In addition to the Spanish Penal Code, the Penal Code of Argentina is representative:

> ARTICLE 45.—Those who take part in the commission of a crime or who provide the perpetrator or perpetrators with help or cooperation without which the crime could not have been committed, shall be sentenced to the full punishment prescribed for the offense. Those ordering another person directly to commit a crime shall be sentenced to the same punishment as the perpetrators.
>
> ARTICLE 46.—Those cooperating in any other manner to the perpetration of the crime ... shall be sentenced to a punishment that ranges from one half to two thirds of the punishment prescribed for the perpetrator. If punishment is life incarceration, incarceration from fifteen to twenty years shall be imposed....

Similarly, pursuant to Section 27 of the German Criminal Code and Article 27(2) of the Portuguese Penal Code, accessories are punished less than perpetrators and those who intentionally "induce" or "determine" another to commit an offense.

3. The rationale for punishing some kinds of complicity less than others is that substantial contributions to the commission of the offense are more blameworthy and dangerous than minor contributions to the crime. Thus, for example, it could be argued that selling ink that will be used for counterfeiting dollar bills is less blameworthy than selling a sophisticated machine that can only be used to counterfeit money. Discriminating between different types of complicity also assumes that providing minor assistance to the perpetrator should often be punished less severely than actually perpetrating the crime. Giving a pen to someone so that they can forge a Picasso drawing is arguably less worthy of condemnation than actually forging the drawing. Do you agree that selling the ink for counterfeiting money is less blameworthy than selling the sophisticated counterfeiting machine? Do you agree that it is more worthy of condemnation to actually forge a Picasso drawing than to provide the forger with a pencil so that he can forge the drawing? If there are differences between these cases, should the law take them into account by punishing some contributions to the crime less than others? Explain.

4. While the distinction between essential accomplices that substantially contribute to the crime and non-essential accomplices that provide minor contributions to the offense is neat in theory, it is sometimes quite difficult to distinguish between essential and non-essential assistance in practice. This is how the Spanish Supreme Court has tried to distinguish between essential and non-essential accomplices:

> This Court has stated in the past that the difference between non-essential complicity and essential complicity is that the non-essential accomplice's contribution is secondary, accessorial and merely auxiliary to the perpetrator's act, whereas the conduct of the essential accomplice is necessary to bringing about the crime. We have examined various factors in order to determine whether conduct is necessary for the crime. On the one hand, we ask whether the assistance was a "conditio sine qua non" of the crime, which would lead to considering as essential complicity a contribution without which the offense could not have been committed. That is, we engage in a thought experiment in which we suppress the accomplice's contribution and ask whether the crime could have been committed without it. We also take into account the so-called "scarce goods theory," which holds that contributing a good or service should be considered essential complicity when the good or service provided is scarce. [Finally], an actor is an essential accomplice if he had the power to prevent the crime by merely refusing to provide whatever assistance he had agreed to provide. On the other hand, an actor is a non-essential accomplice if he provides assistance that facilitates the consummation of the offense, but without which the criminal objective would have likely been achieved anyway. *Sentencia del Tribunal Supremo de Septiembre 24 de 2009.*

5. The most vexing problem inherent in trying to distinguish essential from non-essential contributions is determining whether the offense would have been committed without the accomplice's assistance. How do we know, for example, whether the perpetrator would have killed the victim had the accomplice not furnished him with a gun? Perhaps the perpetrator would have been able to find a gun elsewhere. Or perhaps he would have killed the victim with a knife or a baseball bat. For these reasons, asking what would have happened without the accomplice's help seems useless and speculative. Is there a more promising way of distinguishing between essential and non-essential contributions to the crime? Explain.

6. In the judgment excerpted in Note 4, the Spanish Supreme Court suggests that whether the accomplice's contribution should be considered "essential" or "non-essential" could depend on whether the good or service that she provided was scarce or abundant. If the good or service provided is scarce, then the contribution is essential, for scarce goods or services are—by definition—difficult to obtain. Therefore, providing them makes it considerably easier for the perpetrator to consummate the offense. If, on the other hand, the good or service provided is abundant, then the contribution is non-essential, given that abundant goods are—by definition—easy to obtain. Consequently, providing such goods to the perpetrator does not make it considerably easier for her to consummate the offense, for she could have easily obtained such goods or services elsewhere. This shifts the *locus* of the inquiry from asking what would have happened without the accomplice's help to asking whether the good or service provided was scarce or abundant and, therefore, easy or difficult to obtain. The latter inquiry might be preferable, for determining whether the good or service provided by the accessory is scarce or abundant in a given time and place seems to be less speculative than asking whether a crime would have been committed without the accomplice's help. As the Spanish Supreme Court points out, this theory has come to be known as the "scarce goods theory." It was devised by Enrique Gimbernat Ordeig, one of Spain's leading criminal law theorists. This is how Gimbernat explains his theory:

> From a general perspective, the following goods are not scarce [i.e., are abundant]: a pen, an over the counter medication, twenty dollars, a rope, a hammer, a metal rod, matches (to commit arson), a rock (to commit an assault), a stick (to grab something that is out of reach), a ladder (to gain access to a second floor window in order to burglarize a home), etc. This general classificatory schema must, however, take into account the concrete time and place in which the contribution takes place. A pen used to commit a forgery might be an abundant good in Madrid, but a scarce one in a small village in the African jungle.
>
> From this general point of view, one can classify the following goods as scarce in a normal case (according to a person of average wealth in Spain): a gun, a prescription medication, dynamite, 20,000 dollars, a machine for counterfeiting money ... and, in sum, any object that is very expensive or that—for whatever reason—is considerably difficult to obtain.
>
> Provisionally, then, one can say that giving the perpetrator ... a knife, a rope, a pen, etc., amounts to [non-essential complicity that should be punished less than actually perpetrating the offense]. On the other hand, providing the perpetrator with dynamite, $20,000 ... or with a potentially deadly medication that can only be acquired with a prescription amounts to essential complicity [that should be punished as severely as actually perpetrating the offense]. Enrique Gimbernat Ordeig, Autor y Cómplice en Derecho Penal 128 (B de F, 2ª ed., 2006).

Do you believe that Gimbernat's "scarce goods theory" provides a good test for discriminating between essential and non-essential contributions? Do you agree that providing the perpetrator with a scarce good or service (a gun, dynamite or a difficult to obtain poison) should—all things being equal—be punished more severely than supplying an abundant good to the perpetrator (e.g., giving him matches, a pen or a rope)? Explain.

7. American criminal law makes no formal distinction between accomplices and perpetrators in terms of the maximum amount of punishment that can be imposed on one or the other. Therefore, as a general rule, accomplices may be punished as severely as perpetrators. Nevertheless, the sentencing judge has discretion to punish accomplices less

than perpetrators if she believes that the circumstances surrounding the criminal act warrant making such a determination. The sentencing judge also has discretion to punish some accomplices more or less depending on their personal blameworthiness and other relevant factors. Note, however, that whether to punish some accomplices less severely than others or to punish accomplices in general less severely than perpetrators is entirely up to the sentencing judge. Contrary to what happens in Spain and other European and Latin American countries, there is no mitigation of punishment as a matter of right, even when the contributions of the participant are minor. The United States Sentencing Guidelines do provide for a "downwards adjustment" in offense level if the defendant is a "minimal participant" in the offense. U.S. SENTENCING GUIDELINES MANUAL § 3B1.2 (2007). These guidelines, however, are merely advisory and are therefore not binding on the sentencing judge. *See, United States v. Booker*, 543 U.S. 220 (2005). It thus continues to be the case that accomplices may be punished as severely as perpetrators, even when the conduct giving rise to accomplice liability is minor. Is it fair to punish minor contributions to crime as severely as significant contributions, as American law currently allows? Would you prefer that American law punish minor complicity less than substantial complicity, as many civil law countries do? Explain.

## § 10.07 Complicity: Scholarly Debates

### Joshua Dressler, *Rethinking Complicity Law: Trivial Complicity as a Lesser Offense?*

5 Ohio St. J. Crim. L. 427 (2008)

American accomplice law is a disgrace. It treats the accomplice in terms of guilt and, potentially, punishment, as if she were the perpetrator, even when her culpability is often less than that of the perpetrator and/or her involvement in the crime is tangential.

The subject of accomplice liability has received relatively little scholarly attention in the United States except for a flurry of intellectual activity in the mid-1980s. One of these articles proposed reform of complicity law in the form of what may be characterized as the "causation approach." The thesis of that article was that the criminal law fails to adequately distinguish between accomplices who are critical parties in a crime and those whose involvement is trivial. To alleviate this problem, the article recommended a statutory distinction between "causal" and "non-causal" accomplices: causal accomplices could continue to be convicted of the offense committed by the principal; non-causal accomplices would be convicted of a lesser offense and punished accordingly....

#### II. The Problem

An accomplice is one who, with the requisite mens rea, "aids or abets" the principal in committing an offense. Without listing all of the possibilities, she may be one who: solicits the offense by commanding, without legally coercing, another to commit the offense; procures the offense by offering an incentive to another to commit the crime; provides psychological encouragement to a principal already planning to commit the offense who needs—or does not need—the extra psychological boost; provides an essential—or non-essential—instrumentality used in the crime; provides a significant—or insignificant—service in the commission of the offense; or does nothing at all and thereby fails to make any effort to impede the offense when she has a legal duty to make such an effort. In short (putting the omission example aside), an accomplice is one who provides substantial—or quite trivial-aid in the commission of the crime. And, in states that have enacted the Model Penal Code's complicity provision, accomplice liability is even extended to persons who do not aid, even trivially, but attempt to do so.

Despite the immense variations in participation suggested in the last paragraph, complicity law is binary: a person is or is not an accomplice. Legally speaking, there is no such thing as a "major" or "minor" accomplice. Thus, if the binary switch is turned on—the major or minor actor is deemed to be an accomplice—she and the perpetrator are treated alike in terms of guilt and potential punishment. This occurs because an accomplice, as it is now commonly explained, derives her liability from the principal. If the principal commits no crime, there is no liability for the would-be accomplice to derive, although she might be guilty of some inchoate offense of her own, such as conspiracy or solicitation. If the crime is committed by the principal, the accomplice is guilty of that crime, not of a separate and lesser offense of "aiding and abetting." As Professor Weisberg has nicely put it, "complicity is not a distinct crime, but a way of committing a crime."

For immediate purposes, it is sufficient to note just two troubling features of derivative liability. First, because the accomplice is guilty of the offense committed by the principal, there is a grammatical inaccuracy—and, if you will, legality problem—in her conviction: as an accomplice to murder she will be convicted of the offense of "killing" another person when, in fact, she did not kill the victim; as an accomplice to a rape, she will be convicted of having sexual intercourse with one whom she did not (and perhaps could not) have had sexual relations; as an accomplice to burglary she will be convicted of breaking and entering a structure she may never have seen, much less broken or entered. Second, as the last point suggests, the accomplice and the principal are treated as if they were one; the law ignores their separate identities. It is for this reason that the principal and accomplice are treated alike in terms of guilt and punishment—after all, as far as the law is concerned, they are one and the same person....

It does not take much reflection to realize that accomplices are not always, or perhaps even usually, as deserving of guilt or punishment, or as dangerous, as their principal cohorts. It is similarly evident that not all accomplices—contrast the mastermind behind a bank heist with a loving spouse who brings a midday meal to her criminal-minded husband or a car occupant who merely points at illegal drugs—are equally deserving (or in need) of punishment....

### VII. New Reform Proposals

... [I]f a person is held responsible for a serious offense although her causal participation is minor, complicity law may sometimes still lead to "jaw-dropping" results.

Therefore, an alternative reform proposal is the following: A person is not accountable for the actions of the perpetrator unless ... there is evidence that the accomplice was a substantial participant, not a bit player, in the multi-party crime....

### B. "Substantial Participation" Standard

... The best reform of complicity law may be to distinguish exclusively on the basis of the substantiality of the actor's participation in an offense, without direct consideration of causation principles. A person whom the fact-finder determines was a substantial participant (with the requisite mens rea, of course), and only such a person, would be convicted of the same offense (and subject to the same punishment) as the principal, based on traditional derivative liability principles....

"Substantial participant" concededly is an imprecise term, but certainly no more so that the doctrine of proximate causation, which invites the fact-finder to draw justice-based lines of responsibility. Ultimately, the issue here is whether the accomplice's role in the planning or commission of the offense is sufficiently great that it is just to hold her accountable for—to derive liability for—the offense committed by the principal.

In regard to insubstantial participants in a crime, it would constitute poor policy, whether one applies utilitarian or just-deserts philosophy, to allow such a person to escape criminal liability. Minor assistance should constitute a separate and lesser degree of offense than the crime committed by the principal party.

### VIII. Conclusion

Current complicity law is unjust in various regards, not the least of which is the fact that perpetrators, substantial participants, and tangential accomplices are treated alike in the guilt phase of a criminal trial.

... Lawmakers should also seriously consider a "substantial participation" standard of complicity. This approach would provide a more just outcome than current law, permit line-drawing that conforms to moral intuitions about criminal responsibility, and does so in an uncomplicated manner.

## R.A. Duff, *Is Accomplice Liability Superfluous?*

156 U. Pa. L. Rev. PENNumbra 444 (2008)

### II. Intention, Foresight, and Complicity

... To simplify matters, we can focus on cases in which liability is grounded in the fact that *D* assists (or intends to assist) the commission of the target offense—focusing on assistance, rather than on solicitation or encouragement. Two familiar questions about the appropriate mens rea arise. First, when it is said that *D* must intend to assist or facilitate *P*'s commission of the offense, should that be taken to require a "specific intent"—that is, purpose—to assist or facilitate? Or should it be enough that *D* realizes (or knows) that his intended action will in fact assist or facilitate?... American law typically requires purpose, whereas English law (which has signally failed to develop an adequately clear understanding of intention) requires only knowledge. Second, must *D* also "intend," however intention is interpreted, that the offense be committed; or is it enough that he intends to assist *P*, even if he has no interest in whether *P* succeeds, or even hopes that *P* fails?

... If I make it my purpose to assist the commission of an offense and act as I do in order that the offense will be committed, I make myself nonderivatively responsible for it; my contribution might be less, as a matter of degree, than that of the person who finally does the deed, but my responsibility and liability are neither derivative from his nor different in kind from his. Thus, if the law should require purpose, rather than merely knowledge, both as to the fact that what I do will assist the commission of the crime and as to its actual commission, it does not need a distinct type of accomplice liability. However, two concerns arise here: first, there is good reason to extend the law more broadly than this, to capture some who do what they know will assist the commission of an offense although it is not their purpose to do so; and, second, this should be understood as a distinct type of liability.

*D* supplies *P* with equipment or goods that he knows *P* intends to use for the commission of a crime (he supplies ingredients that he knows *P* will use to make explosives for a terrorist attack, a gun that he knows *P* will use to commit a robbery, a car that he knows *P* will drive while drunk or disqualified, etc.). He claims, plausibly, that it was no part of his purpose to assist *P*'s commission of the offense; his purpose was merely to meet a friend's request for the item in question or to earn the money that *P* offered for it. Should that save him from liability for involvement in *P*'s commission of the crime?[28] Surely not. As well as condemning *P*, morally and legally, for his commission of the crime, we should be able to condemn *D*, both morally and legally, for his contribution to its commission. However, although we should condemn them both, we should also draw a distinction of kind, rather than only of degree, between them, for two reasons.

First, if I act with the (direct) intention of assisting the commission of an offense, I cannot (absent a plea of infancy or insanity) deny responsibility for assisting it or for its commission. If, however, I act in the knowledge that my action will assist its commission, there might be room to admit such knowledge while denying responsibility, by arguing that I had no prospective responsibility, in relation to that aspect of my action, that would give me reason to act differently. A doctor who prescribes contraceptives to a girl of fifteen might know that this will facilitate the commission of an offense of sexual intercourse with a minor, since the girl and her eighteen-year-old boyfriend are more likely to have intercourse more often if she has the contraceptives. But, the doctor might plausibly argue, she should not be held responsible for assisting its commission, since its prospective commission was not a factor that she should have considered in deciding whether to prescribe the contraceptive. Her sole concern was, as it should have been, to provide the treatment that was medically appropriate for her patient.[29] Part of what makes at least some such denials of responsibility morally plausible is, I suggest, the fact of intervening human agency: it is not my business that what I do makes it easier for *P* to commit the crime partly because it is *P*'s business whether he commits the crime (whereas if I act with the intention of assisting *P*'s commission, I make it my business); it is up to *P* whether he commits the crime or not and—at least sometimes—I am not required to guide my actions by my knowledge of what *P* will do.

Second, even when *D* should not be allowed to deny responsibility for the foreseen fact that her action will assist *P*'s commission of an offense, and even when her action does make a genuine contribution to the commission of the offense, there still seems to be a categorical difference, rather than one only of degree, between *D* and *P*. For *D* has not committed herself to the crime's commission (as *P* commits himself by intending to commit the crime); she has not made the crime her own in the way that *P* does; she can still say that, in the end, it is up to *P* rather than to her whether the crime is committed. This might not save her from criminal liability (often it should not). It might not even make her offense less serious than *P*'s (for we must remember that differences that are worth marking are not always differences in degree of guilt). But it does make her relationship to the commission of the offense significantly different.

---

28. It might be argued that we can and should deal with such cases not via any general doctrine of complicity, but through the creation of particular special offenses, for instance of supplying certain kinds of dangerous item. Such offenses do have a place in a rational criminal code, but they do not capture the way in which *D* should also be held responsible in relation to the commission of the primary offense.

29. *See* Gillick v. W. Norfolk & Wisbech Area Health Auth., (1986) 1 A.C. 112, 190 (H.L.) (on appeal from Eng.) (involving a case with similar facts); R.A. DUFF, ANSWERING FOR CRIME 35–36 (2007). Shopkeepers might offer an analogous, though morally less plausible, argument that what their customers do with the goods they sell is not their business. Similarly, hosts who serve drinks to guests who will, they know, then drive home under the influence might analogously argue that it is the guests', not the host's, responsibility to avoid the commission of that offense.

## *Notes and Questions*

1. Professor Dressler points out "accomplices are not always, or perhaps even usually, as deserving of guilt or punishment, or as dangerous, as their principal cohorts." He also argues that "[i]t is similarly evident that not all accomplices—contrast the mastermind behind a bank heist with ... a car occupant who merely points at illegal drugs—are equally deserving (or in need) of punishment." As a result, Dressler proposes that minor participants be punished less than substantial participants. Note that while Dressler's proposal may be novel in America, most European and Latin American penal codes have distinguished between substantial and minor accomplices for quite some time.

2. Dressler acknowledges that one of the weaknesses of his proposal is that "'[s]ubstantial participant' concededly is an imprecise term." He counters by arguing that the term is "no more [imprecise] ... tha[n] the doctrine of proximate causation, which invites the fact-finder to draw justice-based lines of responsibility." Is Dressler's reply to the "imprecision" objection satisfactory? Would you feel comfortable with juries distinguishing between substantial accomplices and minor accomplices on the basis of "justice-based" intuitions? Explain. Perhaps who counts as a "substantial participant" according to Dressler's proposal could be made more precise by applying some of the tests that continental courts and scholars have put forth to distinguish between essential and non-essential complicity (see previous section). This illustrates how useful comparative criminal law can be. Why come up with a theory of substantial vs. minor complicity from scratch when courts and scholars in other jurisdictions have spent decades elaborating such a theory?

3. Professor Duff argues that—all things being equal—a person who purposely assists the commission of a crime is more blameworthy than an actor who knowingly aids the consummation of the offense without actually desiring to help bring about the crime. Do you agree? Why or why not?

4. If Duff is right that purposeful complicity is generally more blameworthy than knowing complicity, there would be sound reasons for—as a general rule—punishing purposeful complicity more severely than knowing complicity. This is indeed what happens in America, for—as was discussed in § 10.03—knowing complicity is not punishable in most states. Furthermore, some states have enacted criminal facilitation statutes that punish knowing assistance less severely than purposeful complicity. But perhaps Duff's proposal is also useful to those who—like Dressler and scholars in Europe and Latin America—are interested in discriminating between substantial and minor participants. The factors cited by courts and scholars to make these distinctions seem to focus on an objective inquiry about the substantiality of the accomplice's contribution. Nevertheless, perhaps the distinction between major and minor accomplices should also take into account the accessory's subjective mental state by, for example, punishing some purposeful accomplices as substantial participants even if their contribution was relatively minor. By the same token, perhaps knowing accomplices should usually be punished for minor complicity, unless their contributions were of great import to the commission of the offense. This is not to suggest that distinguishing between major and minor participants by focusing on the substantiality of their contributions is misguided. Rather, it suggests that the inquiry might be enriched by also taking note of the accomplice's mental state. Of course, this presupposes that the criminal law formally distinguishes between major and minor accomplices, which American law currently does not.

# Chapter 11

# Attempts

## § 11.01 Attempts: Conduct Element— Common Law Approaches

### State v. Duke

District Court of Appeal of Florida, Fifth District, 1998
709 S.2d 580

W. SHARP, Judge.

The state appeals from an order of the trial court which granted a new trial in a criminal case. We are of the opinion that the trial court should have directed a verdict for the defendant, Duke, on the ground that the criminal charges in this case were not proved by sufficient evidence. Accordingly, we reverse and direct that a judgment of acquittal be entered for the appellee, Duke.

Duke was charged with three counts of attempted sexual battery on a child. [Florida law defines the conduct constitutive of the offense in the following manner]:

> 'Sexual battery' means oral, anal, or vaginal penetration by, or union with, the sexual organ of another by any other object;....

With regard to attempt, [Florida law provides]:

> (1) A person who attempts to commit an offense prohibited by law and in such attempt does any act towards the commission of such offense, but fails in the perpetration or is intercepted or prevented in the execution thereof, commits the offense of criminal attempt, ...

The evidence at trial established that Duke communicated on the Internet with a person he thought was a twelve-year-old girl using the name "Niki 012" from Orlando. In fact, the person was an adult male, Detective Irwin, assigned to the Orange County Sex Crimes Unit, who was surfing the Internet "chat rooms" looking for persons attempting to solicit children for sexual acts. Duke and "Niki" had a number of conversations on a number of different days. They discussed participating in various sexual acts in explicit terms.

"Niki" told Duke her mother would be away from home one night and they made plans for Duke to come to her home at a certain time. He was given directions to a parking lot where "Niki" was supposed to meet him. He was also told to flash his car lights so "Niki" would recognize the car. The plan was that she would take him to her home, and they would engage in various sex acts, including cunnilingus, fellatio and perhaps intercourse. As soon as Duke arrived in the parking lot and flashed his lights, he was arrested.

The issue which the state urges us to address in this case ... is whether Duke's conversations with "Niki," his arrangements to have sex with her, and his arrival in the parking lot to rendezvous with her rise to the level of a sufficient overt act to sustain his conviction for attempted sexual battery....

[W]e find the evidence adduced at trial was insufficient to warrant Duke's conviction of attempted sexual battery....

*Morehead v. State* is a controlling decision in this case. In *Morehead,* this court held that in order to prove an attempt crime, some actual overt step must be taken or an act in furtherance of committing the crime must be done. The overt act must reach far enough towards accomplishing the attempted crime as to amount to commencement of consummation of the crime. The overt act must go beyond preparation and planning.

In *Morehead,* the defendant was charged with attempting to escape from the Tomoka Correctional Institute. The state relied on two acts of preparation to establish attempt: the defendant cut his hand to obtain medical treatment off prison grounds, with the plan that his girlfriend would meet him with a gun and help him escape; and he caused a confederate to slip him a gun in the prison, for use in another planned escape effort. The girlfriend and the gun never materialized. This court held that the defendant's escape plans and efforts to implement them did not progress beyond mere preparation and thus did not constitute attempted escape.

In this case, we do not think the proven conduct undertaken by Duke reached the level of an overt act leading to the commission of sexual battery as required by [Florida law]. He discussed sexual acts with "Niki," he intended to commit them with Niki, he planned an occasion where he could carry out those acts, and he arrived at a prearranged meeting point. But we conclude that is not enough to constitute an attempt to commit a sexual battery. We note the difficulty in policing the Internet, and the challenges the cyber world poses to preventing criminal acts against children. This may be an area the Legislature needs to address specifically.

Accordingly, we quash the order granting a new trial and direct that a judgment of acquittal be entered.

**HARRIS, Judge, concurring specially.**

I concur with Judge Sharp that an attempt to commit sexual battery was not proved in this case. It is difficult to see how, under *Morehead v. State* an attempt to commit sexual battery could occur when the victim was not even present. An attempt is not a "one crime fits all facts" offense. But that does not mean that Florida is helpless to protect our children from adult predators. It is a federal offense to cross a state line for the purpose of having sex with a minor. This lends some protection against out-of-state internet predators. It appears that Florida has now criminalized the use of a computer to solicit sex from a minor *or from a person believed to be a minor.* Unfortunately, this matter arose before the effective date of the new offense. In any event, there must be a limit on the reach of attempts or else the crime of attempt will cease to have meaning.

## People v. Rizzo

Court of Appeals of New York, 1927
158 N.E. 888

CRANE, J.

The police of the city of New York did excellent work in this case by preventing the commission of a serious crime. It is a great satisfaction to realize that we have such wide-awake guardians of our peace. Whether or not the steps which the defendant had taken up to the time of his arrest amounted to the commission of a crime, as defined by our law, is, however, another matter. He has been convicted of an attempt to commit the crime of robbery in the first degree and sentenced to State's prison. There is no doubt that he had the intention to commit robbery if he got the chance. An examination, however, of the facts is necessary to determine whether his acts were in preparation to commit the crime if the opportunity offered, or constituted a crime in itself, known to our law as an attempt to commit robbery in the first degree. Charles Rizzo, the defendant, appellant, with three others, Anthony J. Dorio, Thomas Milo and John Thomasello, on January 14th planned to rob one Charles Rao of a payroll valued at about $1,200 which he was to carry from the bank for the United Lathing Company. These defendants, two of whom had firearms, started out in an automobile, looking for Rao or the man who had the payroll on that day. Rizzo claimed to be able to identify the man and was to point him out to the others who were to do the actual holding up. The four rode about in their car looking for Rao. They went to the bank from which he was supposed to get the money and to various buildings being constructed by the United Lathing Company. At last they came to One Hundred and Eightieth street and Morris Park avenue. By this time they were watched and followed by two police officers. As Rizzo jumped out of the car and ran into the building all four were arrested. The defendant was taken out from the building in which he was hiding. Neither Rao nor a man named Previti, who was also supposed to carry a payroll, were at the place at the time of the arrest. The defendants had not found or seen the man they intended to rob; no person with a payroll was at any of the places where they had stopped and no one had been pointed out or identified by Rizzo. The four men intended to rob the payroll man, whoever he was; they were looking for him, but they had not seen or discovered him up to the time they were arrested.

Does this constitute the crime of an attempt to commit robbery in the first degree? The Penal Law, section 2, prescribes, "An act, done with intent to commit a crime, and tending but failing to effect its commission, is 'an attempt to commit that crime.'" The word "*tending*" is very indefinite. It is perfectly evident that there will arise differences of opinion as to whether an act in a given case is one *tending* to commit a crime. "Tending" means to exert activity in a particular direction. Any act in preparation to commit a crime may be said to have a tendency towards its accomplishment. The procuring of the automobile, searching the streets looking for the desired victim, were in reality acts tending toward the commission of the proposed crime. The law, however, has recognized that many acts in the way of preparation are too remote to constitute the crime of attempt. The line has been drawn between those acts which are remote and those which are proximate and near to the consummation. The law must be practical, and, therefore, considers those acts only as tending to the commission of the crime which are so near to its accomplishment that in all reasonable probability the crime itself would have been committed but for timely interference. The cases which have been before the courts express this idea in different language, but the idea remains the same. The act or acts must come or advance very near to the accomplishment of the intended crime. In *People v. Mills* it was said: "Felonious intent alone is not enough, but there must be an overt act shown in order to establish even an attempt. An overt act is one done to carry out the intention, and it must be such as would naturally effect that result, unless prevented by some extraneous cause." In *Hyde v. U. S.* it was stated that the act amounts to an attempt when it is so near to the result that the danger of success is very great. "There must be dangerous proximity to success." Halsbury in his "Laws of England" (Vol. IX, p. 259) says: "An act, in order to be a criminal attempt, must be immediately, and not remotely, connected with and directly tending to the commission of an offence." *Commonwealth v. Peaslee* refers to the acts constituting an attempt as coming *very near* to the accomplishment of the crime.

The method of committing or attempting crime varies in each case so that the difficulty, if any, is not with this rule of law regarding an attempt, which is well understood, but with its application to the facts. As I have said before, minds differ over proximity and the nearness of the approach.

How shall we apply this rule of immediate nearness to this case? The defendants were looking for the payroll man to rob him of his money. This is the charge in the indictment. Robbery is defined in section 2120 of the Penal Law as "the unlawful taking of personal property, from the person or in the presence of another, against his will, by means of force, or violence, or fear of injury, immediate or future, to his person;" and it is made robbery in the first degree by section 2124 when committed by a person aided by accomplices actually present. To constitute the crime of robbery the money must have been taken from Rao by means of force or violence, or through fear. The crime of attempt to commit robbery was committed if these defendants did an act tending to the commission of this robbery. Did the acts above describe come dangerously near to the taking of Rao's property? Did the acts come so near the commission of robbery that there was reasonable likelihood of its accomplishment but for the interference? Rao was not found; the defendants were still looking for him; no attempt to rob him could be made, at least until he came in sight; he was not in the building at One Hundred and Eightieth street and Morris Park avenue. There was no man there with the payroll for the United Lathing Company whom these defendants could rob. Apparently no money had been drawn from the bank for the payroll by anybody at the time of the arrest. In a word, these defendants had planned to commit a crime and were looking around the city for an opportunity to commit it, but the opportunity fortunately never came. Men would not be guilty of an attempt at burglary if they had planned to break into a building and were arrested while they were hunting about the streets for the building not knowing where it was. Neither would a man be guilty of an attempt to commit murder if he armed himself and started out to find the person whom he had planned to kill but could not find him. So here these defendants were not guilty of an attempt to commit robbery in the first degree when they had not found or reached the presence of the person they intended to rob.

For these reasons, the judgment of conviction of this defendant, appellant, must be reversed and a new trial granted.

## *Notes and Questions*

1. Most of the specific offenses listed in the special part of criminal codes criminalize successfully engaging in certain conduct or causing a particular result. Thus, the offense of rape prohibits engaging in non-consensual sexual intercourse. The underlying offense with which the defendant was charged in *Duke* proscribes having sexual contact with a minor. In *Rizzo*, the underlying offense prohibited unlawfully taking the property of another by force or violence. In both cases, the prohibited act is effectively engaging in either the prohibited conduct (having sexual contact with a minor in the case of sexual battery of a minor) or successfully bringing about the proscribed harm (taking the prop-

erty of another in the case of robbery). The special part of criminal codes usually prescribes punishment only for those who complete the conduct described in the definition of the offense. The consequence of this is that those who *try* but *fail* to engage in the conduct proscribed by the offense do not, strictly speaking, perform an act that is prohibited by the law defining the criminal offense. Nevertheless, there are powerful consequentialist and retributive reasons for punishing those who try to engage in criminal conduct but (fortunately) do not succeed. That is, we have good reasons to punish those who try but fail to kill and those who try but fail to rape. The doctrine of attempt liability was created to address this gap in the law. Pursuant to this general doctrine, criminal liability attaches whenever someone tries to commit an offense but fails to successfully consummate it.

2. As both *Duke* and *Rizzo* illustrate, courts often struggle with determining the exact point in time during which conduct crosses the threshold from being a mere act of preparation that generally goes unpunished to being an act of execution of the criminal offense that is typically punished as an attempt. This is the problem inherent in figuring out what the conduct element (*actus reus*) of attempt offenses should be. It is a particularly thorny problem, given that often many events take place between the time during which the actor first contemplates the commission of the offense and the moment in which the offense is completed. Many things happen, for example, between the time that the actor thinks about poisoning the victim and the moment in which the actor actually poisons and kills the victim. When exactly does an actor's conduct become a punishable attempt? When he contemplated killing the victim? When he called a friend to ask for help? When he browsed the web looking for a poison with which to kill the victim? When he bought the poison? When he drove to the victim's home? When he entered the home? When he poisoned the coffee?

3. Until the second half of the twentieth century, there was a generalized consensus in common law jurisdictions that attempts to commit offenses should only be punished if they come dangerously close to completion. Courts and commentators frequently suggested—as the court did in *Rizzo*—that the act must be "dangerously proximate" to completion. Some—like the Florida court in *Duke*—held that the defendant's act "must reach far enough towards accomplishing the attempted crime as to amount to commencement of consummation of the crime." A few courts went as far as holding that the actor must engage in the "last act" prior to consummation of the offense, although this view never mustered much support in America. *See, e.g., R v. Eagleton,* 6 Cox C.C. 559 (Ct. Crim. Law 1855). Note that according to these approaches, defendant should be punished for an attempt only if his conduct is "proximate to" consummating the crime or "comes close to" completing the offense. As a result, the standards applied in these cases are often referred to as "proximity tests" for determining attempt liability. Application of proximity tests generated an acquittal in both *Duke* and *Rizzo*. Do you agree that either or both of these defendants should have been acquitted of attempting to commit the underlying crime that they were charged with? If you believe that either or both of these defendants should have been held liable for an attempt, how would you draw the line between preparation and attempt in a way that captures the kinds of conduct that you believe warrant punishment while also excluding the acts that you deem too remote to justify imposing criminal liability? If you think that either or both of these defendants should have been convicted of an attempt, which of the acts that either of them performed do you believe crossed the threshold between preparation and execution of the criminal conduct?

4. Sometimes the line of demarcation between acts of preparation and attempts was drawn by asking whether defendant's acts unequivocally revealed that a criminal offense was going to be consummated. Attempt liability would be deemed appropriate if the defendant's acts unequivocally revealed that a crime was about to be committed. If, on the

other hand, the acts were compatible with both a non-criminal and a criminal aim, the conduct would be considered "equivocal" and thus not sufficient to ground liability for an attempt. This standard for ascertaining whether a punishable attempt has taken place is often referred to as the "equivocality test." Although this view has not garnered many adherents in America, a handful of states have embraced it. The Wisconsin attempt statute is representative, for it defines attempts as "acts toward the commission of the crime which demonstrate unequivocally … that the actor formed [the intent to commit a crime]." W.S.A. 939.32(3). Similarly, the Puerto Rican Penal Code defines an attempt as conduct that is "unequivocally … directed toward initiating the commission of an offense." CPPR, Article 35. Finally, Delaware criminalizes conduct as an attempt only if it amounts to "an act or omission which leaves no reasonable doubt as to the defendant's intention to commit the crime which the defendant is charged with attempting." 11 Del.C. § 532. Although the Delaware statute does not expressly state that the acts need to be "unequivocal" in order to be punished as an attempt, requiring that the conduct reveal the intention to commit a crime beyond a reasonable doubt is another way of stating that the acts must unequivocally evince that a crime is about to be committed.

5. In principle, focusing on the "unequivocality" of the defendant's conduct may lead to criminalizing conduct as an attempt before the conduct is "dangerously proximate" to completion, for some acts may unequivocally reveal that criminal conduct will take place even if several steps remain to be taken before the offense can be consummated. As one court explained:

> We are mindful of the fact that language appearing in *Stokes v. State* that "whenever the design of a person to commit crime is clearly shown, slight acts done in furtherance of this design will constitute an attempt", has received approval. The statement, however, that slight acts in *furtherance of the design* will be sufficient is not in conflict with the usual statements of the tests applied to aid in drawing the line at the point where preparation leaves off and execution has commenced. It still presupposes some direct act or movement in execution of the design, as distinguished from mere preparation which leaves the intended assailant only in the condition to commence the first direct act toward consummation of his design. The reason for requiring evidence of a direct act, however slight, toward consummation of the intended crime, is, as pointed out by the author in Wharton's Criminal Law, that in the majority of cases up to that time the conduct of the defendant, consisting merely of acts of preparation, has never ceased to be equivocal; and this is necessarily so, irrespective of his declared intent. It is that quality of being equivocal that must be lacking before the act becomes one which may be said to be a commencement of the commission of the crime, or an overt act, or before any fragment of the crime itself has been committed, and this is so for the reason that so long as the equivocal quality remains no one can say with certainty what the intent of the defendant is. …
>
> In the case of *Stokes v. State* … it was held that, the intent being clear, the taking of a loaded gun and going in search of the intended victim constituted an attempt. Justification for the decision in that case may be said to lie in the possibility of the jury's finding under the facts there involved that the preparation for the assault was without any equivocality, and the intent thus being proved, the preparation was sufficient to constitute the overt act. The same reasoning applies to the cases of *People v. Lanzit*, wherein the defendant had prepared a bomb for the purpose of killing his wife; and *People v. Stites*, wherein the defendant had prepared to place dynamite on railway tracks, and in both of which

> convictions were upheld. These cases illustrate the small class of cases where the acts of preparation themselves clearly indicate the certain unambiguous intent and suffice to constitute the attempt. *People v. Miller,* 2 Cal.2d 527 (1935).

Without direct proof of the intent of the defendants in *Duke* and *Rizzo*, did their acts unequivocally indicate that a crime was about to be committed? Explain.

6. While focusing on the unequivocality of defendant's act may sometimes criminalize conduct as an attempt before the proximity tests would, in a few cases the unequivocality standard may criminalize conduct even later than under the proximity tests. Professor Glanville Williams came up with an example that illustrates this quite nicely. Suppose that a defendant approaches a haystack that belongs to another, fills his pipe and lights a match. At the time, the defendant's aim is equivocal, for his next act may be perfectly lawful (lighting the pipe) or evidently criminal (setting the haystack on fire). *See,* Glanville Williams, Criminal Law: The General Part 630 (Steven & Sons, London, 1961). Given that the act is equivocal, lighting the match would not count as an attempt under the equivocality test, *even if it can be demonstrated that the defendant intended to set the haystack on fire.* Note, however, that defendant's conduct would likely be considered an attempt under the proximity theories, for lighting the match next to the haystack is an act that comes dangerously proximate to completion. The act is so close to completion that it is likely to be considered the "last step" before consummation of the crime. If there is proof that the defendant intended to set the haystack on fire, should the defendant be convicted regardless of whether the act of lighting the match is equivocal? Why or why not?

7. Sometimes the actor who attempts to commit a crime has done everything in her power to consummate the offense but fails to do so for circumstances that are beyond her control. This is the case, for example, of a person who shoots at a victim but misses. Such attempts can be called "completed attempts," for in these cases the actor has failed to bring about the desired harm even though she had "completed" or "finished" doing everything she had planned to do in order to achieve her criminal objective. In *People v. Staples,* 85 Cal.Rptr. 589 (1970), a California court of appeals helpfully discussed the nature of completed attempts:

> [There are some] situations where the actor does all acts necessary (including the last proximate act) to commit the substantive crime, but nonetheless he somehow is unsuccessful. This lack of success is either a "failure" or a "prevention" brought about because of some extraneous circumstances, e.g., a malfunction of equipment, a miscalculation of operations by the actor or a situation wherein circumstances were at variance with what the actor believe them to be. Certain convictions for attempted murder illustrate [this] category. Some turn on situations wherein the actor fires a weapon at a person but misses; takes aim at an intended victim and pulls the trigger, but the firing mechanism malfunction; plants on an aircraft a homemade bomb which sputters but does not explode. Another … example is highlighted in *People v. Fulton.* The factual setting and legal reasoning in *Fulton* is well characterized by Justice Kingsley in *People v. Orndorff*: "*Fulton* … involved an alleged Jamaica Switch, practiced on two alleged intended victims. The schemes failed, in one instance because a bank officer told the intended victim that it was a bunco scheme.… [T]he court unanimously held that … [this] instance was a punishable attempt … All three judges lay stress on the element of the procuring cause of failure, saying that it must be "by extraneous circumstances," or "by circumstances independent of any actions of their [defendants'] part." The defendants in *Fulton* did every act in their preconceived plan. It was only the extraneous circumstance of the intended

> victim acquiring knowledge that the defendants' proposal to his was a bunco scheme which resulted in the defendants not obtaining the money. *Id.*

In contrast, sometimes an actor is guilty of an attempt even though she has not done everything that she wanted to do in order to consummate the offense. A person may, for example, be arrested by police officers minutes before she shoots at the victim or just prior to planting the homemade bomb on an aircraft. Such attempts are frequently called "incomplete attempts." Once again, the court's discussion in *People v. Staples* is illustrative:

> [I]t is quite clear that under California law overt act, which, when added to the requisite intent, is sufficient to bring about a criminal attempt, need not be the last proximate or ultimate step towards commission of the substantive crime. "It is not necessary that the overt act proved should have been the ultimate step toward the consummation of the design. It is sufficient if it was 'the first or some subsequent step in a direct movement towards the commission of the offense after the preparations are made.' Police officers need not wait until a suspect, who aims a gun at his intended victim, actually pulls the trigger before they arrest him; nor do these officers need to wait until a suspect, who is forcing the lock of a bank door, actually breaks in before they arrest him for attempted burglary."
>
> This rule makes for a second category of "attempts." The recognition of this separate category is well articulated by Mr. Chief Judge Learned Hand in *United States* v. *Coplon* as follows: "A neat doctrine by which to test when a person, intending to commit a crime which he fails to carry out, has 'attempted' to commit it, would be that he has done all that it is within his power to do, but has been prevented by intervention from outside; in short that he has passed beyond any *locus poenitentiae*. Apparently that was the original notion, and may still be law in England; but it is certainly not now generally the law in the United States, for there are many decisions which hold that the accused has passed beyond 'preparation,' although he has been interrupted before he has taken the last of his intended steps." *Staples*, 85 Cal.Rptr. 589.

8. The distinction between completed and incomplete attempts is helpful in understanding the doctrine of "abandonment" or "renunciation." According to some courts, the defendant's voluntary abandonment of his criminal scheme may be a defense to attempt liability. *See, e.g., State v. Latraverse*, 443 A.2d 890. Renunciation of criminal purpose is not a defense, however, if the plan is abandoned because of circumstances beyond the control of the actor, such as the fact that he could not find the victim, that his plan was detected or that he encountered more resistance than he envisioned. *See, e.g., People v. Staples*. The interplay between the defense of abandonment and the completed/incomplete attempt dichotomy lies in the fact that abandonment can only be a defense to incomplete attempts. It only makes sense to assert that the defendant has "abandoned" or "renounced" his criminal plan if the steps needed to carry out the plan have not been completed. If, on the other hand, the attempt has been completed, referring to defendant's abandonment of the criminal plan is inapposite, for all the steps that were necessary to carry out the plan were taken. In other words, once the attempt is complete, there is nothing left to abandon. As one court has put it, "[s]ince all attempts to commit crimes are failures to do so, a failure excuses a defendant who attempts a crime only when his actual attempt is incomplete" and abandoned instead of when it is complete but "unsuccessful." *Boyles v. State*, 175 N.W.2d 277, 278–279 (1970).

9. After the attempt is completed and it seems that a legally proscribed harm will be caused, the defendant could take steps to try to reverse the harm that will likely take place.

The facts of *State v. Smith,* 409 N.E.2d 1199 (1980), illustrate the issue. The defendant stabbed his uncle twice. Subsequently, the defendant felt deep remorse for what he had done and took his uncle to the hospital with the hope that medical personnel could save his life. Thanks to the medical treatment he received, the uncle survived. The defendant was charged with the attempted murder of his uncle. Defendant claimed that he should be acquitted because he abandoned his criminal purpose when he took his uncle to the hospital. The Court of Appeals of Indiana rejected his claim because:

> [A]bandonment must occur before the crime is completed or the harm is done. In this case the offense charged was attempted murder which is completed ... with the first thrust of Smith's knife. This was followed by a second stabbing and further pursuit of the uncle with the knife. Two attempts were completed and Smith abandoned the third attempt. Remorse, common to many who are imprisoned for crime, is not abandonment. Here, abandonment came too late. *Smith,* 409 N.E.2d 1199.

## § 11.02 Attempts: Conduct Element — Model Penal Code Approach

### People v. Scott

Appellate Court of Illinois, Second District, 2000
318 Ill.App.3d 46

Justice GEIGER delivered the opinion of the court:

The defendant appeals from the February 23, 1999, order of the circuit court of Lake County finding him guilty of attempted predatory criminal sexual assault of a child, attempted aggravated criminal sexual abuse, and two counts of attempted indecent solicitation of a child and sentencing him to 12 years' incarceration. On appeal, the defendant argues that ... the State did not prove him guilty beyond a reasonable doubt of attempted predatory criminal sexual assault [and that] the State did not prove him guilty beyond a reasonable doubt of attempted indecent solicitation of a child....

The charges against the defendant arose from his communications with an undercover Lake County sheriff's detective, Richard White, who met the defendant on the Internet. At the bench trial, Detective White testified that, on July 13, 1998, he was conducting an investigation on the Internet service provider America Online. Detective White used the screen name "XradboyX," the profile of which indicated that the user was named "Ricky" and was born on December 12, 1986. On July 13, 1998, Detective White was in a chat room when he received an instant message from the defendant, who was using the screen name "FarWestBoy." The defendant asked Ricky/XradboyX how old he was. An Internet instant message conversation then ensued, during which Detective White represented that he was 12 years old, and the defendant indicated that he was 34.

The conversation included references to sexual behaviors. Detective White and the defendant agreed to meet later that day at a Denny's restaurant. At the appointed time, Detective White appeared at the location, but the defendant did not.

Detective White testified that, the following day, he received two e-mails from the defendant. In those e-mails, the defendant apologized for not attending the meeting and expressed his desire to continue the exchange of messages. When Detective White logged on to America Online, he received an instant message from the defendant. They engaged in a sexually suggestive computer dialogue for about one hour. During that conversation, Detective White requested that the defendant send him pictures via e-mail of men engaged in sexual conduct. The defendant complied with his request and forwarded images of two young males engaged in acts of sexual penetration. Detective White and the defendant again agreed to meet at the Denny's restaurant.

At the agreed-upon time on July 15, 1998, Lake County detectives arrived at the location. After the defendant arrived, he approached Detective Manis who had been dressed to attempt to match the description of a 12-year-old boy that Detective White had conveyed to the defendant. The defendant asked Detective Manis if he was Ricky. After Detective Manis responded in the affirmative, the defendant stated, "[Y]ou don't look like you're twelve years old." Police officers then arrested the defendant.

Following his arrest, the defendant was taken to the sheriff's department, where he gave oral and written statements to investigators. During the interview, the defendant identified himself as FarWestBoy and admitted his understanding that Ricky/XradboyX was 12 years old. He confirmed that he had driven to the Denny's restaurant to meet Ricky/XradboyX, and that he would have had sex if Ricky/XradboyX had wanted to.

The defendant presented no evidence at the bench trial and moved for a directed verdict. The trial court found the defendant guilty of attempted predatory criminal sexual assault of a child, attempted criminal sexual abuse, and two counts of attempted indecent solicitation of a child. The trial court denied the defendant's post trial motions ...

[One of] the defendant's ... argument[s] on appeal is that the State did not prove him guilty beyond a reasonable doubt of attempted predatory criminal sexual assault of a child because the State did not prove either that he possessed the intent to commit an act of sexual penetration with a child or that he took a substantial step toward the commission of the offense. The State responds that the defendant may be found guilty of the offense of attempt even if the intended victim, a 12-year-old boy, did not in reality exist.

To prove the defendant guilty of attempt, the State is required to establish beyond a reasonable doubt that the defendant intended to commit the offense and that the defendant took a substantial step toward the commission of the offense. The impossibility of completing the offense is not a defense. A person commits predatory criminal sexual assault of a child if the accused is at least 17 years of age and commits an act of sexual penetration with a victim under 13 years of age. For the purposes of that offense, sexual penetration is defined as:

> [A]ny contact, however slight, between the sex organ or anus of one person by an object, the sex organ, mouth or anus of another person, or any intrusion, however slight, of any part of the body of one person or of any animal or object into the sex organ or anus of another person, including but not limited to cunnilingus, fellatio or anal penetration....

We ... turn to the substantial-step element of the crime. What constitutes a substantial step toward the commission of an offense is determined by evaluating the facts and circumstances of each particular case. It is not necessary that a defendant complete the last proximate act to be convicted of attempt. Relying in part on *People v. Montefolka*, the defendant reasons that he did not engage in any behavior of a sexual nature such that a trier of fact could conclude that he committed a substantial step towards engaging in an act of sexual penetration with Ricky/XradboyX.

In *Montefolka,* the court held that the State failed to prove that the defendant had taken a substantial step toward committing aggravated criminal sexual assault even through the defendant broke into the victim's home, restrained her, and told her to take off her underwear. This court has recently decided that the holding from *Montefolka* does not apply to a case where a person communicated via the Internet with an individual he believed to be a minor child, set up a meeting place, and then drove to that meeting at the appointed time. *See People v. Patterson*. In *Patterson,* we held that the defendant's substantial steps were arranging the rendezvous with the intended victim and keeping the appointment by traveling to the meeting at the prearranged time. We further held that it was not necessary for the defendant to commit an act of a sexual nature with the fictional intended victim in order to find that the defendant had completed a substantial step towards committing sexual abuse of a child.

Moreover, we note that *Montefolka* may not be good law. In *People v. Hawkins,* the defendant, relying on *Montefolka,* argued that he had not taken a substantial step towards committing criminal sexual assault although he had entered the victim's house, sat on her bed, took off his shoes, crawled between the sheets, and announced his objective to "kick it" with her. The *Hawkins* court was unpersuaded by the defendant's arguments that he did not remove any clothing or fondle the victim, and it affirmed his conviction of attempted criminal sexual assault. The court further noted that *Montefolka* erroneously focused on the fact that there were additional steps the defendant could have taken to bring him within the ambit of having completed a substantial step. In addition, the court looked to the Model Penal Code for guidance in determining whether the defendant had committed a substantial step.

The Model Penal Code lists types of conduct that shall not, as a matter of law, be held insufficient to support an attempt conviction, so long as the act is strongly corroborative of the actor's criminal purpose. The list includes "enticing or seeking to entice the contemplated victim of the crime to go to the place contemplated for its commission." *Hawkins,* quoting Model Penal Code § 5.01(2) at 296 (1985).

In this case, we similarly hold that the defendant completed a substantial step towards the commission of predatory criminal sexual assault. The defendant engaged in two distinct acts leading to the commission of sexual conduct with Ricky/XradboyX. The first was the Internet communication in which he enticed Ricky/XradboyX to meet with him. The second was driving to the agreed-upon location for the meeting. We agree with the defendant that Internet communication, standing alone, is insufficient to find that the defendant had committed a substantial step towards committing predatory sexual acts with a minor. What we are necessarily concerned with is whether the communications, coupled with the defendant's act of driving to the agreed-upon location, constitute a substantial step.

We see no basis to conclude that a rational trier of fact could not have found that the defendant had committed a substantial step and had possessed the requisite intent. Therefore, we affirm the judgment of the trial court finding the defendant guilty of attempted predatory criminal sexual assault of a child.

## United States v. Jackson

United States Court of Appeals, Second Circuit, 1977
560 F.2d 112

FREDERICK van PELT BRYAN, Senior District Judge:

Robert Jackson, William Scott, and Martin Allen appeal from judgments of conviction entered on November 23, 1976 in the United States District Court for the Eastern District of New York after a trial before Chief Judge Jacob Mishler without a jury.

Count one of the indictment alleged that between June 11 and June 21, 1976 the appellants conspired to commit an armed robbery of the Manufacturers Hanover Trust branch located at 210 Flushing Avenue, Brooklyn, New York. Counts two and three each charged appellants with an attempted robbery of the branch on June 14 and on June 21, 1976, respectively. Count four charged them with possession of two unregistered sawed-off shotguns on June 21, 1976.

After a suppression hearing on July 23, 1976 and a one-day trial on August 30, 1976, Chief Judge Mishler filed a memorandum of decision finding each defendant guilty on all four counts.

Appellants' principal contention is that the court below erred in finding them guilty on counts two and three. While they concede that the evidence supported the conspiracy convictions on count one, they assert that, as a matter of law, their conduct never crossed the elusive line which separates "mere preparation" from "attempt." This troublesome question was recently examined by this court in *United States v. Stallworth*, which set forth the applicable legal principles. For the reasons which follow, we affirm the convictions of all three appellants on all four counts.

### I.

The Government's evidence at trial consisted largely of the testimony of Vanessa Hodges, an unindicted co-conspirator, and of various FBI agents who surveilled the Manufacturers Hanover branch on June 21, 1976. Since the facts are of critical importance in any attempt case, we shall review the Government's proof in considerable detail....

Hodges was arrested on Friday, June 18, 1976 on an unrelated bank robbery charge, and immediately began cooperating with the Government.... [S]he told FBI agents that a robbery of the Manufacturers branch at 210 Flushing Avenue was ... scheduled for the following Monday, June 21. The three black male robbers, according to Hodges, would be heavily armed with hand and shoulder weapons and expected to use a brown four-door sedan equipped with a cardboard license plate as the getaway car. She told the agents that Jackson, who would drive the car, was light-skinned with a moustache and a cut on his lip, and she described Allen as short, dark-skinned with facial hair, and Scott as 5' 9, slim build, with an afro hair style and some sort of defect in his right eye.

At the request of the agents, Hodges called Allen on Saturday, June 19, and asked if he were still planning to do the job. He said that he was ready. On Sunday she called him again. This time Allen said that he was not going to rob the bank that Monday because he had learned that Hodges had been arrested and he feared that federal agents might be watching. Hodges nevertheless advised the agents that she thought the robbery might still take place as planned with the three men proceeding without her.

At about 7:00 A. M. on Monday, June 21, 1976, some ten FBI agents took various surveilling positions in the area of the bank. At about 7:39 A. M. the agents observed a brown four-door Lincoln, with a New York license plate on the front and a cardboard facsimile of a license plate on the rear, moving in an easterly direction on Flushing Avenue past the bank, which was located on the southeast corner of Flushing and Washington Avenues. The front seat of the Lincoln was occupied by a black male driver and a black male passenger with mutton-chop sideburns. The Lincoln circled the block and came to a stop at a fire hydrant situated at the side of the bank facing Washington Avenue, a short distance south of the corner of Flushing and Washington....

[After sighting the Lincoln several more times], [t]he Lincoln was next sighted several minutes later in the same position it had previously occupied on the south side of Flushing Avenue between Waverly and Washington. The front license plate was now missing. The vehicle remained parked there for close to thirty minutes. Finally, it began moving east on Flushing Avenue once more, in the direction of the bank.

At some point near the bank as they passed down Flushing Avenue, the appellants detected the presence of the surveillance agents. The Lincoln accelerated down Flushing Avenue and turned south on Grand Avenue again. It was overtaken by FBI agents who ordered the appellants out of the car and arrested them. The agents then observed a black and red plaid suitcase in the rear of the car. The zipper of the suitcase was partially open and exposed two loaded sawed-off shotguns, a toy nickel-plated revolver, a pair of handcuffs, and masks. A New York license plate was seen lying on the front floor of the car. All of these items were seized.

In his memorandum of decision, Chief Judge Mishler concluded that the evidence against Jackson, Scott, and Allen was "overwhelming" on counts one and four. In contrast, he characterized the question of whether the defendants had attempted a bank robbery as charged in counts two and three or were merely engaged in preparations as "a close one." After canvassing the authorities on what this court one month later called a "perplexing problem," Chief Judge Mishler applied the following two-tiered inquiry formulated in *United States v. Mandujano*:

> First, the defendant must have been acting with the kind of culpability otherwise required for the commission of the crime which he is charged with attempting....
>
> Second, the defendant must have engaged in conduct which constitutes a substantial step toward commission of the crime. A substantial step must be conduct strongly corroborative of the firmness of the defendant's criminal intent.

He concluded that on June 14 and again on June 21, the defendants took substantial steps, strongly corroborative of the firmness of their criminal intent, toward commission of the crime of bank robbery and found the defendants guilty on each of the two attempt counts. These appeals followed.

## II.

"(T)here is no comprehensive statutory definition of attempt in federal law." Fed.R.Crim.P. 31(c), however, provides in pertinent part that a defendant may be found guilty of "an attempt to commit either the offense charged or an offense necessarily included therein if the attempt is an offense." [Federal law] specifically makes attempted bank robbery an offense.

Appellant Scott argues that the very wording of [the Federal bank robbery statute] precludes a finding that the actions charged in counts two and three reached the level of attempts. Relying on *United States v. Baker*, he contends that since the statute only mentions attempted taking and not attempted force, violence, or intimidation, it clearly contemplates that actual use of force, violence, or intimidation must precede an attempted taking in order to make out the offense of attempted bank robbery.

The *Stallworth* court faced a similar statutory construction argument which also relied heavily on *United States v. Baker*, supra. In response to the assertion that the defendants in that case could not be convicted of attempted bank robbery because they neither entered the bank nor brandished weapons, Chief Judge Kaufman stated:

> We reject this wooden logic. Attempt is a subtle concept that requires a rational and logically sound definition, one that enables society to punish malefactors who have unequivocally set out upon a criminal course without requiring law enforcement officers to delay until innocent bystanders are imperiled.

We conclude that Scott's argument is foreclosed by this *Stallworth* holding, with which we are in entire accord.

Appellants Jackson and Allen, however, seek to distinguish the instant case from *Stallworth*. They claim that while the conduct of the defendants in that case could properly support a finding of attempted bank robbery, this is not true in the case at bar.

In *Stallworth*, the Government provided Rodney Campbell, an informant who had participated in numerous bank robberies, with an undercover vehicle outfitted with a tape recorder and monitoring equipment on the understanding that he would aid in apprehending his former accomplices. Campbell rejoined his companions, and he transported the group in his undercover vehicle as they cased several banks in Queens.

On Wednesday, January 21, they began actual preparations for a robbery by stealing ski masks from a department store, surgical gloves from a hospital, and purchasing a hacksaw and roofing nails to "fix" a shotgun. On Thursday, January 22, the gang selected a target bank in Whitestone, had one member enter it and report on its physical layout, and scheduled the robbery for Friday morning.

On Friday morning, January 23, Campbell and company assembled with a revolver, sawed-off shotgun, and other paraphernalia for a hold-up. On their way to the bank in the undercover vehicle they covered their fingers with band aids, their hands with the surgical gloves, and put on the ski masks. Gasoline-soaked newspapers were placed under the seats of the car in preparation for its destruction after the getaway.

The car entered the parking lot of the shopping center in which the bank was located and one Sellers got out. He strolled past the bank several times, peeking in at each opportunity, while the car circled the shopping center. Finally, the vehicle pulled up directly in front of the bank and Sellers, armed with the sawed-off shotgun and positioned at an adjacent liquor store, started to approach the bank. Campbell said "let's go," and the occupants of the car reached for the doors. Immediately, FBI agents and New York City policemen who had staked out the parking lot and were monitoring the gang's conversations moved in and arrested the men.

Chief Judge Kaufman, writing for the court, selected the two-tiered inquiry of *United States v. Mandujano*, supra, "properly derived from the writings of many distinguished jurists," as stating the proper test for determining whether the foregoing conduct constituted an attempt. He observed that this analysis "conforms closely to the sensible definition of an attempt proffered by the American Law Institute's Model Penal Code." That definition, Model Penal Code s 5.01 (Proposed Official Draft 1962), provides:

> Criminal Attempt
>
> (1) Definition of Attempt. A person is guilty of an attempt to commit a crime if, acting with the kind of culpability otherwise required for commission of the crime, he:

(a) purposely engages in conduct which would constitute the crime if the attendant circumstances were as he believes them to be; or

(b) when causing a particular result is an element of the crime, does or omits to do anything with the purpose of causing or with the belief that it will cause such result without further conduct on his part; or

(c) purposely does or omits to do anything which, under the circumstances as he believes them to be, is an act or omission constituting a substantial step in a course of conduct planned to culminate in his commission of the crime.

(2) Conduct Which May Be Held Substantial Step Under Subsection (1)(c). Conduct shall not be held to constitute a substantial step under Subsection (1) (c) of this Section unless it is strongly corroborative of the actor's criminal purpose. Without negating the sufficiency of other conduct, the following, if strongly corroborative of the actor's criminal purpose, shall not be held insufficient as a matter of law:

(a) lying in wait, searching for or following the contemplated victim of the crime;

(b) enticing or seeking to entice the contemplated victim of the crime to go to the place contemplated for its commission;

(c) reconnoitering the place contemplated for the commission of the crime;

(d) unlawful entry of a structure, vehicle or enclosure in which it is contemplated that the crime will be committed;

(e) possession of materials to be employed in the commission of the crime, which are specially designed for such unlawful use or which can serve no lawful purpose of the actor under the circumstances;

(f) possession, collection or fabrication of materials to be employed in the commission of the crime, at or near the place contemplated for its commission, where such possession, collection or fabrication serves no lawful purpose of the actor under the circumstances;

(g) soliciting an innocent agent to engage in conduct constituting an element of the crime.

(3) Conduct Designed to Aid Another in Commission of a Crime. A person who engages in conduct designed to aid another to commit a crime which would establish his complicity under Section 2.06 if the crime were committed by such other person, is guilty of an attempt to commit the crime, although the crime is not attempted by such other person.

(4) Renunciation of Criminal Purpose. When the actor's conduct would otherwise constitute an attempt under Subsection (1)(b) or (1)(c) of this Section, it is an affirmative defense that he abandoned his effort to commit the crime or otherwise prevented its commission, under circumstances manifesting a complete and voluntary renunciation of his criminal purpose. The establishment of such defense does not, however, affect the liability of an accomplice who did not join in such abandonment or prevention.

Within the meaning of this Article, renunciation of criminal purpose is not voluntary if it is motivated, in whole or in part, by circumstances, not present or apparent at the inception of the actor's course of conduct, which increase the probability of detection or apprehension or which make more difficult the accomplishment of the criminal purpose. Renunciation is not complete if it is motivated by a decision to postpone the criminal conduct until a more advantageous time or to transfer the criminal effort to another but similar objective or victim.

The draftsmen of the Model Penal Code recognized the difficulty of arriving at a general standard for distinguishing acts of preparation from acts constituting an attempt. They found general agreement that when an actor committed the "last proximate act," i.e., when he had done all that he believed necessary to effect a particular result which is an element of the offense, he committed an attempt. They also concluded, however, that while the last proximate act is sufficient to constitute an attempt, it is not necessary to such a finding. The problem then was to devise a standard more inclusive than one requiring the last proximate act before attempt liability would attach, but less inclusive than one which would make every act done with the intent to commit a crime criminal. *See* Model Penal Code s 5.01, Comment at 38–39 (Tent. Draft No. 10, 1960).

The draftsmen considered and rejected the following approaches to distinguishing preparation from attempt, later summarized in *Mandujano* :

> (a) The physical proximity doctrine the overt act required for an attempt must be proximate to the completed crime, or directly tending toward the completion of the crime, or must amount to the commencement of the consummation.
>
> (b) The dangerous proximity doctrine a test given impetus by Mr. Justice Holmes whereby the greater the gravity and probability of the offense, and the nearer the act to the crime, the stronger is the case for calling the act an attempt.
>
> (c) The indispensable element test a variation of the proximity tests which emphasizes any indispensable aspect of the criminal endeavor over which the actor has not yet acquired control.
>
> (d) The probable desistance test the conduct constitutes an attempt if, in the ordinary and natural course of events, without interruption from an outside source, it will result in the crime intended.
>
> (e) The abnormal step approach an attempt is a step toward crime which goes beyond the point where the normal citizen would think better of his conduct and desist.
>
> (f) The res ipsa loquitur or unequivocality test an attempt is committed when the actor's conduct manifests an intent to commit a crime.

The formulation upon which the draftsmen ultimately agreed required, in addition to criminal purpose, that an act be a substantial step in a course of conduct designed to accomplish a criminal result, and that it be strongly corroborative of criminal purpose in order for it to constitute such a substantial step. The following differences between this test and previous approaches to the preparation-attempt problem were noted:

> First, this formulation shifts the emphasis from what remains to be done the chief concern of the proximity tests to what the actor has already done. The fact that further major steps must be taken before the crime can be completed does not preclude a finding that the steps already undertaken are substantial. It is expected, in the normal case, that this approach will broaden the scope of attempt liability.
>
> Second, although it is intended that the requirement of a substantial step will result in the imposition of attempt liability only in those instances in which some firmness of criminal purpose is shown, no finding is required as to whether the

> actor would probably have desisted prior to completing the crime. Potentially the probable desistance test could reach very early steps toward crime depending upon how one assesses the probabilities of desistance but since in practice this test follows closely the proximity approaches, rejection of probable desistance will not narrow the scope of attempt liability.
>
> Finally, the requirement of proving a substantial step generally will prove less of a hurdle for the prosecution than the res ipsa loquitur approach, which requires that the actor's conduct must itself manifest the criminal purpose. The difference will be illustrated in connection with the present section's requirement of corroboration. Here it should be noted that, in the present formulation, the two purposes to be served by the res ipsa loquitur test are, to a large extent, treated separately. Firmness of criminal purpose is intended to be shown by requiring a substantial step, while problems of proof are dealt with by the requirement of corroboration (although, under the reasoning previously expressed, the latter will also tend to establish firmness of purpose). Model Penal Code s 5.01, Comment at 47 (Tent. Draft No. 10, 1960).

The draftsmen concluded that, in addition to assuring firmness of criminal design, the requirement of a substantial step would preclude attempt liability, with its accompanying harsh penalties, for relatively remote preparatory acts. At the same time, however, by not requiring a "last proximate act" or one of its various analogues it would permit the apprehension of dangerous persons at an earlier stage than the other approaches without immunizing them from attempt liability. *Id.* at 47–48.

Applying the *Mandujano* test, which in turn was derived in large part from the Model Penal Code's standard, Chief Judge Kaufman concluded that since the *Stallworth* appellants had intended to execute a successful bank robbery and took substantial steps in furtherance of their plan that strongly corroborated their criminal intent, their attempted bank robbery convictions were proper.

In the case at bar, Chief Judge Mishler anticipated the precise analysis which this Court adopted in the strikingly similar *Stallworth* case. He then found that on June 14 the appellants, already agreed upon a robbery plan, drove to the bank with loaded weapons. In order to carry the heavy weekend deposit sacks, they recruited another person. Cardboard was placed over the license, and the bank was entered and reconnoitered. Only then was the plan dropped for the moment and rescheduled for the following Monday. On that day, June 21, the defendants performed essentially the same acts. Since the cameras had already been located there was no need to enter the bank again, and since the appellants had arrived at the bank earlier, conditions were more favorable to their initial robbery plan than they had been on June 14. He concluded that on both occasions these men were seriously dedicated to the commission of a crime, had passed beyond the stage of preparation, and would have assaulted the bank had they not been dissuaded by certain external factors, viz., the breaking up of the weekend deposits and crowd of patrons in the bank on June 14 and the detection of the FBI surveillance on June 21.

We cannot say that these conclusions which Chief Judge Mishler reached as the trier of fact as to what the evidence before him established were erroneous. As in *Stallworth*, the criminal intent of the appellants was beyond dispute. The question remaining then is the substantiality of the steps taken on the dates in question, and how strongly this corroborates the firmness of their obvious criminal intent. This is a matter of degree. *See* Model Penal Code s 5.01, Comments at 47 (Tent. Draft No. 10, 1960).

On two separate occasions, appellants reconnoitered the place contemplated for the commission of the crime and possessed the paraphernalia to be employed in the commission of the crime loaded sawed-off shotguns, extra shells, a toy revolver, handcuffs, and masks which was specially designed for such unlawful use and which could serve no lawful purpose under the circumstances. Under the Model Penal Code formulation, supra at 117–118, approved by the *Stallworth* court, either type of conduct, standing alone, was sufficient as a matter of law to constitute a "substantial step" if it strongly corroborated their criminal purpose. Here both types of conduct coincided on both June 14 and June 21, along with numerous other elements strongly corroborative of the firmness of appellants' criminal intent. The steps taken toward a successful bank robbery thus were not "insubstantial" as a matter of law, and Chief Judge Mishler found them "substantial" as a matter of fact. We are unwilling to substitute our assessment of the evidence for his, and thus affirm the convictions for attempted bank robbery on counts two and three.

The judgments of conviction are affirmed.

## *Notes and Questions*

1. The influence of the Model Penal Code's substantial step test has been considerable. Over half of the states in America follow a version of this test, as well as close to two thirds of the United States Circuit Courts of Appeals.

2. In a sense, *People v. Scott* and *United States v. Jackson* are mirror images of the *Duke* and *Rizzo* cases discussed in the previous section. The court held in *Scott* that a defendant's online communications with a minor and driving to the agreed-upon location for meeting with the minor were sufficient to trigger attempt liability under the Model Penal Code's "substantial step" formulation. In contrast, the *Duke* court applied a common law proximity test to hold that that essentially identical conduct could not trigger liability for an attempt. Which approach do you believe generates the right outcome in this kind of case? Explain.

3. In *Jackson,* the circuit court ruled that either "reconnoiter[ing] the place contemplated for the commission of the crime" or "possess[ing] the paraphernalia to be employed in the commission of the crime" would be enough, standing alone, for an attempted robbery conviction according to the Model Penal Code's substantial step test. This stands in stark contrast with the application of the dangerous proximity test in *Rizzo,* which led to acquitting the defendant of attempted robbery on essentially identical facts to the ones in *Jackson.* This demonstrates that—as the court pointed out in *Jackson*—application of the Model Penal Code's "substantial step" test "is expected, in the normal case ... [to] broaden the scope of attempt liability." Do you see the Model Penal Code's expansion of the scope of attempt liability when compared to the common law proximity tests as a virtue or a defect? Why?

4. As the court explained in *Jackson,* the substantial step test focuses on the substantiality of the acts that the defendant has already performed. If the defendant has performed a substantial act in furtherance of the commission of the offense, his conduct triggers attempt liability even if several more important steps have yet to be taken. This explains why reconnoitering the place where the offense is going to be committed is enough to generate liability for attempted robbery, even though several additional and important steps need to be taken in order to consummate the crime. In contrast, the focus of the proximity tests is on what remains to be done. Therefore, attempt liability is not imposed under these tests if the actor has yet to perform important acts in furtherance

of the crime. This is why the court held in *Rizzo* that reconnoitering the place was not enough to trigger liability for attempted robbery. Although several important steps had been taken, additional significant steps had to be taken in order for the robbery to be successful. Therefore, the actors were still not in "dangerous proximity" to the consummation of the offense.

5. The fact that the Model Penal Code's substantial step test generates attempt liability earlier than the common law proximity tests has important consequences for the police. The substantial step test allows police officers to arrest those who plan to commit an offense at an earlier stage than the proximity tests without running the risk that early apprehension might make it more difficult to hold the defendant liable for an attempt. As the court observed in *Jackson,* the substantial step test "would permit the apprehension of dangerous persons at an earlier stage than the other approaches without immunizing them from attempt liability." Given that under the proximity tests attempt liability is triggered only when the actor comes dangerously close to consummating the offense, police officers have to wait until the offense is about to be committed in order to thwart the crime if they want to maximize the chances of an attempt conviction. This is illustrated by the *Rizzo* case, in which the court praised the police for efficiently foiling a robbery but then explained that the actors could not be held liable for an attempt because the police intervened too early. On the other hand, the substantial step test allows officers to apprehend a suspect fairly early without risking that early apprehension may shield the actor from attempt liability.

6. The differences between the substantial step test and the common law proximity tests have important consequences for the abandonment doctrine as well. Since the proximity tests draw the line between preparation and punishable attempts very close to consummation, the actor may abandon his criminal plan quite late in the process. The opposite is true in the case of the substantial step test. Given that the substantial step test gives rise to attempt liability relatively early, the actor has comparatively little time to renounce his criminal purpose. This, as the Supreme Court of Washington explained in *State v. Workman,* 90 Wash.2d 443 (1978), barely leaves room for the defense of abandonment:

> Once a substantial step has been taken, and the crime of attempt is accomplished, the crime cannot be abandoned. The defendants' attempt to show they abandoned their plan is thus relevant only if the abandonment occurred before a substantial step was taken. Through arguing their theory at trial, they could only have hoped to show they never took a substantial step toward the specific crime. Abandonment is not, however, a true defense to the crime of attempt under our statute that is, a showing of abandonment does not negate the State's allegation that a substantial step occurred. Thus, pursuing the theory of abandonment could only be a strategy for showing why a substantial step was never taken. Defendants could not thereby show whether such a step was taken. We therefore conclude an instruction on abandonment is not necessary as a matter of law to properly define a "substantial step." *Id.*

Note, however, that—contrary to what is the case in Washington—the Model Penal Code contemplates an abandonment defense in § 5.01(4), which prescribes that:

> When the actor's conduct would otherwise constitute an attempt under Subsection (1)(b) or (1)(c) of this Section, it is an affirmative defense that he abandoned his effort to commit the crime or otherwise prevented its commission, under circumstances manifesting a complete and voluntary renunciation of his criminal purpose. § 5.01(4).

Pursuant to this provision, voluntary renunciation is a defense even if the conduct would otherwise constitute an attempt according to the Code. That is, a showing of voluntary abandonment will defeat criminal liability even if the defendant already engaged in a substantial step in furtherance of the offense. The Code's position is a compromise, however, for it prescribes that abandonment is an "affirmative defense." According to § 1.12(4)(a) of the Code, this means that the defendant has the burden of proving voluntary renunciation. Several of the states that have followed the Model Penal Code approach to renunciation hold that the defendant must prove voluntary abandonment by a preponderance of the evidence. *See, e.g., State v. Alston,* 709 A.2d 310 (1998).

7. The following depiction illustrates how criminal liability attaches at different moments depending on whether the Model Penal Code's substantial step test or the common law proximity tests are used to distinguish between preparation and punishable attempts:

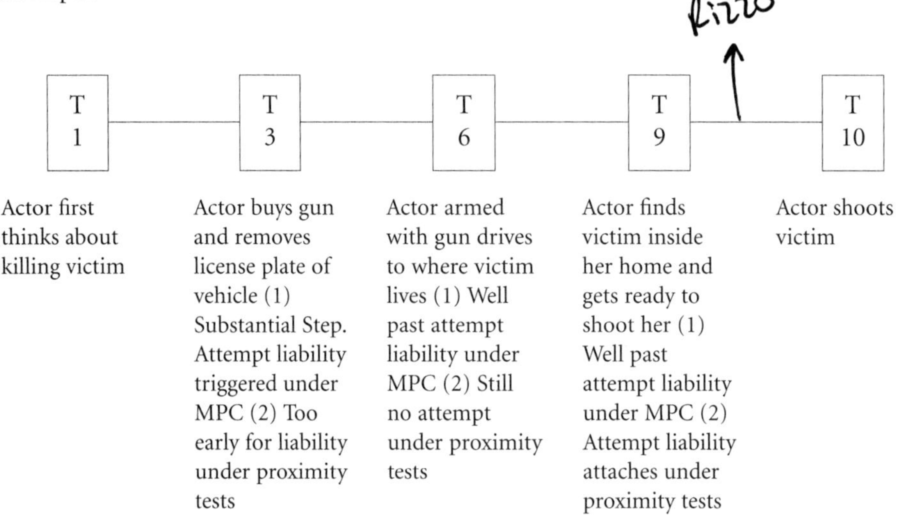
T 1
T 3
T 6
T 9
T 10
Actor first thinks about killing victim
Actor buys gun and removes license plate of vehicle (1) Substantial Step. Attempt liability triggered under MPC (2) Too early for liability under proximity tests
Actor armed with gun drives to where victim lives (1) Well past attempt liability under MPC (2) Still no attempt under proximity tests
Actor finds victim inside her home and gets ready to shoot her (1) Well past attempt liability under MPC (2) Attempt liability attaches under proximity tests
Actor shoots victim

Note that attempt liability is triggered under the substantial step test well before it attaches under the common law proximity tests (T 3 vs. T 9). Also, observe how the different tests impact both when the police may arrest the actor without immunizing him from attempt liability and when the actor may renounce his criminal purpose before crossing the threshold that separates preparation from attempt. In a jurisdiction that applies the substantial step test, the police may arrest the actor without shielding him from attempt liability any time after "T 3." On the other hand, in a jurisdiction that applies a common law proximity test, the police may have to wait to make an arrest until at least "T 8" or "T 9." If they arrest earlier, they run the risk of not being able to secure a conviction for an attempted offense, as *Rizzo* illustrates. Finally, take note of how the actor has a very short amount of time during which he can abandon his criminal plan before his conduct amounts to an attempt under the substantial step test. He can only abandon the conduct with no consequences whatsoever from "T 1" to "T 3." After "T 3," his conduct already counts as a substantial step that generates attempt liability. As a result, voluntary renouncement after "T 3" will no longer be a defense (see *State v. Workman* in Note 5) or it will be an affirmative defense that the defendant will likely have the burden of proving by a preponderance of the evidence (see Model Penal Code and *State v. Alston* in Note 5). In contrast, in a proximity test jurisdiction, the actor may renounce his criminal purpose with absolutely no adverse consequences at any time from "T 1" until at least "T 8" or "T 9."

# § 11.03 Attempts: Subjective Offense Element (*Mens Rea*) — Common Law

## Stennet v. State

Court of Criminal Appeals of Alabama, 1990
564 So.2d 95

TYSON, Judge.

Chinda Urbina Stennet, the appellant, was indicted for the attempted murder of Vicki Pearson. The jury found her guilty of the lesser included offense of attempted manslaughter. The trial judge set sentence at ten years' imprisonment in the penitentiary.

On the evening of April 19, 1988, an argument ensued between the appellant and Vicki Pearson at Pearson's trailer. At some point, the appellant left Pearson's trailer. A short time later, the appellant returned to Pearson's trailer and fired a shotgun twice at the trailer. Although no one was injured by the shots, numerous shotgun pellets hit Pearson's trailer.

The sole issue raised by this appellant is whether the trial judge erred by failing to instruct the jury on the offenses of attempted assault in the second degree and reckless endangerment. We agree that the trial judge should have instructed the jury on the offense of reckless endangerment. The trial judge erroneously instructed the jury on the offense of attempted manslaughter, since we find that attempted manslaughter is not an offense in this state.

[The Alabama attempt statute] provides that "[a] person is guilty of an attempt to commit a crime, if, *with the intent to commit a specific offense,* he does any overt act towards the commission of such offense." The trial judge [also] ... instructed the jury [that] "[a] person commits the crime of manslaughter if ... [h]e *recklessly* causes the death of another person" (emphasis added). Therefore, in order to constitute the offense of attempted manslaughter, one must intend to recklessly cause the death of another. This is impossible because "intentional" and "reckless" are inconsistent terms.

Numerous other courts have considered this question and have also found that there is no such offense as attempted manslaughter. *See People v. Zimmerman,* 360 N.Y.S.2d 127, 128 (1974) ("An attempt is an intentional act. Manslaughter ... is a reckless act. One may not intentionally attempt to cause the death of another human being by a reckless act."); ... *People v. Brown,* 249 N.Y.S.2d 922, 923 (1964) ("There must be an intent to commit a specific crime in order to constitute an attempt. An attempt to commit manslaughter is apparently a contradiction because the specific crime of manslaughter involves no intent and, accordingly, an intention to commit a crime whose distinguishing element is lack of intent is logically repugnant."); ... *State v. Zupetz,* 322 N.W.2d 730 (Minn.1982) ("it seems illogical that someone could intend to cause someone else's death through negligence or even recklessness" because while "[o]ne may reasonably conclude that [the defendant] intentionally behaved in a reckless manner" and "may have intended to kill [the victim]," even so "it makes no sense to say that he intended to kill her by being reckless").

> Recklessness and negligence are incompatible with desire or intention. Where, therefore, in a crime which by definition may be committed recklessly or negligently but not intentionally, the recklessness or negligence relates not to a pure circumstance but to a consequence, it is impossible to conceive of an attempt. Thus

> there can be no attempt to commit involuntary manslaughter. The consequence involved in that crime is the death of the victim and an act done with intent to achieve this, if an attempt at all, is attempted murder. Smith, *Two Problems in Criminal Attempts,* 70 Harv.L.Rev. 422, 434 (1957).

Likewise, under Alabama law, if a person attempts to cause, recklessly or otherwise, the death of another person, that person is guilty of attempted murder. This is because the death of another was the act intended although the attempt to accomplish this result failed. There is no such offense as attempted manslaughter in Alabama since "intent" and "recklessness" are incompatible terms. *See Free v. State,* 455 So.2d 137 (Ala.Crim.App.), *cert. denied* (Ala.1984) ("one cannot recklessly attempt [i.e., intend but fail] to commit murder") ... Thus, the trial judge erred by instructing the jury on the offense of attempted manslaughter, an offense which does not exist in this state....

Defense counsel properly requested an instruction on the offense of reckless endangerment, and we find that the trial judge erroneously refused to give that charge. A person commits the offense of reckless endangerment if he "recklessly engages in conduct which creates a substantial risk of serious physical injury to another person." Ala.Code, § 13A-6-24 (1975). The evidence in this case showed that the appellant fired a shotgun at the victim's trailer while the victim and her family were inside. Under the facts of this case, as established by the evidence presented at trial, there was a rational basis for a verdict convicting the appellant of reckless endangerment. Thus, under these particular circumstances, reckless endangerment was a lesser included offense of attempted murder, and the jury should have been so instructed.

The appellant's conviction for the offense of attempted manslaughter is reversed and the cause is remanded to the trial court.

## People v. Thomas

Supreme Court of Colorado, 1986
729 P.2d 972

LOHR, Justice.

The defendant, John Leago Thomas, Jr., was convicted of attempted reckless manslaughter and first degree assault as the result of a jury trial in Adams County District Court. On appeal, the defendant argued, among other things, that attempted reckless manslaughter is not a cognizable crime in Colorado. The court of appeals agreed with the defendant's argument and reversed the conviction for attempted reckless manslaughter, but affirmed the conviction for first degree assault. We granted certiorari to determine whether attempted reckless manslaughter is a cognizable crime in the state of Colorado. We conclude that it is, and hold that the court of appeals erred in reversing the defendant's conviction for that crime.

### I.

On the evening of February 4, 1981, the defendant received a telephone call from a former girlfriend informing him that she had been raped in her apartment by a man who lived in an apartment upstairs. The defendant arrived at the woman's apartment shortly thereafter, armed with a pistol. He went upstairs and gained entrance into the apartment occupied by the alleged assailant by identifying himself as a policeman. The defendant pointed his gun at the man who, believing the defendant was a police officer, accompanied him back down to the woman's apartment. The woman identified the man as the rapist, and the defendant instructed her to call the police. At that time, the man started to flee to his own apartment, and the defendant gave chase. The defendant fired three shots, two of which struck the fleeing man. The defendant testified that he fired the first shot as a warning when the man was going up the stairs, that he fired a second shot accidentally when the man kicked him while on the stairs, and that the third shot was also a warning shot, fired from the outside of the building near the window of the apartment occupied by the alleged rapist. When the police arrived, they found the defendant still waiting outside, holding the gun.

The jury was instructed on the crimes of attempted first degree murder, first degree assault, and the lesser included offenses of attempted second degree murder, attempted reckless manslaughter, attempted heat of passion manslaughter, and second degree assault. The jury returned verdicts of guilty to the charges of first degree assault and attempted reckless manslaughter, and the trial court entered judgment accordingly.

Upon appeal, the court of appeals sustained the conviction for first degree assault, but reversed the attempted reckless manslaughter conviction on the basis that attempted reckless manslaughter is not a legally cognizable offense in Colorado. We granted certiorari to review that latter conclusion and the resulting reversal of the defendant's conviction for attempted reckless manslaughter.

## II.

### A.

The language of the relevant statutes provides the framework for our analysis. The crime of reckless manslaughter is defined as follows:

> (1) A person commits the crime of manslaughter if:
>
> (a) He recklessly causes the death of another person;....
>
> "Recklessly," the relevant culpable mental state for this crime, is defined [as]
>
> (8) A person acts recklessly when he consciously disregards a substantial and unjustifiable risk that a result will occur or that a circumstance exists.
>
> As applied to the offense of reckless manslaughter, the requisite conscious disregard of a substantial and unjustifiable risk relates to a result, the death of another person.
>
> The inchoate offense of criminal attempt is defined as follows ...:
>
> A person commits criminal attempt if, acting with the kind of culpability otherwise required for commission of an offense, he engages in conduct constituting a substantial step toward the commission of the offense. A substantial step is any conduct, whether act, omission, or possession, which is strongly corroborative of the firmness of the actor's purpose to complete the commission of the offense....

The court of appeals held that "[r]ecklessness is ... a mental culpability which is incompatible with the concept of an intentional act." This is so, the court held, because the "conscious disregard" with respect to risk of death that is essential to reckless manslaughter cannot be equated with the conscious intent to cause death which the court of appeals implicitly determined to be a necessary element of the offense of criminal attempt in this context. On certiorari review, the defendant supports this analysis, contending that "[o]ne cannot intend to cause a specific result ... by consciously disregarding the risk that the result will occur." A careful analysis of the elements of criminal attempt and of reckless manslaughter demonstrates, however, that the court of appeals' analysis and the defendant's supporting arguments are misconceived.

In *People v. Frysig*, we construed the criminal attempt statute in the context of a charge of attempted first degree sexual assault. We held that the intent to commit the underlying offense is an essential element of the crime.

More precisely, in order to be guilty of criminal attempt, the actor must act with the kind of culpability otherwise required for commission of the underlying offense and must engage in the conduct which constitutes the substantial step with the further intent to perform acts which, if completed, would constitute the underlying offense.

In order to complete the offense of reckless manslaughter, it is necessary that the actor cause the death of another person by acting in a manner that involves a substantial and unjustifiable risk of death of that other person and that the actor be conscious of that risk and of its nature when electing to act. Attempted reckless manslaughter requires that the accused have the intent to commit the underlying offense of reckless manslaughter. The "intent to commit the underlying offense" of which *People v. Frysig* speaks is the intent to engage in and complete the risk-producing act or conduct. It does not include an intent that death occur even though the underlying crime, reckless manslaughter, has death as an essential element.

The crime of attempted reckless manslaughter also requires that the risk-producing act or conduct be commenced and sufficiently pursued to constitute a "substantial step toward the commission of the offense." That is, the act or conduct must proceed far enough to be "strongly corroborative of the firmness of the actor's purpose," *Id.*, to complete those acts that will produce a substantial and unjustifiable risk of death of another.

Finally, in order to be guilty of attempted reckless manslaughter the actor must engage in the requisite acts or conduct "with the kind of culpability otherwise required for the commission of the underlying offense," that is, with a conscious disregard of a substantial and unjustifiable risk that the acts or conduct will cause the death of another person. Based upon this analysis, and contrary to the defendant's argument, there is no logical or legal inconsistency involved in the recognition of attempted reckless manslaughter as a crime under the Colorado Criminal Code....

We reverse that part of the court of appeals' judgment overturning the defendant's conviction for attempted reckless manslaughter.

**DUBOFSKY, Justice, specially concurring:**

I join the majority opinion under the facts of this case. *People v. Krovarz,* 697 P.2d 378, 381 n. 9 (Colo.1985), suggests that the analysis employed in that case should not be extended to attempted reckless conduct. The footnote in *Krovarz* reflected the concern of a commentator who observed that allowing one to be charged with attempted murder under the wide range of conduct encompassed within "reckless," without a resulting death, may extend criminal liability for harmful conduct to situations such as driving very fast on the wrong side of the road while going around a curve. Enker, *Mens Rea and Criminal Attempt,* 1977 Am.Bar Found.Res.J. 845, 854. The conduct is not in fact harmful if there is no traffic coming in the opposite direction. *Id.* The commentator suggested that where the actor risks harm, rather than intending harm, the conduct should be penalized under a legislative definition of a substantive crime instead of the common law definition of attempt. *Id.* at 859. Given the facts in this case, however, I am convinced that the defendant came close enough to intending harm that he can be convicted of attempted reckless manslaughter.

## *Notes and Questions*

1. Punishable attempts at common law required proof that the defendant had the "specific intent" to bring about the proscribed harm. In other words, defendant must engage in conduct that risks causing harm with the "intent" or "purpose" of harming the victim. Consequently, a defendant cannot be held liable of attempting the commission of a reckless or negligent result crime. This is the view espoused in *Stennet v. State* and adopted in the vast majority of American jurisdictions.

2. In *People v. Thomas,* the Supreme Court of Colorado adopted a different view. According to the court, an actor may be held liable for an attempted offense as long as he purposely engages in the conduct that creates the risk of harm and acts with the kind of culpability that the underlying offense requires regarding the result. Under this view, a defendant may be convicted of attempted reckless manslaughter if he both *purposely* created the risk *and* he *recklessly* disregarded the risk created by his conduct.

3. The defendant in *Stennet* fired at a trailer twice with a shotgun. Although no one was hurt, defendant was charged with attempted reckless manslaughter. As was pointed out in Note 1, the court ruled that defendant could not be held liable because the state did not prove that she intended to kill the person inside the trailer. What result if the view of attempts adopted in *Thomas* is applied to the facts in *Stennet*? Which approach is preferable? Why?

4. Justice Dubofsky pointed out in his special concurrence in *Thomas* that some commentators are concerned that allowing a conviction for attempted reckless homicide might lead to imposing criminal liability on someone for "driving very fast on the wrong side of the road while going around a curve" even "if there is no traffic coming in the opposite direction." Should someone who engages in that type of conduct be convicted of attempted reckless homicide? Would criminal liability be warranted if there is traffic coming in the opposite direction but no one is harmed by the driver's reckless conduct? Why or why not?

5. The court observed in *Stennet* that the defendant could be held liable for "reckless endangerment" as a result of his conduct. The offense is defined as "recklessly engaging in conduct which creates a substantial risk of serious physical injury to another person." Code of Alabama Section 13A-6-24. Is it more appropriate to convict actors like the defendant in *Stennet* of "attempted reckless manslaughter" or of "reckless endangerment?" Or do you think such actors should escape liability altogether? Why?

6. Reckless endangerment is considered a misdemeanor in Alabama, as it is in most states which criminalize such conduct. The punishment in Alabama for reckless endangerment is a term of imprisonment that cannot exceed one year. In contrast, attempted reckless manslaughter in Colorado is considered a felony and is punished by a term of imprisonment of more than one year but less than three years. If attempted reckless manslaughter were punishable in Alabama (which it is not, according to *Stennet*), it would be punished with a term of imprisonment between one and ten years. How much do you think an actor like the defendant in *Stennet* deserves to be punished? If so, should he be punished for a misdemeanor or a felony? Assuming that such actors should be punished, how much should they be punished? Do you think that the punishment imposed in Alabama for reckless endangerment is appropriate, or should it be higher or lower? Do you think

that Colorado punishes attempted reckless manslaughter appropriately, or should the offense be punished more or less? Explain.

# § 11.04 Attempts: Subjective Offense Element (*Mens Rea*) — Model Penal Code

## Model Penal Code § 5.01. Criminal Attempt.

(1) Definition of Attempt. A person is guilty of an attempt to commit a crime if, acting with the kind of culpability otherwise required for commission of the crime, he:

(a) purposely engages in conduct that would constitute the crime if the attendant circumstances were as he believes them to be; or

(b) when causing a particular result is an element of the crime, does or omits to do anything with the purpose of causing or with the belief that it will cause such result without further conduct on his part; or

(c) purposely does or omits to do anything that, under the circumstances as he believes them to be, is an act or omission constituting a substantial step in a course of conduct planned to culminate in his commission of the crime.

## State v. Nuñez

Court of Appeals of Arizona, Division 1, 1989
159 Ariz. 594

GREER, Judge.

Appellant was indicted on March 2, 1987, on three counts of attempted first degree murder and one count of first degree burglary, all class 2 felonies. Prior to trial, the state alleged that the felonies were of a dangerous nature. After a trial by jury, appellant was found guilty as charged. On November 25, 1987, appellant was sentenced to the presumptive term of 10.5 years on each count, with all counts to run concurrently ... Appellant filed a timely notice of appeal.

The facts, taken in a light most favorable to sustaining the verdict, are as follows. On February 23, 1987, appellant began banging on the front door of L.T. and T.T.'s house. Appellant demanded to speak with L.T., whom he accused of dating his girlfriend. L.T. was asleep, and T.T. refused to open the front door. T.T. telephoned her brother, Richard, to come over and persuade the appellant to leave. When Richard arrived, he found appellant in the front yard. Appellant produced a pistol and shot and injured Richard. He then kicked in the front door, shot both L.T. and T.T., and left the home. On his way off the property, appellant shot Richard one more time. Appellant was followed from the L.T., T.T. home by neighbors, who alerted the police.

The police apprehended appellant some blocks from the L.T., T.T. home after he had disposed of his pistol. The arresting officers noted signs of intoxication and gave appellant a breath test which showed that he had a blood-alcohol level of .11%. At trial, appellant defended on the basis that he was too intoxicated to form the necessary intent for attempted murder. On appeal, appellant raises the following issue:

> Did the trial court erroneously instruct the jury on first degree murder and attempt?....

At trial, the jury was instructed, in part, as follows:

> For the crime of Attempted First Degree Murder, the State must prove that the defendant acted intentionally or knowingly. If you determine that the defendant was intoxicated at the time, you may consider the fact that he was intoxicated in determining whether he could have intentionally or with intent to commit the same crimes (sic). However, you may not consider the fact that he was voluntarily intoxicated in determining whether he could have "knowingly" committed the said crime of attempted first degree murder.

... Appellant acknowledges that first degree murder can be committed with either an intentional or knowing state of mind. However, he claims that, since the attempt statute requires an intentional state of mind, the jury instructions referring to either intentional or knowing attempted first degree murder were erroneous.

In *State v. Galan,* this court considered whether a defendant could commit attempted trafficking in stolen property. Under the trafficking statute, a person need only act recklessly to commit second degree trafficking in stolen property. In discussing whether or not one could intentionally attempt to recklessly traffic in stolen property, this court stated:

> The defendant's argument that an attempt still requires a specific intent which is incompatible with the reckless state of mind does not reckon with all of the language of A.R.S. § 13-1001, the attempt statute. We quote that provision again with emphasis on the words that the defendant's argument ignores:
>
> A person commits attempt if, *acting with the kind of culpability otherwise required for the commission of an offense, such person,*
>
> (1) Intentionally engages in conduct which would constitute an offense if the attendant circumstances were as such person believes them to be.
>
> A common sense reading of the provision leads to the conclusion that the words "intentionally engages in conduct" refers in this case to the actions that make up trafficking like buying property intending to resell it (A.R.S. § 13-2301(B)(3)) and that the words "acting with the kind of culpability otherwise required for the commission of an offense" requires (sic) only that acts be accompanied by a reckless state of mind as to the circumstances attending the status of the property. A contrary conclusion would mean that the words "acting with the kind of culpability otherwise required for the commission of an offense" are superfluous. *Galan,* 134 Ariz. at 591–592, 658 P.2d at 244–45 (emphasis in original) (footnote omitted).

In other words, Galan needed only to intentionally buy property intending to resell it; as to the rest of the elements of the crime, he only needed to act recklessly. The court in *Galan* also noted that the Model Penal Code's proposed definition of attempt, Model Penal Code § 5.01(1), was, in every material respect, like the language of Arizona's attempt statute, A.R.S. § 13-1001(A). *Id.* at 592, 658 P.2d at 245. Quoting from the comments to the Model Penal Code, § 5.01(1), at 27 (Tent. Draft No. 10, 1960), the court stated:

> This section adopts the view that the actor must have for his purpose to engage in the criminal conduct or accomplish the criminal result which is an element of the substantive crime but that his purpose need not encompass all the surrounding circumstances included in the formal definition of the substantive offense. As to them, it is sufficient that he acts with the culpability that is required for commission of a crime. *Galan,* 134 Ariz. at 592, 658 P.2d at 245.

... In *State v. Adams,* the defendant was convicted of attempted second degree murder. On the issue of whether or not there was a cognizable offense in Arizona of attempted reckless manslaughter or attempted negligent homicide, an issue specifically left open in *Galan,* this court stated:

> Clearly, the statute, like the Model Penal Code ... requires the actor to engage in "purposive" conduct. The relevant portion of the intent statute applies to a person who has planned the commission of an offense and intentionally takes any step towards accomplishing the commission of the offense. *Adams,* 155 Ariz. at 120, 745 P.2d at 178.

In addressing this same question, the drafters of the Model Penal Code agreed that there should be no attempt crime for negligent or reckless homicide. The Code goes on to state:

> When, on the other hand, a person actually believes that his behavior will produce the proscribed result, it is appropriate to treat him as attempting to cause the result, whether or not that is his purpose.
>
> Subsection (1)(b) provides that when causing a particular result is an element of the crime, as in homicide offenses or criminally obtaining property, an actor commits an attempt when he does or omits to do anything with the purpose of causing "or with the belief that it will cause" such result without further conduct on his part. Thus, a belief that death will ensue from the actor's conduct, or that property will be obtained, will suffice, as well as would a purpose to bring about those results. If, for example, the actor's purpose were to demolish a building and, knowing that persons were in the building and that they would be killed by the explosion, he nevertheless detonated a bomb that turned out to be defective, he could be prosecuted for attempted murder even though it was no part of his purpose that the inhabitants of the building would be killed. Model Penal Code § 5.01.2, at 301 (1985).

After looking at these authorities and their interpretation of or application to the Arizona attempt statute, we conclude that attempted first degree murder can be knowingly committed and, as such, is an offense in Arizona. *Galan* holds that the Arizona attempt statute does not require a defendant to act intentionally as to all elements of an offense. *Adams* and the Model Penal Code conclude that the attempt statute generally punishes conduct consistent with either an intentional or knowing state of mind.

While cases from other jurisdictions have come to different conclusions regarding jury instructions for attempted murder which refer to a knowing state of mind, *see, i.e., People v. Kraft, supra,* Arizona's statute has not been interpreted to require an intentional state of mind for all elements of the attempted crime. Accordingly, the jury instruction in this case was a correct statement of Arizona law.

For the foregoing reasons, the conviction and sentence are affirmed.

## *Notes and Questions*

1. The Model Penal Code's approach to the *mens rea* of attempts distinguishes between the mental state that must attach regarding conduct, result and circumstance elements. Regarding the conduct element of attempted offenses, the Code prescribes that the actor must either *purposely* "engag[e] in conduct that would constitute the crime" or *purposely* "d[o] or omi[t] to do anything that ... a substantial step" toward the commission of the

offense. The discussion in *State v. Nuñez* regarding the mental state required for the offense of "attempted trafficking in stolen property" is illustrative. According to Arizona law, a person commits the offense of "trafficking in stolen property" if she "recklessly traffics in the property of another that has been stolen." Az. Law § 13-2307. Given that Arizona law—as does the Model Penal Code—prescribes that an actor can only be held liable for an attempt if she *purposely* engages in the proscribed conduct, the court in *Nuñez* pointed out that a person is liable of attempted trafficking in property only if he *purposely* or "intentionally buy[s] property."

2. The court in *Nuñez* observed that both under Arizona law and the Model Penal Code, attempt liability does not require that the actor's purpose encompass all the circumstances included in the definition of the substantive offense. As to the circumstances, attempt liability attaches as long as the person acts with the kind of culpability that the substantive offense requires regarding such circumstances. In the context of the offense of "trafficking in stolen property," the *Nuñez* court concluded that attempt liability merely required proof that the actor was reckless with regard to whether the property that he bought with intent to sell was stolen.

3. Regarding results, attempt liability attaches under the Model Penal Code if the actor has the purpose of bringing about the proscribed harm. Note that § 5.01(1)(B) of the Code also imposes attempt liability when the defendant acts with "the belief that [his act] will cause [the proscribed result]." Consequently, even if he did not intend to cause the result, attempt liability is appropriate under the Code as long as the actor knows that his conduct will bring about the prohibited harm.

## § 11.05 Attempts: Impossible Attempts—Common Law

### People v. Thousand

Court of Appeals of Michigan, 2000
241 Mich. App. 102

SAWYER, Judge.

Defendant was charged with child sexually abusive activity, solicitation to commit third-degree criminal sexual conduct, and attempted distribution of obscene material to a minor. The trial court granted defendant's motion to quash and dismissed the case. The people now appeal, and we affirm in part, reverse in part, and remand.

In December 1998, during an undercover investigation of persons using the Internet to attempt to engage in child sexually abusive activity, Wayne County Sheriff's Deputy William Liczbinski, an adult, entered Internet chat rooms and posed as a minor. While in a chat room, Deputy Liczbinski, posing as a fourteen-year-old girl named "Bekka," began chatting with defendant. During their correspondence, defendant made sexual comments to "Bekka" and sent "her" a picture of his penis via the Internet. Defendant told "Bekka" that he was going to "take [her] back to his home into his bedroom where we can be alone and not be bothered for sexual activity." Defendant and "Bekka" decided to meet at the McDonald's Restaurant located on Van Dyke in the city of Detroit. Defendant told "Bekka" that he would be driving a green Duster, what clothing he would be wearing for the meeting, and that he would be carrying a gift for her, a white teddy bear. When he arrived at the meeting site at the predetermined time, defendant was arrested by sheriff's deputies. Two white teddy bears were found in defendant's automobile.

Defendant moved to quash the information and dismiss the case, arguing that each of the charged offenses required the existence of a minor as the victim or potential victim and that it was undisputed that no minor was actually involved in this matter. The trial court agreed with defendant and granted the motion to quash. The trial court reasoned that the existence of a minor was an element of each offense with which defendant was charged and, because no such minor was involved, it was legally impossible for defendant to have committed or have attempted to commit the charged offenses.

The prosecution's only argument involves whether it is legally or factually impossible for defendant to have committed the charged offenses where the victim was not, in fact, a fourteen-year-old girl as defendant thought, but in fact an adult male. This distinction is critical because, while legal impossibility is a defense to the crime of attempt, factual impossibility is not. Although this is the only issue raised by the prosecution, we believe that the analysis differs with each of the three charged offenses. Accordingly, we will analyze each offense separately.

To begin, the issue of factual versus legal impossibility presents a question like the ancient quandary of whether a glass is half empty or half full. As Professor Joshua Dressler states … the distinction can be very subtle:

> *Ultimately any case of hybrid legal impossibility may reasonably be characterized as factual impossibility.* That is, applying the definition of "factual impossibility" set out above …, in each case *D*'s intended end (e.g., to receive stolen property; to pick a human pocket; to bribe a juror; to kill a human; to hunt a deer out of season) constituted a crime, but she failed to consummate the offense because of some fact of which *D* was unaware or was beyond her control. Thus, by skillful characterization, one can describe virtually any case of hybrid legal impossibility, which is a common law defense, as an example of factual impossibility, which is *not* a defense (emphasis in original).

Professor Dressler summarizes factual impossibility as follows:

> "Factual impossibility" exists when a person's intended end constitutes a crime, but she fails to consummate the offense because of an attendant circumstance unknown to her or beyond her control. Examples of factual impossibility are: (1) a pickpocket putting her hand in the victim's empty pocket; (2) an abortionist beginning the surgical procedure on a nonpregnant woman; (3) an impotent male trying to have nonconsensual sexual intercourse; (4) an assailant shooting into an empty bed where the intended victim customarily sleeps, or pulling the trigger of an unloaded gun aimed at a person who is present.
>
> In each of these examples the actor was mistaken regarding some fact relating to the victim, herself or himself, and/or the method of commission. More specifically, the target offense was not consummated because the actor chose the wrong victim (the pickpocket and abortion cases), the victim was not present (the empty bed case), the actor was not physically capable of committing the offense (the impotency case), or inappropriate means were used to commit the crime (the unloaded gun case). Had the circumstances been as the actors believed them to be, or hoped that they were (e.g., the pocket contained property; the woman was pregnant; the victim was in the bed; the actor was physically capable of having intercourse; the gun was loaded), the crimes would have been consummated.

> It should not be surprising that lawmakers are unsympathetic to claims of factual impossibility. In each of the cases described above, the actor has demonstrated her or his dangerousness (critical to subjectivists) and manifested criminality (important to objectivists). No good reason exists to recognize a defense merely because a person chooses her victim badly, does not use proper means to commit the crime, or for some other reason unrelated to her culpability does not successfully commit the offense.

Dressler summarizes legal impossibility as follows:

> Hybrid legal impossibility (or what courts will simply call "legal impossibility") exists if the actor's goal is illegal (thus, distinguishing itself from pure legal impossibility), but commission of the offense is impossible due to a *factual* mistake by her regarding the *legal* status of some attendant circumstance relevant to her conduct. As the preceding definition implies and as is clarified immediately below, this is a hybrid version of impossibility: the actor's impossibility claim includes both legal and factual aspects to it.
>
> Courts have recognized a defense of legal impossibility or have stated that it would exist if *D:* (1) receives *un* stolen property believing that it was stolen; (2) tries to pick the pocket of a stone image of a human; (3) offers a bribe to a "juror" who is not a juror; (4) tries to hunt deer out of season by shooting a stuffed animal; (5) shoots a corpse believing that it is alive; or (6) shoots at a tree stump believing that it is a human.
>
> Notice that each of the mistakes in these cases affected the legal status of some aspect of the defendant's conduct. A person is not guilty of "receiving stolen property with knowledge that it is stolen" unless the property is "stolen" in character. Likewise, one cannot legally bribe a juror unless the person bribed is a juror. The status of a victim as a "human being," rather than as a corpse, tree stump, or statue, legally is necessary to commit the crime of murder or to "take and carry away the personal property *of another.*" Finally, putting a bullet into a stuffed deer cannot legally constitute the crime of killing a deer out of season.
>
> On the other hand, in each of the preceding examples of hybrid legal impossibility, *D* was mistaken about a fact: whether the property had been stolen; whether a person was a juror; whether the victims were living human beings; or whether the victim was an animal subject to being hunted out of season (emphasis in original).

This brings us back to the original point from Professor Dressler that we quoted: cases may be reasonably characterized as either factually or legally impossible. One distinction we do note between Dressler's examples of legal and factual impossibility is this: in the legal impossibility cases, the intended object of the defendant's actus reus could *not* possibly support the crime, while in the factual impossibility cases the object of the actus reus *could* have been the victim of a crime.

Taking the examples of legal impossibility, the property the defendant intended to receive was not, in fact, stolen and therefore could not form the basis of receiving stolen property; the intended victim of the pickpocket was, in fact, a stone statue, which cannot be the victim of a theft; the person the defendant intended to give money to was not a juror, and therefore could not be a bribed juror; the defendant intended, in fact, to shoot the object that turned out to be a stuffed deer and a stuffed deer cannot be taken out of season; the defendant intended to shoot the object that was, in fact, a corpse or the object that was, in fact, a tree stump and neither a corpse nor a tree stump may be the victim of a homicide. In each of these cases, the defendant accomplished the actual act he set out to do. He received the property he intended to receive, he picked the pocket he intended to pick, he gave money to the person to whom he intended to give the money, and he shot the object he intended to shoot. While upon learning the full facts of the situation, the defendant may be disappointed in the results, he nevertheless committed the act he intended to commit.

Turning to the examples of factual impossibility, if the victim's pocket had had a wallet, the victim would have suffered a theft; if the woman were pregnant, there would have been an abortion; if the defendant had not been impotent, the victim would have been raped; if the victim had been in the location where the defendant shot, or if the gun had been loaded, the victim would have suffered the wound. In each of these cases, the defendant did *not* accomplish the intended task. He did not remove anything from the victim's pocket, he did not abort the fetus, he failed to have intercourse with the victim, and failed to shoot the victim.

Turning then to the case at bar, we believe that defendant's conduct with respect to two of the charges represents legal impossibility and, therefore, the trial court properly dismissed the charges. However, with respect to one of the charges, we believe the trial court improperly dismissed the charge.

First, we consider the offense of solicitation of criminal sexual conduct in the third degree. The form of criminal sexual conduct in the third degree (CSC-3) charged is engaging in sexual penetration with a person under the age of sixteen. We believe that this represents a case of legal impossibility from both the solicitation aspect and the CSC-3 aspect. First, with respect to the CSC-3 element, [Michigan Law] requires that the defendant engage in sexual penetration with a victim who is at least thirteen years of age and under sixteen. While defendant desired to engage in sexual activity with a fourteen-year-old girl, the actual object of his desire was an adult male, Deputy Liczbinski. The person to whom defendant actually made the offer of sexual relations was over the age of sixteen. If defendant had actually engaged in sexual penetration with the person to whom he made the offer (Deputy Liczbinski), he would not have violated [Michigan law]. It is similar to the poaching the stuffed deer case. Just as it is not poaching to shoot a stuffed deer, it is not a violation of [the criminal law] to engage in consensual sexual intercourse with an adult.

Turning to the issue of solicitation, [Michigan criminal law] provides in pertinent part as follows:

> (1) For purposes of this section, "solicit" means to offer to give, promise to give, or give any money, services, or anything of value, or to forgive or promise to forgive a debt or obligation.
>
> * * *
>
> (3) Except as provided in subsection (2), a person who solicits another person to commit a felony, or who solicits another person to do or omit to do an act which if completed would constitute a felony, is punishable as follows....

What is lacking here is defendant's request to another person to commit a crime. "Bekka," the fourteen-year-old female online persona of Deputy Liczbinski, was not asked to commit a crime. That is, while it would be a crime for defendant to engage in sexual intercourse with a fourteen-year-old girl, a fourteen-year-old girl is not committing a criminal offense (or at least not CSC-3) by engaging in sexual intercourse with an adult. Thus, whether we look at this case as defendant asking fourteen-year-old "Bekka" to engage in sexual intercourse with him or as defendant asking Deputy Liczbinski to engage in sexual intercourse with him, he did not ask another person to commit CSC-3. That is, it is legally impossible for a person to [commit the offense charged] by engaging in sexual intercourse with defendant.

For the above reasons, we conclude that the trial court properly dismissed the charge of solicitation to commit criminal sexual conduct.

Turning next to the charge of attempted disseminating or exhibiting sexual material to a minor, we again find the crime to be legally impossible under the facts of this case. [The relevant statute] provides as follows:

> A person is guilty of distributing obscene matter to a minor if that person does either of the following:
>
> (a) Knowingly disseminates to a minor sexually explicit visual or verbal material that is harmful to minors.
>
> (b) Knowingly exhibits to a minor a sexually explicit performance that is harmful to minors.

Further, [Michigan law] defines "minor" as a person under eighteen years of age.

Defendant's conduct at issue is the e-mailing of a picture of his penis to "Bekka." Thus, while defendant believed he was sending the picture to a fourteen-year-old girl named Bekka, he in fact was sending it to an adult male named Deputy Liczbinski. We believe that this, too, falls within the area of legal, rather than factual, impossibility. The e-mail was sent to its intended recipient: a person whose chat-room screen name was "Bekka." Because "Bekka" was, in fact, an adult, an essential requirement of the statute was not met: dissemination to a minor.

In fact, this case is very similar to an example of legal impossibility used by Professor Dressler. Dressler ... posed the question of two cases. In each case, the male defendant had sexual intercourse with a seventeen-year-old female in a jurisdiction where the age of consent was sixteen. Therefore, statutory rape did not occur in either case. However, the first defendant erroneously believed the girl was fifteen and, therefore, believed (erroneously) that he had committed statutory rape. The second defendant, on the other hand, knew the girl was seventeen, but erroneously believed the age of consent was eighteen, thus also incorrectly thinking that he had committed statutory rape. Thereafter, Professor Dressler points out that the second defendant is not guilty of a crime because it is not a crime to commit an act that a person erroneously believes is against the law (called "pure legal impossibility"). Professor Dressler then goes on to point out that the first defendant also is not guilty of statutory rape under a legal impossibility analysis:

> Consider, as well, the hypothetical in subsection [A], *supra,* in which *D1* has intercourse with a female old enough to consent, although he believed that she was underage. This example involves hybrid legal impossibility: *D1* was mistaken about a fact (the girl's age); but her age is of legal significance in that sexual intercourse with a 17-year-old female (her true age) does not constitute statutory rape.

The exact same circumstance exists here: defendant was mistaken about "Bekka's" age, but Bekka's age is of legal significance in that distributing sexually explicit material to an adult does not violate the statute under which defendant was charged.

Therefore, for the above reasons, we conclude that it is legally impossible to [commit the offense at issue] by distributing obscene material to an adult and, therefore, it does not constitute an attempted violation of that statute to distribute obscene material to a person the defendant believes is a minor, but who is, in fact, an adult. Accordingly, the trial court properly dismissed this charge ...

## *Notes and Questions*

1. As the Court of Appeals of Michigan points out, factual impossibility did not amount to a defense at common law. Nevertheless, legal impossibility was usually a defense to attempt liability at common law.

2. Factual impossibility exists when the defendant fails to consummate the offense because of a factual circumstance unknown to her or beyond her control. Examples of factual impossibility would thus be shooting at an empty bed believing that it is occupied, performing an abortion on a non-pregnant woman, and pickpocketing by reaching inside of an empty pocket. In these cases, the defendant cannot commit the offense because she is unaware of a factual circumstance that makes it impossible for her to consummate the offense (the bed is empty, the woman is not pregnant, the pocket is empty). The circumstances that are absent in factual impossibility can be determined without need of making legal judgments. Thus, determining whether a pocket is empty or a woman is pregnant does not require making legal judgments.

3. In contrast, legal impossibility exists when the defendant cannot complete the offense because of a *legal* circumstance unknown to her or beyond her control. Paradigmatic examples are trying to receive stolen property when the property is, in fact, not stolen and attempting to bribe a juror when the person bribed is not really a juror. In both cases, the defendant is unable to commit the crime because she is not aware of a legal circumstance that makes it impossible for the offense to be consummated (that the property is not stolen and that the person is not a juror). Note that determining whether property is stolen requires making a legal judgment about the status of the property. Similarly, determining whether a person is a juror requires making a judgment regarding whether the person meets the legal criteria for being considered a juror.

4. The court claims that the following cases are examples of legal impossibility: "tr[ying] to pick the pocket of a stone image of a human," "tr[ying] to hunt deer out of season by shooting a stuffed animal," "shoot[ing] a corpse believing that it is alive," and "shoot[ing] at a tree stump believing that it is a human." Do you agree? Explain.

5. Suppose that defendant marries for a second time believing that his first marriage was legally valid. In fact, his first marriage was never legally valid and, therefore, his "second" marriage was actually his "first." May the defendant be held liable for "attempted bigamy"? Is this a case of factual or legal impossibility? Explain.

6. Imagine that defendant has sex with the victim believing that the victim had not consented to sex when she in fact had consented to the act. May the defendant be held liable for attempted rape? Is this a case of factual or legal impossibility? Explain. Suppose that defendant has sex with the victim believing that the victim is unconscious when in fact the victim was conscious at the time of the act. Assume that the applicable statute makes it rape to engage in sexual intercourse "when the victim is unconscious." May the defendant be held liable for attempted rape? Why or why not? Is this a case of factual or legal impossibility. Regardless of how you answered this question, should this defendant be treated differently than the defendant who has sex with a victim believing that she's not consenting when in fact she is? Does the common law approach to impossibility treat these two defendants in the same way?

7. The Court concluded that the defendant in the excerpted case could not be held liable of attempting to disseminate sexual materials to a minor and soliciting sex with a minor. The Court reasoned that committing the crimes in both cases was "legally impossible" because, although the defendant thought he was interacting with a minor, he was actually chatting with an adult undercover agent. Do you agree that this is a case of legal impossibility? Regardless of how you answered this question, should defendants like this one be punished for attempting to distribute sexual materials to minors and soliciting sex with a minor? Why or why not?

## § 11.06 Attempts: Impossible Attempts — Model Penal Code

### People v. Thousand

Supreme Court of Michigan, 2001
465 Mich. 149

YOUNG, J.

We granted leave in this case to consider whether the doctrine of "impossibility" provides a defense to a charge of attempt to commit an offense prohibited by [Michigan] law or to a charge of solicitation to commit a felony ... The circuit court granted defendant's motion to quash and dismissed all charges against him on the basis that it was legally impossible for him to have committed any of the charged crimes [Editor's Note: See case excerpted in previous section.]. We conclude that the concept of impossibility, which this Court has never adopted as a defense, is not relevant to a determination whether a defendant has committed attempt under [Michigan law] and that the circuit court therefore erred in dismissing the charge of attempted distribution of obscene material to a minor on the basis of the doctrine of legal impossibility ...

I. FACTUAL AND PROCEDURAL BACKGROUND

[Editor's Note: Facts are omitted. They are the same facts that gave rise to the case excerpted in the previous section.]

III. ANALYSIS

A. THE "IMPOSSIBILITY" DOCTRINE

The doctrine of "impossibility" as it has been discussed in the context of inchoate crimes represents the conceptual dilemma that arises when, because of the defendant's mistake of fact or law, his actions could not possibly have resulted in the commission of the substantive crime underlying an attempt charge. Classic illustrations of the concept of impossibility include: (1) the defendant is prosecuted for attempted larceny after he tries to "pick" the victim's empty pocket; (2) the defendant is prosecuted for attempted rape after he tries to have nonconsensual intercourse, but is unsuccessful because he is impotent; (3) the defendant is prosecuted for attempting to receive stolen property where the property he received was not, in fact, stolen; and (4) the defendant is prosecuted for attempting to hunt deer out of season after he shoots at a stuffed decoy deer. In each of these examples, despite evidence of the defendant's criminal intent, he cannot be prosecuted for the *completed* offense of larceny, rape, receiving stolen property, or hunting deer out of season, because proof of at least one element of each offense cannot be derived from his objective actions. The question, then, becomes whether the defendant can be prosecuted for the *attempted* offense, and the answer is dependent upon whether he may raise the defense of "impossibility."

Courts and legal scholars have drawn a distinction between two categories of impossibility: "factual impossibility" and "legal impossibility." It has been said that, at common law, legal impossibility is a defense to a charge of attempt, but factual impossibility is not. However, courts and scholars alike have struggled unsuccessfully over the years to articulate an accurate rule for distinguishing between the categories of "impossibility."

"Factual impossibility," which has apparently never been recognized in any American jurisdiction as a defense to a charge of attempt, "exists when [the defendant's] intended end constitutes a crime but she fails to consummate it because of a factual circumstance unknown to her or beyond her control." An example of a "factual impossibility" scenario is where the defendant is prosecuted for attempted murder after pointing an unloaded gun at someone and pulling the trigger, where the defendant believed the gun was loaded.

The category of "legal impossibility" is further divided into two subcategories: "pure" legal impossibility and "hybrid" legal impossibility. Although it is generally undisputed that "pure" legal impossibility will bar an attempt conviction, the concept of "hybrid legal impossibility" has proven problematic. As Professor Dressler points out, the failure of courts to distinguish between "pure" and "hybrid" legal impossibility has created confusion in this area of the law. Dressler, *supra,* § 27.07[D][1], p. 351.

"*Pure legal impossibility* exists if the criminal law does not prohibit *D*'s conduct or the result that she has sought to achieve." In other words, the concept of pure legal impossibility applies when an actor engages in conduct that he believes is criminal, but is not actually prohibited by law: "There can be no conviction of criminal attempt based upon D's erroneous notion that he was committing a crime." Perkins & Boyce, *supra,* p. 634. As an example, consider the case of a man who believes that the legal age of consent is sixteen years old, and who believes that a girl with whom he had consensual sexual intercourse is fifteen years old. If the law actually fixed the age of consent at fifteen, this man would not be guilty of attempted statutory rape, despite his mistaken belief that the law prohibited his conduct. See Dressler, *supra,* § 27.07[D][2], pp. 352–353, n. 25.

When courts speak of "legal impossibility," they are generally referring to what is more accurately described as "hybrid" legal impossibility.

Most claims of legal impossibility are of the hybrid variety. *Hybrid legal impossibility* exists if *D*'s goal was illegal, but commission of the offense was impossible due to a factual mistake by her regarding the legal status of some factor relevant to her conduct. This version of impossibility is a "hybrid" because, as the definition implies and as is clarified immediately below, D's impossibility claim includes both a legal and a factual aspect to it.

Courts have recognized a defense of legal impossibility or have stated that it would exist if D receives unstolen property believing it was stolen; tries to pick the pocket of a stone image of a human; offers a bribe to a "juror" who is not a juror; tries to hunt deer out of season by shooting a stuffed animal; shoots a corpse believing that it is alive; or shoots at a tree stump believing that it is a human.

Notice that each of the mistakes in these cases affected the legal status of some aspect of the defendant's conduct. The status of property as "stolen" is necessary to commit the crime of "receiving stolen property with knowledge it is stolen"—i.e., a person legally is incapable of committing this offense if the property is not stolen. The status of a person as a "juror" is legally necessary to commit the offense of bribing a juror. The status of a victim as a "human being" (rather than as a corpse, tree stump, or statue) legally is necessary to commit the crime of murder or to "take and carry away the personal property *of another*." Finally, putting a bullet into a stuffed deer can never constitute the crime of hunting out of season.

On the other hand, in each example of hybrid legal impossibility *D* was mistaken about a fact: whether property was stolen, whether a person was a juror, whether the victims were human or whether the victim was an animal subject to being hunted out of season. [Dressler, *supra*, § 27.07[D][3][a], pp. 353–354 (emphasis in original).]

As the Court of Appeals panel in this case accurately noted, it is possible to view virtually any example of "hybrid legal impossibility" as an example of "factual impossibility"...

It is notable that "the great majority of jurisdictions have now recognized that legal and factual impossibility are 'logically indistinguishable'... and have abolished impossibility as a defense." *United States v. Hsu*, 155 F.3d 189, 199 (C.A.3, 1998). For example, several states have adopted statutory provisions similar to Model Penal Code § 5.01(1), which provides:

> A person is guilty of an attempt to commit a crime if, acting with the kind of culpability otherwise required for commission of the crime, he:
>
> (a) purposely engages in conduct which would constitute the crime if the attendant circumstances were as he believes them to be; or
>
> (b) when causing a particular result is an element of the crime, does or omits to do anything with the purpose of causing or with the belief that it will cause such result without further conduct on his part; or
>
> c) purposely does or omits to do anything which, under the circumstances as he believes them to be, is an act or omission constituting a substantial step in a course of conduct planned to culminate in his commission of the crime.

In other jurisdictions, courts have considered the "impossibility" defense under attempt statutes that did not include language explicitly abolishing the defense. Several of these courts have simply declined to participate in the sterile academic exercise of categorizing a particular set of facts as representing "factual" or "legal" impossibility, and have instead examined solely the words of the applicable attempt statute.

B. ATTEMPTED DISTRIBUTION OF OBSCENE MATERIAL TO A MINOR

The Court of Appeals panel in this case, after examining Professor Dressler's exposition of the doctrine of impossibility, concluded that it was legally impossible for defendant to have committed the charged offense of attempted distribution of obscene material to a minor. The panel held that, because "Bekka" was, in fact, an adult, an essential requirement of the underlying substantive offense was not met (dissemination to a minor), and therefore it was legally impossible for defendant to have committed the crime...

[W]e turn now to the terms of the statute. [The Michigan attempt statute] provides, in relevant part:

> Any person who shall attempt to commit an offense prohibited by law, and in such attempt shall do any act towards the commission of such offense, but shall fail in the perpetration, or shall be intercepted or prevented in the execution of the same, when no express provision is made by law for the punishment of such attempt, shall be punished as follows:

> * * *
>
> 3. If the offense so attempted to be committed is punishable by imprisonment in the state prison for a term less than 5 years, or imprisonment in the county jail or by fine, the offender convicted of such attempt shall be guilty of a misdemeanor....

Under our statute, then, an "attempt" consists of (1) an attempt to commit an offense prohibited by law, and (2) any act towards the commission of the intended offense. We have further explained the elements of attempt under our statute as including "an intent to do an act or to bring about certain consequences which would in law amount to a crime; and ... an act in furtherance of that intent which, as it is most commonly put, goes beyond mere preparation." ...

We are unable to discern from the words of the attempt statute any legislative intent that the concept of "impossibility" provide any impediment to charging a defendant with, or convicting him of, an attempted crime, notwithstanding any factual mistake—regarding either the attendant circumstances or the legal status of some factor relevant thereto—that he may harbor. The attempt statute carves out no exception for those who, possessing the requisite criminal intent to commit an offense prohibited by law and taking action toward the commission of that offense, have acted under an extrinsic misconception.

Defendant in this case is not charged with the substantive crime of distributing obscene material to a minor ... It is unquestioned that defendant could not be convicted of that crime, because defendant allegedly distributed obscene material not to "a minor," but to an adult man. Instead, defendant is charged with the distinct offense of attempt, which requires only that the prosecution prove intention to commit an offense prohibited by law, coupled with conduct toward the commission of that offense. The notion that it would be "impossible" for the defendant to have committed the *completed* offense is simply irrelevant to the analysis. Rather, in deciding guilt on a charge of attempt, the trier of fact must examine the unique circumstances of the particular case and determine whether the prosecution has proven that the defendant possessed the requisite specific intent and that he engaged in some act "towards the commission" of the intended offense.

Because the nonexistence of a minor victim does not give rise to a viable defense to the attempt charge in this case, the circuit court erred in dismissing this charge on the basis of "legal impossibility."

## *Notes and Questions*

1. As the Supreme Court of Michigan pointed out in *Thousand*, "the great majority of jurisdictions have now recognized that legal and factual impossibility are 'logically indistinguishable.'" As a result, most courts have now "abolished impossibility as a defense." The Supreme Court of Michigan followed suit, holding that neither factual nor legal impossibility defeat liability in Michigan and, therefore, that the defendant could be held liable for soliciting sex with a minor and distributing sexual materials to a minor. Do you agree with this outcome or do you prefer the outcome reached by the Court of Appeals in the case (excerpted in the previous section)?

2. The Court pointed out that the drafters of the Model Penal Code also abolished impossibility as a defense. The relevant provision is Model Penal Code § 5.01(1)(c), which provides that an actor is guilty of an attempt if she "purposely does or omits to do anything which, under the *circumstances as he believes them to be*, is an act or omission constituting a substantial step in a course of conduct planned to culminate in his commission

of the crime." Note that according to the Code what matters is if the defendant would have successfully consummated the crime had the circumstances been as she believed them to be.

3. The Model Penal Code's approach to attempts has the consequence of abolishing both factual and legal impossibility as defenses to liability, for in both of these cases the defendant would have consummated the crime had the circumstances been as she believed them to be. Thus, for example, the pickpocket who reaches into an empty pocket (factual impossibility) would have successfully consummated the theft had her belief that there was money inside the pocket been correct. Similarly, one who tries to bribe a person incorrectly believing that she was a juror (legal impossibility) would have completed the crime of bribing a juror had her belief that she was bribing a juror been correct. Do you agree with the Code's treatment of impossible attempts? Why or why not?

4. In *People v. Dlugash,* 395 N.Y.S.2d 419 (1977), the defendant claimed that he could not be held liable of attempted murder for shooting at the body of a dead person even if he believed that the person was alive at the time of the shooting. The Court of Appeals of New York rejected defendant's contention. In doing so, the Court explained that the Model Penal Code abolished the impossibility defense and that the New York legislature followed the Code's approach to this issue. More specifically, the Court opined that:

> [T]he distinction between "factual" and "legal" impossibility was a nice one indeed and the courts tended to place a greater value on legal form than on any substantive danger the defendant's actions posed for society. The approach of the draftsmen of the Model Penal Code was to eliminate the defense of impossibility in virtually all situations. Under the code provision, to constitute an attempt, it is still necessary that the result intended or desired by the actor constitute a crime. However, the code suggested a fundamental change to shift the locus of analysis to the actor's mental frame of reference and away from undue dependence upon external considerations. The basic premise of the code provision is that what was in the actor's own mind should be the standard for determining his dangerousness to society and, hence, his liability for attempted criminal conduct.
>
> In the belief that neither of the two branches of the traditional impossibility arguments detracts from the offender's moral culpability, the [New York] Legislature substantially carried the code's treatment of impossibility into the 1967 revision of the Penal Law. Thus, a person is guilty of an attempt when, with intent to commit a crime, he engages in conduct which tends to effect the commission of such crime. It is no defense that, under the attendant circumstances, the crime was factually or legally impossible of commission, "if such crime could have been committed had the attendant circumstances been as such person believed them to be." Thus, if defendant believed the victim to be alive at the time of the shooting, it is no defense to the charge of attempted murder that the victim may have been dead.

Do you agree with the outcome in *Dlugash*? Was it factually or legally impossible for the defendant in *Dlugash* to consummate the offense? While the answer to this question would be determinative of whether liability could be imposed in this case at common law, distinguishing between factual and legal impossibility is irrelevant under the Model Penal Code because neither form of impossibility defeats liability according to the Code. Do you prefer the common law or Model Penal Code approach to impossibility? Explain.

5. The Model Penal Code's grading provisions allow the court to mitigate punishment or even dismiss the prosecution when the defendant's attempt is extremely unlikely to re-

sult in the commission of the offense. More specifically, Model Penal Code § 5.05(2) provides that:

> (2) **Mitigation.** If the particular conduct charged to constitute a criminal attempt ... is so inherently unlikely to result or culminate in the commission of a crime that neither such conduct nor the actor presents a public danger warranting the grading of such offense under this Section, the Court shall exercise its power under Section 6.12 to enter judgment and impose sentence for a crime of lower grade or degree or, in extreme cases, may dismiss the prosecution.

This provision may be invoked, for example, to dismiss a case against a defendant charged with attempted murder for trying to kill the victim by inserting pins into a voodoo doll. Assuming that such a defendant does not have a violent history, his belief in voodoo and his attempts to cast spells on the victim may not present a "public danger" warranting the imposition of punishment and, therefore, the judge would have discretion to dismiss the charges under § 5.05(2).

## § 11.06 Attempts: Comparative Perspectives

### Günther Jakobs, *Derecho Penal Parte General*

(Marcial Pons Publishers, 1996, pages 866–867)

A person attempts a punishable act when she engages in conduct that—according to her plan—amounts to the commencement of the commission of the offense. The objective element of the offense in attempted crimes is incomplete, [for the result is missing]. [T]he subjective element, however, has to concur in exactly the same way that it should for the consummated crime.... If the consummated offense is punishable on the basis of *dolus eventualis*, then *dolus eventualis* also suffices for attempt liability.

### Hans Heinrich Jescheck & Thomas Weigend, *Tratado de Derecho Penal Parte General*

(Comares, 2002, page 554)

Attempted offenses require proof of the same subjective elements that must be proved had the offense been consummated. Like in the case of consummated offenses, attempted crimes are punishable only if the defendant has the subjective element that the offense requires for each one of the different objective offense elements [i.e., circumstance and conduct].... [Therefore,] attempts may be punishable on the basis of *dolus eventualis*, as long as *dolus eventualis* would also suffice had the offense been consummated.

### Francisco Muñoz Conde & Mercedes García Arán, *Derecho Penal Parte General*

(Tirant Lo Blanch, 8th ed., 2010)

Attempted crimes are offenses that are dependent on other crimes, for all of the elements of attempted offenses refer to the elements of consummated crimes. There is no stand-alone crime of "attempt," but rather attempted murders, thefts, frauds, etc. Therefore, the subjective element required for attempted offenses should be the same as that which is required for the relevant consummated offense....

From the reasons underlying the criminalization of attempts and from the way in which attempts are defined in the Spanish Penal Code, one may infer that there can be no attempted negligent crimes, for these cases do not reveal the desire to engage in criminal conduct. Furthermore, if the consummated offense requires proof of special subjective elements (e.g., intent to dispossess owner of property in larceny), such elements must also be proved in prosecution for the attempted offense.

It is more debatable whether attempted crimes may be punished when the defendant acts with *dolus eventualis* with regard to the result element of the offense. Insofar as the consummated offense allows conviction upon proof of *dolus eventualis,* it would seem that attempt liability could be imposed upon proof of the same subjective element, although in the typical case the defendant will act at least knowingly. The terrorist who places a bomb in a public space with awareness that the bomb might kill someone has engaged in a punishable attempt if the bomb does not explode, or if it explodes but does not harm anyone.

### *Notes and Questions*

1. As the excerpted comparative materials reveal, proof of *dolus eventualis*—the imperfect analogue to recklessness in European Continental jurisdictions—suffices in the majority of civil law countries for the imposition of attempt liability. As long, of course, as *dolus eventuali* would also suffice for liability had the offense been consummated.

2. Professors Muñoz Conde and García Arán point out that a terrorist who places a bomb in a public space without desiring to kill people but being conscious that some people might die as a result of the bomb exploding may be convicted of attempted homicide if the bomb does not detonate or if it explodes and does not kill anyone. Do you find it intuitively appealing to hold the terrorist liable for attempted homicide if the bomb fails to explode? Why or why not? What result if this case is tried under the Model Penal Code? How would the case be decided according to the common law's approach to attempts? Explain.

## § 11.06 Attempts: Scholarly Debates

### Sanford Kadish, *Foreword: Criminal Law and the Luck of the Draw*

84 J. Crim. L. & Criminology 679 (1994)

... I propose to consider what to make of a doctrine of the criminal law that seems to me not rationally supportable notwithstanding its near universal acceptance in Western law, the support of many jurists and philosophers, and its resonance with the intuitions of lawyers and lay people alike. This is the doctrine—the harm doctrine, I'll call it—that reduces punishment for intentional wrongdoers (and often precludes punishment for negligent and reckless wrongdoers) if by chance the harm they intended or risked does not occur. I will also consider a corollary of the harm doctrine which offers a full defense if it so happens that, unbeknownst to the defendants, the harm they intended could not possibly have been done.

Whether the harm doctrine can be justified is, as George Fletcher has said, a "deep, unresolved issue in the theory of criminal liability." Indeed, a German scholar, Björn

Burkhardt, recently concluded his comparative review of the law on this subject with the sobering words that "little progress has been made toward a solution of this issue in the last two hundred years." ...

I should explain at the start what I mean by saying that the harm doctrine is not rationally supportable. I mean that it is a doctrine that does not serve the crime preventive purposes of the criminal law, and is not redeemed by any defensible normative principle....

Of course our criminal law has for centuries included many irrational doctrines—whole Augean stables full. Some of them were that way from the start. Others got that way when changed conditions made them anomalous, like the murder rule requiring the victim to have died within a year and a day of the injury. But these differ from the harm doctrine in that they are widely recognized as insupportable, and their long persistence in the law is simply evidence that the law is slow to change. The harm doctrine is special (although, as we will see, not singular) in that large segments of the legal and lay community regard it as sound.

I will begin by setting out the law that most clearly exhibits the harm doctrine at work. This is the law governing the punishment of failed efforts to do some prohibited harm (the law of attempts) and of actions that create the risk of the harm without producing it (the law of culpable risk creation). These rules are well known and I will only sketch them briefly.

First, the law of attempts. Consider the case of a man who stabbed his son in anger, pleaded guilty and was convicted of a crime equivalent for our purposes to attempted murder. After serving several months of a two year sentence he was paroled. However, three months later his son, who had been hospitalized since the attack, took a turn for the worse and died, whereupon the prosecutor, quite within the law, charged the father with murder, a crime punishable with life imprisonment or death.

What did the father do in jail or on parole that merited the greater punishment? Not a thing. If a good constitution or a good surgeon had saved the son, the father could not have been further punished. The occurrence of the resulting death alone raises the crime and the punishment. In most jurisdictions this same principle operates for all crimes, not just homicidal crimes. In California, for example, an attempt to commit a crime is punishable with half the punishment for the completed crime. Thus, the reward for failing, no matter how hard you try to succeed or how close you come, is a lesser punishment.

Now consider crimes of culpable risk creation—crimes in which a person is punished, not for attempting a harm, but for culpably risking it. The punishment of these crimes is also made to depend on chance. Take the case of Mr. Malone. He and his friend decided to play a game of Russian Roulette in which each took turns spinning the chamber of a revolver, with one round in it, and firing at the other. When Malone's turn came to pull the trigger the gun fired and killed his friend. Malone was convicted of second degree murder, based on the egregious risk to life he needlessly created.

That sounds fair enough. But suppose instead, that the bullet only inflicted a flesh wound, or that the bullet was not in the firing chamber when Malone pulled the trigger. Could Malone then have been convicted of any crime? Perhaps he could have been convicted of some ad hoc statutory offense concerning firearms, but such an offense would carry nothing like the penalty for murder. And if there had been no special statute of this kind, he could not be convicted of any crime at all, since traditionally just recklessly endangering another was itself not criminal—except in specific contexts, like driving a car. Some jurisdictions have in recent years made it criminal to recklessly endanger another person in all situations, but even these statutes treat the offense as a minor one....

Having illustrated the workings of the harm doctrine, the two major tasks I have set for myself lie ahead. First I must make good, if I can, my claim that the doctrine, in all its applications, is not rationally defensible. Second, I need to consider what to make of the durability of this doctrine....

### B. The Argument from the Principle of Desert

... I said at the outset, a practice may be justified by some relevant principle of justice. Now I take the principle that limits punishment to what the offender deserves to be such a principle, and one which those subscribing to the harm doctrine would want to rely on. The question, then, is whether wrongdoers deserve less punishment (or none at all) because the harm they intended or culpably risked happens not to occur, or could not have occurred, for reasons unknown to them.

Isn't desert the same whether or not the harm occurs? It is commonly accepted that punishment is deserved if persons are at fault, and that fault depends on their choice to do the wrongful action, not on what is beyond their control. Reconsider my attempt cases. Would the father who stabbed his son deserve less punishment if a skillful doctor had been available to save the son's life? Would the Russian Roulette player deserve less punishment if the bullet happened to be in another chamber when he fired?

While in principle it's difficult to find good reasons for making desert turn on chance, here's the rub: most of us do in fact make judgments precisely of this kind. Doesn't it seem natural for a parent to want to punish her child more for spilling his milk than for almost spilling it, more for running the family car into a wall than for almost doing so? That's the way our unexamined intuitions run. The sight of the harm arouses a degree of anger and resentment that far exceeds that aroused by apprehension of the harm. What Adam Smith observed of his time is still largely true of ours:

> Our resentment against the person who only attempted to do a mischief, is seldom so strong as to bear us out in inflicting the same punishment upon him, which we should have thought due if he had actually done it. In the one case, the joy of our deliverance alleviates our sense of the atrocity of his conduct; in the other, the grief of our misfortune increases it.

Since he believed that the real demerit is the same in both cases, the person's intentions and actions being equally culpable, Smith concluded that in this respect there is "an irregularity in the sentiments of all men, and a consequent relaxation of discipline in the laws of ... all nations, of the most civilized, as well as of the most barbarous."

What should we make of this paradox? Is there something to be said after all for the popular sentiment that fortuitous results do have a bearing on blameworthiness, something that is missed by treating it simply as an irregularity? Can attributing punishment significance to the occurrence of harm be justified in terms of the desert principle?

Obviously, the foundation of my argument against making punishment turn on the chance happening of harm rests on the incompatibility of luck and desert. But perhaps this assumption is mistaken. A distinguished philosopher, Thomas Nagel, has advanced the paradoxical notion of "moral luck." His point is that we do commonly make and defend judgments of moral desert despite the presence of substantial elements of chance. So if the harm principle is irrational because it makes moral desert turn on chance, then so are many of our considered moral judgments.

Nagel instances four situations in which moral desert turns on chance. Two of the four are based on a determinist premise; namely, that you may be lucky or unlucky in the antecedent factors that determine the kind of person you turn out to be and in how you choose to exercise your will. True enough if one accepts determinism. But, first, that explanation of human action is highly contestable, and second, the criminal law, with its concepts of personal responsibility and desert, plainly rejects it.

A third instance Nagel gives of moral luck is that you may be lucky or not in whether circumstances present you with an occasion to make a moral choice that will reveal your moral shortcomings; for example, luck in whether you are ever presented with the need to choose to betray a friend or break a promise. But I don't believe that this threatens our sense of justice in blaming in the same way that luck in the fortuitous outcome of an action (the harm doctrine) threatens it. The settled moral understanding is that what you deserve is a function of what you choose. It may be that you would not have had occasion to make a choice that revealed your badness if you had better luck. Nonetheless, you did make a choice—nobody made you—and it is that choice for which you are blamed. It is a different matter, however, to say that chance occurrences that follow after you have made your choice determine what you deserve, for that is to rest desert upon factors other than what you chose to do. Fortuity prior to choice, therefore, may be accommodated to our notions of just desert; fortuity thereafter cannot. As I see it, that leaves the harm doctrine, Nagel's fourth instance of moral luck, as the one deep challenge to the desert principle, the singular paradox which Adam Smith early identified.

I turn now to arguments designed to justify the harm doctrine in terms of the principle of desert. They all strike me the way one philosopher found metaphysics—"the finding of bad reasons for what we believe upon instinct." One argument proceeds as follows: our prevailing punishment practice with respect to results is no different than a penal lottery in which the amount of punishment for a crime depends on some such chance event as the drawing of long and short straws. To appreciate this, the argument goes, we need to cease thinking of the lesser punishment for failing to complete the crime as attributable to lesser guilt, and think of it merely as the chance event that determines the losers and winners of the lottery. Thought of as a penal lottery, then, there is no unfairness, for in leaving punishment to chance all attempters are treated alike. They all, in effect, draw straws. If they draw the short straw (that is, they succeed) they get the greater punishment. If they draw the long straw (that is, they fail) they get lesser punishment. There is no unfairness in treating the winners better than the losers so long as the lottery is unrigged.

But even unrigged, the basic injustice of a lottery in allocating punishment remains: to allow one of two offenders equally deserving of punishment to receive less punishment if she wins a lottery detaches punishment from desert. It would be the same if we allowed every equally guilty offender a throw of the dice—a throw of six or less and we halve the punishment. The two offenders end up being punished differently even though they are identical in every non-arbitrary sense. That is what is crucial, not the fact that they both had an equal chance of getting a lesser punishment when they threw the dice.

One might object that while punishing a person more than he deserves is unjust, punishing him less because he lucked out is not. Of course, the offender who lucked out can't complain. But the one who got what would otherwise be his just punishment may well complain, as any child knows who sees his sibling spanked once while he is spanked twice for the same offense. You wouldn't convince the child he wasn't unfairly treated by explaining to him that you left it to chance and he lost. He'd feel wronged, and rightly so. The parent's punishment action was arbitrary, in the sense that punishment of the children was left to chance, and thus forfeited any claim that the child should respect it as fair punishment.

... Finally, I will mention two recent efforts to bring our intuitions about the harm doctrine into harmony with our reason. The first draws upon the recently popular retributive justification of punishment that views punishing the offender as restoring the imbalance of benefits and burdens created by the crime. There is, of course, one readily understandable imbalance produced by most crimes: the criminal profits from a loss he imposes on the victim—he steals or damages the victim's property, he causes the victim to suffer an economic loss, or he injures him physically. If punishment can justifiably be seen as somehow restoring the victim's loss, then less punishment for an attempt, where the victim has suffered no (or, arguably less) loss, could make sense. It is hard to see, however, how inflicting pain on the criminal restores anything—certainly it doesn't restore the victim to his property or compensate him for his economic loss or for his medical expenses and pain and suffering. And even if it somehow did, in the unpalatable sense that the victim received a restorative amount of pleasure from the offender's suffering, it is not the morality of retributive punishment that would have been demonstrated, but the desirability of satisfying the vengeful feelings of the victim, which is not the same thing....

The second recent effort to justify the harm doctrine comes from R.A. Duff. He suggests that in punishing an attempt less than a completed crime the law serves to communicate to the offender that, although subjectively he is as culpable as one who does the harm, in fact all should be grateful that the harm he intended did not come to pass. The lesser punishment communicates the law's judgment that a worse state of affairs would have existed if the offender had achieved his objective—in other words, things are not as bad as they might have been. Perhaps the force of this argument turns on Duff's theory of justified punishment as communication directed towards the offender's repentance, but I find it hard to accept that we need the lesser punishment to keep us (and the offender) aware, for example, that things would be worse if the attempted rapist had succeeded in raping his victim.

## Guyora Binder, *Victims and the Significance of Causing Harm*

28 Pace L. Rev. 713 (2008)

As any mystery reader knows, a dead body is a problem. A death by violence announces the onset of a conflict between two worlds, the clandestine, illicit order of the street, and the public legal order of the state. The consequence of death makes the otherwise shadowed dramas of petty grifters suddenly consequential enough to attract the state's notice. In detective fiction, the interpreting eye of the state is what turns these small-time hustles into a tragic narrative, the beginning and middle needed to account for the victim's bitter end.

The history of Anglo-American criminal law also began with this problem of the unexplained corpse. While ancient Germanic law treated violent disputes as quasi-private matters to be resolved by the parties and their kin, whether in blood or money, Danish and Norman occupiers treated certain acts of violence as matters of public concern. Thus, they charged Anglo-Saxon villages an "ammercement" for each unattributed killing of one of their compatriots there. Eventually, royal courts took jurisdiction over all homicides.

As breaches of the king's peace, violent deaths were offenses against the crown. The sovereign could tolerate the controlled use of force within the household. This was not disorder, but the proper exercise of governing authority. On the other hand, armed conflict among men in public places raised the question of who governed. In a state without a regular armed police force, the outbreak of such violence was an ever-present threat. A killing was particularly problematic because it could not be hidden and might well provoke retaliation. Killing therefore became a pivotal event, transforming what might otherwise remain a private dispute into a public wrong that challenged sovereignty and triggered the jurisdiction of the royal courts. We can think of homicide victims as spectral sentries guarding the frontiers of the ancient criminal law and mutely bearing witness to trespasses against the royal domain.

To this day, criminal law frequently conditions punishment on causing harmful results like death. Intentional killing is generally punished more severely than failed attempts to kill; reckless homicide is punished far more severely than dangerous but non-fatal acts like assault or reckless driving. Much dangerous conduct remains unexamined and unpunished until it leads to harm. Many of us have caught ourselves acting irresponsibly behind the wheel and felt grateful relief that our stupidity or inattention escaped a collision with fate. But who among us has felt remorseful enough to stop a cop and turn ourselves in for our unconsummated calamities? Even in the deepest recesses of conscience we reassure ourselves, "no harm, no foul." If we are thus willing to accept "moral luck" when it favors us, should we not also take the bad with the good?

Yet many criminal law theorists find the punishment of harm puzzling and even, in Sanford Kadish's phrase, "rationally indefensible." They argue that acts should be evaluated only on the basis of the risks they create and the actors' awareness of those risks. One who knowingly imposes an unjustified risk on others acts wrongly, whether or not the risk eventuates in harm....

Philosophers have offered [several] reasons why those who culpably cause harm deserve more punishment than those who culpably impose risk. We may call these the determinist slippery slope, the lottery ticket argument, the remorse analogy, the undeserved gratification argument, and the undeserved status argument.

The determinist slippery slope is retributivist legal philosopher Michael Moore's answer to the moral luck argument. Moore argues that reducing actual harm to a matter of luck places the theorist on a slippery slope towards a deterministic view of choice and character as matters of luck as well. If an actor cannot be blamed for a consequence that would not have occurred under other circumstances, why should he or she be blamed for creating a risk that would have been less under other circumstances? Why should he or she be blamed for a choice he or she would not have made under less tempting circumstances, or with better parenting and education, or different genetic endowments? If we accept the premise of the moral luck argument, that actors deserve punishment only for their choices, we need some way to separate the actor's choices from his or her circumstances. Otherwise, we render the retributivist project of deserved punishment incoherent and unachievable.

For Moore, the concept of action is the ledge that stops the slide down the determinist slope. Moore rejects the claim that action inherently involves risk but only contingently involves harm. Instead, he offers a picture of action as embodied willing. On this view, willing must produce some intended consequence—moving a body part in a desired direction—to count as action at all. So if we require action as a requisite of criminal liability, we are already basing punishment on consequences. Those who object to punishing harm are simply disagreeing about which consequences should matter.

This argument is fine as far as it goes, but it may not take us far enough up the slippery slope to justify punishing harm. Yes, perhaps we can justify conditioning punishment on consequences as unavoidable—at least if we are going to have a liberal state that does not excessively police thought and association. But why must the consequences we punish be harms? That we cannot act without causing consequences does not necessarily mean we choose all the consequences of our actions. While most modern criminal justice systems punish harm more than risk (holding other considerations equal), they still also punish crimes of harmless risk imposition. And by Moore's admission, a wrongful act can fall short of causing harm in any material sense. So his argument that deserved punishment for wrongful choice logically requires conditioning punishment on consequences does not imply any requirement of harmful consequences. Thus, Moore's argument does not identify any reason why ignoring actual harm would violate desert. We must look for some other justification for conditioning punishment on harm....

[Another argument for punishing harmful acts more severely than failed attempts to harm is] the undeserved gratification argument. This argument is rooted in Kant's moral philosophy, which defines a moral act as one determined by a "good will," properly motivated by duties of fair cooperation. An immoral act is determined by a bad will, one that yields to a desire incapable of realization if universalized. Punishment serves to enforce duties of fair cooperation by frustrating such anti-cooperative desires. Kant therefore argued that no penalty should be imposed on a drowning swimmer who wrested a plank from another, because no later penalty could possibly negate his immediate desire to survive. Such a sanction could not constitute punishment because it could not frustrate the desire motivating the crime. Kantian punishment makes the offender's illicit desire self-defeating, thereby illustrating the futility of such a desire if universalized.

On these premises, punishment for intentionally causing harm fairly corrects an offender's undeserved gratification for causing it. If we punished attempts and completed crimes equally, successful offenders would be left more satisfied than unsuccessful attempters. Their regret at having been caught and punished would be mitigated by their pleasure in having achieved their criminal aims. From this viewpoint, we are obliged to punish the successful wrongdoer more than the attempter lest we become complicit in his self-indulgence by permitting his undeserved gratification. H.L.A Hart approved this argument as "the nearest to a rational defense" he knew for the principle that harmful wrongdoing deserves extra punishment.

Yet the undeserved gratification argument appears to justify punishing only purposeful harm, not knowing or reckless harm. If the actor is indifferent to harm rather than seeking it, there is no extra satisfaction to frustrate through additional suffering. It seems that the undeserved gratification argument cannot justify enhanced punishment for causing harm in all cases. A possible response to this objection is that the desiderative attitudes we wish to negate include indifference to the welfare of victims, and we negate this by forcing the indifferent offender to share the victim's suffering. But if we thus punish in order to coerce empathy and remorse, the undeserved gratification argument collapses back into the remorse analogy, which we saw was more about giving victims their due than about properly repaying offenders.

This implication should prompt us to reexamine the Kantian aim of frustrating the offender's gratification in taking advantage of a victim. Does this aim derive primarily from a duty of justice to the offender or a duty of justice to the victim? Presumably, despite paradoxical claims of Kant and Hegel that offenders had a "right to be punished," the offender is hoping for neither punishment nor frustration. If we are obliged to spoil the offender's fun in order to dissociate ourselves from his act, we are apparently concerned about our obligations to victims. The offender humiliates a victim by harming him or her, and the public compounds that humiliation by tolerating it. Kantian morality is a cooperative scheme generating duties on the part of beneficiaries to cooperators who make the benefits possible. If we cannot prevent defectors from exploiting trusting cooperators, we can at least prevent them from enjoying the benefits and laughing at their victims as chumps. So, one reason we have to prevent the offender's undeserved gratification is to prevent the consequent degradation of the victim. And we do this not only to enforce the offender's duty to respect the victim, but also to fulfill our own.

This reinterpretation of the undeserved gratification argument as a display of respect for victims brings us to our final argument for punishing harm: the undeserved status argument. This argument justifies punishment for actual harm as necessary to correct the effects of successful crime on the social status of offenders. It draws on Jean Hampton's expressive account of punishment as "defeat." Hampton presumes that when one person wrongfully harms another, this offender asserts authority over the victim or claims superior honor. The offender thereby marks the victim as a person of lesser status whose interests do not count. A person who suffers such an insult without resistance or retaliation invites more abuse from others. On the other hand, the wrongdoer may gain in status and become an increasing threat to others if his wrong is left unredressed. According to Hampton, punishment is necessary to reverse this undeserved increase in status by humbling the offender. Yet, if the offender's increase in status is undeserved, so is the victim's decrease in status. It seems at least as important to correct that injustice. And insofar as the offender's claim to superiority rests on his subordination of a victim, it seems impossible to decrease the status of the offender without raising the status of the victim. By punishing, we restore the victim's status in much the same way as the victim might do by means of revenge. As our earlier discussion of punishment as a substitute for revenge revealed, however, there are some important differences. On the one hand, the victim cannot show martial honor and courage by personally avenging the wrong. On the other hand, the punitive state can back the humiliation of the offender and the vindication of the victim with its unique authority.

This interpretation of criminal punishment as the state's exercise of a monopoly on vengeance gives the state a special obligation to punish those wrongdoers who actually cause harm. This is because offenders only gain undeserved status by subordinating particular victims. It is humiliating to be injured with impunity, but people tend to take risk much less personally. They are not personally compelled to retaliate against risk or endure loss of face. The conception of state punishment as a substitute for private vengeance implies an undertaking to vindicate particular victims by avenging actual harms, rather than merely deterring the imposition of risk against the public at large. Such deterrence may reduce injury, but does nothing to restore the status of those who have been wrongly injured. Thus, it does not preempt retaliatory violence, nor does it earn the loyalty of victims. The state may only justly claim the loyalty and demand the forbearance of victims if it fulfills its undertaking to vindicate them.

The state's promise to avenge wrongs against each citizen explains its obligation to punish particular harms, rather than maximizing the welfare of all by discouraging the imposition of risk. The citizen's status is not challenged by merely being subjected to risk as part of a population. Only when he or she is subjected to unredressed harm is he or she forced into the dilemma of retaliating or accepting status degradation. Only then is the state obliged to exact retribution on his or her behalf in order to vindicate his or her honor. A failure to do so would represent the betrayal of a fundamental commitment. In wartime we often see citizens maintaining their loyalty to a state even in the face of death. But as the Iraqi civil war illustrates, a state that does not guarantee its citizens' basic civic dignity cannot expect even compliance, let alone heroic self-sacrifice.

Rather than asking whether it is fair or utility-maximizing to punish actual harm, we should ask how doing so supports the criminal law's legitimacy. Once the question is posed in this way, the answer seems almost obvious: punishing harm contributes to the legitimacy of the criminal justice system by vindicating victims. The ability to thus account for the criminal law's otherwise puzzling punishment of actual harm is a strong argument in favor of a political conception of criminal law.

## *Notes and Questions*

1. Suppose that while John is robbing the First National Bank, Mary is robbing the Second National Bank. John and Mary are not accomplices and the only connection between their two robberies is that they coincidentally took place at the same time. Police officers attempted to foil both robberies. John fired his gun intending to kill a police officer. Fortunately for the officer, she was not harmed, given that—unbeknownst to John—she was wearing a bulletproof vest. The police officer dispatched to the scene of Mary's robbery was not as fortunate, as she died when Mary shot her. Note that John is liable only of attempted murder, whereas Mary is liable for a consummated murder. Since completed offenses are punished more severely than attempted crimes in most jurisdictions, John will be punished more harshly than Mary. Do you agree with this outcome or do you believe that both John and Mary should be punished equally? Explain.

2. Did John do everything that he intended to do in order to bring about the death of the police officer? Did Mary do everything that she intended to do in order to kill the officer? If both John and Mary engaged in conduct that was designed to kill a police officer, why should Mary be punished significantly more than John merely because the police officer that John shot was wearing a bulletproof vest, whereas the officer that she shot was not? Is it fair to punish John more than Mary solely because of fortuitous circumstances such as whether the police officer that is shot is wearing protective armor? Why or why not?

3. Many legal and moral philosophers argue that completed attempts should be punished as severely as consummated offenses. They point out that the once the actor has done everything in her power to bring about the result, whether the proscribed harm materializes or not is entirely dependent on fortuitous occurrences that the actor cannot control. If so, they observe that punishing consummated crimes more than attempted offenses is irrational, given that the occurrence of harm is the product of "luck." That is, whether the police officers that John and Mary shot end up dying is a consequence of accidental circumstances that neither John nor Mary control. They cannot control, for example, whether the police officers that they shot were wearing a bulletproof vest or not. Similarly, they cannot control whether the police officers receive good or poor medical assistance after they are injured. This, in a nutshell, is why Professor Kadish argues in the excerpted article that punishing consummated crimes more severely than attempted offenses is "rationally insupportable." Do you agree? Explain.

4. Professor Binder takes issue with those who suggest that punishing completed crimes more severely than attempted offenses is irrational. He observes that whether to punish harm causation more than attempted harm causation is ultimately a question of political philosophy. More specifically, Binder argues that the right query in this context is not whether resulting harm is a product of "luck," but rather whether punishing harm more harshly than attempted harm "supports the criminal law's legitimacy." According to Binder, distinguishing between harm causation and attempted but failed harm creation promotes the legitimacy of the criminal justice system, for the state vindicates the interests of victims when it recognizes victim suffering as an appropriate ground for allocating blame and punishment. Furthermore, Binder points out that people generally feel more indignation when they actually suffer harm than when the are merely exposed to harm that does

not materialize. As a result, he suggests that punishing harm causation is more important to preventing private vengeance than punishing risk creation. Given that people care more about being harmed than about being endangered, the legitimacy of the criminal justice system is enhanced when the state tracks people's intuitions by punishing harm creation more than risk creation. Do you find Professor Binder's justification for punishing completed crimes more harshly than attempted offenses convincing? Why or why not?

# Chapter 12

# Conspiracy

## § 12.01 Conspiracy: In General

### Krulewitch v. United States

Supreme Court of the United States, 1949
336 U.S. 440

Mr. Justice BLACK delivered the opinion of the Court.

A federal district court indictment charged in three counts that petitioner and a woman defendant had (1) induced and persuaded another woman to go on October 20, 1941, from New York City to Miami, Florida, for the purpose of prostitution, in violation of [federal law]; (2) transported or caused her to be transported from New York to Miami for that purpose, in violation of [federal law]; and (3) conspired to commit those offenses in violation of [federal law]. Tried alone, the petitioner was convicted on all three counts of the indictment. The Court of Appeals affirmed. We granted certiorari limiting our review to consideration of alleged error in admission of certain hearsay testimony against petitioner over his timely and repeated objections.

The challenged testimony was elicited by the Government from its complaining witness, the person whom petitioner and the woman defendant allegedly induced to go from New York to Florida for the purpose of prostitution. The testimony narrated the following purported conversation between the complaining witness and petitioner's alleged co-conspirator, the woman defendant. "She asked me, she says, 'You didn't talk yet?' And I says, 'No.' And she says, 'Well, don't,' she says, 'until we get you a lawyer.' And then she says, 'Be very careful what you say.' And I can't put it in exact words. But she said, 'It would be better for us two girls to take the blame than Kay (the defendant) because he couldn't stand it, he couldn't stand to take it."

The time of the alleged conversation was more than a month and a half after October 20, 1941, the date the complaining witness had gone to Miami. Whatever original conspiracy may have existed between petitioner and his alleged co-conspirator to cause the complaining witness to go to Florida in October, 1941, no longer existed when the reported conversation took place in December, 1941. For on this latter date the trip to Florida had not only been made — the complaining witness had left Florida, had returned to New York, and had resumed her residence there. Furthermore, at the time the conversation took place, the complaining witness, the alleged co-conspirator, and the petitioner had been arrested. They apparently were charged in a United States District Court of Florida with the offense of which petitioner was here convicted.

It is beyond doubt that the central aim of the alleged conspiracy — transportation of the complaining witness to Florida for prostitution — had either never existed or had long since ended in success or failure when and if the alleged co-conspirator made the statement attributed to her. The statement plainly implied that petitioner was guilty of the crime for which he was on trial. It was made in petitioner's absence and the Government made no effort whatever to show that it was made with his authority. The testimony thus stands as an unsworn, out-of-court declaration of petitioner's guilt. This hearsay declaration, attributed to a co-conspirator, was not made pursuant to and in furtherance of objectives of the conspiracy charged in the indictment, because if made, it was after those objectives either had failed or had been achieved. Under these circumstances, the hearsay declaration attributed to the alleged co-conspirator was not admissible on the theory that it was made in furtherance of the alleged criminal transportation undertaking.

Although the Government recognizes that the chief objective of the conspiracy—transportation for prostitution purposes—had ended in success or failure before the reported conversation took place, it nevertheless argues for admissibility of the hearsay declaration at one in furtherance of a continuing subsidiary objective of the conspiracy. Its argument runs this way. Conspirators about to commit crimes always expressly or implicitly agree to collaborate with each other to conceal facts in order to prevent detection, conviction and punishment. Thus the argument is that even after the central criminal objectives of a conspiracy have succeeded or failed, an implicit subsidiary phase of the conspiracy always survives, the phase which has concealment as its sole objective. The Court of Appeals adopted this view. It viewed the alleged hearsay declaration as one in furtherance of this continuing subsidiary phase of the conspiracy, as part of 'the implied agreement to conceal.' It consequently held the declaration properly admitted.

We cannot accept the Government's contention. There are many logical and practical reasons that could be advanced against a special evidentiary rule that permits out-of-court statements of one conspirator to be used against another. But however cogent these reasons, it is firmly established that where made in furtherance of the objectives of a going conspiracy, such statements are admissible as exceptions to the hearsay rule. This prerequisite to admissibility, that hearsay statements by some conspirators to be admissible against others must be made in furtherance of the conspiracy charged, has been scrupulously observed by federal courts. The Government now asks us to expand this narrow exception to the hearsay rule and hold admissible a declaration, not made in furtherance of the alleged criminal transportation conspiracy charged, but made in furtherance of an alleged implied but uncharged conspiracy aimed at preventing detection and punishment. No federal court case cited by the Government suggests so hospitable a reception to the use of hearsay evidence to convict in conspiracy cases. The Government contention does find support in some but not all of the state court opinions cited in the Government brief. But in none of them does there appear to be recognition of any such broad exception to the hearsay rule as that here urged. The rule contended for by the Government could have far-reaching results. For under this rule plausible arguments could generally be made in conspiracy cases that most out-of-court statements offered in evidence tended to shield co-conspirators. We are not persuaded to adopt the Government's implicit conspiracy theory which in all criminal conspiracy cases would create automatically a further breach of the general rule against the admission of hearsay evidence ...

Reversed.

**Mr. Justice JACKSON, concurring in the judgment and opinion of the Court.**

This case illustrates a present drift in the federal law of conspiracy which warrants some further comment because it is characteristic of the long evolution of that elastic, sprawling and pervasive offense. Its history exemplifies the 'tendency of a principle to expand itself to the limit of its logic.' The unavailing protest of courts against the growing habit to indict for conspiracy in lieu of prosecuting for the substantive offense itself, or in addition thereto, suggests that loose practice as to this offense constitutes a serious threat to fairness in our administration of justice.

The modern crime of conspiracy is so vague that it almost defies definition. Despite certain elementary and essential elements, it also, chameleon-like, takes on a special coloration from each of the many independent offenses on which it may be overlaid. It is always 'predominantly mental in composition' because it consists primarily of a meeting of minds and an intent.

The crime comes down to us wrapped in vague but unpleasant connotations. It sounds historical undertones of treachery, secret plotting and violence on a scale that menaces social stability and the security of the state itself. 'Privy conspiracy' ranks with sedition and rebellion in the Litany's prayer for deliverance. Conspiratorial movements do indeed lie back of the political assassination, the coup d'etat, the putsch, the revolution, and seizures of power in modern times, as they have in all history.

But the conspiracy concept also is superimposed upon many concerted crimes having no political motivation. It is not intended to question that the basic conspiracy principle has some place in modern criminal law, because to unite, back of a criminal purpose, the strength, opportunities and resources of many is obviously more dangerous and more difficult to police than the efforts of a lone wrongdoer. It also may be trivialized, as here, where the conspiracy consists of the concert of a loathsome panderer and a prostitute to go from New York to Florida to ply their trade ... and it would appear that a simple Mann Act prosecution would vindicate the majesty of federal law. However, even when appropriately invoked, the looseness and pliability of the doctrine present inherent dangers which should be in the background of judicial thought wherever it is sought to extend the doctrine to meet the exigencies of a particular case.

Conspiracy in federal law aggravates the degree of crime over that of unconcerted offending. The act of confederating to commit a misdemeanor, followed by even an innocent overt act in its execution, is a felony and is such even if the misdemeanor is never consummated. The more radical proposition also is well-established that at common law and under some statutes a combination may be a criminal conspiracy even if it contemplates only acts which are not crimes at all when perpetrated by an individual or by many acting severally.

Thus the conspiracy doctrine will incriminate persons on the fringe of offending who would not be guilty of aiding and abetting or of becoming an accessory, for those charges only lie when an act which is a crime has actually been committed.

Attribution of criminality to a confederation which contemplates no act that would be criminal if carried out by any one of the conspirators is a practice peculiar to Anglo-American law. 'There can be little doubt that this wide definition of the crime of conspiracy originates in the criminal equity administered in the Star Chamber.' In fact, we are advised that 'The modern law of conspiracy is almost entirely the result of the manner in which conspiracy was treated by the Court of the Star Chamber. The doctrine does not commend itself to jurists of civil-law countries, despite universal recognition that an organized society must have legal weapons for combatting organized criminality. Most other countries have devised what they consider more discriminating principles upon which to prosecute criminal gangs, secret associations and subversive syndicates.

A recent tendency has appeared in this Court expand this elastic offense and to facilitate its proof. In Pinkerton v. United States, it sustained a conviction of a substantive crime where there was no proof of participation in or knowledge of it, upon the novel and dubious theory that conspiracy is equivalent in law to aiding and abetting....

Of course, it is for prosecutors rather than courts to determine when to use a scatter gun to bring down the defendant, but there are procedural advantages from using it which add to the danger of unguarded extension of the concept.

An accused, under the Sixth Amendment, has the right to trial 'by an impartial jury of the State and district wherein the crime shall have been committed.' The leverage of a conspiracy charge lifts this limitation from the prosecution and reduces its protection to a phantom, for the crime is considered so vagrant as to have been committed in any district where any one of the conspirators did any one of the acts, however innocent, intended to accomplish its object. The Government may, and often does, compel one to defend at a great distance from any place he ever did any act because some accused confederate did some trivial and by itself innocent act in the chosen district. Circumstances may even enable the prosecution to fix the place of trial in Washington, D.C., where a defendant may lawfully be put to trial before a jury partly or even wholly made up of employees of the Government that accuses him.

When the trial starts, the accused feels the full impact of the conspiracy strategy. Strictly, the prosecution should first establish prima facie the conspiracy and identify the conspirators, after which evidence of acts and declarations of each in the course of its execution are admissible against all. But the order of proof of so sprawling a charge is difficult for a judge to control. As a practical matter, the accused often is confronted with a hodgepodge of acts and statements by others which he may never have authorized or intended or even known about, but which help to persuade the jury of existence of the conspiracy itself. In other words, a conspiracy often is proved by evidence that is admissible only upon assumption that conspiracy existed. The naive assumption that prejudicial effects can be overcome by instructions to the jury, all practicing lawyers know to be unmitigated fiction.

The trial of a conspiracy charge doubtless imposes a heavy burden on the prosecution, but it is an especially difficult situation for the defendant. The hazard from loose application of rules of evidence is aggravated where the Government institutes mass trials. Moreover, in federal practice there is no rule preventing conviction on uncorroborated testimony of accomplices, as there are in many jurisdictions, and the most comfort a defendant can expect is that the court can be induced to follow the 'better practice' and caution the jury against 'too much reliance upon the testimony of accomplices.'

A co-defendant in a conspiracy trial occupies an uneasy seat. There generally will be evidence of wrongdoing by somebody. It is difficult for the individual to make his own case stand on its own merits in the minds of jurors who are ready to believe that birds of a feather are flocked together. If he is silent, he is taken to admit it and if, as often happens, co-defendants can be prodded into accusing or contradicting each other, they convict each other. There are many practical difficulties in defending against a charge of conspiracy which I will not enumerate.

Against this inadequately sketched background, I think the decision of this case in the court below introduced an ominous expansion of the accepted law of conspiracy. The prosecution was allowed to incriminate the defendant by means of the prostitute's recital of a conversation with defendant's alleged co-conspirator, who was not on trial. The conversation was said to have taken place after the substantive offense was accomplished, after the defendant, the co-conspirator and the witness had all been arrested, and after the witness and the other two had a falling out. The Court of Appeals sustained its admission upon grounds stated as follows: '* * * We think that implicit in a conspiracy to violate the law is an agreement among the conspirators to conceal the violation after as well as before the illegal plan is consummated. Thus the conspiracy continues, at least for purposes of concealment, even after its primary aims have been accomplished. The statements of the co-conspirator here were made in an effort to protect the appellant by concealing his role in the conspiracy. Consequently, they fell within the implied agreement to conceal and were admissible as evidence against the appellant ...'

I suppose no person planning a crime would accept as a collaborator one on whom he thought he could not rely for help if he were caught, but I doubt that this fact warrants an inference of conspiracy for that purpose. Of course, if an understanding for continuous aid had been proven, it would be embraced in the conspiracy by evidence and there would be no need to imply such an agreement. Only where there is no convincing evidence of such an understanding is there need for one to be implied.

It is difficult to see any logical limit to the 'implied conspiracy,' either as to duration or means, nor does it appear that one could overcome the implication by express and credible evidence that no such understanding existed, nor any way in which an accused against whom the presumption is once raised can terminate the imputed agency of his associates to incriminate him. Conspirators, long after the contemplated offense is complete, after perhaps they have fallen out and become enemies, may still incriminate each other by deliberately harmful, but unsworn declarations, or unintentionally by casual conversations out of court. On the theory that the law will impute to the confederates a continuing conspiracy to defeat justice, one conceivably could be bound by another's unauthorized and unknown commission of perjury, bribery of a juror or witness, or even putting an incorrigible witness with damaging information out of the way.

Moreover, the assumption of an indefinitely continuing offense would result in an indeterminate extension of the statute of limitations. If the law implies an agreement to cooperate in defeating prosecution, it must imply that it continues as long as prosecution is a possibility, and prosecution is a possibility as long as the conspiracy to defeat it is implied to continue.

I do not see the slightest warrant for judicially introducing a doctrine of implied crimes or constructive conspiracies. It either adds a new crime or extends an old one. True, the modern law of conspiracy was largely evolved by the judges. But it is well and wisely settled that there can be no judge-made offenses against the United States and that every federal prosecution must be sustained by statutory authority. No statute authorizes federal judges to imply, presume or construct a conspiracy except as one may be found from evidence. To do so seems to approximate creation of a new offense and one that I would think of doubtful constitutionality even if it were created by Congress. And, at all events, it is one fundamentally and irreconcilably at war with our presumption of innocence.

There is, of course, strong temptation to relax rigid standards when it seems the only way to sustain convictions of evildoers. But statutes authorize prosecution for substantive crimes for most evildoing without the dangers to the liberty of the individual and the integrity of the judicial process that are inherent in conspiracy charges. We should disapprove the doctrine of implied or constructive crime in its entirety and in every manifestation. And I think there should be no straining to uphold any conspiracy conviction where prosecution for the substantive offense is adequate and the purpose served by adding the conspiracy charge seems chiefly to get procedural advantages to ease the way to conviction.

Although a reversal after trials is, of course, regrettable, I cannot overlook the error as a harmless one. But I should concur in reversal even if less sure that prejudice resulted, for it is better that the crime go unwhipped of justice than that this theory of implied continuance of conspiracy find lodgment in our law, either by affirmance or by tolerance. Few instruments of injustice can equal that of implied or presumed or constructive crimes. The most odious of all oppressions are those which mask as justice.

## *Notes and Questions*

1. The crime of conspiracy is a fixture of American law. Conspiracy is relevant to the criminal justice system in several ways. First, conspiracy is a freestanding substantive offense that is consummated when two or more people agree to commit a crime. Second, co-conspirators may be jointly charged and prosecuted. Therefore—as Justice Jackson points out in his concurrence—"[t]he Government may, and often does, compel one to defend at a great distance from any place he ever did any act because some accused confederate did some trivial and by itself innocent act in the chosen district." Third, hearsay statements made by a conspirator during the course—and in furtherance—of the conspiracy are admissible against all co-conspirators. The issue in *Krulewitch* was determining whether the hearsay statements that the government introduced against the defendant were made during the course of the conspiracy.

2. Is conspiracy a kind of inchoate crime similar to attempt? When thought about in these terms, criminalizing conspiracy would be akin to prohibiting an act of preparation that would generally not be punished as an attempt. So conceived, conspiracy might be analogized to other acts of preparation that are criminalized, such as solicitation. In contrast, perhaps conspiracy is best viewed as a stand alone offense that criminalizes conduct for different reasons than those that justify prohibiting inchoate crimes. The distinctive feature of conspiracy that may make it amenable to being analyzed as an offense that differs in kind from traditional inchoate crimes is that it targets group criminality. Thus conceived, the special danger inherent in conspiracies is that—all things being equal—a group of people is more dangerous than a single individual. If this is true, the likelihood of consummating the offense will generally increase when a group of persons agree to commit an offense when compared to the likelihood of consummation of the crime when it is undertaken by a single person.

3. Prosecutors often charge a defendant with both engaging in a substantive crime (e.g., robbery) and conspiring to commit the substantive crime (e.g., conspiracy to commit robbery). If conspiracy is viewed as an inchoate crime akin to attempts and solicitation, then the conspiracy charge should "merge" with the consummated crime. This, in turn, would preclude punishing the defendant for both the substantive offense and conspiring to commit the substantive offense, just as it would bar punishing a defendant for consummating a crime and attempting the same offense. See, e.g., *State v. Malone*, 635 A.2d 596 (N.J. 1993).

4. Nevertheless, conspiracy will not merge with the substantive offense if conspiracy is viewed primarily as a stand-alone offense that seeks to curb the special danger inherent in group criminality. Thus, the Supreme Court of the United States has held that under federal law conspiracy does not merge with the substantive crime, for "[c]ombination in crime makes more likely the commission of crimes unrelated to the original purpose for which the group was formed." As a result, the Court concluded that merging conspiracy with the substantive offense would be inappropriate, given that "the danger which a conspiracy generates is not confined to the substantive offense which is the immediate aim of the enterprise." *Ianelli v. United States*, 420 U.S. 770 (1975). Do you be-

lieve that conspiracy should merge with the substantive offense like the New Jersey Superior Court held in *Malone*, or do you think—as the Supreme Court of the United States held in *Ianelli*—that the offenses should not merge? Explain.

## § 12.02 Conspiracy: Conduct Elements

### United States v. Shabani

Supreme Court of the United States, 1994
513 U.S. 10

Justice O'CONNOR delivered the opinion of the Court.

This case asks us to consider whether ... the [federal] drug conspiracy statute requires the Government to prove that a conspirator committed an overt act in furtherance of the conspiracy. We conclude that it does not.

I

According to the grand jury indictment, Reshat Shabani participated in a narcotics distribution scheme in Anchorage, Alaska, with his girlfriend, her family, and other associates. Shabani was allegedly the supplier of drugs, which he arranged to be smuggled from California. In an undercover operation, federal agents purchased cocaine from distributors involved in the conspiracy.

Shabani was charged with conspiracy to distribute cocaine ... He moved to dismiss the indictment because it did not allege the commission of an overt act in furtherance of the conspiracy, which act, he argued, was an essential element of the offense. The United States District Court for the District of Alaska, Hon. H. Russel Holland, denied the motion, and the case proceeded to trial.... The jury returned a guilty verdict, and the court sentenced Shabani to 160 months' imprisonment.

The United States Court of Appeals for the Ninth Circuit reversed.... The Court of Appeals reasoned that, although the Government must prove at trial that the defendant has committed an overt act in furtherance of a narcotics conspiracy, the act need not be alleged in the indictment because "'[c]ourts do not require as detailed a statement of an offense's elements under a conspiracy count as under a substantive count.'" ...

II

Congress passed the drug conspiracy statute as § 406 of the Comprehensive Drug Abuse Prevention and Control Act of 1970. It provided: "Any person who attempts or conspires to commit any offense defined in this title is punishable by imprisonment or fine or both which may not exceed the maximum punishment prescribed for the offense, the commission of which was the object of the attempt or conspiracy." As amended by the Anti-Drug Abuse Act of 1988, the statute currently provides: "Any person who attempts or conspires to commit any offense defined in this subchapter shall be subject to the same penalties as those prescribed for the offense, the commission of which was the object of the attempt or conspiracy." The language of neither version requires that an overt act be committed to further the conspiracy, and we have not inferred such a requirement from congressional silence in other conspiracy statutes. In *Nash v. United States*, Justice Holmes wrote, "[W]e can see no reason for reading into the Sherman Act more than we find there," and the Court held that an overt act is not required for antitrust conspiracy liability. The same reasoning prompted our conclusion in *Singer v. United States*, that the Selective Service Act "does not require an overt act for the offense of conspiracy."

*Nash* and *Singer* follow the settled principle of statutory construction that, absent contrary indications, Congress intends to adopt the common law definition of statutory terms. We have consistently held that the common law understanding of conspiracy "does not make the doing of any act other than the act of conspiring a condition of liability." ... *Bannon v. United States,* 156 U.S. 464, 468, 15 S.Ct. 467, 469, 39 L.Ed. 494 (1895) ("At common law it was neither necessary to aver nor prove an overt act in furtherance of the conspiracy ...") ...

... [W]e find it instructive that the general conspiracy statute contains an explicit requirement that a conspirator "do any act to effect the object of the conspiracy." In light of this additional element in the general conspiracy statute, Congress' silence in [the drug conspiracy statute] speaks volumes. After all, the general conspiracy statute preceded and presumably provided the framework for the more specific drug conspiracy statute. "*Nash* and *Singer* give Congress a formulary: by choosing a text modeled on [the general conspiracy statute], it gets an overt-act requirement; by choosing a text modeled on the Sherman Act, it dispenses with such a requirement." *United States v. Sassi.* Congress appears to have made the choice quite deliberately with respect to [the drug conspiracy statute]; the same Congress that passed this provision also enacted the Organized Crime Control Act of 1970, ... which contains an explicit requirement that "one or more of [the conspirators] does any act to effect the object of such a conspiracy,".

Early opinions in the Ninth Circuit dealing with the drug conspiracy statute simply relied on our precedents interpreting the general conspiracy statute and ignored the textual variations between the two provisions ...

What the Ninth Circuit failed to recognize we now make explicit: In order to establish a violation of [the drug conspiracy statute], the Government need not prove the commission of any overt acts in furtherance of the conspiracy ...

Shabani reminds us that the law does not punish criminal thoughts and contends that conspiracy without an overt act requirement violates this principle because the offense is predominantly mental in composition. The prohibition against criminal conspiracy, however, does not punish mere thought; the criminal agreement itself is the *actus reus* and has been so viewed since *Regina v. Bass,* [decided in 1705] ("[T]he very assembling together was an overt act"); see also *Iannelli v. United States* ("Conspiracy is an inchoate offense, the essence of which is an agreement to commit an unlawful act") ...

As the District Court correctly noted in this case, the plain language of the statute and settled interpretive principles reveal that proof of an overt act is not required to establish a violation of [the federal drug conspiracy statute]. Accordingly, the judgment of the Court of Appeals is *reversed.*

## People v. Persinger

Appellate Court of Illinois, 1977
49 Ill.App.3d 116

CARTER, Presiding Justice.

The defendant, Harold D. Persinger, was charged by an indictment with the crime of conspiracy as follows:

> Harold Persinger on the 18th day of June, 1975 ... committed the offense of conspiracy, in that he did with the intent to commit the offense of unlawful deliv-

> ery of controlled substance in violation of Illinois [law], he agreed with Ida Frances Persinger to the commission of that offense and performed an act in furtherance of that agreement in that he obtained a prescription for less than 200 grams of a substance containing a derivative of barbituric acid, to-wit: Nembutal, and procured said controlled substance with his Public Aid Medical Card in violation of Illinois [law].

The defendant was tried by the court, without a jury, found guilty, and sentenced to a term of one year to fifteen months. From this adverse judgment the defendant argues on appeal that ... the State failed to prove beyond a reasonable doubt that the defendant entered into an agreement with Ida Persinger with the intent to commit the offense of unlawful delivery ... For the reasons detailed below ... we ... affirm the judgment of the lower court.

The State's evidence consisted primarily of the testimony of witnesses who observed four controlled purchases of pills from Mrs. Ida Persinger at the Persinger residence; testimony from a pharmacist identifying bottles and pills which were sold by Mrs. Persinger as coming from his pharmacy; and the testimony of Mrs. Mary Scammahorn, the mother-in-law of the defendant's son ...

The defendant argues that the evidence presented by the prosecution shows, at best, only his mere presence at the sale on June 23, 1975 and has established only his knowledge of the illegal conduct of his wife. Therefore, the evidence is insufficient to prove that the defendant entered into a conspiracy with his wife to commit the offense of unlawful delivery of a controlled substance in violation of [Illinois law].

Conspiracy, because of its indefiniteness and comprehensiveness has often been the target for criticism. In Krulewitch v. United States, Justice Jackson's concurring opinion referred to conspiracy as an 'elastic, sprawling and pervasive offense, so vague that it almost defies definition.' ...

It is frequently said that the 'gist' or 'essence' of a conspiracy is not the offense that is the object of the agreement, but the making of an unlawful combination of agreement. Recognizing that few conspirators would memorialize the agreement in writing as a contract or even testify as to the existence of an agreement during trial, the courts retreat from precise statements concerning the need for an 'agreement' to statements such as:

a) A common design is the essence of the charge and if it be proved that the defendants pursued by their acts the same object, by the same means, one performing one part and one another, a conspiracy may be inferred if the evidence is sufficient.

b) The guilty knowledge which is an essential element of the crime ... is rarely susceptible of direct and positive proof. It is sufficiently shown if it may be inferred from all the surrounding facts and circumstances involved in the transaction, including the acts and declarations of the accused concerning the same.

c) While common design is the essence of a conspiracy, it is not necessary to prove that common design by direct evidence of an agreement between the conspirators. It is only necessary to show that they pursued a cause tending toward the accomplishment of the object of which the complaint is made.

In essence, because of the clandestine nature of a conspiracy and the foreseeable difficulty of the prosecution's burden of establishing the conspiracy by direct proof, the courts have permitted broad inferences to be drawn of the defendant's conspiratorial intent and agreement from evidence of acts, conduct, and circumstances. Attempting to mitigate the far reaching effects of the conspiracy doctrine, the legislature requires, in addition to the requisite Mens rea, that an overt act in furtherance of the conspiracy be shown. However, this additional requirement rarely imposes any substantial burden on the prosecution for just about any act in furtherance of the unlawful agreement will satisfy this element and this act need not be committed by a particular defendant so long as one of the co-conspirators was involved in the act.

In order to convict the defendant of conspiracy, the State need only prove that the defendant, with the intent that the offense of sale of controlled substance be committed, agreed with his wife to obtain the drugs and that an act was done in furtherance of that agreement. Since no direct evidence was presented of an agreement, our task is to see if there was sufficient circumstantial evidence to inferentially establish the existence of an 'agreement' and not merely raise a suspicion as to its existence.

From a careful examination of the record, especially considering evidence of the defendant's participation in the June 23, 1975 sale; statements to the effect that the defendant was often present when Scammahorn brought drugs; the statement made by the defendant in the bank on May 1, 1975 coupled with the receipt written by the defendant; as well as the quantity, frequency, and duration of the sales to Scammahorn, we believe that the cumulative effect of this evidence is sufficient to justify a finding of guilty on the conspiracy charge.

We emphasize, however, that mere knowledge, acquiescence, approval, or attempt on the part of one to perpetrate the illegal act does not constitute conspiracy. Moreover, a conspiracy cannot be established by evidence of a mere relationship or transaction between the parties. In situations, such as the one at bar, where knowledge might readily be demonstrated, it is nonetheless the finding of intent and an agreement which is required rather than mere knowledge....

Accordingly, the judgment of the Circuit Court of Clay County is affirmed.

## People v. Foster

Supreme Court of Illinois, 1983
99 Ill.2d 48

UNDERWOOD, Justice:

Following a jury trial in the circuit court of McLean County the defendant, James Foster, was convicted of conspiracy to commit robbery, and sentenced to an extended term of six years' imprisonment. Based upon its interpretation of the Illinois conspiracy statute the appellate court reversed .... We granted the State's petition for leave to appeal.

On September 28, 1981, defendant initiated his plan to commit a robbery when he approached John Ragsdale in a Rantoul bar and asked Ragsdale if he was "interested in making some money." Defendant told Ragsdale of an elderly man, A.O. Hedrick, who kept many valuables in his possession. Although Ragsdale stated that he was interested in making money he did not believe defendant was serious until defendant returned to the bar the next day and discussed in detail his plan to rob Hedrick. In an effort to gather additional information, Ragsdale decided to feign agreement to defendant's plan but did not contact the police.

On October 1, defendant went to Ragsdale's residence to find out if Ragsdale was "ready to go." Since Ragsdale had not yet contacted the police he told defendant that he would not be ready until he found someone else to help them. Ragsdale informed the police of the planned robbery on October 3. Defendant and Ragsdale were met at Hedrick's residence the following day and arrested.

The appellate court determined that the conspiracy statute required actual agreement between at least two persons to support a conspiracy conviction. Reasoning that Ragsdale never intended to agree to defendant's plan but merely feigned agreement, the court reversed defendant's conviction.

On appeal to this court the State argues that under the conspiracy statute it suffices if only one of the participants to the alleged conspiracy actually intends to agree to commit an offense. Alternatively, the State contends that there was sufficient evidence to convict defendant even under the appellate court's interpretation of the statute.

The question is whether the Illinois legislature, in amending the conspiracy statute in 1961, intended to adopt the unilateral theory of conspiracy. To support a conspiracy conviction under the unilateral theory only one of the alleged conspirators need intend to agree to the commission of an offense. Prior to the 1961 amendment the statute clearly encompassed the traditional, bilateral theory, requiring the actual agreement of at least two participants. The relevant portion of the former statute is as follows:

"If any *two or more persons* conspire or *agree together* * * * to do any illegal act * * * they shall be deemed guilty of a conspiracy."

The amended version of the statute provides:

"*A person* commits conspiracy when, with intent that an offense be committed, *he agrees* with another to the commission of that offense."

Since the statute is presently worded in terms of "a person" rather than "two or more persons" it is urged by the State that only one person need intend to agree to the commission of an offense …

While impressed with the logic of the State's interpretation of [the conspiracy statute], we are troubled by the committee's failure to explain the reason for deleting the words "two or more persons" from the statute. The committee comments to section 8-2 detail the several changes in the law of conspiracy that were intended by the 1961 amendment. The comments simply do not address the unilateral/bilateral issue. The State suggests that the new language was so clear on its face that it did not warrant additional discussion. We doubt, however, that the drafters could have intended what represents a rather profound change in the law of conspiracy without mentioning it in the comments to section 8-2. …

It is also not without significance that two appellate court panels have construed section 8-2(a) as encompassing the bilateral theory of conspiracy since its amendment in 1961. While it is true that a legislature's failure to amend a statute after judicial interpretation is not conclusive evidence of the correctness of that interpretation, such inaction is suggestive of legislative agreement. We agree with defendant that, here, the legislature's failure to act after the[se] [decisions] lends considerable support to the conclusion that a bilateral theory of conspiracy was intended, particularly since [one of the cases was a] 1975 decision.… For the above reasons we conclude that section 8-2(a) encompasses the bilateral theory of conspiracy.

Our conclusion requires consideration of the State's argument that there was sufficient evidence to convict defendant even under the bilateral theory of conspiracy. We find no basis for this assertion and agree with the appellate court that at best the jury could have found beyond a reasonable doubt only that Ragsdale considered defendant's offer before going to the police.

The judgment of the appellate court is therefore affirmed.

## *Notes and Questions*

1. As the Supreme Court points out in *Shabani,* the conduct element (*actus reus*) of conspiracy at common law was "the agreement" to commit a crime. Thus, at common law a defendant may be held liable for conspiracy even if she did not engage in an act in furtherance of the conspiratorial agreement.

2. In *Persinger,* however, the Supreme Court of Illinois explained that liability under the state conspiracy statute required that—in addition to the conspiratorial agreement—the state prove that the defendant engage in an overt act in furtherance of the conspiracy. The so-called "overt act" requirement has been adopted in a considerable number of jurisdictions. Others, however, follow the common law rule that proof of the agreement is sufficient to establish conspiracy liability even in the absence of an overt act. Which approach is preferable? Why?

3. Note that the court in *Persinger* was careful to point out that proof of knowledge of another's criminal plan does not by itself amount to the sort of agreement that generates liability for conspiracy. In addition to knowledge of another's criminal plan, the actor must have the intent to help achieve the other's criminal objective. The Court was concerned that—in spite of the intent requirement—defendants might be convicted of conspiracy solely on the basis of knowledge of another's criminal plan. The concern is particularly acute when there is a close relationship between the parties, such as husband and wife. Would requiring proof of an overt act allay some of the concerns raised by the Court in *Persinger*? Why or why not?

4. Must there be an actual agreement between the parties in order for conspiracy liability to attach, or would a mistaken belief that there is a true agreement suffice for liability? At common law, proof of an actual agreement was required. Therefore, a defendant could not be held liable for conspiracy if the other conspiring party feigned agreement. This position is usually called the "bilateral theory" of conspiracy. As *Foster* illustrates, the bilateral theory of conspiracy is still followed in several jurisdictions. Nevertheless, some jurisdictions have instead adopted the "unilateral theory" of conspiracy. Under the unilateral theory, conspiracy liability attaches as long as the defendant believed that the other party or parties were actually agreeing to commit the offense, even if the defendant's belief turns out to be mistaken. See, e.g., *Miller v. State,* 955 P.2d 892 (Wyo., 1998).

5. When many parties are involved, it is often difficult to determine whether one or multiple conspiracies exist. That is, it is unclear in some cases involving multiple parties whether there are one or many conspiratorial agreements. The facts of *Kotteakos v. United States,* 328 U.S. 750 (1946), are illustrative. The defendant attempted to fraudulently secure a loan under the National Housing Act. He sought services of one Simon Brown in order to perpetrate the fraud. Brown, in turn, was helping several others engage in similar fraudulent acts. The Government charged the defendant with participating in a single conspiracy. Nevertheless, it admitted to proving "not one conspiracy but some eight or more different ones of the same sort executed through a common key figure, Simon Brown." The defendant was convicted. He appealed, contending that it was prejudicial error to charge him with a single conspiracy. The Supreme Court of the United States reversed:

> The evidence against the other defendants whose cases were submitted to the jury was similar [to the evidence against Kotteakos]. They too had transacted business with Brown relating to National Housing Act loans. But no connection was shown between them and petitioners, other than that Brown had been the instrument in each instance for obtaining the loans. In many cases the other defendants did not have any relationship with one another, other than Brown's connection with each transaction. As the Circuit Court of Appeals said, there were 'at least eight, and perhaps more, separate and independent groups, none of which had any connection with any other, though all dealt independently with Brown as their agent.' As the Government puts it, the pattern was 'that of separate spokes meeting at a common center,' though we may add without the rim of the wheel to enclose the spokes ... The proof therefore admittedly made out a case, not of a single conspiracy, but of several, notwithstanding only one was charged in the indictment. *Id.*

6. The kind of conspiracy illustrated by *Kotteakos* is frequently called a "hub and spoke" conspiracy. This salient feature of hub and spoke conspiracies is that you have a central figure (hub) which enters into several similar agreements with different parties (spokes). The problem in *Kotteakos* was that there was nothing to link the different "spokes" (Kotteakos and the others who entered into agreements with Simon Brown) with each other enough to conclude that the "spokes" were not only in an agreement with the central hub (Simon Brown), but also with each other. To continue with the spoke analogy, what is missing is the "rim of the wheel" that links the scopes to one another.

7. What else does the government need to demonstrate in order to establish the existence of a "rim" that links the "spokes" together? In *Interstate Circuit v. United States,* 306 U.S. 208 (1939), two large movie theater chains sent letters to eight film distributors proposing contracts that would limit the theaters in which the distributors would release their films. The names and addresses of the eight film distributors were included in all of the letters sent. The distributors signed the agreement with the movie theater. The distributors and the movie theaters were charged with engaging in a single conspiracy to violate the Sherman Act (i.e., antitrust laws). The defendants argued that there were multiple conspiracies rather than a single conspiracy. The Supreme Court of the United States found that there was only one conspiracy:

> While the District Court's finding of an agreement of the distributors among themselves is supported by the evidence, we think that, in the circumstances of this case, such agreement for the imposition of the restrictions upon subsequent-run exhibitors was not a prerequisite to an unlawful conspiracy. It was enough that, knowing that concerted action was contemplated and invited, the distributors gave their adherence to the scheme and participated in it. Each distributor was advised that the others were asked to participate; each knew that cooperation was essential to successful operation of the plan. They knew that the plan, if carried out, would result in a restraint of commerce, which, we will presently point out, was unreasonable within the meaning of the Sherman Act, and, knowing it, all participated in the plan. The evidence is persuasive that each distributor early became aware that the others had joined. With that knowledge, they renewed the arrangement and carried it into effect for the two successive years.
>
> It is elementary that an unlawful conspiracy may be and often is formed without simultaneous action or agreement on the part of the conspirators. Acceptance by competitors, without previous agreement, of an invitation to participate in a plan the necessary consequence of which, if carried out, is restraint of in-

> terstate commerce is sufficient to establish an unlawful conspiracy under the Sherman Act.

In *Interstate Circuit*, the rim that connected the spokes (the eight film distributors) to the central hub (the two movie theater chains) was the knowledge that the film distributors had about each other's participation in the common scheme and their awareness that the goal of the movie theaters (obtaining an unlawful competitive edge over other movie theater chains) could only be achieved if most or all of them agreed to the terms proposed by the movie theaters.

8. Another common type of conspiracy is that in which several actors are considered essential links in a criminal chain. Such "chain conspiracies" are often comprised of parties who act separately and who may not be aware of the identities of the other parties. Nevertheless, all parties are aware that the good or service that they provide is essential to the success of the criminal enterprise. If such awareness exists, it is often held that a single conspiracy exists in spite of the fact that the parties may not be aware of each other's identities. In *United States v. Bruno*, 105 F.2d 921 (1939), for example, the government charged drug smugglers, the middlemen and two groups of retailers with engaging in a single drug trafficking conspiracy. The defendants contended that there were multiple conspiracies rather than a single one, for one group of conspirators had no contact whatsoever with other groups of conspirators. The Court of Appeals for the Second Circuit rejected the argument because:

> The evidence allowed the jury to find that there had existed over a substantial period of time a conspiracy embracing a great number of persons, whose object was to smuggle narcotics into the Port of New York and distribute them to addicts both in this city and in Texas and Louisiana. This required the cooperation of four groups of persons; the smugglers who imported the drugs; the middlemen who paid the smugglers and distributed to retailers; and two groups of retailers—one in New York and one in Texas and Louisiana—who supplied the addicts. The defendants assert that there were, therefore, at least three separate conspiracies; one between the smugglers and the middlemen, and one between the middlemen and each group of retailers. The evidence did not disclose any cooperation or communication between the smugglers and either group of retailers, or between the two groups of retailers themselves; however, the smugglers knew that the middlemen must sell to retailers, and the retailers knew that the middlemen must buy of importers of one sort or another. Thus the conspirators at one end of the chain knew that the unlawful business would not, and could not, stop with their buyers; and those at the other end knew that it had not begun with their sellers. That being true, a jury might have found that all the accused were embarked upon a venture, in all parts of which each was a participant, and an abettor in the sense that the success of that part with which he was immediately concerned, was dependent upon the success of the whole. That being true, a jury might have found that all the accused were embarked upon a venture, in all parts of which each was a participant, and an abettor in the sense that the success of that part with which he was immediately concerned, was dependent upon the success of the whole.

Do you agree with the Court's conclusion that a jury could find that there was a single conspiracy in this case? Explain. Does it make sense to claim that there was an "agreement" between the smugglers and the retailers when "the evidence did not disclose any cooperation or communication between the smugglers and either group of retailers"? Why or why not?

# § 12.03 Conspiracy: Subjective Elements

## People v. Lauria

Court of Appeal, Second District, California, 1967
251 Cal.App.2d 471

FLEMING, J.

In an investigation of call-girl activity the police focused their attention on three prostitutes actively plying their trade on call, each of whom was using Lauria's telephone answering service, presumably for business purposes.

On January 8, 1965, Stella Weeks, a policewoman, signed up for telephone service with Lauria's answering service. Mrs. Weeks, in the course of her conversation with Lauria's office manager, hinted broadly that she was a prostitute concerned with the secrecy of her activities and their concealment from the police. She was assured that the operation of the service was discreet and "about as safe as you can get." It was arranged that Mrs. Weeks need not leave her address with the answering service, but could pick up her calls and pay her bills in person.

On February 11, Mrs. Weeks talked to Lauria on the telephone and told him her business was modelling and she had been referred to the answering service by Terry, one of the three prostitutes under investigation. She complained that because of the operation of the service she had lost two valuable customers, referred to as tricks. Lauria defended his service and said that her friends had probably lied to her about having left calls for her. But he did not respond to Mrs. Weeks' hints that she needed customers in order to make money, other than to invite her to his house for a personal visit in order to get better acquainted. In the course of his talk he said "his business was taking messages."

On February 15, Mrs. Weeks talked on the telephone to Lauria's office manager and again complained of two lost calls, which she described as a $50 and a $100 trick. On investigation the office manager could find nothing wrong, but she said she would alert the switchboard operators about slip-ups on calls.

On April 1 Lauria and the three prostitutes were arrested. Lauria complained to the police that this attention was undeserved, stating that Hollywood Call Board had 60 to 70 prostitutes on its board while his own service had only 9 or 10, that he kept separate records for known or suspected prostitutes for the convenience of himself and the police. When asked if his records were available to police who might come to the office to investigate call girls, Lauria replied that they were whenever the police had a specific name. However, his service didn't "arbitrarily tell the police about prostitutes on our board. As long as they pay their bills we tolerate them." In a subsequent voluntary appearance before the grand jury Lauria testified he had always cooperated with the police. But he admitted he knew some of his customers were prostitutes, and he knew Terry was a prostitute because he had personally used her services, and he knew she was paying for 500 calls a month.

Lauria and the three prostitutes were indicted for conspiracy to commit prostitution, and nine overt acts were specified. Subsequently the trial court set aside the indictment as having been brought without reasonable or probable cause. (Pen Code, § 995.) The People have appealed, claiming that a sufficient showing of an unlawful agreement to further prostitution was made.

To establish agreement, the People need show no more than a tacit, mutual understanding between coconspirators to accomplish an unlawful act. Here the People attempted to establish a conspiracy by showing that Lauria, well aware that his codefendants were prostitutes who received business calls from customers through his telephone answering service, continued to furnish them with such service. This approach attempts to equate knowledge of another's criminal activity with conspiracy to further such criminal activity, and poses the question of the criminal responsibility of a furnisher of goods or services who knows his product is being used to assist the operation of an illegal business. Under what circumstances does a supplier become a part of a conspiracy to further an illegal enterprise by furnishing goods or services which he knows are to be used by the buyer for criminal purposes?

The two leading cases on this point face in opposite directions. In *United States v. Falcone*, the sellers of large quantities of sugar, yeast, and cans were absolved from participation in a moonshining conspiracy among distillers who bought from them, while in *Direct Sales Co. v. United States*, a wholesaler of drugs was convicted of conspiracy to violate the federal narcotic laws by selling drugs in quantity to a codefendant physician who was supplying them to addicts. The distinction between these two cases appears primarily based on the proposition that distributors of such dangerous products as drugs are required to exercise greater discrimination in the conduct of their business than are distributors of innocuous substances like sugar and yeast.

In the earlier case, *Falcone*, the sellers' knowledge of the illegal use of the goods was insufficient by itself to make the sellers participants in a conspiracy with the distillers who bought from them. Such knowledge fell short of proof of a conspiracy, and evidence on the volume of sales was too vague to support a jury finding that respondents knew of the conspiracy from the size of the sales alone.

In the later case of *Direct Sales*, the conviction of a drug wholesaler for conspiracy to violate federal narcotic laws was affirmed on a showing that it had actively promoted the sale of morphine sulphate in quantity and had sold codefendant physician, who practiced in a small town in South Carolina, more than 300 times his normal requirements of the drug, even though it had been repeatedly warned of the dangers of unrestricted sales of the drug. The court contrasted the restricted goods involved in *Direct Sales* with the articles of free commerce involved in *Falcone*: "All articles of commerce may be put to illegal ends," said the court. "But all do not have inherently the same susceptibility to harmful and illegal use.... This difference is important for two purposes. One is for making certain that the seller knows the buyer's intended illegal use. The other is to show that by the sale he intends to further, promote, and cooperate in it. This intent, when given effect by overt act, is the gist of conspiracy. While it is not identical with mere knowledge that another purposes unlawful action it is not unrelated to such knowledge.... The step from knowledge to intent and agreement may be taken. There is more than suspicion, more than knowledge, acquiescence, carelessness, indifference, lack of concern. There is informed and interested cooperation, stimulation, instigation. And there is also a 'stake in the venture' which, even if it may not be essential, is not irrelevant to the question of conspiracy."

While *Falcone* and *Direct Sales* may not be entirely consistent with each other in their full implications, they do provide us with a framework for the criminal liability of a supplier of lawful goods or services put to unlawful use. Both the element of *knowledge* of the illegal use of the goods or services and the element of *intent* to further that use must be present in order to make the supplier a participant in a criminal conspiracy. Proof of *knowledge* is ordinarily a question of fact and requires no extended discussion in the present case. The knowledge of the supplier was sufficiently established when Lauria admitted he knew some of his customers were prostitutes and admitted he knew that Terry, an active subscriber to his service, was a prostitute. In the face of these admissions he could scarcely claim to have relied on the normal assumption an operator of a business or service is entitled to make, that his customers are behaving themselves in the eyes of the law. Because Lauria knew in fact that some of his customers were prostitutes, it is a legitimate inference he knew they were subscribing to his answering service for illegal business purposes and were using his service to make assignations for prostitution. On this record we think the prosecution is entitled to claim positive knowledge by Lauria of the use of his service to facilitate the business of prostitution.

The more perplexing issue in the case is the sufficiency of proof of *intent* to further the criminal enterprise. The element of intent may be proved either by direct evidence, or by evidence of circumstances from which an intent to further a criminal enterprise by supplying lawful goods or services may be inferred. Direct evidence of participation, such as advice from the supplier of legal goods or services to the user of those goods or services on their use for illegal purposes, such evidence as appeared in a companion case we decide today … provides the simplest case. When the intent to further and promote the criminal enterprise comes from the lips of the supplier himself, ambiguities of inference from circumstance need not trouble us. But in cases where direct proof of complicity is lacking, intent to further the conspiracy must be derived from the sale itself and its surrounding circumstances in order to establish the supplier's express or tacit agreement to join the conspiracy.

In the case at bench the prosecution argues that since Lauria knew his customers were using his service for illegal purposes but nevertheless continued to furnish it to them, he must have intended to assist them in carrying out their illegal activities. Thus through a union of knowledge and intent he became a participant in a criminal conspiracy. Essentially, the People argue that knowledge alone of the continuing use of his telephone facilities for criminal purposes provided a sufficient basis from which his intent to participate in those criminal activities could be inferred.

In examining precedents in this field we find that sometimes, but not always, the criminal intent of the supplier may be inferred from his knowledge of the unlawful use made of the product he supplies. Some consideration of characteristic patterns may be helpful.

Intent may be inferred from knowledge, when the purveyor of legal goods for illegal use has acquired a stake in the venture.… For example, in *Regina v. Thomas,* a prosecution for living off the earnings of prostitution, the evidence showed that the accused, knowing the woman to be a convicted prostitute, agreed to let her have the use of his room between the hours of 9 p.m. and 2 a.m. for a charge of £3 a night. The Court of Criminal Appeal refused an appeal from the conviction, holding that when the accused rented a room at a grossly inflated rent to a prostitute for the purpose of carrying on her trade, a jury could find he was living on the earnings of prostitution.

In the present case, no proof was offered of inflated charges for the telephone answering services furnished the codefendants.

Intent may be inferred from knowledge, when no legitimate use for the goods or services exists. The leading California case is *People v. McLaughlin*, in which the court upheld a conviction of the suppliers of horse-racing information by wire for conspiracy to promote bookmaking, when it had been established that wire-service information had no other use than to supply information needed by bookmakers to conduct illegal gambling operations …

In *Shaw v. Director of Public Prosecutions*, the defendant was convicted of conspiracy to corrupt public morals and of living on the earnings of prostitution, when he published a directory consisting almost entirely of advertisements of the names, addresses, and specialized talents of prostitutes. Publication of such a directory, said the court, could have no legitimate use and serve no other purpose than to advertise the professional services of the prostitutes whose advertisements appeared in the directory. The publisher could be deemed a participant in the profits from the business activities of his principal advertisers.

Other services of a comparable nature come to mind: the manufacturer of crooked dice and marked cards who sells his product to gambling casinos; the tipster who furnishes information on the movement of law enforcement officers to known lawbreakers ... In such cases the supplier must necessarily have an intent to further the illegal enterprise since there is no known honest use for his goods.

However, there is nothing in the furnishing of telephone answering service which would necessarily imply assistance in the performance of illegal activities. Nor is any inference to be derived from the use of an answering service by women, either in any particular volume of calls, or outside normal working hours. Night-club entertainers, registered nurses, faith healers, public stenographers, photographic models, and free lance substitute employees, provide examples of women in legitimate occupations whose employment might cause them to receive a volume of telephone calls at irregular hours.

3. Intent may be inferred from knowledge, when the volume of business with the buyer is grossly disproportionate to any legitimate demand, or when sales for illegal use amount to a high proportion of the seller's total business. In such cases an intent to participate in the illegal enterprise may be inferred from the quantity of the business done. For example, in *Direct Sales,* the sale of narcotics to a rural physician in quantities 300 times greater than he would have normal use for provided potent evidence of an intent to further the illegal activity. In the same case the court also found significant the fact that the wholesaler had attracted as customers a disproportionately large group of physicians who had been convicted of violating the Harrison Act. In *Shaw v. Director of Public Prosecutions*, almost the entire business of the directory came from prostitutes.

No evidence of any unusual volume of business with prostitutes was presented by the prosecution against Lauria.

Inflated charges, the sale of goods with no legitimate use, sales in inflated amounts, each may provide a fact of sufficient moment from which the intent of the seller to participate in the criminal enterprise may be inferred. In such instances participation by the supplier of legal goods to the illegal enterprise may be inferred because in one way or another the supplier has acquired a special interest in the operation of the illegal enterprise. His intent to participate in the crime of which he has knowledge may be inferred from the existence of his special interest.

Yet there are cases in which it cannot reasonably be said that the supplier has a stake in the venture or has acquired a special interest in the enterprise, but in which he has been held liable as a participant on the basis of knowledge alone.... [It could be argued, for example, that a] supplier who furnishes equipment which he *knows* will be used to commit a serious crime may be deemed from that knowledge alone to have intended to produce the result. Such proof may justify an inference that the furnisher intended to aid the execution of the crime and that he thereby became a participant. For instance, we think the operator of a telephone answering service with positive knowledge that his service was being used to facilitate the extortion of ransom, the distribution of heroin, or the passing of counterfeit money who continued to furnish the service with knowledge of its use, might be chargeable on knowledge alone with participation in a scheme to extort money, to distribute narcotics, or to pass counterfeit money. The same result would follow the seller of gasoline who knew the buyer was using his product to make Molotov cocktails for terroristic use.

Logically, the same reasoning could be extended to crimes of every description. Yet we do not believe an inference of intent drawn from knowledge of criminal use properly applies to the less serious crimes classified as misdemeanors. The duty to take positive action to dissociate oneself from activities helpful to violations of the criminal law is far stronger and more compelling for felonies than it is for misdemeanors or petty offenses.... We believe the distinction between the obligations arising from knowledge of a felony and those arising from knowledge of a misdemeanor continues to reflect basic human feelings about the duties owed by individuals to society. Heinous crime must be stamped out, and its suppression is the responsibility of all ... Venial crime and crime not evil in itself present less of a danger to society, and perhaps the benefits of their suppression through the modern equivalent of the posse, the hue and cry, the informant, and the citizen's arrest, are outweighed by the disruption to everyday life brought about by amateur law enforcement and private officiousness in relatively inconsequential delicts which do not threaten our basic security. The subject has been summarized in an English text on the criminal law: "Failure to reveal a felony to the authorities is now authoritatively determined to be misprision of felony, which is a commonwealth misdemeanour; misprision of treason is punishable with imprisonment for life.... No offence is committed in failing to disclose a misdemeanour....

With respect to misdemeanors, we conclude that positive knowledge of the supplier that his products or services are being used for criminal purposes does not, without more, establish an intent of the supplier to participate in the misdemeanors. With respect to felonies, we do not decide the converse, viz., that in all cases of felony knowledge of criminal use alone may justify an inference of the supplier's intent to participate in the crime. The implications of *Falcone* make the matter uncertain with respect to those felonies which are merely prohibited wrongs.... But decision on this point is not compelled, and we leave the matter open.

From this analysis of precedent we deduce the following rule: the intent of a supplier who knows of the criminal use to which his supplies are put to participate in the criminal activity connected with the use of his supplies may be established by (1) direct evidence that he intends to participate, or (2) through an inference that he intends to participate based on, (a) his special interest in the activity, or (b) the aggravated nature of the crime itself.

When we review Lauria's activities in the light of this analysis, we find no proof that Lauria took any direct action to further, encourage, or direct the call-girl activities of his codefendants and we find an absence of circumstance from which his special interest in their activities could be inferred. Neither excessive charges for standardized services, nor the furnishing of services without a legitimate use, nor an unusual quantity of business with call girls, are present. The offense which he is charged with furthering is a misdemeanor, a category of crime which has never been made a required subject of positive disclosure to public authority. Under these circumstances, although proof of Lauria's knowledge of the criminal activities of his patrons was sufficient to charge him with that fact, there was insufficient evidence that he intended to further their criminal activities, and hence insufficient proof of his participation in a criminal conspiracy with his codefendants to further prostitution. Since the conspiracy centered around the activities of Lauria's telephone answering service, the charges against his codefendants likewise fail for want of proof.

In absolving Lauria of complicity in a criminal conspiracy we do not wish to imply that the public authorities are without remedies to combat modern manifestations of the world's oldest profession. Licensing of telephone answering services under the police power, together with the revocation of licenses for the toleration of prostitution, is a possible civil remedy. The furnishing of telephone answering service in aid of prostitution could be made a crime. Other solutions will doubtless occur to vigilant public authorities if the problem of call-girl activity needs further suppression.

The order is affirmed.

## State v. Gunnison

Supreme Court of Arizona, 1980
127 Ariz. 110

CAMERON, Justice.

On 21 September 1978, defendant Robert Harlan Gunnison, Jr., was found guilty of five counts involving violations of Chapter 12 (sales of securities), Title 44 of the Arizona Revised Statutes.... We granted review ... to answer only one question: Must the State show scienter to prove a criminal conspiracy to sell securities [in violation of Arizona law]?

In 1975, Gunnison was the president of Arizona Realty and Mortgage Trust, a corporation which managed several other corporations, most of which were involved in the development and/or sale of subdivision lots within the State of Arizona and most of which suffered substantial cash flow problems resulting in an inability to construct projected improvements in their subdivisions. Gunnison thus acted as an informal "receiver" for these ailing businesses.

One of the land companies in his control was Consolidated Mortgage Corporation, which had previously been run by Nathan "Ned" Warren. One method by which Consolidated raised money was through liquidation of assets, including wholesale disposal of lots and sales of mortgages they held as mortgagees. Most, if not all, of the mortgages liquidated by Gunnison went to Equitable Mortgage Company, which, in turn, sold the mortgages to the public. Equitable's president was Thomas O'Brien, a friend of both Gunnison and Warren.

Gunnison, O'Brien, Warren and several other participants in the dealings of Equitable and Arizona Realty were indicted by a Pima County Grand Jury for numerous alleged violations of state securities laws and for conspiracy to commit such violations. The defendant was named in 148 counts of the 173 count indictment. The cases of all indicted, with the exception of O'Brien and Gunnison, were disposed of through plea negotiations. On 14 December 1977, O'Brien was convicted, after trial to a jury, of 30 counts. In September of 1978, Gunnison was tried on the five counts.

The defendant waived his right to a jury. The parties stipulated that Gunnison's bench trial would include the testimony given in the O'Brien trial, which had been heard by the same judge, and that the trial court would be governed by the legal principles set forth in the jury instructions given in the O'Brien trial. Gunnison was convicted of all five counts and sentenced to five concurrent prison terms of one to three years. From this judgment and sentence he appeals.

There was extensive argument in the trial court concerning the scienter which the State must prove in order to convict the defendant. Gunnison attempted to show that he did not have the specific intent to commit the crime; that he acted in good faith because he relied on statements made by an attorney and an official of the Corporation Commission that the contemplated sales were "all right."

The trial court, in excluding evidence of good faith in the O'Brien trial, stated:

> "evidence or any comment upon the issue of whether * * * O'Brien knew that his conduct was unlawful * * * is neither relevant or material."

In Gunnison's trial the court restated its position that scienter was not an element of the crime of conspiracy, and that to convict the defendant the State need not prove intentional wrongdoing or "evil motive." ...

The criminal statute under which defendant was prosecuted in Count 1 read in part as follows:

> "A person is guilty of conspiracy in the second degree if, with the intent to commit or to have another person commit, any action constituting any felony other than those listed in subsection A, he conspires with one or more persons to engage in or cause the commission of such." A.R.S. § 13-331(B).

... The crime of conspiracy has been widely regarded as involving a consciously criminal agreement and is for that reason blameworthy and punishable in itself: "conspiracy imports a corrupt agreement between not less than two with guilty knowledge on the part of each." ...

This criminality of intent, together with the increased danger believed to result from group effort, justify the arrest and punishment of conspirators when their crimes are merely inchoate; and without regard to whether a planned offense is ever completed:

> "... For two or more to confederate and combine together to commit or cause to be committed a breach of the criminal laws is an offense of the gravest character, sometimes quite outweighing, in injury to the public, the mere commission of the contemplated crime. It involves deliberate plotting to subvert the laws, educating and preparing the conspirators for further and habitual criminal practices. And it is characterized by secrecy, rendering it difficult of detection, requiring more time for its discovery, and adding to the importance of punishing it when discovered." United States v. Rabinowich.

Conspiracy is a crime that requires a mens rea, or specific intent, even if the crime the conspirators are agreeing to commit does not in itself require such intent.

We agree with the California court that:

> "... even though a conspiracy has as its object the commission of an offense which can be committed without any specific intent, there is no criminal conspiracy absent a specific intent to violate the law. That is, to uphold a conviction for conspiracy to commit a 'public welfare offense' there must be a showing that the accused knew of the law and intended to violate it." People v. Marsh.

Because the trial court in the present case specifically ruled that no intent to violate a known law need be shown for the State to prove a conspiracy charge, and because evidence of good faith was rejected, Gunnison's conspiracy conviction must fall.

## *Notes and Questions*

1. Both of the cases excerpted in this section highlight the generally accepted principle that conspiracy liability only attaches if the defendant has the purpose (i.e., intend) to help his fellow co-conspirators commit the agreed-upon crime. Therefore—as *Lau-*

*ria* illustrates—knowledge of the criminal plans of another not does not typically satisfy the *mens rea* requirements of conspiracy liability. Furthermore, liability for conspiracy demands proof of an intent to consummated the agreed upon offense, even if the underlying crime lacks a *mens rea* requirement. Thus, the court held in *Gunnison* that in order to convict the defendant of conspiracy to sell securities in violation of state law, the prosecution must prove that the defendant intended to violate the laws governing the sale of securities, *even if such laws imposed punishment without proof of criminal intent.*

2. Note that the court in *Lauria* suggested that knowledge alone may be enough to satisfy the *mens rea* of conspiracy when the agreed upon crime is particularly serious. More specifically, the court pointed out that "the operator of a telephone answering service with positive knowledge that his service was being used to facilitate the extortion of ransom ... might be chargeable on knowledge alone with participation in a scheme to extort money." Do you agree that knowledge alone should be enough to trigger conspiracy liability in this case? What if the owner of a guest house knows that a guest will be using his room to sexually molest and torture small children? Would it be appropriate to hold the guest house owner liable as a conspirator to the child molestation on the basis of his knowledge? Why or why not?

3. Note the parallels between the *mens rea* requirements for accomplice and conspiracy liability. Knowing assistance of a crime does not typically give rise to accomplice liability. As a result, the standard mental state required for accomplice liability is purpose (i.e., intent). Nevertheless, courts and commentators often debate whether knowing assistance should on occasion trigger some degree of criminal liability, especially when the offense that is assisted is particularly grave. This has led a handful of jurisdictions to enact "criminal facilitation" statutes that punish knowing assistance of a crime as a free standing offense that is punished less than purposeful complicity. See Chapter 10, § 10.03. Perhaps a similar approach should be taken in the context of conspiracy. The result would be that the operator of the phone answering service that knows that his service is being used to facilitate extortion of a ransom could be held liable for a lesser offense of conspiracy analogous to "criminal facilitation." Is this approach preferable to punishing the owner of the phone answering service as a full blown conspirator to the extortion? Is it preferable to acquitting the owner of the phone answering service because he lacked the purpose to assist the person asking for the ransom? Explain.

## § 12.04 Conspiracy: Accessorial Liability

### Pinkerton v. United States

Supreme Court of the United States, 1946
328 U.S. 640

Mr. Justice DOUGLAS delivered the opinion of the Court.

Walter and Daniel Pinkerton are brothers who live a short distance from each other on Daniel's farm. They were indicted for violations of the Internal Revenue Code. The indictment contained ten substantive counts and one conspiracy count. The jury found Walter guilty on nine of the substantive counts and on the conspiracy count. It found Daniel guilty on six of the substantive counts and on the conspiracy count.... The judgments of conviction were affirmed by the Circuit Court of Appeals. The case is here on a petition for a writ of certiorari which we granted, because one of the questions presented involved a conflict between the decision below and United States v. Sall, decided by the Circuit Court of Appeals for the Third Circuit ...

It is contended that there was insufficient evidence to implicate Daniel in the conspiracy. But we think there was enough evidence for submission of the issue to the jury.

There is, however, no evidence to show that Daniel participated directly in the commission of the substantive offenses on which his conviction has been sustained, although there was evidence to show that these substantive offenses were in fact committed by Walter in furtherance of the unlawful agreement or conspiracy existing between the brothers. The question was submitted to the jury on the theory that each petitioner could be found guilty of the substantive offenses, if it was found at the time those offenses were committed petitioners were parties to an unlawful conspiracy and the substantive offenses charged were in fact committed in furtherance of it.

Daniel relies on United States v. Sall. That case held that participation in the conspiracy was not itself enough to sustain a conviction for the substantive offense even though it was committed in furtherance of the conspiracy. The court held that, in addition to evidence that the offense was in fact committed in furtherance of the conspiracy, evidence of direct participation in the commission of the substantive offense or other evidence from which participation might fairly be inferred was necessary.

We take a different view. We have here a continuous conspiracy. There is here no evidence of the affirmative action on the part of Daniel which is necessary to establish his withdrawal from it. As stated in that case, 'having joined in an unlawful scheme, having constituted agents for its performance, scheme and agency to be continuous until full fruition be secured, until he does some act to disavow or defeat the purpose he is in no situation to claim the delay of the law. As the offense has not been terminated or accomplished, he is still offending. And we think, consciously offending—offending as certainly, as we have said, as at the first moment of his confederation, and consciously through every moment of its existence.' And so long as the partnership in crime continues, the partners act for each other in carrying it forward. It is settled that 'an overt act of one partner may be the act of all without any new agreement specifically directed to that act.' Motive or intent may be proved by the acts or declarations of some of the conspirators in furtherance of the common objective. A scheme to use the mails to defraud, which is joined in by more than one person, is a conspiracy. Yet all members are responsible, though only one did the mailing. The governing principle is the same when the substantive offense is committed by one of the conspirators in furtherance of the unlawful project. The criminal intent to do the act is established by the formation of the conspiracy. Each conspirator instigated the commission of the crime. The unlawful agreement contemplated precisely what was done. It was formed for the purpose. The act done was in execution of the enterprise. The rule which holds responsible one who counsels, procures, or commands another to commit a crime is founded on the same principle. That principle is recognized in the law of conspiracy when the overt act of one partner in crime is attributable to all. An overt act is an essential ingredient of the crime of conspiracy under § 37 of the Criminal Code. If that can be supplied by the act of one conspirator, we fail to see why the same or other acts in furtherance of the conspiracy are likewise not attributable to the others for the purpose of holding them responsible for the substantive offense.

A different case would arise if the substantive offense committed by one of the conspirators was not in fact done in furtherance of the conspiracy, did not fall within the scope of the unlawful project, or was merely a part of the ramifications of the plan which could not be reasonably foreseen as a necessary or natural consequence of the unlawful agreement. But as we read this record, that is not this case.

Affirmed.

## People v. McGee

Court of Appeals of New York, 1979
49 N.Y.2d 48

COOKE, Chief Judge.

Two trials are considered here. Out of one evolve appeals by defendants McGee, Edwards and Tolliver, who were convicted, after a jury trial, of one count of conspiracy in the third degree and 28 counts of bribery in the second degree. From the other, arise appeals by defendants Quamina and Waters, who were convicted, upon a jury verdict, of one count of conspiracy in the third degree and 10 counts of bribery in the second degree. The judgments of conviction were affirmed by five separate orders of the Appellate Division and leave to appeal to this court was granted. For the reasons that follow, the order affirming the judgment of conviction of McGee should be modified to the extent of reversing the conviction on the bribery counts and dismissing the indictment as to those counts, and as so modified, affirmed. The remaining orders affirming the convictions of Quamina, Waters, Edwards and Tolliver should be affirmed.

At the joint trial of Quamina and Waters, the People's theory was that the defendants proposed an arrangement whereby Rochester Police Officers Gerald Luciano and Gustave J. D'Aprile, members of the Vice Squad, would be paid to prevent the arrest of defendants' gambling associates while enforcing the law against competitors. The evidence at trial consisted of the testimony of Luciano, D'Aprile, defendants and others, as well as tape recordings of conversations between the officers and defendants....

II

Defendants McGee, Edwards and Tolliver were later brought into the operation. In October, 1974, Quamina arranged an organizational meeting at which he, Edwards, Tolliver and the officers were present. Edwards, proclaiming himself spokesman for those present as well as McGee, articulated the group's desire to start a black organization, and suggested that the officers could make money if they wanted to be "outlaws". At a subsequent meeting with Edwards, the officers were told that they would receive a percentage of the receipts from assigned numbers writers in exchange for police protection. On November 13, there was a meeting with Edwards and McGee at which the group discussed the scope of police activity, as well as weekly payments to the police. No payments were made at that meeting. During the meeting, McGee indicated that he was in accord with Edwards' goals. At various intervals during the ensuing months, Edwards made payments to the officers....

III

Defendants assert numerous errors in the conduct of the trials, many of which are common to some or all of the defendants. A substantial argument is advanced by McGee alone, however, and that issue is treated first.

McGee argues that the Trial Judge erred in charging the jury that he could be found guilty of the substantive offense of bribery by virtue of his status as a conspirator. After determining that there was sufficient evidence of an agreement among the defendants to go to the jury on the conspiracy count, the court charged that each conspirator could be convicted of bribery on the basis of acts of any one of the coconspirators committed in furtherance of the conspiracy (see Pinkerton v. United States). The court also charged that McGee alone could be convicted of the bribery if he solicited, requested, commanded, importuned or intentionally aided another to engage in that offense (see Penal Law, § 20.00). McGee is correct in his contention that the portion of the charge concerning conspirator liability was erroneous. It is held that liability for the substantive offense may not be independently predicated upon defendant's participation in an underlying conspiracy. As there was no evidence of McGee's complicity in the bribery counts submitted to the jury, and thus no basis for accomplice liability, there must be a reversal of the conviction of bribery and a dismissal of the indictment as to those counts.

In rejecting the notion that one's status as a conspirator standing alone is sufficient to support a conviction for a substantive offense committed by a coconspirator, it is noted that the Legislature has defined the conduct that will render a person criminally responsible for the act of another. Conspicuously absent from section 20.00 of the Penal Law is reference to one who conspires to commit an offense. That omission cannot be supplied by construction. Conduct that will support a conviction for conspiracy will not perforce give rise to accessorial liability. True, a conspirator's conduct in many instances will suffice to establish liability as an accomplice, but the concepts are, in reality, analytically distinct. To permit mere guilt of conspiracy to establish the defendant's guilt of the substantive crime without any evidence of further action on the part of the defendant, would be to expand the basis of accomplice liability beyond the legislative design.

The crime of conspiracy is an offense separate from the crime that is the object of the conspiracy. Once an illicit agreement is shown, the overt act of any conspirator may be attributed to other conspirators to establish the offense of conspiracy and that act may be the object crime. But the overt act itself is not the crime in a conspiracy prosecution; it is merely an element of the crime that has as its basis the agreement. It is not offensive to permit a conviction of conspiracy to stand on the overt act committed by another, for the act merely provides corroboration of the existence of the agreement and indicates that the agreement has reached a point where it poses a sufficient threat to society to impose sanctions. But it is repugnant to our system of jurisprudence, where guilt is generally personal to the defendant, to impose punishment, not for the socially harmful agreement to which the defendant is a party, but for substantive offenses in which he did not participate.

We refuse to sanction such a result and thus decline to follow the rule adopted for Federal prosecutions in Pinkerton v. United States. Accessorial conduct may not be equated with mere membership in a conspiracy and the State may not rely solely on the latter to prove guilt of the substantive offense....

## *Notes and Questions*

1. The *Pinkerton* case is noteworthy because it held that not only are the overt acts of any conspirator attributable to all other co-conspirators, but also that all conspirators are liable for any *substantive* crimes committed by fellow co-conspirators. As such, the *Pinkerton* rule invokes conspiracy as a basis for imposing *accessorial* (i.e., accomplice) liability.

2. Note that the *Pinkerton* rule does not limit the imposition of accomplice liability to substantive crimes committed by co-conspirators that formed part of the original conspiratorial agreement. The rule is much broader, for it imposes accomplice liability on conspirators for any and all substantive crimes that could have been reasonably foreseen as a necessary or natural consequence of the unlawful agreement.

3. The consequence of the *Pinkerton* rule is thus to water down the traditional *mens rea* requirements for accomplice liability in cases in which liability is based on a conspiratorial agreement. The conventionally accepted rule is that an actor must purposely aid the perpetrator in order to be held liable for complicity. Nevertheless, under *Pinkerton* a conspirator may be held liable for substantive offenses that she did not intend to help carry out, as long as such offenses are reasonably foreseeable in light of the conspiratorial agreement. The *Pinkerton* doctrine is similar to the *Luparello* rule for accomplice liability. According to *Luparello,* an accomplice is liable is "not only ... of the particular crime that to his knowledge his confederates are contemplating committing, but he is also liable for the natural and reasonable or probable consequences of any act that he knowingly aided or encouraged." See Chapter 10, § 10.03, Note 6.

4. Like *Luparello,* the *Pinkerton* doctrine has been criticized by many courts and commentators. As *McGee* demonstrates, a considerable number of state courts have refused to follow *Pinkerton.* Instead, these courts hold that an accomplice is liable only if he satisfies the traditional *mens rea* requirements for accomplice liability. That is, liability is triggered only if the accomplice purposely encouraged the perpetrator's conduct. Do you prefer the *Pinkerton* rule or the *McGee* approach to accessorial liability and conspiracy? Explain.

## § 12.05 Conspiracy: Model Penal Code

### Minnesota v. St. Christopher

Supreme Court of Minnesota, 1975
305 Minn. 226

ROGOSHESKE, Justice.

Defendant was found guilty by the court, sitting without a jury, of conspiracy to commit murder and attempted first-degree murder, and sentenced under the conspiracy conviction to a maximum indeterminate term of 20 years' imprisonment. He contends upon this appeal from the judgment ... that he was improperly convicted of conspiracy because the evidence shows that the only party with whom he conspired never intended to aid defendant but merely feigned agreement while cooperating with police.... We affirm the conviction of conspiracy ...

The facts in this case are relatively simple. On March 16, 1974, defendant (who formerly was named Marlin Peter Olson but legally changed his name to Daniel St. Christopher) stated to his cousin, Roger Zobel, that he wanted to kill his mother, Mrs. Marlin Olson, and that he wanted Zobel's help. He would pay him $125,000 over the years, money defendant would get from his father after his mother was dead. Zobel, the key witness against defendant at his trial on the charge of conspiracy, testified that at no time did he ever intend to participate in the murder but that he discussed the matter with defendant on that and subsequent occasions and acted as if he intended to participate in the plan. On March 18, Zobel contacted the police and told them of defendant's plan and they later told him to continue to cooperate with defendant. The plan, which became definite in some detail as early as March 20, was for Zobel to go to the Olson farmhouse on Saturday, March 23, when defendant's father was at the weekly livestock auction. Since defendant's mother was Zobel's aunt, Zobel could gain entrance readily. The idea was for Zobel to break her neck, hide her body in his automobile trunk, and then attack bricks to it and throw it in a nearby river after dark. Later it developed that defendant's father might not go to the sale on Saturday, so a plan was developed whereby defendant would feign car trouble, call his father for help, then signal Zobel when the father was on his way. Police followed defendant on Saturday when he left his apartment and observed him make a number of telephone calls. In one of these he called his father and told him he was having car trouble and asked him to come and help him pay the bill. In a call to Zobel, which was taped, defendant told Zobel that his father was coming and that Zobel should proceed with the plan. Shortly thereafter, police arrested defendant.

During the trial defense counsel, in a motion to dismiss, made it clear to the trial court that he felt defendant could not be convicted of conspiracy. He argued that since Zobel never intended to participate in a murder, he did not really conspire with defendant.... [Nevertheless,] the trial court found defendant guilty of both conspiracy and attempted murder, sentencing defendant for the conspiracy offense to an indeterminate term of 20 years' imprisonment.

We have not found any Minnesota cases in point on the issue of the validity of the conspiracy conviction. However, in two criminal conspiracy cases this court has stated, or at least implied, that a person cannot be guilty of conspiracy where the only person with whom he has conspired or agreed has feigned agreement. The first of these cases is State v. Burns, where this court stated that '(t)o constitute a conspiracy to cheat and defraud, there must be not only a combination, but a common object to cheat and defraud, which each member of the combination intends shall be accomplished by the concerted action of all.'

The more recent Minnesota case is State v. Willman. In that case, there was a true meeting of the minds by both defendant and one Toles followed by an overt act in furtherance of the conspiracy to commit murder in the first degree. Subsequently, Toles changed his mind and contacted the police. In holding that there was sufficient evidence that defendant was guilty of conspiracy, this court arguably implied (but did not hold or even say) that this might not be the case if there had not been a true meeting of the minds or if an overt act had not occurred until after Toles contacted the police.

There is extensive authority from other jurisdictions which supports defendant's contention. The reasoning employed in these cases was summarized in Fridman, Mens Rea in Conspiracy, 19 Modern L.Rev. 276, as follows:

> '... Conspiracy is the agreement of two or more to effect an unlawful purpose. Two people cannot agree unless they both intend to carry out the purpose which is stated to be the object of their combination. Therefore there is no agreement, and consequently no conspiracy, where one of the two never intends to carry out the unlawful purpose.'

... If there had been some evidence to suggest that, contrary to his testimony, Zobel in fact had intended to participate in the conspiracy and had not feigned agreement from the start, then the court as factfinder could have found defendant guilty of conspiracy without rejecting the rule followed in the cited cases. However, the only evidence that the state produced was that Zobel did not intend at any time to participate in the conspiracy and that his agreement was feigned, and the trial court believed his evidence. Therefore, if we accept the rule followed in these cases, we would have to reverse defendant's conviction.

We are persuaded not to accept this rule and base our decision on (a) our belief that the rule is unsound, and (b) our belief that the present conspiracy statute ... authorizes a conviction in this situation.

(a) One criticism by a number of commentators of the rule followed in the cited cases is that the courts have reached their conclusion by using as a starting point the definition of conspiracy as an agreement between two or more persons, a definition which was framed in cases not involving the issue. As one commentator put it, 'if a conspiracy is arbitrarily defined as 'an agreement of intentions and not merely of language (the intentions being unlawful)' the answer to the problem is undoubtedly that where there is no such agreement of intentions then there is no conspiracy.' Fridman, Mens Rea in Conspiracy, 19 Modern L.Rev. 276, 278. In other words, the basis for the rule is a strict doctrinal approach toward the conception of conspiracy as an agreement in which two or more parties not only objectively indicate their agreement but actually have a meeting of the minds.

Addressing the rule to be applied as a policy issue, a number of commentators have come to the conclusion that there should be no requirement of a meeting of the minds. Thus, Fridman points to cases holding that factual impossibility is no defense to a charge of attempt to commit a crime and argues that, because of close connections between the origins and purposes of the law of conspiracy and of attempt, a similar rule should obtain in conspiracy. Specifically, he argues that '(t)he fact that, unknown to a man who wishes to enter a conspiracy to commit some criminal purpose, the other person has no intention of fulfilling that purpose ought to be irrelevant as long as the first man does intend to fulfill it if he can' because 'a man who believes he is conspiring to commit a crime and wishes to conspire to commit a crime has a guilty mind and has done all in his power to plot the commission of an unlawful purpose.'

Professor Glanville Williams makes a somewhat similar argument, basing his opinion on the fact that conspiracy, like attempt, is an inchoate crime and that it is the act of conspiring by a defendant which is the decisive element of criminality, for it makes no difference in logic or public policy that the person with whom the defendant conspires is not himself subject to prosecution. Williams, Criminal Law—The General Part, § 157(a).

The draftsmen of the Model Penal Code take a slightly different approach. They recognize that conspiracy is not just an inchoate crime complementing the law of attempt and solicitation but that it is also a means of striking at the special dangers incident to group activity. A.L.I., Model Penal Code (Tent. Draft No. 10, 1960) § 5.03, Comment. In view of that recognition, it is probably not quite as easy to reject the approach taken by the cases cited, yet this is what the draftsmen have done. The provision which accomplishes this, § 5.03(1), reads as follows:

> 'A person is guilty of conspiracy with another person or persons to commit a crime if with the purpose of promoting or facilitating its commission he:
>
> '(a) agrees with such other person or persons that they or one or more of them will engage in conduct which constitutes such crime or an attempt or solicitation to commit such crime; or
>
> '(b) agrees to aid such other person or persons in the planning or commission of such crime or of an attempt or solicitation to commit such crime.' 10 U.L.A., Model Penal Code, § 5.03(1).

In comments explaining this provision, the reporters state as follows:

> '2. The Conspiratorial Relationship.
>
> 'Unilateral Approach of the Draft. The definition of the Draft departs from the traditional view of conspiracy as an entirely bilateral or multilateral relationship, the view inherent in the standard formulation cast in terms of 'two or more persons' agreeing or combining to commit a crime. Attention is directed instead to each individual's culpability by framing the definition in terms of the conduct which suffices to establish the liability of any given actor, rather than the conduct of a

group of which he is charged to be a part—an approach which in this comment we have designated 'unilateral.'

'One consequence of this approach is to make it immaterial to the guilt of a conspirator whose culpability has been established that the person or all of the persons with whom he conspired have not been or cannot be convicted. Present law frequently holds otherwise, reasoning from the definition of conspiracy as an agreement between two or more persons that there must be at least two guilty conspirators or none. The problem arises in a number of contexts.

'Second: Where the person with whom the defendant conspired secretly intends not to go through with the plan. In these cases it is generally held that neither party can be convicted because there was no 'agreement' between two persons. Under the unilateral approach of the Draft, the culpable party's guilt would not be affected by the fact that the other party's agreement was feigned. He has conspired, within the meaning of the definition, in the belief that the other party was with him; apart from the issue of entrapment often presented in such cases, his culpability is not decreased by the other's secret intention. True enough, the project's chances of success have not been increased by the agreement; indeed, its doom may have been sealed by this turn of events. But the major basis of conspiratorial liability—the unequivocal evidence of a firm purpose to commit a crime—remains the same. The result would be the same under the Draft if the only co-conspirator established a defense of renunciation under Section 5.03(6). While both the Advisory Committee and the Council support the Draft upon this point, it should be noted that the Council vote was 14–11, the dissenting members deeming mutual agreement on the part of two or more essential to the concept of conspiracy.'

(b) We find the scholarly literature persuasive on this subject. The question is whether this court can take the recommended approach. We think the answer lies in the wording of our statute. The Minnesota statute formerly dealing with the crime of conspiracy read as follows

'When two or more persons shall conspire:

(1) To commit a crime;

'Every such person shall be guilty of a misdemeanor.'

This is the most common type of conspiracy statute, and it is understandable that this type of statute lends itself easily to the result reached by the cases because the statute starts with the phrase, 'When two or more persons shall conspire.'

However, the Minnesota statute as it presently reads omits this phrase and is now phrased in unilateral terms similar to those used in the Model Penal Code. The provision reads in part:

'Whoever conspires with another to commit a crime and in furtherance of the conspiracy one or more of the parties does some overt act in furtherance of such conspiracy may be sentenced as follows:'

Because of this wording, we hold that the trial court was free to convict defendant of conspiracy under the facts of this case.

## *Notes and Questions*

1. The Model Penal Code's rejection of the "bilateral" approach to conspiracy stems from the Code drafters' belief that a person who tries to enlist someone else to help him carry

out an offense manifests a "firm purpose to commit a crime" regardless of whether the other party feigns agreement. Such a person is dangerous and in need of correction. This, in turn, provides consequentialist reasons to punish such offenders (i.e., specific deterrence, incapacitation, rehabilitation). Furthermore, such an actor behaves culpably, for culpability depends on the actor's beliefs, not on whether the actor's beliefs are correct. Such culpability provides retributive reasons for punishing actors even when one of the parties feigns agreement. Do you believe that these arguments provide sufficient reasons for imposing complicity liability when one of the parties is feigning agreement? Why or why not?

2. The drafters of the Model Penal Code also rejected the *Pinkerton* view that imposes liability on conspirators for reasonably foreseeable crimes committed by fellow co-conspirators in furtherance of the unlawful agreement. According to the Code drafters, "law would lose all sense of just proportion" if—solely because of his status as a conspirator—a defendant was "held accountable for thousands of additional offenses of which he was completely unaware and which he did not influence at all." Consequently, the Code holds conspirators are as accomplices to the substantive crimes committed by co-conspirators only if they satisfy the subjective and objective elements of the Code's complicity provisions. That is, conspirators will be held liable as accomplices only if they purposely encouraged the perpetrator's conduct.

## § 12.06 Conspiracy: Comparative Perspectives

### Sergio Politoff, *La Conspiración Para Cometer Delitos Previstos en la Ley Sobre Tráfico de Estupefacientes*

Revista Chilena de Derecho, Vol. 24 Num. 3, pp.447–458 (1997)

It is well-known that criminalizing conspiracy is the exception in [Chile's] legal system, and that conspiracy is therefore punishable only when conspiring to commit a certain crime is specifically prohibited by the Penal Code. The approach followed in the Chilean Penal Code—as well as in the Spanish Penal Code of 1848 upon which our Code is based—is to criminalize conspiracy only when the conspirators agree to commit a crime against national security... Therefore—as other scholars have pointed out—conspiracy to commit common crimes is not punishable [in our jurisdiction]. This can be explained by the liberal philosophy that inspired the drafters of the French Penal Code of 1810, which limited the criminalization of complicity to cases in which the agreement was to harm the king or a member of his family.

### Spanish Penal Code—Article 17

1. A conspiracy exists when two or more persons agree to commit a crime....

3. A conspiracy to commit a crime is punishable only when it is expressly prohibited by law.

### *Notes and Questions*

1. As Professor Politoff explains, conspiracy is typically not punishable in civil law jurisdictions. Nevertheless, there are exceptional instances in which conspiring to commit

an offense is criminalized. The paradigmatic cases involve conspiring to commit crimes that threaten national security. These offenses generally include treason, terrorism related offenses and crimes against certain governmental officials. Why do you think civil law jurisdictions shy away from creating a stand-alone offense of conspiracy that criminalizes agreements to commit any criminal offense?

2. The excerpted provision of the Spanish Penal Code is illustrative of how conspiracy is criminalized in European Continental countries. Instead of creating a freestanding offense that punishes all agreements to commit crimes, the Spanish Penal Code criminalizes conspiracy only when a law expressly prohibits the agreement to commit a certain offense. The Spanish Penal Code currently prohibits conspiring to commit the following crimes: kidnapping, human trafficking, robbery, extortion, money laundering, drug trafficking, rebellion, violent crimes against public officers, terrorism related offenses, and treason. Do you prefer Spain's more targeted approach that criminalizes only agreements to commit a relatively small number of serious crimes or America's broad approach that criminalizes agreements to commit any offense regardless of its seriousness? Why?

## § 12.07 Conspiracy: Scholarly Debates

### Phillip E. Johnson, *The Unnecessary Crime of Conspiracy*

61 Cal. L. Rev. 1137 (1973)

The literature on the subject of criminal conspiracy reflects a sort of rough consensus. Conspiracy, it is generally said, is a necessary doctrine in some respects, but also one that is overbroad and invites abuse. Conspiracy has been thought to be necessary for one or both of two reasons. First, it is said that a separate offense of conspiracy is useful to supplement the generally restrictive law of attempts. Plotters who are arrested before they can carry out their dangerous schemes may be convicted of conspiracy even though they did not go far enough towards completion of their criminal plan to be guilty of attempt. Second, conspiracy is said to be a vital legal weapon in the prosecution of "organized crime," however defined. As Mr. Justice Jackson put it, "the basic conspiracy principle has some place in modem criminal law, because to unite, back of a criminal purpose, the strength, opportunities and resources of many is obviously more dangerous and more difficult to police than the efforts of a lone wrongdoer." To deal with such dangerous criminal combinations the government must have the benefit of special legal doctrines which make conviction easier and punishment more severe.

The overbreadth of conspiracy and its potential for abuse have been extensively discussed in the literature. One principal theme of criticism, best illustrated by Mr. Justice Jackson's opinion in *Krulewitch v. United States*, emphasizes the difficulties which the ordinary criminal defendant may face when charged with conspiracy. The advantages which conspiracy provides the prosecution are seen as disadvantages for the defendant so serious that they may lead to unfair punishment unfairly determined. Critics taking this approach typically propose to trim conspiracy doctrine just enough to provide protection for defense interests without disturbing those rules deemed genuinely important for effective law enforcement. The leading reform proposal of this type is the conspiracy section of the American Law Institute's Model Penal Code, some of whose reforms were incorporated in the proposed Federal Criminal Code now before the Senate Subcommittee on Criminal Laws and Procedures of the United States.

Unfortunately, the proposals for legislative or constitutional reforms of conspiracy law are inadequate. It will not do simply to reform conspiracy legislatively by removing its most widely deplored overextensions, or to reform it judicially by engrafting new doctrines derived from the first amendment. Such measures are appropriate for improving a doctrine that is basically sound, but in need of some adjustment at the edges. The law of criminal conspiracy is not basically sound. It should be abolished, not reformed.

The central fault of conspiracy law and the reason why any limited reform is bound to be inadequate can be briefly stated. What conspiracy adds to the law is simply confusion, and the confusion is inherent in the nature of the doctrine. The confusion stems from the fact that conspiracy is not only a substantive inchoate crime in itself, but the touchstone for invoking several independent procedural and substantive doctrines.

We ask whether a defendant agreed with another person to commit a crime initially for the purpose of determining whether he may be convicted of the offense of conspiracy even when the crime itself has not yet been committed. If the answer to that question is in the affirmative, however, we find that we have also answered a number of other questions that would otherwise have to be considered independently. Where there is evidence of conspiracy, the defendant may be tried jointly with his criminal partners and possibly with many other persons whom he has never met or seen, the joint trial may be held in a place he may never have visited, and hearsay statements of other alleged members of the conspiracy may be used to prove his guilt. Furthermore, a defendant who is found guilty of conspiracy is subject to enhanced punishment and may also be found guilty of any crime committed in furtherance of the conspiracy, whether or not he knew about the crime or aided in its commission.

Each of these issues involves a separate substantive or procedural area of the criminal law of considerable importance and complexity. The essential vice of conspiracy is that it inevitably distracts the courts from the policy questions or balancing of interests that ought to govern the decision of specific legal issues and leads them instead to decide those issues by reference to the conceptual framework of conspiracy. Instead of asking whether public policy or the interests of the parties requires a particular holding, the courts are led instead to consider whether the theory of conspiracy is broad enough to permit it. What is wrong with conspiracy, in other words, is much more basic than the overbreadth of a few rules. The problem is not with particular results, but with the use of a single abstract concept to decide numerous questions that deserve separate consideration in light of the various interests and policies they involve.

Although it is true that the confusion that conspiracy introduces into the law has an overall tendency to benefit the prosecution, sometimes it has the opposite effect. Occasionally, use of a conspiracy charge converts a relatively simple case into a monstrosity of conceptual complexity, giving the defense substantial grounds for an appeal. Furthermore, eliminating the substantive crime of conspiracy would not necessarily require the elimination of all the procedural rules that are now associated with it: at most it would require only that the rules be reconsidered on their own merits. In fact, many of these procedural rules are even now applicable in all criminal cases, whether conspiracy is charged or not ...

Conspiracy gives the courts a means of deciding difficult questions without thinking about them. The basic objection to the doctrine is not simply that many of its specific rules are bad, but rather that all of them are ill considered. The first step towards improving a rule of law is to consider the policies it serves. The specific rules of conspiracy, however, are derived more from the logic of an abstract concept than from any realistic assessment of the needs of law enforcement or the legitimate interests of criminal defendants. We need to reconsider the problem of group crime without being distracted by the abstractions that the concept of conspiracy always seems to introduce.

The current revision of the Federal Criminal Code should have resulted in a reassessment of the usefulness of conspiracy as an independent crime, but it has not. The *Working Papers* of the National Commission on Reform of Federal Criminal Laws suggest that the authors of the initial drafts of the proposed Federal Criminal Code wanted to retain conspiracy only as a inchoate offense similar to attempt, but none of the subsequently published drafts of the Code reflect such a limitation. In any case, given the tendency of conspiracy doctrine to expand into new areas of the law, it is doubtful whether any attempt to retain the doctrine in only a limited role can succeed for very long.

Abolition of conspiracy is not an idea whose time has come, because law enforcement interests erroneously regard the doctrine as a vital weapon against organized crime and because critics of conspiracy have attacked it piecemeal rather than in its entirety. This Article is therefore addressed more to the law reformers of the future than to those of the present, and its aim is not so much to settle an argument as to start one.

## Neal Kumar Katyal, *Conspiracy Theory*

112 Yale L. J. 1307 (2003)

* * *

### 1. Extra Punishment for Group Activity

Conspiracy law imposes two additional sanctions on group behavior. First, it takes the punishment a lone offender would receive and authorizes the government to double it when two offenders conspire to commit the same crime. Second, traditionally conspiracy law refused to permit merger, so that when A conspires with B to steal government funds, both are liable for the theft and the offense of conspiracy. The functional case for these doctrines begins by observing that the first method, doubling the total amount of punishment, rarely happens. Doubling is used as a threat to promote information extraction, but cooperating defendants do not receive the full sanction. Total punishment increases (though at a level below doubling), and is justified because of pernicious group dynamics at work in conspiracy ... If government punished crimes equally, whether they were committed by one person or many, no legal incentive to desist from conspiracy would exist. To the contrary, additional co-conspirators would defray the legal risks of getting caught. The formation of such criminal groups, in turn, would threaten society even further because they would be spurred to commit greater crimes. Their behavior in groups would be, on average, more dangerous than their individual activities ...

Nevertheless, how can the exclusion from merger be justified—particularly when criminal attempts merge? Merger is inappropriate because the punishment for an object offense does not capture the harm of carrying out crime as a group. Liability for an attempt, by contrast, may merge with the substantive offense because attempt does not involve the pernicious group. Moreover, by attaching an additional penalty to the completion of a substantive offense, the merger exclusion bolsters marginal deterrence from inchoate to completed criminal conduct....

### 2. Pinkerton

The editors of the Harvard Law Review proclaimed in 1959 that "[n]o court which has taken the Pinkerton approach has offered an adequate rationale for convicting a conspirator for the crimes of his associates." More recently, George Fletcher has claimed that while vicarious liability "might make some sense in the field of torts ... it is patently absurd to think of conspirators controlling each other's acts." Such views have led to the conventional wisdom that Pinkerton liability is some sort of criminal monster.

[One of the benefits of *Pinkerton* is that] the doctrine ... increases ... uncertainty about the sanction [that could be ultimately imposed on conspirators]. Under Pinkerton, a criminal takes her chances when she joins a conspiracy, in that she is liable for all the crimes that are within the scope of the organization. Greater liability will deter some from joining the conspiracy ... Because people are less likely to know the full extent of their liability under Pinkerton, moreover, uncertainty increases and the conditions for trust thus diminish. Psychological experiments have shown that uncertainty leads to less trust; in situations where a bad apple could poison a group, trust is weak. Lawful partnerships operate under similar precepts since each member is liable for what the others do. Such arrangements work well when the members of the firms are homogenous, practice the same trade, have similar educational backgrounds, and are subject to the same ethical rules (such as law firms), but they become unwieldy and inefficient once heterogeneity is introduced. The criminal conspiracy, often composed of relatively heterogeneous members who lack the same reputational mechanisms to secure trust among each other, will face particular problems from joint liability. Put somewhat differently, Pinkerton reverses the well-known advantages of limited liability for corporations.

Furthermore, just as vicarious liability in torts will produce more monitoring, so too will Pinkerton. Here, the major reason why is that the increasing amounts of leverage will result in more instances of cooperation with law enforcement. In the lawful entity context, vicarious liability may force corporations to take wasteful precautions. This is, however, exactly the result we want when the organization is an unlawful one. Monitoring will be driven by the climate of uncertainty about loyalty, so that more monitoring begets less trust, and less trust begets more monitoring. Like a romantic couple where one party suspects the other of infidelity and begins tracking the other's movements, the acts of monitoring themselves may contribute to a cycle of distrust, thereby eliminating many advantages of joint activity....

### 3. Inchoate Liability

Conspiracy, from the time of Lord Coke to the present, has been an inchoate offense. This choice is no doubt disquieting to many. Yet other inchoate doctrines, such as attempt, attach liability at a far later stage in criminal planning, for example, when there is "dangerous proximity to success." And the psychological work on group identity makes the case for why conspiracy law should attach liability at the incipient stage. The argument has to do with complementarity—that the formation of a criminal group, even one that may be far from achieving its success regarding a particular crime, poses dangers to society because it is likely to have engaged in, or will engage in, other crimes. The penalty attaches to confederation for a bad end. Because groups are not only more likely to engage in crime than are individuals, but are also faster at accomplishing them once they set their minds to the task, preventative steps must be commensurate. Conspiracy law does this by attacking the group at the moment it is formed and not waiting until the group comes too close to success in carrying out any particular crime. It focuses not only on the actual harm a group has caused but also on its potential for harm....

Inchoate liability induces members of the group to defect early, for each has already committed a crime at the time of agreement. This gives law enforcement an omnipresent weapon to flip a conspirator, and also a crime with which to prosecute the other members of the group. And, ex ante, the criminal syndicate does not have to worry only about assuring loyalty of all members at the end of a crime but throughout the planning and development as well. Accordingly, the group constantly will need to undertake costly preventative measures in order to minimize the danger from flipped witnesses.

### 4. Impossibility

This year, the U.S. Supreme Court reversed a federal court of appeals and reaffirmed its view that a person can be guilty of conspiracy even when the object of the agreement is impossible. In United States v. Recio, a Nevada police officer stopped two individuals driving a truck and discovered between ten and twelve million dollars in narcotics. One of the individuals cooperated with the government in a sting operation by revealing the criminal plan. The truck was driven to Idaho and the cooperator called a pager number. A caller returned the page and stated that someone would come get the truck. A few hours later, an individual, Mr. Recio, drove up to the truck, got into it, and began driving the truck away. Government agents then arrested Recio. Recio's successful claim before the Ninth Circuit was that he could not be charged with a conspiracy when the drugs had already been seized unless the prosecution could prove that his decision to conspire predated the seizure. Otherwise, Recio stated, the object of the conspiracy, possession of narcotics with intent to distribute, was impossible.

The Recio case is a textbook illustration of the way conspiracy law singles out the agreement as a distinct malady because of the economic and psychological harm of groups. Unlike a substantive offense, as to which factual impossibility may be a defense, the harm of a conspiracy is not confined to the likelihood that the agreement will be successful. Rather, the law of conspiracy aims to punish the criminal agreement out of a recognition that the agreement may produce other, unrelated, harms. Even the impossible agreement may further a malicious group identity, leading the individuals down a path of further criminal activity beyond their initial object. In this respect, impossibility must be contrasted with a mens rea defense: The type of person who believes (wrongly) that an object crime is possible, and intentionally agrees to further it, poses a special danger to society because he breathes life into a joint project dedicated to carrying out a crime—and this project may then grow beyond its original moorings ...

### 5. Withdrawal

Conspiracy law sets a tough standard for withdrawal. A defendant must show "that he has taken affirmative steps ... to disavow or to defeat the objectives of the conspiracy; and ... that he made a reasonable effort to communicate those acts to his co-conspirators or that he disclosed the scheme to law enforcement." The rule is generally justified on the ground that it ensures "that withdrawal did occur and is not simply being invented ex post." But the rule also has a robust ex ante effect.

The "disclosed the scheme to law enforcement" prong of withdrawal aids information extraction because it lowers the sentences of those who provide such information to authorities. As such, the doctrine nicely tracks the trend toward information-based sentencing: Liability attaches not because of what a person did, but because of what a person knew and did not reveal. The "communicate [to] co-conspirators" prong, permitting withdrawal without informing law enforcement, destabilizes conspiracies in two ways. First, because defection from groups is more common when members believe their activities are coming to a close, the withdrawal of one member can prompt defection from the others, thus weakening the group and providing additional opportunities for information extraction. Second, the prong provides an incentive for conspirators to chip away at group identity and to reduce the dangerous effects of group behavior that their presence facilitates. Because conspirators sit in a unique position to influence the behavior of the group, conspiracy law tries to align the incentives of individual members in ways that will reduce the group's criminal behavior. This is done in the shadow of the law—and works even when law enforcement never learns about the operation of the criminal conspiracy.

The effect of withdrawal on sentencing [is also calibrated to produce beneficial outcomes]. Withdrawal ends liability for further substantive offenses, but not the initial liability for the offense of conspiring or other substantive crimes already committed while the person was a member. The withdrawal rule thus bolsters marginal deterrence by imposing a penalty on all conspirators, including withdrawers (thereby deterring some from making an initial agreement), and by providing some benefit for withdrawers, in that they avoid further substantive liability.

## *Notes and Questions*

1. Professor Johnson argues that conspiracy doctrine is so hopelessly confusing that it ought to be abolished. The confusion "stems from the fact that conspiracy is not only a substantive inchoate crime in itself, but the touchstone for invoking several independent procedural and substantive doctrines." This is troubling for Professor Johnson because it makes it difficult to consider the myriad doctrines that are related to complicity on their own merits. As a result, Professor Johnson contends that the different conspiracy doctrines remain under-theorized and ill considered. In sum, he argues that it is inappropriate to use "a single abstract concept to decide numerous questions that deserve separate consideration in light of the various interests and policies they involve." Do you agree with Professor Johnson's criticism of conspiracy law? Why or why not?

2. Professor Katyal takes issue with Professor Johnson's critique of conspiracy law. Rather than abolishing the doctrines related to conspiracy, Professor Katyal suggests that we should embrace conspiracy law as a salutary development. More specifically, he contends that the substantive and procedural rules that conspiracy triggers are an appropriate way of dealing with the special evils inherent in group criminality. According to Katyal, focusing on how the different rules that conspiracy triggers impact group criminality explains many of the features of conspiracy that scholars like Johnson have criticized as unfounded and arbitrary.

3. Thus, for example, Katyal argues that the much criticized *Pinkerton* doctrine may be justified by viewing it as a mechanism for deterring group criminality. Potential conspirators may think twice before joining a conspiracy if they know that they may be held liable not only for the crimes that they personally commit, but also for any reasonably foreseeable crime committed by other conspirators. Similarly, holding that the hearsay statements of fellow conspirators are admissible against all co-conspirators discourages group criminality by making it easier for prosecutors to introduce hearsay statements in cases involving group criminality. This, in turn, places a premium on group criminality when compared to individual criminality. Are you convinced by Professor Katyal's defense of conspiracy and its related doctrines? Why or why not?

4. Professor Katyal explains that the law of conspiracy "sets a tough standard" for withdrawing from the conspiracy. First, a conspirator may withdraw only by taking affirmative steps to defeat the conspiracy or to distance herself from the conspiracy. Second, she must make her efforts known to her fellow co-conspirators or she must notify law enforcement of the conspiratorial scheme. Furthermore, withdrawal only ends liability for

future substantive offenses. Therefore, the conspirator is still liable for the initial conspiracy even if she subsequently withdraws.

5. While the tough withdrawal standards may seem overly harsh to some, Katyal argues that they are appropriate. By not providing a defense to the original conspiracy, the withdrawal rules continue to deter and discourage entering into a conspiratorial agreement in the first place. Nevertheless, by precluding punishment for crimes committed by co-conspirators after the actor disavows herself from the conspiracy, withdrawal encourages conspirators to terminate their participation in the conspiracy as early as possible. Do you agree with Professor Katyal that the withdrawal standards for conspiracy are sound, or do you believe that the standards should be more or less stringent than they currently are? Explain.

# Chapter 13

# Corporate Criminal Liability

## § 13.01 Corporate Criminal Liability: Common Law

### United States v. Basic Construction Co.

United States Court of Appeals, Fourth Circuit, 1983
711 F.2d 570

PER CURIAM:

This is an appeal from a conviction for violation of section 1 of the Sherman Act, 15 U.S.C. § 1. The defendants, Basic Construction Co., Henry S. Branscome, Inc., and Henry Branscome, were charged with conspiring in April of 1978 to rig the bidding for state road paving contracts. A jury found the defendants guilty, and both Basic and Branscome appeal. We affirm.

I.

Basic's principal contention is that the district court gave erroneous jury instructions regarding the criminal liability of a corporation for acts of its employees. With regard to corporate liability, the court instructed the jury as follows:

> A corporation is legally bound by the acts or statements of its agents done or made within the scope of their employment, and within their apparent authority, acts done within the scope of employment and acts done on behalf of or to the benefit of a corporation, and directly related to the performance of the type duties the employee has general authority to perform....
>
> When the act of an agent is within the scope of his employment or within the scope of his apparent authority, the corporation is held legally responsible for it. This is true even though the agent's acts may be unlawful, and contrary to the corporations [sic] actual instructions....
>
> A corporation may be responsible for the action of its agents done or made within the scope of their authority, even though the conduct of the agents may be contrary to the corporation's actual instructions, or contrary to the corporation's stated position.
>
> However, the existence of such instructions and policies, if any be shown, may be considered by you in determining whether the agents, in fact, were acting to benefit the corporation.

At trial, Basic introduced evidence which would have tended to prove that it had a longstanding, well known, and strictly enforced policy against bid rigging. Such evidence tended to show that the bid rigging activities for which it was charged were perpetrated by two relatively minor officials and were done without the knowledge of high level corporate officers. Basic argues that, in light of this evidence, the district court should have instructed the jury that it could consider the evidence of Basic's antitrust compliance policy in deciding whether the company had the requisite intent to violate the Sherman Act.

... Basic argues ... that the government [must] prove that the corporation, presumably as represented by its upper level officers and managers, had an intent separate from that of its lower level employees to violate the antitrust laws. Consequently, Basic asserts that the jury should have been instructed to consider corporate antitrust compliance policies in determining whether Basic had the requisite intent.

We do not [agree].... The instructions given by the district court in the instant case are amply supported by case law.

These cases hold that a corporation may be held criminally responsible for antitrust violations committed by its employees if they were acting within the scope of their authority, or apparent authority, and for the benefit of the corporation, even if, as in *Hilton Hotels* and *American Radiator*, such acts were against corporate policy or express instructions....

In the instant case, the district court properly allowed the jury to consider Basic's alleged antitrust compliance policy in determining whether the employees were acting for the benefit of the corporation. It also properly instructed on the issue of intent in an antitrust prosecution, i.e., that corporate intent is shown by the actions and statements of the officers, directors, and employees who are in positions of authority or have apparent authority to make policy for the corporation.

Accordingly, the convictions are AFFIRMED.

## Vaughan and Sons, Inc. v. State

Court of Criminal Appeals of Texas, 1987
737 S.W.2d 805

ONION, Presiding Judge.

Appellant, Vaughan and Sons, Inc., a Texas corporation, was convicted by a jury of criminally negligent homicide. The information alleged that appellant, acting through two of its agents, caused the death of two individuals in a motor vehicle collision. Punishment was assessed by the trial court at a fine of $5,000.00.

On appeal the appellant contended, inter alia, that the "penal code provisions for prosecution of corporations and other artificial legal entities do not extend to any type of criminal homicide, therefore the trial court erred in failing to grant appellant's motion to set aside the information."

The Court of Appeals agreed and reversed the conviction. The Court of Appeals wrote in part:

> "A superficial reading of the negligent homicide statute construed with the Penal Code definition of 'person' indicates that a corporation could indeed be found guilty of the crime charged. But the actual question before this court is whether a legislative intent plainly appears which includes corporations within the criminal field of negligent homicide by use of the term 'person.'"

After reviewing other statutes, etc., the Court of Appeals concluded:

> "Therefore, without a stronger, clearer indication from the legislature that the policy for holding corporations criminally responsible for homicide has changed, we decline to so hold. We should make haste slowly when it is in the direction of holding either an individual or a corporation criminally liable for a crime, especially one so serious as homicide, when it is committed by someone other than the person charged."

Thus, the Court of Appeals ruled that even though the statutes so state, the Legislature could not have intended to include corporations within the class of culpable parties because corporations are unable to formulate "intent" in their "artificial and soulless" form.

We granted the State's petition for discretionary review to determine the correctness of the holding of the Court of Appeals.

At common law a corporation could not commit a crime. "This position was predicated on the rationale that a corporation had no mind and hence could not entertain the appropriate criminal intent required for all common law crimes. Also, the absence of physical body precluded imprisonment, the primary punishment available at common law. Illegal acts of a corporate agent were not imputed to the corporate entity because they were considered ultra vires and therefore without the authority of the corporation."

The rule that a corporation could not be tried for any criminal offense was once widely accepted, not just in Texas, but throughout the nation. Today, however, the general rule is that a corporation may be held liable for criminal acts performed by its agents acting on its behalf ...

[We begin by discussing the relevant sections of the Texas Penal Code, which provide]:

"(a) *In this Code:*

"(17) 'Individual' means a human being who has been born and is alive.

"(27) *'Person' means an individual, corporation, or association*" (emphasis supplied).

And added to § 1.07(a) in 1979 was (9.1) which provides:

"(9.1) 'Corporation' includes nonprofit corporation, professional association created pursuant to statute, and joint stock companies."

V.T.C.A., Penal Code, § 7.22 (Criminal Responsibility of Corporation or Association), provides:

"(a) If conduct constituting an offense is performed by an agent acting in behalf of a corporation or association and within the scope of his office or employment, the corporation or association is criminally responsible for an offense defined:

"(1) in this code where corporations and associations are made subject thereto;

"(2) by law other than this code in which a legislative purpose to impose criminal responsibility on corporations or associations plainly appears; or

"(3) by law other than this code for which strict liability is imposed, unless a legislative purpose not to impose criminal responsibility on corporations or associations plainly appears.

V.T.C.A., Penal Code, § 19.07 (Criminal Negligence Homicide), provides:

"(a) A *person* commits an offense if he causes the death of an individual by criminal negligence.

"(b) An offense under this section is a Class A misdemeanor" (emphasis supplied)....

The Legislature, recognizing that for years Texas was the only jurisdiction in which corporations bore no general criminal responsibility, and aware of the previous roadblocks in case law to the prosecution of corporations for criminal offenses, enacted statutes to remedy the situation. As earlier noted, the Legislature defined "person" in both the Penal Code and the Code of Criminal Procedure (Article 17A.01(b), V.A.C.C.P.) so as to expressly embrace corporations. To leave no doubt the Legislature also similarly defined "person" in the Code Construction Act (Government Code, § 311.005). In the accusatory and definitional part of most offenses found in the Penal Code the term "person" (as defined elsewhere) is used without qualification. Observe that this was done in V.T.C.A., Penal Code, § 19.01, defining criminal homicide, and in the statute in question in this case, V.T.C.A., Penal Code, § 19.07 (Criminal Negligent Homicide) ...

The intention of the Legislature could hardly be made clearer given the history, the reform intended and the literal meaning of the statutes involved. Taken collectively, the foregoing statutes furnish the basis for overcoming the obstacles which in the past have prevented the criminal prosecution of corporations.

It is the State's contention that a corporation is a "person" under general definitional statute of the Penal Code and Government Code and since the crime of criminally negligent homicide can be committed by a "person", it follows that the crime can be committed by a corporation. We agree....

The Court of Appeals stated that those jurisdictions which have addressed the issue of corporate criminal liability "... are divided as to criminal responsibility for personal crimes such as homicide or rape, though the majority still agrees that a corporation cannot commit a crime requiring specific intent." No authority is cited.

In 18B Amer.Jur.2d, § 2137, pp. 959–960, it is stated:

> "It is now *generally accepted* that a corporation may be indicted for a crime to which a specific intent is essential, and that the intent is essential, and that the intent of its employees or agents may be imputed to the corporations" (emphasis supplied).

In 19 C.J.S., Corporations, § 1363, pp. 1075–1076, it was pointed out that:

> "A corporation may be criminally liable for crimes which involve a specific element of intent as well for those which do not, and, although some crimes require such a personal, malicious intent that a corporation is considered incapable of committing them, nevertheless under the proper circumstances the criminal intent of its agent may be imputed to it so as to render it liable, the requisites of such imputation being essentially the same as those required to impute malice to corporations in civil actions."

After recognizing that some courts have held that a corporation cannot be guilty of homicide in absence of a specific statutory provision, it is stated in 19 C.J.S., Corporations, § 1364, p. 1077:

> "However it has been said that a definition of certain forms of manslaughter may be formulated which would be applicable to a corporation and make it liable for various acts of misfeasance and nonfeasance when resulting in homicide. Thus, a corporation has been held subject to prosecution for involuntary manslaughter where there was nothing in the definition of the crime or the punishment provided which would make it impossible to hold a corporation liable."

An examination of decisional law from other states indicates that where there are corporate criminal responsibility statutes similar to our own Texas statutes, it appears to have been consistently held that a corporation is liable for specific intent crimes and offenses of criminal negligence.

In *Commonwealth of Kentucky v. Fortner LP Gas Co., Inc.*, the indictment involved manslaughter in the second degree. A corporate truck with defective brakes had struck two children, killing one, while they were crossing the highway after alighting from a school bus. The circuit court sustained the motion to dismiss the indictment relying upon *Commonwealth v. Illinois Central Railway Co.* The *Illinois Central* case had been a definitive case on corporate responsibility for criminal conduct for many years. Basically, the holding of that case was that "corporations cannot be indicted for offenses which derive their criminality from evil intention or which consist in a violation of those social duties which appertain to man and subjects." The holding was predicated on two things. One, was that in 1913 there was no separate punishment for corporations provided by Kentucky statute, and two, the court was not willing, in a criminal prosecution, to extend the definition of the word "person" in § 475 of the Kentucky statutes to include corporations. On appeal of the ruling dismissing the indictment the Kentucky Court of Appeals decided that *Illinois Central* must be considered in light of its date, statutory changes and its total holding. The Kentucky Court of Appeals observed that there was now a statute imposing criminal liability upon a corporation, second there was a general statutory definition of "person" which included corporations, and a punishment statute which imposed fines upon a corporation for violation of offenses. The court concluded that these statutes were envisioned in *Illinois Central* which might support an indictment. The order to dismiss the indictment was reversed. Our Texas statutes are almost identical to the Kentucky statutes....

[Furthermore,] In Brickley, *Corporate Criminal Liability*, Vol. I (Evolution of Liability), § 209, p. 31, it was written:

> "As courts gave express recognition to the capacity of corporations to commit crimes requiring general intent, open hostility to retention of a 'fanciful theory in process of abandonment' surfaced and brought to the forefront consideration of the question whether there remained a sound reason for drawing a distinction between imputing general and specific intent to corporations. After all, corporations have been held vicariously liable for intentional torts including assault and battery, libel and malicious prosecution. Because it would be no more difficult theoretically to impute specific intent for a crime than a tort, the only point remaining in dispute was the question whether the corporation lacked capacity to form evil intention. The suggestion that it did was met with little patience. 'The same law that creates the corporation may create the crime, and to assert that the Legislature cannot punish its own creature because it cannot make a creature capable of violating the law does not ... bear discussion.' The proposition simply was untenable.
>
> "Beginning in the late nineteenth and continuing into the early twentieth century, courts wrestling with this issue began breaking down the last barrier to imposing on corporations the full range of liabilities to which natural persons were subject. During this period corporations were found to be properly subject to criminal prosecution for such diverse offenses as ... even manslaughter."

Given the history of corporate criminal liability in Texas prior to the 1974 Penal Code, the various provisions of the 1974 Penal Code and other statutes enacted to bring about a change, the clear statutory language, and the analogous case authority, we reject the reasoning of the Court of Appeals and conclude that a corporation may be criminally prosecuted for the misdemeanor code offense of criminally negligent homicide …

The Court of Appeals judgment is reversed and the cause remanded to that court for consideration of appellant's points of error.

**TEAGUE, Judge, dissenting.**

Please, dear reader, believe me: Contrary to what you might surmise from this Court's majority opinion, the law that addresses corporate criminal liability, as reflected by the many law review articles and court decisions on the subject, is one big mess. I must, however, sadly report: The majority opinion actually does absolutely nothing to clear the air in this area of the law. In fact, I find that the majority opinion will actually add to the confusion that presently exists in this area of our law.

Without any limitation whatsoever, this Court granted the State's petition for discretionary review in order to review the decision of the Texarkana Court of Appeals, which declared that a private corporation in Texas could not be prosecuted for the offense of criminally negligent homicide that had been previously committed by one or more of its employees or agents. Contrary to the court of appeals' decision, the majority opinion of this Court holds generally that a private corporation doing business in Texas can be held strictly and automatically criminally liable for the personal negligent acts of its employees or agents, provided that at a later date the trier of fact finds that the employees' or agents' personal negligent acts were actually criminal. Given this Court's unlimited grant, what the court of appeals stated and held, and what the State argues in its petition for discretionary review, I respectfully dissent to the majority opinion's failure to "put some meat on the bones of that old corporation dog" that it has now discovered exists. I also dissent for other reasons that I will give.

Although I dissent, I nevertheless acknowledge that the law that addresses the civil and criminal liability of a private corporation in Texas and elsewhere has come a long way since the year 1250 when Pope Innocent IV decreed that because a corporation, although apparently then a "person", did not have a soul that could be damned, it could not be excommunicated from the Church …

It is actually not the reasoning that the majority opinion uses to reach its conclusion, that a private corporation doing business in Texas falls within the statutory term "person", that concerns me. What actually concerns me lies in the fact that the majority opinion fails to give the bench and bar of this State any guidance as to how the concept of strict and automatic criminal liability, which it approves, either expressly or implicitly, is to be applied to future criminal cases involving corporate criminal defendants …

The majority opinion, without taking into account the distinction between an offense created on behalf of the public welfare and an offense that is totally unrelated to the public welfare, i.e., making it criminal for a private corporation to be strictly and automatically held criminally responsible for the personal negligent acts of its employees or agents that are later determined by some trier of fact to be criminal negligent acts, holds that the Legislature may enact non-police power legislation to hold a private corporation criminally liable by imputing to the corporation acts of ordinary and personal negligence of its employees that are later determined by some trier of fact to be criminal negligent acts. I find that such cannot occur without violating the due process and due course of law clauses of the respective constitutions because such is unreasonable, arbitrary, and capricious. As previously stated, because § 7.22(a)(1) permits private corporations to be treated differently than humans, it is patently violative of the equal protection clauses …

Again, I emphasize: The criminal liability of the corporation in this instance is not based upon some form of regulatory criminal type statute which can be classified as a "public welfare statute", and I can find no public policy justification in §7.22(a)(1) that might warrant the finding that the corporation's liability is predicated upon a "public welfare statute." I find and conclude that to strictly criminalize a private corporation doing business in Texas for the personal criminal negligent acts of its employees or agents, pursuant to §7.22(a)(1), amounts to arbitrariness and nonsense....

Given the fact that the issue here does not involve the application of the police powers of the State, and also given the fact that imposition of criminal liability usually requires proof that the Appellant corporation itself did something personally criminally wrongful, I ask: As far as the personal act of negligence that caused the death of the victim in this cause, what personal negligent act did the appellant corporation commit, which personal negligent act was later determined to be criminal? How was the corporation put on notice that its truck was going to quit running when it did and at the place it did, after its driver had successfully made a delivery? How could the corporation have predicted that the driver would not take every reasonable precaution to remove the truck from the highway? How could the corporation have predicted that a collision would occur, much less that death would result? Predictability or foreseeability, alas, is nowhere to be found in the majority opinion, which should be entitled "Private Corporations, Beware. Another Almanza the Terrible has been turned loose by an aggressive and assertive majority of this Court to do dastardly deeds to *you* !!!"

For the above and foregoing reasons, I respectfully dissent to the majority opinion.

## *Notes and Questions*

1. Imposition of corporate criminal liability was frowned upon until late in the nineteenth century. The standard argument against corporate criminal liability was that corporations were both incapable of criminal intent or *mens rea* and that punishing corporations would be useless, for such legal entities cannot be imprisoned or otherwise be made to suffer. Both arguments were eventually overcome. Regarding the capacity for a guilty mind, courts began imputing the guilty mind of the corporation's employees to the corporation. Corporate criminal liability was thus—and still is in many jurisdictions—conceived as a form of vicarious criminal liability that draws heavily from tort law *respondeat superior* principles. With regard to punishment sanctions, courts began imposing fines on corporations as a substitute for imprisonment.

2. As both the *Basic Construction Co.* and *Vaughan and Sons* cases illustrate, the *respondeat superior* approach imposes criminal liability on corporations if three requirements are satisfied. First, an employee of the corporation must have committed a criminal act during the course of his employment. Second, the employees must have apparent authority to engage in the kind of act that gave rise to criminal liability. The focus is not on the specific criminal act, for employees are rarely authorized by a corporation to engage in criminal conduct. Rather, the emphasis is on whether the employee had the authority to engage in the general type of act that culminated in the commission of a crime. Thus, for example, the question in *Vaughan and Sons* would not be whether the employee had authority to negligently kill a human being. Obviously, the corporation does not afford its employees such authority. Instead, the question is whether the employee had the authority to drive a vehicle on behalf of the corporation, for that is the general type of conduct that culminated in the commission of the crime. This, of course, the employee in *Vaughan and Sons* was authorized to do. Finally, the employees must act to

benefit the corporation. Once again, the emphasis is not on whether the criminal act itself benefits the corporation, as criminal acts may eventually end up harming the corporate entity. Instead, the focus is on whether the general type of act that the employee performed is of the sort that may benefit the corporation. In *Vaughan and Sons,* for example, the question is not whether negligently killing a person benefits the corporation. It obviously does not. Rather, the question is whether the general act of driving that the defendant was engaged in when he negligently killed the victim may benefit the corporation. Once the inquiry is framed in this manner, it is easy to see that the employee's conduct in *Vaughan and Sons* did benefit the corporate entity. Furthermore, many courts follow the approach adopted in *Basic Construction Co.* that allows for the imposition of corporate criminal liability even if the acts of the employee are contrary to corporate policy or instructions.

3. While corporations are usually held liable for public welfare offenses or crimes related to commercial practices, courts are increasingly willing to hold corporations liable for core non-commercial crimes. The corporate defendant in *Vaughan and Sons,* for example, was held liable for the commission of the crime of negligent homicide. Note, however, that the dissenting justice in *Vaughan and Sons* believes that application of the *respondeat superior* approach to impose liability on corporations for non-public welfare offenses such as negligent homicide is unfair. According to the dissent, the unfairness stems from the fact that the *respondeat superior* approach to corporate criminal liability imposes punishment without fault, for the corporation is held liable for the criminal acts of its employees even if the corporation did not intentionally or negligently facilitate the criminal conduct of its employees. While imposition of such vicarious liability on the corporation is perhaps tolerable when the offense charged is a public welfare offense, the dissent argues that it is unwarranted when the crime charged is a more serious *malum in se* offense such as homicide. Do you agree with the dissent's argument? Why or why not?

## § 13.02 Corporate Criminal Liability: Model Penal Code

### Model Penal Code § 2.07. Liability of Corporations, Unincorporated Associations and Persons Acting, or Under a Duty to Act, in Their Behalf.

(1) A corporation may be convicted of the commission of an offense if:

(a) the offense is a violation or the offense is defined by a statute other than the Code in which a legislative purpose to impose liability on corporations plainly appears and the conduct is performed by an agent of the corporation acting in behalf of the corporation within the scope of his office or employment, except that if the law defining the offense designates the agents for whose conduct the corporation is accountable or the circumstances under which it is accountable, such provisions shall apply; or

(b) the offense consists of an omission to discharge a specific duty of affirmative performance imposed on corporations by law; or

(c) the commission of the offense was authorized, requested, commanded, performed or recklessly tolerated by the board of directors or by a high managerial agent acting in behalf of the corporation within the scope of his office or employment....

(4) As used in this Section: ...

(c) "high managerial agent" means an officer of a corporation or an unincorporated association, or, in the case of a partnership, a partner, or any other agent of a corporation or association having duties of such responsibility that his conduct may fairly be assumed to represent the policy of the corporation or association.

(5) In any prosecution of a corporation or an unincorporated association for the commission of an offense included within the terms of Subsection (1)(a) or Subsection (3)(a) of this Section, other than an offense for which absolute liability has been imposed, it shall be a defense if the defendant proves by a preponderance of evidence that the high managerial agent having supervisory responsibility over the subject matter of the offense employed due diligence to prevent its commission. This paragraph shall not apply if it is plainly inconsistent with the legislative purpose in defining the particular offense ...

## State v. Community Alternatives Missouri, Inc.

Missouri Court of Appeals, Southern District, Division One, 2010
267 S.W.3d 735

JOHN E. PARRISH, Presiding Judge.

Community Alternatives Missouri, Inc., d/b/a Turtle Creek Group Home, (defendant) was convicted of resident neglect following a jury trial. This court affirms.

### I. Criminal Charge

The information alleged that defendant committed the Class D felony of resident neglect. It charged that employees of defendant, "on or about between November 28, 2001, and January 10, 2002, ... neglected Gary Oheim, a resident of a residential facility licensed by the Missouri Department of Mental Health, by failing to provide the services which were reasonable and necessary to maintain the physical and mental health of said Gary Oheim, which presented an imminent danger to the health, safety or welfare of said Gary Oheim." The information charged "that under Section 562.056.1(3), RSMo, Mary Collura engaged in and knowingly tolerated the conduct constituting this offense as a high managerial agent of the defendant and acted within the scope of her employment and in behalf of defendant."

### II. Facts

Defendant is certified by the Missouri Department of Mental Health to provide services to persons who are developmentally disabled or mentally retarded. Defendant is licensed to provide individualized supported living services, residential habilitation services, and day habilitation services. Defendant's responsibilities include providing basic health and safety assurances to its residents.

#### A. Organization and Business Structure

Defendant is a corporation. Defendant's management chain includes a chief executive officer, regional vice presidents, and regional directors. Defendant operates more than 30 group homes, including Turtle Creek Group Home at Bolivar, Missouri (Turtle Creek). Its management chain for the operation of the group homes is divided into three divisions—North, Central, and South. Each division is headed by an executive director, an associate director, and a program coordinator. Turtle Creek is part of defendant's South division. Amy Follis was executive director of that division, Diane Bickham was associate director, and Lisa Martin was program coordinator.

Mary Collura was lead staff person for two of the group homes in the South division, Turtle Creek and Forest Ridge. Lead staff person is a management position. Collura was entrusted with the care, safety, health, and well-being of the residents of Turtle Creek. Collura's responsibilities included managing residents' medical care and supervising the staffs at Turtle Creek and Forest Ridge. Collura attended management meetings with Diane Bickham. She also performed training for the direct support staff for multiple homes within the South division. She gave job evaluations, disciplined support staff, and had authority to write checks on residents' accounts to buy personal items for them. She was provided a company credit card for use in purchasing supplies.

Mary Collura had authority to take residents to the doctor when necessary. She was responsible for getting residents to their appointments on time and for maintaining residents' prescriptions and refills. Her duties included ensuring that residents' medical care was properly documented and relaying medical information regarding residents to case managers with the Department of Mental Health.

B. Care of Gary Oheim

Gary Oheim was a resident of Turtle Creek from February 2001 until his death on January 30, 2002. He was mentally retarded and suffered from cerebral palsy. He was confined to a wheel chair. He could not move himself. He had to be repositioned often to prevent bedsores from developing ... [Ms. Collura was aware of the defendant's proneness to develop bedsores]....

[In light of continuous problems with bedsores,] Oheim was brought to the clinic on January 5, 2002. He was ... seen by Joe Follis. Ms. Collura was also present. Follis asked to see Oheim's hip and asked Collura to lean Oheim forward in his wheelchair, but Collura told Follis that was not necessary. Collura leaned Oheim to the side while he remained seated in the wheelchair. Joe Follis examined Oheim in the wheelchair while Oheim remained fully clothed. Follis testified that he should have known Oheim had bedsores and should have examined for them; that had he done so he would have known Oheim's sores were worsening....

Patty Price was present for Mr. Oheim's January 5 appointment. Price verified that Collura did not show Oheim's buttocks to Follis while Price was in the room with them. Price asked Follis if Oheim needed medicine and was told that he did not.

[Oheim eventually died as a result of complications related to his bedsores.]

III. Defendant's Appeal

... Section 562.056.1(3) states:

> A corporation is guilty of an offense if ...
>
> (3) The conduct constituting the offense is engaged in, authorized, solicited, requested, commanded or knowingly tolerated by the board of directors or by a high managerial agent acting within the scope of his employment and in behalf of the corporation.

[In] Point III [Defendant] asserts that "[t]he trial court erred in sustaining the jury's verdict against [defendant]" because there was not sufficient evidence from which the jury could reasonably find that Mary Collura was a high managerial agent of defendant acting within the scope of her employment and that she neglected Gary Oheim ...

... For defendant, a corporation, to be guilty of [resident neglect], the conduct that constituted the offense must have been "engaged in, authorized, solicited, requested, commanded or knowingly tolerated ... by a high managerial agent acting within the scope of his employment and in behalf of the corporation."

Without copies of the jury instructions, *see* n. 8, *supra*, this court is left to speculate as to the directive given to the jury in this regard. The amended information alleged, however, that Gary Oheim, a resident of a residential facility, licensed by the Missouri Department of Mental Health, was knowingly neglected; that he was not provided "the services which were reasonable and necessary to maintain the physical and mental health of said Gary Oheim, which presented an imminent danger to the health, safety or welfare of said Gary Oheim, and that under Section 562.056.1(3), RSMo, Mary Collura engaged in and knowingly tolerated the conduct constituting this offense as a high managerial agent of the defendant and acted within the scope of her employment and in behalf of the defendant." Point III takes issue only with whether there was sufficient proof that Mary Collura was a high managerial agent of defendant and that her actions were done in the course of her employment by defendant as required by § 562.056.1(3), and that, as such, she knowingly neglected Gary Oheim.

Defendant's argument regarding whether Mary Collura was a high managerial agent and whether the actions she took, or failed to take, occurred on behalf of defendant within the scope of her employment is directed to Ms. Collura's status in defendant's overall corporate structure. Defendant contends it cannot be held liable because Mary Collura lacked corporate-wide authority and lacked authority comparable to a corporate officer within that structure. Defendant contends that for those reasons, requirements imposed by § 562.056.1(3) to hold it criminally liable were not met.

Defendant's statement of facts, albeit with the argumentative subtitle, "Mary Collura Was a Low-Level Employee Lacking Management Authority," acknowledges that defendant operates multiple group homes. Defendant operated "over thirty group homes throughout the State of Missouri." Its operating structure included three divisions designated as North, South, and Central. Turtle Creek was one of 13 group homes located within defendant's South division. Defendant contends that its overall size and operation must be considered in ascertaining Mary Collura's status for purposes of applying § 562.056.1(3).

The state contends that the applicability of § 562.056.1(3) is to be ascertained by examination of Mary Collura's role in the operation of the single group home that is the subject of this case, Turtle Creek. The state suggests that the definition of "high managerial agent" for purposes of determining corporate criminal liability per § 562.056.1(3) involves three circumstances; that for purposes of § 562.056, the term is defined by subsection 3(2) of that statute. The state suggests that the third circumstance the statute prescribes is applicable here; that, under the facts in this case, Mary Collura qualified as a high managerial agent for defendant for purposes of § 562.056; that although she was not designated as an officer of the corporation, the evidence was sufficient for the jury to find that Mary Collura supervised subordinate employees in a managerial capacity; that in that regard, Mary Collura was in a position of authority at Turtle Creek comparable to that of a corporate officer. This court agrees ...

Section 562.056.3 states:

As used in this section:

(1) "Agent" means any director, officer or employee of a corporation ... or *any other person who is authorized to act in behalf of the corporation ...*;

(2) "High managerial agent" means an officer of a corporation or *any other agent in a position of comparable authority with respect to ... the supervision in a managerial capacity of subordinate employees* (emphasis added).

The plain language of the statute provides that a person authorized to act in behalf of a corporation who has managerial authority to supervise subordinate employees, comparable to a corporate officer, is, for purposes of § 562.056, a high managerial agent. Acts of persons who satisfy the definition of "high managerial agent" set forth in § 562.056.3(2) can subject a corporation to criminal liability notwithstanding that he or she is not a member of a corporate board of directors or is not a corporate officer. It is the function within a corporate structure that must be considered, not merely job titles.

A question this appeal presents is whether the definition of "high managerial agent" is to be applied differently with respect to corporations that operate numerous business units than to corporations that operate a single business unit. Is a corporation that operates numerous business units shielded from criminal liability when the same conduct would subject a corporation with a single business unit to criminal liability? This court thinks not.

In *State v. Boone Retirement Center, Inc., supra,* the corporate defendant was held criminally liable for mistreatment of nursing home residents tolerated by the corporation's administrator. The administrator was a managing official of a single residential facility who supervised subordinate employees who provided care for residents. Patients were neglected to the extent that they suffered serious physical disability—ulcers (bedsores) that contributed to the death of two patients. *Boone* held that the corporation was criminally liable, via § 562.056, by reason of combined acts of the administrator of the facility and its nursing director's combined knowledge and actions or inactions with respect to the neglect of the patients who died.

In this case, defendant operated many facilities, or business units, under a single corporate ownership. Each business unit had personnel responsible for the care of the residents at its facility. This court does not perceive the legislative intent that fostered enactment of § 562.056 to have been to treat large corporations with numerous operating units different from those that operate a single or a few business units.

Here, as in *Boone,* an employee was responsible for supervising and managing the care of residents. In *Boone* the responsibility was that of the facility administrator and director of nursing. Here, the employee who had that responsibility was Mary Collura. Mary Collura had comparable responsibility at Turtle Creek with respect to Gary Oheim that the administrator and director of nursing had with respect to the residents at the single facility that was operated by Boone Retirement Center, Inc.

Mary Collura managed and supervised the employees responsible for providing patient care. She determined what medical care would be afforded Gary Oheim pursuant to the business structure prescribed by defendant. She was defendant's "lead staff person" at Turtle Creek. She supervised staff at Turtle Creek. The support staff at Turtle Creek responsible for direct care-giving to residents reported to Collura. Mary Collura gave job evaluations, disciplined support staff through written reprimands, and made recommendations regarding hiring and firing of support staff.

Mary Collura had a company credit card for use in purchasing needed items such as food, cleaning supplies, and gasoline. She had authority to take residents to doctors when she believed it was necessary. She was responsible for getting residents to their appointments. No other authorization was required for her to obtain medical care for residents. Other evidence of Collura's supervisory responsibilities was directives given other staff members that they were not to talk to residents' doctors; that this was Collura's responsibility. At least one staff member testified she was told by defendant's "main office" not to talk to doctors because that was not her responsibility.

Collura was the only manager who was regularly present at Turtle Creek. There was evidence that Collura's corporate supervisor, Lisa Martin, visited Turtle Creek only about once a month, although Martin testified that she tried to visit Turtle Creek once a week.

Collura's acts were undertaken pursuant to defendant's direction and authorization. As such, her activities and directives given others with respect to the care provided Gary Oheim were within the scope of her employment. Her actions were on behalf of defendant. They were done to further defendant's business or interest.

There was sufficient evidence for the jury to have found that Mary Collura was authorized to act in behalf of defendant; that she had managerial responsibility pursuant to which she supervised subordinate employees. In the capacity in which she supervised subordinate employees, the evidence was sufficient to permit the jury to find Mary Collura was an agent in a position of comparable authority as an officer of the corporation. The evidence was likewise sufficient to prove that Mary Collura committed acts or knowingly tolerated conduct of others that presented an imminent danger to the health, safety, and welfare of Gary Oheim. Point III is denied ...

The judgment is affirmed.

## *Notes and Questions*

1. Note that the Model Penal Code distinguishes between the rules that apply for imposing corporate criminal liability for "violations" and offenses defined outside the Code and the rules that apply for assessing corporate criminal liability for true Code offenses (i.e., non-violations). Pursuant to § 2.07(1)(a), liability may be imposed on corporations for Code *violations* as long as the conduct giving rise to the violation was performed by an agent of the corporation acting within the scope of this employment. This is essentially equivalent to the common law *respondeat superior* approach to corporate criminal liability discussed in the previous section. Nevertheless, the Code adopted a significantly different approach to imposing criminal liability on corporations for the commission of true Code offenses (i.e., non-violations). In such cases, according to § 2.07(1)(c), corporations are only liable for the criminal acts of their employees if the board of directors or a high managerial agent "authorized, requested, commanded, performed or recklessly tolerated" the criminal conduct. Compared to the common law *respondeat superior* approach, the Model Penal Code standard narrows considerably the scope of corporate criminal liability. Furthermore, the Model Penal Code standard does not impose true vicarious criminal liability on corporations, for liability is imposed only if the corporation itself—through its board or high managerial agents—authorized or recklessly tolerated the criminal conduct of its employees. Would the corporate defendant in *Vaughan and Sons* be held liable for homicide had the corporation been tried under § 2.07(1)(c) of the Model Penal Code? Explain.

2. A recurrent problem in the context of the Model Penal Code's corporate criminal liability provisions is determining who counts as a "high managerial agent" that may "authorize" or "recklessly tolerate" the employee's criminal conduct. There is no issue if the person who authorizes the conduct is a member of the board of directors or one of the corporation's chief officers. But things get more complicated when the corporate employee manages a sub-division or department of the corporation but is not a member of centralized high-level management. According to the court in *Community Alternatives,* the administrator/manager of each of the corporation's nursing facilities is a "high managerial agent" for the purposes of § 2.07(1)(c) of the Code, because such administrators are in charge of "subordinate employees in a managerial capacity" and they are therefore in a position of managerial authority "comparable to that of a corporate officer," at least with regard to the operations that they supervise. As a result, the court held that the Ms. Collura was a "high managerial agent," given that she was the administrator of the Tur-

tle Creek nursing facility, although she was not a member of the upper level management of the corporation at the centralized level. Do you agree with the court's decision? Why or why not?

3. According to Model Penal Code § 2.07(5), it is an affirmative defense to corporate criminal liability that the high managerial agent employed due diligence to prevent the commission of the offense. This provision has been adopted only in a handful of state jurisdictions. Given that it is an affirmative defense, the corporation has the burden of coming forward with evidence of due diligence. Furthermore, even if the corporation comes forward with such evidence, it also has the burden of proving by preponderance of the evidence that the high managerial agent exercised due diligence to prevent the commission of the offense.

## § 13.03 Corporate Criminal Liability: Comparative Perspectives

### Thomas Weigend, *Societas Delinquere Non Potest*

6 J. Int. Crim. Just. 927 (2008)

#### 2. The German Debate on Corporate Criminal Responsibility

A. History, and a Compromise Solution

While the majority of European states have moved toward recognizing corporate criminal responsibility, Germany, along with a few allies, has so far held out in a position of at least partial denial. Germany recognizes an indirect form of corporate liability for wrongdoing of officers and managers of legal persons, but has so far refrained from making corporations subject to 'genuine' criminal sanctions....

[Nevertheless,] [s]ince 1968, the Code on Administrative Infractions (Gesetz fiber Ordnungswidrigkeiten) permits the imposition of an administrative fine against a legal person if an organ, a representative or a person with control functions of the legal person committed a criminal offence or an administrative infraction by which an obligation of the legal person was violated or the legal person was enriched. In order to impose an administrative fine, it is not necessary to identify an individual officer or representative who did wrong; it only has to be shown that someone acting for the legal person in a capacity designated by the statute committed an offence. The offence can also consist in a culpable lack of supervision over lower-rank employees. The appropriate state agency can thus impose an administrative fine on a legal person when all that is known is the fact that one of its employees committed a criminal or administrative offence on behalf of the legal person and that a responsible officer of the legal person failed to prevent or discourage the commission of that offence through proper supervision of the subordinate. The maximum amount of an administrative fine against the legal person is one million Euro. If the legal person obtained an illicit profit from the offence, the fine can exceed one million Euro and is limited only by the amount of the legal persons gain. The Penal Code also provides for the possibility of confiscating the proceeds of a crime from a legal person when a natural person has committed a criminal offence on its behalf. This legal arrangement basically fulfils the main functions of corporate criminal responsibility. It permits the state to hold the corporation financially responsible for offences committed by its agents on its behalf, and even for offences of mere employees if they were not sufficiently supervised, and to deprive the corporation of any illicit profit it may have drawn from violations committed on its behalf. It can therefore be argued that the Federal Republic of Germany lives up to its commitment under various international conventions to provide for proportional and deterrent sanctions against legal persons.

### B. The Debate Continues

Yet, the debate continues whether 'true' criminal responsibility of legal persons should be introduced into German law. For practical-minded observers, this debate may seem to turn on verbal or perhaps philosophical niceties. But on closer observation, the controversial issues are about the very foundations of criminal law: What are the prerequisites that an entity must fulfil to be able to commit a criminal act? What does the attribution of (criminal) blame pre-suppose? What are the subjective requirements for receiving criminal punishment? I will return to these questions after I have briefly lined out the arguments that German supporters of corporate criminal responsibility pro-pose in support of their cause.

Those who argue in favor of extending the core criminal law to corporations emphasize the penological need for and practical advantages of punishing legal persons in the same way as natural persons. Legal persons, they claim, are in today's economic system responsible for the bulk of business and environmental crime. At the same time, a fragmentation of tasks and responsibilities within business enterprises makes it difficult, if not impossible, to trace criminal violations back to individual actors. Even if that is possible, the requisite mens rea is frequently lacking or impossible to prove against an individual who may only be a small cog in a large wheel. High-level corporate managers, on the other hand, will often deny knowledge of criminal conduct, claiming that individual employees were acting on their own and against company rules. Another ground advanced for holding corporations criminally responsible is that companies encourage criminal conduct by maintaining a corporate culture that condones or even rewards violations of the law. Only criminal sanctions, it is being said, sufficiently affect the legal person to make it change its lawless corporate attitude. With respect to sentencing, the court, when imposing a fine for business-related offences, should be able to take into account the financial means of the corporation rather than just the personal income of the individual corporate officer, as prescribed by German sentencing law....

### D. 'Fundamental' Objections

Given the deficiencies of the two 'models' of corporate criminal responsibility, it is not surprising that a strong group of German theorists oppose the introduction of full-scale corporate liability. These authors argue that corporate criminal responsibility conflicts with basic tenets of German criminal law. They see three fatal deficiencies: corporations cannot act, corporations cannot be blamed, and corporations cannot be subject to criminal punishment.

To understand this argument remember that, according to traditional German doctrine, criminal law is a profoundly moral business. Criminal sanctions, as opposed to civil liability for damages or administrative sanctions, are said to have an inherent element of moral blame, a negative socio-ethical value judgment addressed to the offender and relating to the offence. This negative value judgment can be justified only when the person has acted (or omitted to act) according to his voluntary decision and could have avoided the act of wrongdoing. Attribution of blame, under these high standards, is not a pragmatic tool employed to bring about desired behavior on the part of citizens, but the outcome of a dialogue between the state and the citizen, a dialogue with strong ethical overtones. Seen from this perspective, the problems of corporate criminal responsibility become easily apparent. The criminal law presupposes the existence of and is addressed to a moral agent. His fault is the reason for the law's moral condemnation of his criminal act. A legal person, even though it can be subject to legal obligations, lacks all ingredients of a moral agent in the true sense: it has no moral conscience, it cannot recognize moral or legal norms, and it cannot stop itself from violating such norms. This significant difference suggests prima facie that criminal liability cannot be imposed on corporations, at least not in the same way as they are imposed on natural persons. If one wishes to make corporations criminally liable it would, in any event, be necessary to adapt and transform basic concepts of criminal law so that they 'fit' the special characteristics of a legal person. Whether or not such transformation is possible and, if so, desirable is the issue on which the debate in Germany has centered.

Let us now take a closer look at the requirements for individual criminal responsibility....

### 2. Corporations Cannot be Morally Guilty

Matters become even more complicated when we consider the issue of a corporation's blameworthiness. Schuld—which I will interchangeably translate as 'guilt' or 'blameworthiness'—has been another hot topic of debate in German criminal law theory, especially after the Second World War. As early as in 1952, the Federal Court of Appeals declared in a landmark ruling that a person cannot be found guilty of a crime if he was unable to recognize the fact that his conduct was prohibited. In that judgment, the Court, referring to principles of natural law, declared that 'man is directed toward free, responsible moral self-determination' and that only for that reason moral and legal blame can be imposed on him when he commits a crime. The Federal Constitutional Court has since then repeatedly declared that the rule nulla poena sine culpa, although not specifically mentioned in the German Basic Law of 1949, is an important constitutional principle. According to the Court, this principle is rooted in the protection of human dignity and the right to develop one's personality and is also supported by the fact that the Federal Republic of Germany is a state based on the rule of law. It is easy to see that 'moral self-determination' is not something that can easily be attributed to legal persons. For that reason, the German legislature did not provide for criminal punishment of corporations, but relegated their liability to the law of administrative infractions. In that part of the law, so the theory goes, sanctions, although they can amount to millions of Euro, do not imply moral blame and therefore can be applied to legal persons.

In recent years, however, several theorists have challenged the idea that criminal guilt presupposes moral self-determination and can therefore not be attributed to legal persons. The main lines of argument are similar to those used with respect to a corporation's ability to act. Some authors propose a concept of 'corporate guilt', supposed to reflect popular thinking about the responsibility of corporations for harm caused under their name. Others maintain that the legislature, by providing for administrative sanctions against corporations, has indicated its belief that corporations can act culpably. Beyond that positivistic argument, many authors would be willing to re-define the concept of guilt to fit the conditions of decision-making of a corporation. They argue that although a legal person cannot be said to have a free will in the same way as is postulated for natural persons, a legal person does have a choice to act legally or in violation of the law, a choice that is eventually determined by its organs. One author even suggests that a corporation as such can act intentionally and negligently, depending on the kind of fault.

Other writers would transfer the guilt of officers to the corporation, thereby its organs or employees commit in defectively organising the corporation, sidestepping the question of whether a corporation itself can act culpably.

Yet others have gone so far as to abandon strict adherence to the guilt requirement and would regard the necessity to prove an actor's blameworthiness as only one factor in assessing the legitimacy of a criminal statute. If the evil to be repressed is serious enough and the sanction can generally be termed proportionate, then guilt in any traditional sense need not be a prerequisite for conviction. The proposals to lower the traditional guilt standard have nevertheless met with serious opposition. For example, Ginther Jakobs, one of Germany's leading criminal law theorists, has insisted that blameworthiness presupposes a capacity to comprehend the meaning of a moral norm and to take a position with respect to that norm; even an organ of a legal person, Jakobs maintains, cannot transfer that capacity to the legal person itself.

Jakobs' statement, I think, draws a correct conclusion from a 'personal' concept of guilt. But it remains an open question whether the traditional concept of blameworthiness, which would indeed preclude introduction of corporate criminal responsibility, can be altered when activities of legal persons are concerned. Tatjana Hornle has recently shown that the proclaimed connection between the guilt principle and the dignity of man is not so strict and close as had been assumed. The guilt principle, Hornle says, is necessary to protect the citizen against unwarranted reprobation, which would interfere with his right to freely develop his personality. The protection of the guilt principle is thus needed only to the extent moral reprobation is pronounced by formally convicting a person of a crime. Only when the reprobation inherent in criminal punishment is personal, Hornle concludes, personal guilt is required. If that is correct, the very fact that legal persons do not partake of the autonomy and free will that forms the basis of human dignity means that the 'guilt principle' in its traditional form need not be applied to them. To the extent that sanctions against corporations do not imply moral blame, corporations do not need protection against unwarranted blaming. In other words, sanctions against corporations may neither presume nor express the notion that the corporation has committed a moral wrong in the same sense in which a natural person could have culpably violated a norm. The guilt principle thus not stand in the way of introducing sanctions that do not impose moral blame …

### 1. Concluding Remarks

Let me conclude with a few skeptical relativistic remarks. It seems to me that proponents of corporate criminal responsibility are a little too eager to bridge the doctrinal gaps in their argument in order to reach the desired result. I have grave doubts about the persuasiveness of either of the … theories that have been advanced to justify the imposition of criminal responsibility on legal persons. These theories do not offer a convincing doctrinal basis for transferring corporate officers' guilt to the corporation itself, nor does a corporate obligation of responsible self-organization have sufficiently clear contours to provide a basis for criminal liability.

If one nevertheless wishes to introduce corporate criminal responsibility, it would be necessary to adapt certain concepts associated with a 'moralistic' criminal law to the new world of corporate liability. This adaptation has been easy in jurisdictions that have always been comparatively loose in attributing criminal responsibility, using concepts such as strict and vicarious liability when deemed necessary to reach criminal policy goals. In such jurisdictions, the borderline between civil and criminal liability is typically blurred, and criminal sanctions are freely used in order to reinforce 'civil' or administrative duties. When criminal liability is just one of several tools to enforce compliance with state regulations or adherence to certain standards of care, then corporate criminal liability is perfectly compatible with that general concept of criminal law.

In the continental tradition, by contrast, criminal responsibility has been kept strictly apart from 'mere' civil or administrative liability, distinguished by the moral reprobation exclusively associated with criminal punishment. Corporate criminal responsibility, as we have seen, does not easily fit into such a system because corporations are not moral agents. A certain amount of de-moralization of the criminal law is thus a prerequisite for adoption of corporate criminal responsibility; and routinely imposing criminal sanctions on legal persons would further increase the tendency toward using the criminal law as a utilitarian tool of bringing about compliance. In 'traditional' jurisdictions, the introduction of corporate criminal responsibility and the accompanying transformation of the concept of guilt might even have repercussions on the requirements for holding natural persons criminally liable. If corporations can be criminally punished on the basis of vaguely termed attribution of someone else's wrongful behaviour or of 'defective self-organization', why should those same loose standards not be sufficient to justify criminal punishment of individuals?

What is at stake, eventually, is the 'otherness, the specific character of criminal responsibility. Corporate criminal responsibility is not a problem if we are willing to employ criminal law as one of several means to make people (including corporations) obey the law. It remains an alien concept, however, in a system where criminal responsibility presupposes moral fault and where criminal punishment differs qualitatively from other forms of state intervention by visiting moral reprobation on the offender. Although there seems to exist a strong worldwide trend toward a utilitarian, functional approach, I would take a deep breath before abandoning the special character of criminal law. In our haste to respond to all kinds of undesirable behaviour by imposing criminal sanctions, we may contribute to an inflation of criminal law that may eventually make it ineffectual. My plea therefore is for tolerance: those system that are comfortable with corporate criminal responsibility, use it; but do not force it on those who choose to adhere to a different concept of criminal law that genuinely applies only to individuals.

## *Notes and Questions*

1. For most of the twentieth century, the vast majority of civil law jurisdictions did not impose criminal liability on corporations. Nevertheless, the recent trend is to expand the scope of criminal liability to allow for the punishment of corporate actors. Some countries in Europe and Latin America have, however, have resisted this trend. The most prominent example is Germany. Although Germany does not currently impose criminal liability on corporations, it does provide for the imposition of administrative sanctions on corporate actors. Sometimes corporations that are liable to administrative sanctions are ordered to pay fines of up to one million Euros. Assuming that German corporations may be ordered to pay administrative fines that are equivalent in amount to the fines that American corporations may be ordered to pay as a result of criminal punishment, does it matter that German law calls the fines "administrative sanctions" and American law calls them "criminal punishment"? Why or why not?

2. Professor Weigend believes that the defining feature of criminal punishment is that it expresses moral condemnation. Such moral condemnation is warranted when a being that is capable of self-determination (autonomy) freely chooses to violate legal norms. Punishment is society's way of reacting to the freely willed violation of legal norms. With its imposition, society rejects the offender's action and expresses moral condemnation

for the criminal conduct. Weigend argues that punishing corporations is objectionable because corporations are fictitious entities that are not capable of acting or behaving culpably. While it may make metaphorical sense to say that corporations act, the real actors are the human beings who are charged with making corporate decisions. Therefore, punishment should be imposed on the actors who conduct business on behalf of the corporation rather than on the corporation itself. Do you agree with Weigend's arguments? Explain.

3. More fundamentally, Weigend contends that corporations are not "moral agents" because they lack the capacity for self-determination and autonomy. Since corporations do not have the capacity to act "morally" or "immorally," Weigend suggests that it does not make much sense to punish them. Given that punishment is meant to express moral condemnation, it is pointless to direct such condemnation at business entities that do not have the capacity to behave morally or immorally. Instead, punishment should, once again, be directed at the persons who are capable of autonomy and, therefore, of behaving morally or immorally—the agents of the corporation. Do you agree? Why or why not?

4. Professor Weigend points out that those who view the criminal law as a consequentialist (utilitarian) instrument for producing good consequences will have no trouble justifying the imposition of corporate criminal liability. What does Professor Weigend mean by this? Do you agree? Why or why not?

## § 13.04 Corporate Criminal Liability: Scholarly Debates

### Albert Alschuler, *Two Ways to Think about the Punishment of Corporations*

46 Am. Crim. L. Rev. 453 (2009)

V. Two Conceptions of Corporate Criminal Liability

Misguided though it is, corporate criminal liability is probably here to stay. Much to my regret, we cannot return to the eighteenth century. The question in the twenty-first century is how best to conceptualize this practice. There are two alternatives, which we can call deodand and frankpledge.

A. The Corporation as Deodand

[Editor's Note: Deodand was the practice of punishing animals or objects that have caused harm.]

People indignant about an injury produced by a corporation's employees may treat the corporation as deodand. They may truly personify and hate the corporation. They may hate the mahogany paneling, the Lear jet, the smokestack, the glass tower, and all of the people inside. They—the mahogany and all of them—are responsible for the medical fraud, the oil spill, the price fixing, and the illegal campaign contributions. To superstitious people, villains need not breathe. They may include Exxon, Warner Lambert, and the cable company.

Scholars have advanced refined variations of the deodand position. Dan Kahan declares, "Punishing corporations ... is understood to be the right way for society to repudiate the false valuations that their crimes express. Criminal liability 'sends the message' that people matter more than profits." Endorsing a similar "expressive retributivist" position, Peter Henning observes, "The label 'criminal' has social significance aside from the particular punishment imposed on the offender."

The punishment of corporations can indeed be expressive, and so can the punishment of other things. I myself have repudiated false valuations by punishing my computer. When a family member or colleague has discovered my discipline of the machine, however, I have usually been embarrassed. Expressing one's values by smashing a computer can be therapeutic, but it is not recommended for children or for grownups.

Henning, moreover, is correct that the label "criminal" has a special social significance. He is not alone in arguing that corporate punishment is appropriate because it can stigmatize an entity and affect its reputation in ways that civil liability cannot. The word "criminal" has its distinctive significance, however, because this word means blameworthy. Someone who applies this word to objects and entities that are not blameworthy uses the label falsely. The desired social stigmatization may not materialize, and if it does, it occurs only because, once the label is applied, some members of the public associate blameless things with real criminals. You can fool some of the people all of the time, and that may be enough.

In an essay titled *In Defense of Corporate Criminal Liability*, Lawrence Friedman defends a position like that of Kahan and Henning. He recognizes that from a deterrent or "economic" perspective, "criminal liability fares poorly as compared to civil liability." He also recognizes that, because a corporation has no mind, it cannot be an appropriate target of "pure Kantian retribution." Friedman nevertheless contends that expressive retributivism justifies corporate punishment. "The expressive retributivist's commitment is 'to assert[] moral truth in the face of its denial.'"

Friedman argues that punishing corporations differs from punishing mahogany in two ways. First, echoing a theme of Pamela Bucy, he observes that a corporation has an "identifiable persona" or "ethos" distinct from the personalities of the people who work for it, and second, he notes that a corporation can express itself. The Supreme Court held in *First National Bank of Boston v. Bellotti* that corporations have a constitutional right to speak.

The Supreme Court's argument in *Bellotti*, however, was that the act of incorporation should not cause people to lose a right they would otherwise possess—the right to speak as a group. Imagine, then, an *unincorporated* group with an identifiable persona distinct from those of its members and one that can express itself—a barbershop quartet. Imagine in addition that, without any knowledge on the part of the tenor, bass or baritone, the lead singer of this group has bribed the judge of a music contest, stolen four plaid sports coats, and poisoned the lead singer of a rival quartet. Would Friedman express his commitment to moral truth by convicting and punishing the entire quartet? If not, would the group's incorporation change the outcome?

Or consider another body with a persona distinct from those of its members that speaks as an entity—the Justice Department's Office of Legal Counsel. The release of "torture memos" written by several lawyers of this Office during the administration of President George W. Bush has prompted discussion of whether the lawyers should be prosecuted. The Obama administration's Justice Department has seemed reluctant to proceed. Its willingness to let bygones be bygones appears to be influenced by the political distraction a trial would cause.

No one appears to have considered a less *ad hominem* way of resolving the controversy—exempting the lawyers from prosecution while authorizing a trial of the Office of Legal Counsel itself. If this office were found guilty, it (or perhaps the entire Justice Department) could be placed on probation and required to implement a compliance program, or the Office might enter a deferred prosecution agreement and allow a monitor to review its compliance efforts ...

### B. The Corporation as Frankpledge

[Editor's Note: Frankpledge was the practice of punishing all members of a group when one member of the group has avoided apprehension for a crime.]

Most defenders of corporate criminal liability view it as frankpledge. They justify the punishment of corporations on the ground that innocent managers, anxious to avoid the punishment of innocent shareholders, will act as patrol officers. Everyone will police everyone else and will have appropriate incentives to create a law-observant corporate culture. With the Thompson memorandum, moreover, the parallel to frankpledge becomes sharper still. The group can avoid punishment by delivering the individual wrongdoer to the authorities. Echoing the Norman Kings of England, the Justice Department's Manual for United States Attorneys declares, "Indicting corporations for wrongdoing enables the government to be a force for positive change of corporate culture, and a force to prevent, discover, and punish serious crimes." ...

Our own criminal justice system frequently presses offenders to aid in the apprehension and prosecution of other offenders. Ordinarily, however, it does not create crimes and threaten the innocent simply to gain their cooperation. Our justice system does not, for example, declare a drug dealer's family, friends, and roommates guilty of his crimes simply because declaring them criminals would strongly encourage their cooperation. Even if careful economic analysis could show the imposition of this vicarious liability cost-effective, it would cause most non-economists to gag.

Moreover, as Jennifer Arlen has noted, corporate criminal liability can backfire. It can prompt managers to do less policing than they would if their firms faced only civil liability, for internal policing may produce information that will lead to a firm's indictment and conviction. Consider, for example, the advice a lawyer might give a brokerage firm that is considering whether to tape-record its brokers' calls: "To the extent the proposed recordings deter brokers from committing fraud, they will reduce the firm's potential criminal liability. But if the deterrence is imperfect, some tapes may contain evidence of fraud. These tapes will be subject to subpoena, and when the government obtains them, it may use them to indict the firm and perhaps put it out of business."

I do not think highly of the institution of frankpledge, but it seems less silly than hating an artificial person. Holding the members of a group responsible for the other members' crimes is not as strange as imagining that a legal fiction deserves punishment.

## VI. Some Implications of the Competing Views

This section considers where the "deodand" and "frankpledge" views of corporate criminal liability would take the law. Neither perspective justifies the federal courts' current standard of corporate liability, but the differing perspectives point to differing reforms....

### A. The *Respondeat Superior* Standard of Corporate Liability

Neither the "deodand" view of corporate criminal liability nor the "frankpledge" view justifies the *respondeat superior* standard now employed in the federal courts to determine a corporation's criminal guilt.

#### 1. The Deodand View

A corporation's "ethos" or "persona"—the essence alleged to justify its punishment for "expressive retributive" reasons—is not established by the wrongful act of a single employee, and the isolated wrongful act of a "high managerial agent" may not manifest a corporation's "personality" either. Even the "rude Kukis of Southern Asia," who allegedly punished trees for fatal falls, might have had difficulty hating an otherwise virtuous corporation with tens of thousands of employees whenever one employee did something wrong.

Blaming an entity apparently demands an atmospheric assessment of the entity's *spirit*, and Pamela Bucy has proposed that juries make this assessment. She advocates what she calls "the corporate ethos standard" and says that this standard "directs criminal liability toward only those corporations which are 'deserving' of prosecution as demonstrated by their lawless ethos."

Bucy elaborates:

> To ascertain the ethos of a corporation, and to determine if this ethos encouraged the criminal conduct at issue, the factfinder should examine: the corporate hierarchy, the corporate goals and policies, the corporation's historical treatment of prior offenses, the corporation's efforts to educate and monitor employees' compliance with the law, and the corporation's compensation scheme, especially its policy on indemnification of corporate employees.

Bucy would ask juries to consider whether a corporation's board did its job or instead operated as a figurehead, whether corporate goals were "so unrealistic that they encourage[d] illegal behavior," whether employees were "required to sign a statement each year indicating that they are familiar with pertinent-government regulations *and* indicating that they realize such violations will result in dismissal," whether the corporation had an ombudsman, and more.

A medieval academic similarly might have opposed the indiscriminate punishment of objects that killed people and might have proposed a more careful assessment of each object's ethos. Was an accused wheel well designed? Was it made of the best material? Was it inspected and repaired on a regular basis? Had it previously provided useful service? Had it been involved in prior accidents?

Bucy's proposal provides few standards, invites prosecutors to appeal to the anti-corporate sentiments of some jurors, and probably would yield outcomes based mostly on the jurors' proclivities, the trial lawyers' rhetoric, and how much harm the defendant's agents had caused. The impossibility of translating deodand sentiments into an operational standard of liability reflects the "let's pretend" character of the group-blame concept, and the difficulty of formulating anything other than knee-jerk standards of culpability suggests placing the punishment of organizations on a different basis. The goal of corporate criminal punishment should be instrumental. It should be to induce an appropriate level of monitoring within an organization and nothing else.

### 2. The Frankpledge View

If the goal of group liability is to encourage appropriate monitoring, the issue should be whether the group has monitored appropriately. The Norman inventors of frankpledge, however, did not address this question directly. Instead, they applied a standard of strict liability, presuming a failure to monitor whenever one member of a tithing escaped punishment for a serious crime.

The modern law of corporate criminality similarly employs a strict liability standard, but the modern standard is worse. For one thing, even if the criminal has not escaped, this standard presumes a failure to monitor whenever a member of the group has committed a crime. The group's delivery of the wrongdoer to the authorities may prompt forbearance or leniency, but it does not eradicate the group's responsibility. Moreover, the modern law treats any criminal act by any member of a 10,000-person group as proof of the other members' failure. That position is roughly 1000 times more misguided than treating the wrongful act of any member of a ten-person group as conclusive proof of the other members' default. A teacher who cannot determine which of his students misbehaved may keep an entire class after school, but even the most tyrannical teacher does not detain every student in the school system.

The rule of strict liability arose because people believed that the acts of an agent could be attributed to the agent's principal, and that was that. The rule had no articulated purpose. Courts and legislatures had decided to punish corporations, and they saw no other way to do it. The rule of *respondeat superior* never had a reason, and there is no reason to retain it.

When one rejects deodand mythology and recognizes that the goal of corporate punishment is to ensure an appropriate level of internal policing, the appropriate principle of liability becomes clear. Whether a criminal case against a corporation can be triggered by the criminal act of any employee or only by an act approved or tolerated by a high managerial agent, the defendant should at a minimum be permitted to show as an affirmative defense that it had an appropriate compliance program in place prior to this act. When a corporation implements a suitable compliance program, it does what the authors of the law of corporate criminal liability (at least the non-superstitious authors) meant it to do. The government should ask for no more.

Strict *respondeat superior* liability gives managers an incentive to establish effective compliance programs, but an affirmative defense of due care or appropriate monitoring would give them a stronger incentive. The expected benefits of compliance programs are greater when they can lead to a defense than when they cannot. Contrary to common intuition, strict liability probably weakens rather than strengthens the deterrent force of the criminal law ...

Rewarding firms for establishing compliance programs encourages them to establish compliance programs. In addition, the proposed affirmative defense removes the incentive *not* to monitor that strict *respondeat superior* liability sometimes creates. A firm need not fear that an appropriate compliance program would produce incriminating information that the government could use to destroy it.

The United States Attorneys' Manual lists "the existence and effectiveness of the corporation's pre-existing compliance program" as one of nine factors to be considered in determining whether to file charges. These factors are described as "additional" to "the factors normally considered in the sound exercise of prosecutorial judgment: the sufficiency of the evidence; the likelihood of success at trial; the probable deterrent, rehabilitative, and other consequences of conviction; and the adequacy of noncriminal charges." The listed factors "are intended to be illustrative" rather than "exhaustive," and "the existence of a compliance program is not sufficient, in and of itself, to justify not charging a corporation for criminal misconduct undertaken by its officers, directors, employees, or agents."

## Sara Sun Beale, *A Response to the Critics of Corporate Criminal Liability*

46 Am. Crim. L. Rev. 1481 (2009)

### I. Corporations Are Real

A good deal of scholarship begins from the premise that corporations are fictional entities, which have no existence apart from the various individuals who act on behalf of the fictitious entity. This premise can lead quickly to the conclusion that corporate liability is unjust because it effectively punishes innocent third parties (shareholders, employees, and so forth) for the acts of individuals who commit offenses while in the employ of these fictional entities. What this account misses is the reality that corporations are not fictions. Rather, they are enormously powerful, and very real, actors whose conduct often causes very significant harm both to individuals and to society as a whole. In a variety of contexts, the law recognizes this reality by allowing corporations to own property, make contracts, commit torts, and to sue and be sued. Indeed, the Supreme Court has held that corporations have many constitutional rights under the U.S. constitution.

Moreover, the power now wielded by corporations is both enormous and unprecedented in human history. It misses a lot to compare corporations like Exxon Mobil, Microsoft, or AIG to a horse or a cart that was treated as a deodand under ancient English law. The wealth of the top Fortune 500 corporations is one measure of corporate power. In 2008, annual revenues from the top ten revenue-producing corporations in the U.S. were more than $2.1 trillion; the profits from the ten most profitable U.S. corporations were more than $176 billion. Exxon Mobil topped both lists, recording almost $445 billion in revenue and over $45 billion in profit. Corporations also wield power more directly via their lobbying efforts. Since 1998 Exxon Mobil has spent over $120 million on lobbying, including $29 million in 2009. The U.S. Chamber of Commerce has spent over $477 million since 1998, more than twice the amount of any other corporation or industry group. Other industry groups, like the Pharmaceutical Research and Manufacturers of America, spent hundreds of millions of dollars in the last ten years to lobby on behalf of multiple corporations.

Modern corporations not only wield virtually unprecedented power, but they do so in a fashion that often causes serious harm to both individuals and to society as a whole. In some recent cases, corporate misconduct and malfeasance destabilized the stock market and led to the loss of billions in shareholder equity and the loss of tens (or perhaps even hundreds) of thousands of jobs. Enron was the seventh-most valuable company in the U.S., until the revelation of its use of deceptive accounting devices to shift debt off its books and hide corporate losses led to losses of more than $100 billion in shareholder equity before it filed for bankruptcy. But Enron was not alone in the use of fraudulent accounting practices. The revelation of similar misconduct by other corporations (including Dynergy, Adelphia Communications, WorldCom, and Global Crossing) also led to massive losses. Federal prosecutors have also uncovered widespread wrongdoing in other industries, though the nature of the violations has varied over time. In the past decade, virtually every major pharmaceutical company has pled guilty to or settled charges arising out of serious misconduct. In the previous decade, the 1990s, the most prominent cases concerned antitrust violations. The largest single fine imposed was $500 million for a worldwide scheme to fix the price of vitamins, and fines from the nine most serious antitrust cases of the decade totaled $1.2 billion.

Because of their size, complexity, and control of vast resources, corporations have the ability to engage in misconduct that dwarfs that which could be accomplished by individuals. For example, Siemens, the German engineering giant, paid more than $1.4 billion in bribes to government officials in Asia, Africa, Europe, the Middle East, and Latin America, using its slush funds to secure public works contracts around the world. There is nothing wrong with recognizing that it was Siemens, not simply some of its officers or employees, who should be held legally accountable. U.S. investigators found that the use of bribes and kickbacks were not anomalies, but the corporation's standard operating procedure and part of its business strategy. In my view, Siemens was properly prosecuted and convicted.

Professor Alschuler, echoing other classic critiques, argues that the corporation is a mere fiction that cannot be punished, and that it is innocent shareholders who are forced—wrongly—to bear the direct burden of criminal sanctions, and it is innocent employees, creditors, customers, and communities who must bear the *1485* indirect burdens. This argument misses the mark in several respects. First, the entire point of the corporate form is to create a legal entity that is separate from its shareholders (as well as its employees, creditors, and others). Each corporation has its own assets, as well as its own liabilities. The shareholders of Siemens benefitted from its success when it used bribery and kickbacks to obtain contracts that generated billions of dollars of profit. They would have benefitted if the corporation had brought suit to enforce its contractual rights. On the other hand, if Siemens had breached its contracts or committed torts, no one questions that the corporation would have been liable, though the innocent shareholders would have lost equity. Note, however, that the point of the corporate form is that those losses would have affected the shareholders' equity in the corporation, but not their personal assets, even if the corporation's liabilities exceeded its obligations. Why, then, is it surprising that the corporation should be held liable for fines arising from criminal conduct, even though the fines might have affected the value of the shareholder's equity in Siemens? (Or the interests of Siemens' employees or its creditors?)

Moreover, the argument that it is improper to impose criminal fines that effectively punish the innocent shareholders, employees, creditors, and others, proves far too much. These arguments apply equally to punitive damages, and indeed to any money judgment against a corporation, since such a judgment also reduces the shareholders' equity (as well as the corporation's ability to pay its employees and creditors). Is it conceivable that the need to protect innocent shareholders means they may benefit from the corporation's successes, but never suffer the detriment of any error in judgment, misconduct, or malfeasance that might result in a breach of contract, a tort, or a regulatory violation? Note that the civil damages resulting from the most serious misconduct by employees, such as the oil spill caused by the Exxon Valdez and the explosion that left thousands dead at Bhopal, India, may be hundreds of millions of dollars, or more. These damages, of course, can effectively punish shareholders and other third parties. Do criminal penalties really differ in some fundamental way from other damages that are properly imposed upon corporations?

In my view, it is not possible to distinguish in a meaningful way the innocent third parties in corporate cases (the shareholders, employees, creditors, and so forth) from the innocent third parties who are typically affected by the prosecution of individual defendants. Indeed, the innocents typically suffer more, not less, when individuals are prosecuted. As noted above, the corporation is a distinct legal entity, with its own assets that are distinct from the personal assets of the shareholders. The corporation pays its fines, like any other judgment, from those assets. The punishment falls on the entity, though the effect is felt by the shareholders and others. Similarly, when individual defendants are ordered to pay criminal fines, or imprisoned and unable to earn income, the purpose is to punish the defendant, though the effect is to punish those who are dependent, directly or indirectly, upon the defendant. This includes family members who may be part of an economic unit with the defendant, sharing income and owning property jointly or by the entirety, as well as creditors and in some cases employees. Note that the innocent parties harmed by the punishment of individual defendants are often less able to protect their assets than the shareholders, who have no liability beyond their investment in the shares of the corporation....

Conclusion

The power and the corresponding scale of the wrongs that can be committed by modern corporations are unprecedented. For that reason, it is important for society to have at its disposal the full range of legal tools, including both regulations intended to prevent harm, as well as civil and criminal remedies. Corporate criminal liability is not a unique and anachronistic feature of U.S. law.

## *Notes and Questions*

1. Clearly, Professor Alschuler is no friend of corporate criminal liability. He argues that punishing corporations is equivalent either to punishing an inanimate object (deodand) or to punishing innocent third parties (frankpledge). He argues that both practices are indefensible. The first—punishing an inanimate object—is childish and superstitious. The second—punishing innocent third parties—is unfair. Since punishing corporations does one of these two things, the practice ought to be abandoned. Do you agree with Professor Alschuler's critique of corporate criminal liability? Explain.

2. Alschuler discusses Professor Pamela Bucy's view that corporations have a "corporate ethos" or "personality" that is distinct from the personalities of its employees and shareholders. Do you agree with Professor Bucy that corporations sometimes develop their own corporate ethos or personality and that such corporate personality may take a life of its own that is quite distinct from the personality of its employees and shareholders? Why or why not? Can you name corporations that are generally believed to have a distinctive corporate ethos that transcends the personality of its staff and shareholders?

3. Professor Bucy argues that it is fair to punish corporations when the crimes committed by its employees are a product of a "corporate ethos" or "personality" that is "lawless." When the crimes committed by employees reflect the perverse or flawed corporate ethos of the corporation, punishing the corporation expresses moral condemnation of the corporate ethos. Bucy argues that this way of describing corporate criminal liability is both accurate and morally appealing. Do you find Professor Bucy's account of corporate criminal liability attractive? Explain.

4. Professor Alschuler takes issue with Bucy's defense of corporate criminal liability contending, in essence, that this view merely reflects a more sophisticated—but ultimately unpersuasive—defense of the deodand. That is, a defense of punishing inanimate objects for the harms caused by those who use the object. Ultimately, there is no autonomous corporate ethos. So-called corporate ethos can always be traced back to human conduct and decisions. If there is something wrong or lawless about a particular corporate ethos, this is not the corporation's fault. After all, the corporation is—like a rock or a wheel—an inanimate object that is not capable of anything by itself. In much the same way that it only makes sense to hold the humans who set the rock or wheel in motion liable for the harms caused by the items, it is the humans who were in charged of making decisions that eventually developed into a particular "lawless corporate ethos" that should be held liable for the harms caused by the corporation. Do you find Alschuler's critique of Professor Bucy's "corporate ethos" account of corporate criminal liability convincing? Why or why not?

5. Although Professor Alschuler takes issue with the view that corporations have a personality that is truly different from that of the human actors that run it and fund it, he thinks it is more coherent to think of corporate criminal liability as a way of punishing innocent employees and shareholders for the crimes committed by guilty employees. Pun-

ishing these innocent actors provides incentives for the employees to put compliance programs in place to prevent criminal conduct. Professor Alschuler believes that this instrumental view of corporate criminal liability is coherent and, perhaps, economically/socially efficient. Nevertheless, he argues that it is unfair and that it probably shouldn't even count as true punishment, for it "punishes" people although they have not engaged in conduct that violates legal rules. Do you agree? Explain.

6. Professor Sara Sun Beale believes that Alschuler's equation of punishing corporations with punishing wheels or rocks is profoundly misleading. Corporations can do many things that wheels, rocks and mahogany cannot do. They can buy and sell property, make campaign contributions and exercise First Amendment free speech rights. Therefore, equating corporations with wheels, rocks or other inanimate objects fundamentally misunderstands the nature and role of corporations in contemporary society. Do you agree that drawing analogies between punishing corporations and punishing rocks or wheels—as Alschuler does—is unenlightening?

7. Sun Beale argues that once the power that corporations exercise in our communities is fully understood, it should naturally follow that corporations ought to be held criminally liable for the harms that they cause. If corporations have the privilege of being considered "persons" for the purposes of the First Amendment's right to freedom of speech, they should also be considered "persons" for the purposes of the criminal law's rules regarding perpetration and complicity. Furthermore, Professor Sun Beale contends that if shareholders and employees reap the benefits of corporate acts that they did not participate in, they should also pay for the misdeeds committed by the corporation even if they did not encourage them. Do you find Professor Sun Beale's arguments in favor of corporate criminal liability convincing? Why or why not?

# Part Four

# The Elements of Punishable Crimes II — Absence of Justification

# Chapter 14

# Lesser Evils

## § 14.01 Necessity: Distinguishing Necessity from Duress

### Hunt v. Florida

District Court of Appeal of Florida, Fifth Circuit, 2000
753 So.2d 609

GRIFFIN, J.

This is another appeal arising out of a series of crimes perpetrated by the defendant, Deidre M. Hunt, through her association with Konstantinos X. Fotopoulos.

In the Summer of 1989, Deidre M. Hunt ["Hunt"], then twenty years old, moved to the Daytona Beach area from New Hampshire to live with her boyfriend, but the relationship soon ended. Hunt became acquainted with Lori Henderson ["Henderson"] and Tony Calderoni. After a brief sexual relationship, Tony Calderoni rented Hunt an apartment and provided her a job at "Top Shots," a pool hall he managed for the owner, Konstantinos X. Fotopoulos ["Fotopoulos"]. Soon thereafter, Hunt began an affair with Fotopoulos, who in turn rented her an apartment, gave her money, and bought her clothes.

Fotopoulos was married to Lisa Fotopoulos, and lived with Lisa, her mother, and brother, in her mother's home. Lisa owned a business on the boardwalk in Daytona Beach called "Joyland Amusement Center." Sometime towards the end of October 1989, Lisa learned of Fotopoulos' affair with Hunt and she demanded that Fotopoulos fire Hunt from Top Shots. When he denied the affair, she announced her plan to file for divorce.

On November 1, 1989, while working at Joyland, Lisa was attacked by a man later identified as Teja James. James pointed a gun at Lisa and told her he would shoot her if she did not heed his command. Lisa, however, managed to escape and notified the police. Lisa identified James' photograph and the search began for his capture.

Four days later, Lisa awoke to a loud noise. All she could remember was seeing Fotopoulos with a gun in his hand and a young man, later identified as Bryan Chase, lying shot at the foot of her bed with his finger on the trigger of a gun. Fotopoulos had shot Chase several times after shooting Lisa in the head.

The police responded to the scene and initially classified the crime as a home invasion gone wrong and a self-defense shooting by Fotopoulos. The police soon became suspicious, however, that the incident was somehow related to the events at Joyland. As part of their investigation, the police contacted Hunt and Henderson. While at the police station, Hunt confessed to her involvement during an audio-taped interview.

She informed them of the extent of Fotopoulos' criminal activity, including counterfeiting, stealing cars and bank robberies. Hunt further told the police that Fotopoulos was a "trained assassin," had tortured then killed approximately eight people and owned numerous weapons, including assault rifles, guns, and grenades.

Hunt explained that the elaborate plans to kill Lisa had begun with another murder, that of Kevin Ramsey ["Ramsey"] a month earlier. Ramsey was a former Fotopoulos employee whom Fotopoulos believed was blackmailing him over his counterfeiting enterprise. The police were not aware that Ramsey was missing.

Hunt detailed the events of Ramsey's murder as follows: Fotopoulos, Ramsey and Hunt went out to the woods to an old rifle range. Fotopoulos tied Ramsey to a tree, gave a .22 pistol to Hunt, pointed his AK-47 automatic rifle at her head and demanded she shoot Ramsey. She shot him several times. Hunt informed the police that Fotopoulos videotaped the shooting and still had the tape in his possession. Hunt then guided the police to Ramsey's severely decomposed body....

In the judgment and sentencing order, the lower court made the following findings: The defendant murdered Kevin Ramsey execution-style while his hands were bound behind his back and he was tied to a tree. The evidence at trial showed the defendant murdered Ramsey calmly, after cool reflection, and that the murder of Ramsey was not an act prompted by emotional frenzy, panic, or a fit of rage. The evidence showed the defendant and codefendant Fotopoulos had a prearranged design to murder Ramsey.... The Court finds this is proof beyond a reasonable doubt of heightened premeditation and deliberate ruthlessness.

The court sentenced Hunt on count I of the Indictment for the first-degree murder of Kevin Ramsey to life imprisonment with twenty-five years before the possibility of parole ...

Hunt has raised two related issues on appeal, namely that the lower court erred in refusing to give either of two requested jury instructions directed at her contention that the only reason she killed Kevin Ramsey was that Fotopoulos had a gun pointed at her head and that she killed Ramsey to avoid being killed. The first of these proposed instructions was designed to supplement the standard instruction on premeditation to include the requirement that premeditation be uninfluenced by a dominating passion sufficient to obscure reason. The second was an instruction that necessity is a defense to homicide.

We find no merit to Hunt's claim that she was entitled to a "necessity" instruction. We agree with the State that the necessity defense does not apply in this case; rather the facts support a claim of duress [which at common law is not a defense to homicide]. The Supreme Court described the difference in *United States v. Bailey*:

> Common law historically distinguished between the defenses of duress and necessity. Duress was said to excuse criminal conduct where the actor was under an unlawful threat of imminent death or serious bodily injury, which threat caused the actor to engage in conduct violating the literal terms of the criminal law. While the defense of duress covered the situation where the coercion had its source in the actions of other human beings, the defense of necessity, or choice of evils, traditionally covered the situation where physical forces beyond the actor's control rendered illegal conduct the lesser of two evils. Thus, where A destroyed a dike because B threatened to kill him if he did not, A would argue that he acted under duress, whereas if A destroyed the dike in order to protect more valuable property from flooding, A could claim a defense of necessity....

Affirmed.

## *Notes and Questions*

1. As the court points out in Hunt, the defense of "necessity" — also known as "choice of evils" or "lesser evils" — is traditionally distinguished from the defense of duress. While both necessity and duress apply when the actor causes harm in order to avoid harm to herself or others, necessity traditionally applies when the harm that threatens the actor originates in natural causes. In contrast, the defense of duress typically applies when the threatened harm results as a consequence of human conduct. Given that the purported harm faced by the defendant in *Hunt* originated in the threats made by Fotopoulus, the court held that the appropriate defense was duress rather than necessity.

2. Another important difference between necessity and duress is that necessity is usually considered a justification, whereas duress is often described as an excuse. As a result, an actor that is justified pursuant to necessity does not engage in wrongful conduct. That is, his conduct is — all things being considered — a permissible thing to do under the circumstances. A classic example of conduct that is justified pursuant to necessity is that of an actor who breaks the window of a car belonging to another in order to save a child who is suffocating inside the vehicle. Given that the harm prevented by the conduct (death of the child) outweighs the evil caused by the conduct (harm to the vehicle), breaking the window is justified and, therefore, not wrongful. On the other hand, an actor that is excused pursuant to the duress defense engages in wrongful conduct that is nevertheless not punishable. Although such conduct is not lawful, the excused actor is nevertheless exonerated because he cannot be fairly expected to conform his conduct to the mandates of law. This is the case, for example, of an actor who is told that she will be killed if she refuses to rob a bank. If the actor robs the bank in order to avoid being killed, her conduct remains wrongful but is nevertheless excused because a person of reasonable moral firmness would have likely done the same thing under the circumstances.

3. Why does American law generally refuse to justify conduct pursuant to the necessity defense when the threatened harm originates in the conduct of a human being? Suppose that the curator at the Museum of Modern Art is told by a group of thugs that a bomb will be detonated inside the building if she does not help them steal a famous Picasso from the museum. Assuming that the threat is credible and that dozens of people would die if the bomb is detonated, should the curator be justified or excused if she helps the thugs steal the painting in order to avoid the deaths of many innocent human beings? Explain. Note that the conventional approach to the necessity/duress distinction would lead to the conclusion that stealing the painting in order to save dozens of lives should be excused pursuant to the duress defense, for the source of the threat is human conduct. Do you agree with this conclusion, or should stealing the painting in these circumstances be justified pursuant to the necessity defense regardless of whether the threat originates in human conduct? Why?

## § 14.02 Necessity: Triggering Conditions — The Imminence of the Threat

### Commonwealth v. Leno

Supreme Judicial Court of Massachusetts, 1993
415 Mass. 835

ABRAMS, Justice.

Massachusetts is one of ten States that prohibit distribution of hypodermic needles without a prescription. In the face of those statutes the defendants operated a needle exchange program in an effort to combat the spread of acquired immunodeficiency syndrome (AIDS). As a result, the defendants were charged with and convicted of (1) unauthorized possession of instruments to administer controlled substances, and (2) unlawful distribution of an instrument to administer controlled substances. On appeal, the defendants challenge the judge's refusal to instruct the jury on the defense of necessity. We allowed the defendants' application for direct appellate review. We affirm.

We set forth the relevant facts. In June, 1991, the defendants were arrested and charged with sixty-five counts of unauthorized possession of hypodermic needles and fifty-two counts of unauthorized possession of syringes. Each defendant also was charged with one count of distributing an instrument for the administration of a controlled substance. The defendants told the police they were exchanging clean syringes and needles for dirty, possibly contaminated, ones to prevent the spread of AIDS.

Defendant Leno is a fifty-five year old grandfather, who had been addicted to alcohol, cocaine, heroin, or various pills from age twelve to forty-five. At the time of trial, he was in his tenth year of recovery from addiction; his health insurance covered his treatment. Leno learned of needle exchange programs from a National AIDS Brigade lecturer. Leno worked for needle exchange programs in Boston, in New Haven, Connecticut, and in New York City. Leno started a needle exchange program in Lynn in September, 1990, after realizing that "in my own back yard ... people were dying of AIDS ... and this particular service was not offered to them." Leno testified that he believed that by providing clean needles to addicts he was helping to stem the spread of AIDS, he was helping addicts, especially the homeless, to reach recovery, and that he was not helping addicts continue their habit.

Defendant Robert Ingalls said that he is fifty-three years old and works as a landscaper. He joined Leno in operating a needle exchange program in Lynn as a matter of conscience: "I would have had a hard time with my conscience if I didn't do it without good reason. I [knew] people were dying of AIDS ... and when [Leno] told me what he was doing, I thought well, maybe, you could save a few lives.... [I]t's sort of an irresistible opportunity for me, if you can save a life."

The two defendants legally purchased new sterile needles over-the-counter in Vermont. The defendants were at a specific location on Union Street in Lynn from 5 P.M. to 7 P.M. every Wednesday evening in 1991 until they were arrested June 19. They accepted dirty needles in exchange for clean needles; they exchanged between 150 and 200 needles each night, for fifty to sixty people. The defendants did not charge for the service or for the materials.

The defendants offered expert testimony on AIDS and needle exchange programs. Doctor Ernest Drucker of the Montefiore Medical Center in the Bronx, who is also a professor of epidemiology at Einstein College of Medicine and an authority on the treatment of drug users and the relationship between intravenous drug use and AIDS, stated that: the sharing of needles by infected drug users transmits the AIDS virus; the mortality rate of persons diagnosed with human immunodeficiency virus (HIV) ten years ago is very high, in that fewer than five per cent still are alive; there is no cure for AIDS; studies of needle exchange programs revealed no evidence that such programs cause people who are not drug addicts to become addicts, but that evidence indicates that needle exchange programs bring some addicts into drug and AIDS treatment programs who would not otherwise be there; he could not think of any harmful effects caused by needle exchange programs, and no studies found harmful effects; needle exchange programs save lives; and AIDS accounts for three times as many deaths as all other drug-related causes, such as overdosing, combined.

Elaine O'Keefe, director of the AIDS Division of the New Haven (Connecticut) health department, which has run a needle exchange program for several years, said that the program has shown only positive results. She noted that: a Yale University research study found that the program had significantly reduced needle sharing and produced an estimated reduction of 33% in incidence of new infections among program participants; at the beginning of the program about 60% of the needles turned in were contaminated by the HIV virus, but that percentage decreased dramatically over time, leading O'Keefe to conclude that the program had reduced the risk of infection; the needle exchange program is saving the lives of "[d]rug users, sexual partners, mostly women, and children who are born of them."

Kathleen Gallagher, director of the AIDS surveillance program of the Massachusetts Department of Public Health, testified that AIDS is a very serious epidemic in Massachusetts and elsewhere, that the AIDS fatality rate is "essentially 100%," that so far more than 5,000 people in Massachusetts were diagnosed as having AIDS, and that many more are infected by HIV but are still asymptomatic. In 1991, 31% of new AIDS cases were intravenous drug users. When sexual partners and children were included, 38% of AIDS cases were associated with intravenous drug use. Fifty percent of Massachusetts women with AIDS contracted the disease through intravenous drug use.

Brian Condron, research director for the Massachusetts Legislature's joint committee on health care, stated that the Legislature had considered repeal of the prescription requirement and needle exchange legislation for several years, with different branches and committees giving approval of some of the bills at different times. The Legislature had not repealed the prescription requirement by the time of trial.

*Discussion.* The defendants do not deny that they violated the provisions of the statutes restricting the possession and distribution of hypodermic needles; rather, they contend that the judge's refusal to instruct the jury on the defense of necessity was error. We disagree.

"[T]he application of the defense [of necessity] is limited to the following circumstances: (1) the defendant is faced with a clear and imminent danger, not one which is debatable or speculative; (2) the defendant can reasonably expect that his [or her] action will be effective as the direct cause of abating the danger; (3) there is [no] legal alternative which will be effective in abating the danger; and (4) the Legislature has not acted to preclude the defense by a clear and deliberate choice regarding the values at issue." ... We have emphasized that a person asserting the necessity defense must demonstrate that the danger motivating his or her unlawful conduct is imminent, and that he or she acted out of necessity at all times that he or she engaged in the unlawful conduct. The analysis of whether a danger is imminent does not call for a comparison of competing harms. *Commonwealth v. Hutchins*, 410 Mass. 726, 731, 575 N.E.2d 741 (1991) ...

The prevention of possible future harm does not excuse a current systematic violation of the law in anticipation of the eventual over-all benefit to the public.... The defendants did not show that the danger they sought to avoid was clear and imminent, rather than debatable or speculative. The defense of necessity "[does] not deal with nonimminent or debatable harms ... [it is inapplicable when] the hazards are long term, [and] the danger is not imminent." ...

Judgments affirmed.

### *Notes and Questions*

1. Do you think that the needle exchange program established by the defendants in *Leno* likely saved lives? If so, shouldn't distributing the hypodermic needles be justified regardless of whether the harm averted by the program was imminent? Explain.

2. Why is an actor justified pursuant to necessity only if the harm averted by his conduct was imminent? Shouldn't it suffice that the threatened harm was likely to happen regardless of whether it was imminent? Why or why not?

3. Suppose that a person hiking in a remote mountain range hears an official weather report that states that a dangerous storm will impact the area within the next 12 to 15 hours. Thirty minutes later, the hiker finds a cabin that would provide him with shelter and supplies that would likely keep him alive when the storm hits. If he continues to hike, he may or may not find similar shelter. If he does not find similar shelter, he will likely die when the storm impacts the area. Should breaking into the shelter be justified pursuant to the necessity defense? What result if the rule discussed by the Court in *Leno* is applied to the case? Would anything be gained by requiring the hiker to wait until the storm is about to begin before breaking into the shelter? Explain.

## § 14.03 Necessity: Limiting Conditions — The Necessity of Causing Harm

### Stodghill v. State

Supreme Court of Mississippi, 2005
892 So.2d 236

WALLER, Presiding Justice, for the Court.

The Amite County Circuit Court convicted George C. Stodghill of a misdemeanor conviction of first offense driving under the influence of alcohol. The trial court imposed a sentence of forty-eight hours in jail and a $1000 fine, but suspended both due to mitigating circumstances. A divided Court of Appeals reversed the conviction and remanded for further findings and we granted the State's petition for a writ of certiorari. Finding the circuit court's conviction of Stodghill was correct, we reverse the judgment of the Court of Appeals and affirm the judgment of the circuit court.

FACTS

George Stodghill and his girlfriend, Carla Kenny, spent a weekend in a secluded country cabin with his adult son and daughter and their spouses. On the night of June 10, the group held an outdoor barbeque, during which everyone consumed different amounts of alcohol. Stodghill consumed three bourbons before he and Kenny went to bed around 9:30.

Stodghill testified that he awoke from his sleep to discover Kenny staggering around the room. He said she collapsed onto the floor outside their bedroom trembling, sweating, and exhibiting seizure-like symptoms. Hope Armstrong, Stodghill's daughter, called 911 on the cellular phone but was unable to communicate the address of the cabin due to poor reception. After making another 911 call, the operator confirmed the location of the cabin. Armstrong testified,

> [T]hey asked me where I was, and I told them … that I was on Finn Road and asked my father what the address was, and he told me … the McGehee house, and I remember the dispatcher saying it was the yellow house; that it used to be yellow. And my father said "Yes, that's the house."

She testified that they waited "a little while" before her father decided to drive Kenny to the hospital, rather than wait on the ambulance. Despite the fact that Stodghill helped confirm the location to the 911 operator, he testified that he decided to take Kenny to the hospital, because Armstrong had been unable to get through to 911 on the second phone call and he knew the ambulance was not coming.

While Stodghill was on the way to the hospital, State Trooper Scott Clark pulled Stodghill over after he noticed that Stodghill was speeding and crossing the center line. Stodghill's eyes were bloodshot, his breath smelled of alcohol, and when he got out of the car, he staggered as he walked. Clark noticed that Kenny was pale and covered with a blanket. After Clark requested Stodghill to submit to a portable breath test, Stodghill refused and explained that he was taking his sick girlfriend to the hospital. Clark then called an ambulance for Kenny. Soon after the ambulance arrived, Armstrong and her husband drove up to the scene. Clark testified that he did not offer them a sobriety test, because he detected nothing that made him suspect their ability to drive was impaired. He then released Stodghill's car to Armstrong and her husband, and allowed them to go on to the hospital.

After the ambulance arrived, Stodghill agreed to undergo the standard field sobriety tests. After failing the field sobriety tests, Clark arrested Stodghill for driving under the influence. Clark took Stodghill to the sheriff's department where he refused to submit to an Intoxilyzer 5000 breath test.

Stodghill elected to proceed to trial and defended upon the ground of necessity. The trial court found Stodghill guilty and imposed a sentence of forty-eight hours in jail and a $1000 fine but suspended both due to the mitigating circumstances. At a hearing on a Motion for New Trial, the court further explained it found necessity an inadequate defense, because Stodghill had failed to exhaust all possible alternatives before driving a vehicle after consuming alcohol. The Court of Appeals reversed and remanded the case for further fact-finding by the trial court.

## ANALYSIS

The State petitioned for writ of certiorari, requesting that we reverse the Court of Appeals' decision. The State argues that because Stodghill ignored other alternatives to driving drunk, the trial court correctly found that Stodghill could not use the affirmative defense of necessity to avoid conviction. We granted the petition solely on the issue of whether the Court of Appeals erred when it found the trial court's holding was unsupported by the evidence.

In *Knight v. State*, 601 So.2d 403, 405 (Miss.1992), the Court adopted the defense of necessity and held that when a "person reasonably believes that he is in danger of physical harm[,] he may be excused for some conduct which ordinarily would be criminal." The defense is also available where the defendant reasonably acts out of fear of "imminent danger of death or serious bodily harm" to others. *See McMillan v. City of Jackson,* 701 So.2d 1105, 1106–07 (Miss.1997). To prove that he had an objective need to commit a crime excusable by the defense of necessity, a defendant must prove three essential elements: (1) the act charged was done to prevent a significant evil; (2) there must was no adequate alternative; and (3) the harm caused was not disproportionate to the harm avoided. Factors such as intoxication or abnormality are irrelevant to the inquiry into objective reasonableness "since the 'reasonable man' standard postulates a sane and sober man."

In denying Stodghill's Motion for a New Trial, the trial court stated that because there were adequate alternatives to driving Kenny to the hospital while intoxicated, Stodghill failed to prove the affirmative defense of necessity. The Court of Appeals reversed the trial court, holding that the trial court "never found exactly, or even generally, what alternatives were available and whether or not they were adequate under the circumstances." However, the Court of Appeals failed to cite (and we have not found) any authority requiring a trial court to make an on-the-record justification for judgments in these types of cases. When a defendant attempts to prove an affirmative defense, such as necessity, it is his burden to prove that such circumstances exist so as to substantiate such a defense.

Though the record is scant, it fully supports the trial court's finding that Stodghill had at least one adequate alternative at his disposal the night he chose to drive Kenny to the hospital while under the influence of alcohol. At the cabin, Armstrong and her husband were present when Kenny began exhibiting signs of sickness. Officer Clark testified that at the scene of the arrest, the Armstrongs appeared to be sober, while Stodghill was too impaired to pass the field sobriety tests Clark administered. Clark's testimony demonstrates that, rather than driving while intoxicated, Stodghill could have asked either his daughter or her husband to drive Kenny to the hospital.

In light of the grave danger posed to the public by drunken drivers, we are reluctant to extend the defense of necessity in all but the most exceptional circumstances of driving under the influence of alcohol. We are troubled by the prospect of those who are alcohol-impaired attempting to justify heinous endangerment to the public simply because they are stranded and have created their own emergency by way of irresponsible drinking....

There was adequate evidence in the record for the trial court to find Stodghill did not satisfy the elements of the necessity defense. We therefore affirm the trial court's finding that there were reasonable alternatives available to Stodghill other than driving under the influence of alcohol. We reverse the Court of Appeals' judgment and affirm the judgment of the circuit court.

## *Notes and Questions*

1. Was the harm that the defendant was trying to avert (death or serious bodily injury to his girlfriend Kenny) imminent? If so, why did the Court hold that he was not entitled to a necessity defense?

2. Would the defendant have been entitled to a necessity defense if he had asked his daughter and her husband to drive Kenny to the hospital and they had both refused? Explain.

3. As the Supreme Cour of Mississippi explains in *Stodghill,* causing a harm is justified pursuant to necessity only if it is necessary in order to avoid an even greater harm. Causing harm is necessary only if it is the only way of avoiding an even greater injury. That is, inflicting harm is not necessary if the actor could have avoided the threatened harm

by engaging in a less harmful course of action. Or—as the court puts it in *Stodghill*—causing a harm is not necessary if the defendant had other reasonable (and less harmful) alternatives that would have successfully prevented the threatened harm from taking place.

## § 14.04 Necessity: Limiting Conditions—Proportionality

### People v. Unger

Supreme Court of Illinois, 1977
66 Ill.2d 333

RYAN, Justice.

Defendant, Francis Unger, was charged with the crime of escape, and was convicted following a jury trial before the circuit court of Will County. Defendant was sentenced to a term of three to nine years to be served consecutively to the remainder of the sentence for which he was imprisoned at the time of the escape. The conviction was reversed upon appeal and the cause was remanded for a new trial over the dissent of one justice. We granted leave to appeal and now affirm the judgment of the appellate court.

At the time of the present offense, the defendant was confined at the Illinois State Penitentiary in Joliet, Illinois. Defendant was serving a one- to three-year term as a consequence of a conviction for auto theft in Ogle County. Defendant began serving this sentence in December of 1971. On February 23, 1972, the defendant was transferred to the prison's minimum security, honor farm. It is undisputed that on March 7, 1972, the defendant walked off the honor farm. Defendant was apprehended two days later in a motel room in St. Charles, Illinois.

At trial, defendant testified that prior to his transfer to the honor farm he had been threatened by a fellow inmate. This inmate allegedly brandished a six-inch knife in an attempt to force defendant to engage in homosexual activities. Defendant was 22 years old and weighed approximately 155 pounds. He testified that he did not report the incident to the proper authorities due to fear of retaliation. Defendant also testified that he is not a particularly good fighter.

Defendant stated that after his transfer to the honor farm he was assaulted and sexually molested by three inmates, and he named the assailants at trial. The attack allegedly occurred on March 2, 1972, and from that date until his escape defendant received additional threats from inmates he did not know. On March 7, 1972, the date of the escape, defendant testified that he received a call on an institution telephone. Defendant testified that the caller, whose voice he did not recognize, threatened him with death because the caller had heard that defendant had reported the assault to prison authorities. Defendant said that he left the honor farm to save his life and that he planned to return once he found someone who could help him. None of these incidents were reported to the prison officials. As mentioned, defendant was apprehended two days later still dressed in his prison clothes.

The State introduced prior statements made by the defendant which cast some doubt on his true reasons for leaving the prison farm. In these statements, defendant indicated that he was motivated by a desire for publicity concerning the sentence on his original conviction, which he deemed to be unfair, as well as fear of physical abuse and death.

Defendant's first trial for escape resulted in a hung jury. The jury in the second trial returned its verdict after a five-hour deliberation. The following instruction (People's Instruction No. 9) was given by the trial court over defendant's objection.

> 'The reasons, if any, given for the alleged escape are immaterial and not to be considered by you as in any way justifying or excusing, if there were in fact such reasons.'

The appellate court majority found that the giving of People's Instruction No. 9 was reversible error. Two instructions which were tendered by defendant but refused by the trial court are also germane to this appeal. Defendant's instructions Nos. 1 and 3 were predicated upon the affirmative defenses of compulsion and necessity. Defendant's instructions Nos. 1 and 3 read as follows:

> 'It is a defense to the charge made against the Defendant that he left the Honor Farm of the Illinois State Penitentiary by reason of necessity if the accused was without blame in occasioning or developing the situation and reasonably believed such conduct and necessary to avoid a public or private injury greater than the injury which might reasonably result from his own conduct.'
>
> 'It is a defense to the charge made against the Defendant that he acted under the compulsion of threat or menace of the imminent infliction of death or great bodily harm, if he reasonably believed death or great bodily harm would be inflicted upon him if he did not perform the conduct with which he is charged.'

The principal issue in the present appeal is whether it was error for the court to instruct the jury that it must disregard the reasons given for defendant's escape and to conversely refuse to instruct the jury on the statutory defenses of compulsion and necessity. In the appellate court the defendant successfully asserted that the giving of People's Instruction No. 9 was tantamount to directing a verdict against the defendant. The State contends that, under the facts and circumstances of this case, the defenses of compulsion and necessity are, as a matter of law, unavailable to defendant ...

Proper resolution of this appeal requires some preliminary remarks concerning the law of compulsion and necessity as applied to prison escape situations. Traditionally, the courts have been reluctant to permit the defenses of compulsion and necessity to be relied upon by escapees. This reluctance appears to have been primarily grounded upon considerations of public policy. Several recent decisions, however, have recognized the applicability of the compulsion and necessity defenses to prison escapes. In People v. Harmon, the defense of duress was held to apply in a case where the defendant alleged that he escaped in order to avoid repeated homosexual attacks from fellow inmates. In People v. Lovercamp, a limited defense of necessity was held to be available to two defendants whose escapes were allegedly motivated by fear of homosexual attacks.

As illustrated by Harmon and Lovercamp, different courts have reached similar results in escape cases involving sexual abuse, though the question was analyzed under different defense theories. A certain degree of confusion has resulted from the recurring practice on the part of the courts to use the terms 'compulsion' (duress) and 'necessity' interchangeably, though the defenses are theoretically distinct. It has been suggested that the major distinction between the two defenses is that the source of the coercive power in cases of compulsion is from human beings, whereas in situations of necessity the pressure on the defendant arises from the forces of nature. Also, as noted in the dissenting opinion in the appellate court, the defense of compulsion generally requires an impending, imminent threat of great bodily harm together with a demand that the person perform the specific criminal act for which he is eventually charged. Additionally, where the defense of compulsion is successfully asserted the coercing party is guilty of the crime.

It is readily discernible that prison escapes induced by fear of homosexual assaults and accompanying physical reprisals do not conveniently fit within the traditional ambits of either the compulsion or the necessity defense. However, it has been suggested that such cases could best be analyzed in terms of necessity. One commentator has stated that the relevant consideration should be whether the defendant chose the lesser of two evils, in which case the defense of necessity would apply, or whether he was unable to exercise a free choice at all, in which event compulsion would be the appropriate defense.

In our view, the defense of necessity, as defined by our statute, is the appropriate defense in the present case. In a very real sense, the defendant there was not deprived of his free will by the threat of imminent physical harm which, according to the Committee Comments, appears to be the intended interpretation of the defense of compulsion as set out in section 7-11 of the Criminal Code. Rather, if defendant's testimony is believed, he was forced to choose between two admitted evils by the situation which arose from actual and threatened homosexual assaults and fears of reprisal. Though the defense of compulsion would be applicable in the unlikely event that a prisoner was coerced by the threat of imminent physical harm to perform the specific act of escape, no such situation is involved in the present appeal. We, therefore, turn to a consideration of whether the evidence presented by the defendant justified the giving of an instruction on the defense of necessity.

The defendant's testimony was clearly sufficient to raise the affirmative defense of necessity. That defense is defined by statute (Ill.Rev.Stat.1971, ch. 38, par. 7-13):

> 'Conduct which would otherwise be an offense is justifiable by reason of necessity if the accused was without blame in occasioning or developing the situation and reasonably believed such conduct was necessary to avoid a public or private injury greater than the injury which might reasonably result from his own conduct.'

Defendant testified that he was subjected to threats of forced homosexual activity and that, on one occasion, the threatened abuse was carried out. He also testified that he was physically incapable of defending himself and that he feared greater harm would result from a report to the authorities. Defendant further testified that just prior to his escape he was told that he was going to be killed, and that he therefore fled the honor farm in order to save his life. Through the State's evidence cast a doubt upon the defendant's motives for escape and upon the reasonableness of defendant's assertion that such conduct was necessary, the defendant was entitled to have the jury consider the defense on the basis of his testimony. It is clear that defendant introduced some evidence to support the defense of necessity. As previously mentioned, that is sufficient to justify the giving of an appropriate instruction.

The State, however, would have us apply a more stringent test to prison escape situations. The State refers to the Lovercamp decision, where only a limited necessity defense was recognized. In Lovercamp, it was held that the defense of necessity need be submitted to the jury only where five conditions had been met.

Those conditions are:

> '(1) The prisoner is faced with a specific threat of death, forcible sexual attack or substantial bodily injury in the immediate future;
>
> (2) There is no time for a complaint to the authorities or there exists a history of futile complaints which make any result from such complaints illusory;

(3) There is no time or opportunity to resort to the courts;

(4) There is no evidence of force or violence used towards prison personnel or other 'innocent' persons in the escape; and

(5) The prisoner immediately reports to the proper authorities when he has attained a position of safety from the immediate threat.'

The State correctly points out that the defendant never informed the authorities of his situation and failed to report immediately after securing a position of safety. Therefore, it is contended that, under the authority of Lovercamp, defendant is not entitled to a necessity instruction. We agree with the State and with the court in Lovercamp that the above conditions are relevant factors to be used in assessing claims of necessity. We cannot say, however, that the existence of each condition is, as a matter of law, necessary to establish a meritorious necessity defense.

The preconditions set forth in Lovercamp are, in our view, matters which go to the weight and credibility of the defendant's testimony. The rule is well settled that a court will not weigh the evidence where the question is whether an instruction is justified. The absence of one or more of the elements listed in Lovercamp would not necessarily mandate a finding that the defendant could not assert the defense of necessity.

By way of example, in the present case defendant did not report to the authorities immediately after securing his safety. In fact, defendant never voluntarily turned himself into the proper officials. However, defendant testified that he intended to return to the prison upon obtaining legal advice from an attorney and claimed that he was attempting to get money from friends to pay for such counsel. Regardless of our opinion as to the believability of defendant's tale, this testimony, if accepted by the jury, would have negated any negative inference which would arise from defendant's failure to report to proper authorities after the escape. The absence of one of the Lovercamp preconditions does not alone disprove the claim of necessity and should not, therefore, automatically preclude an instruction on the defense. We therefore reject the contention that the availability of the necessity defense be expressly conditioned upon the elements set forth in Lovercamp....

Therefore, the judgment of the appellate court is affirmed, and the cause is remanded to the circuit court of Will County for further proceedings in accordance with the views expressed herein.

UNDERWOOD, Justice, dissenting:

My disagreement with my colleagues stems from an uneasy feeling that their unconditional recognition of necessity as a defense to the charge of escape carries with it the seeds of future troubles. Unless narrowly circumscribed, the availability of that defense could encourage potential escapees, disrupt prison discipline, and could even result in injury to prison guards, police or private citizens. For these reasons courts have been quite reluctant to honor the defenses of duress, necessity or compulsion in prison escapes, and, until recent years, they were uniformly held insufficient to justify escapes. As Mr. Justice Stengel noted in his dissenting opinion in the appellate court: "Until (People v. Lovercamp, 43 Cal.App.3d 823, 118 Cal.Rptr. 110 (1974)), no reviewing court had ever upheld a defense of necessity in ordinary adverse situations such as threats from fellow inmates."

Lovercamp, however, imposed well-defined conditions which must be met before a defendant is entitled to have the defense of necessity submitted to the jury ...

I am not totally insensitive to the sometimes brutal and unwholesome problems faced by prison inmates, and the frequency of sexually motivated assaults. Prisoner complaints to unconcerned or understaffed prison administrations may produce little real help to a prisoner or may actually increase the hazard from fellow inmates of whose conduct complaint has been made. Consequently, and until adequate prison personnel and facilities are realities, I agree that a necessity defense should be recognized. The interests of society are better served, however, if the use of that defense in prison-escape cases is confined within well-defined boundaries such as those in Lovercamp. In that form it will be available, but with limitations precluding its wholesale use.

It is undisputed that defendant here did not meet those conditions. He did not complain to the authorities on this occasion even though, following an earlier threat and demand by a fellow inmate that defendant submit to homosexual activity, defendant had requested and been granted a transfer to the minimum security honor farm. Nor did he immediately report to the authorities when he had reached a place of safety. Rather, he stole a truck some nine hours after his escape, drove to Chicago, and later drove to St. Charles, using the telephone to call friends in Canada. This conduct, coupled with his admitted intent to leave in order to gain publicity for what he considered an unfair sentence, severely strain the credibility of his testimony regarding his intention to return to the prison.

Since defendant's conduct does not comply with conditions such as those in Lovercamp which, in my judgment, should be required before a necessity defense may be considered by a jury, I believe the trial court did not err in its instructions.

I would accordingly reverse the appellate court and affirm the judgment of the trial court.

## Commonwealth v. Hutchins

Supreme Judicial Court of Massachusetts, 1991
410 Mass. 726

O'CONNOR, Justice.

The defendant was convicted of drug offenses at a bench trial in the District Court ... In a jury session of the District Court, the charges were first amended to charges of cultivation of THC (a chemical found in marihuana) and of marihuana, and of possession of both substances with intent to distribute. Subsequently, the charges were reduced to simple possession or cultivation of THC and marihuana, and the defendant waived trial by jury.

Before trial, the defendant filed a motion to dismiss the complaints "on the ground that any possession of controlled substances by the [d]efendant is within the [d]efense of [m]edical [n]ecessity." The motion states that counsel "wishes to present a clear record for the reviewing court," and therefore requests the court to "state that it is denying the [d]efendant the right to assert a defense of medical necessity as a matter of law." This, the motion states, would "prevent the [d]efendant from having to call witnesses, many of whom [would be] paid medical experts, from Boston and Washington D.C. in an idle ceremony where such witnesses will not be allowed to testify." After a hearing, a judge complied, and endorsed the motion, "10/24/85 Motion denied. Def[endant] will not be allowed to introduce [evidence] re defense of medical necessity." Following a bench trial, the defendant was convicted of both reduced charges, and appealed. The defendant's sentences were stayed pending appeal. Due to missing transcripts and exhibits, there was a delay of over four years in docketing the case in the Appeals Court. Ultimately, the appeal was docketed, and we transferred the case to this court on our own initiative. We now affirm the convictions.

In support of his motion, as an offer of proof, the defendant submitted affidavits, excerpts from his medical records, literature on a disease known as progressive systemic sclerosis (scleroderma) and on the medicinal uses of marihuana and other materials. Through these materials, the defendant offered to prove the following facts: The defendant is a forty-seven year old man who has been diagnosed as having scleroderma accompanied by Raynaud's phenomenon, related to his service in the Navy. Scleroderma is a chronic disease that results in the buildup of scar tissue throughout the body. The cause of scleroderma is not known and no effective treatment or cure has been discovered. In the most severe cases, scleroderma may result in death. The defendant's medical history includes episodes of fatigue, hypertension, loss of appetite, weight loss of up to twenty-five pounds, diarrhea, nausea, vomiting, reflux of food and stomach acid into the mouth, reduced motility and constriction of the esophagus, extreme difficulty and pain in swallowing, and swollen, painful joints and extreme sensitivity to the cold in his hands and feet. He also suffers from severe depression, related at least in part to his disease, and was briefly hospitalized after attempting suicide. As a result of his illness, the defendant has been unable to work since 1978.

According to the offer of proof, the defendant's medical condition has been unsuccessfully treated with numerous medications and therapies by physicians of the Veterans Administration. The constriction of his esophagus has been treated by dilation and in 1974 was so severe that his treating physician advised him to have his esophagus surgically removed and replaced with a piece of his own intestine. The defendant has informed his treating physicians that since 1975, with some success, he has used marihuana, in lieu of antidepressants and surgery, to alleviate certain symptoms of his illness including nausea, loss of appetite, difficulty in eating, drinking or swallowing, loss of motility of the esophagus, spasticity, hypertension, and anxiety. Two of his treating physicians state that, although they are unable to "confirm [the defendant's] claim that his use of mari[h]uana has caused his remarkable remission, ... it does appear that his use of mari[h]uana does alleviate the previously mentioned symptoms." These two physicians also state that "there appears to be a sufficient basis to conduct a scientific and medical investigation into the possible use of mari[h]uana to treat the disease of scleroderma." A research study of its therapeutic potential and medical uses indicates that the use of marihuana, indeed, may be effective to treat loss of appetite, nausea, vomiting, and weight loss and may relieve severe anxiety and depression. One of the defendant's other treating physicians, however, does not find that marihuana "had any effect in [the defendant's] case" and that he is "unaware of any published or unpublished evidence of [a] beneficial effect of mari[h]uana in this condition." Through correspondence with his physicians, the Veterans Administration, and members of the Massachusetts Legislature and the United States Congress, the defendant has made numerous, albeit unsuccessful, attempts lawfully to obtain either a prescription for marihuana or permission to participate in a research study on the use of marihuana to treat scleroderma. The Massachusetts Legislature has considered a bill providing for the use of marihuana in therapeutic research on more than one occasion, but no such statute has been enacted in the Commonwealth. The Veterans Administration has determined that presently there is no research study on the use of marihuana to treat scleroderma and therefore will not dispense marihuana for the defendant's treatment....

Our question ... is whether, if the defendant were able to prove by admissible evidence at trial the facts contained in the offer of proof, a properly instructed fact finder could determine that the defendant had established the defense which he asserts.

"Under the common law defense of justification by necessity, a crime committed under the pressure of imminent danger may be excused if the harm sought to be avoided far exceeds the harm resulting from the crime committed." "In essence, the 'competing harms' defense exonerates one who commits a crime under the 'pressure of circumstances' if the harm that would have resulted from compliance with the law significantly exceeds the harm actually resulting from the defendant's violation of the law. At its root is an appreciation that there may be circumstances where the value protected by the law is, as a matter of public policy, eclipsed by a superseding value which makes it inappropriate and unjust to apply the usual criminal rule." ...

[T]he first question [in necessity cases is thus] always ... whether the harm that would have resulted from compliance with the law significantly outweighs the harm that reasonably could result from the court's acceptance of necessity as an excuse in the circumstances presented by the particular case....

We mention two illustrative cases. In *Commonwealth v. Thurber,* the defendant was convicted of escape from the Massachusetts Correctional Institution at Concord. At the trial, the defendant presented evidence that he had escaped because his life was in imminent danger at the prison. In discussing the necessity defense, we quoted with approval a statement in a California case of the circumstances in which an escape from prison might be excused, one of the circumstances being that the escape be accomplished without violence, and another being that "[t]he prisoner immediately reports to the proper authorities when he has attained a position of safety from the immediate threat." *People v. Lovercamp*. In *Thurber,* we "[a]ssum[ed] that we would apply the doctrine [of necessity] as a justification for escape in a proper case." The extent of public harm likely to attend a peaceful escape from prison, followed by the prisoner's prompt submission to the authorities, would be minimal compared to the likely harm to the prisoner, as demonstrated by the defendant's evidence in *Thurber,* if he were to comply with the law. Common sense tells us that, in the absence of a clear and specific contrary statutory expression, the court would not frustrate legislative intent in a *Thurber*-type situation by recognizing a necessity defense.

*Commonwealth v. Iglesia,* 403 Mass. 132, 525 N.E.2d 1332 (1988), provides another illustration. There, the defendant was charged with unlawfully carrying a firearm. He testified that he was attacked by a man with a gun, that he wrested the gun from the man, and that he immediately went to the police station with it. Again, as we did in *Commonwealth v. Thurber,* we "assume[d] ... that, when 'a defendant seizes a firearm from one who had expressed an immediate intention to use it, and flees to a place of safe-keeping,' such possession might be lawful." In *Iglesia,* as in *Thurber,* the likely harm to society that would be likely to result from recognition of a necessity defense, carefully limited as to circumstances, would be significantly outweighed by the potential harm to the defendant, if his evidence were to be believed, if he were to comply with the law. It is fair to assume, in the absence of a specifically expressed contrary legislative intent, that judicial recognition of a necessity defense in the circumstances of the *Iglesia* case would not contradict any legislative policy determination.

Accepting the defendant's offer of proof, and assuming, as we do without decision, that the circumstances referred to above as enumerated in *Schuchardt, Hood,* and *Brugmann* obtain, nevertheless we rule that the defendant's proffered evidence does not raise the defense of necessity. In our view, the alleviation of the defendant's medical symptoms, the importance to the defendant of which we do not underestimate, would not clearly and significantly outweigh the potential harm to the public were we to declare that the defendant's cultivation of marihuana and its use for his medicinal purposes may not be punishable. We cannot dismiss the reasonably possible negative impact of such a judicial declaration on the enforcement of our drug laws, including but not limited to those dealing with marihuana, nor can we ignore the government's overriding interest in the regulation of such substances. Excusing the escaped prisoner in the circumstances presented by *Thurber,* or the carrier of a gun in the circumstances of *Iglesia,* is quite different from excusing one who cultivates and uses marihuana in the circumstances of this case.

Judgments affirmed.

**LIACOS, Chief Justice (dissenting, with whom NOLAN, Justice, joins).**

I believe that a jury, not a judge, ordinarily should be allowed to determine whether medical necessity is a defense to a charge of possession or cultivation of marihuana. "The defendant[ ] presented sufficient evidence to raise such a defense. Neither the judge below nor this court should substitute its judgment for the sound deliberation of the jury."

The court today engages in speculative judicial fact finding by concluding that "the alleviation of the defendant's medical symptoms, the importance to the defendant of which we do not underestimate, would not clearly and significantly outweigh the potential harm to the public were we to declare that the defendant's cultivation of marihuana and its use for his medicinal purposes may not be punishable. We cannot dismiss the reasonably possible negative impact of such a judicial declaration on the enforcement of our drug laws, including but not limited to those dealing with marihuana, nor can we ignore the government's overriding interest in the regulation of such substances." While I recognize that the public has a strong interest in the enforcement of drug laws and in the strict regulation of narcotics, I do not believe that the interest would be significantly harmed by permitting a jury to consider whether the defendant cultivated and used marihuana in order to alleviate agonizing and painful symptoms caused by an illness. The court seems to suggest that we should not condone the use of marihuana, regardless of a particular individual's reasons for using the drug. Although the court appears to recognize the defense by taking this position, it fails to give sufficient consideration to the rationale behind the common law defense of necessity. That rationale is based on the recognition that, under very limited circumstances, "the value protected by the law is, as a matter of public policy, eclipsed by a superseding value which makes it inappropriate and unjust to apply the usual criminal rule."

The superseding value in a case such as the present one is the humanitarian and compassionate value in allowing an individual to seek relief from agonizing symptoms caused by a progressive and incurable illness in circumstances which risk no harm to any other individual. In my view, the harm to an individual in having to endure such symptoms may well outweigh society's generalized interest in prohibiting him or her from using the marihuana in such circumstances. On a proper offer of proof I would recognize the availability of a necessity defense when marihuana is used for medical purposes.

To recognize a medical necessity defense based on the use of marihuana for medical purposes would not allow *every* defendant charged with possessing or cultivating marihuana to present such a defense to the jury. Instead, "the application of the defense [would be] limited to the following circumstances: (1) the defendant is faced with a clear and imminent danger, not one which is debatable or speculative; (2) the defendant can reasonably expect that his [or her] action will be effective as the direct cause of abating the danger; (3) there is [no] legal alternative which will be effective in abating the danger; and (4) the Legislature has not acted to preclude the defense by a clear and deliberate choice regarding the values at issue." The defendant's offer of proof satisfied all the elements of a necessity defense. The judge erred in not allowing the defendant to present evidence of medical necessity to a jury of his peers....

I dissent.

## The Queen v. Dudley and Stephens

House of Lords, 1884
14 Queens Bench Division 273

At the trial before Huddleston, B., at the Devon and Cornwall Winter Assizes, November 7, 1884, the jury, at the suggestion of the learned judge, found the facts of the case in a special verdict which stated "that on July 5, 1884, the prisoners, Thomas Dudley and Edward Stephens, with one Brooks, all able-bodied English seamen, and the deceased also an English boy, between seventeen and eighteen years of age, the crew of an English yacht, a registered English vessel, were cast away in a storm on the high seas 1600 miles from the Cape of Good Hope, and were compelled to put into an open boat belonging to the said yacht. That in this boat they had no supply of water and no supply of food, except two 1 lb. tins of turnips, and for three days they had nothing else to subsist upon. That on the fourth day they caught a small [p. 274] turtle, upon which they subsisted for a few days, and this was the only food they had up to the twentieth day when the act now in question was committed. That on the twelfth day the turtle were entirely consumed, and for the next eight days they had nothing to eat. That they had no fresh water, except such rain as they from time to time caught in their oilskin capes. That the boat was drifting on the ocean, and was probably more than 1000 miles away from land. That on the eighteenth day, when they had been seven days without food and five without water, the prisoners spoke to Brooks as to what should be done if no succour came, and suggested that some one should be sacrificed to save the rest, but Brooks dissented, and the boy, to whom they were understood to refer, was not consulted. That on the 24th of July, the day before the act now in question, the prisoner Dudley proposed to Stephens and Brooks that lots should be cast who should be put to death to save the rest, but Brooks refused consent, and it was not put to the boy, and in point of fact there was no drawing of lots. That on that day the prisoners spoke of their having families, and suggested it would be better to kill the boy that their lives should be saved, and Dudley proposed that if there was no vessel in sight by the morrow morning the boy should be killed. That next day, the 25th of July, no vessel appearing, Dudley told Brooks that he had better go and have a sleep, and made signs to Stephens and Brooks that the boy had better be killed. The prisoner Stephens agreed to the act, but Brooks dissented from it. That the boy was then lying at the bottom of the boat quite helpless, and extremely weakened by famine and by drinking sea water, and unable to make any resistance, nor did he ever assent to his being killed. The prisoner Dudley offered a prayer asking forgiveness for them all if either of them should be tempted to commit a rash act, and that their souls might be saved. That Dudley, with the assent of Stephens, went to the boy, and telling him that his time was come, put a knife into his throat and killed him then and there; that the three men fed upon the body and blood of the boy for four days; that on the fourth day after the act had been committed the boat was picked up by a passing vessel, and the prisoners were rescued, still alive, but in the lowest state of prostration. That they were carried to the port of Falmouth, and committed for trial at Exeter. That if the men had not fed upon the body of the boy they would probably not have survived to be so picked up and rescued, but would within the four days have died of famine. That the boy, being in a much weaker condition, was likely to have died before them. That at the time of the act in question there was no sail in sight, nor any reasonable prospect of relief. That under these circumstances there appeared to the prisoners every probability that unless they then fed or very soon fed upon the boy or one of themselves they would die of starvation. That there was no appreciable chance of saving life except by killing some one for the others to eat. That assuming any necessity to kill anybody, there was no greater necessity for killing the boy than any of the other three men. But whether upon the whole matter by the jurors found the killing of Richard Parker by Dudley and Stephens be felony and murder the jurors are ignorant, and pray the advice of the Court thereupon, and if upon the whole matter the Court shall be of opinion that the killing of Richard Parker be felony and murder, then the jurors say that Dudley and Stephens were each guilty of felony and murder as alleged in the indictment." ...

The judgment of the Court (Lord Coleridge, C.J., Grove and Denman, JJ., Pollock and Huddleston, B-B.) was delivered by LORD COLERIDGE, C.J.

The two prisoners, Thomas Dudley and Edwin Stephens, were indicted for the murder of Richard Parker on the high seas on the 25th of July in the present year. They were tried before my Brother Huddleston at Exeter on the 6th of November, and under the direction of my learned Brother, the jury returned a special verdict, the legal effect of which has been argued before us, and on which we are now to pronounce judgment.

The special verdict as, after certain objections by Mr. Collins to which the Attorney General yielded, it is finally settled before us is as follows. (His Lordship read the special verdict as above set out.) From these facts, stated with the cold precision of a special verdict, it appears sufficiently that the prisoners were subject to terrible temptation, to sufferings which might break down the bodily power of the strongest man and try the conscience of the best. Other details yet more harrowing, facts still more loathsome and appalling, were presented to the jury, and are to be found recorded in my learned Brother's notes. But nevertheless this is clear, that the prisoners put to death a weak and unoffending boy upon the chance of preserving their own lives by feeding upon his flesh and blood after he was killed, and with the certainty of depriving him of any possible chance of survival. The verdict finds in terms that "if the men had not fed upon the body of the boy they would probably not have survived," and that, "the boy being in a much weaker condition was likely to have died before them." They might possibly have been picked up next day by a passing ship; they might possibly not have been picked up at all; in either case it is obvious that the killing of the boy would have been an unnecessary and profitless act. It is found by the verdict that the boy was incapable of resistance, and, in fact, made none; and it is not even suggested that his death was due to any violence on his part attempted against, or even so much as feared by, those who killed him. Under these circumstances the jury say that they are ignorant whether those who killed him were guilty of murder, and have referred it to this Court to determine what is the legal consequence which follows from the facts which they have found.

There remains to be considered the real question in the case—whether killing under the circumstances set forth in the verdict be or be not murder. The contention that it could be anything else was, to the minds of us all, both new and strange, and we stopped the Attorney General in his negative argument in order that we might hear what could be said in support of a proposition which appeared to us to be at once dangerous, immoral, and opposed to all legal principle and analogy. All, no doubt, that can be said has been urged before us, and we are now to consider and determine what it amounts to. First it is said that it follows from various definitions of murder in books of authority, which definitions imply, if they do not state, the doctrine, that in order to save your own life you may lawfully take away the life of another, when that other is neither attempting nor threatening yours, nor is guilty of any illegal act whatever towards you or any one else. But if these definitions be looked at they will not be found to sustain this contention....

Now, except for the purpose of testing how far the conservation of a man's own life is in all cases and under all circumstances an absolute, unqualified, and paramount duty, we exclude from our consideration all the incidents of war. We are dealing with a case of private homicide, not one imposed upon men in the service of their Sovereign and in the defence of their country. Now it is admitted that the deliberate killing of this unoffending and unresisting boy was clearly murder, unless the killing can be justified by some well-recognised excuse admitted by the law. It is further admitted that there was in this case no such excuse, unless the killing was justified by what has been called "necessity." But the temptation to the act which existed here was not what the law has ever called necessity. Nor is this to be regretted. Though law and morality are not the same, and many things may be immoral which are not necessarily illegal, yet the absolute divorce of law from morality would be of fatal consequence; and such divorce would follow if the temptation to murder in this case were to be held by law an absolute defence of it. It is not so. To preserve one's life is generally speaking a duty, but it may be the plainest and the highest duty to sacrifice it. War is full of instances in which it is a man's duty not to live, but to die. The duty, in case of shipwreck, of a captain to his crew, of the crew to the passengers, of soldiers to women and children, as in the noble case of the Birkenhead; these duties impose on men the moral necessity, not of the preservations but of the sacrifice of their lives for others, from which in no country, least of all, it is to be hoped, in England, will men ever shrink as indeed, they have not shrunk. It is not correct, therefore, to say that there is any absolute or unqualified necessity to preserve one's life. "Necesse est ut eam, non ut vivam," is a saying of a Roman officer quoted by Lord Bacon himself with high eulogy in the very chapter on necessity to which so much reference has been made. It would be a very easy and cheap display of commonplace learning to quote from Greek and Latin authors, from Horace, from Juvenal, from Cicero, from Euripides, passage after passages, in which the duty of dying for others has been laid down in glowing and emphatic language as resulting from the principles of heathen ethics; it is enough in a Christian country to remind ourselves of the Great Example whom we profess to follow. It is not needful to point out the awful danger of admitting the principle which has been contended for. Who is to be the judge of this sort of necessity? By what measure is the comparative value of lives to be measured? Is it to be strength, or intellect, or what? It is plain that the principle leaves to him who is to profit by it to determine the necessity which will justify him in deliberately taking another's life to save his own. In this case the weakest, the youngest, the most unresisting, was chosen. Was it more necessary to kill him than one of the grown men? The answer must be "No"—

"So spake the Fiend, and with necessity,

The tyrant's plea, excused his devilish deeds."

It is not suggested that in this particular case the deeds were devilish, but it is quite plain that such a principle once admitted might be made the legal cloak for unbridled passion and atrocious crime. There is no safe path for judges to tread but to ascertain the law to the best of their ability and to declare it according to their judgment; and if in any case the law appears to be too severe on individuals, to leave it to the Sovereign to exercise that prerogative of mercy which the Constitution has intrusted to the hands fittest to dispense it.

It must not be supposed that in refusing to admit temptation to be an excuse for crime it is forgotten how terrible the temptation was; how awful the suffering; how hard in such trials to keep the judgment straight and the conduct pure. We are often compelled to set up standards we cannot reach ourselves, and to lay down rules which we could not ourselves satisfy. But a man has no right to declare temptation to be an excuse, though he might himself have yielded to it, nor allow compassion for the criminal to change or weaken in any manner the legal definition of the crime. It is therefore our duty to declare that the prisoners' act in this case was wilful murder, that the facts as stated in the verdict are no legal justification of the homicide; and to say that in our unanimous opinion the prisoners are upon this special verdict guilty, of murder.

[The defendants were sentenced to death. Nevertheless, the Crown subsequently commuted the sentence to six months imprisonment].

## Notes and Questions

1. The central element of the necessity defense is that the actor's conduct must avert a greater harm than the one that it causes. This is why necessity is sometimes called "lesser evils," for conduct is justified pursuant to this defense only if it inflicts a lesser evil than the one averted. This strict proportionality requirement distinguishes necessity from self-defense. While conduct is justified as the lesser evil only when the harm caused is strictly proportional to the one averted, self-defense justifies conduct as long as the harm inflicted is not grossly disproportional than the harm caused. As a result, necessity authorizes the infliction of less harm than that which is threatened, whereas self-defense tolerates the infliction of more harm than is averted. Thus, for example, self-defense would allow causing death in order to avoid serious bodily injury, whereas the lesser evils defense would not.

2. Sometimes it is difficult to determine whether the actor's conduct averts a greater harm than the one inflicted. The three cases excerpted in this section are illustrative. In *Unger* the court had to decide if the harm averted by escaping from prison is greater than the evil inflicted by the escape. The question is complicated, for it is unclear what precisely is the harm inherent in escaping from prison. Is it frustrating the administration of justice? Is it disobeying state authority? Even after the harm is appropriately defined, it is difficult to quantify it in a way that makes it possible to compare it with the harm averted by escaping from prison. Do you believe that necessity justifies a prisoner's escape in order to avoid being assaulted by fellow inmates? Assuming that such a prisoner should be exonerated, is the right ground for acquittal that his conduct is justified because it inflicts a lesser evil or is it that he ought to be excused for engaging in admittedly wrongful conduct because he cannot be fairly expected to remain in prison knowing that he would likely be assaulted by fellow inmates? See, generally, George P. Fletcher, *Should Intolerable Prison Conditions Generate a Justification or Excuse for Escape*? 26 U.C.L.A. L Rev. 1355 (1979). Note that the court in *Unger*—as well as the courts in the other cases excerpted in this section—sometimes stated that necessity "excuses" conduct. This reveals conceptual confusion, as necessity is a justification that negates the wrongfulness of the actor's conduct.

3. The defendant in *Hutchins* broke the drug laws in order to obtain marijuana to "treat loss of appetite, nausea, vomiting, and weight loss" that resulted as a consequence of scleroderma. How would you describe the evil inflicted by breaking the laws against possession of marijuana? What was the evil averted by engaging in the unlawful use of marijuana? A majority of the court in *Hutchins* concluded that the evil inflicted by the defendant's action was not outweighed by the benefits reaped by engaging in the conduct. The dissenting judge took issue with the majority's conclusion, contending that "the harm to an individual in having to endure such symptoms may well outweigh society's generalized interest in prohibiting him or her from using the marihuana in such circumstances." Who has the better part of this argument? Explain.

4. Perhaps the thorniest problem regarding the balancing of evils required by the necessity defense is whether killing an innocent human being can ever be regarded as the lesser evil. This is the issue that the court faced in the (in)famous *Dudley and Stephens* case. The defendants argued that killing the cabin boy was justified because cannibalizing him allowed them to survive. Expressed in mathematical terms, the defendants argued that killing one innocent person is justified if doing so saves two or more persons. The court rejected the argument. In doing so, the court expressed doubts about whether the comparative value of human lives could be determined objectively. Furthermore, the court pointed out the "awful danger" inherent in "admitting the principle" that it may sometimes be justified to sacrifice an innocent person for the wellbeing of many more. What do you think are the "awful dangers" that the court had in mind when it made this statement? Do you think that it may sometimes be justified to kill an innocent person in order to save many more? Why or why not?

5. In *U.S. v. Holmes,* 26 F.Cas. 360 (1842), a ship struck an iceberg and started to sink. A group of passengers and crewmembers boarded a lifeboat. Unfortunately, the lifeboat started to leak. Several hours later, the defendant crewmember helped force 12 men out of the lifeboat in order to slow the sinking of the lifeboat. Upon reaching shore, defendant was charged and convicted of murdering one of the persons he helped throw overboard. Interestingly, the court noted that the crewmembers did not draw lots or consult the people in the lifeboat as to how to proceed. This suggests that the result might have been different had the people who were thrown overboard agreed to some sort of procedure for randomly selecting which persons to sacrifice. Do you agree that it would have been justified to throw some people overboard pursuant to some kind of previously agreed upon procedure for determining whom to sacrifice? Explain. Suppose that all of the occupants of the lifeboat agree to sacrificing those who are chosen by lot, but the chosen ones then back out of the agreement. Would it be justified for the rest to enforce the agreement by forcing the chosen ones overboard in spite of their objections? Why or why not?

6. In a relatively recent judgment of the Court of Appeals of England and Wales, the court authorized severing conjoined twins in a way that would kill the weaker of the twins in order to save the stronger. *A (Children), Re,* [2000] EWCA Civ 254 (22 September 2000). The weaker twin would not have survived much longer regardless of what was done. Both twins would have surely died within several months had surgery not been performed. The thorny issues raised by the case were compounded by the fact that the parents of the twins refused to authorize the operation, contending that they could not choose to kill one of their daughters in order to save the other. Lord Justice Ward explained his decision in the following manner:

> The analytical problem is to determine what may, and what may not, be placed in each scale and what weight is then to be given to each of the factors in the scales.
>
> > (i) The universality of the right to life demands that *the right* to life be treated as equal. The intrinsic value of their human life is equal. So the right of each goes into the scales and the scales remain in balance.
> >
> > (ii) The question which the court has to answer is whether or not the proposed treatment, the operation to separate, is in the best interests of the twins. That enables me to consider and place in the scales of each twin the worthwhileness of the treatment. That is a quite different exercise from the proscribed (because it offends the sanctity of life principle) consideration of the worth of one life compared with the other. When considering the worthwhileness of the treatment, it is legitimate to have regard to the actual condition of each twin and hence the actual balance sheet of advantage and

> disadvantage which flows from the performance or the non-performance of the proposed treatment. Here it is legitimate, as John Keown demonstrates, and as the cases show, to bear in mind the actual quality of life each child enjoys and may be able to enjoy. In summary, the operation will give Jodie the prospects of a normal expectation of relatively normal life. The operation will shorten Mary's life but she remains doomed for death. Mary has a full claim to the dignity of independence which is her human entitlement. In the words of the Rabbinical scholars involved in the 1977 case in Philadelphia, Mary is "designated for death" because her capacity to live her life is fatally compromised. The prospect of a full life for Jodie is counterbalanced by an acceleration of certain death for Mary. That balance is heavily in Jodie's favour.
>
> (iii) I repeat that the balancing exercise I have just conducted is *not* a balancing of the Quality of life in the sense that I value the potential of one human life above another. I have already indicated that the value of each life in the eyes of God and in the eyes of law is equal....
>
> (iv) In this unique case it is, in my judgment, impossible not to put in the scales of each child the manner in which they are individually able to exercise their right to life. Mary may have a right to life, but she has little right to be alive. She is alive because and only because, to put it bluntly, but nonetheless accurately, she sucks the lifeblood of Jodie. She will survive only so long as Jodie survives. Jodie will not survive long because constitutionally she will not be able to cope. Mary's parasitic living will be the cause of Jodie's ceasing to live. If Jodie could speak, she would surely protest, "Stop it, Mary, you're killing me". Mary would have no answer to that. Into my scales of fairness and justice between the children goes the fact that nobody but the doctors can help Jodie. Mary is beyond help.

> Hence I am in no doubt at all that the scales come down heavily in Jodie's favour. The best interests of the twins is to give the chance of life to the child whose actual bodily condition is capable of accepting the chance to her advantage even if that has to be at the cost of the sacrifice of the life which is so unnaturally supported. I am wholly satisfied that the least detrimental choice, balancing the interests of Mary against Jodie and Jodie against Mary, is to permit the operation to be performed.

Lord Justice Ward suggests that one of the reasons that the balance of evils shifts decidedly in favor of killing Mary in order so save Jodie is that Mary was "doomed for death" regardless of whether the operation was performed. In contrast, Jodie was likely to lead a relatively long life if she was severed from her twin sister. Do you agree that killing Mary is the lesser evil under the circumstances? Explain.

# § 14.05 Necessity: The Problem of Civil Disobedience

## United States v. Schoon

United States Court of Appeals, Ninth Circuit, 1991
971 F.2d 193

BOOCHEVER, Circuit Judge:

Gregory Schoon, Raymond Kennon, Jr., and Patricia Manning appeal their convictions for obstructing activities of the Internal Revenue Service Office in Tucson, Arizona, and failing to comply with an order of a federal police officer. Both charges stem from their activities in protest of United States involvement in El Salvador. They claim the district court improperly denied them a necessity defense. Because we hold the necessity defense inapplicable in cases like this, we affirm.

I.

On December 4, 1989, thirty people, including appellants, gained admittance to the IRS office in Tucson, where they chanted "keep America's tax dollars out of El Salvador," splashed simulated blood on the counters, walls, and carpeting, and generally obstructed the office's operation. After a federal police officer ordered the group, on several occasions, to disperse or face arrest, appellants were arrested.

At a bench trial, appellants proffered testimony about conditions in El Salvador as the motivation for their conduct. They attempted to assert a necessity defense, essentially contending that their acts in protest of American involvement in El Salvador were necessary to avoid further bloodshed in that country. While finding appellants motivated solely by humanitarian concerns, the court nonetheless precluded the defense as a matter of law, relying on Ninth Circuit precedent. The sole issue on appeal is the propriety of the court's exclusion of a necessity defense as a matter of law.

II.

A district court may preclude a necessity defense where "the evidence, as described in the defendant's offer of proof, is insufficient as a matter of law to support the proffered defense." To invoke the necessity defense, therefore, the defendants colorably must have shown that: (1) they were faced with a choice of evils and chose the lesser evil; (2) they acted to prevent imminent harm; (3) they reasonably anticipated a direct causal relationship between their conduct and the harm to be averted; and (4) they had no legal alternatives to violating the law....

The district court denied the necessity defense on the grounds that (1) the requisite immediacy was lacking; (2) the actions taken would not abate the evil; and (3) other legal alternatives existed. Because the threshold test for admissibility of a necessity defense is a conjunctive one, a court may preclude invocation of the defense if "proof is deficient with regard to any of the four elements."

While we could affirm substantially on those grounds relied upon by the district court, we find a deeper, systemic reason for the complete absence of federal case law recognizing a necessity defense in an indirect civil disobedience case. As used in this opinion, "civil disobedience" is the wilful violation of a law, undertaken for the purpose of social or political protest. Indirect civil disobedience involves violating a law or interfering with a government policy that is not, itself, the object of protest. Direct civil disobedience, on the other hand, involves protesting the existence of a law by breaking that law or by preventing the execution of that law in a specific instance in which a particularized harm would otherwise follow. This case involves indirect civil disobedience because these protestors were not challenging the laws under which they were charged. In contrast, the civil rights lunch counter sit-ins, for example, constituted direct civil disobedience because the protestors were challenging the rule that prevented them from sitting at lunch counters. Similarly, if a city council passed an ordinance requiring immediate infusion of a suspected carcinogen into the drinking water, physically blocking the delivery of the substance would constitute direct civil disobedience: protestors would be preventing the execution of a law in a specific instance in which a particularized harm—contamination of the water supply—would otherwise follow.

While our prior cases consistently have found the elements of the necessity defense lacking in cases involving indirect civil disobedience, we have never addressed specifically whether the defense is available in cases of indirect civil disobedience. Indeed, some other courts have appeared doubtful. *See, e.g., United States v. Seward* ("[Necessity] is obviously not a defense to charges arising from a typical protest."); *United States v. Kroncke* ("None of the cases even suggests that the defense of necessity would be permitted where the actor's purpose is to effect a change in governmental policies which, according to the actor, may in turn result in a future saving of lives."). Today, we conclude, for the reasons stated below, that the necessity defense is inapplicable to cases involving indirect civil disobedience.

### III.

Necessity is, essentially, a utilitarian defense. It therefore justifies criminal acts taken to avert a greater harm, maximizing social welfare by allowing a crime to be committed where the social benefits of the crime outweigh the social costs of failing to commit the crime.

What all the traditional necessity cases have in common is that the commission of the "crime" averted the occurrence of an even greater "harm." In some sense, the necessity defense allows us to act as individual legislatures, amending a particular criminal provision or crafting a one-time exception to it, subject to court review, when a real legislature would formally do the same under those circumstances. For example, by allowing prisoners who escape a burning jail to claim the justification of necessity, we assume the lawmaker, confronting this problem, would have allowed for an exception to the law proscribing prison escapes.

Because the necessity doctrine is utilitarian, however, strict requirements contain its exercise so as to prevent nonbeneficial criminal conduct. For example, "'[i]f the criminal act cannot abate the threatened harm, society receives no benefit from the criminal conduct.'" Similarly, to forgive a crime taken to avert a lesser harm would fail to maximize social utility. The cost of the crime would outweigh the harm averted by its commission. Likewise, criminal acts cannot be condoned to thwart threats, yet to be imminent, or those for which there are legal alternatives to abate the harm.

Analysis of three of the necessity defense's four elements leads us to the conclusion that necessity can never be proved in a case of indirect civil disobedience. We do not rely upon the imminent harm prong of the defense because we believe there can be indirect civil disobedience cases in which the protested harm is imminent.

### A.

#### I. Balance of Harms

It is axiomatic that, if the thing to be averted is not a harm at all, the balance of harms necessarily would disfavor any criminal action. Indirect civil disobedience seeks first and foremost to bring about the repeal of a law or a change of governmental policy, attempting to mobilize public opinion through typically symbolic action. These protestors violate a law, not because it is unconstitutional or otherwise improper, but because doing so calls public attention to their objectives. Thus, the most immediate "harm" this form of protest targets is the *existence* of the law or policy. However, the mere existence of a constitutional law or governmental policy cannot constitute a legally cognizable harm …

The protest in this case was in the form of indirect civil disobedience, aimed at reversal of the government's El Salvador policy. That policy does not violate the Constitution, and appellants have never suggested as much. There is no evidence that the procedure by which the policy was adopted was in any way improper; nor is there any evidence that appellants were prevented systematically from participating in the democratic processes through which the policy was chosen. The most immediate harm the appellants sought to avert was the existence of the government's El Salvador policy, which is not in itself a legally cognizable harm. Moreover, any harms resulting from the operation of this policy are insufficiently concrete to be legally cognizable as harms for purposes of the necessity defense.

Thus, as a matter of law, the mere existence of a policy or law validly enacted by Congress cannot constitute a cognizable harm. If there is no cognizable harm to prevent, the harm resulting from criminal action taken for the purpose of securing the repeal of the law or policy necessarily outweighs any benefit of the action.

2. Causal Relationship Between Criminal Conduct and Harm to be Averted

This inquiry requires a court to judge the likelihood that an alleged harm will be abated by the taking of illegal action. In the sense that the likelihood of abatement is required in the traditional necessity cases, there will never be such likelihood in cases of indirect political protest. In the traditional cases, a prisoner flees a burning cell and averts death, or someone demolishes a home to create a firebreak and prevents the conflagration of an entire community. The nexus between the act undertaken and the result sought is a close one. Ordinarily it is the volitional illegal act alone which, once taken, abates the evil.

In political necessity cases involving indirect civil disobedience against congressional acts, however, the act alone is unlikely to abate the evil precisely because the action is indirect. Here, the IRS obstruction, or the refusal to comply with a federal officer's order, are unlikely to abate the killings in El Salvador, or immediately change Congress's policy; instead, it takes another *volitional* actor not controlled by the protestor to take a further step; Congress must change its mind.

3. Legal Alternatives

A final reason the necessity defense does not apply to these indirect civil disobedience cases is that legal alternatives will never be deemed exhausted when the harm can be mitigated by congressional action. As noted above, the harm indirect civil disobedience aims to prevent is the continued existence of a law or policy. Because congressional action can *always* mitigate this "harm," lawful political activity to spur such action will always be a legal alternative. On the other hand, we cannot say that this legal alternative will always exist in cases of direct civil disobedience, where protestors act to avert a concrete harm flowing from the operation of the targeted law or policy …

B.

… The real problem here is that litigants are trying to distort to their purposes an age-old common law doctrine meant for a very different set of circumstances. What [indirect civil disobedience] cases are really about is gaining notoriety for a cause—the defense allows protestors to get their political grievances discussed in a courtroom. It is precisely this political motive that has left some courts, like the district court in this case, uneasy. Because these attempts to invoke the necessity defense "force the courts to choose among causes they should make legitimate by extending the defense of necessity," and because the criminal acts, themselves, do not maximize social good, they should be subject to a *per se* rule of exclusion.

Thus, we see the failure of any federal court to recognize a defense of necessity in a case like ours not as coincidental, but rather as the natural consequence of the historic limitation of the doctrine. Indirect protests of congressional policies can never meet all the requirements of the necessity doctrine. Therefore, we hold that the necessity defense is not available in such cases.

AFFIRMED.

**FERNANDEZ, Circuit Judge, concurring:**

I agree with much of what the majority says regarding the application of the necessity defense to this type of case.

I do not mean to be captious in questioning whether the necessity defense is grounded on pure utilitarianism, but fundamentally, I am not so sure that this defense of justification should be grounded on utilitarian theory alone rather than on a concept of what is right and proper conduct under the circumstances. *See, e.g.,* G. Fletcher, Rethinking Criminal Law, 759–875 (1978). *Cf.,* J. Thomson, Rights, Restitution and Risk, 78–116 (1986) (some reflections on the trolley problem). At any rate this doubt would not prevent me from joining in the majority's opinion.

## *Notes and Questions*

1. The necessity defense is often invoked by protesters who break a law by engaging in civil disobedience. Nevertheless, as the Ninth Circuit Court of Appeals explains in *Schoon,* most acts of civil disobedience fail to meet most—if not all—of the elements of the necessity defense. The imminence requirement is often not satisfied, for the acts that are being protested frequently threaten future rather than immediate harm. This is the case, for example, with protests against nuclear power plants, for the harm threatened by such plants will take place at some indefinite point in time, if it takes place at all. Even in the few cases in which the harm being protested against is imminent, it is unclear whether the acts of civil disobedience will actually avert the threatened harm. Finally, there are often legal alternatives available that may be used as a tool for preventing the threatened harm. Thus, for example, the threat from nuclear power plants may be curbed by engaging in lawful efforts to change the existing legislation that authorizes the operation of such plants.

2. The court in *Schoon* distinguished between direct and indirect civil disobedience. A person engages in an act of civil disobedience if she breaks the law that she is seeking to change. This is what Rosa Parks did when she refused to take a seat in the back of the bus, for the law that she violated was precisely the law or policy that she was protesting against. In contrast, someone who refuses to pay taxes as a way of protesting against a war being waged by the government in a foreign country is an act of indirect civil disobedience, for the law that is infringed (tax law) is not the law or policy that is being protested against (the law authorizing military intervention in the foreign country). Did the defendant in *Schoon* engage in an act of direct or indirect civil disobedience? Explain.

3. The court argued in *Schoon* that "[i]ndirect protests of congressional policies can never meet all the requirements of the necessity doctrine." Nevertheless, the court's holding leaves the door open for a subsequent finding that some acts of *direct* civil disobedience may meet the requirements of the choice of evils defense. Do you agree acts of indirect civil disobedience never meet the requirements of the necessity defense? Why or why not? Assuming that indirect civil disobedience should never be justified pursuant to necessity, do you nevertheless believe that the choice of evils defense may justify some acts of direct civil disobedience? If so, when should necessity justify acts of direct civil disobedience? Explain.

# § 14.06 Necessity: Model Penal Code

## Model Penal Code § 3.02. Justification Generally: Choice of Evils.

(1) Conduct that the actor believes to be necessary to avoid a harm or evil to himself or to another is justifiable, provided that:

> (a) the harm or evil sought to be avoided by such conduct is greater than that sought to be prevented by the law defining the offense charged; and
>
> (b) neither the Code nor other law defining the offense provides exceptions or defenses dealing with the specific situation involved; and
>
> (c) a legislative purpose to exclude the justification claimed does not otherwise plainly appear.

(2) When the actor was reckless or negligent in bringing about the situation requiring a choice of harms or evils or in appraising the necessity for his conduct, the justification afforded by this Section is unavailable in a prosecution for any offense for which recklessness or negligence, as the case may be, suffices to establish culpability.

### *Notes and Questions*

1. The Model Penal Code choice of evils provision essentially reflects the common law approach to the defense. Therefore, an actor is justified pursuant to necessity only if the harm or evil sought by the conduct is greater than the evil inflicted. Furthermore, the defense is not available if the legislature expressly or tacitly foreclosed the possibility of invoking necessity as a defense to a certain crime or group of crimes.

2. Although the Code's approach to necessity is similar to the common law approach to the defense, it "rejects any limitations on necessity cast in terms of particular evils to be avoided or particular evils to be avoided." Furthermore, as the Code drafters pointed out:

> It would be particularly unfortunate to exclude homicidal conduct from the scope of the defense. For, recognizing that the sanctity of life has a supreme place in the hierarchy of values, it is nonetheless true that conduct that results in taking life may promote the very value sought to be protected by the law of homicide. Suppose, for example, that the actor makes a breach in a dike, knowing that this will inundate a farm, but taking the only course available to save a whole

> town. If he is charged with homicide of the inhabitants of the farm house, he can rightly point out that the object of the law of homicide is to save life, and that by his conduct he has effected a net saving of innocent lives. The life of every individual must be taken in such a case to be of equal value and the numerical preponderance in the lives saved compared to those sacrificed surely should establish legal justification for the act. *Model Penal Code and Commentaries § 3.02, page 14–15.*

Do you agree with the Code drafters that killing innocent human beings may be justified pursuant to the lesser evils defense if doing so saves more lives than the ones sacrificed? How would *Dudley & Stephens* be decided if § 3.02 of the Model Penal Code applied? What result if the Model Penal Code was applied in the conjoined twins case? Explain.

## § 14.07 Necessity: Comparative Perspectives

### Aviation Security Case

Federal Constitutional Court (Germany)
Judgment of the First Senate of 15 February 2006

A.

The constitutional complaint challenges the armed forces' authorization by the Aviation Security Act to shoot down, by the direct use of armed force, aircraft that are intended to be used as weapons in crimes against human lives.

I.

On 11 September 2001, four passenger planes of US American airlines were hijacked in the United States of America by an international terrorist organization and caused to crash. Two of the planes hit the World Trade Center in New York, one crashed into the Pentagon, the Ministry of Defense of the United States of America. The crash of the fourth plane occurred southeast of Pittsburgh in the state of Pennsylvania, after, possibly, the intervention of passengers on board had resulted in a change of the plane's course. More than 3,000 persons in the planes, in the area of the World Trade Center, and in the Pentagon died in the attacks.

On 5 January 2003, an armed man captured a sports plane, circled above the banking district of Frankfurt/Main and threatened to crash the plane into the high-rise of the European Central Bank if he was not granted the possibility of making a phone call to the United States of America. A police helicopter and two jet fighters of the German Air Force took off and circled the powered glider. The police ordered major alert, the city center of Frankfurt was cleared, high-rises were evacuated. Slightly more than half an hour after the capture, it was evident that the hijacker was a mentally confused person acting on his own. After his demand had been complied with, he landed on Rhein Main Airport and did not resist his arrest.

Both incidents caused a large number of measures aimed at preventing unlawful interference with civil aviation, at improving the security of civil aviation as a whole and at protecting it, in doing so, also from dangers that are imminent where aircraft ... are taken command of by people who want to abuse them for objectives that are unrelated to air traffic ...

Since 1 October 2003, a "National Air Security Center" ... which has been established in Kalkar on the Lower Rhine, has been operational. It is intended to ensure coordinated, swift cooperation of all authorities of the Federation and the Länder in charge of questions of aviation security as a central information hub in order to guarantee security in the German air space. In the National Air Security Center, members of the Federal Armed Forces, the Federal Police and the Deutsche Flugsicherung (German Air Navigation Services) survey the air space.

The main function of the center is to avert dangers that emanate from so-called renegade planes, which are civil aircraft that have been taken command of by people who want to abuse them as weapons for a targeted crash. Once an aircraft has been classified as a renegade—be it by NATO, be it by the National Air Security Center itself—the responsibility for the measures required for averting such danger in the German air space rests with the competent authorities of the Federal Republic of Germany.

The legal basis for these measures is laid down in the Act on the New Regulation of Aviation Security Functions ... of 11 January 2005 ...

The operations that are permissible in accordance with the Aviation Security Act and the principles that apply as regards their choice are specified in §§ 14 and 15 of the Aviation Security Act. Pursuant to § 15.1 of the Aviation Security Act, operations intended to prevent the occurrence of an especially grave accident ... may be taken only if the aircraft from which the danger of such accident emanates has previously been checked by the armed forces in the air space and if it has then been unsuccessfully tried to warn and to divert it. If this prerequisite has been met, the armed forces may, pursuant to § 14.1 of the Aviation Security Act, force the aircraft off its course in the air space, force it to land, threaten to use armed force, or fire warning shots.

The principle of proportionality applies to the choice among these measures.... Pursuant to § 14.3 of the Aviation Security Act, the direct use of armed force against the aircraft is permissible only if the occurrence of an especially grave accident cannot be prevented even by such measures. This, however, only applies where it must be assumed under the circumstances that the aircraft is intended to be used as a weapon against human lives, and where the direct use of armed force is the only means to avert this imminent danger. Pursuant to § 14.4 sentence 1 of the Aviation Security Act, the exclusive competence for ordering this measure rests with the Federal Minister of Defense, or in the event of the Minister of Defense having to be represented, with the member of the Federal Government who is authorized to represent the Minister....

II.

With their constitutional complaint, the complainants directly challenge the Aviation Security Act because, as they argue, it permits the state to intentionally kill persons who have not become perpetrators but [are] victims of a crime.

The complainants put forward that § 14.3 of the Aviation Security Act, which under the conditions specified in the law authorizes to shoot down aircraft, violates their rights under ... the Basic Law [of Germany]....

[II].

Article 2.2 sentence 1 of the Basic Law guarantees the right to life as a liberty right.... With this right, the biological and physical existence of every human being is protected against encroachments by the state from the point in time of its coming into being until the human being's death, independently of the individual's circumstances of life and of his or her physical state and state of mind. Every human life as such has the same value....

Although it constitutes an ultimate value within the order of the Basic Law..., also this right is nevertheless subject to the constitutional requirement of the specific enactment of a statute pursuant to Article 2.2 sentence 3 of the Basic Law.

[III].

The challenged provision of § 14.3 of the Aviation Security Act does not live up to [constitutional] standards.

It encroaches upon the scope of protection of the fundamental right to life, which is guaranteed by Article 2.2 sentence 1 of the Basic Law, of the crew and of the passengers of an aircraft affected by an operation pursuant to § 14.3 of the Aviation Security Act and also of those who want to use the plane against the lives of people in the sense of this provision. Recourse to the authorization to use direct armed force against an aircraft pursuant to § 14.3 of the Aviation Security Act will virtually always result in its crash. The consequence of the crash, in turn, will with near certainty be the death, and consequently the destruction of the lives, of all people on board the aircraft....

[T]he provision.... infringes Article 2.2 sentence 1 of the Basic Law as regards substance to the extent that it not only affects those who want to abuse the aircraft as a weapon but also persons who are not responsible for causing the major aerial incident presumed under § 14.3 of the Aviation Security Act (b)....

The fundamental right to life guaranteed by Article 2.2 sentence 1 of the Basic Law is subject to the requirement of the specific enactment of a statute pursuant to Article 2.2 sentence 3 of the Basic Law ... The Act, however, that restricts the fundamental right must in its turn be regarded in the light of the fundamental right and of the guarantee of human dignity under Article 1.1 of the Basic Law, which is closely linked with it.

Human life is the vital basis of human dignity as the essential constitutive principle, and as the supreme value, of the constitution.... All human beings possess this dignity as persons, irrespective of their qualities, their physical or mental state, their achievements and their social status.... It cannot be taken away from any human being. What can be violated, however, is the claim to respect which results from it.... This applies irrespective, inter alia, of the probable duration of the individual human life.... on the human being's claim to respect of his or her dignity (even after death).

In view of this relation between the right to life and human dignity, the state is prohibited, on the one hand, from encroaching upon the fundamental right to life by measures of its own, thereby violating the ban on the disregard of human dignity. On the other hand, the state is also obliged to protect every human life. This duty of protection demands of the state and its bodies to shield and to promote the life of every individual, which means above all to also protect it from unlawful attacks, and interference, by third.... Also this duty of protection has its foundations in Article 1.1 sentence 2 of the Basic Law, which explicitly obliges the state to respect and protect human dignity.

What this obligation means in concrete terms for state action cannot be definitely determined once and for all....

[T]he obligation to respect and protect human dignity generally precludes making a human being a mere object of the state.... What is thus absolutely prohibited is any treatment of a human being by public authority which fundamentally calls into question his or her quality of a subject, his or her status as a legal entity.... by its lack of the respect of the value which is due to every human being for his or her own sake, by virtue of his or her being a person.... When it is that such a treatment occurs must be stated in concrete terms in the individual case in view of the specific situation in which a conflict can arise ...

According to these standards, § 14.3 of the Aviation Security Act is also incompatible with Article 2.2 sentence 1 in conjunction with Article 1.1 of the Basic Law to the extent that the shooting down of an aircraft affects people who, as its crew and passengers, have not exerted any influence on the occurrence of the non-warlike aerial incident assumed under § 14.3 of the Aviation Security Act.

In the situation in which these persons are at the moment in which the order to use direct armed force against the aircraft involved in the aerial incident pursuant to § 14.4 sentence 1 of the Aviation Security Act is made, it must be possible, pursuant to § 14.3 of the Aviation Security Act, to assume with certainty that the aircraft is intended to be used against human lives. As has been stated in the reasoning for the Act, the aircraft must have been converted into an assault weapon by those who have brought it under their command ... ; the aircraft itself must be used by the perpetrators in a targeted manner as a weapon for the crime, not merely as an auxiliary means for committing the crime, against the lives of people who stay in the area in which the aircraft is intended to crash....

In such an extreme situation, which is, moreover, characterized by the cramped conditions of an aircraft in flight, the passengers and the crew are typically in a desperate situation. They can no longer influence the circumstances of their lives independently from others in a self-determined manner.

This makes them objects not only of the perpetrators of the crime. Also the state which in such a situation resorts to the measure provided by § 14.3 of the Aviation Security Act treats them as mere objects of its rescue operation for the protection of others. The desperateness and inescapability which characterize the situation of the people on board the aircraft who are affected as victims also exist vis-à-vis those who order and execute the shooting down of the aircraft. Due to the circumstances, which cannot be controlled by them in any way, the crew and the passengers of the plane cannot escape this state action but are helpless and defenseless in the face of it with the consequence that they are shot down in a targeted manner together with the aircraft and as result of this will be killed with near certainty. Such a treatment ignores the status of the persons affected as subjects endowed with dignity and inalienable rights.

By [using] their killing ... as a means to save others, they are treated as objects and at the same time deprived of their rights; with their lives being disposed of unilaterally by the state, the persons on board the aircraft, who, as victims, are themselves in need of protection, are denied the value which is due to a human being for his or her own sake ...

Also the assessment that the persons who are on board a plane that is intended to be used against other people's lives within the meaning of § 14.3 of the Aviation Security Act are doomed anyway cannot remove its nature of an infringement of their right to dignity from the killing of innocent people in a situation that is desperate for them which an operation performed pursuant to this provisions as a general rule involves. Human life and human dignity enjoy the same constitutional protection regardless of the duration of the physical existence of the individual human being.... Whoever denies this or calls this into question denies those who, such as the victims of a hijacking, are in a desperate situation that offers no alternative to them, precisely the respect which is due to them for the sake of their human dignity....

The idea that the individual is obliged to sacrifice his or her life in the interest of the state as a whole in case of need if this is the only possible way of protecting the legally constituted body politic from attacks which are aimed at its breakdown and destruction ... also does not lead to a different result. In this context, the Senate need not decide whether, and should the occasion arise, under which circumstances such a duty of taking responsibility, in solidarity, over and above the mechanisms of protection provided in the emergency constitution can be derived from the Basic Law. For in the area of application of § 14.3 of the Aviation Security Act the issue is not averting attacks aimed at abolishing the body politic and at eliminating the state's legal and constitutional system.

[As a result, the Aviation Security Act was struck down as unconstitutional].

## *Notes and Questions*

1. Do you agree with the German Federal Constitutional Court that it is unlawful to shoot down a hijacked commercial plane headed towards a heavily populated area because by doing so the innocent passengers are used "as a means to save others" and "are treated as objects"? Why or why not?

2. The German court concludes that shooting down the plane denies the passengers "the value which is due to a human being for his or her own sake" because "their lives [are] disposed of unilaterally by the state" in order to save others. Do you agree that shooting down the plane devalues the lives of the plane's passengers? Explain.

3. The Court also concluded that it was irrelevant to the balancing of evils that the passengers were going to surely die regardless of whether the government shoots down the plane or not. The conclusion is justified by pointing out that "[h]uman life and human dignity enjoy the same constitutional protection regardless of the duration of the physical existence of the individual human being." Do you agree that the fact that the passengers are going to die regardless of whether the government downs the plane is immaterial to assessing whether shooting down the plane is justified? Why or why not?

4. Suppose that the inhabitants of a heavily populated building facing a 9/11-type situation have the capacity to shoot down the hijacked plane that is headed towards them. Would they be justified if they shoot down the plane? Explain. If they are justified in shooting down the plane, does it follow that the government should also be justified if it downs the plane on their behalf? Why or why not?

5. Assume that you are a passenger in a hijacked plane headed towards a heavily populated area in a 9/11-type scenario. Would you consent to the government shooting down the plane seconds before it crashes into its target? Why or why not? Do you think that most people in such circumstances would consent to the government shooting down the plane? If so, could downing the plane be justified according to some theory of implied consent?

6. How would the German case be decided under the Model Penal Code? Why? What result if the rule put forth in *Dudley & Stephens* was applied to the German case? Explain.

## § 14.08 Necessity: Scholarly Debates

### Kimberly Kessler Ferzan, *Torture Necessity and the Union of Law and Philosophy*

33 Rutgers L. J. 183 (2004)

If law professors are thought to be intellectuals in ivory towers, philosophers build those towers to new heights. Thus, the question arises as to how the union of these two fields ... could contribute to issues of "contemporary relevance" as we claim it will do.

In my view, not only do both of these disciplines have much to say about issues of contemporary relevance, but the sum of these two disciplines is stronger than their individual parts. While law frequently foots in reality, many of its presuppositions are, at root, philosophical. We are thus more prepared to address the challenges of our times when we combine these fields.

Indeed, consider the memoranda, written by departments within the Bush Administration, opining as to the permissibility of torture. In August 2002, the Justice Department's Office of Legal Counsel (OLC) authored a memorandum that was signed by Jay. S. Bybee, then-head of the OLC, and now a Ninth Circuit judge, advising White House counsel Alberto Gonzales as to the conditions under which it would be legal to torture. The motivation for the memorandum was a post-September 11, 2001, request by the Central Intelligence Agency for legal guidance as to how it could permissibly interrogate key al Qaeda leaders. This memorandum in turn formed the basis for a March 2003 memorandum authored by the Department of Defense. Both memoranda contain a number of legal arguments, including the claim that shall be our focus: that the justification of necessity might be available as a defense to violations of ... the federal statute that criminalizes torture.

The defense of necessity is a catch-all justification wherein a defendant has a defense to a crime when the commission of that crime constitutes the lesser evil. Necessity is commonly thought to be a justification, wherein we view the defendant's act to be right or permissible, as opposed to wrongful but excused because of a peculiarity of the actor or the actor's situation. The rationale for the defense is that the legislature cannot provide specific defenses for all the circumstances in which we would want the defendant to act, and thus, the defendant should be permitted to choose the lesser evil in those instances where had the legislature considered the situation, it would have authorized the defendant's conduct. The necessity defense is implicated in different classes of cases ranging from those generic cases wherein one may cause some small harm to another in order to avoid a great harm; to instances of civil disobedience; to the hard cases that involve torture or the taking of innocent lives, such as the classic Regina v. Dudley and Stephens.

The torture memoranda make a number of legal claims about the viability of the necessity defense. First, they state that the defense, although not codified, has been recognized by the Supreme Court. Second, the authors assert that "the necessity defense can justify the intentional killing of one person to save two others." The authors also cite to the LaFave and Scott hornbook for other elements of the necessity defense, including its applicability to all harms; the requirement of justificatory intent; the fact that the balance of evils is assessed from what the defendant reasonably believed, but that the actual balancing is itself an objective question decided by the court; and the requirement that other alternatives not be available. In light of these elements, the memoranda conclude that the necessity defense could be successfully maintained. For instance, the Department of Justice memorandum notes the significance of the September 11 attacks and the presence of al Qaeda sleeper cells intent on making other such attacks, and concludes that "a detainee may possess information that could ... equal or surpass the September 11 attacks in their magnitude. Clearly any harm that might occur during an interrogation would pale insignificance (sic) compared to the harm avoided by preventing such attack, which could take hundreds of thousands of lives."

The claim that torture may be justified—that is, that it is right or permissible to torture another human being—is and should be immediately controversial. When our government claims that its agents may legally engage in such conduct, such a claim should be subjected to significant scrutiny. How can law and philosophy help us to better understand the issues at hand?

From a lawyer's standpoint, the memoranda's claims are themselves problematic. First, it is actually an open question whether the Supreme Court recognizes the necessity defense as a matter of federal common law. The authority cited in the memorandum, United States v. Bailey, was called into question by United States v. Oakland Cannabis Buyers' Cooperative. Secondly, while the memoranda claim that necessity is a defense to intentional killings—that claim is also controversial. The memoranda endorse the Model Penal Code's necessity test, thus ignoring the traditional common law bar on necessity as a defense to homicide. Thus, any lawyer addressing the torture memoranda would question whether the memoranda are overreaching.

While the memoranda are controversial even at the level of hornbook law, their approach can also be analyzed from the perspective of criminal law theory. Paul Robinson, a leading criminal law scholar, contends that we must focus on criminal law's structure and function. Specifically, Robinson distinguishes between ex ante rules of conduct that are directed toward citizens, and ex post rules of adjudication that determine whether the violation of the conduct rule warrants criminal liability.

Consider the torture memoranda at this more macroscopic level. Necessity, as a justification, sets forth an ex ante rule of conduct. It tells citizens what they may or may not do. Can the executive branch have a policy that torture is necessary? Notice that such a policy conflicts with the underlying structure of the defense. As Alan Dershowitz has noted, "(t)he point of the necessity defense is to provide a kind of 'interstitial legislation', to fill 'lacunae' left by legislative and judicial incompleteness. It is not a substitute legislative or judicial process for weighing policy options by state agencies faced with long-term systemic problems." Hence, we should question whether the executive should have a long-standing policy as to a determination delegated to citizens by the legislature only in cases of emergency.

On the other hand, we must question whether legislation is appropriate. According to Meir Dan-Cohen, there is an acoustic separation in criminal law—there is what we tell citizens we want them to do, and what we really want them to do. In light of this separation, Michael Moore has argued that a "flat ban on torture" is the appropriate legislative approach, even if the legislature truly desires for its citizens to torture in dire emergencies. While we cannot resolve what the appropriate approach is here, it is apparent that we better understand the meaning of these memoranda, for citizens and state, for legislature and executive, when we come to this question armed with the tools of criminal law theory.

And yet, we can take even another step back. The necessity justification appears to be patently consequentialist. That is, it tells us that we may engage in criminal conduct in those instances in which we will do more good than harm. But to say that the necessity defense is simply a matter of consequentalist balancing is to ignore deeper moral questions about the defense.

First, we might wonder whether there are, at the very least, deontological constraints on the consequentalist calculus. That is, while most people believe it is permissible to turn the infamous runaway trolley so that it kills one lone worker instead of five, we reject that a surgeon can kill one person and use his organs to save five others. As theorists note, the appropriation of the victim in the second case is what distinguishes it from the first. Thus, we must ask how torture fits within this paradigm. Are we using the terrorist as a means to our ends? Does torture tread where deontology tells us we must not go? After all, the interrogator can only gain information by intentionally torturing his victim.

Another question is commensurability—how can we compare torture to other harms? Certainly, we can compare harms if the torture of one is used to prevent the torture of one hundred. But once we venture beyond preventing torture, we must ask how we are to compare torture to death and other harms, especially given that the intentional infliction of severe harm is a particularly egregious wrong.

Finally, we must ask whether the fact that the victim is a terrorist is relevant. While necessity allows harms to innocents (although perhaps not the killing of innocents), a terrorist is someone who is, in some sense, a culpable cause of the peril. The more relevant the culpability of the victim, the more essential it is that we seek a high degree of certainty that the victim is a terrorist before engaging in this behavior.

The outcry over these memoranda was more than legal—it was moral. In defense of the Justice Department authors, University of Chicago law professors Eric Posner and Adrian Vermeule claimed that the DOJ attorneys were in the business of giving legal advice—not moral advice—as to the permissibility of torture. According to Posner and Vermeule, moral condemnation was simply not an appropriate reaction to the work of "legal technicians."

As we can see, the memoranda's authors had to engage in more than legal analysis. The necessity defense directly implicates consequentialist balancing, and forces us to examine when good consequences may justify an otherwise wrongful act.

My criminal law textbook includes Public Committee Against Torture in Israel v. Government of Israel, and thus, our class discussion includes the availability of necessity as a defense to torture. To press the question, I often ask my students whether it would be permissible, not to torture the terrorist, but to torture the terrorist's innocent baby. The answer to this question has changed since September 11, 2001. There is now a strong contingent of students who believe that in order to prevent another attack of that magnitude, such conduct would be permissible. These are our "legal technicians" of tomorrow. And there is no doubt that to confront this challenge, we have much to learn from the union of law and philosophy.

## Larry Alexander, *Deontology at the Threshold*

37 San Diego L. Rev. 893 (2000)

### I. Introduction

In his 1989 law review article, Torture and the Balance of Evils, later republished as Chapter Seventeen in Placing Blame, Michael Moore declares himself to be a "threshold deontologist." What he means is this: There are some acts that are morally wrong despite producing a net positive balance of consequences; but if the positive balance of consequences becomes sufficiently great—especially if it does so by averting horrible consequences as opposed to merely making people quite well off—then one is morally permitted, and perhaps required, to engage in those acts that are otherwise morally prohibited. Thus, one may not kill or torture an innocent person in order to save two or three other innocent people from death or torture—even though purely consequentialist considerations might dictate otherwise. However, if the number of innocent people who can be saved from death or torture gets sufficiently large, then what was morally proscribed—the killing or torture of an innocent person—becomes morally permissible or mandatory. At a certain number of lives at risk—the Threshold—consequentialist moral principles override deontological ones. Says Moore:

> It just is not true that one should allow a nuclear war rather than killing or torturing an innocent person. It is not even true that one should allow the destruction of a sizable city by a terrorist nuclear device rather than kill or torture an innocent person. To prevent such extraordinary harms extreme actions seem to me to be justified.

Does allowing consequentialist concerns to override deontological prohibitions at the Threshold collapse deontology into consequentialism? Moore denies this.

A consequentialist is committed by her moral theory to saying that torture of one person is justified whenever it is necessary to prevent the torture of two or more. The [deontological] view, even as here modified, is not committed to this proposition. To justify torturing one innocent person requires that there be horrendous consequences attached to not torturing that person—the destruction of an entire city, or, perhaps, of a lifeboat or building full of people. On this view, in other words, there is a very high threshold of bad consequences that must be threatened before something as awful as torturing an innocent person can be justified. Notwithstanding, Moore does admit that there is a psychological danger that people, once told that deontological prohibitions give way to consequentialist considerations at some point, will be much too quick to allow those consequentialist considerations to dominate. After all, if one can kill or torture to prevent the killing or torturing of N, it is hard to see why one should not kill or torture to prevent the killing or torturing of N-1, or N-2, and so on, right down to the point where the number saved is only slightly larger than the number harmed. However, this psychological point, which may suggest that people should not be told that consequentialist considerations can ever override deontological prohibitions, in no way undermines the moral truth that at some point, deontological prohibitions do give way.

Moore acknowledges that threshold deontology might appear arbitrary and irrational. As he puts it, "Why should goodness of consequences not count at all and then, at some point, count enormously in the sense that it fully determines the rightness of action?" Moore's answer to this question is that consequences always count, even below the threshold, but until the threshold is reached, consequentialist principles are outweighed by deontological ones. He analogizes the deontological norms to a dam, and the consequentialist considerations to water building up behind it. Eventually, if enough water builds up, it will reach and exceed the dam's height—which is analogous to the threshold of threshold deontology. "There is nothing arbitrary about thinking both that there is no spillover until the threshold of the dam's height is reached, and that each bit of water always counts in determining whether water will spill over the dam or not."

Finally, Moore attempts to deflect the charge that any number for the Threshold (other than the number pure consequentialism would select) will be arbitrary. May we torture an innocent to save 500, or will 450 do? And if 450, why not 449? Moore replies that apparent arbitrariness cannot be the basis of any powerful objection to threshold deontology because:

> [T]his is no more than the medieval worry of how many stones make a heap. Our uncertainty whether it takes three, or four, or five, etc., does not justify us in thinking that there are no such things as heaps. Similarly, preventing the torture of two innocents does not justify my torturing one, but destruction of an entire city does.

Moore is surely not alone in holding that threshold deontology is the correct description of our moral reality. Thomas Nagel, in his essay War and Massacre, put forward a similar position, though one that smacks more of a moral dilemma than as a moral guide....

Even Robert Nozick, perhaps the most significant modern advocate of deontological (cum libertarian) side constraints, concedes the possibility of a threshold at which consequentialist considerations could override deontological prohibitions. The question of whether these side constraints are absolute, or whether they may be violated in order to avoid catastrophic moral horror, and if the latter, what the resulting structure might look like, is one I hope largely to avoid.

It is my aim here to raise some doubts about the threshold deontologist's picture of morality. I am going to do so, not by a direct frontal attack on its plausibility, but by assuming at first that it is correct and then doing what Moore, Nagel, and Nozick (the latter self-consciously) eschew—namely, examining threshold deontology's structure in some detail. That structure turns out to produce a number of anomalous results. It seems, for example, more plausible to reject the existence of deontological thresholds and to assume instead either that deontological side constraints are absolute, or, as Nagel has hinted, that morality is thoroughly dilemmatic. I shall reach no strong conclusions on any of these points, however, since my principal aim is not to persuade you of any position other than that the structure of threshold deontology merits serious attention—attention that it has not heretofore received.

### IV. The Arbitrariness of Deontological Thresholds

... What I intend to do now is drop the assumption that N is not arbitrary in a morally problematic way. That assumption, I believe, is incorrect. Recall that Moore believes that locating N, while difficult, is no different in kind from the sorites problem of identifying the number of stones required to make a heap. I believe, on the contrary, that the moral arbitrariness of N is not a sorites problem, and that such arbitrariness seriously threatens Moore's picture of deontological thresholds.

My demonstration of N's arbitrariness will borrow heavily from a recent article by Anthony Ellis. Ellis puts forward three propositions that a threshold deontologist might accept:

> (1) There is some number [N] at which the act that was wrong becomes right....
>
> (2) There is no non-arbitrary way of specifying [N].
>
> (3) The difference between what is morally right and what is morally wrong cannot be arbitrary.

The three propositions are inconsistent, so one must be rejected. The threshold deontologist presumably must hold (1), so that leaves rejecting either (2) or (3). And (3) seems plausible, so (2) appears the most eligible for rejection.

Is (2) correct? Ellis canvasses several arguments that might be raised against (2). First, someone might assert that the threshold for killing to save lives is ten, and then defend that choice of N against the charge of arbitrariness by pointing out that the death of ten is worse than the death of nine. But, says Ellis, this cannot rebut the charge of arbitrariness. As Ellis puts it, "[W]hat needs to be explained is why a given level of harm generates the [threshold], and this is not explained by pointing out that this level is greater than some lesser level."

Neither is it a satisfactory defense of the non-arbitrariness of N to appeal to the idea of judgment. Ellis's response to this tack, which response I endorse, is worth quoting at length:

> This response seems—to speak plainly—to be little more than bluff and rhetoric. There can be judgment only where there is something to be judged about. And that does not simply mean that there must be an issue to be resolved, but that there must be considerations capable of resolving the issue (or—at the very least—bearing intelligibly upon its resolution). And the problem here is to see what considerations could do that. It is not enough simply to assert that we have to weigh the wrongness of the action against the badness of the consequences of refraining from it. That is not the solution, but the problem. What we need an account of is how that weighing can be carried out—an account of what considerations judgment is supposed to be exercised upon, and how that exercise works upon them. Put simply, we need to be told not merely that locating N requires judgment, but how judgment is to take into account the relevant considerations of lives and rights.

A third response that Ellis rejects is one that argues that the problem of locating N is merely epistemological. For example, many people hold such a view about the morality of abortion. Such people believe that we know that at some point between conception and birth, the fetus becomes a "person" (i.e., morally protectable), but that we do not know exactly where this point is. Ellis replies that even if the fetus becomes a person at a precise point in time, and it does so by virtue of something that we cannot understand (e.g., ensoulment by God), the same thing cannot be true for locating N.

The present suggestion is that there is a reason why [N] is just here but one which we do not know, or cannot understand. But the suggestion seems bizarre. It is hard to believe, after all, that there is anything more that we could learn about the scale of harm which [N] ... involves, and its relation to the harm involved in other [situations], which could even be relevant to our moral decision. Locating N is not an epistemological problem.

The reason locating N is arbitrary, Ellis argues, is that it involves the weighing of incommensurables. Deontologists treat killing an innocent person for others' benefit as intrinsically wrong. Consequences are immaterial insofar as one is a deontologist. On the other hand, for the consequentialist, consequences are all that matter. The only thing that is intrinsically wrong for her is the act-type "failure to promote the best consequences."

Consequentialism and deontology may be incommensurable in two ways. One might say that both deontological norms and consequentialist ones apply to every choice, but neither is weightier than the other. When they generate conflicting prescriptions, then they create moral dilemmas. But this will not help the threshold deontologist locate N because the threshold deontologist holds, not that there are moral dilemmas where consequentionalism and deontology conflict, but that deontology should reign below N and consequentialism above it. That is an entirely different picture from one of moral dilemma.

The other sense in which deontology and consequentialism might be incommensurable is if no consequentialist considerations could ever outweigh deontological ones (or vice versa). But this would lead to regarding deontological (or consequentionalist) norms as absolute. The threshold deontologist obviously must reject this account as well, for on it, just as on the moral dilemma account, there is no N.

The threshold deontologist must regard deontological and consequentialist norms as being capable of being weighed against each other—that is, as being commensurable. For the threshold deontologist's claim is that at N, consequences justify acts that are otherwise intrinsically wrong. But it is difficult to see how consequences could do this unless consequences and intrinsic wrongness were commensurable on some scale.

If the specification of N is arbitrary—and I believe that Ellis has shown that it must be—then perhaps the threshold deontologist should reject either the third proposition (that the difference between what is morally right and morally wrong cannot be arbitrary), or the first proposition (that there is a specific number N at which wrong acts become right) mentioned above.

I believe it is clear that the threshold deontologist—as opposed, perhaps, to someone who viewed morality as thoroughly dilemmatic—cannot accept that moral rightness is arbitrary and thus must accept the third proposition. That leaves the threshold deontologist with the possibility of rejecting the first proposition. Indeed, Moore himself regards the problem of specifying N for threshold deontology as analogous to the classic sorites problem of specifying N for rocks in a "heap." Just as there may be no specific N for "heapness," there may be no specific N for killing, torturing, or rescuing, and so forth, in order to save lives, avoid pain, and so forth. As Ellis puts this argument, killing one to save one may be wrong, killing one to save two may be wrong (but less so), and so on, "[b]ut ... as we proceed through the series of acts the act gets less wrong until, at some later points, it is right; but there was never any point at which it became right. There is in the series no last case of rightness." Just as if we start with a totally bald man and add hairs to his head, eventually he would be hirsute without there being any specific number of hairs that marks the point where baldness ceases and hirsuteness begins, so too with the morality of killings to save lives.

Now this analogy requires that there be degrees of wrongness. In the typical sorites example, we have a vague predicate (e.g., "bald" or "orange") and a smooth continuum (e.g., from bald to hirsute, or from orange to red), and it does make sense there to refer to degrees of baldness or to degrees of orangeness. However, in the case of threshold deontology, there is a radical discontinuity at the point of N. So in order to make use of the sorites analogy, the threshold deontologist must reject the idea that there are discontinuities as we move from deontologically forbidden to consequentially required.

Suppose the threshold deontologist rejects discontinuous change and accepts that there are diminishing degrees of wrongness as we make the consequences of abiding by deontological norms more and more dire. Can he then, as in the case of vague predicates, avail himself of the sorites analogy and deny that there is a specific number N that marks the threshold? He cannot. Denying that there is a specific cutoff point in threshold deontology is arbitrary and troubling in a way that is disanalogous to typical sorites examples....

... Take an analogy. There is no precise cutoff between, say, red and orange, and if we wanted one we should have to specify it arbitrarily. But we could not put it just anywhere within the colour spectrum. We should be faced with specifying an arbitrary point, but within a non-arbitrary range. That is not what we are faced with in morality. Specifying a range where the transition from wrong to right takes place would be no less arbitrary than would be specifying a precise cutoff. And if, to make the analogy with the transition from red to orange yet closer, it was said that the limits of the range are somewhat vague, this would still leave the position unaltered. The concession that the range is a vague range makes it no less arbitrary.

Why is the threshold deontologist's location of N disanalogous to the problem of vague predicates, such as red and orange?

In the transition from red to orange we find a range of cases about which we are unsure (itself a vague range) and ranges of cases (vague again) about which we are quite sure. Now those ranges are given by a deep and wide agreement in judgements, and that agreement settles any questions that might arise about the proper description of any point on that part of the colour spectrum. It could not be like this in morality. It is not just that we do not find agreement in judgements here. (Though we don't, and this is to be expected on my account.) If that were all that it is, then we could simply conclude that, where there is not such agreement, the matter is indeterminate, not yet decided. The problem is that in morality such judgements cannot be settled by group agreement....

Suppose that everyone did in fact agree, on the number 50 say, but no-one could give any reason why it should be 50 and not some other number. This would not tell us anything about moral theory; it would simply be an utterly bizarre mystery. And if we found agreement on a vague range—again with no-one able to give any reason to justify this range rather than some other—then this might be less dramatic but it would be just as mysterious. It would be senseless to think that this agreement could make any contribution to settling the moral question.

Thus, the threshold deontologist cannot utilize the sorites analogy and deny that there is any specific N that marks the threshold. And I have already shown that any specific N must be arbitrary. If one then accepts the third proposition and denies that the difference between the morally right and morally wrong can be arbitrary, threshold deontology would then be an untenable position. The three propositions are not jointly compatible, yet the threshold deontologist must accept them all.

### V. Threshold Deontology as Indirect Consequentialism

Perhaps, however, I am mistaken in thinking that threshold deontologists like Moore are really deontologists at all, even if a softer type than Kantian absolutists. Suppose that threshold deontologists are actually thoroughgoing consequentialists for whom deontological restrictions are at bottom merely heuristics for the indirect pursuit of the Good. This would explain Moore's rather cavalier treatment of how N is to be specified. Moore could believe that following rules that prohibit killings or torturings of some as means to save others from greater harm would ultimately produce better consequences than having each person weigh the predicted consequences of each choice. The reasons are familiar—cognitive limits and biases, coordination difficulties, and decision costs. On the other hand, a moral rule which tells us not to kill or torture unless the consequences of not doing so are catastrophic, but that leaves catastrophic undefined, might produce better consequences than one that absolutely forbids killings and torture, or one that specifies the precise number of saved lives that justify killing or torture. The absolute rule might be followed too well. The rule with a specific threshold may look too arbitrary (because it is arbitrary), and people might start reasoning down the slippery slope from an arbitrary N to pure consequentialist balancing, which by hypothesis is undesirable.

A rule with an exception for catastrophes, but that leaves catastrophes unspecified, may then be optimal in terms of consequences. Of course, the matter is an empirical one and like all indirect consequentialist rules cannot be confidently formulated from one's armchair. Still, the account that sees threshold deontology as an indirect consequentialist strategy is plausible, and it can explain why the inability to specify N non-arbitrarily is not a problem but a virtue.

In the end, however, I doubt that Moore—or Nagel or Nozick for that matter—want to grasp this lifeline. Nothing in what Moore or the others have written suggests that they are consequentialists at the level of their deepest moral beliefs. To the contrary, I believe that their deontological positions are at least as fundamental are their consequentialist ones. If I am correct, then the arbitrariness of N cannot be dismissed by Moore in the way that an indirect consequentialist might.

VI. Conceptualizing the Conflict Between Deontology and Consequentialism

... Moore's picture of threshold deontology as a deontological dam holding back a consequentialist body of water ultimately treats the deontological and consequentialist conceptions as commensurable. Dams and bodies of water can be compared along the dimension of height, so that the dam either will, or will not, be higher than the water. But deontology and consequentialism are incommensurable because they are fundamentally opposed conceptions of what morality is about. One sees the individual as inviolate, an end in himself, and the opposite of a resource for the betterment of the world. The other sees the individual in exactly the opposite way.

The threshold deontologist would have us believe that we switch from not being resources for others to being resources for others when N is reached. When N is looked at like that, however, it seems downright implausible that the moral universe is so constituted. There may be thresholds at which new phenomena emerge, but it is quite another thing to have thresholds at which things become their opposites.

## *Notes and Questions*

1. The thorniest problem in the context of the necessity defense is how to non-arbitrarily balance the evils that are in conflict. This raises the commensurability problem that Professor Ferzan discusses in the excerpted article. How can we, for example, compare the harm caused by torture with the harm brought about when we let an innocent person die? How do we compare the relative value of human lives? Should all human lives be valued equally in the consequentialist calculus or should some lives count more than others? Should the life of a scientist who is on the verge of developing a vaccine for cancer be valued more than the life of a law professor? Explain.

2. Ferzan asks "whether it would be permissible, not to torture the terrorist, but to torture the terrorist's innocent baby" in order to prevent a 9/11-type event. Would it? Why or why not?

3. As Professor Alexander points out, many non-consequentialists consider themselves "threshold deontologists." A threshold deontologist believes that non-consequentialist rules that prohibit engaging in certain conduct yield when following the non-consequentialist rule would have catastrophic consequences. Thus, Michael Moore claims that the non-consequentialist rule against torture or against the taking of innocent life gives way when torturing or killing innocents avoids a harm of catastrophic magnitude. Do you share Moore's intuitions that torturing and killing innocents is morally wrong unless doing so is necessary to avoid a catastrophe? Or do you believe that torturing people or killing innocents is wrong even in order to avoid a catastrophe?

4. Alexander argues that there is no non-arbitrary way to determine when deontological norms give way to consequentialist considerations. Deontology holds that certain

acts (e.g., torture) are categorically wrong regardless of whether they produce good consequences. In contrast, consequentialism holds that no act is categorically wrong, for the wrongfulness of an act depends on whether it brings about good consequences. Given that these two rules originate in "fundamentally opposed conceptions of what morality is about," it is difficult to see how deontology and consequentialism can be combined in the way that threshold deontology requires. If it is categorically wrong to torture even when doing so is necessary to save N number of lives, it is odd to claim that it suddenly becomes permissible to torture someone to save N+1 lives. Do you agree with Alexander's criticism of threshold deontology? Explain.

# Chapter 15

# Defensive Force Justifications

## § 15.01 Defensive Force: Imminent Wrongful Aggression

### State v. Norman

Supreme Court of North Carolina, 1989
324 N.C. 253

MITCHELL, Justice.

The defendant was tried at the 16 February 1987 Criminal Session of Superior Court for Rutherford County upon a proper indictment charging her with the first degree murder of her husband. The jury found the defendant guilty of voluntary manslaughter. The defendant appealed from the trial court's judgment sentencing her to six years imprisonment.

The Court of Appeals granted a new trial, citing as error the trial court's refusal to submit a possible verdict of acquittal by reason of perfect self-defense. Notwithstanding the uncontroverted evidence that the defendant shot her husband three times in the back of the head as he lay sleeping in his bed, the Court of Appeals held that the defendant's evidence that she exhibited what has come to be called "the battered wife syndrome" entitled her to have the jury consider whether the homicide was an act of perfect self-defense and, thus, not a legal wrong.

We conclude that the evidence introduced in this case would not support a finding that the defendant killed her husband due to a reasonable fear of imminent death or great bodily harm, as is required before a defendant is entitled to jury instructions concerning either perfect or imperfect self-defense. Therefore, the trial court properly declined to instruct the jury on the law relating to self-defense. Accordingly, we reverse the Court of Appeals.

At trial, the State presented the testimony of Deputy Sheriff R.H. Epley of the Rutherford County Sheriff's Department, who was called to the Norman residence on the night of 12 June 1985. Inside the home, Epley found the defendant's husband, John Thomas Norman, lying on a bed in a rear bedroom with his face toward the wall and his back toward the middle of the room. He was dead, but blood was still coming from wounds to the back of his head. A later autopsy revealed three gunshot wounds to the head, two of which caused fatal brain injury. The autopsy also revealed a .12 percent blood alcohol level in the victim's body.

Later that night, the defendant related an account of the events leading to the killing, after Epley had advised her of her constitutional rights and she had waived her right to remain silent. The defendant told Epley that her husband had been beating her all day and had made her lie down on the floor while he slept on the bed. After her husband fell asleep, the defendant carried her grandchild to the defendant's mother's house. The defendant took a pistol from her mother's purse and walked the short distance back to her home. She pointed the pistol at the back of her sleeping husband's head, but it jammed the first time she tried to shoot him. She fixed the gun and then shot her husband in the back of the head as he lay sleeping. After one shot, she felt her husband's chest and determined that he was still breathing and making sounds. She then shot him twice more in the back of the head. The defendant told Epley that she killed her husband because "she took all she was going to take from him so she shot him."

The defendant presented evidence tending to show a long history of physical and mental abuse by her husband due to his alcoholism. At the time of the killing, the thirty-nine-year-old defendant and her husband had been married almost twenty-five years and had several children. The defendant testified that her husband had started drinking and abusing her about five years after they were married. His physical abuse of her consisted of frequent assaults that included slapping, punching and kicking her, striking her with various objects, and throwing glasses, beer bottles and other objects at her. The defendant described other specific incidents of abuse, such as her husband putting her cigarettes out on her, throwing hot coffee on her, breaking glass against her face and crushing food on her face. Although the defendant did not present evidence of ever having received medical treatment for any physical injuries inflicted by her husband, she displayed several scars about her face which she attributed to her husband's assaults.

The defendant's evidence also tended to show other indignities inflicted upon her by her husband. Her evidence tended to show that her husband did not work and forced her to make money by prostitution, and that he made humor of that fact to family and friends. He would beat her if she resisted going out to prostitute herself or if he was unsatisfied with the amounts of money she made. He routinely called the defendant "dog," "bitch" and "whore," and on a few occasions made her eat pet food out of the pets' bowls and bark like a dog. He often made her sleep on the floor. At times, he deprived her of food and refused to let her get food for the family. During those years of abuse, the defendant's husband threatened numerous times to kill her and to maim her in various ways.

The defendant said her husband's abuse occurred only when he was intoxicated, but that he would not give up drinking. She said she and her husband "got along very well when he was sober," and that he was "a good guy" when he was not drunk. She had accompanied her husband to the local mental health center for sporadic counseling sessions for his problem, but he continued to drink.

In the early morning hours on the day before his death, the defendant's husband, who was intoxicated, went to a rest area off I-85 near Kings Mountain where the defendant was engaging in prostitution and assaulted her. While driving home, he was stopped by a patrolman and jailed on a charge of driving while impaired. After the defendant's mother got him out of jail at the defendant's request later that morning, he resumed his drinking and abuse of the defendant.

The defendant's evidence also tended to show that her husband seemed angrier than ever after he was released from jail and that his abuse of the defendant was more frequent. That evening, sheriff's deputies were called to the Norman residence, and the defendant complained that her husband had been beating her all day and she could not take it anymore. The defendant was advised to file a complaint, but she said she was afraid her husband would kill her if she had him arrested. The deputies told her they needed a warrant before they could arrest her husband, and they left the scene.

The deputies were called back less than an hour later after the defendant had taken a bottle of pills. The defendant's husband cursed her and called her names as she was attended by paramedics, and he told them to let her die. A sheriff's deputy finally chased him back into his house as the defendant was put into an ambulance. The defendant's stomach was pumped at the local hospital, and she was sent home with her mother.

While in the hospital, the defendant was visited by a therapist with whom she discussed filing charges against her husband and having him committed for treatment. Before the therapist left, the defendant agreed to go to the mental health center the next day to discuss those possibilities. The therapist testified at trial that the defendant seemed depressed in the hospital, and that she expressed considerable anger toward her husband. He testified that the defendant threatened a number of times that night to kill her husband and that she said she should kill him "because of the things he had done to her."

The next day, the day she shot her husband, the defendant went to the mental health center to talk about charges and possible commitment, and she confronted her husband with that possibility. She testified that she told her husband later that day: "J.T., straighten up. Quit drinking. I'm going to have you committed to help you." She said her husband then told her he would "see them coming" and would cut her throat before they got to him.

The defendant also went to the social services office that day to seek welfare benefits, but her husband followed her there, interrupted her interview and made her go home with him. He continued his abuse of her, threatening to kill and to maim her, slapping her, kicking her, and throwing objects at her. At one point, he took her cigarette and put it out on her, causing a small burn on her upper torso. He would not let her eat or bring food into the house for their children.

That evening, the defendant and her husband went into their bedroom to lie down, and he called her a "dog" and made her lie on the floor when he lay down on the bed. Their daughter brought in her baby to leave with the defendant, and the defendant's husband agreed to let her baby-sit. After the defendant's husband fell asleep, the baby started crying and the defendant took it to her mother's house so it would not wake up her husband. She returned shortly with the pistol and killed her husband.

The defendant testified at trial that she was too afraid of her husband to press charges against him or to leave him. She said that she had temporarily left their home on several previous occasions, but he had always found her, brought her home and beaten her. Asked why she killed her husband, the defendant replied: "Because I was scared of him and I knowed when he woke up, it was going to be the same thing, and I was scared when he took me to the truck stop that night it was going to be worse than he had ever been. I just couldn't take it no more. There ain't no way, even if it means going to prison. It's better than living in that. That's worse hell than anything."

The defendant and other witnesses testified that for years her husband had frequently threatened to kill her and to maim her. When asked if she believed those threats, the defendant replied: "Yes. I believed him; he would, he would kill me if he got a chance. If he thought he wouldn't a had to went to jail, he would a done it."

Two expert witnesses in forensic psychology and psychiatry who examined the defendant after the shooting, Dr. William Tyson and Dr. Robert Rollins, testified that the defendant fit the profile of battered wife syndrome. This condition, they testified, is characterized by such abuse and degradation that the battered wife comes to believe she is unable to help herself and cannot expect help from anyone else. She believes that she cannot escape the complete control of her husband and that he is invulnerable to law enforcement and other sources of help.

Dr. Tyson, a psychologist, was asked his opinion as to whether, on 12 June 1985, "it appeared reasonably necessary for Judy Norman to shoot J.T. Norman?" He replied: "I believe that ... Mrs. Norman believed herself to be doomed ... to a life of the worst kind of torture and abuse, degradation that she had experienced over the years in a progressive way; that it would only get worse, and that death was inevitable...." Dr. Tyson later added: "I think Judy Norman felt that she had no choice, both in the protection of herself and her family, but to engage, exhibit deadly force against Mr. Norman, and that in so doing, she was sacrificing herself, both for herself and for her family."

Dr. Rollins, who was the defendant's attending physician at Dorothea Dix Hospital when she was sent there for evaluation, testified that in his opinion the defendant was a typical abused spouse and that "[s]he saw herself as powerless to deal with the situation, that there was no alternative, no way she could escape it." Dr. Rollins was asked his opinion as to whether "on June 12th, 1985, it appeared reasonably necessary that Judy Norman would take the life of J.T. Norman?" Dr. Rollins replied that in his opinion, "that course of action did appear necessary to Mrs. Norman."

Based on the evidence that the defendant exhibited battered wife syndrome, that she believed she could not escape her husband nor expect help from others, that her husband had threatened her, and that her husband's abuse of her had worsened in the two days preceding his death, the Court of Appeals concluded that a jury reasonably could have found that her killing of her husband was justified as an act of perfect self-defense. The Court of Appeals reasoned that the nature of battered wife syndrome is such that a jury could not be precluded from finding the defendant killed her husband lawfully in perfect self-defense, even though he was asleep when she killed him. We disagree.

The right to kill in self-defense is based on the necessity, real or reasonably apparent, of killing an unlawful aggressor to save oneself from *imminent* death or great bodily harm at his hands. Our law has recognized that self-preservation under such circumstances springs from a primal impulse and is an inherent right of natural law.

In North Carolina, a defendant is entitled to have the jury consider acquittal by reason of *perfect* self-defense when the evidence, viewed in the light most favorable to the defendant, tends to show that at the time of the killing it appeared to the defendant and she believed it to be necessary to kill the decedent to save herself from imminent death or great bodily harm. That belief must be reasonable, however, in that the circumstances as they appeared to the defendant would create such a belief in the mind of a person of ordinary firmness. Further, the defendant must not have been the initial aggressor provoking the fatal confrontation. A killing in the proper exercise of the right of *perfect* self-defense is always completely justified in law and constitutes no legal wrong ...

The defendant in the present case was not entitled to a jury instruction on ... self-defense. The trial court was not required to instruct on ... self-defense unless evidence was introduced tending to show that at the time of the killing the defendant reasonably believed herself to be confronted by circumstances which necessitated her killing her husband to save herself from *imminent* death or great bodily harm. No such evidence was introduced in this case ...

The killing of another human being is the most extreme recourse to our inherent right of self-preservation and can be justified in law only by the utmost real or apparent necessity brought about by the decedent. For that reason, our law of self-defense has required that a defendant claiming that a homicide was justified and, as a result, inherently lawful by reason of perfect self-defense must establish that she reasonably believed at the time of the killing she otherwise would have immediately suffered death or great bodily harm.

has to be immediate/imminent danger

Only if defendants are required to show that they killed due to a reasonable belief that death or great bodily harm was imminent can the justification for homicide remain clearly and firmly rooted in necessity. The imminence requirement ensures that deadly force will be used only where it is necessary as a last resort in the exercise of the inherent right of self-preservation. It also ensures that before a homicide is justified and, as a result, not a legal wrong, it will be reliably determined that the defendant reasonably believed that absent the use of deadly force, not only would an unlawful attack have occurred, but also that the attack would have caused death or great bodily harm. The law does not sanction the use of deadly force to repel simple assaults.

The term "imminent," as used to describe such perceived threats of death or great bodily harm as will justify a homicide by reason of perfect self-defense, has been defined as "immediate danger, such as must be instantly met, such as cannot be guarded against by calling for the assistance of others or the protection of the law." Our cases have sometimes used the phrase "about to suffer" interchangeably with "imminent" to describe the immediacy of threat that is required to justify killing in self-defense.

The evidence in this case did not tend to show that the defendant reasonably believed that she was confronted by a threat of imminent death or great bodily harm. The evidence tended to show that no harm was "imminent" or about to happen to the defendant when she shot her husband. The uncontroverted evidence was that her husband had been asleep for some time when she walked to her mother's house, returned with the pistol, fixed the pistol after it jammed and then shot her husband three times in the back of the head. The defendant was not faced with an instantaneous choice between killing her husband or being killed or seriously injured. Instead, *all* of the evidence tended to show that the defendant had ample time and opportunity to resort to other means of preventing further abuse by her husband. There was no action underway by the decedent from which the jury could have found that the defendant had reasonable grounds to believe either that a felonious assault was imminent or that it might result in her death or great bodily injury. Additionally, no such action by the decedent had been underway immediately prior to his falling asleep ...

Dr. Tyson ... testified that the defendant "believed herself to be doomed ... to a life of the worst kind of torture and abuse, degradation that she had experienced over the years in a progressive way; that it would only get worse, and that death was inevitable." Such evidence of the defendant's speculative beliefs concerning her remote and indefinite future, while indicating she had felt generally threatened, did not tend to show that she killed in the belief—reasonable or otherwise—that her husband presented a threat of *imminent* death or great bodily harm. Under our law of self-defense, a defendant's subjective belief of what might be "inevitable" at some indefinite point in the future does not equate to what she believes to be "imminent." Dr. Tyson's opinion that the defendant believed it was necessary to kill her husband for "the protection of herself and her family" was similarly indefinite and devoid of time frame and did not tend to show a threat or fear of *imminent* harm....

We are not persuaded by the reasoning of our Court of Appeals in this case that when there is evidence of battered wife syndrome, neither an actual attack nor threat of attack by the husband at the moment the wife uses deadly force is required to justify the wife's killing of him in perfect self-defense. The Court of Appeals concluded that to impose such requirements would ignore the "learned helplessness," meekness and other realities of battered wife syndrome and would effectively preclude such women from exercising their right of self-defense ...

The Court of Appeals suggests that ... [an instruction regarding self-defense was appropriate in the case] because the jury, based on the evidence of the decedent's intensified abuse during the thirty-six hours preceding his death, could have found that the decedent's passive state at the time of his death was "but a momentary hiatus in a continuous reign of terror by the decedent [and] the defendant merely took advantage of her first opportunity to protect herself." Requiring jury instructions on perfect self-defense in such situations, however, would still tend to make opportune homicide lawful as a result of mere subjective predictions of indefinite future assaults and circumstances. Such predictions of future assaults to justify the defendant's use of deadly force in this case would be entirely speculative, because there was no evidence that her husband had ever inflicted any harm upon her that approached life-threatening injury, even during the "reign of terror." It is far from clear in the defendant's poignant evidence that any abuse by the decedent had ever involved the degree of physical threat required to justify the defendant in using deadly force, even when those threats were imminent. The use of deadly force in self-defense to prevent harm other than death or great bodily harm is excessive as a matter of law.

As we have stated, stretching the law of self-defense to fit the facts of this case would require changing the "imminent death or great bodily harm" requirement to something substantially more indefinite than previously required and would weaken our assurances that justification for the taking of human life remains firmly rooted in real or apparent necessity. That result in principle could not be limited to a few cases decided on evidence as poignant as this. The relaxed requirements for perfect self-defense proposed by our Court of Appeals would tend to categorically legalize the opportune killing of abusive husbands by their wives solely on the basis of the wives' testimony concerning their subjective speculation as to the probability of future felonious assaults by their husbands. Homicidal self-help would then become a lawful solution, and perhaps the easiest and most effective solution, to this problem. In conclusion, we decline to expand our law of self-defense beyond the limits of immediacy and necessity which have heretofore provided an appropriately narrow but firm basis upon which homicide may be justified and, thus, lawful by reason of perfect self-defense ...

For the foregoing reasons, we conclude that the defendant's conviction for voluntary manslaughter and the trial court's judgment sentencing her to a six-year term of imprisonment were without error. Therefore, we must reverse the decision of the Court of Appeals which awarded the defendant a new trial.

**MARTIN, Justice, dissenting.**

... At the heart of the majority's reasoning is its unsubstantiated concern that to find that the evidence presented by defendant would support an instruction on self-defense would "expand our law of self-defense beyond the limits of immediacy and necessity." Defendant does not seek to expand or relax the requirements of self-defense and thereby "legalize the opportune killing of allegedly abusive husbands by their wives," as the majority overstates. Rather, defendant contends that the evidence as gauged by the existing laws of self-defense is sufficient to require the submission of a self-defense instruction to the jury. The proper issue for this Court is to determine whether the evidence, viewed in the light most favorable to the defendant, was sufficient to require the trial court to instruct on the law of self-defense. I conclude that it was ...

A defendant is entitled to an instruction on self-defense when there is evidence, viewed in the light most favorable to the defendant, that these four elements existed at the time of the killing:

(1) it appeared to defendant and he believed it to be necessary to kill the deceased in order to save himself from death or great bodily harm; and

> (2) defendant's belief was reasonable in that the circumstances as they appeared to him at the time were sufficient to create such a belief in the mind of a person of ordinary firmness; and
>
> (3) defendant was not the aggressor in bringing on the affray, i.e., he did not aggressively and willingly enter into the fight without legal excuse or provocation; and
>
> (4) defendant did not use excessive force, i.e., did not use more force than was necessary or reasonably appeared to him to be necessary under the circumstances to protect himself from death or great bodily harm ...

The first element requires that there be evidence that the defendant believed it was necessary to kill in order to protect herself from serious bodily harm or death; the second requires that the circumstances as defendant perceived them were sufficient to create such a belief in the mind of a person of ordinary firmness. Both elements were supported by evidence at defendant's trial.

Evidence presented by defendant described a twenty-year history of beatings and other dehumanizing and degrading treatment by her husband. In his expert testimony a clinical psychologist concluded that defendant fit "and exceed[ed]" the profile of an abused or battered spouse, analogizing this treatment to the dehumanization process suffered by prisoners of war under the Nazis during the Second World War and the brainwashing techniques of the Korean War. The psychologist described the defendant as a woman incarcerated by abuse, by fear, and by her conviction that her husband was invincible and inescapable:

> Mrs. Norman didn't leave because she believed, fully believed that escape was totally impossible. There was no place to go. He, she had left before; he had come and gotten her. She had gone to the Department of Social Services. He had come and gotten her. The law, she believed the law could not protect her; no one could protect her, and I must admit, looking over the records, that there was nothing done that would contradict that belief. She fully believed that he was invulnerable to the law and to all social agencies that were available; that nobody could withstand his power. As a result, there was no such thing as escape.

When asked if he had an opinion whether it appeared reasonably necessary for Judy Norman to shoot her husband, this witness responded:

> Yes.... I believe that in examining the facts of this case and examining the psychological data, that Mrs. Norman believed herself to be doomed ... to a life of the worst kind of torture and abuse, degradation that she had experienced over the years in a progressive way; that it would only get worse, and that death was inevitable; death of herself, which was not such, I don't think was such an issue for her, as she had attempted to commit suicide, and in her continuing conviction of J.T. Norman's power over her, and even failed at that form of escape. I believe she also came to the point of beginning to fear for family members and her children, that were she to commit suicide that the abuse and the treatment that was heaped on her would be transferred onto them.

This testimony describes defendant's perception of circumstances in which she was held hostage to her husband's abuse for two decades and which ultimately compelled her to kill him. This testimony alone is evidence amply indicating the first two elements required for entitlement to an instruction on self-defense.

In addition to the testimony of the clinical psychologist, defendant presented the testimony of witnesses who had actually seen defendant's husband abuse her. These witnesses described circumstances that caused not only defendant to believe escape was impossible, but that also convinced *them* of its impossibility. Defendant's isolation and helplessness were evident in testimony that her family was intimidated by her husband into acquiescing in his torture of her. Witnesses also described defendant's experience with social service agencies and the law, which had contributed to her sense of futility and abandonment through the inefficacy of their protection and the strength of her husband's wrath when they failed. Where torture appears interminable and escape impossible, the belief that only the death of the oppressor can provide relief is reasonable in the mind of a person of ordinary firmness, let alone in the mind of the defendant, who, like a prisoner of war of some years, has been deprived of her humanity and is held hostage by fear....

Defendant's intense fear, based on her belief that her husband intended not only to maim or deface her, as he had in the past, but to kill her, was evident in the testimony of witnesses who recounted events of the last three days of the decedent's life. This testimony could have led a juror to conclude that defendant reasonably perceived a threat to her life as "imminent," even while her husband slept. Over these three days, her husband's anger was exhibited in an unprecedented crescendo of violence. The evidence showed defendant's fear and sense of hopelessness similarly intensifying, leading to an unsuccessful attempt to escape through suicide and culminating in her belief that escape would be possible only through her husband's death....

By his barbaric conduct over the course of twenty years, J.T. Norman reduced the quality of the defendant's life to such an abysmal state that, given the opportunity to do so, the jury might well have found that she was justified in acting in self-defense for the preservation of her tragic life ...

If the evidence in support of self-defense is sufficient to create a reasonable doubt in the mind of a rational juror whether the state has proved an intentional killing without justification or excuse, self-defense must be submitted to the jury. This is such a case.

## *Notes and Questions*

1. A person may justifiably use force against a wrongful aggressor in order to protect her person, property or habitation. Force may also be used against a wrongful aggressor in order to protect a third party from an unlawful attack. These cases share four elements in common. First, the use of force is triggered by the existence of an imminent wrongful attack. Second, the use of force is justified only if it's necessary to avert the wrongful attack. Third, the use of force is justifiable only if it is in some way proportional to the averted harm. Finally, justification follows only if the actor reasonably believed that the use of force was necessary to repel the wrongful attack. This section focuses on the requirement that the defensive force be triggered by an "imminent wrongful aggression." The remaining requirements are discussed in subsequent sections.

2. The *Norman* case illustrates the traditional view that force is justified pursuant to self-defense only if the defendant reasonably believes such force to be necessary to repel an "imminent" attack. The North Carolina Supreme Court concluded that Judy Norman's killing of her husband could not be justified as self-defense because a spouse cannot engage in an "imminent aggression" while she is asleep. The dissenting judge disagreed, analogizing Judy Norman's situation to that of a hostage who is continuously under attack until she is released. So conceived, the fact that the spouse fell asleep should be viewed—as the Court of Appeals suggested—as "a momentary hiatus in a continuous

reign of terror by the decedent." According to the dissent, just like a hostage may seek freedom by using force against her kidnappers even while they are asleep, Judy Norman may terminate her abuse by attacking her abusive husband even while he was sleeping. The majority, on the other hand, argued that expanding the meaning of "imminence" to justify killing sleeping abusers should be resisted because it presents the danger of "legaliz[ing] the opportune killing of abusive husbands by their wives solely on the basis.... [of] subjective speculation as to the probability of future felonious assaults by their husbands." Who has the better part of this argument? Why?

3. Note that several experts testified that they believed that Judy Norman suffered from what psychologists call "battered woman syndrome" (BWS). People who suffer from BWS often experience a feeling of "learned helplessness" that makes them think that they are powerless to prevent future abuses. Such evidence is generally admissible because it may help the factfinder assess whether the battered woman's belief that force was necessary was "objectively reasonable." The reasons justifying the admissibility of BWS evidence were summarized in *State v. Kelly*, 97 N.J. 178 (1984):

> The crucial issue of fact on which [BWS] testimony would bear is why, given such allegedly severe and constant beatings, combined with threats to kill, [a battered woman does not leave her spouse]. Whether raised by the prosecutor as a factual issue or not, our own common knowledge tells us that most of us, including the ordinary juror, would ask himself or herself just such a question. And our knowledge is bolstered by the experts' knowledge, for the experts point out that one of the common myths, apparently believed by most people, is that battered wives are free to leave. To some, this misconception is followed by the observation that the battered wife is masochistic, proven by her refusal to leave despite the severe beatings; to others, however, the fact that the battered wife stays on unquestionably suggests that the "beatings" could not have been too bad for if they had been, she certainly would have left. The expert could clear up these myths, by explaining that one of the common characteristics of a battered wife is her inability to leave despite such constant beatings; her "learned helplessness"; her lack of anywhere to go; her feeling that if she tried to leave, she would be subjected to even more merciless treatment; her belief in the omnipotence of her battering husband; and sometimes her hope that her husband will change his ways.

Invoking this line of cases, the Court of Appeals suggested that a jury could find that—as a result of her learned helplessness—Judy Norman believed that it was necessary to kill her husband in order to prevent subsequent aggressions. The North Carolina Supreme Court, however, explained that no amount of BWS evidence is enough to justify killing a person while she is asleep. That is, someone in a non-confrontational situation (i.e., while the person is sleeping or is otherwise not confronting the defendant) cannot—as a matter of law—reasonably believe that force is necessary to repel an "imminent" attack. Do you agree? Explain.

4. It is important to distinguish evidence of the abusive spouse's history of violence and proof of the defendant's prior attempts to flee from expert testimony regarding BWS and learned helplessness. Evidence of an abusive spouse's history of violence is clearly relevant to determining whether the defendant's belief that killing her spouse was necessary to prevent an attack is objectively reasonable. Knowledge of someone else's history of violence would influence any reasonable person's beliefs regarding whether that person presents a threat. Furthermore, this evidence may be—and often will be—presented without the need for expert testimony. Both the defendant and others who know the abusive spouse may testify about prior acts of violence committed by the spouse. Finally, this ev-

idence may be admissible regardless of whether the defendant suffers from BWS, for the prior abuses may be offered to prove that the defendant's belief that she was being attacked was reasonable rather than to establish that she suffered from BWS. The same can be said about evidence of defendant's prior attempts to flee from her spouse. This evidence is clearly relevant to assessing whether using force against the abusive spouse was necessary. It is also admissible without the need of expert testimony and even if not presented to prove that the defendant suffered from BWS. Regarding the former, both the defendant and those who witnessed her attempts to escape the relationship are capable of testifying about this matter. With regard to the latter, defendant's attempts to flee are relevant to whether force is necessary regardless of whether the defendant suffered from BWS.

In contrast to these types of evidence, it is unclear whether evidence of BWS is relevant to assessing whether the defendant's belief that the use of force was necessary was objectively reasonable. There is a sense in which BWS evidence sounds more in the language of insanity than in the language of justification. So conceived, BWS may be viewed as evidence that demonstrates why defendant failed to perceive facts in the way that a reasonable person would perceive them. In other words, BWS evidence may not demonstrate that defendant's beliefs were objectively reasonable. Rather, it may reveal that—in spite of being unreasonable—defendant's beliefs were understandable in light of BWS. Additionally, note that BWS evidence is only admissible via expert testimony, for discussion of psychological phenomena requires specialized knowledge that laypeople lack.

5. Assuming that Judy Norman deserves to be acquitted, there are two ways of explaining why she should not be punished. On the one hand, it may be argued that killing her spouse was the right thing to do under the circumstances and, therefore, she had a right to kill her husband while he was sleeping. This amounts to asserting that killing the sleeping spouse in this case was justified and, thus, not wrongful. On the other hand, it may be contended that killing her husband was not the right thing do to under the circumstances and, therefore, she did not have a right to kill her spouse while he was asleep. Nevertheless, she should be acquitted because—in spite of the wrongfulness of her act—we could not have fairly expected her to behave in a different manner. This is equivalent to asserting that the killing should be excused rather than justified. Which rationale for acquitting Judy Norman do you find more persuasive? Why?

6. Assuming that Judy Norman's killing ought to be justified pursuant to self-defense, should we broaden what counts as an "imminent attack" in a way that may encompass killings in non-confrontational situations or is it better to abandon the "imminent attack" requirement altogether? Broadening the meaning of "imminence" can be achieved by arguing—as the Court of Appeals did in *Norman*—that some battered women cases present a "continuing attack" that can be analogized to hostage taking or kidnapping. The problem with doing so is that to conclude that someone who is sleeping is "imminently attacking" someone else does violence to the conventionally accepted meaning of "imminence." Perhaps we are willing do adopt an artificial meaning of imminence, but we should acknowledge that in doing so we are—at least partially—redefining the meaning of imminence. In contrast, one may simply bite the bullet and claim that the imminence requirement should be abandoned. Adopting this position would require making some other element the triggering condition for the use of defensive force. The most obvious candidate would be the requirement that force be "necessary" to repel an aggression. Perhaps we should justify pursuant to self-defense all killings that are "necessary" to repel aggressions, regardless of whether the aggressions are imminent or not. In the context of the *Norman* case, application of this view would lead to asking whether killing the sleeping spouse was the only way (i.e., "necessary") of preventing attacks that would surely

take place in the future. If the question is answered affirmatively, then the conduct ought to be justified even if the husband was not imminently attacking Judy Norman when she killed him. If the goal is to acquit defendants like Norman, do you prefer broadening imminence beyond its conventionally accepted meaning or abandoning the imminence requirement altogether? Explain. This issue is revisited in the "Scholarly Debates" section of this Chapter (§ 15.07).

7. In addition to being imminent, the aggression that triggers the right to use defensive force must also be "wrongful." But when is an attack "wrongful" in the sense required by self-defense? This question has generated considerable debate in the scholarly literature. While there are some cases in which it is unclear whether an aggression is wrongful, there are some instances in which attacks are obviously wrongful. If the attack amounts to a criminal offense, the aggression is clearly wrongful. What about an attack that satisfies the elements of an offense but is excused? There seems to be general agreement that such excused attacks also count as the sort of wrongful aggression that triggers a right to self-defense. The paradigmatic example would be that of an insane assailant that attacks an innocent person. See, e.g., Luis E. Chiesa and George P. Fletcher, 'Self-Defense and the Psychotic Aggressor' in Paul Robinson, Kimberly Ferzan, Stephen Garvey (eds), Criminal Law Conversations (Oxford, 2010). However, a minority of scholars think that excused aggression should not trigger the right to use force in self-defense. See, e.g., Kimberly Kessler Ferzan, 'Culpable Aggression: The Basis for Moral Liability to Defensive Killing', [2012] Ohio State J. Crim. L. 669.

8. Another particularly complicated case is that of an aggression that does not satisfy the voluntary act requirement. Think, for example, of a person who attacks you while sleepwalking or someone who violently thrusts their body toward you while they're having a seizure. These acts do not satisfy criminal law's act requirement and thus do not give rise to criminal liability. Do they, however, count as wrongful aggressions that trigger the right to use self-defense? There is scant case law on the subject. Even if such "acts" do not count as wrongful aggressions, using force to repel them should be justified pursuant to some other justification, such as lesser evils/necessity.

## § 15.02 Defensive Force: The Necessity of Using Force and the Retreat Doctrine

### Richards v. State

District Court of Appeals of Florida, Second District, 2010
39 So.3d 431

ALTENBERND, Judge.

John Rynell Richards, the Defendant, appeals his judgment and sentence for attempted murder in the second degree. He argues that the trial court improperly used an outdated jury instruction concerning his defense of the justifiable use of deadly force and that, accordingly, it committed an error when it told jurors he had a duty to retreat before using deadly force. The State concedes that the instruction was improper. We agree that the use of the outdated instruction was an error in this case. We reverse and remand for a new trial.

In October 2007, the Defendant was in a park in St. Petersburg with three friends. All four were homeless and were spending their time imbibing alcohol. This activity was detrimental to their recollection of the events of the day, and each recalled the events somewhat differently.

It is undisputed that the Defendant stabbed one of his friends, Mr. Russell. The other two friends testified at trial for the State. They generally explained that the Defendant, Mr. Russell, and a third member of the group were sitting on a park bench with Mr. Russell in the middle. The Defendant pulled out a knife and began waving it around. When Mr. Russell complained about this, the Defendant bit him on the arm. Mr. Russell tried to get the Defendant to stop biting him by grabbing the Defendant's face. When Mr. Russell did this, the Defendant cut Mr. Russell's ear with the knife and stabbed him in the neck.

Several officers responded to the scene. They testified that the Defendant was visibly intoxicated and made several loud statements upon being apprehended. He admitted stabbing the victim and claimed the victim was trying to kill him. At some point, he also said he had stabbed Mr. Russell because he thought Mr. Russell was going to attack him.

The officers testified that they had to forcibly subdue the Defendant to arrest him. They struggled with him and eventually forced him to the ground and put him in handcuffs. They claimed the Defendant was injured during the struggle and got cut on his head during the arrest.

The Defendant testified and told a very different story. According to him, the group was in the park that night, but they were not sitting close to one another. He and Mr. Russell were sitting on opposite ends of the same bench. The other two friends were sitting nearby.

The Defendant claimed that Mr. Russell wanted the Defendant to give him a beer. When Mr. Russell persisted in his requests for beer, they began arguing. Mr. Russell punched him in the face, grabbed him by the throat, and slammed him into the bench. Mr. Russell still had the Defendant by the throat when the Defendant pulled out his knife and stabbed Mr. Russell.

The Defendant claimed that he stabbed Mr. Russell because he feared for his life. After the incident, he got on his bicycle and pedaled away to wait for the police. When the police arrived, he waved them over to where he was standing.

The Defendant said his injuries that night were not the result of any altercation with the police, but were the result of Mr. Russell's attack. He claimed that Mr. Russell cut his face, blackened his eye, and bruised or cracked some of his ribs. His throat and neck were also sore for several days. He also claimed Mr. Russell had cracked the bench when he slammed him into it. The trial court admitted a picture of the bench on which the attack allegedly occurred. It was broken.

At the end of the case, the trial court instructed the jury on the justifiable use of deadly force, using the standard instruction that was applicable to offenses occurring prior to October 1, 2005. The instruction stated:

> The defendant cannot justify the use of force likely to cause death or great bodily harm unless he used every reasonable means within his power and consistent with his own safety to avoid the danger before resorting to that force.
>
> The fact that the defendant was wrongfully attacked cannot justify his use of force likely to cause death or great bodily harm if, by retreating, he could have avoided the need to use that force. However, if the defendant was placed in a

> position of imminent danger of death or great bodily harm, and it would have increased his own danger to retreat, then his use of force likely to cause death or great bodily harm was justifiable.

It is undisputed that this instruction was improper because the Florida legislature eliminated the duty to retreat in 2005.... The trial court should have instructed the jury that:

> If the defendant was not engaged in an unlawful activity and was attacked in any place where [he] had a right to be, [he] had no duty to retreat and had the right to stand [his] ground and meet force with force, including deadly force, if [he] reasonably believed that it was necessary to do so to prevent death or great bodily harm to [himself] or to prevent the commission of a forcible felony. *See* Fla. Std. Jury Instr. (Crim.) 3.6(f).

... The Defendant's sole defense at trial was that he acted in self-defense. According to him, he was in a public park with a group of acquaintances when Mr. Russell initiated the attack against him. If the jury accepted his version of the facts, the Defendant may not have had a legal duty to retreat before using deadly force. The outdated jury instructions effectively negated his defense.

We agree with the Fourth District that this error rises to the level of fundamental error ... Accordingly, we reverse and remand for a new trial.

## *Notes and Questions*

1. Assuming that there is an imminent wrongful aggression, use of force is lawful only if it is necessary to avert the attack. Force is necessary when there are no less harmful alternatives that may avert the attack with equal possibility of success. The necessity of the use of force is often confused with the proportionality of the force. If a pickpocket steals your wallet, is running away from you and the only way to stop him is to shoot him in the leg, shooting the pickpocket is necessary, although likely disproportional. It is necessary because it is the only means that you have available to stop the aggression. It is likely disproportional, however, because the harm threatened (loss of a wallet) is considerably less serious than the harm inflicted (serious bodily injury).

2. An issue related to the necessity of the use of force is the so-called "retreat" doctrine. According to the doctrine, a person has a duty to retreat before resorting to the use of deadly force if retreating could safely avert the attack. Nonetheless, the general rule is that there is no duty to retreat if non-deadly force is used to repel the aggression. The one glaring exception to the retreat doctrine is that there is no duty to retreat when you are attacked in your home. That is, a person attacked in her home may meet deadly force with deadly force even if retreating would avert the attack. This is typically called the "castle doctrine." This is the view generally followed at common law. Also—as the Court explained in *Richards*—this was the view followed in Florida prior to the enactment of the state "Stand Your Ground" statute in 2005. The standard common law position was summarized by the Florida Supreme Court in the pre "stand your ground" decision of *Weiand v. State,* 732 So.2d 1044 (1999):

> Under Florida statutory and common law, a person may use deadly force in self-defense if he or she reasonably believes that deadly force is necessary to prevent imminent death or great bodily harm. Even under those circumstances, however, a person may not resort to deadly force without first using every reasonable means within his or her power to avoid the danger, including re-

treat. The duty to retreat emanates from common law, rather than from our statutes.

There is an exception to this common law duty to retreat "to the wall," which applies when an individual claims self-defense in his or her own residence. An individual is not required to retreat from the residence before resorting to deadly force in self-defense, so long as the deadly force is necessary to prevent death or great bodily harm.

The privilege of nonretreat from the home, part of the "castle doctrine," has early common law origins. In the [*Tomlins* case], the defendant claimed self-defense when attacked in his home by his son. In reversing the defendant's conviction because the duty to retreat instruction was given, Justice Cardozo explained the historical basis of the privilege of nonretreat from the home:

> It is not now and never has been the law that a man assailed in his own dwelling is bound to retreat. If assailed there, he may stand his ground and resist the attack. He is under no duty to take to the fields and the highways, a fugitive from his own home. More than 200 years ago it was said by Lord Chief Justice Hale: In case a man "is assailed in his own house, he need not flee as far as he can, as in other cases of the defendant, for he hath the protection of his house to excuse him from flying, as that would be to give up the protection of his house to his adversary by flight." *Flight is for sanctuary and shelter, and shelter, if not sanctuary, is in the home.... The rule is the same whether the attack proceeds from some other occupant or from an intruder.*

3. Support for the retreat doctrine has waned considerably in recent years. Several states have now enacted so-called "stand your ground" laws, which allow actors to use deadly force without having to retreat even if retreating would prevent the threatened harm from taking place. The Florida statute discussed in *Richards* is representative. According to this law:

> A person who is not engaged in an unlawful activity and who is attacked in any other place where he or she has a right to be has no duty to retreat and has the right to stand his or her ground and meet force with force, including deadly force if he or she reasonably believes it is necessary to do so to prevent death or great bodily harm to himself or herself or another or to prevent the commission of a forcible felony.

Do you believe that "stand your ground" laws that allow you to meet "force with force" even when you could easily prevent the harm by retreating are justified or do you prefer the traditional common law "retreat doctrine"?

4. Stand your ground statutes became the subject of great controversy as a result of the criminal proceedings related to George Zimmerman's killing of Trayvon Martin in February of 2012. Before the shooting, Zimmerman placed a now infamous call to 911 in which he stated:

> Hey we've had some break-ins in my neighborhood, and there's a real suspicious guy, uh, [near] Retreat View Circle, um, the best address I can give you is 111 Retreat View Circle. This guy looks like he's up to no good, or he's on drugs or something. It's raining and he's just walking around, looking about.

Subsequently, the 911 dispatcher asked Zimmerman for clarification regarding his location. The following conversation ensued:

Zimmerman: No you go in straight through the entrance and then you make a left ... uh you go straight in, don't turn, and make a left. Shit he's running.

Dispatcher: He's running? Which way is he running?

Zimmerman: Down towards the other entrance to the neighborhood.

Dispatcher: Which entrance is that that he's heading towards?

Zimmerman: The back entrance ... fucking [unintelligible]

Dispatcher: Are you following him?

Zimmerman: Yeah

Dispatcher: Ok, we don't need you to do that.

Zimmerman: Ok

While it's unclear exactly what happened next, an altercation that resulted in Zimmerman shooting and killing Trayvon Martin ensued. Zimmerman was eventually arrested. He explained to the police that he killed Martin in self-defense. Do you believe that George Zimmerman "stood his ground" or did he do something different from standing his ground? Explain.

5. The police eventually released Zimmerman without pressing charges, claiming that there was no evidence to refute Zimmerman's self-defense claim. Furthermore, they alleged that Zimmerman could not even be prosecuted, for the state's "stand your ground" law provides immunity from prosecution. A flurry of national protests ensued, most of which focused on the racial aspects of the case. Many claimed that Zimmerman concluded that Trayvon Martin was dangerous and about to attack him merely because Martin was black and wearing a hoodie. Faced with widespread protests, the state eventually decided to charge Zimmerman with murder. Zimmerman's defense argued that Trayvon Martin was the initial aggressor and that Zimmerman thus acted in self-defense. He was ultimately acquitted, presumably because the defense was able to raise reasonable doubt as to whether the killing was in self-defense. While the Florida stand your ground statute played a role in the police's initial decision to release Zimmerman and not move forward with the case, the statute did not play a meaningful role during the course of the trial and was never expressly relied upon by the defense.

6. There is a fine line between "standing your ground" and causing or provoking another person to use force against you. While the former is lawful in many jurisdictions, the latter is often unlawful. As a result, it is often stated that the person who claims the right to use justifiable force must not have provoked the conditions that create her own defense. This, in turn, leads to broad statements such as that the person who purports to use justifiable force must be "free from fault" if the force is to be ultimately justified. See, e.g., *United States v. Peterson*, 483 F.2d 1222, 1231 (1973). In the context of self-defense, it has been stated that a person loses the right to self-defense if he engages in an "affirmative unlawful act [that is] reasonably calculated to produce an affray foreboding injurious or fatal consequences." *Id.* As a result, provoking or causing the conditions of your defense can and does often lead to losing the opportunity to plead the defense. It is unclear, however, what amount of provocation is enough to deny the right to plead a particular defense. As was mentioned above, some courts like to assert that the defendant must be entirely free from fault. However, as Professor Dressler has observed, this is very likely an "overstatement." Joshua Dressler, *Understanding Criminal Law* 266 (4th, Lexis, 2006). Other courts tone down the rhetoric, stating that self-defense situations often feature "fault on both sides." *State v. Corchado*, 453 A.2d 427, 433 (1982).

# § 15.03 Defensive Force: The Proportionality of the Force Used and Defense of Property and Habitation

## People v. Ceballos

Supreme Court of California, 1974
12 Cal.3d 470

BURKE, Justice.

Don Ceballos was found guilty by a jury of assault with a deadly weapon.... He appeals from the judgment, contending primarily that his conduct was not unlawful because the alleged victim was attempting to commit burglary when hit by a trap gun mounted in the garage of defendant's dwelling and that the court erred in instructing the jury. We have concluded that the former argument lacks merit, that the court did not commit prejudicial error in instructing the jury, and that the judgment should be affirmed.

Defendant lived alone in a home in San Anselmo. The regular living quarters were above the garage, but defendant sometimes slept in the garage and had about $2,000 worth of property there.

In March 1970 some tools were stolen from defendant's home. On May 12, 1970, he noticed the lock on his garage doors was bent and pry marks were on one of the doors. The next day he mounted a loaded .22 caliber pistol in the garage. The pistol was aimed at the center of the garage doors and was connected by a wire to one of the doors so that the pistol would discharge if the door was opened several inches.

The damage to defendant's lock had been done by a 16-year-old boy named Stephen and a 15-year-old boy named Robert. On the afternoon of May 15, 1970, the boys returned to defendant's house while he was away. Neither boy was armed with a gun or knife. After looking in the windows and seeing no one, Stephen succeeded in removing the lock on the garage doors with a crowbar, and, as he pulled the door outward, he was hit in the face with a bullet from the pistol ...

Defendant, testifying in his own behalf, admitted having set up the trap gun. He stated that after noticing the pry marks on his garage door on May 12, he felt he should 'set up some kind of a trap, something to keep the burglar out of my home.' When asked why he was trying to keep the burglar out, he replied, '... Because somebody was trying to steal my property ... and I don't want to come home some night and have the thief in there ... usually a thief is pretty desperate ... and ... they just pick up a weapon ... if they don't have one ... and do the best they can.'

When asked by the police shortly after the shooting why he assembled the trap gun, defendant stated that 'he didn't have much and he wanted to protect what he did have.'

As heretofore appears, the jury found defendant guilty of assault with a deadly weapon. An assault is 'an unlawful attempt, coupled with a present ability, to commit a violent injury on the person of another.'

Defendant contends that had he been present he would have been justified in shooting Stephen since Stephen was attempting to commit burglary, that ... defendant had a right to do indirectly what he could have done directly, and that therefore any attempt by him to commit a violent injury upon Stephen was not 'unlawful' and hence not an assault. The

People argue that ... as a matter of law a trap gun constitutes excessive force, and that in any event the circumstances were not in fact such as to warrant the use of deadly force.

The issue of criminal liability under statutes such as Penal Code section 245 where the instrument employed is a trap gun or other deadly mechanical device appears to be one of first impression in this state, but in other jurisdictions courts have considered the question of criminal and civil liability for death or injuries inflicted by such a device ...

In the United States, courts have concluded that a person may be held criminally liable under statutes proscribing homicides and shooting with intent to injure, or civilly liable, if he sets upon his premises a deadly mechanical device and that device kills or injures another. However, an exception to the rule that there may be criminal and civil liability for death or injuries caused by such a device has been recognized where the intrusion is, in fact, such that the person, were he present, would be justified in taking the life or inflicting the bodily harm with his own hands.

Allowing persons, at their own risk, to employ deadly mechanical devices imperils the lives of children, firemen and policemen acting within the scope of their employment, and others. Where the actor is present, there is always the possibility he will realize that deadly force is not necessary, but deadly mechanical devices are without mercy or discretion. Such devices 'are silent instrumentalities of death. They deal death and destruction to the innocent as well as the criminal intruder without the slightest warning. The taking of human life (or infliction of great bodily injury) by such means is brutally savage and inhuman.'

It seems clear that the use of such devices should not be encouraged. Moreover, whatever may be thought in torts, the foregoing rule setting forth an exception to liability for death or injuries inflicted by such devices 'is inappropriate in penal law for it is obvious that it does not prescribe a workable standard of conduct; liability depends upon fortuitous results.' We therefore decline to adopt that rule in criminal cases.

Furthermore, even if that rule were applied here, as we shall see, defendant was not justified in shooting Stephen....

Where the character and manner of the burglary do not reasonably create a fear of great bodily harm, there is no cause for exaction of human life or for the use of deadly force. The character and manner of the burglary could not reasonably create such a fear unless the burglary threatened, or was reasonably believed to threaten, death or serious bodily harm.

In the instant case the asserted burglary did not threaten death or serious bodily harm, since no one but Stephen and Robert was then on the premises. A defendant is not protected from liability merely by the fact that the intruder's conduct is such as would justify the defendant, were he present, in believing that the intrusion threatened death or serious bodily injury. There is ordinarily the possibility that the defendant, were he present, would realize the true state of affairs and recognize the intruder as one whom he would not be justified in killing or wounding.

We thus conclude that defendant was not justified ... in shooting Stephen to prevent him from committing burglary. Our conclusion is in accord with dictum indicating that there may be no privilege to use a deadly mechanical device to prevent a burglary of a dwelling house in which no one is present ...

Several cases contain broad language relating to justification for killing where a person acts in defense of his habitation or property to prevent 'a felony', but in those cases also it does not appear that any issue was raised or decided as to the nature of the felony coming within that doctrine.

We recognize that our position regarding justification for killing ... differs from the position of ... the Restatement Second of Torts, regarding the use of deadly force to prevent a 'felony ... of a type ... involving the breaking and entry of a dwelling place'. But in view of the supreme value of human life, we do not believe deadly force can be justified to prevent all felonies of the foregoing type, including ones in which no person is, or is reasonably believed to be, on the premises except the would-be burglar....

Defendant also does not, and could not properly, contend that the intrusion was in fact such that, were he present, he would be justified under Civil Code section 50 in using deadly force. That section provides, 'Any necessary force may be used to protect from wrongful injury the person or property of oneself....' This section also should be read in the light of the common law, and at common law in general deadly force could not be used solely for the protection of property. "The preservation of human life and limb from grievous harm is of more importance to society than the protection of property." Thus defendant was not warranted under Civil Code section 50 in using deadly force to protect his personal property ...

At common law an exception to the foregoing principle that deadly force could not be used solely for the protection of property was recognized where the property was a dwelling house in some circumstances. 'According to the older interpretation of the common law, even extreme force may be used to prevent dispossession (of the dwelling house).' Also at common law if another attempted to burn a dwelling the owner was privileged to use deadly force if this seemed necessary to defend his 'castle' against the threatened harm. Further, deadly force was privileged it if was, or reasonably seemed, necessary to protect the dwelling against a burglar.

Here we are not concerned with dispossession or burning of a dwelling, and, as heretofore concluded, the asserted burglary in this case was not of such a character as to warrant the use of deadly force ...

We conclude that as a matter of law the exception to the rule of liability for injuries inflicted by a deadly mechanical device does not apply under the circumstances here appearing.

The judgment is affirmed.

## *Notes and Questions*

1. Force used in defense of self, property or others must be proportional to the threatened harm. There is no requirement, however, that the force inflict a lesser evil than the one averted. An actor may thus inflict more harm than the harm with which he is threatened, as long as the force used is not grossly disproportional to the harm caused. A person may, for example, kill in order to prevent rape or serious bodily injury.

2. As *Ceballos* illustrates, a person may not use deadly force in order to prevent harm to property interests. Furthermore, the use of trap guns or other contraptions that may endanger vital interests to protect property or habitation is generally deemed unlawful, for such mechanical devices are not able to discriminate between wrongful intruders and lawful visitors and the force unleashed by the devices may be grossly disproportional to the harm threatened by an intruder. A trap gun that is triggered by the opening of a door cannot, for example, discriminate between the burglar who opens the door to commit a crime inside the dwelling and the fire fighter who opens the door to put out a fire inside the home.

3. Do you agree that deadly force may not be used to protect property interests? Suppose, for example, that a burglar steals the Mona Lisa from the Louvre. If the only way of preventing the theft of the painting is to use deadly force against the thieves, should the use of such force be considered justified? Why or why not?

4. Note that the court in *Ceballos* points out that the defendant would not be justified in using deadly force against he burglar even if he had been present when the burglary took place. According to the Court, deadly force is lawful only to protect against death or the infliction of serious bodily injury. Given that there was no indication that the burglar who was injured by the trap gun in *Ceballos* was armed or was intent on causing death or serious bodily injury, the court concluded that using deadly force against him would have been unwarranted even had the defendant been present when the burglary took place.

5. As was noted in *Ceballos,* there is some authority for the proposition that deadly force may be used to protect "habitation." However, the court construed this position narrowly, suggesting that deadly force to protect habitation is lawful only when the defensive force is necessary to prevent "dispossession" of the dwelling. A threat of dispossession may exist, for example, if someone attempts to set the actor's dwelling on fire. Nevertheless, since the burglar in *Ceballos* was not attempting to dispossess the owner of his dwelling, using deadly force against him was unjustified.

6. While some jurisdictions—in accordance with *Ceballos*—hold that deadly force is unlawful to protect habitation unless the actor is threatened with dispossession, others argue that such force may be used to protect habitation even when faced with threats less serious than disposition. Furthermore, some states have enacted so-called "Make My Day" statutes, which allow actors to use deadly force to prevent even slight attacks against habitation. The Colorado statute is representative:

> ... [A]ny occupant of a dwelling is justified in using any degree of physical force, including deadly physical force, against another person when that other person has made *an unlawful entry* into the dwelling, and when the occupant has a reasonable belief that such other person has committed a crime in the dwelling in addition *to the uninvited entry,* or is committing or intends to commit a crime against a person or property in addition to the uninvited entry, and when the occupant reasonably believes that such other person might use any physical force, no matter how slight, against any occupant. Section 18-1-704.5, C.R.S.

Assuming that the use of trap guns is lawful as long as the force used would have been justified had defendant been present when the burglary was being committed, what result in *Ceballos* had the Colorado "Make My Day" statute applied?

## § 15.04 Defensive Force: The Reasonableness of the Belief That Force Is Necessary

### People v. Goetz

Court of Appeals of New York, 1986
68 N.Y.2d 96

Chief Judge WACHTLER.

A Grand Jury has indicted defendant on attempted murder, assault, and other charges for having shot and wounded four youths on a New York City subway train after one or two of the youths approached him and asked for $ 5. The lower courts, concluding that the prosecutor's charge to the Grand Jury on the defense of justification was erroneous, have dismissed the attempted murder, assault and weapons possession charges. We now reverse and reinstate all counts of the indictment.

The precise circumstances of the incident giving rise to the charges against defendant are disputed, and ultimately it will be for a trial jury to determine what occurred. We feel it necessary, however, to provide some factual background to properly frame the legal issues before us. Accordingly, we have summarized the facts as they appear from the evidence before the Grand Jury. We stress, however, that we do not purport to reach any conclusions or holding as to exactly what transpired or whether defendant is blameworthy. The credibility of witnesses and the reasonableness of defendant's conduct are to be resolved by the trial jury.

On Saturday afternoon, December 22, 1984, Troy Canty, Darryl Cabey, James Ramseur, and Barry Allen boarded an IRT express subway train in The Bronx and headed south toward lower Manhattan. The four youths rode together in the rear portion of the seventh car of the train. Two of the four, Ramseur and Cabey, had screwdrivers inside their coats, which they said were to be used to break into the coin boxes of video machines.

Defendant Bernhard Goetz boarded this subway train at 14th Street in Manhattan and sat down on a bench towards the rear section of the same car occupied by the four youths. Goetz was carrying an unlicensed .38 caliber pistol loaded with five rounds of ammunition in a waistband holster. The train left the 14th Street station and headed towards Chambers Street.

It appears from the evidence before the Grand Jury that Canty approached Goetz, possibly with Allen beside him, and stated "give me five dollars". Neither Canty nor any of the other youths displayed a weapon. Goetz responded by standing up, pulling out his handgun and firing four shots in rapid succession. The first shot hit Canty in the chest; the second struck Allen in the back; the third went through Ramseur's arm and into his left side; the fourth was fired at Cabey, who apparently was then standing in the corner of the car, but missed, deflecting instead off of a wall of the conductor's cab. After Goetz briefly surveyed the scene around him, he fired another shot at Cabey, who then was sitting on the end bench of the car. The bullet entered the rear of Cabey's side and severed his spinal cord ...

On December 31, 1984, Goetz surrendered to police in Concord, New Hampshire, identifying himself as the gunman being sought for the subway shootings in New York nine days earlier. Later that day, after receiving Miranda warnings, he made two lengthy statements, both of which were tape recorded with his permission. In the statements, which are substantially similar, Goetz admitted that he had been illegally carrying a handgun in New York City for three years. He stated that he had first purchased a gun in 1981 after he had been injured in a mugging. Goetz also revealed that twice between 1981 and 1984 he had successfully warded off assailants simply by displaying the pistol.

According to Goetz's statement, the first contact he had with the four youths came when Canty, sitting or lying on the bench across from him, asked "how are you," to which he replied "fine". Shortly thereafter, Canty, followed by one of the other youths, walked over to the defendant and stood to his left, while the other two youths remained to his right, in the corner of the subway car. Canty then said "give me five dollars". Goetz stated that he knew from the smile on Canty's face that they wanted to "play with me". Although he was certain that none of the youths had a gun, he had a fear, based on prior experiences, of being "maimed".

Goetz then established "a pattern of fire," deciding specifically to fire from left to right. His stated intention at that point was to "murder [the four youths], to hurt them, to make them suffer as much as possible". When Canty again requested money, Goetz stood up, drew his weapon, and began firing, aiming for the center of the body of each of the four. Goetz recalled that the first two he shot "tried to run through the crowd [but] they had nowhere to run". Goetz then turned to his right to "go after the other two". One of these two "tried to run through the wall of the train, but he had nowhere to go". The other youth (Cabey) "tried pretending that he wasn't with [the others]" by standing still, holding on to one of the subway hand straps, and not looking at Goetz. Goetz nonetheless fired his fourth shot at him. He then ran back to the first two youths to make sure they had been "taken care of". Seeing that they had both been shot, he spun back to check on the latter two. Goetz noticed that the youth who had been standing still was now sitting on a bench and seemed unhurt. As Goetz told the police, "I said '[you] seem to be all right, here's another'", and he then fired the shot which severed Cabey's spinal cord. Goetz added that "if I was a little more under self-control I would have put the barrel against his forehead and fired." He also admitted that "if I had had more [bullets], I would have shot them again, and again, and again." ...

We [think] that neither the prosecutor's charge to the Grand Jury on justification nor the information which came to light while the motion to dismiss was pending required dismissal of any of the charges in the second indictment.

Penal Law article 35 recognizes the defense of justification, which "permits the use of force under certain circumstances". One such set of circumstances pertains to the use of force in defense of a person, encompassing both self-defense and defense of a third person. Penal Law section 35.15 (1) sets forth the general principles governing all such uses of force: "[a] person may ... use physical force upon another person when and to the extent he reasonably believes such to be necessary to defend himself or a third person from what he reasonably believes to be the use or imminent use of unlawful physical force by such other person".

Section 35.15 (2) sets forth further limitations on these general principles with respect to the use of "deadly physical force": "A person may not use deadly physical force upon another person under circumstances specified in subdivision one unless (a) He reasonably believes that such other person is using or about to use deadly physical force or (b) He reasonably believes that such other person is committing or attempting to commit a kidnapping, forcible rape, forcible sodomy or robbery".

Thus, consistent with most justification provisions, Penal Law section 35.15 permits the use of deadly physical force only where requirements as to triggering conditions and the necessity of a particular response are met. As to the triggering conditions, the statute requires that the actor "reasonably believes" that another person either is using or about to use deadly physical force or is committing or attempting to commit one of certain enumerated felonies, including robbery. As to the need for the use of deadly physical force as a response, the statute requires that the actor "reasonably believes" that such force is necessary to avert the perceived threat.

Because the evidence before the second Grand Jury included statements by Goetz that he acted to protect himself from being maimed or to avert a robbery, the prosecutor correctly chose to charge the justification defense in section 35.15 to the Grand Jury. The prosecutor properly instructed the grand jurors to consider whether the use of deadly physical force was justified to prevent either serious physical injury or a robbery, and, in doing so, to separately analyze the defense with respect to each of the charges. He elaborated upon the prerequisites for the use of deadly physical force essentially by reading or paraphrasing the language in Penal Law section 35.15. The defense does not contend that he committed any error in this portion of the charge.

When the prosecutor had completed his charge, one of the grand jurors asked for clarification of the term "reasonably believes". The prosecutor responded by instructing the grand jurors that they were to consider the circumstances of the incident and determine "whether the defendant's conduct was that of a reasonable man in the defendant's situation". It is this response by the prosecutor—and specifically his use of "a reasonable man"—which is the basis for the dismissal of the charges by the lower courts. As expressed repeatedly in the Appellate Division's plurality opinion, because section 35.15 uses the term "he reasonably believes", the appropriate test, according to that court, is whether a defendant's beliefs and reactions were "reasonable to him". Under that reading of the statute, a jury which believed a defendant's testimony that he felt that his own actions were warranted and were reasonable would have to acquit him, regardless of what anyone else in defendant's situation might have concluded. Such an interpretation defies the ordinary meaning and significance of the term "reasonably" in a statute, and misconstrues the clear intent of the Legislature, in enacting section 35.15, to retain an objective element as part of any provision authorizing the use of deadly physical force.

Penal statutes in New York have long codified the right recognized at common law to use deadly physical force, under appropriate circumstances, in self-defense. These provisions have never required that an actor's belief as to the intention of another person to inflict serious injury be correct in order for the use of deadly force to be justified, but they have uniformly required that the belief comport with an objective notion of reasonableness. The 1829 statute, using language which was followed almost in its entirety until the 1965 recodification of the Penal Law, provided that the use of deadly force was justified in self-defense or in the defense of specified third persons "when there shall be a reasonable ground to apprehend a design to commit a felony, or to do some great personal injury, and there shall be imminent danger of such design being accomplished." ...

In People v. Lumsden, we approved a charge to the jury which instructed it to consider whether the circumstances facing defendant were such "as would lead a reasonable man to believe that [an assailant] is about to kill or to do great bodily injury". We emphatically rejected the position that any belief by an actor as to the intention of another to cause severe injury was a sufficient basis for his use of deadly force, and stated specifically that a belief based upon "mere fear or fancy or remote hearsay information or a delusion pure and simple" would not satisfy the requirements of the statute."

In 1961 the Legislature established a Commission to undertake a complete revision of the Penal Law and the Criminal Code. The impetus for the decision to update the Penal Law came in part from the drafting of the Model Penal Code by the American Law Institute.... The drafting of the general provisions of the new Penal Law, including the article on justification, was particularly influenced by the Model Penal Code. While using the Model Penal Code provisions on justification as general guidelines, however, the drafters of the new Penal Law did not simply adopt them verbatim.

The provisions of the Model Penal Code with respect to the use of deadly force in self-defense reflect the position of its drafters that any culpability which arises from a mistaken belief in the need to use such force should be no greater than the culpability such a mistake would give rise to if it were made with respect to an element of a crime. Accordingly, under Model Penal Code section 3.04 (2) (b), a defendant charged with murder (or attempted murder) need only show that he "[believed] that [the use of deadly force] was necessary to protect himself against death, serious bodily injury, kidnapping or [forcible] sexual intercourse" to prevail on a self-defense claim. If the defendant's belief was wrong, and was recklessly, or negligently formed, however, he may be convicted of the type of homicide charge requiring only a reckless or negligent, as the case may be, criminal intent....

New York did not follow the Model Penal Code's equation of a mistake as to the need to use deadly force with a mistake negating an element of a crime, choosing instead to use a single statutory section which would provide either a complete defense or no defense at all to a defendant charged with any crime involving the use of deadly force. The drafters of the new Penal Law adopted in large part the structure and content of Model Penal Code section 3.04, but, crucially, inserted the word "reasonably" before "believes".

The plurality below agreed with defendant's argument that the change in the statutory language from "reasonable ground," used prior to 1965, to "he reasonably believes" in Penal Law § 35.15 evinced a legislative intent to conform to the subjective standard contained in Model Penal Code section 3.04. This argument, however, ignores the plain significance of the insertion of "reasonably". Had the drafters of section 35.15 wanted to adopt a subjective standard, they could have simply used the language of section 3.04. "Believes" by itself requires an honest or genuine belief by a defendant as to the need to use deadly force. Interpreting the statute to require only that the defendant's belief was "reasonable to him," as done by the plurality below, would hardly be different from requiring only a genuine belief; in either case, the defendant's own perceptions could completely exonerate him from any criminal liability.

We cannot lightly impute to the Legislature an intent to fundamentally alter the principles of justification to allow the perpetrator of a serious crime to go free simply because that person believed his actions were reasonable and necessary to prevent some perceived harm. To completely exonerate such an individual, no matter how aberrational or bizarre his thought patterns, would allow citizens to set their own standards for the permissible use of force. It would also allow a legally competent defendant suffering from delusions to kill or perform acts of violence with impunity, contrary to fundamental principles of justice and criminal law.

We can only conclude that the Legislature retained a reasonableness requirement to avoid giving a license for such actions. The plurality's interpretation, as the dissenters below recognized, excises the impact of the word "reasonably." ...

In People v. Collice, we rejected the position that section 35.15 contains a wholly subjective standard. The defendant in Collice asserted, on appeal, that the trial court had erred in refusing to charge the justification defense. We upheld the trial court's action because we concluded that, even if the defendant had actually believed that he was threatened with the imminent use of deadly physical force, the evidence clearly indicated that "his reactions were not those of a reasonable man acting in self-defense". Numerous decisions from other States interpreting "reasonably believes" in justification statutes enacted subsequent to the drafting of the Model Penal Code are consistent with Collice, as they hold that such language refers to what a reasonable person could have believed under the same circumstances.

Goetz ... argues that the introduction of an objective element will preclude a jury from considering factors such as the prior experiences of a given actor and thus, require it to make a determination of "reasonableness" without regard to the actual circumstances of a particular incident. This argument, however, falsely presupposes that an objective standard means that the background and other relevant characteristics of a particular actor must be ignored. To the contrary, we have frequently noted that a determination of reasonableness must be based on the "circumstances" facing a defendant or his "situation". Such terms encompass more than the physical movements of the potential assailant. As just discussed, these terms include any relevant knowledge the defendant had about that person. They also necessarily bring in the physical attributes of all persons involved, including the defendant. Furthermore, the defendant's circumstances encompass any prior experiences he had which could provide a reasonable basis for a belief that another person's intentions were to injure or rob him or that the use of deadly force was necessary under the circumstances.

Accordingly, a jury should be instructed to consider this type of evidence in weighing the defendant's actions. The jury must first determine whether the defendant had the requisite beliefs under section 35.15, that is, whether he believed deadly force was necessary to avert the imminent use of deadly force or the commission of one of the felonies enumerated therein. If the People do not prove beyond a reasonable doubt that he did not have such beliefs, then the jury must also consider whether these beliefs were reasonable. The jury would have to determine, in light of all the "circumstances", as explicated above, if a reasonable person could have had these beliefs.

The prosecutor's instruction to the second Grand Jury that it had to determine whether, under the circumstances, Goetz's conduct was that of a reasonable man in his situation was thus essentially an accurate charge....

Accordingly, the order of the Appellate Division should be reversed, and the dismissed counts of the indictment reinstated.

## *Notes and Questions*

1. An actor may only use force in self-defense if she reasonably believes that the force is necessary to thwart a wrongful attack. As the Court of Appeals of New York explains in *Goetz,* it is thus legally irrelevant whether an actual attack takes place. Force is justified regardless of whether an actual aggression takes place as long as the defendant *reasonably believed* that an attack was about to take place and force was necessary to repel the aggression. Therefore, defendant will—as a general rule—be held liable for the crime charged if he unreasonably believed that force was necessary to thwart an attack.

2. The actor's belief that force is necessary to repel wrongful aggression must be objectively reasonable. As a result, the defendant's subjective belief that force is necessary is not enough to justify defensive force. Note that the defendant in *Goetz* sought the dismissal of the charges contending that the prosecutor erroneously failed to explain to the grand jury that his conduct was justified pursuant to self-defense as long as it seemed *reasonable to him* that using force was necessary to thwart a wrongful attack. Nevertheless, the prosecutor explained to the grand jury that that defensive force is justified only if it is objectively reasonable, not if it is reasonable to the defendant. The high court of New York agreed with the state and therefore reinstated the charges against Goetz, concluding that the belief that justifies defensive force must be an objectively reasonable belief that force is necessary to avert wrongful aggression. A subjective belief that force is necessary will not do if it is deemed to be objectively unreasonable according to societal standards.

3. The defendant in *Goetz* also argued that evidence regarding his prior experiences should be relevant to determining whether his belief that force was necessary was objectively reasonable. This was of particular importance in the case, for Goetz had been mugged several times in the past. The prior muggings were the reason why he bought a gun and also

explain why he was afraid that the youths were going to mug him. The Court of Appeals agreed that evidence of prior experiences that are relevant to assessing the defendant's state of mind at the time of the use of force are relevant to determining whether his belief that force was necessary was objectively reasonable. The Court further explained that the standard that should be employed to assess whether the defendant's belief is reasonable is whether a reasonable person *in the defendant's situation* would have also believed that using force was necessary to thwart wrongful aggression. An assessment of what a reasonable person would believe "in the defendant's situation" allows the fact finder to take into consideration past experiences of the defendant that are relevant to assessing his frame of mind at the time of the incident. As was discussed in § 15.01 of this Chapter, this is also relevant in battered women cases, where courts routinely hold that evidence of prior spousal abuse and battered woman syndrome is admissible to assessing the objective reasonableness of the woman's belief that force was necessary to avert a wrongful attack from her spouse.

4. Although unreasonable force does not generally trigger a full or partial defense to liability, the partial defense of "imperfect self-defense" mitigates murder to the less serious offense of manslaughter in some jurisdictions. See, e.g., *Swann v. United States*, 548 A.2d 928, 930–931 (D.C. 1994). In the states that allow for an imperfect self-defense mitigation, the partial defense applies when the defendant honestly but unreasonably believed that the force was necessary to avert wrongful aggression or when she reasonably believed that using some force was necessary but she unreasonably used more force than was necessary to thwart the attack.

# § 15.05 Defensive Force: Model Penal Code

## Model Penal Code § 3.04. Use of Force in Self-Protection.

(1) **Use of Force Justifiable for Protection of the Person.** Subject to the provisions of this Section and of Section 3.09, the use of force upon or toward another person is justifiable when the actor believes that such force is immediately necessary for the purpose of protecting himself against the use of unlawful force by such other person on the present occasion.

(2) **Limitations on Justifying Necessity for Use of Force ...**

(b) The use of deadly force is not justifiable under this Section unless the actor believes that such force is necessary to protect himself against death, serious bodily injury, kidnapping or sexual intercourse compelled by force or threat; nor is it justifiable if:

(i) the actor, with the purpose of causing death or serious bodily injury, provoked the use of force against himself in the same encounter; or

(ii) the actor knows that he can avoid the necessity of using such force with complete safety by retreating or by surrendering possession of a thing to a person asserting a claim of right thereto or by complying with a demand that he abstain from any action that he has no duty to take, except that:

(A) the actor is not obliged to retreat from his dwelling or place of work, unless he was the initial aggressor or is assailed in his place of work by another person whose place of work the actor knows it to be; and

(B) a public officer justified in using force in the performance of his duties or a person justified in using force in his assistance or a person justified in using force in making an arrest or preventing an escape is not obliged to desist from efforts to perform such duty, effect such arrest or prevent such escape because of resistance or threatened resistance by or on behalf of the person against whom such action is directed.

## Model Penal Code § 3.05. Use of Force for the Protection of Other Persons.

(1) Subject to the provisions of this Section and of Section 3.09, the use of force upon or toward the person of another is justifiable to protect a third person when:

(a) the actor would be justified under Section 3.04 in using such force to protect himself against the injury he believes to be threatened to the person whom he seeks to protect; and

(b) under the circumstances as the actor believes them to be, the person whom he seeks to protect would be justified in using such protective force; and

(c) the actor believes that his intervention is necessary for the protection of such other person....

## Model Penal Code § 3.06. Use of Force for Protection of Property.

(1) **Use of Force Justifiable for Protection of Property.** Subject to the provisions of this Section and of Section 3.09, the use of force upon or toward the person of another is justifiable when the actor believes that such force is immediately necessary:

(a) to prevent or terminate an unlawful entry or other trespass upon land or a trespass against or the unlawful carrying away of tangible, movable property, provided that such land or movable property is, or is believed by the actor to be, in his possession or in the possession of another person for whose protection he acts; or

(b) to effect an entry or re-entry upon land or to retake tangible movable property, provided that the actor believes that he or the person by whose authority he acts or a person from whom he or such other person derives title was unlawfully dispossessed of such land or movable property and is entitled to possession, and provided, further, that:

(i) the force is used immediately or on fresh pursuit after such dispossession; or

(ii) the actor believes that the person against whom he uses force has no claim of right to the possession of the property and, in the case of land, the circumstances, as the actor believes them to be, are of such urgency that it would be an exceptional hardship to postpone the entry or re-entry until a court order is obtained....

(3) **Limitations on Justifiable Use of Force....**

(d) **Use of Deadly Force.** The use of deadly force is not justifiable under this Section unless the actor believes that:

(i) the person against whom the force is used is attempting to dispossess him of his dwelling otherwise than under a claim of right to its possession; or

(ii) the person against whom the force is used is attempting to commit or consummate arson, burglary, robbery or other felonious theft or property destruction and either:

(A) has employed or threatened deadly force against or in the presence of the actor; or

(B) the use of force other than deadly force to prevent the commission or the consummation of the crime would expose the actor or another in his presence to substantial danger of serious bodily injury....

(5) **Use of Device to Protect Property.** The justification afforded by this Section extends to the use of a device for the purpose of protecting property only if:

(a) the device is not designed to cause or known to create a substantial risk of causing death or serious bodily injury; and

(b) the use of the particular device to protect the property from entry or trespass is reasonable under the circumstances, as the actor believes them to be; and

(c) the device is one customarily used for such a purpose or reasonable care is taken to make known to probable intruders the fact that it is used ...

## Model Penal Code § 3.11. Definitions.

In this Article, unless a different meaning plainly is required:

(1) "unlawful force" means force, including confinement, that is employed without the consent of the person against whom it is directed and the employment of which constitutes an offense or actionable tort or would constitute such offense or tort except for a defense (such as the absence of intent, negligence, or mental capacity; duress; youth; or diplomatic status) not amounting to a privilege to use the force. Assent constitutes consent, within the meaning of this Section, whether or not it otherwise is legally effective, except assent to the infliction of death or serious bodily injury.

(2) "deadly force" means force that the actor uses with the purpose of causing or that he knows to create a substantial risk of causing death or serious bodily injury. Purposely firing a firearm in the direction of another person or at a vehicle in which another person is believed to be constitutes deadly force. A threat to cause death or serious bodily injury, by the production of a weapon or otherwise, so long as the actor's purpose is limited to creating an apprehension that he will use deadly force if necessary, does not constitute deadly force ...

## *Notes and Questions*

1. According to § 3.04(1), force is justified in self-defense only if it is necessary to prevent *unlawful force*. Unlawful force is defined in § 3.11. According to this provision, force is "unlawful" for the purposes of self-defense if it amounts to a tort or crime. Furthermore, the provision clarifies that excused force is considered unlawful. Nevertheless, it makes clear that justified (i.e., privileged) force is not "unlawful" and, therefore, cannot be justifiably defended against. This is compatible with the traditional understanding of the kind of aggression that may trigger the use of justifiable defensive force.

2. The Model Penal Code justifies force pursuant to self-defense as long as the defendant subjectively believed that the use of force was necessary. Therefore—as the Court of Appeals of New York pointed out in *Goetz*—the Code does not require that the defendant's belief that force is necessary be reasonable in order to justify her conduct. Nevertheless, as the Explanatory Note observes, a defendant who negligently be-

lieved that force was necessary when it actually was not may be held liable for a negligent version of the crime charged (if such an offense exists). Similarly, a defendant who recklessly believes that force is necessary when it really is not may be held liable for a reckless version of the offense (assuming, once again, that such an offense exists). This stands in stark contrast with the traditional common law approach, which leads to the imposition of liability for the offense charged if the defendant's belief is unreasonable (except in prosecutions for homicide in states that apply the "imperfect self-defense" doctrine).

3. Note that the § 3.04 justifies force in self-defense as long as the actor believes it is *immediately necessary* to thwarting a wrongful aggression. As a result, the Code does not require that the defendant believe that force is necessary to repel an *imminent* attack. In doing so, the Model Penal Code adopted a novel position regarding the "imminent attack" requirement. While not entirely doing away with the imminence requirement as the critics of the *Norman* case would do, the Code relaxes the requirement by requiring merely proof that the force was "immediately necessary" to preventing future harm. The "immediacy" requirement imposes some temporal limits on when force can be used, but the limits are considerably less rigid than what a strict requirement of imminence would impose.

4. The Code addresses the issue regarding provocation of the conditions that give rise to self-defense in § 3.04(2)(b)(i). Observe that the Code only denies a self-defense claim when the defendant "with the purpose of causing death or serious bodily injury, provoked the use of force against himself in the same encounter." As a result, a defendant who recklessly provokes the use of force against him does not automatically lose the right to use force in self-defense under the Code. This is considerably more lenient to the defendant than the traditional common law approach, which often is stated to require that the defendant be entirely "free from fault" in order to plead self-defense.

5. The common law "duty to retreat" doctrine is adopted by the Code pursuant to § 3.04(b)(ii)(a), along with the traditional "castle doctrine" exception. The Code thus rejects the "stand your ground" doctrine that has become fashionable in some states in recent years.

6. The issue of "defense of others" is addressed in § 3.05 of the Code. As the provision points out, the rules governing defense of others are essentially the same as those that justify self-defense. The actor must reasonably believe that using force is necessary to prevent a wrongful attack upon the third party. In such instances, force is justified if the third party that the actor defends would have been justified in using the same amount of force to repel the attack.

7. The Code's approach to "defense of property" basically tracks what was held in *Ceballos*. Pursuant to § 3.06(3), deadly force may not be used to protect property, unless it is necessary to prevent "dispossession" of the actor's dwelling or force is necessary in order to prevent a series of enumerated property crimes when they are committed in a way that presents a risk of death or serious bodily injury. Furthermore, use of trap guns and other mechanical devices to protect property is lawful only if they are not designed to cause death or serious bodily injury.

# § 15.06 Defensive Force: Comparative Perspectives

## B. Sharon Byrd, *Till Death do Us Part: A Comparative Law Approach to Justifying Lethal Self-Defense by Battered Women*

1991 Duke J. Comp. & Int'l L. 169

III. GERMAN THEORY

A. Development of the Necessity Defense Approach

German courts have taken a different route from U.S. courts in providing the battered woman with a defense to a criminal charge. Whereas U.S. courts have tended toward acquittal based on some version of self-defense or toward punishment mitigation based on heat of passion, German courts have been more favorable to the defense of necessity in battered woman cases. Self-defense is problematic in these cases, since usually the victim is not attacking at the moment the defendant acts. In many U.S. jurisdictions a prerequisite of perfect self-defense is the victim's reasonable belief that he is being attacked. Under German law, self-defense is the response to a "present, wrongful attack." Rather than expand upon the concept of an "attack" to include a general danger of a future attack, the courts have viewed the situation created by the victim as an "ongoing danger" that the defendant can repel even in cases in which the victim's life is at stake. This Part examines the development of German law and legal theory on this issue and considers whether it can provide some insight for U.S. courts in battered woman cases.

In a 1926 case, the Reichsgericht affirmed the decision of a lower court in acquitting the defendant for killing his father in a battering case. In that case, the defendant's mother had a serious heart condition and the family doctor had warned the defendant that extreme emotional upheaval could result in either the mother's having a stroke or committing suicide. Twenty hours before the defendant's act, his father had seriously mistreated the defendant's mother and sister and shortly before had threatened to repeat the mistreatment of the day before, "but twice as bad." The defendant shot and killed his father while he was still in bed playing with the family dog.

At the time of this case neither the Strafgesetzbuch nor the courts clearly distinguished between necessity as a justification and as an excuse, although the distinction was not foreign to the German literature. The court considered three possible defenses provided for in the old version of the Strafgesetzbuch:

> (Duress):
>
> A punishable act does not exist if the actor was coerced to commit the act through irresistible force or through a threat that involved a present and otherwise unavoidable danger for the life or limb of the actor or of one of his relatives....
>
> (Self-defense):
>
> A punishable act does not exist if the act was required in self-defense. Self-defense is the defense that is necessary to ward off a present, wrongful attack from oneself or another. Excessive self-defense is not punishable if the actor exceeded the limits of defensive action in a state of consternation, fear or fright.
>
> (Necessity):
>
> A punishable act does not exist if the act, in a case other than self-defense, was committed during a state of necessity for which the actor was not responsible

> and which could not have been avoided otherwise and in order to save the life or limb of the actor or one of his relatives from a present danger.

The court rejected duress since it required that the defendant be coerced by another individual through a threat or through force to commit a criminal act and that the coercion be exerted at the time of the act. It also rejected self-defense because it required that the defendant be responding to an immediate attack by the victim. The court referred to both of these defenses as requiring "dangers of the moment," as opposed to necessity which also included "situations of longer duration." On appeal, the prosecutor had argued that necessity was inapplicable, since it required dangers caused by natural events. The court explicitly rejected this argument: "The dangerous state—be it of a momentary or lasting nature—can have its basis in the blameworthy ... conduct of humans, indeed in their generally existing dangerousness for those around them."

Another issue raised on appeal was that the danger presented by the victim was not imminent, since the last harm had occurred twenty hours before the defendant's act, and at the time of the act the victim was lying in bed. This question is of considerable relevance in battering cases because usually the victim is physically stronger than the defendant. If so, waiting for the next attack means sacrificing all possibility of self-defense. The court dismissed this argument, saying that the imminence of the danger is neither to be judged by the initiation of the actual attack nor directly prior to it, but rather in light of an ongoing danger that could erupt at any time and that then could no longer be avoided.

Today the Strafgesetzbuch provides a justification for otherwise wrongful acts undertaken in a state of necessity. The justification applies if the interest saved substantially outweighs the interest harmed, and the threat to the interest saved was otherwise unavoidable. The code also provides an excuse for individuals who have saved their own interests in a necessity situation, or those of a relative or close friend, regardless of the comparative value of the interests involved. In addition, a new justificatory defense for criminal acts, referred to as "defensive necessity," has found its way into the leading theoretical literature on criminal law. It is this defense that offers a possible alternative to self-defense in battering cases. Although it is codified in the Bürgerliches Gesetzbuch, the scholarly literature has discussed extensively its applicability in the criminal law. To understand the real nature of the interrelationship between a traditional lesser evils defense, referred to as "aggressive" necessity, and the German variation embodied in "defensive" necessity, it is necessary to examine the relevant codifications.

### B. Aggressive and Defensive Necessity

The German Bürgerliches Gesetzbuch includes two sections on necessity. Section 904, corresponding to the traditional lesser evils defense in the criminal law, reads as follows:

> (Necessity) The owner of property is not justified in prohibiting another person from interfering with that property if that interference is necessary to avoid a present danger and the harm avoided thereby is disproportionately large in relation to the damage suffered by the owner of the property. The owner can demand restitution for the damage suffered.

Although this section defines the situation in which the property owner is not justified, the German courts interpret it as a justification for the party causing the damage. The duty to restore the owner to his or her original position or, under U.S. tort principles, to pay damages does not undercut the justification but rather is the Vincent v. Lake Erie Transportation Co. addition to the decision in Ploof v. Putnam.

The § 904 defense is an "aggressive" necessity defense, since it justifies damaging the interest of an uninvolved third party to save one's own interest. The paradigm case is Ploof v. Putnam. In order to save a ship from destruction in a sudden storm, the plaintiff attempted to moor the ship at the defendant's dock. The danger threatening the ship was not caused by the defendant nor did it emanate from the defendant's property but rather from natural causes. Still the court held that the plaintiff had a right to moor the ship and damage or destroy the defendant's dock, just as § 904 of the German Bürgerliches Gesetzbuch provides a justification for an individual to damage someone else's property even though that property is not causing the threatened danger.

The complementary defense is contained in § 228 of the Bürgerliches Gesetzbuch:

> (Necessity) One who damages or destroys another's property in order to avert a danger emanating from it to oneself or another does not act wrongfully if the damage or destruction is necessary to avoid the danger and is not disproportionate thereto. If the actor is responsible for the danger, he is liable for the damages.

The § 228 defense refers to "defensive" necessity. This justification permits one to damage another's property in cases in which the danger is caused by that property. If the Ploof v. Putnam facts were altered such that the ship were a mere boat that was already docked at defendant's wharf when a sudden storm arose, and the boat was causing damage to the dock, the defendant would be justified under defensive necessity in releasing the boat from its moorings and thereby destroying it to avert damage to the dock. Although one might see this defense as a version of self-defense (defense of property) rather than necessity, such an interpretation would be fallacious. The primary difference between the two defenses is that self-defense is triggered by a present attack whereas defensive necessity is triggered by an imminent danger.

A closer look at aggressive and defensive necessity also reveals the complementary nature of the standards employed for balancing the interests involved. In cases of aggressive necessity, the actor may justifiably damage the property of an uninvolved third party only in cases in which the interest thereby saved is of disproportionately greater value than the interest damaged. In cases of defensive necessity, the actor is justified in damaging the danger-causing property in all cases except when the value of that property is disproportionately high in comparison to the value of the property saved. Thus in the case of Ploof v. Putnam, the ship owner may damage or destroy the dock to save the ship under an aggressive necessity theory in cases in which the ship is of much greater value than the dock, whereas the dock owner may damage or destroy the boat to save the dock under a defensive necessity theory in cases in which the boat is not of much greater value....

## IV. THE DEFENSIVE NECESSITY SOLUTION

### A. The Defensive Necessity Argument

The major problem with applying self-defense to the battered woman case in which the defendant killed her sleeping spouse is that traditionally self-defense is the response to a present wrongful attack. Including the killing of an aggressor while he is sleeping within self-defense thereby extends the justification far beyond its conceptual origin. However, some cases exist in which the battered wife's response seems every bit as justified as the response of one acting in self-defense. The fact that U.S. courts are prepared to consider self-defense as a justification for the killing indicates a willingness to justify the battered woman that is perhaps completely appropriate but conceptually unclear. Rather than base the defense on the objective existence of an attack, the courts must rely upon the defendant's beliefs in the necessity of using defensive force. In determining whether those beliefs are reasonable, a subjective standard must be applied in the total absence of any attack. Although the subjective standard of reasonableness is completely appropriate for determining the defendant's blameworthiness for making a mistake as to the necessity of using defensive force, it is not a substitute for determining whether the objective elements of a justification are fulfilled in the particular case. For this reason alone, many courts may be unwilling to apply the subjective standard.

The necessity or lesser evils defense generally requires not a present attack but a situation of imminent danger. It is exactly this distinction that separates the battered woman case from the typical self-defense case. Even though it is very difficult to maintain that the defendant in these cases was being attacked, the fact that her spouse has placed her in a general situation of danger is more plausible. A dangerous situation can be ongoing and need not represent a sudden threat posed by another's voluntary, aggressive conduct. If the spouse's slumber is merely a momentary pause in a battering relationship that threatens great bodily harm or death, then an imminent danger, though not a present attack, can exist objectively. Courts, therefore, do not have to rely on purely subjective evaluations in affirming the dangerous situation. The first step in a battered woman case should be to show a situation of necessity rather than self-defense.

The traditional necessity situation is one in which there is an imminent danger that can be avoided only through harming another uninvolved individual's interests. Taking someone else's car to drive an accident victim to the hospital or breaking into someone's cabin to gain shelter from a blizzard are typical examples of the type of case in which the defense is appropriate. In these cases the danger emanates from some extraneous source and the rights of an uninvolved third party are violated to save one's own or someone else's interests. Since the defensive measure is essentially an attack on a third party's interests, German literature refers to it as "aggressive" necessity. A violation in aggressive necessity is justified only if an interest of more, or considerably more, value is saved than harmed. Therefore, one cannot take another person's car to get to a business appointment on time or break into another person's cabin to relax from a strenuous hike. In battering cases, if the woman's life is in danger and she can avoid the danger by doing something less harmful than killing her husband, such as fettering him for several hours, then she would be justified under a theory of aggressive necessity in taking the lesser measure. If the only possibility of avoiding a future, threatened attack on her life is to kill her husband, however, then she could not be justified under aggressive necessity since the two values, her life versus his, are equal.

However, defensive necessity turns the balancing test around in cases in which the danger emanates not from some extraneous source, but rather from the individual who is harmed by the defensive action. The fact that the individual harmed causes the danger provides a sound reason for inverting the interest balancing test, particularly in cases in which the danger is intentional. Thus although one may not take another person's car to avoid being late for a business appointment, if the car owner has intentionally kept the other person from being on time, perhaps to secure the advantages of the business deal for himself, then the defensive action seems more reasonable. If the cabin owner has immobilized the hiker's only means of transportation, perhaps in the hopes that he will be injured leaving the mountainous area after dark, then breaking into the cabin to rest before continuing the journey the next day is also more understandable.

In the battered woman cases, clearly a danger emanates from the batterer. He has created a general situation of danger that, upon his awakening, can result in serious bodily harm or death for his spouse. In addition, the danger created for the woman is a product of her husband's voluntary actions. In such cases, the battered woman should be justified under a defensive necessity theory in acting before the actual attack takes place, particularly when waiting would mean that she no longer would be able to respond effectively. The law cannot legitimately require an individual to risk serious injury or death at the hands of someone who is intentionally creating the relevant ongoing danger. Under a theory of defensive necessity, the test is not whether the woman's interest is greater than that of her husband's, but rather only whether his interest is disproportionately large in comparison to hers. In life versus life cases it is not greater, and the battered woman would be justified in sacrificing his to avert an imminent danger to hers.

One final requirement of either type of necessity defense is that the danger be otherwise unavoidable. The U.S. law of self-defense refers to this requirement as the retreat rule. Under German law, an individual does not have to retreat before using deadly force when exercising self-defense, but must retreat from a danger if possible before damaging another person's interests in a situation of necessity. The reason for this distinction lies in the attitude expressed by the victim, or initial aggressor, in a self-defense case, of disrespect for the individual rights of the defender. The attack not only creates a danger for the self-defender but also represents an affront to his personal integrity. Requiring the individual attacked to flee rather than stand up for his rights would deny this integrity. In a necessity situation, however, the danger-causing party does not express this disregard. The focus, therefore, is upon salvaging rightful interests and minimizing losses. If retreat is possible, then both the interests of the actor and the victim can be saved. Since under U.S. law retreat is also required before employing deadly force in self-defense, this distinction between the two types of defensive force defenses is irrelevant to the instant analysis.

In a battered woman case, arguably the woman could have fled, thereby avoiding the danger, rather than take her husband's life. In cases in which she could have taken this measure, it would be appropriate to deny her the defensive necessity justification. Retreat is necessary under both legal systems, however, only when it can be undertaken with complete safety. If the battered woman fears for the safety of her children when left alone with the batterer or exposes herself to similar or greater danger through fleeing, then she should not be required to retreat before exercising defensive force. Evidence of previous attempts to flee with the result of being followed and more brutally beaten by the batterer or of unsuccessful efforts to obtain police intervention would indicate the exact nature of the particular situation. Usually the battered spouse does not turn to deadly force upon the first confrontation, has been exposed to so many repeated beatings over years of marriage to the batterer that the situation is characterized by its cyclic nature. Adequate evidence of the problems with retreat, therefore, is generally available for the judge or jury to determine as an objective matter whether it was a feasible alternative or not. If it were not objectively possible, it still may be the case that the battered woman, because of what is described as "learned helplessness," did not recognize the viability of this course of action. In such cases a subjective standard of reasonableness should be applied to determine her culpability for incorrectly evaluating the situation.

## *Notes and Questions*

1. As Professor Byrd points out, Germany (and other European and Latin American countries) distinguishes between two different kinds of justifiable necessity. Aggressive necessity applies when the actor harms a person or thing that is not the source of the

threat that his conduct averts. Thus, for example, a hiker who breaks into a cabin in order to seek refuge from a harsh winter storm engages in an act of "aggressive" necessity, for she harms a person (owner of the cabin) or thing (the cabin itself) that is not the source of the threat to the hiker's wellbeing (the source of the threat is the winter storm). In contrast, a hiker who shoots at an aggressive dog that is eating his limited food supply engages in an act of "defensive" necessity, given that he is harming the thing that is the source of the threat.

2. As Professor Byrd also points out, defensive necessity typically applies in circumstances in which an element of defense of self or property is missing, but the force appears to be otherwise justifiable. Once again, the example of the hiker who shoots the aggressive dog is a good example. Shooting the dog looks a lot like an act that is made in "defense of property." Nevertheless, it may be argued that shooting the dog is not justified pursuant to defense of property, for the dog's attack does not amount to the kind of "unlawful force" or wrongful aggression that triggers the right to use defensive force. The reason why the dog's attack fails to qualify as wrongful aggression is because dogs—unlike humans—are incapable of acting "unlawfully" or "wrongfully." The quality of an act being "wrongful" or "unlawful" attaches only to human acts, for laws are addressed to persons, not animals or things. Since the dog's attack fails to satisfy the "unlawful force" requirement that triggers "defense of property," another claim of justification must be invoked in order to justify the conduct. In Germany—as in other European and Latin American countries—the solution is to describe the case as one of justifiable "defensive" necessity that applies when the actor directs the attack towards the source of the threat but the threat fails to satisfy all of the triggering conditions for self-defense or defense of property. It is unclear how the hiker's shooting of the aggressive dog would be treated under American law. While the inclination might be to think of such cases as straightforward instances of "defense of property," this is problematic, for—as the European Continental approach to the question shows—it is difficult to assert that the dog's attack amounts to the kind of "unlawful aggression" that triggers the right to self-defense or defense of property.

3. Distinguishing between aggressive and defensive necessity is important in European and Latin American countries because different standards of proportionality apply depending on which defense is invoked. In cases of aggressive necessity (hiker breaks into cabin to seek shelter from storm), the conduct is justified only if the defendant causes less harm than the harm averted. This is the classic proportionality requirement in lesser evil cases. Nevertheless, defensive necessity (hiker shoots aggressive dog to prevent him from eating his limited food supply), allows the defendant to cause slightly more harm than the harm averted, but not as much harm as she would be able to inflict pursuant to defense of self or property. Therefore, defensive necessity justifies conduct even if the defendant does not choose the lesser evil, as long as she inflicts an equal or slightly greater harm than the one thwarted. A Spanish scholar explains the rules that govern the use of force pursuant to defensive necessity in the following way:

> [Defensive necessity] is a special kind of necessity in which the force is used against a thing or person that is the source of the danger, although the thing or person does not act in a way that amounts to a "wrongful aggression" that triggers the use of force in self-defense ...
>
> [Although the Spanish Penal Code does not expressly codify justifiable defensive necessity], it is possible for courts to invoke it by analogy in light of the features it shares with self-defense and with lesser evils. Given that in cases of defensive necessity the actor uses force against the source of the threat, the proportionality requirement is modified, and—like in cases of self-defense—it is possible to

> cause [slightly] more harm than the one averted. However, since the human, animal or natural source of the threat in these cases does not count as a "wrongful aggression", there has to be a more stringent proportionality requirement that—similar to the proportionality requirement in classic lesser evils cases—does not allow the defendant to cause noticeably more harm than the one averted.... Furthermore, given the [special nature of defensive necessity cases], the defendant has a more stringent duty to retreat than she has in self-defense cases.

Diego Manuel Luzón Peña, *Lecciones de Derecho Penal Parte General* 433–434 (2nd Ed., 2012).

4. Professor Byrd argues that perhaps the best way of looking at a case like Judy Norman's in which a battered woman kills her abuser in a non-confrontational situation is as an instance of justifiable defensive necessity. This would require us to acknowledge that killing the sleeping abuser is not justified pursuant to self-defense, for the "imminent wrongful aggression" that triggers the right to use such force is missing. Byrd argues that this is precisely the sort of case in which it makes sense to apply the defensive necessity justification, since the defendant harms the source of the threat (the abusive spouse) in circumstances in which self-defense cannot be invoked because of the lack of a present/actual aggression. Note that the traditional lesser evils defense could not be invoked to justify the conduct, because the harm prevented (death of defendant) is not greater than the one averted (death of spouse). Nonetheless, defensive necessity is applicable, for under the more lenient proportionality requirements that apply in this context, a defendant is justified as long as she causes equal or slightly greater harm than the one averted. Since Norman inflicted a harm that is equal (husband's death) to the harm averted (her death), she satisfies the more lax proportionality standards of defensive necessity. Do you find Professor Byrd's solution to the *Norman* case appealing? Why or why not? Does it matter whether we conclude that Norman's killing of her sleeping husband was justified pursuant to self-defense or pursuant to (defensive) necessity? Explain.

## § 15.07 Defensive Force: Scholarly Debates

### George P. Fletcher, *Domination in the Theory of Justification and Excuse*

57 U. Pitt. L. Rev. 553 (1996)

... III. Domination and Imminence

The central debate in the theory of self-defense for the last decade has been whether we should maintain a strict requirement of imminence in assessing which attacks trigger a legitimate defensive response. The traditional rule confronts a critique favoring relaxation of the rule primarily to make it easier for battered women to assert a claim of self-defense in cases of doubtful imminence. The typical case in dispute is like the Norman case. One in which the battered woman kills her batterer when he is asleep or otherwise quiescent. In her trial for the 1985 killing, Judy Norman was held to the strict imminence requirement and, as might be expected, her claim of self-defense failed. She was convicted of manslaughter, sentenced to six years in prison but released three months into her term after the governor commuted her sentence.

To many critics it seems that Judy Norman had no practicable, reasonable choice. Her shooting her husband in the head was a necessary response under the circumstances. Thus, the argument goes, there must be something wrong with the imminence requirement. The critique of the imminence requirement is buttressed by additional considerations:

1. The shift in language in the Model Penal Code from imminence to "immediately necessary."

2. Hypothetical cases involving long range latent dangers that make killing necessary even though the attack does not seem to be imminent.

3. The subjectivist interpretation of self-defense that seems to make the interpretation of imminence dependent on the perceptions of the defender.

A number of these objections would be satisfied by recognizing an excuse of self-defense based on necessary action where there is no practicable alternative. Under this standard, Judy Norman would have been excused and acquitted.

The more difficult questions arise in the context of justification. Does the imminence requirement belong in a properly constructed standard of justifiable self-defense? And if it does, is it proper to condition the interpretation of imminence on the power relationship between the parties? Does it follow that the battered wife, subject to the domination of her husband, should be allowed a broader interpretation of imminence?

In response to these questions, I confess that the existing literature of criminal law has done a woefully inadequate job in constructing a case for the imminence requirement. The traditional rule, arguably based on patriarchy, hardly persuades feminist critics. Needed is an argument of principle about why only imminent attacks—those about to happen—should trigger a right of self-defense ...

The significance of the imminence requirement in cases of self-defense ... [is that] when an attack against private individuals is imminent, the police are no longer in a position to intervene and exercise the state's function of securing public safety. The individual right to self-defense kicks in precisely because immediate action is necessary. Individuals do not cede a total monopoly of force to the state. They reserve the right when danger is imminent and otherwise unavoidable to secure their own safety against aggression.

Several implications follow from this account of the imminence requirement. First, the requirement properly falls into the domain of political rather than moral theory. The issue is the proper allocation of authority between the state and the citizen. When the requirement is not met, when individuals engage in preemptive attacks against suspected future aggressors, we fault them on political grounds. They exceed their authority as citizens; they take "the law into their own hands." Precisely because the issue is political rather than moral, the requirement must be both objective and public. There must be a signal to the community that this is an incident in which the law ceases to protect, that the individual must secure his or her own safety.

Now so far as the issue is objective, the interpretation of attacks as imminent depends exclusively on the qualities of the attack—on its proximity to success and on the danger latent in the threatened use of force. The background relationships of the parties, whether one is dominant and the other subordinate, should not matter. This seems to be obvious in relations between states. Whether Egypt is engaged in an imminent attack against Israel depends exclusively on what they are doing. The general power relationship between the parties might have some bearing on the interpretation of the danger expressed by amassing troops at the border. But whether one state does the bidding of the other should not give the subordinate party either an advantage or disadvantage. If this proposition applies as between Israel and Egypt, it should also govern the relations between Judy Norman and her battering husband.

In cases like Norman, however, an additional element seems to influence those who seek to relax the law in favor of the battered wife who strikes back. The political issue at stake in interpreting the requirement of imminence is whether the state's authority to keep the peace should yield to the individual's authority to use force in self-protection. The argument is often made that in these cases, the state fails to exercise its protective function. Judy Norman in fact sought protection from social agencies and she failed to receive it. In other cases, the police fail to intervene to protect those who are victimized at home. In these situations, where there is a gap between the theory of state protection and the reality of police indifference, it becomes difficult to assess whether the courts of the state should be required to recognize a broader than usual right of self-defense. The problem, it seems, is to formulate a precise test of how badly the police have failed and to determine a proportionate adjustment in the law of self-defense.

This is about as good a case as I can make for the view that the underlying relationship of dominance and subordination should not bear on the analysis of self-defense as a justification. The deeper point that I have established, I hope, is that because the requirement of imminence is political rather than moral, the element of self-defense known as an "imminent attack" must actually occur in the real world. The attack signals to the community that the defensive response is not a form of aggression but a legitimate response in the name of self-protection. Self-defense becomes compatible with the state's supposed monopoly over the use of force precisely because the community can understand the exceptional nature of self-defense in response to imminent attacks....

V. Domination as It Bears on Excuses

The question remains: How should the law bring relief to people like Judy Norman?... My view, which I have expressed many times, is that the law should make greater use of excusing conditions. The prior relationship between the parties should bear on aspects of self-defense that sound in the theory of excuses, namely the recognition that the action is wrongful but nonetheless not a fit basis for blaming and punishing the person who resorts to violence.

Two features of self-defense properly appeal to criteria that negate the blameworthiness of the defender. One is the theory of necessity. Where there is no reasonable choice but to attack someone who is sleeping or otherwise in a quiescent mode, the proper argument is not that the attack is right and lawful, but that the actor is not properly subject to blame for acting on the instinct of self-preservation. A prior relationship of dominance bears upon the analysis of necessity, for it assists us in understanding whether reasonable alternatives permitted an escape from the situation without resorting to the use of deadly force.

Relations of dominance also enter into the analysis of mistaken belief in the imminence of an attack. A good example is State v. Wanrow, in which the defendant suspected a man named Wesler of having molested her son and violated her daughter. When confronted with these charges, Wesler went to the home of Yvonne Wanrow's friend. Wesler, "a large man who was visibly intoxicated, entered the home and when told to leave declined to do so." A quarrel ensued. Wanrow, who was 5'4" and then on crutches, had a pistol in her purse. Suddenly Wesler appeared behind her. "She testified to being gravely startled by this situation and to having then shot and killed Wesler in what amounted to a reflex action." Yvonne Wanrow was convicted of second-degree murder.

The conviction was reversed partly because the trial court had admitted into evidence the tape recording of a telephone call in which Wanrow's friend made statements that apparently incriminated the defendant by making the shooting appear vengeful rather than defensive. For our purposes, the more interesting grounds for reversal are the defects asserted in the instruction quoted above. The instruction directs the jury to consider only those circumstances occurring "at or immediately before the killing." The Supreme Court of Washington responds: "This is not now, and never has been, the law of self-defense in Washington. On the contrary, the justification of self-defense is to be evaluated in light of all the facts and circumstances known to the defendant, including those known substantially before the killing."

In particular, the court noted, the decedent's reputation for aggressive behavior, so far as it was known to the defendant, should enter into an assessment of the "degree of force which ... a reasonable person in the same situation ... seeing what [s]he sees and knowing what [s]he knows, then would believe to be necessary." Note that the prior relationship of the parties, including factors leading to the aggressor's dominating behavior, bear properly only on the reasonable perception of danger. This is the aspect of self-defense that, as I have argued, should be considered grounds for excuse rather than justification. If Yvonne Wanrow was mistaken about the danger that the decedent represented, she could try to invoke the relationship of the parties in assessing whether her mistake was reasonable and therefore compatible with an excuse.

In an additional, arguably redundant paragraph, the court notes the concentration of the disputed instruction on the male gender as though the standard "to be applied is that applicable to an altercation between two men." This arguably deprived the defendant of the equal protection of the laws. A correct instruction would enable "the jury to consider her actions in the light of her own perceptions of the situation, including those perceptions which were the product of our nation's long and unfortunate history of sex discrimination."

These last lines have spawned a great deal of misunderstanding. There is no doubt, as I have argued since the early 1970s, that excusing conditions should focus on the individual circumstances of the person asserting the excuse. If a female defender is substantially weaker than her assailant, this factor obviously should enter into the analysis of whether her perception of danger is reasonable under the circumstances. The problem, in my view, is not the "history of sex discrimination" (however malign that history may have been) but rather the unfortunate history of a system of criminal law that has paid too little attention to rendering justice in individual cases of excusable criminal actions.

## Richard A. Rosen, *On Self-Defense, Imminence and Women who Kill their Batterers*

71 N.C. L. Rev. 371 (1993)

... *Imminence and Necessity*

In self-defense, the concept of imminence has no significance independent of the notion of necessity. It is, in other words, a "translator" of the underlying principle of necessity, not the principle itself. Society does not require that the evil avoided be an imminent evil because it believes that an imminent evil is the only type of evil that should be avoided, nor because an imminent threatened harm is necessarily worse than a non-imminent one. Rather, imminence is required because, and only because, of the fear that without imminence there is no assurance that the defensive action is necessary to avoid the harm. If the harm is not imminent then surely the actor can take steps that will alleviate the necessity for responding with fatal force.

At the trial level imminence operates as a condition precedent for a finding of necessity. The legislature, or in common-law jurisdictions, the appellate courts, have made an *a priori* decision that a killing to prevent a non-imminent threatened harm cannot in any case be a necessary killing, and the jury (or judge in a bench trial) must decide guilt or innocence in light of this determination.

Because imminence serves only to further the necessity principle, if there is a conflict between imminence and necessity, necessity must prevail. If action is *really* necessary to avert a threatened harm, society should allow the action, or at least not punish it, even if the harm is not imminent. Conversely, even if the harm is imminent, society should not permit defensive action if such action is not necessary.

While the criminal law in this country tends to follow the latter proposition, at least to some degree, it ignores the former. Thus, generally the law requires that a person avoid using force, especially lethal force, if an alternative to avoiding a threat is available, even if the threat poses an imminent danger. The law does not, however, allow a person to use force of any degree to ward off a danger that is not deemed imminent, no matter how necessary the protective action may be.

On a theoretical level, this choice seems questionable. In cases where the principle, i.e., necessity, is present, and the translator, i.e., imminence, is not, this choice mandates ignoring the principle because of the absence of the translator. If imminence is required only to ensure necessity, how can the law discount necessity even when it presents itself without imminence? This course permits imminence to act as an inhibitor, interfering with the underlying norm instead of furthering it.

One can argue, of course, that lethal force can never be necessary unless the threatened harm is imminent, but it is not difficult to imagine situations in which this is not the case. For example, Robinson postulates the situation of a hostage who is told that he will be executed at some date in the future; in the interim he is kept in captivity in perfect safety. Although the threatened harm is not imminent, it is reasonably certain to happen. The hostage discovers an opportunity to escape, but can do so safely only by killing the captor. Should the law brand the hostage a criminal if he kills his captor in order to escape? Robinson argues that it should not, and his position seems unassailable. In this situation the captor is at fault, the killing is proportional to the harm threatened, and the killing is necessary to protect an innocent person's life. The escaped hostage easily could be considered a hero rather than a criminal. Clearly, then, a killing can be necessary even though the harm threatened is not imminent....

*Did She Really Need To Kill?*

The first reaction of many people to a non-confrontational killing of a batterer, as in *Norman,* is that the killing could not have been necessary because the defendant simply could have seized the opportunity to flee. Why alter the law of self-defense when the victim of the abuse could have merely walked out the door? Under this argument, the time lapse between the abuse and the killing, and the resulting lack of imminent danger, conclusively demonstrate that the killing was not necessary.

The obvious response to this argument is that a jury would certainly remain free, even without a strict imminence requirement, to decide that the killing was not really necessary and, therefore, could convict the defendant upon such a finding. Eliminating the imminence requirement in a specific case does not mandate a specific verdict, it merely permits the jury to make the decision on necessity without the interference (or assistance) of the imminence requirement. Nor does its elimination make the question of imminence irrelevant. Imminence remains, as do the other factors in the case, relevant to the jury's core inquiry: Was the killing necessary?

One cannot rest on this counterargument alone, however, because this objection does raise a subsidiary question about the consideration the law should give to the possibility of flight in a situation where the woman has an opportunity to flee. As discussed earlier, part of what first struck me about *Norman* was the conviction that Ms. Norman did not have a realistic alternative to her lethal action, that the only way she could really be safe was to kill her husband.

J.T. Norman's abuse of his wife was prolonged and vicious. Over the years, whenever he was drunk, he brutally beat her, often inflicting serious injuries. He used his fists, bottles, ashtrays, and even a baseball bat. Mr. Norman forced his wife to prostitute herself to support him. When she was pregnant he kicked her down the stairs, causing the premature birth of her child. When she ran away, he tracked her, caught **393* her, and beat her. He frequently threatened to kill her.

In the days immediately preceding the killing, the abuse Ms. Norman suffered became more constant and vicious, and the threats to kill her became more frequent and, by all accounts, more believable. Ms. Norman called the police. The officers told her that she would have to take out a warrant, but she told them that her husband would kill her if she did. The officers left, but returned when they received a call that she had taken an overdose of pills. When the ambulance arrived, Mr. Norman tried to interfere, saying, "Let the bitch die ... She ain't nothing but a dog ... She don't deserve to live," and threatened to kill her, her mother, and her grandmother.

The day after she was released from the hospital, Ms. Norman sought help at a counseling center. When she returned home and told her husband that he must stop drinking or she would have him committed, he told her that he would cut her throat if he saw someone coming for him. During the day, he threatened twice to cut off her breast, and his threats to kill her continued until he took a nap late that afternoon, forcing her to lie on the floor by the bed.

The point of this grisly recitation is not to demonstrate that Mr. Norman deserved to be killed because of his past misdeeds, nor to provide substance for a "battered women's syndrome" defense, which would focus on the impact this abuse had on Ms. Norman's psyche. Rather, the narrative lends credence to the notion that, given this history, a reasonable person could have believed that the only way to stop Mr. Norman from killing or greatly harming his wife was to kill him.

Other than the use of lethal force, Ms. Norman's options were limited. One choice was to do nothing—to sleep on the floor as her husband commanded her and to await whatever lay ahead. Another option was to arm herself and wait until the next attack before killing her husband. Yet another was to call for help. Finally, she could have just fled into the night. Each of these choices carried a realistic chance of great harm or death to Ms. Norman. Given her husband's past behavior and threats, doing nothing offered an assurance that she would suffer at least great bodily harm during one of his drunken attacks.

Similarly, it does not strain the imagination to calculate the risk Ms. Norman would have taken had she decided to wait until the next attack before wielding her weapon. *Perhaps* she would have been able to extract the gun from its hiding place in time to protect herself. *Perhaps* she would have been able to shoot her husband before he reached her. *Perhaps* the first shot would have been effective enough to stop him. Unless all three of these conditions were met, however, she could easily have been a dead woman.

As with her other options, calling for help or flight carried a serious risk of death or great bodily harm. Newspaper and television news reports are filled with stories of spurned men who often go to extraordinary lengths to pursue the women who reject them, who often hurt these women and sometimes kill them. The professional literature recently has developed evidence to support the contention that a woman who is already being battered by an abusive man, and who tries to leave or get help, is placing her life at risk. In fact, the time of most danger for the woman is when she attempts to leave; women are often killed when, and because, they attempt to escape. Efforts to involve outside agencies, including the police, similarly escalate the risk to the woman. Threats may turn into force, and non-deadly force into deadly force. As for Ms. Norman, her husband had told her explicitly that he would maim her or kill her if she tried to alter the situation, and can one honestly maintain that she was unreasonable in believing him?

Ms. Norman was not, of course, a total captive. In Robinson's hostage example, discussed earlier in this Article, the captive can only escape by killing the captor. Even if flight would have been risky for Ms. Norman, there was at least a chance that she could have crept out of town, masked her identity, and fled to Alaska to establish a new life. One could argue, therefore, that the killing of her husband was not absolutely necessary. The difficulty with such an argument is that it is based on an erroneous premise—that the law *always* requires absolute necessity before granting the privilege of self-defense. In fact, the law *never* requires the necessity to be absolute before allowing self-defense. The possibility always exists that a person attacking another with a gun will change his mind, or miss, or have a heart attack before pulling the trigger. If a reasonable person in the situation, however, would believe that deadly force was needed, the law permits the use of fatal defensive force. Similarly, the mere possibility of retreat is not determinative so long as a reasonable person would believe that the retreat would not provide safety.

Take the analysis one step further, however, and assume that Ms. Norman could have escaped safely from her house and fled to Alaska, where she could change her identity and live happily, and safely, ever after. If society required her to do this, the end result most likely would be one less dead body, a result not always possible when the aggressor is coming after the victim at the moment she kills in self-defense. The simple answer to this proposition is that society does not now, nor has it ever, required completely innocent people to behave in this fashion. No matter how clear it was to Gary Cooper that somebody would end up dead if he did not leave before the train carrying his enemy arrived at "High Noon," our culture allows him to stay in town and affords him the right to kill in self-defense when the bad guys come after him. Even when retreat is required, which is not all that often, one must only physically move to a place of temporary safety. Renunciation of personal and family identity is not demanded.

There may come a time when society will develop mechanisms, in the criminal justice system or elsewhere, that would effectively guarantee women in Ms. Norman's position refuge and safety. When, or if, that occurs, society could, and should, require that women choose a nonlethal option by requiring either imminence of the threatened harm or a retreat/flight alternative. That time, however, certainly has not arrived.

### *Imminence, Necessity, and the Jury*

Using a necessity rule instead of an imminence rule imports no new norms into the law of self-defense; it merely changes the locus of decision making. Under the current criminal justice scheme, the legislature, or, in common-law jurisdictions, judges, already have decided that a killing to prevent a non-imminent threatened harm can never be a necessary killing. In light of this predetermined conclusion jurors must then decide the case.

Removing or modifying the imminence rule shifts the locus of decisionmaking to jurors, allowing them to weigh the evidence and make their own decision on necessity in a suitable case.

Such a shift is not without risks. One reasonable concern is that a jury would be encouraged to make *ad hoc* decisions based upon its estimation of the relative worth of the individuals involved. The danger also exists that increasing the discretion given to jurors will simultaneously increase the opportunity for bias, arbitrariness, or discrimination to influence the jurors' decision making. After all, it arguably was the Crown's distrust of jurors' proclivities in homicide cases that led to the medieval development of strict rules for self-defense.

Although there is no way to eliminate these risks, they do not appear to be overly troubling in cases of nonconfrontational killings of batterers. Aside from eliminating the imminence requirement, the law of self-defense would remain as it now stands. Jurors would still be instructed that the use of deadly defensive force is justified only in those situations in which such force reasonably appears to be necessary. Jurors would still be instructed on the proportionality principle: that deadly force can be used only in the face of a threat of serious bodily injury or death. Jurors would still be instructed on the fault principle: that the defendant must not be culpable in the creation of the life-threatening situation and that the defendant may use deadly force only if her belief in the necessity for its use is objectively reasonable. Jurors would still be instructed that the defendant must have acted out of fear, not revenge or spite, and that deadly force may be used only if the defendant reasonably believed, and the evidence supported the reasonableness of the belief, that the force was *necessary* to prevent the harm threatened ...

One need not replace imminence with necessity in every case in which self-defense is claimed, nor, for that matter, in every case in which a woman kills a batterer. Because imminence effectively translates the necessity principle in a significant number of cases, it is both useful and appropriate to continue to utilize it in those cases.

To accomplish this goal, the trial judge could instruct the jury that a killing in self-defense must be in response to an imminent danger unless the defendant is able to meet an initial burden of production by presenting substantial evidence that the killing was necessary even though the danger was not imminent. If, and only if, the defendant meets this burden of production would imminence be eliminated as a *sine qua non* for self-defense. Only then would the jury be instructed solely on necessity, with the imminence of the threat constituting only one factor among many to be considered. This procedure would retain the imminence requirement in those cases in which it is a translator of the necessity principle, but would remove it when it acts as a potential inhibitor.

This approach would serve several functions. On the theoretical side, the use of the unmodified necessity principle where appropriate would allow for a degree of individual justice without diluting the overall integrity of society's notions of self-defense. On the practical side, most self-defense cases will remain unchanged. In nonconfrontational situations outside of the battered woman scenario, society usually provides other reasonably feasible alternatives to homicidal self-help. Thus, even though the changes in self-defense law this Article advocates are not limited theoretically to cases in which women kill their batterers, few defendants in generic self-defense cases could meet even a minimal burden of production on a claim that self-defense was warranted even though the danger threatened was not imminent.

Even the impact on trials in which the defendant successfully meets the initial burden of production should not be overwhelming. Most courts, as the trial court did in *Norman*, already admit evidence about prior abuse and threats, as well as testimony about battered women's syndrome. Replacing imminence with necessity in an appropriate case should not alter this. Rather, it would permit the jury to consider this evidence not only in the context of why the woman did not leave, but also in determining whether the abuse and threats produced a reasonable fear of death.

One further change, however, is needed. In appropriate cases, the jury should be allowed to consider evidence of the availability and efficacy of alternatives to the use of lethal force to kill a batterer in a nonconfrontational setting as well as the woman's knowledge of these alternatives. Because, in a case involving a nonconfrontational killing, in which a woman has the *time* to avoid the harm, evidence about whether she had a realistic *chance* to avoid death or serious physical abuse without killing (or without obliterating her identity) and whether society had provided her with information about these alternatives, is indisputably relevant. The jury cannot make an informed decision on this issue without being informed of the defendant's alternatives. Assuming that the fate awaiting Ms. Norman (and others similarly situated) was reasonably certain death or grave bodily harm had she not acted as she did, the jury should know that society presently provides her with no reasonable alternatives that would even minimally protect her for more than a brief time.

## Notes and Questions

1. Professor Fletcher suggests that defendants like Judy Norman should be excused rather than justified. Thus, Fletcher contends that Judy Norman acted wrongfully, but that we should nevertheless excuse her because we could not fairly expect her to behave in a different way. In contrast, Professor Rosen suggests that imminence be considered one—amongst many—factors that are relevant to determining whether the use of force was necessary to thwart an attack. If force is deemed by the fact finder to be necessary to repel an attack even if the aggression was not yet imminent, Rosen argues that the defendant should be justified rather than excused. As a result, he suggests that Judy Norman should have been justified if it is concluded that killing her sleeping husband was the only way of preventing future attacks. Who has the better part of this argument? Explain.

2. Professor Rosen argues that "[i]n self-defense, the concept of imminence has no significance independent of the notion of necessity." Professor Fletcher seems to agree, as he points out that "[t]he significance of the imminence requirement in cases of self-defense ... [is that] when an attack against private individuals is imminent, the police are no longer in a position to intervene and exercise the state's function of securing public safety." Therefore, Fletcher argues that "[t]he individual right to self-defense kicks in precisely because immediate action is necessary." Do you agree that the sole purpose of requiring that force be used to thwart an "imminent" attack is to guarantee that the use of force is "necessary"? Why or why not? Can you think of a purpose for the imminence requirement other than making sure that the use of defensive force is necessary?

3. Contrary to what Rosen and Fletcher argue in the excerpted articles, Professor Kimberly Ferzan argues that imminence is not merely a proxy for necessity. Instead, she observes that the imminence requirement qualifies the kind of threats that can amount to "wrongful aggressions" that trigger the right to use force in self-defense. According to Ferzan, only "imminent" attacks can logically count as "aggressions." Consequently, if an attack is non-imminent, it simply cannot count as an "aggression" that triggers the right to use force in self-defense, even if using force is necessary to prevent a future attack. Ferzan observes:

> The critical question is not when the defender needs to act but what kind of threat triggers the right to self-defense. Theorists who propose that we switch what "imminence" modifies—shifting focus from "imminent threats" to "immediately necessary"—ask the wrong question. The necessity of the defender's action to preserve her life may have nothing to do with the current culpability or capabilities of the putative aggressor. But the need to act remains. Therefore, the true question that animates the debate over the imminence requirement is what type of threats trigger the right to self-defense. The correct question is not when does the defender need to act but at what point is it fair to construe the putative aggressor as posing a threat?
>
> Recall that there are two senses of the word, "threat." One sense of the word threat is a forthcoming battery. But threats may also be far more inchoate. In the latter sense, the possession of nuclear weapons by North Korea is a threat to the United States and a sleeping husband is a threat to a battered woman. The concept of threat may be further extended—if two people are stuck in a cave with limited oxygen, each poses a "threat" to the other simply because one individual's survival is dependent on limiting the chances of the other's.
>
> While our mere existence in some sense "threatens" others, those who wish to reject the status quo have never been regarded as self-defenders. After all, it seems that no one individual has a stronger claim to the right to life, existence, or thriving than another. Thus, the right to self-defense cannot be this broad....
>
> What we seek from our quest for "threats" is the concept of aggression. It is aggression that triggers the right to a defensive response. Indeed, while the adage "the best defense is a good offense" may be true, it is, by its own terms, offensive behavior, not defensive behavior. Self-defense is only understandable as a response to another's aggressive conduct ...
>
> Aggression is ... morally relevant for domestic criminal law. Theorists who adopt a forfeiture approach to self-defense claim that the actor loses her right to life when she poses an unjust threat. Moreover, some scholars claim that self-defense is justifiable only when it is intended to repel a present threat. Thus, the moral assessment of both the aggressor's and the defender's rights hinges on some notion of aggression.
>
> Our understanding of aggression contains several elements, one of which is action. The imminence requirement is best understood as the actus reus of aggression ...
>
> For self-defense, however, the action serves a different purpose. The aggressor's action "starts it." We can only understand defense by comparison with offense. The aggressor's action signifies the breach of the community rules and the lack of equal respect for the defender. It is this action that makes self-defense understandable.
>
> When the right to self-defense is broadened to any person that might potentially inflict harm, we blur the distinction between offense and defense. Two nations may have great disdain for each other and accumulate significant weaponry in case these weapons must be used. But once inchoate threats are sufficient to justify self-defense, then both nations are authorized to attack the other. We then have no ability to distinguish self-defensive conduct from aggressive conduct.

Kimberly Kessler Ferzan, *Defending Imminence: From Battered Women to Iraq*, 46 Arizona L. Rev. 213 (2004).

Do you agree with Ferzan's claim that imminence is not merely a proxy for necessity, but also an essential feature of the sort of "aggression" that allows society to determine who "started" the attack and, therefore, who has the right to defend against the attack? Explain.

4. Note that Ferzan claims that if we eliminate the imminence requirement "[w]e then have no ability to distinguish self-defensive conduct from aggressive conduct." This insight proves particularly revealing if one slightly modifies the *Norman* case. Suppose that Judy Norman's husband wakes up when his wife is about to shoot and kill him. Would he be justified in using force in defense of self to prevent Judy Norman from killing him? In this modified hypothetical, who is the aggressor and who is the defender? Who "started" the attack in this tweaked version of *Norman*, Judy Norman or her husband? Ferzan would likely argue that, given that the sleeping husband was not imminently attacking Judy Norman, the line between "attacker" and "defender" is blurred in this case. This, in turn, may give us reasons to hold on to an imminence requirement in self-defense cases even when force seems to be necessary in spite of the absence of an imminent attack. Without such requirement, we simply won't be able to tell whether Judy Norman's force is truly being used defensively or if it is actually being used aggressively. Do you find this argument in favor of requiring imminence in cases like *Norman* persuasive? Why or why not?

# Chapter 16

# Law Enforcement Authority

## § 16.01 Law Enforcement Authority: Common Law Approach and Constitutional Limitations

### Tennessee v. Garner

Supreme Court of the United States, 1985
471 U.S. 1

Justice WHITE delivered the opinion of the Court.

This case requires us to determine the constitutionality of the use of deadly force to prevent the escape of an apparently unarmed suspected felon. We conclude that such force may not be used unless it is necessary to prevent the escape and the officer has probable cause to believe that the suspect poses a significant threat of death or serious physical injury to the officer or others.

I

At about 10:45 p.m. on October 3, 1974, Memphis Police Officers Elton Hymon and Leslie Wright were dispatched to answer a "prowler inside call." Upon arriving at the scene they saw a woman standing on her porch and gesturing toward the adjacent house. She told them she had heard glass breaking and that "they" or "someone" was breaking in next door. While Wright radioed the dispatcher to say that they were on the scene, Hymon went behind the house. He heard a door slam and saw someone run across the backyard. The fleeing suspect, who was appellee-respondent's decedent, Edward Garner, stopped at a 6-feet-high chain link fence at the edge of the yard. With the aid of a flashlight, Hymon was able to see Garner's face and hands. He saw no sign of a weapon, and, though not certain, was "reasonably sure" and "figured" that Garner was unarmed. He thought Garner was 17 or 18 years old and about 5'5" or 5'7" tall. While Garner was crouched at the base of the fence, Hymon called out "police, halt" and took a few steps toward him. Garner then began to climb over the fence. Convinced that if Garner made it over the fence he would elude capture, Hymon shot him. The bullet hit Garner in the back of the head. Garner was taken by ambulance to a hospital, where he died on the operating table. Ten dollars and a purse taken from the house were found on his body.

In using deadly force to prevent the escape, Hymon was acting under the authority of a Tennessee statute and pursuant to Police Department policy. The statute provides that "[i]f, after notice of the intention to arrest the defendant, he either flee or forcibly resist, the officer may use all the necessary means to effect the arrest." Tenn.Code Ann. § 40-7-108 (1982). The Department policy was slightly more restrictive than the statute, but still allowed the use of deadly force in cases of burglary. The incident was reviewed by the Memphis Police Firearm's Review Board and presented to a grand jury. Neither took any action.

Garner's father then brought this action in the Federal District Court for the Western District of Tennessee, seeking damages under 42 U.S.C. § 1983 for asserted violations of Garner's constitutional rights. The complaint alleged that the shooting violated the Fourth, Fifth, Sixth, Eighth, and Fourteenth Amendments of the United States Constitution. It named as defendants Officer Hymon, the Police Department, its Director, and the Mayor and city of Memphis. After a 3-day bench trial, the District Court entered judgment for all defendants. It dismissed the claims against the Mayor and the Director for lack of evidence. It then concluded that Hymon's actions were authorized by the Tennessee statute, which in turn was constitutional. Hymon had employed the only reasonable and practicable means of preventing Garner's escape. Garner had "recklessly and heedlessly attempted to vault over the fence to escape, thereby assuming the risk of being fired upon."

The Court of Appeals for the Sixth Circuit affirmed with regard to Hymon, finding that he had acted in good-faith reliance on the Tennessee statute and was therefore within the scope of his qualified immunity ...

The Court of Appeals reversed and remanded. It reasoned that the killing of a fleeing suspect is a "seizure" under the Fourth Amendment, and is therefore constitutional only if "reasonable." The Tennessee statute failed as applied to this case because it did not adequately limit the use of deadly force by distinguishing between felonies of different magnitudes—"the facts, as found, did not justify the use of deadly force under the Fourth Amendment." Officers cannot resort to deadly force unless they "have probable cause ... to believe that the suspect [has committed a felony and] poses a threat to the safety of the officers or a danger to the community if left at large."

The State of Tennessee, which had intervened to defend the statute appealed to this Court....

## II

Whenever an officer restrains the freedom of a person to walk away, he has seized that person. While it is not always clear just when minimal police interference becomes a seizure, there can be no question that apprehension by the use of deadly force is a seizure subject to the reasonableness requirement of the Fourth Amendment.

### A

A police officer may arrest a person if he has probable cause to believe that person committed a crime. Petitioners and appellant argue that if this requirement is satisfied the Fourth Amendment has nothing to say about *how* that seizure is made. This submission ignores the many cases in which this Court, by balancing the extent of the intrusion against the need for it, has examined the reasonableness of the manner in which a search or seizure is conducted. To determine the constitutionality of a seizure "[w]e must balance the nature and quality of the intrusion on the individual's Fourth Amendment interests against the importance of the governmental interests alleged to justify the intrusion." We have described "the balancing of competing interests" as "the key principle of the Fourth Amendment." Because one of the factors is the extent of the intrusion, it is plain that reasonableness depends on not only when a seizure is made, but also how it is carried out.

Applying these principles to particular facts, the Court has held that governmental interests did not support a lengthy detention of luggage an airport seizure not "carefully tailored to its underlying justification," surgery under general anesthesia to obtain evidence, or detention for fingerprinting without probable cause. On the other hand, under the same approach it has upheld the taking of fingernail scrapings from a suspect, an unannounced entry into a home to prevent the destruction of evidence, administrative housing inspections without probable cause to believe that a code violation will be found, and a blood test of a drunken-driving suspect. In each of these cases, the question was whether the totality of the circumstances justified a particular sort of search or seizure.

B

The same balancing process applied in the cases cited above demonstrates that, notwithstanding probable cause to seize a suspect, an officer may not always do so by killing him. The intrusiveness of a seizure by means of deadly force is unmatched. The suspect's fundamental interest in his own life need not be elaborated upon. The use of deadly force also frustrates the interest of the individual, and of society, in judicial determination of guilt and punishment. Against these interests are ranged governmental interests in effective law enforcement. It is argued that overall violence will be reduced by encouraging the peaceful submission of suspects who know that they may be shot if they flee. Effectiveness in making arrests requires the resort to deadly force, or at least the meaningful threat thereof. "Being able to arrest such individuals is a condition precedent to the state's entire system of law enforcement."

Without in any way disparaging the importance of these goals, we are not convinced that the use of deadly force is a sufficiently productive means of accomplishing them to justify the killing of nonviolent suspects. The use of deadly force is a self-defeating way of apprehending a suspect and so setting the criminal justice mechanism in motion. If successful, it guarantees that that mechanism will not be set in motion. And while the meaningful threat of deadly force might be thought to lead to the arrest of more live suspects by discouraging escape attempts, the presently available evidence does not support this thesis. The fact is that a majority of police departments in this country have forbidden the use of deadly force against nonviolent suspects. If those charged with the enforcement of the criminal law have abjured the use of deadly force in arresting nondangerous felons, there is a substantial basis for doubting that the use of such force is an essential attribute of the arrest power in all felony cases. Petitioners and appellant have not persuaded us that shooting nondangerous fleeing suspects is so vital as to outweigh the suspect's interest in his own life.

The use of deadly force to prevent the escape of all felony suspects, whatever the circumstances, is constitutionally unreasonable. It is not better that all felony suspects die than that they escape. Where the suspect poses no immediate threat to the officer and no threat to others, the harm resulting from failing to apprehend him does not justify the use of deadly force to do so. It is no doubt unfortunate when a suspect who is in sight escapes, but the fact that the police arrive a little late or are a little slower afoot does not always justify killing the suspect. A police officer may not seize an unarmed, nondangerous suspect by shooting him dead. The Tennessee statute is unconstitutional insofar as it authorizes the use of deadly force against such fleeing suspects.

It is not, however, unconstitutional on its face. Where the officer has probable cause to believe that the suspect poses a threat of serious physical harm, either to the officer or to others, it is not constitutionally unreasonable to prevent escape by using deadly force. Thus, if the suspect threatens the officer with a weapon or there is probable cause to believe that he has committed a crime involving the infliction or threatened infliction of serious physical harm, deadly force may be used if necessary to prevent escape, and if, where feasible, some warning has been given. As applied in such circumstances, the Tennessee statute would pass constitutional muster.

III

A

It is insisted that the Fourth Amendment must be construed in light of the common-law rule, which allowed the use of whatever force was necessary to effect the arrest of a fleeing felon, though not a misdemeanant. As stated in Hale's posthumously published Pleas of the Crown:

"[I]f persons that are pursued by these officers for felony or the just suspicion thereof... shall not yield themselves to these officers, but shall either resist or fly before they are apprehended or being apprehended shall rescue themselves and resist or fly, so that they cannot be otherwise apprehended, and are upon necessity slain therein, because they cannot be otherwise taken, it is no felony." 2 M. Hale, Historia Placitorum Coronae 85 (1736).

Most American jurisdictions also imposed a flat prohibition against the use of deadly force to stop a fleeing misdemeanant, coupled with a general privilege to use such force to stop a fleeing felon.

The State and city argue that because this was the prevailing rule at the time of the adoption of the Fourth Amendment and for some time thereafter, and is still in force in some States, use of deadly force against a fleeing felon must be "reasonable." It is true that this Court has often looked to the common law in evaluating the reasonableness, for Fourth Amendment purposes, of police activity. On the other hand, it "has not simply frozen into constitutional law those law enforcement practices that existed at the time of the Fourth Amendment's passage." Because of sweeping change in the legal and technological context, reliance on the common-law rule in this case would be a mistaken literalism that ignores the purposes of a historical inquiry.

B

It has been pointed out many times that the common-law rule is best understood in light of the fact that it arose at a time when virtually all felonies were punishable by death. "Though effected without the protections and formalities of an orderly trial and conviction, the killing of a resisting or fleeing felon resulted in no greater consequences than those authorized for punishment of the felony of which the individual was charged or suspected." Courts have also justified the common-law rule by emphasizing the relative dangerousness of felons.

Neither of these justifications makes sense today. Almost all crimes formerly punishable by death no longer are or can be. And while in earlier times "the gulf between the felonies and the minor offences was broad and deep," today the distinction is minor and often arbitrary. Many crimes classified as misdemeanors, or nonexistent, at common law are now felonies. These changes have undermined the concept, which was questionable to begin with, that use of deadly force against a fleeing felon is merely a speedier execution of someone who has already forfeited his life. They have also made the assumption that a "felon" is more dangerous than a misdemeanant untenable. Indeed, numerous misdemeanors involve conduct more dangerous than many felonies.

There is an additional reason why the common-law rule cannot be directly translated to the present day. The common-law rule developed at a time when weapons were rudimentary. Deadly force could be inflicted almost solely in a hand-to-hand struggle during which, necessarily, the safety of the arresting officer was at risk. Handguns were not carried by police officers until the latter half of the last century. Only then did it become possible to use deadly force from a distance as a means of apprehension. As a practical matter, the use of deadly force under the standard articulation of the common-law rule has an altogether different meaning—and harsher consequences—now than in past centuries.

One other aspect of the common-law rule bears emphasis. It forbids the use of deadly force to apprehend a misdemeanant, condemning such action as disproportionately severe.

In short, though the common-law pedigree of Tennessee's rule is pure on its face, changes in the legal and technological context mean the rule is distorted almost beyond recognition when literally applied....

IV

The District Court concluded that Hymon was justified in shooting Garner because state law allows, and the Federal Constitution does not forbid, the use of deadly force to prevent the escape of a fleeing felony suspect if no alternative means of apprehension is available. This conclusion made a determination of Garner's apparent dangerousness unnecessary. The court did find, however, that Garner appeared to be unarmed, though Hymon could not be certain that was the case. Restated in Fourth Amendment terms, this means Hymon had no articulable basis to think Garner was armed.

In reversing, the Court of Appeals accepted the District Court's factual conclusions and held that "the facts, as found, did not justify the use of deadly force." We agree. Officer Hymon could not reasonably have believed that Garner—young, slight, and unarmed—posed any threat. Indeed, Hymon never attempted to justify his actions on any basis other than the need to prevent an escape. The District Court stated in passing that "[t]he facts of this case did not indicate to Officer Hymon that Garner was 'non-dangerous.'" This conclusion is not explained, and seems to be based solely on the fact that Garner had broken into a house at night. However, the fact that Garner was a suspected burglar could not, without regard to the other circumstances, automatically justify the use of deadly force. Hymon did not have probable cause to believe that Garner, whom he correctly believed to be unarmed, posed any physical danger to himself or others.

The dissent argues that the shooting was justified by the fact that Officer Hymon had probable cause to believe that Garner had committed a nighttime burglary. While we agree that burglary is a serious crime, we cannot agree that it is so dangerous as automatically to justify the use of deadly force. The FBI classifies burglary as a "property" rather than a "violent" crime. Although the armed burglar would present a different situation, the fact that an unarmed suspect has broken into a dwelling at night does not automatically mean he is physically dangerous. This case demonstrates as much. In fact, the available statistics demonstrate that burglaries only rarely involve physical violence. During the 10-year period from 1973–1982, only 3.8% of all burglaries involved violent crime ...

The judgment of the Court of Appeals is affirmed, and the case is remanded for further proceedings consistent with this opinion.

**Justice O'CONNOR, with whom THE CHIEF JUSTICE and Justice REHNQUIST join, dissenting.**

The Court today holds that the Fourth Amendment prohibits a police officer from using deadly force as a last resort to apprehend a criminal suspect who refuses to halt when fleeing the scene of a nighttime burglary. This conclusion rests on the majority's balancing of the interests of the suspect and the public interest in effective law enforcement. Notwithstanding the venerable common-law rule authorizing the use of deadly force if necessary to apprehend a fleeing felon, and continued acceptance of this rule by nearly half the States, the majority concludes that Tennessee's statute is unconstitutional inasmuch as it allows the use of such force to apprehend a burglary suspect who is not obviously armed or otherwise dangerous. Although the circumstances of this case are unquestionably tragic and unfortunate, our constitutional holdings must be sensitive both to the history of the Fourth Amendment and to the general implications of the Court's reasoning. By disregarding the serious and dangerous nature of residential burglaries and the longstanding practice of many States, the Court effectively creates a Fourth Amendment right allowing a burglary suspect to flee unimpeded from a police officer who has probable cause to arrest, who has ordered the suspect to halt, and who has no means short of firing his weapon to prevent escape. I do not believe that the Fourth Amendment supports such a right, and I accordingly dissent ...

II

For purposes of Fourth Amendment analysis, I agree with the Court that Officer Hymon "seized" Garner by shooting him. Whether that seizure was reasonable and therefore permitted by the Fourth Amendment requires a careful balancing of the important public interest in crime prevention and detection and the nature and quality of the intrusion upon legitimate interests of the individual. In striking this balance here, it is crucial to acknowledge that police use of deadly force to apprehend a fleeing criminal suspect falls within the "rubric of police conduct ... necessarily [involving] swift action predicated upon the on-the-spot observations of the officer on the beat." The clarity of hindsight cannot provide the standard for judging the reasonableness of police decisions made in uncertain and often dangerous circumstances. Moreover, I am far more reluctant than is the Court to conclude that the Fourth Amendment proscribes a police practice that was accepted at the time of the adoption of the Bill of Rights and has continued to receive the support of many state legislatures. Although the Court has recognized that the requirements of the Fourth Amendment must respond to the reality of social and technological change, fidelity to the notion of *constitutional*—as opposed to purely judicial—limits on governmental action requires us to impose a heavy burden on those who claim that practices accepted when the Fourth Amendment was adopted are now constitutionally impermissible....

A proper balancing of the interests involved suggests that use of deadly force as a last resort to apprehend a criminal suspect fleeing from the scene of a nighttime burglary is not unreasonable within the meaning of the Fourth Amendment. Admittedly, the events giving rise to this case are in retrospect deeply regrettable. No one can view the death of an unarmed and apparently nonviolent 15-year-old without sorrow, much less disapproval. Nonetheless, the reasonableness of Officer Hymon's conduct for purposes of the Fourth Amendment cannot be evaluated by what later appears to have been a preferable course of police action. The officer pursued a suspect in the darkened backyard of a house that from all indications had just been burglarized. The police officer was not certain whether the suspect was alone or unarmed; nor did he know what had transpired inside the house. He ordered the suspect to halt, and when the suspect refused to obey and attempted to flee into the night, the officer fired his weapon to prevent escape. The reasonableness of this action for purposes of the Fourth Amendment is not determined by the unfortunate nature of this particular case; instead, the question is whether it is constitutionally impermissible for police officers, as a last resort, to shoot a burglary suspect fleeing the scene of the crime ...

IV

The Court's opinion sweeps broadly to adopt an entirely new standard for the constitutionality of the use of deadly force to apprehend fleeing felons. Thus, the Court "lightly brushe[s] aside," a long-standing police practice that predates the Fourth Amendment and continues to receive the approval of nearly half of the state legislatures. I cannot accept the majority's creation of a constitutional right to flight for burglary suspects seeking to avoid capture at the scene of the crime. Whatever the constitutional limits on police use of deadly force in order to apprehend a fleeing felon, I do not believe they are exceeded in a case in which a police officer has probable cause to arrest a suspect at the scene of a residential burglary, orders the suspect to halt, and then fires his weapon as a last resort to prevent the suspect's escape into the night. I respectfully dissent.

## *Notes and Questions*

1. The Tennessee statute that was struck down in *Garner* prescribed that:

> "If, after notice of the intention to arrest the defendant, he either flee[s] or forcibly resist[s], the officer may use all the necessary means to effect the arrest."

The only limitation on the use of force pursuant to this statute is that it be "necessary" to effect the arrest. Therefore, the law authorized police officers to use deadly force to make an arrest, as long as such force was the only way (i.e., necessary) of effecting the arrest. Application of the statute would justify the killing of the suspect in *Garner,* as he was fleeing from the police and the only way of detaining him was by shooting at him. As the Court observed in *Garner*, the statute closely tracked the common law approach to justifying force pursuant to law enforcement authority. At common law, police officers could use deadly force as long as it was necessary to prevent the escape of a person suspected of committing a felony. Nonetheless, deadly force could not be used to prevent the escape of a person who is merely suspected of committing a misdemeanor. Although the force used in *Garner* to prevent the suspect's escape was lawful both under the Tennessee statute and the common law approach to law enforcement authority, the United States Supreme Court struck it down, arguing that the use of deadly force under the circumstances of the case ran afoul the Fourth Amendment.

2. The Fourth Amendment of the Constitution of the United States provides that:

> The right of the people to be secure in their persons, houses, papers, and effects, against unreasonable searches and seizures, shall not be violated, and no Warrants shall issue, but upon probable cause, supported by Oath or affirmation, and particularly describing the place to be searched, and the persons or things to be seized.

The Supreme Court held in *Garner* that a fleeing suspect who is killed by the police is "seized" for the purposes of the Fourth Amendment. Therefore, the killing of the fleeing felon is constitutional only if it satisfies the substantive requirements that must be observed under the Fourth Amendment in order to seize a person. At a minimum, the Fourth Amendment requires that such seizures be "reasonable." Note, however, that the Fourth Amendment does not state that the seizure is lawful only if it is made pursuant to "probable cause." Instead, the Amendment provides that *no warrants shall issue* unless they are supported by probable cause (to believe that the person to be seized has committed a crime or is about to commit an offense). Given that the officer who killed the suspect in *Garner* was not acting pursuant to a warrant, his seizure may, in principle, be justified as long as it was reasonable, even if not supported by probable cause. Nonetheless, the

Supreme Court concluded in *Garner* that deadly force to detain a fleeing felon may only be used if the officer has *probable cause* to believe that the fleeing suspect poses a significant threat of death or serious physical injury to the officer or others. Does the Fourth Amendment's text support this conclusion? Explain.

3. Contrary to what the majority concluded, Justice O'Connor argued in dissent that using force under the circumstances of the case was reasonable even if there was no probable cause to believe that the fleeing felon posed a risk of death or serious bodily injury to the police or others. More specifically, she argues that a police officer who has "probable cause to arrest a suspect at the scene of a residential burglary, orders the suspect to halt, and then fires his weapon as a last resort to prevent the suspect's escape into the night" does not act "unreasonably" for the purposes of the Fourth Amendment. Do you agree? Why or why not?

4. After the Tennessee statute was struck down in *Garner,* the Tennessee legislature amended the law to read as follows:

> [A police] officer may use deadly force to effect an arrest only if all other reasonable means of apprehension have been exhausted or are unavailable, and where feasible, the officer has given notice of the officer's identity as an officer and given a warning that deadly force may be used unless resistance or flight ceases, and:
>
> (1) The officer has probable cause to believe the individual to be arrested has committed a felony involving the infliction or threatened infliction of serious bodily injury; or
>
> (2) The officer has probable cause to believe that the individual to be arrested poses a threat of serious bodily injury, either to the officer or to others unless immediately apprehended.

Subsection (2) describes exactly the kind of circumstances under which the use of deadly force to apprehend a fleeing suspect would be permissible under the Fourth Amendment as construed by the Supreme Court *Garner.* Nevertheless, Subsection (1) authorizes the use of deadly force if the police officer believes that the suspect has committed a felony that involves the actual or threatened infliction of serious bodily injury. Is deadly force authorized under this Subsection constitutional under *Garner*? Explain.

5. In *Scott v. Harris,* the United States Supreme Court was once again asked to assess the constitutionality of the use of deadly force by the police to apprehend a suspect. The police ordered the suspect to pull over because he was speeding. Instead, the suspect sped away. A high-speed chase ensued. The suspect engaged in reckless driving maneuvers in order to flee from the police. After viewing a video of the chase (you can see it too, as it's on YouTube), the Court described the suspect's driving in the following manner:

> [In the video] we see respondent's vehicle racing down narrow, two-lane roads in the dead of night at speeds that are shockingly fast. We see it swerve around more than a dozen other cars, cross the double-yellow line, and force cars traveling in both directions to their respective shoulders to avoid being hit. We see it run multiple red lights and travel for considerable periods of time in the occasional center left-turn-only lane, chased by numerous police cars forced to engage in the same hazardous maneuvers just to keep up.... What we see on the video ... closely resembles a Hollywood-style car chase of the most frightening sort, placing police officers and innocent bystanders alike at great risk of serious injury.

One of the police officers pursuing the suspect "decided to attempt to terminate the episode by employing a Precision Intervention Technique ('PIT') maneuver, which causes the fleeing vehicle to spin to a stop." The officer then proceeded to apply "his push bumper to the rear of respondent's vehicle," which resulted in the suspect "losing control of his vehicle, which left the roadway, ran down an embankment, overturned, and crashed." The suspect suffered a serious injury and was rendered quadriplegic. The injured suspect sued the police for violation of his Fourth Amendment rights, arguing that the use of force was unlawful pursuant to *Garner.* Was the police officer's use of force constitutional under *Garner*? Explain.

6. According to the plaintiff in *Harris,* deadly force is lawful pursuant to *Garner* only if:

> (1) The suspect ... posed an immediate threat of serious physical harm to the officer or others;
>
> (2) deadly force [was] necessary to prevent escape; and
>
> (3) [if] feasible, the officer [gave] the suspect some warning.

Do you agree with the plaintiff's reading of *Garner*? Why or why not? A majority of the Supreme Court disagreed with the plaintiff's interpretation of *Garner's* core holding. According to the Court:

> Respondent's argument falters at its first step; *Garner* did not establish a magical on/off switch that triggers rigid preconditions whenever an officer's actions constitute "deadly force." *Garner* was simply an application of the Fourth Amendment's "reasonableness" test to the use of a particular type of force in a particular situation. *Garner* held that it was unreasonable to kill a "young, slight, and unarmed" burglary suspect by shooting him "in the back of the head" while he was running away on foot and when the officer "could not reasonably have believed that [the suspect] ... posed any threat," and "never attempted to justify his actions on any basis other than the need to prevent an escape". Whatever *Garner* said about the factors that *might have* justified shooting the suspect in that case, such "preconditions" have scant applicability to this case, which has vastly different facts. "*Garner* had nothing to do with one car striking another or even with car chases in general.... A police car's bumping a fleeing car is, in fact, not much like a policeman's shooting a gun so as to hit a person." Nor is the threat posed by the flight on foot of an unarmed suspect even remotely comparable to the extreme danger to human life posed by respondent in this case. Although respondent's attempt to craft an easy-to-apply legal test in the Fourth Amendment context is admirable, in the end we must still slosh our way through the factbound morass of "reasonableness." Whether or not Scott's actions constituted application of "deadly force," all that matters is whether Scott's actions were reasonable.

Do you agree with the Supreme Court's reading of *Garner*? Is it true that *Garner* did not trigger special and relatively strict rules governing the use of force pursuant to law enforcement authority whenever deadly force is used to effect an arrest? Explain.

7. After explaining that *Garner* did not establish a rigid test for determining whether the use of force to detain a fleeing suspect is lawful under the Fourth Amendment, the Court proceeded to assess whether the use of force in *Harris* was reasonable under the totality of the circumstances of that particular case. The Court concluded that:

> A police officer's attempt to terminate a dangerous high-speed car chase that threatens the lives of innocent bystanders does not violate the Fourth Amendment, even when it places the fleeing motorist at risk of serious injury or death. The car chase that respondent initiated in this case posed a substantial and im-

> mediate risk of serious physical injury to others; no reasonable jury could conclude otherwise. Scott's attempt to terminate the chase by forcing respondent off the road was reasonable.

Do you agree that the use of force in *Harris* was reasonable and, therefore, constitutional (it might be helpful to watch the video)? Could the Court have reached the same conclusion by applying the standards set forth in *Garner*?

8. It is interesting to note that the majority opinion in *Harris* did not once mention the terms "probable cause." Instead, it focused solely on whether the force used in the case was "reasonable." As was pointed out in Note 2, this is actually consistent with the wording of the Fourth Amendment, given that probable cause is textually linked to the requirements governing the issuing of warrants rather than to the general requirements governing warrantless seizures (or searches). With regard to the more general inquiry about the lawfulness of warrantless searches or seizures, the Fourth Amendment merely requires that the search or seizure be reasonable. As a result, the Supreme Court has concluded that certain warrantless seizures (and searches) are lawful even if they are based on less than probable cause. See, e.g., *Terry v. Ohio*, 392 U.S. 1 (1968). This way of approaching the Fourth Amendment in general and the constitutionality of force used pursuant to law enforcement authority in particular is more compatible with the "reasonableness-centered" approach adopted by the dissenters in *Garner* than with the more rigid "probable cause" centered approach adopted by the majority.

## § 16.02 Law Enforcement Authority: Model Penal Code

### Model Penal Code § 3.07. Use of Force in Law Enforcement

(1) Use of Force Justifiable to Effect an Arrest. Subject to the provisions of this Section and of Section 3.09, the use of force upon or toward the person of another is justifiable when the actor is making or assisting in making an arrest and the actor believes that such force is immediately necessary to effect a lawful arrest ...

(a) The use of force is not justifiable under this Section unless:

(i) the actor makes known the purpose of the arrest or believes that it is otherwise known by or cannot reasonably be made known to the person to be arrested; and

(ii) when the arrest is made under a warrant, the warrant is valid or believed by the actor to be valid.

(b) The use of deadly force is not justifiable under this Section unless:

(i) the arrest is for a felony; and

(ii) the person effecting the arrest is authorized to act as a peace officer or is assisting a person whom he believes to be authorized to act as a peace officer; and

(iii) the actor believes that the force employed creates no substantial risk of injury to innocent persons; and

(iv) the actor believes that:

(A) the crime for which the arrest is made involved conduct including the use or threatened use of deadly force; or

(B) there is a substantial risk that the person to be arrested will cause death or serious bodily injury if his apprehension is delayed.

(5) Use of Force to Prevent Suicide or the Commission of a Crime.

(a) The use of force upon or toward the person of another is justifiable when the actor believes that such force is immediately necessary to prevent such other person from committing suicide, inflicting serious bodily injury upon himself, committing or consummating the commission of a crime involving or threatening bodily injury, damage to or loss of property or a breach of the peace, except that:

(i) any limitations imposed by the other provisions of this Article on the justifiable use of force in self-protection, for the protection of others, the protection of property, the effectuation of an arrest or the prevention of an escape from custody shall apply notwithstanding the criminality of the conduct against which such force is used; and

(ii) the use of deadly force is not in any event justifiable under this Subsection unless:

(A) the actor believes that there is a substantial risk that the person whom he seeks to prevent from committing a crime will cause death or serious bodily injury to another unless the commission or the consummation of the crime is prevented and that the use of such force presents no substantial risk of injury to innocent persons; or

(B) the actor believes that the use of such force is necessary to suppress a riot or mutiny after the rioters or mutineers have been ordered to disperse and warned, in any particular manner that the law may require, that such force will be used if they do not obey.

(b) The justification afforded by this Subsection extends to the use of confinement as preventive force only if the actor takes all reasonable measures to terminate the confinement as soon as he knows that he safely can, unless the person confined has been arrested on a charge of crime.

## *Notes and Questions*

1. The Model Penal Code provision on use of force pursuant to law enforcement authority is quite similar to the Tennessee statute after it was amended following the Supreme Court's decision in *Garner*. Note that according to § 3.07(1)(b)(iv)(a), deadly force may be used if "the crime for which the arrest is made involved conduct including the use or threatened use of deadly force." Suppose that a police officer uses deadly force to detain an unarmed fleeing felon suspected of having just committed a homicide in circumstances in which using such force was the only way to prevent the suspect's escape. Is the use of such force justified pursuant to the Model Penal Code? Would the use of such force conform to Fourth Amendment requirements according to *Garner*?

2. Regardless of what the Supreme Court held in *Garner,* do you believe that the rule prescribed in the Model Penal Code that authorizes the use of deadly force when it is necessary to effect an arrest of a person who is suspected of committing a crime that includes the actual or threatened use of deadly force is reasonable? That is, do you believe that police officers that use deadly force in the circumstances described in § 3.07(1)(b)(iv)(a) behave reasonably? Explain. Do you believe that the constitutional

validity of a provision like this one is more likely to be upheld under *Harris* than under *Garner*? Why?

## § 16.03 Law Enforcement Authority: Comparative Perspectives

### Spanish Supreme Court

Judgment of November 4, 1994

[Force used to prevent crime is lawful if:] (1) the person who uses force is a governmental agent who is authorized to use force or violence in order to discharge her duties, and (2) the use of force is the product of the governmental agent's attempt to fulfill the duties imposed on her by law. [Furthermore, the force is lawful solely if:] the officer needs to use violent methods in order to discharge her duties (i.e., requirement that use of violence be necessary in the abstract), (2) the officer uses the least dangerous form of violence available to her and inflicts the least amount of harm that discharging her duty requires under the circumstances (i.e., requirement that the use of violence be necessary in the concrete case), and (3) the force used by the officer is proportional to the threat represented by the offense that originally triggered the officer's involvement.

### Case Montero Aranguren v. Venezuela

Judgment of July 5, 2006
Inter-American Court of Human Rights

The use of force by state security forces is exceptional and should only be used when doing so is proportional to the threatened harm. Therefore, this Court has decided that the use of such force is justified only when the governmental agents have exhausted other less harmful methods of social control. The use of deadly force by state authorities is even more exceptional. Therefore, state use of firearms against citizens should, as a general rule, be prohibited. The exceptional use of such methods should be expressly regulated by law. Furthermore, such statutes should be strictly construed against the use of such force, so that these methods are only employed when they are absolutely necessary and proportional to the threat or force that the conduct attempts to thwart. Any killing that is the product of excessive force is automatically arbitrary [and, hence, unlawful].

According to the basic principles that regulate the government's use of deadly force and firearms against the citizenry, firearms can only be used: (1) in self-defense or defense of others, (2) in cases in which such force is necessary to neutralize a threat of imminent death or serious bodily injury, (3) when the force is necessary to prevent the commission of a particularly serious offense that poses a significant threat to the life of the officer or third parties, or (4) when the use of force is necessary to detain a person that poses the kind of danger described in (3) and who resists arrest. In the latter case, the use of such force is justified only when less extreme means would be ineffective to neutralize the threat. In sum, governmental agents may only use deadly force [and weapons] when doing so is unavoidable in order to protect life.

### *Notes and Questions*

1. Compare and contrast the approach adopted by the Spanish Supreme Court in the excerpted case to assess whether the use of force pursuant to law enforcement authority is justified with the framework adopted by the Supreme Court of the United States. Which approach more strictly circumscribes the instances in which police officers may justifiably use force? Explain.

2. How would *Garner* and *Scott* be decided under the framework provided by the Spanish Supreme Court in the excerpted case? Why? Do you find the Spanish approach preferable to the United States Supreme Court's approach? Why or why not?

3. Compare the approach to justifying force pursuant to law enforcement authority adopted by the Inter-American Court of Human Rights in the excerpted case with the framework adopted by the Supreme Court of the United States. Which approach more strictly circumscribes the instances in which police officers may justifiably use force? Explain.

4. How would *Garner* and *Scott* be decided under the framework provided by the Inter-American Court of Human Rights in the excerpted case? Why? Do you find the approach preferable to the United States Supreme Court's approach? Why or why not?

5. Is the approach adopted in the Model Penal Code to regulate force used by law enforcement authorities more, equally, or less strict than the approach adopted in Spain and by the Inter-American Court of Human Rights? Explain. Is the Code's approach preferable to either of the frameworks highlighted in the current section? Why or why not?

## § 16.04 Law Enforcement Authority: Scholarly Debates

### Rachel A. Harmon, *When Is Police Violence Justified?*

102 Nw. U. L. Rev. 1119 (2008)

... I. Inadequacy and Indeterminacy in Police Use of Force Law

Police violence never arises in a vacuum. During an arrest, an officer might give verbal commands to a suspect to stop, to keep his hands visible, to turn around and place his hands against the wall, to submit to a pat-down, to put his hands behind his back for handcuffing, to come along to the car, to get in, to get booked at the station. Most suspects are compliant and require no more than a guiding arm, but those who refuse or resist, and occasionally those who do not, may provoke a forcible response. Subjects of police uses of force often respond with allegations of law enforcement brutality. Sometimes these allegations are baseless, a product of misunderstanding what might justify lawful force or of false accusation. Other times they represent a just demand for recognition and redress for damaged bodies and spirits.

Courts typically confront allegations of excessive force during arrest in federal civil suits under 42 U.S.C. § 1983, which makes individuals liable for depriving others of their constitutional rights while acting under color of law. Using this statute, subjects of police uses of force claim that the force violated their constitutional right under the Fourth Amendment "to be secure in their persons ... against unreasonable ... seizures." Federal prosecutors also charge federal, state, and local law enforcement officers with violating the Fourth Amendment by using excessive force under the criminal equivalent to § 1983, 18 U.S.C. § 242, which makes it a crime to willfully deprive any person of his or her federal or constitutional rights while acting under color of law. Since 1961, when contemporary § 1983 litigation began, the law of police violence has been dominated by thousands of § 1983 suits alleging excessive force by police officers and hundreds of federal criminal convictions of police officers for the same.

Clearly, when the law confronts claims under these statutes that an officer used too much force during an arrest, the central question for federal liability is what constitutes constitutionally excessive force under the Fourth Amendment. Despite the legal and social importance of this question, however, the federal courts have said relatively little about how to determine what constitutes an inappropriate use of force. The Supreme Court has addressed the question directly three times, in Tennessee v. Garner in 1985, in Graham v. Connor in 1989, and recently, in April 2007, in Scott v. Harris. In this Part, I argue that the doctrine articulated in these cases is deeply problematic. It provides unprincipled, indeterminate, and sometimes simply misleading guidance to lower courts, police officers, jurors, and members of the public because it fails to articulate a systematic conceptual framework for assessing police uses of force. It does not delineate the legitimate interests that justify police uses of force, and it does not answer adequately the most basic questions about police uses of force: when a police officer may use force against a citizen, how much force he may use, and what kinds of force are permissible.

### A. Garner, Graham, and Scott

Edward Garner was an eighth grader in Memphis, Tennessee when police officer Elton Hymon saw him fleeing across the yard of a house that had been reported to have a prowler. Hymon called out to Garner. When he then saw Garner start over a fence, Hymon shot him in the back of the head, killing Garner to prevent his escape. Although Hymon believed Garner was unarmed, he also believed that Garner would easily outrun him if he made it over the fence. Cleamtree Garner, Edward's father, sued the officer, the Memphis Police Department, its director, the mayor, and the city of Memphis in federal district court for monetary damages under 42 U.S.C. § 1983.

Using an approach developed in the context of evaluating government searches and seizures conducted without probable cause, the Supreme Court in Garner stated that determining the reasonableness of police uses of force requires balancing an individual's interests against those of the government by looking at the "totality of the circumstances." The Court then considered the interests that arise in cases like Garner's. On the one hand, the average individual has an "unmatched" interest in his own life, and the individual and society have an interest in the "judicial determination of guilt and punishment." The Court took both of these interests to counsel against permitting deadly force. On the other hand, the government's interest in effectively enforcing its criminal laws counsels in its favor. On balance, the Court reasoned, where the suspect is "nonviolent," the government's interests in effecting the arrest are insufficient to justify killing a suspect.

Lower court cases following Garner have taken the decision to establish a bright-line rule for the use of force against fleeing suspects that deadly force is justified—which is to say constitutionally reasonable—only against dangerous felons in flight:

> Where the officer has probable cause to believe that the suspect poses a threat of serious physical harm, either to the officer or to others, it is not constitutionally unreasonable to prevent escape by using deadly force. Thus, if the suspect threatens the officer with a weapon or there is probable cause to believe that he has com-

> mitted a crime involving the infliction or threatened infliction of serious physical harm, deadly force may be used if necessary to prevent escape, and if, where feasible, some warning has been given.

Only four years later, in Graham v. Connor, the Court considered police uses of force more broadly. Whereas Garner addressed police uses of force against fleeing felons, Graham described a general standard for evaluating police uses of force, and treated Garner as a particular application. Considering its importance, Graham's analysis of what "reasonable" force means in the context of police violence was quite short. Graham appeared to instruct courts to balance the intrusion on the individual's interests with the government's competing interests, and specified that courts must do so under "the facts and circumstances of each particular case, including [1] the severity of the crime at issue, [2] whether the suspect poses an immediate threat to the safety of the officers or others, and [3] whether he is actively resisting arrest ... or [4] [whether he is] attempting to evade arrest by flight." The Court's only additional counsel was that reasonableness is an objective inquiry and should be considered from the officer's perspective at the time, taking into consideration the often "tense, uncertain, and rapidly evolving" nature of the circumstances in which police use force.

Although the test articulated in Graham appears to come directly from Garner, the Court in Garner weighed the government's interests against those of the suspect as a means to develop a rule to guide and govern police practices, just as the Court had done in prior seizure cases. In Graham, the Court provided no rule, and instead recommended the weighing technique to lower courts—and presumably to officers—as a primary method for evaluating individual uses of force. Graham's use of the balancing test, list of relevant circumstances or factors, and description of the objective perspective from which uses of force should be evaluated have dominated federal cases involving the reasonableness of police uses of force since 1989. And yet, as guidance regarding what constitutes reasonableness, Graham's instruction is woefully inadequate: While Graham mentions at least one government interest that may weigh in favor of using force, the right to make an arrest, it does not further delimit the scope of relevant government interests that may justify force. Nor has the Court done so since. Thus, the lower courts are without guidance about what purposes police uses of force may serve, which is to say which government interests may be placed on the scale. Instead, Graham permits courts to consider any circumstance in determining whether force is reasonable without providing a standard for measuring relevance, it gives little instruction on how to weigh relevant factors, and it apparently requires courts to consider the severity of the underlying crime in all cases, a circumstance that is sometimes irrelevant and misleading in determining whether force is reasonable. Thus, Graham has largely left judges and juries to their intuitions, and what direction it does give sometimes steers them off course.

Consider, for example, the last three factors cited by Graham. Whether the suspect poses a threat, actively resists, or flees are all questions of central importance in evaluating the reasonableness of the use of force against him. But these are questions with binary answers: either the suspect poses a threat or not; flees or not; resists or not. Moreover, these binaries are often incompatible: a fleeing suspect does not resist; a fighting suspect does not flee. By stating these factors in such terms, Graham provides a weak tool for evaluating the use of force, particularly in the common complex encounters that result in nondeadly uses of force by officers.

The use of force, and especially the use of nondeadly force, is often not a singular event but a series of choices made by an officer, sometimes in quick succession, over the course of an interaction. Officers have their bodies and a few basic weapons that together provide a spectrum of options, ranging from verbal persuasion or a guiding hand to a baton blow to the head or a shooting. Reasonable force is properly measured on a sliding scale, where more force is justified to counter an increased threat, taking into account the conditions of the interaction. For example, a come-along hold or wristlock might induce compliance in a mildly resistant suspect. If circumstances allow, police officers should employ lesser uses of force rather than escalate to throwing, kicking, hitting, or stunning a suspect. In simply listing circumstances under which force may be justified, the Graham factors fail to specify how to evaluate whether an officer's actions were justified in a particular situation, including whether they were reasonable given the spectrum of possible responses. They do not tell us how much force is justified or what kind of force is reasonable.

The Graham factors also fail to answer the question of when the officer's force is appropriate. Timing is crucial to any meaningful account of what is reasonable force. If a threat to the officer or a state interest has not yet manifested itself, no force is justified. If force occurs after the threat terminates, it is excessive regardless of what took place before it. Although two of the four Graham factors imply that timing may be relevant—whether an "immediate threat to the safety of the officers" existed and whether someone was "actively resisting" at the time of a use of force—Graham's vague "totality of the circumstances" approach falls critically short in addressing this crucial matter because it suggests that timing is one factor to be considered among many, when it is often simply dispositive. As a consequence, Graham may misfire in cases in which force is mistimed.

Since Graham, juries have assessed police violence hundreds, if not thousands, of times. And yet the lower courts have failed to develop significantly the law of reasonable seizures. There has been no substantial advance over the Supreme Court's formulation, no further attempt at a test or a structure, almost nothing to help officers, victims, juries, or the public understand the nature of legitimate police force. This is not to say that courts have not made law. They have made lots of it. Nevertheless, in a country that has since seen Rodney King, Abner Louima, Amadou Diallo, and many other victims of police uses of force, the federal courts have added little analysis to the Supreme Court's brief and inadequate statement in Graham about what factors are relevant in determining the reasonableness of a seizure and why. Instead, the lower federal courts have recited Graham as if it were a mantra and then gone on to try to make sense of the facts of individual cases using intuitions about what is reasonable for officers to do. Nor has the academy filled the lacuna. Although some academics have noted that the Graham standard lacks content, none have offered a meaningful alternative to fill the gap.

After almost twenty years of silence on the subject, the Supreme Court again confronted directly the constitutionality of the use of force by a police officer in Scott v. Harris. In this case, a deputy sheriff from the Coweta County Sheriff's Office was monitoring traffic on a highway in Georgia when Victor Harris passed him traveling seventy-three miles-per-hour in a fifty-five mile-per-hour zone. When Harris did not respond to the police car's lights, the deputy pursued him, and a high speed chase ensued. After hearing a radio call about the pursuit, a second deputy, Chuck Scott, joined the chase without knowing the nature of the underlying offense. Eventually, in order to stop Harris, Scott rammed Harris's car with his police cruiser. Harris lost control, left the roadway, ran his vehicle down an embankment, and crashed. Harris suffered serious injuries and is now a quadriplegic.

Using § 1983 and state law, Harris sued Scott, other members of the sheriff's department, and the county. The defendants all sought summary judgment. Using the Supreme Court's analysis in Graham, the district court granted some of those motions, but denied summary judgment on the Fourth Amendment claim against Scott, in which Harris alleged that

Scott unreasonably seized him when Scott rammed Harris's car. The court of appeals affirmed. In an opinion joined by eight Justices, the Supreme Court reversed, concluding that Scott's actions did not violate the Fourth Amendment. Using a video of the pursuit, the Court notably rejected the version of the facts adopted by the lower courts and substituted its own assessment of Harris's conduct leading up to the collision. In doing so, the Court discarded a central premise of the lower court opinions—that, in the light most favorable to the plaintiff, Harris posed little threat to pedestrians and other motorists—and found instead that Harris "plac[ed] police officers and innocent bystanders alike at great risk of serious injury." This factual premise became the basis for the Court's conclusion that Scott's seizure of Harris by ramming Harris's car was not unreasonable.

The Court reasoned that the government's interest in protecting passing pedestrians, civilian motorists, and officers involved in the chase outweighed the risk of injury that Scott posed to Harris by ramming his car. Although Scott eliminated the "lesser probability of injuring or killing numerous bystanders" by creating "the perhaps larger probability of injuring or killing a single person," the Court found this outcome justified by the number of lives Harris put at risk and the fact that, while Harris was largely responsible for the risks he himself faced, the endangered civilians and officers "were entirely innocent."

Scott's Fourth Amendment reasonableness analysis represents a significant departure from both Garner and Graham. Prior to Scott, most lower courts analyzed police uses of vehicles to exert force during high speed chases under Garner's rule. Other courts used Graham because they did not take such collisions to constitute deadly force. In Scott itself, the district court found that under the facts alleged by Harris, Scott's use of force could be considered unreasonable under Graham. The Eleventh Circuit reached the same result using Garner. Scott argued in his brief to the Supreme Court that Graham rather than Garner governed Scott's actions because it was not clear from Scott's perspective that he was using deadly force, and that even if the Garner rule did apply, he could satisfy it. Harris contended that Garner prohibited Scott's use of force, but that even under Graham, ramming Harris's car was constitutionally unreasonable. All considered Graham and Garner to be the relevant governing precedents.

By contrast, the majority opinion expressly rejected Harris's attempt to frame the question whether Scott's use of force was excessive in terms of the Garner test for determining whether deadly force is permitted against a fleeing suspect. The Court stated that Garner could not be applied to the "vastly different facts" of Scott's use of force, noting in particular two distinctions between Garner and Scott. First, Garner involved shooting a gun instead of striking one car with another; and second, the threat posed by the unarmed fleeing suspect in Garner was remote compared to the "extreme danger" posed by Harris's flight. But Scott went beyond holding Garner inapplicable to Scott's facts. Instead, the Court rejected the idea that Garner provided a rule at all. It noted that Garner did not set "rigid preconditions" for the use of deadly force, and instead was simply a fact-based analysis of reasonableness in the circumstances of that case. Moreover, it raised doubt about whether the distinction between deadly and nondeadly force on which Garner is premised has constitutional relevance. Rather, the Court emphasized that in this case—and in future ones—"all that matters is whether [the officer's] actions were reasonable," a determination for which there is no test beyond a case-specific "slosh" through "the factbound morass of 'reasonableness.'"

In a paragraph, then, the Supreme Court waved away what every federal court since Garner—including the Supreme Court itself—had taken to be clear criteria for determining the reasonableness of the use of deadly force against fleeing suspects during an arrest. The Graham factors got even less respect. Although the Scott Court engaged in the weighing advocated by Graham, Scott simply does not acknowledge the sentence from Graham that has driven the analysis in thousands of cases since 1989: that the "proper application" of the reasonableness test involves consideration of "the severity of the crime at issue, whether the suspect poses an immediate threat to the safety of the officers or others, and whether he is actively resisting arrest or attempting to evade arrest by flight." Nor does it even cite Graham in its analysis of the reasonableness of Scott's actions. Instead it ends where Graham starts, by stating that the Fourth Amendment analysis requires balancing "the nature or quality of the intrusion on the individual's Fourth Amendment interests against the importance of the governmental interests alleged to justify the intrusion." Thus, the Court not only emasculated Garner, but in the same paragraph—without comment or analysis—implicitly dismissed the factors articulated in Graham as central to analyzing reasonableness. In doing so, the Court reduced the Fourth Amendment regulation of reasonable force to its vaguest form: an ad hoc balancing of state and individual interests unconstrained by any specific criteria.

The Court easily could have reached the same outcome in Scott without undermining Garner and Graham. Given its rejection of the lower courts' factual basis, it could have concluded simply that Scott satisfied Garner's clear charge that "[w]here the officer has probable cause to believe that the suspect poses a threat of serious physical harm, either to the officer or to others, it is not constitutionally unreasonable to prevent escape by using deadly force." This would have been inconsistent with the view of the Eleventh Circuit in Scott and some other federal courts that Garner specified other preconditions for deadly force, including that the force be necessary to prevent escape and that a warning be given if possible. But it would have retained Garner's primary command—untouched by Graham—that deadly force demands dangerousness.

Nor is Scott's outcome necessarily inconsistent with Graham. At the time of Scott's use of force, Harris was—in the view of the Supreme Court if not the lower courts—criminally evading the officers by driving extremely recklessly, even feloniously so, posing a threat to civilians and officers. Given this interpretation of Harris's conduct, the Court could have read Graham to mean that, whether or not Scott's use of force would have been justified when the chase began, from the "perspective of a reasonable officer" in Scott's position at the time he used force, "the severity of the crime at issue" was the seriousness of Harris's criminal conduct during flight, rather than the original traffic violation. Moreover, it could have found that it was the threat this conduct posed that demonstrated "an immediate threat to the safety of the officers or others" that might have justified substantial force....

Why did the Court instead back away from Graham and Garner? Scott presented the Court with some of the inherent weaknesses of these two cases. Both Graham and Garner appear to demand consideration of the underlying crime of which Harris was initially suspected in evaluating Scott's use of force, and both lower courts emphasized that the force was unreasonable in large part because Harris was suspected only of speeding. The Scott Court may have believed that the initial traffic offense was irrelevant to the use of force but have been unable to articulate a principle for why this consideration was immaterial in this case but not in others. In addition, the relationship between Garner's test and Graham's factors in a case like Scott was at best unclear at the time of Scott, as is evidenced by the differing focuses of the lower court opinions and briefs. Rather than fixing the problems by refining its framework for analyzing uses of force, however, the Court retreated from guiding lower courts, relying instead on a balancing test that depends on lower court judges' intuitions about what matters to reasonableness. Thus, the Court did not resolve the question of when the seriousness of the underlying crime matters. Moreover, even the little guidance Scott provides to lower courts about what to consider in implementing the weighing test is unhelpful. The Court announced, for example, that "culpability is relevant to the reasonableness of the seizure," but said little about how, when, or why. In sum, in Scott, the Court rid itself of the clear rule of Garner, establishing instead a much narrower rule for most high speed chase cases; deemphasized, if not eliminated, any significant instruction to lower courts facing future cases about what to consider in evaluating police violence; and remained near silent about how to balance the interests of officers, suspects, and others. After Scott, courts must "slosh" their way through the "factbound morass" without galoshes or a compass, which is to say, with almost no direction at all about what constitutes reasonable force.

### B. The Consequences of an Impoverished Use of Force Doctrine

The consequences of the Supreme Court's problematic use of force doctrine are profound and significant. By eliminating what guidance Garner and Graham provided and by failing to articulate principles to shape lower court determinations, Scott increases the likelihood that lower courts will decide use of force cases inconsistently. For example, some courts may continue to apply Garner to situations involving nondangerous suspects fleeing on foot; others may take Scott to eliminate even this application of Garner. Scott also makes it more likely that lower courts will use inappropriate criteria in reaching results: some lower courts may take the Supreme Court's declaration that a suspect's culpability is relevant to the relative strength of the government's interest to mean that wrongdoing by the suspect may be used to justify force against the suspect during the arrest, even if that force was more than was necessary under the circumstances immediately facing the officer.

More importantly, however, Scott almost surely makes the outcome of lower court decisions about the reasonableness of police uses of force more difficult to predict. Scott does not confine its recommended analysis to high speed chases. Instead, it appears to encourage lower courts to dispense with mandatory consideration of Graham's factors and to engage in ad hoc balancing in all cases of alleged unreasonable force, whether deadly or not. As a result, after Scott, it is difficult to imagine what specific circumstances federal courts will emphasize as relevant when they weigh individual and societal interests, and what balance they will strike. Scott, even more than Graham and Garner, makes almost all future cases indeterminate....

A better constitutional framework for evaluating uses of force would put the police on notice of whether a particular use of force is constitutional before the federal courts have addressed the constitutionality of that precise use of force. Such a standard would not only compensate for and indirectly deter unconstitutional uses of force by holding officers accountable ex post, it also could reduce such uses of force ex ante by providing legal guidelines for training officers to use force constitutionally. Currently, nearly all officers receive training about the legal standards governing the use of force. But while officers receive elaborate training about how to use force, and detailed legal instruction about when they may search or seize persons, cars, and things, the legal training they receive about when to use force mirrors current law: it often constitutes little more than an exhortation to act reasonably. Even if officers are told the outcomes of specific cases, the law provides them little basis for extrapolating from those cases guidance for the new circumstances they continually face. If courts could articulate the reasoning that informs judicial intuition about excessive force, officers might be influenced by that reasoning in regulating their own actions or—often just as importantly—in discouraging the excessive use of force by a peer.

The imprecise current legal framework shapes the decisions not only of judges and officers but also of jurors. Jurors are routinely asked to make legal decisions about excessive force. And juries often get the closest cases: on the civil side, those not suitable for qualified immunity and not clear enough to motivate settlement; and in the criminal context, those in which evidence of guilt is not strong enough to induce a plea. Moreover, they are asked to determine whether the defendant's actions were unreasonable under the Constitution without any access to precedent. Instead, courts provide jury instructions distilling principles from the existing case law, jury instructions that sometimes provide exceptionally little help in shaping a determination about excessiveness. Because many of those instructions have in recent years referred to the Graham factors, factors not even recognized in Scott, or to the Garner rule, weakened in Scott, after Scott, those instructions inevitably will become even vaguer.

The weakness of Supreme Court doctrine will affect the general public as well. The public cares deeply about police violence, and there has long been an active public conversation about the use of force by police officers, a conversation that often becomes heated—even violent—in the wake of a controversial use of force. The law often provides grist for this mill in the form of a prosecutor who refuses to bring criminal charges or a court that grants summary judgment to the defendant, or more rarely in the form of a jury verdict. Because there is no clear legal framework that regulates the use of force, these legal decisions have little communicative value. The government cannot cite any well-reasoned, concrete, and accessible standard to justify to the public its prosecutorial and political decisions in salient cases of police violence. Nothing in Graham, Garner, or Scott explains how uses of force, and the politicians, police officials, and police officers who are politically accountable for them, should be judged. One might argue that the public rarely understands the intricacies of the law, and that the outcome of litigation rarely provides a useful basis for holding political actors accountable. But, even for the lawyers who transform public concern about violent policing into litigation or legislative efforts, the Supreme Court has provided a barren legal scheme, filled with judicial intuitions about what matters in police uses of force, but devoid of a satisfactory structure with which others can engage.

## *Notes and Questions*

1. Professor Harmon argues that *Scott* is in tension with *Garner*. Can you explain why she argues that these two cases represent quite different approaches to assessing the constitutionality of force used pursuant to law enforcement authority? Do you agree with her that there is significant tension between these two cases or do you believe that they can be reconciled rather easily?

2. An aspect of *Scott*—and to a lesser extent *Garner* and *Graham*—that Professor Harmon finds particularly troubling is the indeterminacy of the standards provided in these cases to guide juries and judges in making determinations regarding whether police officers have used excessive force in violation of the Fourth Amendment. Do you agree that the standards provided in these cases are too indeterminate? Do you believe that the standards provided in the Model Penal Code to govern the use of force pursuant to law enforcement authority are more determinate and, therefore, more helpful to judges and juries than the standards put forth by the Supreme Court in these cases? Explain.

3. Given that Professor Harmon believes that the standards developed by the Supreme Court to govern the use of force by governmental authorities are too indeterminate, she suggests the following framework as an alternative mode of analysis:

> [I believe that] the concepts that structure justification defenses can and should be imported, subject to appropriate modifications, into the Fourth Amendment

> doctrine regulating police violence. Specifically, the law of justification defenses permits individuals to use force to serve particular well-defined interests, such as to protect themselves or others, under specific, carefully delineated conditions, i.e., when that force is necessary to protect against an imminent threat to one of those interests and is proportional to that threat. Analogously, I contend that the Fourth Amendment permits police uses of force only to serve directly the state's distinct interests in (1) facilitating its institutions of criminal law, most commonly by enabling a lawful arrest; (2) protecting public order; and (3) protecting the officer from physical harm. Moreover, even if one of these interests is at stake, a use of force should be considered unreasonable—and therefore unconstitutional under the Fourth Amendment—unless it is a response to an imminent threat to one of these interests, the force reasonably appears necessary in both degree and kind to protect the interest, and the harm the force threatens is not substantially disproportionate to the interest it protects. In this way, the substructure of justification defenses can be used to analyze whether a police use of force is constitutional.

Is Professor Harmon's framework for assessing the constitutionality of force used by police officers more determinate than the standards provided by the Supreme Court in *Garner* and its progeny? Why or why not? Regardless of your answer to the previous question, do you believe that the proposed framework is an improvement over the one proposed by the Supreme Court? Is it more appealing than the Model Penal Code approach to justifying force pursuant to law enforcement authority? Explain.

4. How would *Garner, Scott* and *Graham* be decided if the framework proposed by Professor Harmon is applied? Why? Is it easier to decide whether force was justified in these cases if you apply Professor Harmon's framework, or is the framework equally or more difficult to apply than the one adopted by the Supreme Court in the aforementioned cases? Explain.

5. Compare Professor Harmon's framework with the approaches adopted by the Spanish Supreme Court and the Inter-American Court of Human Rights. Is Professor Harmon's framework more determinate than either of these other two approaches? Regardless of your answer to the previous question, do you believe that Harmon's proposed framework is superior to either or both of these approaches? Explain.

## Part Five

# The Elements of Punishable Crimes III — Absence of Excuse

# Chapter 17

# Duress

## § 17.01 Duress: Human v. Natural Threats

### United States v. Hayes

United States Court of Appeals for the Armed Forces, 2012
70 M.J. 454

Chief Judge BAKER delivered the opinion of the Court.

A military judge sitting as a general court-martial at the U.S. Naval Academy, Annapolis, Maryland convicted Appellee, pursuant to his pleas, of eleven specifications of selling military property without authority and ten specifications of larceny of military property, in violation of Articles 108 and 121, Uniform Code of Military Justice (UCMJ). Appellee was sentenced to confinement for thirty-six months, forfeiture of all pay and allowances, dismissal, and a $28,000 fine. The convening authority approved the adjudged sentence but suspended all confinement in excess of twelve months.

On review, the United States Navy-Marine Corps Court of Criminal Appeals (NMCCA) set aside the findings of guilty and the sentence and remanded for rehearing. [The government now challenges this determination] ...

I. BACKGROUND

A. Facts

Appellee was a twenty-six-year-old midshipman first class at the U.S. Naval Academy when he stole laboratory equipment from the Naval Academy and sold it on eBay. The acts took place on ten separate occasions between October 2008 and February 2009. The equipment was located in an engineering lab in Rickover Hall onboard the U.S. Naval Academy. In his stipulation of fact and during the plea colloquy with the military judge, Appellee explained how he typically sold the equipment: he would list the equipment on eBay, wait until the highest bidder won the auction, steal the equipment from the lab, mail it to the bidder, and finally receive electronic payment from PayPal. Appellee stated that he earned about $13,000 from the sales.

During his plea colloquy, the military judge asked Appellee with respect to each charge "[w]ere there any circumstances which forced you to take this item?" or words to that effect. Likewise, the military judge asked Appellee "could you have avoided ... doing this?" or other words to the same effect. Appellee stated that no one forced him to steal the equipment and that he had no justification or excuse for doing so.

During an unsworn statement during presentencing, Appellee explained the background for what he had done, including the pressure he felt regarding his mother's financial and personal well-being. During his first year at the Academy, his mother, Mrs. Jackson, "would call and she would ask if there was any way I could help out" since she was "short on money." By his junior year, Appellee was receiving "daily" phone calls from Mrs. Jackson saying that "she didn't want to lose her house" and that "it was [Appellee's] responsibility to help her because [he was] her eldest son." Appellee talked to a chaplain and a counselor about his situation, and they told him he needed to focus on graduating and that his mother was "an adult, she needs to take care of herself." His mother's calls continued and "it got to a point where she would—she would call crying and—and then say that she didn't want to live any more and that she, you know, was thinking about taking her life." Appellee stated that he "didn't know how to handle that," that his father could not help because he had passed away, and that he was worried his younger brothers and sisters "were going to lose their mom."

During his unsworn statement, Appellee also described the first time he stole equipment from the lab:

> [I]t was purely curiosity, you know ... how much things were worth, and I was like, "Well, my mom needs money, there's all these extra things laying around." I know it wasn't right, but in my state of mind I just—I just couldn't differentiate the difference between doing the right thing for—for home or doing the right thing that's going to make the phone calls stop, or doing the right thing for being a Midshipman.

Appellee also described what he did with the money after he sold the equipment:

> I used the money, and I'd go home every weekend, and whether—whatever my mom needed I was doing, whether it was just taking her out to dinner or taking all my brothers and sisters out for ice cream, I mean just being there. I'm not—I didn't know how to deal with somebody who's threatening to end their life or threatening to, you know, not be there anymore. And that's—that's the pressure that I was feeling at that time, sir....

At presentencing Appellee submitted a signed letter from his mother stating that at that time she had made frequent phone calls to her son making him feel guilty for not helping out. She stated that, when Appellee was "not doing what I thought was his job, I made him feel guilty and increased the pressure with constant phone calls and telling him my thoughts about ending my life." She noted that when her son "feared for my safety he came home and helped me out financially."

The military judge did not reopen the providence inquiry following Appellee's unsworn statement and did not reject the guilty plea. The military judge also did not ask defense counsel whether he had discussed any potential defenses with his client.

### B. NMCCA Decision

On appeal to the NMCCA, Appellee argued that his presentencing statement raised matters inconsistent with his plea and thus the military judge had erroneously failed to reopen the providence inquiry to inquire into potential duress and mental responsibility defenses raised by Appellee's unsworn statement during sentencing. The NMCCA agreed with Appellee and held that his unsworn statement raised a possible defense of duress because it "sets forth matter clearly inconsistent with his admission of culpability." The court noted that Appellee had indicated that "he was under apprehension and fearful that his mother would commit suicide, and ... that he committed his acts in order to prevent that from happening, indicating some immediacy in his mind as to the prospective threat." The court also noted that, because the military judge had not inquired into the issue, the court lacked "adequate facts on the record to resolve the conflict [so that it could] only speculate and cannot be confident that the appellant was not under duress when he committed the acts to which he pled guilty." *Id.* The court did not directly discuss whether the threat of suicide could be included in the duress defense, but clearly its decision is based on the assumption that the threat of suicide could provide the predicate for a duress defense. The NMCCA remanded Appellee's case for rehearing. *Id.*

II. DISCUSSION

... C. Threat of Suicide as Duress

... The Government contends that, as a matter of law, an individual's suicide threat cannot give rise to a duress defense since it does not constitute an unlawful act against a third party. The Government derives its third party argument from the rule's requirement that the accused reasonably apprehend "that the accused or another innocent person would be immediately killed or would immediately suffer serious bodily injury." Here, the Government argues, the mother's conduct was not directed against "another innocent person." The Government finds the requirement for an "unlawful act" as the predicate for duress from dicta found in *United States v. Washington,* 57 M.J. 394 (C.A.A.F.2002). Specifically, the plurality opinion states: "R.C.M. 916(h) should be viewed in a manner consistent with the requirement in prevailing civilian law that the threat emanate from the unlawful act of another person." However, as the Government also acknowledges, this Court's case law can be read to support an opposite result as well.

This Court has not squarely addressed the issue of whether a threat of suicide could present a duress defense. Two of our cases that discuss threats emanating from non-third-parties, *United States v. Rankins,* and Washington, for example, addressed inapposite factual scenarios. The plurality's ruling in *Rankins,* for example, considered whether an accused, who missed movement because she was afraid that her husband would have a heart attack in her absence, could raise a duress defense. This Court did not address suicide or specify what was meant by a presumed requirement that the harm contemplated by R.C.M. 916(h) come from a third party. Because the threat in *Rankins* was caused by her husband's health and not human action, the plurality's statement in dicta that the "plain language" of R.C.M. 916(h) indicates that the duress defense "applies only to cases where the coercion is asserted by third persons" is not determinative in this case.

In *United States v. Jeffers,* the Court again indirectly addressed the issue of suicide, appearing to include the threat of suicide within the duress defense. Though the issue raised in that case did not directly address whether a suicide threat could form a valid basis for a duress defense, the Court did note that the "military judge properly instructed the members that duress was a defense to appellant's failure to obey his commander's order."

In Washington, the Court addressed the issue somewhat more directly when it affirmed an accused's conviction for disobedience of a lawful order for refusing an anthrax vaccine. The Court explained that the President's guidance on the duress defense in R.C.M. 916(h) must be read not in isolation but rather:

> [I]n conjunction with the guidance on disobedience of lawful orders and the essential purposes of military law. In that context, the military judge correctly ruled that the duress defense in R.C.M. 916(h) should be viewed in a manner consistent with the requirement in prevailing civilian law that the threat emanate from the unlawful act of another person.

The Court noted earlier in the opinion that the military judge had rejected the defense of duress as unavailable because "it requires an unlawful threat from a human being, and that the defense of necessity was unavailable because it requires a threat from a natural physical force—neither of which was present in this case."

In summary, review of this Court's case law indicates that, while dicta might support one position or another, this Court has not been faced with the direct question posed [in this case]. Another reason the law is unclear is that, with respect to suicide, R.C.M. 916 is susceptible to a number of possible interpretations. We now conclude, as the CCA did below, that R.C.M. 916 does not foreclose the possibility that a threat of suicide could provide the basis for a duress defense....

[T]he conclusion that the threat of suicide could provide the basis for a duress defense is supported by the Supreme Court's holding in Dixon. The defense allows an individual to avoid liability "'because coercive conditions or necessity negates a conclusion of guilt even though the necessary *mens rea* was present.'" An accused "ought to be excused when he is the victim of a threat that a person of reasonable moral strength could not fairly be expected to resist." To exclude suicide from the defense would, as Appellee puts it, shift the analysis from that of whether a person of reasonable moral strength could resist to a mere "head-counting exercise."

Second, the plain language of R.C.M. 916(h) does not preclude a duress defense based on the threat of suicide. A person who commits suicide may indeed "be ... killed"—a person who kills himself is killed by his or her own hand. And a person who threatens suicide is indeed "threatened," for the threatening is done by him or herself. It is not uncommon for the drafters of statutes to use the passive voice to focus on an event that occurred rather than on a particular subject....

Third, this conclusion is consistent with the scant federal case law that has addressed the issue. In *Toney*, the United States Court of Appeals for the Seventh Circuit noted in passing its approval of the trial judge's instruction that "fear of suicide of another is not a sufficient basis for coercion, unless the defendant took reasonable alternative steps to avoid the suicide." Although neither *Toney* nor *Stevison* raised a direct challenge to the issue of whether a threat of suicide is included in the defense of duress, they did offer approval for including the threat of suicide in the duress defense. This definition of duress/coercion requires three elements: "(1) an immediate threat of death or serious bodily injury, (2) a well-grounded fear that the threat will be carried out, and (3) no reasonable opportunity to avoid the threatened harm." In addition, four federal courts of appeals have defined duress in a manner that includes the threat of suicide.

For the foregoing reasons, we do not foreclose the possibility of a duress defense in the context of a suicide threat as a matter of law. We do not decide the question of what circumstances would give rise to such a defense since this question is not before the Court.

[Editor's Note: Although the Court ruled that the NMCCA did not err in concluding that a threat fo suicide could trigger the duress defense, the decision of the NMCCA was reversed on other grounds.]

STUCKY, Judge (concurring in the result):

... I am ... unwilling to join the majority's dictum that the threat of suicide may give rise to a duress or necessity defense.

Duress is a special defense, long recognized in our jurisprudence, which may excuse criminal conduct when the actor's participation in the offense was caused by a reasonable apprehension that he or another innocent party would immediately suffer death or serious bodily injury if he did not commit the offense. The parties argue over whether Appellee's mother was an innocent party. The term "innocent party," as used in the duress defense does not require a determination of whether the act threatened—in this case, suicide—was criminal but rather requires that the person who is threatened with death or severe bodily injury not be the person who is threatening the act. *See* Dressler, *supra* § 23.01[B] ("another person threatened to kill or grievously injure the actor or a third party"); 2 LaFave, *supra* § 9.7(a). Although a person threatening suicide may be innocent in some colloquial or moral sense of the word, that person is not innocent as that term has been interpreted in the duress defense situation. Therefore, as a matter of law, this case does not raise a duress defense.

## *Notes and Questions*

1. Self-defense and necessity are justification defenses. That is, society acquits those who act in self-defense and those who cause a harm to prevent even greater harm because such courses of conduct are, all things being considered, appropriate under the circumstances. Given that self-defense and necessity are justification defenses, they negate the wrongfulness of the conduct. Duress, on the other hand, is usually classified as an excuse defense. We acquit those who act under duress because we cannot fairly expect such actors to behave differently. Nevertheless, given that those who act under duress do not generally prevent a greater harm than the one that they inflict, such conduct is typically considered wrongful. Suppose that a person is told that his child will be shot and killed if he does not cause serious bodily injury to an innocent third party. Assuming that the actor inflicts serious bodily injury to an innocent person in order to prevent harm to his child, his conduct would be excused pursuant to the duress defense. Note, however, that such conduct remains—all things being considered—wrongful, for the actor does not have a right to harm an innocent third party.

2. As the Court pointed out in *Hayes,* the traditional view is that the excuse of duress is triggered when an actor faces a threat that originates in the acts of a human being. Although there is support in American scholarly literature for expanding the defense of duress to encompass "situational" or "circumstantial" duress that is the product of natural acts, American courts and codes continue to reject broadening the defense in this manner.

3. The rationale most commonly offered for limiting duress to cases of human threats is that it is still possible to prosecute the actor who issued the threat for the criminal conduct committed by the excused actor. In contrast, when the threats originate in natural acts (i.e., "situational duress"), excusing the actor who engages in the crime necessarily entails that no one would be prosecuted for the criminal conduct. This outcome is deemed unacceptable. The *Dudley and Stephens* case illustrates this matter quite nicely. Since the threat facing the crewmembers (starvation) originated in natural events (capsizing of the boat), American duress law would not excuse the killing of the cabin boy. The result would be justified on the grounds that excusing the crewmembers would leave the killing of the cabin boy unpunished and that is an unwelcome outcome. In contrast, if a person had told the crewmembers that they would be shot and killed unless they kill the cabin boy, they would have a valid duress defense in some American jurisdictions. Excusing such a killing is acceptable in these jurisdictions because someone will still be held accountable for the killing of the cabin boy—the person who issued the threats.

4. Are you persuaded that duress should not be expanded to encompass situational or circumstantial threats that do not originate in the acts of human beings? Explain. Is it

fair (or efficient) to punish someone for yielding to natural pressures that would prove insurmountable to an average person? Why or why not? Assuming that it is unfair to punish in such circumstances, do you believe that such actors should nevertheless be held criminally liable because excusing the conduct would leave the harm caused go unpunished? Explain.

5. The government contended in *Hayes* that duress is triggered when an actor succumbs to an unlawful threat. The government thus argued that the defendant was not entitled to a duress defense in this case, for the mother's threat to commit suicide does not amount to an "*unlawful* threat," given that committing suicide is not a crime. This is essentially the view of duress defended in the dissenting opinion. In contrast, a majority of the members of the Court of Appeals rejected the government's contention, arguing that the essential element of duress is that the actor succumbs to a threat that originates in a human act, regardless of whether the threat is "unlawful." Who has the better part of this argument? Explain. Regardless of how you answered this question, do you believe that a threat to commit suicide should trigger the duress defense? Why or why not?

6. The Court in *Hayes* pointed out that—even if duress could be triggered by a suicide threat—the defense will only succeed if the actor yields to "an immediate threat of death or serious bodily injury." Did the defendant in this case succumb to an "immediate" threat? Regardless of how this question is answered, should duress only be triggered by imminent threats or should it also be triggered by non-imminent threats that a person of reasonable firmness would succumb to? It is to this issue that we now turn.

## § 17.02 Duress: Imminent vs. Non-Imminent Threats

### Anguish v. State

Court of Appeals of Texas, Houston (1st Dist.), 1999
991 S.W.2d 883

TIM TAFT, Justice.

A jury found appellant, Gaylord William Anguish, guilty of robbery and theft of an automobile. The jury assessed appellant's punishment for the robbery at five years in prison, and for the theft at two years in prison and a $1,000 fine. We address whether threats made four days before appellant committed the offenses constituted imminent threats necessary to raise the affirmative defense of duress. We affirm.

#### Facts

On December 3, 1990, appellant stole a van from a child care center. He drove the van to a drive-through bank window where he threatened to blow up the bank. The teller placed all the money she had, approximately $15,000, in the drawer. Appellant took the money and drove away. The bank's security guard followed appellant to an apartment complex parking lot and then arrested him ...

#### B. Relevance of Threats Four Days Before Robbery

In his first, third, fourth, and fifth points of error, appellant argues that the trial court erred by excluding his testimony, and quashing a subpoena for witnesses, both of whom would have established his affirmative defense of duress. To place appellant's contentions in context, we will examine his claims of duress as a whole, the portion of his claims that the trial court permitted him to present to the jury, and the portion of his claims that the trial court excluded. We will then analyze the trial court's ruling that appellant's evidence of the threat was inadmissible as irrelevant because the alleged threat was not an imminent threat of harm. Finally, we will consider appellant's innovative waiver theory.

### 1. Appellant's Claims of Duress

Appellant claimed to have learned that a Federal Bureau of Investigation (FBI) agent was having an extra-marital affair, and that the FBI agent and his lover conspired to kill the lover's husband. After appellant attempted to confront the FBI agent with his knowledge of the matter, appellant's house was burglarized and he began receiving threatening telephone calls. He reported these incidents to the Harris County Sheriff's Department and the FBI, but neither agency took any action.

Four days before appellant committed the charged offenses, he was threatened by two men he found waiting for him in the back seat of his car. One man put a gun to appellant's head while the other showed appellant a photograph of his wife and daughter in bed. The men told appellant that they were watching him, threatened to kill his family, instructed him not to tell anyone, and then instructed him to rob a bank. Based upon law enforcement agencies' previous inaction, appellant believed that reporting the latest threat would be useless.

Appellant believed the men's motive for urging him to rob the bank was their desire to discredit him and discourage him from conducting future investigations of the FBI agent or the agent's lover. During the three years after the charged offenses, appellant suffered several additional burglaries, an attempted kidnapping, arson, and further telephone threats against him and his family.

### 2. Evidence Admitted

Appellant was permitted to introduce evidence that: (1) although his house was burglarized twice and he received threatening telephone calls, his reports of these matters were not taken seriously by law enforcement agencies; (2) four days before appellant committed the charged offenses, two men threatened to harm him and his family if he did not rob a bank; and (3) he robbed the bank because he was afraid that the men would carry out their threats and he did not think that law enforcement agencies would help him.

### 3. Evidence Excluded

In his first point of error, appellant argues that the trial court erred by excluding the content of the two men's threats, including that they: (1) told him they were watching him; (2) instructed him to rob a bank; (3) threatened to kill his family; and (4) instructed him not to tell anyone about their threats....

### 4. Imminence of Threats

The trial court ruled that the threat appellant claims compelled him to commit the robbery was not an imminent threat and was therefore inadmissible evidence, based upon its lack of relevance.

Duress is an affirmative defense to prosecution when an accused establishes that he "engaged in the proscribed conduct because he was compelled to do so by threat of *imminent* death or serious bodily injury to himself or another." TEX. PENAL CODE ANN. § 8.05(a). When a trial court determines that the threat the accused contends compelled his commission of the offense was not imminent, the trial court properly excludes evidence of the threat.

The Court of Criminal Appeals has not construed the term "imminent" in the context of a section 8.05 duress claim, but has interpreted the term in the context of aggravated robbery and aggravated rape. *Devine v. State,* 786 S.W.2d 268, 270–71 (Tex.Crim.App.1989) (threat to robbery victim five days before offense not imminent); *Blount v. State,* 542 S.W.2d 164, 166 (Tex.Crim.App.1976) (threat to kill rape victim if she told anyone was conditional, future threat, and not imminent). In these contexts, the Court of Criminal Appeals has determined that an imminent threat is a present threat of harm....

We join in this interpretation and conclude that, in applying it to the affirmative defense of duress, an imminent threat has two components of immediacy. First, the person making the threat must intend and be prepared to carry out the threat immediately. Second, carrying out the threat must be predicated upon the threatened person's failure to commit the charged offense immediately.

In the present case, the alleged threat was made four days before appellant committed the robbery. The specific threat was that appellant rob a bank or he and his family would be killed. The record does not reflect that the persons making this threat either intended or were prepared to carry it out immediately. Further, there was no evidence that the persons making the threat gave appellant a time by which he was to commit the robbery, much less that he was to commit the robbery immediately. Therefore, the threat that appellant claims compelled him to commit the robbery fails on both components of immediacy. Accordingly, we conclude the threat was not an imminent threat, as required by section 8.05.

Appellant argues that this Court should extend the definition of imminent to include the situation of an accused who, when threatened, believes that no law enforcement agency will protect him. We acknowledge that in most situations where the threat is imminent, no law enforcement agency is able to provide protection. However, a threat is not rendered imminent solely because law enforcement agencies are unable to provide protection. We therefore decline to adopt appellant's extension of the definition of immanency.

Having found that the alleged threat against appellant was not of *imminent* death of serious bodily injury unless appellant *immediately* committed the bank robbery, we conclude that appellant's testimony concerning the threat was irrelevant, and thus inadmissible. Therefore, the trial court's rulings excluding appellant's testimony and quashing appellant's subpoenas were proper....

We affirm the judgment of the trial court.

## United States v. Contento-Pachón

United States Court of Appeals, Ninth Circuit, 1984
723 F.2d 691

BOOCHEVER, Circuit Judge.

This case presents an appeal from a conviction for unlawful possession with intent to distribute a narcotic controlled substance in violation of [federal law]. At trial, the defendant attempted to offer evidence of duress and necessity defenses. The district court excluded this evidence on the ground that it was insufficient to support the defenses. We reverse because there was sufficient evidence of duress to present a triable issue of fact.

### I. Facts

The defendant-appellant, Juan Manuel Contento-Pachon, is a native of Bogota, Colombia and was employed there as a taxicab driver. He asserts that one of his passengers, Jorge, offered him a job as the driver of a privately-owned car. Contento-Pachon expressed an interest in the job and agreed to meet Jorge and the owner of the car the next day.

Instead of a driving job, Jorge proposed that Contento-Pachon swallow cocaine-filled balloons and transport them to the United States. Contento-Pachon agreed to consider the proposition. He was told not to mention the proposition to anyone, otherwise he would "get into serious trouble." Contento-Pachon testified that he did not contact the police because he believes that the Bogota police are corrupt and that they are paid off by drug traffickers.

Approximately one week later, Contento-Pachon told Jorge that he would not carry the cocaine. In response, Jorge mentioned facts about Contento-Pachon's personal life, including private details which Contento-Pachon had never mentioned to Jorge. Jorge told Contento-Pachon that his failure to cooperate would result in the death of his wife and three year-old child.

The following day the pair met again. Contento-Pachon's life and the lives of his family were again threatened. At this point, Contento-Pachon agreed to take the cocaine into the United States.

The pair met two more times. At the last meeting, Contento-Pachon swallowed 129 balloons of cocaine. He was informed that he would be watched at all times during the trip, and that if he failed to follow Jorge's instruction he and his family would be killed.

After leaving Bogota, Contento-Pachon's plane landed in Panama. Contento-Pachon asserts that he did not notify the authorities there because he felt that the Panamanian police were as corrupt as those in Bogota. Also, he felt that any such action on his part would place his family in jeopardy.

When he arrived at the customs inspection point in Los Angeles, Contento-Pachon consented to have his stomach x-rayed. The x-rays revealed a foreign substance which was later determined to be cocaine.

At Contento-Pachon's trial, the government moved to exclude the defenses of duress and necessity. The motion was granted. We reverse.

### A. Duress

There are three elements of the duress defense: (1) an immediate threat of death or serious bodily injury, (2) a well-grounded fear that the threat will be carried out, and (3) no reasonable opportunity to escape the threatened harm. Sometimes a fourth element is required: the defendant must submit to proper authorities after attaining a position of safety ...

The trial court found Contento-Pachon's offer of proof insufficient to support a duress defense because he failed to offer proof of two elements: immediacy and inescapability. We examine the elements of duress.

*Immediacy*: The element of immediacy requires that there be some evidence that the threat of injury was present, immediate, or impending. "[A] veiled threat of future unspecified harm" will not satisfy this requirement. The district court found that the initial threats were not immediate because "they were conditioned on defendant's failure to cooperate in the future and did not place defendant and his family in immediate danger."

Evidence presented on this issue indicated that the defendant was dealing with a man who was deeply involved in the exportation of illegal substances. Large sums of money were at stake and, consequently, Contento-Pachon had reason to believe that Jorge would carry out his threats. Jorge had gone to the trouble to discover that Contento-Pachon was married, that he had a child, the names of his wife and child, and the location of his residence. These were not vague threats of possible future harm. According to the defendant, if he had refused to cooperate, the consequences would have been immediate and harsh.

Contento-Pachon contends that he was being watched by one of Jorge's accomplices at all times during the airplane trip. As a consequence, the force of the threats continued to restrain him. Contento-Pachon's contention that he was operating under the threat of immediate harm was supported by sufficient evidence to present a triable issue of fact.

*Escapability* : The defendant must show that he had no reasonable opportunity to escape. The district court found that because Contento-Pachon was not physically restrained prior to the time he swallowed the balloons, he could have sought help from the police or fled. Contento-Pachon explained that he did not report the threats because he feared that the police were corrupt. The trier of fact should decide whether one in Contento-Pachon's position might believe that some of the Bogota police were paid informants for drug traffickers and that reporting the matter to the police did not represent a reasonable opportunity of escape.

If he chose not to go to the police, Contento-Pachon's alternative was to flee. We reiterate that the opportunity to escape must be reasonable. To flee, Contento-Pachon, along with his wife and three year-old child, would have been forced to pack his possessions, leave his job, and travel to a place beyond the reaches of the drug traffickers. A juror might find that this was not a reasonable avenue of escape. Thus, Contento-Pachon presented a triable issue on the element of escapability.

*Surrender to Authorities* : As noted above, the duress defense is composed of at least three elements. The government argues that the defense also requires that a defendant offer evidence that he intended to turn himself in to the authorities upon reaching a position of safety. Although it has not been expressly limited, this fourth element seems to be required only in prison escape cases. Under other circumstances, the defense has been defined to include only three elements.

The Supreme Court in *United States v. Bailey,* noted that "escape from federal custody ... is a continuing offense and ... an escapee can be held liable for failure to return to custody as well as for his initial departure." This factor would not be present in most crimes other than escape.

In cases not involving escape from prison there seems little difference between the third basic requirement that there be no reasonable opportunity to escape the threatened harm and the obligation to turn oneself in to authorities on reaching a point of safety. Once a defendant has reached a position where he can safely turn himself in to the authorities he will likewise have a reasonable opportunity to escape the threatened harm.

That is true in this case. Contento-Pachon claims that he was being watched at all times. According to him, at the first opportunity to cooperate with authorities without alerting the observer, he consented to the x-ray. We hold that a defendant who has acted under a well-grounded fear of immediate harm with no opportunity to escape may assert the duress defense, if there is a triable issue of fact whether he took the opportunity to escape the threatened harm by submitting to authorities at the first reasonable opportunity.

### B. Necessity

The defense of necessity is available when a person is faced with a choice of two evils and must then decide whether to commit a crime or an alternative act that constitutes a greater evil. *United States v. Richardson,* 588 F.2d 1235, 1239 (9th Cir.1978), *cert. denied,* 441 U.S. 931, 99 S.Ct. 2049, 60 L.Ed.2d 658, 440 U.S. 947, 99 S.Ct. 1426, 59 L.Ed.2d 636

(1979). Contento-Pachon has attempted to justify his violation of 21 U.S.C. § 841(a)(1) by showing that the alternative, the death of his family, was a greater evil.

Traditionally, in order for the necessity defense to apply, the coercion must have had its source in the physical forces of nature. The duress defense was applicable when the defendant's acts were coerced by a human force. This distinction served to separate the two similar defenses....

Contento-Pachon's acts were allegedly coerced by human, not physical forces. In addition, he did not act to promote the general welfare. Therefore, the necessity defense was not available to him. Contento-Pachon mischaracterized evidence of duress as evidence of necessity. The district court correctly disallowed his use of the necessity defense.

### II. Conclusion

Contento-Pachon presented credible evidence that he acted under an immediate and well-grounded threat of serious bodily injury, with no opportunity to escape. Because the trier of fact should have been allowed to consider the credibility of the proffered evidence, we reverse. The district court correctly excluded Contento-Pachon's necessity defense.

**COYLE, District Judge (dissenting in part and concurring in part):**

In order to establish a defense of duress, the trial court in this case required Contento-Pachon to show (1) that he or his family was under an immediate threat of death or serious bodily injury; (2) that he had a well grounded fear that the threat would be carried out; and (3) that he had no reasonable opportunity to escape the threat. Applying this three-part test, the trial court found that the defendant's offer of proof was insufficient to support a defense of duress. The government argues that this holding should be affirmed and I agree ...

In granting the government's motion in limine excluding the defense of duress, the trial court specifically found Contento-Pachon had failed to present sufficient evidence to establish the necessary elements of immediacy and inescapability. In its Order the district court stated:

> The first threat made to defendant and his family about three weeks before the flight was not immediate; the threat was conditioned upon defendant's failure to cooperate in the future and did not place the defendant and his family in immediate danger or harm. Moreover, after the initial threat and until he went to the house where he ingested the balloons containing cocaine, defendant and his family were not physically restrained and could have sought help from the police or fled. No such efforts were attempted by defendant. Thus, defendant's own offer of proof negates two necessary elements of the defense of duress.

In cases where the defendant's duress has been raised, the courts have indicated that the element of immediacy is of crucial importance. The trial court found that the threats made against the defendant and his family lacked the requisite element of immediacy. This finding is adequately supported by the record. The defendant was outside the presence of the drug dealers on numerous occasions for varying lengths of time. There is no evidence that his family was ever directly threatened or even had knowledge of the threats allegedly directed against the defendant.

Moreover, the trial court found that the defendant and his family enjoyed an adequate and reasonable opportunity to avoid or escape the threats of the drug dealers in the weeks before his flight. Until he went to the house where he ingested the balloons containing cocaine, defendant and his family were not physically restrained or prevented from seeking help. The record supports the trial court's findings that the defendant and his family could have sought assistance from the authorities or have fled. Cases considering the defense of duress have established that where there was a reasonable legal alternative to violating the law, a chance to refuse to do the criminal act and also to avoid the threatened danger, the defense will fail. Duress is permitted as a defense only when a criminal act was committed because there was no other opportunity to avoid the threatened danger.

Because the district court's decision granting the government's motion *in limine* is fully and adequately supported by the record, I cannot agree that the district court abused its discretion and I therefore respectfully dissent.

I agree with the majority, however, that the district court properly excluded Contento-Pachon's necessity defense.

## *Notes and Questions*

1. As the *Anguish* case illustrates, at common law it was often stated that duress would only excuse conduct if the threat that triggered the defense was imminent. Is the common law rule sound? Suppose that someone credibly threatens to kill you and your family if you do not rob the First National Bank within the next thirty-six hours. Assume that they also credibly threaten to kill you and your family if you go to the police for help. Is the threat in this hypothetical case "imminent," as the term is defined in *Anguish*? Would you yield to the threats and rob the bank without alerting the police or would you risk death to you and your family by refusing to rob the bank or alerting the police? Does a person who yields to such threats deserve punishment? Would imposing punishment on those who yield to this kind of threat deter others in similar circumstances from succumbing to the threats? Explain.

2. Both the majority and the dissenting opinions in *Contento Pachón* agree that duress is triggered by an "immediate" (i.e., "present" or "imminent") threat. They part ways, however, on whether the threat faced by the defendant in the case was "immediate." According to the majority, the threat was immediate because:

> Jorge had gone to the trouble to discover that Contento-Pachon was married, that he had a child, the names of his wife and child, and the location of his residence. These were not vague threats of possible future harm. According to the defendant, if he had refused to cooperate, the consequences would have been immediate and harsh.

In contrast, the dissent argued that the threat in this case was not immediate. More specifically, the dissent contended that:

> The trial court found that the threats made against the defendant and his family lacked the requisite element of immediacy. This finding is adequately supported by the record. The defendant was outside the presence of the drug dealers on numerous occasions for varying lengths of time. There is no evidence that his family was ever directly threatened or even had knowledge of the threats allegedly directed against the defendant.

Which argument do you find more persuasive? Why?

3. Put yourself in *Contento-Pachón's* situation. Imagine that you live in the Bogotá of the early 1980s, one of the most dangerous cities in the world at the time. The country is waging an internal war with the FARC (the local guerrilla groups) and overridden by drug kingpins who amassed more power than governmental forces. Many police officers were paid off by the drug cartels. A drug trafficker approaches you and threatens to kill

your child and spouse if you don't swallow balloons full of drugs and smuggle them into the United States. What would you do? Would you go to the police? Would you smuggle the drugs? Would you resist the threat and tell the trafficker that you simply won't do it? Does someone who yields to such threats and thus decides to smuggle drugs into the country deserve to be punished? Would punishing such an actor have an appreciable deterrent effect on similarly situated individuals? Explain. Does your answer to any of these questions depend on whether or not the threat faced by the actor is "immediate"?

## § 17.03 Duress: May Coercion Excuse Homicide?

### People v. Anderson

Supreme Court of California, 2002
122 Cal.Rptr.2d 587

CHIN, J.

Over two centuries ago, William Blackstone, the great commentator on the common law, said that duress is no excuse for killing an innocent person: "And, therefore, though a man be violently assaulted, and hath no other possible means of escaping death, but by killing an innocent person, this fear and force shall not acquit him of murder; for he ought rather to die himself than escape by the murder of an innocent." (2 Jones's Blackstone (1916) p. 2197.)

We granted review to decide whether these words apply in California. We conclude that, as in Blackstone's England, so today in California: fear for one's own life does not justify killing an innocent person. Duress is not a defense to murder ...

#### A.The Facts and Procedural History

Defendant was charged with kidnapping and murdering Margaret Armstrong in a camp area near Eureka called the South Jetty. Defendant and others apparently suspected the victim of molesting two girls who resided in the camp. Ron Kiern, the father of one of the girls, pleaded guilty to Armstrong's second degree murder and testified at defendant's trial.

The prosecution evidence showed that a group of people, including defendant and Kiern, confronted Armstrong at the camp. Members of the group dragged Armstrong to a nearby field, beat her, put duct tape over her mouth, tied her naked to a bush, and abandoned her. Later, defendant and Kiern, in Kiern's car, saw Armstrong going naked down the street away from the jetty. The two grabbed Armstrong, forced her into the car, and drove away. They then put Armstrong into a sleeping bag, wrapped the bag with duct tape, and placed her, screaming, into the trunk of Kiern's car.

Witnesses testified that defendant picked up a large rock, brought it to the trunk, and handed it to Kiern. Kiern appeared to hit Armstrong with the rock, silencing her. Kiern testified that defendant said Armstrong had to die. After they put her into the trunk, defendant dropped a small boulder onto her head. Kiern also said that defendant picked up the rock again, handed it to Kiern, and told him to drop it on Armstrong or something would happen to his family. Kiern dropped the rock but believed it missed Armstrong. Kiern and defendant later commented to others that Armstrong was dead.

The evidence indicated that defendant and Kiern disposed of Armstrong's body by rolling it down a ravine. One witness testified that Kiern stated he had stepped on her neck until it crunched to ensure she was dead before putting her in the ravine. The body was never found.

Defendant testified on his own behalf. He said he had tried to convince Kiern to take Armstrong to the hospital after she had been beaten. When he and Kiern saw her going down the road beaten and naked, Kiern grabbed her and put her in the backseat of the car. Back at camp, Kiern put Armstrong in the sleeping bag and bound it with duct tape. At Kiern's instruction, defendant opened the trunk and Kiern put Armstrong inside. Kiern told defendant to retrieve a certain rock the size of a cantaloupe. Defendant said, "Man, you are out of your mind for something like that." Kiern responded, "Give me the rock or I'll beat the shit out of you." Defendant gave him the rock because Kiern was bigger than he and he was "not in shape" to fight. When asked what he thought Kiern would have done if he had said no, defendant replied: "Punch me out, break my back, break my neck. Who knows." Kiern hit Armstrong over the head with the rock two or three times. Kiern's wife was standing there yelling, "Kill the bitch."

Defendant testified that later they left in Kiern's car. They pulled over and Kiern opened the trunk. Armstrong was still moaning and moving around. Defendant tried to convince Kiern to take her to a hospital, but Kiern refused. Defendant got back into the car. A few minutes later, Kiern closed the trunk, got in the car, and said, "She's dead now. I stomped on her neck and broke it."

A jury convicted defendant of first degree murder and kidnapping. Based primarily on his testimony that Kiern threatened to "beat the shit out of" him, defendant contended on appeal that the trial court erred in refusing to instruct the jury on duress as a defense to the murder charge. The Court of Appeal concluded that duress is not a defense to first degree murder and affirmed the judgment. We granted defendant's petition for review to decide to what extent, if any, duress is a defense to a homicide-related crime, and, if it is a defense, whether the trial court prejudicially erred in refusing a duress instruction.

## II. Discussion

### A. Whether Duress Is a Defense to Murder

At common law, the general rule was, and still is today, what Blackstone stated: duress is no defense to killing an innocent person. "Stemming from antiquity, the nearly 'unbroken tradition' of Anglo-American common law is that duress never excuses murder, that the person threatened with his own demise 'ought rather to die himself, than escape by the murder of an innocent.'"

The basic rationale behind allowing the defense of duress for other crimes "is that, for reasons of social policy, it is better that the defendant, faced with a choice of evils, choose to do the lesser evil (violate the criminal law) in order to avoid the greater evil threatened by the other person." (LaFave, Criminal Law, *supra*, § 5.3, p. 467.) This rationale, however, "is strained when a defendant is confronted with taking the life of an innocent third person in the face of a threat on his own life.... When the defendant commits murder under duress, the resulting harm—i.e., the death of an innocent person—is at least as great as the threatened harm—i.e., the death of the defendant." (*U.S. v. LaFleur, supra,* 971 F.2d at p. 205.) We might add that, when confronted with an apparent kill-an-innocent-person-or-be-killed situation, a person can always choose to resist. As a practical matter, death will rarely, if ever, inevitably result from a choice not to kill. The law should require people to choose to resist rather than kill an innocent person.

A state may, of course, modify the common law rule by statute ...

[Nevertheless,] no reason appears for the Legislature to have silently abrogated the common law rule. The reasons for the rule applied as well to 19th-century California as to Blackstone's England. They apply, if anything, with greater force in California today. A person can always choose to resist rather than kill an innocent person. The law must encourage, even require, everyone to seek an alternative to killing. Crimes are often committed by more than one person; the criminal law must also, perhaps especially, deter those crimes. California today is tormented by gang violence. If duress is recognized as a defense to the killing of innocents, then a street or prison gang need only create an internal reign of terror and murder can be justified, at least by the actual killer. Persons who know they can claim duress will be more likely to follow a gang order to kill instead of resisting than would those who know they must face the consequences of their acts. Accepting the duress defense for any form of murder would thus encourage killing. Absent a stronger indication than the [applicable statutes], we do not believe the Legislature intended to remove the sanctions of the criminal law from the killing of an innocent even under duress....

Accordingly, we conclude that duress is not a defense to any form of murder. Our conclusion that duress is no defense to murder makes it unnecessary to decide whether the evidence would have warranted duress instructions in this case.

We affirm the judgment of the Court of Appeal.

**Concurring and Dissenting Opinion by KENNARD, J.**

... The majority concludes that the trial court did not err because, under California law, duress is not a defense to second degree murder, or to any form of murder, whether or not the particular form of murder is punishable by death. I disagree. Applying established rules of statutory construction, I would hold that duress is unavailable as a defense only when the offense is capital murder—that is, first degree murder with a special circumstance—and that duress is available as a defense to all noncapital forms of murder, including murder in the second degree. Because no substantial evidence of duress was presented here, however, I agree with the majority that defendant was not entitled to have the trial court instruct the jury on that defense ...

III

... The majority's discussion appears to assume that murder necessarily involves a *choice* to take an innocent life. Second degree murder, however, does not require an intent to kill. A person who engages in a provocative act or who drives with great recklessness may be convicted of second degree murder under an implied malice theory. Yet, under the majority's construction, section 26 does not allow a duress defense even in situations of unintentional implied malice killings.

Imagine, for example, this scenario: Two armed robbers fleeing the scene of a store robbery force their way into a car that is leaving the parking lot. One robber holds a gun to the driver's head, while the other places a gun against the head of the driver's wife. They order the driver to take off at high speed and not to stop or slow down for stop signs or signal lights, threatening immediate death to the driver and his wife. If the driver complies, and an accident ensues resulting in the death of an innocent person, the driver could be prosecuted for second degree murder on an implied malice theory, and, under the majority's construction of section 26, the driver could not assert duress as a defense. I doubt that our Legislature intended to withhold the defense of duress under these or similar circumstances.

The majority expresses concern that if defendants can assert a duress defense to noncapital murder, the defense may be used to excuse killings by gang members. But most if not all gang-motivated killings are capital murder because it is a special circumstance that "the defendant intentionally killed the victim while the defendant was an active participant in a criminal street gang ... and the murder was carried out to further the activities of the criminal street gang." Moreover, the defense of duress is not available to a defendant who recklessly or intentionally placed himself in a situation where coercion to commit criminal acts could reasonably be anticipated. Because persons who join criminal street gangs or terrorist organizations can anticipate pressure to commit crimes, the defense would usually be unavailable to those individuals. (See *State v. Scott* (1992) 250 Kan. 350, 827 P.2d 733, 739–740 [defendant who voluntarily **796* joined drug-selling organization barred from asserting duress when coerced into torturing fellow gang member]; Rutkowski, *A Coercion Defense for the Street Gang Criminal: Plugging the Moral Gap in Existing Law, supra,* 10 Notre Dame J., L. Ethics & Pub. Pol'y. At p. 186, fn. 239 ["Most jurisdictions hold that intentionally placing oneself in the position where one would likely be the subject of coercion will defeat a duress defense."].)

IV

Because, as I have concluded, duress is a defense to noncapital murder, a defendant charged with noncapital murder is entitled to a jury instruction on the defense if there is substantial evidence to support it. This means "'evidence from which a jury composed of reasonable [people] could have concluded that there was [duress] sufficient to negate the requisite criminal intent.'" [In California,] the defense of duress is only available to defendants who present evidence of threats or menace sufficient to show a reasonable and actual belief that their life was presently and immediately endangered if participation was refused.

Here, defendant failed to present substantial evidence of duress. He testified that Ron Kiern told him, "Give me the rock or I'll beat the shit out of you" and that he complied because he feared that Kiern, a stronger and bigger man, would beat him severely. Yet, Kiern did not threaten him with death, and there was no history of violence between the two men despite their long acquaintance. In addition, defendant voluntarily joined Kiern in the initial attack on the victim, thereby placing himself in the situation where he should have anticipated that Kiern would pressure him to commit further acts of violence. Throughout the day, defendant made no use of opportunities to leave Kiern and to obtain help for the victim.

Because defendant presented insufficient evidence of duress to warrant a jury instruction on that defense, I agree with the majority that the Court of Appeal properly affirmed defendant's conviction.

## Notes and Questions

1. As the Supreme Court of California pointed out in *Anderson*, at common law duress was not a defense to homicide. Citing from LaFave's influential criminal law hornbook, the Court explains that duress defeats liability because "it is better that the defendant, faced with a choice of evils, choose to do the lesser evil (violate the criminal law) in order to avoid the greater evil threatened by the other person."

2. The Court in *Anderson*—and Professor LaFave—treats the duress defense as a species of the lesser evils defense. Given that killing an innocent human being in order to save oneself does not inflict a lesser evil than the one averted, the Court concludes that duress is unavailable in homicide prosecutions. Do you find this argument persuasive? Why or why not? If duress defeats liability because the coerced actor chooses the lesser evil, why aren't these cases merely treated as instance of justifiable "necessity" (lesser evils)

rather than as a distinct defense? Is there an explanation for why duress ought to defeat criminal liability that does not focus on whether the harm caused by the defendant was the lesser evil? Explain.

3. In the dissenting opinion, Judge Kennard asks the reader to imagine that both a driver and her spouse are being held at gunpoint and "order[ed] to take off at high speed and not to stop or slow down for stop signs or signal lights." If the driver yields to the threat and an accident that causes the death of an innocent person ensues, should the driver be held liable for homicide or should he be excused pursuant to duress? At common law, the driver would be held liable for homicide (in this case, second degree murder based on a theory of implied malice), given that duress is unavailable in prosecutions for homicide. Judge Kennard suggests that the driver should be allowed to plead duress. Do you agree with Judge Kennard? Explain.

4. A substantial minority of American jurisdictions now allow defendants to plead duress as a defense to homicide. The change was sparked by the Model Penal Code's novel approach to the defense. The next section discusses the Code's duress provision.

## § 17.04 Duress: Model Penal Code

### Model Penal Code § 2.09

(1) It is an affirmative defense that the actor engaged in the conduct charged to constitute an offense because he was coerced to do so by the use of, or a threat to use, unlawful force against his person or the person of another, that a person of reasonable firmness in his situation would have been unable to resist.

(2) The defense provided by this Section is unavailable if the actor recklessly placed himself in a situation in which it was probable that he would be subjected to duress. The defense is also unavailable if he was negligent in placing himself in such a situation, whenever negligence suffices to establish culpability for the offense charged.

(3) It is not a defense that a woman acted on the command of her husband, unless she acted under such coercion as would establish a defense under this Section. [The presumption that a woman acting in the presence of her husband is coerced is abolished.]

(4) When the conduct of the actor would otherwise be justifiable under Section 3.02, this Section does not preclude such defense.

### Commonwealth v. Markman

Supreme Court of Pennsylvania, 2007
916 A.2d 586

Justice SAYLOR.

This is a direct appeal from a sentence of death imposed by the Cumberland County Court of Common Pleas, following Appellant Beth Ann Markman's conviction of the first-degree murder of Leslie White and related charges. We affirm in part, reverse in part, and remand.

#### I. Background

During the summer of 2000, shortly after graduating from high school, Leslie White, the victim in this case, began working in the photo shop of a Wal-Mart store in Silver

Springs Township, Cumberland County. Throughout the course of the events leading to her death, White lived at home with her parents and drove her new black Jeep Cherokee to work, as well as to her classes at Harrisburg Area Community College ("HACC"), where she was a freshman. White had a particular interest in art and photography, and was pursuing studies in these subjects. The prior year, her parents gave her a camera costing approximately $600, which she continued to use.

During her first day of employment at Wal-Mart on August 2, 2000, White met Appellant's co-defendant, William Housman, who also started working at the store that day. White and Housman struck up a friendship, which eventually became romantic in nature. Unbeknownst to White, however, Housman had been involved with Appellant for some time, and was living with her in a trailer park in Newville, Cumberland County. In fact, Appellant and Housman had cohabited for nearly two years, including a period of time in which they previously had resided in Virginia. Some time in August of 2000, Appellant discovered that Housman was dating White, which led to a series of escalating arguments between Appellant and Housman. Around this time, Appellant's friends and co-workers noticed that Appellant began showing dark bruising around her eyes, neck, and arms, which Appellant attributed to fights between herself and Housman. Several individuals testified that Appellant also became increasingly temperamental, and expressed her anger toward White by referring to her as a "f___ing bitch" and stating that she would "kick her ass" or "kill her" if she ever got hold of her. At one point, Appellant called White at work, and White appeared frightened immediately afterward.

By the end of August, when Appellant realized that Housman had not terminated his relationship with White, she evicted him from the trailer and changed the lease to reflect her name only. She also called the domestic violence hotline to obtain a protection-from-abuse order due to her fear that Housman might retaliate, and mentioned an incident in which he had previously broken into the trailer. No order was issued, however, because Appellant failed to attend the requisite in-person interview. Moreover, approximately two weeks later, in mid-September of 2000, Appellant and Housman reconciled and she permitted him to move back in. Still, Appellant did not place Housman's name back on the lease, and she told her probation officer that Housman would have to earn back her trust. Appellant's probation officer testified that Appellant wanted White to come to the trailer so that Housman could finally terminate his affair with White in Appellant's presence.

... [O]n October 4, 2000, at approximately 5:30 p.m., Appellant was seen driving her car, with Housman in the front passenger's seat, to a local Sheetz gas station/convenience store. They parked, proceeded to the pay phone, and called White at Wal-Mart to lure her to the trailer (at this time Appellant's trailer did not have telephone service). Housman placed the call and stated, falsely, that his father had died; he asked White to come to the trailer to console him. According to Appellant, Housman told White that Appellant had gone out of town, and hence, only he (Housman) would be at the trailer when White arrived. This ploy was effective, as White became concerned that Housman might be suicidal over the supposed loss of his father. Thus, she left her shift early at 6:16 p.m. and drove her jeep to the trailer to comfort him.

When White arrived, Housman admitted her into the living room, and the two began to talk. Appellant remained in the bedroom with the door closed, and White initially did not know she was there. Subsequently, while White and Housman were sitting on the couch conversing, Appellant came out of the bedroom and stood by the front door. Appellant testified that she did this because she was having trouble breathing due to her asthma, and needed fresh air. She also stated that, just before coming out of the bedroom, she heard White cry out because Housman had hit her on the hand with a hammer, and her hand appeared swollen. In any event, shortly after coming out of the bedroom and standing by the door, Appellant acted together with Housman to subdue White, binding her hands and feet with speaker wire, and placing a large piece of cloth in her mouth, as well as a tight gag over her mouth and around the back of her neck to secure the cloth. With White bound and gagged, Housman and Appellant stepped outside to smoke a cigarette and discuss the situation. Upon returning to the trailer, Appellant held the victim down, while Housman strangled her with speaker wire and the crook of his arm, killing her. During the struggle, White reached up and scratched Appellant on the neck, leaving dark red marks. According to the medical examiner, White died of asphyxiation caused by Housman's strangulating actions together with the blockage of air due to the cloth stuffed in her mouth. [Appellant was charged with first-degree murder of White]....

Appellant testified in her defense, and asserted that she had been physically abused by Housman during the course of their relationship. She repeated her specific allegations of coercion on the night of the murder, placing them in the context of a broader pattern of longstanding physical abuse by Housman. She also added significant details concerning the crime, including an assertion that Housman had terrorized her for two full days prior to the murder, during which time he had cut her clothes off with a knife, repeatedly raped her, and threatened to "put a .45 in [her] head" or "send [her] home in pieces to [her] daughter" if she did not do as he instructed or tried to escape the trailer, and ordered her to write a letter to White stating that she (Appellant) had moved to Virginia and was no longer involved with Housman. She stated as well that, when she and Housman went to the Sheetz convenience store, she was not aware that Housman was planning to call White until he actually called her, and that when they returned to the trailer, she tried to escape twice, but each time Housman prevented her from doing so in a violent manner. Appellant stated further that, even after White was bound and gagged, she (Appellant) did not know that Housman actually planned to kill her. In this regard, Appellant testified that when she and Housman returned to the trailer after smoking a cigarette, White's gag had slipped down from her mouth and White requested some water. When Appellant went to the kitchen to get her a glass of water, Appellant heard screaming as Housman began to choke White. According to Appellant, at that point Housman ordered her to come back to the living room and pull the gag back up over White's mouth. Appellant complied and, after Housman continued to strangle White, it ultimately became apparent that White had died. Appellant maintained that she obeyed Housman during this time and did not attempt to prevent him from choking White because she was afraid that he might kill her as well....

Based in part upon the above testimony, Appellant requested an instruction on the defense of duress. The trial court refused this request, and the jury ultimately found both defendants guilty on all charges, including first-degree murder.... [Appellant was sentenced to death].

### IV. Appellant's other claims

#### *A. Duress instruction*

First, Appellant maintains that the trial court erroneously refused her request for a jury instruction on the defense of duress. Duress is a defense to criminal culpability. It is codified in the Crimes Code as follows:

> (a) **General Rule.**—It is a defense that the actor engaged in the conduct charged to constitute an offense because he was coerced to do so by the use of, or a threat to use, unlawful force against his person or the person of another, which

> a person of reasonable firmness in his situation would have been unable to resist.
>
> (b) **Exception.**—The defense provided by subsection (a) of this section is unavailable if the actor recklessly placed himself in a situation in which it was probable that he would be subjected to duress. The defense is also unavailable if he was negligent in placing himself in such a situation, whenever negligence suffices to establish culpability for the offense charged.

Although at common law duress was not available as to a charge of first-degree murder, Section 309 does not create an exception for any particular offense. In drafting this provision—which replaces the common law test for duress, the General Assembly could have placed an express exception for murder into the statutory text, as some other states have done. Because the Legislature chose not to include such an exception, we conclude that it did not intend to preserve the common law rule in this regard. Accordingly, the defense of duress is available in this Commonwealth as to a charge of first-degree murder. The question remains, then, whether the trial court committed legal error or abused its discretion in removing the question of duress from the jury after the issue was properly raised....

Here, Appellant's trial testimony set out at length the basis for her claim of duress, including that Housman repeatedly battered her and placed a knife to her throat or side and threatened her with death if she did not do as he instructed. These assertions have already been adequately set out at length ... We find this evidence sufficient to raise a question of fact as to whether Appellant was subjected to duress under Section 309(a), and thus, to confer upon Appellant a *prima facie* entitlement to a jury instruction on the issue.

This does not end our analysis, however, because the trial court justified its refusal to give the requested charge on the grounds that the Section 309(b) exception applied. As set forth above, this exception precludes the defense where the actor recklessly places himself in a situation where duress is probable....

Notably, it is the *trier of fact* that must determine whether the defendant acted recklessly. Thus, an appellate court will only affirm a trial judge's removal of the duress issue from the jury on the basis of the recklessness exception where there can be no reasonable dispute that this exception applies....

[In the present case], Appellant's testimony and post-arrest statement provided evidence that she was subjected to duress by Housman during and immediately prior to the kidnapping and homicide. On the other hand, Appellant failed to take advantage of potential opportunities to escape Housman's control. For example, while standing at the payphone, Housman had allegedly placed the knife back in his pocket; thus, Appellant may have been able to run into the store and ask that the police be called. Furthermore, after returning to her trailer, Appellant did not flee the scene when she went to the kitchen to obtain the cloth gag, when she and Housman went outside to smoke a cigarette, or when Housman was choking White and Appellant was close enough to the front door to run out of the trailer and seek help.... [T]hese missed opportunities raise a question of fact as to whether Appellant acted recklessly. It cannot be overlooked, however, that there was also evidence to the effect that: Appellant had been subjected to terrorization, assaults, and death threats over a two-day period immediately prior to these events; she had already tried to escape through both the front and back doors of the trailer, and each time had been violently restrained from doing so by Housman; and Housman was at all relevant times in close proximity to Appellant and in possession of a hunting knife ... We conclude, therefore, that there was conflicting evidence on the issue of whether Appellant was reckless, and thus, Appellant's actions did not remove the duress issue from the jury's purview....

Accordingly, the jury should have been informed of the elements of the defense of duress and its recklessness exception, and allowed to resolve these factual issues—at least with respect to the charges of homicide, kidnapping, and unlawful restraint...

## State v. Toscano

Supreme Court of New Jersey, 1977
378 A.2d 755

PASHMAN, J.

Defendant Joseph Toscano was convicted of conspiring to obtain money by false pretenses in violation of N.J.S.A. 2A:98-1. Although admitting that he had aided in the preparation of a fraudulent insurance claim by making out a false medical report, he argued that he had acted under duress. The trial judge ruled that the threatened harm was not sufficiently imminent to justify charging the jury on the defense of duress. After the jury returned a verdict of guilty, the defendant was fined $500.

The Appellate Division affirmed the conviction. It stressed that defendant had ample opportunity between the time of the threat and the commission of the allegedly coerced act to report the matter to the police or to avoid participation in the conspiracy altogether. Relying on [prior case law], it also concluded that defendant failed to satisfy the threshold condition that the threatened harm be "present, imminent and impending."

We granted certification to consider the status of duress as an affirmative defense to a crime. We hold that duress is an affirmative defense to a crime other than murder, and that it need not be based upon an alleged threat of immediate bodily injury. Under the standard announced today, we find that this defendant did allege sufficient facts to warrant charging the jury on his claim of duress. Accordingly, we reverse his conviction and remand for a new trial.

### I

On April 20, 1972, the Essex County Grand Jury returned a 48-count indictment alleging that eleven named defendants and two unindicted co-conspirators had defrauded various insurance companies by staging accidents in public places and obtaining payments in settlement of fictitious injuries. The First Count of the indictment alleged a single conspiracy involving twelve different "staged" accidents over a span of almost three years. In the remaining counts, the participants were charged with separate offenses of conspiracy, obtaining money by false pretenses and receiving fraudulently obtained money.

Dr. Joseph Toscano, a chiropractor, was named as a defendant in the First Count and in two counts alleging a conspiracy to defraud the Kemper Insurance Company (Kemper). Prior to trial, seven of the eleven defendants pleaded guilty to various charges, leaving defendant as the sole remaining defendant charged with the conspiracy to defraud Kemper. Among those who pleaded guilty was William Leonardo, the architect of the alleged general conspiracy and the organizer of each of the separate incidents. Although the First Count was dismissed by the trial judge at the conclusion of the State's case, the evidence did reveal a characteristic modus operandi by Leonardo and his cohorts which is helpful in understanding the fraudulent scheme against Kemper. Typically, they would stage an accident or feign a fall in a public place. A false medical report for the "injured" person, together with a false verification of employment and lost wages, would then be submitted to the insurer of the premises. The same two doctors were used to secure the medical reports in every instance except that involving the claim against Kemper. Likewise, the confirmations of employment and lost wages were secured from the same pool of friendly employers. The insurance companies made cash payments to resolve the claims under their "quick settlement" programs, usually within a few weeks after the purported accidents. Leonardo took responsibility for dividing the funds to the "victims" of the accidents, to the doctors and employers, taking a substantial portion for himself.

Michael Hanaway, an unindicted co-conspirator who acted as the victim in a number of these staged accidents, testified that defendant was drawn into this scheme largely by happenstance. On January 6, 1970, Hanaway staged a fall at E. J. Korvette's in Woodridge, New Jersey under the direction of Leonardo and Frank Neri, another defendant who pleaded guilty prior to trial. Dr. Miele, one of the two doctors repeatedly called upon by Leonardo to provide fraudulent medical reports, attested to Hanaway's claimed injuries on a form supplied by the insurer. Hanaway was subsequently paid $975 in settlement of his claim by the Underwriters Adjusting Company on behalf of Korvette's insurer.

In the meantime, however, the same trio performed a similar charade at the R.K.O. Wellmont Theater in Montclair, New Jersey. Kemper, which insured the R.K.O. Theater, was immediately notified of Hanaway's claim, and Dr. Miele was again enlisted to verify Hanaway's injuries on a medical report. However, because the R.K.O. accident occurred on January 8, 1970 only two days after the Korvette's incident Dr. Miele confused the two claims and mistakenly told Kemper's adjuster that he was treating Hanaway for injuries sustained at Korvette's. When Hanaway learned of the claims adjuster's suspicions, he informed William Leonardo who, in turn, contacted his brother Richard (a co-defendant at trial) to determine whether Toscano would agree to verify the treatments.

The State attempted to show that Toscano agreed to fill out the false medical report because he owed money to Richard Leonardo for gambling debts. It also suggested that Toscano subsequently sought to cover up the crime by fabricating office records of non-existent office visits by Hanaway. Defendant sharply disputed these assertions and maintained that he capitulated to William Leonardo's demands only because he was fearful for his wife's and his own bodily safety. Since it is not our function here to assess these conflicting versions, we shall summarize only those facts which, if believed by the jury, would support defendant's claim of duress.

Defendant first met Richard Leonardo in 1953 as a patient and subsequently knew him as a friend. Defendant briefly encountered the brother, William, in the late 1950s at Caldwell Penitentiary when Toscano served as a prison guard. Although William was an inmate, the doctor did not know him personally. Through conversations with some police officers and William's brother and father, however, he did learn enough about William to know of his criminal record. In particular, Richard told him many times that William was "on junk," that he had a gang, that "they can't keep up with the amount of money that they need for this habit," and that he himself stayed away from William.

Thus, when William first called the defendant at his office, asking for a favor, he immediately cut off the conversation on the pretext that he was with a patient. Although William had not specifically mentioned the medical form at that time, defendant testified that he was "nauseated" by "just his name." A few days later, on a Thursday evening, he received another call in his office. This time Leonardo asked defendant to make out a report for a friend in order to submit a bill to a claims adjuster. He was more insistent, stating that defendant was "going to do it," but defendant *428 replied that he would not and could not provide the report. Once again the doctor ended the conversation abruptly by claiming, falsely, that he was with other persons.

The third and final call occurred on Friday evening. Leonardo was "boisterous and loud" repeating, "You're going to make this bill out for me." Then he said: "Remember, you just moved into a place that has a very dark entrance and you leave there with your wife.... You and your wife are going to jump at shadows when you leave that dark entrance." Leonardo sounded "vicious" and "desperate" and defendant felt that he "just had to do it" to protect himself and his wife. He thought about calling the police, but failed to do so in the hope that "it would go away and wouldn't bother me any more."

In accordance with Leonardo's instructions, defendant left a form in his mailbox on Saturday morning for Leonardo to fill in with the necessary information about the fictitious injuries. It was returned that evening and defendant completed it. On Sunday morning he met Hanaway at a pre-arranged spot and delivered a medical bill and the completed medical report. He received no compensation for his services, either in the form of cash from William Leonardo or forgiven gambling debts from Richard Leonardo. He heard nothing more from Leonardo after that Sunday.

Shortly thereafter, still frightened by the entire episode, defendant moved to a new address and had his telephone number changed to an unlisted number in an effort to avoid future contacts with Leonardo. He also applied for a gun permit but was unsuccessful. His superior at his daytime job with the Newark Housing Authority confirmed that the quality of defendant's work dropped so markedly that he was forced to question defendant about his attitude. After some conversation, defendant explained that he had been upset by threats against him and his wife. He also revealed the threats to a co-worker at the Newark Housing Authority.

After defendant testified, the trial judge granted the State's motion to exclude any further testimony in connection with defendant's claim of duress, and announced his decision not to charge the jury on that defense. He based his ruling on two decisions by the former Court of Errors and Appeals, State v. Palmieri, supra, and State v. Churchill, supra, which referred to the common law rule that a successful claim of duress required a showing of a "present, imminent and impending" threat of harm. As he interpreted these decisions, the defendant could not satisfy this standard by establishing his own subjective estimate of the immediacy of the harm. Rather, the defendant was obliged to prove its immediacy by an objective standard which included a reasonable explanation of why he did not report the threats to the police. Since Toscano's only excuse for failing to make such a report was his doubts that the police would be willing or able to protect him, the court ruled that his subjective fears were irrelevant.

After stating that the defense of duress is applicable only where there is an allegation that an act was committed in response to a threat of present, imminent and impending death or serious bodily harm, the trial judge charged the jury:

> Now, one who is standing and receiving instructions from someone at the point of a gun is, of course, in such peril. One can describe such threat as being imminent, present and pending, and a crime committed under those circumstances, or rather conduct engaged in under those circumstances, even though criminal in nature, would be excused by reason of the circumstances in which it was committed.
>
> Now, where the peril is not imminent, present and pending to the extent that the defendant has the opportunity to seek police assistance for himself and his wife as well, the law places upon such a person the duty not to acquiesce in the unlawful demand and any criminal conduct in which he may thereafter engage may not be excused. Now, this principle prevails regardless of the subjective estimate

> he may have made as to the degree of danger with which he or his wife may have been confronted. Under the facts of this case, I instruct you, as members of the jury, that the circumstances described by Dr. Toscano leading to his implication in whatever criminal activities in which you may find he participated are not sufficient to constitute the defense of duress.

II

The trial judge's formulation of the law of duress appears in harmony with recent decisions of this Court. Nevertheless, while these cases offer some support for following the common law rule tacitly approved in Palmieri and Churchill, we question whether those precedents should be controlling under the instant facts....

III

Since New Jersey has no applicable statute defining the defense of duress, we are guided only by common law principles which conform to the purposes of our criminal justice system and reflect contemporary notions of justice and fairness.

At common law the defense of duress was recognized only when the alleged coercion involved a use or threat of harm which is "present, imminent and pending" and "of such a nature as to induce a well grounded apprehension of death or serious bodily harm if the act is not done."

It was commonly said that duress does not excuse the killing of an innocent person even if the accused acted in response to immediate threats. Aside from this exception, however, duress was permitted as a defense to prosecution for a range of serious offenses ...

To excuse a crime, the threatened injury must induce "such a fear as a man of ordinary fortitude and courage might justly yield to." Although there are scattered suggestions in early cases that only a fear of death meets this test, an apprehension of immediate serious bodily harm has been considered sufficient to excuse capitulation to threats. Thus, the courts have assumed as a matter of law that neither threats of slight injury nor threats of destruction to property are coercive enough to overcome the will of a person of ordinary courage. A "generalized fear of retaliation" by an accomplice, unrelated to any specific threat, is also insufficient.

More commonly, the defense of duress has not been allowed because of the lack of immediate danger to the threatened person. When the alleged source of coercion is a threat of "future" harm, courts have generally found that the defendant had a duty to escape from the control of the threatening person or to seek assistance from law enforcement authorities.

Assuming a "present, imminent and impending" danger, however, there is no requirement that the threatened person be the accused. Although not explicitly resolved by the early cases, recent decisions have assumed that concern for the well-being of another, particularly a near relative, can support a defense of duress if the other requirements are satisfied ...

The insistence under the common law on a danger of immediate force causing death or serious bodily injury may be ascribed to its origins in early cases dealing with treason, to the proclivities of a "tougher-minded age," or simply to judicial fears of perjury and fabrication of baseless defenses. We do not discount the latter concern as a reason for caution in modifying this accepted rule, but we are concerned by its obvious shortcomings and potential for injustice. Under some circumstances, the commission of a minor criminal offense should be excusable even if the coercive agent does not use or threaten force which is likely to result in death or "serious" bodily injury. Similarly, it is possible that authorities might not be able to prevent a threat of future harm from eventually being carried out ... Warnings of future injury or death will be all the more powerful if the prospective victim is another person, such as a spouse or child, whose safety means more to the threatened person than his own wellbeing. Finally, as the drafters of the Model Penal Code observed, "long and wasting pressure may break down resistance more effectively than a threat of immediate destruction." s 2.09, Comment at 8 (Tent.Draft No. 10, 1960).

Commentators have expressed dissatisfaction with the common law standard of duress. Stephen viewed the defense as a threat to the deterrent function of the criminal law, and argued that "it is at the moment when temptation is strongest that the law should speak most clearly and emphatically to the contrary." Stephen, 2 History of the Criminal Law in England 107 (1883). A modern refinement of this position is that the defense should be designed to encourage persons to act against their self-interest if a substantial percentage of persons in such a situation would do so. Hall, General Principles of Criminal Law (2 ed. 1960), 446–47. This standard would limit its applicability to relatively minor crimes and exclude virtually all serious crimes unless committed under threat of imminent death. Id. at 448.

Others have been more skeptical about the deterrent effects of a strict rule. As the Alabama Supreme Court observed in an early case:

> That persons have exposed themselves to imminent peril and death for their fellow man, and that there are instances where innocent persons have submitted to murderous assaults, and suffered death, rather than take life, is well established; but such self-sacrifice emanated from other motives than the fear of legal punishment.

Building on this premise, some commentators have advocated a flexible rule which would allow a jury to consider whether the accused actually lost his capacity to act in accordance with "his own desire, or motivation, or will" under the pressure of real or imagined forces ...

The drafters of the Model Penal Code and the New Jersey Penal Code sought to steer a middle course between these two positions by focusing on whether the standard imposed upon the accused was one with which "normal members of the community will be able to comply" They stated:

> ... law is ineffective in the deepest sense, indeed it is hypocritical, if it imposes on the actor who has the misfortune to confront a dilemmatic choice, a standard that his judges are not prepared to affirm that they should and could comply with if their turn to face the problem should arise. Condemnation in such case is bound to be an ineffective threat; what is, however, more significant is that it is divorced from any moral base and is injust. Where it would be both 'personally and socially debilitating' to accept the actor's cowardice as a defense, it would be equally debilitating to demand that heroism be the standard of legality. (Model Penal Code s 2.09, Comment at 7 (Tent.Draft No. 10, 1960).

Thus, they proposed that a court limit its consideration of an accused's "situation" to "stark, tangible factors which differentiate the actor from another, like his size or strength or age or health," excluding matters of temperament. They substantially departed from the existing statutory and common law limitations requiring that the result be death or serious bodily harm, that the threat be immediate and aimed at the accused, or that the crime committed be a non-capital offense. While these factors would be given evidential weight, the failure to satisfy one or more of these conditions would not justify the trial judge's withholding the defense from the jury.

Both the Prosecutor and the Attorney General substantially approve of the modifications suggested by the drafters of the model codes. However, they would allow the issue to be submitted to the jury only where the trial judge has made a threshold determination that the harm threatened was "imminent." Defendant, in a rather cryptic fashion, refers us to New York's statutory definition of duress, New York Penal Code s 40.00 (1970), which requires a showing of coercion by the use or threatened imminent use of unlawful force. However, he advocates leaving the question of immediacy to the jury.

For reasons suggested above, a per se rule based on immediate injury may exclude valid claims of duress by persons for whom resistance to threats or resort to official protection was not realistic. While we are hesitant to approve a rule which would reward citizens who fail to make such efforts, we are not persuaded that capitulation to unlawful demands is excusable only when there is a "gun at the head" of the defendant. We believe that the better course is to leave the issue to the jury with appropriate instructions from the judge.

Although they are not entirely identical, under both model codes defendant would have had his claim of duress submitted to the jury. Defendant's testimony provided a factual basis for a finding that Leonardo threatened him and his wife with physical violence if he refused to assist in the fraudulent scheme. Moreover, a jury might have found from other testimony adduced at trial that Leonardo's threats induced a reasonable fear in the defendant. Since he asserted that he agreed to complete the false documents only because of this apprehension, the requisite elements of the defense were established. Under the model code provisions, it would have been solely for the jury to determine whether a "person of reasonable firmness in his situation" would have failed to seek police assistance or refused to cooperate, or whether such a person would have been, unlike defendant, able to resist.

Exercising our authority to revise the common law, we have decided to adopt this approach as the law of New Jersey. Henceforth, duress shall be a defense to a crime other than murder if the defendant engaged in conduct because he was coerced to do so by the use of, or threat to use, unlawful force against his person or the person of another, which a person of reasonable firmness in his situation would have been unable to resist.

We have deliberately followed the language of the proposed New Jersey Penal Code in stating our holding and we expect trial judges to frame their jury charges in the same terms. The defendant shall have the burden of producing sufficient evidence to satisfy the trial judge that the fact of duress is in issue. Such evidence may appear in the State's case or that of the defendant. No longer will there be a preliminary judicial determination that the threats posed a danger of "present, imminent and impending" harm to the defendant or to another. In charging the jury, however, the trial judge should advert to this factor of immediacy, as well as the gravity of the harm threatened, the seriousness of the crime committed, the identity of the person endangered, the possibilities for escape or resistance and the opportunities for seeking official assistance. He should also emphasize that the applicable standard for judging the defendant's excuse is the "person of reasonable firmness in (the accused's) situation." ...

IV

Defendant's conviction of conspiracy to obtain money by false pretenses is hereby reversed and remanded for a new trial.

## *Notes and Questions*

1. The Pennsylvania duress statute discussed by the Court in *Markman* is identical to § 2.09(1) & (2) of the Model Penal Code. As the Court pointed out, under this statute—

and all statutes that track the Model Penal Code's approach to duress—duress is a defense to all crimes. As a result, such provisions may excuse the commission of a homicide, as long as a person of reasonable firmness in the actor's situation would have also committed homicide in order to avert the threat.

2. Note, however, that some duress provisions based on Model Penal Code § 2.09 expressly prescribe that the defense is unavailable in homicide prosecutions. Sometimes such statutes preclude invoking duress as a defense to other serious crimes. The Colorado duress provision is representative:

> **§ 18-1-708. Duress**
>
> A person may not be convicted of an offense, other than a class 1 felony, based upon conduct in which he engaged at the direction of another person because of the use or threatened use of unlawful force upon him or upon another person, which force or threatened use thereof a reasonable person in his situation would have been unable to resist. This defense is not available when a person intentionally or recklessly places himself in a situation in which it is foreseeable that he will be subjected to such force or threatened use thereof. The choice of evils defense, provided in section 18-1-702, shall not be available to a defendant in addition to the defense of duress provided under this section unless separate facts exist which warrant its application.

3. As the New Jersey Supreme Court explained in *Toscano,* the Model Penal Code's approach to duress does not require that the threat that compels the defendant to act be "imminent." Instead, it merely requires proof that a reasonable person in the actor's situation would have also committed the offense, even if the threat is not technically "imminent" or "immediate." Do you agree with the Code's rejection of the "imminence" limitation to the duress defense, or do you prefer the common law's strict adherence to the imminence requirement in this context? Why?

4. Recall that whether force could be used only when faced with an imminent threat generated considerable debate in the context of self-defense (see Chapter 16.01). Some courts and scholars argued that allowing defensive force to thwart non-imminent threats should never be justified. Note, however, that the role of imminence in duress may plausibly be different than its role in self-defense. If duress is—as most scholars argue—an excuse rather than a justification, limiting the defense to instances in which the actor yields to an imminent threat is questionable. An actor ought to be excused when, in light of the circumstances of the case, she could not have been fairly expected to abstain from committing the offense. The defining feature of excuses, then, is whether a person of ordinary fortitude would have also committed the crime if she were in the defendant's shoes. Whether or not the conduct is in response to an imminent threat is, therefore, not essential. What is determinative is whether we can fairly blame the person for having engaged in what admittedly amounts to an unjustified act, regardless of whether the person was faced with an imminent or non-imminent threat.

5. Duress excuses crime under the Model Penal Code only if a "person of reasonable firmness" in the actor's "situation" would have also yielded to the threats. How objective is the "person of reasonable firmness" standard? That is, is the conduct of a "person of reasonable firmness" supposed to be judged by appealing to societal expectations regarding conduct or should it focus more on what could be fairly expected of the defendant in light of his particular strengths and limitations? If the standard is objective and focuses on societal expectations of reasonable moral fortitude, how many features of the

actor's "situation" can be taken into account without transforming the standard into a subjective one? Addressing this issue, the New Jersey Supreme Court pointed out in *Toscano* that:

> [The Model Penal Code drafters] proposed that a court limit its consideration of an accused's "situation" to "stark, tangible factors which differentiate the actor from another, like his size or strength or age or health," excluding matters of temperament. They substantially departed from the existing statutory and common law limitations requiring that the result be death or serious bodily harm, that the threat be immediate and aimed at the accused, or that the crime committed be a non-capital offense. While these factors would be given evidential weight, the failure to satisfy one or more of these conditions would not justify the trial judge's withholding the defense from the jury.

In *State v. B.H.*, 870 A.2d 273 (2005), the New Jersey Supreme Court further elaborated on the nature of the "person of reasonable firmness standard." The defendant in the case wanted to present evidence of battered woman syndrome to buttress her duress claim. Reaffirming the view that the standard is ultimately objective in nature, but that it allows the fact finder to take into account certain characteristics of the defendant and his situation, the Court observed that:

> In making [an] assessment [of what a person of reasonable firmness in the actor's situation would do], the jury must consider objectively such factors as the gravity of the threat, the proximity of the impending harm being threatened, opportunities for escape, likely execution of the threat, and the seriousness of the crime defendant committed. A defendant's personal timidity or lack of firmness in the face of intimidation does not serve as the measure for his or her conduct. Community expectations prevail in judging a defendant's response to a threat when that response involves engaging in criminal action toward, or affecting, an innocent third person—not the one who posed the threat to the defendant. With the defense of duress, a defendant is neither held to a standard of heroism, nor is defendant allowed to rely on his or her idiosyncratic mental and emotional weaknesses.

Turning to the facts of the case in *B.H.*, the Court explained that although evidence of battered woman syndrome (BWS) is admissible to assess whether the defendant believed that she was threatened, such evidence is inadmissible to determine what a "person of reasonable firmness" in the defendant's "situation" would have done. That is, the Court concluded that BWS is not part of the actor's "situation" for the purposes of the "person of reasonable firmness" standard. The Court explained:

> Because [the New Jersey duress statute] embodies an objective standard for the evaluation of a defendant's conduct in response to a threat by another, we can discern no place for battered woman syndrome evidence in that assessment. In applying the statute's objective measure, it is a person of reasonable firmness that the jury must consider. The jury must evaluate objectively the defendant's criminal conduct toward a third person, and whether a person of ordinary strength and willpower would refuse to do the criminal act even in the face of the harm threatened. The idiosyncratic fact that the defendant may be susceptible to the demands of her abuser because she suffers from battered woman syndrome becomes irrelevant in that assessment. The issue is whether a person of reasonable firmness in her situation would have been able to resist the threat from her abuser. Expert testimony on the syndrome is inconsistent

> with the objective standard. Other jurisdictions also have held such evidence not relevant to an objective "person of reasonable firmness" standard, reasoning that the evidence simply explains why a particular defendant would succumb to coercion when a person without a background of being battered would not.

Do you agree with the Court's conclusion that asking whether a "person of reasonable firmness that suffers from BWS" would have also succumbed to the threat is incompatible with the objective nature of the standard? Why or why not?

## § 17.05 Duress: Comparative Perspectives

### Prosecutor v. Drazen Erdemovic

International Criminal Tribunal for the former Yugoslavia, 1997
Case No. IT-96-22-A, Judgment on Appeal, P 10 (Oct. 7, 1997)

[Editor's Note: Drazen Erdemovic was charged with systematically killing Muslim men and children in July 1995 as a member of the Bosnian Serb army. Initially, he refused to take part in the shootings, but his superiors threatened to kill him if he did not comply. At trial, Erdemovic confessed that he succumbed to the threats and killed nearly seventy people. Ultimately, the question before the ICTY Appeals Chamber was whether the defense of duress is available when the offense charged is a crime against humanity.]

**Joint Separate Opinion of Judge Mcdonald and Judge Vohrah**

**III. Can Duress be a Complete Defence in International Law to the Killing of Innocents?**

... As to the first preliminary question addressed to the parties in this appeal, "[i]n law, may duress afford a complete defence to a charge of crimes against humanity and/or war crimes such that, if the defence is proved at trial, the accused in entitled to an acquittal?" ...

**B. Customary International Law (Article 38(1)(b) of ICJ Statute)**

The Prosecution submits that "under international law duress cannot afford a complete defence to a charge of crimes against humanity and war crimes when the underlying offence is the killing of an innocent human being." The Prosecution contends that the relevant case-law of the post-Second World War military tribunals does not recognise duress as a defence to a charge involving the killing of innocent persons. Given also that there is no conventional international law which resolves the question of duress as a defence to murder, it is the submission of the Prosecution that customary international law, as contained in the decisions of the post-World War Two military tribunals, clearly precludes duress as such a defence. Although the Prosecution does not confine its arguments to the specific question as to whether duress is a complete defence for a soldier who has been charged under international law with killing innocent persons, we would, however, so limit our inquiry in this appeal....

We find that the only express affirmation of the availability of duress as a defence to the killing of innocent persons in post-World War Two military tribunal cases appears in the Einsatzgruppen case before a United States military tribunal. There the tribunal stated:

> Let it be said at once that there is no law which requires that an innocent man must forfeit his life or suffer serious harm in order to avoid committing a crime which he condemns. The threat, however, must be imminent, real and inevitable. No court will punish a man who, with a loaded pistol at his head, is compelled to pull a lethal lever.

In our view, however, the value of this authority is cast into some considerable doubt by the fact that the United States military tribunal in the Einsatzgruppen case did not cite any authority for its opinion that duress may constitute a complete defence to killing an innocent individual. The military tribunal certainly could not have relied on any authority from the common law of the United States in which it has been established since the 1890s that duress is no defence to murder in the first degree. Moreover, even if the tribunals views regarding duress as a defence to murder had been supportable in its time, these views cannot presently constitute good authority in light of the development of the law. Rule 916 (h) of the Manual for Courts-Martial United States 1984 now clearly provides that duress is a defence "to any offence except killing an innocent person".

The laws of all but a handful of state jurisdictions in the United States definitively reject duress as a complete defence for a principal in the first degree to murder. The comments of the most qualified publicists, recognised as a subsidiary source of international law in Article 38(1)(d) of the ICJ Statute, are also informative. Two years after the Einsatzgruppen decision in the opus classicum on international law, Professor Hersch Lauterpacht wrote that "[n]o principle of justice and, in most civilised communities, no principle of law permits the individual person to avoid suffering or even to save his life at the expense of the life—or, as revealed in many war crimes trials, of a vast multitude of lives—of or sufferings, on a vast scale, of others" and, in particular, that there is "serious objection to this [contrary] reasoning of the Tribunal" in the Einsatzgruppen case.

We, accordingly, find that the Einsatzgruppen decision is in discord with the preponderant view of international authorities. There is no other precedent in the case-law of international post-World War Two military tribunals which could be cited as authority for the proposition that duress is a complete defence to the killing of innocent persons in international law....

.... To the extent that the domestic decisions and national laws of States relating to the issue of duress as a defence to murder may be regarded as state practice, it is quite plain that this practice is not at all consistent. The defence in its Notice of Appeal surveys the criminal codes and legislation of 14 civil law jurisdictions in which necessity or duress is prescribed as a general exculpatory principle applying to all crimes. The surveyed jurisdictions comprise those of Austria, Belgium, Brazil, Greece, Italy, Finland, the Netherlands, France, Germany, Peru, Spain, Switzerland, Sweden and the former Yugoslavia. Indeed, the war crimes decisions cited in the Separate Opinion of Judge Cassese are based upon the acceptance of duress as a general defence to all crimes in the criminal codes of France, Italy, Germany, the Netherlands and Belgium.

In stark contrast to this acceptance of duress as a defence to the killing of innocents is the clear position of the various countries throughout the world applying the common law. These common law systems categorically reject duress as a defence to murder. The sole exception is the United States where a few states have accepted Section 2.09 of the United States Penal Code which currently provides that duress is a general defence to all crimes....

In order to arrive at a general principle relating to duress, we have undertaken a limited survey of the treatment of duress in the world's legal systems. This survey is necessarily modest in its undertaking and is not a thorough comparative analysis. Its purpose is to derive, to the extent possible, a "general principle of law" as a source of international law.

### 1. Duress as a Complete Defence

(a) Civil law systems.

The penal codes of civil law systems, with some exceptions, consistently recognise duress as a complete defence to all crimes. The criminal codes of civil law nations provide that an accused acting under duress "commits no crime" or "is not criminally responsible" or "shall not be punished". We would note that some civil law systems distinguish between the notion of necessity and that of duress. Necessity is taken to refer to situations of emergency arising from natural forces. Duress, however, is taken to refer to compulsion by threats of another human being.

(b) Common law systems

England. In England, duress is a complete defence to all crimes except murder, attempted murder and, it would appear, treason. Although there is no direct authority on whether duress is available in respect of attempted murder, the prevailing view is that there is no reason in logic, morality or law in granting the defence to a charge of attempted murder whilst withholding it in respect of a charge of murder.

United States and Australia

The English position that duress operates as a complete defence in respect of crimes generally is followed in the United States and Australia with variations in the federal state jurisdictions as to the precise definition of the defence and the range of offences for which the defence is not available.

[Editor's Note: The judges survey the law of other common law jurisdictions, including Canada and several African countries and concludes that duress is not generally considered a defense to homicide in common law systems.]

### … 4.What is the Applicable Rule?

The rules of the various legal systems of the world are, however, largely inconsistent regarding the specific question whether duress affords a complete defence to a combatant charged with a war crime or a crime against humanity involving the killing of innocent persons. As the general provisions of the numerous penal codes set out above show, the civil law systems in general would theoretically allow duress as a complete defence to all crimes including murder and unlawful killing.

On the other hand, there are laws of other legal systems which categorically reject duress as a defence to murder. Firstly, specific laws relating to war crimes in Norway and Poland do not allow duress to operate as a complete defence but permit it to be taken into account only in mitigation of punishment. Secondly, the Ethiopian Penal Code of 1957 provides in Article 67 that only "absolute physical coercion" may constitute a complete defence to crimes in general. Where the coercion is "moral", which we would interpret as referring to duress by threats, the accused is only entitled to a reduction of penalty. This reduction of penalty may extend, where appropriate, even to a complete discharge of the offender from punishment. Thirdly, the common law systems throughout the world, with the exception of a small minority of jurisdictions of the United States which have adopted without reservation Section 2.09 of the United States Model Penal Code, reject duress as a defence to the killing of innocent persons....

### D. The Rule Applicable to this Case ...

... [T]he law should not be the product or slave of logic or intellectual hair-splitting, but must serve broader normative purposes in light of its social, political and economic role. It is noteworthy that the authorities we have just cited issued their cautionary words in respect of domestic society and in respect of a range of ordinary crimes including kidnapping, assault, robbery and murder. Whilst reserving our comments on the appropriate rule for domestic national contexts, we cannot but stress that we are not, in the International Tribunal, concerned with ordinary domestic crimes. The purview of the International Tribunal relates to war crimes and crimes against humanity committed in armed conflicts of extreme violence with egregious dimensions. We are not concerned with the actions of domestic terrorists, gang-leaders and kidnappers. We are concerned that, in relation to the most heinous crimes known to humankind, the principles of law to which we give credence have the appropriate normative effect upon soldiers bearing weapons of destruction and upon the commanders who control them in armed conflict situations. The facts of this particular case, for example, involved the cold-blooded slaughter of 1200 men and boys by soldiers using automatic weapons. We must bear in mind that we are operating in the realm of international humanitarian law which has, as one of its prime objectives, the protection of the weak and vulnerable in such a situation where their lives and security are endangered. Concerns about the harm which could arise from admitting duress as a defence to murder were sufficient to persuade a majority of the House of Lords and the Privy Council to categorically deny the defence in the national context to prevent the growth of domestic crime and the impunity of miscreants. Are they now insufficient to persuade us to similarly reject duress as a complete defence in our application of laws designed to take account of humanitarian concerns in the arena of brutal war, to punish perpetrators of crimes against humanity and war crimes, and to deter the commission of such crimes in the future? If national law denies recognition of duress as a defence in respect of the killing of innocent persons, international criminal law can do no less than match that policy since it deals with murders often of far greater magnitude. If national law denies duress as a defence even in a case in which a single innocent life is extinguished due to action under duress, international law, in our view, cannot admit duress in cases which involve the slaughter of innocent human beings on a large scale. It must be our concern to facilitate the development and effectiveness of international humanitarian law and to promote its aims and application by recognising the normative effect which criminal law should have upon those subject to them. Indeed, Security Council resolution 827 (1993) establishes the International Tribunal expressly as a measure to "halt and effectively redress" the widespread and flagrant violations of international humanitarian law occurring in the territory of the former Yugoslavia and to contribute thereby to the restoration and maintenance of peace.

It might be urged that although the civil law jurisdictions allow duress as a defence to murder, there is no evidence that crimes such as murder and terrorism are any more prevalent in these societies than in common law jurisdictions. We are not persuaded by this argument. We are concerned primarily with armed conflict in which civilian lives, the lives of the most vulnerable, are at great risk. Historical records, past and recent, concerned with armed conflict give countless examples of threats being brought to bear upon combatants by their superiors when confronted with any show of reluctance or refusal on the part of the combatants to carry out orders to perform acts which are in clear breach of international humanitarian law. It cannot be denied that in an armed conflict, the frequency of situations in which persons are forced under duress to commit crimes and the magnitude of the crimes they are forced to commit are far greater than in any peacetime domestic environment . . .

### 2. An Exception Where the Victims Will Die Regardless of the Participation of the Accused?

It was suggested during the hearing of 26 May 1997 that neither the English national cases nor the post-World War Two military tribunal decisions specifically addressed the situation in which the accused faced the choice between his own death for not obeying an order to kill or participating in a killing which was inevitably going to occur regardless of whether he participated in it or not. It has been argued that in such a situation where the fate of the victim was already sealed, duress should constitute a complete defence. This is because the accused is then not choosing that one innocent human being should die rather than another. In a situation where the victim or victims would have died in any event, such as in the present case where the victims were to be executed by firing squad, there would be no reason for the accused to have sacrificed his life. The accused could not have saved the victims life by giving his own and thus, according to this argument, it is unjust and illogical for the law to expect an accused to sacrifice his life in the knowledge that the victims will die anyway.

For the reasons given below we would reject [this] approach.

### 3. Rejection of Utilitarianism and Proportionality Where Human Life Must Be Weighed

The [aforementioned] approach proceeds from the starting point of strict utilitarian logic based on the fact that if the victim will die anyway, the accused is not at all morally blameworthy for taking part in the execution; there is absolutely no reason why the accused should die as it would be unjust for the law to expect the accused to die for nothing. It should be immediately apparent that the assertion that the accused is not morally blameworthy where the victim would have died in any case depends entirely again upon a view of morality based on utilitarian logic. This does not, in our opinion, address the true rationale for our rejection of duress as a defence to the killing of innocent human beings. The approach we take does not involve a balancing of harms for and against killing but rests upon an application in the context of international humanitarian law of the rule that duress does not justify or excuse the killing of an innocent person. Our view is based upon a recognition that international humanitarian law should guide the conduct of combatants and their commanders.

There must be legal limits as to the conduct of combatants and their commanders in armed conflict.

In accordance with the spirit of international humanitarian law, we deny the availability of duress as a complete defence to combatants who have killed innocent persons. In so doing, we give notice in no uncertain terms that those who kill innocent persons will not be able to take advantage of duress as a defence and thus get away with impunity for their criminal acts in the taking of innocent lives.

(a) Proportionality. The notion of proportionality is raised with great frequency in the limited jurisprudence on duress. [According to the aforementioned] approach, the killing of the victims by the accused is apparently proportional to the fate faced by the accused if the victims were going to die anyway.

Proportionality is merely another way of referring to the utilitarian approach of weighing the balance of harms and adds nothing to the debate when it comes to human lives having to be weighed and when the law must determine, because a certain legal consequence will follow, that one life or a set of lives is more valuable than another. The Prosecution draws attention to the great difficulty in judging proportionality when it is human lives which must be weighed in the balance:

> [O]ne immediately sees even from a philosophical point of view the immensely difficult balancing which a court would have to engage in such a circumstance. It would be really a case of a numbers game, if you like, of: "Is it better to kill one person and save ten? Is it better to save one small child, let us say, as opposed to elderly people? Is it better to save a lawyer as opposed to an accountant?" One could engage in all sorts of highly problematical philosophical discussions.

These difficulties are clear where the court must decide whether or not duress is a defence by a straight answer, "yes" or "no". Yet, the difficulties are avoided somewhat when the court is instead asked not to decide whether or not the accused should have a complete defence but to take account of the circumstances in the flexible but effective facility provided by mitigation of punishment.

[Editor's Note: The judges then conclude that Erdemovic should not be allowed to plead duress as a complete defense to the crime charged, but that duress can be taken into account to mitigate punishment.]

### Separate and Dissenting Opinion of Judge Cassese

### ... II. Duress

*(OR: THE QUESTION OF WHETHER INTERNATIONAL CRIMINAL LAW UPHOLDS THE COMMON-LAW APPROACH TO DURESS IN CASE OF KILLING)*

#### A. Introduction

I also respectfully disagree with the conclusions of the majority of the Appeals Chamber concerning duress, as set out in the Joint Separate Opinion of their Honours Judge McDonald and Judge Vohrah and on the following grounds:

(i) after finding that no specific international rule has evolved on the question of whether duress affords a complete defence to the killing of innocent persons, the majority should have drawn the only conclusion imposed by law and logic, namely that the general rule on duress should apply—subject, of course, to the necessary requirements. In logic, if no exception to a general rule be proved, then the general rule prevails. Likewise in law, if one looks for a special rule governing a specific aspect of a matter and concludes that no such rule has taken shape, the only inference to be drawn is that the specific aspect is regulated by the rule governing the general matter;

(ii) instead of this simple conclusion, the majority of the Appeals Chamber has embarked upon a detailed investigation of "practical policy considerations" and has concluded by upholding "policy considerations" substantially based on English law. I submit that this examination is extraneous to the task of our Tribunal. This International Tribunal is called upon to apply international law, in particular our Statute and principles and rules of international humanitarian law and international criminal law. Our International Tribunal is a court of law; it is bound only by international law. It should therefore refrain from engaging in meta-legal analyses. In addition, it should refrain from relying exclusively on notions, policy considerations or the philosophical underpinnings of common-law countries, while disregarding those of civil-law countries or other systems of law. What is even more important, a policy-oriented approach in the area of criminal law runs contrary to the fundamental customary principle nullum crimen sine lege. On the strength of international principles and rules my conclusions on duress differ widely from those of the majority of the Appeals Chamber. I shall set out below the legal reasons which I believe support my dissent.

In short, I consider that: (1) under international criminal law duress may be generally urged as a defence, provided certain strict requirements are met; when it cannot be admitted as a defence, duress may nevertheless be acted upon as a mitigating circumstance; (2) with regard to war crimes or crimes against humanity whose underlying offence is murder or more generally the taking of human life, no special rule of customary international law has evolved on the matter; consequently, even with respect to these offences the general rule on duress applies; it follows that duress may amount to a defence provided that its stringent requirements are met. For offences involving killing, it is true, however, that one of the requirements (discussed at paragraph 42 below)—proportionality—would usually not be fulfilled.

Nevertheless, in exceptional circumstances this requirement might be met, for example, when the killing would be in any case perpetrated by persons other than the one acting under duress (since then it is not a question of saving your own life by killing another person, but of simply saving your own life when the other person will inevitably die, which may not be proportionate as a remedy); (3) the Appeals Chamber should therefore remit the case to a Trial Chamber on the issue of duress (as well as on the issue that the plea was not informed), directing the Trial Chamber to enter a not-guilty plea on behalf of Drazen Erdemovic (and then to satisfy itself, in trial proceedings, whether or not the Appellant acted under duress and consequently, whether or not he is excused).

Before I dwell on the specific question of duress in relation to crimes involving the taking of innocent lives, I consider it useful, and indeed necessary, briefly to expound the general notion of duress and the conditions for its applicability in international criminal law.

### B. Notion And Requirements Of Duress

Duress, namely acting under a threat from a third person of severe and irreparable harm to life or limb, entails that no criminal responsibility is incurred by the person acting under that threat. Duress is often termed "necessity", both in national legislation and in cases relating to war crimes or crimes against humanity. I too will have occasion to use these two terms as equivalent. However, as rightly pointed out in the British Manual of Military Law, from a technical viewpoint, necessity proper also covers situations other than those where one is faced with threats or compulsion of a third party, for instance the condition where a person "in extremity of hunger kills another person to eat him". In other words, necessity is a broader heading than duress, encompassing threats to life and limb generally and not only when they emanate from another person ...

Let us now turn to the conditions applicable to the defence of duress. The relevant case-law is almost unanimous in requiring four strict conditions to be met for duress to be upheld as a defence, namely:

(i) the act charged was done under an immediate threat of severe and irreparable harm to life or limb;

(ii) there was no adequate means of averting such evil;

(iii) the crime committed was not disproportionate to the evil threatened (this would, for example, occur in case of killing in order to avert an assault). In other words, in order not to be disproportionate, the crime committed under duress must be, on balance, the lesser of two evils;

(iv) the situation leading to duress must not have been voluntarily brought about by the person coerced.

In addition, the relevant national legislation supports the principle that the existence in law of any special duty on the part of the accused towards the victim may preclude the possibility of raising duress as a defence....

[Editor's Note: After discussing several cases—mostly from civil law jurisdictions—that allow duress to be raised as a defense to murder, Judge Cassese addressed what he calls the "proportionality" element of duress:]

The third criterion—proportionality (meaning that the remedy should not be disproportionate to the evil or that the lesser of two evils should be chosen)—will, in practice, be the hardest to satisfy where the underlying offence involves the killing of innocents. Perhaps—although that will be a matter for a Trial Chamber or a Judge to decide—it will never be satisfied where the accused is saving his own life at the expense of his victim, since there are enormous, perhaps insurmountable, philosophical, moral and legal difficulties in putting one life in the balance against that of others in this way: how can a judge satisfy himself that the death of one person is a lesser evil that the death of another? Conversely, however, where it is not a case of a direct choice between the life of the person acting under duress and the life of the victim—in situations, in other words, where there is a high probability that the person under duress will not be able to save the lives of the victims whatever he does—then duress may succeed as a defence. Again, this will be a matter for the judge or court hearing the case to decide in the light of the evidence available in this regard. The court may decide, in a given case, that the accused did not do all he could to save the victims before yielding to duress, or that it is too speculative to assert that they would have died in any event. The important point, however—and this is the fundamental source of my disagreement with the majority—is that this question should be for the Trial Chamber to decide with all the facts before it. The defence should not be cut off absolutely and a priori from invoking the excuse of duress by a ruling of this International Tribunal whereby, in law, the fact of acting under duress can never be a defence to killing innocents. This is altogether too dogmatic and, moreover, it is a stance unsupported by international law, where there is no rule to this effect; in international law there only exists a general rule stating that duress may be a defence when certain requirements are met.

These inferences, which I have drawn from the case-law, find support in the following considerations:

Firstly, it is extremely difficult to meet the requirements for duress where the offence involves killing of innocent human beings. This I infer from the fact that courts have very rarely allowed the defence of duress to succeed in cases involving unlawful killing even where they have in principle admitted the applicability of this defence. But for the Italian and German cases mentioned above, which stand out as exceptional, the only cases where national courts have upheld the plea of duress in relation to violations of international humanitarian law relate to offences other than killing. In this connection mention can be made of the well-known cases brought before United States Military Tribunals sitting at Nuremberg, Flick and Farben, as well as a few German cases. To my mind, this bears out the strong reluctance of national courts to make duress available in case of offences involving killing. The reason for this restrictive approach no doubt has its roots in the fundamental importance of human life to law and society. As the German Court of Assize of Arnsberg rightly pointed out in Wetzling et al., the right to life is one of the most fundamental and precious human rights, and any legal system is keen to safeguard it at the utmost; it follows that any legal endorsement of attacks on, or interference with, this right must be very strictly construed and only exceptionally admitted.

Secondly, it is a relevant consideration that the crime would have been committed in any case by a person other than the one acting under duress. This is borne out by a comparison of two different sets of cases. In cases such as Hölzer et al., where the accused did not raise any issue that the victims would have died in any event, and where he therefore raised duress simply as a choice between his life or that of his victim, the defence has been refused in principle, applying the classical formula that you are not entitled to save your own life at the expense of others. However, where the accused has been charged with participation in a collective killing which would have proceeded irrespective of whether the accused was a participant, the defence has in principle been allowed. In such cases, if duress failed as a defence, this was because the courts were not satisfied that duress had in fact been exerted on the accused—not because the remedy was disproportionate to the harm to be avoided. As far as the proportionality requirement is concerned, in all these cases the harm caused by not obeying the illegal order would not have been much greater than the harm which would have resulted from obeying it. This notion was manifestly the underlying idea in all the cases where duress was upheld by Italian and German courts after the Second World War. Arguably, the same reasoning was applied by the Judge-Advocate in the Jepsen case when he accepted that, in principle, duress could be a defence where the underlying offence is killing, because, on the accused's version of the facts, he could do nothing to save the lives of the victims and by refusing to obey the order would have only added the forfeiture of his life to theirs. However, the court, i.e., the jury, evidently did not believe Jepsen's account and convicted him (see paragraph 23, supra).

Thus the case-law seems to make an exception for those instances where—on the facts—it is highly probable, if not certain, that if the person acting under duress had refused to commit the crime, the crime would in any event have been carried out by persons other than the accused. The commonest example of such a case is where an execution squad has been assembled to kill the victims, and the accused participates, in some form, in the execution squad, either as an active member or as an organiser, albeit only under the threat of death. In this case, if an individual member of the execution squad first refuses to obey but has then to comply with the order as a result of duress, he may be excused: indeed, whether or not he is killed or instead takes part in the execution, the civilians, prisoners of war, etc., would be shot anyway. Were he to comply with his legal duty not to shoot innocent persons, he would forfeit his life for no benefit to anyone and no effect whatsoever apart from setting a heroic example for mankind (which the law cannot demand him to set): his sacrifice of his own life would be to no avail. In this case the evil threatened (the menace to his life and his subsequent death) would be greater than the remedy (his refraining from committing the crime, i.e., from participating in the execution).

In sum, the customary rule of international law on duress, as evolved on the basis of case-law and the military regulations of some States, does not exclude the applicability of duress to war crimes and crimes against humanity whose underlying offence is murder or unlawful killing. However, as the right to life is the most fundamental human right, the rule demands that the general requirements for duress be applied particularly strictly in the case of killing of innocent persons....

### D. Application To The Judgement Under Appeal

... [I]n applying the conclusions of law which I have reached above, in my view the Trial Chamber to which the matter is remitted must first of all determine whether the situation leading to duress was voluntarily brought about by the Appellant. In particular, the Trial Chamber must satisfy itself whether the military unit to which he belonged and in which he had voluntarily enlisted (the 10th Sabotage Unit) was purposefully intent upon actions contrary to international humanitarian law and the Appellant either knew or should have known of this when he joined the Unit or, if he only later became aware of it, that he then failed to leave the Unit or otherwise disengage himself from such actions. If the answer to this be in the affirmative, the Appellant could not plead duress. Equally, he could not raise this defence if he in any other way voluntarily placed himself in a situation he knew would entail the unlawful execution of civilians.

If, on the other hand, the above question be answered in the negative, and thus the Appellant would be entitled to urge duress, and the Trial Chamber must then satisfy itself that the other strict conditions required by international criminal law to prove duress are met in the instant case, namely:

(i) whether Appellant acted under a threat constituting imminent harm, both serious and irreparable, to his life or limb, or to the life or limb of his family, when he killed approximatively 70 unarmed Muslim civilians at the Branjevo farm near Pilica in Bosnia on 16 July 1995;

(ii) whether Appellant had no other adequate means of averting this harm other than executing the said civilians;

(iii) whether the execution of the said civilians was proportionate to the harm Appellant sought to avoid. As I have stated above, this requirement cannot normally be met with respect to offences involving the killing of innocents, since it is impossible to balance one life against another.

However, the Trial Chamber should determine, on its assessment of the evidence, whether the choice faced by Appellant was between refusing to participate in the killing of the Muslim civilians and being killed himself or participating in the killing of the Muslim civilians who would be killed in any case by the other soldiers and thus being allowed to live. If the Trial Chamber concludes that it is the latter, then Appellant's defence of duress will have succeeded.

## *Notes and Questions*

1. Note that in the vast majority of common law jurisdictions duress may not be invoked as a defense to homicide. *A fortiori*, in these jurisdictions duress will not be a defense to a crime against humanity that—like the offense charged in *Erdemovic*—involves the killing of dozens of human beings. In contrast, most civil law jurisdictions allow defendants to plead duress as a defense to homicide. Therefore—as Judge Cassese argues—it is likely that in these jurisdictions a defendant like Erdemovic would be allowed to invoke duress as a defense to the killing of many innocent civilians.

2. Perhaps the most obvious reason why duress is not a defense to homicide in most common law countries is that in many of these jurisdictions duress is a defense only if the actor causes a lesser evil. This sounds in the language of justification. Given that it is often held that it may never be justified to take innocent life, common law jurisdictions that frame the duress inquiry in lesser evil terms will usually conclude that the defense is unavailable in homicide prosecutions. On the other hand, arguing that duress is a defense to homicide is much easier in civil law countries, for duress is conventionally viewed in these jurisdictions as an excuse. Therefore, the defendant who pleads duress in civil law

countries is seldom required to show that his conduct inflicted a lesser evil. Rather, he has to demonstrate that he yielded to a threat that a reasonable person in his position would have also succumbed to. Did Judges McDonald and Vohrah treat duress as a justification or an excuse in *Erdemovic*? Did Judge Cassese treat duress as a justification or an excuse? Explain.

3. Would the defendant in *Erdemovic* be allowed to plead duress in an American jurisdiction that follows the Model Penal Code's approach to the defense? Is the Model Penal Code's approach to duress more compatible with the traditional approach to the defense adopted in most common law jurisdictions or with the conventionally accepted view of the defense in civil law jurisdictions? Explain.

4. In his dissenting opinion, Judge Cassese argues that for a defendant to successfully plead duress "the crime committed under duress must be, on balance, the lesser of two evils." As a result, he argues that duress will often fail as a defense to homicide, for the killing of an innocent human being is unlikely to be the lesser of two evils. Nevertheless, he suggested that Erdemovic's killing of innocent civilians might have been the lesser of two evils, given that the civilians were going to die regardless of whether he killed them or not. Therefore, had he refused to kill them, the civilians would have died and—additionally—Erdemovic would have been killed. By yielding to the threat, however, the same number of civilians died, but at least he was not killed. Consequently, Cassese argued that by succumbing to the threat Erdemovic arguably chose the lesser of two evils, for less people died than had he resisted the threats. Is Cassese's view of duress more compatible with the defense being considered a justification or an excuse? Are you persuaded by Cassese's argument in favor of a possible acquittal in this case? Why or why not? Is there an alternative argument that better explains why it may make sense to acquit a defendant like Erdemovic?

## § 17.06 Duress: Scholarly Debates

### Luis E. Chiesa, *Duress, Demanding Heroism and Proportionality*

41 Vand. J. Trans. L. 741 (2008)

#### 4. Understandability and the Capacity to Prevent the Harm Threatened from Occurring

[An] important consideration to take into account when deciding whether to exempt a coerced actor from penal liability is whether he could have avoided harming his victims by choosing to resist the threats. This factor appeared to be determinative for Judge Cassese in Erdemovic; in his dissenting opinion, he argued that a coerced actor who kills innocent human beings should be relieved of criminal responsibility if "it is highly probable, if not certain, that if the person acting under duress had refused to commit the crime, the crime would in any event have been carried out by persons other than the accused."

Judge Cassese's position assumes that, in these instances, deciding to kill the innocent people constitutes the lesser evil because "the evil threatened (the menace to [the life of the coerced actor] and his subsequent death) would be greater than the remedy (his refraining from committing the crime, i.e., from participating in the execution)." Therefore, he suggests that this type of case invites a variation of the justification commonly known as the "choice of evils" defense.

An example in Judge Cassese's dissent illustrates this lesser evil argument. Suppose that "a driver of a van … transporting victims to a place of execution … is told by the executioners he must shoot one of the victims or he himself will be shot." Assuming that "[t]he victims who are at the execution site will certainly die in any event," shooting the innocent victim would constitute the lesser evil because:

> (1) If the driver resists the threats, he will be killed. Shortly thereafter, the innocent person that he was ordered to kill will die anyway. Thus, two people will die if the driver resists the threat;
>
> (2) If the driver yields to the threat, his life will be spared, but an innocent victim will die. Thus, one person will die if he capitulates to the threat.
>
> (3) Two people will die if the driver resists the threats, and one will die if he gives way to the coercion. Therefore, the decision to succumb to the threat and kill the innocent victim would constitute the lesser evil.

Based on this logic, Judge Cassese concludes that, even though "the crime committed under duress must be, on balance, the lesser of two evils," someone who is coerced into "participating in the killing of … civilians who would be killed in any case by the other[s]" has a valid duress defense.

Judge Cassese's contention is objectionable because it presupposes an oversimplified calculus of what constitutes the lesser evil. In addition to comparing the number of people that would have been killed had the coerced actor resisted the threats with the amount of people that would have been killed had the actor yielded to the coercion, one should also take into consideration that, by giving way to the threats, the actor is aiding someone else in the commission of a wrongful and heinous act. This collaboration in the perpetration of a crime is, in and of itself, an evil that should weigh against yielding to the threats. Thus, as the philosopher Frances Kamm has suggested, these types of decisions are "not merely a matter of weighing the lives saved versus the life lost," for the agent's moral integrity is compromised by his forced involvement in the production of evil.

Similarly, Professor Robinson has stated that "the harm to the social order inherent in unjustified aggression" should be taken into account when balancing evils. Scholars in continental legal traditions also argue that the evil inherent in human collaboration with wrongful conduct is a relevant consideration in deciding which conduct constitutes the lesser evil. One Spanish criminal law scholar has asserted that when balancing evils one must keep in mind that:

> [T]he law compares "evils", not "personal interests." [This is crucial], since the gravity of an "evil" is not only determined by the value of the "personal interest" harmed, but by the way in which it is harmed as well. Since a harm produced by nature does not allow for an assessment of anything else besides the personal interest harmed, the gravity of the "evil" in such a case is equal to the importance of the injured interest. However, the "evil" caused [by the conduct of another] entails not only the harming of a personal interest, but, additionally, a perturbation of the social order.… Thus, [a valid lesser evils defense requires that the personal interest saved] be sufficiently more important [than the one harmed] to compensate for the additional [harm] that the [perturbation of the social order entails].

Therefore, it may not be true, as Judge Cassese suggests, that killing "x" people is necessarily a lesser evil than killing "x + 1" people. When engaging in this delicate balancing of interests, one must take into account not only the lives at stake but also the evil that the coerced actor's aggression represents. Thus, in the case of a coerced actor who saves her own life by killing many people who would have died soon anyway, one must weigh not only the number of lives sacrificed and saved but also the evil inherent in the actor's collaboration with the wrongful conduct of the coercer. It is nevertheless unclear whether this additional consideration tilts the balance decisively against justifying the coerced actor's conduct constituted as the lesser of two evils.

Fortunately, there is no need to engage in this delicate balancing act. The fact that the coerced actor's victims would have died soon anyway is relevant to determining whether the actor's conduct generates sufficient understanding among the public to warrant an exemption from criminal liability. Although this fact is not necessarily determinative when examining whether the actor's conduct is justified as a choice of the lesser evil, it is decisive when evaluating whether her action should be excused because of the coercion.

Thus, although a coerced actor who harms an innocent victim may act wrongfully despite the fact that she could not have prevented the harm, this fact provides a sound reason to excuse her conduct. There is no need to inquire whether the harm caused was proportional to the harm averted in order to determine whether to excuse the coerced actor. Because the actor effectively lacked the capacity to prevent the harm threatened from occurring, punishing the actor for deciding to save her own life instead of dying to protect innocent people who were going to die anyway would be unfair. In sum, yielding to the coercive threats in this case is wrongful but perfectly understandable and, hence, not punishable ...

[As a result,] Erdemovic should have prevailed on a plea of duress. Because he could not have prevented the deaths of his victims even if he had resisted coercion, it is unfair to punish him for choosing to yield to the coercion in order to save his own life. Hence, although the fact that he lacked the capacity to prevent the death of the civilians should not be considered a sufficient reason to justify his conduct, it offers compelling grounds for excusing his admittedly wrongful act.

## Thomas Weigend, *Kill or Be Killed: Another Look at Erdemovic*

10 J. Int. Crim. Just. 1219 (2012)

### Duress as a Justification

Opinions are divided as to whether duress provides a justification or an excuse—and as to whether that makes any difference. My claim is that duress may, depending on the circumstances, justify the actor's conduct or excuse him, and that the distinction between these two situations makes a great difference.

### A. Duress and the Logic of Justification

An act that would otherwise be criminal is justified if the law prefers the commission of the crime to any alternative outcome of the situation. For example, in the case of self-defence the law prefers that the assailant be hit than the victim of the attack being killed or injured. Any ground of justification affords the actor a right to do what would otherwise be a crime; and at the same time, it confers a legal obligation upon the victim of the justified act—for example, the assailant who has created a situation of self-defence—to suffer his loss in silence. The reason for that expectation may be either the prior unlawful conduct of the affected person (as in the self-defence situation or when a police officer arrests an escaped prisoner) or a general obligation of extending minimal solidarity to one's fellow persons.

The obligation of solidarity explains the justification of acts of necessity. If I need to break my absent neighbour's window and take his fire extinguisher in order to stop a fire from burning down my house, I am justified by necessity; and the reason that my neighbour is not allowed to stop my action is the law's expectation that he should give up his minor property interest in order to avoid a much greater harm to my property. The reason for my neighbour's obligation lies not simply in the fact that the (otherwise) criminal act is the 'lesser evil' and its commission creates a net gain (his window is broken, but my house still stands), because he is not responsible for contributing to achieving 'net gains'. The law may oblige him to give up his minor interest only if that sacrifice is demanded by a rule of minimal solidarity among fellow men; this implies that the value differential between the interest affected and the interest saved must be so great as to trigger this obligation.

Given this general understanding of a justification, may a situation of duress ever *justify* the criminal conduct of a person who has been coerced by another person to commit the crime? In looking for an answer, we have to assume an *Erdemović*-like situation where there exists no alternative for the actor to avoid the conflict. The actor will certainly be killed or severely injured unless he carries out the order to commit a crime. Assume Erdemović had (credibly) been told that his wife and small child would be killed unless he tortured a Muslim prisoner; if he had then given in to the coercion and had tortured the prisoner, thereby saving the lives of his loved ones, can we say that he was justified? I think that the answer should be yes. Hard as it may appear on the prisoner, the law expects him to suffer the torture if that is the only means to save two lives—the balance of interests is so strong in favour of Erdemović taking the required action that the prisoner's interests in his health and dignity must cease. We may conclude that a person committing a crime under duress *can* be justified; but justification requires that a clearly superior interest be saved by the commission of the crime, because only under that condition can the victim of the offence fairly be expected to sacrifice his interest.

### B. Counter Arguments

Two arguments have been advanced against this conclusion. In their joint opinion in *Erdemović*, Judges McDonald and Vorah quote no less an authority than James F. Stephen-for the proposition that:

> It is, of course, a misfortune for a man that he should be placed between two fires [i.e., to be killed by the threatener if he disobeys, or be convicted by the law if he obeys], but it would be a much greater misfortune for society at large if criminals could confer impunity upon their agents by threatening them with death or violence if they refused to execute their commands. If impunity could be so secured a wide door would be open to collusion, and encouragement would be given to associations of malefactors, secret or otherwise.

But is it true that wicked superiors can 'confer impunity' on their subordinates—and presumably on themselves as a result—by coercing them into executing their unlawful commands? This may have been the case at the time when Sir James Stephen wrote his treatise, but in the meantime the concepts of indirect perpetration, accessorial liability, and—as a last resort—command responsibility have developed such that at least the superior would not escape punishment, because his criminal liability does not depend on the subordinate's punishability. As far as the subordinate in the unfortunate position of Dražen Erdemović is concerned, he is certainly punishable if he colludes with the superior, knowing that the threat of being killed for disobedience has been made for show only. If, on the other hand, the threat to the soldier's life is real, it remains technically true that the commander's unlawful coercion is the *cause* of the soldier's impunity, but the *reason* for that result is the justifying effect of the situation of duress.

Luis Chiesa has formulated another objection to justifying a person acting under duress. He claims that, when gauging the proportionality of the harm caused, 'one should also take into consideration that, by giving way to the threats, the actor is aiding someone else in the commission of a wrongful and heinous act' and that 'one must weigh not only the number of lives sacrificed and saved but also the evil inherent in the actor's collaboration with the wrongful conduct of the coercer'. But does a woman 'collaborate' with a gunman who points a gun at her head, does she 'aid' him when she carries out the gunman's orders? The terms chosen by Chiesa to describe the situation seem strangely inapposite. In purely objective terms, one can say that the act of the coerced woman causes the result that the coercer wishes to occur; but would 'aiding' and 'collaboration' not require more than that, would there not have to be at least a minimal amount of approval and willing collusion with the coercer's plans?

Several German writers have come to a similar conclusion as Chiesa by considering the position of the victim of the coerced assault. Should the victim not be permitted to defend himself against the coerced woman's attack? The answer lies in the principle of minimal solidarity and the ensuing high standard of proportionality for justification by duress. Returning to Erdemović, if he is threatened with torture unless he beats up an innocent civilian, that civilian may lawfully resist Erdemović's assault in self-defence even if the injuries Erdemović has been threatened with are more serious than those Erdemović would cause to the civilian. But if, as in the example given above, Erdemović's family was certain to die if Erdemović did not carry out the unlawful command, then the victim has no right to defend himself.

### C. Can Killing be Justified?

Do these considerations change when the victim's *life* is at stake? May duress ever justify killing? Several considerations speak against an affirmative answer. The least convincing among them is the 'sanctity of life', cited by English courts as an argument for an absolute ban of the defence of duress against charges of murder. If, as in the paradigmatic necessity case of *Dudley and Stephens*, the lives of three men can be saved by killing one, the 'sanctity of life' is not a good argument for criminally prohibiting the killing and thus to prevent the saving of three lives. Nor is, in a secular state, the religious postulate that man should not play God by deciding who is to live and who is to die a reliable foundation for a criminal conviction for murder; this applies especially where the actor saved several lives by sacrificing one person.

But any appeal to duress as a justification must end at the limits of the solidarity principle. We may all be willing to offer our property or even to suffer some temporary pain in order to save a life; but most of us would—behind a veil of ignorance—resist giving up our life for the sake of others, even for the greater good of society. Nor is there a good reason for the law to demand or expect the sacrifice of a person's life, even if several others could thereby be saved. Therefore, killing a person cannot be justified even where the killer is himself coerced at gunpoint and will eventually be killed if he does not carry out the command to shoot. Even a crude utilitarian calculus does not trump every individual's right to live. If we assume that a group of ten soldiers is told that they will all be executed unless they kill one innocent prisoner, they are not justified when they shoot the man, because the law cannot demand the victim to give up his life for the lives of the soldiers.

But in the *Erdemović* situation, there is a further complication that should give us pause. The Muslim prisoners were lined up to be shot, with their hands tied behind their backs, and given the large number of Serb soldiers present and willing to execute the prisoners, their lives were inescapably doomed. If Erdemović had been a hero and had joined the ranks of the prisoners, they would have been killed, at most a few minutes later, by other soldiers. Because of this state of affairs, Judges Cassese and Stephen thought that the requirement of proportionality was fulfilled. As Judge Cassese eloquently stated the matter:

> Thus the case-law seems to make an exception for those instances where—on the facts—it is highly probable, if not certain, that if the person acting under duress had refused to commit the crime, the crime would in any event have been carried out by persons other than the accused. The commonest example of such a case is where an execution squad has been assembled to kill the victims, and the accused participates, in some form, in the execution squad, either as an active member or as an organiser, albeit only under the threat of death. In this case, if an individual member of the execution squad first refuses to obey but has then to comply with the order as a result of duress, he may be excused: indeed, whether or not he is killed or instead takes part in the execution, the civilians, prisoners of war, etc., would be shot anyway. Were he to comply with his legal duty not to shoot innocent persons, he would forfeit his life for no benefit to anyone and no effect whatsoever apart from setting a heroic example for mankind (which the law cannot demand him to set): his sacrifice of his own life would be to no avail. In this case the evil threatened (the menace to his life and his subsequent death) would be greater than the remedy (his refraining from committing the crime, i.e., from participating in the execution).

But is it appropriate to compare Erdemović's actual conduct (the shooting of 70 innocent Muslim men) with something that never happened (Erdemović refusing to shoot and then being killed along with the prisoners) and then to exonerate him on the basis of this hypothetical course of events? Wouldn't that open the floodgates for the familiar argument, 'If I hadn't done it someone else would have done it; therefore I'm innocent?' If we insist—as we did above—that none of the victims may be demanded by law to offer their lives in order to save Erdemović, doesn't that create an absolute barrier to justifying Erdemović's actual conduct, regardless of what might have happened if he had refused to shoot? Assume that Erdemović is one of very few specialists in a technique requisite to kill 70 innocent men hiding away in a subterranean cave. If Erdemović, who is threatened with his own death, refuses to apply that technique, the commanders need two weeks to find and fly in another specialist. Would we then still readily accept Erdemović's plea that 'the victims would have died anyway, so I was justified in killing them in order to save my life'? We would at least have doubts, and these doubts may increase the longer the remaining life span of the victims becomes.

The critical factor in the *Erdemović* situation may thus not be the fact that Erdemović could have been replaced as a member of the execution squad but the fact that the victims had, under the circumstances, only a few more seconds or perhaps minutes to live, regardless of Erdemović's decision. Was their remaining life span so short that their lives should not enter into the proportionality calculus at all? Is that calculus then 'Erdemović's life compared with nothing'? May, in other words, the law demand a person to give up the last—rather unpleasant—three minutes of his life in order to save a young man's life who has a reasonably bright and long future before him if he is allowed to shoot the victims?

In Germany, this question has been debated extensively in connection with a statute that would have permitted the air force to shoot down any airplane abducted by terrorists and assumed to be flying, as in the 11 September situation, into a building or other place where it would kill any number of victims on the ground. This law would have given state agents a licence to kill the innocent passengers of the abducted plane on the same rationale as proposed here for the *Erdemović* conundrum: the passengers are doomed in any event and their last few minutes until the hijacked plane crashes are not worth living.

The German Federal Constitutional Court rejected this argument and held that the relevant provision of the statute violated the constitutional protection of the right to life as well as the guarantee of human dignity. The Court explicitly refused to discount the value of a human life because the passengers were not expected to live for more than another few minutes. If one follows this line of thought, there can be no justification in the *Erdemović* situation, because even the few seconds the prisoners had yet to live count as much as any other life and they cannot be deemed to have lost the protection of the law. Although this absolutist position has the great advantage of precluding any line drawing according to the number of minutes or hours left to live, it puts theory before reality. If one could ask one of the prisoners whether he agreed to be shot now by Erdemović rather than two minutes later by another soldier, if that sacrifice would save Erdemović's life, most prisoners would probably be glad to give up their last two minutes of agony, even if they didn't care too much about Erdemović's personal fate.

I therefore tend to regard Erdemović's deed as justified, based on the specific, extraordinary facts stipulated by the parties. But I would be hard-placed to define a general rule on when a remaining life span is so negligible that it does not count any more, so that a person who saves his own life by killing another person may be justified. Certainly, justification would not extend to a situation in which the actor would afford the victims another day or even a few hours of their lives by remaining passive. The test might be whether a reasonable victim would tend to insist on staying alive even for the short time still available.

## Notes and Questions

1. Both of the articles excerpted in this section discuss the plausibility of Judge Cassese's contention that the defendant in Erdemovic may have chosen the lesser evil when he capitulated to the threats. More specifically, both readings address the issue of whether the fact that the victims would have died regardless of whether the defendant yielded to the threat is a sufficient reason to justify killing the civilians. Professor Weigend contends that Erdemovic's killing of the civilians is likely justified if the civilians were going to soon die anyway because:

> If one could ask one of the prisoners whether he agreed to be shot now by Erdemović rather than two minutes later by another soldier, if that sacrifice would save Erdemović's life, most prisoners would probably be glad to give up their last two minutes of agony, even if they didn't care too much about Erdemović's personal fate.

Do you agree that most prisoners would agree to be shot now by Erdemovic rather than two minutes later by someone else if they knew that allowing Erdemovic to shoot them now would spare Erdemovic's life? Would *you* agree to be killed earlier by a person if you knew that you would die anyway in a couple of minutes and that allowing that person to kill you earlier would likely save that person's life? Assuming that both of these questions are answered affirmatively, does it follow that killing the prisoners (or you) is justified in these cases rather than excused? Explain.

2. The first article excerpted in this section argues that balancing evils in duress cases is more complicated than simply counting the number of lives at stake or determining whether

the victims are going to die anyway. According to the article, a special harm inherent in duress—which is not present in standard lesser evils cases—is that the coerced actor collaborates or is complicit in the wrongful acts of another. Therefore, the coerced actor's conduct amounts to an instance in which the "right" (resisting the wrongful coercion) yields to the "wrong" (the unlawful coercion itself). The legal system should not be indifferent to this, given that—as the doctrine of self-defense illustrates—it is appropriate for the law to communicate to the citizenry that those who are in the "right" should not yield to those who are in the "wrong" (unlawful aggressors). By the same token, it is appropriate for the law—at least in the realm of justification—to communicate that yielding to the "wrong" is discouraged. In the context of *Erdemovic*, this provides an argument against justifying the defendant's conduct, for doing so would communicate approval of those who yield to the "wrong." This, however, is precisely the sort of conduct that the law of justification ought to discourage. Do you find this argument persuasive? Why or why not?

3. Professor Weigend takes issue with the aforementioned argument. He argues that it is odd to describe the coerced actor who yields to the unlawful threat as a person who "collaborates" with or "aids" the wrongful aggressor. According to Weigend, "aiding" and "collaboration" require more than yielding to coercion. In addition, Weigend contends that there needs to be "at least a minimal amount of approval and willing collusion with the coercer's plans." Do you agree that the coerced actor "aids" the unlawful coercer only if he "approves" the coercer's plans? Explain. Does the law of complicity define "aiding" the perpetrator as "approving" of her plan or does it define "aiding" the perpetrator as intentionally engaging in conduct that helps the perpetrator? Did Erdemovic "intentionally engage in conduct" that helped the coercer carry out their murderous plan? Did Erdemovic purposely yield to the "wrong" represented by the coercer's threats? Is it inappropriate to capitulate to such threats regardless of whether the victims are going to die anyway or is it appropriate to capitulate to such threats if the victims are going to die anyway?

4. Professor Weigend suggests that if Erdemovic's killing of the civilians is justified—as he argues it might be—"then the victim[s] ha[ve] no right to defend [themselves]" against Erdemovic's conduct. Do you agree that the victims in Erdemovic should not be able to use force to prevent Erdemovic from killing them? Explain. Would the victims have a right to kill Erdemovic if they knew that they were going to die two minutes later? Why or why not?

5. In the first article excerpted in this section it is argued that—contrary to what Judge Cassese and Professor Weigend argue—the fact that Erdemovic lacked the capacity to prevent the death of the civilians should not be considered a sufficient reason to justify his conduct. Nevertheless, the article suggests that this fact does offer compelling grounds for excusing Erdemovic's admittedly wrongful act. Because he could not have prevented the deaths of his victims even if he had resisted coercion, it is unfair to punish him for choosing to yield to the coercion in order to save his own life. Hence, Erdemovic should have prevailed on a plea of duress. Do you agree that there are sound reasons for acquitting Erdemovic? If so, is it better to classify the killing of civilians in this case as justified or excused? Why?

# Chapter 18

# Insanity

## § 18.01 Insanity: The M'Naghten Test

### Maas v. Territory

Supreme Court of the Territory of Oklahoma, 1901
63 P. 960

BURWELL, J.

The appellant was tried and convicted of the crime of murder, in the district court of Blaine county, and sentenced to life imprisonment at hard labor. From this sentence he appealed to this court, and contends that the trial court erred in two of its instructions to the jury upon the defense of insanity, and these instructions we will now consider:

> "Instruction 28. In this case it is claimed for the defendant that, at the time of the commission of the act, his mind and judgment were affected by an insane delusion, or by insanity, and to such an extent as to render him of unsound mind, and not responsible for his acts.
>
> "Instruction 29. In reference to this point, you are instructed that although you may believe from the evidence that the defendant, at the time of the killing of his wife, Martha Maas, was affected by an insanity, or was laboring under an insane delusion, yet this would not exempt him from liability for his acts, if the jury believe from the evidence, beyond a reasonable doubt, that he intentionally fired the shot or shots which killed the deceased, and that he knew and was conscious at the time that what he was doing was wrong, and punishable by the law of this territory."

To the giving of each of these instructions the defendant saved an exception. If these two instructions stood alone, unaided by any other, it might be said that they were insufficient to present fully the question of insanity; but when considered in connection with the other instructions requested by the defendant, and given, they are a correct statement of the law.

Instruction 28 is merely a statement of the defendant's contention, and instruction 29 states the rule of law applicable thereto. Before discussing the general rules of law regarding insane persons, we will notice the express provisions of our own statutes. Section 5372, St. 1893, provides: "An act done by a person in a state of insanity cannot be punished as a public offense, nor can a person be tried, adjudged to punishment or punished for a public offense while he is insane." Section 1852, St. 1893: "All persons are capable of committing crimes except those belonging to the following classes: *** Lunatics, insane persons, and all persons of unsound mind, including persons temporarily or partially deprived of reason, upon proof that, at the time of committing the act charged against them, they were incapable of knowing its wrongfulness."

Now, it is contended by the appellant's counsel that the statute recognizes two classes: (1) That one who is a lunatic or insane cannot, under any circumstances, be punished for an act done by him; and (2) that one of unsound mind, including persons temporarily or partially deprived of reason, cannot be punished for a criminal act upon proof that at the time of committing the act charged against him he was incapable of knowing its wrongfulness. This position is incorrect. We think that the language, "upon proof that at the time of committing the act charged against them they were incapable of knowing its wrongfulness," modifies "lunatics" and "insane persons," as well as "persons of unsound mind" and "persons temporarily or partially deprived of reason." In other words, the language, "upon proof that at the time of committing the act charged against them they were incapable of knowing its wrongfulness," modifies all of subdivision 4 of section 1852 which precedes it; and an insane person or a lunatic, before he can be excused from the consequences of an act which is declared to be a crime, on the ground of insanity or lunacy, must introduce his proof to show that, at the time of the commission of the act charged, he did not, by reason of his insanity or lunacy, have sufficient understanding to know that the act was wrong.

Under this section of the statute, the test of responsibility is fixed at the point where one has the mental capacity to know that the act is wrong, and if one has sufficient mental capacity to distinguish between right and wrong, as applied to the particular act, and to understand the nature and consequences of such act, he is responsible for the same; and it is immaterial what standard scientific men may fix, or by what rules the medical profession determines that one is a lunatic or insane, he is in law insane or a lunatic, or of unsound mind, or temporarily or partially deprived of reason, to such an extent as will excuse him from punishment, only when he has not the capacity to know the wrongfulness of the particular act, but the knowledge of the wrongfulness of an act also embraces capacity to understand the nature and consequences of the same. But no matter what the condition of a defendant's mind at the time of committing an act which the statute declares to be criminal, he can only be excused, where his defense is lunacy, insanity, or unsoundness of mind, upon proof that he was incapable of knowing its wrongfulness, and the duty of establishing this proof is upon the defendant. But to what extent?

Upon this point the authorities differ. Two states, New Jersey and Delaware, follow the rule that the defendant must prove his insanity beyond a reasonable doubt before he can be acquitted. But perhaps two-thirds of the states follow the rule that the defendant must prove his insanity by a preponderance of the evidence. Among the states following this rule are Alabama, Arkansas, California, Connecticut, Georgia, Idaho, Iowa, Kentucky, Louisiana, Maine, Massachusetts, Minnesota, Missouri, North Carolina, Ohio, Pennsylvania, South Carolina, Texas, Virginia, West Virginia, and Nevada, and this is the rule in England. One of the best-considered cases which follows this rule is State v. Lewis (Nev.) 22 Pac. 241, written by Chief Justice Hawley. This opinion is clear and logical, and shows great research and a thorough understanding of the subject. But with the development of criminal law, and the advancement of civilization, the rules which once governed the defense of insanity are being relaxed so as to give defendants the fullest opportunity to present the truth to the court and jury, that full justice may be done; and, while it is true that this defense is sometimes successfully manufactured and imposed upon courts and juries, the adjudicated cases show no greater abuse of this defense than of the defense of alibi or self-defense.

The defense of insanity, when successfully made, appeals to the tenderest sentiments and mercies of the jury, but when feigned and detected it invites their utmost contempt; and, while juries are always ready to deal kindly with one who is so unfortunate as to be dethroned of his reason to such an extent that he cannot distinguish between right and wrong, they are also, as a rule, quick to punish a guilty defendant who tries to escape the consequences of his act through fraud and deceit. Therefore, viewing this defense from every standpoint, we see no good reason why the defense of insanity should be singled out and governed by rules as to burden of proof different from those applicable to other cases, and we feel constrained to enunciate the rule as to the burden of proof, where the defense is insanity, to be this: Every person is presumed to be sane, or of sound mind, and able to distinguish between right and wrong, as applied to the particular act, and to understand the nature and consequences of such act; and the burden is upon the defendant in the first instance to overcome this presumption by introducing sufficient evidence to raise a reasonable doubt as to his sanity. When this is done, then the state must prove the defendant's sanity beyond a reasonable doubt, in order to secure a conviction; and if, taking the evidence all together, the jury entertain a reasonable doubt as to the defendant's sanity, he should be acquitted. As has been well said by some of our ablest jurists, to doubt the defendant's sanity is to doubt his intent, and where one has not capacity to form an intent there can be no crime. Hence the above rule, which is now the settled law of the following states: Illinois, Indiana, Kansas, Michigan, Mississippi, New Hampshire, New York, and Nebraska. Some of the authorities go to the extent of holding that the defendant is not required to introduce sufficient evidence to raise a reasonable doubt of his sanity, but, if he introduces any evidence tending to prove insanity in the slightest degree, that the state must then prove his sanity beyond a reasonable doubt. This rule is manifestly unjust to the state. A defendant is presumed to be sane, and this presumption continues until a reasonable doubt of his sanity is raised by competent evidence, and, under our statutes, the burden of raising this doubt is placed upon the defendant.

Section 5227, St. 1893, provides: "Upon a trial for murder, the commission of the homicide by the defendant being proved, the burden of proving circumstances of mitigation, or that justify or excuse it, devolves upon him, unless the proof on the part of the prosecution tends to show that the crime committed only amounts to manslaughter, or that the defendant was justifiable or excusable." This statute was originally adopted in California, and has been repeatedly construed by the supreme court of that state. The early cases laid down the rule that in all trials for murder, the commission of the homicide being proved, the burden of proving circumstances of mitigation, or that justify or excuse the killing, devolves upon the defendant, and that such mitigation, justification, or excuse must be proved by a preponderance of evidence; but the later cases have repudiated this doctrine, and now hold that this section of the statute simply casts upon the defendant the burden of introducing sufficient evidence to raise a reasonable doubt of his guilt of murder, and this is the construction which we adopt. If the proof on the part of the prosecution tends to show that the crime committed only amounts to manslaughter, or that the defendant was justifiable or excusable, no evidence need be introduced by him; but, if the proof of the territory does not tend to show justification, excuse, or mitigation, then the burden is on the defendant to introduce sufficient evidence to raise a reasonable doubt as to his guilt of murder. Therefore, under our statute, a defendant is required to do more than introduce some evidence tending to prove his insanity. He must introduce sufficient evidence to raise a reasonable doubt of his sanity before the prosecution is required to introduce any evidence upon that subject. There was no error in the instructions complained of, and the instructions on the question of insanity, when considered all together, state the law fully and very liberally for the defendant …

The case should be affirmed, and the judgment of the trial court carried into execution. It is so ordered.

## *Notes and Questions*

1. A person who commits a crime while she is legally insane is excused. Nonetheless, a person held not guilty by reason of insanity may be committed to a mental institution until she is no longer a menace to society. Therefore, as opposed to what happens to defendants who are excused pursuant to some other defense (e.g., duress), those who are excused by reason of insanity may be deprived of their freedom in spite of their acquittal. Furthermore, given that the deprivation of liberty that may follow from an insanity acquittal is predicated on the need to protect society from a dangerous individual rather than on the interest in exacting retribution or bringing about an optimal level of deterrence, the insane offender may very well end up spending more time in confinement if he successfully pleads insanity than if he actually pleads guilty. If he pleads guilty, he will—in principle—be released after serving his sentence. In contrast, if he is acquitted by reason of insanity, he may be held indefinitely. If this is the case, what incentive is there for a defendant to plead insanity? In which cases—if any—would it make sense to raise the insanity defense? Should a defendant that is committed following an acquittal by reason of insanity be released after his commitment has exceeded the amount of time that he would have spent imprisoned had he been held guilty of the offense charged? Why or why not?

2. The *Maas* case illustrates the legal test for insanity applied in the majority of American jurisdictions. This rule traces back its origins to the English case of *M'Naghten*, 8 Eng.Rep. 718 (1843). According to the so-called *M'Naghten* rule, mental disease or defect is a defense only if it prevents the defendant either from understanding the nature of his act or from comprehending the wrongfulness of his conduct. A frequently cited example of the former is that of a person who is squeezing his spouse's neck while actually believing that he is squeezing lemons. If this belief was brought about by a mental disease or defect, it would preclude the imposition of liability under *M'Naghten* because it prevents the defendant from understanding what he is doing. An example of the latter would be the case of a paranoid schizophrenic who kills her spouse because she hallucinated that her spouse was poisoning her food. The defendant may be acquitted under *M'Naghten* because her mental disease or defect prevented her from understanding that killing her spouse was wrong. Finally, note that insanity is a defense only if the impairment of the cognitive capabilities of the defendant is brought about by a "mental disease or defect." As a result, other types of impairments—such as those that may arise as a consequence of environmental factors or cultural forces—do not generally give rise to an insanity defense, even if they prevent the defendant form knowing that what he is doing is wrong.

3. The Court in *Maas* concluded that the state had the burden of disproving insanity beyond a reasonable doubt. While this rule is followed in many state jurisdictions, others place the burden of proving insanity by a preponderance of the evidence on the defendant. The Supreme Court of the United States upheld the validity of shifting the burden of proving insanity to the defendant in *Leland v. Oregon*, 343 U.S. 790 (1952).

4. As the Court points out in *Maas,* insanity generates an acquittal under the *M'Naghten* approach when the mental condition suffered by the defendant causes him to be unable to distinguish right from wrong. A question that has generated considerable debate in this context is whether a defendant who knows that his conduct is against the law but believes—because of mental disease or defect—that his act is not morally wrong

satisfies the *M'Naghten* legal test for insanity. This kind of defendant would not be acquitted if the *M'Naghten* approach to insanity exculpates those who are unable to know "legal" right from "legal" wrong because of mental disease or defect. In contrast, insanity would exculpate in this type of case if the defense applies when mental disease or defect prevents the defendant from distinguishing "moral" right from "moral" wrong. In the oft-cited case of *State v. Crenshaw,* 659 P.2d. 488 (1983), the Supreme Court of Washington had to choose between these two definitions of "wrong." The defendant in *Crenshaw* suspected "thought [that his wife] had been unfaithful." According to his testimony, he sensed "it wasn't the same Karen ... she'd been with someone else." As a result, defendant beat his wife unconscious and stabbed her twenty-four times. He then left, came back with an ax and "decapitated his wife with such force that the ax marks cut into the concrete floor under the carpet and splattered blood throughout the room." Defendant then proceeded to hide the body and clean the room of blood and fingerprints with a bucket and sponge. Defendant was charged with murdering his wife. Defense counsel raised the defense of insanity, claiming that the defendant "followed the Moscovite religious faith, and that it would be improper for a Moscovite not to kill his wife if she committed adultery." The defendant had a history of mental problems and had been hospitalized in the past as a result of this. A jury convicted him of the crime charged. On appeal, the defendant contended that the jury was improperly instructed on the insanity defense. More specifically, he argued that the following instruction did not accurately convey to the meaning of "wrong" in the context of the insanity defense:

> Instruction 10:
>
> For a defendant to be found not guilty by reason of insanity you must find that, as a result of mental disease or defect, the defendant's mind was affected to such an extent that the defendant was unable to perceive the nature and quality of the acts with which the defendant is charged or was unable to tell right from wrong with reference to the particular acts with which defendant is charged.
>
> What is meant by the terms "right and wrong" refers to knowledge of a person at the time of committing an act that he was acting contrary to the law.

Defendant argued that "the trial court erred in defining 'right and wrong' as legal right and wrong rather than in the moral sense." The Supreme Court of Washington rejected this argument, observing that:

> The definition of the term "wrong" in the *M'Naghten* test has been considered and disputed by many legal scholars ...
>
> This court's view has been that "when *M'Naghten* is used, all who might possibly be deterred from the commission of criminal acts are included within the sanctions of the criminal law."
>
> > [O]nly those persons "who have lost contact with reality so completely that they are beyond any of the influences of the criminal law," may have the benefit of the insanity defense in a criminal case.
> >
> > *State v. McDonald.*
>
> Given this perspective, the trial court could assume that one who knew the illegality of his act was not necessarily "beyond any of the influences of the criminal law," thus finding support for the statement in instruction 10....
>
> Alternatively, the statement in instruction 10 may be approved because, in this case, legal wrong is synonymous with moral wrong. This conclusion is premised on two grounds.

First, in discussing the term "moral" wrong, it is important to note that it is society's morals, and not the individual's morals, that are the standard for judging moral wrong under *M'Naghten.* If wrong meant moral wrong judged by the individual's own conscience, this would seriously undermine the criminal law, for it would allow one who violated the law to be excused from criminal responsibility solely because, in his own conscience, his act was not morally wrong. This principle was emphasized by Justice Cardozo:

> The anarchist is not at liberty to break the law because he reasons that all government is wrong. The devotee of a religious cult that enjoins polygamy or human sacrifice as a duty is not thereby relieved from responsibility before the law ...
>
> *People v. Schmidt*

More recently the Arizona Supreme Court stated:

> We find no authority upholding the defendant's position that one suffering from a mental disease could be declared legally insane if he knew that the act was morally and legally wrong but he personally believed that act right. We believe that this would not be a sound rule, because it approaches the position of exonerating a defendant for his personal beliefs and does not take account of society's determination of defendant's capacity to conform his conduct to the law.
>
> *State v. Corley.*

There is evidence on the record that Crenshaw knew his actions were wrong according to society's standards, as well as legally wrong. Dr. Belden testified:

> I think Mr. Crenshaw is quite aware on one level that he is in conflict with the law *and with people.* However, this is not something that he personally invests his emotions in.

We conclude that Crenshaw knew his acts were morally wrong from society's viewpoint and also knew his acts were illegal. His personal belief that it was his duty to kill his wife for her alleged infidelity cannot serve to exculpate him from legal responsibility for his acts.

5. Note that the Supreme Court of Washington in *Crenshaw* distinguished between three different ways of defining "wrong" for the purposes of insanity. First, the defense could only apply if defendant is unaware that his act is legally wrong. This is the narrowest reading insanity, for it would preclude those who are aware that the conduct is unlawful but unaware that it is immoral from raising the defense. Second, insanity could apply when the defendant is aware that his conduct is unlawful, but unaware that his conduct is morally wrong according to societal standards. Finally, the defense could apply when the actor is aware that his conduct is both unlawful and against societal morality, but he believes that the conduct is morally required for personal and idiosyncratic reasons. According to the Court in *Crenshaw,* the first two ways of defining "wrong" for the purposes of insanity are acceptable. However, the Court believes that the third alternative is intolerable, for it would provide a defense to those who decide to commit crimes even though they are aware that doing so is both against the law and contrary to shared standards of morality. Providing a defense to such actors is unjustifiable both from the perspectives of retribution and deterrence. Do you agree with the Court that such defendants should not be able to plead insanity? Why or why not?

6. Do you agree with the outcome in *Crenshaw*? That is, do you believe that the insanity defense should be unavailable for defendants like *Crenshaw*? Explain. Do you believe that

the defendant in *Crenshaw* knew that killing his wife was "legally" wrong? Why? Do you believe that he knew that killing his wife was contrary to societal morality? Why? Do you believe that he thought that killing his wife was morally appropriate according to his honestly held religious beliefs? If so, why should he be punished when he believed that what he did was morally appropriate?

7. Although the Court in *Crenshaw* held that an actor's personal religious beliefs that engaging in a criminal act is morally required may not generate an insanity acquittal, it observed that insanity may exculpate if the defendant believes that God ordered him to commit the crime. This has come to be known as the "deific decree" doctrine. Although the doctrine is discussed in the literature, it is unclear how many jurisdictions actively apply it. The Court explained the reasoning underlying the doctrine in the following way:

> A narrow exception to the societal standard of moral wrong has been drawn for instances wherein a party performs a criminal act, knowing it is morally and legally wrong, but believing, because of a mental defect, that the act is ordained by God: such would be the situation with a mother who kills her infant child to whom she is devotedly attached, believing that God has spoken to her and decreed the act. Although the woman knows that the law and society condemn the act, it would be unrealistic to hold her responsible for the crime, since her free will has been subsumed by her belief in the deific decree.

Turning to the facts of the case, the Court concluded that:

> [The deific decree] exception is not available to Crenshaw, however. Crenshaw argued only that he followed the Moscovite faith and that Moscovites believe it is their duty to kill an unfaithful wife. This is not the same as acting under a deific command. Instead, it is akin to "[t]he devotee of a religious cult that enjoins ... human sacrifice as a duty [and] is *not* thereby relieved from responsibility before the law". Crenshaw's personal "Moscovite" beliefs are not equivalent to a deific decree and do not relieve him from responsibility for his acts.

Do you agree that someone who believes that God commanded him to commit a crime should be acquitted by reason of insanity even if he knows that his conduct is both against the law and contrary to social morality? Explain. Should it make a difference whether the actor believes that God or his religious beliefs compelled him to commit the offense? According to the deific decree doctrine, this distinction matters, for only those who believe they are compelled by God to commit the offense will get the benefit of an acquittal. This explains why the defendant in *Crenshaw* was not able to successfully plead insanity. Do you agree with this outcome?

# § 18.02 Insanity: Dissatisfaction with M'Naghten and the Rise of the Irresistible Impulse Test

## Smith v. United States

Court of Appeals of District of Columbia, 1929
36 F.2d 548

VAN ORSDEL, Associate Justice.

Appellant, defendant below, was convicted of the crime of murder in the first degree, and was sentenced to death. From the judgment, this appeal was taken.

It is conceded that defendant committed the crime charged. No good purpose, therefore, would be subserved in reciting the horrible circumstances attending the conception and perpetration of the crime. A single question of law is presented for our consideration. The sole defense interposed on behalf of the defendant was insanity, and counsel for defendant requested the court to submit to the jury the following prayer:

> 'The jury are instructed that if they believe from the evidence that at the time of committing the acts charged in the indictment the defendant was suffering from such a perverted and deranged condition of his mental faculties as rendered him incapable of distinguishing between right and wrong, or unconscious at such time of the nature of the act charged in the indictment while committing the same, or where through conscious of them and able to distinguish between right and wrong, and to know the acts were wrong, yet his will, the governing power of his mind, was, otherwise than voluntarily, so completely destroyed that his action was not subject to it but beyond his control, it will be their duty to acquit the defendant, and in such case their verdict shall be not guilty.'

No objection was made by counsel for the government to the granting of the prayer. Indeed counsel suggested his willingness that it should be granted. The trial justice, however, denied the prayer, and in his general charge defined insanity as follows:

> 'I want to tell you what the legal definition of sanity and insanity is in connection with the charge of the commission of a crime. That is the definition by which you and I are both bound. I want to say to you that a person may be insane and criminally responsible, just as a person may be insane and civilly responsible for that which he does. These are the limits within which the jury must act in this case. You are instructed that the term 'insanity,' as used in this defense, means that you must find, before you may reach a verdict of not guilty because of insanity, that the defendant was laboring under such a defect of reason from disease of the mind as not to know the nature and quality of what he was doing—that is to say, not to know what he was doing—or, if he did know it, that he did not know that he was doing wrong. If you have no reasonable doubt but that the defendant did know what he was doing, the nature and quality of what he was doing, and if you have no reasonable doubt but that he did know that he was doing wrong, then you may not find a verdict of not guilty because of insanity, because if he did know what he was doing, if he did know what he was doing was wrong, then in the eyes of the law he was a man of sound mind and legally responsible for what he was doing.'

Laying aside the objectionable negative style of the charge, we think it erroneous in point of law, in that it ignores the modern well-established doctrine of 'irresistible impulse.'

The English rule, followed by the American courts in their early history, and still adhered to in some of the states, was that the degree of insanity which one must possess at the time of the commission of the crime in order to exempt him from punishment must be such as to totally deprive him of understanding and memory. This harsh rule is no longer followed by the federal courts or by most of the state courts. The modern doctrine is that the degree of insanity which will relieve the accused of the consequences of a criminal act must be such as to create in his mind an uncontrollable impulse to commit the offense charged. This impulse must be such as to override the reason and judgment and obliterate the sense of right and wrong to the extent that the accused is deprived of the power to choose between right and wrong. The mere ability to distinguish right from wrong is no longer the correct test either in civil or criminal cases, where the defense of insanity is interposed. The accepted rule in this day and age, with the great advancement in medical science as an enlightening influence on this subject, is that the accused must be capable, not only of distinguishing between right and wrong, but that he was not impelled to do the act by an irresistible impulse, which means before it will justify a verdict of acquittal that his reasoning powers were so far dethroned by his diseased mental condition as to deprive him of the will power to resist the insane impulse to perpetrate the deed, though knowing it to be wrong.

In *Insurance Company v. Rodel*, the court charged the jury in part as follows: 'It is not every kind or degree of insanity which will so far excuse the party taking his own life as to make the company insuring liable; to do this, the act of self-destruction must have been the consequence of insanity, and the mind of the deceased must have been so far deranged as to have made him incapable of using a rational judgment in regard to the act which he was committing. If he was impelled to the act by an insane impulse, which the reason that was left him did not enable him to resist, or if his reasoning powers were so far overthrown by his mental condition that he could not exercise his reasoning faculties on the act which he was about to do, the company is liable.'...

[W]e have no hesitation in declaring [the irresistible impulse test] to be the law of this District that, in cases where insanity is interposed as a defense, and the facts are sufficient to call for the application of the rule of irresistible impulse, the jury should be so charged.

Objection is made by counsel for the government that the facts in this case were not sufficient to call for the allowance of the prayer requested by counsel for the defense. We think this objection is not well taken. One of the physicians who was examined as a witness on the issue of insanity testified 'that he would not say that a person who killed his daughter was per se of unsound mind; that the witness believed that at the time the defendant grabbed his daughter he knew what he was doing; and probably appreciated that he was doing wrong,' whereupon counsel for the government propounded the following question: 'You say that he did? A. He appreciated it, but he was unable to—he knew the right and wrong, but he was unable to carry it through. Q. You mean he was unable to carry the right through and refrain from doing the wrong? A. Yes.' Another physician testified as follows: 'Q. Do you think that, at the time he committed that act, he had full recognition of what he was doing, namely, killing his daughter, was wrong? A. Of course, he had the idea, but he was incapable of doing as he would like to do.' The defendant himself testified 'that after he grabbed her he felt that he would give anything if he could stop, but that he could not.' A physician who testified for the prosecution 'stated that it would be difficult to say if, after the commencement of the act, the defendant was in such a mental state that he could discontinue it.'

Considering the evidence as a whole, we are of opinion that it was error to refuse the prayer requested by the defense, and, regardless of the gravity of the offense, or the probable guilt or innocence of the accused, a fundamental principle of law is involved, and a new trial should be granted; in other words, the defendant has been deprived of a substantial right which the law accords him, and which is essential to a fair and impartial trial.

The judgment is reversed, and the cause is remanded for a new trial.

## *Notes and Questions*

1. As the Court of Appeals points out in *Smith*, under the irresistible impulse test, a defendant has a valid insanity claim if his mental disease or defect "deprive[s] him of the will power to resist the insane impulse to perpetrate the deed, though knowing it to be wrong." Do you agree that those who "can't control their impulse to commit crime" because of mental disease or defect should be acquitted pursuant to insanity? Explain. Is the irresistible impulse test superior to *M'Naghten*? Why or why not?

2. When does mental disease "deprive" an actor of "his will power to resist" the "impulse to perpetrate the deed"? A frequently invoked standard for determining when an impulse is "irresistible" enough to warrant a finding of insanity is the "policeman at the elbow" test. One court explained the test in the following way:

> The "policeman at the elbow" test ... is ... that there is no irresistible impulse unless the offense would have been committed had a policeman been present at the time, and the test for irresistible impulse stated in the 1953 edition of TM 8-240 ... is ... whether "the compulsion generating the illness was so strong that the act would have been committed even though the circumstances were such that the accused could expect to be detected and apprehended forthwith when the offense was committed," possess an identical core of meaning having to do with whether the prospect of penal sanctions would have deterred the accused from the conduct in question.

3. A problem with the irresistible impulse test is that it is often very difficult—if not impossible—to distinguish between those who "can't" control their impulses and those who simply "won't". Think of a drug-addict who is deciding whether to use drugs again. If he succumbs to his urge to use drugs, is his conduct the produce of an "irresistible" impulse or could he have resisted the urge? In other words, was it the case that the drug-addict "can't" resist the urge to use drugs or that he "won't" resist it? If it were the former, criminal liability would seem inappropriate. If it is the latter, however, punishment may be appropriate. How are we supposed to decide whether such actors "can't" or "won't" resist their urges? The "policeman at the elbow" test would require asking whether the drug-addict would have used cocaine in front of a police officer. If the answer is "no," then the impulse is not "irresistible" and, therefore, the insanity defense would not apply. Does this standard provide an adequate test for distinguishing between those who "can't" and those who "won't" resist their impulses? Explain.

## § 18.03 Insanity: Model Penal Code— Combining the M'Naghten and the Irresistible Impulse Tests

### Blake v. United States

United States Court of Appeals, Fifth Circuit, 1969
407 F.2d 908

BELL, Circuit Judge:

The significant assignments of error presented on this appeal center on the defense of insanity and the legal standards which are applicable thereto in a criminal trial in the federal courts. Because of the importance of the questions in light of developing medico-legal concepts in the field of behavioral science, this court, *sua sponte*, ordered en banc consideration of the case. We reverse for retrial on a definition of insanity more nearly attuned to present day concepts of psychiatry.

Blake was charged with bank robbery, 18 U.S.C.A. § 2113. He was arrested on the day following the robbery and his trial began some six months later. The evidence that he committed the robbery was overwhelming; his principal defense was insanity at the time of the commission of the offense. He was convicted and his motion for new trial denied. He was thereafter sentenced and this appeal followed ...

II.

[The defendant] asserted that the definition of insanity given the jury in charge for determining the issue of not guilty by reason of insanity was outmoded and prejudicial ...

III.

We come then to the definition of insanity given in charge. The district court charge was based on the dictum in Davis v. United States, on the second appearance of the case in the Supreme Court ...

We are asked once again to review the Davis definition to the end of holding that the district court committed reversible error in giving it in charge. Blake urges that such a charge is unduly restrictive and that it was prejudicial to him. The government denies that the charge was prejudicial but states that the Davis definition could be improved by converting it into more up-to-date language. This overlooks the fact that the district court here updated the language. The real issue is the government's opposition to the substitution of a standard or measure of substantiality for the complete lack of mental capacity measure of Davis. It urges that 'substantial' is an imprecise and phantom-like term. The other side of the coin is that rarely if ever is one completely lacking in mental capacity. The government insists on the absolutes of Davis. The district court, following our decisions, charged the absolutes.

These positions point up the difference between the Davis standard and that of the Model Penal Code as adopted by the American Law Institute. The Davis standard is as follows:

> 'The term 'insanity' as used in this defence means such a perverted and deranged condition of the mental and moral faculties as to render a person incapable of distinguishing between right and wrong, or unconscious at the time of the nature of the act he is committing, or where, though conscious of it and able to dis-

> tinguish between right and wrong and know that the act is wrong, yet his will, by which I mean the governing power of his mind, has been otherwise than voluntarily so completely destroyed that his actions are not subject to it, but are beyond his control.' 165 U.S. at 378, 17 S.Ct. at 362.

Section 4.01 of the ALI Model Penal Code is as follows:

> '(1) A person is not responsible for criminal conduct if at the time of such conduct as a result of mental disease or defect he lacks substantial capacity either to appreciate the criminality (wrongfulness) of his conduct or to conform his conduct to the requirements of law.
>
> '(2) As used in this Article, the terms 'mental disease or defect' do not include an abnormality manifested only by repeated criminal or otherwise antisocial conduct.'

The federal courts of appeals have given extensive consideration to the problem of adapting the definition of insanity as it is to be applied in administering the defense of insanity to the expanding knowledge available from medical science. One prime question has been that of a test couched in terms of substantial lack of mental capacity as distinguished from a complete lack of capacity. The dissenting opinions in our Carter case, supra, 325 F.2d 697, and the decisions of other circuits contain elaborate discussions of the problem of definition beginning with McNaghten's Rule, 1843, 10 Cl. and F. 200, 210, 8 Eng.Rep. 718, 722. They are filled with references to the applicable treatises, both of law and medicine.

The upshot is that the Second, Fourth, Sixth, Seventh and Tenth Circuits have adopted the substantiality test of the Model Penal Code. The District of Columbia Circuit has adopted a substantiality test although not stated in Model Penal Code terms.... The First and Ninth Circuits have open minds on the question.

The facts of this case point up the difference in the standards. Here the facts are such, read favorably to the government as they must be, as not to show complete mental disorientation under the absolutes of Davis. The record does show evidence which, if believed, would indicate that Blake suffered from a severe mental disease which the jury might have found impaired his control over the conduct in question. He could not prevail under a Davis charge. He might have prevailed under a substantial lack of capacity type charge.

We think that a substantiality type standard is called for in light of current knowledge regarding mental illness. A person, as Blake here, may be a schizophrenic or may merely have a sociopathic personality. The evidence could go either way. He may or may not have been in a psychotic episode at the time of the robbery. But, he was not unconscious, incapable of distinguishing right and wrong nor was his will completely destroyed in the terms of Davis definition. Modifying the lack of mental capacity by the adjective 'substantial', still leaves the matter for the jury under the evidence, lay and expert, to determine mental defect vel non and its relationship to the conduct in question.

We have concluded that this is an appropriate case for adopting a definition of insanity which will serve as a vehicle to enable the court and jury to give effect to the defense of insanity in terms of what is now known about diseases of the mind. We conclude also that such a definition must be in less than the absolute terms of Davis. A substantial lack of capacity is a more nearly adequate standard. We treat the Davis test as a dictum and in no event is it a stricture on our supervisory power to adopt a new standard.

The question remains as to the specifics of the standard. The federal courts of appeals as well as the state courts serve as separate laboratories in the development of the law, and it is at once apparent that we are somewhat late in this field. Much can be gained from what has been developed in the other laboratories. As noted, the ALI Model Penal Code standard in varying forms has been adopted in five of the federal circuits. Moreover, that same substantiality standard has been adopted in five states....

We have concluded to adopt the Model Penal Code standard and to require it or an approximation of it as a matter of uniformity in this circuit. We think it lends itself as a uniform standard.

At the same time, we must notice that the circuits adopting the Model Penal Code standard have varied it in some degree. For example, the Sixth Circuit expressly refused to adopt the second paragraph of the Model Penal Code standard, § 401(2), while the Second, Fourth, and Seventh Circuits did adopt the contents of the paragraph as a part of the standard. The Tenth Circuit did not address itself to the question. We have determined to follow the Second, Fourth, and Seventh Circuit opinions in this regard.

We follow the Second and Seventh Circuits, in the same opinions, in substituting the alternative term 'wrongfulness' as used in the first paragraph of the Model Penal Code for 'criminality'. The Second Circuit concluded that it was a broader term in that it would include the case where the perpetrator appreciated that his conduct was criminal but, because of a delusion, believed it to be morally justified.

In sum, we adopt the following standard as a definition for use in defining insanity in this circuit where the defense of insanity is in issue:

> '(1) A person is not responsible for criminal conduct if at the time of such conduct as a result of mental disease or defect he lacks substantial capacity either to appreciate the wrongfulness of his conduct or to conform his conduct to the requirements of law.
>
> '(2) As used in this Article, the terms 'mental disease or defect' do not include an abnormality manifested only by repeated criminal or otherwise antisocial conduct.'

This leaves two questions: First, shall Blake have the benefit of the new standard? We hold that he should ... Here we think that Blake was prejudiced by the Davis definition of insanity given in charge to the extent of being entitled to a new trial under the new definition.

Second, is the new standard to apply retroactively?... The new definition of insanity is to apply prospectively only, i.e., from the date of this decision, except as to those cases new on appeal.

Reversed and remanded for further proceedings not inconsistent herewith.

## *Notes and Questions*

1. The Model Penal Code's formulation of insanity combines the *M'Naghten* and irresistible impulse tests. Furthermore—as the Court of Appeals noted in *Blake*—the Code's approach to the defense is broader than both *M'Naghten* and the irresistible impulse test insofar as it does not require proof that the defendant *lacked* the ability to distinguish right from wrong or to control his conduct. Rather, the Code's formulation merely requires proof that the actor did not have "substantial capacity" to appreciate the wrongfulness of his conduct or to conform his acts to the mandates of law. The difference is of significance, for it is quite difficult to prove that a person was "absolutely" unaware of the wrongfulness of his acts or that it was "totally" impossible to control his urges. Instead, the Code requires proof that the relevant cognitive or volitional capabil-

ities of the defendant were "substantially" impaired. This standard is considerably easier to satisfy. Which of these two approaches is preferable? Why?

2. Model Penal Code § 4.01(1) prescribes that insanity exculpates if the mental disease or defect deprives the actor of substantial capacity to appreciate the "criminality" of his conduct. Note, however, that the drafters included the term "wrongfulness" in parentheticals as a way of signaling that the proper approach might be to exculpate as long as the defendant lacks substantial capacity to appreciate the "moral" wrongfulness of his conduct, even if he is aware of its "criminality." By doing so, the Model Penal Code drafters deliberately refused to take a position regarding the appropriate way of defining "wrong" for the purposes of the insanity defense (i.e., legal vs. moral wrong). The Code drafters thus decided to leave the resolution of the issue to state courts and legislatures.

3. Shortly after the publication of the Model Penal Code, a substantial number of jurisdictions adopted the Code's insanity formulation either judicially or legislatively. Nevertheless, the trend eventually halted and started moving in the opposite direction. That is, many jurisdictions moved away from the Code's approach to insanity, usually by returning to the *M'Naghten* rule. In fact, fifteen years after *Blake* was decided, the Court of Appeals for the Fifth Circuit abandoned the Model Penal Code formulation of insanity in *United States v. Lyons,* 731 F.2d 243 (1984). The Court of Appeals justified its decision by pointing out that:

> Because the concept of criminal responsibility in the federal courts is a congeries of judicially-made rules of decision based on common law concepts, it is usually appropriate for us to reexamine and reappraise these rules in the light of new policy considerations. We last examined the insanity defense in *Blake v. United States,* where we adopted the ALI Model Penal Code definition of insanity: that a person is not responsible for criminal conduct if, at the time of such conduct and as a result of mental disease or defect, he lacks substantial capacity either to appreciate the wrongfulness of his conduct or to conform his conduct to the requirements of the law. Following the example of sister circuits, we embraced this standard ... because we concluded that then current knowledge in the field of behavioral science supported such a result. Unfortunately, it now appears our conclusion was premature—that the brave new world that we foresaw has not arrived.
>
> Reexamining the *Blake* standard today, we conclude that the volitional prong of the insanity defense—a lack of capacity to conform one's conduct to the requirements of the law—does not comport with current medical and scientific knowledge, which has retreated from its earlier, sanguine expectations. Consequently, we now hold that a person is not responsible for criminal conduct on the grounds of insanity only if at the time of that conduct, as a result of a mental disease or defect, he is unable to appreciate the wrongfulness of that conduct.
>
> We do so for several reasons. First, as we have mentioned, a majority of psychiatrists now believe that they do not possess sufficient accurate scientific bases for measuring a person's capacity for self-control or for calibrating the impairment of that capacity. "The line between an irresistible impulse and an impulse not resisted is probably no sharper than between twilight and dusk." *American Psychiatric Association Statement on the Insanity Defense,* 11 (1982) [APA Statement]. Indeed, Professor Bonnie states:
>
>> There is, in short, no objective basis for distinguishing between offenders who were undeterrable and those who were merely undeterred, between the impulse that was irresistible and the impulse not resisted, or between substantial impairment of capacity and some lesser impairment.

> In addition, the risks of fabrication and "moral mistakes" in administering the insanity defense are greatest "when the experts and the jury are asked to speculate whether the defendant had the capacity to 'control' himself or whether he could have 'resisted' the criminal impulse." Moreover, psychiatric testimony about volition is more likely to produce confusion for jurors than is psychiatric testimony concerning a defendant's appreciation of the wrongfulness of his act. It appears, moreover, that there is considerable overlap between a psychotic person's inability to understand and his ability to control his behavior. Most psychotic persons who fail a volitional test would also fail a cognitive test, thus rendering the volitional test superfluous for them....
>
> One need not disbelieve in the existence of Angels in order to conclude that the present state of our knowledge regarding them is not such as to support confident conclusions about how many can dance on the head of a pin. In like vein, it may be that some day tools will be discovered with which reliable conclusions about human volition can be fashioned. It appears to be all but a certainty, however, that despite earlier hopes they do not lie in our hands today. When and if they do, it will be time to consider again to what degree the law should adopt the sort of conclusions that they produce. But until then, we see no prudent course for the law to follow but to treat all criminal impulses—including those not resisted—as resistible. To do otherwise in the present state of medical knowledge would be to cast the insanity defense adrift upon a sea of unfounded scientific speculation, with the palm awarded case by case to the most convincing advocate of that which is presently unknown—and may remain so, because unknowable.

Note that the Court of Appeals' main objection to the Model Penal Code's insanity formulation is the difficulty in distinguishing between an "irresistible" impulse and an impulse "not resisted." That is, the Court was concerned with the difficulty inherent in telling apart those who "can't" control their conduct from those that "won't" control it. These are the same critiques that can be leveled against the "irresistible impulse" test. Do you find these objections convincing? Why or why not?

4. The trend away from the Model Penal Code's insanity formulation was provoked, at least in part, by the massive public outcry in the wake of John Hinckley's acquittal by reason of insanity for attempting to assassinate then President Reagan. Not only did many jurisdictions revert to the *M'Naghten* rule in the wake of the controversial Hinckley acquittal, but a handful of states actually abolished the insanity defense altogether. The Idaho insanity statue, for example, prescribes that "[m]ental condition shall not be a defense to any charge of criminal conduct." Idaho Code § 18-207(1).

## § 18.04 Insanity: Comparative Perspectives

### Diego Manuel Luzón Peña, *Lecciones de Derecho Penal: Parte General*

Tirant Lo Blanch, 2012, pages 526–527

When the effects of the mental disease or defect partially—but not entirely—preclude the actor from knowing the wrongfulness of his conduct or conforming his conduct to the mandates of law, there will nevertheless be an attenuation of the actor's culpability if his mental disease or defect makes it harder—although not impossible—for him to behave in accordance to law ... This may happen in some instances of mild psychotic episodes and more frequently in psychotic and neurotic episodes that do not impair the actor's volition or cognitive capabilities to the extent required by the defense of insanity. The Spanish Penal Code allows for two distinct kinds of mitigation in this type of "partial insanity" case. [If the actor's capacities were significantly impaired by mental disease or defect that nevertheless fails to meet the requirements for a full insanity defense], the judge may apply a partial or "imperfect" insanity defense that [authorizes a downward departure below the range of punishment prescribed for the offense charged]. [If, on the other hand, the actor's capacities were compromised—albeit not significantly—by mental disease or defect], the judge may mitigate punishment by imposing a sentence within the lower bounds of the range of punishment prescribed for the offense charged.

## Hans Heinrich Jescheck & Thomas Weigend, *Lehrbuch des Strafrechts. Allgemeiner Teil*

5th ed. 1996, p. 443

The doctrine of "diminished responsibility" primarily has the purpose of allowing courts to deal adequately with minor degrees of feeblemindedness, of acts committed under the influence of an affect, of alcohol and drugs, or of psychopathy, neurosis or anomalous urges. The biological prerequisites of diminished responsibility are the same as [lack of responsibility due to mental illness]. The difference lies in the psychological criteria: the actor's ability to recognize the unlawfulness of his act or his ability to control himself is not absent but significantly reduced. This is not a kind of "half-culpability" inserted between full criminal responsibility and lack of responsibility. The actor is in fact criminally responsible; but the sentence may be reduced because of the actor's reduced ability either to recognize the unlawfulness of his conduct or to adapt his conduct to that insight.

## Eugenio Raúl Zaffaroni, Alejandro Slokar & Alejandro Alagia, *Derecho Penal: Parte General*

Ediar, 2000, pages 707–708

It is patently incorrect to negate that there are degrees of blameworthiness and, therefore, of culpability. Once it is recognized that blameworthiness is a matter of degrees, it is obvious that there are some mentally diseased actors who are capable of understanding the wrongfulness of their conduct and controlling their acts, but who are nevertheless less capable of doing so than a mentally sound individual. In such cases, the actor's culpability is "diminished", although not totally excluded ...

These cases of "diminished responsibility" are instances in which the actor's culpability for engaging in the act is reduced and, therefore, mitigation of punishment is warranted.... Given that these cases feature actors who behave less culpably than their mentally sane counterparts, the mitigation of punishment in these instances must be automatic rather than discretionary. This must be the case, for imposing punishment that does not adequately reflect the defendant's blameworthiness violates the principle of proportionality. As a result, instances of "diminished responsibility" must generate an automatic mitigation of punishment ...

[It is argued whether in cases of "diminished responsibility" the judge is authorized to impose punishment that falls below the range prescribed for the offense charged]. Some have observed that the judge must be authorized to do so, for punishment should always correspond to the culpability of the accused. If the culpability of the accused warrants less punishment than what the lower bound of the range prescribes, the judge should be free to make a downward departure from the range.

## *Notes and Questions*

1. The readings excerpted in this section illustrate how the doctrine of "diminished responsibility" is conceived in Spain, Germany and Argentina, respectively. The excerpts reveal the widespread support that the doctrine commands in civil law jurisdictions. Pursuant to the doctrine of diminished responsibility, insanity should not be viewed as an "all-or-nothing" defense that either leads to an outright acquittal or to the full-fledged imposition of criminal responsibility. Rather, insanity is a matter of degrees, given that an actor's volitional and cognitive capabilities may be more or less impaired depending on the seriousness of the mental disease or defect suffered by the actor. As a result, an actor who is aware that his conduct is wrongful and is able to control his conduct but nevertheless suffers from a mental disease or defect that significantly impairs his capacity to distinguish right from wrong or control his urges should be punished considerably less than someone who suffers from no mental disease or defect. Do you find this position attractive? Why or why not?

2. There is disagreement regarding whether diminished responsibility should lead to a discretionary or mandatory mitigation of punishment. In some jurisdictions—like Germany—mitigation is discretionary. Although mitigation in Germany is discretionary, if the court does decide to do so, the mitigation in punishment may be quite substantial. According to Article 49 of the German Penal Code, punishment in these cases may be mitigated in the following manner:

> (1) If mitigation is prescribed or permitted under this provision, then the following shall apply to such mitigation:
>
> 1. Imprisonment for not less than three years shall take the place of imprisonment for life;
>
> 2. In cases of imprisonment for a fixed term, at most three-fourths of the maximum term provided may be imposed ...
>
> 3. An increased minimum term of imprisonment shall be reduced:
>
> in the case of a minimum term of ten or five years, to two years;
>
> in case of a minimum term of three or two years, to six months;
>
> in case of a minimum term of one year, to three months;
>
> in other cases to the statutory minimum.
>
> (2) If the court may in its discretion mitigate the punishment pursuant to a norm which refers to this provision, then it may reduce the punishment to the statutory minimum or impose a fine instead of imprisonment.

In other jurisdictions—like Spain—mitigation of punishment in cases of diminished responsibility is mandatory. It is also interesting to note that the Spanish Penal Code allows for substantial mitigation pursuant to an "incomplete" or "partial" insanity defense if the mental disease significantly impaired the actor's volitional or cognitive capacities. In this case, the judge may impose a sentence that falls below the range of punishment prescribed for the offense. If the impairment is less substantial, the Spanish Penal Code calls for imposing a sentence within the lower bound of the range of punishment prescribed for the offense.

3. The closest American analogue to the civil law doctrine of "diminished responsibility" is "diminished capacity." The difference is that in most jurisdictions the American doctrine of diminished capacity merely serves to negate "premeditation" or "deliberation" in order to reduce a first-degree murder to a second-degree murder. As a result—contrary to what occurs in civil law jurisdictions—diminished capacity in the United States is not generally conceived as a doctrine that mitigates liability for any and all offenses. Nevertheless, the United States Sentencing Guidelines do authorize federal judges to make a downward departure in punishment in cases of diminished capacity for a broad range of offenses. The relevant statute prescribes that:

> A downward departure may be warranted if:
>
> (1) the defendant committed the offense while suffering from a significantly reduced mental capacity; and
>
> (2) the significantly reduced mental capacity contributed substantially to the commission of the offense.
>
> Similarly, if a departure is warranted under this policy statement, the extent of the departure should reflect the extent to which the reduced mental capacity contributed to the commission of the offense.
>
> However, the court may not depart below the applicable guideline range if:
>
> (1) the significantly reduced mental capacity was caused by the voluntary use of drugs or other intoxicants;
>
> (2) the facts and circumstances of the defendant's offense indicate a need to protect the public because the offense involved actual violence or a serious threat of violence;
>
> (3) the defendant's criminal history indicates a need to incarcerate the defendant to protect the public; or
>
> (4) the defendant has been convicted of an offense under chapter 71, 109A, 110, or 117, of title 18, United States Code.

Note that the excerpted guideline provision states that the court "may not" depart from the guideline range if defendant engaged in a violent offense that reveals a need to protect the public. As a result, the provision may not authorize downward departures for very serious offenses. Furthermore, the Federal Sentencing Guidelines are merely advisory rather than mandatory, pursuant to the Supreme Court's decision in *United States v. Booker*, 542 U.S. 220 (2005). Therefore, federal judges are not required to make downward departures even in the case of non-violent offenses. Should American courts adopt a broader approach to diminished capacity that applies to all offenses similar to what civil law jurisdictions require pursuant to their doctrine of diminished responsibility? Why or why not?

## § 18.05 Insanity: Scholarly Debates

### Stephen Morse, *Rationality and Responsibility*

74 S. Cal. L. Rev. 251 (2000)

... I. RESPONSIBILITY

... The law's concept of responsibility follows from its view of the person and the nature of law itself. Unless human beings are rational creatures who can understand the applicable rules and standards, and can conform to those legal requirements through intentional action, the law would be powerless to affect human behavior. Legally responsible agents are therefore people who have the general capacity to grasp and be guided by good reason in particular legal contexts. They must be capable of rational practical reasoning. The law presumes that adults are so capable and that the same rules may be applied to all people with this capacity. The law does not presume that all people act for good reason all the time. It is sufficient for responsibility that the agent has the general capacity for rationality, even if the capacity is not exercised on a particular occasion. Indeed, it is my claim that lack of the general capacity for rationality explains precisely those cases, such as infancy or certain instances of severe mental disorder or dementia, in which the law now excuses agents or finds them not competent to perform some task.

The general capacity for rationality in a particular context is thus the primary criterion of responsibility and its absence is the primary excusing condition. A general capacity is nothing more than an underlying ability to engage in certain behavior. English speakers, for example, have the general capacity to speak English, even when they are silent or are speaking a different language.... People often engage in legally relevant behavior for non-rational, irrational, and foolish reasons, but this does not excuse them or render them nonresponsible if they are generally capable of rationality.

I have claimed that rationality is the defining criterion of legal (and moral) responsibility, but it is not self-defining. It is a normative concept that can take on various meanings according to differing moral and political judgments about how society should govern itself. Accepting rationality as the defining criterion therefore does not entail a commitment to any particular view of what rationality requires. "Thick" and "thin" versions are possible, which would narrow or expand respectively the numbers of citizens who would be considered responsible. For example, if rationality is deemed to require the emotional capacity to empathize with the feelings of others, then people who lack this capacity, such as psychopaths, would not be considered rational. Which capacities and how much of such capacities are necessary can only be decided on normative grounds.

Although there cannot be an a priori, incontrovertible answer to such normative questions, some guidance is available concerning the content of the capacity for rationality. I do not have an exalted or complicated notion of rationality—itself a congeries of skills rather than a unitary capacity. At the very least, rationality must include the ability, in Susan Wolf's words, "to be sensitive and responsive to relevant changes in one's situation and environment—that is, to be flexible." By this account, rationality is the ability to perceive accurately, to get the facts right, to form justifiable beliefs, and to reason instrumentally, including weighing the facts appropriately and according to a minimally coherent preference-ordering. Rationality includes the general ability to recognize and be responsive to the good reasons that should guide action. Put yet another way, it is the ability to act for good reasons. There is good reason not to act (or to act) if doing so (or not doing so) will be unjustifiably harmful or maladaptive ...

In sum, the general capacity for rationality is the precondition for liberty and autonomy. A lack of this capacity explains virtually all cases of criminal law excuses and virtually all the mental health laws that treat some people with mental disorders differently from people without disorders....

### III.

Should a history of deprivation furnish an excuse to crime? How should the law respond to crimes motivated by disorders of desire? Should psychopathy provide an excuse? How should the law respond to newly discovered psychological syndromes? Should the criminal law adopt a generic partial-responsibility excusing condition? Should results matter to desert? Is involuntary civil commitment justified for some people with mental disorders? The model of responsibility Part I describes is at the heart of much of the analysis, but my views are also animated by a strong political preference for permitting maximum liberty and autonomy.

Understanding that the capacity for rationality is the fundamental criterion of criminal responsibility for intentional action clarifies a number of important criminal law questions. Let us begin with the oft-stated claim that a history of deprivation that plays a causal role in criminal conduct should itself be an excusing condition. Causation per se is not an excusing condition, however. If it were, everyone or no one would be excused because all behavior is caused. Deprivation should provide an excuse only if it severely diminishes the agent's capacity for rationality, but there is little reason to believe that this is true for most people who have had an unfortunate history of deprivation. Indeed, to believe otherwise threatens to patronize and stigmatize such people. In cases in which rationality is diminished, the excusing condition should be irrationality, not deprivation. Nor is there reason to believe that deprived people are often in a sufficiently hard-choice condition to justify a compulsion excuse. Deprivation is not compulsion per se, and if a deprived person is compelled by a sufficient threat, duress will be the excusing doctrine. In contrast, if deprivation produces a situation in which otherwise wrongful conduct is right or permissible under the circumstances because the balance of evils is positive, the agent will be justified. For example, an agent may justifiably steal to avoid starvation because it is preferable to commit theft than to starve. As a matter of social justice, our society must try harder to prevent avoidable deprivation among needy citizens, but excusing responsible agents will not accomplish this goal.

How should the law respond to criminal conduct motivated by "disorders" of desire, such as "addictions," so-called "pathological" or "compulsive" gambling, "deviant" sexual desires, and the like? [C]ontrary to popular belief, [I suggest that] there is no problem of compulsion or volition in such cases, but in some cases the desire may be so intense that it undermines the capacity for rationality. Nonetheless, an irrationality excuse is problematic because virtually all sufferers from disorders of desire have quiescent periods during which their capacity for rationality is not undermined and during which they recognize future dangers. They arguably have the duty at that time to take those steps necessary to suppress the desire or to ensure that they will not be in a position to act wrongly or dangerously when they become irrational. Thus, they may be held legally responsible if they offend to satisfy the desire.

Some disorders of desire, such as addiction, may sometimes produce a lifestyle with so much physical and psychological stress that the addict's general capacity for rationality is impaired, even when the desire is not at its peak. Such cases should be treated like "settled insanity" and an excuse like legal insanity should obtain. Whether many or few addicts would be excused under such a regime would depend on a normative judgment about how much the general capacity for rationality must be undermined to warrant a full excuse. In cases of lesser impairment, a generic partial responsibility excuse, discussed below, might apply to addicts and others with disorders of desire. Finally, if those with such desires are considered criminally responsible, as they usually are, it is difficult to justify a regime of preventive civil detention on the ground that such people cannot control themselves. I am not sure what it means to be unable to control oneself, but if this condition warrants preventive detention, it should also furnish an excuse to crime. After all, could it possibly be fair to blame and to punish those who genuinely cannot control themselves?

Although the law does not furnish an excusing condition to psychopaths, people who lack a conscience and the capacity for empathy, I believe that they are morally irrational and should be excused. Unless an agent is able to understand what the victim will feel and is able to at least feel the anticipation of unpleasant guilt for unjustifiably harming another, the agent lacks the capacity to grasp and be guided by the primary rational reasons for complying with legal and moral norms. What could be a better reason not to harm another than full, emotional understanding of another's pain? People who lack such understanding are, in my opinion, incapable of moral rationality and not part of our moral community. They should not be held responsible, but if they are dangerous, they should be civilly confined to protect society.

The alleged discovery of new psychological or psychiatric syndromes, such as battered-victim syndrome or abused-child syndrome, has motivated claims for new excusing conditions. Once again, however, even if a syndrome is valid and played a causal role in the criminal conduct, causation per se is not an excuse. Thus, the law should not adopt a new excuse each time a causal variable for crime, such as a syndrome, is discovered. The proper way to understand these claims is that many syndromes may potentially undermine rationality, which is a genuine excusing condition. Indeed, in many cases, the defendant's rationality does appear diminished, but the insanity defense is unlikely to obtain because most new syndrome sufferers remain firmly in contact with reality and more substantial irrationality is usually necessary for a successful plea of legal insanity. Consequently, there is no extant excusing doctrine to cover these cases and mitigation must be considered solely and discretionarily at sentencing or through executive clemency or pardon. As I shall argue, this result is unfair and can be remedied by the adoption of a generic partial excuse.

Before turning to the partial-responsibility proposal, let me comment briefly on the attempts by some advocates to use new syndromes to support alleged justifications, such as self-defense, under conditions in which traditional self-defense would not obtain. The argument is that the reasonable person should be "subjectified," that is, the law should grant a justification if the person acted as a "reasonable syndrome sufferer." But this move would obliterate objectivity and the important distinction between justification and excuse. It is also internally incoherent. By definition, the syndrome sufferer, who has a mental abnormality, is unreasonable in those areas of his or her life in which the syndrome is operating. The impulse to adopt a justification in these cases is understandable, but it would produce unwise policy and should be resisted.

Contrary to my earlier writing on this subject, I now believe that the law should adopt a generic partial excusing condition, "Guilty But Partially Responsible," based on diminished rationality. Mitigating doctrines in the law of homicide, such as provocation and passion, or extreme mental or emotional disturbance, reflect the recognition that many defendants suffer from substantially impaired rationality that is nonetheless insufficient to support an insanity claim. There is no reason whatsoever that such impaired rationality is true only of homicide defendants. Indeed, the criteria of such doctrines are potentially fully applicable to the mental states of defendants accused of any crime. Because rationality is the touchstone of responsibility and culpability, the law should offer a formal, doctrinal partial excuse rather than leave mitigation primarily to the discretion of sentencing judges. Although responsibility is a continuum concept and an agent's level of responsibility depends on facts about the agent's capacity for rationality, we have only limited epistemic ability to make the fine-grained responsibility judgments that are theoretically possible. Thus, as the mitigating doctrines within homicide law demonstrate, one generic partial excuse with a legislatively mandated reduction in sentence would be a workable scheme that would improve the quality of justice in criminal cases. Such a partial excuse would apply and would be a rational, just response in many cases in which new syndrome claims are made....

## Christopher Slobogin, *An End to Insanity: Recasting the Role of Mental Disability in Criminal Cases*

86 Va. L. Rev. 1199 (2000)

INSANITY defense jurisprudence has long been in a state of chaos. Some have responded to this unfortunate situation by calling for abolition of the defense, while others have tinkered further with its scope. This Article proposes what amounts to an intermediate position. It argues that insanity should be eliminated as a separate defense, but that the effects of mental disorder should still carry significant moral weight. More specifically, mental illness should be relevant in assessing culpability only as warranted by general criminal law doctrines concerning mens rea, self-defense and duress.

While a few scholars and courts have toyed with this idea, it has yet to be fully endorsed or coherently defended by any of them. This Article provides such a defense. It contends that, both morally and practically, the most appropriate manner of recognizing mental illness's mitigating impact in criminal cases is to recast mental disorder as a factor relevant to the general defenses, rather than treat it as a predicate for a special defense.

The starting point for this claim is the retributive principle that blameworthiness should be the predominant guidepost of the criminal law. One can imagine a system, as Lady Wootton has, which is agnostic about culpability and focused on prevention and treatment. In such a world we would not need to talk about the insanity defense, because autonomy or its absence would be relevant, if at all, only in determining whether a person has sufficient control to avoid offending in the future. The reason Lady Wootton's approach has not gained significant ground is that a world in which the government imposes harsh penalties without considering blameworthiness is morally repugnant to many people. The human urge to condemn those who have done wrong is strong; at the same time, it is considered fundamentally unfair to visit such condemnation on a person who is not "culpable." Even if that noninstrumental position is wrong—because moral condemnation is the role of spiritual rather than secular entities, because culpability is not a necessary basis for condemnation, or because "hard" determinists are right that everything we do is inevitable and culpability is thus a meaningless concept—the state should act as if blameworthiness can be measured, to enhance the perception that our decisions about conduct matter and concomitantly encourage law-abiding behavior.

Accepting blameworthiness as the touchstone of the criminal law means that individual culpability must be assessed. That is where the kind of inquiry the insanity defense mandates comes into play. It is meant to help us decide who among those who commit criminal acts deserve to be the subject of criminal punishment.

The central assertion of this Article, however, is that the insanity defense does not adequately carry out this definitional task. At least in its modern guises, the insanity defense is overbroad. Instead, mental disorder should be relevant to criminal culpability only if it supports an excusing condition that, under the subjective approach to criminal liability increasingly accepted today, would be available to a person who is not mentally ill. The three most prominent such conditions would be: (1) a mistaken belief about circumstances that, had they occurred as the person believed, would amount to a legal justification; (2) a mistaken belief that conditions exist that amount to legally recognized duress; and (3) the absence of intent to commit crime (that is, the lack of mens rea, defined subjectively in terms of what the defendant actually knew or was aware of).

Before justifying this position, some examples of how it would apply in well-known actual and hypothetical cases should be provided. As a prime example of the first excusing condition, consider the famous M'Naghten case, from whence much of current insanity defense jurisprudence derives. In 1843, Daniel M'Naghten killed the secretary of Prime Minister Peel, apparently believing the secretary was Peel and that killing Peel would bring an end to a campaign of harassment against him. He was found insane by the trial court judges. Whether M'Naghten would have been acquitted under the proposed approach would depend upon whether he believed the harassment would soon lead to his death or serious bodily harm and whether he thought there was any other way to prevent that occurrence. Because in his paranoid state he feared he would be assassinated by his enemies and had on several occasions unsuccessfully applied to the police for protection, he may have had such a defense. But if the circumstances in which he thought he was involved would not amount to self-defense, no acquittal would result (although a conviction of manslaughter rather than murder might have been appropriate, analogous to the result under the modern theory of "imperfect" self-defense as it has developed in connection with provocation doctrine).

Now consider the case of John Hinckley, who convinced a jury that he was insane when he tried to kill President Reagan. If, as even his defense attorneys asserted, John Hinckley shot President Reagan simply because he believed Reagan's death would somehow unite him with actress Jodi Foster, he would be convicted under the proposed approach. Regardless of how psychotic Hinckley may have been at the time of the offense, he would not have an excuse under the proposed regime, because killing someone to consummate a love affair is never justified, nor is it deserving even of a reduction in charge.

Two other recent cases furnish additional exemplars of how the proposed regime might work in practice. Jeffrey Dahmer killed and cannibalized thirteen individuals. The jury was right to convict him. As sick as his actions were, even he never thought they were justified, and he would not be excused under the proposal. Lorena Bobbitt, who cut off her husband's penis because he repeatedly beat her, was found insane. Whether she would have a complete defense under the proposal would depend on the extent to which she thought she had other ways of forestalling the beating and whether the option she chose was disproportionate to that threat. On the facts presented at trial, even on her own account her act would probably not be considered necessary by the factfinder, and she would therefore have been convicted of some version of assault.

In these cases, then, whether a defense existed under the proposed approach would depend upon self-defense principles, applied to the circumstances as the defendant believed them to be. A second variety of cases can be analyzed in terms of a similarly subjectified version of duress, which traditionally has excused crimes that are coerced by serious threats to harm the perpetrator. For instance, some people with mental illness who commit crimes claim they were commanded by God to do so. If the perceived consequences of disobeying the deity were lethal or similarly significant, such a person would deserve acquittal, perhaps even if the crime charged were homicide. On the other hand, contrary to Judge Cardozo's famous hypothetical suggestion, the mere fact that the defendant honestly believed God ordained a crime would not automatically be an excuse.

The third type of excuse that might apply when people with mental illness commit crime—lack of mens rea—is extremely rare. M'Naghten, Hinckley, Dahmer, Bobbitt and Cardozo's hypothetical defendant all intended to carry out their criminal acts. Indeed, most people with mental disorder who cause harm mean to do so, albeit sometimes for reasons that seem irrational. Nonetheless, when mens rea is defined subjectively, there are at least four possible lack-of-mens rea scenarios: involuntary action, mistake as to results, mistake as to circumstances, and ignorance of the law.

First, a person may engage in motor activity without intending it to occur (for example, a reflex action which results in a gun firing and killing someone). The criminal law typically classifies such events as involuntary acts. Although mental disorder usually does not eliminate conscious control over bodily movements associated with crime, when it does (for example, in connection with epileptic seizures), a defense would exist if one accepts the premise that culpability requires intent.

Second, a person may intentionally engage in conduct but intend a different result than that which occurs (such as when firing a gun at a tree kills a person due to a ricochet). Distortions of perception caused by mental illness might occasionally lead to such accidental consequences; for instance, a mentally ill person driving a car may inadvertently hit someone because his "voices" and hallucinations prevent him from perceiving the relevant sounds and visual cues. In such situations a subjectively defined mens rea doctrine would absolve him of criminal liability for any harm caused.

Closely related is the situation in which a person intentionally engages in conduct and intends the physical result that occurs, but is under a misapprehension as to the attendant circumstances (such as when a person intentionally shoots a gun at what he thinks is a dummy but which in fact is a real person). Of the various mens rea defenses, mental illness is most likely to play a role here (in what has sometimes been labeled the "mistake of fact" defense). For instance, a person who believes he is shooting the devil when in fact he is killing a person, or a person who exerts control over property he delusionally believes to be his, would be acquitted of homicide and theft, respectively, if mens rea is subjectively defined. Another, more subtle example of this type of mens rea defense is most likely to arise in connection with a person who is mentally retarded rather than mentally ill. Like a young child, such a person may kill not realizing that a life has been ended, because of an incomplete conception of what life is; for instance, the offender may believe the victim will rejuvenate like a cartoon character. Mens rea, subjectively defined, would be absent in such a case because murder requires not only an intentional killing, but also that the offender understands that the victim is a human being who is capable of dying.

Finally, a person may intentionally engage in conduct and intend the result, under no misapprehension as to the attendant circumstances, but still not intend to commit a crime because of an inadequate understanding of what crime is. There are actually two versions of this type of mens rea requirement. First, the person may not be aware of the concept of crime (as might be true of a three-year-old). Second, the person may understand that criminal prohibitions exist but believe that his specific act is legally permissible (such as might occur when a person from a different country commits an act that would be perfectly legal in his culture, although illegal in ours). The first situation might be called "general" ignorance of the law, while the second might be called "specific" ignorance of the law. Outside of the insanity and infancy contexts, neither type of ignorance has been recognized as an excuse for mala in se crimes. However..., a subjectively defined mens rea doctrine should excuse at least general ignorance of the law, a position that would acquit those rare individuals who intentionally carry out criminal acts without understanding the concepts of good and evil.

In short, the proposal would treat people with mental disorder no differently from people who are not mentally ill, assuming (and this is admittedly a big assumption) a modern criminal justice system that adopts a subjective approach to culpability. [This proposal is justified from] three perspectives: historical, moral, and instrumental. First, as a historical matter, the insanity defense was the only method of mitigating culpability for unreasonable actions; now that other aspects of criminal law doctrine have taken on this role, the defense has lost much of its raison d'etre. Ironically, the scope of the insanity defense began expanding at roughly the same time developments in other parts of the criminal law rendered the original defense redundant in many respects. Second, and most importantly, the proposal captures the universe of mentally disordered individuals who should be excused. The expansion of the defense that has occurred in modern times, whether it encompasses anyone with an "abnormal" condition or is limited to those who are viewed as "irrational," does not adequately distinguish those we excuse from those we do not. Third, the proposal has several practical advantages, including enhancing respect for people with mental illness, facilitating treatment, and promoting the legitimacy of the criminal justice system.

## *Notes and Questions*

1. Professor Morse argues that insanity should focus on whether a mental condition significantly impairs the actor's "capacity for rationality" rather than on whether mental disease or defects impair an actor's capacity to distinguish right from wrong or to control his conduct. More specifically, Morse contends that law is a system of rules that is designed to guide the conduct of individuals. It does so by providing persons with reasons for action. The crime of homicide, for example, provides persons with a legally relevant reason to abstain from killing other people. Similarly, the law of theft provides people with legally relevant reasons to abstain from taking the property of others without consent. In order for the law to successfully guide conduct, the addressees of legal norms must be capable of being guided by reasons. This is why law is not directed at animals or inanimate objects. Given that such entities fail to possess the minimum cognitive capabilities that are necessary to be guided by reasons, legal norms cannot influence their conduct. A human being's capacity to be guided by reasons may be impaired by mental disease or defect. When the impairment significantly reduces or eliminates a human's capacity for rationality, punishing the individual ceases to make sense. Given that such persons are not capable of being guided by reasons, it is pointless to hold them liable for failing to grasp the legally relevant reasons that legislatively defined offenses provide against engaging in certain conduct. This, in turn, provides us with powerful reasons to excuse those who commit crimes when their capacity for rationality is significantly undermined as a result of mental disease or defect. Are you persuaded by Professor Morse's account of when and why insanity should excuse criminal conduct? Would it be better to define insanity as a mental disease or defect that substantially impairs an actor's capacity for rationality or do you prefer to define it according to the *M'Naghten* or the Model Penal Code standards for insanity? Why?

2. Professor Morse argues that addiction should not generally be considered the type of mental disease or defect that triggers the insanity excuse. He contends that although addicts are often irrational, they also—as a general rule—have moments of quiescence during which they have the capacity for rationality and, thus, the capacity to be guided by reasons. It is during these moments that they should seek help to prevent future antisocial conduct. The failure to seek help during these moments of quiescence is culpable and, therefore, worthy of punishment. Nevertheless, Professor Morse suggests that addiction "may sometimes produce a lifestyle with so much physical and psychological stress that the ad-

dict's general capacity for rationality is impaired, even when the desire is not at its peak." In such cases there are no real moments of quiescence during which the actor fully regains the capacity for rationality. As a result, Morse believes that these addicts suffer from what he calls "settled insanity" that should generate a full-blown excuse. Do you agree with Morse's distinction between addicts that should not be excused because they have moments of quiescence and addicts that ought to be excused because they lack such moments of serenity and are therefore in a state of "settled insanity"? Explain. If you disagree with Morse, when—if ever—should addiction excuse conduct? Why?

3. A particularly thorny problem that arises in the context of insanity is whether psychopaths should be excused. The standard legal answer to this question is that such actors should not escape punishment. This is usually done by defining "mental disease or defect" in a way that excludes psychopathy. Subsection (2) of § 4.01 of the Model Penal Code is representative:

> (2) As used in this Article, the terms 'mental disease or defect' do not include an abnormality manifested only by repeated criminal or otherwise antisocial conduct.

Some scholars—like Professor Morse—argue that it is a mistake to exclude psychopathy from the kind of mental disease or defects that may trigger the insanity defense. Morse defines psychopathy as a mental condition causes people to "lack a conscience and the capacity for empathy." According to Morse, psychopaths cannot "understand what the victim will feel" and are thus unable to "feel the anticipation of unpleasant guilt for unjustifiably harming another" that normal people feel when they contemplate harming others. Lacking the capacity to fully understand another's pain, psychopaths cannot truly understand why it is wrong to harm others. As a result, Morse observes that such agents "lack the capacity to grasp and be guided by the primary rational reasons for complying with legal and moral norms." Are you persuaded by Morse's argument in favor of excusing (some) psychopaths?

4. Professor Morse is highly critical of the way in which American criminal law typically deals with what he calls "partially responsible" actors. As was pointed out in § 17.04, in most states diminished capacity mitigates liability for a small number of offenses but does not amount to a general partial defense to all crimes. Furthermore, even in the few jurisdictions adopt a broader view of diminished capacity, mitigation is discretionary rather than mandatory. Morse takes issue with this position, suggesting that it "would improve the quality of justice in criminal cases" to adopt a "generic partial excuse with a legislatively mandated reduction in sentence." Observe that—as was pointed out in the "Comparative Perspectives" section—this is the approach championed in many civil law jurisdictions.

5. While Professor Slobogin does not suggest that insanity should be irrelevant to criminal liability, he believes the freestanding excuse of insanity should be abolished. In its place, Slobogin argues for what he calls a more "subjectified" view of justification defenses, duress and *mens rea* related doctrines.

6. Slobogin argues that insane offenders may be excused if, because of mental disease or defect, they subjectively believe that they are acting in self-defense and they would have a valid claim of self-defense had the circumstances been as they (incorrectly) believed them to be. An example would be an insane person who shoots another incorrectly believing that the person was about to attack him. Similarly, an insane offender would be excused if, because of a mental condition, he subjectively believed that he was acting under coercion when—had the circumstances been as he believed them to be—

he would have a valid duress defense. Slobogin suggests that insane offenders who believe that God commands them to commit an offense would fall in this category. Finally, an insane actor may be excused when his mental disease or defect causes him to believe that he is not committing a crime because he is mistaken about certain facts. An example would be that of an insane person who shoots a person believing that he is shooting at an alien. Slobogin believes that his proposal "captures the universe of mentally disordered individuals who should be excused" while simultaneously denying exculpation to mentally diseased people who should not be excused (e.g., Hinckley, Bobbitt, etc.). Do you agree? Why or why not? Is Slobogin's proposal more attractive than excusing those who satisfy the *M'Naghten* or the Model Penal Code standards of insanity? Explain.

# Chapter 19

# Mistake of Law

## § 19.01 Mistake of Law: *Ignorantia Legis, Neminem Excusat*

### Hoover v. State

Supreme Court of Alabama, 1877
59 Ala. 57

STONE, J.

In *Green v. The State,* at the present term, we entered into an elaborate discussion of section 4189 of the Code of 1876, which prohibits, under severe penalties, intermarriage and living in adultery or fornication between white and colored persons, and declares such marriages void. We are satisfied with the arguments then used, sustained, as the opinion was, by the highest authority, and will not repeat or review it here. The marriage being absolutely void, the offending parties must be treated as unmarried persons, and their sexual cohabitation as fornication within the statute.

The act "to establish a new penal code," Pamph. Acts 121, approved February 23, 1866, contains the section which is now 4189 of the Code of 1876. That section was carried into the Code of 1867 as section 3602. It was approved in the adoption of each of the Codes of 1867 and 1876. The enactment of the statute "to establish a new penal code," was a constitutional enactment of all the provisions contained therein.—*Dew v. Cunningham,* 28 Ala. 466.

The Circuit Court did not err in refusing to receive testimony that, before the alleged marriage, the probate judge counselled the defendant it was lawful for him to marry a white woman. The maxim, *ignorantia legis, neminem excusat,* is a stern, but inflexible and necessary rule of law, that has no exceptions in judicial administration, and the former erroneous ruling of this court furnishes no excuse which we can recognize.—*Boyd v. The State,* December term, 1876; S. C. 4 Otto, 645.

It is very true that to constitute a crime, there must be both an act and an intent. But, in such a case as this, it is enough if the act be knowingly and intentionally committed. The law makes the act the offence, and does not go farther, and require proof that the offenders intended, by the prohibited act, to violate the law. The act being intentionally done, the criminality necessarily follows.

There is no error in the record, but we consider this a case for executive clemency, on condition there be given satisfactory assurance of a discontinuance of this very gross offence against morals and decorum. Should the crime be repeated or continued, the law should lay a heavy restraining hand on the offenders.

Affirmed.

## *Notes and Questions*

1. It is important to distinguish mistakes of law from mistakes of fact. A person is under a mistake of fact when he knows that doing *X* is prohibited but does not know that he is doing *X*. Take, for example, the case of a person who shoots at a human being mistakenly believing that he is shooting at quail. This is a classic case of mistake of fact, for the person knows that shooting at human beings is prohibited, but he does not know—because of his mistaken belief—that he is actually shooting at a human being (he thinks he is shooting at quail). Mistakes of fact are often relevant to criminal liability. The rules governing when mistake of fact defeats liability were discussed in Chapter 9.

2. A person acts under a mistake of law when he knows that he is doing *X*, but he mistakenly believes that doing *X* is not prohibited. In the context of the previous example, a person who knows that he is shooting at a human being but mistakenly believes that doing so is lawful acts under a mistake of law. Another example would be that of a person who knows that he is engaging in sexual intercourse with a person who is fifteen years of age, but he mistakenly believes that doing so is not prohibited because the legal age of consent is fourteen when it is in fact sixteen. In contrast, a person who knows that engaging in sexual intercourse with a person under sixteen is prohibited but mistakenly believes that the victim is seventeen when she in fact is fifteen acts under a mistake of fact.

3. It is also important to distinguish mistakes of criminal law from mistakes of non-criminal law. A person who receives stolen goods incorrectly believing that receipt of such property is not prohibited makes a mistake about the criminal law because she ignores what the penal law criminalizes. This is the kind of mistake of law addressed in this Chapter. In contrast, a person makes a mistake of non-criminal law when she receives abandoned goods incorrectly believing that she is not receiving stolen property because abandoned goods belong to the person who found them. In fact, abandoned goods in that jurisdiction belong to the state. In this case, the actor is not mistaken about what the criminal law prohibits, for she knows that receiving stolen goods is against the penal law. Nevertheless, she incorrectly believes that the goods are not stolen because she makes a mistake about the rules governing property law (i.e., she makes a mistake about non-criminal law). Mistakes of non-criminal law are analogous to mistakes of fact and are thus treated quite often in the same way as mistakes of fact are. The distinction was further explored in Note 3 of § 9.01 of this casebook. The remainder of this chapter focuses on mistakes of criminal law. For the sake of brevity, the rest of the chapter treats "mistake of law" as synonymous with "mistake of criminal law."

4. The *Hoover* case illustrates the traditional common law approach to mistake of law. Regardless of how reasonable the mistake is, mistakes of law are never a defense at common law. This is so even if the actor was mistaken about the law because—as occurred in *Hoover*—he relied on the advice of a legal official that was subsequently ruled to be incorrect.

5. Although American law still refuses to exculpate based on mistake of law in the vast majority of cases, there are now several exceptions to the general principle that mistake of law may never defeat criminal liability. The rest of this chapter explores the few cases in which mistake of law is relevant to the criminal law.

# § 19.02 Mistake of Law: Negating (Some) *Mens Rea*

## Cheek v. United States

Supreme Court of the United States, 1991
498 U.S. 192

Justice WHITE delivered the opinion of the Court.

Title 26, § 7201 of the United States Code provides that any person "who willfully attempts in any manner to evade or defeat any tax imposed by this title or the payment thereof" shall be guilty of a felony. Under 26 U.S.C. § 7203, "[a]ny person required under this title ... or by regulations made under authority thereof to make a return ... who willfully fails to ... make such return" shall be guilty of a misdemeanor. This case turns on the meaning of the word "willfully" as used in §§ 7201 and 7203.

I

Petitioner John L. Cheek has been a pilot for American Airlines since 1973. He filed federal income tax returns through 1979 but thereafter ceased to file returns. He also claimed an increasing number of withholding allowances—eventually claiming 60 allowances by mid-1980—and for the years 1981 to 1984 indicated on his W-4 forms that he was exempt from federal income taxes. In 1983, petitioner unsuccessfully sought a refund of all tax withheld by his employer in 1982. Petitioner's income during this period at all times far exceeded the minimum necessary to trigger the statutory filing requirement.

As a result of his activities, petitioner was indicted for 10 violations of federal law. He was charged with six counts of willfully failing to file a federal income tax return for the years 1980, 1981, and 1983 through 1986, in violation of § 7203. He was further charged with three counts of willfully attempting to evade his income taxes for the years 1980, 1981, and 1983 in violation of 26 U.S.C. § 7201. In those years, American Airlines withheld substantially less than the amount of tax petitioner owed because of the numerous allowances and exempt status he claimed on his W-4 forms. The tax offenses with which petitioner was charged are specific intent crimes that require the defendant to have acted willfully.

At trial, the evidence established that between 1982 and 1986, petitioner was involved in at least four civil cases that challenged various aspects of the federal income tax system. In all four of those cases, the plaintiffs were informed by the courts that many of their arguments, including that they were not taxpayers within the meaning of the tax laws, that wages are not income, that the Sixteenth Amendment does not authorize the imposition of an income tax on individuals, and that the Sixteenth Amendment is unenforceable, were frivolous or had been repeatedly rejected by the courts. During this time period, petitioner also attended at least two criminal trials of persons charged with tax offenses. In addition, there was evidence that in 1980 or 1981 an attorney had advised Cheek that the courts had rejected as frivolous the claim that wages are not income.

Cheek represented himself at trial and testified in his defense. He admitted that he had not filed personal income tax returns during the years in question. He testified that as early as 1978, he had begun attending seminars sponsored by, and following the advice of, a group that believes, among other things, that the federal tax system is unconstitutional. Some of the speakers at these meetings were lawyers who purported to give professional opinions about the invalidity of the federal income tax laws. Cheek produced a letter from an attorney stating that the Sixteenth Amendment did not authorize a tax on wages and salaries but only on gain or profit. Petitioner's defense was that, based on the indoctrination he received from this group and from his own study, he sincerely believed that the tax laws were being unconstitutionally enforced and that his actions during the 1980–1986 period were lawful. He therefore argued that he had acted without the willfulness required for conviction of the various offenses with which he was charged.

In the course of its instructions, the trial court advised the jury that to prove "willfulness" the Government must prove the voluntary and intentional violation of a known legal duty, a burden that could not be proved by showing mistake, ignorance, or negligence. The court further advised the jury that an objectively reasonable good-faith misunderstanding of the law would negate willfulness, but mere disagreement with the law would not. The court described Cheek's beliefs about the income tax system and instructed the jury that if it found that Cheek "honestly and reasonably believed that he was not required to pay income taxes or to file tax returns," a not guilty verdict should be returned.

After several hours of deliberation, the jury sent a note to the judge that stated in part:

> "'We have a basic disagreement between some of us as to if Mr. Cheek honestly & reasonably believed that he was not required to pay income taxes.
>
> ....
>
> "'Page 32 [the relevant jury instruction] discusses good faith misunderstanding & disagreement. Is there any additional clarification you can give us on this point?'"

The District Judge responded with a supplemental instruction containing the following statements:

> "[A] person's opinion that the tax laws violate his constitutional rights does not constitute a good faith misunderstanding of the law. Furthermore, a person's disagreement with the government's tax collection systems and policies does not constitute a good faith misunderstanding of the law."

At the end of the first day of deliberation, the jury sent out another note saying that it still could not reach a verdict because "'[w]e are divided on the issue as to if Mr. Cheek honestly & reasonably believed that he was not required to pay income tax.'" When the jury resumed its deliberations, the District Judge gave the jury an additional instruction. This instruction stated in part that "[a]n honest but unreasonable belief is not a defense and does not negate willfulness," and that "[a]dvice or research resulting in the conclusion that wages of a privately employed person are not income or that the tax laws are unconstitutional is not objectively reasonable and cannot serve as the basis for a good faith misunderstanding of the law defense." The court also instructed the jury that "[p]ersistent refusal to acknowledge the law does not constitute a good faith misunderstanding of the law." Approximately two hours later, the jury returned a verdict finding petitioner guilty on all counts.

Petitioner appealed his convictions, arguing that the District Court erred by instructing the jury that only an objectively reasonable misunderstanding of the law negates the statutory willfulness requirement. The United States Court of Appeals for the Seventh Circuit rejected that contention and affirmed the convictions. In prior cases, the Seventh Circuit had made clear that good-faith misunderstanding of the law negates willfulness only if the defendant's beliefs are objectively reasonable; in the Seventh Circuit, even actual ignorance is not a defense unless the defendant's ignorance was itself objectively reasonable. In its opinion in this case, the court noted that several specified beliefs, including the beliefs that the tax laws are unconstitutional and that wages are not income, would not be objectively reasonable. Because the Seventh Circuit's interpretation of "willfully" as used in these statutes conflicts with the decisions of several other Courts of Appeals, we granted certiorari.

II

The general rule that ignorance of the law or a mistake of law is no defense to criminal prosecution is deeply rooted in the American legal system. Based on the notion that the law is definite and knowable, the common law presumed that every person knew the law. This common-law rule has been applied by the Court in numerous cases construing criminal statutes.

The proliferation of statutes and regulations has sometimes made it difficult for the average citizen to know and comprehend the extent of the duties and obligations imposed by the tax laws. Congress has accordingly softened the impact of the common-law presumption by making specific intent to violate the law an element of certain federal criminal tax offenses. Thus, the Court almost 60 years ago interpreted the statutory term "willfully" as used in the federal criminal tax statutes as carving out an exception to the traditional rule. This special treatment of criminal tax offenses is largely due to the complexity of the tax laws. In *United States v. Murdock,* the Court recognized that:

> "Congress did not intend that a person, by reason of a bona fide misunderstanding as to his liability for the tax, as to his duty to make a return, or as to the adequacy of the records he maintained, should become a criminal by his mere failure to measure up to the prescribed standard of conduct."

The Court held that the defendant was entitled to an instruction with respect to whether he acted in good faith based on his actual belief. In *Murdock,* the Court interpreted the term "willfully" as used in the criminal tax statutes generally to mean "an act done with a bad purpose," or with "an evil motive".

Subsequent decisions have refined this proposition.... [In] *United States v. Pomponio* ... [we held that] willfulness in this context simply means a voluntary, intentional violation of a known legal duty. We concluded that after instructing the jury on willfulness, "[a]n additional instruction on good faith was unnecessary."

III

Cheek accepts the *Pomponio* definition of willfulness, but asserts that the District Court's instructions and the Court of Appeals' opinion departed from that definition. In particular, he challenges the ruling that a good-faith misunderstanding of the law or a good-faith belief that one is not violating the law, if it is to negate willfulness, must be objectively reasonable. We agree that the Court of Appeals and the District Court erred in this respect.

A

Willfulness, as construed by our prior decisions in criminal tax cases, requires the Government to prove that the law imposed a duty on the defendant, that the defendant knew of this duty, and that he voluntarily and intentionally violated that duty. We deal first with the case where the issue is whether the defendant knew of the duty purportedly imposed by the provision of the statute or regulation he is accused of violating, a case in which there is no claim that the provision at issue is invalid. In such a case, if the Government proves actual knowledge of the pertinent legal duty, the prosecution, without more, has satisfied the knowledge component of the willfulness requirement. But carrying this burden requires negating a defendant's claim of ignorance of the law or a claim that because of a misunderstanding of the law, he had a good-faith belief that he was not violating any of the provisions of the tax laws. This is so because one cannot be aware that the law imposes a duty upon him and yet be ignorant of it, misunderstand the law, or believe that the duty does not exist. In the end, the issue is whether, based on all the evidence, the Government has proved that the defendant was aware of the duty at issue, which cannot be true if the jury credits a good-faith misunderstanding and belief submission, whether or not the claimed belief or misunderstanding is objectively reasonable.

In this case, if Cheek asserted that he truly believed that the Internal Revenue Code did not purport to treat wages as income, and the jury believed him, the Government would not have carried its burden to prove willfulness, however unreasonable a court might deem such a belief. Of course, in deciding whether to credit Cheek's good-faith belief claim, the jury would be free to consider any admissible evidence from any source showing that Cheek was aware of his duty to file a return and to treat wages as income, including evidence showing his awareness of the relevant provisions of the Code or regulations, of court decisions rejecting his interpretation of the tax law, of authoritative rulings of the Internal Revenue Service, or of any contents of the personal income tax return forms and accompanying instructions that made it plain that wages should be returned as income.

We thus disagree with the Court of Appeals' requirement that a claimed good-faith belief must be objectively reasonable if it is to be considered as possibly negating the Government's evidence purporting to show a defendant's awareness of the legal duty at issue. Knowledge and belief are characteristically questions for the factfinder, in this case the jury. Characterizing a particular belief as not objectively reasonable transforms the inquiry into a legal one and would prevent the jury from considering it. It would of course be proper to exclude evidence having no relevance or probative value with respect to willfulness; but it is not contrary to common sense, let alone impossible, for a defendant to be ignorant of his duty based on an irrational belief that he has no duty ...

It was therefore error to instruct the jury to disregard evidence of Cheek's understanding that, within the meaning of the tax laws, he was not a person required to file a return or to pay income taxes and that wages are not taxable income, as incredible as such misunderstandings of and beliefs about the law might be. Of course, the more unreasonable the asserted beliefs or misunderstandings are, the more likely the jury will consider them to be nothing more than simple disagreement with known legal duties imposed by the tax laws and will find that the Government has carried its burden of proving knowledge.

### B

Cheek asserted in the trial court that he should be acquitted because he believed in good faith that the income tax law is unconstitutional as applied to him and thus could not legally impose any duty upon him of which he should have been aware. Such a submission is unsound, not because Cheek's constitutional arguments are not objectively reasonable or frivolous, which they surely are, but because the *Murdock-Pomponio* line of cases does not support such a position. Those cases construed the willfulness requirement in the criminal provisions of the Internal Revenue Code to require proof of knowledge of the law. This was because in "our complex tax system, uncertainty often arises even among taxpayers who earnestly wish to follow the law," and "'[i]t is not the purpose of the law to penalize frank difference of opinion or innocent errors made despite the exercise of reasonable care.'"

Claims that some of the provisions of the tax code are unconstitutional are submissions of a different order. They do not arise from innocent mistakes caused by the complexity of the Internal Revenue Code. Rather, they reveal full knowledge of the provisions at issue and a studied conclusion, however wrong, that those provisions are invalid and unenforceable. Thus in this case, Cheek paid his taxes for years, but after attending various seminars and based on his own study, he concluded that the income tax laws could not constitutionally require him to pay a tax.

We do not believe that Congress contemplated that such a taxpayer, without risking criminal prosecution, could ignore the duties imposed upon him by the Internal Revenue Code and refuse to utilize the mechanisms provided by Congress to present his claims of invalidity to the courts and to abide by their decisions. There is no doubt that Cheek, from year to year, was free to pay the tax that the law purported to require, file for a refund and, if denied, present his claims of invalidity, constitutional or otherwise, to the courts. Also, without paying the tax, he could have challenged claims of tax deficiencies in the Tax Court with the right to appeal to a higher court if unsuccessful. Cheek took neither course in some years, and when he did was unwilling to accept the outcome. As we see it, he is in no position to claim that his good-faith belief about the validity of the Internal Revenue Code negates willfulness or provides a defense to criminal prosecution under §§ 7201 and 7203. Of course, Cheek was free in this very case to present his claims of invalidity and have them adjudicated, but like defendants in criminal cases in other contexts, who "willfully" refuse to comply with the duties placed upon them by the law, he must take the risk of being wrong.

We thus hold that in a case like this, a defendant's views about the validity of the tax statutes are irrelevant to the issue of willfulness and need not be heard by the jury, and, if they are, an instruction to disregard them would be proper. For this purpose, it makes no difference whether the claims of invalidity are frivolous or have substance. It was therefore not error in this case for the District Judge to instruct the jury not to consider Cheek's claims that the tax laws were unconstitutional. However, it was error for the court to instruct the jury that petitioner's asserted beliefs that wages are not income and that he was not a taxpayer within the meaning of the Internal Revenue Code should not be considered by the jury in determining whether Cheek had acted willfully.

## IV

For the reasons set forth in the opinion above, the judgment of the Court of Appeals is vacated, and the case is remanded for further proceedings consistent with this opinion.

**Justice BLACKMUN, with whom Justice MARSHALL joins, dissenting.**

It seems to me that we are concerned in this case not with "the complexity of the tax laws," but with the income tax law in its most elementary and basic aspect: Is a wage earner a taxpayer and are wages income?

The Court acknowledges that the conclusively established standard for willfulness under the applicable statutes is the "'voluntary, intentional violation of a known legal duty.'" That being so, it is incomprehensible to me how, in this day, more than 70 years after the institution of our present federal income tax system with the passage of the Income Tax Act of 1913 any taxpayer of competent mentality can assert as his defense to charges of statutory willfulness the proposition that the wage he receives for his labor is not income, irrespective of a cult that says otherwise and advises the gullible to resist income tax collections. One might note in passing that this particular taxpayer, after all, was a licensed pilot for one of our major commercial airlines; he presumably was a person of at least minimum intellectual competence....

This Court's opinion today, I fear, will encourage taxpayers to cling to frivolous views of the law in the hope of convincing a jury of their sincerity. If that ensues, I suspect we have gone beyond the limits of common sense.

While I may not agree with every word the Court of Appeals has enunciated in its opinion, I would affirm its judgment in this case. I therefore dissent.

## *Notes and Questions*

1. The *Cheek* case illustrates one of the few instances in which mistake of law may defeat criminal liability. The exception crafted in *Cheek* is of very narrow application. According to the case, some statutes that prohibit "willfully" engaging in certain conduct require the prosecution to prove that the defendant was aware that his conduct was prohibited by law. The doctrine is predicated on a broad reading of the *mens rea* term "willfully." According to the Supreme Court, "willfully" in the context of the tax law means, among other things, "that the defendant knew of [the duty imposed by law], and that he voluntarily and intentionally violated that duty." Mistake of law is relevant to negate willfulness so defined, for it negates that the actor knew of the duty imposed by law. Furthermore—as the Supreme Court points out in *Cheek*—good faith mistakes of law defeat liability in such cases even if they are unreasonable, for any honestly held belief in the lawfulness of the conduct negates knowledge about the conduct's unlawfulness. Do you agree with how the Court defines "willfulness" in this context? Are you persuaded that both reasonable and unreasonable mistakes of law should defeat liability in prosecutions under the tax law for crimes that require "willfulness" as the relevant *mens rea*? Explain.

2. The Court held that the defendant in *Cheek* must be acquitted if the jury concludes that he honestly believed that "he was not a person required to file a return or to pay income taxes" or that "wages are not taxable income." An acquittal would be warranted if the defendant honestly held such beliefs even if they were unreasonable and "incredible as such misunderstandings of and beliefs about the law might be." Do you agree with this outcome? Why or why not?

3. The *Cheek* doctrine is particularly stringent in cases in which defendant is charged with a willful violation of the tax laws. As the Supreme Court pointed out, "[t]his special treatment of criminal tax offenses is largely due to the complexity of the tax laws." Furthermore, the *Cheek* doctrine is more easily defensible when the defendant is charged with a *malum prohibitum* crime (e.g., tearing the tag off a mattress). Given that the conduct in such cases is not inherently wrongful, a defendant who is unaware that the law prohibits such conduct is not particularly blameworthy. In contrast, application of the *Cheek* standard in cases in which the crime charged is *malum in se* (e.g., theft) is more problematic, for in these instances the criminalized conduct is inherently wrongful and, therefore, the defendant's lack of awareness of the criminality of the conduct appears to be worthy of condemnation. As a result of these considerations, it is unclear whether "willfulness" is construed as broadly as it was in *Cheek* when the defendant is charged with willful violations of non-tax statutes. There is authority to suggest that grossly unreasonable beliefs in the lawfulness of the conduct do not negate willfulness in at least some non-tax law related contexts. This is particularly the case when the offense charged is *malum in se.* See, e.g., *Bryan v. United States,* 524 U.S. 184 (1998) (construing "willfulness" more narrowly than in *Cheek* in prosecution for dealing in firearms without a federal license), *United States v. Petrie,* 302 F.3d 1280 (11th Cir., 2002) (construing "willfulness" more narrowly than in *Cheek* in prosecution for conspiracy to money launder), *United*

*States v. Mathes,* 151 F.3d 251 (5th Cir., 1998) (construing "willfulness" more narrowly than in *Cheek* in prosecution for willfully failing to pay child support).

4. While the Supreme Court held in *Cheek* that a good faith mistake of law may negate the *mens rea* of "willfulness" in some contexts, in the vast majority of cases mistake of law does not negate the mental state required by the offense. In such instances, mistake of law is generally irrelevant to criminal liability, even if reasonable. However, there are a few cases in which mistake of law does defeat liability although it does not negate *mens rea.* When this occurs, mistake of law provides the defendant with an excuse for having engaged in conduct that unjustifiably satisfies both the objective and subjective elements of the offense. In these cases, mistake of law amounts to a general excuse defense similar to duress or insanity. That is, an actor exculpated because of mistake of law in these instances behaves wrongfully and, therefore, not justifiably. His conduct remains unlawful and may thus generate other forms of non-penal liability. Furthermore, it may not be lawfully assisted by third parties and may be lawfully resisted by others. Nevertheless, mistake of law excuses conduct in very specific circumstances in which the actor cannot be fairly expected to know that what he is doing is against the law. The remaining sections explore mistake of law as an excuse.

## § 19.03 Mistake of Law: Due Process and Mistake of Law

### Lambert v. California

Supreme Court of the United States, 1957
355 U.S. 225

Mr. Justice DOUGLAS delivered the opinion of the Court.

Section 52.38(a) of the Los Angeles Municipal Code defines 'convicted person' as follows:

> 'Any person who, subsequent to January 1, 1921, has been or hereafter is convicted of an offense punishable as a felony in the State of California, or who has been or who is hereafter convicted of any offense in any place other than the State of California, which offense, if committed in the State of California, would have been punishable as a felony.'

Section 52.39 provides that it shall be unlawful for 'any convicted person' to be or remain in Los Angeles for a period of more than five days without registering; it requires any person having a place of abode outside the city to register if he comes into the city on five occasions or more during a 30-day period; and it prescribes the information to be furnished the Chief of Police on registering.

Section 52.43(b) makes the failure to register a continuing offense, each day's failure constituting a separate offense.

Appellant, arrested on suspicion of another offense, was charged with a violation of this registration law. The evidence showed that she had been at the time of her arrest a resident of Los Angeles for over seven years. Within that period she had been convicted in Los Angeles of the crime of forgery, an offense which California punishes as a felony. Though convicted of a crime punishable as a felony, she had not at the time of her arrest registered under the Municipal Code. At the trial, appellant asserted that § 52.39 of the Code denies her due process of law and other rights under the Federal Constitution, unnecessary to enumerate. The trial court denied this objection. The case was tried to a jury which found appellant guilty. The court fined her $250 and placed her on probation for three years. Appellant, renewing her constitutional objection, moved for arrest of judgment and a new trial. This motion was denied. On appeal the constitutionality of the Code was again challenged. The Appellate Department of the Superior Court affirmed the judgment, holding there was no merit to the claim that the ordinance was unconstitutional. The case is here on appeal ... [W]e now hold that the registration provisions of the Code as sought to be applied here violate the Due Process requirement of the Fourteenth Amendment.

The registration provision, carrying criminal penalties, applies if a person has been convicted 'of an offense punishable as a felony in the State of California' or, in case he has been convicted in another State, if the offense 'would have been punishable as a felony' had it been committee in California. No element of willfulness is by terms included in the ordinance nor read into it by the California court as a condition necessary for a conviction.

We must assume that appellant had no actual knowledge of the requirement that she register under this ordinance, as she offered proof of this defense which was refused. The question is whether a registration act of this character violates due process where it is applied to a person who has no actual knowledge of his duty to register, and where no showing is made of the probability of such knowledge.

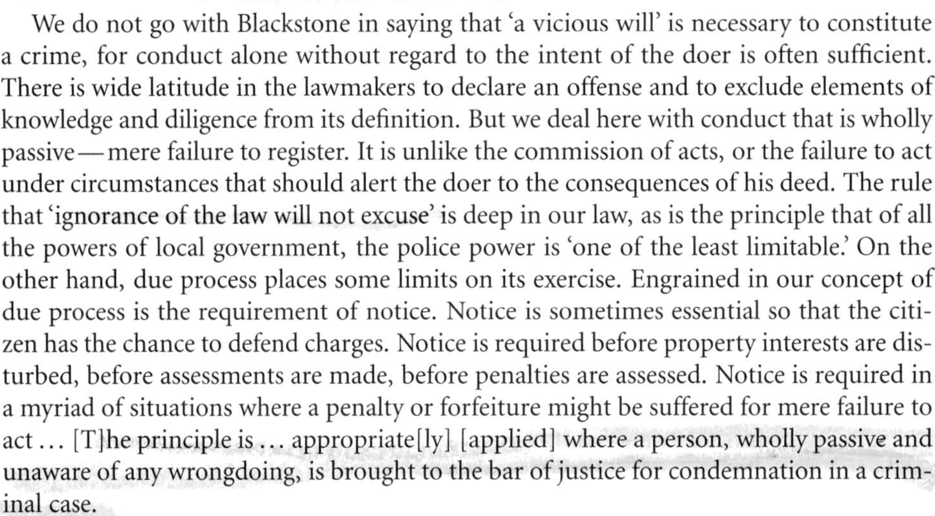

We do not go with Blackstone in saying that 'a vicious will' is necessary to constitute a crime, for conduct alone without regard to the intent of the doer is often sufficient. There is wide latitude in the lawmakers to declare an offense and to exclude elements of knowledge and diligence from its definition. But we deal here with conduct that is wholly passive—mere failure to register. It is unlike the commission of acts, or the failure to act under circumstances that should alert the doer to the consequences of his deed. The rule that 'ignorance of the law will not excuse' is deep in our law, as is the principle that of all the powers of local government, the police power is 'one of the least limitable.' On the other hand, due process places some limits on its exercise. Engrained in our concept of due process is the requirement of notice. Notice is sometimes essential so that the citizen has the chance to defend charges. Notice is required before property interests are disturbed, before assessments are made, before penalties are assessed. Notice is required in a myriad of situations where a penalty or forfeiture might be suffered for mere failure to act ... [T]he principle is ... appropriate[ly] [applied] where a person, wholly passive and unaware of any wrongdoing, is brought to the bar of justice for condemnation in a criminal case.

Registration laws are common and their range is wide. Many such laws are akin to licensing statutes in that they pertain to the regulation of business activities. But the present ordinance is entirely different. Violation of its provisions is unaccompanied by any activity whatever, mere presence in the city being the test. Moreover, circumstances which might move one to inquire as to the necessity of registration are completely lacking. At most the ordinance is but a law enforcement technique designed for the convenience of law enforcement agencies through which a list of the names and addresses of felons then residing in a given community is compiled. The disclosure is merely a compilation of former convictions already publicly recorded in the jurisdiction where obtained. Nevertheless, this appellant on first becoming aware of her duty to register was given no opportunity to comply with the law and avoid its penalty, even though her default was entirely innocent. She could but suffer the consequences of the ordinance, namely, conviction with the imposition of heavy criminal penalties thereunder. We believe that actual knowledge of the duty to register or proof of the probability of such knowledge and subsequent failure to comply are necessary before a conviction under the ordinance can stand. As Holmes wrote in The Common Law, 'A law which punished conduct which would not be blameworthy in the average member of the community would be too severe for that community to bear.' Its severity lies in the absence of an opportunity either to avoid the consequences of the law or to defend any prosecution brought under it. Where a person did not know of the duty to register and where there was no proof of the probability of such knowledge, he may not be convicted consistently with due process. Were it otherwise, the evil would be as great as it is when the law is written in print too fine to read or in a language foreign to the community.

Reversed.

## *Notes and Questions*

1. As the Supreme Court pointed out in *Lambert,* the Due Process clauses of the Fifth and Fourteenth Amendments of the United States Constitution sometimes bar the imposition of criminal liability when the defendant is unaware that his conduct is prohibited by law. That is, in a limited set of circumstances, a defendant is constitutionally allowed to plead mistake of law even when the offense charged prescribes no *mens rea* and the local law does not allow for mistake of law to be pleaded as an excuse.

2. The rationale underlying the Court's decision in *Lambert* is that in a very limited set of cases, a defendant may have absolutely no reason to know that his conduct is criminal and may thus be deprived of fair warning and notice if he is prosecuted for engaging in such conduct. The facts of *Lambert* are illustrative. According to the Court, the ordinance requiring convicts to register with the city of Los Angeles did not criminalize affirmative conduct. Instead, it merely criminalized being present in the city for five days without registering. Furthermore, the Court pointed out that "circumstances which might move one to inquire as to the necessity of registration [were] completely lacking" in this case. Finally, actors who eventually become aware of their duty to register are given "no opportunity to comply with the law and avoid its penalty, even though [their] default was entirely innocent." As a result, the Court concluded that many innocent people might be convicted under this law although they had no reason to believe that such passive conduct was criminal. Such convictions are fundamentally unfair, deprive actors of notice and fair warning and, therefore, violate the Due Process clauses of the Fifth and Fourteenth Amendments. Are you persuaded by the Court's analysis? Why or why not?

3. The Court held that convictions under the statute challenged in *Lambert* could stand only if the prosecution proves either "actual knowledge of the duty to register" or "proof of the probability of such knowledge" and a "subsequent failure to comply." Note that a defendant's good faith belief that there is no duty to register is not enough to defeat liability under the statute, for the prosecution may secure a conviction by proving that there was a probability that the defendant knew about the duty to register. That is, a defendant's unreasonable but honestly held belief that there is no duty might not be enough to trigger the *Lambert* rule, for in such cases it could be held that a reasonable person would have been able to know that the duty existed by making reasonable efforts to find out.

4. Narrowly construed, the constitutional problems discussed in *Lambert* arise solely when the challenged law criminalizes *malum prohibitum* conduct and imposes strict liability for a failure to act in circumstances that would not move a reasonable person to inquire as to whether the duty to act existed. The universe of cases in which this narrow

rule will come into play is quite small. Nevertheless, the fair warning and notice principles that underpin the Supreme Court's holding in *Lambert* may be implicated in other circumstances. The most obvious cases are instances in which the government either does not adequately publicize the enactment of a criminal law or when the defendant believes that the conduct is lawful because he relies on an official interpretation of law that is later overturned. In such cases it might plausibly be argued that the defendant lacked fair warning that the conduct was prohibited. These are the concerns that undergird the Model Penal Code's approach to mistake of law, which is discussed in the next section.

## § 19.04 Mistake of Law: Model Penal Code

### Haggren v. State

Court of Appeals of Alaska, 1992
829 P.2d 842

MANNHEIMER, Judge.

J. Michael Haggren was convicted of the strict liability violation of operating a commercial drift gill net within 600 feet of a set gill net. Haggren now appeals both his conviction and his sentence. We affirm.

According to the written findings entered by Superior Court Judge Charles K. Cranston, Haggren was fishing with a drift net approximately 250 feet offshore from a shore fishery lease issued by the City of Kenai to Frank Canady. As Haggren was fishing, Canady placed a set net in the water and began to fish. Believing that the two nets were so close they might become entangled, Canady asked Haggren to pull his gear out of the water and move. Haggren refused. The nets did in fact become entangled, prompting Canady to cut Haggren's net. Canady kept the approximately 1,200 fish that were in Haggren's net.

When Haggren saw Canady on the shore, preparing to set his net, Haggren called the Alaska State Trooper dispatcher. This conversation occurred:

HAGGREN: Is this [Fish & Wildlife] Protection?

DISPATCHER: Yes, it is.

HAGGREN: Yeah, I'd like a clarification on a regulation.

DISPATCHER: Ah, what would you like, sir?

HAGGREN: It's on commercial fishing.

DISPATCHER: What is your question, sir?

HAGGREN: In regards to the distance between set nets and drift nets. The distance between set netters and drift netters is 600 feet. Is it the first net in the water that has the right of way?

After conferring with Fish & Wildlife Patrol Officer Titus, the dispatcher responded that the first net in the water had the right of way. Officer Titus later testified that he based his response on the assumption that there was 600 feet between the set net and the drift net. Officer Titus testified that, had he known all the circumstances, his response would have been that Haggren was obliged to stay 600 feet from the set net.

Judge Cranston found that, even though Haggren had been the first to deploy his net in the area, Haggren had violated 5 AAC 21.335 when, following Canady's deployment of the set net, Haggren had continued to operate his drift net within 600 feet of Canady's set net.

Haggren argues that, because his net was the first in the water, he had priority and it was Canady who was obliged to deploy his set net more than 600 feet from Haggren's drift net. This court recently adopted a rule of "first in time, first in right" when we interpreted a related regulation, which provides: "No set gill net may be set or operated within 600 feet of another set gill net". *Clucas v. State*. However, Haggren was charged with violating 5 AAC 21.335(a), a regulation worded in a significantly different way:

> Minimum Distance Between Units of Gear.
>
> (a) No part of a commercial drift gill net or set gill net may be set or operated within 600 feet of any part of another commercial set gill net.

With respect to two competing commercial set gill nets, this regulation is identical to the one interpreted in Clucas. However, between a competing commercial drift gill net and set gill net, the regulation operates differently: it is the conduct of the drift net fisherman that is regulated. A person operating a commercial drift gill net may neither set the net nor continue its operation within 600 feet of a commercial set gill net. Judge Cranston correctly interpreted the regulation; Haggren violated 5 AAC 21.335(a) when he refused to move his drift net after Canady deployed his set net.

Haggren also argues that, even if 5 AAC 21.335(a) invariably gives set netters priority over drift netters, he still should not be convicted because he reasonably relied on the mistaken advice of the State Troopers that the first net in the water had priority. Generally, a defendant's mistake—even a reasonable mistake—about what the law requires is not a defense to a criminal (or, as here, a quasi-criminal) charge. Ostrosky v. State. The legislature has enacted a limited "mistake of law" defense covering situations when a person acts in the reasonable belief that the conduct is required or authorized by a court order, or to carry out court process, or to assist a police officer in carrying out his or her official duties. AS 11.81.420. However, none of these exceptions applies to Haggren's case.

In Ostrosky, this court indicated a willingness to entertain an expanded "reasonable mistake of law" defense as a matter of common law. However, the facts presented in Ostrosky—a litigant's reliance on a decision of the superior court—fall within the defense established by the legislature. AS 11.81.420(b)(1). Moreover, even under the expansive formulation of the "mistake of law" defense proposed by the Model Penal Code, Haggren's conduct in this case would not be excused.

The broadest formulation of the "reasonable mistake of law" defense is found in Model Penal Code § 2.04(3)(b) (Official Draft, 1962). The Model Penal Code provision suggests that

> a defendant be excused from criminal liability if he or she acted in reasonable reliance on a mistaken "official statement of law ... contained in (i) a statute or other enactment, (ii) a judicial decision, opinion, or judgment, (iii) an administrative order or grant of permission, or (iv) an official interpretation of the public officer or body charged by law with responsibility for the interpretation, administration, or enforcement of the law defining the offense."

At his trial, Haggren relied upon his conversation with the State Troopers to argue that he was affirmatively misled about the requirements of the regulation. He also testified that he was aware of a memorandum opinion issued by this court which purportedly held that a drift net fisherman has priority over a set net fisherman who arrives later.

We hold that Haggren cannot rely on a mistaken interpretation of the law provided by the State Trooper dispatcher or the Fish and Wildlife Protection officer whom the dispatcher consulted. As noted above, Haggren's claim is not cognizable under the "mistake of law" defense contained in AS 11.81.420(b). Even under the Model Penal Code's broad formulation of the "mistake of law" defense, a defendant cannot rely on an interpretation of the law provided by a police officer who happens to be available. The defendant must show that he or she relied on an "official interpretation" provided by "the public officer or body charged by law with ... enforcement of the law defining the offense." We interpret this language to refer to a formal interpretation of the law issued by the chief enforcement officer or agency; it does not encompass extemporaneous legal advice or interpretations given by a subordinate officer ...

Haggren also claims that he relied on a memorandum opinion of this court. Both Alaska Appellate Rule 214(d) and Court of Appeals Order No. 3 state that unpublished opinions have no precedential effect and are not to be cited as legal authority. Given this, we doubt that it would ever be reasonable for a defendant to rely on a statement of law contained in an unpublished decision of this court (unless the defendant was a party to the case). Moreover, even if a memorandum opinion could be relied upon to establish a defendant's reasonable mistake of law, Haggren has misinterpreted the memorandum opinion he alluded to in district court; the ruling in that case does not apply to the facts of Haggren's case.

Finally, we note the general rule suggested in W. LaFave & A. Scott, Substantive Criminal Law (1986), § 5.1(a), Vol. 1, pp. 575–77, that mistake of law should constitute a defense only if the mistake negates the existence of the culpable mental state required to establish the crime. This rule is incorporated in the Model Penal Code, § 2.04(1), and it is supported by the statutes listed in the Commentary to the Model Penal Code. This interpretation of the defense would make it unavailable in a strict liability prosecution like Haggren's.

The judgement of the district court is AFFIRMED.

## *Notes and Questions*

1. As the Court correctly points out in *Haggren,* the § 2.04 of the Model Penal Code provides an excuse to those who mistakenly believe that their conduct is lawful pursuant to their reliance on an official statement of law contained in a statute, judicial or administrative decision, or an official interpretation of the public officer or body charged by law with responsibility for the interpretation of the relevant statute. The problem in *Haggren* was that the defendant relied on the interpretation of the statute made by a subordinate officer in the Department of Fish and Wildlife Protection. According to the Court, this is not the kind of official interpretation that actors may rely on pursuant to the Model Penal Code. The only interpretation that counts as "official" under the Code is that of the "chief enforcement officer or agency" in charge of enforcing the law. As a result, reliance on "extemporaneous legal advice or interpretations given by a subordinate officer" does not trigger application of the Model Penal Code's mistake of law provision. Do you agree with the outcome of the case or do you think that reliance on a subordinate public officer's interpretation of the relevant law should generate an excuse?

2. An oft-cited case in this context is *People v. Marrero,* 69 N.Y.2d 382 (1987). The defendant in *Marrero* was charged with criminal possession of a weapon. He raised the mistake of law defense, claiming that he was a Federal corrections officer in Danbury,

Connecticut, and "that there were various interpretations of fellow officers and teachers, as well as the peace officer statute itself, upon which he relied for his mistaken belief that he could carry a weapon with legal impunity." Construing the New York mistake of law statute—which closely tracks the Model Penal Code's analogous provision—the New York Court of Appeals rejected the defendant's contention. In doing so, it explained that:

> It was early recognized that the "official statement" mistake of law defense was a statutory protection against prosecution based on reliance of a statute that did *in fact* authorize certain conduct. "It seems obvious that society must rely on some statement of the law, and that conduct which *is in fact* 'authorized' * * * should not be subsequently condemned. The threat of punishment under these circumstances can have no deterrent effect unless the actor doubts the validity of the official pronouncement—*a questioning of authority that is itself undesirable.*" While providing a narrow escape hatch, the idea was simultaneously to encourage the public to read and rely on official statements of the law, not to have individuals conveniently and personally question the validity and interpretation of the law and act on that basis. If later the statute was invalidated, one who mistakenly acted in reliance on the authorizing statute would be relieved of criminal liability. That makes sense and is fair. To go further does not make sense and would create a legal chaos based on individual selectivity.
>
> In the case before us, the underlying statute never *in fact authorized* the defendant's conduct; the defendant only thought that the statutory exemptions permitted his conduct when, in fact, the primary statute clearly forbade his conduct. Moreover, by adjudication of the final court to speak on the subject in this very case, it turned out that even the exemption statute did not permit this defendant to possess the weapon. It would be ironic at best and an odd perversion at worst for this court now to declare that the same defendant is nevertheless free of criminal responsibility.
>
> The "official statement" component in the mistake of law defense in both paragraphs (a) and (d) adds yet another element of support for our interpretation and holding. Defendant tried to establish a defense under Penal Law § 15.20(2)(d) as a second prong. But the interpretation of the statute relied upon must be "officially made or issued by a public servant, agency or body legally charged or empowered with the responsibility or privilege of administering, enforcing or interpreting such statute or law." We agree with the People that the trial court also properly rejected the defense under Penal Law § 15.20(2)(d) since none of the interpretations which defendant proffered meets the requirements of the statute. The fact that there are various complementing exceptions to section 15.20, none of which defendant could bring himself under, further emphasizes the correctness of our view which decides this case under particular statutes with appropriate precedential awareness.
>
> It must also be emphasized that, while our construction of Penal Law § 15.20 provides for narrow application of the mistake of law defense, it does not, as the dissenters contend, "rule out *any* defense based on mistake of law." To the contrary, mistake of law is a viable exemption in those instances where an individual demonstrates an effort to learn what the law is, relies on the validity of that law and, later, it is determined that there was a *mistake in the law itself.*
>
> The modern availability of this defense is based on the theory that where the government has affirmatively, albeit unintentionally, misled an individual as to

> what may or may not be legally permissible conduct, the individual should not be punished as a result. This is salutary and enlightened and should be firmly supported in appropriate cases. However, it also follows that where, as here, the government is not responsible for the error (for there is none except in the defendant's own mind), mistake of law should not be available as an excuse.

3. In a sense, the outcome of *Marrero* is unremarkable. If the Fish and Wildlife police officer who advised the defendant in *Haggren* was capable of issuing an "official" interpretation of law pursuant to the Model Penal Code's mistake provision, it is sensible to conclude that the defendant in *Marrero* could not rely on interpretations made by "fellow officers and teachers." Nevertheless, there is a sense in which the outcome of *Marrero* is not easily explained. Pursuant to § 265.20 of the New York Penal Law, the offense of criminal possession of a weapon "shall not apply" to "peace officers as defined in § 2.10 of the criminal procedure law." Subsection 25 of § 2.10 of the criminal procedure law prescribes, in turn, that "correction officers of any state correctional facility or of any penal correctional institution" are "peace officers." Doesn't the most natural reading of this provision lend support to the defendant's claim in *Marrero* that he was a "peace officer" exempted from the weapons statute? After all, he was a Federal correctional officer in Connecticut and the statute defines "peace officers" as encompassing "correction officers ... of *any* penal correctional institution." In spite of the plausibility of this reading of the criminal procedure law, the New York Appellate Division concluded—by a 3–2 margin—that the aforementioned statute only included *state* correctional officers as peace officers. Although *Marrero* accepted the interpretation of the statute, he argued that he should nevertheless be excused, for he relied on what appeared to be an extremely plausible—even natural—reading of the applicable law. Therefore, he argued that he acted pursuant to a "mistaken belief ... founded upon an official statement of the law contained in ... a *statute* or other enactment" which gives rise to a mistake of law defense under both the Model Penal Code and New York Penal Law. The majority, of course, rejected the argument, holding that the mistake of law provision applies only when the actor relies on a statute that is later struck down as unconstitutional rather than when the defendant makes his own interpretation of the statute, however natural his interpretation may be. Are you persuaded by the reasons provided by the Court to reject the defendant's argument? The dissent was not. More specifically, the dissenting judge contended that:

> It is difficult to imagine a case more squarely within the wording of Penal Law § 15.20(2)(a) or one more fitted to what appears clearly to be the intended purpose of the statute than the one before us. For this reason it is helpful to discuss the statute and its apparent intended effect in the light of what defendant contends was his mistaken belief founded on an official statement of the law contained in a statute.
>
> Defendant stands convicted after a jury trial of criminal possession of a weapon in the third degree for carrying a loaded firearm without a license (Penal Law § 265.02). He concedes that he possessed the unlicensed weapon but maintains that he did so under the mistaken assumption that his conduct was permitted by law. Although at the time of his arrest he protested that he was a Federal corrections officer and exempt from prosecution under the statute, defendant was charged with criminal possession of a weapon in the third degree. On defendant's motion before trial the court dismissed the indictment, holding that he was a peace officer as defined by CPL 2.10(26) and, therefore, exempted by Penal Law § 265.20 from prosecution under Penal Law § 265.02. The People appealed and the Appellate Division reversed and reinstated the indictment by a 3–2 vote.

> Defendant's appeal to this court was dismissed for failure to prosecute and the case proceeded to trial. The trial court rejected defendant's efforts to establish a defense of mistake of law under Penal Law § 15.20(2)(a). He was convicted and the Appellate Division has affirmed.
>
> Defendant's mistaken belief that, as a Federal corrections officer, he could legally carry a loaded weapon without a license was based on the express exemption from criminal liability under Penal Law § 265.02 accorded in Penal Law § 265.20(a)(1)(a) to "peace officers" as defined in the Criminal Procedure Law and on his reading of the statutory definition for "peace officer" in CPL 2.10(26) as meaning a correction officer "of *any* penal correctional institution" (emphasis added), including an institution not operated by New York State. Thus, he concluded erroneously that, as a corrections officer in a Federal prison, he was a "peace officer" and, as such, exempt by the express terms of Penal Law § 265.20(a)(1)(a). This mistaken belief, based in good faith on the statute defining "peace officer" (CPL 2.10[26]), is, defendant contends, the precise sort of "mistaken belief * * * founded upon an official statement of the law contained in * * * a statute or other enactment" which gives rise to a mistake of law defense under Penal Law § 15.20(2)(a). He points out, of course, that when he acted in reliance on his belief he had no way of foreseeing that a court would eventually resolve the question of the statute's meaning against him and rule that his belief had been mistaken, as three of the five-member panel at the Appellate Division ultimately did in the first appeal.
>
> The majority, however, has accepted the People's argument that to have a defense under Penal Law § 15.20(2)(a) "a defendant must show that the statute *permitted his conduct,* not merely that he believed it did". Here, of course, defendant cannot show that the statute permitted his conduct. To the contrary, the question has now been decided by the Appellate Division and it is settled that defendant was not exempt under Penal Law § 265.20(a)(1)(a). Therefore, the argument goes, defendant can have no mistake of law defense. While conceding that reliance on a statutory provision which is later found to be invalid would constitute a mistake of law defense (*see,* Model Penal Code § 2.04 [3][b][i]), the People's flat position is that "one's mistaken reading of a statute, no matter how reasonable or well intentioned, is not a defense".
>
> Nothing in the statutory language suggests the interpretation urged by the People and adopted by the majority: that Penal Law § 15.20(2)(a) is available to a defendant *not* when he has mistakenly read a statute *but only* when he has correctly read and relied on a statute which is later invalidated. Such a construction contravenes the general rule that penal statutes should be construed against the State and in favor of the accused and the Legislature's specific directive that the revised Penal Law should not be strictly construed but "must be construed according to the fair import of [its] terms to promote justice and effect the objects of the law" (Penal Law § 5.00).

The majority was not persuaded. It was particularly preoccupied that the dissent's interpretation of the mistake of law provision would allow defendants to plead mistake of law whenever they make mistaken personal interpretations of the statute. They contend that allowing such claims to be made would be contrary to the very limited mistake of law excuse that both the Model Penal Code and New York Penal Law intended to create. More specifically, the majority argues that:

> Strong public policy reasons underlie the legislative mandate and intent which we perceive in rejecting defendant's construction of New York's mistake of law

> defense statute. If defendant's argument were accepted, the exception would swallow the rule. Mistakes about the law would be encouraged, rather than respect for and adherence to law. There would be an infinite number of mistake of law defenses which could be devised from a good-faith, perhaps reasonable but mistaken, interpretation of criminal statutes, many of which are concededly complex. Even more troublesome are the opportunities for wrongminded individuals to contrive in bad faith solely to get an exculpatory notion before the jury. These are not in terrorem arguments disrespectful of appropriate adjudicative procedures; rather, they are the realistic and practical consequences were the dissenters' views to prevail. Our holding comports with a statutory scheme which was not designed to allow false and diversionary stratagems to be provided for many more cases than the statutes contemplated. This would not serve the ends of justice but rather would serve game playing and evasion from properly imposed criminal responsibility.

Who has the better part of this argument? Why?

4. While cases in which an actor relies on an official statement of law that is later overturned rarely arise, the issue is dealt with in a few published opinions. Perhaps the most famous one is *Cox v. State of Louisiana,* 379 U.S. 559 (1965). The defendant in *Cox* was convicted of violating a law that criminalized picketing near a courthouse. He claimed mistake of law as a defense, arguing that the police chief told him and other fellow protesters that they could lawfully "conduct the demonstration on the far side of the street." The government did not contradict this statement. Instead, it conceded that "the officials gave Cox and his group some time to demonstrate across the street from the courthouse." The defendant thus contended that it would violate due process to convict him of the charged offense when he relied on the official interpretation of the statute made by the police chief. The Supreme Court of the United States agreed with the defendant, observing that:

> In Raley v. Ohio, this Court held that the Due Process Clause prevented conviction of persons for refusing to answer questions of a state investigating commission when they relied upon assurances of the commission, either express or implied, that they had a privilege under state law to refuse to answer, though in fact this privilege was not available to them. The situation presented here is analogous to that in Raley, which we deem to be controlling. As in Raley, under all the circumstances of this case, after the public officials acted as they did, to sustain appellant's later conviction for demonstrating where they told him he could 'would be to sanction an indefensible sort of entrapment by the State—convicting a citizen for exercising a privilege which the State had clearly told him was available to him.' The Due Process Clause does not permit convictions to be obtained under such circumstances.

5. According to § 2.04(3)(a) of the Model Penal Code, an actor may also raise a mistake of law defense when:

> The statute or other enactment defining the offense is not known to the actor and has not been published or otherwise reasonably made available prior to the conduct alleged.

In modern times it will seldom be the case that the state fails to publish legislation that criminalizes certain conduct. Nevertheless—as one commentator has noted—lack of notice because of a failure to publicize a law may still be a problem "[p]articularly in smaller communities" where "local ordinances may never be printed or otherwise made generally available." Wayne R. LaFave, 1 *Substantive Criminal Law* § 5.6 (West, 2nd ed.,

2013). It may also be an issue with regard to state administrative rules that create crimes, for "[many] states have not attempted a systematic publication and codification of their administrative regulations." *Id.*

## § 19.05 Mistake of Law: Comparative Perspectives

### German Penal Code

*Section 17 Mistake of Law*

If upon commission of the act the perpetrator lacks the appreciation that he is doing something wrong, he acts without guilt if he was unable to avoid this mistake. If the perpetrator could have avoided the mistake, the punishment may be mitigated pursuant to Section 49 subsection (1).

### Helmut Frister, *Derecho Penal: Parte General*

Hammurabi, 2012, pages 380–385

[In the context of Section 17 of the German Penal Code], [a]n actor does not know that his conduct is wrong when he is unaware that his conduct is against the law ... It is not necessary that he know that his conduct violates the criminal law.... A person who drives without a license incorrectly believing that such conduct amounts to an administrative infraction instead of a criminal offense nevertheless acts with knowledge that his conduct is "wrong" [for the purposes of Section 17]. Similarly, whether the actor believes that his conduct is morally justified is irrelevant in this context, as long as he is aware that his conduct is against the law. An actor who damages property in order to protest against a nuclear power plant does not act under a mistake of law solely because he believes that his conduct is morally justified or even obligatory ... Conversely, a person who believes that his conduct is morally worthy but thinks that the conduct is not against the law acts under a mistake of law. Two siblings that engage in sexual intercourse without knowing that doing so is prohibited by law act under a mistake of law even if they think that their conduct is worthy of significant moral condemnation....

Most scholars believe that an actor is aware that his conduct is wrong in the sense of Section 17 as long as he believes that it is possible that the conduct is illegal ... The consequence of this is that the actor must abstain from engaging in the conduct as soon as he has doubts about whether the conduct is legal ... I believe that this is incorrect and unjustifiable. Given that the state is responsible for any vagueness and obscurities in the laws, the citizen should be able to plead mistake of law even if he had doubts about whether the conduct was prohibited.... When, however, the actor fails to make reasonable efforts to find out what the law requires of him, his mistake should be classified as avoidable and would thus only generate a discretionary mitigation of punishment rather than a full fledged excuse....

Actors must make an effort to inform themselves about the applicable law if they are to be fully excused pursuant to Section 17. This is pointed out in German case law, which requires that the actor "employ all of his cognitive efforts to dispel any lingering doubts regarding the possible unlawfulness of his conduct". Furthermore, the case law points out that it may sometimes be necessary for the actor to seek counsel....

In cases [involving everyday activities such as driving], citizens are not expected to seek legal counsel before they act. It suffices in such instances for them to inform themselves of the rules that govern the kind of activity that they are engaging in. Nevertheless, to assess the legality of engaging in more complex activities, citizens are expected to seek legal counsel. Once he seeks such counsel, however, the law expects nothing more of the citizen. That is, the actor is not expected to question the accuracy of the information provided by counsel. As a result, if a person seeks legal counsel and the advice he receives is that it is lawful for him to engage in the conduct, his mistake of law is generally unavoidable and—therefore—fully excused.

## *Notes and Questions*

1. In sharp contrast to the American approach to mistake of law, German criminal law—and the criminal laws of the vast majority of civil law jurisdictions—provide for a general mistake of law excuse that applies whenever an actor fails to appreciate that his conduct is unlawful and his failure to do so is deemed "unavoidable." An actor's failure to appreciate the unlawfulness of his conduct is "unavoidable" pursuant to § 17 of the German Penal Code when a reasonable person in the actor's situation would have also believed that his conduct was lawful. Note that—unlike the Model Penal Code—the German Penal Code does not enumerate the (few) instances in which mistake of law provides an excuse. Rather, the German Penal Code merely prescribes that mistake of law is a defense when reasonable. If the mistake of law is unreasonable—which it will be in the vast majority of cases—then the actor may not be excused, but punishment may be discretionally mitigated. Do you prefer the more lenient German approach to mistake of law over the much stricter American approach to the issue? Why or why not?

2. As Professor Frister points out in the excerpted reading, "if a person seeks legal counsel and the advice he receives is that it is lawful for him to engage in the conduct, his mistake of law is generally unavoidable and—therefore—fully excused." This is undoubtedly the context in which the civil law approach to mistake of law deviates most significantly from the American approach to the doctrine. Reliance on legal counsel is seldom—if ever—grounds for a mistake of law excuse in America, both at common law and under the Model Penal Code. The American approach to this issue is illustrated by the decision of the Court of Criminal Appeals of Texas in *Gallegos v. State,* in which it was stated that:

> The State is correct in its assertion that reliance upon the advice of counsel does not constitute a permissible mistake of law. It is no defense to prosecution that the actor was ignorant of the provisions of any law, unless he acted in reasonable reliance upon an official statement of the law by an administrative agency or an interpretation of the law found in a court opinion. Appellant relied upon the advice of his attorney. Because his mistake of law was not based upon an official statement or interpretation of the law by a court or an administrative agency, he is not entitled to a mistake of law defense. 825 S.W.2d 577 (Tex. App. 1992)

At least one state, however, holds that mistake of law based on reasonable reliance on legal counsel may generate an excuse. Pursuant to the New Jersey mistake of law statute, an actor may raise mistake of law as a defense if:

> The actor otherwise diligently pursues all means available to ascertain the meaning and application of the offense to his conduct and honestly and in good faith concludes his conduct is not an offense in circumstances in which a law-abiding and prudent person would also so conclude. *N.J.Stat.Ann. 2C:2-4*

Note that the New Jersey statute is as broad as the German Penal Code's mistake of law provision, for it provides a defense to any actor who mistakenly believes his conduct is lawful as long as the mistake is reasonable. Mistakes of law based on legal counsel's advice will often be reasonable and, therefore, excusable. Do you think that—as is the case in Germany and New Jersey—mistake of law based on reasonable reliance on legal counsel should excuse or do you agree with the common law and Model Penal Code's refusal to excuse such conduct? Why?

## § 19.06 Mistake of Law: Scholarly Debates

### Dan Kahan, *Ignorance of the Law Is an Excuse— But Only for the Virtuous*

96 Mich. L. Rev. 127 (1997)

#### I. Marrero: The Impudence of Legal Knowledge

Who exactly is the mistake of law doctrine afraid of? The answer suggested by the classic view is the strategically heedless. Were mistake of law a defense, a person bent on violating the rights of others ... could evade punishment by remaining studiously ignorant of his legal duties.

But the specter of strategic heedlessness is a fairly obvious piece of misdirection. To be sure, strict liability for mistakes of law takes the profit out of deliberate ignorance, but it's such a wildly overinclusive solution to that problem that it's impossible to view the strategically heedless as more than a bit player in the mistake of law drama. The real protagonist is someone else; to see who, consider People v. Marrero.

[A DISCUSSION OF THE FACTS OF MARRERO FOLLOWS. THE FACTS WERE SUMMARIZED AND DISCUSSED IN § 17.04, NOTES 2 & 3]

The New York Court of Appeals's reason for denying a mistake of law defense [in *Marrero*] was the ... utility of knowledge principle. The point of punishing the legally mistaken, the court explained, is "to encourage the societal benefit of individuals' knowledge of and respect for the law." Were Marrero to be afforded a defense, "[m]istakes about the law would be encouraged."

There's nothing persuasive in this account. The anxiety of strategic heedlessness obviously rang false in Marrero's individual case. Marrero hadn't deliberately shielded himself from legal knowledge; rather he had tenaciously attempted to ferret it out, displaying exactly the type of dedication to legal learning that the utility of knowledge purports to value.

Nor would an excuse for Marrero have promoted strategic heedlessness in others. Marrero sought to present a reasonable mistake of law defense. Had the court sided with Marrero, it would have been establishing, in effect, a negligence standard with respect to the existence or meaning of the law defining who counts as a "peace officer" under the New York gun possession statute. Under such a standard, heedlessness would be a foolish strategy, for a lawbreaker who deliberately failed to take reasonable steps to learn the law would be deemed negligent and hence denied a defense.

In fact, if the goal were truly to maximize private knowledge of law, a negligence standard would be unambiguously superior to a strict liability standard. This is so because the value of learning the law is always higher when the law excuses reasonable mistakes of law than when it doesn't.

A person will take reasonable steps to learn the law when the expected benefit of having legal information exceeds the expected cost of obtaining it. This benefit can take a number of forms. If a person invests in learning the law, she might discover that some course of conduct that she would otherwise have engaged in—for example, carrying an unlicensed handgun—is unlawful and consequently not worth undertaking given the penalty. Alternatively, she might learn that some course of conduct that she otherwise would have forgone is in fact perfectly legal and hence worth engaging in after all. But unless she believes the possibility of some such benefit is sufficiently high, she won't bother to invest in learning the law and will instead rely on her untutored judgment about what the law happens to be.

The probability of realizing a benefit sufficient to defray the cost of legal research will always be higher when the law excuses reasonable mistakes of law than when it doesn't. As Marrero himself discovered, even after a person takes reasonable steps to learn the law, there always remains some residual risk that a court will disagree with that person's conclusions. In a regime that imposes strict liability, that person will be punished notwithstanding her reasonable effort to learn the law; the prospect that one's legal information will turn out to be incorrect thus diminishes the value of obtaining such information ex ante. Under a negligence standard, however, reasonable mistakes of law are a defense; accordingly, once a person takes reasonable steps to learn the law, she is insured against punishment even if it turns out that her information is mistaken. Because the expected value of having legal information is thus higher under a negligence standard than under a strict liability standard, more individuals will conclude that investing in legal knowledge is worthwhile if the law in fact excuses reasonable mistakes.

The relative effects of strict liability and negligence in promoting legal knowledge expose the first crack in the classic conception of the mistake of law doctrine. Both strict liability and negligence punish the heedless; however, negligence rewards all, and strict liability only some, of the citizens who take reasonable steps to learn the law's commands. In other words, if the goal is only to protect society from the legally stupid, either strict liability or negligence will suffice; but if society genuinely aspires to make its citizens legally wise, it should pick negligence. The steadfast refusal of the law to excuse reasonable mistakes, then, displays much more ambivalence about private learning of the law [than what is generally assumed].

This ambivalence is laid bare by a second holding in Marrero. Marrero grounded his reasonable mistake of law defense in a New York statute that was meant to liberalize the common law position on when such mistakes excuse. That statute [was modeled on § 2.04 of the Model Penal Code] ...

Marrero's mistake clearly didn't entitle him to a defense under this standard: the "statement of the law ... contained in" the New York procedural code, and on which Marrero relied, was not "afterward determined to be invalid or erroneous"; only Marrero's private understanding of that statement was. As construed by the court of appeals, section 15.20(2), like section 2.04(3) of the Model Penal Code, excuses reasonable reliance only on the mistakes of courts, legislatures, and other official interpreters, and not reasonable reliance on a private citizen's own mistakes.

But was it proper for the court of appeals to read the language of section 15.20(2) as if it were identical to section 2.04(3)? That depends on how far one thinks the New York legislature was trying to go in modifying the common law position. The court of appeals concluded that the legislature meant to go as far as the drafters of the Model Penal Code, who decided to permit reasonable mistake as a defense only when a citizen was misled by a government official; the court of appeals concluded that the legislature, contrary to the literal meaning of the statutory text, did not intend to take the additional step of excusing even reasonable private misreadings of statutes because the idea that the legislature meant to do something that outrageous was, to the court, all but unthinkable ...

By now it should be clear who the mistake of law doctrine is really afraid of. It's not, or at least not only, the strategically heedless, but also the impudently inquisitive—the lay interpreter who isn't content to rely on her untutored judgment, supplemented by what officials tell her the law means, but who insists on inspecting the law for herself and forming her own admittedly reasonable view about what the law is saying. It is not that person's deliberate ignorance of, but rather her exacting attention to, the law's fine points that we must regard as a "false and diversionary stratagem," a form of "game playing and evasion" that we should construe the law to discourage. But this question remains: What exactly makes this person's diligent efforts to decode the law so unwelcome?...

... Marrero came out the way it did [because] Marrero ignored the law's injunction to do what's right rather than what one thinks is legal. New York's restrictive gun possession law embodies its citizens' strong antipathy toward, and fear of, handguns. But rather than defer to those norms, Marrero decided to be strategic, availing himself of what must have appeared even to him to be a largely fortuitous gap in the law. That's the attitude that made the court see in Marrero's efforts to decode the law not an earnest and laudable attempt to obey but rather a "false and diversionary stratagem[ ]," a form of "game playing and evasion." Other facts, not even mentioned by the court, also likely played a role: that the policy of the federal prison at which Marrero worked forbade guards to carry guns either on or off duty; that Marrero had supplied his girlfriend and another companion with guns, even though they clearly had no grounds for believing their possession to be lawful; and that Marrero menacingly reached for his weapon when the police approached him in the Manhattan club. These facts might not have been formally relevant to the court's disposition, but they no doubt helped the court to see Marrero as a Holmesian bad man. And in the eyes of the court, a Holmesian bad man is plenty bad enough to be designated a criminal....

### III. Cheek: A Defense for the Virtuous

Not every mistake of law, however, displays bad character. When a person makes the kind of error that even a morally virtuous person could make, then her ignorance of the law should be an excuse. That is the moral of Cheek v. United States.

Cheek neglected to file tax returns for several years. His defense to charges of criminal tax evasion was that he honestly believed he owed no tax on the salary he earned as a pilot for American Airlines. Cheek claimed to have formed this belief on the basis of lectures by members of a tax protest group, who persuaded him that wages were not taxable income for purposes of the federal tax code and that any form of income tax violated the Constitution. After being instructed that these beliefs were not a defense, the jury convicted.

But the Supreme Court reversed. Reaffirming precedents of over a half century's standing, the Court held that a person can be convicted of criminal tax evasion only if he "intentional[ly] violat[es] ... a known legal duty." Under this standard, Cheek's mistaken beliefs about the unconstitutionality of income taxes would not be a defense, the Court reasoned, because a person who declines to comply with the law on that basis is nevertheless aware that he has a duty to pay under the tax code. However, a person who honestly believes—however unreasonably—that wages or any other species of income aren't taxable under the code would have a defense, for in that circumstance he couldn't be said to "know" that he had a duty to pay. The Court remanded the case for retrial under this standard....

It is at this point that the complexity of the tax code becomes relevant. The obligation to pay a tax on one's salary or wages is a simple matter; ignorance of it displays such a gross degree of inattention to civic duty that one can justly be blamed for that very lack of knowledge. But the tax code extends far beyond the obligation to pay tax on one's wages or salaries: it encompasses as well one's duty to pay tax on barter transactions, to recognize taxable gains associated with swapping comparable mortgage portfolios, and to make withholdings from the wages of once-weekly maids. Good persons—from the "average citizen" to the prospective Supreme Court Justice—can make mistakes about these duties, which involve no independent moral obligation and which aren't a matter of common civic knowledge. A mistake of law defense protects these excusably inattentive actors from punishment. Of course, it might protect some culpably inattentive ones from punishment, too, insofar as courts are obliged, as a matter of statutory construction, to treat all mistakes of law alike. Excusing the vicious Cheek for his ignorance was thus necessary to avoid condemning many virtuous ones for theirs.

Another way to see this point is to reflect on the difference in how we typically regard marginally legal behavior in the tax field and how we regard it in other domains of criminal law. When the law implements independent moral norms, members of society are likely to view marginally legal behavior with disapproval. Because of the persistent incompleteness of law relative to morality, persons who deliberately try to skirt the line of what separates, say, legal from illegal drug distribution, or mere sharp dealing from fraud, strike us (usually) as morally bad persons. Punishing them if they miscalculate gives them exactly what they deserve and helps to reinforce for the rest of us what being good entails. But society feels differently about persons who try to find "loopholes" in the tax code; we don't condemn those persons, but instead compensate them with hundreds of dollars an hour, and honor them with status and respect. Giving them an excuse for ignorance of law implements the widely shared (but by no means uncontentious) judgment that persons like that shouldn't be deemed criminals when they make honest mistakes....

Of course, the tax code isn't the only complex body of criminally enforceable law that doesn't implement independent moral norms; the same can be said for banking law, broadcasting law, and election law, among others. If the point of strict liability is to punish individuals who are culpably inattentive to society's moral norms, then we should expect to see courts fashioning exceptions to the mistake of law doctrine for all manner of malum prohibitum offenses.

Which is exactly what we do see. Structuring banking transactions so as to avoid having to report them is not "obviously 'evil'" or "inevitably nefarious." There's "nothing inherently wrong in making" a campaign contribution without disclosing it to the government. There's nothing about broadcasting on a CB radio without an FCC license that's "likely to create danger" or otherwise make a "reasonable man ... aware that he [is doing something] forbidden." Exporting and importing "amphibious vehicles, pressure-breathing suits, [and] aerial cameras" can be done "innocently" and thus can't be analogized to distribution of illicit "substances which are known generally to be controlled by government regulation, such as heroin or like drugs." In all of these settings, and in various others, courts have recognized mistake of law as a defense because the underlying conduct violates no moral norms independent of the law that prohibits it.

Still, courts don't invariably recognize mistake of law defenses for crimes of this kind. As a statement of black letter law, the rule that ignorance of law excuses malum prohibitum—but not malum in se—crimes is overbroad; indeed, it takes no real detective work to find cases that say just the opposite—that ignorance of law is no excuse "whether the crime charged is malum prohibitum or malum in se"—although that proposition too is (as I've just shown) wildly overstated. So why do courts permit mistake of law as a defense only selectively across malum prohibitum crimes?

... [One circumstance in which] matters are different [is] when, say, the defendant is a sophisticated participant in a "closely regulated" industry; we expect "repeat players" to be attentive to the rules of the game. Matters are different, too, when someone is engaged in behavior that, while not strictly speaking immoral, nevertheless exposes the public to unusually high risks: it might not occur to someone who is transporting "[p]encils, dental floss, [or] paper clips" that his conduct is subject to stringent safety regulations, but if it doesn't to someone who is transporting "dangerous or deleterious devices ... or obnoxious waste materials," then he's missing a critical faculty of moral perception. In these particular settings, ignorance of a malum prohibitum obligation, no less than ignorance of a malum in se one, expresses a culpable failure to attune oneself to basic civic norms.

The second circumstance in which judges might be tempted to deny that malum prohibitum crimes get special treatment is when they want to avoid the burden of explaining why they really view the conduct in question as malum in se. It goes without saying that the line between prohibitum and in se will often be blurry. It should go without saying as well that drawing the line will often be a controversial and even politically perilous task for a court to undertake. It's inconvenient to declare the transporting of alcohol during and immediately after Prohibition to be intrinsically immoral; it's risky to be seen as jumping into the fray when management ejects a union official from company property. Life is much easier for a court in these and like cases when it can simply invoke a rule—"ignorance of the law is never an excuse, for malum prohibitum offenses or malum in se ones"—that spares it the burden of justifying the denial of a defense. But against the background of all the malum prohibitum crimes that now do get mistake of law defenses, the invoking of such a rule serves only to conceal, and does not genuinely eliminate, the need for the court to make contentious, context-specific judgments about which actors have characters good enough to be excused for their mistakes of law.

That such discretion must be exercised, moreover, completes the indictment of the classic conception of the mistake of law doctrine.... [H]ad it been accepted by courts that the law ought to judge persons only by the conformity of their actions to the standard laid down by law and not by the conformity of their characters to an extralegal conception of moral virtue—courts would never have perceived the need to reform the doctrine upon the advent of malum prohibitum crimes. Moreover, had courts been intent on conserving the positivistic character of the law as a descriptive matter, they would never have reformed it by making an exception for malum prohibitum crimes, much less only for certain of them. For one can determine whether a particular species of conduct—whether possessing a gun, distributing a drug, or neglecting to pay a tax—is malum in se or malum prohibitum only by appraising that conduct in light of moral norms external to positive law. Once it is acknowledged that an important component of the law depends on this kind of appraisal, a person who "want[s] to know the law," even if she wants to know "nothing else," has no choice but to view the world through a good person's eyes.

## *Notes and Questions*

1. Professor Kahan provocatively argues that the purpose of the stringent American approach to mistake of law is not to encourage people to inform themselves of what the law requires of them. That this is not the purpose of the mistake of law doctrine in America should be evident when the defense is denied to actors who—like the defendant in *Marrero*—seek to inform themselves of what the law requires. Rather than encouraging citizens to inform themselves of the law, Kahan argues that the mistake of law doctrine seeks to prevent citizens from trying to "game" the law by finding reasonable "loopholes" in legal regulations and exploiting them.

2. Actors who try to game the system or find legal loopholes to take advantage of them should not be excused—as they generally are not under the conventional understanding of mistake of law in America. They are not excused, Kahan argues, because it is blameworthy for actors to seek to inform themselves of the law merely for the purpose of gaming it or exploiting loopholes in the law. This is why the defendant in *Marrero* was denied a defense. He sought a loophole in New York's gun laws by construing "peace officer" in a way that was beneficial to him. In doing so, he revealed both that he was aware that he may not be an exempted "peace officer" within the meaning of the statute and that he was interested in learning about the law in order to game the system or find a loophole rather than in order to become a more virtuous citizen. The two character traits revealed by Marrero's conduct are worthy of condemnation and, therefore, his conduct should not be excused. Are you persuaded by Kahan's account of why the defendant in *Marrero* should not be able to plead mistake of law? Explain.

3. Professor Kahan compares the conduct in *Marrero* with the conduct in *Cheek.* According to Kahan, the defendant in *Cheek* was able to claim mistake of law as a defense to a charge of violating the tax laws because seeking loopholes in the tax laws is not conduct that the vast majority of Americans deem to be worthy of condemnation. As a matter of fact, the opposite is generally true. Most people encourage others to seek loopholes in the tax laws and attempt to game the system. Therefore, trying to game the tax laws—as the defendant attempted to do in *Cheek*—is generally believed to be less blameworthy than trying to game gun laws, as the defendant attempted to do in *Marrero.* This explains why the defendant in *Cheek* was allowed to plead mistake of law as a defense, while the defendant in *Marrero* was not. Do you agree with Kahan's way of justifying the holdings in these two cases? Why or why not?

4. More broadly, Kahan's account of mistake of law leads to generally allowing the defense to be pleaded in prosecutions for *malum prohibitum* offenses, but disallowing it in most prosecutions for *malum in se* offenses. The reason for this is that trying to exploit loopholes in *malum prohibitum* offenses (e.g., tax laws) does not seem generally blameworthy, while trying to do so in *malum in se* offenses (e.g., gun laws) seems considerably more worthy of condemnation. Do you agree? Explain.

# Part Six
# Specific Offenses

# Chapter 20

# Homicide

## § 20.01 Murder

### Hern v. State

Supreme Court of Nevada, 1981
97 Nev. 529

MANOUKIAN, Justice:

Appellant Hern was convicted by jury of first degree murder. From the judgment and sentence fixing his punishment at life imprisonment without the possibility of parole, he appeals. The sole issue requiring our consideration is whether the homicide committed by appellant constituted first or second degree murder. On review of the record, we affirm.

On February 17, 1979, Hern beat to death Curtis Wayne Fausett, three years of age, the son of Kimla Huddleston. Hern had lived with Huddleston since January of 1978. During the evening of February 17, Huddleston left for her employment, leaving Hern in charge of Curtis.

Although the record shows generally that Hern's relationship with Curtis was equivalent to a father-son relationship, it also reveals that Hern had physically beaten the child on a number of prior occasions to such an extent as to constitute child abuse. Indeed, he had agreed with Huddleston to refrain from any physical discipline of the child. On the date in question, however, and during the mother's absence, when Curtis spilled some milk, Hern began to "spank" the child. The "spanking" transcended the limits of reasonable discipline and developed into a severe beating which is the undisputed cause of the child's death. The medical cause of death was internal hemorrhaging.

Appellant contends that there was no evidence introduced at trial to establish that Curtis' death was a result of a willful deliberate, and premeditated act on his part, as required by [Nevada's definition of first-degree murder]. Specifically, he claims that if he is guilty of murder at all, it must be murder in the second degree ...

The determination of the degree of crime is almost invariably left to the discretion of the jury. On appeal, we are confined to reviewing the evidence most favorably in support of its determination ... The issue is not whether this court would have found beyond a reasonable doubt that appellant was guilty of first degree murder, but whether the jury, acting reasonably, could have been convinced to that certitude by the evidence it had a right to consider....

We turn now to determine whether respondent met its burden in proving first degree murder or whether a verdict for a lesser included degree was required.

Murder, and this includes murder of the first degree as well as murder in the second degree, is defined as the "unlawful killing of a human being with malice aforethought." The critical question confronting us is whether, upon a review of the evidence most favorably in support of the judgment, a reasonable interpretation indicates a sufficiency of evidence to establish that the homicide was murder of the first degree, as distinguished from murder in the second degree. To make this determination, we must clearly distinguish the two degrees of murder.

Although leaving much to the discretion of the jury, the legislature, in defining degrees of murder, requires the exercise of that discretion to be sufficiently supported by the facts. [The relevant provision prescribes that:]

2. Murder of the first degree is murder which is:

(a) Perpetrated by means of poison, or lying in wait, torture, or by any other kind of willful, deliberate and premeditated killing;

(b) Committed in the perpetration or attempted perpetration of rape, kidnaping, arson, robbery, burglary or sexual molestation of a child under the age of 14 years....

[Furthermore, Nevada homicide law] defines murder of the second degree as comprehending "all other kinds of murder."

The homicide under consideration was clearly not perpetrated by any of the specifically characterized means, such as poisoning, nor was it committed in the perpetration of any of the enumerated felonies. Therefore, to constitute first degree murder, it must fall within the category of "any other kind of willful, deliberate, or premeditated killing."

Malice is not synonymous with either deliberation or premeditation. To view it otherwise would obliterate the distinction between the two degrees of murder. Malice aforethought is an element of the crime of murder, but malice aforethought and premeditated homicide is murder in the first degree; intentional homicide without premeditation is, in the absence of legally cognizable provocation or mitigating circumstances, murder in the second degree.

It is clear from the statute that all three elements, willfulness, deliberation, and premeditation, must be proven beyond a reasonable doubt before an accused can be convicted of first degree murder.

Hern testified that he remembered grabbing the child and starting to spank him and that his next memory was standing over the child's body. In addition to this testimony, a defense psychiatrist testified that being a child abuse victim himself, appellant may not have had the intent to kill the child or the ability to premeditate. Other testimony was introduced showing that Hern evidenced affection for the victim. From this, the appellant concludes that insufficient evidence was presented to convict him of first degree murder. We remain unpersuaded.

Prosecution testimony was presented that appellant lied to paramedics at the scene concerning the circumstances surrounding the death. Other evidence involved an admission by appellant that he beat and kicked the victim prior to the child's death. Immediately upon being informed of the child's death, and in the presence of the appellant, the mother yelled at Hern, "Now you finally did it, you killed him." The autopsy, analyzed by Dr. Giles Sheldon Green, a Clark County medical examiner, showed that Curtis died of internal hemorrhage resulting from injury to the liver. External examination of the child's body further disclosed approximately thirty bruises, including to the head, chest, penis, abdomen, back, buttock, thighs and lower legs, anus and arms. Based on the abrasions and bruises he observed on the child's body, Dr. Green concluded that Curtis was a victim of child abuse.

From the appellant's instant and previous abuse of Curtis, leading inexorably to his death, the jury could find that premeditation, or fixed purpose to kill, requisite for first degree murder, was formed prior to his death. Therefore, it was permissible for the jury to find that Hern formed an intent to kill through the extreme physical abuse, and that appellant caused the death with premeditation. The nature and extent of the injuries, coupled with repeated blows, constitutes substantial evidence of willfulness, premeditation and deliberation.

Premeditation is generally established by circumstantial evidence. Direct evidence is not required. Malice aforethought, and premeditation may be deduced from the circumstances of the killing, such as the use of certain means calculated to produce death. The jury must be given the prerogative to make logical inferences derived from the evidence. We should not, and will not, interfere with a jury determination which is supported by substantial evidence. Any other result would leave prosecutors, defenders and judges without guidance in such cases. If the result were to the contrary, then absent direct evidence of premeditation, a first degree murder conviction would be most difficult, if not impossible, to obtain if the victim is a child who has not been killed with a gun or other dangerous weapon but severely beaten, as in the instant case …

The conviction for first degree murder is affirmed.

## Simpkins v. State

Court of Special Appeals of Maryland, 1991
596 A.2d 655

WILNER, Chief Judge.

This case arises from the tragic, senseless death of two year-old Brandy Simpkins. She died of starvation—or, as the medical examiner testified, malnutrition and dehydration. As a result, Brandy's parents—Alan Simpkins and Grace Geisler—were charged with first degree, premeditated murder. After trial before the Circuit Court for Baltimore City, sitting without a jury, they were each convicted of second degree murder.

In this appeal, both appellants contest the evidentiary basis for the murder convictions …

### The Murder Convictions

Brandy lived with her parents and her four year-old sister, Heather. A houseguest, John Monte, had been living with the family for just under two weeks. Mr. Monte normally slept on a mat in Brandy's room, but for the two nights prior to her death he had slept downstairs. On Monday morning, December 18, 1989, as Ms. Geisler hurriedly left the house to deal with some problem involving Heather, Mr. Monte recalled that he had not seen Brandy since the previous Saturday night, and so he went to her room to check on her. He found her in the crib, quite still. Alarmed, he awoke Mr. Simpkins and called 911 for assistance. When the police arrived, they found Brandy in her crib dead, clad only in a diaper.

Dr. Frank Peretti, from the medical examiner's office, also came to the home that afternoon. From his observations of Brandy, from pictures that were taken of the child, and from an autopsy, Dr. Peretti opined that the cause of death was malnutrition and dehydration. There was no evidence of disease or trauma. According to Dr. Peretti, Brandy had not been given food or drink for three to five days. Her stomach contained no food—only 4 cc ("that's about the size of a fingernail," he said) of thin, mucoid material, which the stomach itself secretes; there "were no contents whatsoever in the small and large bowels except for ten grams of tan brown feces located in the rectum." She was found in a diaper that had 370 grams—about three-quarters of a pound—of layered fecal material in it, leading Dr. Peretti to believe that the diaper had not been changed for four to six days. As a result, Brandy had an extensive diaper rash that covered her entire genital area and that Dr. Peretti found to be "very, very severe." The condition of the body indicated that death had occurred more than 24 hours before its discovery.

The malnutrition was both acute and chronic. Dr. Peretti stated that children are born with about a quarter-inch of subcutaneous fat, which becomes thicker as they grow. Brandy had less than one-sixteenth inch of fat; there was no fat around the kidneys, where there is usually an accumulation of fat. This condition, he stated, accrued over time.

The circumstances under which Brandy was permitted to starve to death were in some dispute. One thing, however, is abundantly clear: it was not because of appellants' inability to provide food. Their kitchen refrigerator was crammed full of food, and they and Heather apparently ate quite well. Mr. Monte testified that he and Ms. Geisler went grocery shopping on December 11 or 12 and spent over $100 on food. The only thing Ms. Geisler needed but did not buy that day was milk.

Other evidence bearing on Brandy's short and pathetic life was presented. According to Mr. Monte, although appellants paid considerable attention to Heather—took meals with her and played with her—Brandy was left in her crib most of the time. Monte said that she cried a lot, wanting to get out of the crib, but he was forbidden to remove her except on the occasions when *he* fed her. Brandy was not allowed to play with Heather and Heather was not allowed in Brandy's room.

Dr. Branson, a pediatrician who had treated Brandy on earlier occasions, testified that Brandy had missed her two-month and four-month immunizations. In August, 1988, when she was a year old, Brandy was hospitalized for failure to thrive because (1) she had lost more than one pound in the previous six months despite Ms. Geisler's assurance that the child had a healthy appetite and was eating heartily, (2) she was dehydrated, and (3) there was "serious infection in her system." Brandy gained weight well during her 10-day stay; Ms. Geisler was told to bring the child back for a check-up three weeks after her discharge, which she failed to do. Although children normally begin walking between nine and twelve months, at 16 months, Brandy was still not walking. On August 9, 1989, Dr. Branson saw Brandy for the last time. She then weighed 24 pounds three ounces and, although late for a number of her shots, appeared to be in good health. When she died four months later, she weighed only 21½ pounds.

Appellants defend against the second degree murder conviction on the ground that the State failed to prove they acted, or failed to act, with malice toward Brandy. They assert, quite correctly, that "[m]alice is the indispensable ingredient of murder; by its presence, homicide is murder; in its absence, homicide is manslaughter." This element, they say, was lacking here.

As the Court noted in *Ross v. State*, the term "malice" has been used "as a type of legal shorthand to embrace the elements of (1) the presence of the required malevolent state of mind, and (2) the absence of legally adequate justification, excuse or circumstances of mitigation." There are four "qualifying malevolent states of mind," from which "malice" may be inferred: "(1) the intent to kill, (2) the intent to do grievous bodily harm, (3) the intent to do an act under circumstances manifesting extreme indifference to the value of human life (depraved heart), or (4) the intent to commit a dangerous felony." Although, as noted, the State initially charged that appellants intentionally killed Brandy, near the end of trial the prosecutor informed the court that the State was proceeding "on the charges of second degree murder under the theory of depraved heart," and it was upon that theory that the convictions rested.

In *Robinson v. State,* the Court, said of this theory:

> "A depraved heart murder is often described as a wanton and wilful killing. The term 'depraved heart' means something more than conduct amounting to a high or unreasonable risk to human life. The perpetrator must [or reasonably should] realize the risk his behavior has created to the extent that his conduct may be termed willful. Moreover, the conduct must contain an element of viciousness or contemptuous disregard for the value of human life which conduct characterizes that behavior as wanton."

Continuing, the Court added: "The critical feature of 'depraved heart' murder is that the act in question be committed 'under circumstances manifesting extreme indifference to the value of human life.'"

In announcing its verdict, the trial court found that "the indifference and the lack of care that has been demonstrated in the evidence presented ... over the past week shows a level of lack of care that is uncommon to cases of this sort" and declared itself satisfied from the evidence "that the element of viciousness or contemptuous disregard for human life has been established in this case...." The argument, essentially, is that this finding is clearly erroneous, unsupported by substantial evidence.

Most cases prosecuted under a "depraved heart" theory involve affirmative conduct—firing a gun or driving a car or boat into a crowd, for example. But "depraved heart" murder has also been found in cases of malicious omission, including situations where a parent has maliciously allowed a small child to die of exposure or of malnutrition and dehydration.

The development of a "depraved heart" theory to support murder convictions in child exposure or starvation cases started in England ...

In one of the earliest cases, *Regina v. Walters*, the defendant was charged with murder for having abandoned her newborn infant to the elements. Justice Coltman, sitting in the Oxford Circuit, instructed the jury, in pertinent part:

> "If a party do any act with regard to a human being helpless and unable to provide for itself, which must necessarily lead to its death, the crime amounts to murder.... But if the circumstances are not such, that the party must have been aware that the result would be death, that would reduce the offence to the crime of manslaughter, provided the death was occasioned by an unlawful act, but not such as to imply a malicious mind. There have been cases where it has been held, that persons leaving a child exposed and without any assistance, and under circumstances where no assistance was likely to be rendered, and thereby causing the death of the child, were guilty of murder."

This instruction would appear to permit a murder conviction to be based on a "depraved heart" theory, as it does not require a finding of an express intent that the child die.

[Editor's Note: After surveying additional English cases, the court turned its attention to American cases.]

In *Lewis v. State*, a case arising from the death of a 10 year-old child, in part through starvation and exposure, the issue on appeal was whether the evidence supported murder as opposed to manslaughter. [T]he court affirmed the murder conviction, stating in relevant part, "Death ensuing in consequence of the willful omission of a duty will be murder; death ensuing in consequence of the negligent omission of a duty will be manslaughter" and

> "[w]here a sick or weak person is exposed to cold with an intent to destroy him, this may amount 'to willful murder, under the rule that he who willfully and deliberately does any act which apparently endangers another's life and thereby occasions his death shall, unless he clearly prove to the contrary, be adjudged to kill him of malice *prepense.*'"

Similarly, in *Pallis v. State*, involving the abandonment and exposure of an infant who, fortunately, was rescued, the court affirmed a conviction of assault with intent to murder, [stating]:

> "If the exposure or neglect of an infant or other dependent person, resulting in death, is an act of mere carelessness, wherein danger to life does not clearly appear, the homicide is only manslaughter; whereas, if the exposure or neglect is of a dangerous kind, it is murder. For example, if from an infant of tender years the person under obligation to provide for it willfully withholds needful food or any other needful thing, *though not with intent to kill,* and by reason thereof the child dies, he commits murder."

... Several courts have affirmed murder convictions based expressly on an "implied malice" or "depraved heart" theory. *State v. Crocker* (upholding a murder conviction on a "depraved indifference" theory where the defendant knocked his stepson unconscious and then left him untreated and/or withheld food from him).

Most of these cases—English and American—tend to be fact-specific. It is evident from all of them that mere neglect, despite its awful consequence, is not enough to establish malice and thus to support a conviction of murder. We believe, however, that ... the court's finding of malice in this case is supported by the evidence. Where a young child, incapable of self-help, is knowingly, deliberately, and unnecessarily placed in confinement and left alone for up to five days without food, drink, or attention and death ensues from that lack, malice may be inferred. A rational trier of fact could reasonably find that death is at least a likely, if not a certain, consequence of such conduct, that any normal adult would understand and appreciate the likelihood of that consequence, and that the conduct is therefore willful and wanton, manifesting "viciousness or contemptuous disregard for the value of human life...." This is essentially a restatement of the view expressed by Justice Coltman 150 years ago in *Regina v. Walters,* which we believe to be an accurate statement of the current law.

In urging that their conduct over that fateful December weekend amounted only to neglect and not to wantonness, appellants point to what they regard as "indisputable evidence that long term care was provided for Brandy," which, they say is "impossible to reconcile" with ill-will. Moreover, they stress evidence that "there was no specific assignment of responsibility" between them for Brandy's care, and that her neglect arose from the fact that they were too busy arguing with each other that weekend to care for their child. We reject both of these arguments as utterly specious. In the first place, there was no "indisputable evidence" that either defendant provided reasonable long-term care for Brandy. There is no evidence that Mr. Simpkins provided any care at all for her, and Dr. Branson's testimony showed, at best, a rather cavalier and uncaring attitude on the part of Ms. Geisler as to Brandy's health and welfare. Indeed, as noted in our discussion below of Ms. Geisler's statement, there was evidence that she was aware of Brandy's condition on

December 17—the day before the child was discovered dead—but did nothing to help her. As to assignments of responsibility, the law itself imposes a duty on *both* parents to care and nurture their minor children. Md.Fam.Law Code Ann. § 5-203(b) makes the parents of a minor child "jointly and severally responsible for the child's support, care, nurture, welfare, and education." Subject to supervening court orders, they may decide by agreement who, if either, shall be the primary care-giver, but the ultimate legal responsibility for the required care is and remains on them both. The evidence here fully justified the verdict.

## *Notes and Questions*

1. The common law of murder originally distinguished only between murder and manslaughter, without further subdividing murder into degrees or manslaughter into voluntary and involuntary manslaughter. In 1794, however, the Pennsylvania state legislature passed a homicide statute that distinguished between murder in the first degree and murder in the second degree. Furthermore, the statute discriminated between voluntary and involuntary manslaughter. The Pennsylvania murder statute became a model for criminal law reform throughout the country. It remains an important model today, as a significant number of American jurisdictions continue to divide murder into degrees and manslaughter into voluntary and involuntary versions of the crime.

2. As the cases excerpted in this section illustrate, murder was defined at common law as the unlawful killing of a person with *malice* aforethought. The term "aforethought" is now deemed superfluous, with the result that any killing with malice is regarded as murder at common law.

3. In jurisdictions that distinguish between first and second-degree murder, the distinction is often made on the basis of whether the killing was "premeditated" or not. The purpose of dividing murder into degrees is to distinguish between the most serious and heinous kinds of killings and less heinous—although still very serious—types of killings. Liability for murder in the first-degree is reserved for the former kind of killing, whereas liability for murder in the second-degree applies to the latter type of killing.

4. When exactly does a killing count as "premeditated," so as to trigger liability for murder in the first-degree under the Pennsylvania Model of murder? More specifically, does "premeditation" require that the defendant reflect about the killing for some time before engaging in the homicidal act, or may premeditation be formed in an instant? If the conventionally accepted meaning of "premeditation" is of any guidance, the term implies deliberate reflection for some time prior to engaging in the act. Defining premeditation as something that can occur in an instant would thus seem to do violence to the conventionally accepted meaning of the term. Nevertheless, some courts have held that premeditation can be formed in an instant. In *State v. Flores*, 418 N.W.2d 150 (1988), for example, the trial court instructed the jury that:

> Premeditation means that Defendant considered, planned, prepared for, or determined to commit the act before he committed it. *Premeditation may be formed at anytime, (sic) moment or instant before the killing. Premeditation means thought of beforehand for any length of time, no matter how short.*

The defendant alleged that the instruction was erroneous, for it failing to properly explain the distinction between premeditation and intent to kill. The Minnesota Supreme Court rejected defendant's contention, observing that:

In *State v. Marsyla,* this court [stated]:

> "All the time needed for premeditation or deliberation is that required to form the intent to kill. Thus, the following instruction was sustained in *State v. Prolow*:
>
> > "The 'premeditation may be formed at any time, moment or instant before the killing. Premeditation means thought of beforehand for any length of time, no matter how short. There need be no appreciable space of time between the intention of killing and the act of killing. They may be as instantaneous as the successive thoughts of the mind.'"...

In a prosecution for murder in the first degree, extensive planning and calculated deliberation need not be shown by the prosecution. The requisite "plan" to commit first degree murder "can be formulated virtually instantaneously by a killer."

The trial court evidently relied on *[these cases]* in formulating its instruction on premeditation. We find that the trial court's instruction, read as a whole, was not error.

Although the view that deliberation may be formed in an instant is followed in a handful of jurisdictions, most state courts hold that premeditation requires that some appreciable amount of time elapse between the moment the intent to kill is formulated and the time of the killing. In *State v. Guthrie,* 461 S.E.2d 163 (1995), for example, the Supreme Court of Appeals of West Virginia overruled cases in which it held that premeditation could be formed in an instant. According to the Court, overruling such cases was justified because:

> [W]ithin the parameters of our current homicide statutes the [instant premeditation approach to] premeditation and deliberation is confusing, if not meaningless. To allow the State to prove premeditation and deliberation by only showing that the intention came "into existence for the first time at the time of such killing" completely eliminates the distinction between the two degrees of murder. Hence, we feel compelled in this case to attempt to make the dichotomy meaningful by making some modifications to our homicide common law.
>
> Premeditation and deliberation should be defined in a more careful, but still general way to give juries both guidance and reasonable discretion. Although premeditation and deliberation are not measured by any particular period of time, there must be some period between the formation of the intent to kill and the actual killing, which indicates the killing is by prior calculation and design. As suggested by the dissenting opinion in *Green v. State*: "True, it is not necessary to prove premeditation existed for any definite period of time. But it is necessary to prove that it did exist." This means there must be an opportunity for some reflection on the intention to kill after it is formed. The accused must kill purposely after contemplating the intent to kill. Although an elaborate plan or scheme to take life is not required, our *[previous]* notion of instantaneous premeditation and momentary deliberation is not satisfactory for proof of first degree murder. In *Bullock v. United States,* the court discussed the need to have some appreciable time elapse between the intent to kill and the killing:
>
> > "To speak of premeditation and deliberation which are instantaneous, or which take no appreciable time, is a contradiction in terms. It deprives the statutory requirement of all meaning and destroys the statutory distinction be-

tween first and second degree murder. At common law there were no degrees of murder. If the accused had no overwhelming provocation to kill, he was equally guilty whether he carried out his murderous intent at once or after mature reflection. Statutes like ours, which distinguish deliberate and premeditated murder from other murder, reflect a belief that one who meditates an intent to kill and then deliberately executes it is more dangerous, more culpable or less capable of reformation than one who kills on sudden impulse; or that the prospect of the death penalty is more likely to deter men from deliberate than from impulsive murder. The deliberate killer is guilty of first degree murder; the impulsive killer is not. The quoted part of the charge was therefore erroneous."

Thus, there must be some evidence that the defendant considered and weighed his decision to kill in order for the State to establish premeditation and deliberation under our first degree murder statute. This is what is meant by a ruthless, cold-blooded, calculating killing. Any other intentional killing, by its spontaneous and nonreflective nature, is second degree murder.

We are asked to overrule the language appearing in [previous decisions] so that there might be some clarity and coherence to the law of homicide. We naturally are reluctant to overrule prior decisions of this Court. No court likes to acknowledge a mistake, and adherence to precedent is based on deeper reasons than *amour propre;* rather, it is in fact a cornerstone of Anglo-American adjudication. Additionally, the more recent a precedent, the more authoritative it is because there is less likelihood of significantly changed circumstances that would provide a "special justification" for reassessing the soundness of the precedent. Nevertheless, the circumstances of this case are different, and we agree with the defendant that the language in our opinion in *Schrader* virtually eliminates the distinction in this State between first and second degree murder, equating as it does premeditation with the formation of the intent to kill. We have tried to clarify the difference between the degrees of murder in the preceding paragraphs. We find that *Schrader* wrongly equated premeditation with intent to kill.... To the extent that the *Schrader* opinion is inconsistent with our holding today, it is overruled....

Finally, we feel obligated to discuss what instruction defining premeditation is now acceptable. [We propose the following]:

"'The jury is instructed that murder in the first degree consists of an intentional, deliberate and premeditated killing which means that the killing is done after a period of time for prior consideration. The duration of that period cannot be arbitrarily fixed. The time in which to form a deliberate and premeditated design varies as the minds and temperaments of people differ, and according to the circumstances in which they may be placed. Any interval of time between the forming of the intent to kill and the execution of that intent, which is of sufficient duration for the accused to be fully conscious of what he intended, is sufficient to support a conviction for first degree murder.'"

Do you prefer the "instantaneous premeditation" approach or do you prefer the approach that requires that some appreciable amount of time pass between the formulation of the intent to kill and the killing itself? Why? Does the instruction proposed by the Court of Appeals of West Virginia in *Guthrie* adequately distinguish between premeditation and intent to kill? Explain.

5. While many courts treat "premeditation" and "deliberation" as synonymous, some hold that the terms are not interchangeable. In *State v. West,* 844 S.W.2d 144 (1992), the Supreme Court of Tennessee defined the terms in the following way:

> The element of premeditation requires a previously formed design or intent to kill. Deliberation, on the other hand, requires that the killing be done with a cool purpose—in other words, that the killer be free from the passions of the moment. Moreover ... the fact that "premeditation can be formed in an instant" must be viewed in contrast to the element of deliberation, which obviously cannot be formed "instantaneously." While it remains true that no specific length of time is required for the formation of a cool, dispassionate intent to kill, *[our previous decisions]* require more than a "split-second" of reflection in order to satisfy the elements of premeditation and deliberation. Without evidence that the killing was willful, malicious, premeditated, and deliberate, this Court cannot uphold a conviction for first degree murder.

Regardless of whether deliberation and premeditation are defined differently, the relevant issues in a prosecution for first-degree murder based on premeditation or deliberation remain the same. First, may premeditation be formed in an instant? As was previously discussed, most states hold that it may not, but a few jurisdictions do allow for an instantaneous form of premeditation. Second, if the jurisdiction rejects "instantaneous premeditation," did an appreciable amount of time elapse between the formulation of the intent to kill and the killing itself? It is not material whether this second inquiry is couched in "premeditation" or "deliberation" terms.

6. While premeditation is the element that is most often invoked by prosecutors to charge a defendant with first-degree murder, there are other types of killings that may be considered first-degree murder without proof of premeditation. The Nevada murder statute cited in the first of the two leading cases excerpted in this section (*Hern v. State*) lists a number of killings that are automatically classified as first-degree murder without the need to prove premeditation. The statute prescribes that killings are automatically considered first-degree murder if they are:

> (a) Perpetrated by means of poison, or lying in wait, torture ... [or]
>
> (b) Committed in the perpetration or attempted perpetration of rape, kidnaping, arson, robbery, burglary or sexual molestation of a child under the age of 14 years....

Observe that subsection (a) lists killings in which premeditation can easily be inferred from the mode of perpetration of the offense. Subsection (b), on the other hand, classifies so-called "felony murders" as first-degree murder. The felony murder rule is discussed in § 20.02.

7. In states that distinguish between second and first-degree murders, second-degree murders are usually defined as any malicious killing that is not premeditated and is not otherwise listed as first-degree murder. In most cases, a second-degree murder will thus be a malicious but unpremeditated killing. As the second leading case excerpted in this section illustrates (*Simpkins v. State*), in the context of the common law definition of murder, a prosecutor may prove malice by showing that the defendant had:

(1) intent to kill,

(2) intent to cause serious bodily injury,

(3) a "depraved heart" or extreme indifference to the value of human life, or by proving

(4) felony murder.

In the first kind of case (intent to kill), courts frequently state that malice is "express." In the remaining three instances, it is frequently asserted that malice is "implied." No significant practical implications follow from the distinction between express and implied malice.

8. The most problematic kind of malice is that of so-called "depraved heart" murder. The problem arises because it is difficult to distinguish between reckless killings that do not evince a "depraved heart" and reckless killings that do. While the latter would be classified as (second-degree) murder, the former would only give rise to liability for manslaughter. As the court observed in *Simpkins,* the kind of recklessness that triggers liability for "depraved heart" murder is frequently described as conduct that reveals extreme indifference to human life. Therefore, the court pointed out that "[t]he perpetrator must [or reasonably should] realize the risk his behavior has created to the extent that his conduct may be termed willful." Furthermore, "the conduct must contain an element of viciousness or contemptuous disregard for the value of human life which conduct characterizes that behavior as wanton." Does the court define the mental state that characterizes "depraved heart" murder in a way that sufficiently distinguishes it from traditional "recklessness"? Explain. The issue has vexed courts for decades. One court explained that the difference between depraved heart recklessness and standard recklessness is that "depraved-heart murder involves a higher degree of recklessness from which malice or deliberate design may be implied." *Windham v. Mississippi,* 602 So.2d 798 (1992). Is this formulation of depraved heart murder more or less helpful than the one put forth in *Simpkins*? Why? Ultimately, it appears that depraved heart murders are simply killings in which the defendant's recklessness is so culpable that it can be equated with purposeful killings in terms of blameworthiness. A more specific definition is, however, elusive.

9. The vagueness inherent in drawing the line between depraved heart murder based on some kind of extreme recklessness and manslaughter predicated on standard recklessness has led to constitutional attacks on the distinction. This was the case in *Brown v. Commonwealth,* 975 S.W.2d 922 (1998), in which the Supreme Court of Kentucky observed that:

> [O]ther jurisdictions faced with this issue have held that the phrase "extreme indifference to human life" does not render a wanton murder statute void for vagueness. In *State v. Robinson,* Appellant argued that the statute setting forth the offense of depraved heart second-degree murder, the unintentional but reckless killing under circumstances manifesting extreme indifference to human life, was void for vagueness because it did not adequately distinguish itself from reckless involuntary manslaughter. In upholding the statute, the Kansas Supreme Court stated:
>
>> We hold that depraved heart second-degree murder requires a conscious disregard of the risk, sufficient under the circumstances, to manifest extreme indifference to the value of human life. Recklessness that can be assimilated to purpose or knowledge is treated as depraved heart second-degree murder, and less extreme recklessness is punished as manslaughter. Conviction of depraved heart second-degree murder requires proof that the defendant acted recklessly under circumstances manifesting extreme indifference to the value of human life. This language describes a kind of culpability that differs in degree but not in kind from the ordinary recklessness required for manslaughter.
>
> The Court concluded that, "[a] jury is expected to decipher many difficult phrases without receiving specific definitions, such as the term 'reasonable doubt.' The phrase 'extreme indifference to the value of human life' is not so vague as to be unconstitutionally void."
>
> Similarly, in *State v. Dow,* the Supreme Court of New Hampshire held that the words "extreme indifference to the value of human life" contained in the gov-

> erning statute were not unconstitutionally void for vagueness. "The words 'extreme indifference to the value of human life' are easily understood. They are the equivalent of what is sometimes referred to as 'depraved heart murder,' which has long been a part of the law."
>
> We are of the opinion that the phrase "extreme indifference to human life" are words of common understanding, and further that the Commentary to the Penal Code sufficiently sets forth the type of conduct that will sustain a wanton murder conviction. As such, the General Assembly was not required to include a precise definition of the phrase within KRS 507.020(1)(b). It is the duty of the trier of fact to determine, under the given circumstances, whether a defendant's conduct rises to the culpable mental state equivalent to intentional murder. Therefore, we conclude that the statutory language in question in KRS 507.020(1)(b) is sufficient to withstand constitutional challenges for both vagueness and separation of powers.

Do you agree that the phrase "extreme indifference to human life" is not impermissibly vague? What exactly is it that makes an act one that manifests "extreme" indifference to human life? Is it that the act is extremely dangerous from an objective perspective? That the actor was subjectively aware of the act and did not care about the consequences of continuing to engage in the act? Both? Explain.

## § 20.02 Felony Murder

### People v. Stamp

Court of Appeal, Second District, Division 3, California, 1969
82 Cal.Rptr. 598

COBEY, Associate Justice.

These are appeals by Jonathan Earl Stamp, Michael John Koory and Billy Dean Lehman, following jury verdicts of guilty of robbery and murder, both in the first degree. Each man was given a life sentence on the murder charge together with the time prescribed by law on the robbery count.

Defendants appeal their conviction of the murder of Carl Honeyman who, suffering from a heart disease, died between 15 and 20 minutes after Koory and Stamp held up his business, the General Amusement Company, on October 26, 1965, at 10:45 a.m. Lehman, the driver of the getaway car, was apprehended a few minutes after the robbery; several weeks later Stamp was arrested in Ohio and Koory in Nebraska.

Broadly stated, the grounds of this appeal are: (1) insufficiency of the evidence on the causation of Honeyman's death; (2) inapplicability of the felony-murder rule to this case; (3) errors in the choice of instructions given and refused; and (4) erroneous admission in evidence of the extrajudicial confessions of Stamp and Koory and the incriminating statement of Lehman.

On this appeal appellants primarily rely upon their position that the felony-murder doctrine should not have been applied in this case due to the unforeseeability of Honeyman's death.

THE FACTS

Defendants Koory and Stamp, armed with a gun and a blackjack, entered the rear of the building housing the offices of General Amusement Company, ordered the employees they found there to go to the front of the premises, where the two secretaries were working. Stamp, the one with the gun, then went into the office of Carl Honeyman, the owner and manager. Thereupon Honeyman, looking very frightened and pale, emerged from the office in a 'kind of hurry.' He was apparently propelled by Stamp who had hold of him by an elbow.

The robbery victims were required to lie down on the floor while the robbers took the money and fled out the back door. As the robbers, who had been on the premises 10 to 15 minutes, were leaving, they told the victims to remain on the floor for five minutes so that no one would 'get hurt.'

Honeyman, who had been lying next to the counter, had to use it to steady himself in getting up off the floor. Still pale, he was short of breath, sucking air, and pounding and rubbing his chest. As he walked down the hall, in an unsteady manner, still breathing hard and rubbing his chest, he said he was having trouble 'keeping the pounding down inside' and that his heart was 'pumping too fast for him.' A few minutes later, although still looking very upset, shaking, wiping his forehead and rubbing his chest, he was able to walk in a steady manner into an employee's office. When the police arrived, almost immediately thereafter, he told them he was not feeling very well and that he had a pain in his chest. About two minutes later, which was 15 to 20 minutes after the robbery had occurred, he collapsed on the floor. At 11:25 he was pronounced dead on arrival at the hospital. The coroner's report listed the immediate cause of death as heart attack.

The employees noted that during the hours before the robbery Honeyman had appeared to be in normal health and good spirits. The victim was an obese, sixty-year-old man, with a history of heart disease, who was under a great deal of pressure due to the intensely competitive nature of his business. Additionally, he did not take good care of his heart.

Three doctors, including the autopsy surgeon, Honeyman's physician, and a professor of cardiology from U.C.L.A., testified that although Honeyman had an advanced case of atherosclerosis, a progressive and ultimately fatal disease, there must have been some immediate upset to his system which precipitated the attack. It was their conclusion in response to a hypothetical question that but for the robbery there would have been no fatal seizure at that time. The fright induced by the robbery was too much of a shock to Honeyman's system. There was opposing expert testimony to the effect that it could not be said with reasonable medical certainty that fright could ever be fatal.

## SUFFICIENCY OF THE EVIDENCE RE CAUSATION

... A review of the facts as outlined above shows that there was substantial evidence of the robbery itself, that appellants were the robbers, and that but for the robbery the victim would not have experienced fright which brought on the fatal heart attack.

## APPLICATION OF THE FELONY-MURDER RULE

Appellants' contention that the felony-murder rule is inapplicable to the facts of this case is also without merit. Under the felony-murder rule ... a killing committed in either the perpetration of or an attempt to perpetrate robbery is murder of the first degree. This is true whether the killing is willful, deliberate and premeditated, or merely accidental or unintentional, and whether or not the killing is planned as a part of the commission of the robbery....

The doctrine presumes malice aforethought on the basis of the commission of a felony inherently dangerous to human life. This rule is a rule of substantive law in California and not merely an evidentiary shortcut to finding malice as it withdraws from the jury the requirement that they find either express malice or the implied malice which is manifested in an intent to kill. Under this rule no intentional act is necessary other than the attempt to or the actual commission of the robbery itself. When a robber enters a place with a deadly weapon with the intent to commit robbery, malice is shown by the nature of the crime.

There is no requirement that the killing occur, 'while committing' or 'while engaged in' the felony, or that the killing be 'a part of' the felony, other than that the few acts be a part of one continuous transaction. Thus the homicide need not have been committed 'to perpetrate' the felony. There need be no technical inquiry as to whether there has been a completion or abandonment of or desistence from the robbery before the homicide itself was completed.

The doctrine is not limited to those deaths which are foreseeable. Rather a felon is held strictly liable for all killings committed by him or his accomplices in the course of the felony. As long as the homicide is the direct causal result of the robbery the felony-murder rule applies whether or not the death was a natural or probable consequence of the robbery. So long as a victim's predisposing physical condition, regardless of its cause, is not the only substantial factor bringing about his death, that condition, and the robber's ignorance of it, in no way destroys the robber's criminal responsibility for the death. So long as life is shortened as a result of the felonious act, it does not matter that the victim might have died soon anyway. In this respect, the robber takes his victim as he finds him ...

The judgment is affirmed.

## *Notes and Questions*

1. According to the original understanding of the felony murder rule, killings that take place during the commission of a felony are automatically classified as murder, thus relieving the prosecution of the burden of proving premeditation or malice. Malice is inferred from the decision to commit the underlying felony. Consequently, under the traditional view of felony murder, the prosecution does not need to prove intent to kill, intent to cause serious bodily injury or extreme indifference to the value of human life. As a result—at least in principle—a defendant may be held liable for murder under the felony murder rule for negligent and even accidental (i.e., non-negligent) killings that take place during the commission of the felony. An extreme example of this is the *Stamp* case, in which the defendant was held liable for murder although the victim's death as a result of a heart attack was not reasonably foreseeable. So construed, the felony murder rule imposes liability without fault and is, therefore, objectionable on retributive grounds. These and other objections to the felony murder rule are discussed in more detail in the Scholarly Debates section of this Chapter.

2. Given that extreme versions of the felony murder rule may give rise to murder liability for acts that may not deserve being punished as murder, some courts have devised a series of doctrines that are designed to limit the application of the felony murder rule to cases in which the imposition of liability for murder seems appropriate. One particularly common limitation on the felony murder rule is the doctrine that limits its application to deaths that occur during the commission of an "inherently dangerous felony." Pursuant to this rule, a death that occurs during the commission of an armed robbery would likely trigger the application of the rule, but a death caused during the perpetration of a simple non-violent theft would likely not. An interesting issue that arises in the context

of the "inherently dangerous felony" limitation is whether the determination of what counts as an inherently dangerous crime should be made in the abstract or taking into account the circumstances of the concrete case. Is, for example, the felony of "unlawful possession of a firearm" inherently dangerous? The answer depends on whether the offense is viewed in the abstract or not. In the abstract, it could be argued that the crime is not inherently dangerous, for one can imagine multiple ways of commission of the offense that do not present any appreciable danger to human life (e.g., a person safely—but unlawfully—keeps a firearm inside a safe that cannot be accessed by anyone). Nevertheless, the felony may sometimes be inherently dangerous if the focus is the concrete mode of commission of the offense (e.g., gang member unlawfully brings a weapon to a brawl against a rival gang). In *Hines v. State,* 578 S.E.2d 868 (2003), the Supreme Court of Georgia had to answer this very question. The Court concluded that—under the circumstances of the case—unlawful possession of a firearm was an inherently dangerous felony that triggered the application of the felony murder rule. In doing so, the Court observed that:

> A felony is "inherently dangerous" when it is "'dangerous per se'" or "'by its circumstances create[s] a foreseeable risk of death.'" Depending on the facts, possession of a firearm by a convicted felon can be an inherently dangerous felony.
>
> In *Ford v. State,* the defendant was a convicted felon who was unloading a handgun when it accidentally discharged, went through the floor, and killed an occupant of the apartment below. A jury convicted Ford for felony murder based on his felonious possession of a firearm. This Court reversed, finding that, because no evidence showed the defendant knew there was an apartment below him or that the victim was present, his possession of a firearm could not support a conviction for felony murder.
>
> In contrast to *Ford,* Hines intentionally fired his shotgun intending to hit his target. He had been drinking before he went hunting, and there was evidence that he had been drinking while hunting. He knew that other hunters were in the area and was unaware of their exact location. He also knew that other people visited the area in which he was hunting. He took an unsafe shot at dusk, through heavy foliage, at a target eighty feet away that he had not positively identified as a turkey. Under these circumstances, we conclude that Hines's illegal possession of a firearm created a foreseeable risk of death. Accordingly, Hines's violation of the prohibition against convicted felons possessing firearms was an inherently dangerous felony that could support a felony murder conviction.

Are you persuaded by the Court's reasoning? Do you believe that an intoxicated hunter who kills a person while attempting to shoot an animal deserves to be punished as a murderer or does he deserve to be punished less severely, perhaps with the punishment that is reserved for reckless or negligent homicide? Explain. Note that the outcome in *Hines* was made possible by looking at how the offense was actually committed. Other courts, however, adopt a stricter view that focuses on whether the offense is inherently dangerous *per se* (i.e., in the abstract). An offense is inherently dangerous in the abstract when every possible form of commission of the offense is dangerous. Had this approach been adopted in *Hines,* unlawful possession of a gun would not be inherently dangerous, for the offense can be—and is often—committed in a non-dangerous way. The Supreme Court of California adopted the stricter *per se* approach in *People v. Phillips,* 414 P.2d 353 (1998), in which it was held that the felony of "grand theft" was not inherently dangerous in the abstract. The defendant committed grand theft by fraudulently claiming that he could cure cancer. The victim's parents removed her daughter from proper medical care and instead paid the defendant so that he could cure their daughter of cancer. The defendant did not cure the daughter and she eventually died as a result of her failure to get appropriate medical treatment. The defendant was charged with felony murder based on the underlying crime of grand theft. In rejecting the application of the felony murder rule, the Court explained that:

> We have held … that only such felonies as are in themselves 'inherently dangerous to human life' can support the application of the felony murder rule. We have ruled that in assessing such peril to human life inherent in any given felony 'we look to the elements of the felony in the abstract, not the particular 'facts' of the case.'
>
> We have thus recognized that the felony murder doctrine expresses a highly artificial concept that deserves no extension beyond its required application. Indeed the rule itself has been abandoned by the courts of England, where it had its inception. It has been subjected to severe and sweeping criticism. No case to our knowledge in any jurisdiction has held that because death results from a course of conduct involving a felonious perpetration of a fraud, the felony murder doctrine can be invoked.
>
> Admitting that grand theft is not inherently dangerous to life, the prosecution asks us to encompass the entire course of defendant's conduct so that we may incorporate such elements as would make his crime inherently dangerous. In so framing the definition of a given felony for the purpose of assessing its inherent peril to life the prosecution would abandon the statutory definition of the felony as such and substitute the factual elements of defendant's actual conduct. In the present case the Attorney General would characterize that conduct as 'grand theft medical fraud,' and this newly created 'felony,' he urges, clearly involves danger to human life and supports an application of the felony murder rule.
>
> To fragmentize the 'course of conduct' of defendant so that the felony murder rule applies if any segment of that conduct may be considered dangerous to life would widen the rule beyond calculation. It would then apply not only to the commission of specific felonies, which are themselves dangerous to life, but to the perpetration of Any felony during which defendant may have acted in such a manner as to endanger life.
>
> The proposed approach would entail the rejection of our holding in Williams. That case limited the felony murder doctrine to such felonies as were themselves inherently dangerous to life. That decision eschews the prosecution's present sweeping concept because, once the Legislature's own definition is discarded, the number or nature of the contextual elements which could be incorporated into an expanded felony terminology would be limitless. We have been, and remain, unwilling to embark on such an uncharted sea of felony murder.

What result if the *Hines* approach to whether a felony is inherently dangerous were applied to the facts in *Phillips*? Which is the better approach? Why?

3. As an outgrowth of the inherently dangerous felony limitation, most states now specifically enumerate the felonies that trigger the felony murder rule. These are usually limited to crimes that are inherently dangerous. Once again, the Nevada murder statute discussed in the previous section is representative. The statute prescribes that a killing is murder in the first degree if it is:

> (b) Committed in the perpetration or attempted perpetration of rape, kidnaping, arson, robbery, burglary or sexual molestation of a child under the age of 14 years.…

4. Another doctrine that some courts apply in order to limit the felony murder rule is the so-called "merger" doctrine. According to this doctrine, the felony murder rule applies when the death results as a consequence of a felony that is not "assaultive" in nature. If, on the other hand, the felony is assaultive in nature, then the assaultive felony "merges" with the homicide and will thus not trigger the application of the felony murder rule. An obvious example would be that of a person who recklessly (but without "depraved heart") kills another person. May the felony of reckless homicide be used to trigger the felony murder rule and thus hold the defendant liable for murder rather than reckless homicide? The answer must be "no," for holding otherwise would virtually eliminate liability for non-murder homicides, given that the non-murder homicides would always amount to a felony that triggers liability for murder instead of liability for the less serious homicide. For similar reasons, most jurisdictions hold that "assault" or "battery" may not be used as felonies that trigger application of the felony murder rule. Since most homicides also amount to assaults, allowing assault to trigger the felony murder rule would basically eliminate liability for manslaughter, given that the assault would almost always trigger liability for felony murder. The more complicated case arises when the felony is not assault or a lesser form of homicide, but often involves assaultive conduct. Think, for example, of a death that results as a consequence of an armed robbery. Should this felony trigger the felony murder rule or should it merge with the homicide because it is assaultive in nature? Most courts hold that robbery (and other offenses that are not specifically directed at causing physical harm to the victim) does not trigger the merger rule and, therefore, may be invoked as a predicate felony that generates felony murder liability. The result is usually justified by pointing out that the underlying felony (in this case, robbery) is independent of the assault of the victim. More specifically, the purpose of the underlying felony is not to cause physical harm. In the case of robbery, the purpose is to take the victim's property. Consequently, the potential physical harm that might be caused to the victim is tangential or incidental to the ultimate objective of taking her property. Given that the felony (e.g., robbery) has a purpose that is different than physically harming the victim, the merger doctrine does not apply. The Supreme Court of Georgia explained this result in the following manner:

> [W]e generally do not apply the ... merger rule "to any felony murder conviction in which the underlying felony was not the aggravated assault of the murder victim." Indeed, in several cases ... we have "reiterated that the modified merger rule does not apply when the underlying felony, such as armed robbery, is independent of the killing itself." Here, the indictment charged Grimes with attempted armed robbery by "brandishing a knife and demanding money," and the evidence supports his conviction for felony murder in the commission of that attempted armed robbery. Because the underlying felony—that attempted armed robbery—was independent of the killing itself, the ... merger rule ... does not apply, and Grimes was properly convicted of felony murder. *Grimes v. State,* 293 Ga. 559 (2013).

As the Court pointed out, the consequence of this position is that the merger doctrine will usually apply only when the underlying felony is a kind of homicide or assault. Under this approach, crimes such as kidnapping and forcible rape would not trigger the merger doctrine and would thus still serve as predicate felonies for the purposes of the felony murder rule.

5. Some courts hold that the felony murder rule applies only if death was a "natural and probable" consequence of the defendant's act. See, e.g., *Commonwealth v. Gordon,* 422 Mass. 816 (1996). According to this approach, an actor may be held liable for a death

that occurs during the commission of a felony only if the death was reasonably foreseeable in light of the actor's conduct. The approach has found its way to more modern statutory formulations of the felony murder rule. In the Puerto Rico 2004 Penal Code, for example, a death that occurred during the commission of one of the statutorily enumerated felonies generated liability for felony murder only if it was a "natural consequence" of the act. Similarly, the Wisconsin homicide statute prescribed that "whoever causes death as a natural and probable consequence of the commission of a felony is guilty of second-degree murder." This statutory provision was construed by the Court of Appeals of Wisconsin in *State v. Noren,* 371 N.W.2d 381 (1985), in which the defendant claimed that causing the death was not a "natural and probable consequence" of striking the intoxicated victim's head three times with his fist. The Court observed that:

> The phrase "natural and probable" has not been defined under the felony-murder statute. The parties concede that to be a natural consequence of a felony, death must be proximately caused by the defendant's conduct. The test of cause is whether the defendant's conduct was a substantial factor in causing the death. It is undisputed on appeal that Noren's conduct caused Lebakken's death. The critical issue therefore is whether death was a probable consequence of striking Lebakken's head.
>
> Although the parties agree that "probable" relates to the foreseeability of death, they disagree about how foreseeabledeath must be. We agree that foreseeability requires different degrees of certainty in different contexts. To constitute negligence, harm must be probable rather than merely possible. Negligent homicide requires that conduct create a high probability of death or great bodily harm. "High probability" is defined as a probability that the ordinary person, having in mind all the circumstances, including the seriousness of the consequences, would consider unreasonable. It does not mean that the mathematical probability of the consequences must be greater than fifty percent. Death caused by conduct evincing a depraved mind requires that the defendant's conduct be imminently dangerous to human life. "Imminently dangerous" means that the conduct is dangerous in and of itself; it must have been inherently, apparently, and consciously dangerous to life and not such as might casually produce death by misadventure.
>
> The statutory requirement that death be a probable consequence of a felony is intended to limit felony-murder liability to situations where the defendant's conduct creates some measure of foreseeable risk of death.

Turning to the facts of the case, the Court concluded that:

> Noren argues that striking a person's head three times with a fist is not inherently dangerous. He relies on *Beauregard v. State,* where our supreme court stated that striking a person's head with a gun barrel generally would not cause death. The state argues that striking a very intoxicated person who has a respiratory disease is inherently dangerous. According to this argument, the specific traits of the victim must be considered when deciding whether conduct is dangerous. The state also argues that one who commits a violent crime takes his victim as he finds him.
>
> We agree that generally death is not the natural and probable result of a blow with a hand. Our inquiry is not complete, however, because the particular traits of the victim also must be considered. Conduct that is unlikely to cause the death of a healthy adult may be dangerous to others. Only special attributes that the defendant was aware of may be considered. Conduct does not become inher-

> ently dangerous on the basis of latent danger. The truism that a defendant takes his victim as he finds him, therefore, does not apply to this case. The proposition applies in tort law when assessing damages. It also applies in criminal law when deciding the issue of causation. The unknown qualities of a victim, however, are irrelevant to the issue of foreseeability of death.
>
> Applying the ... test to this case, we conclude that sufficient evidence supports Noren's conviction. Although Lebakken's respiratory disease was irrelevant to the issue of inherent danger, his extreme intoxication was a factor that distinguished him from a healthy adult. Striking an intoxicated person exposes him to familiar risks that a sober person would not face. He may fall and fatally strike his head. He also may asphyxiate from vomit while unconscious. Although Lebakken did not die from either of these causes, the jury could consider such possibilities when determining whether Noren's conduct was inherently dangerous. We conclude that a reasonable jury could have been convinced beyond a reasonable doubt that his conduct was inherently dangerous.

Do you agree with the outcome of the case? Why or why not? What result if the "natural and probable consequences" limitation had been applied in the leading case excerpted in this section (*People v. Stamp*)? Explain.

6. May a felon be held liable for murder under the felony murder rule when someone kills a co-felon or an innocent third party while attempting to thwart the commission of the felony? The paradigmatic example is that of a police officer who kills a co-felon in an attempt to prevent the felony from taking place. The officer may also accidentally kill an innocent third party while attempting to thwart the crime. Some courts hold that co-felons are liable for murder under the felony murder rule for such deaths as long as they were "reasonably foreseeable." This has come to be known as the "proximate causation" approach to this issue. In contrast, a majority of jurisdictions hold that felons may only be held liable under the felony murder rule for deaths caused by fellow co-felons. This is known as the "agency" approach to the problem. Both theories were discussed by the Supreme Court of Illinois in *People v. Lowery,* 178 Ill.2d 462 (1997), in which it was observed that:

> At issue in this appeal is whether the felony-murder rule applies where the intended victim of an underlying felony, as opposed to the defendant or his accomplice, fired the fatal shot which killed an innocent bystander. To answer this question, it is necessary to discuss the theories of liability upon which a felony-murder conviction may be based. The two theories of liability are proximate cause and agency.
>
> In considering the applicability of the felony-murder rule where the murder is committed by someone resisting the felony, Illinois follows the "proximate cause theory." Under this theory, liability attaches under the felony-murder rule for any death proximately resulting from the unlawful activity—notwithstanding the fact that the killing was by one resisting the crime.
>
> *People v. Payne* is exemplary of Illinois' first application of the proximate cause theory. In *Payne,*the armed robbers approached the home of two brothers. One of the brothers fired a gun, attempting to prevent the robbery, and one of the robbers also fired. The second brother was killed by the gunfire, but it could not be determined whether his brother or the robber fired the fatal shot. The court found this fact to be immaterial and confirmed the defendant's murder conviction, stating:

> "It reasonably might be anticipated that an attempted robbery would meet with resistance, during which the victim might be shot either by himself or someone else in attempting to prevent the robbery, and those attempting to perpetrate the robbery would be guilty of murder."

> More recently, this court followed the reasoning of *Payne* in *People v. Hickman*. In *Hickman*, a police officer killed another police officer while attempting to apprehend cofelons fleeing from the scene of a burglary. This court held that the shot that killed the police officer was in opposition to the escape of the fleeing burglars and was a direct and foreseeable consequence of defendant's actions.

> Alternatively, the majority of jurisdictions employ an agency theory of liability. Under this theory, "the doctrine of felony murder does not extend to a killing, although growing out of the commission of the felony, if directly attributable to the act of one other than the defendant or those associated with him in the unlawful enterprise." Thus, under the agency theory, the felony-murder rule is inapplicable where the killing is done by one resisting the felony.

Which theory—agency or proximate cause—do you find more appealing? Why?

## § 20.03 Voluntary Manslaughter

### State v. Gounagias

Supreme Court of Washington, 1915
153 P. 9

ELLIS, J.

The defendant was tried upon an information charging him with murder in the first degree. The jury returned a verdict of guilty as charged. The defendant's motion for a new trial was overruled. Judgment was entered upon the verdict. The defendant appealed ...

Counsel for the appellant in his opening statement disclaimed any intention of asking an acquittal, but started to detail certain circumstances which he expected to prove in mitigation to reduce the offense from murder to manslaughter. On objection by the state he was not permitted to proceed with this part of the statement. In the progress of the defense counsel offered to prove by the appellant that on the 19th day of April, 1914, the Greek Easter, the appellant, who was then living in the same house with the deceased, had taken several glasses of beer, and either because of the beer, or of some drug therein, had become helpless and almost unconscious, when the deceased, after making many insulting remarks concerning the appellant and his wife, who lived in the old country, finally, while the appellant lay helpless on the floor, committed upon him the unmentionable crime [Editor's Note: The crime of sodomy], and went away, leaving the appellant in a state of semiconsciousness; that the appellant thereafter moved to another house, and on the next day, meeting George on the street, upbraided him for his action and asked him why he had done it, to which George in substance laughingly replied, 'You're all right, it did not hurt you;' that the appellant then, in order to avoid the disgrace of the matter, asked George to say nothing about it to their countrymen; that thereafter, wherever the appellant went, he could hear remarks and see signs made by his countrymen indicating that George had circulated the story, so that the appellant was continuously ridiculed and subjected to insulting remarks and gestures on the part of his fellow countrymen; that these things so preyed upon his mind that he became sick and afflicted with severe headaches, and that the headache on May 6th, which was so severe as to prevent his working, was induced by this cause; that when he entered the coffeehouse at about 11 o'clock on the evening of May 6th there were about 10 men there, who began making laughing remarks and suggestive gestures, which in the appellant's weakened condition so excited and enraged him that he lost all control of his reason and rushed from the house, with the design of avenging himself by killing George. The appellant also offered to prove by other witnesses that Dan George had in fact circulated the report of his treatment of the appellant, and that by reason thereof the insulting remarks, signs, and gestures were often made in the appellant's presence. These offers were made in the absence of the jury, and the evidence was by the court excluded. The appellant was asked in the presence of the jury, 'Why did you kill Dan George?' The court, evidently understanding that in answer to this question he would repeat the story which had been excluded, did not permit him to answer, further than to say that he first thought of killing George 'at the moment when I saw those inhuman things at 11 o'clock.'...

The court instructed the jury as to the necessary elements of murder in the first and second degrees, but refused to instruct as to manslaughter. There are many assignments of error, but they are all directed to the exclusion of the offered evidence, which it is claimed should have been admitted in mitigation of the offense from murder to manslaughter, and to the refusal of the court to instruct as to manslaughter upon such evidence. The solution of these questions will sufficiently dispose of all the errors assigned.

The Criminal Code of 1909, which is now in force, defines and classifies homicide ... as follows:

> 'Homicide is the killing of a human being by the act, procurement or omission of another and is either (1) murder, (2) manslaughter, (3) excusable homicide, or (4) justifiable homicide.'

Murder in the first degree ... is defined as:

> 'The killing of a human being, unless it is excusable or justifiable, is murder in the first degree when committed either—
>
> '(1) With a premeditated design to effect the death of the person killed, or of another; or
>
> '(2) By an act imminently dangerous to others and evincing a depraved mind, regardless of human life, without a premeditated design to effect the death of any individual; or
>
> '(3) Without a design to effect death, by a person engaged in the commission of, or in an attempt to commit, or in withdrawing from the scene of, a robbery, rape, burglary, larceny or arson in the first degree ...

Murder in the second decree is defined by section 2393 as:

> 'The killing of a human being, unless it is excusable or justifiable, is murder in the second degree when—
>
> '(1) Committed with a design to effect the death of the person killed or of another, but without premeditation ...

Section 2395 defines manslaughter as follows:

> 'In any case other than those specified in sections 2392, 2393 and 2394, homicide, not being excusable or justifiable, is manslaughter. * * *'...

A reading of the foregoing sections of the Code makes it manifest that the general definition of manslaughter contained in section 2395, by a process of elimination through the definitions of first and second degree murder, includes the killing of a human being without justification or excuse when: (1) Committed *without* design to effect death and *without* premeditation; or (2) perpetrated by a person engaged in the commission of, or in an attempt to commit, or in withdrawing from the scene of a crime *other than a felony*.... It is obvious that, under the admitted facts of this case as testified to by the appellant himself, his crime could not by any construction of the evidence be reduced to the degree of manslaughter. The killing was with the admitted design to effect death, and was not in any manner connected with the commission of any other crime less than a felony. Clearly, therefore, the evidence which was offered and excluded was not admissible for the purpose of proving, because under other admitted facts it did not tend to prove, manslaughter.

But it does not follow that the evidence offered was properly excluded. Obviously, if the evidence tended to mitigate the crime from murder in the first degree to murder in the second degree, it should have been admitted. If it had that tendency, it would have been admissible at common law, as tending to reduce the crime from murder to manslaughter; but, as we have seen, under our present statute a killing with intent to produce death, but without premeditation, is murder in the second degree. If, therefore, the offered evidence had any tendency to negative premeditation and deliberation, which are essentials of murder in the first degree, it should have been admitted.

The appellant contends that what would be such reasonable provocation as to be competent evidence in mitigation, and what would be a reasonable cooling time after such provocation, are always questions for the jury.

The doctrine of mitigation is briefly this: That if the act of killing, though intentional, be committed under the influence of sudden, intense anger, or heat of blood, obscuring the reason, produced by an adequate or reasonable provocation, and before sufficient time has elapsed for the blood to cool and reason to reassert itself, so that the killing is the result of temporary excitement rather than of wickedness of heart or innate recklessness of disposition, then the law, recognizing the standard of human conduct as that of the ordinary or average man, regards the offense so committed as of less heinous character than premeditated or deliberate murder. Measured as it must be by the conduct of the average man, what constitutes adequate cause is incapable of exact definition.

What is a reasonable cooling time is ... generally a question for the jury ... All courts agree that the time necessary for cooling is a reasonable time. The question of reasonable time is always a conclusion to be drawn from all of the facts and circumstances of the particular case ...

As stated in 2 Bishop's New Criminal Law (8th Ed.) § 712:

> 'We have no rule for determining how much time is necessary for cooling; in the nature of things, it must depend much on what is special to the particular case. Commonly the time in which an ordinary man under like circumstances would cool is deemed reasonable.'

We apprehend that the true rule is precisely the same as that in other cases where reasonableness of human conduct is necessarily measured by the conduct of the ordinary or average man in like situation, so frequently announced and applied in cases where the ultimate question is one of negligence. It is only where it can be said that, giving to the evidence every reasonable inference that can be drawn from it favorable to the defendant, the minds of reasonable men could not differ in the conclusion that a reasonable cooling time had elapsed, the question is one for the court. Wanting this inevitable conclusion both from the evidence and inference therefrom, the question is always one for the jury upon proper instructions....

Measured by these principles, in which we have adopted the most liberal views expressed by any court, did the court err in refusing to admit the offered evidence of provocation? For the purpose of this discussion we must, of course, assume that the offered evidence was true. There can be no doubt that the original outrage committed by the deceased would have been a sufficient provocation to take the case to the jury, if the appellant, immediately upon realizing its perpetration, had sought out and slain the deceased. There can be little doubt that, had the appellant slain the deceased when, on meeting him the next day, the deceased impudently treated the outrage as inconsequential, the question of provocation would have been for the jury. No court would be warranted in saying that such callous conduct, while the original wrong was but a day old, would have no reasonable tendency to produce immediate, uncontrollable anger, destroying the capacity for cool reflection in the average man. In such a case evidence of both the previous conduct and the insolent behavior of deceased on the subsequent meeting would have been admissible.

The appellant, however, did neither of these. On the meeting the next day, notwithstanding the insolence of the deceased, he admittedly condoned the offense, requesting that deceased preserve silence. It may even be conceded that, had the appellant met the deceased immediately after first discovering from words and gestures of others that deceased had circulated the story of the outrage and then, smarting under this added injury, had killed him, evidence of the whole transaction should have been submitted to the jury to determine the adequacy of the provocation. We have, however, been cited to no case, independent of a governing statute, in which it has been held that the immediate provocation, when referable for its provocative force to some antecedent outrage known to the accused from the beginning, was held sufficient to take the case to the jury, when not the act of or participated in by the deceased. At least one court has asserted that provocative words or acts, to have a reasonable tendency to produce a mitigating degree of anger and excitement in the ordinary man, must be the words or acts of the victim at the time and place of the killing.

We are not prepared to go so far, since it would seem but natural that, on first seeing the gestures and hearing the words of others indicating that the story had been circulated, the appellant would as certainly know that the deceased was responsible for its circulation as if he had been present and participating in the demonstrations, and that such knowledge would be as suddenly exasperating when *at first acquired* the one way as the other. But even this assumption does not meet the case in hand. According to the offered evidence the appellant let these things pass repeatedly for many days without molesting the deceased, even to the extent of a remonstrance. The offered evidence makes it clear that the appellant knew and appreciated for days before the killing the full meaning of the words, signs, and vulgar gestures of his countrymen, which, as the offer shows, he had encountered from day to day for about three weeks following the original outrage, wherever he went. The final demonstration in the coffeehouse was nothing new. It was exactly what the appellant, from his experience for the prior three weeks, must have anticipated. To say that it alone tended to create the sudden passion and heat of blood essential to mitigation is to ignore the admitted fact that the same thing had created no such condition on its repeated occurrence during the prior three weeks. To say that these repeated demonstrations, coupled with the original outrage, *culminated* in a sudden passion and heat of blood when he encountered the same character of demonstration in the coffeehouse on the night of the killing, is to say that sudden passion and heat of blood in the mitigative sense may be a cumulative result of repeated reminders of a single act of provocation occurring weeks before, and this, whether that provocation be regarded as the original outrage or the spreading of the story among appellant's associates, both of which he knew and fully realized for three weeks before the fatal night. This theory of the cumulative effect of reminders of former wrongs, not of new acts of provocation by the deceased, is contrary to the idea of sudden anger as understood in the doctrine of mitigation. In the nature of the thing *sudden* anger cannot be cumulative. A provocation which does not cause instant resentment, but which is only resented after being thought upon and brooded over, is not a provocation sufficient in law to reduce intentional killing from murder to manslaughter, or under our statute to second degree murder, which includes every inexcusable, unjustifiable, unpremeditated, intentional killing.

> 'Provocation which would not naturally cause instant resentment, however, but which would have to be thought and brooded over after it is given, in order to produce rage or anger, is not, in contemplation of law, a provocation sufficient to reduce an intentional killing from murder to manslaughter.' Wharton, Homicide (3d Ed.) § 172, p. 273;

The evidence offered had no tendency to prove sudden anger and resentment. On the contrary, it did tend to prove brooding thought, resulting in the design to kill. It was therefore properly excluded....

The cumulative effect of the original outrage and the humiliation suffered by the appellant by reason of being subjected to continual reminders of it, though wholly inadmissible as tending to prove sudden anger in mitigation, might, nevertheless, have tended to produce a weakened mental and physical state amounting to temporary insanity or moral irresponsibility at the time of the commission of the homicide. The appellant, however, not only failed to plead insanity as required by our statute, but expressly disclaimed that defense.

We are constrained to hold that upon the offer of evidence for the purpose of mitigation the court must, as a preliminary question, decide as a matter of law whether the offered evidence has any tendency to prove mitigating circumstances. If it has any such tendency, it must be admitted, and the questions of sufficient provocation and cooling time are then solely for the jury. If it has no such tendency, there is no error in its rejection. Upon all authority we are convinced that the evidence here had no such tendency. It was properly rejected.

The judgment is affirmed.

## *Notes and Questions*

1. At common law, an intentional killing committed "in the heat of passion" was considered (voluntary) manslaughter rather than murder. Passion thus negates the "malicious" nature of the killing, therefore reducing what would otherwise be murder to the less serious offense of manslaughter. As *Gounagias* illustrates, in order to successfully mitigate murder to manslaughter pursuant to this partial defense, the defendant must have (1) acted in the heat of passion, (2) that is the product of adequate or sufficient provocation, and (3) acted before he had a reasonable time to cool off.

2. With regard to the heat of passion itself, the defendant may only plead mitigation if he subjectively acted while experiencing a sudden and passionate anger or other strong emotion. Defendants who kill without being in this heightened emotional state may not plead the passion mitigation even if the victim engaged in acts of provocation that would have stirred the passions of an average person.

3. Only passion that is the product of "adequate or sufficient" provocation suffices to mitigate murder to manslaughter. Originally, only a very limited number of acts counted as adequate provocation. The classic cases were instances of mutual combat, assault and battery, commission of a serious offense against a close family member, unlawful arrest and witnessing spousal adultery. Therefore, minor assaults, learning about—without personally witnessing—adultery, and unfaithfulness of someone who is not the legal spouse of the actor did not amount adequate provocation as a matter of law. Finally—and more importantly—words alone never amounted to sufficient provocation at early common law, no matter how offensive.

4. The more modern trend is to move away from enumerating the kinds of acts that can give rise to adequate provocation. Instead, modern formulations provide that provocation is adequate if it is "sufficient to lead a reasonable person to act in an irrational manner" (Tennessee Code Annotated § 39-13-211), or if it "would cause a reasonable person to lose control" (*People v. Tierney,* 703 N.W.2d 204 [2005]). In spite of this trend, a significant number of jurisdictions continue to hold that words alone may not amount to adequate provocation. The Supreme Judicial Court of Massachusetts approach to passion in *Commonwealth v. Bins,* 465 Mass. 348 (2013) is representative of the current state of the doctrine:

> "Voluntary manslaughter is unlawful homicide arising not from malice, but 'from the frailty of human nature,' as in a case of 'sudden passion induced by reasonable provocation, sudden combat, or excessive force in self-defense.'" "Reasonable provocation is provocation that 'would have been likely to produce in an ordinary person such a state of passion, anger, fear, fright, or nervous excitement as would eclipse his capacity for reflection or restraint.'" "[T]he jury must be able to infer that a reasonable person would have become sufficiently provoked." Words alone are insufficient to produce the requisite passion in a reasonable person. Physical contact may be, but is not necessarily, sufficient.

Do you agree that words alone should always be insufficient to trigger the passion mitigation? Explain.

5. Given that the defense is triggered by a sudden heat of passion, courts typically hold that the mitigation is unavailable when the defendant killed after she had enough time to cool off. There is no precise amount of time that must pass in order to conclude that the actor had enough time to cool off. Rather, the test is whether a reasonable person would have had sufficient time to do so. As the Supreme Court of Nevada explained in *Allen v. State,* 98 Nev. 354 (1982):

> Whether the interval between the provocation and the killing is sufficient for the passions of a reasonable person to cool is not measured exclusively by any precise time. What constitutes a sufficient cooling-off period also depends upon the magnitude of the provocation and the degree to which passions are aroused.

This is why the defendant in *Gounagias* was unable to successfully plead passion. Since he killed several weeks after he was sodomized, the court held that—as a matter of law—enough time had elapsed between the provocative act and the killing for the defendant to cool off. It is always the case that the passage of time leads to "cooling off"? Did the defendant's passion in *Gounagias* recede or increase with the passage of time? Why?

6. Is passion a partial excuse or a partial justification to conduct? Some scholars argue that passion is a partial justification to conduct. Under this approach, passion mitigates punishment because the victim contributes to her own demise by engaging in the provocative conduct. The victim's causal contribution to her death is thus seen as something that

diminishes the wrongfulness of the act. See, e.g., Vera Bergelson, *Justification or Excuse: Exploring the Meaning of Provocation*, 42 Texas Tech L. Rev. 307 (2009). In contrast, other scholars argue that provocation is better viewed as a partial excuse that mitigates liability because passion impairs the actor's choice-making capabilities. This approach focuses on the defendant's cognitive and volitional impairments rather than on the victim's causal contribution to the crime. Joshua Dressler, *Rethinking Heat of Passion: A Defense in Search of a Rationale*, 73 J. Crim. L. & Criminology 421, 442 (1982). The discussion is not only of theoretical import. Sorting out whether passion is a partial excuse or a partial justification is relevant to determining whether a provoked defendant who kills someone other than the person who provoked her should be able to plead passion as mitigation. Think of an enraged person who goes on a shooting spree right after witnessing her spouse commit adultery. May the person plead passion as mitigation if during the shooting spree she kills someone other than the adulterous spouse? This is the problem of "misdirected retaliation." If passion is viewed as a partial excuse that is afforded to those who lose self-control, such a killing should be mitigated regardless of the fact that retaliation was misdirected. As long, of course, as the defendant actually lost the capacity to control her acts. In contrast, if the defense is viewed primarily as a partial justification that focuses on the victim's contribution to her own demise, there should be no mitigation in cases of misdirected retaliation. Given that the person who is killed in these instances was not the person who provoked the attack, mitigation would be unwarranted in these cases. Several states disallow passion as a defense in cases of misdirected retaliation. Others allow it. Which is the better view? Why?

7. Some feminist scholars have argued in favor of significantly narrowing the provocation defense. Others have gone as far as calling for the abolition of the defense. See, e.g., Celia Wells, *Provocation: The Case for Abolition, in* RETHINKING ENGLISH HOMICIDE LAW 85 (Andrew Ashworth & Barry Mitchell eds., 2000). According to these scholars, the problem with provocation law is that it has a negative impact on women, for the vast majority of defendants who successfully plead passion are males who are charged with killing their female partners in intimate settings. As a result, provocation disproportionately (and unjustifiably) favors violent men who kill their female partners at the expense of passive women who endure assaults from their violent partners. As Professor Victoria Nourse pointed out, in provocation cases "men are by far the most frequent victimizers, and women the most frequent victims." Victoria Nourse, *Passion's Progress: Modern Law Reform and the Provocation Defense,* 106 Yale L. J. 1331 (1997).

## § 20.06 Involuntary Manslaughter

### Cook v. State

Court of Special Appeals of Maryland, 1997
702 A.2d 971

ROBERT C. MURPHY, Judge.

Appellant, Robert Cook, was convicted by a jury sitting in the Circuit Court for Montgomery County (Beard, J., presiding) of second degree murder, involuntary manslaughter, and use of a handgun in commission of a crime of violence. He was sentenced to thirty years imprisonment for the second degree murder conviction, into which the manslaughter conviction was merged, and a consecutive fifteen-year term for the use of a handgun conviction. Appellant noted a timely appeal and presents [this question] for our review:

> I. Did the trial court fail to adequately distinguish second degree depraved heart murder and involuntary manslaughter in its instructions to the jury?

FACTS

Appellant and Kathryn Burns, the victim, had a stormy relationship. They were living together when on May 12, 1996, appellant shot the victim once in the upper back, which caused severe internal bleeding. The victim died as a result of that single wound. The record discloses that on the morning of May 12, the victim drank several beers before leaving the apartment she shared with appellant to go to her job at Country Nursery in Burtonsville. Dawn Hale, appellant's daughter, was visiting and during the day, she and appellant decided to cook dinner for the victim as it was Mother's Day. At approximately 4:45 p.m., the victim called the apartment, spoke to Ms. Hale, and informed her that she was running late and would be home in about one-half hour ...

At trial, Ms. Hale testified that about one hour after the victim telephoned, she had not yet returned to the apartment. Appellant was upset and left the apartment. According to Ms. Hale, appellant returned to the apartment twenty minutes later and handed a pipe, approximately three-feet in length, to her, telling her to rub her hands up and down it. Ms. Hale did so and rubbed the pipe on her shirt, noticing that it had glass on it. Appellant was angry and was yelling. A short while later, appellant and Ms. Hale left the apartment to look for the victim. As they drove in appellant's tow truck, they saw the victim travelling in her car. Appellant pulled in front of the victim's car, Ms. Hale got out of the tow truck and into the victim's car. The victim wanted to go to the liquor store to purchase additional beer. At appellant's direction, Ms. Hale reported to two police officers that the victim was driving drunk. Eventually, Ms. Hale returned to appellant's tow truck and when they drove past a house, appellant yelled something out the window. Ms. Hale was unable to discern what he said. Appellant and Ms. Hale then returned to the apartment.

When appellant and Ms. Hale entered the apartment, they found the victim sitting on the bed in the bedroom. According to Ms. Hale, the victim was "very quiet" and "looked upset." Ms. Hale added that the victim had been drinking. Ms. Hale described appellant as "[v]ery, very angry." She stated that appellant yelled at the victim over being late and accused her of sleeping with Mr. Palomo. Appellant and the victim had been drinking beer throughout the day and in Ms. Hale's estimation, both were drunk.

Ms. Hale had appellant leave the bedroom and was attempting to speak with the victim when appellant returned and, again, yelled at the victim. Ms. Hale was able to get appellant to leave the bedroom. She then spoke with the victim, telling her that she did not want to be in the middle of their dispute, when appellant retrieved a gun from the linen closet. Appellant entered the bedroom, threw the gun on the bed, and said to Ms. Hale, "Well, then shoot us." Appellant again left the bedroom.

The victim picked up the gun, looked at it, and pulled back the hammer. Ms. Hale asked the victim to put the gun away and the victim placed it under the bed. When appellant returned to the bedroom, Ms. Hale picked up the gun and gave it to him, telling him to put it away. Appellant took the gun and asked who had pulled the hammer back. The victim stated that she had done so. Appellant put the hammer back down and began to leave the bedroom. He returned and questioned the victim as to why she had pulled the hammer back, asking if she wanted to kill herself. The victim simply shrugged, continued to smoke a cigarette and drink her beer.

Appellant pulled the hammer back and began waving the gun around. Ms. Hale testified that appellant waved the gun in front of the victim's face and yelled at her that she should go ahead and kill herself. Appellant refused Ms. Hale's requests to lay the gun down. According to Ms. Hale, appellant pointed the gun behind the victim, toward a pillow, and it went off. He removed the cylinder rod from the gun and handed the gun to Ms. Hale, telling her to get rid of it. The victim laid back on the bed and it was only then that Ms. Hale realized that the victim had been shot. At appellant's direction, Ms. Hale called for an ambulance, informing the operator that the gun had gone off while appellant was cleaning it.

DISCUSSION

I.

The trial court instructed the jury on the crime of second degree depraved heart murder, explaining that

> [i]t is the killing of another person while acting with an extreme disregard for human life.
>
> And in order to convict the defendant of second degree murder, the State must prove that the conduct of the defendant caused the death of the victim; that the defendant's conduct created a very high degree of risk to the life of the victim; and that the defendant, conscious of such risk, acted with extreme disregard of the life endangering consequences.

The court also instructed the jury on involuntary manslaughter, stating:

> In order to convict the defendant of involuntary manslaughter, the State must prove: one, that the conduct of the defendant caused the death of the victim; and that the defendant conscious of the risk, acted in a grossly negligent manner, that is, in a manner that created a high degree of risk to human life.

Appellant claims that the court's instructions failed to adequately distinguish between second degree depraved heart murder and involuntary manslaughter. He stresses that, in defining second degree murder, the trial court did not use the word "malice," but relied upon words that were almost identical to those it used to define involuntary manslaughter. Appellant argues that under these circumstances, explaining the malice element of depraved heart murder was critical. Appellant concedes that he failed to object to the instructions given by the trial court on the grounds he raises on appeal, but asks this Court to address his contentions as plain error....

This Court has commented that the distinction between second degree depraved heart murder and involuntary manslaughter of the gross criminal negligence variety is "a very blurred line." We explained that "[t]here is little distinction between ... [the *mens rea* of involuntary manslaughter] and the *mens rea* of depraved heart murder." We turn to the cases from the Court of Appeals to divine the distinction between these crimes.

In *Robinson v. State,* [the Court of Appeals] defined depraved heart murder [as]:

> the form [of murder] that establishes that the wilful doing of a dangerous and reckless act with wanton indifference to the consequences and perils involved, is just as blameworthy, and just as worthy of punishment, when the harmful result ensues, as is the express intent to kill itself. This highly blameworthy state of mind is not one of mere negligence.... It is not merely even one of gross criminal negligence.... It involves rather the deliberate perpetration of a knowingly dangerous act with reckless and wanton unconcern and indifference as to whether anyone is harmed or not.

The Court further stated:

> "A depraved heart murder is often described as a wanton and wilful killing. The term 'depraved heart' means something more than conduct amounting to a high or unreasonable risk to human life. The perpetrator must [or reasonably should] realize the risk his behavior has created to the extent that his conduct may be termed wilful. Moreover, the conduct must contain an element of viciousness or contemptuous disregard for the value of human life which conduct characterizes the behavior as wanton."

It is this level of blameworthiness that fills the place of intent to kill and, thus, malice.

In *State v. Albrecht,* the Court of Appeals, set forth the elements of involuntary manslaughter:

> "It is well settled in this State that where a charge of involuntary manslaughter is predicated on negligently doing some act lawful in itself, the negligence necessary to support a conviction must be gross or criminal, *viz.,* such as manifests a wanton or reckless disregard of human life. A causal connection between such gross negligence and death must exist to support a conviction, although it is not essential that the ultimate harm which resulted was foreseen or intended. On the other hand whether an accused's conduct constituted gross negligence must be determined by the conduct itself and not by the resultant harm. Nor can criminal liability be predicated on every careless act merely because its carelessness results in injury to another."

The Court further stated, "In determining whether a defendant's actions constituted gross negligence, we must ask whether the accused's conduct, 'under the circumstances, amounted to a disregard of the consequences which might ensue and indifference to the rights of others, and so was a wanton and reckless disregard for human life.'"

In the present case, there is no need for inclusion of the word "malice" in the instruction on second degree depraved heart murder as it is the high level of blameworthiness, *i.e.,* the high degree of risk to the victim and the defendant's conscious disregard of the life endangering consequences, which takes the place of malice that must be present in offenses requiring an intent to kill. In addition, although both instructions explained that the defendant's conduct had to create a high degree of risk to the life of the victim, the instruction on depraved heart murder also explained that the defendant had to be conscious of the risks and act with extreme disregard for the life endangering consequences. In contrast, in instructing the jury on involuntary manslaughter, the court explained that the defendant had to act only in a grossly negligent manner, that is, a manner creating a high degree of risk to human life. The instructions, thus, adequately conveyed the fine distinction between the two crimes ... We perceive no error, plain or otherwise, committed by the trial court in its jury instructions on second degree depraved heart murder and involuntary manslaughter.

Judgments Affirmed.

## *Notes and Questions*

1. Whereas killings with malice are murder, non-malicious killings are considered manslaughter at common law. As was discussed in the previous section, intentional killings are manslaughter when they take place while defendant was in the heat of passion. In such cases, passion negates malice in spite of the defendant's intent to kill. Furthermore,

when the defendant lacks intent to kill and the other forms of malice (intent to cause serious bodily injury, depraved heart or felony murder), the killing is considered involuntary manslaughter. Involuntary manslaughter is the least serious kind of homicide at common law and, therefore, is punished considerably less than murder and voluntary manslaughter. Liability for involuntary manslaughter is usually imposed when the defendant causes the death of a person with criminal negligence or recklessness.

2. The thorniest issue in this context is distinguishing reckless killings that evince enough "indifference to the value of human life" to warrant being punished as a "depraved heart murder" from reckless killings that are less serious and therefore should be punished as involuntary manslaughter. This is the issue raised by *Cook v. State.* The Court explained in *Cook* that depraved heart murder involves conduct that generates a "high degree of risk to the life of the victim." Furthermore, the Court stated that "the defendant had to be conscious of the risks" created by his act. Finally, the Court asserted that the defendant must also act "with extreme disregard for the life endangering consequences." In contrast, the Court pointed out that involuntary manslaughter involves "grossly negligent" conduct that creates "a high degree of risk to human life." What's the difference between these two standards? According to *Cook,* is a reckless killing a depraved heart murder or is it involuntary manslaughter? Is the degree of risk created in depraved heart cases higher, lower or equal than the degree of risk created in involuntary manslaughter cases? Is a defendant who was aware that his conduct created a high risk of death automatically liable for depraved heart murder or must it also be demonstrated that he acted "with extreme disregard to the value of human life"? Is there a difference between "extreme disregard to the value of life" and "disregard to the value of human life"?

3. While courts will often state that the criminal negligence that triggers liability for involuntary manslaughter requires something more than civil law negligence, it is not clear what exactly that "something more" is. It is also unclear whether courts and juries are capable of non-arbitrarily distinguishing between traditional negligence and criminal negligence. The issue was explored in more detail in Chapter 8, § 8.04.

## § 20.07 Homicide: Model Penal Code

### Model Penal Code § 210

§ 210.1. Criminal Homicide.

(1) A person is guilty of criminal homicide if he purposely, knowingly, recklessly or negligently causes the death of another human being.

(2) Criminal homicide is murder, manslaughter or negligent homicide.

§ 210.2. Murder.

(1) Except as provided in Section 210.3(1)(b), criminal homicide constitutes murder when:

(a) it is committed purposely or knowingly; or

(b) it is committed recklessly under circumstances manifesting extreme indifference to the value of human life. Such recklessness and indifference are presumed if the actor is engaged or is an accomplice in the commission of, or an attempt to commit, or flight after committing or attempting to commit robbery, rape or deviate sexual intercourse by force or threat of force, arson, burglary, kidnapping or felonious escape.

(2) Murder is a felony of the first degree [but a person convicted of murder may be sentenced to death, as provided in Section 210.6].

§ 210.3. Manslaughter.

(1) Criminal homicide constitutes manslaughter when:

(a) it is committed recklessly; or

(b) a homicide which would otherwise be murder is committed under the influence of extreme mental or emotional disturbance for which there is reasonable explanation or excuse. The reasonableness of such explanation or excuse shall be determined from the viewpoint of a person in the actor's situation under the circumstances as he believes them to be.

(2) Manslaughter is a felony of the second degree.

§ 210.4. Negligent Homicide.

(1) Criminal homicide constitutes negligent homicide when it is committed negligently.

(2) Negligent homicide is a felony of the third degree.

## People v. Casassa

Court of Appeals of New York, 1980
49 N.Y.2d 668

ASEN, Judge.

The significant issue on this appeal is whether the defendant, in a murder prosecution, established the affirmative defense of "extreme emotional disturbance" which would have reduced the crime to manslaughter in the first degree.

On February 28, 1977, Victoria Lo Consolo was brutally murdered. Defendant Victor Casassa and Miss Lo Consolo had been acquainted for some time prior to the latter's tragic death. They met in August, 1976 as a result of their residence in the same apartment complex. Shortly thereafter, defendant asked Miss Lo Consolo to accompany him to a social function and she agreed. The two apparently dated casually on other occasions until November, 1976 when Miss Lo Consolo informed defendant that she was not "falling in love" with him. Defendant claims that Miss Lo Consolo's candid statement of her feelings "devastated him."

Miss Lo Consolo's rejection of defendant's advances also precipitated a bizarre series of actions on the part of defendant which, he asserts, demonstrate the existence of extreme emotional disturbance upon which he predicates his affirmative defense. Defendant, aware that Miss Lo Consolo maintained social relationships with others, broke into the apartment below Miss Lo Consolo's on several occasions to eavesdrop. These eavesdropping sessions allegedly caused him to be under great emotional stress. Thereafter, on one occasion, he broke into Miss Lo Consolo's apartment while she was out. Defendant took nothing, but, instead, observed the apartment, disrobed and lay for a time in Miss Lo Consolo's bed. During this break-in, defendant was armed with a knife which, he later told police, he carried "because he knew that he was either going to hurt Victoria or Victoria was going to cause him to commit suicide."

Defendant's final visit to his victim's apartment occurred on February 28, 1977. Defendant brought several bottles of wine and liquor with him to offer as a gift. Upon Miss Lo Consolo's rejection of this offering, defendant produced a steak knife which he had brought with him, stabbed Miss Lo Consolo several times in the throat, dragged her body to the bathroom and submerged it in a bathtub full of water to "make sure she was dead." ...

On March 8, 1977, defendant was indicted and charged with murder in the second degree ...

Defendant waived a jury and proceeded to trial before the County Court.... The defendant did not contest the underlying facts of the crime. Instead, the sole issue presented to the trial court was whether the defendant, at the time of the killing, had acted under the influence of "extreme emotional disturbance". The defense presented only one witness, a psychiatrist, who testified, in essence, that the defendant had become obsessed with Miss Lo Consolo and that the course which their relationship had taken, combined with several personality attributes peculiar to defendant, caused him to be under the influence of extreme emotional disturbance at the time of the killing.

In rebuttal, the People produced several witnesses. Among these witnesses was a psychiatrist who testified that although the defendant was emotionally disturbed, he was not under the influence of "extreme emotional disturbance" within the meaning of ... the Penal Law because his disturbed state was not the product of external factors but rather was "a stress he created from within himself, dealing mostly with a fantasy, a refusal to accept the reality of the situation."

The trial court in resolving this issue noted that the affirmative defense of extreme emotional disturbance may be based upon a series of events, rather than a single precipitating cause. In order to be entitled to the defense, the court held, a defendant must show that his reaction to such events was reasonable. In determining whether defendant's emotional reaction was reasonable, the court considered the appropriate test to be whether in the totality of the circumstances the finder of fact could understand how a person might have his reason overcome. Concluding that the test was not to be applied solely from the viewpoint of defendant, the court found that defendant's emotional reaction at the time of the commission of the crime was so peculiar to him that it could not be considered reasonable so as to reduce the conviction to manslaughter in the first degree. Accordingly, the trial court found defendant guilty of the crime of murder in the second degree. The Appellate Division affirmed, without opinion.

On this appeal defendant contends that the trial court erred in failing to afford him the benefit of the affirmative defense of "extreme emotional disturbance". It is argued that the defendant established that he suffered from a mental infirmity not arising to the level of insanity which disoriented his reason to the extent that his emotional reaction, from his own subjective point of view, was supported by a reasonable explanation or excuse. Defendant asserts that by refusing to apply a wholly subjective standard the trial court misconstrued ... the Penal Law. We cannot agree.

Section 125.25 (subd. 1, par. (a)) of the Penal Law provides that it is an affirmative defense to the crime of murder in the second degree where "(t)he defendant acted under the influence of extreme emotional disturbance for which there was a reasonable explanation or excuse." This defense allows a defendant charged with the commission of acts which would otherwise constitute murder to demonstrate the existence of mitigating factors which indicate that, although he is not free from responsibility for his crime, he ought to be punished less severely by reducing the crime upon conviction to manslaughter in the first degree.

In enacting [this provision],the Legislature adopted the language of the manslaughter provisions of the Model Penal Code. The only substantial distinction between the New York statute and the Model Penal Code is the designation by the Legislature of "extreme emotional disturbance" as an "affirmative defense", thus placing the burden of proof on this issue upon defendant. The Model Penal Code formulation, however, as enacted by the Legislature, represented a significant departure from the prior law of this State.

The "extreme emotional disturbance" defense is an outgrowth of the "heat of passion" doctrine which had for some time been recognized by New York as a distinguishing factor between the crimes of manslaughter and murder. However, the new formulation is significantly broader in scope than the "heat of passion" doctrine which it replaced.

For example, the "heat of passion" doctrine required that a defendant's action be undertaken as a response to some provocation which prevented him from reflecting upon his actions. Moreover, such reaction had to be immediate. The existence of a "cooling off" period completely negated any mitigating effect which the provocation might otherwise have had. In *Patterson*, however, this court recognized that "(a)n action influenced by an extreme emotional disturbance is not one that is necessarily so spontaneously undertaken. Rather, it may be that a significant mental trauma has affected a defendant's mind for a substantial period of time, simmering in the unknowing subconscious and then inexplicably coming to the fore." This distinction between the past and present law of mitigation, enunciated in *Patterson*, was expressly adopted by the trial court and properly applied in this case.

The thrust of defendant's claim, however, concerns a question arising out of another perceived distinction between "heat of passion" and "extreme emotional disturbance" which was not directly addressed in *Patterson*, to wit: whether, assuming that the defense is applicable to a broader range of circumstances, the standard by which the reasonableness of defendant's emotional reaction is to be tested must be an entirely subjective one. Defendant relies ... upon the language of the statute to support his claim that the reasonableness of his "explanation or excuse" should be determined solely with reference to his own subjective viewpoint. Such reliance is misplaced ...

Section 125.25 (subd. 1, par. (a)) of the Penal Law states it is an affirmative defense to the crime of murder that "(t)he defendant acted under the influence of extreme emotional disturbance for which there was a reasonable explanation or excuse, the reasonableness of which is to be determined from the viewpoint of a person in the defendant's situation under the circumstances as the defendant believed them to be." Whether the language of this statute requires a completely subjective evaluation of reasonableness is a question that has never been decided by this court, although it has been raised in our lower courts with diverse results....

Consideration of the Comments to the Model Penal Code, from which the New York statute was drawn, are instructive. The defense of "extreme emotional disturbance" has two principal components (1) the particular defendant must have "acted under the influence of extreme emotional disturbance", and (2) there must have been "a reasonable explanation or excuse" for such extreme emotional disturbance, "the reasonableness of which is to be determined from the viewpoint of a person in the defendant's situation under the circumstances as the defendant believed them to be". The first requirement is wholly subjective i. e., it involves a determination that the particular defendant did in fact act under extreme emotional disturbance, that the claimed explanation as to the cause of his action is not contrived or sham.

The second component is more difficult to describe i. e., whether there was a reasonable explanation or excuse for the emotional disturbance. It was designed to sweep away "the rigid rules that have developed with respect to the sufficiency of particular types of provocation, such as the rule that words alone can never be enough", and "avoids a merely arbitrary limitation on the nature of the antecedent circumstances that may justify a mitigation" "The ultimate test, however, is objective; there must be 'reasonable' explanation or excuse for the actor's disturbance". In light of these comments and the necessity of articulating the defense in terms comprehensible to jurors, we conclude that the determination whether there was reasonable explanation or excuse for a particular emotional disturbance should be made by viewing the subjective, internal situation in which the defendant found himself and the external circumstances as he perceived them at the time, however inaccurate that perception may have been, and assessing from that standpoint whether the explanation or excuse for his emotional disturbance was reasonable, so as to entitle him to a reduction of the crime charged from murder in the second degree to manslaughter in the first degree. We recognize that even such a description of the defense provides no precise guidelines and necessarily leaves room for the exercise of judgmental evaluation by the jury. This, however, appears to have been the intent of the draftsmen. "The purpose was explicitly to give full scope to what amounts to a plea in mitigation based upon a mental or emotional trauma of significant dimensions, with the jury asked to show whatever empathy it can."

By suggesting a standard of evaluation which contains both subjective and objective elements, we believe that the drafters of the code adequately achieved their dual goals of broadening the "heat of passion" doctrine to apply to a wider range of circumstances while retaining some element of objectivity in the process. The result of their draftsmanship is a statute which offers the defendant a fair opportunity to seek mitigation without requiring that the trier of fact find mitigation in each case where an emotional disturbance is shown or as the drafters put it, to offer "room for argument as to the reasonableness of the explanations or excuses offered." ...

In the end, we believe that what the Legislature intended in enacting the statute was to allow the finder of fact the discretionary power to mitigate the penalty when presented with a situation which, under the circumstances, appears to them to have caused an understandable weakness in one of their fellows....

We conclude that the trial court, in this case, properly applied the statute. The court apparently accepted, as a factual matter, that defendant killed Miss Lo Consolo while under the influence of "extreme emotional disturbance", a threshold question which must be answered in the affirmative before any test of reasonableness is required. The court, however, also recognized that in exercising its function as trier of fact, it must make a further inquiry into the reasonableness of that disturbance. In this regard, the court considered each of the mitigating factors put forward by defendant, including his claimed mental disability, but found that the excuse offered by defendant was so peculiar to him that it was unworthy of mitigation. The court obviously made a sincere effort to understand defendant's "situation" and "the circumstances as defendant believed them to be", but concluded that the murder in this case was the result of defendant's malevolence rather than an understandable human response deserving of mercy. We cannot say, as a matter of law, that the court erred in so concluding. Indeed, to do so would subvert the purpose of the statute.

In our opinion, this statute would not require that the jury or the court as trier of fact find mitigation on any particular set of facts, but, rather, allows the finder of fact the opportunity to do so, such opportunity being conditional only upon a finding of extreme emotional disturbance in the first instance. In essence, the statute requires mitigation to be afforded an emotionally disturbed defendant only when the trier of fact, after considering a broad range of mitigating circumstances, believes that such leniency is justified. Since the trier of fact found that defendant failed to establish that he was acting "under the influence of extreme emotional disturbance for which there was a reasonable explanation or excuse", defendant's conviction of murder in the second degree should not be reduced to the crime of manslaughter in the first degree....

Accordingly, the order of the Appellate Division should be affirmed.

## *Notes and Questions*

1. Given that the Model Penal Code rejects the common law's approach to *mens rea*, the concept of "malice" plays no role in the grading of homicide offenses under the code. Instead, murder is defined as killings that are purposeful, knowing or reckless with gross indifference to the value of human life. A significant number of American jurisdictions follow the Code in this regard and have thus have abandoned "malice" as the defining element of murder.

2. Although the Model Penal Code eschews malice from its definition of murder, the kinds of killings that may give rise to murder liability under the Code are quite similar than those that would give rise to murder liability at common law. Purposeful killings are identical to "intent-to-kill" killings. Knowing killings overlap to a certain extent with "intent to cause serious bodily injury" killings. Reckless killings that evince "gross indifference to the value of human life" are very similar to "depraved heart" killings. Finally, although the Code does not automatically classify killings that occur during the commission of a felony as murder, it creates a presumption of acting recklessly with gross indifference to the value of human life in these cases. If the presumption is not rebutted, the defendant will be held liable for murder in much the same way as he would under the common law felony murder rule. Nevertheless, the Code's approach is more lenient than the traditional felony murder rule, for it allows defendants to rebut the presumption of recklessness with gross indifference to human life. If the presumption is rebutted, the defendant may not be held liable for murder even if the death took place during the perpetration of a felony. The Code's reformulation of the felony murder rule has not garnered support in American jurisdictions.

3. It is important to note that the Mode! Penal Code does not classify murder into degrees. This differs quite substantially from the influential Pennsylvania Model that distinguished between first and second-degree murders primarily on the basis of premeditation. In contrast with the Pennsylvania Model, premeditation plays no role in the Model Penal Code's approach to homicide.

4. The Code punishes reckless killings as manslaughter, which is a less serious offense than murder. Nevertheless, if the actor's recklessness evinces a gross indifference to the value of human life, liability for murder is imposed rather than manslaughter. The line between standard recklessness and recklessness with gross indifference to human life is fuzzy. The difference seems to be normative. Reckless killings should trigger murder liability if the circumstances surrounding the act suggest that the killing is as worthy of condemnation as a purposeful or knowing killing. In contrast, the killing should be considered manslaughter if the circumstances surrounding the act reveal that it is not as blameworthy as purposeful and knowing killings. It is unclear if juries can make these distinctions in a non-arbitrary manner. See, e.g., Francis X. Shen, Morris B. Hoffman, Owen D. Jones, Joshua D. Greene & René Marois, *Sorting Guilty Minds,* 86 N.Y.U. L. Rev. 1306 (2011) (arguing that empirical studies reveal that laypeople are not capable of distinguishing between recklessness and knowledge and, *a fortiori,* between recklessness and recklessness with gross indifference to the value of human life).

5. Perhaps the most novel aspect of the Model Penal Code's approach to homicide is the partial defense of "extreme emotional disturbance" (EED) that mitigates what would otherwise be murder to manslaughter. The EED mitigation is the Code's alternative to the common law's heat of passion partial defense. As the *Casassa* case illustrates, EED is considerably broader than the common law's heat of passion mitigation. As a result, the Code's EED provision does away with "the rigid rules that have developed with respect

to the sufficiency of particular types of provocation such as the rule that words alone can never be enough." Furthermore, the EED mitigation might apply even if the defendant's response is not "sudden" or "immediate." That is, the Code doesn't automatically disallow the defense once a "cooling period" has elapsed. Instead, it recognizes that—as the Court of Appeals of New York pointed out in *Casassa*—"(a)n action influenced by an extreme emotional disturbance is not one that is necessarily so spontaneously undertaken." It therefore allows for a showing that the mental disturbance has "affected a defendant's mind for a substantial period of time, simmering in the unknowing subconscious and then inexplicably coming to the fore." Which doctrine of partial mitigation—EED or heat of passion—do you find more appealing? What result if the Code's EED provision had been applied in *Gounagias* (§ 20.03)?

6. Although the Code's EED provision is considerably broader than the common law's heat of passion mitigation, the defendant may successfully plead the EED partial defense only if there is a "reasonable explanation or excuse" for her emotional disturbance. As the Court pointed out in *Casassa*, this standard allows for taking into account "the subjective, internal situation in which the defendant found himself and the external circumstances as he perceived them at the time, however inaccurate that perception may have been." This standard is considerably more subjective than the reasonableness standard in self-defense and duress. Nevertheless, the inquiry is not entirely subjective. Ultimately, the jury must also ask "whether the explanation or excuse for his emotional disturbance was reasonable so as to entitle him to a reduction of the crime charged from murder ... to manslaughter." Stated differently, mitigation under the EED provision is warranted when, "after considering a broad range of mitigating circumstances", the trier of fact "believes that [mitigation] is justified." Does the EED provision strike the right balance between subjective and objective components of "reasonableness" in this context? Do you believe that the Court's explanation of how to determine whether there is "reasonable explanation or excuse" for the emotional disturbance is workable? Explain. Could you come up with a better standard for making this determination?

## § 20.08 Homicide: Comparative Perspectives

### George P. Fletcher, *Rethinking Criminal Law*

(reprint, Oxford, 2000)

§ 4.5.2 The standard Form of Criminal Homicide

In France, Germany and the Soviet Union, the standard form of criminal homicide is defined simply as intentionally killing another human being. Of course it is implicit that the killing be without provocation. The rough analogue to this standard offense in the United States is second-degree murder. The major difference is that this standard form of the crime cannot be established in Continental jurisdictions either (1) on a theory of reckless homicide, or (2) felony-murder. Yet at least as to reckless homicide sufficient to constitute killing with malice in the United States, this nominal difference is highly misleading. Both Soviet and German law take an indirect intention (*dolus eventualis*) to be sufficient to constitute intentional killing. The technical definition of indirect intention is that if the actor engages in life-endangering behavior, his killing is intentional if he "reconciles himself' or "makes peace" with the likelihood of death. Thus, intentional killing is committed with "manifest indifference to the value of human life," even conduct of minimal risk can qualify as intentional homicide. Thus if the suspect fires at a moving car with people in it and a passenger is hit by the bullet, his killing is likely to be treated as intentional. A large number of killings that would he classified as reckless murder in the United States would meet the Continental criteria of *dolus eventualis.*

The penalties for this standard form of homicide vary widely among Continental jurisdictions. In France, the maximum prescribed by statute is imprisonment for life, in Germany, imprisonment for a maximum of only five years, and in the Soviet Union, imprisonment for ten years.

### § 4.5.3 Aggravated Homicide

The techniques for defining aggravated homicide vary widely, but the point of all systems of grading is to define the most heinous forms of killing. The analogue to this offense in the United States is not only first degree murder, but the newly cast offenses of capital murder—namely, those cases of egregious murder subject to the death penalty. To elicit the underlying patterns in these diverse legislative systems, we shall consider three factors that shape the definition of aggravated homicide.

#### A. The Motive of the Slaying

The German code contains the most detailed listing of the motives that are sufficient to classify a killing as aggravated homicide. Two of these enumerated motives are unusual features of German legislation an intentional killing is regarded as aggravated if committed (1) for the sake of the pleasure gained in killing, or (2) for the sake of sexual satisfaction.

The latter ground was initially interpreted narrowly to require a perverse sexual interest in necrophilia, in recent years the courts and commentators have broadened the interpretation to include cases of killing to overcome the resistance of a rape victim. This relation brings the German standard in line with the theory of felony-murder in rape eases that once prevailed in the English courts. The German Courts would say that there is an intent to kill in these cases, but as we have seen, the standard of "intent" is interpreted loosely to encompass dangerous conduct in which the rapist is indifferent to the risk of death.

The third motive mentioned in the German code, killing for a pecuniary motive is widely shared in several legislative schemes. In the [Soviet] code, it is specifically listed as an aggravating factor sufficient to warrant the imposition of the death penalty. It also appears prominently as a ground for capital punishment in the United States. For example, in the Georgia statute upheld by the United States Supreme court, the ten aggravating circumstances include "The purpose of receiving money or any other thing of monetary value." When the required motive is so defined, the actor must kill for the direct purpose of gain, a killing incidental to a robbery is insufficient. The Georgia provision appears to require a purpose to receive a concrete thing of value. The German provision is interpreted flexibly to include cases of eliminating a competing heir or a creditor.

After listing these three motives, the German statute concludes with a catchall clause covering all cases of intentional killing for "base motives". As elaborated in the case law, these "base motives" include vengeance and jealousy, avoiding arrest, and racial hatred. The Soviet statute avoids a catchall clause of this sort, but includes another broad consideration that is peculiar to the Soviet legal style. A sufficient ground for classifying an intentional homicide as aggravated and thus subject to the death penalty, is killing "for hooliganistic purposes". The notion of "hooliganism" in Soviet law is closely associated with violations of public order and the proper mode of socialist life, and is typified by drunk and disorderly behavior in public. A good example of the USSR Supreme Court's construing this provision is the case of *A* who went to a restaurant with some friends and became drunk and boisterous after having had too much to drink. His friend *G* tried to quiet him down. As they left the restaurant and started down the street, *A* lagged behind the others, then he attacked *G* and stabbed him twice. This was a killing that, in the Court's view, was motivated by "hooliganistic motives". The important criminological significance of this doctrine is that it fashions a framework in which drunkenness serves not to excuse the homicide, but to aggravate it. Soviet criminologists regard the link between intoxication and violent criminality as so strong that it is understandable that especially repressive measures would be taken against drunken killings.

### B. The Manner of Killing

Considerable consensus prevails on the manner of killing sufficient to qualify homicide as aggravated and therefore subject to the most serious penalty under the law. Virtually all systems include a reference to killings that are especially cruel or barbaric. French law takes an intentional killing to be subject lo the death penalty if it is committed by "torture or barbarous acts." German and Soviet law refer generally to "cruelty" and "special cruelty" as aggravating circumstances. In its listing of aggravating criteria sufficient for capital punishment, the Model Penal Code includes a general clause referring to murders that are "especially heinous, atrocious or crucl, manifcsting exceptional depravity." Some states have included this highly emotional language in their listing of grounds sufficient for the death penalty, and the Supreme Court has upheld the clause against a challenge of excessive vagueness.

Another general means regarded as sufficient for aggravated murder is killing by ambush or lying-in-wait. Killing secretively, by exploiting the victim's vulnerability, lies at die core the English law or homicide. The analogous concept of *guet-apens* is of ancient vintage in the French law of homicide. In the Penal Code of 1810, it appears as one of the two grounds (along with premeditation) for classifying an intentional killing as the capital crime of *assassinat*. German law employs an analogous, but slightly different notion of "surreptitious killing." This manner of killing, sufficient for aggravated homicide, includes cases of inducing a victim to enter an ambush (but perhaps not all instances of lying-in-wait). It goes beyond the analogous, common-law and French concepts by encompassing the killing of another person, particularly a spouse, in his or her sleep. The German commentators stress the element of breach of trust as the underlying element that renders [these] killings so heinous.

Another common standard for qualifying a homicide as among the most grave offenses is whether the act of killing endangers a large number or people. This is described in German law as killing by "socially dangerous means", in the [Soviet Union], as killing by "means dangerous to many people". The same consideration is expressed in California's defining the use of "a destructive device or explosive" as sufficient for classifying a murder as one in the first degree. In addition, several jurisdictions in the United States refer to creating a "great risk of death to many persons" as one of the aggravating circumstances to be considered in assessing the death penalty.

France is the only one of the three foreign systems under study that relies on the notion of "premeditation" as a distinguishing mark of aggravated homicide. This prominent feature, as well as the general de-emphasis of motives in the analysis of aggravated homicide, brings into focus the general similarity of style between the French and Anglo-American laws of homicide

C. Felony Murder

The similarity of French and American law is further borne out by their being the only systems among all those under study that maintain a comprehensive rule of felony murder. French Penal Code § 304 provides that intentional homicide should be punished capitally if the homicide "precedes, accompanies, or follows another felony." The only requirement is that of "concomitance," spatial and temporal, between the felony and the homicide. Yet the French rule is less sweeping than the American fe1ony murder rule, for it encompasses only cases of intentional homicide.

The German and Soviet statutes both contain a clause for classifying an intentional homicide as aggravated if it is committed in connection with another felony. Yet both provisions expressly capture a limitation on the rule that, as I have argued, was implicit in the English common law of felony-murder. The homicide must serve either to facilitate or to conceal the ancillary felony. This limitation presumably excludes all cases of killing by third parties as well as killings committed by one confederate against another unless killing the confederate would serve to conceal the felony. The grounds for capital murder in thc United States often include a ground of felony murder, sometimes with the limitation that the killing must he intentional, yet the connection required between the felony and the homicide is typically only one of temporal and spatial concomitance, as in the French law of capital murder It would have been far preferable to follow the model of German and Soviet legislation and require, as a condition for the death penalty, that the intentional homicides serve to facilitate or conceal the felony. The soviet law of aggravated homicide includes one exceptional case of felony-murder in the sweeping sense characteristic of legislation in the United States. If an intentional killing is committed concomitantly with a rape, then the killing is subject to the death penalty regardless of whether the object of the killing is to further or to conceal the rape.

## *Notes and Questions*

1. Note that most civil law countries distinguish between the most serious kinds of homicide on the basis of some criteria other than premeditation. Professor Fletcher identifies two features that serve as aggravating factors in most civil law jurisdictions: the reasons for the killing (motive) and the manner of killing. Regarding motive, Fletcher points out that many continental countries aggravate homicide when it's committed for a pecuniary purpose, for sadistic reasons, or to get sexual gratification. With regard to the manner of the killing, Professor Fletcher points out that homicides committed in especially cruel manners are usually aggravated, as well as those that are perpetrated with devices capable of causing widespread harm. Would it be better for American law to discriminate between degrees of homicide based on these considerations (motive and manner of commission) rather than on the basis of premeditation? Explain.

2. As Professor Fletcher points out, civil law jurisdictions do not have an equivalent doctrine to the felony murder rule. While the criminal laws of some continental jurisdictions may sometimes aggravate homicides committed during the perpetration of a felony, they only do so if the killing was intentional. Nevertheless, accidental or negligent killings during a felony would not automatically be classified as the most serious kind of homicide simply because they took place during the commission of a crime. That is, killing during crime in continental jurisdictions do not give rise to strict liability for the killing, as the more extreme versions of the American felony murder rule would do. Do you prefer the American or continental approach to grading killings during felonies? Why?

# § 20.09 Homicide: Scholarly Debates

## Kevin Cole, *Killing during Crime: Toward a Discriminating Theory of Strict Liability*

28 Am. Crim. L. Rev. 73 (1990)

[A] consequentialist punishment strategy ... justifies distinguishing between felony murders and simple murders. That is because we can plausibly predict that potential felony murderers, viewed as a class, will require more punishment to deter them from crime than will potential simple murderers. And that increment in punishment is best achieved by treating felony murder as a form of strict liability offense.

1. Taking Felony Murders (More) Seriously

The felony-murder rule threatens greater punishment of potential felony murderers than potential simple murderers face. As to many felony murderers, this point is quite straightforward. Without the felony-murder rule, a robber who killed negligently might be guilty of manslaughter, and even a robber who killed intentionally might be guilty only of second-degree murder if premeditation was not present; in most formulations, however, the felony-murder rule makes both guilty of first-degree murder, imposing greater punishment on felony murderers. For robbers who might kill intentionally and with premeditation, the felony-murder rule still increases threatened punishment in another way. Though the possible punishment for the offense does not necessarily increase, the potential killer's expected disutility from committing the crime—the pertinent inquiry in assessing the deterrent force of the criminal law, as the focus is on the potential criminal's likely punishment at the time the criminal decides whether to commit crime—increases because the felony-murder rule eliminates the possibility that the criminal will be apprehended but nevertheless escape punishment by raising a false mens rea claim.

Potential felony murderers quite plausibly do need a greater threat of punishment to achieve optimal deterrence than do potential simple murderers. That is so for several reasons. The first relates to how the potential felony murderers' approach to risk likely compares with that of the paradigm potential simple murderer.

Society comprises people who respond to risk in dramatically different ways. In discussing risk, three characteristics require attention: the estimation of risk; the preference for risk; and the attention to risk. Some people systematically overestimate the chance that ill will befall them; others, often found in Las Vegas, misestimate risk in precisely the opposite direction. Still others estimate risk accurately, but differ in their risk preferences. If you offer a room of people the option either of receiving one dollar outright or of having one chance to roll a six with a die for a six-dollar prize, people will chose different options; some mathematicians will prefer a chance to roll the die even when the potential payoff is reduced to $5. And finally, some people are more likely than others to reflect on the costs and benefits of their actions, and reflection is more likely in some situations than in others ...

The pool of potential felony murderers ... predictably will differ from the pool of potential simple murderers. Respecting attention to risk, some felons undoubtedly commit predicate felonies with limited forethought. But to the extent the felony-murder rule targets the career criminal, it identifies a class that commits crime for monetary gain and therefore likely evaluates, in some crude way, the likelihood of benefit before undertaking crime. Unlike bar fights and other assaults that might result in simple murders, robbery and burglary require some planning. That these crimes will generally occur after a deliberative process suggests that a greater percentage of these criminals will be subject to deterrence than will potential simple murderers. Put from the other direction, because the class of potential simple murderers is statistically likely to include a greater percentage of nonadverters than is the class of potential felony murderers, we might expect that an efficient punishment system would target felony murder for greater penalties than simple murder.

The financial motivation of many of the felony-murder predicates is likewise important in evaluating the likely risk attitudes of potential felony and simple murderers. Even when compared with simple murderers who *do* advert to the risks associated with their crime, the career criminals targeted by the felony-murder rule place less value on killing *simpliciter* than will the relevant class of potential simple murderers. Felons will generally view resulting death simply as a means of ensuring escape or silencing witnesses, both of which are simply means to financial reward. If the cost of causing death is increased, we might expect these felons to regard causing death as inconsistent with their own motivation—committing a financially beneficial crime. Regarding simple murderers, however, this separation of death from motive will often be impossible to effect. When someone has decided to kill for killing's sake under a system of high penalties, we should expect that increased penalties will often fail to change the killer's decision.

Because of this characteristic of potential felony murderers, a consequentialist quite plausibly could favor harsher penalties for potential felony murderers than for potential simple murderers. If potential felony murderers commit crime in part because of a deliberative process that is more susceptible to influence through threatened sanction than is the thought process of potential simple murderers, then the optimal penalties for potential felony murderers are likely to be higher than will be the optimal penalties for potential simple murderers, because higher penalties for potential simple murderers will not yield the same increase in deterrence when applied to a targeted class that is less responsive to threatened punishment ...

Apart from risk considerations, incapacitation provides a further justification for imposing more serious penalties on felony murderers than on simple murderers. Simple killings occur in a variety of situations; many of them might be expected not to recur frequently, somewhat reducing our anxiety about releasing the simple murderer back into society. Felony murders, on the other hand, occur during the course of a situation (the felony) brought on by the killers themselves. Since recidivism rates among felons are high, we can plausibly predict that felony murderers are more likely than simple murderers to kill again, since felony murderers as a class are more likely to put themselves into future situations posing the same incentives to kill to which they previously succumbed....

[Also], the felon's liability for another crime regardless whether death results means that potential felony murderers must be threatened with higher penalties just to achieve the same deterrent threat available through lower penalties for simple murder. That conclusion follows from two likely phenomena—the relatively greater harshness of the earlier parts of a serious criminal sentence and the tendency of most people to discount the future.

The early part of a criminal sentence is when much of its damage is done. Stigma is associated with the fact of conviction, and extra stigma is associated with being forced to spend *any* time in prison. Employment opportunities and family relationships are immediately placed under serious strain. And the prisoner suffers the pain of adjusting to a new environment of restraints on liberty and threats on well-being. All these deprivations may well occur within the first year of a prison term. Thus, a five-year prison term cannot be assumed to be five times worse than a one-year term, since many of the costs associated with the first year will not be incurred in successive years.

Discounting exaggerates the effects of the disproportionate occurrence of pain during a prison sentence. For even if every year of prison carried the same quantum of suffering, potential criminals are likely to value their immediate future more highly than their distant future, much as people value cash today more highly than the firm promise of cash in the future. From the vantage of a potential felony murderer, spending 20 years in jail for armed robbery and a killing is not four times worse than spending five years in jail for simple armed robbery. If the criminal discounts the future at a 20-percent annual rate, the criminal will perceive a proposed 20-year sentence as only 1.7 times more painful than a proposed 5-year sentence.

Both the discounting phenomenon and the front-loaded nature of imprisonment show that treating simple murder and felony murder "the same" is actually a way of treating them differently. From a deterrence perspective, treating murder monolithically effectively affords potential felony murderers with fewer—not more—incentives to abstain from killing. Regardless how convincing the case seems in favor of *greater* threats for potential felony murderers, a system punishing felony murderers less seriously than simple murderers would certainly seem odd.

### 2. Strict Liability

Establishing a consequentialist case for threatening greater punishments for potential felony murderers than for potential simple murderers does not make the case for the felony-murder rule. It remains to show why the strict liability quality of the felony-murder rule has special deterrent value, and why that deterrent effect could not be adequately achieved simply by other means, like increasing the penalties for felony murderers but observing mens rea requirements.

The increased deterrent threat flowing from the strict liability aspects of the felony-murder rule was examined above. To establish the increased deterrent value of the felony-murder rule requires the additional showing that felons might act in response to this increased threat. Holding felons strictly liable for deaths that occur during their felonies plausibly deters killings during felonies in two ways. First, as to what might be called subjectively culpable killings—killings that are reckless, knowing, or purposeful, in the terms of the Model Penal Code—the felony-murder rule eliminates the possibility that a felon contemplating such life-threatening conduct will believe that the consequences of such action can be avoided by falsely claiming after the fact that the death was subjectively nonculpable. If claims of accident are declared irrelevant, the felon will know that, if caught, punishment will ensue for any killing that occurred during the felony. Removing the chance that the felon could kill, be caught, and still escape proper punishment for the killing should affect the felon's decision whether to engage in life-threatening conduct, altering the expected disutility of the defendant's crime.

Second, regarding both negligent and less culpable killings—and to some extent regarding subjectively culpable killings—strict liability may promote increased care on the part of the felon in structuring the felony so as to minimize the risk of death or other injury. Aware that any killings resulting from a robbery will increase punishment dramatically, a robber might choose to minimize the risk of accident by using unloaded guns in effecting robberies. Or a robber might avoid acts so threatening as to provoke a self-defensive response from a victim who might otherwise have simply complied with a demand for money—for example, the robber might deliver the now stereotypical "Give me your wallet and no one will get hurt" line. Or a robber, facing the use of self-defensive force, might opt for flight rather than pursue the crime at the now apparent risk of death ...

## Guyora Binder, *The Culpability of Felony Murder*

83 Notre Dame L. Rev. 965 (2008)

[C]riminal law theorists have almost unanimously condemned felony murder as a form of strict liability, imposing undeserved punishment for causing death without culpability. Courts, obliged to impose felony murder liability despite these criticisms, have sought to defend it as a useful deterrent. Do these deterrence rationales justify felony murder liability? I will argue that they do not ...

[C]riminal law theorist Kevin Cole has argued that a small risk of felony murder liability may be more salient to potential felons than a slight increase in liability for the underlying felony. Such intuitions about the salience of severe penalties also support the widespread assumption that a small chance of capital punishment must deter murder. However, despite some recent claims to the contrary, this assumption has never been confirmed empirically ...

Legal scholar Kevin Cole offers three deterrence arguments for enhancing the penalty for culpable killers based on their participation in enumerated felonies. First, he speculates that felons may be more deterrable because their predicate felonies involve planning and calculation. This assumption is dubious, however, based on criminologist Jack Katz's research on armed robbers. Katz shows that their crimes are sometimes impulsive and are often pursued for expressive rather than instrumental reasons. If robbers act against their own welfare to enact a role or claim a reputation, they are unlikely to be unusually responsive to deterrent threats. Second, Cole speculates that those who culpably cause death in the course of felonies may be more likely to do so again than those who culpably cause death in the course of other activities. He offers no empirical support for this intuition and it is hard to see why it should be so. Third, he argues that felons are harder to deter from culpable killing because they already face a stiff sentence for the underlying felony. An additional sentence for homicide will have a lower marginal disutility ... This is a clever argument, but it directly contradicts Cole's earlier argument that felons are easier to deter from homicide because they calculate. Moreover, if we are concerned with cost-efficient deterrence, arguably we should ration punishment to those who will be most easily deterred rather than those who are hardest to deter.

Courts sometimes claim that deterring culpable killing by felons justifies strict liability, reasoning that punishment is more certain if the prosecution need not prove the killer's culpability. If this argument presumes that prosecutors will charge only culpable killers, it identifies no incentives for them to do so. And if determining culpability on the basis of prosecutorial suspicion rather than jury conviction really serves utility, why do so only in this class of cases? So let us instead interpret the argument that strict liability deters culpable killing by felons as presuming that faultless as well as culpable felons will indeed be punished for causing death under such a rule. Thus construed, the argument is that strict liability for causing harm in the course of otherwise beneficial activities always has the benefit of deterring culpable harm but comes at the cost of also deterring the beneficial underlying conduct. However, since the underlying activity of committing felonies is also harmful, there is no cost to deterring it. Kevin Cole offers a version of this argument.

While this cleaned-up argument for strict liability as a deterrent to negligence has a certain intuitive appeal, it has two problems. First, it proves too much: it appears to justify strict murder liability for causing death in the course of any crime, not just a few very serious and dangerous felonies. But there is a deeper problem that undermines every form of the argument that felony murder liability deters negligent killing by felons. This is that, as we shall later see, the punishment lottery argument not only disfavors murder liability as a way of deterring felonies, but it also disfavors punishing any harm as a way of deterring the imposition of risk. Thus, the most efficient deterrent for negligent conduct—by felons or anyone else—is attaching a small but certain penalty to each negligent act, rather than imposing murder liability on the much smaller number of negligent acts that happen to result in death. Deterrence theory favors punishing risk rather than harm. With apologies to Herbert Wechsler, architect of the Model Penal Code, when the end is to rationalize the law of homicide, deterrence theory is the wrong place to start.

Even if deterrence rationales for felony murder made sense on their own terms, they would not justify the imposition of felony murder liability. Felony murder liability can only be justified if it is deserved. In making this claim I take no position on the controversy as to whether punishment is ultimately justified by desert or utility. Even if we punish to advance the public welfare by preventing crime, we can best do so by restricting punishment to the deserving. Most people obey the criminal law because they approve its demands and see themselves as law abiding rather than because they fear punishment. Legal scholar Louis Seidman illustrates this by pointing to high levels of compliance with obligations of military service during wartime, despite the fact that such service is often more burdensome than incarceration. Seidman reasons that punishment motivates compliance more by threatening to impose deserved blame than by threatening to inflict suffering. By eroding the law's moral authority and obscuring its commands, undeserved punishment may therefore provoke more crime than it deters. Moreover, the anxiety aroused by the prospect of undeserved punishment may outweigh the security provided by any reduction in crime. As I have elsewhere shown, Jeremy Bentham's utilitarianism was centrally concerned with assuring citizens they would not be oppressed by public officials. Thus, even if systematically punishing the undeserving deterred crime, that would not mean it would maximize utility. Other things being equal, punishment discourages crime more effectively, and with less damage to public confidence in government, when it is deserved. Thus even utilitarian defenders of felony murder must meet its critics on the ground of desert and refute the claim that it imposes punishment without culpability.

The widespread view of felony murder as strict liability rests on three contestable premises: the myth of the common law felony murder rule … ; a narrowly formalistic conception of strict liability; and the cognitive conception of culpability. The myth of a common law rule imposing liability for all unintended deaths in the course of all felonies supports the prevailing view of felony murder as a strict liability crime. Murder liability for truly accidental death during felonies neither violent nor dangerous would have constituted strict liability on any definition of that contested term. Yet … history summarized above reveals that felony murder has generally been predicated on a narrow class of dangerous felonies, and has usually required an act of violence or an act foreseeably dangerous to human life. Once we acknowledge felony murder's relatively benign history, we can see that the validity of the strict liability charge depends on what we mean by "strict liability."

The meaning of strict liability is contested, particularly in criminal law. Broadly speaking, "strict liability" means liability without moral fault. In private and regulatory law, where there are social costs of profitable activities to be distributed, strict liability may be useful and not unfair. In criminal law, however, where liability implies blame and imposes uncompensated suffering, liability without moral fault seems contradictory. In this area of law, "strict liability" is an epithet implying "undeserved punishment." Accordingly, the power to define the concept of strict liability is the power to define the limits of legitimate criminal law making.

The drafters of the Model Penal Code developed an influential scheme for defining and analyzing offense elements that includes a technical definition of strict liability. In this scheme, a criminal offense consists of one or more objective elements, with a culpable mental state corresponding to each. Thus every offense must involve at least one act or omission and possibly additional circumstance and result elements. To be guilty the offender must have a culpable mental state of negligence, recklessness, knowledge, or purpose with respect to each of these objective elements. According to this scheme, failure to require proof of a culpable mental state with respect to each objective element makes an offense strict liability.

Criminal law theorist Ken Simons has dubbed this esoteric conception (punishment for an offense containing an objective element without a corresponding mental state) "formal" strict liability. He calls the more familiar conception (liability without moral fault) "substantive" strict liability. Formal strict liability need not entail substantive strict liability. Thus, a legislature may impose deserved punishment for carelessly causing harm by two different means: by conditioning punishment on awareness of risk, or by conditioning it on particularly dangerous conduct that the legislature regards as culpable per se. The second approach does not require proof of a culpable mental state with respect to the proscribed harm, and adds an additional objective element—the dangerous conduct—without a corresponding culpable mental state. As such, it imposes strict liability in the formal sense, but not in the substantive sense.

If felony murder requires no proof of any culpable mental state with respect to death, it imposes strict liability in the formal sense. Yet it may nevertheless condition liability on moral fault by substituting a per se culpability rule for a culpability standard. A legislature may conclude that certain conduct poses a significant enough risk of death that its commission implies negligence or recklessness with respect to death. By providing notice of this judgment through a statutory rule, the legislature estops a defendant from pleading ignorance of this risk. A dangerous felonies limitation provides such a per se rule. Another way of conditioning felony murder liability on conduct inherently dangerous to life is to condition the element of "killing" on violent methods of causing death, as eighteenth-century English law did. In these ways, felony murder rules can substantively require culpability with respect to a risk of death, even when they do not do so formally. Finally, a felony murder rule can require a foreseeable risk of death as part of the proof of causation rather than as a separate mental element. Although formally a crime of strict liability, such a felony murder rule nevertheless requires culpability.

The charge that felony murder liability is a form of strict liability may have a different meaning, however. A critic of felony murder rules might concede that they effectively condition murder liability on negligence with respect to a risk of death, but object that negligence is not a legitimate form of culpability. According to the Model Penal Code's influential definitions of culpable mental states, the imposition of risk is negligent when the actor should be aware that she is imposing a substantial and unjustifiable risk. Thus a requirement of negligence can be satisfied by conduct a reasonable person would recognize as dangerous, even if the actor fails—presumably unreasonably—to advert to the danger. For example, an armed robber who threatens a victim with a loaded gun might simply expect that he can control the weapon, the victim will obey, the robbery will go according to plan, and no one will get hurt—and so might never advert to the various ways creating such a volatile situation could result in death. The motel clerk killer described in the introduction is such a robber. For criminal law theorists with a strictly cognitive view of culpability, such unreasonably inadvertent risk imposition is merely stupid, but not morally culpable. On this cognitive view, if criminal negligence does not require actual awareness of risk, it cannot be a form of culpability. It follows that, if felony murder is conditioned on negligent imposition of a risk of death, it imposes strict liability, even in the substantive sense. The negligent actor might be morally at fault for a wrongful act that inadvertently causes harm, but not for the harm itself.

The defender of negligence liability may respond in one of two ways: either she may insist that negligence is a form of cognitive culpability, or she may offer some alternative conception of culpability. If she takes the first approach, she may define negligence as actual awareness of some unjustified risk less substantial than that required for recklessness. Or she might argue that negligence is a second order cognitive failure. Thus, one who fails to inform herself about the risks of an activity or who impairs her own capacity to perceive risks might be seen as cognitively culpable for resulting harms. Some commentators have tried to develop cognitive accounts of unreasonable failure to perceive risks. According to these accounts, actors are cognitively culpable if they are aware of facts from which they would infer risk if they thought about it. We might say they have notice rather than knowledge of risk, or that their knowledge of risk is "tacit." This might describe an unreflective armed robber like our motel clerk killer. If asked, he might acknowledge that a gun pointed at a victim might go off if he fumbles it, or if the victim, a witness, or a law enforcement officer startles him, or that one of these parties might pull a gun and fire, perhaps hitting a bystander.

Yet I am not sure this hypothetical knowledge or notice really suffices to justify holding the robber culpable for a foreseeable death. After all, he might never pose questions to himself about how things might go wrong. He might habitually act, not on the basis of reasoned expectations about the consequences of his actions, but instead on the basis of desired or wished for consequences. This certainly seems true of many bank robbers, for example, who perform their dramas on camera and in front of dozens of witnesses, and consequently face an eighty percent prospect of apprehension. In other words, the risks robbers unthinkingly impose on themselves are far greater and more apparent than the risks they impose on others. But when someone systematically tries to enact unrealistic fantasies rather than thinking about likely consequences, does her moral fault really depend upon tacit knowledge of risk? Or does it depend, as some "character theorists" claim, on a faulty process of practical reasoning that dismisses risk as irrelevant? If so, negligence seems to depend on character or motivation, not just on cognition.

This reasoning pushes us to broaden our conception of culpability beyond the cognitive, so as to include the robber's negligence toward victims. On the expressive theory of culpability explored [in this article], the robber's moral fault lies in the social meaning of her actions, the implication that her desires should have priority over the safety of others. On such a view the actor is at fault not for the unexamined and yet tacit cognitive implications of her action, but instead for the unexamined and yet tacit normative implications of her actions. So it seems that the legitimacy of the negligence component of felony murder liability will also depend on the choice between cognitive and expressive theories of culpability discussed in the next subpart.

[In sum,] [c]ritics of felony murder tend to elide the difference between formal and substantive strict liability. By calling felony murder a strict liability offense, critics create the impression that felony murder rules impose liability without moral fault. Often, however, their objection really concerns only the form of the offense definition. In other cases, the charge of strict liability disguises an objection to conditioning criminal liability on negligence.

## *Notes and Questions*

1. Professor Kevin Cole argues that imposing strict liability for murder when actors kill during the course of a felony may be justified on consequentialist grounds. According to Cole, people who decide to engage in the kind of felony that typically triggers the felony murder rule are often career-type criminals who are more likely to plan their crime in advance. These—as opposed to emotional or angry killers—are precisely the kinds of people that one can expect will consider the possible punishment that will be imposed if they get caught while committing the crime. Consequently, raising the cost of engaging in a felony by ratcheting up punishment if a person is killed during the commission of the felony may cause potential felons to either abstain from engaging in the felony in the first place or take additional precautions to ensure that no one is hurt during the commission of the felony. Furthermore, Cole believes holding felons strictly liable for killings that occur during the consummation of the offense may also discourage felons from engaging in such crimes by putting them on notice that they will not be able to escape murder liability by raising a *mens rea* related defense. This raises the cost of engaging in the felony even more. Are you persuaded by Professor Cole's arguments in favor of felony murder liability?

2. Professor Guyora Binder is not persuaded by Cole's consequentialist defense of felony murder liability. Regarding Professor Cole's description of the typical felon, Binder points out that research reveals that "crimes are sometimes impulsive and are often pursued for expressive rather than instrumental reasons." Therefore, "if robbers act against their own welfare to enact a role or claim a reputation, they are unlikely to be unusually responsive to deterrent threats." Furthermore, Professor Binder points out that empirical research suggests that—contrary to what Cole seems to imply—"the most efficient deterrent for negligent conduct—by felons or anyone else—is attaching a small but certain penalty to each negligent act." As a result, Binder suggests that devoting additional resources to heightened enforcement and policing of existing laws is likely to be more effective than devoting such resources to ratcheting up punishment for killings that take place during felonies. Finally, Binder contends that imposing strict liability for murder whenever a killing takes place during the commission of a felony is objectionable regardless of whether it is justified from a consequentialist perspective. Even if imposing such punishment is efficient (which Binder denies), he argues that doing so is unfair because such punishment is not deserved. This, in turn, provides a decisive reason against the more extreme form of felony murder that imposes murder liability without proof of fault for killings committed during felonies. Who has the better part of this argument? Why?

# Chapter 21

# Rape

## § 21.01 Rape: Objective Elements of the Offense— Force vs. Non-Consent

### United States v. Webster

United States Coast Guard Court of Military Review, 1993
37 M.J 670

EDWARDS, Judge:

In a trial before members, Appellant pled not guilty to all charges and specifications. Nevertheless, he was convicted of violating two separate lawful general regulations (four specifications), rape (one specification), assault consummated by a battery (two specifications), indecent assault (three specifications), and communicating indecent language to another (two specifications), in violation of Articles 92, 120, 128, and 134, Uniform Code of Military Justice [hereinafter UCMJ]. The convening authority approved the adjudged sentence of reduction to pay grade E-1, forfeiture of $500.00 pay per month for two months, confinement for two months, and a bad conduct discharge.

Appellant submits [in assignment I] ... that the evidence was insufficient as a matter of law to find Appellant guilty of rape beyond a reasonable doubt.

The case having been fully briefed and argued, we affirm in part and reverse in part.

I.
THE ALLEGED RAPE

A.

Although styled as a challenge purely to the legal sufficiency of the evidence, Appellant also challenges the factual sufficiency of the evidence upon which he was found guilty of rape, contending that the government failed to establish that the act of sexual intercourse was accomplished by force and without the consent of Petty Officer T, the alleged victim. The test for legal sufficiency is whether, considering the evidence in a light most favorable to the government, the trier of fact rationally could find the existence of every element of the alleged offense beyond a reasonable doubt. The test for factual sufficiency is whether, after weighing the evidence in the record of trial and making allowances for our not having observed the witnesses personally, we are convinced of Appellant's guilt beyond a reasonable doubt.

As is common in trials where rape is charged, the description given by the participants presents differing versions of the events that transpired. There is agreement, however, on certain basic facts. At the time of the alleged rape, both Appellant and Petty Officer T were assigned to Coast Guard Station Hatteras Inlet, North Carolina. Petty Officer T resided in an off-base apartment in Frisco, North Carolina. Appellant was a Machinery Technician Second Class (E-5). Petty Officer T was a Boatswain's Mate Third Class (E-4). Although Appellant was senior in rate to Petty Officer T, the nature of their duty assignments was such that when underway on a Search and Rescue (SAR) case, he was subject to her orders as Boat Coxswain. Neither was married. Prior to the events in question, they had seen each other socially, had held hands and kissed, and Appellant had declared his love for Petty Officer T.

Based upon Petty Officer T's testimony, on an uncertain date in July of 1991, Appellant visited Petty Officer T in her apartment. No one else was present. They sat together on a couch and talked for about an hour and a half. During this period, they eventually began to hold hands and kiss.

When Petty Officer T observed her cat using a litter box in her bedroom, she arose from the couch and went to close the bedroom door. Appellant followed her. He asked her if they could go into the bedroom together. Petty Officer T said, "no." Appellant then asked Petty Officer T if they could go into the closet instead. Again, she said, "no." Appellant then pulled Petty Officer T to the living room floor. She arose and asked Appellant to leave. Appellant told her that he would do so. Petty Officer T walked toward the front door, which was located in the kitchen area of her apartment. Appellant followed her, but, rather than departing, he placed his hands on Petty Officer T's arms and backed her up against a kitchen counter. Beginning when Appellant started to push Petty Officer T backwards, she told him "no" approximately five more times. In some fashion, Petty Officer T next found herself sitting on the counter.

Petty Officer T had been wearing a bikini, a shirt, and a pair of boxer shorts. While she was sitting on the counter, Appellant pulled the shorts down, pushed the bikini bottom to the side, and inserted his fingers into Petty Officer T's vagina. Thereafter, he inserted his penis into Petty Officer T's vagina. She asked Appellant not to ejaculate inside her vagina. Appellant complied with her request and withdrew before ejaculating. After each had cleaned up, Appellant spoke a few words to her and departed.

Petty Officer T testified she did nothing to assist him in completing the act of sexual intercourse. She was not sexually aroused. Although there were instances in which Appellant had no more than one hand on Petty Officer T, she never attempted to flee. She did, however, feel that she could not move. She did not scream. Petty Officer T did not attempt to hit or otherwise physically repel Appellant, and she testified that she considered herself a "very peaceful person." Petty Officer T was angry with Appellant for what he was doing to her, but was never afraid that he might harm her, nor did he make any threats.

Petty Officer T did not report this incident to anyone until some time much later. As was his right, Appellant elected not to testify. However, in a somewhat unusual fashion, the members were apprised of a different version of the events of July 1991 in Petty Officer T's apartment. During the government's case in chief, a Coast Guard Intelligence Special Agent was called. He testified about an interview of Appellant conducted in October of 1991. During the interview, Appellant admitted that sexual intercourse had occurred, in much the same fashion as testified to by Petty Officer T. The critical distinction in this second version is that concerning Petty Officer T's consent. As related by the Special Agent, Petty Officer T had conveyed her actual consent to intercourse through her actions. Although Petty Officer T would say "No, stop, we can't," while they were kissing and fondling each other, she responded favorably to his actions. According to Appellant's statement to the agent, these included her continuing to kiss Appellant after both had entered the kitchen, fondling his penis with her hand before he lifted or helped her onto the counter, rubbing his head during intercourse, and allowing him to ejaculate into her hand.

B.

There are three elements of rape, *viz.*, that the accused committed an act of sexual intercourse with a certain female, that the female was not the accused's wife, and that the act of sexual intercourse was done by force and without the female's consent.

Before this Court, Appellant's brief cites [several] cases in support of his argument against finding legal and factual sufficiency.

*United States v. Townsend, supra,* decided by another panel of this Court, although factually similar in some respects to the instant case, is distinguishable. The purported victim in *Townsend* willingly left an enlisted club with the accused late at night, and went to and then into an otherwise deserted office building with him. She freely participated in a "french-kiss" with the accused. Although she then protested against going further, when subsequently directed to "lay down" on a conference room floor, she did comply. Even after the alleged rape had occurred, she was more concerned that the accused's "buddy" would learn about the sexual intercourse, than she was upset that it had occurred at all.

Although fitting the so-called "date rape" classification, *Bonano-Torres* involved a male Staff Sergeant and a female Specialist who apparently had not dated each other prior to an evening of dining and drinking while on a temporary assignment. On returning to their hotel, the Sergeant gained access to the victim's room in order to use the bathroom. The victim lay down on the bed and was drifting in and out of an alcohol-induced state of unconsciousness or sleep. She became aware of the Sergeant, naked, in bed with her, kissing her and massaging her breast. She told him she did not want to engage in this activity because he was married, and she kept turning her head and moving his hands. After he stopped his overtures, she again passed out or fell asleep, but similar sequences of events occurred until she finally permitted him to have intercourse so he would leave her alone and let her sleep. The Army Court of Military Review set aside the finding of rape, holding that, under Article 120, UCMJ, rape requires "proof of lack of consent *and* force" and that the force required is more than that merely incidental to the act of intercourse.

On certification to the Court of Military Appeals, the government contended that the court below incorrectly considered resistance by the victim to be an element of the offense of rape. The Court rejected this argument as misconstruing the holding of the court below and declined to extract from the lower court's opinion an "inflexible rule establishing resistance as a necessary element of [rape]" in cases not involving constructive force. The Court agreed that force is required by Article 120, UCMJ, and that the conduct of the attacker and the victim need to be considered in determining whether the force used is sufficient to meet this requirement. Noting that the explanation ... stops short of explaining what is sufficient force, the Court affirmed, stating "we find no legal error in the holding by the court below of insufficient force in this case *to the extent that it is based on the totality of the circumstances evidenced in this record.*"

At trial, Appellant's counsel argued vigorously that Petty Officer T's version of events was implausible. In two instances, he even alluded to the favorable testimony of the Special Agent. Yet, following proper instruction by the military judge, the members, who had had the opportunity to observe Petty Officer T while she testified, convicted Appellant of rape. Applying the test of *Jackson v. Virginia, supra,* we are convinced that the government easily satisfied its burden of presenting legally sufficient proof of rape. With respect to factual sufficiency, the issue is a closer one. As did the trial court, we reject Appellant's version of events that would lead one to conclude that Petty Officer T was a willing participant in the act of intercourse. Nevertheless, we must be convinced beyond a reasonable doubt that, under the "totality of circumstances evidenced in this record," the act of intercourse constituted rape.

Neither *Bonano-Torres* nor *Townsend* specifically addresses the determination of force and lack of consent in the "date rape" or "acquaintance rape" situation. Of course, neither Article 120, UCMJ, nor 45, Part IV, MCM, makes any distinction among any types of rape. Nevertheless, in making our own determination of factual sufficiency in this case, we need not disregard the much greater research and understanding which date or acquaintance rape has received in recent years.

The characteristics of date or acquaintance rape may include (1) kissing, "necking," and fondling but no consent by the victim to subsequent sexual intercourse; (2) passive resistance by the victim to the sexual advances of her attacker; (3) the attacker's disregard of the victim's statement that she does not desire to engage in sexual intercourse; (4) the absence of physical threats by the attacker to his victim; (5) the failure of the victim to seize opportunities to escape from her attacker; (6) the failure of the victim to scream or cry out; (7) little or no observable physical injury to the victim; and (8) the failure of the victim to report the rape promptly.

Review of these apparently not uncommon characteristics of date rape helps to illuminate this troubling area, and amply supports the actions of the various legislatures that have modified the statutory provisions concerning lack of consent and resistance to force, but does not answer the critical questions which we must decide. Did Appellant employ force more than that incidental to the act of intercourse and did Petty Officer T make "her lack of consent reasonably manifest by taking such measures of resistance as [were] called for by the circumstances"?

There is no evidence that Petty Officer T had engaged in intercourse with Appellant, under any circumstances, prior to the July, 1991, incident. On that day, she did hold hands with and kiss Appellant for a period of time; however, even under Appellant's version of events, she consistently and repeatedly told him "no" when in the living room and broke off physical contact and went into the kitchen. According to Petty Officer T, when Appellant pulled her to the floor, she immediately stood up and asked him to leave and she continued to say "no" and to resist his physical advances in the kitchen. Despite the absence of threats by Appellant and Petty Officer T's lack of fear, we find there was more force applied by Appellant than that incidental to the act of intercourse. Petty Officer T's failure either to cry out or to attempt to flee, or to strike Appellant, do not lead us to believe that her resistance was insufficient to make her lack of consent reasonably manifest. Accordingly, considering the totality of circumstances, we find that the charged act of sexual intercourse "was done by force and without her consent." ...

Accordingly, the sentence is affirmed.

## State in the Interest of M.T.S.

Supreme Court of New Jersey, 1992
609 A.2d 1266

HANDLER, J.

Under New Jersey law a person who commits an act of sexual penetration using physical force or coercion is guilty of second-degree sexual assault. The sexual assault statute does not define the words "physical force." The question posed by this appeal is whether the element of "physical force" is met simply by an act of non-consensual penetration involving no more force than necessary to accomplish that result.

That issue is presented in the context of what is often referred to as "acquaintance rape." The record in the case discloses that the juvenile, a seventeen-year-old boy, engaged in consensual kissing and heavy petting with a fifteen-year-old girl and thereafter engaged in actual sexual penetration of the girl to which she had not consented. There was no evidence or suggestion that the juvenile used any unusual or extra force or threats to accomplish the act of penetration.

The trial court determined that the juvenile was delinquent for committing a sexual assault. The Appellate Division reversed the disposition of delinquency, concluding that non-consensual penetration does not constitute sexual assault unless it is accompanied by some level of force more than that necessary to accomplish the penetration. We granted the State's petition for certification.

I

The issues in this case are perplexing and controversial. We must explain the role of force in the contemporary crime of sexual assault and then define its essential features. We then must consider what evidence is probative to establish the commission of a sexual assault. The factual circumstances of this case expose the complexity and sensitivity of those issues and underscore the analytic difficulty of those seemingly-straightforward legal questions.

On Monday, May 21, 1990, fifteen-year-old C.G. was living with her mother, her three siblings, and several other people, including M.T.S. and his girlfriend. A total of ten people resided in the three-bedroom town-home at the time of the incident. M.T.S., then age seventeen, was temporarily residing at the home with the permission of the C.G.'s mother; he slept downstairs on a couch. C.G. had her own room on the second floor. At approximately 11:30 p.m. on May 21, C.G. went upstairs to sleep after having watched television with her mother, M.T.S., and his girlfriend. When C.G. went to bed, she was wearing underpants, a bra, shorts, and a shirt. At trial, C.G. and M.T.S. offered very different accounts concerning the nature of their relationship and the events that occurred after C.G. had gone upstairs. The trial court did not credit fully either teenager's testimony.

C.G. stated that earlier in the day, M.T.S. had told her three or four times that he "was going to make a surprise visit up in [her] bedroom." She said that she had not taken M.T.S. seriously and considered his comments a joke because he frequently teased her. She testified that M.T.S. had attempted to kiss her on numerous other occasions and at least once had attempted to put his hands inside of her pants, but that she had rejected all of his previous advances.

C.G. testified that on May 22, at approximately 1:30 a.m., she awoke to use the bathroom. As she was getting out of bed, she said, she saw M.T.S., fully clothed, standing in her doorway. According to C.G., M.T.S. then said that "he was going to tease [her] a little bit." C.G. testified that she "didn't think anything of it"; she walked past him, used the bathroom, and then returned to bed, falling into a "heavy" sleep within fifteen minutes. The next event C.G. claimed to recall of that morning was waking up with M.T.S. on top of her, her underpants and shorts removed. She said "his penis was into [her] vagina." As soon as C.G. realized what had happened, she said, she immediately slapped M.T.S. once in the face, then "told him to get off [her], and get out." She did not scream or cry out. She testified that M.T.S. complied in less than one minute after being struck; according to C.G., "he jumped right off of [her]." She said she did not know how long M.T.S. had been inside of her before she awoke.

C.G. said that after M.T.S. left the room, she "fell asleep crying" because "[she] couldn't believe that he did what he did to [her]." She explained that she did not immediately tell her mother or anyone else in the house of the events of that morning because she was "scared and in shock." According to C.G., M.T.S. engaged in intercourse with her "without [her] wanting it or telling him to come up [to her bedroom]." By her own account, C.G. was not otherwise harmed by M.T.S.

At about 7:00 a.m., C.G. went downstairs and told her mother about her encounter with M.T.S. earlier in the morning and said that they would have to "get [him] out of the house." While M.T.S. was out on an errand, C.G.'s mother gathered his clothes and put them outside in his car; when he returned, he was told that "[he] better not even get near the house." C.G. and her mother then filed a complaint with the police.

According to M.T.S., he and C.G. had been good friends for a long time, and their relationship "kept leading on to more and more." He had been living at C.G.'s home for about five days before the incident occurred; he testified that during the three days preceding the incident they had been "kissing and necking" and had discussed having sexual intercourse. The first time M.T.S. kissed C.G., he said, she "didn't want him to, but she did after that." He said C.G. repeatedly had encouraged him to "make a surprise visit up in her room."

M.T.S. testified that at exactly 1:15 a.m. on May 22, he entered C.G.'s bedroom as she was walking to the bathroom. He said C.G. soon returned from the bathroom, and the two began "kissing and all," eventually moving to the bed. Once they were in bed, he said, they undressed each other and continued to kiss and touch for about five minutes. M.T.S. and C.G. proceeded to engage in sexual intercourse. According to M.T.S., who was on top of C.G., he "stuck it in" and "did it [thrust] three times, and then the fourth time [he] stuck it in, that's when [she] pulled [him] off of her." M.T.S. said that as C.G. pushed him off, she said "stop, get off," and he "hopped off right away."

According to M.T.S., after about one minute, he asked C.G. what was wrong; she replied with a back-hand to his face. He recalled asking C.G. what was wrong a second time, and her replying, "how can you take advantage of me or something like that." M.T.S. said that he proceeded to get dressed and told C.G. to calm down, but that she then told him to get away from her and began to cry. Before leaving the room, he told C.G., "I'm leaving ... I'm going with my real girlfriend, don't talk to me ... I don't want nothing to do with you or anything, stay out of my life ... don't tell anybody about this ... it would just screw everything up." He then walked downstairs and went to sleep.

On May 23, 1990, M.T.S. was charged with conduct that if engaged in by an adult would constitute second-degree sexual assault of the victim, contrary to N.J.S.A. 2C:14-2c(1) ...

Following a two-day trial on the sexual assault charge, M.T.S. was adjudicated delinquent. After reviewing the testimony, the court concluded that the victim had consented to a session of kissing and heavy petting with M.T.S. The trial court did not find that C.G. had been sleeping at the time of penetration, but nevertheless found that she had not consented to the actual sexual act. Accordingly, the court concluded that the State had proven second-degree sexual assault beyond a reasonable doubt. On appeal, following the imposition of suspended sentences on the sexual assault and the other remaining charges, the Appellate Division determined that the absence of force beyond that involved in the act of sexual penetration precluded a finding of second-degree sexual assault. It therefore reversed the juvenile's adjudication of delinquency for that offense.

## II

The New Jersey Code of Criminal Justice, N.J.S.A. 2C:14-2c(1), defines "sexual assault" as the commission "of sexual penetration" "with another person" with the use of "physical force or coercion." An unconstrained reading of the statutory language indicates that both the act of "sexual penetration" and the use of "physical force or coercion" are separate and distinct elements of the offense. Neither the definitions section of N.J.S.A. 2C:14-1 to -8, nor the remainder of the Code of Criminal Justice provides assistance in interpreting the words "physical force." The initial inquiry is, therefore, whether the statutory words are unambiguous on their face and can be understood and applied in accordance with their plain meaning. The answer to that inquiry is revealed by the conflicting decisions of the lower courts and the arguments of the opposing parties. The trial court held that "physical force" had been established by the sexual penetration of the victim without her consent. The Appellate Division believed that the statute requires some amount of force more than that necessary to accomplish penetration.

The parties offer two alternative understandings of the concept of "physical force" as it is used in the statute. The State would read "physical force" to entail any amount of sexual touching brought about involuntarily. A showing of sexual penetration coupled with a lack of consent would satisfy the elements of the statute. The Public Defender urges an interpretation of "physical force" to mean force "used to overcome lack of consent." That definition equates force with violence and leads to the conclusion that sexual assault requires the application of some amount of force in addition to the act of penetration.

Current judicial practice suggests an understanding of "physical force" to mean "any degree of physical power or strength used against the victim, even though it entails no injury and leaves no mark." Model Jury Charges, Criminal 3 (revised Mar. 27, 1989). Resort to common experience or understanding does not yield a conclusive meaning. The dictionary provides several definitions of "force," among which are the following: (1) "power, violence, compulsion, or constraint exerted upon or against a person or thing," (2) "a general term for exercise of strength or power, esp. physical, to overcome resistance," or (3) "strength or power of any degree that is exercised without justification or contrary to law upon a person or thing."

Thus, as evidenced by the disagreements among the lower courts and the parties, and the variety of possible usages, the statutory words "physical force" do not evoke a single meaning that is obvious and plain. Hence, we must pursue avenues of construction in order to ascertain the meaning of that statutory language. Those avenues are well charted. When a statute is open to conflicting interpretations, the court seeks the underlying intent of the legislature, relying on legislative history and the contemporary context of the statute. With respect to a law, like the sexual assault statute, that "alters or amends the previous law or creates or abolishes types of actions, it is important, in discovering the legislative intent, to ascertain the old law, the mischief and the proposed remedy." We also remain mindful of the basic tenet of statutory construction that penal statutes are to be strictly construed in favor of the accused. Nevertheless, the construction must conform to the intent of the Legislature.

The provisions proscribing sexual offenses found in the Code of Criminal Justice, N.J.S.A. 2C:14-2c(1), became effective in 1979, and were written against almost two hundred years of rape law in New Jersey. The origin of the rape statute that the current statutory offense of sexual assault replaced can be traced to the English common law. Under the common law, rape was defined as "carnal knowledge of a woman against her will." American jurisdictions generally adopted the English view, but over time states added the requirement that the carnal knowledge have been forcible, apparently in order to prove that the act was against the victim's will. As of 1796, New Jersey statutory law defined rape as "carnal knowledge of a woman, forcibly and against her will." Those three elements of rape—carnal knowledge, forcibly, and against her will—remained the essential elements of the crime until 1979.

Under traditional rape law, in order to prove that a rape had occurred, the state had to show both that force had been used and that the penetration had been against the woman's will. Force was identified and determined not as an independent factor but in relation to the response of the victim, which in turn implicated the victim's own state of mind. "Thus, the perpetrator's use of force became criminal only if the victim's state of mind met the statutory requirement. The perpetrator could use all the force imaginable and no crime would be committed if the state could not prove additionally that the victim did not consent." Although the terms "non-consent" and "against her will" were often treated as equivalent, under the traditional definition of rape, both formulations squarely placed on the victim the burden of proof and of action. Effectively, a woman who was above the age of consent had actively and affirmatively to withdraw that consent for the intercourse to be against her will. As a Delaware court stated, "If sexual intercourse is obtained by milder means, or with the consent or silent submission of the female, it cannot constitute the crime of rape."

The presence or absence of consent often turned on credibility. To demonstrate that the victim had not consented to the intercourse, and also that sufficient force had been used to accomplish the rape, the state had to prove that the victim had resisted. According to the oft-quoted Lord Hale, to be deemed a credible witness, a woman had to be of good fame, disclose the injury immediately, suffer signs of injury, and cry out for help. Courts and commentators historically distrusted the testimony of victims, "assuming that women lie about their lack of consent for various reasons: to blackmail men, to explain the discovery of a consensual affair, or because of psychological illness." Evidence of resistance was viewed as a solution to the credibility problem; it was the "outward manifestation of nonconsent, [a] device for determining whether a woman actually gave consent."

The resistance requirement had a profound effect on the kind of conduct that could be deemed criminal and on the type of evidence needed to establish the crime. Courts assumed that any woman who was forced to have intercourse against her will necessarily would resist to the extent of her ability. In many jurisdictions the requirement was that the woman have resisted to the utmost. "Rape is not committed unless the woman oppose the man to the utmost limit of her power." "[A] mere tactical surrender in the face of an assumed superior physical force is not enough. Where the penalty for the defendant may be supreme, so must resistance be unto the uttermost." Other states followed a "reasonableness" standard, while some required only sufficient resistance to make non-consent reasonably manifest.

At least by the 1960s courts in New Jersey followed a standard for establishing resistance that was somewhat less drastic than the traditional rule. In State v. Harris, the Appellate Division recognized that the "to the uttermost" test was obsolete. "The fact that a victim finally submits does not necessarily imply that she consented. Submission to a compelling force, or as a result of being put in fear, is not consent." Nonetheless, the "resistance" requirement remained an essential feature of New Jersey rape law. Thus, in 1965 the Appellate Division stated: "[W]e have rejected the former test that a woman must resist 'to the uttermost.' We only require that she resist as much as she possibly can under the circumstances."

The judicial interpretation of the pre-reform rape law in New Jersey, with its insistence on resistance by the victim, greatly minimized the importance of the forcible and assaultive aspect of the defendant's conduct. Rape prosecutions turned then not so much on the forcible or assaultive character of the defendant's actions as on the nature of the victim's response. "[I]f a woman assaulted is physically and mentally able to resist, is not terrified by threats, and is not in a place and position that resistance would have been useless, it must be shown that she did, in fact, resist the assault." Under the pre-reform law, the resistance offered had to be "in good faith and without pretense, with an active determination to prevent the violation of her person, and must not be merely passive and perfunctory." That the law put the rape victim on trial was clear.

The resistance requirement had another untoward influence on traditional rape law. Resistance was necessary not only to prove non-consent but also to demonstrate that the force used by the defendant had been sufficient to overcome the victim's will. The amount of force used by the defendant was assessed in relation to the resistance of the victim. See, e.g., Tex.Penal Code Ann.§ 21.02 (1974) (repealed 1983) (stating that "the amount of force necessary to negate consent is a relative matter to be judged under all the circumstances, the most important of which is the resistance of the female"). In New Jersey the amount of force necessary to establish rape was characterized as "'the degree of force sufficient to overcome any resistance that had been put up by the female.'" Resistance, often demonstrated by torn clothing and blood, was a sign that the defendant had used significant force to accomplish the sexual intercourse. Thus, if the defendant forced himself on a woman, it was her responsibility to fight back, because force was measured in relation to the resistance she put forward. Only if she resisted, causing him to use more force than was necessary to achieve penetration, would his conduct be criminalized. Indeed, the significance of resistance as the proxy for force is illustrated by cases in which victims were unable to resist; in such cases the force incident to penetration was deemed sufficient to establish the "force" element of the offense.

The importance of resistance as an evidentiary requirement set the law of rape apart from other common-law crimes, particularly in the eyes of those who advocated reform of rape law in the 1970s. However, the resistance requirement was not the only special rule applied in the rape context. A host of evidentiary rules and standards of proof distinguished the legal treatment of rape from the treatment of other crimes. Many jurisdictions held that a rape conviction could not be sustained if based solely on the uncorroborated testimony of the victim. Often judges added cautionary instructions to jury charges warning jurors that rape was a particularly difficult charge to prove. Courts in New Jersey allowed greater latitude in cross-examining rape victims and in delving into their backgrounds than in ordinary cases. Rape victims were required to make a prompt complaint or have their allegations rejected or viewed with great skepticism. Some commentators suggested that there be mandatory psychological testing of rape victims.

During the 1970s feminists and others criticized the stereotype that rape victims were inherently more untrustworthy than other victims of criminal attack. Reformers condemned such suspicion as discrimination against victims of rape. They argued that "[d]istrust of the complainant's credibility [had] led to an exaggerated insistence on evidence of resistance," resulting in the victim rather than the defendant being put on trial. Reformers also challenged the assumption that a woman would seduce a man and then, in order to protect her virtue, claim to have been raped. If women are no less trustworthy than other purported victims of criminal attack, the reformers argued, then women should face no additional burdens of proving that they had not consented to or had actively resisted the assault.

To refute the misguided belief that rape was not real unless the victim fought back, reformers emphasized empirical research indicating that women who resisted forcible intercourse often suffered far more serious injury as a result. That research discredited the assumption that resistance to the utmost or to the best of a woman's ability was the most reasonable or rational response to a rape.

The research also helped demonstrate the underlying point of the reformers that the crime of rape rested not in the overcoming of a woman's will or the insult to her chastity but in the forcible attack itself—the assault on her person. Reformers criticized the conception of rape as a distinctly sexual crime rather than a crime of violence. They emphasized that rape had its legal origins in laws designed to protect the property rights of men to their wives and daughters. Although the crime had evolved into an offense against women, reformers argued that vestiges of the old law remained, particularly in the understanding of rape as a crime against the purity or chastity of a woman. The burden of protecting that chastity fell on the woman, with the state offering its protection only after the woman demonstrated that she had resisted sufficiently.

That rape under the traditional approach constituted a sexual rather than an assaultive crime is underscored by the spousal exemption. According to the traditional reasoning, a man could not rape his wife because consent to sexual intercourse was implied by the marriage contract. Therefore, sexual intercourse between spouses was lawful regardless of the force or violence used to accomplish it.

Critics of rape law agreed that the focus of the crime should be shifted from the victim's behavior to the defendant's conduct, and particularly to its forceful and assaultive, rather than sexual, character. Reformers also shared the goals of facilitating rape prosecutions and of sparing victims much of the degradation involved in bringing and trying a charge of rape. There were, however, differences over the best way to redefine the crime. Some reformers advocated a standard that defined rape as unconsented-to sexual intercourse; others urged the elimination of any reference to consent from the definition of rape. Nonetheless, all proponents of reform shared a central premise: that the burden of showing non-consent should not fall on the victim of the crime. In dealing with the problem of consent the reform goal was not so much to purge the entire concept of consent from the law as to eliminate the burden that had been placed on victims to prove they had not consented.

Similarly, with regard to force, rape law reform sought to give independent significance to the forceful or assaultive conduct of the defendant and to avoid a definition of force that depended on the reaction of the victim. Traditional interpretations of force were strongly criticized for failing to acknowledge that force may be understood simply as the invasion of "bodily integrity." In urging that the "resistance" requirement be abandoned, reformers sought to break the connection between force and resistance.

### III

... Since the 1978 reform, the Code has referred to the crime that was once known as "rape" as "sexual assault." The crime now requires "penetration," not "sexual intercourse." It requires "force" or "coercion," not "submission" or "resistance." It makes no reference to the victim's state of mind or attitude, or conduct in response to the assault. It eliminates the spousal exception based on implied consent. It emphasizes the assaultive character of the offense by defining sexual penetration to encompass a wide range of sexual contacts, going well beyond traditional "carnal knowledge." Consistent with the assaultive character, as opposed to the traditional sexual character, of the offense, the statute also renders the crime gender-neutral: both males and females can be actors or victims.

The reform statute defines sexual assault as penetration accomplished by the use of "physical force" or "coercion," but it does not define either "physical force" or "coercion" or enumerate examples of evidence that would establish those elements. Some reformers had argued that defining "physical force" too specifically in the sexual offense statute might have the effect of limiting force to the enumerated examples. The task of defining "physical force" therefore was left to the courts ...

The Legislature's concept of sexual assault and the role of force was significantly colored by its understanding of the law of assault and battery. As a general matter, criminal battery is defined as "the unlawful application of force to the person of another." The application of force is criminal when it results in either (a) a physical injury or (b) an offensive touching. Any "unauthorized touching of another [is] a battery." Thus, by eliminating all references to the victim's state of mind and conduct, and by broadening the definition of penetration to cover not only sexual intercourse between a man and a woman but a range of acts that invade another's body or compel intimate contact, the Legislature emphasized the affinity between sexual assault and other forms of assault and battery.

The intent of the Legislature to redefine rape consistent with the law of assault and battery is further evidenced by the legislative treatment of other sexual crimes less serious than and derivative of traditional rape. The Code redefined the offense of criminal sexual contact to emphasize the involuntary and personally-offensive nature of the touching. Sexual contact is criminal under the same circumstances that render an act of sexual penetration a sexual assault, namely, when "physical force" or "coercion" demonstrates that it is unauthorized and offensive. N.J.S.A. 2C:14-3(b). Thus, just as any unauthorized touching is a crime under traditional laws of assault and battery, so is any unauthorized sexual contact a crime under the reformed law of criminal sexual contact, and so is any unauthorized sexual penetration a crime under the reformed law of sexual assault.

The understanding of sexual assault as a criminal battery, albeit one with especially serious consequences, follows necessarily from the Legislature's decision to eliminate non-consent and resistance from the substantive definition of the offense. Under the new law, the victim no longer is required to resist and therefore need not have said or done anything in order for the sexual penetration to be unlawful. The alleged victim is not put on trial, and his or her responsive or defensive behavior is rendered immaterial. We are thus satisfied that an interpretation of the statutory crime of sexual assault to require physical force in addition to that entailed in an act of involuntary or unwanted sexual penetration would be fundamentally inconsistent with the legislative purpose to eliminate any consideration of whether the victim resisted or expressed non-consent.

We note that the contrary interpretation of force—that the element of force need be extrinsic to the sexual act—would not only reintroduce a resistance requirement into the sexual assault law, but also would immunize many acts of criminal sexual contact short of penetration. The characteristics that make a sexual contact unlawful are the same as those that make a sexual penetration unlawful. An actor is guilty of criminal sexual contact if he or she commits an act of sexual contact with another using "physical force" or "coercion." N.J.S.A. 2C:14-3(b). That the Legislature would have wanted to decriminalize unauthorized sexual intrusions on the bodily integrity of a victim by requiring a showing of force in addition to that entailed in the sexual contact itself is hardly possible.

Because the statute eschews any reference to the victim's will or resistance, the standard defining the role of force in sexual penetration must prevent the possibility that the establishment of the crime will turn on the alleged victim's state of mind or responsive behavior. We conclude, therefore, that any act of sexual penetration engaged in by the defendant without the affirmative and freely-given permission of the victim to the specific act of penetration constitutes the offense of sexual assault. Therefore, physical force in excess of that inherent in the act of sexual penetration is not required for such penetration to be unlawful. The definition of "physical force" is satisfied under N.J.S.A. 2C:14-2c(1) if the defendant applies any amount of force against another person in the absence of what a reasonable person would believe to be affirmative and freely-given permission to the act of sexual penetration.

Under the reformed statute, permission to engage in sexual penetration must be affirmative and it must be given freely, but that permission may be inferred either from acts or statements reasonably viewed in light of the surrounding circumstances. Persons need not, of course, expressly announce their consent to engage in intercourse for there to be affirmative permission. Permission to engage in an act of sexual penetration can be and indeed often is indicated through physical actions rather than words. Permission is demonstrated when the evidence, in whatever form, is sufficient to demonstrate that a reasonable person would have believed that the alleged victim had affirmatively and freely given authorization to the act.

Our understanding of the meaning and application of "physical force" under the sexual assault statute indicates that the term's inclusion was neither inadvertent nor redundant. The term "physical force," like its companion term "coercion," acts to qualify the nature and character of the "sexual penetration." Sexual penetration accomplished through the use of force is unauthorized sexual penetration. That functional understanding of "physical force" encompasses the notion of "unpermitted touching" derived from the Legislature's decision to redefine rape as a sexual assault. As already noted, under assault and battery doctrine, any amount of force that results in either physical injury or offensive touching is sufficient to establish a battery. Hence, as a description of the method of achieving "sexual penetration," the term "physical force" serves to define and explain the acts that are offensive, unauthorized, and unlawful.

That understanding of the crime of sexual assault fully comports with the public policy sought to be effectuated by the Legislature. In redefining rape law as sexual assault, the Legislature adopted the concept of sexual assault as a crime against the bodily integrity of the victim. Although it is possible to imagine a set of rules in which persons must demonstrate affirmatively that sexual contact is unwanted or not permitted, such a regime would be inconsistent with modern principles of personal autonomy. The Legislature recast the law of rape as sexual assault to bring that area of law in line with the expectation of privacy and bodily control that long has characterized most of our private and public law. In interpreting "physical force" to include any touching that occurs without permission we seek to respect that goal.

Today the law of sexual assault is indispensable to the system of legal rules that assures each of us the right to decide who may touch our bodies, when, and under what circumstances. The decision to engage in sexual relations with another person is one of the most private and intimate decisions a person can make. Each person has the right not only to decide whether to engage in sexual contact with another, but also to control the circumstances and character of that contact. No one, neither a spouse, nor a friend, nor an acquaintance, nor a stranger, has the right or the privilege to force sexual contact.

We emphasize as well that what is now referred to as "acquaintance rape" is not a new phenomenon. Nor was it a "futuristic" concept in 1978 when the sexual assault law was enacted. Current concern over the prevalence of forced sexual intercourse between persons who know one another reflects both greater awareness of the extent of such behavior and a growing appreciation of its gravity. Notwithstanding the stereotype of rape as a violent attack by a stranger, the vast majority of sexual assaults are perpetrated by someone known to the victim. One respected study indicates that more than half of all rapes are committed by male relatives, current or former husbands, boyfriends or lovers. Similarly, contrary to common myths, perpetrators generally do not use guns or knives and victims generally do not suffer external bruises or cuts. Although this more realistic and accurate view of rape only recently has achieved widespread public circulation, it was a central concern of the proponents of reform in the 1970s.

The insight into rape as an assaultive crime is consistent with our evolving understanding of the wrong inherent in forced sexual intimacy. It is one that was appreciated by the Legislature when it reformed the rape laws, reflecting an emerging awareness that the definition of rape should correspond fully with the experiences and perspectives of rape victims. Although reformers focused primarily on the problems associated with convicting defendants accused of violent rape, the recognition that forced sexual intercourse often takes place between persons who know each other and often involves little or no violence comports with the understanding of the sexual assault law that was embraced by the Legislature. Any other interpretation of the law, particularly one that defined force in relation to the resistance or protest of the victim, would directly undermine the goals sought to be achieved by its reform.

IV

In a case such as this one, in which the State does not allege violence or force extrinsic to the act of penetration, the factfinder must decide whether the defendant's act of penetration was undertaken in circumstances that led the defendant reasonably to believe that the alleged victim had freely given affirmative permission to the specific act of sexual penetration. Such permission can be indicated either through words or through actions that, when viewed in the light of all the surrounding circumstances, would demonstrate to a reasonable person affirmative and freely-given authorization for the specific act of sexual penetration …

In short, in order to convict under the sexual assault statute in cases such as these, the State must prove beyond a reasonable doubt that there was sexual penetration and that it was accomplished without the affirmative and freely-given permission of the alleged victim. As we have indicated, such proof can be based on evidence of conduct or words in light of surrounding circumstances and must demonstrate beyond a reasonable doubt that a reasonable person would not have believed that there was affirmative and freely-given permission. If there is evidence to suggest that the defendant reasonably believed that such permission had been given, the State must demonstrate either that defendant did not actually believe that affirmative permission had been freely-given or that such a belief was unreasonable under all of the circumstances. Thus, the State bears the burden of proof throughout the case.

In this case, the Appellate Division [erred in concluding that that non-consensual penetration accomplished with no additional physical force or coercion is not criminalized under the sexual assault statute].

We acknowledge that cases such as this are inherently fact sensitive and depend on the reasoned judgment and common sense of judges and juries. The trial court concluded that the victim had not expressed consent to the act of intercourse, either through her words or actions. We conclude that the record provides reasonable support for the trial court's disposition.

Accordingly, we reverse the judgment of the Appellate Division and reinstate the disposition of juvenile delinquency for the commission of second-degree sexual assault.

## *Notes and Questions*

1. Is rape a crime against bodily integrity or a crime against sexual autonomy? Note that if rape is viewed as a violent crime against bodily integrity, the force requirement makes sense. The use (or threatened use) of force signals the attack on bodily integrity. If, however, rape is a crime against sexual autonomy, the force requirement is more difficult to make sense of, given that non-consensual sexual intercourse violates sexual autonomy regardless of whether it is accomplished by the use of force.

2. Even if rape is viewed primarily as a crime against sexual autonomy, the force requirement might still be justified for evidentiary reasons. That is, requiring force might be viewed as a way of making sure that the victim did not in fact consent. One of the chief concerns in rape prosecutions is that the defendant may be convicted solely on the basis of the victim's testimony that the sex was not consensual. Unfortunately, there are seldom any witnesses in rape cases other than the alleged perpetrator and victim. Therefore, rape prosecutions often pit two radically different accounts of what transpired, with the victim alleging that the sex was non-consensual and the defendant contending that it was consensual. This is what happened in both of the leading cases excerpted in this section. Requiring the prosecution to prove force in these cases may be viewed as a way of guaranteeing that the sex was truly non-consensual. While in non-forcible sex cases there might be doubts as to whether the sex was consensual, in forcible sex cases there will seldom be any doubt. Forcible sex is almost by definition non-consensual. So conceived, force would thus be an evidentiary proxy for non-consent. The problem with this view is that it will always benefit the defendant at the expense of the victim, at least if rape is viewed as a crime against sexual autonomy. It always benefits the defendant because the defendant will often be acquitted although he engaged in non-consensual sex if the sex was not forcible. This would leave many instances of non-consensual sex unpunished.

3. The history of rape is inextricably linked to the history of sexism and gender (in)equality. Many features of rape law reveal a male-centered conception of the crime. As the Supreme Court of New Jersey pointed out in *M.T.S.*, at common law a husband could not legally rape his wife. This so-called marital exemption led to the obviously sexist and unpalatable outcome of leaving a husband who forces his wife to engage in sexual intercourse unpunished. According to the Court in *M.T.S.*, "a man could not rape his wife because consent to sexual intercourse was implied by the marriage contract." Consequently, "sexual intercourse between spouses was lawful regardless of the force or violence used to accomplish it." The marital exemption has been repealed in many jurisdictions.

4. The sexist nature of the original understanding of the crime of rape is also revealed by the procedural hurdles that rape victims had to overcome in order to successfully prosecute the perpetrators. An example of such hurdles is the "fresh complaint rule." According to this rule, it is admissible to offer "proof that the violated victim complained within a reasonable time to someone she would ordinarily turn to for sympathy, protection and advice." *State v. Balles,* 47 N.J. 331, 338 (1966). Such proof is inadmissible, however, if the victim did not complain within a "reasonable time." This doctrine has been criticized for perpetuating "sexist notions of how the 'normal' woman responds to rape." *People v. Brown,* 883 P.2d 949 (1994). Another rule that has been attacked as sexist was the requirement that a victim's testimony regarding rape had to be corroborated in order for a conviction to stand. As a consequence of this rule, a defendant could not be convicted of rape solely on the basis of the victim's testimony. Finally, many have decried as sexist certain evidentiary rules that allowed the defendant to introduce evidence of prior sexual acts of the victim as proof that the victim consented to the sexual act for which the

defendant is charged with rape. These doctrines have now been reformed or abandoned in most jurisdictions. As a result, many states now hold that a rape conviction based solely on the victim's uncorroborated testimony may (but need not) stand and that a rape victim's complaint may be admissible even if it's not "fresh." Furthermore, a great deal of jurisdictions have adopted "rape-shield statutes" that bar the defendant from asking the victim about prior sexual acts during cross-examination. Feminist critics of rape laws have been instrumental in achieving these reforms. Do you agree that all of these substantive and procedural bars or hurdles to securing rape convictions should be repealed? Should some of these hurdles be repealed but others not? Why?

5. The military court in *Webster* and the Supreme Court of New Jersey in *M.T.S.* championed radically different definitions of "force" in the context of rape prosecutions. For the *Webster* court, the force required by the crime is force that is "more than that incidental to the act of intercourse." In contrast, the Court in *M.T.S.* held that "any act of sexual penetration engaged in by the defendant without the affirmative and freely-given permission of the victim to the specific act of penetration constitutes the offense of sexual assault." Consequently, the Court concluded that—contrary to what the military court held in *Webster*—"physical force in excess of that inherent in the act of sexual penetration is not required for such penetration to be unlawful." The broad definition of force put forth by the Court in *M.T.S.* would thus generate liability for rape whenever "the defendant applies any amount of force against another person in the absence of what a reasonable person would believe to be affirmative and freely-given permission to the act of sexual penetration." Which definition of force do you prefer? Why? Does *M.T.S.*'s definition of "force" make the force element superfluous? That is, did the court in *M.T.S.* define force in a way in which it is synonymous with non-consent, thus collapsing the elements of "force" and "non-consent"? The Court in *M.T.S.* asserted that it was mindful of the "basic tenet of statutory construction that penal statutes are to be strictly construed in favor of the accused." Did the Court in *M.T.S.* strictly construe the "force" element in favor of the accused? Explain.

6. The Court in *Webster* required that the victim make "her lack of consent reasonably manifest by taking such measures of resistance as [were] called for by the circumstances." This resistance requirement is conceptually distinct from the force requirement. Force is usually construed—as the Court did in *Webster*—to mean something in addition to the force inherent in the non-consensual sexual penetration. In contrast, the resistance requirement has traditionally been viewed as the proof that was legally required to prove the victim's non-consent. Therefore, a sexual act that was not resisted in the way that the law required was simply treated as a sexual act that was legally consented to and, therefore, not punishable. The old common law rule was that the victim had to "resist to the utmost" in order for a rape conviction to stand. The more contemporary trend is to require that the victim resist to the extent that a reasonable person would resist. This version of the rule allows for convictions to stand in certain cases in which the victim did not resist, provided that it is concluded that resistance would have been futile or counterproductive in light of the defendant's conduct. In contrast, according to *M.T.S.*, the prosecution must prove that the sexual act "was accomplished without the affirmative and freely-given permission of the alleged victim." The victim is thus not required to resist in order for a rape conviction to stand. It is sufficient that the victim did not "affirmatively and freely" give permission to the act. Which is the better view? Why?

7. Force and resistance are not required when the victim is incapable of consent. This typically occurs when the victim is under a certain age (statutory rape), when her capacity to consent is impaired because of mental disease or defect, when she is so grossly

intoxicated that she cannot meaningfully consent to sex, and when she is otherwise unconscious. Given that the law presumes that in these cases the victim is incapable of consent, it is rape to engage in sexual intercourse in these instances regardless of whether the victim nominally consents to sex. The California rape statute is representative:

> Section 261 (a) Rape is an act of sexual intercourse accomplished with a person not the spouse of the perpetrator, under any of the following circumstances:
>
> > (1) Where a person is incapable, because of a mental disorder or developmental or physical disability, of giving legal consent, and this is known or reasonably should be known to the person committing the act ...
> >
> > (3) Where a person is prevented from resisting by any intoxicating or anesthetic substance, or any controlled substance, and this condition was known, or reasonably should have been known by the accused....
> >
> > (4) Where a person is at the time unconscious of the nature of the act, and this is known to the accused....

When is a person "unconscious of the nature of the act" in rape cases? Obvious instances are when the person is asleep or in an actual state of unconsciousness, such as a coma. But what about a person who is induced to engage in a sexual act by fraudulent misrepresentations? Is such a person "unconscious of the nature of the act"? The next section addresses this question.

## § 21.02 Rape: Objective Elements of the Offense — Consent and Rape by Fraud

### Suliveres v. Commonwealth

Supreme Judicial Court of Massachusetts, 2007
449 Mass. 112

COWIN, J.

In *Commonwealth v. Goldenberg*, we concluded that it is not rape when consent to sexual intercourse is obtained through fraud or deceit. In determining [this we focused on the state] definition of rape as sexual intercourse compelled "by force and against [the] will" of the victim, [and] we stated that "[f]raud cannot be allowed to supply the place of the force which the statute makes mandatory." In the present case, the Commonwealth asks us to overrule the *Goldenberg* decision and hold that misrepresentations can in fact substitute for the requisite force. Because the *Goldenberg* case has been the law for nearly one-half century, during which the Legislature has had ample opportunity to change the rape statute and has not done so, we decline to overrule our decision in *Goldenberg*.

*Relevant law.* The crime of rape is defined in G.L. c. 265, § 22(*b*): "Whoever has sexual intercourse or unnatural sexual intercourse with a person and compels such person to submit by force and against his will, or compels such person to submit by threat of bodily injury, shall be punished...." This definition has changed over time, but the requirement that the act be "by force and against [the] will" of the victim has remained constant for two hundred years. We have said that "by force" and "against [the] will" are "two separate elements each of which must independently be satisfied."

In *Commonwealth v. Goldenberg, supra,* we considered, as a matter of first impression, whether rape could be committed by fraud. The *Goldenberg* case involved a woman who had gone to the defendant, a physiotherapist, to procure an abortion. The defendant told her that, as part of the procedure, he "had to have intercourse" with her and that it would "help it some way." He then proceeded to have intercourse with her. We noted that "it could not be found beyond a reasonable doubt that the intercourse was without her consent," and that the evidence "negatived the use of force." Thus, the only way the defendant could have been convicted was if his fraudulent representation that the intercourse was medically necessary could both invalidate the consent and supply the requisite "force." We concluded, however, that "[f]raud cannot be allowed to supply the place of the force which the statute makes mandatory".

*Facts.* We turn now to the facts of the present case, viewed in the light most favorable to the Commonwealth. On the night in question, the defendant had sexual intercourse with the complainant by impersonating her longtime boy friend, his brother. According to the complainant, while she was asleep alone in the bedroom she shared with her boy friend, the defendant entered the room, and she awoke. In the dark room, the complainant assumed that the defendant was her boy friend returning home from work, and addressed him by her boy friend's name. He got into the bed and had intercourse with her. The complainant was "not fully awake" at the time of penetration. During the intercourse, she believed that the man was her boy friend, and had she known it was the defendant, she "would have never consented."

The defendant was indicted for rape and tried before a jury in the Superior Court. At trial, the main issue was whether the complainant knew at the time the identity of the person with whom she was having sex. The defense was that the sex was fully consensual. The defendant told an investigating police officer that the complainant had come to him while he was asleep in another room and had invited him to her bedroom to have sex with her. The Commonwealth argued that the defendant had procured the complainant's consent to sex fraudulently by impersonating her boy friend.

*Procedural history.* The defendant moved for a required finding of not guilty at the close of the Commonwealth's evidence, but the motion was denied. The jury were unable to reach a verdict, and the judge declared a mistrial. The defendant then moved to dismiss the indictment, arguing that the Commonwealth had failed to present sufficient evidence to support a guilty verdict at trial, and that any subsequent retrial would thus violate common-law principles of double jeopardy …

*Standard of review.* In determining whether the Commonwealth presented sufficient evidence to support a finding of guilt so as to permit a subsequent retrial without violating double jeopardy principles, we apply the familiar standard: "whether, after viewing the evidence in the light most favorable to the prosecution, *any* rational trier of fact could have found the essential elements of the crime beyond a reasonable doubt" (emphasis in original).

*Discussion.* Taking the evidence in the light most favorable to the Commonwealth, we assume that the defendant fraudulently induced the complainant to have intercourse. However, as noted above, the rule of *Commonwealth v. Goldenberg,* is that intercourse where consent is achieved by fraud does not constitute rape. That rule compels the conclusion that there was no evidence of rape in this case, and we decline to overrule the *Goldenberg* decision.

*The rule of the* Goldenberg *decision.* For all purposes relevant to this case, the crime of rape is defined by statute as nonconsensual intercourse achieved "by force." The Commonwealth, advancing the same argument that was rejected in the *Goldenberg* decision, contends that the defendant's fraud should be allowed to satisfy the requirement of force. In requesting that we overrule the *Goldenberg* case, the Commonwealth asks us to read "force" out of the statute in cases involving misrepresentation as to identity. Yet we have never suggested that force is not an element of the crime, or that "by force" is synonymous with lack of consent. Because "[n]o portion of the statutory language may be deemed superfluous," we are not free, any more than we were in the *Goldenberg* case, to adopt the Commonwealth's proposed interpretation ...

*Whether the* Goldenberg *decision is distinguishable.* [T]he Commonwealth attempts to distinguish the *Goldenberg* decision on the ground that it involved "fraud in the inducement" while the present case is one of "fraud in the factum." We find this argument unpersuasive. Assuming that there is a distinction that is meaningful in the context of sexual intercourse, we examine the concepts involved. The term "fraud in the factum" typically refers to "the rare case when there has been fraud as to the essential nature of [a legal] instrument or an essential element of it." "Fraud in the inducement," by contrast, occurs "when a misrepresentation leads another to enter into a transaction with a false impression of the risks, duties, or obligations involved," but there is no fraud as to the essential nature of the transaction. In the context of rape, by analogy, "fraud in the factum" must mean that the victim is defrauded as to the nature of the act performed, rather than the reason for doing it. Compare *Boro v. Superior Court* (fraud in factum where victim consents to doctor's penetration of her with medical instrument but he then penetrates her with his penis), with *State v. Bolsinger* (fraud in inducement where defendant touched victims' genitals on pretext of medical examination because they were "touched in exactly the manner represented to them"). In the present case, there is no claim that the complainant did not know she was consenting to a sex act; rather, just as in the *Goldenberg* case, her consent was induced by fraud as to the circumstances surrounding the act. Thus, the present case involves "fraud in the inducement," as did *Goldenberg,* and is squarely controlled by that decision.

*Conclusion.* Fraudulently obtaining consent to sexual intercourse does not constitute rape as defined in our statute. Accordingly, the defendant's motion for a required finding of not guilty should have been granted. This case is remanded to the county court for entry of an appropriate order by the single justice barring a subsequent retrial on double jeopardy grounds.

## Notes and Questions

1. As the *Suliveres* case illustrates, fraudulently obtaining consent through false misrepresentations seldom vitiates consent to the extent required by rape. When it does, however, it is usually in cases of "fraud in the factum." Fraud in the factum occurs when the defendant's fraudulent misrepresentation lead the victim to incorrectly believe that she is consenting to an act that is not sexual intercourse. The most cited example is that of a gynecologist who represents to the patient that he is going to perform a medical procedure when he in fact he engages in sexual intercourse with the victim. In such cases, the victim consents to a medical procedure rather than to sexual intercourse. As a result, many courts argue that the actor may be held liable for rape because the victim is "unconcious" of the nature of the act that she is consenting to. In contrast, fraud in the inducement is typically held to not give rise to liability for rape. The reason typically afforded in favor of this conclusion is that in cases of fraud in the inducement the victim is aware that she is consenting to sex, although she is deceived as to some collateral matter.

2. In the oft-cited case of *Boro v. Superior Court,* the defendant falsely told the victim that he was a doctor and that she was infected with a deadly disease that could only be treated by either having a very expensive surgical procedure or by engaging in sexual intercourse with an anonymous donor that would deposit the disease-curing serum when he ejaculated inside of her. Given that the victim did not have much money, she consented to having sex with the "anonymous" donor. The anonymous donor was the defendant, who was subsequently prosecuted for perpetrating a rape by fraud. Was the victim unconscious of the nature of the act to the extent that the defendant could be successfully prosecuted for rape? The court concluded that the act could not be punished as rape, observing that:

> Our research discloses sparse California authority on [whether fraud vitiates consent in rape cases]. A victim need not be totally and physically unconscious in order [for rape to occur]. In *People v. Minkowski,* the defendant was a physician who "treated" several victims for menstrual cramps. Each victim testified that she was treated in a position with her back to the doctor, bent over a table, with feet apart, in a dressing gown. And in each case the "treatment" consisted of the defendant first inserting a metal instrument, then substituting an instrument which "felt different"—the victims not realizing that the second instrument was in fact the doctor's penis. The precise issue before us was never tendered in *People v. Minkowski* because the petitioner there *conceded* the sufficiency of evidence to support the element of consciousness.
>
> The decision is useful to this analysis, however, because it exactly illustrates certain traditional rules in the area of our inquiry. Thus, as a leading authority has written, "if deception causes a misunderstanding as to the fact itself (fraud in the *factum*) there is no legally-recognized consent because what happened is not that for which consent was given; whereas consent induced by fraud is as effective as any other consent, so far as direct and immediate legal consequences are concerned, if the deception relates not to the thing done but merely to some collateral matter (fraud in the inducement)."
>
> The victims in *Minkowski* consented, not to sexual intercourse, but to an act of an altogether different nature, penetration by medical instrument. The consent was to a pathological, and not a carnal, act, and the mistake was, therefore, in the *factum* and not merely in the inducement.
>
> Another relatively common situation in the literature on this subject—discussed in detail … is the fraudulent obtaining of intercourse by impersonating a spouse. As Professor Perkins observes, the courts are not in accord as to whether the crime of rape is thereby committed. "[T]he disagreement is not in regard to the underlying principle but only as to its application. Some courts have taken the position that such a misdeed is fraud in the inducement on the theory that the woman consents to exactly what is done (sexual intercourse) and hence there is no rape; other courts, with better reason it would seem, hold such a misdeed to be rape on the theory that it involves fraud in the *factum* since the woman's consent is to an innocent act of marital intercourse while what is actually perpetrated upon her is an act of adultery. Her innocence seems never to have been questioned in such a case and the reason she is not guilty of adultery is because she did not consent to adulterous intercourse. Statutory changes in the law of rape have received attention earlier and need not be repeated here."
>
> In California, of course, we have by statute adopted the majority view that such fraud is in the *factum*, not the inducement, and have thus held it to vitiate con-

> sent. It is otherwise, however, with respect to the conceptually much murkier statutory offense with which we here deal, and the language of which has remained essentially unchanged since its enactment in 1872.
>
> The language itself could not be plainer. It defines rape to be "an act of sexual intercourse" with a nonspouse, accomplished where the victim is "at the time unconscious of the nature of the act ..." .... Moreover, courts of this state have previously confronted the general rule that fraud in the inducement does not vitiate consent. [In] *Mathews* [we] found section 266 (fraudulent procurement of a female for illicit carnal connection) inapplicable where the facts showed that the defendant, impersonating an unmarried woman's paramour, made sexual advances to the victim with her consent. While the facts demonstrate classic fraud in the *factum*, a concurring opinion in *Mathews* specifically decried the lack of a California statutory prohibition against fraudulently induced consent to sexual relations in circumstances other than those specified in section 261, subdivision (5) and then—section 268. 163 Cal. App. 3d 1224 (1985)

Turning to the facts of the case, the Court concluded that from the victim's testimony it "was clear that she precisely understood the 'nature of the act,' but, motivated by a fear of disease, and death, succumbed to petitioner's fraudulent blandishments." Although the Court condemned what it called the "heartless cruelty of petitioner's scheme," it held that the scheme simply did not give rise to liability for rape. Do you agree with the outcome in *Boro*? Why or why not?

3. Even if it is conceded that the defendant in *Boro* should have been acquitted of rape, was his conduct nevertheless worthy of condemnation and punishment? If so, would it be appropriate for a legislature to create a separate offense criminalizing sex obtained by fraud? Assuming that creating such an offense is appropriate, should it be punished more, less or the same as rape? What would be the costs and benefits of enacting such a statute?

4. Note that the Court in *Boro* pointed out that many jurisdictions have held that impersonating to be the victim's spouse should be considered "fraud in the factum" and, therefore, give rise to liability for rape. Nevertheless, jurisdictions that apply this rule often hold that the rule applies only when the actor impersonates being the spouse of the victim, not when he impersonates being the victim's boyfriend. Does the distinction between these two cases make sense? What result if the *Boro* analysis of fraud in the factum vs. fraud in the inducement is applied to the facts that gave rise to the *Suliveres* case? Explain.

## § 21.03 Rape: Objective Elements of the Offense—Consent and Threats/Abuse of Authority

### State v. Thompson

Supreme Court of Montana, 1990
243 Mont. 28

SHEEHY, Justice.

On May 25, 1989, the defendant Gerald Roy Thompson was charged with two counts of sexual intercourse without consent and one count of sexual assault. Subsequently, Thompson moved to dismiss Counts I and II of the information, those counts charging defendant with sexual intercourse without consent. Thompson moved to dismiss Counts

I and II of the information on the specific ground that the probable cause affidavit was insufficient. On September 1, 1989, the District Court, Tenth Judicial District, Judith Basin County, granted Thompson's motion and dismissed Counts I and II of the information for lack of probable cause in the supporting affidavit. The State now appeals the District Court. We affirm.

The State raised the following issue on appeal: Did the District Court err when it granted defendant's motion to dismiss Counts I and II of the information charging defendant with sexual intercourse without consent for failure to state offenses?

The defendant, Gerald Roy Thompson, the principal and boys basketball coach at Hobson High School, was accused of two counts of sexual intercourse without consent, and one count of sexual assault. This appeal only concerns the two counts of sexual intercourse without consent. The information, filed with the District Court, alleged the defendant committed the crime of sexual intercourse without consent, and stated the following:

**Count I**

On or between September, 1986 and January, 1987 in Judith Basin County, Montana, the defendant knowingly had sexual intercourse without consent with a person of the opposite sex; namely Jane Doe, by threatening Jane Doe that she would not graduate from high school and forced Jane Doe to engage in an act of oral sexual intercourse.

**Count II**

On or between February, 1987 and June, 1987 in Judith Basin County, Montana, the defendant knowingly had sexual intercourse without consent with a person of the opposite sex; namely Jane Doe, by threatening Jane Doe that she would not graduate from high school and forced Jane Doe to engage in act of oral sexual intercourse.

The affidavits filed in support of this information contained facts and allegations supporting the two counts of sexual intercourse without consent. In essence, they alleged that the threats "caused Jane Doe great psychological pain and fear."

The State contended that fear of the power of Thompson and his authority to keep her from graduating forced Jane Doe into silence until after she graduated from high school in June of 1987. On November 25, 1988, Jane Doe filed a letter with the Hobson School Board describing the activities against her by Thompson. After investigations by both the school board and the Judith Basin County prosecutor's office, the prosecutor filed an information on May 25, 1989. The information charged Thompson with two counts of sexual intercourse without consent, both felonies in violation of § 45-5-503, MCA, and with one count of attempted sexual assault, a felony ...

The District Court granted Thompson's motion, due to the fact the State failed to meet the element of "without consent" under § 45-5-501, MCA.

I

Did the District Court err when it granted defendant's motion to dismiss Counts I and II of the information charging defendant with sexual intercourse without consent for failure to state offenses?

We agree with the District Court that the facts in the information, in regards to Counts I and II, fail to state offenses ...

The allegations in the affidavit, however, do not indicate a probability that Thompson committed the crime of sexual intercourse without consent.

Thompson was charged with two counts of alleged sexual intercourse without consent under § 45-5-503, MCA. Section 45-5-503, MCA, states the following:

> A person who knowingly has sexual intercourse without consent with a person of the opposite sex commits the offense of sexual intercourse without consent ...

The phrase "without consent"—the key element of the crime—has a very specific definition in Montana's criminal code. This phrase is defined in § 45-5-501, MCA, which states in pertinent part:

> As used in 45-5-503 and 45-5-505, the term "without consent" means:
>
> (i) the victim is compelled to submit by force or by threat of imminent death, bodily injury, or kidnapping to be inflicted on anyone; ...

Section 45-5-501, MCA, makes it clear that the element of "without consent" is satisfied if submission of the victim is obtained either by force or by threat of imminent death, bodily injury, or kidnapping. No other circumstances relating to force or threat eliminate consent under the statute.

Thompson challenged the probable cause affidavit in the District Court, contending it failed to state any fact or circumstance showing that Jane Doe's submission to an alleged act of sexual intercourse was obtained by force or by any of the threats listed in § 45-5-501, MCA. In contrast, the State argues that Thompson's actions constitute sexual intercourse through force or threats. The District Court, in its opinion and order, agreed with Thompson's contentions, and found that the facts in the affidavit supporting the information failed to show the element of "without consent." ...

In contrast, the State argues the District Court's definition of force is too limited. The State ... argues that intimidation and fear may constitute force. The State also contends that Thompson, in his position of authority as the principal, intimidated Jane Doe into the alleged acts. Furthermore, the State argues the fear and apprehension of Jane Doe show Thompson used force against her. We agree with the State that Thompson intimidated Jane Doe; however, we cannot stretch the definition of force to include intimidation, fear, or apprehension. Rather, we adopt the District Court's definition of force.

Other jurisdictions, such as California, have expanded the definition of force, beyond its physical connotation. *People v. Cicero* (1984), 157 Cal.App.3d 465, 204 Cal.Rptr. 582. The California Supreme Court adopted the following reasoning to expand the word force:

> ... the fundamental wrong at which the law of rape is aimed is not the application of physical force that causes physical harm. Rather, the law of rape primarily guards the integrity of a women's will and the privacy of her sexuality from an act of intercourse undertaken without her consent. Because the fundamental wrong is the violation of a woman's will and sexuality, the law of rape does not require that "force" cause physical harm. Rather, in this scenario, "force" plays merely a supporting evidentiary role, as necessary only to ensure an act of intercourse has been undertaken against a victim's will.

The California Supreme Court's definition of the word force is too broad under Montana's definition of the crime. Until the legislature adopts a definition for the word "force", we must adopt the ordinary and normal definition of the word "force" as set forth by the District Court.

The State in its information and accompanying affidavit complain that Thompson deprived Jane Doe of consent to the sexual act by threatening that he would prevent her from graduating from high school. The threat required in § 45-5-501, MCA, is "a threat of imminent death, bodily injury, or kidnapping to be inflicted on anyone ..." The District Court found that something more than a threat is necessary to satisfy the statutory requirement. A threat one will not graduate from high school is not one of the threats listed under § 45-5-501, MCA. The State argues that the definition "threat of bodily injury" includes psychological impairment. Unfortunately, the statute sets forth bodily injury, not psychological impairment. A threat that eventually leads to psychological impairment is not sufficient under the statute. The statute only addresses the results of three specific kinds of threats, and psychological impairment is not one of them.

The State urges this Court to adopt the definitions of threat set forth in § 45-2-101(68), MCA. Section 45-2-101(68), MCA, has no application in regard to the crime of sexual intercourse without consent. Section 45-5-501, MCA, plainly and succinctly lays out the types of threats necessary to make the victim act "without consent."

Under § 45-5-501, MCA, the threat also must be of "*imminent* death, bodily injury, or kidnapping." Thompson's threats cannot be considered imminent. The alleged sexual act and threat occurred in December of 1986. Jane Doe graduated from Hobson High School in June of 1987. Clearly, Thompson's alleged threats were not imminent ...

This case is one of considerable difficulty for us, as indeed it must have been for the District Court judge. The alleged facts, if true, show disgusting acts of taking advantage of a young person by an adult who occupied a position of authority over the young person. If we could rewrite the statutes to define the alleged acts here as sexual intercourse without consent, we would willingly do so. The business of courts, however, is to interpret statutes, not to rewrite them, nor to insert words not put there by the legislature. With a good deal of reluctance, and with strong condemnation of the alleged acts, we affirm the District Court.

### *Notes and Questions*

1. Do you believe that the defendant in *Thompson* engaged in conduct that should give rise to criminal liability? If so, should the defendant in *Thompson* be punished for rape or should he be held liable for a less serious offense? Since the defendant did not use physical force against the victims, the court held that he could not be held liable for rape. The Court explained that under Montana law a conviction for rape could only be secured if consent was negated by threats of physical force and threats to not allow the victims to graduate simply do not amount to "physical force." But could defendant have been held liable for rape if the offense was defined simply as engaging in non-consensual sexual intercourse? That is, do you believe that the sex in this case was non-consensual even if there was no threat of physical force? What result if the case had been tried in New Jersey and force was defined in the way that *State in the Interest of M.T.S.* held it should?

2. In *Commonwealth v. Milnarich,* 518 Pa. 247 (1988), an adult guardian of a 14-year-old female threatened to send her back to a juvenile detention facility if she refused to perform oral sex on him. The victim acquiesced and the adult guardian was subsequently charged with rape. The Pennsylvania Supreme Court concluded that the facts did not amount to rape. According to the Court:

> The gravamen of common law rape was the non-volitional participation of the woman in the act, either because of being overpowered by force or being confronted with imminent threat of serious bodily injury or both. In either of these instances the victim's submission was deemed not to be the product of her will and the nonconsensual quality of her participation was established ...

> The critical distinction [between rape and non-rape] is where the compulsion overwhelms the will of the victim in contrast to a situation where the victim can make a deliberate choice to avoid the encounter even though the alternative may be an undesirable one. Indeed, the victim in this instance apparently found the prospect of being returned to the detention home a repugnant one. Notwithstanding, she was left with a choice and therefore the submission was a result of a deliberate choice and was not an involuntary act. This is not in any way to deny the despicable nature of appellee's conduct or even to suggest that it was not criminal. We are merely constrained to recognize that it does not meet the test of "forcible compulsion" set forth in [the relevant rape provisions].

A dissenting judge vehemently disagreed with the majority in *Milnarich.* The dissent explained:

> The crime of rape is accomplished when a person "engages in sexual intercourse with another person not his spouse ... by threat of forcible compulsion that would prevent resistance by a person of reasonable resolution."
>
> The gravamen of rape is to take what would not be given except for "forcible compulsion," or "threats" of forcible compulsion.
>
> That all threats, however compelling in the mind of the actor, leave a choice in the victim is not to be denied. If one yields their bodily integrity for small reason the law may imply their consent. What reasons are small and what sufficient to compel assent are subject to interpretation under the circumstances of the occasion. Not every threat is necessarily such that it presents an illegal choice to persons of reasonable resolution.
>
> The question here is whether the return of a person to confinement qualifies as a threat of forcible compulsion sufficient to overcome reasonable resolve. If it is such, then whether fact finders could find that it in fact overcame reasonable resolution, given the circumstances, remains for them to decide.
>
> Three members of this Court have decided, however, that the question cannot be put, because to their minds the victim had choices that could be exercised, choices that would have obviated the occasion. To my mind, under the circumstances here, that view is an arcane quibble.
>
> A person may well believe that one who secured her release could return her to confinement. Confinement in a detention facility is, among other things, a *punishment* provided by law, which by its very nature is a serious loss in the life of a person: a condition only imposed, as a last resort, by proper judicial officers. Its purposes and unpleasantness were not designed as an adjunct for would-be rapists.
>
> Here the threats were employed to deprive the victim of her freedom; to institutionalize her if she did not yield. The size of the dread imposed upon her is certainly a question for fact finders to determine, and not a question of law that implies there could be no forcible compulsion in such a threat. The question is not whether she could make a choice to yield or be confined, but whether the law should allow such a choice at all. The purpose of law is to narrow the choices that may be offered to compel others in order to gain an end of one's own. Certainly, we should be spared, where possible, choices imposed by others that require surrender or certain punishment.
>
> The threat of confinement, that a victim could believe possible, is objectively a threat of forcible compulsion that could, as here, overcome a person's reason-

> able resolve. It ought not be a choice one may legally impose upon another. The actor believed it sufficient to gain his end and so did the jury. Under any standard we ought not to countenance, as a game of choices, so clear and deliberate a threat.

Who has the better part of this argument? Assuming that the acts of the defendant should be punished, should they be punished as severely as rape or less harshly? Why?

## § 21.04 Rape: Subjective Elements of the Offense — Mistake of Fact

### Commonwealth v. López

Supreme Judicial Court of Massachusetts, 2001
433 Mass. 722

SPINA, J.

The defendant, Kenny Lopez, was convicted on two indictments charging rape and one indictment charging indecent assault and battery on a person over the age of fourteen years. We granted his application for direct appellate review. The defendant claims error in the judge's refusal to give a mistake of fact instruction to the jury. He asks us to recognize a defendant's honest and reasonable belief as to a complainant's consent as a defense to the crime of rape, and to reverse his convictions and grant him a new trial. Based on the record presented, we decline to do so, and affirm the convictions.

1. *Background.* We summarize facts that the jury could have found. On May 8, 1998, the victim, a seventeen year old girl, was living in a foster home in Springfield. At approximately 3 P.M., she started walking to a restaurant where she had planned to meet her biological mother. On the way, she encountered the defendant. He introduced himself, asked where she was going, and offered to walk with her. The victim met her mother and introduced the defendant as her friend. The defendant said that he lived in the same foster home as the victim and that "they knew each other from school." Sometime later, the defendant left to make a telephone call. When the victim left the restaurant, the defendant was waiting outside and offered to walk her home. She agreed.

The two walked to a park across the street from the victim's foster home and talked for approximately twenty to thirty minutes. The victim's foster sisters were within earshot, and the victim feared that she would be caught violating her foster mother's rules against bringing "a guy near the house." The defendant suggested that they take a walk in the woods nearby. At one point, deep in the woods, the victim said that she wanted to go home. The defendant said, "trust me," and assured her that nothing would happen and that he would not hurt her. The defendant led the victim down a path to a secluded area.

The defendant asked the victim why she was so distant and said that he wanted to start a relationship with her. She said that she did not want to "get into any relationship." The defendant began making sexual innuendos to which the victim did not respond. He grabbed her by her wrist and began kissing her on the lips. She pulled away and said, "No, I don't want to do this." The defendant then told the victim that if she "had sex with him, [she] would love him more." She repeated, "No, I don't want to. I don't want to do this." He raised her shirt and touched her breasts. She immediately pulled her shirt down and pushed him away.

The defendant then pushed the victim against a slate slab, unbuttoned her pants, and pulled them down. Using his legs to pin down her legs, he produced a condom and asked her to put it on him. The victim said, "No." The defendant put the condom on and told the victim that he wanted her to put his penis inside her. She said, "No." He then raped her, and she began to cry. A few minutes later, the victim made a "jerking move" to her left. The defendant became angry, turned her around, pushed her face into the slate, and raped her again. The treating physician described the bruising to the victim's knees as "significant." The physician opined that there had been "excessive force and trauma to the [vaginal] area" based on his observation that there was "a lot of swelling" in her external vaginal area and her hymen had been torn and was "still oozing." The doctor noted that in his experience it was "fairly rare" to see that much swelling and trauma.

The defendant told the victim that she "would get in a lot of trouble" if she said anything. He then grabbed her by the arm, kissed her, and said, "I'll see you later." The victim went home and showered. She told her foster mother, who immediately dialed 911. The victim cried hysterically as she spoke to the 911 operator.

The defendant's version of the encounter was diametrically opposed to that of the victim. He testified that the victim had been a willing and active partner in consensual sexual intercourse. Specifically, the defendant claimed that the victim initiated intimate activity, and never once told him to stop. Additionally, the defendant testified that the victim invited him to a party that evening so that he could meet her friends. The defendant further claimed that when he told her that he would be unable to attend, the victim appeared "mildly upset."

Before the jury retired, defense counsel requested a mistake of fact instruction as to consent. The judge declined to give the instruction, saying that, based "both on the law, as well as on the facts, that instruction is not warranted." Because the defendant's theory at trial was that the victim actually consented and not that the defendant was "confused, misled, or mistaken" as to the victim's willingness to engage in sexual intercourse, the judge concluded that the ultimate question for the jury was simply whether they believed the victim's or the defendant's version of the encounter. The decision not to give the instruction provides the basis for this appeal.

*Mistake of fact instruction.* The defendant claims that the judge erred in failing to give his proposed mistake of fact instruction. The defendant, however, was not entitled to this instruction. In *Commonwealth v. Ascolillo*, we held that the defendant was not entitled to a mistake of fact instruction, and declined to adopt a rule that "in order to establish the crime of rape the Commonwealth must prove *in every case* not only that the defendant intended intercourse but also that he did not act pursuant to an honest and reasonable belief that the victim consented" Neither the plain language of our rape statute nor this court's decisions prior to the *Ascolillo* decision warrant a different result.

A fundamental tenet of criminal law is that culpability requires a showing that the prohibited conduct (actus reus) was committed with the concomitant mental state (mens rea) prescribed for the offense. The mistake of fact "defense" is available where the mistake negates the existence of a mental state essential to a material element of the offense. In determining whether the defendant's honest and reasonable belief as to the victim's consent would relieve him of culpability, it is necessary to review the required elements of the crime of rape.

[The Commonwealth rape] statute follows the common-law definition of rape, and requires the Commonwealth to prove beyond a reasonable doubt that the defendant committed (1) sexual intercourse (2) by force or threat of force and against the will of the victim....

Although the Commonwealth must prove lack of consent, the "elements necessary for rape do not require that the defendant intend the intercourse be without consent." Historically, the relevant inquiry has been limited to consent in fact, and no mens rea or knowledge as to the lack of consent has ever been required.

A mistake of fact as to consent, therefore, has very little application to our rape statute. Because G.L. c. 265, § 22, does not require proof of a defendant's knowledge of the victim's lack of consent or intent to engage in nonconsensual intercourse as a material element of the offense, a mistake as to that consent cannot, therefore, negate a mental state required for commission of the prohibited conduct. Any perception (reasonable, honest, or otherwise) of the defendant as to the victim's consent is consequently not relevant to a rape prosecution.

This is not to say, contrary to the defendant's suggestion, that the absence of any mens rea as to the consent element transforms rape into a strict liability crime. It does not. Rape, at common law and pursuant to G.L. c. 265, § 22, is a general intent crime, and proof that a defendant intended sexual intercourse by force coupled with proof that the victim did not in fact consent is sufficient to maintain a conviction.

Other jurisdictions have held that a mistake of fact instruction is necessary to prevent injustice. New Jersey, for instance, does not require the force necessary for rape to be anything more than what is needed to accomplish penetration. See *In re M.T.S.*, 129. Thus, an instruction as to a defendant's honest and reasonable belief as to consent is available in New Jersey to mitigate the undesirable and unforeseen consequences that may flow from this construction. By contrast, in this Commonwealth, unless the putative victim has been rendered incapable of consent, the prosecution must prove that the defendant compelled the victim's submission by use of physical force; nonphysical, constructive force; or threat of force. Proof of the element of force, therefore, should negate any possible mistake as to consent.

We also have concerns that the mistake of fact defense would tend to eviscerate the long-standing rule in this Commonwealth that victims need not use any force to resist an attack. A shift in focus from the victim's to the defendant's state of mind might require victims to use physical force in order to communicate an unqualified lack of consent to defeat any honest and reasonable belief as to consent. The mistake of fact defense is incompatible with the evolution of our jurisprudence with respect to the crime of rape.

We are cognizant that our interpretation is not shared by the majority of other jurisdictions. States that recognize a mistake of fact as to consent generally have done so by legislation. Some State statutes expressly require a showing of a defendant's intent as to nonconsent. Alaska, for example, requires proof of a culpable state of mind. "Lack of consent is a 'surrounding circumstance' which under the Revised Code, requires a complementary mental state as well as conduct to constitute a crime." *Reynolds v. State*. Because no specific mental state is mentioned in Alaska's statute governing sexual assault in the first degree, the State "must prove that the defendant acted 'recklessly' regarding his putative victim's lack of consent." So understood, an honest and reasonable mistake as to consent would negate the culpability requirement attached to the element of consent. *See* Colo.Rev.Stat. § 18-3-402(1) (1999) ("Any actor who knowingly inflicts sexual intrusion or sexual penetration on a victim commits sexual assault ..."); Or.Rev.Stat. §§ 161.115(2) (1999) ("Except as provided in [Or.Rev.Stat. § ] 161.105, if a statute defining an offense does not prescribe a culpable mental state, culpability is nonetheless required and is established only if a person acts intentionally, knowingly, recklessly or with criminal negligence"); Tex.Penal Code § 22.021(a)(1)(A)(i) (West Supp.2001) ("A person commits an offense if the person ... intentionally or knowingly ... causes the penetration of the anus or female sexual organ of another person by any means, without that person's consent").

The New Jersey statute defines sexual assault (rape) as "any act of sexual penetration engaged in by the defendant without the affirmative and freely-given permission of the victim to the specific act of penetration." *In re M.T.S.* A defendant, by claiming that he had permission to engage in sexual intercourse, places his state of mind directly in issue. The jury must then determine "whether the defendant's belief that the alleged victim had freely given affirmative permission was reasonable."

The mistake of fact "defense" has been recognized by judicial decision in some States. In 1975, the Supreme Court of California became the first State court to recognize a mistake of fact defense in rape cases. See *People v. Mayberry*. Although the court did not make a specific determination that intent was required as to the element of consent, it did conclude that, "[i]f a defendant entertains a reasonable and bona fide belief that a prosecutrix [*sic*] voluntarily consented ... to engage in sexual intercourse, it is apparent he does not possess the wrongful intent that is a prerequisite under Penal Code section 20 to a conviction of ... rape by means of force or threat." Thus, the intent required is an intent to engage in nonconsensual sexual intercourse, and the State must prove that a defendant intentionally engaged in intercourse and was at least negligent regarding consent.

Other State courts have employed a variety of different constructions in adopting the mistake of fact defense. See *State v. Smith* ("We arrive at that result, however, not on the basis of our penal code provision relating to a mistake of fact ... but on the ground that whether a complainant should be found to have consented depends upon how her behavior would have been viewed by a reasonable person under the surrounding circumstances"); *State v. Koonce* (construing rape statute to require defendant acted at least recklessly as to consent).

However, the minority of States sharing our view is significant. See *People v. Witte* ("whether the defendant intended to commit the offense[s] without the victim's consent is not relevant, the critical question being whether the victim did, in fact, consent. This involves her mental state, not the defendant's"); *State v. Christensen* ("[D]efendant's awareness of a putative sexual abuse victim's lack of consent is not an**969 element of third-degree sexual abuse.... [I]t follows from this premise that a defendant's mistake of fact as to that consent would not negate an element of the offense")....

This case does not persuade us that we should recognize a mistake of fact as to consent as a defense to rape in *all* cases. Whether such a defense might, in some circumstances, be appropriate is a difficult question that we may consider on a future case where a defendant's claim of reasonable mistake of fact is at least arguably supported by the evidence. This is not such a case.

Judgments affirmed.

## *Notes and Questions*

1. As is pointed out in *López,* it may be argued that there is little need for a mistake of fact defense regarding consent in rape prosecutions if the governing statute requires that force be used to compel the victim to engage in sexual intercourse. It is difficult to imagine a scenario in which a defendant who uses force to compel a victim to have sex can in good faith believe that the victim is consenting to the act. This, in a nutshell, is what the

Supreme Judicial Court of Massachusetts held in *López*. Given that the state rape statute requires that the victim be compelled to have sex by the use (or threatened use) of force, the Court concluded that there was no need for a mistake of fact defense regarding consent, for any claim that the victim consented to intercourse is negated by the fact that force had to be used to compel the victim to submit to the actor's demands for sex. Do you find this argument persuasive? Why or why not?

2. The need for a mistake of fact defense becomes considerably stronger when the governing rape statute either does not require the use of force or defines force in a way that the force inherent in the sexual act itself satisfies the force requirement. As the Court pointed out in *López*, this is what happens in New Jersey. Pursuant to the Supreme Court of New Jersey's decision in *State in the Interest of M.T.S.* (excerpted in § 21.01 of this Chapter), "any act of sexual penetration engaged in by the defendant without the affirmative and freely-given permission of the victim to the specific act of penetration" is punished as rape. When rape is defined in this manner, some defendants may plausibly claim that they simply were not aware that the victim had not consented. As a result of this, some courts allow defendants to plead mistake of fact when prosecuted under these statutes. Therefore, in *M.T.S.*, the Supreme Court of New Jersey held that it is a defense to rape that the defendant reasonably—albeit mistakenly—believed that the victim had freely given affirmative permission to engaging in sexual intercourse.

3. As the Court pointed out in *López*, a majority of jurisdictions currently allow a defendant to plead mistake of fact regarding consent as a defense to rape. In most of these jurisdictions, mistake is a defense only if it is reasonable. An unreasonable mistake regarding consent would thus generate full liability for rape. Nevertheless, a minority of jurisdictions require the prosecution to prove that the defendant acted "recklessly" with regard to the victim's consent. That is, they require that the prosecution show that the defendant was aware that there was a substantial risk that the victim was not consenting to the sexual intercourse. The Supreme Court of Alaska explained the rationale underlying this approach in *Reynolds v. State*, 664 P.2d 621 (1983):

> [T]he [Alaska] legislature has substantially enhanced the risk of conviction in ambiguous circumstances by eliminating the requirement that the state prove "resistance" and by substantially broadening the definitions of "force" and "physical injury." We are satisfied, however, that the legislature counteracted this risk through its treatment of mens rea. It did this by shifting the focus of the jury's attention from the victim's resistance or actions to the defendant's understanding of the totality of the circumstances. Lack of consent is a "surrounding circumstance" which under the Revised Code, requires a complementary mental state as well as conduct to constitute a crime. No specific mental state is mentioned in [the Alaska rape statute] governing the surrounding circumstance of "consent." Therefore, the state must prove that the defendant acted "recklessly" regarding his putative victim's lack of consent. This requirement serves to protect the defendant against conviction for first-degree sexual assault where the circumstances regarding consent are ambiguous at the time he has intercourse with the complaining witness. While the legislature has substantially reduced the state's burden of proof regarding the actus reus of the offense, it has at the same time made it easier for the defendant to argue the defense of mistake of fact. The Alaska rule is more favorable to [the defendant] than the rule [that allows defendants to plead reasonable mistake of fact as a defense to rape] ...

> [As a result], [i]n order to prove [rape], the state must prove that the defendant knowingly engaged in sexual intercourse and recklessly disregarded his victim's lack of consent.

Why did the Supreme Court of Alaska state that the rule they adopted in *Reynolds* is more favorable to defendants than the traditional rule that reasonable mistakes of fact regarding consent defeat liability but unreasonable mistakes do not? Which of these approaches to mistake of fact regarding consent do you prefer? Why?

4. Many American courts hold that rape by engaging in sexual intercourse with a child under the legal age of consent (statutory rape) is a strict liability crime. In these jurisdictions, proof that the defendant mistakenly believed that the victim was over the legal age of consent is not material to rape liability. In *Garnett v. State,* 332 Md. 571 (1993), for example, the defendant argued that he should not be convicted of the crime of "engaging in sexual intercourse with a person under 14 years of old (statutory rape)" because he mistakenly believed that the victim was 16 years old. The court rejected defendant's argument, explaining that "Maryland's [statutory] rape statute defines a strict liability offense that does not require the State to prove *mens rea;* it makes no allowance for a mistake-of-age defense." A considerable number of states have similarly held that statutory rape is a strict liability offense and mistake of fact is thus no defense to liability. See, e.g., *Jenkins v. State,* 110 Nev. 865 (1994). Other courts, however, have held that statutory rape is not a strict liability crime and thus defendant must be allowed to raise mistake of fact regarding the victim's age as a defense. See, e.g., *State v. Guest,* 583 P.2d 836 (1978).

## § 21.04 Rape: Model Penal Code

### Model Penal Code § 213

#### Section 213. 1. Rape and Related Offenses

1. ***Rape.*** A male who has sexual intercourse with a female not his wife is guilty of rape if:

(a) he compels her to submit by force or by threat of imminent death, serious bodily injury, extreme pain or kidnapping, to be inflicted on anyone; or

(b) he has substantially impaired her power to appraise or control her conduct by administering or employing without her knowledge drugs, intoxicants or other means for the purpose of preventing resistance; or

(c) the female is unconscious; or

(d) the female is less than 10 years old.

Rape is a felony of the second degree unless (i) in the course thereof the actor inflicts serious bodily injury upon anyone, or (ii) the victim was not a voluntary social companion of the actor upon the occasion of the crime and had not previously permitted him sexual liberties, in which cases the offense is a felony of the first degree.

2. ***Gross Sexual Imposition.*** A male who has sexual intercourse with a female not his wife commits a felony of the third degree if:

(a) he compels her to submit by any threat that would prevent resistance by a woman of ordinary resolution; or

(b) he knows that she suffers from a mental disease or defect which renders her incapable of appraising the nature of her conduct; or

(c) he knows that she is unaware that a sexual act is being committed upon her or that she submits because she mistakenly supposes that he is her husband.

**§ 213.2. Deviate Sexual Intercourse by Force or Imposition.**

(1) **By Force or Its Equivalent.** A person who engages in deviate sexual intercourse with another person, or who causes another to engage in deviate sexual intercourse, commits a felony of the second degree if:

(a) he compels the other person to participate by force or by threat of imminent death, serious bodily injury, extreme pain or kidnapping, to be inflicted on anyone; or

(b) he has substantially impaired the other person's power to appraise or control his conduct, by administering or employing without the knowledge of the other person drugs, intoxicants or other means for the purpose of preventing resistance; or

(c) the other person is unconscious; or

(d) the other person is less than 10 years old.

(2) **By Other Imposition.** A person who engages in deviate sexual intercourse with another person, or who causes another to engage in deviate sexual intercourse, commits a felony of the third degree if:

(a) he compels the other person to participate by any threat that would prevent resistance by a person of ordinary resolution; or

(b) he knows that the other person suffers from a mental disease or defect which renders him incapable of appraising the nature of his conduct; or

(c) he knows that the other person submits because he is unaware that a sexual act is being committed upon him.

**§ 213.3. Corruption of Minors and Seduction.**

(1) **Offense Defined.** A male who has sexual intercourse with a female not his wife, or any person who engages in deviate sexual intercourse or causes another to engage in deviate sexual intercourse, is guilty of an offense if:

(a) the other person is less than [16] years old and the actor is at least [four] years older than the other person; or

(b) the other person is less than 21 years old and the actor is his guardian or otherwise responsible for general supervision of his welfare; or

(c) the other person is in custody of law or detained in a hospital or other institution and the actor has supervisory or disciplinary authority over him; or

(d) the other person is a female who is induced to participate by a promise of marriage which the actor does not mean to perform.

**§ 213.6. Provisions Generally Applicable to Article 213.**

(1) **Mistake as to Age.** Whenever in this Article the criminality of conduct depends on a child's being below the age of 10, it is no defense that the actor did not know the child's age, or reasonably believed the child to be older than 10. When criminality depends on the child's being below a critical age other than 10, it is a defense for the actor to prove by a preponderance of the evidence that he reasonably believed the child to be above the critical age …

## *Notes and Questions*

1. The Supreme Court of Pennsylvania in *Commonwealth v. Milnarich,* 498 A.2d 395 (1985), explained the Model Penal Code's approach to rape in the following manner:

> The common law definition of rape was determined to be unsatisfactory. It was found inadequate not because of its insistence that force or violence be an essential element but because of its inordinate emphasis on "lack of consent." This element of the offense had been construed to require a woman to resist to the utmost. Therefore, whether she resisted sufficiently was deemed an issue for the jury in most cases where the charge was rape. The rule worked to the unfair disadvantage of the woman who, when threatened with violence, chose quite rationally to submit to her assailant's advances rather than risk death or serious bodily injury.
>
> Because of the often unjust result achieved by the common law definition, the American Law Institute determined to find a more satisfactory approach. The original draft of the Model Penal Code proposed the establishment of separate crimes of "rape" and "intercourse without legally effective consent." The proposed crimes were defined as follows:
>
> Section 207.4. Rape and Related Offenses.
>
> (1) *Rape by Force or Its Equivalent.* A male who has carnal knowledge of a female not his wife commits a felony of the second degree if:
>
> > (a) *He compels her to submit by force or violence or out of fear that death or serious physical injury or extreme pain is about to be inflicted on her or a member of her family, or by threat to commit any felony of the first degree;* or
> >
> > (b) For the purpose of preventing resistance he administers to her or employs, without her knowledge or consent, drugs, intoxicants, or other substance or force resulting in a major deficiency of the victim's power to appraise or control behavior; or
> >
> > (c) The female is unconscious or physically powerless to resist; or
> >
> > (d) The female is less than 10 years old (whether or not the actor is aware of that).
> >
> > An offense within this subsection shall constitute a felony of the first degree if the actor inflicts serious physical injury upon the victim, or if the victim is not a voluntary social companion of the actor and has not previously permitted him sexual liberties.
>
> (2) *Intercourse Without Legally Effective Consent.* A male who has carnal knowledge of a female not his wife, in situations not covered by subsection (1), commits a felony of the third degree if:
>
> > (a) *He compels her to submit by any intimidation* [which would prevent resistance by a woman of ordinary resolution] [reasonably calculated to prevent resistance]; or
> >
> > (b) He knows that her submission is due to substantially complete incapacity to appraise or control her own behavior, but this paragraph shall not apply where a woman over 18 years of age loses that capacity as a result of voluntary use of [intoxicants or] drugs in the company of the actor; or
> >
> > (c) He knows that the female submits because she is unaware that a sexual act is being committed upon her or because she falsely supposes that he is her husband; or

> (d) The female is less than 16 years old and the actor is at least 5 [?] years older than she is; but it shall be a defense under this paragraph if the actor proves that the girl was a prostitute.
>
> ....

> Model Penal Code, § 207.4 (Tentative Draft No. 4 1955) (emphasis added). The Commentary explained that paragraph (a) of subsection (1) was intended to cover "the classic rape cases, where the woman [had been] overpowered by violence or the threat of it." By requiring only that the victim be "compelled to submit," and not that she resist "to the utmost," it was intended to eliminate to a great extent the requirement that a woman struggle when struggle would be useless and dangerous. Subsection (2), on the other hand, was designed to emphasize the absence of voluntary consent. The Comment stated:
>
> > As the gravity of the threat diminishes, the situation gradually changes from one where compulsion overwhelms the will of the victim to a situation where she can make a deliberate choice to avoid some alternative evil. The man may threaten to disclose an illicit affair, to foreclose the mortgage on her parent's farm, to cause her to lose her job, or to deprive her of a valued possession. The situation may move into a shadow area between coercion and bargain. A bargain for gain is not within the present section; but subsection 2(a) is designed to reach all situations of actual compulsion, i.e., where the female's submission is determined by fear of harm, with an objective test of the efficiency of the coercive element.
>
> Under this proposed statute, subsection (1) was designed to cover sexual intercourse accomplished by physical force or by threats which instilled fear of grave physical consequences to the victim or a member of her family, or fear of the perpetration of a serious crime. Subsection (2), on the other hand, sought to criminalize intercourse obtained by psychological duress rather than physical violence or threats thereof.
>
> These definitions were modified when a corresponding provision was inserted into the Proposed Official Draft of the Model Penal Code. It was there proposed as follows [Editor's Note: Court then cited model penal code's actual provision, which is excerpted at the beginning of this section of the chapter.]
>
> [The current draft] continued the distinction between "classic rape cases" involving force and situations where force was not present but the other person had not freely consented. The latter situation, which the proposed statute designated as "Gross Sexual Imposition," was defined as intercourse compelled "by *any threat* that would prevent resistance by a woman of ordinary resolution."

2. Perhaps the most novel feature of the Model Penal Code's rape provision is that it distinguishes between what it calls "rape" (§ 213.1(1)) and "gross sexual imposition" (§ 213.1(2)). Rape is defined similarly to how it was defined at common law. Nevertheless, the Code's "gross sexual imposition" provision criminalizes cases in which consent to sex is gained by making threats of non-physical harm as long as such threats "would prevent resistance by a woman of ordinary resolution." Defendants who abuse their authority by threatening those under their supervision with significant non-physical harm would likely be held liable of gross sexual imposition. The defendants in the *Thompson* (principal who threatened students with not graduating unless they performed oral sex) and *Milnarich* (adult guardian who threatened juvenile under his control with being sent to juvenile detention unless she performed oral sex) cases would likely be held liable for

gross sexual imposition as defined under the Model Penal Code. Is it appropriate to hold such defendants liable for gross sexual imposition or would it be preferable to not punish such conduct? Assuming that it is appropriate to hold such defendants criminally liable, is it preferable to punish them for the more serious crime of rape or the less serious offense of gross sexual imposition? Explain.

3. Note that the Model Penal Code allows defendants to raise a mistake of fact claim regarding the age of the victim in sexual assault cases. In contrast with its general approach to mistake of law, the Code treats a mistake regarding a victim's age in sexual assaults cases as an "affirmative defense," and thus places the burden of proving mistake on the defendant by a preponderance of the evidence. Moreover, the Code requires that the defendant prove that his mistake was reasonable. Observe, however, that the Code completely disallows such claims when the defendant is charged with engaging in sexual intercourse with a child under the age of 10. In such cases, the offense becomes one of strict liability. Do you agree with the Code's approach to mistake regarding the victim's age in sexual assault cases? Is it appropriate to require the defendant to prove the mistake by a preponderance of the evidence? Why does the Code require that this kind of mistake be reasonable in order to defeat liability, when for other offenses it suffices that the mistake "negatives the purpose, knowledge, belief, recklessness or negligence required to establish a material element of the offense"?

4. Observe that while the Model Penal Code's rape provisions may be preferable to the common law approach to rape, the Code still adopts evidently sexist positions. The most obvious flaw in the Code's approach is that it retains the now discredited marital exemption. Many also criticize the Code's failure to criminalize non-consensual sexual intercourse when it is not forcible. While the Code does create the lesser offense of gross sexual imposition, it remains the case that the prosecution must prove either force, threats or incapacity to consent in order to obtain a conviction for either rape, gross sexual imposition or deviate sexual intercourse. Finally, note that the Code only criminalizes sex that is obtained as a result of what courts usually call "fraud in the factum" or when the defendant impersonates being the spouse of the victim. The Code does not, however, criminalize sex obtained as a result of what courts would call fraud in the inducement. Consequently, the defendants in both *Suliveres* (defendant impersonates being the victim's boyfriend) and *Boro* (defendant falsely claims that having sex with donor would cure deadly disease) would not be punished if they were prosecuted under the Model Penal Code. Do you agree with this outcome or do you believe that the Code should also criminalize fraud in the inducement?

5. The American Law Institute is in the process of revising the Model Penal Code's rape provisions. While the issues highlighted in the previous note are being addressed by the commission tasked with reforming the provisions, it remains to be seen what changes will ultimately be made.

# § 21.04 Rape: Comparative Perspectives

## M.C. v. Bulgaria

European Court of Human Rights, 2003
Official Summary of Judgment

### 1. Principal facts

The applicant, M.C., is a Bulgarian national born in 1980 who alleged that she was raped by two men, A. and P., aged 20 and 21, when she was 14 years old, the age of consent for sexual intercourse in Bulgaria.

M.C. claimed that, on 31 July 1995, she went to a disco with the two men and a friend of hers. She then agreed to go on to another disco with the men. On the way back, A. suggested stopping at a reservoir for a swim. M.C. remained in the car. P. came back before the others, allegedly forcing M.C. to have sexual intercourse with him. M.C. maintained that she was left in a very disturbed state. In the early hours of the following morning, she was taken to a private home. She claimed that A. forced her to have sex with him at the house and that she cried continually both during and after the rape. She was later found by her mother and taken to hospital where a medical examination found that her hymen had been torn.

A. and P. both denied raping M.C.

The criminal investigations conducted found insufficient evidence that M.C. had been compelled to have sex with A. and P. The proceedings were terminated on 17 March 1997 by the District Prosecutor, who found that the use of force or threats had not been established beyond reasonable doubt. In particular, no resistance on the applicant's part or attempts to seek help from others had been established. The applicant appealed unsuccessfully.

Written expert opinions submitted to the European Court of Human Rights by M.C. identified "frozen fright" (traumatic psychological infantilism syndrome) as the most common response to rape, where the terrorised victim either submits passively to or dissociates her or himself psychologically from the rape. Of the 25 rape cases analysed, concerning women in Bulgaria aged between 14 and 20, 24 of the victims had responded to their aggressor in this way.

### 3. Summary of the judgment

#### Complaints

M.C. complained that Bulgarian law and practice do not provide effective protection against rape and sexual abuse, as only cases where the victim resists actively are prosecuted. She submitted that Bulgaria has a positive obligation under the European Convention on Human Rights to protect the individual's physical integrity and private life and to provide an effective remedy. She also complained that the authorities had not effectively investigated the events in question. She relied on Article 3 (prohibition of degrading treatment), Article 8 (right to respect for private life), Article 13 (right to an effective remedy) and Article 14 (prohibition of discrimination).

#### Decision of the Court

*Articles 3 and 8 of the Convention*

The Court reiterated that, under Articles 3 and 8 of the Convention, Member States had a positive obligation both to enact criminal legislation to effectively punish rape and to apply this legislation through effective investigation and prosecution.

The Court then observed that, historically, proof of the use of physical force by the perpetrator and physical resistance on the part of the victim was sometimes required under domestic law and practice in rape cases in a number of countries. However, it appeared that this was no longer required in European countries. In common-law jurisdictions, in Europe and elsewhere, any reference to physical force had been removed from legislation and/or case-law. Although in most European countries influenced by the continental legal tradition, the definition of rape contained references to the use of violence or threats of violence by the perpetrator, in case-law and legal theory, it was lack of consent, not force, that was critical in defining rape.

The Court also noted that the Member States of the Council of Europe had agreed that penalising non-consensual sexual acts, whether or not the victim had resisted, was necessary for the effective protection of women against violence and had urged the implementation of further reforms in this area. In addition, the International Criminal Tribunal for the former Yugoslavia had recently found that, in international criminal law, any sexual penetration without the victim's consent constituted rape, reflecting a universal trend towards regarding lack of consent as the essential element of rape and sexual abuse. As *[an amicus curiae] had submitted, victims of sexual abuse—in particular, girls below the age of majority—often failed to resist for a variety of psychological reasons or through fear of further violence from the perpetrator. In general, law and legal practice concerning rape were developing to reflect changing social attitudes requiring respect for the individual's sexual autonomy and for equality. Given contemporary standards and trends, Member States' positive obligation under Articles 3 and 8 of the Convention requires the penalisation and effective prosecution of any non-consensual sexual act, even where the victim had not resisted physically.*

The applicant alleged that the authorities' attitude in her case was rooted in defective legislation and reflected a practice of prosecuting rape perpetrators only where there was evidence of significant physical resistance. In the absence of case-law explicitly dealing with the question, the Court considered it difficult to arrive at safe general conclusions on the issue. However, the Bulgarian Government were unable to provide copies of judgments or legal commentaries clearly disproving the applicant's allegations of a restrictive approach in the prosecution of rape. Her claim was therefore based on reasonable arguments which had not been disproved.

The presence of two irreconcilable versions of the facts obviously called for a context-sensitive assessment of the credibility of the statements made and for verification of all the surrounding circumstances. Little was done, however, to test the credibility of the version of events put forward by P. and A.—even the assertion that the applicant, aged 14, had started caressing A. minutes after having had sex for the first time in her life with another man—or to test the credibility of the witnesses called by the accused or the precise timing of the events. Neither were the applicant and her representative able to question witnesses, whom she had accused of perjury. The authorities had therefore failed to explore the available possibilities for establishing all the surrounding circumstances and did not assess sufficiently the credibility of the conflicting statements made.

The reason for that failure appeared to be that the investigator and prosecutor considered that a "date rape" had occurred, and, in the absence of "direct" proof of rape such as traces of violence and resistance or calls for help, that they could not infer proof of lack of consent and, therefore, of rape from an assessment of all the surrounding circumstances. While the prosecutors did not exclude the possibility that the applicant might not have consented, they adopted the view, in the absence of proof of resistance, that it could not be concluded that the perpetrators had understood that the applicant had not consented. They did not assess evidence that P. and A. had deliberately misled the applicant in order to take her to a deserted area, thus creating an environment of coercion, or judge the credibility of the versions of the facts proposed by the three men and witnesses called by them.

The Court considered that the Bulgarian authorities should have explored all the facts and should have decided on the basis of an assessment of all the surrounding circumstances. The investigation and its conclusions should also have been centred on the issue of non-consent. Without expressing an opinion on the guilt of P. and A., the Court found that the effectiveness of the investigation of the applicant's case and, in particular, the approach taken by the investigator and the prosecutors fell short of Bulgaria's positive obligations under Articles 3 and 8 of the Convention—viewed in the light of the relevant modern standards in comparative and international law—to establish and apply effectively a criminal-law system punishing all forms of rape and sexual abuse.

## *Notes and Questions*

1. The European Court of Human Rights looked to the law of different jurisdictions in order to determine whether a consensus had emerged regarding the kinds of acts that should be punished as rape. The Court summarized the law of the different jurisdictions it surveyed as follows:

> 88. In the legal systems of a number of European States, rape and sexual assault are "gender-neutral" offences, whereas in other countries rape may only be committed by a man against a woman.
>
> 89. The minimum age of consent for sexual activity in most States is 14, 15 or 16 years. In some countries, there is a different age of consent for sexual acts without penetration and for sexual acts with penetration, or different penalties depending on the age of the victim. The approaches vary significantly from one country to another.
>
> 90. Article 375 §§ 1 and 2 of the Belgian Criminal Code (referred to by Interights), as amended in 1989, read:
>
>> "Any act of sexual penetration, of whatever nature and by whatever means, committed on a person who does not consent to it shall constitute the crime of rape.
>>
>> In particular, there is no consent where the act is forced by means of violence, coercion or ruse or was made possible by the victim's disability or physical or mental deficiency."
>
> 91. Article 241 § 1 of the Czech Criminal Code (Law no. 140/1961, as amended) provides:
>
>> "A person who coerces another into an act of sexual penetration or a similar sexual act through violence or the threat of imminent violence or by taking advantage of the person's helplessness shall be liable to imprisonment for a term of two to eight years."
>
> 92. Sections 216(1) and 217 of the Danish Penal Code (referred to by the intervener) provide:
>
>> "Any person who coerces [another into having] sexual intercourse by violence or under threat of violence shall be guilty of rape and liable to imprisonment

for a term not exceeding eight years. The placing of a person in such a position that the person is unable to resist shall be equivalent to violence ..."

"Any person who by means of unlawful coercion (according to section 260 of this Act) other than violence or the threat of violence procures sexual intercourse for himself, shall be liable to imprisonment for a term not exceeding four years."

93. Chapter 20, sections 1 and 3, of the Finnish Penal Code (as amended in 1998) provides:

"Section 1: Rape

(1) A person who coerces another into having sexual intercourse by the use or threat of violence shall be sentenced for rape to imprisonment for at least one year and at most six years.

(2) A person shall also be guilty of rape if he/she takes advantage of the incapacity of another to defend himself/herself and has sexual intercourse with him/her, after rendering him/her unconscious or causing him/her to be in a state of incapacity owing to fear or another similar reason ...

Section 3: Coercion into having sexual intercourse

(1) If the rape, in view of the low level of violence or threat and the other particulars of the offence, is deemed to have been committed under mitigating circumstances, the offender shall be sentenced for coercion into having sexual intercourse to imprisonment for at most three years.

(2) A person who coerces another into having sexual intercourse by a threat other than that referred to in section 1(1) shall be guilty of coercion into having sexual intercourse."

94. Articles 222-22, 222-23 and 227-25 of the French Criminal Code provide:

"Sexual aggression is any sexual assault committed by violence, coercion, threats or surprise."

"Any act of sexual penetration, whatever its nature, committed against another person by violence, coercion, threats or surprise, shall be considered rape. Rape shall be punishable by fifteen years' imprisonment."

"A sexual offence committed without violence, coercion, threats or surprise by an adult on the person of a minor under 15 years of age shall be punished by five years' imprisonment and a fine of 75,000 euros."

95. The following information about French case-law on rape may be gathered from the authoritative publication *Juris-Classeur* (2002):

(i) The words "violence, coercion, threats or surprise" are given a broad meaning in practice. For example, in one case it was stated that the fact that the victim was begging the perpetrator to stop, without further resistance, where she had previously agreed to enter his car and to be kissed by him, was sufficient to establish that there was rape The victim's refusal may be inferred from the circumstances, such as paralysing shock, as a result of which the victim could not protest or escape....

96. The relevant part of Article 177 (Sexual coercion; Rape) of the German Criminal Code reads:

"1. Anyone who coerces another person:

(1) by force,

(2) by the threat of immediate danger to life or limb, or

(3) by exploiting a situation in which the victim is defenceless and at the mercy of the actions of the perpetrator into submitting to sexual acts performed by the perpetrator or by a third person or into performing such acts on the perpetrator or on the third person, shall be punished by imprisonment for not less than one year."

97. Article 197 § 1 of the Hungarian Criminal Code (Law no. 4 of 1978) provides:

> "A person who by violent action or a direct threat to life or limb forces a person to have sexual intercourse, or uses a person's incapacity to defend himself/herself or to express his/her will to have sexual intercourse shall be guilty of a serious offence punishable by imprisonment for two to eight years."

98. In Ireland, section 2(1) of the Criminal Law (Rape) Act 1981 and section 9 of the Criminal Law (Rape) (Amendment) Act 1990 (referred to by the intervener) provide:

> "A man commits rape if (a) he has sexual intercourse with a woman who at the time of intercourse does not consent and (b) at the time he knows she does not consent or is reckless as to whether or not she is consenting."
>
> "It is hereby declared that in relation to an offence that consists of or includes the doing of an act to a person without the consent of the person, any failure or omission by that person to offer resistance to the act does not of itself constitute consent to that act."

99. Article 180 § 1 of the Slovenian Criminal Code reads:

> "Anyone who compels a person of the same or the opposite sex to submit to sexual intercourse by force or the threat of imminent attack on life and limb shall be sentenced to imprisonment from one to ten years."

100. In the United Kingdom, section 1(1) of the Sexual Offences (Amendment) Act 1976 (referred to by the intervener) provides:

> "[A] man commits rape if (a) he has unlawful sexual intercourse with a woman who at the time of intercourse does not consent to it; and (b) at that time he knows that she does not consent to the intercourse or is reckless as to whether she consents to it."

In light of these foreign statutes, do you agree with the European Court of Human Right's conclusion that "any reference to physical force had been removed from legislation and/or case-law" of the European and Anglo-American jurisdictions surveyed? Although the Court conceded that the language of these statutes suggests that proof of force is still required in many jurisdictions in order to secure a rape conviction, it asserted that "in case-law and legal theory, it was lack of consent, not force, that was critical in defining rape."

2. Review once more the statutes excerpted in the previous note. Which statute or statutes do you think define rape and rape related crimes in the best manner? Why?

3. Look back at the rape statutes discussed in the leading cases excerpted in the previous sections of this Chapter. Which of these statutes—as construed by the court deciding the case in which the statute is invoked—would satisfy the "positive obligations under Articles 3 and 8 of the [European Convention of Human Rights]" that requires jurisdic-

tions to "establish and apply effectively a criminal-law system punishing all forms of rape and sexual abuse"? Would the Model Penal Code's rape and rape related provisions satisfy the requirements imposed pursuant to the aforementioned articles? Explain.

# § 21.04 Rape: Scholarly Debates

## Susan Estrich, *Rape*

95 Yale L. J. 1087 (1986)

### V. TOWARD A BROADER UNDERSTANDING

The conduct that one might think of as "rape" ranges from the armed stranger who breaks into a woman's home to the date she invites in who takes silence for assent. In between are literally hundreds of variations: the man may be a stranger, but he may not be armed; he may be armed, but he may not be a stranger; he may be an almost, rather than a perfect, stranger—a man who gave her a ride or introduced himself through a ruse; she may say yes, but only because he threatens to expose her to the police or the welfare authorities; she may say no, but he may ignore her words.

In 1985, the woman raped at gunpoint by the intruding stranger should find most of the legal obstacles to her complaint removed. That was not always so: As recently as ten years ago, she might well have faced a corroboration requirement, a cautionary instruction, a fresh complaint rule, and a searing cross-examination about her sexual past to determine whether she had nonetheless consented to sex. In practice, she may still encounter some of these obstacles; but to the extent that the law communicates any clear message, it is likely to be that she was raped.

But most rapes do not as purely fit the traditional model, and most victims do not fare as well. Cases involving men met in bars or at work or at airports let alone cases involving ex-boyfriends, still lead some appellate courts to enforce the most traditional views of women in the context of the less traditional rape. And in the system, considerations of prior relationship and the circumstances of the initial encounter, as well as force and resistance and corroboration, seem to reflect a similarly grounded if not so clearly stated view of the limits of rape law.

In thinking about rape, it is not as difficult to decide which rapes are more serious or which rapists deserving of more punishment: Weapons, injury, and intent—the traditional grading criteria of the criminal law—are all justifiable answers to these questions. Most jurisdictions that have reformed their rape laws in the last ten years have focused on creating degrees of rape-aggravated and unaggravated-based on some combination of the presence of weapons and injury. While *mens rea* or mistake needs to be addressed more clearly in some rape laws, and bodily injury more carefully defined in others, these are essentially problems of draftsmanship which are hardly insurmountable.

The more difficult problem comes in understanding and defining the threshold for liability—where we draw the line between criminal sex and seduction. Every statute still uses some combination of "force," "threats" and "consent" to define the crime. But in giving meaning to those terms at the threshold of liability, the law of rape must confront the powerful norms of male aggressiveness and female passivity which continue to be adhered to by many men and women in our society.

The law did not invent the "no means yes" philosophy. Women as well as men have viewed male aggressiveness as desirable and forced sex as an expression of love; women as well as men have been taught and have come to believe that when a woman "encourages" a man, he is entitled to sexual satisfaction. From the sociological surveys to prime time television, one can find ample support in society and culture for even the most oppressive views of women, and the most expansive notions of seduction enforced by the most traditional judges.

But the evidence is not entirely one-sided. For every prime time series celebrating forced sex, there seems to be another true confession story in a popular magazine detailing the facts of a date rape and calling it "rape." College men and women may think that the typical male is forward and primarily interested in sex, but they no longer conclude that he is the desirable man. The old sex manuals may have lauded male sexual responses as automatic and uncontrollable, but some of the newer ones no longer see men as machines and even advocate sensitivity as seductive.

We live, in short, in a time of changing sexual mores—and we are likely to for some time to come. In such times, the law can cling to the past or help move us into the future. We can continue to enforce the most traditional views of male aggressiveness and female passivity, continue to adhere to the "no means yes" philosophy and to the broadest understanding of seduction, until and unless change overwhelms us. That is not a neutral course, however; in taking it, the law (judges, legislators, or prosecutors) not only reflects (a part of) society, but legitimates and reenforces those views.

Or we can use the law to move forward. It may be impossible—and even unwise—to try to use the criminal law to change the way people think, to push progress to the ideal. But recognition of the limits of the criminal sanction need not be taken as a justification for the *status quo.* Faced with a choice between reenforcing the old and fueling the new in a world of changing norms, it is not necessarily more legitimate or neutral to choose the old. There are lines to be drawn short of the ideal: The challenge we face in thinking about rape is to use the power and legitimacy of law to reenforce what is best, not what is worst, in our changing sexual mores.

In the late eighteenth and early nineteenth centuries, the judges of England waged a successful campaign against duelling. While "the attitude of the law" was clear that killing in a duel was murder, the problem was that for some, accepting a challenge remained a matter of "honour," and juries would therefore not convict. "Some change in the public attitude toward duelling, coupled with the energy of judges in directing juries in strong terms, eventually brought about convictions, and it was not necessary to hang many gentlemen of quality before the understanding became general that duelling was not required by the code of honour."

There has been "some change in the public attitude" about the demands of manhood in heterosexual relations, as in duelling. If the "attitude of the law" is made clearer—and that is, in essence, what this Article is about—then it may not be necessary to prosecute too many "gentlemen of quality" before the understanding becomes general that manly honor need not be inconsistent with female autonomy.

In a better world, I believe that men and women would not presume either consent or nonconsent. They would ask, and be certain. There is nothing unromantic about showing the kind of respect for another person that demands that you know for sure before engaging in intimate contact. In a better world, women who said yes would be saying so from a position of equality, or at least sufficient power to say no. In a better world, fewer women would bargain with sex because they had nothing else to bargain with; they would be in at least as good a position to reject demands for sexual access as men are to reject demands for money.

If we are not at the point where it is appropriate for the law to presume nonconsent from silence, and the reactions I have received to this Article suggest that we are not, then at least we should be at the point where it is legitimate to punish the man who ignores a woman's explicit words of protestations. I am quite certain that many women who say yes—whether on dates or on the job—would say no if they could; I have no doubt that women's silence is sometimes the product not of passion and desire but of pressure and pain. But at the very least the criminal law ought to say clearly that women who actually say no must be respected as meaning it; that nonconsent means saying no; that men who proceed nonetheless, claiming that they thought no meant yes, have acted unreasonably and unlawfully.

So, too, for threats of harm short of physical injury, and for deception and false pretenses as methods of seduction. The powerlessness of women and the value of bodily integrity are great enough to argue that women deserve more comprehensive protection for their bodies than the laws of extortion or fraud provide for money. But if going so far seems too complicated and fraught with difficulty, as it does to many, then we need not. For the present, it would be a significant improvement if the law of rape in any state prohibited exactly the same threats as that state's law of extortion and exactly the same deceptions as that state's law of false pretenses or fraud.

In short, I am arguing that "consent" should be defined so that "no means no." And the "force" or "coercion" that negates consent ought be defined to include extortionate threats and deceptions of material fact. As for *mens rea*, unreasonableness as to consent, understood to mean ignoring a woman's words, should be sufficient for liability: Reasonable men should be held to know that no means no, and unreasonable mistakes, no matter how honestly claimed, should not exculpate. Thus, the threshold of liability—whether phrased in terms of "consent," "force" or "coercion," or some combination of the three, should be understood to include at least those non-traditional rapes where the woman says no or submits only in response to lies or threats which would be prohibited were money sought instead. The crime I have described would be a lesser offense than the aggravated rape in which life is threatened or bodily injury inflicted, but it is, in my judgment, "rape." One could, I suppose, claim that as we move from such violent rapes to "just" coerced or nonconsensual sex, we are moving away from a crime of violence toward something else. But what makes the violent rape different—and more serious—than an aggravated assault is the injury to personal integrity involved in forced sex. That same injury is the reason that forced sex should be a crime even when there is no weapon or no beating. In a very real sense, what does make rape different from other crimes, at every level of the offense, is that rape is about sex and sexual violation. Were the essence of the crime the use of the gun or the knife or the threat, we wouldn't need—and wouldn't have—a separate crime.

Conduct is labeled as criminal "to announce to society that these actions are not to be done and to secure that fewer of them are done." As a matter of principle, we should be ready to announce to society our condemnation of coerced and nonconsensual sex and to secure that we have less of it. The message of the substantive law to men, and to women, should be made clear.

That does not mean that this crime will, or should, be easy to prove. The constitutional requirement of proof beyond a reasonable doubt may well be difficult to meet in cases where guilt turns on whose account is credited as to what was said. If the jury is in doubt, it should acquit. If the judge is uncertain, he should dismiss.

The message of the substantive law must be distinguished from the constitutional standards of proof. In this as in every criminal case, a jury must be told to acquit if it is in doubt. The requirement of proof beyond a reasonable doubt rests on the premise that it is better that ten guilty should go free than that one innocent man should be punished. But if we should acquit ten, let us be clear that the we are acquitting them not because they have an entitlement to ignore a woman's words, not because what they allegedly did was right or macho or manly, but because we live in a system that errs on the side of freeing the guilty.

## Stephen Schulhofer, *Taking Sexual Autonomy Seriously: Rape Law and Beyond*

11 Law & Philosophy 35 (1992)

[The] conflict over the problem of how to treat silence and ambiguity [toward sex in the context of rape law] spotlights radical disagreement about what autonomy and consent are, empirically and conceptually. We don't know what most women feel when their response to a sexual initiative is neither clearly affirmative nor clearly negative. More importantly, society and law can mean many things by "willingness" or "consent". The argument that the silent person cannot be unwilling, because any unwilling person would object, is most plausible if unwillingness means having an aversion or revulsion. But there are other possibilities. A woman considering a sexual initiative (like any other person considering a course of action) may feel emphatically negative, enthusiastically positive, indifferent, uncertain, or ambivalent. The present problem is not only to determine which of these feelings most often corresponds to silence, but also to determine which of these feelings should count as "nonconsent" (that is, operationally, which should render sexual contact impermissible).

Traditional rape law has been quite attuned to these concerns about the ambiguity of willingness and sexual desire. But because it has seen these concerns through the lens of protection against violence, their relevance has been transformed. Precisely because "the woman's attitude may be deeply ambivalent", it was hard to see her as a victim of forcible compulsion. The very conception of rape implied coercing someone to do something repugnant. From this perspective even a verbal no might not signal what nonconsent was once thought to mean, a sort of abhorrence. Reformers who insist that "no means no" question one application of this approach but they in essence legitimate its basic conception of consent by stressing the emphatic expression of an unambiguous preference. Rather than challenging the prevailing paradigm, they reinforce it by equating nonconsent with a clearly crystallized negative attitude.

The autonomy perspective suggests different ways of thinking about what nonconsent should mean. Consider this parable. A hospitalized athlete, suffering from chronic knee problems, consults a surgeon, who recommends an operation. The athlete is not sure. If the operation is successful, he will enjoy a long, fulfilling career with his team. But there are imponderables. The operation carries a risk of a burdensome infection that can be hard to cure. The procedure may not produce the expected benefits. In any event, it is sure to be stressful in the short run. The athlete hesitates. There are clear advantages, clear disadvantages, and lots of uncertainties. What to do? Maybe he should postpone this big step for a while, see how things go without it. The surgeon is encouraging: "Try it. You'll like it". Still the athlete is unsure.

Now our surgeon becomes impatient. He has spent a lot of time with this case. The athlete's hesitation is becoming tiresome and annoying. So the surgeon signals an anesthesiologist to ready the drugs that will flow through an intravenous tube already in place.

One last time the surgeon (a sensitive, modern male) reminds the athlete, "You don't have to go ahead with this. If you really want me to stop, just say so." But the athlete, his brain still clouded with doubts, fears, hopes, and uncertainties, says nothing. So the surgeon starts the anesthesia and just does it.

Consent? Of course not. But why not? The athlete was not compelled to submit. Nobody forced him. His "attitude may be deeply ambivalent", but surgical patients are almost always like that. Surely his silence proves that he was not unwilling. If he really objected, all he had to do was say so!

There are, to be sure, important contextual differences between surgery and sexual intimacy. But even allowing for those differences, it would not be implausible to find "consent" by the patient, provided we could get ourselves to think of illegal surgery as an offense requiring "forcible compulsion", and to think of "nonconsent" in this context as revulsion, aversion, or a clearly crystallized negative attitude.

We do not see matters this way because we are not thinking about a crime of violence. We are thinking about an offense against the patient's autonomy. Moral and intellectual autonomy as well as physical, bodily autonomy must be respected. Both dimensions are important. The athlete's freedom of choice might have been impaired by confinement, time pressure, or professional authority. But even if his intellectual autonomy was unconstrained, even if he remained free to choose, his physical autonomy was unquestionably violated because no choice was ever made. In the surgical context, at least, nonconsent cannot mean aversion or a crystallized negative decision, because in our society this kind of intrusion on the person requires unambiguous, positive permission. Nonconsent is simply anything that is not positive consent, anything that is not an affirmative, crystallized expression of willingness. To treat the athlete as a victim is not, of course, to patronize him. It is merely to recognize an obvious violation of the physical autonomy of his person.

Why aren't the same conceptions of autonomy and nonconsent just as appropriate for acts of sexual intimacy? Are the differences in context, and in social and psychological meanings, relevant to the result?

One could imagine a world that required affirmative permission even for a kiss or a hug between intimates. "May I kiss you?" would be respectful but may sound quaint to modern ears. In many social contexts, men and women can justifiably infer positive willingness even without express consent. Conversely, a kiss or hug known to be unwelcome is undoubtedly battery, a clear offense against the physical autonomy of the person.

What if a man kisses a woman when he knows that she is ambivalent? Should ambivalence in this context, the absence of positive consent, count as nonconsent? My impression of both law and existing social etiquette is that it does not, at least not always. Respect for the individual (and sensitivity to the potentially overbearing character of male physical and social power) arguably should prompt a rethinking of cultural attitudes here. For now there is probably no clear social consensus that a kiss violates the autonomy of an ambivalent recipient.

But intercourse is not a kiss. In our society voluntary touching, hugging, and kissing occur frequently between all sorts of acquaintances and even between virtual strangers (at public ceremonies, for example). Attitudes about such casual, superficial physical contacts have no bearing on the meaning and appropriate limitations on intimate genital contact and, especially, sexual intercourse. These intimate contacts unquestionably involve profound intrusions on the physical and emotional integrity of the individual. For such intrusions, as for surgery, actual permission, nothing less than a crystallized attitude of positive willingness, should ever count as consent.

Though I have no doubt about what autonomy ought to mean in this context, my approach might seem inconsistent with some of existing social practice. Since the cases (and massive numbers of judges, prosecutors, and juries) have so often insisted on clear, unequivocal objections to intercourse, in effect equating ambivalence with consent, affirmative permission obviously has not been considered necessary. Intercourse has been treated like a kiss.

But this minimalist attitude toward consent surely does not flow from a casual attitude about the physical and psychological significance of intercourse. On the contrary, present culture recognizes intercourse as a major intrusion on physical autonomy in just the way I have posited. Why then the minimalist attitude toward consent? Its source, I suggest, is the pervasive association of "rape" with violent misconduct. When the charge is "forcible compulsion", it can be plausible to view the victim's ambivalence as an appropriate defense, as a kind of "consent". But there is still, as in surgery, an unambiguous intrusion on the bodily integrity of the person. As in surgery, nothing less than affirmative permission can warrant such action. The unwarranted contact may not be rape, but it is still a grave personal intrusion that criminal law can appropriately reach.

In sum, intercourse in the face of verbal objections, ambivalence, or silence is intercourse without consent, and it represents a clear offense against the physical autonomy of the person. Even in the complete absence of force, such behavior is "nonviolent sexual misconduct" and should be punished as such.

## *Notes and Questions*

1. Professor Estrich claims that at the very least "criminal law ought to say clearly that women who actually say no must be respected as meaning it." As a result, she argues that "nonconsent means saying no" regardless of whether force is used or whether the victim physically resists or not. The consequence of this is that "men who proceed ... claiming that they thought no meant yes, have acted unreasonably and unlawfully" and are therefore deserving of punishment. Do you agree with Estrich's claims? Explain.

2. Another claim put forth by Professor Estrich is that sex that is obtained as a result of "threats of harm short of physical injury" ought to be punished. This would lead to criminalizing conduct in cases such as *Thompson* and *Milnarich* (§21.03). Estrich also suggests that sex that is secured by "deception and false pretenses" should be criminalized. This would lead to punishing *both* sex that is obtained by what courts have called fraud in the factum and fraud in the inducement. Consequently, Estrich's proposal would likely lead to punishing the defendants in both *Suliveres* (defendant impersonated being victim's boyfriend) and *Boro* (defendant fraudulently claimed that having sex with donor would cure deadly illness). In all of these cases, however, Professor Estrich argues that "[t]he crime ... would be a lesser offense than the aggravated rape in which life is threatened or bodily injury inflicted." Nonetheless, she claims that these crimes should still be considered "rape." Do you agree with the how these cases would be decided if Estrich's approach to rape is adopted? Why or why not?

3. Professor Estrich explains that in an ideal world "men and women would not presume either consent or nonconsent." Instead, "[t]hey would ask, and be certain" that the woman is consenting to the sexual act. This view is what has come to be known as the "affirmative consent" approach to rape. Under this view, engaging in sexual intercourse with a person who does not affirmatively convey consent is rape even if the victim never said "no." In other words, this approach views silence as non-consent, whereas under the traditional view silence is viewed as consent. Are you persuaded that having sex with a per-

son who remains silent but does not resist in any way should be considered rape? Explain.

4. Professor Schulhofer is one of the leading proponents of the view that having sex without first obtaining the affirmative consent of the victim should be considered rape. He compares having sex without first obtaining affirmative consent with performing surgery without securing the patient's affirmative permission. Schulhofer suggests that in much the same way as operating on a patient who does not resist the surgery but does not affirmatively consent to it is a battery, it should be rape to have sexual intercourse with a person who remains silent throughout the act even if the person never resists. Do you find Schulhofer's argument persuasive? Explain.

# Index